Basic Accounting
for Managerial and Financial
Control

Basic Accounting
for Managerial and Financial
Control

Second Edition

Albert Slavin
Northeastern University

Isaac N. Reynolds
The University of North Carolina

Johnn T. Miller
Chabot College

DRYDEN PRESS
HINSDALE, ILLINOIS

Copyright © 1968, 1972 by Holt, Rinehart and Winston, Inc.
All rights reserved
Library of Congress Catalog Card Number: 71-167807
ISBN: 0-03-086122-5
Printed in the United States of America
 4567890   032   98765

Preface

This book is designed for use primarily in the first-year accounting course. It is arranged, however, to meet several needs. For the first-year basic accounting course every chapter can be used. For a graduate-level MBA survey course, all chapters, with some careful deletions in certain chapters, constitute a high-level course. For the many schools that teach only one course in elementary accounting, Chapters 1–18 provide excellent coverage of basic accounting. By carefully integrating the managerial uses of accounting with the traditional subject matter of financial accounting, the book provides students of business administration with the basic concepts and uses of accounting, and accounting majors with a broad foundation for advanced study. The primary objective of the text is to present the managerial and financial uses of accounting concomitantly with fundamental accounting practices and theory, thus providing a balanced approach to both the structural form and uses of accounting information.

A new edition of a book provides the author(s) with the opportunity to update the text, to tighten and polish the treatment of basic concepts and subject matter, and to reorganize the material along sounder pedagogical lines, emphasizing conceptual matter and de-emphasizing topics that have declined in importance. All these objectives have been accomplished in this revision.

In this second edition, the emphasis on certain procedural details has been reduced, thereby providing needed time and space for a continuing development of the uses of accounting as an aid in the formulation and administration of management policies and controls, in financial management and analysis, and in budgetary controls and procedures. Several of these areas are not included in the typical elementary text. From the outset the text attempts to stress the analysis and the interpretation of financial statements, as well as managerial accounting concepts, principles, and standards. Citations from the publications of the American Accounting Association and the American Institute of Certified Public Accountants are used to a greater extent than in the first edition and are interwoven with the pertinent text discussions.

The book is divided into four parts:

1. Basic Concepts and Methodology: Service and Merchandising Businesses
2. Income Measurement and Valuation Problems Related to Sources and Uses of Invested Capital
3. Financial Reporting: Analysis and Interpretive Problems
4. Cost Accumulation, Cost Control, and Financial Planning

Part 1 (Chapters 1–6) covers the basic accounting cycle, introduces the various ways of processing a mass of data, and includes a discussion of automatic data processing.

Part 2 (Chapters 7–15) covers the accounting for cash; the measurement and control of receivables, inventory, and plant and equipment; contributed capital, short-term business financing, including an extended discussion of simple and compound interest; and managerial and financial debt and investment decisions.

Part 3 (Chapters 16–19) covers corporate financial reporting, business combinations and consolidated statements, changing price levels, and sources and uses of funds.

Part 4 (Chapters 20–25) introduces cost accumulation and control for general merchandising operations, job order and process cost systems, standard costs and direct costing, cost control in managerial decisions, capital budgeting, quantitative techniques for decision making, and federal income taxes.

The specific new materials that have been added in this edition include the following:

1. Chapter 6 has been expanded to include flow charting, added emphasis on the computer as a tool in the total information process, and a basic introduction to the program language BASIC.
2. Compound interest is introduced midway in the text (Chapter 13) and is used in several other chapters.
3. Two new chapters have been added—Chapter 17 "Corporate Financial Reporting: Business Combinations and Consolidated Statements" and Chapter 18 "Corporate Financial Reporting: Changing Price Levels."
4. In Chapter 22, added emphasis has been placed on cost and revenue behavior patterns.
5. In Chapter 23, a great deal of new material has been added on quantitative techniques for decision making.

As in the first edition, the end-of-chapter material is divided into five parts: (1) questions for class discussion, (2) short exercises, (3) class demonstration problems designed for the use of the instructor, (4) problems, and (5) three differently indicated kinds of decision problems: accounting policy decision problems, financial policy decision problems, and managerial policy decision problems. The demonstration problems, averaging three to a chapter, exemplify the highlights of each chapter. The questions and exercises are designed either for class discussion or for outside assignment; they test the student's understanding of the chapter contents. The problems stress both theory and practice and are graded by level of difficulty and approximate completion time. The decision problems are also correlated to the chapter material but are set within a broader business background and furnish a specific business orientation for in-depth analysis and class discussion.

An optional self-study guide, prepared by Johnn T. Miller, not only tests the student's comprehension of the text but also reduces the amount of class time required to cover the individual chapters. Demonstration problems with their solutions, self-testing quizzes, and short exercises are included in the self-study guide as a supplementary aid to an understanding of the text discussions. Also available are working papers for the exercises and problems. A short practice set, The Pineland Wholesale Furniture Company, containing narrative and working papers, furnishes a review of the fundamentals established in Part 1.

The use of color in the text, the marginal notations underscoring accounting concepts, the chapter summaries, the wide margins, and a comprehensive index greatly enhance the usefulness of the book. The discussions and problems in the text and all the supplementary materials have been classroom tested over a sustained period by the authors, and those in the first edition by professors in schools throughout the world.

Boston, Massachusetts   ALBERT SLAVIN
Chapel Hill, North Carolina   ISAAC N. REYNOLDS
Fremont, California   JOHNN T. MILLER
January 1972

Contents

Part 2   Income Measurement and Valuation Problems Related
to Sources and Uses of Invested Capital

Part 4   Cost Accumulation, Cost Control, and Financial Planning

Basic Concepts and Methodology: Service and Merchandising Businesses

part

1

1

The Accounting
Equation and the
Statement of
Financial Position

Accounting is the language of business; it provides the kinds of information that managers and other interested persons must have in order to make business decisions. Accounting is therefore of valuable service to complex modern business.

Basic Accounting for Managerial and Financial Control is designed as an introduction to the field of accounting as a whole. The text starts with basic concepts and methodology; then shifts to specific data processing methods, income measurement, valuation problems related to the sources and uses of invested capital, and the analysis and interpretation of financial reports; and concludes with cost accumulation, cost control, and financial planning.

ROLE AND FUNCTION OF ACCOUNTING

To understand and appreciate accounting and its role in business management, the accounting function must be thought of as the *information management* function in an organization. It is concerned with the collection and classification of data for the purpose of assisting managers and others in making business decisions. Accordingly, accounting and business management are inextricably linked. To speak and understand the language of business, one must know something about accounting.

The usefulness of accounting, however, is not limited to business; it is applicable to many different units in our society—political units, such as school districts, cities, states, and the Federal government; social units, such as clubs, fraternities; religious units; and many others. This is why the study of accounting is important, irrespective of whether the student ultimately becomes an accountant, enters business management, or follows almost any other career.

Accounting may be described as the process of identifying, meas-

3

uring, recording, and reporting information, mostly of a financial nature, on the activities of a business enterprise or other entity in society. These four processes of accounting are not *arbitrarily* accomplished; rather, they are carried out according to "generally accepted accounting principles." A major purpose of this text is to acquaint the student with generally accepted accounting principles so that he may apply the knowledge he gains to an understanding of the financial accounting reports of organizations in general and to apply this knowledge to the specific organization with which he is associated.

The difference between accounting and bookkeeping is confusing to many people. Bookkeeping is generally thought of as one segment of accounting—the recording segment. The actual recording of the transactions of a business is the "bookkeeping" and is performed by a person known as the "bookkeeper." The accountant, on the other hand, is responsible for the entire operation of the accounting system with which he works. This responsibility includes identifying the events pertaining to the organization that must be recorded, their measurement or quantification, and the system by which the events are recorded and reported. Thus, an accountant, instead of being strictly a technician, must be concerned with and have a broad understanding of the environment in which his organization operates. This understanding is essential if he is to succeed in identifying and supplying relevant information about the activities of an entity to its management.

In the case of a business organization, the activities to be identified, measured, and recorded are centered around the past, present, and future efforts of the business entity to earn an income. In some other type of organization, such as a school or a governmental unit, the main concern may be with keeping a record of the money received and its subsequent disbursement. In a medical facility, this information may be expanded to include the number of patients served and the care they receive. For each unit, the management, together with the accountant, must identify the broad areas of information needs relevant to the operation of the unit. It is then the responsibility of the accountant to identify specifically, or to pinpoint, these needs in terms of events and to set up and operate a system to measure, record, and report these events in a form meaningful to management.

This text is concerned almost exclusively with business organizations and the business environment. Thus, an added benefit from the study of accounting is the gaining of a broader as well as a deeper understanding of business units and how different economic events affect them.

An objective of accounting for all units is that the accounting function should aid in the protection of the enterprise from errors in data and from misappropriations. This is often referred to as the *internal control function.*

THE ENTITY CONCEPT

In order to provide meaningful decision-making information about a business unit, the accountant must maintain a separate set of records for each business enterprise of an owner. The focal point of attention is not the owner but the *economic unit*, which has well-defined boundaries. For example, suppose that John

Goodwin owns a grocery store, a hardware store, and a service station, and that in addition he has a car, a residence, some stocks and bonds, and other personal items of value. These are shown in a graphic form:

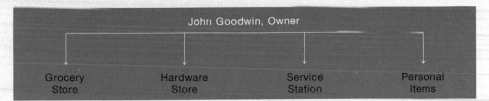

If the accountant's total attention is focused on John Goodwin, he may lose sight of the individual economic units. Thus, in this case, the accounting information for all Goodwin's activities lumped together is useless in making decisions for any single unit. ▼ In order to accomplish the accounting objectives mentioned in the preceding paragraph, a set of records must be provided for each of the individual business units, and the focal point of attention must be the individual unit rather than the owner. ▼ This is referred to as the _entity concept_.

Accounting Concept: ▼
Business Entity.

ASSETS

The _assets_ of a business are everything of value found in the business. The word _value_ is used here in the sense of future usefulness to a continuing business enterprise; it does not indicate the cost of replacing the asset or how much it would bring in if offered for sale. Cash, notes and accounts receivable (amounts owed to the business through transactions on credit), land, buildings, and high-grade, readily marketable stocks or bonds of other companies (_marketable securities_) are examples of assets in a business. An asset is recorded at its full cost even though it has not been fully paid for in cash; the amount of any debt or claim against the asset is shown as a _liability_.

EQUITIES: LIABILITIES AND OWNER'S EQUITY

The _equities_ represent claims against, or rights in, the assets of a business. The two major classifications of individuals who have equities in a business are the _creditors_ (liability holders) and the _owner_.

The liabilities of a business are everything owed to creditors. Liabilities represent the claims of the creditors of the business unit. _Accounts payable_ and _notes payable_, which are amounts owed by the business through purchases on credit, are some liabilities that a business may have. Wages owed to employees is another example.

The _owner's equity_ (_capital_ and _proprietorship_ are alternative terms) represents the proprietor's, the partners', or the stockholders' claims against the assets of a business, or the _excess_ of all assets over all liabilities. This excess is also referred to as _net assets_.

THE ACCOUNTING EQUATION

Because equities, by definition, represent the total claims against assets, then assets must equal equities. This relationship is shown:

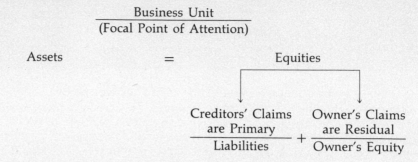

The equities of the unit are broken down into the *primary claims,* those of the creditors, and the *residual claims,* those of the owner. Since assets are derived primarily from these two sources, the truth of the equation is reinforced. Another source is a *gift* of assets, which increases the owner's equity.

The following equation, then, is the *basic accounting equation,* which expresses the financial position of any business unit at all times.

$$\text{Assets} = \text{Liabilities} + \text{Owner's Equity}$$

Business assets owned equal sources of business assets. The equation must be modified slightly to indicate the particular kind of business organization: *single proprietorship, partnership,* or *corporation.* For example, in a corporation the equation would be

$$\text{Assets} = \text{Liabilities} + \text{Stockholders' Equity}$$

and in a partnership the equation would be

$$\text{Assets} = \text{Liabilities} + \text{Partners' Equity}$$

The various forms of business organization will be considered in more detail later in this chapter.

The equation may be restated for various analytical purposes in the following manner:

$$\text{Assets} - \text{Liabilities} = \text{Owner's Equity}$$

The use of this particular form of the equation will be discussed later.

The term *net assets* often is used in business; it may be expressed as follows:

$$\text{Total Assets} - \text{Total Liabilities} = \text{Net Assets}$$

The relationship expressed by the accounting equation is fundamental to the development of accounting records. In essence, *bookkeeping* is the process of recording changes in the terms of the equation during business operations.

THE STATEMENT OF FINANCIAL POSITION

The *statement of financial position, or position statement,* is an expression of the accounting equation (Figure 1-1). The statement of financial position summarizes the assets, liabilities, and owner's equity of a business unit as of a specific time. This statement is often called a *balance sheet,* but the more descriptive term is used in this text. An *account form* of position statement with the accounting equation is shown below.

A variant form of the same statement, the *report form,* is shown in Figure 1-2. Both statements are good illustrations of the accounting equation.

The heading of a statement of financial position usually contains three lines of information:

1. The name of the business
2. The name of the statement
3. The date of the statement

The date given in the example shows that it reveals the financial position of the firm as of the close of business on December 31, 1973.

Figure 1-1. Account-Form Position Statement

| ASSETS | = | LIABILITIES + STOCKHOLDERS' EQUITY |

MURROW CLOTHING STORE
Statement of Financial Position
December 31, 1973

Assets			Liabilities and Stockholders' Equity		
Current Assets			Current Liabilities		
Cash	$ 325		Accounts Payable	$12,060	
Marketable Securities	1,900		Notes Payable	2,060	
Accounts Receivable	11,025		Accrued Wages		
Notes Receivable	2,520		Payable	970	
Merchandise Inventory	14,750		Total Current		
Prepaid Insurance	275		Liabilities		$15,090
Office Supplies	26		Long-Term Liabilities		
Store Supplies	89		Bank Loan Payable		
Total Current Assets		$30,910	(due June 1, 1978)	$ 4,000	
Plant and Equipment			Mortgage Payable	10,000	
Land	$ 3,000		Total Long-Term		
Building	10,000		Liabilities		14,000
Store Equipment	2,500		Total Liabilities		$29,090
Delivery Equipment	3,250		Stockholders' Equity		
Total Plant and			Capital Stock	$20,000	
Equipment		18,750	Retained Earnings	570	
			Total Stockholders'		
			Equity		20,570
			Total Liabilities and		
			Stockholders'		
Total Assets		$49,660	Equity		$49,660

Figure 1-2. Report-Form Position Statement

MURROW CLOTHING STORE
Statement of Financial Position
December 31, 1973

Assets

Current Assets		
Cash	$ 325	
Marketable Securities	1,900	
Accounts Receivable	11,025	
Notes Receivable	2,520	
Merchandise Inventory	14,750	
Prepaid Insurance	275	
Office Supplies	26	
Store Supplies	89	
Total Current Assets		$30,910
Plant and Equipment		
Land	$ 3,000	
Building	10,000	
Store Equipment	2,500	
Delivery Equipment	3,250	
Total Plant and Equipment		18,750
Total Assets		$49,660

Liabilities and Stockholders' Equity

Current Liabilities		
Accounts Payable	$12,060	
Notes Payable	2,060	
Accrued Wages Payable	970	
Total Current Liabilities		$15,090
Long-Term Liabilities		
Bank Loan Payable (due June 1, 1978)	$ 4,000	
Mortgage Payable	10,000	
Total Long-Term Liabilities		14,000
Total Liabilities		$29,090
Stockholder's Equity		
Capital Stock	$20,000	
Retained Earnings	570	
Total Stockholders' Equity		20,570
Total Liabilities and Stockholders' Equity		$49,660

Dollar signs are used on formal typed or printed statements at the top of each column of figures. A new column is created whenever a line is drawn for addition, subtraction, or other reasons. A double rule is drawn under any amount that is the final result of a series of calculations.

Need for Classification in a Statement of Financial Position

Note that the assets and liabilities in the statement of financial position for the Murrow Clothing Store are *classified*. A financial statement should be classified so as to be of maximum value to an analyst, banker, creditor, employee, or other interested person; It can be made more easily understandable by the manner in which the items are arranged. The kind of classifications and the order of arrangement to be shown in the statement depend on tradition, the nature of the business activity, and the expected use of the document.

Classification of Assets—Current

Current assets consist of cash and other assets that are expected to be converted into cash or to be used in the operation of the business within one year. Current assets are usually listed in the order of their probable *liquidity*, or their expected conversion into cash. The current assets, listed in order of liquidity, of the Murrow Clothing Store are the following:

Cash. Cash is any item that a bank will accept as a deposit and that is immediately available and acceptable as a means of payment. Cash includes coins, currency, checks, bank drafts, money orders, and demand deposits in commercial banks.

Marketable Securities. Businesses that have a temporary excess of cash on hand and want to earn interest on it may buy promises to pay issued by other companies (usually referred to as *commercial paper*) or by governmental agencies or institutions (called *notes* or *bonds*). Many finance companies, for example, sell short-term notes that will usually mature within 60 days to six months. The United States government also issues short-term Treasury notes and certificates of indebtedness that are often acquired by businesses with excess cash to invest temporarily. Also, high-grade industrial bonds and stocks may be purchased as temporary investments.

Accounts Receivable. Accounts receivable represent the amounts due from customers for services rendered or for merchandise, or for any asset, sold on credit (*open account*). A business with a limited number of customers could list them individually in the statement of financial position. If the debtors are numerous, however, the individual names are eliminated and the statement shows the total amount of accounts receivable in one figure. A record for each customer must be kept in a subsidiary ledger.

Notes Receivable. A note receivable is a formal written promise by a customer to pay a fixed amount of money on demand or on a specific date. Since the note is usually transferable by endorsement to another party or to a bank, it represents an asset that can be converted readily into cash.

Merchandise Inventory. Businesses that offer products for sale must have them readily available. All the merchandise on hand at any given moment is called the *merchandise inventory.* Merchandise inventories are found on retail store shelves and in stockrooms or warehouses.

Prepaid Items. Prepaid items are current assets which have been acquired and not used up at the statement date. A physical inventory usually is taken of these assets at the statement date so that the cost of the unconsumed portion may be shown. Some common prepaid items are described in the following paragraphs.

unexpired paid : assets

Prepaid Insurance. Every business must protect itself against hazards. Consequently, businesses take out insurance policies for protection. The cost of this type of protection, which is listed on the statement, is called an "insurance premium" and is paid in advance. Insurance policies commonly are issued against such hazards as fire, burglary, personal injury, business interruption, and injury to employees (workmen's compensation).

a date
what is left
: assets =
unexpired cost

e.g. $600 ¹/₁₀
– $201 expired cost
$700 unexpired cost

Office Supplies. Supplies required in an office such as stamps, stationery, and typewriter and adding machine ribbons are grouped under the title Office Supplies and are current assets of the business.

Store Supplies. Store supplies include wrapping paper, twine, paper bags, and similar items used in a store. They are also classified as current assets.

No asset that will be used in the general operation of the business should be included in the merchandise inventory.

Classification of Assets—Plant and Equipment

Plant and equipment comprises assets used over a long period of time in the operation of the business. The caption "Equipment" may be used if the business does not own its land and building, that is, its *plant*. These assets are customarily listed on the statement of financial position according to the degree of permanency; the most permanent item is listed first. Some typical plant and equipment assets are the following:

permanent

Land. Land is shown separately on the statement of financial position, although land and the buildings are usually sold together. Land and buildings are classified separately because the buildings will deteriorate through usage, whereas the land will not.

less permanent

Buildings. In order for a building to appear on the statement of financial position, it must be owned by the business.

Store Equipment. Showcases, counters, and shelves are typical permanent items of store equipment used in selling the merchandise inventory.

Delivery Equipment. Delivery equipment consists of trucks and cars used for the delivery of products to the customer.

Classification of Liabilities—Current

paid within a year

The term *current liabilities* is used principally to designate obligations whose *liquidation* (payment or settlement) is reasonably expected to require the use of current assets or the creation (substitution) of other current liabilities.[1]

All liabilities to be paid within a one-year period are classified as current. In general, current liabilities are listed on the statement of financial position in their probable order of liquidation; those that, on the average, will be paid first are shown first, those to be paid next are next, and so on. Typical current liabilities are the following:

[1] AICPA, *Accounting Principles*, Vol. II. Chicago: Commerce Clearing House, Inc., 1970, p. 6011.

Accounts Payable. Accounts payable represent amounts owed to creditors resulting from purchases on open account, or on credit. If creditors are few, their names may be listed separately on the statement of financial position. If creditors are numerous, the statement of financial position shows only the total amount of accounts payable. A separate record is kept for each creditor.

Notes Payable. A note payable is a formal written promise to pay money to a creditor for value received. A *trade note payable* arises from the purchase of merchandise or services used in the course of business. A note payable to a bank arises when a company borrows money from a bank for business use. Generally these two items are *short-term* and are classified as current liabilities, unless the note is for more than one year.

Accrued Liabilities. Accrued wages payable and accrued interest payable are typical *accrued liabilities,* which are debts that are owed because of the passage of time but that will be paid in the future. These items are customarily placed last among the current liabilities.

Classification of Liabilities—Long-Term

Debts that are not due for at least a year are called *long-term,* or *fixed,* liabilities. A mortgage payable is a typical long-term liability. If a part of a long-term liability is due within a year from the statement of financial position date, the amount of that part should be shown as a current liability. There is no particular order in which long-term liabilities appear in the position statement; however, size may be one criterion as to the order that these items may appear under the long-term liability section.

Mortgage Payable. A mortgage payable is a debt owed by the business that is secured by a specific asset or assets. The legal document by which the debt is secured is called a *mortgage.* A business may arrange a long-term loan with a bank, for example, and give a mortgage on its land and building to the bank as security. If the business fails to meet the terms of payment of the mortgage, the bank can take necessary legal action to take possession of the asset, or to sell it and satisfy the mortgage claim from the proceeds of the sale. Any balance remaining from the sale of the asset reverts to the business.

Bonds Payable. As a means of raising funds, corporations issue *bonds,* which are long-term promises to repay loans. These obligations may or may not be secured by assets of the borrowing company. Many corporations have excellent credit ratings and therefore do not need to offer specific security for loans.

Owner's Equity on the Statement of Financial Position

The form of a business organization determines the manner of reporting the owner's equity on the statement of financial position. The three common forms of business organization are (1) corporations, (2) single proprietorships, and (3) partnerships. The ownership interest in each of these organizational forms is disclosed in a slightly different manner on the statement of financial position.

A corporation is a separate legal entity, created by a *charter* from the state in which it is organized, that is owned by several *stockholders*. Each stockholder owns a certain portion of the corporation, expressed in *shares of stock. Stock certificates* are issued to him as evidence of his ownership. The *investments*, or contributions to the business, of all the stockholders are grouped under the term *capital stock*. Shares may be issued at *par*, which is the face value decided upon by the organizers and stated in the charter, or at a *premium* or *discount*.

The primary advantage of the corporation to its owners is that the stockholders' personal assets cannot be taken by creditors to satisfy the debts of the business; only the assets of the business itself can be taken. There are also other significant legal advantages, which will be studied in later chapters. In turn, corporations are subject to special governmental regulation and taxation. Because the corporate form is the most important form of business ownership today, it is stressed throughout this text. Moreover, the use of the simple form of corporate ownership accentuates the entity concept of accounting. However, at the end of each introductory chapter the procedures applicable to the single proprietorship are presented. Corporations and partnerships are discussed in detail in later chapters.

The profits of the corporation may be distributed to the stockholders in the form of *dividends*, or they may be retained in the corporation. The part that is kept is referred to as *retained earnings*. Retained earnings are not a part of the capital stock, but are a part of the total stockholders' equity. They represent the accumulated undistributed earnings of the corporation—that is, the total profits of the business from the date it was organized less the total dividends and losses that have been sustained during the same period. Retained earnings must be accounted for separately from the capital stock because of the legal restrictions placed on the original capital contributions of corporations.

Corporation. The owners' equity section of a position statement for a corporation is shown as

Stockholders' Equity		
Capital Stock	$20,000	
Retained Earnings	570	
Total Stockholders' Equity		$20,570

Single Proprietorship. Many businesses are owned by individuals; they are referred to as *single proprietorships*. If a business is small and its operations are comparatively simple, the single-proprietorship form of ownership offers several advantages over the corporate form: The owner has a more direct control of the business, he does not have to report to several stockholders, and the business is not subject to the special regulations and taxes for corporations. But his personal assets can be taken as payment of the debts of the business. Careful management will, of course, minimize the chances of such an event.

If Douglas Murrow owned the Murrow Clothing Store as a single proprietorship, his equity would be shown on the statement of financial position as follows:

Owner's Equity
Douglas Murrow, Capital $20,570

The owner's equity for the single proprietorship is listed with the name of the proprietor, followed by the word "Capital." The total owner's equity may be shown as one item because there are no legal restrictions on withdrawals by a single proprietor as there are for the stockholders of a corporation.

Partnership. Often several individuals find it advantageous to form a business by establishing a *partnership.* In this case, the owners are the *partners* of the business. The advantages of a partnership are similar to those of a single proprietorship, with the added advantages of a greater amount of capital from several partners and the different abilities that the partners can bring to the management of the business. The primary disadvantage of the partnership is that each partner is personally responsible for all the debts of the business.

If Douglas Murrow and John Wells owned the Murrow Clothing Store as partners, their equity would be shown on the statement of financial position as follows:

Partners' Equity
Douglas Murrow, Capital $10,085
John Wells, Capital   10,485
Total Partners' Equity $20,570

Management Studies of the Statement of Financial Position

To provide information that will be of maximum assistance in decision making, an accountant must present financial data in a form and manner that make them meaningful and useful. The absolute amounts contained in the statement of financial position for the Murrow Clothing Store are quite useful to management, but they tell only part of the story. For example, a total current asset amount of $30,910 indicates a certain purchasing-power command over goods and services, but how adequate is this amount for the Murrow Clothing Store? The data begin to become more meaningful when they are compared with other related information of this or past years. The following relationships revealed by position statements are critical in making managerial decisions.

The Current Ratio

The relationship of current assets to current liabilities gives some indication of the firm's ability to pay its current debts as they mature. This relationship is called the *current ratio;* it is computed by dividing the current assets by the current liabilities. The current ratio of the Murrow Clothing Store is computed as in Figure 1-3.

Figure 1-3. Computation of the Current Ratio

$$\frac{\text{Current Assets}}{\text{Current Liabilities}} = \frac{\$30,910}{\$15,090} = 2.05 \text{ to } 1$$

The Murrow Clothing Store has $2.05 of current assets for every $1 of current liabilities. This means that even if the current assets of the company were to shrink in value by as much as 50 percent, the short-term creditors could still be paid in full.

In the past, as a rule of thumb, a current ratio of 2 to 1 has been considered evidence of the satisfactory current financial condition of a company. Analysts, however, generally agree that no one ratio is sufficient and that certain other factors must be considered, such as the nature of the business, the season of the year, the composition of the specific items in the current assets category, and the quality of the management of the company.

Grantors of credit emphasize the relative convertibility of the current assets into cash. To illustrate, assume that the Amber Company and the Battle Company have the following current ratios:

	Amber Company	Battle Company
Current Assets		
Cash	$ 500	$ 2,000
Accounts Receivable	700	22,000
Merchandise Inventory	28,800	6,000
Total Current Assets	$30,000	$30,000
Current Liabilities		
Accounts Payable	$15,000	$15,000
Current Ratio	2 : 1	2 : 1

Although each company has a current ratio of 2 to 1, the Battle Company is apparently in a far better position to meet its obligations. The Amber Company first must sell its $28,800 merchandise inventory, then it must convert the resulting receivables into cash; or it can sell its inventory for cash as a single lot, probably for less than the stated value. The Battle Company has $24,000 in cash and receivables and only $6,000 in merchandise inventory, hence there is no conversion problem connected with the sale of inventory. The Amber Company thus may have a favorable current ratio but may be unable to pay its current liabilities due to an unfavorable distribution of the current assets.

Acid-Test Ratio

A supplementary test of the ability of a business to meet its current obligations is the acid-test ratio, which is expressed as follows:

$$\text{Acid-Test Ratio} = \frac{\text{Quick Assets}}{\text{Current Liabilities}}$$

Quick assets include only cash, readily marketable securities, and receivables. The acid-test ratio for the Murrow Clothing Store is computed as follows:

$$\frac{\text{Quick Assets}}{\text{Current Liabilities}} = \frac{(\$325 + \$1,900 + \$11,025 + \$2,520)}{\$15,090}$$

$$= \frac{\$15,770}{\$15,090}$$

$$= 1.05 \text{ to } 1$$

If the analyst is not satisfied with the current ratio as an indicator of liquidity, he may use the acid-test ratio, which does not consider merchandise inventory and prepaid items. If the quick assets are larger than the current liabilities (that is, if the acid-test ratio is better than 1 to 1), there is evidence of a strong short-term credit position and assurance that the company is able to meet its currently maturing obligations.

Working Capital

A term frequently used in financial-statement analysis is *working capital*, or *circulating capital*. Working capital is the difference between the current assets and the current liabilities. The working capital of the Murrow Clothing Store is

Current Assets — Current Liabilities = Working Capital
$30,910   — $15,090   = $15,820

The business has an excess of $15,820 to use in operations after the current assets are converted into cash and the current liabilities are paid.

An interesting comparison may be made relative to working-capital analysis, assuming the following information:

	Line	Carson Company	Dickinson Company
Current Assets	(a)	$200,000	$800,000
Current Liabilities	(b)	100,000	600,000
Working Capital	(a − b)	$100,000	$200,000
Current Ratio	(a ÷ b)	2:1	1.33:1

The Dickinson Company has twice as much working capital as the Carson Company, but its debt-paying ability is not as satisfactory. The relationship between current assets and current liabilities may be more significant than their difference.

Working capital flows through the business in a regular pattern; this flow may be diagramed as illustrated on the following page. As funds flow into the business, the management of the Murrow Clothing Store must make decisions about when, how much, and for what purpose the funds are to be used or put back into the flow cycle. This is the point at which management must apply its skill in making effective use of available working capital.

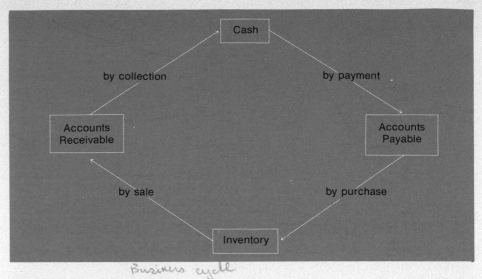

Business cycle

Ratio Analysis—Limitations

A particular ratio may be satisfactory under one set of circumstances and entirely unsatisfactory under another set of circumstances. Ratios are generalizations and reflect conditions that exist only at a particular time. The ratios change continually with the continuing operations of the business. Sole reliance on ratio analysis may at times give a misleading indication of financial condition. Often nonfinancial information must be analyzed in order to get a true picture, including the quality of the employees and employee-management relations. Understanding and correct interpretation of ratios, however, reduce the area over which subjective judgment must be exercised and thus aid the analyst in making sound decisions.

The ratios and comparisons discussed in this and subsequent chapters are valuable managerial aids, provided the user is aware of their limitations. The Murrow Clothing Store's current ratio of 2.05 to 1, computed in Figure 1-3, shows the relationship between two groups of items as of a given moment of time only. The ratio may fluctuate considerably during the course of the year. Furthermore, the ratio may have little meaning unless it is related to the entire business unit. It is like one small section of a painting, which has little meaning without the rest of the picture. If one states, for example, that Paul Clifford is an excellent student, we know very little about him. If we are told that he is 22 years old, is in the upper 5 percent of his class, and is president of Beta Gamma Sigma and captain of the basketball team, we know a good deal more about him. Similarly, if we state that both the Atwater Company and the Excel Company have current ratios of 2 to 1, it does not mean too much until the acid-test ratio and specific composition of the current assets are known.

SUMMARY

Accounting is the process of recording the financial transactions of a business, classifying them in an orderly manner, summarizing them in the form of reports and statements useful to management, and interpreting the results and the significance of the statements and reports. The primary objectives of accounting are (a) to provide meaningful information about the business enterprise for interested parties and (b) to safeguard the properties of the enterprise by the establishment of an adequate and reliable system of accounting.

For data recording purposes, each business enterprise is to be considered a separate unit, or entity, with the affairs of the business and the personal affairs of the owners being kept entirely separate (the *entity concept*). Three primary components of the business entity about which accounting provides information are (a) *assets*, or the properties of the business, (b) *liabilities*, or the amounts that the business owes, and (c) *owners' equity*, or the claims that the owners have on the properties of the business.

The *accounting equation*, the fundamental model upon which accounting is built, states that assets equal equities. In an expanded form this equation is referred to as the *statement of financial position*, or balance sheet, which summarizes the assets, liabilities, and owners' equity of a business entity at a specific point in time. To be of maximum use, the individual items reflected on this statement must be classified in an orderly and meaningful manner. Assets are generally classified as (a) *current assets*, or cash and other assets that will be converted to cash or will be consumed in the operations of the business within one year, and (b) *plant and equipment*, or physical assets that have a relatively long life and are used in the operation of the business. Liabilities are typically classified as (a) *current liabilities*, or obligations whose liquidation requires the use of a current asset or the creation of another current liability within a year, and (b) *long-term liabilities*, or obligations that are not due within the next year.

The three most common forms of business organization are *single proprietorships*, *partnerships*, and *corporations*.

For accounting information to be of maximum use, absolute amounts classified in a meaningful manner and analyses setting forth the significance of the information so classified must be provided. Three tools often used in analyzing accounting information are (a) the *current ratio*, which is computed by dividing the current assets by the current liabilities; (b) the *acid-test ratio*, which is computed by dividing the quick assets by the current liabilities; and (c) *working capital*, or the excess of current assets over current liabilities. These tools give some indication of the firm's ability to meet its current obligations as they mature.

QUESTIONS

Q1-1. Discuss the role of accounting in society.

Q1-2. What is the entity concept? Identify the ways in which this concept aids the accounting function.

Q1-3. Define and give three examples of each of the following terms: (a) assets, (b) liabilities, (c) owner's equity.

Q1-4. What are current assets? Give five examples. In what order should these items be listed on the statement of financial position?

Q1-5. What is the purpose of the statement of financial position?

Q1-6. What is plant and equipment? Give five examples.

Q1-7. What are current liabilities? Give five examples.

Q1-8. Give the equation for: (a) the current ratio, (b) the acid-test ratio, (c) working capital.

Q1-9. What is the major purpose of each item listed in Question 1-8?

Q1-10. On December 31, 1973, the Anson Company had a current ratio of 3 to 1, and the Baker Company had a current ratio of 2 to 1. Is the Anson Company in a better financial position to pay its accounts payable when they are due than the Baker Company is? Discuss.

EXERCISES

E1-1. Assume that a firm has the following items at the end of the year:

Total Assets	$305,000	Retained Earnings	$32,500
Total Long-Term Liabilities	45,600	Current Assets	50,000
Capital Stock	100,000		

Compute the amount of current liabilities.

E1-2. The books of the Ames Company contain the following items:

Retained Earnings	$50,000	Accounts Receivable	$4,500
Cash	30,000	Accounts Payable	3,200
Capital Stock	75,000	Prepaid Insurance	800

Select the current assets and prepare in good form the Current Assets section of the statement of financial position as of December 31, 1973.

E1-3. The books of the Boston Company contain the following items:

Cash	$ 5,850	Bonds Payable (due July 1, 1993)	$50,000
Land	10,000	Delivery Equipment	10,000
John Barnes, Capital	100,000	Office Supplies	1,000
Building	160,000		

Select the plant and equipment items and prepare in good form the Plant and Equipment section of the statement of financial position as of December 31, 1973.

E1-4. The books of the Caye Company contain the following items:

Accounts Receivable	$ 3,420	Accrued Wages Payable	$ 1,230
Accounts Payable	12,860	Retained Earnings	42,680
Notes Receivable	1,950	Bonds Payable (due July 1, 1993)	30,000
Notes Payable	2,000		

Select the current liabilities and prepare in good form the Current Liabilities section of the statement of financial position as of December 31, 1973.

E1-5. The following condensed statement was prepared for the Dawson Company as of December 31, 1973:

DAWSON COMPANY
Statement of Financial Position
December 31, 1973

Assets

Current Assets	$ 30,000
Plant and Equipment	100,000
Total Assets	$130,000

Liabilities and Stockholders' Equity

Current Liabilities		$ 7,500
Long-Term Liabilities		30,000
Total Liabilities		$ 37,500
Stockholders' Equity		92,500
Total Liabilities and Stockholders' Equity		$130,000

(a) Compute (1) the current ratio and (2) the working capital. (b) Explain the significance of each to management.

E1-6. Assume that the Dawson Company (see Exercise E1-5) has the following current assets: cash, $2.000; marketable securities, $1,500; accounts receivable, $14,000; merchandise inventory, $10,000; and prepaid insurance, $2,500. Compute the acid-test ratio and explain its significance to management.

E1-7. Assume that a firm has total assets of $260,000 and total liabilities of $142,000 at the end of the year. Compute the owner's equity.

E1-8. Assume that a firm has current assets, $47,500; current liabilities, $15,000; long-term liabilities, $50,000; and stockholders' equity, $100,000 at the end of the year. Compute the amount of plant and equipment.

E1-9. The following financial information is available for the Agustian Company as of December 31, 1973:

Marketable Securities	$10,000	Accounts Payable	$ 35,000
Accounts Receivable	40,000	Cash on Hand	2,000
Wages Payable	60,000	Cash in Bank	125,000
Buildings	60,000	Retained Earnings	?
Prepaid Insurance	1,000	Land	20,000
Inventories	80,000	Bonds Payable	150,000
Capital Stock	50,000		

Prepare a statement of financial position for the Agustian Company.

E1-10. The following statement of financial position was prepared by the bookkeeper of the Hoosery Company:

HOOSERY COMPANY
Statement of Financial Position
For the Year Ended December 31, 1973

Assets

Current Assets		
Cash	$ 2,000	
Accounts Receivable	6,000	
Building	12,000	
Merchandise Inventory	3,000	
Total Current Assets		$23,000
Plant and Equipment		
Marketable Securities	$ 3,000	
Store Equipment	1,500	
Office Supplies	100	
Delivery Equipment	1,350	
Total Plant and Equipment		5,950
Total Assets		$28,950

Liabilities and Owner's Equity

Current Liabilities		
Accounts Payable	$ 6,600	
Notes Payable (due June 1, 1974)	2,000	
Notes Payable (due July 1, 1994)	1,000	
Total Current Liabilities		$ 9,600
Long-Term Liabilities		
Mortgage Payable (due May 1, 1995)	$ 8,000	
Accrued Wages and Salaries Payable	250	
Total Long-Term Liabilities		8,250
Total Liabilities		$17,850
Owner's Equity		
B. A. Hoosery, Capital		11,100
Total Liabilities and Assets		$28,950

List the errors in this statement.

DEMONSTRATION PROBLEMS

DP1-1. (*Corporate account-form statement of financial position*) The following alphabetical list is taken from the records of the Jason Company at December 31, 1973:

Accounts Payable	$ 25,000	Merchandise Inventory	$ 60,000
Accounts Receivable	38,000	Mortgage Payable (due July 1, 1993)	180,000
Building	300,000	Notes Payable	10,000
Capital Stock	200,000	Notes Receivable	8,000
Cash	150,000	Prepaid Insurance	2,000
Delivery Equipment	40,000	Retained Earnings	194,000
Land	15,000	Wages Payable	4,000

Required: Prepare an account-form statement of financial position.

DP1-2. (*Liabilities and owner's equity—single-proprietorship statement of financial position*) Refer to Problem DP1-1. Assume that the Jason Company is a single proprietorship, operated by John T. Jason.

Required: Show how the right side of an account-form statement of financial position would appear.

DP1-3. (*Liabilities and partners' equity—partnership statement of financial position*) Again refer to Problem DP1-1. Assume that the Jason Company is a partnership owned and operated by Ray M. Jason and John T. Jason and that the two partners have equities as shown:

Ray M. Jason	$170,000
John T. Jason	224,000
Total	$394,000

Required: Show how the right side of the statement of financial position would appear.

DP1-4. (*Ratio analysis*) Using the data in Problem DP1-1, compute the current ratio, working capital, and acid-test ratio for the Jason Company. Explain the significance of each to management.

P1-1. On December 31, 1973, the assets, liabilities, and stockholders' equity of the Johnson Company are as follows:

Assets (in alphabetical order)		
Accounts Receivable		$ 19,000
Building		50,000
Cash		20,000
Equipment		60,000
Land		10,000
Marketable Securities		45,000
Merchandise Inventory		20,000
Supplies		9,000
Liabilities (in alphabetical order)		
Accounts Payable		20,000
Bonds Payable (due July 1, 1995)		45,000
Dividends Payable		4,000
Interest Payable		6,000
Stockholders' Equity		
Capital Stock		150,000
Retained Earnings		?

Required: Prepare a properly classified account-form statement of financial position.

P1-2. The following is an alphabetical list of the assets, liabilities, and owner's equity of the Mitre Company, a single proprietorship, as of December 31, 1973:

Accounts Payable	$ 15,500
Accounts Receivable	17,300
Building	100,000
Cash	65,000
Delivery Equipment	22,400
Land	10,600
Long-Term Notes Payable (due August 1, 2000)	75,000
Marketable Securities	4,800
Merchandise Inventory	33,500
Mortgage Payable (due March 1, 1985)	40,000
Notes Payable	5,250
Peter Mitre, Capital	?
Prepaid Insurance	1,000
Salaries Payable	500

Required: Prepare a properly classified report-form statement of financial position.

P1-3. (*Financial policy decision problem*) The following list contains all the current assets and current liabilities of the Lawter Company as of December 31, 1973. The list also contains some noncurrent items.

Accounts Payable	$ 4,800	Merchandise Inventory	$50,000
Accounts Receivable	12,200	Mortgage Payable (due July 1, 2000)	75,000
Cash	5,500	Notes Payable (due July 1, 1974)	19,400
Land	20,000	Prepaid Insurance	2,400
Marketable Securities	5,500	Salaries Payable	1,000

Required:

1. Compute the current ratio, the acid-test ratio, and the working capital.
2. Assume that you are the loan officer of a bank to which the Lawter Company has applied for a 90-day loan of $15,000. Would you grant the loan? Why? Compute the current ratio,

acid-test ratio, and working capital for the Lawter Company immediately following the receipt of the loan.

P1-4. The following lists show selected statement totals for four different firms: W, X, Y, and Z. In each case, the amount is omitted for one total.

	W	X	Y	Z
Current Assets	$100,000	$ 72,000	$?	$ 20,000
Plant and Equipment	200,000	130,000	71,500	200,000
Current Liabilities	50,000	10,000	5,000	10,750
Long-term Liabilities	75,000	?	25,500	61,400
Capital Stock	175,000	50,000	100,000	?
Retained Earnings	?	20,000	6,500	10,850

Required: In each case, compute the missing figure.

P1-5. The assets, liabilities, and owner's equity of the Toomes Company as of December 31, 1973, are as follows:

Cash	$ 5,600	Building	$13,000
Accounts Receivable	15,200	Land	5,000
Notes Receivable	3,000	Accounts Payable	10,000
Merchandise Inventory	5,600	Notes Payable	7,500
Office Supplies	200	Mortgage Payable (due Feb. 1, 1986)	8,000
Prepaid Insurance	400	Wesley J. Toomes, Capital	26,000
Store Equipment	3,500		

Required:

1. Prepare a report-form statement of financial position.
2. Compute the current ratio, the acid-test ratio, and the working capital.

P1-6. (*Accounting policy decision problem*) Since his graduation from Central High School ten years ago, Joseph Hudson has been employed by small businesses such as grocery stores, drugstores, and service stations. He has developed a good reputation among his various employers for his honesty, industriousness, and dependability. Many of his employers' customers have praised his friendliness, sincerity, and fairness in handling their transactions.

Hudson has often thought of having his own business; his dream is now materializing. He plans to lease a building and some equipment from Claude Walters. The building is on the outskirts of town but very near a developing middle-class residential area. Moreover, a relatively busy new highway, which connects the city with a nearby lake, is in front of the building. Hudson believes that the building will be an excellent location for a combination service station, grocery, and soda fountain.

The building to be leased has adequate downstairs space for all the needs of the business, including a storage area. The building also contains a spacious five-room upstairs apartment, which Hudson plans to use as a home for his family of three (his wife and two children). A shady, grassy area is behind the building, and he plans to enclose it with a fence so that the children will have a safe place to play.

Hudson has decided that the front of the building needs to be changed in order to make it more attractive and that the entire interior (downstairs and upstairs) needs painting. Because the building is made of brick, only the outside trim will require painting. All this work is to be done by a local contractor.

The lease, which provides for the use of the building and lot, includes a clause permitting the purchase of the premises or the renewal of the lease in five years. A deposit is required on signing the lease and a fixed rental must be paid at the beginning of each month.

Much of the equipment needed by the service station and grocery is leased along with the building. However, arrangements must be made for supplementary equipment and for all the equipment for the soda fountain. Individual pieces of equipment may be either purchased or leased. Hudson prefers to purchase all the equipment if his personal savings and his available lines of credit permit.

Several years ago, Hudson purchased an old pickup truck that he has used almost exclusively for fishing and hunting trips. In order to save money now, he plans to use this truck as needed in the operation of the service station. He will still use it for sporting trips when he can spare the time. Someday he hopes to buy a new truck for the station.

Hudson's wife, Alice, has remarked about some of the advantages of their forthcoming living and working arrangements. She says it will be so much easier to get gas for the car and to have it serviced that she will surely not forget these needs as she usually does. She will also save time and money when shopping for groceries. It will be very convenient for the children to get ice cream and drinks, as all they will need to do is to go downstairs. Mrs. Hudson also plans to let one of the service station mechanics clean the children's yard occassionally when business at the station is slack. She also plans to help by working in the store for two or three hours each day, or whenever she is needed.

In view of the encouragement Hudson has received from neighbors and the flow of automobile traffic in the area, he expects a large amount of business. Consequently, he plans to hire two employees to attend the service station during each of the two 8-hour shifts (7 AM to 3 PM; 3 PM to 11 PM). More will be hired when the need arises. The remainder of the business will be open from 9 AM to 7 PM; in the beginning he expects to employ one cashier, one stock attendant, one grocery attendant, and one soda-fountain attendant. He and Alice plan to work wherever they are needed, except that Alice will not work in the service station area. Hudson will also supervise the entire business.

Required:

1. Identify the meaning of the entity concept.
2. Identify and discuss the relevance of this concept to Joseph Hudson's plans.
3. Discuss the problems regarding the entity concept that Hudson will undoubtedly encounter.
4. Of the expenditures that Hudson will make while organizing and operating his business, which are properly classifiable as business expenditures and which as personal expenditures? Explain why you classified each one as you did.
5. Suggest some ways of resolving the difficulties or problems that you identified in requirement 3.

2

Basic Methodology—
Position Statement
Accounts

To obtain the data needed to prepare statements of financial position, an orderly accounting system must be developed. This chapter describes several possible systems, leading up to a discussion of the one in general use in modern business.

In this and the following two chapters, *service businesses*, which sell services rather than merchandise, will be used as examples. Service businesses are good first illustrations of the operation of an accounting system because they do not offer the added complications of the inventories required in *merchandising businesses*.

All businesses go through a period of organization, during which the owners make an investment, acquire plant and equipment, and get ready to operate. The transactions involved in the organization of the Whitside Realty Corporation follow.

1973

July 1 The Whitside Realty Corporation was organized by John Whitside, Ronald Raymond, and James Baker. The charter (proper legal authorization) was received from the Secretary of State, and capital stock in the amount of $50,000 was issued at par (sold for face amount) for cash; that is, the stockholders—Whitside, Raymond, and Baker—made an investment of $50,000 in the business. Whitside invested $40,000; Raymond, $6,000; and Baker, $4,000.

5 Purchased land and building for $30,000 in cash. The land was appraised at $5,000; the building, at $25,000.

10 Purchased furniture on account from the Jones Company for $8,000.

20 Paid the Jones Company $5,000 on account.

25 The corporation found that part of the furniture was not of the type that it wanted. It sold furniture that had cost $1,800 to James Hill for $1,800 on account. Hill promised to pay this amount in 30 days.

31 Collected $1,000 from James Hill on account.

The following discussion is based on these transactions.

24

PREPARATION OF A STATEMENT OF FINANCIAL POSITION AFTER EACH TRANSACTION

Since the statement of financial position is an expanded variation of the accounting equation, it is obvious that the total of the separate sides are always equal. A possible solution to the problem of accumulating data is the preparation of a statement of financial position immediately after each transaction.

Issuance of Capital Stock

The statement of financial position shown in Figure 2-1 would be prepared after the three stockholders incorporate their business and the capital stock of $50,000 has been issued. (In this chapter, the account form of position statement is used to show the effect of each transaction on each side of the accounting equation.)

Figure 2-1. After Original Investment

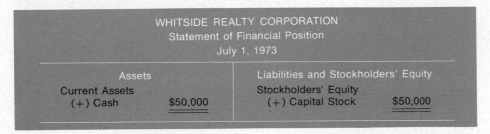

WHITSIDE REALTY CORPORATION	
Statement of Financial Position	
July 1, 1973	
Assets	**Liabilities and Stockholders' Equity**
Current Assets	Stockholders' Equity
(+) Cash $50,000	(+) Capital Stock $50,000

This transaction involves an increase of an asset, Cash, accompanied by an increase in a stockholders' equity item, Capital Stock. The plus and minus signs show the direction of change of each item in the transaction; *they would not be part* of an actual statement.

Purchase of Land and Building

A statement of financial position prepared after the land and building are purchased appears in Figure 2-2.

Figure 2-2. After Purchase of Land and Building

WHITSIDE REALTY CORPORATION				
Statement of Financial Position				
July 5, 1973				
Assets			**Liabilities and Stockholders' Equity**	
Current Assets			Stockholders' Equity	
( ) Cash		$20,000	Capital Stock	$50,000
Plant and Equipment				
(+) Land	$ 5,000			
(+) Building	25,000			
Total Plant and Equipment		30,000		
Total Assets		$50,000	Total Stockholders' Equity	$50,000

This transaction involves increases of assets, Land and Building, accompanied by a decrease of an asset, Cash, with no change occurring in the stockholders' equity.

Purchase of Furniture on Account

The statement prepared after the corporation purchases furniture on account from the Jones Company is shown in Figure 2-3.

Figure 2-3. After Purchase of Furniture on Account

WHITSIDE REALTY CORPORATION
Statement of Financial Position
July 10, 1973

Assets			Liabilities and Stockholders' Equity	
Current Assets			Current Liabilities	
Cash		$20,000	(+) Accounts Payable	$ 8,000
Plant and Equipment			Stockholders' Equity	
Land	$ 5,000		Capital Stock	50,000
Building	25,000			
(+) Furniture	8,000			
Total Plant and Equipment		38,000	Total Liabilities and	
Total Assets		$58,000	Stockholders' Equity	$58,000

This transaction involves an increase of an asset, Furniture, accompanied by an increase of a liability, Accounts Payable, with no change occurring in the stockholders' equity.

Payment of Accounts Payable

The statement of financial position appearing in Figure 2-4 is prepared after the corporation pays $5,000 in cash to the Jones Company on account.

Figure 2-4. After Partial Payment of Accounts Payable

WHITSIDE REALTY CORPORATION
Statement of Financial Position
July 20, 1973

Assets			Liabilities and Stockholders' Equity	
Current Assets			Current Liabilities	
(−) Cash		$15,000	(−) Accounts Payable	$ 3,000
Plant and Equipment			Stockholders' Equity	
Land	$ 5,000		Capital Stock	50,000
Building	25,000			
Furniture	8,000			
Total Plant and Equipment		38,000	Total Liabilities and	
Total Assets		$53,000	Stockholders' Equity	$53,000

The transaction reflected in this statement involves a decrease of a liability, Accounts Payable, accompanied by a decrease of an asset, Cash.

Sale of Furniture on Account

After the corporation sells the furniture on account to James Hill, the statement of financial position shown in Figure 2-5 is prepared.

Figure 2-5. After Sale of Furniture on Account

WHITSIDE REALTY CORPORATION Statement of Financial Position July 25, 1973				
Assets			**Liabilities and Stockholders' Equity**	
Current Assets			Current Liabilities	
Cash	$15,000		Accounts Payable	$ 3,000
(+) Accounts Receivable	1,800		Stockholders' Equity	
Total Current Assets		$16,800	Capital Stock	50,000
Plant and Equipment				
Land	$ 5,000			
Building	25,000			
(−) Furniture	6,200			
Total Plant and Equipment		36,200	Total Liabilities and	
Total Assets		$53,000	Stockholders' Equity	$53,000

    1. The amount of money to be received from James Hill is reflected as an asset, Accounts Receivable. It is a current asset because it is collectible within a year.

    2. This transaction involves an increase of an asset, Accounts Receivable, accompanied by a decrease of an asset, Furniture. It is similar in nature to the transaction of July 5 (Figure 2-2).

    3. The furniture was sold at·cost. If it had been sold at a price above its cost, a stockholders' equity item, Retained Earnings, would have been increased by the amount of the gain.

Collection of Accounts Receivable

After James Hill makes a payment of $1,000, the statement of financial position shown in Figure 2-6 is prepared.

    As in Figure 2-5, this transaction involves an increase of an asset, Cash, accompanied by a decrease of an asset, Accounts Receivable.

    The method of accumulating accounting data illustrated thus far gives the desired results, but in most instances the time and expense involved would prohibit its use. In addition, a statement of financial position prepared after each transaction is not needed by those who use accounting information as a guide to action. A statement of financial position prepared at the end of each month is usually sufficient.

Figure 2-6. After Collection of Accounts Receivable

WHITSIDE REALTY CORPORATION
Statement of Financial Position
July 31, 1973

Assets			Liabilities and Stockholders' Equity	
Current Assets			Current Liabilities	
(+) Cash	$16,000		Accounts Payable	$ 3,000
(−) Accounts Receivable	800		Stockholders' Equity	
Total Current Assets		$16,800	Capital Stock	50,000
Plant and Equipment				
Land	$ 5,000			
Building	25,000			
Furniture	6,200			
Total Plant and Equipment		36,200	Total Liabilities and	
Total Assets		$53,000	Stockholders' Equity	$53,000

Figure 2-7. Expanded Accounting Equation

WHITSIDE REALTY CORPORATION
Expanded Accounting Equation Revealing Financial Position
For Month Ended July 31, 1973

Date	Business Transaction	Cash +	Accounts Receivable +	Land +	Building +	Furniture =	Accounts Payable +	Capital Stock
1973								
July 1	Issued capital stock for $50,000 in cash.	+ $50,000				=		+ $50,000
5	Purchased land and building for $30,000 in cash. Land is appraised at $5,000; building, at $25,000.	−30,000		+ $5,000	+ $25,000			
	Balances	$20,000 +		$5,000 +	$25,000	=		$50,000
10	Purchased furniture on account from the Jones Company for $8,000.					+ $8,000 =	+ $8,000	
	Balances	$20,000 +		$5,000 +	$25,000 +	$8,000 =	$8,000 +	$50,000
20	Paid the Jones Company $5,000 on account.	−5,000					−5,000	
	Balances	$15,000 +		$5,000 +	$25,000 +	$8,000 =	$3,000 +	$50,000
25	Sold furniture at cost to James Hill for $1,800 on account.		+ $1,800			−1,800		
	Balances	$15,000 +	$1,800	$5,000 +	$25,000 +	$6,200 =	$3,000 +	$50,000
31	Collected $1,000 from James Hill on account.	+ 1,000	−1,000					
	Balances	$16,000 +	$ 800	$5,000 +	$25,000 +	$6,200 =	$3,000 +	$50,000

EXPANSION OF THE ACCOUNTING EQUATION

Since the procedure described in the foregoing section is cumbersome, a better methodology is called for. Using the basic accounting equation, developed in Chapter 1, it is possible to show how each transaction will affect the statement of financial position and yet have all six of the transactions combined in one document. In Figure 2-7, the balances are brought down after each transaction and form an equation from which a formal statement similar to Figure 2-6 could be prepared.

After each transaction, the total of the Asset columns equals the total of the Liabilities and Stockholders' Equity columns. For example, after the July 25 transaction, the asset total of $53,000 ($15,000 + $1,800 + $5,000 + $25,000 + $6,200) equals the liabilities and stockholders' equity total of $53,000 ($3,000 + $50,000). A formal statement of financial position could be prepared from Figure 2-7 after the July 31 transaction by simply arranging the various assets, liabilities, and stockholders' equity items in the form illustrated in Figure 2-6.

Although this method tends to shorten the accounting process, it is unsuitable for most companies because it cannot easily be expanded to provide for a large number of asset and liability items. For example, it would be virtually impossible to use this procedure in a company that has 50 assets and 25 liabilities.

A SEPARATE PAGE FOR EACH COMPONENT OF THE ACCOUNTING EQUATION

One answer to the problem of an expanded number of assets and liabilities is to designate a separate page for each asset, liability, and stockholders' equity item. Using the six transactions of the Whitside Realty Corporation, this method may be illustrated as follows:

ASSET PAGES

Cash		Page 101
1973		
July 1	Contribution of stockholders	+$50,000
5	Purchase of land and building	− 30,000
20	Payment to Jones Company on account	− 5,000
31	Collection from James Hill	+ 1,000
	(Cash on hand $16,000)	

Accounts Receivable (James Hill)		Page 111
1973		
July 25	Sale of furniture on account	+$1,800
31	Collection on account	− 1,000
	(Balance due $800)	

Land		Page 151
1973		
July 5	Purchase of land	+$5,000

Building	Page 152
1973	
July 5 Purchase of building	+$25,000

Furniture	Page 157
1973	
July 10 Purchase of furniture on account	+$8,000
20 Sale of furniture at cost	− 1,800
(Furniture on hand $6,200)	

LIABILITY PAGES

Accounts Payable (Jones Company)	Page 201
1973	
July 10 Purchased furniture on account	+$8,000
20 Payment on account	− 5,000
(Balance due $3,000)	

STOCKHOLDERS' EQUITY PAGES

Capital Stock	Page 251
1973	
July 1 Issued capital stock to three stockholders	+$50,000

A comment about the page numbering system should be made. The pages could be numbered 1, 2, 3, 4, 5, 6, 7; but if the numbers are to have a specific meaning—for example, 100–199 for assets, 200–249 for liabilities, and 250–299 for stockholders' equity items—and if expansion is contemplated (the insertion of new pages for new items), then the numbering system should be something like the one shown.

At the end of a designated period, the *balance*, or final amount, of each page may be obtained by adding the plus items and the minus items and subtracting the total of the minus items from the total of the plus items. These balances can then be arranged as a formal statement of financial position as shown in Figure 2-6.

This procedure does permit unlimited expansion, but the use of the plus and minus signs contributes to mathematical errors, and there is no economical way to run a mathematical check on the accuracy of the items contained in the accounting equation. Something else needs to be done to the system.

DIVISION OF SEPARATE PAGES INTO COLUMNS— CREATION OF ACCOUNTS

A possible solution to the problem is the division of the pages, referred to in accounting as *accounts*, into two sections by drawing a line down the middle of the page and using both sides to record financial information pertaining to the particular item for which the account is maintained. The accounting equation

Assets = Liabilities + Stockholders' Equity

suggests the following arrangement: Assets appear on the left side of the equation; therefore, the left side of the account is used to record increases of assets, and the opposite side, the right side, is used to record decreases. Similarly, since liabilities and the stockholders' equity appear on the right side of the accounting equation, the right side is used to record increases in liability and stockholders' equity accounts, and the opposite side, the left side, is used to record decreases.

A diagram of this kind of account is shown:

		Account Title				Account Number
Date	Explanation	Amount	Date	Explanation		Amount
	Use this side to record increases in assets and decreases in liability and stockholders' equity items.			Use this side to record decreases in assets and increases in liability and stockholders' equity items.		

Again using the six transactions of the Whitside Realty Corporation, the added feature of the accounting system is demonstrated. Before the information is placed in the accounts, each transaction is analyzed in the light of the foregoing suggestions for recording the information.

1973
July 1 The Whitside Realty Corporation was organized and capital stock was issued for cash in the amount of $50,000. Cash, an asset, is increased by $50,000, and Capital Stock, a stockholders' equity item, is likewise increased. The $50,000 is placed on the left side of the asset account, Cash, to indicate that it has been increased, and the same figure is placed on the right side of the Stockholders' Equity account to indicate that it also has been increased.

      5 Purchased land and building for $30,000 in cash. The land was appraised at $5,000; the building, at $25,000. Both land and building are assets; thus, the $5,000 and the $25,000 are placed on the left sides of the Land and Building Accounts, respectively, to reflect increases. The Cash account is decreased by $30,000; thus, this amount is placed on the right side of the Cash account.

     10 Purchased furniture on account from the Jones Company for $8,000. The asset Furniture is increased by $8,000; this amount is placed on the left side of the Furniture account. A liability account, Accounts Payable, is increased by the amount due the Jones Company; $8,000 is placed on the right side of the Accounts Payable account to indicate that it has been increased.

     20 Paid the Jones Company $5,000 on account. The liability Accounts Payable is decreased and the asset Cash is also decreased. The $5,000 is placed on the left side of the Accounts Payable account to record the decrease; the same figure is placed on the right side of the asset account, Cash, to reflect the decrease.

     25 Sold furniture that cost $1,800 to James Hill for $1,800 on account. The asset Accounts Receivable is increased by $1,800 and the asset Furniture is decreased by $1,800. The increase in the asset Accounts Receivable is shown by placing the amount on the left side of the Accounts Receivable account; and the decrease in the asset Furniture is shown by placing the amount on the right side of the Furniture account.

31 Collected $1,000 from James Hill on account. The asset Cash is increased by $1,000; the asset Accounts Receivable is decreased by $1,000. The increase of the asset Cash is shown by placing the $1,000 on the left side of the Cash account; the decrease of the asset Accounts Receivable is shown by placing the $1,000 on the right side of the Accounts Receivable account.

These transactions would appear in the accounts as shown:

Cash — Acct. No. 101

Date		Explanation	Amount	Date		Explanation	Amount
1973				1973			
July	1	Issuance of Capital Stock[1]	50,000	July	5	Purchased land & building	30,000
	31	Collection from Hill	1,000		20	Payment to Jones Co.	5,000
		(16,000)	51,000				35,000

Accounts Receivable (James Hill) — Acct. No. 111

Date		Explanation	Amount	Date		Explanation	Amount
1973				1973			
July	25	Sold furniture on account	1,800	July	31	Collection on account	1,000
		(800)					

Land — Acct. No. 151

Date		Explanation	Amount	Date		Explanation	Amount
1973							
July	5	Purchased land	5,000				

Building — Acct. No. 152

Date		Explanation	Amount	Date		Explanation	Amount
1973							
July	5	Purchased building	25,000				

Furniture — Acct. No. 157

Date		Explanation	Amount	Date		Explanation	Amount
1973				1973			
July	10	Purchased furniture on account	8,000	July	25	Sold furniture on account	1,800
		(6,200)					

Accounts Payable (Jones Company) — Acct. No. 201

Date		Explanation	Amount	Date		Explanation	Amount
1973				1973			
July	20	Paid on account	5,000	July	10	Purchased furniture on account	8,000
						(3,000)	

[1] After the journal is introduced, it will be evident that explanations in ledger accounts are rarely needed.

	Capital Stock					Acct. No. 251
Date	Explanation	Amount	Date		Explanation	Amount
			1973 July	1	Issued for cash	50,000

After all the information is recorded, the accounts are *footed*; that is, each amount column containing more than one entry is totaled in small pencil figures under the last amount on each side—see how the Cash account is handled. Then the balance of each account is determined by subtracting the smaller amount from the larger; the balance is then placed in the Explanation column of the side with the larger amount. As a check on the accuracy of the work in relation to the accounting equation, the total of the balances on the left sides of the accounts is compared to the total of the balances on the right sides. If the totals agree, it is presumed that the accounting is correct up to this point. This listing of account balances is called a _trial balance_ (illustrated in Figure 2-8). After the trial balance

Figure 2-8. Trial Balance

	WHITSIDE REALTY CORPORATION Trial Balance July 31, 1973		
Acct. No.	Account Title	Left-Side Balances	Right-Side Balances
101	Cash	$16,000	
111	Accounts Receivable	800	
151	Land	5,000	
152	Building	25,000	
157	Furniture	6,200	
201	Accounts Payable		$ 3,000
251	Capital Stock		50,000
	Totals	$53,000	$53,000

is found to be correct, a statement of financial position similar to Figure 2-6 can be prepared.

TOOLS OF ACCOUNTING

Before the final stage of the basic accounting methodology is discussed, the following accounting tools should be considered:

1. The T account
2. Debits and credits
3. The formal account

The T Account

The simplest form of any account is called a "T account" because of its shape. Owing to its simplicity, this form best clarifies the effects of transactions on a given account. As indicated in the preceding section, each account consists of a left side and a right side, with the title of the account written across the top. The left side of an account is called the *debit* side, and the right side of an account is called the *credit* side.

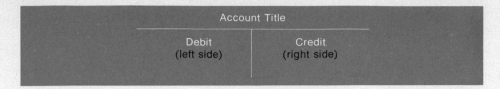

Account Title	
Debit (left side)	Credit (right side)

The terms "debit" and "credit" originally had a more specific meaning, related to *debtor* and *creditor* accounts; today they may be used as nouns, verbs, or adjectives depending on whether one is talking about an amount on the left side (*a debit*) or right side (*a credit*), the process of placing an amount on the left side (*to debit*) or the right side (*to credit*), or the characteristics of information on the left side (*a debit entry*) or the right side (*a credit entry*).

Substituting the terms "debit" and "credit" for the longer analytical description in the preceding section, the following rules may be stated:

Debit to record:	Credit to record:
An increase of an asset	A decrease of an asset
A decrease of a liability	An increase of a liability
A decrease in the stockholders' equity	An increase in the stockholders' equity

The relationship of the rules of debit and credit to the statement of financial position and to the accounting equation may be illustrated as follows:

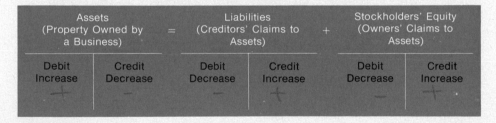

Assets (Property Owned by a Business)		=	Liabilities (Creditors' Claims to Assets)		+	Stockholders' Equity (Owners' Claims to Assets)	
Debit Increase	Credit Decrease		Debit Decrease	Credit Increase		Debit Decrease	Credit Increase

The abbreviation for credit is *Cr.*; for debit it is *Dr.*

The Formal Ledger Account

In actual business practice, the T account is expanded to a formal *ledger account*. A *ledger account* is a statistical device used for sorting accounting information into homogeneous groupings; it typically consists of two sides, with columns on each side for (1) the date, (2) an explanation, (3) the page number of the source from which the amount was transferred (called the *folio column*), and (4) the amount. A standard form of the ledger account is shown; the folio column is indicated by an F.

Cash							Acct. No. 101	
Date	Explanation	F	Debit	Date	Explanation	F	Credit	
						ͨ		

A variation of the T form is the three-money-column form, with Debit, Credit, and Balance columns. After each entry, the balance of the account may be computed and entered in the Balance column. This form is useful when frequent reference is made to the balance of the account.

A three-money-column account form is shown below.

Cash					Acct. No. 101
Date	Explanation	F	Debit	Credit	Balance

The book that contains all the accounts of a business is called the *ledger*.

DEVELOPMENT OF THE GENERAL JOURNAL AND POSTING

In the preceding sections of this chapter, the six transactions of the Whitside Realty Corporation were analyzed in terms of their effect on asset, liability, and stockholders' equity accounts, and the information was entered directly into the accounts. Records can be kept in this manner; however, most businesses need more detailed information as well as a means of ensuring a properly functioning and systematic procedure for the recording of transactions. The desired additional information includes a chronological record of transactions and a complete history of each transaction recorded *in one place.* It is often necessary to view a transaction in its entirety, including reference to the underlying documents and supporting papers. Since every entry consists of at least one debit and one credit, the transaction is recorded on different ledger pages. If the ledger contains many accounts, it may be difficult to reconstruct the complete transaction.

The recording process is commonly divided into two parts:

1. *Journalizing,* or recording transactions in a book called a *journal.* The record of a transaction in the journal is called a *journal entry.*

2. *Posting,* or transferring amounts in the journal to the correct accounts in the ledger.

Entering Transactions in the Journal

The following entry, in the basic form of a journal, the *general journal,* shows the July 1 transaction of the Whitside Realty Corporation.

GENERAL JOURNAL   Page 1

Date 1973	Debit — Credit — Explanation	F	Debit	Credit
July 1	Cash		50000 —	
	Capital Stock			50000 —
	To record the issuance of capital stock to John Whitside, Ronald Raymond, and James Baker.			

(A) → *1973*
(B) → *July*
(C) → *1*
(D) → *Cash*
(F) → *Capital Stock*
(H) → explanation
(E) → *50000 —*
(G) → *50000 —*

(A)   The year is written in small figures at the top of the Date column. It should be written in that position on every page of the journal.

(B)   The month of the first transaction recorded on this page is entered. It is not necessary to write the month again on this page unless it changes.

(C)   The day of each transaction is entered.

(D)   The title of the account debited is placed in the Explanation column against the date line. In order to eliminate confusion, it is important that the account title written in the journal entry should be the exact title of the account as it appears in the ledger.

(E)   The amount of the debit is entered in the Debit money column.

(F)   The title of the account credited is indented approximately ½ inch from the Date column.

(G)   The amount of the credit is entered in the Credit money column.

(H)   The explanation is entered on the next line, indented an additional ½ inch. The explanation should contain all the essential information as well as a reference to the source document from which the information was obtained—inspection report, receiving report, checkbook, and so on. (Since source documents are not illustrated in the first part of this text, the explanations of the illustrative journal entries do not always contain references to such documents.)

In journals, ledger accounts, and trial balances, the use of two zeros or a dash in the cents column is a matter of choice. Thus, an amount may be written 2,357.00 or 2,357.—. Many accountants feel that a dash is more easily written than two zeros, and that the use of dashes facilitates the addition of the cents column.

In a statement of financial position and other statements it is preferable, for the sake of appearance, to use zeros. In the interest of space and time, the zero column will be omitted in most of the journals, ledgers, and statements that are illustrated in the remaining pages of this book.

Dollar signs need not be written in journals and ledger accounts. They should be used in statements of financial position and other formal statements.

Posting from the General Journal

It should be emphasized that the journal does not *replace* the ledger account. The journal is called a *book of original entry* because it is necessary first to journalize the transaction and then to post to the proper accounts in the ledger (the *book of final entry*).

Figure 2-9 illustrates the posting of the July 1 entry from the general journal of the corporation to its ledger. Posting normally should be done once a day.

Figure 2-9. Posting Flow Chart

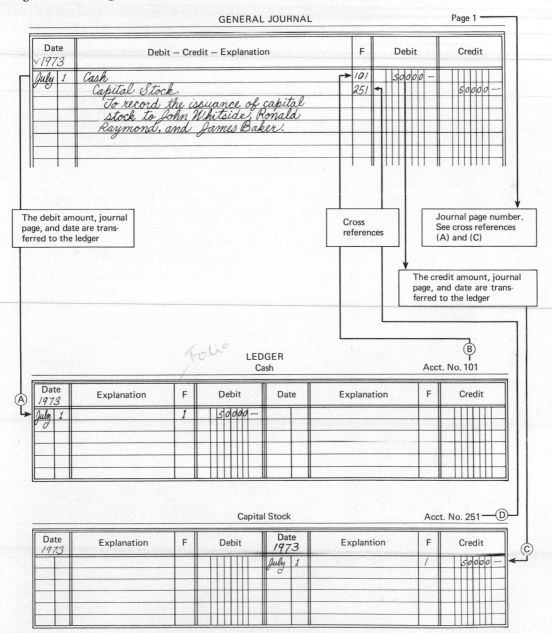

Explanations of encircled letters in Figure 2-9 follow:

(A)   The debit amount, $50,000; the journal page, 1; and the date, July 1, are entered on the debit side of the Cash account in the ledger. The year, 1973, is written at the top of the Date column. Dollar signs are not used in journals or ledgers.

(B)   The ledger account number for the debit entry, 101, is entered in the folio (F) column of the journal to cross reference the journal and ledger.

(C)   The credit amount, $50,000; the journal page, 1; and the date, July 1, are entered on the credit side of the Capital Stock account in the ledger. The year, 1973, is written at the top of the Date column.

(D)   The ledger account number for the credit entry, 251, is entered in the folio column of the journal to complete the cross referencing. It follows that the cross reference in the journal also indicates that the posting to the ledger has been completed.

(E)   It should be observed that explanations are not usually used in the Explanation columns of the ledger accounts. The cross reference to the journal page from which the information was recorded permits any interested individual to quickly find a complete story of the transaction. Short explanations are used in the ledger accounts only when it is deemed that they will be especially useful in particular transactions.

The Accounting Sequence for the Whitside Realty Corporation

The stage of accounting methodology used in actual practice is illustrated with the six transactions of the Whitside Realty Corporation. The steps in the accounting sequence are:

1. Journalizing
2. Posting
3. Preparing a trial balance
4. Preparing a statement of financial position

Journalizing. The six transactions of the Whitside Realty Corporation appear in the general journal as follows:

GENERAL JOURNAL				Page 1	
1973 July	1	Cash	101	50,000	
		Capital Stock	251		50,000
		To record the issuance of capital stock to John Whitside, Ronald Raymond, and James Baker.			
	5	Land	151	5,000	
		Building	152	25,000	
		Cash	101		30,000
		To record purchase of land and building for cash.			
	10	Furniture	157	8,000	
		Accounts Payable—Jones Company	201		8,000
		To record purchase of furniture on account.			
	20	Accounts Payable—Jones Company	201	5,000	
		Cash	101		5,000
		To record payment on account.			
	25	Accounts Receivable—James Hill	111	1,800	
		Furniture	157		1,800
		To record sale of furniture at cost on account.			
	31	Cash	101	1,000	
		Accounts Receivable—James Hill	111		1,000
		To record collection on account.			

Posting. The transactions are posted from page 1 of the general journal to the ledger accounts shown. The cross references are entered in both the journal and the accounts.

LEDGER

Cash — Acct. No. 101

1973					50,000	1973				1	30,000
July	1			1	50,000	July	5			1	30,000
	31		16,000	1	1,000		20			1	5,000
					51,000						35,000

Accounts Receivable—James Hill — Acct. No. 111

1973					1,800	1973				1	1,000
July	25		800	1	1,800	July	31			1	1,000

Land — Acct. No. 151

1973					5,000
July	5			1	5,000

Building — Acct. No. 152

1973					25,000
July	5			1	25,000

Furniture — Acct. No. 157

1973					8,000	1973				1	1,800
July	10		6,200	1	8,000	July	25			1	1,800

Accounts Payable—Jones Company — Acct. No. 201

1973					5,000	1973				1	8,000
July	20			1	5,000	July	10		3,000	1	8,000

Capital Stock — Acct. No. 251

						1973				1	50,000
						July	1			1	50,000

After all the journal entries are posted, the accountant foots each account as shown in the ledger above.

The system under discussion is called *double-entry accounting* because it requires that each record of a transaction have debits and credits of equal amount. Every transaction does not necessarily have a single debit and a single credit. For example, the July 5 entry of the corporation involves two debits totaling $30,000 and one credit of $30,000. This is called a *compound entry*. Regardless of the number of accounts debited and credited in a single transaction, the total amount of all the debits and the total amount of all the credits must be equal. It follows that the totals of the debit and credit balances in all the accounts must also be equal.

THE TRIAL BALANCE

As stated previously, it is customary to prepare a trial balance to test the equality of the debit and credit balances in the ledger before a formal statement of financial position is prepared. The July 31, 1973, trial balance of the Whitside Realty Corporation is shown.

	WHITSIDE REALTY CORPORATION Trial Balance July 31, 1973		
Acct. No.	Account Title	Debits	Credits
101	Cash	$16,000	
111	Accounts Receivable	800	
151	Land	5,000	
152	Building	25,000	
157	Furniture	6,200	
201	Accounts Payable		$ 3,000
251	Capital Stock		50,000
	Totals	$53,000	$53,000

Although the trial balance proves the equality of debits and credits, this does not mean that the accounting is always proved to be correct. A full transaction could be omitted, the debit and credit amounts of an entry could be identically incorrect, a wrong account could be debited or credited, or both the debit and credit amounts for a given transaction could be posted twice. If the trial balance is in balance, however, the accountant considers this strong presumptive evidence of accuracy and proceeds from that point.

The trial balance is useful to the accountant in preparing periodic financial statements. The accountant could prepare a statement of financial position directly from the accounts, as was done in a previous stage, but the trial balance furnishes a convenient summary of the information used in the preparation of the statement of financial position.

If a trial balance does not balance, the following steps should be followed in the indicated sequence to locate the error.

1. Find the difference between the trial balance totals.
2. Examine the trial balance for balances that may be in the wrong column.
3. Readd the trial balance columns.
4. Check the trial balance figures against those appearing in the ledger to see whether the amounts correspond and whether they have been entered in the proper columns.

5. Check the additions on each side of each ledger account and recompute the balances.
6. Check postings from journal to ledger.

The trial balance may not balance because of a single error. Time and effort may be saved by applying the following special tests after step 1:

1. Errors in the amount of $0.01, $0.10, $1, $10, $100, and so on, may be due to errors in addition or subtraction.
2. If the trial balance difference is divisible by 2, the error may be due to a debit amount entered as a credit amount, or vice versa.
3. If the trial balance difference is divisible by 9 or 99, the error may be due to a transposition of figures ($83.41 posted as $38.41) or a slide ($1.05 posted as $105.00).

Statement of Financial Position

The next step in the accounting sequence is the preparation of the formal statement of financial position for the Whitside Realty Corporation (Figure 2-10). Note that Figure 2-10 is the same as Figure 2-6.

Figure 2-10. Formal Statement of Financial Position

WHITSIDE REALTY CORPORATION
Statement of Financial Position
July 31, 1973

Assets			Liabilities and Stockholders' Equity	
Current Assets			Current Liabilities	
Cash	$16,000		Accounts Payable	$ 3,000
Accounts Receivable	800		Stockholders' Equity	
Total Current Assets		$16,800	Capital Stock	50,000
Plant and Equipment				
Land	$ 5,000			
Building	25,000			
Furniture	6,200			
Total Plant and Equipment		36,200	Total Liabilities and	
Total Assets		$53,000	Stockholders' Equity	$53,000

PROCEDURES APPLICABLE TO A SINGLE PROPRIETORSHIP

Many small service businesses are single proprietorships. Among these are professional offices conducted by doctors, lawyers, accountants, engineers, and so on. The only difference between the single-proprietorship form of business organization and that of the corporation relative to the example of the Whitside Realty Corporation is the investment by the owners. If John Whitside had created a single-proprietorship form of realty business and had invested $50,000 in cash, the following journal entry would have been made:

GENERAL JOURNAL				Page 1

1973 July	1	Cash
		    John Whitside, Capital
		        To record investment by proprietor to form
		        a realty business to be called the Whitside
		        Realty Company.
			50,000	50,000

All the other entries would be recorded in the same way regardless of the form of business organization. The statement of financial position prepared at July 31, 1973, for the Whitside Realty Company, a single proprietorship, would be similar to Figure 2-10 with the exception of the owner's equity section, which would appear as follows:

Owner's Equity	
John Whitside, Capital	$50,000

SUMMARY

To fulfill the function of providing timely and meaningful information to management and other interested parties, accounting must provide an effective system for recording the various business transactions and for summarizing these transactions in useful statements and reports.

Since each business transaction has an effect on the statement of financial position, a new statement could be prepared after each transaction. This method is costly and inefficient. The use of an expanded accounting equation to accumulate data from which a statement of financial position can be prepared at the appropriate time is impractical because of the number of accounts normally maintained by a concern. Separate pages maintained for asset, liability, and owner's equity items permit unlimited expansion but the process is susceptible to arithmetical errors. An *account*, formed by dividing a page into two sections by a vertical line, is a device for recording the increases and decreases in an individual asset, liability, or owner's equity item in a systematic and orderly manner. The left side of an account is called the *debit* side and the right side is called the *credit* side. A debit entry records an increase in an asset account or a decrease in a liability or owner's equity account. A credit entry records a decrease in an asset account or an increase in a liability or owner's equity account. A book that contains a group of accounts is referred to as a *ledger*.

Because of the difficulty of recreating transactions when they are recorded only in accounts, each transaction is first listed in chronological order in a book of original entry called a *journal*. After an entry is recorded in the journal, each debit and credit amount is transferred from the journal to the related account in the ledger, a process known as *posting*. After all the entries for a specified period are recorded in the journal and posted to the ledger accounts, the balances of the accounts are computed and listed on a *trial balance*, which is a check of the equality of the debit and credit balances in the ledger. A statement of financial position can then be easily prepared from the trial balance.

The only difference between the single proprietorship and the corporation relative to the transactions discussed is the recording of the investment by the owners. In a corporation, the investment is credited to Capital Stock, whereas in the single proprietorship it is credited to the proprietor's capital account.

QUESTIONS

Q2-1. What is a business transaction? Give eight examples.

Q2-2. In practice, why is a statement of financial position not prepared after the occurrence of each transaction?

Q2-3. What is the difference between the terms *debit* and *credit?*

Q2-4. What is the function of (a) the general journal? (b) the ledger?

Q2-5. A balanced trial balance is a correct trial balance. Discuss.

Q2-6. Robert Hanson purchased furniture on account from the Jones Company. Hanson debited the Furniture account for $800, and erroneously credited the Accounts Receivable account for $800. (a) What effect would the error have on the debit and credit total of the trial balance taken at the end of the period? (b) What accounts in the trial balance would be incorrectly stated?

Q2-7. What does the term *ledger account* mean? Indicate two forms of the account. State the reasons and circumstances for using each form.

Q2-8. Why are statements of financial position classified as to assets and liabilities?

Q2-9. Give an example of a transaction that would result in: (a) an increase of an asset accompanied by an increase in the owner's equity; (b) an increase of an asset accompanied by an increase of a liability; (c) an increase of an asset accompanied by a decrease of an asset; (d) a decrease of an asset accompanied by a decrease of a liability.

EXERCISES

E2-1. The following transactions were engaged in by the Carson Corporation during the month of February 1973:

1973

Feb. 1 Received a charter and issued all authorized capital stock at par for $120,000 in cash.

2 Purchased land and buildings for $10,000 in cash and a 20-year mortgage payable for $50,000. The land was appraised at $8,000 and the building at $52,000.

3 Purchased service supplies from the Belk Company for $4,000 on account.

28 Sold a portion of the lot purchased on February 2 for its approximate cost of $3,500. The buyer, the Gulf Sands Company, paid $1,200 in cash and issued a 90-day note for $2,300.

1. Journalize the transactions.
2. Post to formal ledger accounts. (Assign appropriate numbers to accounts.)
3. Take a trial balance.
4. Prepare a classified account-form statement of financial position.

E2-2. The Brown Corporation engaged in the following transactions during the first week of operations:

1973

May 1 Issued capital stock at par to the four incorporators for $25,000 in cash.

3 Purchased office equipment from White and Sons for $4,000 on account.

5 Purchased land for a future building site at a cost of $20,000; paid $5,000 down and issued a mortgage note payable in 10 years for the balance.

Prepare a classified account-form statement of financial position after each transaction.

E2-3. The following T accounts were taken from the ledger of the Rawson Company:

Cash

1973		1973	
June 20	30,000	June 23	4,000
		29	2,000
		30	16,000

Marketable Securities (U.S. Treasury Notes)

1973	
June 29	2,000

Office Supplies

1973	
June 23	4,000

Land

1973	
June 30	5,000

Building

1973	
June 30	15,000

Mortgage Payable

	1973	
	June 30	4,000

Capital Stock

	1973	
	June 20	30,000

Analyze these accounts and describe each transaction.

E2-4. The following transactions are among those of the Paulson Corporation for 1973:

1973

Nov. 2   The Paulson Corporation was incorporated and capital stock with a par value of $100,000 was issued for cash.

    8   Purchased a plot of land for $15,000 in cash.

   11   Purchased a cabin at a nearby location and moved it to the land owned by the corporation. The cabin will serve as a business office. The total cash paid by the corporation was $6,000.

   30   Invested $4,000 in marketable securities (U.S. government bonds).

Journalize the transactions and post to ledger accounts. (Assign appropriate numbers to accounts.)

E2-5. The following statements of financial position were prepared immediately following each of three transactions engaged in by the Catz Company:

CATZ COMPANY
Statement of Financial Position
July 1, 1973

Assets		Owner's Equity	
Current Assets		Owner's Equity	
Cash	$45,000	John Catz, Capital	$45,000

CATZ COMPANY
Statement of Financial Position
July 3, 1973

Assets			Liabilities and Owner's Equity	
Current Assets			Long-Term Liabilities	
Cash		$39,000	Mortgage Payable	$49,000
Plant and Equipment			Owner's Equity	
Land	$ 5,000		John Catz, Capital	45,000
Building	50,000			
Total Plant and Equipment		55,000	Total Liabilities and	
Total Assets		$94,000	Owner's Equity	$94,000

CATZ COMPANY
Statement of Financial Position
July 5, 1973

Assets			Liabilities and Owner's Equity	
Current Assets			Current Liabilities	
Cash	$39,000		Accounts Payable	$ 1,000
Office Supplies	1,000		Long-Term Liabilities	
Total Current Assets		$40,000	Mortgage Payable	49,000
Plant and Equipment			Total Liabilities	$50,000
Land	$ 5,000		Owner's Equity	
Building	50,000		John Catz, Capital	45,000
Total Plant and Equipment		55,000	Total Liabilities and	
Total Assets		$95,000	Owner's Equity	$95,000

Date and describe each transaction.

E2-6. The following are among the transactions of the Amity Corporation:

1973
Dec. 1 Capital stock of $10,000 par value was issued for cash.

4 Purchased land for $6,000 in cash.

8 Purchased marketable securities (U.S. government bonds) for $1,500 in cash.

14 Purchased service supplies from Washington & Son Company for $515 on account.

18 Sold the land for $6,000 in cash.

31 Paid $515 to Washington & Son Company on account.

Journalize the transactions, post to T accounts, and prepare a trial balance. (Assign appropriate numbers to accounts.)

E2-7. The following trial balance was prepared by the Joe Dawson Company. The trial balance is not in balance and the accounts are not in the proper order, but the account balances are correct.

JOE DAWSON COMPANY
Trial Balance
December 31, 1973

Account Title	Debits	Credits
Cash	$60,000	
Joe Dawson, Capital		$ 85,000
Accounts Payable	10,000	
Notes Payable	5,000	
Land		4,000
Building		60,000
Accounts Receivable		7,000
Notes Receivable		6,000
Service Supplies	3,000	
Mortgage Payable		40,000
Totals	$78,000	$202,000

1. Prepare a corrected trial balance showing the accounts in proper order.
2. Prepare a classified report-form statement of financial position.

E2-8. The William Miller Company had the following ledger accounts at November 30, 1973:

Cash   Acct. No. 101

55,000	3,000
400	1,000
	2,500

Notes Receivable   Acct. No. 112

1,500	400

Service Supplies	Acct. No. 161
4,000	1,500

Land	Acct. No. 151
10,000	

Accounts Payable	Acct. No. 201
2,500	7,000
	3,000

William Miller, Capital	Acct. No. 251
	55,000

1. Compute the account balances.
2. Prepare a trial balance.
3. Prepare an account-form statement of financial position.

DEMONSTRATION PROBLEMS

DP2-1. (*Development of an accounting system—corporation*) The following transactions occurred at the Eason Company during its first month of operations:

1973
March 1 Received a corporate charter and issued all its authorized stock for $75,000 in cash.

2 Purchased land and building for $40,000. The company paid $10,000 in cash and issued a 20-year mortgage payable for the balance. The land was appraised at $12,000 and the building at $28,000.

3 Purchased furniture from the Garwood Company for $7,500 on account.

15 Paid the Garwood Company $2,500 on account.

20 Sold a portion of the land purchased on March 2 at its approximate cost of $4,500 to the Hill Realty Company on account.

31 Received $3,000 in cash and a 90-day note for $1,500 from the Hill Realty Company.

Required:

Using these six transactions, illustrate the five stages discussed in the text:
1. Prepare a statement of financial position after each transaction.
2. Record the transactions in an expanded accounting equation.
3. Record the transactions on separate pages, not divided. (Number the pages.)
4. Record the transactions on separate pages, divided into Debit and Credit columns.
5. Journalize the transactions, post to formal ledger accounts, take a trial balance, and prepare a classified account-form statement of financial position.

DP2-2. (*Transactions peculiar to single proprietorships*) Assume that the Eason Company in Problem DP2-1 is a single proprietorship owned and operated by Robert Eason.

Required: Which transactions would be different under this assumption? Journalize the transactions.

DP2-3. (*Development of an accounting system—single proprietorship*) Dr. Thurber Easter prepared to open a dental office and engaged in the following transactions:

1973

July 1   Opened a bank account, under the business name of Dr. Thurber B. Easter in the amount of $30,000.

2   Purchased land and building for $20,000. Paid $5,000 in cash and issued a 10-year mortgage payable for the balance. The land was appraised at $3,500; the building, at $16,500.

3   Purchased dental equipment and furniture from the Perro Company for $7,500 on account.

12   Dr. Easter wrote a check on his personal bank account (not his business account) for $2,500 in part payment of the Perro Company account.

15   It was discovered that part of the furniture purchased on July 3 was not satisfactory for his office needs, so Dr. Easter sold it on account to an attorney, Samuel Shaffner, at its cost of $1,000.

31   Received $700 from Shaffner on account.

Required:

Using these six transactions, illustrate the five stages discussed in the text.
1. Prepare a statement of financial position after each transaction.
2. Record the transactions in an expanded accounting equation.
3. Record the transactions on separate pages, not divided. (Number the pages.)
4. Record the transactions on separate pages, divided into Debit and Credit columns.
5. Journalize the six transactions, post to formal ledger accounts, take a trial balance, and prepare a report-form statement of financial position.

PROBLEMS

P2-1. The transactions of the newly organized Gooddeal Services, Inc., for the week of April 1 to 6, 1973, are given:

1973

April 1   Received a charter and issued all its authorized capital stock at par for $100,000 in cash.

2   Purchased land and building at a cost of $90,000. Paid $20,000 in cash and issued a 20-year mortgage payable for the balance. The land is appraised at $18,000; the building, at $72,000.

3   Purchased furniture for $2,000 from the Comfort Chair Company on account.

4   Purchased office supplies (stationery, stamps, and envelopes) for $800 in cash.

5   Some of the furniture was found to be defective and was returned to the Comfort Chair Company. The account was reduced by $400.

6   Paid the balance due the Comfort Chair Company.

Required: Prepare a classified statement of financial position after each transaction.

P2-2. Successive statements of financial position for the Hull Clinic are given after each of six transactions.

HULL CLINIC
Statement of Financial Position.
August 1, 1973

Assets		Liabilities and Owner's Equity	
Current Assets		Owner's Equity	
Cash	$65,000	Benjamin Hull, Capital	$65,000

HULL CLINIC
Statement of Financial Position
August 2, 1973

Assets			Liabilities and Owner's Equity	
Current Assets			Long-Term Liabilities	
Cash		$ 58,000	Mortgage Payable	$ 43,000
Plant and Equipment			Owner's Equity	
Land	$ 7,500		Benjamin Hull, Capital	65,000
Building	42,500	50,000	Total Liabilities and	
Total Assets		$108,000	Owner's Equity	$108,000

HULL CLINIC
Statement of Financial Position
August 3, 1973

Assets			Liabilities and Owner's Equity	
Current Assets			Current Liabilities	
Cash	$58,000		Accounts Payable	$ 3,000
Medical Supplies	3,000	$ 61,000	Long-Term Liabilities	
Plant and Equipment			Mortgage Payable	43,000
Land	$ 7,500		Total Liabilities	$ 46,000
Building	42,500	50,000	Owner's Equity	
			Benjamin Hull, Capital	65,000
			Total Liabilities and	
Total Assets		$111,000	Owner's Equity	$111,000

HULL CLINIC
Statement of Financial Position
August 4, 1973

Assets			Liabilities and Owner's Equity	
Current Assets			Current Liabilities	
Cash	$58,000		Accounts Payable	$ 3,000
Notes Receivable	1,500		Long-Term Liabilities	
Medical Supplies	3,000	$ 62,500	Mortgage Payable	43,000
Plant and Equipment			Total Liabilities	$ 46,000
Land	$ 6,000		Owner's Equity	
Building	42,500	48,500	Benjamin Hull, Capital	65,000
			Total Liabilities and	
Total Assets		$111,000	Owner's Equity	$111,000

HULL CLINIC
Statement of Financial Position
August 5, 1973

Assets			Liabilities and Owner's Equity	
Current Assets			Current Liabilities	
Cash	$58,000		Accounts Payable	$ 1,000
Notes Receivable	1,500		Long-Term Liabilities	
Medical Supplies	3,000	$ 62,500	Mortgage Payable	43,000
Plant and Equipment			Total Liabilities	$ 44,000
Land	$ 6,000		Owner's Equity	
Building	42,500	48,500	Benjamin Hull, Capital	67,000
			Total Liabilities and	
Total Assets		$111,000	Owner's Equity	$111,000

HULL CLINIC
Statement of Financial Position
August 7, 1973

Assets			Liabilities and Owner's Equity	
Current Assets			Current Liabilities	
Cash	$59,500		Accounts Payable	$ 1,000
Medical Supplies	3,000	$ 62,500	Long-Term Liabilities	
Plant and Equipment			Mortgage Payable	43,000
Land	$ 6,000		Total Liabilities	$ 44,000
Building	42,500	48,500	Owner's Equity	
			Benjamin Hull, Capital	67,000
			Total Liabilities and	
Total Assets		$111,000	Owner's Equity	$111,000

Required: Study the successive statements of financial position to determine what transactions have occurred. Prepare a list of these transactions, giving the date and description of each.

P2-3. The following account numbers and titles were designed for the Hilton Car Rental System, a single proprietorship:

101	Cash		150	Office Equipment
111	Accounts Receivable		300	Accounts Payable
120	Land		310	Notes Payable
130	Building		500	Charles Hilton, Capital
140	Automobiles			

During the first month of operation the following transactions occurred:

1973

Jan. 1 Hilton deposited $95,000 in cash in a bank account in the name of the business, Hilton Car Rental System, a single proprietorship.

3 Purchased land for $5,000 and a building on the lot for $30,000. A cash payment of $15,000 was made, and a promissory note was issued for the balance.

4 Purchased 15 new automobiles at $2,300 each from the Allied Motor Company. A down payment of $20,000 in cash was made; the balance was promised to be paid in 30 days.

5 Sold one automobile to one of the company's employees at cost. The employee paid $1,000 in cash and agreed to pay the balance within 30 days.

1973
Jan. 6 One automobile proved to be defective and was returned to the Allied Motor Company. The amount due was reduced by $2,300.

11 Purchased a cash register and office desks for $1,850 in cash.

31 Paid $6,000 in cash to the Allied Motor Company on account.

Required: 1. Journalize the transactions.
2. Post to T accounts (provide account numbers).

P2-4. The transactions listed are those of the Samuels Company, which was organized on January 1, 1973:

1973
Jan. 1 Capital stock with a par value of $30,000 was issued for cash.

4 Purchased land for $4,000 in cash.

6 Purchased repair parts from George Watson for $1,000 on account.

8 Purchased a more suitable piece of land for $5,000 in cash.

11 Sold the land acquired on January 4 for $4,000. The buyer, Peter Lorence, agreed to pay for the land within 10 days.

19 Paid George Watson $1,000 on account.

20 Received $4,000 from Peter Lorence.

27 Purchased additional repair parts for $700 in cash.

31 Invested $3,000 in cash in marketable securities (U.S. government bonds).

Required: 1. Journalize these transactions.
2. Post to ledger accounts. (Assign numbers to accounts.)
3. Prepare a trial balance.

P2-5. The Gunderson Stenographic Service, a newly formed company owned and operated by Atwater Gunderson, plans to provide typing, duplicating, and stenographic services to the tenants of the office building it owns and to other clients. The ledger accounts as of October 31, 1973, are not in the proper order.

Cash		Land	
65,000	53,200	10,000	
	1,500		
	450		
	1,050		
	300		
	125		

Office Supplies		Accounts Payable	
100		125	735
450		110	110

Maintenance Supplies		Mortgage Payable	
500			50,000
435			

Prepaid Insurance		Atwater Gunderson, Capital	
1,500			65,000

Machine		Delivery Equipment	
20,600		1,050	

Building		Office Equipment	
72,000		600	

Required:

1. Determine the account balances and prepare a trial balance as of October 31, 1973, in the proper order.
2. Prepare a statement of financial position.

P2-6. The Barker Garage was incorporated on March 20, 1973. During the first several days of operations, its part-time bookkeeper (a high school student who had a few months' instruction in bookkeeping) recorded the transactions and rendered the following unbalanced trial balance as of March 31, 1973:

BARKER GARAGE
Trial Balance
March 31, 1973

Account Title	Debits	Credits
Accounts Payable	$ 18,550	
Accounts Receivable		$10,000
Building	50,000	
Capital Stock	75,000	
Cash	15,500	
Furniture	6,000	
Land		12,000
Marketable Securities		9,600
Mortgage Payable		20,000
Notes Payable	10,350	
Notes Receivable		18,000
Service Supplies	2,800	
Totals	$178,200	$69,600

Required:

1. Assuming that the amounts are correct but that the bookkeeper did not understand the proper debit-credit position of some accounts, prepare a trial balance showing the accounts in correct statement of financial-position order.
2. Prepare a report-form statement of financial position.

P2-7. (*Accounting policy decision problem*) The Blake Corporation has been operating for a period of years. In September 1973 the accountant of the company disappeared, taking the records with him.

You are hired to reconstruct the accounting records, and with this in mind you make an inventory of all company assets. By checking with banks, counting the materials on hand, investigating the ownership of buildings and equipment, and so on, you develop the following information as of October 31, 1973:

Account Title	Balance	Account Title	Balance
Land	$15,000	Marketable Securities	$ 5,000
Equipment	25,000	Inventories	14,000
Buildings	30,000	Cash on Hand	3,000
Accounts Receivable	10,000	Cash in Banks	53,000

Statements from creditors and unpaid invoices found in the office indicate that $40,000 is owed to trade creditors. There is a $10,000 long-term mortgage (30 years) outstanding.

Interviews with the board of directors and a check of the capital stock record book indicate that there are 1,000 shares of capital stock outstanding and that the stockholders have contributed $30,000 to the corporation. No record is available regarding past retained earnings.

Required:

1. Prepare a trial balance and a statement of financial position as of October 31, 1973.
2. Write a report to management indicating a simple accounting system that could be used and why you recommend such a system.

P2-8. (*Financial policy decision problem*) Accounts included in the trial balance of the William Braxton Company as of September 30, 1973, were as follows:

Acct. No.	Account Title	Balance
101	Cash	$24,215
111	Accounts Receivable	11,785
150	Office Supplies	1,220
200	Land	?
250	Building	?
300	Furniture and Fixtures	8,000
350	Machines	60,000
400	Delivery Equipment	3,210
600	Accounts Payable	3,750
650	Notes Payable	25,000
700	Taxes Payable	103
800	William Braxton, Capital	?

Land and building were acquired at a cost of $30,000. It was determined that one third of the total cost should be applied to the cost of land.

The following transactions were completed during the month of October:

1973
Oct. 2 Paid in full a liability of $110 to the Doozier Company.

3 Collected in full an account receivable of $670 from the Parkside Mills Corporation.

4 Purchased office supplies from the Baxter Corporation for $400 on account.

8 Braxton made an additional investment of $16,000 in cash in the business.

10 Collected $1,000 from the Johnson Company on account.

11 Purchased a machine from the National Business Machine Company for $22,000; a cash payment of $2,000 was made, the balance to be paid within 30 days.

15 Paid in full a liability of $400 to the Pace Company.

20 Paid $10,000 in cash to the National Business Machine Company in partial settlement of the liability of October 11. Issued a note payable for the balance.

31 Collected in full an account receivable of $300 from the Durham Company.

Required:

1. Journalize these transactions.
2. Enter the balances of September 30, 1973, to ledger accounts, post the October entries, and determine the new balances.
3. Prepare a trial balance as of October 31, 1973.
4. Prepare a statement of financial position.
5. Compute the following:
   a. Working capital
   b. Current ratio
   c. Acid-test ratio
6. Write a brief report to management indicating the ability of the William Braxton Company to meet its short-term debt.

Basic Methodology—
Income Statement
Accounts

In the previous chapter, changes in the stockholders' equity caused by stockholder investments were discussed. Other changes may be caused by _revenues, expenses_, and _dividends_ to stockholders. These changes, and the statements on which they are reflected, are explained in this chapter.

REVENUES

The term _revenue_ describes the source of inflows of assets received in exchange for services rendered, sales of products or merchandise, gains from sales or exchanges of assets other than stock in trade, and earnings from interest and dividends on investments. It does _not include_ increases arising from owners' contributions or from borrowed funds. For revenue to be earned, it does not have to be collected immediately in cash; it is sufficient that claims for cash on customers or clients exist.

Revenue accounts are created to accumulate the amounts earned during a _specified_ period of time; the typical accounting period is one year. Often, however, progressive statements are prepared each month for the information of the management. The title of a revenue account should indicate the nature of the particular revenue; examples are Commissions Earned, Sales, Interest Earned, Dividends Earned, Accounting Fees Earned, and Garage Repair Revenue.

Revenue accounts are _credited_ to record _increases_; the particular asset that is received is _debited_. To illustrate the journalizing of revenue transactions, several companies that earned different kinds of revenue are considered.

First, suppose that on August 1, 1973, the Whitside Realty Corporation sells a house and lot and receives a commission of $500 in cash; this can be recorded as follows:

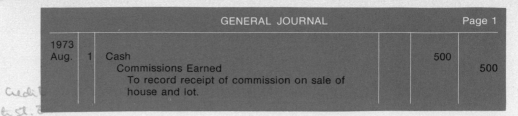

GENERAL JOURNAL			Page 1	
1973 Aug.	1	Cash	500	
		Commissions Earned		500
		To record receipt of commission on sale of house and lot.		

Next, assume that on July 30, 1973, I. N. Malvin, CPA, bills the Anderson Company for $1,000 for an annual audit that he had performed; his journal entry might look like this:

GENERAL JOURNAL			Page 1	
1973 July	30	Accounts Receivable	1,000	
		Accounting Fees Earned		1,000
		To record billing of following client for audit performed: Anderson Company $1,000		

Suppose that on January 2, 1973, the Georgetown Rental Agency receives $750 in cash for January rent:

GENERAL JOURNAL			Page 1	
1973 Jan.	2	Cash	750	
		Rent Earned		750
		To record rental receipts for month of January, 1973.		

EXPENSES

Expenses are costs of the materials used and services received during a specified period and used in the production of revenue during that same period. Examples of *expense accounts* are Salaries Expense, Rent Expense, and Office Expense. Expenses are recorded by a debit to the appropriate expense account and a credit to the Cash account, to a liability account, or possibly to some other type of account.

With a few special exceptions, which will be considered in later chapters, expenses are recorded when they are paid. The recording process for expenses is illustrated by the following transactions, which took place at the Mason Company.

1973
Jan. 2   Paid $400 in rent for the month of January.

10   Purchased an advertisement in the local newspaper for $75 in cash.

1973

Jan. 15   Paid semimonthly salaries of $600.

   20   Had some office machinery repaired at a cost of $45.

These transactions are recorded in the general journal as follows:

GENERAL JOURNAL			Page 1	
1973				
Jan.	2	Rent Expense	400	
		Cash		400
		To record payment of rent for month of January, 1973.		
	10	Advertising Expense	75	
		Cash		75
		To record payment for advertising.		
	15	Salaries Expense	600	
		Cash		600
		To record payment of semimonthly salaries.		
	20	Repairs Expense—Office Equipment	45	
		Cash		45
		To record payment of repairs to office equipment.		

BASIC OPERATING CONCEPTS

▼ The total expenses for a period are deducted from the total revenues to measure the _net income_ (profit) for the period, which in turn reflects the increase in the stockholders' equity resulting from business operations. ▼ This may be expressed in equation form:

Accounting Concept: ▼
Measurement of Net Income

$$\text{Total revenues} - \text{Total expenses} = \text{Net income}$$

If the expenses for a period exceed the revenues for that period, a _net loss_ results, and the stockholders' equity is decreased. The equation now becomes

$$\text{Total expenses} - \text{Total revenues} = \text{Net loss}$$

▼ It is necessary to distinguish between an _expense_ and a _cost_. A _cost_ is the amount paid or payable in either cash or the equivalent, for goods, services, or other assets purchased. When a cost no longer has asset status—that is, when its potential to produce revenue is lost—it is said to be expired and thus to have become an _expense_. ▼ From this statement the following conclusions are warranted:

Accounting Concept: ▼
Expenses Compared with Costs

Expenses = Expired costs (used up in producing revenue)

Assets = Unexpired costs (to be used to produce future revenue)

For example, rent paid in advance for three months is an asset, Prepaid Rent. As time passes, this becomes Rent Expense. The required adjusting process is discussed in detail in the next chapter.

A _disbursement_ is a payment in cash or by check. Hence, a machine may be acquired at a cost of $10,000; the transaction is completed by a disbursement in the form of a check for $10,000; and as the machine is used in operations it loses part of its service value, or *depreciates.* This is an element of expense, Depreciation Expense.

The basic objective of operating a business is to produce a net income, which results from receiving more from a customer for services rendered than the total expense of producing the services to the business; a loss is incurred when the expense of the services to the enterprise is more than the income received from the customer for the services rendered.

Most businesses cannot keep the detailed records necessary to indicate the expense of each service rendered and therefore cannot determine the net income or net loss from each transaction. Even when it is possible, the clerical costs involved in getting the information would not justify the end result. For example, a lawyer bills his client for $1,000 for services performed. How much did it cost the lawyer to perform the service and how much net income did he make on this *one* transaction? The lawyer might total the number of hours he devoted to the case and arrive at an expense in terms of time spent. But how about the rent for his office? the secretary's salary? the telephone bill? the electricity bill?

Accounting Concept: ▼
Matching of Expenses
against Revenue for a
Time Period

Since the determination of each expense involved in rendering service for a particular client would require a considerable amount of recordkeeping, accounting has evolved another and easier method for accomplishing the same result. No attempt is made to determine the cost of each service; instead, records of revenue and expense are kept for a period of time. ▼ At the end of the period, the expenses are matched against the revenue to determine the net income or net loss for that period. This information is contained in a financial statement called an *income statement*, discussed and illustrated later in this chapter. ▼

DIVIDENDS

Dividends are distributions of net income regardless of whether that income is earned in the current period or in past periods. Although dividends reduce the stockholders' equity, they are *not* expenses; they are not declared and paid for the purpose of producing revenue. A dividend may be recorded by a debit to a special Dividends account and a credit to Cash, or to a liability account if it is to be paid at a date subsequent to the date of declaration. For example, suppose that the Zephran Corporation declared and paid a regular quarterly cash dividend of $1,000 to its stockholders on November 10, 1973, this transaction would be recorded in the general journal of the Zephran Corporation as follows:

GENERAL JOURNAL				Page 1
1973 Nov. 10	Dividends		1,000	
	Cash			1,000
	To record declaration and payment of fourth quarterly dividend.			

EXPANDED RULES FOR DEBITS AND CREDITS

Since new types of accounts have been introduced, the rules for debiting and crediting accounts are expanded and restated:

Debit in order to record:	Credit in order to record:
1. An increase of an asset	1. A decrease of an asset
2. An increase of an expense	2. A decrease of an expense
3. An increase of dividends	3. A decrease of dividends
4. A decrease of a liability	4. An increase of a liability
5. A decrease in the stockholders' equity	5. An increase in the stockholders' equity
6. A decrease of revenue	6. An increase in revenue

The relationship of the rules of debits and credits to the accounting equation may be diagrammed as follows:

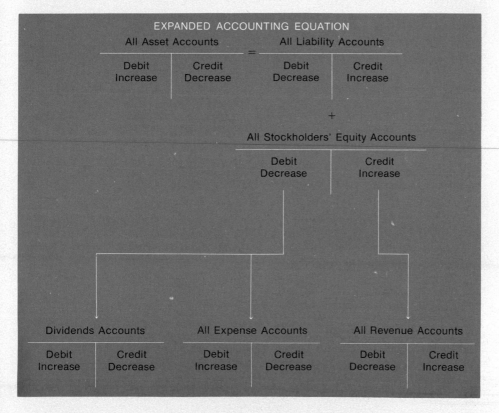

It is evident from the expanded accounting equation that a *decrease* in the stockholders' equity is debited. Note that when the decrease in the stockholders' equity is recorded in an expense account, the expense account is *increased* (debited);

that is, the expense account is designed to *accumulate* a decrease that is later transferred to the stockholders' equity accounts. The specific relationship between the expense accounts and the stockholders' equity accounts is further illustrated as follows:

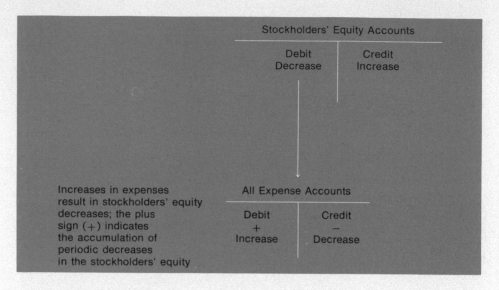

THE GENERAL LEDGER AND SUBSIDIARY LEDGERS

Accounts that are incorporated in the statement of financial position and the income statement are kept in a separate book called the *general ledger*. This ledger may actually be a loose-leaf binder, a bound book, cards in open trays, or some other form. Accounts are usually arranged in the sequence in which they will appear in the financial statements—that is, assets, liabilities, stockholders' equity, revenue, and expenses. These accounts are referred to collectively as *general ledger accounts*.

The Accounts Receivable Ledger

Many businesses have a large number of customers, and detailed information must be kept of transactions with each one. A separate account thus is required for each customer. If the general ledger were to include all the customers' accounts, it would become too large and unwieldy. Consequently, only one account, Accounts Receivable, is maintained in the general ledger. This account shows the combined increases and decreases in the amounts due from all customers. The individual customer accounts are kept in a separate, or *subsidiary*, ledger called the *accounts receivable ledger*. The Accounts Receivable account, referred to as a controlling account, is a summary account in the general ledger and takes the place of the individual customers' accounts in the subsidiary ledger. After all the transactions for the period have been entered, the balance of the Accounts Receivable account in the general ledger should be equal to the sum of the individual account balances in the subsidiary ledger.

The Accounts Payable Ledger

Many businesses have a large number of individual creditors. Consequently, only one account, Accounts Payable, is kept in the general ledger. This account shows the increases and decreases in amounts due to creditors. The individual creditors' accounts are kept in a subsidiary ledger called the *accounts payable ledger.* Accounts Payable, another controlling account, is a summary account in the general ledger. This account takes the place of the individual creditors' accounts kept in the subsidiary ledger. After all the transactions for the period have been entered, the balance of the Accounts Payable account in the general ledger should be equal to the sum of the individual account balances in the subsidiary ledger.

Controlling Accounts

As mentioned above, the Accounts Receivable and Accounts Payable accounts appearing in the general ledger are referred to as controlling accounts. A *controlling account,* by definition, is any account in the general ledger that controls or is supported by a number of other accounts in a separate ledger. These accounts contain summary totals of many transactions, the details of which appear in subsidiary ledgers. The accounts receivable ledger is sometimes referred to as the *customers' ledger;* the accounts payable ledger, as the *creditors' ledger.* Other controlling accounts and their appropriate subsidiary ledgers may be established when enough homogeneous general ledger accounts are created to make it necessary to relegate these accounts to a separate ledger.

Posting to the General Ledger and the Subsidiary Ledgers

To illustrate the method of posting from the general journal to the general and subsidiary ledgers, the following transaction is considered:

On August 1, 1973, Bookkeeping Services, Inc., billed the following clients for professional services performed:

Jay Johnson	$550
O. M. Omar	120
C. W. Wayne	230

This information is recorded and posted as indicated in Figure 3-1 (see page 62).

Entries to the Accounts Payable controlling account and the accounts payable ledger are handled similarly.

Figure 3-1. Posting to Control and Subsidiary Accounts

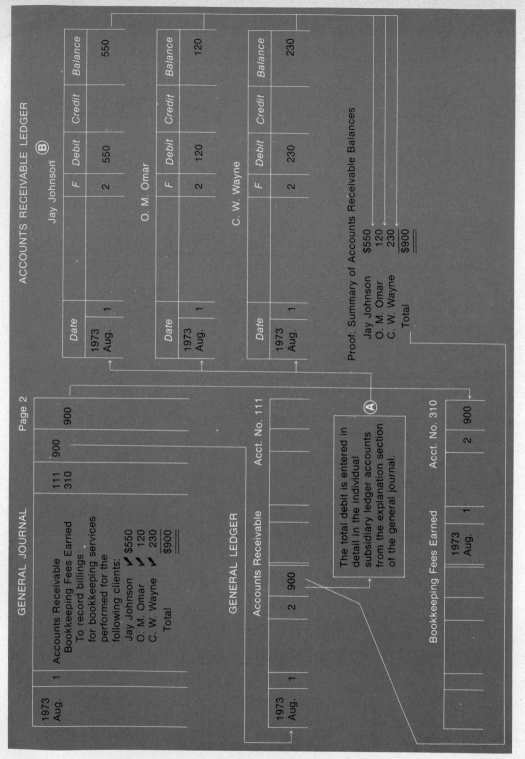

Figure 3-1 (continued)

(A) Figure 3-1 shows the detailed posting of the $900 debit to the Accounts Receivable account in the general ledger and to the subsidiary ledger accounts. Each customer is debited for the amount shown in the explanation of the general journal entry; the balance is extended to the Balance column; the journal page number is entered in the folio (F) column; and the date is entered. After each posting has been completed, a check mark (✔) is entered to the left of each amount in the Explanation column of the general journal to indicate that the amount has been posted to the proper subsidiary ledger account. A check mark is used rather than a page number because subsidiary accounts are generally not numbered but are kept in alphabetical order.

After only a cursory study, it may seem that this dual accounting for accounts receivable would result in double debits that will be incorrectly reflected in the trial balance. Note carefully, however, that only one debit goes into the Accounts Receivable controlling account for later incorporation in the trial balance. The amounts entered in the accounts receivable ledger will not go in the trial balance, but the total of the uncollected balances at the end of a period will be compared with the single balance of the Accounts Receivable controlling account as a check on the accuracy of both the accounts receivable ledger and the Accounts Receivable controlling account in the general ledger.

(B) It should be observed that the balance form of ledger account is used for the accounts receivable ledger. This particular form is customarily used in subsidiary ledgers for two reasons:

1. The balances have to be referred to quite often.
2. The form is adaptable to machine accounting, which is frequently employed for accounts receivable accounting.

THE ACCOUNTING SEQUENCE

Ten steps in the accounting sequence are illustrated through the example of a newly incorporated business called the Nelson Garage. These steps are: (1) selecting a chart of accounts, (2) journalizing the transactions, (3) posting to the general and subsidiary ledgers, (4) preparing a trial balance, (5) preparing a schedule of accounts receivable, (6) preparing a schedule of accounts payable, (7) preparing the financial statements, (8) closing and ruling the revenue and expense accounts, (9) balancing and ruling the position-statement accounts, and (10) taking a post-closing trial balance. An explanation of each step in the sequence is presented along with the accounting procedure for that step.

Selecting a Chart of Accounts

The first step in establishing an efficient accounting system that will satisfy the needs of management, governmental agencies, and other interested groups is the construction of a *chart of accounts*. A separate account should be set up for each item that appears in the financial statements to make the statements easier to prepare. The classification and the order of the items in the chart of accounts corresponds to those of the statements.

Account titles should be carefully selected to suit the needs of the business, and should indicate clearly and precisely the nature of the accounts to ensure proper recording of transactions. However, titles are not standardized; for example, one accountant may use Unexpired Insurance and another Prepaid Insurance Premiums in the same context.

The accountant of the Nelson Garage, expecting the company to grow rapidly, sets up the following chart of accounts—the accounts that he expects to use during the first month of operations are listed with numbers skipped to provide for future expansion.

NELSON GARAGE
Chart of Accounts

Statement of Financial Position Accounts
Assets (100–299)

Current Assets Accounts (100–199)
- 101   Cash
- 121   Accounts Receivable
- 131   Garage Parts and Supplies
- 141   Prepaid Insurance

Plant and Equipment (200–299)
- 201   Land
- 221   Automotive Tools and Equipment

Liabilities and Stockholders' Equity Accounts (300–499)

Current Liabilities (300–399)
- 301   Accounts Payable
- 302   Notes Payable

Stockholders' Equity (400–499)
- 401   Capital Stock
- 411   Retained Earnings
- 421   Dividends

Income Statement Accounts (500–999)

Revenue (500–599)
- 501   Garage Repair Revenue

Expenses (600–699)
- 601   Rent Expense—Garage Building
- 602   Rent Expense—Automotive Tools and Equipment
- 604   Salaries Expense
- 608   Electricity and Water Expense
- 609   Garage Parts and Supplies Used

Clearing and Summary Accounts (900–999)
- 901   Revenue and Expense Summary

In this example, a three-digit system is used to number the accounts; a larger business with a number of departments or branches may use four or more digits. Notice that Accounts 100–299 represent assets; Accounts 300–499 represent liabilities and stockholders' (owner's) equity; and that Accounts 500–999 represent income statement accounts. The more detailed breakdown for current assets, plant and equipment, current liabilities, for example, can be seen in the chart. As stated previously, the gaps between the assigned account numbers allow for additional accounts as they are needed by the business for recording purposes.

Analyzing Transactions and Journalizing

The transactions of the Nelson Garage that occurred during January, 1973, are given. Before making entries in the journal, the accountant must analyze each transaction in terms of the basic system of debits and credits that has already been outlined. Following the first five transactions listed, a description of the analytical thinking that must precede the journalizing of these transactions is given as a guide to future action.

1973

Jan. 2 The charter for the Nelson Garage was received on this date, and all the authorized capital stock was issued to three stockholders at par for $30,000 in cash. An asset, cash, is received; to record an increase of an asset, it must be debited; therefore, the Cash account is debited for $30,000. The stockholders have a claim against the business; the increase in the stockholders' equity account, Capital Stock, is shown by a credit to that account.

3 Rented a temporary garage and paid $300 for rent for January. Since all the rent will have expired by the time the financial statements are prepared, it is considered an expense of the month of January. An increase of an expense account is recorded by a debit; therefore, the Rent Expense–Garage Building account is debited. The decrease of the asset cash is recorded by a credit to Cash. A single rent account may be sufficient for all rented buildings and equipment. In this case, the accountant felt that managerial analyses required a separate Rent Expense account for the garage building.

4 Rented automotive tools and equipment pending purchase of its own. Rent in the amount of $80 was paid for January. As in the preceding transaction, all this rent will have expired before the financial statements are prepared; therefore it is considered an expense of January. An increase of an expense account is recorded by a debit—in this case to Rent Expense–Automotive Tools and Equipment. The decrease of the asset cash is recorded by a credit to Cash. Again, a single Rent Expense account may have been sufficient.

5 Purchased garage parts and supplies from the Southern Supply Company for $400 on account. The Garage Parts and Supplies account is an asset and is increased by the transaction; the increase in the asset is shown by a debit to Garage Parts and Supplies. Since the purchase was on credit, a liability is created. To record the increase in the liability, the Accounts Payable account is credited. The amount payable to the particular creditor, the Southern Supply Company, must be shown in the books. A note should be made in the Explanation column of the journal to the effect that the creditor is the Southern Supply Company, so that the amount can be posted to the accounts payable ledger.

6 Performed garage repairs for several cash customers; received $1,000 in cash. Cash, an asset, is received; to record the increase of the asset, the Cash account must be debited. The particular source of this asset is a revenue. To record an increase in the revenue, Garage Repairs Revenue is credited.

10 Purchased land as a prospective building site for $10,000. Paid $4,000 in cash and issued a one-year note for the balance.

12 Made repairs on George Shipman's car for $40. Shipman asked that a charge account be opened in his name; he promises to settle the account within 30 days. This was authorized by the service manager.

1973

Jan. 15 Paid $800 in salaries for first half of month.

20 Performed garage repairs for cash customers for $2,000.

25 Repairs were made on Jay Munson's truck for $60. A charge account was opened in his name.

28 Made repairs on Robert Batson's car for $120. A charge account was opened in his name.

29 Purchased garage parts and supplies from the Delco Supply House for $250 on account.

30 Paid the Southern Supply Company $300 on account.

31 Paid electricity and water bills for January, totaling $80.

31 Made garage repairs for cash customers for $1,800.

31 Paid $900 in salaries for the last half of the month.

31 Paid a $300 cash dividend to the three stockholders.

31 Purchased automotive tools and equipment for $4,000 in cash. The list price was $5,000.

31 Paid a premium of $600 on a 12-month comprehensive insurance policy; the policy becomes effective on February 1, 1973.

31 Received a check for $10 from George Shipman as part payment of his account.

31 Took a physical inventory of garage parts and supplies; it showed that there were parts and supplies costing $375 on hand, thus indicating that $275 (January 5 purchase $400, plus January 29 purchase $250, minus inventory, $375) worth of garage parts and supplies had been used, becoming an expense. Originally, as parts and supplies were purchased, they were debited to an asset account. Now, as the amount used becomes known, an entry is made debiting an expense account, Garage Parts and Supplies Used, to show that the expense account has been increased, and crediting an asset account, Garage Parts and Supplies, to show that the asset account has been decreased. (This type of transaction is normally recorded in an *adjusting entry*, explained in Chapter 4. It is presented here to broaden the scope of this illustration.)

The results of this analytical reasoning are presented in the following general journal. Note that space is left between entries to ensure that they are separate and distinct.

GENERAL JOURNAL				Page 1	
1973 Jan.	2	Cash	101	30,000	
		Capital Stock	401		30,000
		To record issuance of capital stock for cash.			
	3	Rent Expense—Garage Building	601	300	
		Cash	101		300
		To record payment of rent on garage building for month of January, 1973.			
	4	Rent Expense—Automotive Tools and Equip.	602	80	
		Cash	101		80
		To record payment of rent for automotive tools and equipment for month of January, 1973.			

subsidiary ledger are kept under alphabetical order (handwritten)

GENERAL JOURNAL			Page 1 (cont.)

1973 Jan.	5	Garage Parts and Supplies	131	400	
		Accounts Payable	301		400
		To record purchase of parts and supplies on account.			
		Southern Supply Co. ✔ $400			
	6	Cash	101	1,000	
		Garage Repair Revenue	501		1,000
		To record collections from cash customers for services rendered.			
	10	Land	201	10,000	
		Cash	101		4,000
		Notes Payable	302		6,000
		To record purchase of land.			
	12	Accounts Receivable	121	40	
		Garage Repair Revenue	501		40
		To record billing for repairs rendered:			
		George Shipman ✔ $40			
	15	Salaries Expense	604	800	
		Cash	101		800
		To record payment of semimonthly salaries.			

Besides enter 301, also enter in Southern Supply Co. (handwritten)

GENERAL JOURNAL			Page 2

1973 Jan.	20	Cash	101	2,000	
		Garage Repair Revenue	501		2,000
		To record collections from cash customers for services rendered.			
	25	Accounts Receivable	121	60	
		Garage Repair Revenue	501		60
		To record billing for repair services rendered:			
		Jay Munson ✔ $60			
	28	Accounts Receivable	121	120	
		Garage Repair Revenue	501		120
		To record billing for repair services rendered:			
		Robert Batson ✔ $120			
	29	Garage Parts and Supplies	131	250	
		Accounts Payable	301		250
		To record purchase of parts and supplies on account:			
		Delco Supply House ✔ $250			
	30	Accounts Payable	301	300	
		Cash	101		300
		To record payment:			
		Southern Supply Company ✔ $300			
	31	Electricity and Water Expense	608	80	
		Cash	101		80
		To record payment of electricity and water bills for month of January.			

GENERAL JOURNAL			Page 2 (cont.)
1973			
Jan. 31 Cash	101	1,800	
Garage Repair Revenue	501		1,800
To record collections from cash customers for services rendered.			
31 Salaries Expense	604	900	
Cash	101		900
To record payment of salaries for last half of January.			
31 Dividends	421	300	
Cash	101		300
To record payment of dividends to stockholders.			

GENERAL JOURNAL			Page 3
1973			
Jan. 31 Automotive Tools and Equipment	221	4,000	
Cash	101		4,000
To record purchase of tools and equipment at a cost of $4,000 (list price, $5,000).			
31 Prepaid Insurance	141	600	
Cash	101		600
To record payment of insurance premium for 12 months. Insurance is effective February 1, 1973.			
31 Cash	101	10	
Accounts Receivable	121		10
To record collection to apply on account: George Shipman ✔ $10			
31 Garage Parts and Supplies Used	609	275	
Garage Parts and Supplies	131		275
To record cost of parts and supplies used during month of January.			

Posting to the Ledgers

As the transactions are posted to the ledger, the account numbers are entered in the general journal folio (F) column. At the same time, the number of the journal page from which the entry is posted is entered in the folio (F) column of the ledger account.

The timing of the posting process is a matter of personal preference and expediency. All postings, however, must be completed before financial statements can be prepared. It is advisable to keep accounts with customers and creditors up to date, so that the account balances are readily available. Because of this, it is probably the best rule to post from the journal to the ledgers on a daily basis.

The three posted ledgers are shown:

GENERAL LEDGER

Cash   Acct. No. 101

1973					1973				
Jan.	2		1	30,000	Jan.	3		1	300
	6		1	1,000		4		1	80
	20		2	2,000		10		1	4,000
	31		2	1,800		15		1	800
	31	23,450	3	10		30		2	300
				34,810		31		2	80
						31		2	900
						31		2	300
						31		3	4,000
						31		3	600
									11,360

Accounts Receivable   Acct. No. 121

1973					1973				
Jan.	12		1	40	Jan.	31		3	10
	25		2	60					
	28	210	2	120					
				220					

Garage Parts and Supplies   Acct. No. 131

1973					1973				
Jan.	5		1	400	Jan.	31		3	275
	29	375	2	250					
				650					

Prepaid Insurance   Acct. No. 141

1973				
Jan.	31		3	600

Land   Acct. No. 201

1973				
Jan.	10		1	10,000

Automotive Tools and Equipment   Acct. No. 221

1973				
Jan.	31		3	4,000

Accounts Payable   Acct. No. 301

1973					1973				
Jan.	30		2	300	Jan.	5		1	400
						29	350	2	250
									650

GENERAL LEDGER (Cont.)

Notes Payable   Acct. No. 302

| | | | | | | 1973 | | | | 1 | 6,000 |
| | | | | | | Jan. | 10 | | | | |

Capital Stock   Acct. No. 401

| | | | | | | 1973 | | | | 1 | 30,000 |
| | | | | | | Jan. | 2 | | | | |

Retained Earnings   Acct. No. 411

Dividends   Acct. No. 421

| 1973 | | | | | 2 | 300 | | | | | |
| Jan. | 31 | | | | | | | | | | |

Garage Repair Revenue   Acct. No. 501

						1973				1	1,000
						Jan.	6			1	40
							12			2	2,000
							20			2	60
							25			2	120
							28			2	1,800
							31				5,020

Rent Expense—Garage Building   Acct. No. 601

| 1973 | | | | | 1 | 300 | | | | | |
| Jan. | 3 | | | | | | | | | | |

Rent Expense—Automotive Tools and Equipment   Acct. No. 602

| 1973 | | | | | 1 | 80 | | | | | |
| Jan. | 4 | | | | | | | | | | |

Salaries Expense   Acct. No. 604

1973					1	800					
Jan.	15				2	900					
	31					1,700					

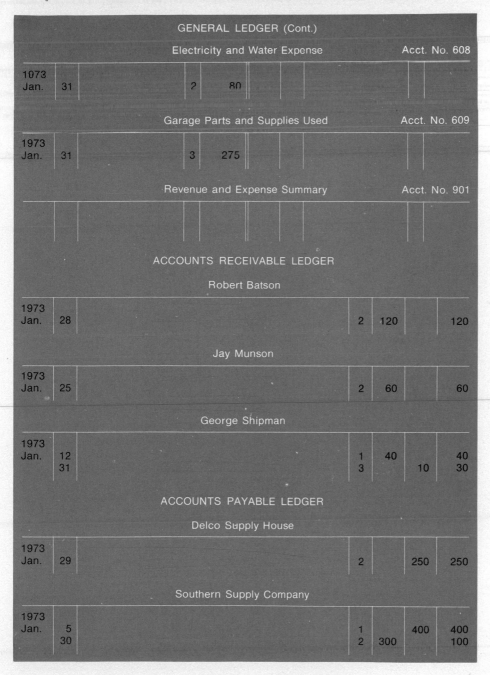

GENERAL LEDGER (Cont.)

Electricity and Water Expense — Acct. No. 608

| 1973 Jan. | 31 | | | 2 | 80 | | | | |

Garage Parts and Supplies Used — Acct. No. 609

| 1973 Jan. | 31 | | | 3 | 275 | | | | |

Revenue and Expense Summary — Acct. No. 901

ACCOUNTS RECEIVABLE LEDGER

Robert Batson

| 1973 Jan. | 28 | | | | | 2 | 120 | | 120 |

Jay Munson

| 1973 Jan. | 25 | | | | | 2 | 60 | | 60 |

George Shipman

| 1973 Jan. | 12 | | | | | 1 | 40 | | 40 |
| | 31 | | | | | 3 | | 10 | 30 |

ACCOUNTS PAYABLE LEDGER

Delco Supply House

| 1973 Jan. | 29 | | | | | 2 | | 250 | 250 |

Southern Supply Company

| 1973 Jan. | 5 | | | | | 1 | | 400 | 400 |
| | 30 | | | | | 2 | 300 | | 100 |

Preparing a Trial Balance

After the accounts in the general ledger are footed and the balances are obtained, the following trial balance is taken:

NELSON GARAGE
Trial Balance
January 31, 1973

Acct. No.	Account Title	Debits	Credits
101	Cash	$23,450	
121	Accounts Receivable	210	
131	Garage Parts and Supplies	375	
141	Prepaid Insurance	600	
201	Land	10,000	
221	Automotive Tools and Equipment	4,000	
301	Accounts Payable		$ 350
302	Notes Payable		6,000
401	Capital Stock		30,000
421	Dividends	300	
501	Garage Repair Revenue		5,020
601	Rent Expense–Garage Building	300	
602	Rent Expense–Automotive Tools and Equipment	80	
604	Salaries Expense	1,700	
608	Electricity and Water Expense	80	
609	Garage Parts and Supplies Used	275	
	Totals	$41,370	$41,370

Preparing a Schedule of Accounts Receivable

The fact that the trial balance is in balance is presumptive evidence of accuracy of the accounting up to this point; the accountant therefore takes the next step, that of preparing a *schedule of accounts receivable.*

At the end of a designated accounting period (one month in this example), the total of all the balances of customers' accounts should agree with the balance of the Accounts Receivable controlling account in the general ledger. A schedule of accounts receivable usually is prepared to check this agreement. The schedule of accounts receivable taken from the Nelson Garage's accounts receivable ledger shows that the total of all customers' accounts is $210, which agrees with the balance of the Accounts Receivable controlling account:

NELSON GARAGE
Schedule of Accounts Receivable
January 31, 1973

Robert Batson	$120
Jay Munson	60
George Shipman	30
Total Accounts Receivable	$210

Preparing a Schedule of Accounts Payable

The next step is similar to the preceding one; it involves the preparation of a *schedule of accounts payable.*

At the end of the accounting period, the total of the balances of the individual creditors' accounts should equal the balance of the Accounts Payable controlling account. The schedule of accounts payable taken from the Nelson Garage's accounts payable ledger shows that the total of the creditors' accounts is $350, which agrees with the balance of the Accounts Payable controlling account.

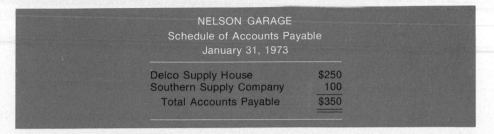

NELSON GARAGE
Schedule of Accounts Payable
January 31, 1973

Delco Supply House	$250
Southern Supply Company	100
Total Accounts Payable	$350

Preparing the Financial Statements from the Trial Balance

The income statement, the statement of retained earnings, and the statement of financial position are usually prepared at the end of an accounting period. The first two have not yet been illustrated.

The Income Statement. The income statement shown in Figure 3-2 was prepared from the trial balance of the Nelson Garage.

The heading of the income statement gives:

1. The name of the business
2. The name of the statement
3. The period covered by the statement

Figure 3-2. Income Statement

NELSON GARAGE
Income Statement
For the Month Ended January 31, 1973

Revenue		
Garage Repair Revenue		$5,020
Expenses		
Rent Expense–Garage Building	$ 300	
Rent Expense–Automotive Tools and Equipment	80	
Salaries Expense	1,700	
Electricity and Water Expense	80	
Garage Parts and Supplies Used	275	
Total Expenses		2,435
Net Income		$2,585

It is important that the period covered be specified clearly. The date January 31, 1973, is not sufficient; it, alone, does not indicate whether the net income of $2,585 was earned in one day, one month, or one year ending January 31, 1973.

The analyst must know how long a period of time it took for the firm to earn the $2,585.

The determination of net income for the Nelson Garage at this level should not be interpreted as being definitive. For example, a corporation is subject to income taxes; but the accounting for income taxes and certain other more complex problems are deferred to later chapters.

There is no standard order for listing accounts in the income statement.

The Statement of Retained Earnings. Since the corporation is a creature of the law, there are certain legal restrictions on it, including a requirement that the net income retained in a business be recorded separately from the Capital Stock account. The typical title of the account used to accumulate this information is Retained Earnings. *The statement of retained earnings* shows the changes in that part of the stockholders' equity designated as "retained earnings"; it should cover the same period as the income statement. Since by definition retained earnings are the accumulation of all past net income less any dividends paid out, it follows that net income and dividends for a period must be reflected in the statement. The first end-of-period statement of retained earnings of the Nelson Garage is shown in Figure 3-3.

Figure 3-3. Statement of Retained Earnings for New Business

NELSON GARAGE	
Statement of Retained Earnings	
For the Month Ended January 31, 1973	
Net Income for January, 1973	$2,585
Deduct Dividends	300
Retained Earnings, January 31, 1973	$2,285

The heading of the statement of retained earnings is similar to that of the income statement.

For a business that has been in existence prior to the current period, there would be an additional item in the statement of retained earnings, the beginning-of-period balance. For example, the statement of the Bebol Company is shown in Figure 3-4.

Figure 3-4. Complete Statement of Retained Earnings

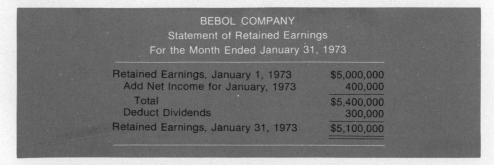

BEBOL COMPANY	
Statement of Retained Earnings	
For the Month Ended January 31, 1973	
Retained Earnings, January 1, 1973	$5,000,000
Add Net Income for January, 1973	400,000
Total	$5,400,000
Deduct Dividends	300,000
Retained Earnings, January 31, 1973	$5,100,000

The Statement of Financial Position. Since the retained earnings of the Nelson Garage, as of January 31, 1973, have now been determined (Figure 3-3), it is possible to prepare the formal statement of financial position as shown in Figure 3-5.

Figure 3-5. Formal Statement of Financial Position

NELSON GARAGE
Statement of Financial Position
January 31, 1973

Assets			Liabilities and Stockholders' Equity		
Current Assets			Current Liabilities		
Cash	$23,450		Accounts Payable	$ 350	
Accounts Receivable	210		Notes Payable	6,000	
Garage Parts and Supplies	375		Total Current Liabilities		$ 6,350
Prepaid Insurance	600		Stockholders' Equity		
Total Current Assets		$24,635	Capital Stock	$30,000	
Plant and Equipment			Retained Earnings	2,285	
Land	$10,000		Total Stockholders'		
Automotive Tools and Equipment	4,000		Equity		32,285
Total Plant and Equipment		14,000	Total Liabilities and		
Total Assets		$38,635	Stockholders' Equity		$38,635

Note that the heading of the statement of financial position contains the single date *January 31, 1973*. This statement reveals the financial position as of the close of business on January 31. It is analogous to a still photograph, whereas the income statement and statement of retained earnings are like moving pictures— they show the changes that have taken place during a specific period.

Closing and Ruling the Revenue and Expense Accounts

The revenue, expense, and dividends accounts are used to measure part of the changes that take place in retained earnings during a specified period of time. For this reason, these accounts are often called *temporary owner's equity accounts*, or *nominal accounts*. At the end of an accounting period, these accounts must be emptied—or *closed*—so that they may be used to accumulate the changes in retained earnings for the next period. Therefore, *closing entries* are made to transfer the final effects of the temporary stockholders' equity accounts to the Retained Earnings account, which is a *permanent*, or *real*, account. The term *real* is applied to the accounts that appear in the statement of financial position; these accounts are not closed at the end of a period.

The Closing Procedure. To simplify the transfer of revenue and expense account balances, an intermediate *summary account,* called Revenue and Expense Summary, is used. The balances of all revenue and expense accounts are transferred to this account. The Revenue and Expense Summary account, the balance of which reveals the net income or loss for the period, is then closed by transferring its balance to the Retained Earnings account, a part of the stockholders' equity. This action is justified because net income or net loss accrues to the owners. Since the Dividends account is not an expense account, it is not closed to the Revenue and Expense Summary account; rather, it is closed directly to the Retained Earnings account. After the revenue and expense accounts are closed, they are ruled to indicate that they have zero balances and that they are now available to accumulate information for measuring the changes in retained earnings in the next accounting period.

The closing procedure is illustrated in Figure 3-6.

Figure 3-6. The Closing Procedure

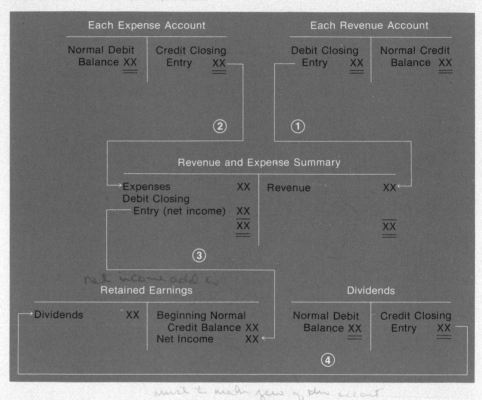

Entry ①—The revenue accounts are closed.
Entry ②—The expense accounts are closed.
Entry ③—The Revenue and Expense Summary account is closed.
Entry ④—The Dividends account is closed.

The caption *Closing Entries* is written in the middle of the first unused line in the general journal under the transactions of the period, and the closing entries are begun directly under that. They are posted immediately to the general ledger. As indicated in Figure 3-6, the closing entries are made in the following sequence:

Entry 1. All the revenue accounts are debited in a compound entry, and the sum of the revenue items is credited to the Revenue and Expense Summary account.

Entry 2. All the expense accounts are credited in a second compound entry, and the sum of the expense items is debited to the Revenue and Expense Summary account.

Entry 3. After entries 1 and 2 are posted, a credit balance in the Revenue and Expense Summary account represents net income, a debit balance, net loss. The balance of the account is transferred to the Retained Earnings account.

Entry 4. The Dividends account is closed directly to the Retained Earnings account by a debit to Retained Earnings and a credit to Dividends.

Unlike regular transaction entries, which require analysis and judgment, the closing process is purely mechanical and involves only the shifting and summarizing of previously determined amounts. The closing journal entries of the Nelson Garage on January 31, 1973, are shown in Figure 3-7.

Figure 3-7. Closing Entries

GENERAL JOURNAL					Page 4
		Closing Entries			
		①			
1973					
Jan.	31	Garage Repair Revenue	501	5,020	
		Revenue and Expense Summary	901		5,020
		To close revenue to summary account.			
		②			
	31	Revenue and Expense Summary	901	2,435	
		Rent Expense—Garage Building	601		300
		Rent Expense—Automotive Tools and			
		Equipment	602		80
		Salaries Expense	604		1,700
		Electricity and Water Expense	608		80
		Garage Parts and Supplies Used	609		275
		To close expenses to summary account.			
		③			
	31	Revenue and Expense Summary	901	2,585	
		Retained Earnings	411		2,585
		To transfer net income to retained earnings.			
		④			
	31	Retained Earnings	411	300	
		Dividends	421		300
		To close dividends to retained earnings.			

The closing journal entries are posted to the ledger accounts indicated in the journal (see Figures 3-8 and 3-9). Closing entries are indicated by the words *Closing Entry* in the Explanation columns of the nominal accounts as shown in Figure 3-8.

Ruling the Closed Nominal Accounts. After the closing entries have been posted, the temporary stockholders' equity accounts consist of equal debit and credit totals; that is, they have zero balances. These accounts (revenue, expense, and dividend) are ruled to separate the amounts entered during one accounting period from

Figure 3-8. The Nominal Accounts Are Closed and Ruled

GENERAL LEDGER										

Dividends — Acct. No. 421

1973					1973					
Jan.	31		2	300	Jan.	31	Closing Entry	4	300	

Garage Repair Revenue — Acct. No. 501

1973					1973					
Jan.	31	Closing Entry	4	5,020	Jan.	6		1	1,000	
						12		1	40	
						20		2	2,000	
						25		2	60	
						28		2	120	
						31		2	1,800	
									5,020	
				5,020					5,020	

Rent Expense—Garage Building — Acct. No. 601

1973					1973					
Jan.	3		1	300	Jan.	31	Closing Entry	4	300	

Rent Expense—Automotive Tools and Equipment — Acct. No. 602

1973					1973					
Jan.	4		1	80	Jan.	31	Closing Entry	4	80	

Salaries Expense — Acct. No. 604

1973					1973					
Jan.	15		1	800	Jan.	31	Closing Entry	4	1,700	
	31		2	900						
				1,700						
				1,700					1,700	

Electricity and Water Expense — Acct. No. 608

1973					1973					
Jan.	31		2	80	Jan.	31	Closing Entry	4	80	

Garage Parts and Supplies Used — Acct. No. 609

1973					1973					
Jan.	31		3	275	Jan.	31	Closing Entry	4	275	

Revenue and Expense Summary — Acct. No. 901

1973					1973					
Jan.	31	Expenses	4	2,435	Jan.	31	Revenue	4	5,020	
	31	Closing Entry	4	2,585						
				5,020						
				5,020					5,020	

the amounts to be entered during the next. Each side is totaled; and the equal debit and credit totals are written on the first available full line. Double rules are then drawn across all the columns, except the Explanation columns, to signify that the accounts have a zero balance. If an account has only one debit and one credit, it is unnecessary to foot the account; double rules are drawn below the individual amounts. Figure 3-8 shows the posting of the closing entries and the ruling of the nominal accounts.

Balancing and Ruling the Open Real Accounts

To simplify computations in the statement of financial position accounts during the following accounting period, and to set apart the amounts from each accounting period, it is customary to bring down the balances of the real accounts, which are still open. The procedure is as follows:

1. The balance of the account is computed. The amount is transferred to the money column on the opposite side, dated as of the last day of the accounting period. The word *Balance* is entered in the Explanation column, and a check mark is placed in the folio (F) column.
2. The equal debit and credit footings are entered on the next unused full line.
3. Double rules are drawn across all the columns, except the Explanation columns.
4. The balance is written under the rules on the appropriate side, dated as of the first day of the new accounting period. The word *Balance* is written in the Explanation column, and a check mark is placed in the folio (F) column. It is not necessary to balance and rule an account that contains only one amount. Balancing an account, unlike adjusting and closing, does not involve journalizing or posting since the balance of the account does not change.

The real accounts of the Nelson Garage are shown in Figure 3-9. Note the placement of rules and balances.

Figure 3-9. The Real Accounts Are Balanced and Ruled

GENERAL LEDGER

Cash   Acct. No. 101

1973 Jan.					1973 Jan.				
2			1	30,000	3			1	300
6			1	1,000	4			1	80
20			2	2,000	10			1	4,000
31			2	1,800	15			1	800
31		23,450	3	10	30			2	300
				34,810	31			2	80
					31			2	900
					31			2	300
					31			3	4,000
					31			3	600
									11,360
					31	Balance	✔		23,450
				34,810					34,810
1973 Feb.	1	Balance	✔	23,450					

Figure 3-9 (continued)

Accounts Receivable — Acct. No. 121

1973							1973						
Jan.	12			1	40		Jan.	31			3		10
	25			2	60			31	Balance		✔		210
	28		210	2	120								210
					220								220
1973													
Feb.	1	Balance		✔	210								

Garage Parts and Supplies — Acct. No. 131

1973							1973						
Jan.	5			1	400		Jan.	31			3		275
	29		375	2	250			31	Balance		✔		375
					650								375
													650
1973													
Feb.	1	Balance		✔	375								

Prepaid Insurance — Acct. No. 141

1973					
Jan.	31			3	600

Land — Acct. No. 201

1973					
Jan.	10			1	10,000

Automotive Tools and Equipment — Acct. No. 221

1973					
Jan.	31			3	4,000

Accounts Payable — Acct. No. 301

1973							1973						
Jan.	30		✔	2	300		Jan.	5			1		400
	31	Balance			350			29		350	2		250
					650								650
							1973						
							Feb.	1	Balance		✔		350

Notes Payable — Acct. No. 302

				1973					
				Jan.	10			1	6,000

Figure 3-9 (continued)

					Capital Stock				Acct. No. 401
					1973 Jan.	2		1	30,000

					Retained Earnings				Acct. No. 411
1973 Jan.	31		4	300	1973 Jan.	31		4	2,585
	31	Balance	✔	2,285			2,285		
				2,585					2,585
					1973 Feb.	1	Balance	✔	2,285

Taking a Post-Closing Trial Balance

After the closing entries have been posted, and the accounts are ruled and balanced, a *post-closing trial balance* is taken from the general ledger. Since the only accounts with open balances are the real accounts, the accounts and amounts in the post-closing trial balance are the same as in the statement of financial position. The post-closing trial balance tests the debit and credit equilibrium of the general ledger before the accounts are used during the next accounting period. Its use, however, is optional, and a comparison of the general ledger account balances with the statement of financial position will serve the same purpose. In any case, it is absolutely essential to start a new period with the accounts in proper balance; even though the trial balance at the end of the new period would indicate an error, errors made in previous accounting periods are very difficult to trace.

The post-closing trial balance of the Nelson Garage is shown:

	NELSON GARAGE Post-Closing Trial Balance January 31, 1973		
Acct. No.	Account Title	Debits	Credits
101	Cash	$23,450	
121	Accounts Receivable	210	
131	Garage Parts and Supplies	375	
141	Prepaid Insurance	600	
201	Land	10,000	
221	Automotive Tools and Equipment	4,000	
301	Accounts Payable		$ 350
302	Notes Payable		6,000
401	Capital Stock		30,000
411	Retained Earnings		2,285
	Totals	$38,635	$38,635

PROCEDURES APPLICABLE TO A SINGLE PROPRIETORSHIP

Since many service-type businesses are single proprietorships, the procedures discussed in this chapter that affect this form of business organization must be considered. If the Nelson Garage had been started by John Nelson as a single proprietorship, the following accounting differences would apply.

On January 2, 1973, Nelson would make the entire investment of $30,000, instead of three stockholders making an investment in a corporation. This investment by the single proprietor would be recorded in the journal as follows:

GENERAL JOURNAL				Page 1
1973 Jan.	2	Cash	30,000	
		John Nelson, Capital		30,000
		To record investment by proprietor in a business to be called the Nelson Garage.		

The only other regular transaction that would be recorded differently in a single proprietorship is the dividend paid by the corporation on January 31, 1973. A comparable situation in the case of the single proprietor would be his withdrawal of cash (or some other asset) in *anticipation* of the net income that he expects to earn. If Nelson withdraws $300, the transaction would be recorded as follows:

GENERAL JOURNAL				Page 1
1973 Jan.	31	John Nelson, Drawing	300	
		Cash		300
		To record withdrawal by proprietor in anticipation of earned income.		

A special account, *John Nelson, Drawing*, would be debited for all withdrawals in anticipation of income, and Cash would be credited; at the end of the period the drawing account would be credited for the net income that is actually earned.

All the other regular transactions of the Nelson garage would be recorded in exactly the same manner for a single proprietorship as for a corporation.

The only other recording difference between the two forms of business organization is in the closing process. After the revenue and expense accounts are closed, the Revenue and Expense Summary and John Nelson, Drawing accounts will appear as follows:

Revenue and Expense Summary				John Nelson, Drawing	
Expenses	2,435	Revenue	5,020	300	
		2,585			

Entries ③ and ④ are made in the journal of the single proprietorship to complete the closing process, in addition to entries ① and ② as shown on page 77.

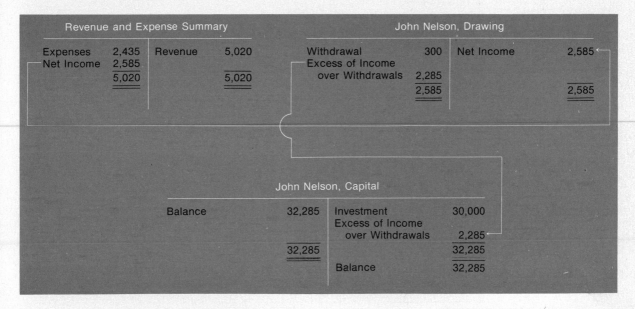

GENERAL JOURNAL				Page 4
		Closing Entries for a Single Proprietorship		
		③		
1973 Jan.	31	Revenue and Expense Summary	2,585	
		John Nelson, Drawing		2,585
		To close net income to Drawing account.		
		④		
	31	John Nelson, Drawing	2,285	
		John Nelson, Capital		2,285
		To close balance of Drawing account to capital.		

The effect of these entries is shown in the following T accounts:

Revenue and Expense Summary				John Nelson, Drawing			
Expenses	2,435	Revenue	5,020	Withdrawal	300	Net Income	2,585
Net Income	2,585			Excess of Income			
	5,020		5,020	over Withdrawals	2,285		
					2,585		2,585

John Nelson, Capital			
Balance	32,285	Investment	30,000
		Excess of Income	
		over Withdrawals	2,285
	32,285		32,285
		Balance	32,285

The net income, or net loss, is transferred to the proprietor's drawing account. This is consistent with the analysis of the withdrawal; since the drawing account is debited for withdrawals in anticipation of income, it should also be credited with the net income actually earned during the period. If the resulting balance of the account is a credit, it indicates that earnings have exceeded withdrawals, so that additional withdrawals can be made. A debit balance indicates an excess of withdrawals over earnings and the possible need for additional investments to cover the deficiency.

Because there are no legal restrictions on the earnings of a single proprietorship, as there are on those of a corporation, the balance of the drawing account is usually closed into the proprietor's capital account at the end of the accounting period.

The statement of financial position of a single proprietorship would be the same as that of a corporation, except for the Owner's Equity section. For a single proprietorship, this section appears as shown:

Owner's Equity	
John Nelson, Capital	$32,285

Because no Retained Earnings account is required for a single proprietorship, a statement of retained earnings would not be prepared; instead, a statement of owner's equity would be made. The statement of owner's equity for the Nelson Garage as a single proprietorship owned and operated by John Nelson is shown as

NELSON GARAGE	
Statement of Owner's Equity	
For the Month Ended January 31, 1973	
John Nelson, Original Investment. January 2, 1973	$30,000
Add Net Income for January, 1973	2,585
Total	$32,585
Deduct Withdrawals	300
John Nelson, Capital, January 31, 1973	$32,285

A statement of owner's equity for a single proprietorship with a beginning balance and an additional investment during January is shown as

JAMES CLARK SERVICES	
Statement of Owner's Equity	
For the Month Ended January 31, 1973	
James Clark, Capital, January 1, 1973	$500,000
Add Net Income for January, 1973	100,000
Additional Investment	200,000
Total	$800,000
Deduct Withdrawals	50,000
James Clark, Capital, January 31, 1973	$750,000

INTERRELATIONSHIP OF THE FINANCIAL STATEMENTS

There is a significant interrelationship between the statement of financial position, the statement of retained earnings, and the income statement, as illustrated in Figure 3-10. The income statement shows the net amount remaining after revenues have been matched with expenses for a given period. This amount, the net income, is transferred to the statement of retained earnings, which shows part of the changes that have taken place in stockholders' equity as a result of the operations

Figure 3-10. Interrelationship of Financial Statements

RELAT CORPORATION Statement of Financial Position January 1, 1973		
Total Assets		$100,000
Total Liabilities		$ 18,000
Stockholders' Equity		
Capital Stock	$70,000	
Retained Earnings	12,000	
Total Stockholders' Equity		82,000
Total Liabilities and		
Stockholders' Equity		$100,000

RELAT CORPORATION Statement of Financial Position January 31, 1973		
Total Assets		$150,000
Total Liabilities		$ 28,000
Stockholders' Equity		
Capital Stock	$70,000	
Retained Earnings	52,000	
Total Stockholders' Equity		122,000
Total Liabilities and		
Stockholders' Equity		$150,000

one-month interval

RELAT CORPORATION Statement of Retained Earnings For the Month Ended January 31, 1973	
Retained Earnings, January 1, 1973	$12,000
Add Net Income for January, 1973	50,000
Total	$62,000
Deduct Dividends	10,000
Retained Earnings, January 31, 1973	$52,000

RELAT CORPORATION Income Statement For the Month Ended January 31, 1973	
Revenues (totals)	$400,000
Expenses (totals)	350,000
Net Income	$ 50,000

of a period. The end-of-the period balance of retained earnings is transferred to the end-of-period statement of financial position, which presents information as of a moment of time—that is, at the end of the accounting period. The income statement and the statement of retained earnings help to account for the changes in the stockholders' equity during the interval between statements of financial position. For this reason, it is helpful if the statements are prepared in this order: income statement, statement of retained earnings, and statement of financial position.

Summary totals are used so that the statements can be presented on one page. This procedure is not acceptable for the problems; details should be given on all statements.

1. The date of the first statement of financial position is also the beginning date of the statement of retained earnings and the income statement.

(*For the Month Ended January 31, 1973*, means the period beginning January 1 and ending January 31.)

2. The date of the second statement of financial position (January 31, 1973), is also the ending date of the statement of retained earnings and the income statement.
3. The retained earnings in the first statement of financial position ($12,000) is the same as the beginning amount in the statement of retained earnings.
4. The net income ($50,000) is transferred from the income statement to the statement of retained earnings.
5. The end-of-period retained earnings ($52,000) is transferred from the statement of retained earnings to the statement of financial position dated January 31, 1973.

SUMMARY

Revenue describes the source of the inflow of assets resulting from services rendered, sales of products or merchandise, gains from sales or exchanges of assets other than stock in trade, and earnings from interest and dividends on investments. *Expenses* are the costs of goods and services used in the production of revenue. A debit records an increase in an expense and a decrease in revenue; whereas a credit records an increase in revenue and a decrease in an expense. *Net income* is the excess of total revenue over total expenses for a specified period of time. It reflects the increase in the owner's equity resulting from business operations. A *net loss* is the excess of total expenses over total revenue for a definite time period. It reflects the decrease in owner's equity resulting from business operations. *Dividends* are distributions of net income, earned in the current period or a prior period, to stockholders. Thus, dividends reduce the owner's equity. A debit records an increase in dividends and a credit records a decrease in dividends.

A *chart of accounts* is a classified listing of all the accounts used by a firm. The *general ledger* contains the statement of financial position and income statement accounts. When there are many homogenous accounts (such as customer's accounts) in the general ledger, a *subsidiary ledger* can be opened to maintain the individual accounts. A *controlling account* in the general ledger summarizes the changes recorded in the subsidiary ledger. A transaction involving a controlling account must be posted to the general ledger and to the appropriate account in the related subsidiary ledger.

The accounting sequence discussed may be summarized as follows: (a) At the end of an accounting period, after all the transactions have been properly recorded and posted and the balances of the accounts have been obtained, a trial balance is taken. (b) After this step, a schedule listing the balances of the individual accounts of each subsidiary ledger is compiled; the total of these balances as shown on the schedule should agree with the related controlling account in the general ledger. (c) Three statements are now prepared from the trial balance— an *income statement*, which summarizes the expenses and revenue for a specific time period, showing the net income or net loss accruing to the owners; a *statement of retained earnings*, which shows the changes in that part of stockholder's equity designated as retained earnings; and a *statement of financial position*. (d) The revenue and expense accounts are closed to the Revenue and Expense Summary account, which is then closed to the Retained Earnings account. The Dividends account is also closed to the Retained Earnings account. The revenue, expense, and dividends accounts are set up to measure part of the changes that take place in Retained Earnings during a specified period of time and therefore must be closed, or emptied, at the end of that accounting period. (e) After the closing entries are posted and the accounts are balanced and ruled, a *post-closing trial balance* is prepared to test the equality of debits and credits before the accounts are used during the next accounting period.

    In a single proprietorship, a drawing account is debited for all withdrawals of earnings. At the end of an accounting period, the Revenue and Expense Summary account is closed to the drawing account and the drawing account is closed to the proprietor's capital account. In a single proprietorship, a *statement of owner's equity* replaces the statement of retained earnings prepared in a corporation. It shows the changes that have taken place in the proprietor's capital account over a specified period of time.

QUESTIONS

Q3-1. Define the term *revenue*. Does the receipt of cash by a business indicate that revenue has been earned? Explain. List ten small businesses and professions, and name the major source of revenue for each.

Q3-2. Define the term *expense*. Does the payment of cash by a business indicate that an expense has been incurred? Explain. Distinguish between a dividend and an expense.

Q3-3. The accountant for J. A. Williams, owner of a parking-lot business, listed the parking lot at a cost of $10,000 on the financial position statement. Williams argues that this amount should be $18,000 because he has recently been offered $18,000 for the lot. Discuss.

Q3-4. What item is common to each of the following: (1) the income statement and the statement of owner's equity; (2) the statement of owner's equity and the statement of financial position as of the beginning of an accounting period; and (3) the statement of owner's equity and the statement of financial position as of the end of an accounting period?

Q3-5. Robert Hanlon purchased electrical supplies on account from the Wilson Company for $350, and from Jackson, Inc., for $100. Hanlon debited Electrical Supplies, $450, and erroneously credited Accounts Receivable for $450 in the general ledger. The credit postings to the accounts payable ledger were properly made. (a) What effect would the error have on the debit and credit totals of the trial balance taken at the end of the month? (b) What accounts in the trial balance would be incorrectly stated? (c) Would the error be discovered? How?

Q3-6. List the advantages to management of a division of the general and subsidiary ledgers and the use of controlling accounts. Is it equally advantageous to exclude the schedules of accounts receivable and accounts payable from the general ledger trial balance? Explain.

Q3-7. The following transaction occurred on June 15, 1973:

Received bills representing charges for truck maintenance and repairs as follows: Beacon Hill Garage, $150; Uptown Garage, $225.

Showing the proper general journal and general and subsidiary ledger accounts, prepare flow charts as shown in Figure 3-1 to illustrate posting from the general journal to the general ledger and the accounts payable ledger.

Q3-8. Assume that your firm has 1,000 charge customers. (a) Why would you want to keep your posting up to date? (b) Is it true that posting depends on previous journalizing? (c) Does journalizing, in turn, depend on earlier procedures in the complete accounting system? Explain.

Q3-9. What is the purpose of closing the books? Using T accounts for Revenue, Expenses, Dividends, Revenue and Expense Summary, and Retained Earnings, diagram the closing process.

Q3-10. Distinguish between single proprietorship and corporate accounting for investments and withdrawals, giving examples.

Q3-11. Draw a diagram showing the interrelationship of the statement of financial position, statement of retained earnings, and income statement.

Q3-12. The balance of retained earnings of the Hanson Company on December 31, 1973, was $1,000 less than on December 31, 1972. Give two possible reasons for the decrease.

EXERCISES

E3-1. Some of the possible effects of a transaction are listed:

1. An asset increase accompanied by an asset decrease
2. An asset increase accompanied by an owner's equity increase
3. An asset increase accompanied by a liability increase
4. An asset increase accompanied by a revenue increase
5. An asset decrease accompanied by a liability decrease
6. An asset decrease accompanied by owner equity decrease
7. An asset decrease accompanied by an expense increase
8. An expense increase accompanied by a liability increase

Using the identifying numbers to the left of the listed combinations, indicate the effect of each of the following transactions:

Example: Issued capital stock for cash. Answer: (2)

a. Paid an account payable.
b. Borrowed money from a bank and issued a note.
c. Collected an account receivable.
d. Collected a commission on a sale made today.
e. Paid for an ad in a newspaper.

E3-2. The following cash receipt transactions occurred at the Alton Realty Corporation during the month of July, 1973:

1973
July 1 Issued capital stock for $75,000 in cash.

7 Received a commission of $1,400 from the sale of a house and lot.

8 Received $3,500 in cash from the issuance of a note payable to a bank.

13 Received $750 in interest from U.S. government bonds.

20 Received $250 in cash for rent of part of a building for July, 1973.

Journalize the revenue transactions only.

E3-3. The following were among the cash payment transactions at the Baltimore Garage during the month of September, 1973:

1973
Sept. 3 Paid $4,000 for a truck.

       7 Paid $860 for salaries for the month.

       9 Paid $3,000 in settlement of an account.

      12 Paid $400 for a typewriter.

      16 Declared and paid a $1,000 cash dividend to stockholders.

      22 Paid $175 for rent of the office for September.

Journalize the expense transactions only.

E3-4. The October, 1973, transactions of the Biltmore Travel Service are given:

1973
Oct.   1 Paid $150 for an advertisement in the Travel section of the New York Times.

       2 Arranged a round-the-world trip for Mr. and Mrs. Hooker J. Sander. A commission
          of $175 in cash was collected from the steamship company.

       3 Arranged fly-now, pay-later European trips for several clients. The Transatlantic
          Airway System agreed to a commission of $600 for services rendered, payment to
          be made at the end of the month.

       4 Another advertisement was placed in the New York Times for $250, payment to be
          made in 10 days.

      16 Benjamin B. Biltmore, owner of the Biltmore Travel Service, withdrew $400 from the
          business for his personal use.

      19 Collected $600 from the Transatlantic Airway System.

Following the example given for the October 1 transaction, analyze each transaction and
prepare the necessary journal entry.

Example:
Oct. 1   a. Advertising is an operating expense. Expenses are recorded by debits. Debit
            Advertising Expense for $150.
         b. The asset Cash was decreased. Decreases of assets are recorded by credits. Credit
            Cash for $150.
         c. Journal entry:
            Advertising Expense   150
                Cash   150

E3-5. The Cash account in the general ledger of Grossman's Repair Shop is given:

	Cash		Acct. No. 101
(1)	1,000	(3)	600
(2)	400	(5)	500
(4)	500		

Item 1 is Grossman's original investment on June 1. Items 2 and 4 are cash receipts, and items
3 and 5 are cash payments made during June.
a. What is the balance of the account to be shown in the trial balance as of the end of June?
b. Will Grossman's income statement for the month of June reflect a net loss of $200—the
   excess of payments ($1,100) over receipts other than the original investment ($900)? Explain.

E3-6. The following transactions occurred at the Adden Rug Cleaning Company:

1973

Sept. 1 Billed customers for $285 for rug cleaning work, as follows:

Charles Abbott	$ 75
Morgan Hooley	120
Arthur Rogers	90
Total	$285

30 Received $135 on account from the following customers:

Charles Abbott	$ 25
Morgan Hooley	60
Arthur Rogers	50
Total .	$135

a. Prepare general journal entries to record the transactions.
b. Post to general ledger and accounts receivable ledger accounts. (Assign appropriate numbers to general ledger accounts.)
c. Prepare a schedule of accounts receivable.

E3-7. On July 1, 1973, the Alden Plumbing Company purchased plumbing supplies on account as follows:

Allan Company	$ 300
Jackson Company	100
Warren, Inc.	600
Total	$1,000

On July 15, 1973, the Alden Plumbing Company paid its creditors as follows:

Allan Company	$200
Jackson Company	40
Warren, Inc.	150
Total	$390

a. Prepare general journal entries to record the transactions.
b. Post to general ledger and accounts payable ledger accounts. (Assign appropriate numbers to general ledger accounts.)
c. Prepare a schedule of accounts payable.

E3-8. As of December 31, 1973, the ledger of the Duncan Company contained the following accounts and account balances, among others: Cash, $60,000; Accounts Receivable, $20,000; Retained Earnings, $62,500; Commissions Earned, $50,000; Rent Earned, $6,000; Salaries Expense, $35,000; Office Expense, $5,000; Miscellaneous Expense, $12,000; Dividends, $6,000. (All the nominal accounts are included.)

Journalize the closing entries.

E3-9. Financial information for three different corporations is given:

a. Net income for 1973	$ 22,800
Retained earnings at beginning of year	100,000
Dividends declared and paid in 1973	15,000
Retained earnings at end of year	?
b. Net income for 1973	$?
Retained earnings at beginning of year	160,000
Dividends declared and paid in 1973	20,000
Retained earnings at end of year	155,000

c. Net loss sustained in 1973　　　　　　　　$ 5,000
　　Retained earnings at beginning of year　　　?
　　Dividends declared and paid in 1973　　7,600
　　Retained earnings at end of year　　　265,000

Supply the missing figures.

E3-10. Financial information for three different single proprietorships is given:

a. Net income for 1973　　　　　　　　　$50,000
　　Owner's equity at the beginning of year　　?
　　Owner's equity at the end of year　　95,000
　　Withdrawals by owner during 1973　　8,500
b. Net income for 1973　　　　　　　　$?
　　Owner's equity at beginning of year　　70,000
　　Owner's equity at end of year　　68,000
　　Withdrawals by owner during 1973　　6,200
c. Net loss sustained in 1973　　　　$ 7,800
　　Owner's equity at beginning of year　　30,000
　　Owner's equity at end of year　　19,800
　　Withdrawals by owner during 1973　　?

Supply the missing figures. (Assume that no additional investments were made during 1973.)

DEMONSTRATION PROBLEMS

DP3-1. (*Journalizing, posting, trial balance, and schedule of accounts receivable*) The chart of accounts of the Watson Corporation includes the following accounts and identifying numbers: Cash, 101; Accounts Receivable, 111; Cleaning Supplies, 135; Store Equipment, 164; Capital Stock, 251; Cleaning Revenue, 301; Miscellaneous General Expense, 712; Wages Expense, 714.

1973
Dec.　1　Issued capital stock for $3,000 in cash to start a cleaning business.

　　　3　Purchased store equipment for $800 in cash.

　　10　Paid $50 in cash for cleaning supplies.

　　15　Billed the following customers for cleaning work for the first half of month:

　　　　　　　　　　　　G. Jamieson　　$125
　　　　　　　　　　　　W. Nixon　　　　100
　　　　　　　　　　　　J. Zarba　　　　　50

　　15　Paid $200 in salaries.

　　21　Paid $90 for miscellaneous general expenses.

　　26　Received cash from the following customers to apply on account:

　　　　　　　　　　　　G. Jamieson　　$100
　　　　　　　　　　　　W. Nixon　　　　　60
　　　　　　　　　　　　J. Zarba　　　　　25

　　31　Paid $250 in salaries.

　　31　Billed the following customers for cleaning work for the second half of the month:

　　　　　　　　　　　　G. Jamieson　　$190
　　　　　　　　　　　　J. Zarba　　　　　80

　　31　Received $420 from cash customers for the month.

Required:

1. Journalize the transactions.
2. Open accounts and post from the journal to the appropriate ledgers. (Assign appropriate numbers to general ledger accounts.)
3. Take a trial balance.
4. Prepare a schedule of accounts receivable.

DP3-2. (*Journalizing, posting, and statements*) Dr. Ransome T. Tyler opened an office for the general practice of dentistry. During the month of October, 1973, the following transactions occurred.

1973

Oct. 1   Invested $2,000 in the business.

3   Purchased dental supplies on account, as follows:

Safety Dental Supply Company	$350
Sanitary Supply Company	400

3   Paid $300 for the October rent.

7   Paid $200 for miscellaneous general expenses.

9   Received $1,200 in cash for professional services rendered.

10   Purchased office equipment from Dental Equipment Company for $5,000 on account.

15   Paid $200 to the Safety Dental Supply Company on account, and $300 to the Sanitary Supply Company.

26   Mailed statements to the following clients for services rendered:

R. Beale	$45
P. Witty	75

31   Paid $1,000 in cash and issued a note payable for $4,000 to the Dental Equipment Company.

31   Received $20 in cash from R. Beale and $50 from P. Witty.

Required:

1. Journalize the transactions.
2. Post to the general ledger, accounts receivable ledger, and accounts payable ledger. (Assign numbers to the general ledger accounts.)
3. Take a trial balance.
4. Prepare schedules of accounts receivable and accounts payable as of October 31, 1973.
5. Prepare an income statement, a statement of owner's equity, and a statement of financial position.
6. Journalize the closing entries and post them.
7. Prepare a post-closing trial balance.

DP3-3. (*Closing entries and post-closing trial balance*) The trial balance of the Carter Corporation on December 31, 1973, is given:

CARTER CORPORATION
Trial Balance
December 31, 1973

Acct. No.	Account Title	Debits	Credits
101	Cash	$50,000	
111	Accounts Receivable	4,000	

Acct. No.	Account Title	Debits	Credits
121	Supplies	$ 1,800	
221	Equipment	20,000	
301	Accounts Payable		$ 4,000
401	Capital Stock		50,000
411	Retained Earnings, January 1, 1973		14,850
421	Dividends	2,000	
501	Commissions Earned		15,000
511	Rent Earned		5,000
601	Salaries Expense	6,700	
602	Advertising Expense	1,000	
603	Supplies Used	1,600	
604	Miscellaneous Expense	1,750	
	Totals	$88,850	$88,850

Required:

1. Set up T accounts for Retained Earnings, Dividends, and each revenue and expense account listed in the trial balance. Enter the account balances.
2. Journalize the closing entries and post to the T accounts.
3. Prepare a post-closing trial balance.

PROBLEMS

P3-1. (*Accounting policy decision problem*) Jay Moser decided to open his own office. Transactions for the month of March, 1973, were:

1973

March 1   Deposited $10,000 in a checking account under the business name, Jay Moser, Attorney-at-Law.

3   Paid $200 for the first month's rent on his office.

5   Purchased office equipment for $720. Paid $220 in cash and issued a note payable for the balance.

6   Paid $120 for a one-year insurance policy on the office equipment, effective March 1, 1973.

7   Paid $100 in cash for office supplies.

8   Billed the following clients for services rendered:

J. Bates	$100
S. Canner	50
C. Faler	50

10   Withdrew $300 for personal use.

15   Received cash from the following clients:

J. Bates	$50
S. Canner	50

18   Received $500 in cash for services rendered not previously billed.

31   Paid $375 for miscellaneous general expenses for March.

Required: 1. Journalize the transactions.
2. Suggest a chart of accounts for Jay Moser and explain why the particular numbers are used in the chart.

P3-2. James Lunn, a master electrician, completed the following transactions during the month of August, 1973:

1973

Aug. 1 Transferred $16,500 from his personal savings and opened a business checking account.

1 Paid $250 for rent for the month.

1 Paid $2,000 in cash for store equipment to the Best Equipment Company.

1 Purchased electrical supplies for $1,500 on account, as follows:

Burnett Supply Company	$ 100
Mystic Wire Company	300
Ray Electrical Supply Company	1,100

2 Paid a $200 premium on a one-year comprehensive insurance policy, effective August 1, 1973.

4 Purchased a truck for $3,100 from Bennett Motor Company, giving $1,100 in cash and a note payable for the balance.

8 Received $800 in cash for a completed wiring job.

12 Paid the following creditors:

Burnett Supply Company	$ 50
Mystic Wire Company	200
Ray Electrical Supply Company	400

15 Invested an additional $2,000 in cash in the business.

20 Received $60 in cash for the rental of his truck.

23 Received $400 in cash for a completed wiring job.

26 Paid $30 for telephone service.

27 Paid $165 for gas, oil, and other truck expenses.

28 Withdrew $250 for personal use.

30 Paid the *Weekly Mercury* $25 for advertising space.

31 Billed customers for completed work, as follows:

Arlex Company	$95
James Phillips	45
Raymond Wills	60

Required:

1. Open the following accounts in the general ledger: Cash 101, Accounts Receivable 111, Electrical Supplies 135, Prepaid Insurance 140, Truck 162, Store Equipment 164, Accounts Payable 201, Notes Payable 204, James Lunn, Capital 251, James Lunn, Drawing 252, Electrical Service Revenue 301, Rental Revenue 302, Advertising Expense 618, Rent Expense 703, Telephone and Telegraph Expense 709, Truck Expense 710.
2. Open customers' accounts in the accounts receivable ledger.
3. Open creditors' accounts in the accounts payable ledger.
4. Record all the transactions in the general journal.
5. Post from the general journal to the appropriate ledgers.
6. Prepare a trial balance from the general ledger.
7. Prepare a schedule of accounts receivable.
8. Prepare a schedule of accounts payable.

P3-3. The Shule Service and Repair Tool Shop was incorporated on September 1, 1973, and capital stock was issued for $21,000 in cash. During the month of September, the Corporation completed the following transactions:

1973

Sept. 1 Paid a $300 premium on a one-year comprehensive insurance policy, effective September 1, 1973.

1 Paid $450 for the September rent.

2 Purchased store equipment for $3,000 in cash.

2 Purchased shop supplies on account as follows:

Alex Supply Company	$1,200
Cambridge Supply House	600
Mystic Tool Company	400

5 Purchased an automobile for $3,100 from Hosmer's Motor Company, giving $800 in cash and a note payable for the balance.

9 Received $600 in cash for servicing and repairing tools.

10 Paid $50 in cash for advertising space in the *Cambridge Weekly.*

15 Paid cash for gas, oil, and other automobile expenses for two weeks, $68.

15 Paid $1,700 to the following creditors:

Alex Supply Company	$900
Cambridge Supply House	500
Mystic Tool Company	300

18 Received $800 in cash for repairing tools.

20 Paid $500 in cash on the note given for the purchase of the automobile.

21 Declared and paid a $250 dividend.

22 Paid $35 for telephone service.

23 Paid $18 for a new battery for the automobile. (Debit Automobile Expense.)

24 Billed customers $500 for service and repair work, as follows:

Harris Jones	$225
William Meserve	175
Patrick Robinson	100

25 Paid $15 for cleaning the shop.

25 Received $450 in cash for servicing tools.

26 Purchased additional shop supplies on account, as follows:

Alex Supply Company	$225
Cambridge Supply House	150

27 Paid $58 for electric service.

28 Purchased a typewriter and an adding machine for $450.

29 Received $325 on account from the following customers:

Harris Jones	$100
William Meserve	150
Patrick Robinson	75

1973

Sept. 30 Paid $55 for gas, oil, and other automobile expenses for two weeks.

30 Received $350 from customers for repair work not previously billed.

30 Paid $100 in cash for advertising space in a local magazine.

30 Received a promissory note from Harris Jones for the balance due on his account.

Required:

1. Open the following accounts in the general ledger: Cash, 101; Accounts Receivable, 111; Notes Receivable, 115; Shop Supplies, 136; Prepaid Insurance, 140; Automobile, 162; Store Equipment, 164; Office Equipment, 165; Accounts Payable, 201; Notes Payable, 204; Capital Stock, 251; Dividends, 252; Repair Service Revenue, 301; Advertising Expense, 618; Rent Expense, 703; Heat and Light Expense, 705; Telephone and Telegraph Expense, 709; Automobile Expense, 710; Miscellaneous General Expense, 712.
2. Open customers' accounts in the accounts receivable ledger.
3. Open creditors' accounts in the accounts payable ledger.
4. Record all the transactions in the general journal.
5. Post to the appropriate ledgers.
6. Prepare a trial balance.
7. Prepare a schedule of accounts receivable.
8. Prepare a schedule of accounts payable.

P3-4. The trial balance of the Doolittle Parking Lot shows the accounts in alphabetical order:

DOOLITTLE PARKING LOT

Trial Balance

December 31, 1973

Account Title	Debits	Credits
Accounts Payable		$ 1,000
Accounts Receivable	$ 6,500	
Cash	21,800	
Capital Stock		20,000
Dividends	950	
Equipment Maintenance Expense	1,200	
Heat and Light Expense	800	
Interest Earned		600
Land	5,000	
Notes Payable		2,000
Notes Receivable	1,500	
Parking Fees Earned		19,650
Salaries Expense	4,500	
Retained Earnings, January 1, 1973		1,250
Supplies on Hand	700	
Supplies Used	1,450	
Telephone Expense	100	
Totals	$44,500	$44,500

Required:

1. Prepare a trial balance in proper statement order.
2. Prepare an income statement, a statement of retained earnings, and a statement of financial position.
3. Journalize the closing entries.

P3-5. The following statements have been prepared for the H. Hobson Company:

H. HOBSON COMPANY
Income Statement
For the Month Ended January 31, 1973

Revenue		
Storage Fees		$2,485
Expenses		
Office Rent Expense	$ 300	
Salaries Expense	1,000	
Miscellaneous Expenses	335	1,635
Net Income		$ 850

H. HOBSON COMPANY
Statement of Financial Position
January 31, 1973

Assets			Liabilities and Stockholders' Equity		
Current Assets			Current Liabilities		
Cash	$1,000		Accounts Payable		$ 300
Repair Parts	500		Stockholders' Equity		
Total Current Assets		$1,500	Capital Stock	$3,000	
Plant and Equipment			Retained Earnings	1,700	
Land	$1,000		Total Stockholders' Equity		4,700
Building	2,500				
Total Plant and Equipment		3,500	Total Liabilities and		
Total Assets		$5,000	Stockholders' Equity		$5,000

During January, the Company declared and paid a dividend of $100.

> Required:

Prepare a statement of retained earnings for the H. Hobson Company for the month of January, 1973, and the closing entries as of January 31, 1973.

P3-6. Allen Finner, a master plumber, opened his own shop. During the month of March, 1973, he completed the following transactions:

1973
March 1   Invested $4,000 in cash in the business.

2   Paid $50 rent for the month of March.

4   Purchased plumbing supplies on account, as follows:

Massachusetts Plumbing Company	$500
Plumbers, Inc.	150
Rice Plumbing Company	250

6   Purchased a used truck for $2,016 from the Barrs Motor Company, giving $216 in cash and a note payable for the balance.

9   Paid $600 in cash for shop equipment.

10   Paid $180 in cash for a one-year insurance policy on the shop equipment and truck, effective March 10, 1973.

14   Received $350 for a completed plumbing job.

1973
March 18 Paid creditors on account, as follows:

Massachusetts Plumbing Company	$30
Plumbers, Inc.	15
Rice Plumbing Company	20

    20 Finner withdrew $175 for his personal use.

Use the following account numbers and titles:

11	Cash	55	Notes Payable
15	Accounts Receivable	61	Allen Finner, Capital
21	Plumbing Supplies	62	Allen Finner, Drawing
31	Prepaid Insurance	71	Rental Revenue
41	Truck	81	Plumbing Revenue
45	Shop Equipment	91	Rent Expense
51	Accounts Payable	92	Telephone and Telegraph Expense

Required: 1. Journalize the transactions.
2. Post to the appropriate ledger accounts.
3. Take a trial balance.
4. Prepare schedule of accounts payable.

P3-7. The following transactions occurred during January, 1973, at the Dodd Roof Repair Company.

1973
Jan. 1 Issued capital stock for $12,000 in cash.

    5 Paid $200 for two days' rental of a derrick and pulley assembly used on a repair job.

    9 Purchased U.S. government bonds for $5,000 in cash.

  11 Collected $1,300 on completion of roofing repair work.

  20 Signed an agreement with Hampton College to repair dormitory roofs for $3,000. The work is to be completed during February and March.

  25 Paid a cash dividend of $250 to stockholders.

  28 Paid $450 for repair materials used on jobs during the month.

  30 Paid $1,800 in salaries and wages.

  31 Completed roofing repair work for Willard J. Evans in the amount of $1,600. Evans promised to pay for the work on February 10.

Use the following account titles and numbers:

11	Cash	41	Repair Service Revenue
15	Marketable Securities	51	Salaries and Wages Expense
18	Accounts Receivable	53	Repair Materials Expense
31	Capital Stock	55	Rental Expense
32	Retained Earnings	61	Revenue and Expense Summary
33	Dividends		

Required: 1. Journalize the transactions.
2. Post to general ledger accounts.
3. Take a trial balance.
4. Prepare an income statement, a statement of retained earnings, and a statement of financial position.
5. Prepare and post the closing entries.
6. Rule the accounts that have no balances.
7. Take a post-closing trial balance.

P3-8. The following information is taken from the books of the Gunn Company:

GUNN COMPANY
Statement of Retained Earnings
For the Year Ended December 31, 1973

Retained Earnings, January 1, 1973	$ 50,000
Net Income for 1973	100,000
Total	$150,000
Deduct Dividends	35,000
Retained Earnings, December 31, 1973	$115,000

The expenses for 1973 were: Salaries, $50,500; Advertising Expense, $10,000; Office Expense, $8,000; and Miscellaneous Expense, $18,000. The revenue came from only one source, Commissions Earned.

Required: Prepare a formal income statement for the Gunn Company. Show your computations of the amounts that are not given.

4

The
End-of-Period
Process

A complete but simple service company illustration, the transactions of the Nelson Garage, was used in Chapter 3. A similar but more complex illustration is used in this chapter to introduce the following elements: (1) *adjustments*—continuous transactions that, for convenience, are not recorded until the end of the period, (2) the *worksheet*—an orderly method of collecting information for the preparation of formal financial statements, and (3) further managerial analysis.

THE ACCOUNTING METHOD

Two accounting methods are found in practice: the cash basis and the accrual basis.

The Cash Basis

Under the cash basis of accounting, revenue is recognized when the cash is received, and the revenue is recorded at that time. Expenses are recognized in the period of payment. Recognition of revenue and expenses during an accounting period is based on an inflow and outflow of cash—a matching of cash receipts and cash disbursements to determine operating results during an accounting period. This method of accounting is obviously simple in application; but in most cases it does not properly measure net income because, for example, it does not recognize uncollected revenue items as being earned and unpaid expense items as being incurred until actual payment is made. Hence, it matches only some of the revenues and expenses for a given period. There are instances, however, particularly in small professional and service businesses, in which the cash basis of accounting is used with acceptable results. Hybrid systems, or modifications of the cash-basis system, are often found in practice.

The Accrual Basis

The accrual basis of accounting is founded on the principle that if the net income of a business for a given period of time is to be measured properly, all the revenue earned during that period and all the related expenses assignable to the period must be considered. Revenues are recognized at the time of sale, and expenses are usually recognized at the time the services are received and used in the production of revenue. ▼ This process of matching the revenue of a period with the expenses of that period, regardless of when, whether, or how much cash has been received or paid, is the central goal of the accrual basis of accounting and underlies all the discussions in this text. ▼

Accounting Concept: ▼
Matching Revenue and
Expenses

The difference in net income resulting from the use of each method is best illustrated by an example. The Dee Company, which does landscape gardening, performed work during August for which it charged $1,000. It received $600 on August 15 and $400 on September 10. Wages (the only expense) of $550 were paid on August 31. No work was performed during September.

| | Cash Basis | | Accrual Basis | |
	August	September	August	September
Revenue	$600	$400	$1,000	$-0-
Expense	550	-0-	550	-0-
Net Income	$ 50	$400	$ 450	$-0-

The accrual basis of accounting gives more useful results because revenue is reflected in the period to which it properly belongs; that is, the period in which it was earned. Net income is the difference between revenue earned and expenses incurred during the accounting period. The accrual method, by matching expenses incurred with revenue earned for the period, presents the better measurement of net income. Since the accrual basis of accounting results in more useful financial statements, most businesses keep their books on this basis.

THE NEED FOR ADJUSTING ENTRIES

▼ During the accounting period, regular business transactions are recorded as they occur. At the end of the period, the accountant may find that the ledger accounts are incomplete: some new accounts must be brought into the books and other accounts must be brought up to date. The journal entries necessary to accomplish this are referred to as *adjusting entries*. Periodic adjustment of the ledger accounts is indispensable if the financial statements are to reflect the realistic position of the company—its assets and equities—as of the end of the period, and the results of its operations—revenue earned and expenses incurred—during the period.

Accounting Procedure: ▼
Adjusting Entries

It is impractical and sometimes impossible to record the day-to-day changes in certain accounts. For example, when the premium payment is made on an insurance policy, the asset Prepaid Insurance is debited. At the end of the accounting period, however, only part of the balance of the Prepaid Insurance account represents an asset. The amount that has expired with the passage of time is an expense because it represents the cost of insurance protection. At the end of the accounting period, therefore, Prepaid Insurance contains both an asset and an expense element. An adjustment is necessary to record the correct amount of Insurance Expense and to reduce Prepaid Insurance. This type of adjusting entry will be referred to as a *short-term cost* apportionment adjustment. ▼

An adjusting entry may be required to record previously unrecorded data. Assume, for example, that a company paid wages on March 28 for the two-week period that ended on that date. However, the employees worked on March 29, 30, and 31. If March 31 is the end of the accounting period, recognition must be given to this unrecorded but incurred expense as well as to the corresponding increase in liabilities, so that the financial statements may show the liability and the proper assignment of the expense to the period. This type of adjustment is referred to as an *accrued expense* adjustment.

Adjusting entries may be entered initially in the worksheet with formal recording in the journal deferred until the closing entries are made, or they may be recorded in the journal first and then applied to the worksheet.

A distinction is usually made between adjusting entries and entries that record regular business transactions. Regular business transactions start and complete their cycles within an accounting period. Adjusting entries deal with the transactions that transpire continuously and may be termed *continuous transactions.* It is neither feasible nor necessary to record these continuing changes during the period; rather, they are recorded at the end of each accounting period by means of *summary* adjusting entries. The nature of the adjusting entries varies. The adjusting entry for wages, for example, records a change that has already taken place—the increase in a liability incurred but unrecorded. The adjusting entry for Supplies Expense, on the other hand, recognizes the partial consumption of an item that was recorded at the time of acquisition in an asset account.

THE PROCESS OF RECORDING ADJUSTMENTS

The various kinds of continuous transactions, or adjustments, may be summarized in the following five groups:

1. *Short-term cost apportionments:* recorded cost that must be apportioned usually between two accounting periods, which could be a month, a quarter, but usually a year. Examples: supplies, prepaid insurance, and prepaid rent.

2. *Short-term revenue apportionments:* recorded revenue that will usually be apportioned between two accounting periods. Examples: rent collected in advance and magazine subscriptions collected in advance.

3. *Long-term cost apportionments:* a type of adjustment similar to short-term cost apportionment except that the recorded cost will usually be apportioned between three or more accounting periods. Example: the cost of a building.

4. *Accrued expenses:* unrecorded expenses incurred in a given period. Example: wages earned by employees after the last pay day in an accounting period.

5. *Accrued revenues:* unrecorded revenues earned in a given period. Example: interest earned on a note receivable held for 30 days in the current period but not due until sometime in the next period.

The Connolly Trucking Company started business on June 1, 1973. As a convenience in illustrating the end-of-period procedures, it is assumed that the books are closed on June 30 (books are customarily closed annually). The trial balance taken from the Connolly Trucking Company's general ledger is shown in Figure 4-1.

Figure 4-1 Trial Balance

CONNOLLY TRUCKING COMPANY
Trial Balance
June 30, 1973

Acct. No.	Account Title	Debits	Credits
101	Cash	$ 5,250	
111	Accounts Receivable	550	
112	Notes Receivable	1,440	
131	Office Supplies	230	
141	Prepaid Insurance	2,160	
142	Prepaid Rent	1,500	
201	Office Equipment	1,400	
211	Trucks	13,000	
301	Accounts Payable		$ 200
302	Notes Payable		8,000
321	Unearned Rent		600
401	Capital Stock		12,000
402	Dividends	500	
501	Trucking Revenue		7,465
601	Heat and Light Expense	40	
602	Maintenance and Repairs Expense	375	
603	Telephone and Telegraph Expense	95	
604	Gas and Oil Expense	525	
605	Wages Expense	1,200	
	Totals	$28,265	$28,265

The adjusting entries are journalized and posted to the accounts. The separate discussion of each adjusting entry is identified by the letter used to cross reference the debit and credit adjustments in the Adjustments columns of the *worksheet*, shown in Figure 4-4.

Short-Term Cost Apportionment Adjustments—a, b, and c

There are three steps in adjusting the mixed account involving a short-term cost apportionment.

1. Determining the balance of each account to be adjusted
2. Determining the amount of the asset or expense elements in each account
3. Recording the adjusting entries

(a)

On June 1, the Connolly Trucking Company paid $1,500 in cash for three months' rent.

Step 1. The general ledger shows the following balance in the account:

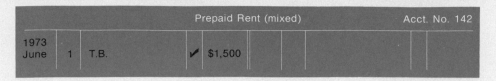

The abbreviation T.B. indicates that the figure is the same figure as shown in the Trial Balance (Figure 4-1) for this particular account.

Step 2. The amount of expense applicable to June is $500 ($1,500 ÷ 3 months). On June 30, therefore, Prepaid Rent is a mixed account consisting of

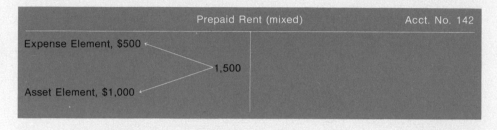

Step 3. The timing of the journalizing of the adjustments should be delayed until the formal financial statements are prepared and presented to management for its use. Here, however, as a basic teaching device, the adjusting entries for the Connolly Trucking Company are made as each adjustment is explained.

The required adjusting entry is

			GENERAL JOURNAL		Page 4	
1973 June	30	Rent Expense		142	500	
		Prepaid Rent		606		500
		To record rent expense for June.				

The expense element is thus removed from the mixed account, as shown by the posting below in the ledger accounts:

			Prepaid Rent (asset)			Acct. No. 142		
1973 June	1	T.B.	✔	1,500	1973 June	30	(adjustment)	4	500

			Rent Expense (expense)		Acct. No. 606
1973 June	30	(adjustment)	4	500	

Prepaid Rent ($1,000) is classified in the statement of financial position as a current asset, and Rent Expense ($500) appears in the income statement as an expense.

(b)

The Connolly Trucking Company paid a premium of $2,160 for a comprehensive three-year insurance policy, effective June 1, 1973.

Step 1. Prepaid Insurance, before adjustment, shows a balance of $2,160. The title Prepaid Insurance classifies it as basically an asset account, but it is in fact a mixed account.

Step 2. An analysis of the account shows that the expense element for the month of June is $60 ($2,160 ÷ 36 mos.), and that the unused portion of $2,100 is the asset prepayment benefiting future periods.

Step 3. The following adjusting entry is made:

GENERAL JOURNAL				Page 4
1973				
June 30	Insurance Expense	607	60	
	Prepaid Insurance	141		60
	To record insurance			
	expense for June.			

This information is shown in the following ledger accounts:

Prepaid Insurance (asset)   Acct. No. 141

1973					1973				
June	1	T.B.	✔	2,160	June	30	(adjustment)	4	60

Insurance Expense (expense)   Acct. No. 607

1973				
June	30	(adjustment)	4	60

Prepaid Insurance ($2,100) is classified in the statement of financial position as a current asset, and Insurance Expense ($60) appears in the income statement as an expense.

(c)

Step 1. On the trial balance (Figure 4-1), Office Supplies has a debit balance of $230, representing a purchase made on June 6.

Step 2. The inventory taken on June 30 showed $60 worth of unused supplies; therefore, the expense element is $170 ($230 − $60).

Step 3. The expense of $170 needs to be removed from the mixed account by the following adjusting entry and the adjustment information is posted to the accounts shown below the journal entry:

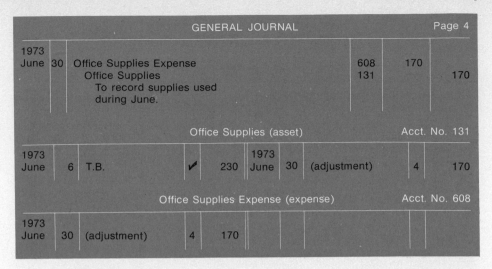

		GENERAL JOURNAL			Page 4
1973					
June	30	Office Supplies Expense	608	170	
		Office Supplies	131		170
		To record supplies used during June.			

				Office Supplies (asset)			Acct. No. 131
1973				1973			
June	6	T.B.	✔ 230	June	30	(adjustment)	4 170

				Office Supplies Expense (expense)		Acct. No. 608
1973						
June	30	(adjustment)	4 170			

Office Supplies ($60) is classified in the statement of financial position as a current asset and Office Supplies Expense ($170) appears in the income statement as an expense.

Short-Term Revenue Apportionment Adjustment—d

The same three steps are followed in making short-term revenue apportionments of amounts originally recorded in mixed liability accounts.

(d)

On June 1, the Connolly Trucking Company signed a contract for the use of its trucks on a part-time basis and received an advance payment of $600 for six months' rent. At that time, Cash was debited and a liability account, Unearned Rent, was credited for $600. On June 30, only the portion earned in the month of June is transferred from Unearned Rent to Rent Earned; the unearned portion remains in Unearned Rent as a liability because the Connolly Trucking Company must provide the use of its truck on a part-time basis for another five months.

Step 1. The amount in the T account is taken from the trial balance, Figure 4-1:

			Unearned Rent (mixed)		Acct. No. 321
			1973		
			June	1	T.B. ✔ 600

Step 2. The rent actually earned in June is $100 ($600 ÷ 6 mos.); on June 30, Unearned Rent is a mixed account and consists of

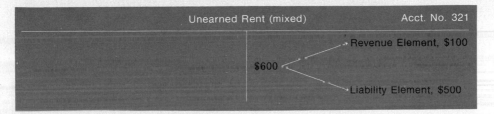

Step 3. The following adjusting entry is made:

		GENERAL JOURNAL			Page 4

1973
June
	30	Unearned Rent
		    Rent Earned
		        To record revenue earned from rental of
		        trucks during June.
			321
			511
				100	
					100

The revenue element is removed from the mixed account as follows:

		Unearned Rent (liability)						Acct. No. 321	
1973 June	30	(adjustment)	4	100	1973 June	1	Balance	✔	600

		Rent Earned (revenue)						Acct. No. 511	
					1973 June	30	(adjustment)	4	100

Rent Earned ($100) appears in the income statement as a revenue item, and Unearned Rent ($500) appears in the statement of financial position as a current liability.

Long-Term Cost Apportionment Adjustment—Depreciation—e and f

Two of the remaining adjusting entries involve the recording of long-term asset cost expiration. Three steps similar to the short-term cost apportionments are followed:

(e)

Step 1. The trial balance, Figure 4-1, shows a balance in the Office Equipment account of $1,400.

Step 2. The equipment, acquired on June 1, is estimated to have a useful life of 10 years, or 120 months, and a *salvage value* of $200 at the end of that period. Salvage, or *residual*, value is the estimated price for which an asset may

Accounting Procedure: ▼
Depreciation

be sold when it is no longer serviceable to the business. In effect, the use of office equipment for 10 years has been purchased at a net cost of $1,200 ($1,400 − $200). A portion of this cost expires in each accounting period during the useful life of the equipment. ▼ This periodic expired cost, called *depreciation expense,* requires no periodic cash outlay, but nevertheless is a continuous expense of operating the business. The portion of the cost of an asset assigned to the accounting period is called *depreciation.* There are a number of methods that may be used in calculating the periodic depreciation charge. ▼ Depreciation expense for the month of June is computed in this case by using the *straight-line method,* in which a uniform portion of the cost is assigned to each period.

$$\frac{\text{Cost} - \text{Salvage value}}{\text{Estimated months of useful life}} = \text{Depreciation for month}$$

The depreciation expense for the office equipment in June is computed as $10.

$$\frac{\$1,400 - \$200}{120} = \$10$$

Step 3. The following adjusting entry is made:

GENERAL JOURNAL					Page 4
1973 June	30	Depreciation Expense–Office Equipment	609	10	
		Accumulated Depreciation–			
		Office Equipment	201A		10
		To record depreciation for June.			

Both of the foregoing accounts are new accounts. The second is called an "Asset Valuation" account or <u>*contra-asset account*</u> because its balance is deducted from Office Equipment to show the book value, or carrying value, of the asset. Office Equipment could be credited directly because the depreciation represents a decrease in the asset; but this procedure is undesirable because it fails to disclose information that is useful to management. Depreciation is an estimate; it is informative to keep asset costs separate from estimated reductions in cost. When separate accounts are used, the original cost and the accumulated depreciation can be determined readily. The June 30 adjusting information is shown in the following ledger accounts:

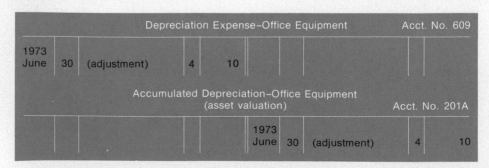

Depreciation Expense–Office Equipment								Acct. No. 609
1973 June	30	(adjustment)	4	10				

Accumulated Depreciation–Office Equipment (asset valuation)								Acct. No. 201A
					1973 June	30	(adjustment)	4	10

Depr. Ep. - O.E. = 10 - debit
Acd. Dep. O.E. = 10 - credit

In the statement of financial position (Figure 4-8), the asset valuation account Accumulated Depreciation–Office Equipment is deducted from Office Equipment; the remainder is the *undepreciated cost*; that is, the portion of the cost of the asset that is not yet charged to expense. Depreciation Expense–Office Equipment ($10) is shown in the income statement as an expense.

(f)

Step 1. On June 1, the Connolly Trucking Company purchased two trucks for business use, each costing $6,500. Because the useful life of the trucks is limited, a portion of the cost is allocable to the month of June. It is estimated that their useful life is five years, or 60 months, at the end of which time each truck will have a salvage value of $500.

Step 2. The computation and recording of the depreciation expense for the trucks is similar to that for the office equipment. The depreciation expense for June for the two trucks is calculated by the straight-line method as follows:

$$\frac{\text{Cost of } \$6{,}500 - \text{Salvage value of } \$500}{60 \text{ months}}$$

= $100 depreciation per month for each truck, or $200 for two trucks

Step 3. The following adjusting entry is made on June 30 and posted to the accounts shown below the journal entry:

GENERAL JOURNAL				Page 4
1973				
June 30	Depreciation Expense–Trucks	610	200	
	Accumulated Depreciation–Trucks	211A		200
	To record depreciation for June.			

Depreciation Expense–Trucks
(expense)   Acct. No. 610

1973								
June	30	(adjustment)	4	200				

Accumulated Depreciation–Trucks
(asset valuation)   Acct. No. 211A

				1973				
				June	30	(adjustment)	4	200

The classification of these accounts in the financial statements is shown in Figures 4-7 and 4-8.

The Accumulated Depreciation accounts are used to accumulate the periodic charges made to expense and to segregate the deduction for the asset valuation. Depreciation Expense shows the expired cost for the accounting period and is closed along with the other expense accounts in an entry that transfers the total expense to Revenue and Expense Summary. Assume that the same adjusting entry for trucks is made on July 31. After it is posted, the general ledger T accounts for Trucks, Depreciation Expense–Trucks, and Accumulated Depreciation–Trucks appear as follows:

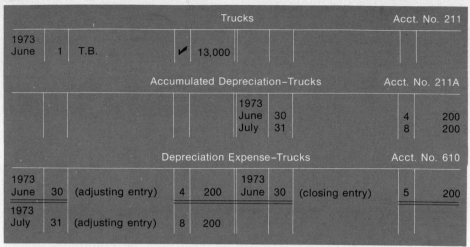

Trucks									Acct. No. 211
1973 June	1	T.B.	✔	13,000					

				Accumulated Depreciation–Trucks					Acct. No. 211A
				1973 June	30			4	200
				July	31			8	200

					Depreciation Expense–Trucks				Acct. No. 610
1973 June	30	(adjusting entry)	4	200	1973 June	30	(closing entry)	5	200
1973 July	31	(adjusting entry)	8	200					

The cost of the trucks and the accumulated depreciation are shown on the statement of financial position at July 31 as follows:

Equipment		
Trucks	$13,000	
Deduct Accumulated Depreciation–Trucks	400	$12,600

Accrued Expense Adjustment—g and h

Accrued expenses are expenses that have been incurred in a given period but have not yet been paid. The accountant's job at the end of the accounting period is to record the expense in the proper period of incurrence and also to record the accompanying liability. The accrued expense adjustment described in (g) is that of unrecorded wages expense of $150.

(g)

Step 1. Wages Expense contains two debits of $600 each, representing wages paid biweekly to employees through June 27.

Step 2. The employees earned wages of $150 for work on June 28, 29, and 30, the last three days of the accounting period. Although the company will not pay the employees again until July 11, it has nevertheless incurred $150 of wages expense for these three days, and a $150 liability exists as of June 30.

Step 3. The following adjusting entry is made on June 30 and posted to the accounts shown below the journal entry:

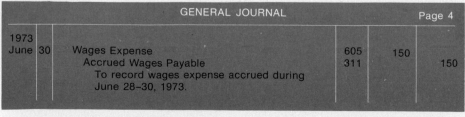

GENERAL JOURNAL						Page 4
1973 June	30	Wages Expense		605	150	
		Accrued Wages Payable		311		150
		To record wages expense accrued during June 28–30, 1973.				

Wages Expense (expense)				Acct. No. 605	
1973 June	13		2	600	
	27		3	600	
	30	(adjustment)	4	150	

Accrued Wages Payable (liability)				Acct. No. 311	
		1973 June	30	(adjustment)	4	150

Wages Expense ($1,350) is shown in the income statement as an expense; Accrued Wages Payable ($150) is shown in the statement of financial position as a current liability.

(h)

Step 1. On June 12, the Connolly Trucking Company borrowed $8,000 from the bank and signed a 45-day, 6-percent interest-bearing note payable. This transaction was recorded in the general journal by debiting Cash and crediting Notes Payable for $8,000.

Step 2. The cost of the use of the $8,000—interest expense—continues throughout the 45 days because interest expense accumulates with the passage of time. The total interest expense plus the $8,000 principal amount will be paid to the bank on July 27, the *maturity*, or due, date. However, unpaid interest expense on an interest-bearing note payable for the 18-day period from June 12 through June 30 must be recognized by an adjusting entry debiting Interest Expense and crediting Accrued Interest Payable for $24.

The formula for computing interest is

Figure 4-2. Interest Formula

$$\text{Principal} \times \text{Interest rate} \times \frac{\text{Elapsed time in days}}{360} = \text{Interest}$$

The unpaid interest expense accrued on June 30 is computed as follows:

$$\$8,000 \times 0.06 \times \frac{18}{360} = \$24$$

The principal multiplied by the interest rate equals the total interest for one year ($8,000 × 0.06 = $480); the interest for a year ($480) multiplied by the elapsed fraction of a year ($^{18}/_{360}$ or $^{1}/_{20}$) is the interest expense for 18 days ($480 × $^{1}/_{20}$), or $24. The use of 360 days in the formula is consistent with commercial practice, the primary reason being simplicity of calculation.

Step 3. The formal adjusting entry is made on June 30 and posted to the accounts indicated on page 112.

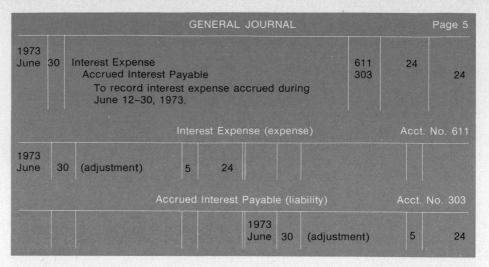

Interest Expense ($24) is reported as an expense in the income statement; Accrued Interest Payable ($24) appears as a current liability in the statement of financial position. This entry gives rise to an *accrued liability.* This term refers to the liability for an expense incurred during one accounting period but payable in a future accounting period. Expenses incurred for which invoices have not yet been received—telephone, heat, light, water, and so on—are also in this category. These may be recorded by debits to appropriate expense accounts and a credit to Accrued Accounts Payable.

Accrued Revenue Adjustment—i

Accrued revenue items are items that have been earned in a given period but for which cash collections have not yet been received. The accountant's job at the end of the accounting period is to record the revenue in the proper period in which it is earned and also to record the accompanying receivable, an asset. The accrued revenue adjustment described in (i) is that of unrecorded earned interest of $4.

(i)

Step 1. The Connolly Trucking Company loaned $1,440 to one of its customers, who signed a 30-day, 5-percent interest-bearing note dated June 10. An entry was made debiting Notes Receivable and crediting Cash for $1,440.

Step 2. The company earned interest on the loan for 20 days in June (June 10 through June 30); it will be received on the maturity date, July 10, when the amount due (principal plus total interest) is paid by the customer. Interest earned, like interest expense, accrues with the passage of time. The 20 days' interest earned by June 30 is recorded by an adjusting entry debiting Accrued Interest Receivable and crediting Interest Earned for $4. Using the formula shown in Figure 4-2, the computation of the interest is

$$\$1,440 \times 0.05 \times \frac{20}{360} = \$4$$

Step 3. The formal adjusting entry is made on June 30 and posted to the accounts indicated below:

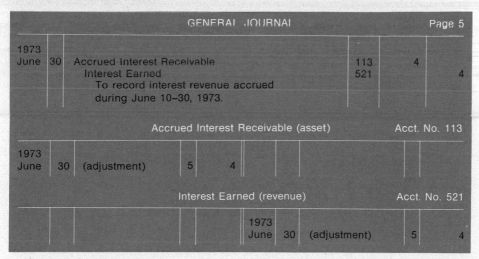

GENERAL JOURNAL					Page 5	
1973						
June	30	Accrued Interest Receivable	113	4		
		Interest Earned	521			4
		To record interest revenue accrued during June 10–30, 1973.				

Accrued Interest Receivable (asset)				Acct. No. 113		
1973						
June	30	(adjustment)	5	4		

Interest Earned (revenue)				Acct. No. 521		
			1973			
			June	30	(adjustment)	5	4

Accrued Interest Receivable ($4) is a current asset in the statement of financial position. Interest Earned is a revenue item in the income statement.

Income Tax Expense Adjustment—j

The income tax expense adjustment is similar to the accrued expense adjustment. A single proprietor or a partner combines his net income from his proprietorship or partnership interest with his income from other sources and computes his tax as an individual taxpayer; he does not pay a tax on his business entity as such. A corporation, however, is taxed as a separate entity, and its financial statements must show the tax and the liability for the tax.

(j)

Step 1. It is difficult to determine precisely the tax related to the taxable income for the month of June because the annual taxable income, on which the tax is based, is not yet known. Nevertheless, the business must make the best possible estimate.

Step 2. The Connolly Trucking Company estimates its income taxes for the month of June to be $1,900.

Step 3. The income tax estimate is journalized on June 30 and posted to the accounts indicated below:

GENERAL JOURNAL					Page 5	
1973						
June	30	Income Tax Expense	611	1,900		
		Income Taxes Payable	331			1,900
		To record estimated taxes for June.				

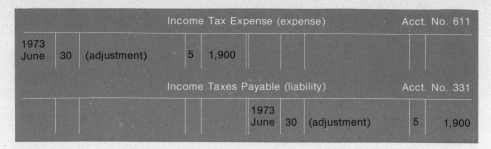

The income tax expense of $1,900 appears in the income statement; it is deducted from net income before income taxes to determine net income after income taxes (Figure 4-7); Income Taxes Payable appears in the statement of financial position as a current liability.

THE WORKSHEET

The worksheet is a device used by the accountant to facilitate the preparation of the formal financial statements; it is not a substitute for the financial statements. Although the worksheet is not indispensable, it would be difficult in most instances to prepare the statements directly from the journals and ledgers since that would often require consolidating material from books, cards, and other documents. The worksheet bridges the gap between the accounting records and the formal statements and serves as a convenient device to calculate the effect of the adjustments and to determine the net income, or net loss, before the adjustments are formally entered in the books and posted to the ledger. It furnishes the accountant with a preview of the final statements. Many businesses do not formally close their books at the end of every accounting period; thus, the worksheet substitutes for the formal procedure of recording and posting the usual adjusting and closing entries.

Preparing the Worksheet

There are four steps in the preparation of the worksheet:

Step 1. The worksheet is headed to show the name of the company, the name of the statement, and the accounting period; the column headings are entered; the trial balance account titles and amounts are entered either directly from the general ledger or from a prepared listing, if available. The account titles are entered in the space provided and the amounts are entered in the first pair of money columns. The worksheet of the Connolly Trucking Company after completion of Step 1 appears in Figure 4-3.

Step 2. The adjustments are entered on the worksheet generally before they are formally journalized. This procedure is followed partly to hasten the preparation of the formal financial statements.

The adjustments are keyed for identification (cross referencing) as they are entered in the Adjustments columns. Any additional accounts required by the adjusting entries are added below the trial balance. (Alternatively, they may

Figure 4-3. Worksheet, Step 1, Trial Balance Entered

CONNOLLY TRUCKING COMPANY
Worksheet
For the Month Ended June 30, 1973

Acct. No.	Account Title	Trial Balance		Adjustments		Adjusted Trial Balance		Income Statement		Position Statement	
		Dr.	Cr.	Dr.	Cr.	Dr.	Cr.	Dr.	Cr.	Dr.	Cr.
101	Cash	5,250									
111	Accounts Receivable	550									
112	Notes Receivable	1,440									
131	Office Supplies	230									
141	Prepaid Insurance	2,160									
142	Prepaid Rent	1,500									
201	Office Equipment	1,400									
211	Trucks	13,000									
301	Accounts Payable		200								
302	Notes Payable		8,000								
321	Unearned Rent		600								
401	Capital Stock		12,000								
402	Dividends	500									
501	Trucking Revenue		7,465								
601	Heat and Light Expense	40									
602	Maintenance and Repairs Expense	375									
603	Telephone and Telegraph Expense	95									
604	Gas and Oil Expense	525									
605	Wages Expense	1,200									
	Totals	28,265	28,265								

Trial balance before adjustments.

be listed in sequence with the other accounts without amounts in the Trial Balance columns.) In entry (a), for example, Rent Expense is debited for $500. Since this account does not appear in the trial balance, the title is written on the line immediately below the trial balance totals and the amount is entered directly in the Adjustments Debit column on the same line; the $500 also is entered in the Adjustments Credit column opposite Prepaid Rent. In this adjustment, only one of the accounts involved had to be written in below the trial balance. In entry (e), however, both the debited and credited accounts had to be written in. After all the adjustments are entered, the Adjustments columns are added as a proof of their equality. The worksheet following the completion of Step 2 is illustrated in Figure 4-4.

Step 3. The amounts extended to the Adjusted Trial Balance columns result from combining the amounts in the Trial Balance columns with the amounts in the Adjustments columns as follows:

a. If there are no adjustments to an account, a debit trial balance amount is extended to the Debit column of the adjusted trial balance, and a credit trial

Figure 4-4. Worksheet, Step 2, Adjustments Entered

CONNOLLY TRUCKING COMPANY
Worksheet
For the Month Ended June 30, 1973

Acct. No.	Account Title	Trial Balance Dr.	Trial Balance Cr.	Adjustments Dr.	Adjustments Cr.	Adjusted Trial Balance Dr.	Adjusted Trial Balance Cr.	Income Statement Dr.	Income Statement Cr.	Position Statement Dr.	Position Statement Cr.
101	Cash	5,250									
111	Accounts Receivable	550									
112	Notes Receivable	1,440									
131	Office Supplies	230			(c) 170						
141	Prepaid Insurance	2,160			(b) 60						
142	Prepaid Rent	1,500			(a) 500						
201	Office Equipment	1,400									
211	Trucks	13,000									
301	Accounts Payable		200								
302	Notes Payable		8,000								
321	Unearned Rent		600	(d) 100							
401	Capital Stock		12,000								
402	Dividends	500									
501	Trucking Revenue		7,465								
601	Heat and Light Expense	40									
602	Maintenance and Repairs Expense	375									
603	Telephone and Telegraph Expense	95									
604	Gas and Oil Expense	525									
605	Wages Expense	1,200		(g) 150							
		28,265	28,265								
606	Rent Expense			(a) 5C0							
607	Insurance Expense			(b) 60							
608	Office Supplies Expense			(c) 170							
511	Rent Earned				(d) 100						
609	Depreciation Expense–Office Equipment			(e) 10							
201A	Accumulated Depreciation–Office Equipment				(e) 10						
610	Depreciation Expense–Trucks			(f) 200							
211A	Accumulated Depreciation–Trucks				(f) 200						
311	Accrued Wages Payable				(g) 150						
611	Interest Expense			(h) 24							
303	Accrued Interest Payable				(h) 24						
113	Accrued Interest Receivable			(i) 4							
521	Interest Earned				(i) 4						
612	Income Tax Expense			(j) 1,900							
331	Income Taxes Payable				(j) 1,900						
				3,118	3,118						

Letters are used to cross reference the debit and credit adjustments.

Additional accounts for the adjustments.

Adjustments are entered in these columns.

balance amount is extended to the Credit column of the adjusted trial balance.

b. If the account in the trial balance has a debit balance, add its debit adjustments and subtract its credit adjustments. The balance, if a debit, is extended to the Adjusted Trial Balance Debit column; if a credit, it is extended to the Credit column.

c. If the account in the trial balance has a credit balance, add its credit adjustments and subtract its debit adjustments. The adjusted balance is extended to the proper Adjusted Trial Balance column.

d. For the accounts listed below the trial balance totals, the adjustment amount is extended directly to the appropriate Adjusted Trial Balance column.

Upon completion of Step 3, the account balances will be the same as the balances of the accounts in the general ledger after the adjusting entries have been journalized and posted. Each line on the worksheet represents a general ledger account and functions in the same manner as to the debit and credit position. For example, after adjustment the Prepaid Rent account appears in the general ledger as follows:

		Prepaid Rent						Acct. No. 142	
1973 June	1	T.B.	✔	1,500	1973 June	30	(adjusting entry)	4	500

The balance is a debit of $1,000, which is the amount shown opposite Prepaid Rent in the Adjusted Trial Balance Debit column of the worksheet.

The worksheet following the completion of Step 3 is shown in Figure 4-5.

Step 4. The amounts in the Adjusted Trial Balance columns are extended either to the Income Statement columns or to the Position Statement columns, depending on their statement classification. Expense and revenue accounts are entered in the Income Statement columns; asset, liability, and stockholders' equity accounts are entered in the Position Statement columns. The four columns then are totaled. The difference between the totals of the Income Statement columns is the net income, or net loss, for the period; a net income is indicated if the total of the Credit column exceeds the total of the Debit column. The excess is entered in the Income Statement Debit column and in the Position Statement Credit column just below the column totals. This procedure records on the worksheet the increase in the stockholders' equity resulting from an excess of revenue over expenses during the period. A net loss is indicated if the total of the Income Statement Debit column exceeds that of the Income Statement Credit column. A loss is shown on the worksheet in the Income Statement Credit column and the Position Statement Debit column just below the column totals. The designation Net Income or Net Loss for the Month, whichever is pertinent, is entered in the Account Title column on the same line. The worksheet following the completion of Step 4 is illustrated in Figure 4-6.

If the differences between the Income Statement Debit and Credit columns (net income) and the Position Statement Debit and Credit columns are not the same, an error has been made. The totaling and ruling of the last four columns of the worksheet (Step 4) is illustrated in Figure 4-6. Note that balancing the last four columns provides only a limited proof of the accuracy of the worksheet—proof that the equality of debits and credits has been maintained throughout its preparation. The extension of the Cash account debit into the Income Statement Debit column, for example, would not destroy the debit-credit relationship of the worksheet, although statements prepared from that worksheet would be inaccurate. Note also that the total of the Position Statement Debit column need not correspond with the total assets reported in the statement. Accumulated Depreciation–Trucks, for example, is extended to the Position Statement Credit

Figure 4-5. Worksheet, Step 3, Adjusted Trial Balance Entered

CONNOLLY TRUCKING COMPANY
Worksheet
For the Month Ended June 30, 1973

Acct. No.	Account Title	Trial Balance Dr.	Trial Balance Cr.	Adjustments Dr.	Adjustments Cr.	Adjusted Trial Balance Dr.	Adjusted Trial Balance Cr.	Income Statement Dr.	Income Statement Cr.	Position Statement Dr.	Position Statement Cr.
101	Cash	5,250				5,250					
111	Accounts Receivable	550				550					
112	Notes Receivable	1,440				1,440					
131	Office Supplies	230			(c) 170	60					
141	Prepaid Insurance	2,160			(b) 60	2,100					
142	Prepaid Rent	1,500			(a) 500	1,000					
201	Office Equipment	1,400				1,400					
211	Trucks	13,000				13,000					
301	Accounts Payable		200				200				
302	Notes Payable		8,000				8,000				
321	Unearned Rent		600	(d) 100			500				
401	Capital Stock		12,000				12,000				
402	Dividends	500				500					
501	Trucking Revenue		7,465				7,465				
601	Heat and Light Expense	40				40					
602	Maintenance and Repairs Expense	375				375					
603	Telephone and Telegraph Expense	95				95					
604	Gas and Oil Expense	525				525					
605	Wages Expense	1,200		(g) 150		1,350					
		28,265	28,265								
606	Rent Expense			(a) 500		500					
607	Insurance Expense			(b) 60		60					
608	Office Supplies Expense			(c) 170		170					
511	Rent Earned				(d) 100		100				
609	Depreciation Expense–Office Equipment			(e) 10		10					
201A	Accumulated Depreciation–Office Equipment				(e) 10		10				
610	Depreciation Expense–Trucks			(f) 200		200					
211A	Accumulated Depreciation–Trucks				(f) 200		200				
311	Accrued Wages Payable				(g) 150		150				
611	Interest Expense			(h) 24		24					
303	Accrued Interest Payable				(h) 24		24				
113	Accrued Interest Receivable			(i) 4		4					
521	Interest Earned				(i) 4		4				
612	Income Tax Expense			(j) 1,900		1,900					
331	Income Taxes Payable				(j) 1,900		1,900				
				3,118	3,118	30,553	30,553				

Balances from the trial balance, adjusted by the amounts in Adjustments columns, are extended here.

column because it represents a position statement account with a credit balance. It is neither an asset nor a liability, but rather a deduction from Trucks, which is extended into the Position Statement Debit column. Since plus and minus symbols are not used on the worksheet, a deduction from an amount in a Debit column is effected by positioning the item to be deducted in the Credit column.

The worksheet may be varied in form—particularly with respect to the number of columns—to meet specific needs of the user. In Figure 5-3, for example, the columns for the adjusted trial balance are omitted.

Figure 4-6. Worksheet, Step 4, Remaining Extensions Made

CONNOLLY TRUCKING COMPANY
Worksheet
For the Month Ended June 30, 1973

Acct. No.	Account Title	Trial Balance		Adjustments		Adjusted Trial Balance		Income Statement		Position Statement	
		Dr.	Cr.	Dr.	Cr.	Dr.	Cr.	Dr.	Cr.	Dr.	Cr.
101	Cash	5,250				5,250				5,250	
111	Accounts Receivable	550				550				550	
112	Notes Receivable	1,440				1,440				1,440	
131	Office Supplies	230			(c) 170	60				60	
141	Prepaid Insurance	2,160			(b) 60	2,100				2,100	
142	Prepaid Rent	1,500			(a) 500	1,000				1,000	
201	Office Equipment	1,400				1,400				1,400	
211	Trucks	13,000				13,000				13,000	
301	Accounts Payable		200				200				200
302	Notes Payable		8,000				8,000				8,000
321	Unearned Rent		600	(d) 100			500				500
401	Capital Stock		12,000				12,000				12,000
402	Dividends	500				500				500	
501	Trucking Revenue		7,465				7,465		7,465		
601	Heat and Light Expense	40				40		40			
602	Maintenance and Repairs Expense	375				375		375			
603	Telephone and Telegraph Expense	95				95		95			
604	Gas and Oil Expense	525				525		525			
605	Wages Expense	1,200		(g) 150		1,350		1,350			
		28,265	28,265								
606	Rent Expense			(a) 500		500		500			
607	Insurance Expense			(b) 60		60		60			
608	Office Supplies Expense			(c) 170		170		170			
511	Rent Earned				(d) 100		100		100		
609	Depreciation Expense–Office Equipment			(e) 10		10		10			
201A	Accumulated Depreciation–Office Equipment				(e) 10		10				10
610	Depreciation Expense–Trucks			(f) 200		200		200			
211A	Accumulated Depreciation–Trucks				(f) 200		200				200
311	Accrued Wages Payable				(g) 150		150				150
611	Interest Expense			(h) 24		24		24			
303	Accrued Interest Payable				(h) 24		24				24
113	Accrued Interest Receivable			(i) 4		4				4	
521	Interest Earned				(i) 4		4		4		
612	Income Tax Expense			(j) 1,900		1,900		1,900			
331	Income Taxes Payable				(j) 1,900		1,900				1,900
				3,118	3,118	30,553	30,553	5,249	7,569	25,304	22,984
	Net Income for the Month							2,320			2,320
								7,569	7,569	25,304	25,304

The difference between the Income Statement columns is net income.

Net income is transferred to the Position Statement Credit column.

The Preparation of Financial Statements from the Worksheet

The income statement is prepared from the amounts in the Income Statement columns of the worksheet; the statement of financial position and the statement of retained earnings are prepared from the amounts in the Position Statement columns of the worksheet. In preparing the financial statements, care should be taken to use each amount just once, and in its proper debit and credit relationship.

Figure 4-7. Income Statement

CONNOLLY TRUCKING COMPANY		Exhibit A
Income Statement		
For the Month Ended June 30, 1973		

			Percent
Revenue			
Trucking Revenue		$7,465	
Interest Earned		4	
Rent Earned		100	
Total Revenues		$7,569	100.0
Expenses			
Heat and Light Expense	$ 40		0.5
Maintenance and Repairs Expense	375		5.0
Telephone and Telegraph Expense	95		1.3
Gas and Oil Expense	525		6.9
Wages Expense	1,350		17.8
Rent Expense	500		6.6
Insurance Expense	60		0.8
Office Supplies Expense	170		2.3
Depreciation Expense–Office Equipment	10		0.1
Depreciation Expense–Trucks	200		2.6
Interest Expense	24		0.3
Total Expenses		3,349	44.2
Net Income before Income Taxes		$4,220	55.8
Income Tax Expense		1,900	25.1
Net Income after Income Taxes—To Exhibit C		$2,320	30.7

Figure 4-8. Statement of Financial Position

CONNOLLY TRUCKING COMPANY			Exhibit B
Statement of Financial Position			
June 30, 1973			

Assets			
			Percent
Current Assets			
Cash		$ 5,250	21.3
Accounts Receivable		550	2.2
Notes Receivable		1,440	5.9
Accrued Interest Receivable		4	–0–
Office Supplies		60	0.2
Prepaid Insurance		2,100	8.5
Prepaid Rent		1,000	4.1
Total Current Assets		$10,404	42.2
Equipment			
Office Equipment	$ 1,400		
Deduct Accumulated Depreciation	10	$ 1,390	5.7
Trucks	$13,000		
Deduct Accumulated Depreciation	200	12,800	52.1
Total Equipment		14,190	57.8
Total Assets		$24,594	100.0

Figure 4-8 (continued)

Liabilities and Stockholders' Equity			
Current Liabilities			
Accounts Payable	$ 200		0.8
Notes Payable	8,000		32.5
Accrued Interest Payable	24		0.1
Accrued Wages Payable	150		0.6
Unearned Rent	500		2.1
Income Taxes Payable	1,900		7.7
Total Current Liabilities		$10,774	43.8
Stockholders' Equity			
Capital Stock	$12,000		48.8
Retained Earnings–Exhibit C	1,820		7.4
Total Stockholders' Equity		13,820	56.2
Total Liabilities and Stockholders' Equity		$24,594	100.0

Figure 4-9. Statement of Retained Earnings

CONNOLLY TRUCKING COMPANY Exhibit C	
Statement of Retained Earnings	
For the Month Ended June 30, 1973	
Net Income for Month of June, 1973—Exhibit A	$2,320
Deduct Dividends	500
Retained Earnings, June 30, 1973—To Exhibit B	$1,820

It is not emphasized by the statements, but the relationship is present. In the statement of financial position, for example, Accumulated Depreciation–Trucks, with a credit balance of $200, is deducted from Trucks, which has a debit balance. Net income (or loss) appears in both the income statement and the statement of retained earnings.

The financial statements of the Connolly Trucking Company for June are shown in Figures 4-7, 4-8, and 4-9. The computation and significance of the items in the Percent columns are discussed later in this chapter. The designations used to identify and cross reference the financial statements are as follows:

Exhibit A for the income statement
Exhibit B for the statement of financial position
Exhibit C for the statement of retained earnings

Since the company was organized on June 1, 1973, it had no beginning balance in the Retained Earnings account; therefore, this item does not appear in the statement.

RECORDING THE ADJUSTMENTS IN THE GENERAL JOURNAL

The formal adjusting entries should not be recorded in the general journal and posted to the general ledger until after the financial statements have been prepared. The adjusting entries should be taken directly from the Adjustments columns of the worksheet and dated as of the last day of the accounting period.

The caption "Adjusting Entries" is written in the general journal on the line following the last regular general journal entry. After the adjusting entries have been posted, the general ledger account balances will correspond with the amounts in the Adjusted Trial Balance columns of the worksheet. Although the adjusting entries for the Connolly Trucking Company have already been made as they were introduced, to add realism to the accounting job, they are collected and repeated in Figure 4-10.

Figure 4-10. Adjusting Entries

GENERAL JOURNAL				Page 4
1973				
		Adjusting Entries		
June 30	Rent Expense	606	500	
	Prepaid Rent	142		500
	To record rent expense for June.			
30	Insurance Expense	607	60	
	Prepaid Insurance	141		60
	To record insurance expense for June.			
30	Office Supplies Expense	608	170	
	Office Supplies	131		170
	To record supplies used during June.			
30	Unearned Rent	321	100	
	Rent Earned	511		100
	To record revenue earned from rental of trucks during June.			
30	Depreciation Expense–Office Equipment	609	10	
	Accumulated Depreciation–Office Equipment	201A		10
	To record the depreciation for June.			
30	Depreciation Expense–Trucks	610	200	
	Accumulated Depreciation–Trucks	211A		200
	To record the depreciation for June.			
30	Wages Expense	605	150	
	Accrued Wages Payable	311		150
	To record wages expense accrued during June.			

GENERAL JOURNAL				Page 5
1973				
June 30	Interest Expense	611	24	
	Accrued Interest Payable	303		24
	To record interest expense accrued during June.			
30	Accrued Interest Receivable	113	4	
	Interest Earned	521		4
	To record interest revenue accrued during June.			
30	Income Tax Expense	612	1,900	
	Income Taxes Payable	331		1,900
	To record estimated taxes for June.			

THE RESULT OF ADJUSTING ENTRIES

When all the adjusting entries are recorded in the journal and posted to the general ledger, the mixed elements in the accounts have been eliminated. Accounts consisting of asset and expense elements and accounts containing liability and revenue elements are apportioned so that each element is recorded in a separate account; advance payments for goods and services to be consumed in the future are shown in the appropriate asset accounts; advance receipts for future revenue are shown in liability accounts; and all other supplementary data not previously recorded but necessary for the preparation of financial statements are available in the ledger. The general ledger should contain all the accounts and amounts— expense, revenue, asset, liability, and stockholders' equity—necessary for the presentation of the financial position of the company as of the end of the accounting period and the results of its operations for the period then ended. Failure to adjust a mixed asset or liability account results in incorrect financial statements; failure to disclose all information may result in misleading financial statements. ▼ The need for adjustment, however, and the need for full disclosure do not apply to insignificant, immaterial, or trivial matters. ▼ The box of paper clips in the bookkeeper's desk as of the position-statement date is an asset of the company, although it has been charged to expense. It is possible, but impractical, to ascertain the asset value of the unused clips and make a corresponding adjusting entry. Because of the insignificance of the unused paper clips, failure to make the adjustment will have no material effect on the financial statements and cannot mislead the user of such statements. A similar situation exists with respect to other items of supply or services.

Accounting Concept: ▼
Materiality

The accountant is faced with the problem of determining the line between what is material and what is immaterial—making a value judgment. An item costing $100 may be material in a small business, whereas an item costing $1,000 may be insignificant in a multimillion-dollar business. It is not misleading to combine several insignificant items of expense or revenue into one account; it is misleading, however, to combine a significant loss from a lawsuit with an operating expense account. It may be necessary to disclose an item of an essential nature, regardless of its amount.

CLOSING ENTRIES RECORDED DIRECTLY FROM THE WORKSHEET

The caption *Closing Entries* is written in the middle of the first unused line on the journal page under the adjusting entries. The closing entries are recorded (Figure 4-11) and are then posted to the general ledger. They are made directly from the worksheet in the following sequence:

Entry 1. Each account in the Income Statement Credit column is debited, and the sum of the debits is credited to the Revenue and Expense Summary account.

Entry 2. Each account in the Income Statement Debit column is credited,

Figure 4-11. Closing Entries

GENERAL JOURNAL		Page 5

1973				
		Closing Entries		
June	30	Trucking Revenue	501	7,465	
		Rent Earned	511	100	
		Interest Earned	521	4	
		Revenue and Expense Summary	902		7,569
		To close.			
	30	Revenue and Expense Summary	902	5,249	
		Heat and Light Expense	601		40
		Maintenance and Repairs Expense	602		375
		Telephone and Telegraph Expense	603		95
		Gas and Oil Expense	604		525
		Wages Expense	605		1,350
		Rent Expense	606		500
		Insurance Expense	607		60
		Office Supplies Expense	608		170
		Depreciation Expense–Office Equipment	609		10
		Depreciation Expense–Trucks	610		200
		Interest Expense	611		24
		Income Tax Expense	612		1,900
		To close.			
	30	Revenue and Expense Summary	902	2,320	
		Retained Earnings	403		2,320
		To transfer net income to			
		Retained Earnings.			
	30	Retained Earnings	403	500	
		Dividends	402		500
		To close.			

and the sum of the credits is debited to the Revenue and Expense Summary account.

Entry 3. The balance of Revenue and Expense Summary, which, after posting entries 1 and 2, represents the net income or the net loss as shown on the worksheet, is transferred to Retained Earnings.

Entry 4. The balance of the Dividends account is closed into Retained Earnings: The amount of this entry is the amount on the Dividends account line in the Position Statement Debit column of the worksheet.

THE GENERAL LEDGER

The general ledger of the Connolly Trucking Company is reproduced after the adjusting entries and the closing entries have been posted. In reproducing the general ledger, exact dates are used when the information is given in the previous discussion. Otherwise the date of June 30 and the balance of the account as taken from the trial balance in Figure 4-1 are inserted because the detailed transactions were omitted from this example. The symbols T.B. for trial balance, A.E. for adjusting entry, and C.E. for closing entry are shown in the Explanation column as an aid in tracing the amounts to their sources. A check mark indicates that the amount was not posted from the journal.

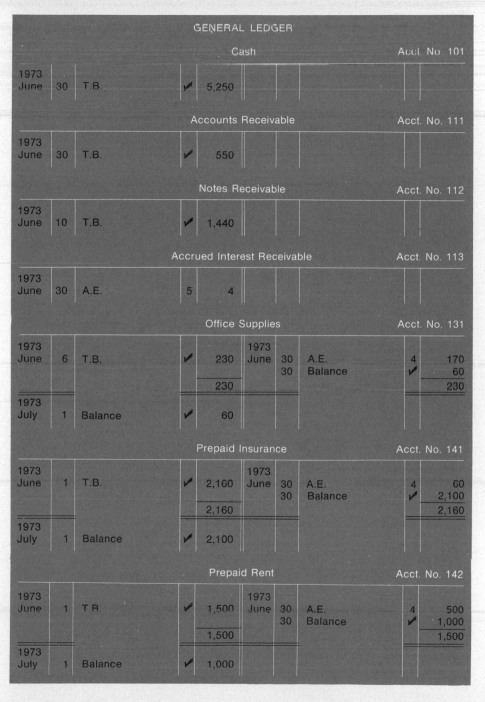

GENERAL LEDGER

Cash   Acct. No. 101

| 1973 June | 30 | T.B. | ✔ | 5,250 | | | | | |

Accounts Receivable   Acct. No. 111

| 1973 June | 30 | T.B. | ✔ | 550 | | | | | |

Notes Receivable   Acct. No. 112

| 1973 June | 10 | T.B. | ✔ | 1,440 | | | | | |

Accrued Interest Receivable   Acct. No. 113

| 1973 June | 30 | A.E. | 5 | 4 | | | | | |

Office Supplies   Acct. No. 131

1973 June	6	T.B.	✔	230	1973 June	30	A.E.	4	170
						30	Balance	✔	60
				230					230
1973 July	1	Balance	✔	60					

Prepaid Insurance   Acct. No. 141

1973 June	1	T.B.	✔	2,160	1973 June	30	A.E.	4	60
						30	Balance	✔	2,100
				2,160					2,160
1973 July	1	Balance	✔	2,100					

Prepaid Rent   Acct. No. 142

1973 June	1	T.B.	✔	1,500	1973 June	30	A.E.	4	500
						30	Balance	✔	1,000
				1,500					1,500
1973 July	1	Balance	✔	1,000					

Office Equipment — Acct. No. 201

Date		Ref		Amount	Date		Ref		Amount
1973 June	1	T.B.	✔	1,400					

Accumulated Depreciation–Office Equipment — Acct. No. 201A

Date		Ref		Amount	Date		Ref		Amount
					1973 June	30	A.E.	4	10

Trucks — Acct. No. 211

Date		Ref		Amount	Date		Ref		Amount
1973 June	1	T.B.	✔	13,000					

Accumulated Depreciation–Trucks — Acct. No. 211A

Date		Ref		Amount	Date		Ref		Amount
					1973 June	30	A.E.	4	200

Accounts Payable — Acct. No. 301

Date		Ref		Amount	Date		Ref		Amount
					1973 June	30	T.B.	✔	200

Notes Payable — Acct. No. 302

Date		Ref		Amount	Date		Ref		Amount
					1973 June	12	T.B.	✔	8,000

Accrued Interest Payable — Acct. No. 303

Date		Ref		Amount	Date		Ref		Amount
					1973 June	30	A.E.	5	24

Accrued Wages Payable — Acct. No. 311

Date		Ref		Amount	Date		Ref		Amount
					1973 June	30	A.E.	4	150

Unearned Rent — Acct. No. 321

Date		Item		Amount	Date		Item		Amount
1973 June	30	A.E.	4	100	1973 June	1	T.B.	✔	600
	30	Balance	✔	500					
				600					600
					1973 July	1	Balance	✔	500

Income Taxes Payable — Acct. No. 331

Date		Ref		Amount	Date		Ref		Amount
					1973 June	30	A.E.	5	1,900

Capital Stock　　　　　　　　　　　Acct. No. 401

					1973				
					June	1	T.B.	✔	12,000

Retained Earnings　　　　　　　　Acct. No. 403

1973					1973				
June	30	C.E.	5	500	June	30	C.E.	5	2,320
	30	Balance	✔	1,820					
				2,320					2,320
					1973				
					July	1	Balance	✔	1,820

Dividends　　　　　　　　　　　　Acct. No. 402

1973					1973				
June	30	T.B.	✔	500	June	30	C.E.	5	500

Trucking Revenue　　　　　　　　Acct. No. 501

1973					1973				
June	30	C.E.	5	7,465	June	30	T.B.	✔	7,465

Interest Earned　　　　　　　　　Acct. No. 521

1973					1973				
June	30	C.E.	5	4	June	30	A.E.	5	4

Rent Earned　　　　　　　　　　　Acct. No. 511

1973					1973				
June	30	C.E.	5	100	June	30	A.E.	4	100

Heat and Light Expense　　　　　Acct. No. 601

1973					1973				
June	30	T.B.	✔	40	June	30	C.E.	5	40

Maintenance and Repairs Expense　　Acct. No. 602

1973					1973				
June	30	T.B.	✔	375	June	30	C.E.	5	375

Telephone and Telegraph Expense　　Acct. No. 603

1973					1973				
June	30	T.B.	✔	95	June	30	C.E.	5	95

Gas and Oil Expense　　　　　　　Acct. No. 604

1973					1973				
June	30	T.B.	✔	525	June	30	C.E.	5	525

Wages Expense — Acct. No. 605

1973 June	13		✔	600	1973 June	30	C.E.	5	1,350
	27		✔	600					
	30	A.E.	4	150					
				1,350					1,350

Rent Expense — Acct. No. 606

| 1973 June | 30 | A.E. | 4 | 500 | 1973 June | 30 | C.E. | 5 | 500 |

Insurance Expense — Acct. No. 607

| 1973 June | 30 | A.E. | 4 | 60 | 1973 June | 30 | C.E. | 5 | 60 |

Office Supplies Expense — Acct. No. 608

| 1973 June | 30 | A.E. | 4 | 170 | 1973 June | 30 | C.E. | 5 | 170 |

Depreciation Expense–Office Equipment — Acct. No. 609

| 1973 June | 30 | A.E. | 4 | 10 | 1973 June | 30 | C.E. | 5 | 10 |

Depreciation Expense–Trucks — Acct. No. 610

| 1973 June | 30 | A.E. | 4 | 200 | 1973 June | 30 | C.E. | 5 | 200 |

Interest Expense — Acct. No. 611

| 1973 June | 30 | A.E. | 5 | 24 | 1973 June | 30 | C.E. | 5 | 24 |

Income Tax Expense — Acct. No. 612

| 1973 June | 30 | A.E. | 5 | 1,900 | 1973 June | 30 | C.E. | 5 | 1,900 |

Revenue and Expense Summary — Acct. No. 902

1973 June	30	C.E.	5	5,249	1973 June	30	C.E.	5	7,569
	30	C.E.	5	2,320					
				7,569					7,569

THE POST-CLOSING TRIAL BALANCE

The post-closing trial balance of the Connolly Trucking Company, taken from the general ledger, is shown in Figure 4-12.

Figure 4-12. Post-Closing Trial Balance

	CONNOLLY TRUCKING COMPANY Post-Closing Trial Balance June 30, 1973		
Acct. No.	Account Title	Debits	Credits
101	Cash	$ 5,250	
111	Accounts Receivable	550	
112	Notes Receivable	1,440	
113	Accrued Interest Receivable	4	
131	Office Supplies	60	
141	Prepaid Insurance	2,100	
142	Prepaid Rent	1,000	
201	Office Equipment	1,400	
201A	Accumulated Depreciation–Office Equipment		$ 10
211	Trucks	13,000	
211A	Accumulated Depreciation–Trucks		200
301	Accounts Payable		200
302	Notes Payable		8,000
303	Accrued Interest Payable		24
311	Accrued Wages Payable		150
321	Unearned Rent		500
331	Income Taxes Payable		1,900
401	Capital Stock		12,000
403	Retained Earnings		1,820
	Totals	$24,804	$24,804

THE ACCOUNTING CYCLE

In this and the preceding chapter, the complete *accounting cycle* of a service business concern has been presented. The cycle consists of a series of steps, as follows:

1. *Selecting an appropriate chart of accounts*, which consists of selecting those accounts that are likely to be needed for financial statements and designating a numerical system for these accounts.
2. *Journalizing,* which consists of analyzing and recording transactions in chronological order in the journal.
3. *Posting,* which is transferring debits and credits to the appropriate ledgers and to the proper accounts in the ledgers.
4. *Preparing a trial balance,* or summarizing the general ledger accounts to test the equality of debits and credits.

5. *Preparing a schedule of accounts receivable,* which is summarizing the accounts receivable ledger accounts and reconciling the total with the balance of the Accounts Receivable controlling account in the general ledger.
6. *Preparing a schedule of accounts payable,* which is summarizing the accounts payable ledger accounts and reconciling the total with the balance of the Accounts Payable controlling account in the general ledger.
7. *Preparing the worksheet,* or assembling and classifying information in columnar form to facilitate the preparation of financial statements.
8. *Preparing the financial statements* from the worksheet; these are the income statement, statement of financial position, and statement of retained earnings.
9. *Adjusting the books,* or recording and posting the adjusting entries from the worksheet.
10. *Closing the books,* which is recording and posting the closing entries from the income statement columns of the worksheet.
11. *Balancing and ruling the real accounts* and bringing the balances forward for the new accounting period.
12. *Taking a post-closing trial balance,* or totaling the open-account balances to prove the equality of the debits and credits in the general ledger.
13. *Analyzing and interpreting the financial statements* by developing percentages, ratios, and other indicators, to make the statements more meaningful.

THE PURPOSE OF SPLIT ENTRIES

The adjusting entries are recorded in the general journal and posted to the general ledger. Three of the adjusting entries—g, h, and i—involve the accrual of previously unrecorded revenue or expense items assignable to June and require a split form of entry in July when the transaction cycle culminates in the receipt or payment of cash.

Paying the Accrued Wages Payable

The next regular pay day at the Connolly Trucking Company is on July 11. On July 1, Wages Expense had a zero balance as a result of the closing entries on June 30 but the Accrued Wages Payable account had a credit balance of $450 as a result of the adjusting entries. Assuming that the biweekly wages again amounted to $600, the entry on July 11 to record this payment is

GENERAL JOURNAL				Page 5
1973 July	11	Accrued Wages Payable	150	
		Wages Expense	450	
		Cash		600
		To record the payment of biweekly wages.		

The result of this entry is to split the biweekly wages of $600 so that $150, which was recognized as a June expense, is debited to Accrued Wages Payable and $450 is recorded as an expense in July. Accrued Wages Payable now has a zero balance.

Paying the Accrued Interest Payable

On the maturity date of the note payable, July 27 (45 days including 18 days accrued in June), the Connolly Trucking Company pays the bank $8,060, the maturity value. The amount consists of $8,000 principal plus $60, which is 45 days' interest at 6 percent on $8,000, calculated as follows:

$$\$8,000 \times 0.06 \times \frac{45}{360} = \$60$$

The entry to record the payment to the bank is

GENERAL JOURNAL			Page 5
1973 July 27	Notes Payable	8,000	
	Accrued Interest Payable	24	
	Interest Expense	36	
	Cash		8,060
	To record the payment of a note payable.		

The adjusting entry on June 30 allocated 18 days' interest expense ($24) on the note to the month of June. The July entry splits the total interest of $60 so that the $24 liability applicable to June is cancelled and the remaining $36 ($60 − $24) is recorded as interest expense for 27 days in July.

Receiving the Accrued Interest Receivable

On the maturity date of the note receivable, July 10 (30 days, including 20 days accrued in June), the Connolly Trucking Company receives the maturity value, $1,446. The maturity value is determined by adding to the principal, $1,440, 30 days' interest at 5 percent, or $6, computed as follows:

$$\$1,440 \times 0.05 \times \frac{30}{360} = \$6$$

The entry to record the receipt from the customer is

GENERAL JOURNAL			Page 5
1973 July 10	Cash	1,446	
	Notes Receivable		1,440
	Accrued Interest Receivable		4
	Interest Earned		2
	To record the collection of a note receivable.		

On June 30, the adjusting entry accrued 20 days' interest earned on the note, or $4, in June. The total interest earned of $6 is split by the July entry so that the $4 asset, Accrued Interest Receivable, is cancelled and the balance of $2 ($6 − $4) is entered as interest earned in July.

ANALYZING THE FINANCIAL STATEMENTS

The financial statements are not ends in themselves. Additional information and insight about the business may be obtained by analyzing the relationships within and between the statements to make them more meaningful to management, creditors, and other interested persons. For this purpose percentages are useful.

A percentage analysis of the income statement and statement of financial position of the Connolly Trucking Company is shown in Figure 4-7 and Figure 4-8. In the income statement, the total revenue ($7,569) is 100 percent. Each expense item is expressed as a percentage of the total revenue. The reader can see the distribution of each revenue dollar—that is, the percentage of revenue that has been absorbed by each expense item. Rent Expense, for example, absorbed 6.6 cents of each revenue dollar, and 25.1 cents of each revenue dollar was absorbed by income tax expense.

In the statement of financial position, the total asset amount is used as the base (100 percent), and the percentage of each asset to the total assets is determined by dividing the individual asset by the total assets. Similarly, the percentage of each liability and stockholders' equity item is expressed as a percentage of the total liabilities and stockholders' equity, and is computed by dividing the individual items by the amount of total liabilities and stockholders' equity. Thus,

$$\frac{\text{Cash}}{\text{Total assets}} = \frac{\$5,250}{\$24,594} = 21.3\%$$

$$\frac{\text{Notes payable}}{\text{Total liabilities and stockholders' equity}} = \frac{\$8,000}{\$24,594} = 32.5\%$$

Percentage computations also are are made to show the relationship of subtotals to the related totals. The analysis shows that total current assets are 42.2 percent of total assets, and total current liabilities are 43.8 percent of total liabilities and stockholders' equity.

EQUITY RATIOS

A significant measure of the stability of a business is the percentage relationship of the equities of the creditors and the owners in the total assets. These equity ratios for the Connolly Trucking Company are computed as follows:

1. Creditors' interest in assets:

$$\frac{\text{Total liabilities}}{\text{Total assets}} = \frac{\$10,774}{\$24,594} = 43.8\%$$

2. Stockholders' interest in assets:

$$\frac{\text{Total stockholders' equity}}{\text{Total assets}} = \frac{\$13,820}{\$24,594} = 56.2\%$$

The creditors have an equity of 43.8 cents and the stockholders have an equity of 56.2 cents of each asset dollar. Many analysts consider the equity ratios equal in importance to the current ratio as indicators of credit strength and sound management. There are no universally accepted percentage relationships to serve as guides for the equity ratios, but it is generally felt that the larger the owner's equity, the stronger the financial condition of the business. A company may, for example, borrow money on a long-term note for working capital purposes. The loan increases the current assets and creates a more favorable current ratio; but it also reduces the stockholders' equity ratio, signaling a possible overdependence on outside sources for financial needs.

SUMMARY

The cash basis and the accrual basis are both found in accounting practice. By the cash basis, revenue is considered to be earned and is recorded when payment is received; expenses are considered to have been incurred and are recorded only at the time of payment. *Accrual accounting* is based on the principle that revenue is realized at the time of the sale of goods and services and expenses are recognized at the time they are incurred. The timing of the cash receipt or cash payment is irrelevant to this matching process.

The proper allocation of the accounts is deferred to the end of the accounting period, at which time the accountant may find that some new accounts must be brought into the books and other accounts brought up to date. This periodic adjustment of the ledger is accomplished by making adjusting entries, which are necessary whenever financial statements are to be prepared.

Adjustments are needed under the following conditions:

1. *Short-Term Cost Apportionment Adjustment.* When an account contains both an asset and an expense element; for example, when a portion of the insurance premiums previously debited to Prepaid Insurance has expired.
2. *Long-Term Cost Apportionment Adjustment.* When a depreciable plant asset is acquired. Part of the service cost of the plant asset will expire over time and it should be recognized as depreciation expense.
3. *Accrued Expense Adjustments.* When previously unrecorded expense data are to be entered; for example, on recognition of the incurred expense and corresponding liability for amounts due employees for services received but not recorded.
4. *Short-Term Revenue Apportionment Adjustment.* When amounts previously received and recorded in a liability account are earned; for example, when an amount is transferred from Unearned Rent to Rent Earned.
5. *Accrued Revenue Adjustment.* When previously unrecorded revenue and asset increases are recognized; for example, Interest Earned and Accrued Interest Receivable on an outstanding interest-bearing note from a customer.

The worksheet is an orderly means of collecting information for the preparation of formal financial statements. It may be varied in form, especially in the number of columns. The steps in its preparation consist of (1) entering the trial balance in the Trial Balance columns, (2) entering the adjusting entries in the Adjustments columns, (3) extending the combined amounts to the Adjusted Trial Balance columns, (4) extending the amounts in the Adjusted Trial Balance columns to either the Income Statement or the Position Statement columns, depending on their statement classification, (5) totaling the columns and entering the excess—the net income or net loss for the period—below the column totals.

The steps in the accounting cycle are (1) selecting the appropriate chart of accounts, (2) journalizing, (3) posting, (4) preparing a trial balance, (5) preparing a schedule of accounts receivable, (6) preparing a schedule of accounts payable, (7) preparing the worksheet, (8) preparing the financial statements, (9) adjusting the books, (10) closing the books, (11) balancing and ruling the accounts, (12) taking a post-closing trial balance, and (13) analyzing and interpreting the financial statements.

QUESTIONS

Q4-1. (a) What are the essential differences between the cash basis and the accrual basis of accounting? (b) Under what conditions is it appropriate to use the cash basis? (c) Under what conditions is it inappropriate to use the cash basis?

Q4-2. (a) What purpose is served by adjusting entries? (b) What events make them necessary? (c) How do they affect the work of the accountant? (d) How does the time period covered by the income statement affect the adjusting entries? (e) How do adjusting entries differ from other entries? (f) What is a mixed account? (g) What are the results of the adjusting entries?

Q4-3. (a) What is the purpose and function of the worksheet? (b) Can the work of the accountant be completed without the use of the worksheet? (c) Where do the amounts on the worksheet come from? (d) What determines the number of columns to be used in the preparation of a worksheet? (e) Why are the parts of each entry in the Adjustments columns cross-referenced with either numbers or letters? (f) How is the amount to be extended into another column determined? (g) What determines the column into which an amount is to be extended? (h) Is the worksheet foolproof? (i) Does the worksheet eliminate the need for formal financial statements? (j) Does the worksheet eliminate the need for recording the adjusting entries on the books?

Q4-4. (a) Do you agree with the statement that "items of little or no consequence may be dealt with as expediency may suggest"? (b) Do you agree with the statement that "problems of materiality are easily resolved and, in any case, are not very important"?

Q4-5. (a) What is meant by the accounting cycle? (b) What are the steps in the complete cycle? (c) Is it possible for the bookkeeper to vary the sequence in which he performs the steps of the cycle?

Q4-6. Is it possible to prepare the formal financial statements from a four-column worksheet consisting of the trial balance amounts and all the necessary adjustments?

Q4-7. What is the purpose and function of the Percent columns in the financial statements?

Q4-8. (a) When would the amounts for Depreciation Expense and for Accumulated Depreciation in the adjusted trial balance be the same? (b) When would these amounts be different?

E4-1. Prepare adjusting entries from the following information pertaining to the accounts of Electrical Control Corporation at the end of June, 1973:

a. Accrued rent receivable, $180.
b. Accrued interest payable, $36.
c. Accrued taxes payable, $70.
d. Accrued wages payable, $340.
e. A trenching machine was rented during June from Equipment Rental, Inc., at the rate of $15 per hour; the machine was used for a total of 60 hours during the month and the corporation had paid $390 to Equipment Rental, Inc., for the rent of the machine.
f. Accrued interest on municipal bonds owned, $75.
g. As of June 30, the unbilled service fees for completed work amounted to $480.
h. The company signed an order form on June 30, 1973, to purchase a trenching machine for $12,000. *No entry until take the machine.*

E4-2. John D. Rock, an electrician, prepares monthly financial statements. The following transactions occurred during December, 1973:

1973
Dec. 15 Billed customers $900 for services rendered this month.

  17 Purchased $550 worth of electrical supplies on account.

  31 Received $410 in cash from customers billed on December 15.

  31 Paid $300 on account for electrical supplies purchased on December 17.

   The electrical supplies inventory on December 31 was $100. Journalize the transactions, assuming that Rock keeps his books (a) on the cash basis; (b) on the accrual basis. (c) What is the net income on the cash basis? on the accrual basis? (d) Which method should Rock use? Why?

E4-3. The Ames Company purchased a new truck on January 1, 1973, for $5,200. It had an estimated useful life of four years and a trade-in value at the end of that time of $400. (a) What is the depreciation expense for 1973? (b) What is the balance in the Accumulated Depreciation–Delivery Equipment account at the end of 1973? 1974? (c) What will the carrying value of the truck be in the statement of financial position of December 31, 1973? December 31, 1974? (d) Why is depreciation expense credited to Accumulated Depreciation–Delivery Equipment rather than directly to Delivery Equipment? *maintain cost & delivery account*

E4-4. The trial balance of the Barden Company on December 31, 1973, included the following account balances before adjustments:

Prepaid Insurance	$ 900
Prepaid Advertising Supplies	800
Prepaid Rent	1,200
Office Supplies	1,500
Office Equipment	3,300

Data for adjustments on December 31, 1973, were

a. On November 1, 1973, the company purchased a two-year comprehensive insurance policy for $900.
b. Advertising supplies on hand totaled $300.
c. On September 1, 1973, the company paid one year's rent in advance.
d. The office supplies inventory was $720.
e. The office equipment was purchased on July 1, 1973, and has an estimated useful life of 10 years and a salvage value of $300.

Make the adjusting entries.

E4-5. The White Company employs three sales clerks at a weekly salary of $100 each. They are paid on Friday, the last day of a five-day work week. Make the adjusting entry, assuming that the accounting period ended on Tuesday.

E4-6. The statements of financial position of the Dewey Company as of December 31, 1973 and 1974, showed Office Supplies at $1,350 and $1,500, respectively. During 1974, office supplies totaling $2,200 were purchased. What was the Office Supplies Expense for the year 1974?

E4-7. The balances of the Prepaid Insurance account of the Burton Company were:

December 31, 1973	$930
December 31, 1974	520

The income statement for 1974 showed insurance expense of $1,150. What were the expenditures for insurance premiums during 1974?

E4-8. Make the additional closing entries indicated by the following accounts:

John Sobel, Capital		John Sobel, Drawing	
	40,000	10,000	

Revenue and Expense Summary	
125,000	150,000

E4-9. The Jernigan Company's adjusted trial balance, taken from the worksheet for the year ended December 31, 1973, was as follows:

Cash	$ 15,700	
Accounts Receivable	11,400	
Machinery and Equipment	32,900	
Accumulated Depreciation		$ 12,000
Accounts Payable		3,040
Notes Payable		7,600
William Jernigan, Capital		32,360
William Jernigan, Drawing	5,000	
Service Revenue		50,000
Heat and Light Expense	1,000	
Wages Expense	35,000	
Depreciation Expense	4,000	
Totals	$105,000	$105,000

(a) Enter the adjusted trial balance on a worksheet; (b) complete the worksheet; (c) prepare an income statement with a Percent column, a statement of financial position with a Percent column, a statement of owner's equity, and the closing entries.

E4-10. The Hume Magazine Company credited Subscription Revenue for $24,000 received from subscribers to its new monthly magazine. All subscriptions were for 12 issues. The initial issue was mailed during October, 1973. Make the adjusting entry on December 31, 1973.

E4-11. Make the end-of-year adjusting entries for the Rex Hall Company for the following items:

a. The debit balance of the Prepaid Insurance account is $720. Of this amount, $600 is expired.

b. Accrued salaries and wages payable total $150.

c. The Office Supplies account has a debit balance of $180; $30 worth is on hand.

d. Depreciation on store equipment is $200; on office equipment, $175.

e. Accrued interest receivable is $95.

f. Accrued interest payable is $60.

g. Unearned Rent has a credit balance of $2,600, of which $2,400 was earned during the past year.

E4-12. From the account balances given, prepare the adjusting entries:

Account	Amount in Trial Balance	Balance After Adjustment
Prepaid Insurance	$1,800	$ 600
Prepaid Interest	200	50
Unearned Rent	700	200
Accumulated Depreciation–Building	7,000	10,000
Salaries and Wages Payable	–0–	450
Accrued Interest Receivable	–0–	110
Accrued Interest Payable	–0–	90

E4-13. The Surf Company debits the cost of all office supplies purchased to Office Supplies Expense. Office supplies inventories were:

> January 1, 1973 $820
> December 31, 1973   570

Supplies used during the year totaled $2,570. What was the cost of office supplies purchased during 1973?

E4-14. The Finn Company issued a 60-day, 6-percent note for $500, dated July 1, to a supplier of merchandise. On July 16, the company received a 30-day, 4-percent note for $750 from a customer. Make the necessary adjusting entries on July 31.

E4-15. The income statement of the Cuney Company for the three-month period ended March 31, 1973, shows net income before income taxes of $20,000. Assuming an income tax rate of 48 percent, make the necessary adjusting entry.

E4-16. Upon examining the books and records of the Fine Company on December 31, 1973, you find the following: (a) The inventory of office supplies on hand is $150; some partially filled cans of duplicating fluid valued at $3.50 were not inventoried. (b) Included in Miscellaneous Expense was a charge of $500 for uninsured losses from a fire. Indicate the adjustments, if any, that should be made, and why.

E4-17. The Sun Company received a 30-day, 6-percent note for $500 from a customer on September 15. On September 20, the company borrowed $1,800 from the bank on its own 30-day, 6-percent note. Make entries to adjust the books on September 30, and to record the collection and payment of the notes on their respective due dates.

E4-18. The statement of financial position of the Mitre Company at December 31, 1973, shows the following totals:

> Current Assets $13,000
> Total Assets   40,000
> Current Liabilities   6,000
> Total Liabilities   16,000

Prepare analyses that will make these summary totals more meaningful to a reader of the statement.

DEMONSTRATION PROBLEMS

DP4-1. (*Worksheet*) The general ledger of Bowling Palace, Inc., showed the following balances at December 31, 1973. The books are closed annually on December 31. The company obtains revenue from its bowling alleys and from a refreshments stand that is leased on a concession basis.

Cash	$19,000	Dividends	$ 7,200
Bowling Supplies	7,200	Bowling Revenue	45,600
Prepaid Insurance	6,000	Concession Revenue	5,750
Prepaid Rent	6,500	Wages Expense	13,000
Bowling Equipment	50,000	Repair Expense	2,625
Accumulated Depreciation	12,250	Heat and Light Expense	2,100
Mortgage Payable	28,000	Telephone and Telegraph Expense	275
Capital Stock	15,000	Miscellaneous Expense	920
Retained Earnings	8,220		

Supplementary data:

a. Bowling supplies on hand based on physical count totaled $525.
b. The balance of the Prepaid Insurance account represents the premium on a three-year insurance policy, effective January 1, 1973.
c. Rent expense for the year was $6,000.
d. The bowling equipment has an expected useful life of 10 years and salvage value of $1,000. No equipment was acquired during the year.
e. Salaries earned by employees but unpaid on December 31 were $125.

Required: 1. Record the trial balance on a worksheet.
2. Complete the worksheet.
3. Why is the difference between the totals of the Income Statement columns and the totals of the Position Statement columns the same amount?

DP4-2. (*Adjusting entries*) Certain unadjusted account balances from the trial balance of the Foley Company, a systems consulting firm, for the year ended December 31, 1973, are given:

Account Title	Debits	Credits
Accounts Receivable	$20,000	
Notes Receivable	9,000	
Prepaid Insurance	1,080	
Office Supplies	620	
Automobiles	10,000	
Accumulated Depreciation–Automobiles		$ 2,000
Notes Payable		3,000
Revenue–Consulting Fees		240,000
Advertising Expense	900	
Rent Expense	20,000	
Salaries Expense	24,500	
Property Taxes Expense	1,675	
Heat and Light Expense	1,200	
Interest Earned		300
Rent Earned		1,200

Adjustment data on December 31 are as follows:

1. Office supplies on hand totaled $50.
2. Depreciation for the year was $1,000.
3. Estimated heat and light expense not recorded was $125.
4. Of the amount shown for Interest Earned, $100 was unearned as of December 31, 1973.
5. The balance of the Prepaid Insurance account consists of $360 for the premium on a three-year policy dated July 1, 1973, and $720 for premiums on a three-year policy dated January 1, 1973.

6. Advertising supplies on hand were $70.
7. The balance of the notes payable account represents a 6-percent interest bearing note dated January 1, 1973, due July 1, 1974.
8. The rent is $2,000 a month.
9. Salaries earned but not paid were $650.
10. Property taxes accrued were $95.
11. On January 1, 1973, the Foley Company subleased a section of its rented space. The lease with the tenant specifies a minimum yearly rental of $1,200 payable in 12 installments at the beginning of each month. The maximum annual rental is 5-percent of sales. The rental adjustment, if any, is due on January 15. The tenant reported sales of $26,500 for 1973.
12. Included in Revenue–Consulting Fees are advance payments of $7,500 by clients for services to be rendered early in 1974.

Required: a. Record the adjusting entries.
b. Indicate the financial statement classification of each account in each entry.
c. Show the amount reported on the financial statements. Present the data in schedule form as shown (Item 1 is done as an example):

Item No.	Adjusting Journal Entries December 31, 1973	Dr.	Cr.	Financial Statement Classification	Amount Reported on Financial Statement
1	Office Supplies Exp. Office Supplies	570	570	Expenses Current Assets	$570 50

DP4-3. (*Financial statements; closing entries*) Boerner Decorators' adjusted trial balance, taken from the worksheet for the month ended July 31, 1973, was as follows:

Cash	$ 600	
Accounts Receivable	900	
Decorating Supplies	2,000	
Prepaid Insurance	1,200	
Building	10,000	
Accumulated Depreciation–Building		$ 5,700
Land	3,000	
Accounts Payable		2,000
Note Payable		1,200
Bank Loan Payable (due June 1, 1975)		3,600
Capital Stock		1,500
Retained Earnings		690
Dividends	475	
Service Revenue		7,950
Heat and Light Expense	120	
Telephone and Telegraph Expense	40	
Wages Expense	800	
Decorating Supplies Expense	3,200	
Insurance Expense	160	
Depreciation Expense–Building	240	
Income Tax Expense	750	
Accrued Wages Payable		70
Interest Expense	25	
Accrued Interest Payable		50
Income Taxes Payable		750
Totals	$23,510	$23,510

Required: 1. An income statement with a Percent column.
2. A position statement with a Percent column.
3. A statement of retained earnings.
4. Closing entries.
5. The company needs additional cash to increase its volume of business. Suggest alternative means of raising money and the advantages and disadvantages of each alternative.

PROBLEMS

P4-1. (*Accounting policy decision problem*) Nelson Stout, a Certified Public Accountant, began practice on July 1, 1973. He kept his accounts on the accrual basis. At the end of the year, the following adjusted trial balance was taken from his worksheet:

Cash	$ 250	
Accounts Receivable	1,300	
Office Supplies	50	
Accrued Salaries Payable		$ 40
Nelson Stout, Capital		1,400
Nelson Stout, Drawing	3,400	
Professional Fees		8,400
Rent Expense	1,200	
Insurance Expense	150	
Office Salaries Expense	3,100	
Miscellaneous Expense	390	
Totals	$9,840	$9,840

An examination of the worksheet shows the following adjustments:

Office Salaries Expense	40	
Accrued Salaries Payable		40
Miscellaneous Expense	30	
Office Supplies		30

Required: 1. Prepare an income statement to determine Stout's net income on the accrual basis of accounting.
2. Prepare an income statement to determine Stout's net income on the cash basis of accounting.
3. Which method of accounting should Stout use? Why?

P4-2. Following is the trial balance of the Sir-Park Corporation for the month of May, 1973, the first month of operations.

SIR-PARK CORPORATION
Trial Balance
May 31, 1973

Cash	$2,500	
Accounts Receivable	800	
Garage Supplies	450	
Prepaid Insurance	325	
Accounts Payable		$ 85
Capital Stock		3,600
Dividends	350	
Garage Revenue		1,300
Advertising Expense	125	
Miscellaneous Expenses	230	
Telephone and Telegraph Expense	75	
Wages Expense	130	
Totals	$4,985	$4,985

Supplementary data on May 31 were:

a. Garage supplies on hand were $300.
b. Expired insurance was $250.
c. Wages earned by employees but not paid were $70.

> Required: 1. Record the trial balance on a worksheet.
> 2. Complete the worksheet for the month of May.
> 3. Determine the net income for the month on the cash basis of accounting.

P4-3. Listed below are the account balances taken from the Trial Balance and Adjusted Trial Balance columns of the worksheet of the Fountain Company for the 12-month period ended June 30, 1973, the first year of operations.

Account Title	Trial Balance	Adjusted Trial Balance
Cash	$ 1,200	$ 1,200
Accounts Receivable	2,000	2,000
Office Supplies	1,750	500
Store Supplies	1,500	100
Prepaid Insurance	1,800	600
Prepaid Rent	2,400	600
Equipment	20,600	20,600
Accounts Payable	7,000	7,000
Capital Stock	19,650	19,650
Dividends	3,500	3,500
Service Revenue	15,500	15,500
Wages Expense	5,500	5,570
Miscellaneous Expense	1,900	1,900
Office Supplies Expense		1,250
Store Supplies Expense		1,400
Insurance Expense		1,200
Rent Expense		1,800
Depreciation Expense–Equipment		2,000
Accumulated Depreciation–Equipment		2,000
Accrued Wages Payable		70

> Required: Reconstruct the Trial Balance, Adjustments, and Adjusted Trial Balance columns of the worksheet.

P4-4. Selected transactions of the Eason Sales Company for 1973 are given:

1973

January 1 Purchased a four-year insurance policy for $3,600.

July 1 Bought two trucks for $11,500. The trucks are expected to last five years, at the end of which time their salvage value will be $750 each.

December 31 Paid $900 rent for the three-month period ending March 31, 1974.

   31 Purchased office supplies for $350.

> Required: 1. Make journal entries to record the transactions.
> 2. Make the adjusting entries as of December 31, 1973. The company closes its books annually on December 31.
> 3. What adjusting entries would be made if the Eason Sales Company was on the cash basis?

P4-5. Certain account balances from the trial balance of the Dune Company as of June 30, 1973, the end of its fiscal year, are given:

Account Title	Debits	Credits
Office Supplies	$ 450	
Prepaid Insurance	3,600	
Prepaid Advertising	4,200	
Unearned Rent		$ 600
Rent Expense	2,000	

Examination of the records as of June 30 shows the following:

1. Office supplies on hand totaled $175.
2. A three-year comprehensive insurance policy was purchased on July 1, 1972, at a premium cost of $3,600.
3. The monthly rent expense is $200.
4. Included in Prepaid Advertising is a payment of $200 for ads to appear during July, 1973. The balance is for ads that appeared in prior months.
5. A portion of the floor space was subleased at $50 a month on September 1, 1972. The tenant paid a year's rent in advance on signing the lease.

    Required: Record the adjusting entries as of June 30, 1973. The books are closed annually.

P4-6. (*Financial policy decision problem*) Following is the trial balance of the Anson Print Company at October 31, 1973. The Company began operations on September 1, 1973. Its fiscal year ends on October 31.

ANSON PRINT COMPANY
Trial Balance
October 31, 1973

Account Title	Debits	Credits
Cash	$ 7,100	
Notes Receivable	2,000	
Accounts Receivable	3,400	
Office Supplies	750	
Printing Supplies	1,000	
Prepaid Rent	2,400	
Printing Equipment	12,000	
Accounts Payable		$ 3,600
Notes Payable		2,200
Lars Anson, Capital		17,000
Lars Anson, Drawing	500	
Printing Revenue		8,335
Heat and Light Expense	80	
Telephone Expense	45	
Maintenance Expense	260	
Wages Expense	1,600	
Totals	$31,135	$31,135

Other data:

1. A physical count shows that (a) office supplies on hand total $375 and (b) printing supplies on hand are $600.
2. The monthly rental is $600.

3. Printing equipment acquired on September 1 has an estimated useful life of five years and a salvage value of $1,200.
4. Wages of employees earned but not paid are $300.
5. The note payable is a one-year note, signed on September 1, and bears interest at 6 percent.
0. The notes receivable account represents a 60-day 5-percent interest-bearing note signed by a customer on October 1.

Required: 1. Prepare adjusting entries.
2. Why did Anson accept the note from the customer?

P4-7. After analyzing the accounts and other records of Bynum, Inc., the following information is made available for the year ended December 31, 1973:

1. The Office Supplies account has a debit balance of $350. Office supplies on hand at December 31 total $110.
2. The Prepaid Rent account has a debit balance of $5,200. Included in this amount is $400 paid in December for the succeeding January; $4,800 has expired.
3. The Prepaid Insurance account has a debit balance of $1,380. It consists of the following policies purchased during 1973:

Policy No.	Date of Policy	Life of Policy	Premiums
A 5321	January 1	3 years	$960
E 452	April 1	2 years	240
X 321	August 1	1 year	180

4. The Prepaid Advertising account has a debit balance of $1,200. Included in this amount is $200 paid to a local monthly magazine for advertising space in its January and February, 1974, issues.
5. At the close of the year three notes receivable were on hand, as follows:

Date	Face Value	Time of Note	Interest Rate
November 16	$5,500	90 days	4 percent
December 4	3,000	60 days	6 percent
December 10	2,500	30 days	none

6. At the close of the year two notes payable were outstanding, as follows:

Date	Face Value	Time of Note	Interest Rate
September 15	$8,000	180 days	6 percent
November 3	5,000	90 days	4 percent

7. Salaries and wages accrued totaled $1,020.
8. The Rent Earned account has a credit balance of $7,200. This amount represents payment on a one-year lease effective May 1, 1973.
9. The Store Equipment account has a debit balance of $11,500. The equipment has an estimated useful life of 10 years and a salvage value of $1,000. All store equipment was acquired prior to January 1, 1973.
10. The Truck account has a debit balance of $5,000. The truck was purchased on June 15, 1972, and has an estimated life of five years and salvage value of approximately $400.
11. Property taxes accrued were $850.
12. Estimated income taxes for the year were $2,500.

Required: Prepare the adjusting journal entries required at December 31.

P4-8. The bookkeeper for the Ronson Company prepared the following condensed income statement for the year ended December 31, 1973, and the condensed statement of financial position as of that date.

Income Statement

Revenue from Services		$31,500
Operating Expenses		
Insurance Expense	$ 1,050	
Miscellaneous Expense	3,800	
Office Supplies Expense	350	
Wages Expense	12,000	17,200
Net Income		$14,300

Statement of Financial Position

Assets

Cash	$ 3,500
Accounts Receivable	8,400
Equipment	30,500
Total Assets	$42,400

Liabilities and Owner's Equity

Accounts Payable	$ 8,400
Stanley Ronson, Capital	34,000
Total Liabilities and Owner's Equity	$42,400

The following items were overlooked entirely by the bookkeeper in the preparation of the statements:

1. The depreciation of equipment (acquired January 1, 1973): estimated life, 10 years; no salvage value
2. Wages earned but unpaid, $600
3. Office supplies on hand, $125 (purchases during 1973 were debited to Office Supplies Expense)
4. Unexpired insurance premiums, $425
5. Heat and light invoices for December, $225

> Required: 1. What adjustments are needed?
> 2. Prepare revised financial statements.
> 3. Prepare a schedule reconciling the revised amount of owner's equity with the amount shown in the original statement.

P4-9. On August 1, 1973, Isaac Bostain opened a repair shop. During August, the following transactions were completed:

1973

August 1   Transferred $1,000 from his personal savings account to a checking account under the name of Bostain Fixery.

     2   Paid $50 for office supplies.

     3   Purchased second-hand office equipment for $150 in cash.

     4   Issued a check for $50 for August rent.

     5   Paid a premium of $24 for an insurance policy on the equipment, effective August 1.

1973

August   6   Purchased supplies on account to be used in repair work, as follows:

Andrews Supply Company	$ 35
Bonica's, Inc.	30
Fixlt Supply Company	60
House of Berezin	20
Total	$145

17   Received $950 for repair work completed.

20   Additional repair work was completed, and bills were sent out, as follows:

Leo Bonner and Company	$105
William Curtis	35
Arnold Johnson	28
Peter Kent	60
Total	$228

22   Paid $20 for the telephone service for the month.

25   Paid the following creditors:

Andrews Supply Company	$20
Bonica's, Inc.	10
Fixit Supply Company	30
House of Berezin	10
Total	$70

27   Received cash from customers to apply on account, as follows:

Leo Bonner and Company	$50
William Curtis	10
Arnold Johnson	10
Peter Kent	20
Total	$90

30   Bostain withdrew $300 in cash for his personal use.

Supplementary adjustment data as of August 31, 1973, were:

1. The insurance premium paid on August 5 is for one year.
2. A physical count shows that (1) office supplies on hand total $25, and (2) repair supplies on hand are $65.
3. The office equipment has an estimated useful life of five years with no salvage value.

Required:

1. Open the following accounts in the general ledger: Cash, 101; Accounts Receivable, 111; Office Supplies, 136; Repair Supplies, 137; Prepaid Insurance, 140; Office Equipment, 163; Accumulated Depreciation–Office Equipment, 163A; Accounts Payable, 201; Isaac Bostain, Capital, 251; Isaac Bostain, Drawing, 252; Repair Revenue, 301; Insurance Expense, 702; Rent Expense, 703; Office Supplies Expense, 708; Telephone and Telegraph Expense, 709; Repair Supplies Expense, 712; Depreciation Expense–Office Equipment, 717; Revenue and Expense Summary, 902.
2. Open accounts in the accounts receivable ledger for Leo Bonner and Company, William Curtis, Arnold Johnson, and Peter Kent.
3. Open accounts in the accounts payable ledger for the Andrews Supply Company; Bonica's, Inc.; the Fixit Supply Company; and the House of Berezin.
4. Record all the transactions in the general journal, post to the appropriate ledgers and enter the general ledger account balances directly in the Trial Balance columns of the worksheet.
5. Enter the adjustment data in the Adjustments columns of the worksheet.

6. Complete the worksheet.
7. Prepare an income statement, a statement of financial position, and a statement of owner's equity (include percentage analyses and equity ratios).
8. Prepare a schedule of accounts receivable.
9. Prepare a schedule of accounts payable.
10. Prepare adjusting journal entries in the general journal.
11. Post the adjusting journal entries from the general journal to the general ledger.
12. Prepare closing entries in the general journal and post to the general ledger.
13. Balance and rule the accounts.
14. Prepare a post-closing trial balance.

P4-10. (*Accounting policy decision problem*) The closing entries and post-closing trial balance of the Fulton Realty Company, as of December 31, 1973, are given below. A yearly accounting period is used. Tyson Fulton, the proprietor, had a capital balance of $15,000 on January 1, 1973; he made one additional investment during the year.

GENERAL JOURNAL   Page 12

		Closing Entries		
1973				
Dec.	31	Rental Revenue	5,500	
		Commission Revenue	21,600	
		Revenue and Expense Summary		27,100
	31	Revenue and Expense Summary	20,050	
		Rent Expense		1,800
		Insurance Expense		400
		Supplies Expense		150
		Commission Expense		16,500
		Depreciation Expense–Office Equipment		1,000
		Miscellaneous Expense		200
	31	Revenue and Expense Summary	7,050	
		Tyson Fulton, Drawing		7,050
	31	Tyson Fulton, Drawing	2,050	
		Tyson Fulton, Capital		2,050

FULTON REALTY COMPANY
Post-Closing Trial Balance
December 31, 1973

Account Title	Debits	Credits
Cash	$5,300	
Office Supplies	150	
Prepaid Insurance	1,600	
Office Equipment	16,000	
Accumulated Depreciation–Office Equipment		$ 2,000
Bank Loans Payable		1,000
Tyson Fulton, Capital		20,050
	$23,050	$23,050

Required: 1. An income statement for 1973.
2. A statement of owner's equity.
3. Fulton believes that the income statement should show a deduction of a reasonable amount for his services to the business. Comment.

5

Merchandising— Determining and Interpreting the Results of Operations

Accounting for businesses that render a service to customers or clients has been discussed up to this point. In this and subsequent chapters, accounting for businesses that buy and sell *merchandise*, or goods, is examined. The principles developed thus far, however, apply to all types of business enterprise, whether service, merchandising, or manufacturing.

ACCOUNTS FOR A MERCHANDISING BUSINESS

The principal difference in the accounts of a merchandising business from those of a service business is that a merchandising business has to account for the purchase of goods, their handling, and their sale; it has to account not only for operating expenses but also for the cost of goods that it has sold. The income statement for a merchandising business, therefore, shows an operating income only if the goods are sold for more than their cost plus all other expenses necessary in operating the business. Since a merchandising business is involved in many activities that are not found in service businesses, additional accounts are needed to report the financial position and operating results of the enterprise. By using separate accounts, detailed information is made available; by combining some of these accounts, additional useful information is made available. The functions of the merchandising accounts and their classifications in the financial statements are discussed and illustrated in this chapter.

The Sales Account

A sale of merchandise, like a sale of service, is recorded by a credit to a revenue account as shown.

TRANSACTION:

Sold merchandise for $200 on account.

JOURNAL ENTRY:

Accounts Receivable	200	
Sales		200

The debit to Accounts Receivable (or to Cash if the sale is for cash) records an increase in an asset. The credit to Sales, a revenue account, records an increase in the stockholders' equity. This credit constitutes a recovery of the cost of the merchandise sold as well as the profit. However, each individual sale cannot be divided into a return of cost and a profit. To do so would require such extensive records as to make the accounting impracticable. Therefore, the entire sales price of the goods is recorded as revenue and the entire cost of goods purchased and sold becomes a deduction from revenue.

The Sales Returns and Allowances Account

A customer may return merchandise because it is not exactly what he ordered; or the customer may be entitled to a reduction of the price, or *allowance*, for defective or broken goods that he retains. The effect of the entry to record a return or allowance is the opposite of a sale; that is, either Cash or the customer's account is credited, and Sales Returns and Allowances is debited. The latter account is used, rather than Sales, so that a record may be available of the amount of returns and allowances.

TRANSACTION:

The customer returned $10 worth of the merchandise (see the previous transaction).

JOURNAL ENTRY:

Sales Returns and Allowances	10	
Accounts Receivable		10

The Sales Discounts Account

The customer may be allowed a *discount*, or reduction in price, if he pays within a limited period of time. Since the effect of a discount is to reduce the amount actually received from the sale, Sales Discounts is debited for the amount of the discount. Sales Discounts is a contra account to Sales and is used for the same reason that prompts the use of Sales Returns and Allowances—to supply management with valuable information about the business. When discounts are offered, the customer is in fact being offered the choice of paying (1) the full amount of the invoice or (2) the full amount reduced by the amount of the discount. The seller, however, does not know at the time of the sale whether the customer is going to avail himself of the discount. The customer is charged, therefore, with the full amount of the sale. If the customer pays within the discount period, payment is recorded under the *gross price method* as shown.

TRANSACTION:

The customer (see the previous transactions) paid his invoice within the discount period, deducting the 2-percent sales discount.

JOURNAL ENTRY:

Cash	186.20	
Sales Discounts	3.80	
Accounts Receivable		190.00

COMPUTATION:

Gross sale price	$200.00
Merchandise returned	10.00
	$190.00
2% discount	3.80
Cash received	$186.20

An alternative procedure, the *Sales discounts not taken method,* is discussed later in this chapter.

The following partial income statement of the King Corporation, whose accounts are used for illustrative purposes in this chapter, shows the classification of the Sales and contra Sales Accounts.

KING CORPORATION		Exhibit A
Income Statement		
For the Year Ended December, 31, 1973		
Sales Revenue		
Sales		$124,200
Deduct Sales Returns and Allowances	$2,400	
Sales Discounts	1,800	4,200
Net Sales Revenue		$120,000

The Purchases Account

It is customary in a merchandising business to use a separate Purchases account for all merchandise bought for resale. The account is *not* used for the purchase of operating supplies, for example, or for store equipment used in operations. The Purchases account is debited for the cost of the goods bought, shown on a document from the seller called an *invoice,* and therefore provides a record of the cost of the goods purchased during the period—not a record of the goods on hand. During the year, Purchases will always have a debit balance; the usual credits to the account are to close the account or to correct errors requiring offsetting debits to some other account(s).

TRANSACTION:

Purchased merchandise for $800 on account.

JOURNAL ENTRY:

Purchases	800	
Accounts Payable		800

The Transportation In Account

The invoice price of goods may include the cost of transporting the goods from the seller's place of business to that of the buyer. If so, no separation is made, and the entire purchase price is debited to Purchases. If the cost of transportation is not included, the carrier is paid directly by the buyer, who debits the amount to Transportation In. This account is added to Purchases in the income statement to determine the *delivered cost of merchandise.*

The following terms are used in connection with the transportation of merchandise:

a. _F.O.B._ (free on board) *destination* means that the seller pays the freight cost to the buyer's location. (Sometimes the buyer pays the cost and deducts the amount from his payment to the seller.)

b. _F.O.B. shipping point_ means that the buyer pays the freight cost from the point of shipment to the destination.

TRANSACTION:

Freight charges of $50 were paid upon delivery of merchandise (see the previous transaction); terms of the purchase were F.O.B. shipping point.

JOURNAL ENTRY:

Transportation In	50	
Cash		50

The Purchases Returns and Allowances Account

Goods bought for resale may be defective, broken, or not of the quality ordered. Either they may be returned for credit, or the seller may make an adjustment by reducing the original price.

TRANSACTION:

Returned $100 worth of defective merchandise to the vendor.

JOURNAL ENTRY:

Accounts Payable	100	
Purchases Returns and Allowances		100

Purchases Returns and Allowances is a contra account to Purchases. The same result could be accomplished by crediting Purchases, but it is useful to management to have the books show total Purchases as well as total Purchases

Returns and Allowances. Analysis of the Purchases Returns and Allowances account may indicate the need for changes in the procedures of ordering and handling merchandise.

The Purchases Discounts Account

The Purchases Discounts account is used to record deductions from the purchase price of goods for payment made within the discount period specified by the seller. At the time of the purchase, the buyer may not know whether he will avail himself of the discount; the account with the seller (Accounts Payable) is therefore credited for the gross purchase price. As in the case of merchandise sales, an alternative procedure, the *discounts lost method*, is discussed later in the chapter.

TRANSACTION:

Paid for merchandise (see the previous transactions) within the discount period and deducted the allowed discount of 1 percent.

JOURNAL ENTRY:

Accounts Payable	700	
Cash		693
Purchases Discounts		7

purchase discount
Loss — expense

COMPUTATION:

Gross purchase	$800
Merchandise returned	100
	$700
1% discount	7
Cash paid	$693

The Merchandise Inventory Account

The system of accounting for merchandise inventory described in this chapter is called the *periodic inventory method*. A slightly different variation which yields a constant inventory balance, called the *perpetual inventory system*, is described in Chapter 9.

Merchandise purchased is recorded at cost in Purchases; merchandise sold is recorded at selling price in Sales. Therefore, an account is needed to show the merchandise actually on hand at the end of the accounting period. The amount is determined by making a list of the goods on hand, usually based on an actual count showing physical quantities and their cost. This *ending inventory* is entered in the books and becomes the beginning inventory of the next period. The amount in the ledger account will not be changed until the end of the next accounting period because the Merchandise Inventory account is not used during the period. Since the account remains open, its balance—the beginning inventory—appears in the trial balance at the end of the period and is transferred to Revenue and

Expense Summary when the books are closed. Concurrently, the new ending merchandise inventory is entered as a debit to Merchandise Inventory and a credit to Revenue and Expense Summary. After the closing entries are posted, the Merchandise Inventory account in the general ledger of the King Corporation appears as shown below.

Merchandise Inventory		Acct. No. 121
1972 Dec. 31 (A) 15,400	1973 Dec. 31 C.E.	(B) 15,400
1973 Dec. 31 (C) 11,480		

(A) The debit amount of $15,400 is the cost of the merchandise inventory on hand at December 31, 1972 (the beginning inventory).

(B) The credit posting of $15,400 closes the account temporarily and transfers the balance to Revenue and Expense Summary.

(C) The debit posting of $11,480 is the cost of the merchandise inventory on hand at December 31, 1973 (the ending inventory); this amount will remain unchanged in the account until the books are closed again on December 31, 1974.

THE FUNCTIONS OF THE MERCHANDISE ACCOUNTS

The following T accounts define the functions of the merchandise accounts and their locations in the financial statements. The accounts are presented in their income statement sequence. The description *Balance* in each account refers to the balance before the closing entries have been posted. After the closing entries are posted, all the merchandise accounts, except Merchandise Inventory, are closed.

Sales	
Debited	**Credited**
At the end of the accounting period to close the account.	During the accounting period for the sales price of goods sold.
	Balance A credit representing cumulative sales for the period to date.
	Statement Classification In the income statement, the first item under sales revenue.

Sales Returns and Allowances

Debited	Credited
During the accounting period for unwanted merchandise returned by customers and allowances for defective or broken goods.	At the end of the accounting period to close the account.

Balance

A debit representing cumulative sales returns and allowances for the period to date.

Statement Classification

In the income statement, a deduction from sales revenue.

Sales Discounts

Debited	Credited
During the accounting period for the amounts that the customers may deduct from the gross sales price if payment is made within the period established by the seller.	At the end of the accounting period to close the account.

Balance

A debit representing cumulative sales discounts allowed for the period to date.

Statement Classification

In the income statement, a deduction from sales revenue.

Merchandise Inventory

Debited	Credited
At the end of each accounting period for the merchandise actually on hand.	At the end of each accounting period for merchandise that was on hand at the beginning of the period, in order to remove the old inventory from the account.

Balance

A debit representing the cost of goods on hand at the beginning of the period.

Statement Classification

1. In the position statement, under current assets.
2. In the income statement, in the cost of goods sold section, the beginning inventory is added to Purchases and the ending intory is subtracted from the cost of merchandise available for sale.

Purchases

Debited

During the accounting period for the purchase price of goods bought for resale.

Balance

A debit representing cumulative purchases for the period to date.

Statement Classification

In the income statement, added to the beginning inventory under the Cost of Goods Sold.

Credited

At the end of the accounting period to close the account.

Transportation In

Debited

During the accounting period for delivery costs—freight or cartage—on merchandise purchases.

Balance

A debit representing cumulative costs for the period to date incurred by the buyer for the delivery of merchandise.

Statement Classification

In the income statement, in the cost of goods sold section, added to Purchases.

Credited

At the end of the accounting period to close the account.

Purchases Returns and Allowances

Debited

At the end of the accounting period to close the account.

Credited

During the accounting period for unwanted merchandise returned by the buyer to the seller or allowances received for defective or broken merchandise.

Balance

A credit representing cumulative purchases returns and allowances for the period to date.

Statement Classification

In the income statement, in the cost of goods sold section, as a deduction from the gross cost of merchandise purchased.

Purchases Discounts	
Debited	**Credited**
At the end of the accounting period to close the account.	During the accounting period for the amounts that the buyer may deduct from the gross purchase price of merchandise if payment is made within the period established by the seller.
	Balance
	A credit representing cumulative purchases discounts taken for the period to date.
	Statement Classification
	In the income statement, in the cost of goods sold section, as a deduction from the gross cost of merchandise purchased.

COST OF GOODS SOLD AND GROSS MARGIN ON SALES

The cost of goods sold is the difference between the cost of the goods available for sale during a period and the cost of the unsold goods on hand at the end of the period. The term does not identify an active account for the recording of transactions but rather the result of adding and subtracting the balances of several accounts. The computation is shown as

Cost of goods sold = Beginning inventory + Net cost of purchases
                                                    − Ending inventory

Net cost of purchases is the total cost of purchases, plus transportation in, less returns, allowances, and discounts.

The income statement of the King Corporation is shown in Figure 5-1. It was prepared from the worksheet in Figure 5-3.

The income statement of the King Corporation shows all the accounts needed to derive the cost of goods sold of $67,200.

The *gross margin on sales* of $52,800 is what is left after the cost of goods sold of $67,200 is deducted from the net sales revenue of $120,000. The term *gross* indicates that the operating expenses necessary to the conduct of the business must still be deducted to arrive at the *net operating margin*. If the gross margin on sales is less than the operating expenses, the difference is a net operating loss for the period.

Figure 5-1. Income Statement

KING CORPORATION
Exhibit A

Income Statement
For the Year Ended December 31, 1973

				Percent
Gross Sales Revenue			$124,200	
Deduct: Sales Returns and Allowances		$ 2,400		
Sales Discounts		1,800	4,200	
Net Sales Revenue			$120,000	100.0
Cost of Goods Sold				
Merchandise Inventory, January 1, 1973		$15,400		
Purchases	$63,580			
Transportation In	4,800			
Gross Purchases	$68,380			
Deduct: Purchases Returns and Allowances	$1,500			
Purchases Discounts	3,600	5,100		
Net Cost of Purchases		63,280		
Cost of Merchandise Available for Sale		$78,680		
Deduct Merchandise Inventory, December 31, 1973		11,480		
Cost of Goods Sold			67,200	56.0
Gross Margin on Sales			$ 52,800	44.0
Deduct Operating Expenses				
Selling Expenses				
Salesmen's Salaries Expense	$12,000			10.0
Transportation Out Expense	2,400			2.0
Advertising Expense	3,000			2.5
Total Selling Expenses		$17,400		14.5
General and Administrative Expenses				
Rent Expense	$ 6,000			5.0
Property Tax Expense	7,800			6.5
Heat and Light Expense	2,160			1.8
Miscellaneous General Expense	480			.4
Insurance Expense	1,920			1.6
Supplies Expense	2,040			1.7
Depreciation Expense–Machinery and Equipment	3,600			3.0
Total General and Administrative Expenses		24,000		20.0
Total Operating Expenses			41,400	34.5
Net Operating Margin			$ 11,400	9.5
Other Revenue				
Interest Earned	$ 125			
Rent Earned	300	$ 425		
Other Expenses				
Interest Expense	$ 75			
Loss on Sale of Equipment	100	175	250	
Net Income Before Income Taxes			$ 11,650	
Income Taxes			5,825	
Net Income			$ 5,825	

THE OPERATING EXPENSE ACCOUNTS

Operating expenses are salaries, postage, telephone and telegraph, heat and light, insurance, advertising, and any other costs incurred for goods or services used in operating the business. The breakdown of operating expenses into a number of detailed accounts facilitates analyses and comparisons that aid in the management of the business. The amount of detail shown depends on the size and type of the business and on the needs and wishes of the management.

The operating expenses are often subdivided into *selling* and *general and administrative*. The expenses incurred in packaging the product, advertising it, making the sale, and delivering the product are classified as selling expenses. Salesmen's salaries, commissions, and supplies used in the Sales department are examples of expenses incurred in making the sale. Expenses of delivering the product include freight paid by the seller (transportation out) and the expense of operating motor vehicles. Expenses such as rent, taxes, and insurance, to the extent that they are incurred in selling the product, are also classified as selling expenses. All other expenses are classified as general and administrative, including office expenses, executive salaries, and the portion of rent, taxes, and insurance applicable to the administrative function of the business. The expenses that are common to both selling and administrative functions may be apportioned on some equitable basis. If an apportionment is not practicable, the account should be classified under the function it serves most broadly. In Figure 5-1, the operating expense accounts that are entirely related to selling are classified as such; all the others are classified as general and administrative. The total operating expenses of $41,400 are deducted from the gross margin on sales of $52,800 to arrive at the net operating margin of $11,400.

If the operating expense accounts in the general ledger are too numerous, it is advisable to remove them to subsidiary selling expense and general and administrative expense ledgers. Two controlling accounts are substituted in the general ledger—Selling Expense and General and Administrative Expense—in place of the accounts that have been removed. The function of controlling accounts is explained in Chapter 3.

OTHER REVENUE AND OTHER EXPENSES

The Other Revenue and Other Expenses sections of the income statement serve a valuable function; they enable the derivation of the net operating margin undistorted by extraneous items and link the net operating margin for the period with the net income for that period.

Other Revenue

Some common examples of items classified as other revenue are gains from the sale of securities, dividends on shares of stock owned, gains from a settlement with an insurance company for fire damage, and gains from the sale of plant and equipment. In Figure 5-1, the King Corporation shows $125 in interest earned and $300 in rent earned under Other Revenue.

Other Expenses

Nonoperating expenses such as interest on money borrowed from the bank or notes given to creditors for the purchase of merchandise, uninsured property losses, or losses from the sale of plant and equipment are shown under other expenses. In the income statement in Figure 5-1, the King Corporation shows $75 in interest expense and $100 from a loss on a sale of equipment under Other Expenses.

The King Corporation added $250, the excess of other revenue over other expenses, to the net operating margin. If other expenses exceed other revenue, the expenses are listed first and the excess is deducted from the net operating margin.

In the absence of other revenue or other expenses, net operating margin becomes net income and net operating loss becomes net loss.

THE COMPLETION OF THE WORKSHEET

The procedure for completing the worksheet in a merchandising business is similar to that in a service business, with the obvious exception of the handling of the merchandise inventories.

At the end of the period, the balance of the Merchandise Inventory account, the beginning inventory of $15,400, is extended to the Income Statement Debit column of the worksheet because it is part of the cost of merchandise available for sale. The ending inventory, $11,480, is shown in the Income Statement Credit column because it is a deduction from the cost of merchandise available for sale and in the Position Statement Debit column because it is an asset. This treatment, which preserves the equality of debits and credits in the worksheet, is shown in Figure 5-2.

Figure 5-2. Partial Worksheet

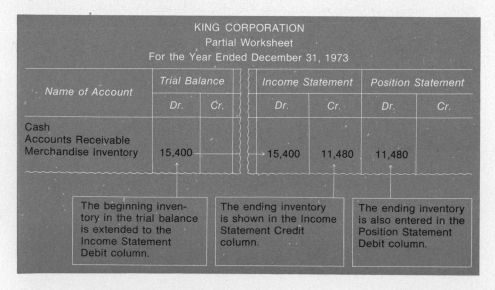

The worksheet of the King Corporation is shown in Figure 5-3. There are a number of possible variations in the form; for instance, the Adjusted Trial Balance columns are omitted in this example. The combined Trial Balance and Adjustment column amounts are extended directly to the proper Income Statement or Position Statement columns.

Figure 5-3. Worksheet

Acct. No.	Account Title	Trial Balance Dr.	Trial Balance Cr.	Adjustments Dr.	Adjustments Cr.	Income Statement Dr.	Income Statement Cr.	Position Statement Dr.	Position Statement Cr.
	KING CORPORATION — Worksheet — For the Year Ended December 31, 1973								
101	Cash	7,200						7,200	
111	Accounts Receivable	39,800						39,800	
121	Merchandise Inventory	15,400				15,400	11,480	11,480	
131	Office Supplies	3,240			(b) 2,040			1,200	
141	Prepaid Insurance	3,740			(a) 1,920			1,820	
151	Machinery and Equipment	70,100						70,100	
151A	Accumulated Depreciation–Machinery and Equipment		7,200		(c) 3,600				10,800
201	Accounts Payable		17,700						17,700
202	Notes Payable		7,300						7,300
221	Mortgage Payable		20,000						20,000
301	Capital Stock		60,000						60,000
302	Retained Earnings		5,150						5,150
303	Dividends	1,000						1,000	
401	Sales Revenue		124,200				124,200		
402	Sales Returns and Allowances	2,400				2,400			
403	Sales Discounts	1,800				1,800			
501	Purchases	63,580				63,580			
502	Transportation In	4,800				4,800			
503	Purchases Returns and Allowances		1,500				1,500		
504	Purchases Discounts		3,600				3,600		
601	Salesmen's Salaries Expense	12,000				12,000			
602	Transportation Out Expense	2,400				2,400			
603	Advertising Expense	3,000				3,000			
701	Rent Expense	6,000				6,000			
702	Property Tax Expense	7,800				7,800			
703	Heat and Light Expense	2,160				2,160			
704	Miscellaneous General Expense	480				480			
801	Interest Earned		125				125		
802	Rent Earned		300				300		
821	Interest Expense	75				75			
822	Loss on Sale of Equipment	100				100			
		247,075	247,075						
705	Insurance Expense			(a) 1,920		1,920			
706	Office Supplies Expense			(b) 2,040		2,040			
707	Depreciation Expense–Machinery and Equipment			(c) 3,600		3,600			
708	Income Tax Expense			(d) 5,825		5,825			
709	Income Taxes Payable				(d) 5,825				5,825
				13,385	13,385	135,380	141,205	132,600	126,775
	Net Income for the Year					5,825			5,825
						141,205	141,205	132,600	132,600

Trial Balance Columns

The account balances in the trial balance are taken from the general ledger of the King Corporation as of December 31, 1973.

Adjustment Columns

Supplementary records show the following information as of December 31, 1973:

    a. Insurance that has expired is $1,920.
    b. Office supplies on hand total $1,200.
    c. Depreciation on machinery and equipment is computed at $3,600.
    d. Income tax expense is estimated to be $5,825.

Income Statement Columns

All the account balances that enter into the measurement of net income are extended to the Income Statement columns. The income statement accounts that enter into the determination of gross margin are shown in Figures 5-3 and 5-4.

Figure 5-4. Abstract from the Worksheet

Acct. No.	Account Title	Income Statement Dr.	Income Statement Cr.
121	Merchandise Inventory	15,400	11,480
401	Sales Revenue		124,200
402	Sales Returns and Allowances	2,400	
403	Sales Discounts	1,800	
501	Purchases	63,580	
502	Transportation In	4,800	
503	Purchases Returns and Allowances		1,500
504	Purchases Discounts		3,600
	Totals of the foregoing items	87,980	140,780

The computation is accomplished on the formal income statement (Figure 5-1), resulting in a gross margin on sales of $52,800. The difference between the worksheet abstract column totals in Figure 5-4 ($140,780 − $87,980 = $52,800) is the same as the gross margin on sales because all the accounts that enter into the determination of the gross margin are listed. Similar examples could be made from the other sections of the income and position statements.

Position Statement Columns

All the amounts that are used to prepare the statements of financial position and retained earnings are extended to the Position Statement columns.

THE COMPLETED FINANCIAL STATEMENTS

Figure 5-5 shows the classified statement of financial position and Figure 5-6 shows the statement of retained earnings. These statements and the income statement (Figure 5-1) were prepared after the completion of the worksheet.

Figure 5-5. Statement of Financial Position

KING CORPORATION Statement of Financial Position December 31, 1973		Exhibit B
Assets		**Percent**
Current Assets		
Cash	$ 7,200	6.0
Accounts Receivable	39,800	32.9
Merchandise Inventory	11,480	9.4
Office Supplies	1,200	1.0
Prepaid Insurance	1,820	1.6
Total Current Assets	$ 61,500	50.9
Plant and Equipment		
Machinery and Equipment	$70,100	
Deduct Accumulated Depreciation	10,800	
Total Plant and Equipment	59,300	49.1
Total Assets	$120,800	100.0
Liabilities and Stockholders' Equity		
Current Liabilities		
Accounts Payable	$17,700	14.7
Notes Payable	7,300	6.0
Income Taxes Payable	5,825	4.8
Total Current Liabilities	$ 30,825	25.5
Long-Term Liabilities		
Mortgage Payable	20,000	16.6
Total Liabilities	$ 50,825	42.1
Stockholders' Equity		
Capital Stock	$60,000	49.7
Retained Earnings—Exhibit C	9,975	8.2
Total Stockholders' Equity	69,975	57.9
Total Liabilities and Stockholders' Equity	$120,800	100.0

Figure 5-6. Statement of Retained Earnings

KING CORPORATION Statement of Retained Earnings For the Year Ended December 31, 1973	Exhibit C
Retained Earnings, January 1, 1973	$ 5,150
Add Net Income for the Year—Exhibit A	5,825
Total	$10,975
Deduct Dividends	1,000
Retained Earnings, December 31, 1973	$ 9,975

Figure 5-7. Use of the Worksheet in Making Closing Entries in the Journal

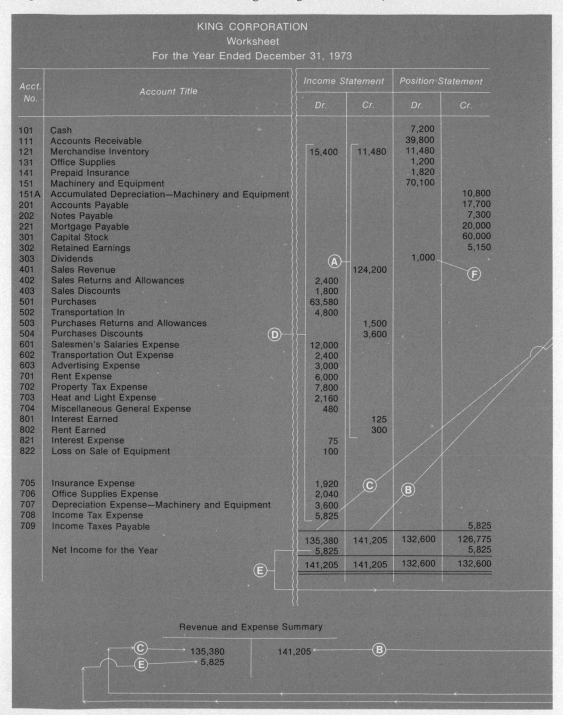

KING CORPORATION
Worksheet
For the Year Ended December 31, 1973

Acct. No.	Account Title	Income Statement		Position Statement	
		Dr.	Cr.	Dr.	Cr.
101	Cash			7,200	
111	Accounts Receivable			39,800	
121	Merchandise Inventory	15,400	11,480	11,480	
131	Office Supplies			1,200	
141	Prepaid Insurance			1,820	
151	Machinery and Equipment			70,100	
151A	Accumulated Depreciation—Machinery and Equipment				10,800
201	Accounts Payable				17,700
202	Notes Payable				7,300
221	Mortgage Payable				20,000
301	Capital Stock				60,000
302	Retained Earnings				5,150
303	Dividends			1,000	
401	Sales Revenue		124,200		
402	Sales Returns and Allowances	2,400			
403	Sales Discounts	1,800			
501	Purchases	63,580			
502	Transportation In	4,800			
503	Purchases Returns and Allowances		1,500		
504	Purchases Discounts		3,600		
601	Salesmen's Salaries Expense	12,000			
602	Transportation Out Expense	2,400			
603	Advertising Expense	3,000			
701	Rent Expense	6,000			
702	Property Tax Expense	7,800			
703	Heat and Light Expense	2,160			
704	Miscellaneous General Expense	480			
801	Interest Earned		125		
802	Rent Earned		300		
821	Interest Expense	75			
822	Loss on Sale of Equipment	100			
705	Insurance Expense	1,920			
706	Office Supplies Expense	2,040			
707	Depreciation Expense—Machinery and Equipment	3,600			
708	Income Tax Expense	5,825			
709	Income Taxes Payable				5,825
		135,380	141,205	132,600	126,775
	Net Income for the Year	5,825			5,825
		141,205	141,205	132,600	132,600

Ⓐ Ⓕ Ⓓ Ⓒ Ⓑ Ⓔ

Revenue and Expense Summary

Ⓒ 135,380   141,205 Ⓑ
Ⓔ 5,825

GENERAL JOURNAL   Page 12

1973 Dec.					
31		Merchandise Inventory	121	11,480	
		Sales Revenue	401	124,200	
		Purchases Returns and Allowances	503	1,500	
(A)		Purchases Discounts	504	3,600	
		Interest Earned	801	125	
		Rent Earned	802	300	
(B)		Revenue and Expense Summary	901		141,205
		To record the ending inventory and close the revenue accounts.			
(C)					
31		Revenue and Expense Summary	901	135,380	
		Merchandise Inventory	121		15,400
		Sales Returns and Allowances	402		2,400
		Sales Discounts	403		1,800
		Purchases	501		63,580
		Transportation In	502		4,800
		Salesmen's Salaries Expense	601		12,000
		Transportation Out Expense	602		2,400
		Advertising Expense	603		3,000
		Rent Expense	701		6,000
(D)		Property Tax Expense	702		7,800
		Heat and Light Expense	703		2,160
		Miscellaneous General Expense	704		480
		Interest Expense	821		75
		Loss on Sale of Equipment	022		100
		Insurance Expense	705		1,920
		Office Supplies Expense	706		2,040
		Depreciation Expense— Machinery and Equipment	707		3,600
		Income Tax Expense	708		5,825
		To close the beginning inventory and the expense accounts.			
31		Revenue and Expense Summary	901	5,825	
(E)		Retained Earnings	302		5,825
		To transfer net income to Retained Earnings.			
31		Retained Earnings	302	1,000	
(F)		Dividends	303		1,000
		To close dividends to retained earnings.			

(A)   Each account in the Credit column of the Income Statement columns is debited in the journal.

(B)   The total of the Credit column is credited to the Revenue and Expense Summary in the journal.

(C)   The total of the Debit column of the Income Statement columns is debited to the Revenue and Expense Summary.

(D)   Each account in the Debit column is then credited.

(E)   The net income is debited to the Revenue and Expense Summary and credited to Retained Earnings.

(F)   If dividends have been declared, that amount which is found in the Position Statement column of the worksheet is debited to Retained Earnings and credited to Dividends.

CLOSING ENTRIES

The procedure for recording the closing entries in a merchandising business is essentially the same as in a service business (illustrated on pages 76 and 77). The closing entries, including the closing of the beginning merchandise inventory and the recording of the ending inventory, are shown in Figure 5-7. Another important reason for presenting the beginning and ending merchandise inventories in the Income Statement columns of the worksheet is the utility of using the worksheet in making the closing entries. Figure 5-7 illustrates how the Income Statement columns can be used to record these entries.

After the closing entries are posted, all the revenue and expense accounts have zero balances. The remaining accounts—the open Position Statement accounts—are ruled and balanced, and a post-closing trial balance is prepared.

INTERIM FINANCIAL STATEMENTS

Financial statements are prepared at least once a year, at which time the adjusting and closing entries are recorded and posted to the general ledger. The closing of the books at intervals of less than one year is not customary but has been assumed in this text as a convenience in illustrating the periodic summary. Financial statements, however, may be prepared at frequent intervals—monthly or quarterly—without the formal recording and posting of the adjusting and closing entries.

Financial statements may be produced at regular or intermittent intervals during the accounting period for external reasons, such as the establishment of credit for a bank loan, or for the internal use of managers and stockholders. They are referred to as *interim statements* and are prepared with the aid of the worksheet. The general ledger accounts balances as of the end of the interim period are entered on the worksheet, the adjustments are listed, the adjusted balances are extended to the appropriate Income Statement and Position Statement columns, and formal statements are prepared.

The amounts in the Trial Balance columns of the worksheet represent the cumulative general ledger totals for the year to date and the adjustments are for the same interval; hence, the amounts in the interim income statement are for the year to date. However, if monthly income statements are desired, the amounts on the statements for the previous months are deducted from the amounts on the current statement, thereby providing year to-date figures as well as results of the current period. The amounts in the Position Statement columns of the worksheet are the correct amounts for the statement of financial position as of the close of the current period.

The preparation of interim statements requires a determination of the cost of the merchandise on hand. Taking a detailed physical inventory, however, is costly and time-consuming and may not be necessary. Alternative methods of determining the ending inventory, such as the gross margin method of inventory valuation and the perpetual inventory system, are discussed in Chapter 9.

MANAGERIAL RATIO ANALYSIS

The financial statements of the King Corporation are analyzed to illustrate some additional ratios commonly used by the management in the analysis of the financial statements. The following amounts used in the illustrations are taken from the December 31, 1972, statement of financial position:

Stockholders' equity	$93,200
Total liabilities	58,600
Current assets	71,500
Current liabilities	29,000

Figures are rounded when it is necessary.

Rate of Return on Stockholders' Equity

The relationship between earnings and the stockholders' investment is a significant measure of the profitability of a business. The rate of return on the stockholders' equity is computed as shown.

Net income for the year 1973	(A)	$ 5,825
Average stockholders' equity Balance, January 1, 1973	(B)	$ 93,200
Balance, December 31, 1973	(C)	69,975
Total	(D)	$163,175
Average (line D ÷ 2)	(E)	$ 81,588
Rate of return on stockholders' equity (line A ÷ line E)		7.1%

Earnings for 1973 were 7.1 cents for each dollar of the stockholders' equity. The average stockholders' equity is computed so that the computation is not based on either the beginning-of-year or the end-of-year stockholders' equity. A further refinement is to compute the average by using the month-end balance for each month in the period covered by the analysis. This practice should be followed for any ratios involving amounts that fluctuate during the period to avoid distortion.

Rate of Return on Total Investments

The relationship of the earnings of a corporation to its total resources is another important indication of profitability. It is computed as shown.

Net income for the year 1973		(A)	$ 5,825
Average total liabilities:			
Balance, January 1, 1973	$ 58,600		
Balance, December 31, 1973 (Figure 5-5)	50,825		
Total	$109,425		
Average total liabilities ($109,425 ÷ 2)		(B)	$ 54,713
Average stockholders' equity (above)		(C)	81,588
Total average equities		(D)	$136,301
Rate of return on total investments (line A ÷ line D)		(E)	4.3%

The King Corporation earned 4.3 cents for each dollar invested in the company—whether by outside creditors or by stockholders. Since total equities are equal to total assets, it also may be said that the King Corporation earned 4.3 cents on each dollar of assets used in the business.

Operating Ratio

An indication of the amount expended during a period in relationship to the revenue of the period is important to management. The computation is shown below.

Net sales revenue	(A)	$120,000
Cost of goods sold	(B)	$ 67,200
Total operating expenses	(C)	41,400
Total revenue deductions	(D)	$108,600
Operating ratio (line D ÷ line A)		90.5%

The operating ratio shows that 90.5 cents of each sales dollar was absorbed by the operations of the King Corporation, or that costs and expenses of 90.5 cents were incurred to generate a dollar of sales revenue.

Net Operating Margin Ratio

The net operating margin ratio is a complement of the operating ratio; it shows the relationship of the net operating margin to sales (other revenue and other expenses are excluded).

$$\frac{\text{Net Operating Margin}}{\text{Net Sales Revenue}} = \frac{\$11,400}{\$120,000} = 9.5\%$$

The King Corporation earned 9.5 cents for each dollar of net sales. This ratio must be considered together with the rate of return on the stockholders' equity in appraising the earning power of a business. A high net operating margin ratio is not necessarily a favorable indication if it is accompanied by a low rate of return on the stockholders' equity.

Turnover of Merchandise Inventory

The quantity of goods to be kept on hand is a major business decision. It is considered good management to carry as little as possible and to turn it over as rapidly as possible. Good management must guard against excessive inventories, the consequences of which could be an abnormal drain on working capital that could lead to financial difficulties. The greater the inventory, the greater is the amount of money tied up, extra space required, and extra handling costs, as well as an increased possibility of loss through shrinkage, style changes, or other factors. Inadequate inventories, on the other hand, may result in higher costs due to buying in smaller quantities and the possible loss of business if what the customer wants is not on hand. Good management, therefore, requires a careful evaluation of all these factors in establishing inventory levels.

One of the ratios used in inventory analysis is the inventory turnover—the relationship between inventory and either net sales or cost of goods sold. Since the net sales figure is given at selling price and the inventory is given at cost, the ratio is computed by dividing the cost of goods sold rather than net sales by the average inventory. The figure used may be the average of the beginning and ending inventories of the period or, preferably, the average for the months involved to minimize the effect of seasonal fluctuations. Although high turnover is usually a sign of good management, this ratio varies widely from one industry to another. A wholesaler of automobile parts and accessories may average five inventory turnovers per year as compared with thirty-five or more for a wholesaler of meat and poultry. Also, a high-volume, low-margin business would have to turn over its inventory more often than a similar business having a low-volume, high-margin policy.

The inventory turnover is computed as shown.

Cost of goods sold	(A)	$67,200
Average merchandise inventory:		
January 1, 1973	(B)	$15,400
December 31, 1973	(C)	11,480
Total	(D)	$26,880
Average (line D ÷ 2)	(E)	$13,440
Turnover of inventory (line A ÷ line E)		5.0

The King Corporation sold and replaced its merchandise inventory five times during the year; that is, the cost of merchandise sold was five times greater than the average cost of merchandise on hand.

Working Capital Turnover

The relationship between working capital and sales tests the efficiency with which the working capital is used. The computation is made as shown.

	January 1, 1973	December 31, 1973
Average working capital:		
Current assets	$71,500	$ 61,500
Current liabilities	29,000	30,825
Working capital	$42,500	$ 30,675
Average working capital		
($42,500 + $30,675 = $73,175 ÷ 2)		$ 36,588
Net sales revenue		$120,000
Working capital turnover ($120,000 ÷ $36,588)		3.28

The King Corporation sold $3.28 worth of merchandise for each dollar of working capital. Care must be used in drawing any conclusions from this ratio because of the number of continuously changing elements (current assets, current liabilities, and sales) that it interrelates.

Percentage Analysis—King Corporation

The ratio of each revenue deduction to net revenue, each asset to total assets, each equity to total equities, and the several subtotals to the related totals are also significant. These percentages may be determined readily from the Percent columns of the King Corporation statements and are therefore not reproduced here. This form of analysis is called *vertical analysis* because the percentages relate to amounts usually shown in columnar statement form.

In Figure 5-1, the amounts of the items listed under other revenue and other expenses are not converted to percentages of net sales revenue because they are not part of the normal operating business cycle and there is no direct relationship between these amounts and net sales revenue.

The Percent column in the income statement of the King Corporation is a *common-size* income statement—each item is stated as a percentage of net sales revenue. It may also be called a *revenue-dollar* statement because it is identical in proportion to the common-size statement. For example, the distribution of the net sales dollar in Figure 5-1 may be expressed as follows:

Cost of Goods Sold	$0.560
Selling Expenses	0.145
General and Administrative Expenses	0.200
Net Operating Margin	0.095
Net Sales Revenue	$1.000

In addition to the analyses already illustrated and discussed, other ratios and percentages furnish useful managerial information. Some relationships of the King Corporation are illustrated on page 169.

$$\text{Sales returns and allowances to sales revenue} = \frac{\$2,400}{\$124,200} = 1.9\%$$

$$\text{Sales discounts to sales revenue} = \frac{\$1,800}{\$124,200} = 1.5\%$$

$$\text{Purchases returns and allowances to purchases} = \frac{\$1,500}{\$63,580} - 2.4\%$$

$$\text{Purchases discounts to purchases} = \frac{\$3,600}{\$63,580} = 5.7\%$$

These ratios serve as tools for controlling various accounts. If, for example, sales returns and allowances have previously been approximately one-half of 1 percent, then management ought to determine the causes of the increase to 1.9 percent.

UNCOLLECTIBLE ACCOUNTS

To measure properly the bad debt losses attributable to sales of a given period and the net realizable value of Accounts Receivable which should be shown on the statement of financial position, it is necessary to make the following end-of-period adjusting entry:

Bad Debts Expense	500	
Allowance for Doubtful Accounts		500
To record the bad debt expense for the year.		

Bad Debts Expense is shown on the income statement as a general and administrative expense and Allowance for Doubtful Accounts is shown on the statement of financial position as follows:

Accounts Receivable	$7,500	
Deduct Allowance for Doubtful Accounts	500	$7,000

When an account is discovered to be uncollectible, it is written off against Allowance for Doubtful Accounts as follows:

Allowance for Doubtful Accounts	75	
Accounts Receivable—James Dunker		75
To write off the uncollectible account of James Dunker.		

A more detailed discussion of the accounting for bad debts and uncollectible accounts is deferred to Chapter 8.

CASH DISCOUNTS—IMPLICATIONS TO MANAGEMENT

Cash discounts are computed on the net sales price; the conditions of payment are stated on the invoice. Some typical conditions follow.

Net cash	Payment is due in full upon delivery of the goods.
Net 30, or n/30	The full amount shown on the invoice is due within 30 days from the date of the invoice.
2/10, n/30	A 2-percent discount may be taken, provided payment is made within 10 days from the invoice date; otherwise the full invoice price is due in 30 days.
2/EOM, n/60	A 2-percent discount may be taken, provided payment is made by the end of the month (EOM) in which the goods are billed; the full amount is due in 60 days from the end of the month.
1/10 prox, n/60 or 1/10 EOM, n/60	A 1-percent discount may be taken, provided payment is made by the tenth of the following month; the full amount is due in 60 days from the end of the month. *Prox* is an abbreviation of *proximal*, or nearest. These terms are designed for buyers who prefer making payments during the first ten days of the month to spreading them throughout.

When the terms of the sale—or of the purchase—are, for example, 2/10, n/30, it is important to recognize the magnitude of the discount offered. This can be done best if the discount is converted into its equivalent annual interest rate. If the buyer of merchandise pays within 10 days from the date shown on the invoice, he may deduct 2 percent from the invoice price, or he may take an additional 20 days, or 30 days in all, before paying. The cost of the additional 20 days is high, however, because the loss of the 2-percent discount amounts to one-tenth of 1 percent per day (2% ÷ 20), or 36 percent per 360-day year (0.1% × 360). The prudent businessman should therefore, take all cash discounts, even if he has to borrow the money to do so.

TRADE DISCOUNTS

Another type of discount is the *trade discount*, which, unlike the cash discount, is not recorded in the accounts. A trade discount is a percentage reduction from a list price. The seller prints a catalog in which the prices of the various articles are shown. The actual price charged may differ from the list price because of the class of buyer (wholesalers, retailers, and so on), the quantity ordered, or changes in the catalog. The granting of trade discounts eliminates the need for frequent reprinting of catalogs or printing different lists for different classes of buyers. If more than one discount is given—a so-called *chain discount*—each discount is applied successively to arrive at the invoice price. Thus, the actual price of an item listed at $300 less trade discounts of 20 percent, 10 percent, and 5 percent is $205.20.

MANAGEMENT CONTROL—THE EXCEPTION PRINCIPLE

The control principle of management by exception involves isolating those amounts or accounts that indicate operating inefficiencies and focus attention on the areas that might require corrective action. Since only exceptions from the norm require such corrective action, management's task is simplified and expedited by separating from the mass of data the exceptional items for further study.

The alternative method for recording cash discounts, the discounts lost method, illustrates the principle of management by exception. Under the gross price procedure discussed earlier in this chapter, the volume of discounts granted or taken is accumulated in the Sales Discounts and Purchases Discounts accounts. Management is interested primarily, however, not in the amount of discounts taken, since it assumes that all available discounts are taken, but rather in the exceptions—that is, the discounts not taken.

Sales Discounts Not Taken — *revenue*

Assume that a $1,000 sale is made on April 1, with terms of 2/10, n/30, and that payment is received on April 10. The entries, recorded net of discount, are

1973			
Apr. 1	Accounts Receivable	980	
	Sales		980
10	Cash	980	
	Accounts Receivable		980

If the payment was received on April 25, the entry would be

1973			
Apr. 25	Cash	1,000	
	Accounts Receivable		980
	Sales Discounts Not Taken		20

Sales Discounts Not Taken is classified as other revenue in the income statement.

Management should make a careful analysis of Sales Discounts Not Taken. A customer who fails to take advantage of discount terms of 2/10, n/30, for example, is foregoing savings equivalent to an annual rate of 36 percent. This indicates an unwillingness or an inability to pay debts promptly, significant information in granting credit or evaluating possible losses from uncollectible accounts.

DISCOUNTS LOST METHOD

The rationale for the alternative method of recording purchases discounts under the discounts lost method is the same as for the recording of sales discounts. Purchases are recorded at net of discount, and discounts lost are entered in a special account.

To illustrate the accounting for discounts lost by the discounts lost method, assume that a purchase of $5,000 in merchandise is received on July 1, with terms of 2/10, n/30, and that the invoice is paid on July 10. Purchases and Accounts Payable are recorded *net of discount* as shown on page 172.

```
1973
July  1  Purchases                    4,900
              Accounts Payable                    4,900
      10  Accounts Payable            4,900
              Cash                                4,900
```

If the invoice was not paid until July 15, the entries would be

```
1973
July  1  Purchases                    4,900
              Accounts Payable                    4,900
      15  Accounts Payable            4,900
          Purchases Discounts Lost     100
              Cash                                5,000
```

Under the discounts lost procedure, the debit to Purchases is $4,900 whether or not the discount is lost, and the loss of $100 appears in a separate general and administrative expense account, isolating the amount for the detection of possible laxities in procedures. The loss of available discounts may indicate a weakness in the organization, such as lack of bank credit or slowness in processing invoices for payment. The cost of goods purchased is not increased when discounts are lost; the amount is classified under other expenses.

There are some disadvantages to recording purchases at the net price: (1) the amount of discounts taken is not reported separately in the income statement; (2) statements from creditors do not agree with the net amounts recorded in the accounts payable ledger; (3) the amounts entered on individual inventory record cards may not agree with the net amounts entered as purchases since the inventory may be carried at invoice price; (4) the additional information may not justify the increased clerical costs and inconveniences; (5) an adjusting entry is needed at the end of the period to record lapsed discounts by debiting Purchases Discounts Lost and crediting Accounts Payable.

SUMMARY

Additional accounts are needed to report the financial position and operating results of a business that buys and sells merchandise. These accounts, either singly or in combination, provide additional useful information.

Net sales revenue is determined from the Sales account less the Sales Returns and Allowances and the Sales Discount accounts. The net cost of goods purchased is determined from the Purchases and Transportation In accounts less the Purchases Returns and Allowances and Purchases Discounts accounts. The cost of goods sold is equal to beginning inventory plus net purchases minus ending inventory. The gross margin is the difference between the net sales and the cost of goods sold. The operating expenses, subdivided into selling and general and administrative, are deducted from the gross margin on sales to arrive at the net operating margin. Items of a nonrecurring nature are recorded in separate accounts and classified under Other Revenue and Other Expenses and their difference is added to or deducted from the net operating margin to arrive at net income for the period.

Again, the worksheet is used to facilitate the preparation of the financial statements. The income statement accounts that enter into the determination of gross margin are extended to the Income Statement columns. The beginning inventory in the Trial Balance Debit column is extended to the Income Statement Debit column; the ending inventory is entered directly into the Income Statement Credit column and the Position Statement Debit column.

Significant information is made available to management by certain ratios and by showing the percentage distributions of the financial statement items. Ratios such as the rate of return on the stockholders' equity, the rate of return on the total investments, and the net operating margin ratio focus on the profitability of the company. The operating ratio and the turnover of merchandise inventory emphasize the effectiveness of a company's inventory management policies and the level of costs and expenses required to generate a dollar of sales revenue.

The principle of management by exception involves isolating those amounts or accounts that indicate operating inefficiencies. Management's task is simplified and expedited by separating from the mass of data only the exceptional items for further study. This is illustrated by the practice of recording sales and purchases at net amounts and recording sales discounts not taken and purchases discounts lost in separate accounts.

QUESTIONS

Q5-1. (a) What is the function of the Sales account? (b) the Sales Returns and Allowances account? (c) the Sales Discount account?

Q5-2. (a) What is the function of the Purchases account? (b) the Purchases Returns and Allowances account? (c) the Purchases Discounts account? (d) the Transportation In account?

Q5-3. (a) What is the function of the Merchandise Inventory account? (b) How is its amount determined? (c) In which columns of the worksheet is the beginning inventory shown? (d) the ending inventory?

Q5-4. (a) How is the cost of goods sold determined? (b) Why is the cost of goods sold not recorded at the time of the sale? (c) What is the relationship between the cost of goods sold and the gross margin on sales?

Q5-5. Why is it desirable to show the following items separately on the income statement: (a) operating expenses and other expenses? (b) net operating margin and other revenue?

Q5-6. (a) How does the procedure of closing the books of a merchandising business differ from that of closing the books of a service business? (b) What advantage is gained by including merchandise inventory, beginning and ending, in the closing entries rather than in the adjusting entries? (c) List the various uses that an accountant can make of the worksheet.

Q5-7. (a) What is the purpose of interim statements? (b) For whom are they prepared? (c) How are they prepared? (d) What special problems do they create?

Q5-8. Is it true that (a) management need not concern itself with the normal results but only with the exceptions? (b) only the big exceptions require corrective action? (c) The alternative method for recording cash discounts illustrates the principle of management by exception. Can you think of any other alternative recording methods that further illustrate this principle? (d) What are the disadvantages of recording purchases at the net price?

Q5-9. (a) What is meant by *inventory turnover*? (b) "The greater the turnover of inventory, the greater the gross margin on sales." Is this statement correct? Explain. (c) What is the significance to management of the turnover of merchandise inventory? (d) Is there an advantage in using monthly inventories to compute the turnover?

Q5-10. What ratios or percentages would aid in answering the following questions: (a) Is the net income satisfactory? (b) Are the operating expenses excessive? (c) Does the net income represent a reasonable return on the company's total resources? (d) Does the net income represent a reasonable return on the stockholders' equity? (e) Is the company maintaining an efficient relationship between working capital and sales? (f) Are the total selling expenses excessive? (g) Is the merchandise on hand excessive?

Q5-11. Assume that a merchandise transaction was made on September 4. In each case determine the latest possible payment date to allow the discount deduction. (a) 1/10, n/30; (b) 2/EOM, n/60; (c) 1/10 EOM, n/60.

Q5-12. Discuss the significance of each of the following: (a) the rate of return on stockholders' equity; (b) the rate of return on total investments; (c) the operating ratio; (d) the turnover of inventory; and (e) the working capital turnover.

Q5-13. (a) Distinguish between a cash discount and a trade discount. (b) Why are trade discounts used in quoting prices? (c) What are the advantages, if any, of recording purchases of merchandise at the invoice amount less cash discount, or net, over recording the full, or gross, invoice amount? (d) Explain the term *2/10, n/30*. (e) Discuss and illustrate alternative income statement presentations of Purchases Discounts and Sales Discounts.

EXERCISES

E5-1. During the year 1973, the Howard Sales Company purchased merchandise costing $14,000. Calculate the cost of goods sold for the year under each of the following assumptions regarding the beginning and ending merchandise inventory balances:

a. No beginning or ending inventory
b. A beginning inventory of $12,000; no ending inventory
c. A beginning inventory of $15,000 and an ending inventory of $19,000
d. No beginning inventory; an ending inventory of $4,000

E5-2. From the following information taken from the books of the Watts Company, prepare a partial income statement through gross margin on sales:

Merchandise Inventory, January 1, 1973	$ 2,000
Merchandise Inventory, January 31, 1973	1,500
Sales	14,500
Transportation In	450
Purchases Discounts	370
Sales Returns and Allowances	230
Purchases	6,300
Sales Discounts	150
Purchases Returns and Allowances	110

E5-3. Journalize the following transactions on the books of the buyer and the seller.

a. On June 1, the Appleby Manufacturing Company in New York sold merchandise to the Saenz Company in Boston for $875; terms 2/10, n/30, F.O.B. destination. The Saenz Company paid $50 freight on the shipment. On June 5, the Saenz Company returned some unsatisfactory merchandise and received credit for $25. On June 10, the Saenz Company mailed a check to the Appleby Manufacturing Company for the net amount due.
b. Assume the same facts as in (a), except that the terms were F.O.B. shipping point.

E5-4. The accounts and balances in the Income Statement columns of Thomas Kelly's worksheet for the year ended December 31, 1973 are given:

Account Title	Income Statement	
	Dr.	Cr.
Merchandise Inventory	6,000	6,500
Sales		15,300
Sales Returns and Allowances	50	
Sales Discounts	350	
Purchases	7,000	
Transportation In	200	
Purchases Returns and Allowances		100
Purchases Discounts		500
Selling Expenses	1,800	
General Expenses	3,000	
Totals	18,400	22,400
Net Income	4,000	
	22,400	22,400

The Position Statement Debit column of the worksheet showed $1,000 for Thomas Kelly, Drawing. (a) Journalize the closing entries. (b) Show the Merchandise Inventory and Revenue and Expense Summary accounts after the closing entries have been posted. (c) What difference, if any, is there between the closing entries of a trading business and those of a nontrading business? (d) May the Revenue and Expense Summary account be eliminated? Explain.

E5-5. On November 5, Robert Gunther, who uses the net price procedure, purchased merchandise for $2,000; terms 2/10, n/30. The invoice was paid on December 1. (a) Record the purchase and the payment of the invoice. (b) Is the net cost of merchandise the same under both the gross and the net procedure? Show your computations. (c) Assume that Gunther takes advantage of all purchases discounts. Is there any advantage in his using the gross price method of recording the purchase of merchandise?

E5-6. John Mack, who uses the net price procedure, sold merchandise on June 1 for $3,000; terms 1/10, n/30. The customer paid the invoice on June 20. (a) Record the sale and the collection of the account receivable. (b) Would net sales revenue be the same under both the gross and the net procedure? Show your computations. (c) Compare and contrast the significance to management of the Sales Discounts Not Taken account and the Sales Discount account.

E5-7. The Arthur Madrid Company grants customer discounts on partial payments made within the discount period. On May 5, the Company sold merchandise to Paul Yochum for $1,000; terms 3/10, n/30. On May 15, the Company received $500 to apply on account; on June 4, a check was received for the balance of the invoice. (a) Record the transactions for the A. Madrid Company using (1) the net price procedure and (2) the gross price procedure. (b) Make the corresponding journal entries for Paul Yochum.

E5-8. The following information is taken from John Silva's books as of December 31, 1973:

Trial Balance		Adjustment Data	
1. Prepaid Insurance	$1,200	Expired Insurance	$ 700
2. Rent Expense	4,800	Rent paid in advance	1,000
3. Wages Expense	8,700	Accrued wages	200
4. Interest Expense	150	Accrued interest	25
5. Unearned Rent	3,600	Rent earned	3,000
6. Interest Earned	1,200	Unearned interest	300

For each account: (a) prepare the adjusting entry; (b) state the amount to be shown in the income statement; (c) state the amount to be shown in the statement of financial position.

E5-9. The following items are taken from John Dap's trial balance on December 31. The books are closed annually on December 31. All the store equipment was acquired three years ago.

	Debits	Credits
Notes Receivable (90-day, 4-percent note, dated December 1)	$ 4,000	
Prepaid Insurance (one-year policy, dated Aug. 1)	360	
Prepaid Rent (payable one year in advance on Sept. 1)	4,800	
Store Equipment (10-year life; salvage value $500)	15,500	
Notes Payable (120-day, 6-percent note, dated November 1)		$2,000
Rent Earned (one-year lease commencing April 1)		2,400

Prepare the adjusting entries.

E5-10. Complete the partial worksheet given:

Account Title	Trial Balance			Income Statement		Position Statement	
	Dr.	Cr.		Dr.	Cr.	Dr.	Cr.
Cash	4,000					4,000	
Accounts Receivable	11,000					11,000	
Merchandise Inventory							
Beginning inventory	$ 8,000						
Ending inventory	10,000						

E5-11. (*Financial policy decision problem*) The following information was taken from the financial statements of the Greer Company.

	December 31, 1972	December 31, 1973
Net income		$ 5,000
Stockholders' equity	$48,000	53,000
Total liabilities	42,000	40,000
Cost of goods sold		60,000
Total operating expenses		45,000
Merchandise inventory	16,000	14,000
Current assets	37,000	39,000
Sales revenue		114,000
Sales discounts		1,000
Sales returns and allowances		3,000
Current liabilities	19,000	13,000

a. Compute the following ratios:
  1. The rate of return on the stockholders' equity
  2. The rate of return on the total investments
  3. The operating ratio
  4. The net operating margin ratio
  5. The turnover of merchandise inventory
  6. The working capital turnover
b. As a bank officer, would you approve a request by the company for a two-year loan for $5,000?

E5-12. From the following information, prepare a partial income statement for the Henry Company.

Net operating margin	$7,500
Gain from the sale of a truck	200
Interest paid on bank loan	100
Loss from theft (uninsured)	300
Payment for land taken under eminent domain	700
Rent earned from leasing facilities	400

E5-13. Record the following transactions:

a. A check for $1,960 was issued in payment for equipment purchased 26 days ago; terms 2/30, n/60; the equipment was entered on the books at the invoice price.
b. A $245 collection was received on account from T. Hayes; the customer had incorrectly taken a 2-percent discount after the expiration of the discount period.
c. A freight charge of $105 was paid on the equipment.

E5-14. The Whalen Company closes its books annually on December 31. An examination of its insurance policies show

Policy No.	Unexpired Premium— January 1, 1973	Remaining Life— January 1, 1973
3954	$126	21 months
4872	98	14 months
670	48	6 months

The policies purchased during 1973 were

Policy No.	Date of Policy	Life of Policy	Prepaid Premium
65412	March 1	2 years	$144
8941	August 1	3 years	180
4624	November 1	5 years	420

a. What was the balance of the Prepaid Insurance account as of January 1, 1973? The Whalen Company debits Prepaid Insurance for all purchases of insurance policies.
b. What was the adjusting entry necessary on December 31, 1973?
c. Reproduce the T accounts for Prepaid Insurance and Insurance Expense as they would appear in the general ledger after the closing entries have been posted on December 31, 1973.
d. Assuming that no additional premiums are paid during 1974, what will be the adjusting entry on December 31, 1974?

E5-15. On January 1, 1971, the Fraga Company entered into a 10-year lease for the rental of a factory from the Kane Investment Corporation. The terms of the lease provided for a rental adjustment whereby the Fraga Company would pay the Kane Investment Corporation for any increase in real estate taxes in excess of a base assessment of $100,000 and a tax rate of $57 per $1,000 of assessed valuation. Make the adjusting entries for the Fraga Company for 1971, 1972, and 1973, assuming the following:

Year	Assessment	Tax Rate Per $1,000
1971	$100,000	$60
1972	100,000	62
1973	105,000	63

E5-16. The statement of financial position of the Dixon Company at December 31, 1972 showed

Accrued Interest Receivable	$3,360
Unearned Interest Revenue	380

During 1973 interest collected in cash amounted to $6,240. The statement of financial position at December 31, 1973, showed

Accrued Interest Receivable	$2,960
Unearned Interest Revenue	250

Compute the amount of interest earned that should appear on the income statement for 1973.

E5-17. The following information was taken from the records of the Montoya Company at September 30, 1973, the end of the fiscal year:

a. On April 1, $3,360 was collected as subscription revenue for one year; Unearned Subscription Revenue was credited.
b. On March 1, 1973, a one-year, 6-percent note for $3,000 was received from a customer.
c. The company has a 5-percent mortgage note payable outstanding with a face value of $500,000; the interest on this note is payable semiannually on March 1 and September 1.
d. The store supplies inventory on September 30, 1972, was $6,250; acquisitions of $18,550 for the year were charged to Stores Supplies; a physical count on September 30, 1973 disclosed store supplies costing $8,500 on hand.
     Make the adjusting entries.

DEMONSTRATION PROBLEMS

DP5-1. (*Cash discounts: gross and net price procedures*) The following transactions were completed by the Hillery Company during November, 1973:

1973
Nov. 1 Sold merchandise on account to the Abel Company for $700; terms 2/10, n/30.

   5 Purchased merchandise from the Jones Company for $800; terms 1½/10, n/30.

   6 Purchased merchandise on account from the Fox Corporation for $650; terms 1/10, n/30, F.O.B. shipping point.

   6 Sold merchandise to the Hancock Corporation for $1,000; terms 1/10, n/30.

   10 Paid freight charges of $20 on the merchandise purchased from the Fox Corporation.

   11 Received payment from the Abel Company, less the cash discount.

   12 Received a $50 credit (gross amount) for defective merchandise returned to the Fox Corporation.

   15 Paid the Fox Corporation.

   25 Paid the Jones Company. Received payment from the Hancock Corporation.

     Required:

1a. Journalize. the transactions, using the gross price method.
 b. Prepare the cost of goods sold section of the income statement. Assume the following inventories: November 1, $500; November 30, $850.

2a. Journalize the transactions, using the net price procedure.
 b. Prepare the cost of goods sold section of the income statement. Assume inventories as
    in 1(b).
3. Under the net price procedure, how are Purchases Discounts Lost and Sales Discounts
    Not Taken classified in the income statement?

DP5-2. (*Worksheet and financial statements*) The trial balance of the Sousa Company for the
year 1973 is shown:

SOUSA COMPANY
Trial Balance
December 31, 1973

Account Title	Debits	Credits
Cash	$ 38,250	
Accounts Receivable	166,500	
Merchandise Inventory	50,000	
Office Supplies	21,000	
Prepaid Insurance	23,100	
Store Equipment	217,750	
Accumulated Depreciation–Store Equipment		$ 35,200
Accounts Payable		57,000
Notes Payable		31,500
Capital Stock		259,100
Retained Earnings		60,000
Dividends	20,000	
Sales		499,200
Sales Returns and Allowances	10,000	
Sales Discounts	9,200	
Purchases	295,000	
Transportation In	15,000	
Purchases Returns and Allowances		6,000
Purchases Discounts		9,000
Salesmen's Salaries Expense	38,400	
Transportation Out Expense	4,800	
Advertising Expense	14,400	
Rent Expense	19,200	
Heat and Light Expense	7,200	
Miscellaneous Expense	7,200	
Totals	$957,000	$957,000

Supplementary data on December 31, 1973, are given:

a. Merchandise inventory, $42,000
b. Unexpired insurance, $14,000
c. Office supplies on hand, $8,000
d. Depreciation on store equipment, $4,800
e. Estimated income taxes for the year, $24,000

Required: 1. Complete the worksheet.
         2. Prepare an income statement with a percent analysis.
         3. Prepare a position statement with a percent analysis.
         4. Prepare a statement of retained earnings.
         5. Explain the significance of the percent analyses.

DP5-3. (*Financial statement analysis*) The statement of financial position of the Callaway Company as of December 31, 1973 is shown:

CALLAWAY COMPANY

Statement of Financial Position

December 31, 1973

Assets

Current Assets		
Cash	$20,000	
Marketable Securities	10,000	
Accounts Receivable	20,000	
Notes Receivable	6,000	
Merchandise Inventory	40,000	
Prepaid Insurance	4,000	
Total Current Assets		$100,000
Plant and Equipment		
Store Equipment	$65,000	
Deduct Accumulated Depreciation	15,000	
Total Plant and Equipment		50,000
Total Assets		$150,000

Liabilities and Owner's Equity

Current Liabilities		
Accounts Payable	$19,000	
Notes Payable	16,000	
Accrued Wages Payable	5,000	
Total Current Liabilities		$ 40,000
Long-Term Liabilities		
Mortgage Payable (due December 31, 1979)		70,000
T. Callaway, Capital		40,000
Total Liabilities and Owner's Equity		$150,000

Additional data are given:

a.	T. Callaway, Capital, January 1, 1973	$ 30,000
b.	Net sales	120,000
c.	Net income	12,000
d.	Cost of goods sold	60,000
e.	Merchandise inventory, January 1, 1973	50,000
f.	Total operating expenses	48,000

Required:

1. Compute the following (show all your computations): (a) current ratio, (b) working capital, (c) operating ratio, (d) acid-test ratio, (e) rate of return on the owner's equity, (f) turnover of merchandise inventory, (g) net operating margin ratio.
2. Explain the significance of the ratios to: (a) Callaway, (b) the holder of the mortgage, (c) the holder of the note payable.
3. What additional data are needed for a more comprehensive analysis of Callaway's financial statements?

DP5-4. (*Closing entries*) The following account balances were taken from the Income Statement columns of John Failler's worksheet for the year ended December 31, 1973.

Account Title	Income Statement	
	Debit	Credit
Merchandise Inventory	8,800	9,500
Sales		23,100
Sales Returns and Allowances	275	
Sales Discounts	450	
Purchases	7,115	
Transportation In	375	
Purchases and Returns and Allowances		225
Purchases Discounts		640
Selling Expenses	1,700	
General Expenses	3,600	
Totals	22,315	33,465
Net Income	11,150	
	33,465	33,465

The Position Statement Debit column showed a balance of $3,000 in the J. Failler, Drawing account.

Required: Prepare closing journal entries.

PROBLEMS

P5-1. The accountant of the Jay Bertelsen Corporation prepared the following trial balance at December 31, 1973:

JAY BERTELSEN CORPORATION
Trial Balance
December 31, 1973

Account Title	Debits	Credits
Cash	$ 1,500	
Accounts Receivable	48,700	
Prepaid Insurance	2,500	
Merchandise Inventory	55,000	
Store Equipment	30,400	
Accumulated Depreciation–Store Equipment		$ 6,000
Accounts Payable		9,000
Notes Payable		20,000
Capital Stock		50,000
Retained Earnings		11,000
Dividends	10,400	
Sales		182,000
Purchases	85,000	
Advertising Expense	3,700	
Miscellaneous Selling Expense	4,000	
Wages Expense	29,000	
Miscellaneous General Expense	5,900	
Rent Expense	2,400	
Interest Expense	500	
Interest Earned		300
Rent Earned		700
Totals	$279,000	$279,000

Additional data are given:

1. Included in Advertising Expense is a charge of $800 for space in the January, 1974, issue of a monthly periodical.
2. The Prepaid Insurance account consists of premiums paid on the following policies:

Policy No.	Date of Policy	Life of Policy	Premium
A938	January 1, 1973	6 months	$1,000
J672	September 1, 1973	3 years	1,200
N531	October 1, 1973	1 year	300
Total			$2,500

3. The Store Equipment account consists of the following acquisitions:

Purchase Date	Cost	Useful Life	Salvage Value
Prior to January 1, 1973	$22,000	10 years	$2,000
April 1, 1973	1,400	10 years	200
July 1, 1973	1,000	5 years	100
October 1, 1973	6,000	15 years	600
Total	$30,400		

4. A physical count of store supplies shows $250 worth on hand at December 31, 1973. At the time of purchase, Miscellaneous General Expense was debited.
5. On October 1, the Jay Bertelsen Corporation rented some of its equipment to the Jones Company for eight months under the following terms: $175 per month payable in two payments of $700 each on October 1, 1973, and February 1, 1973.
6. Wages earned by employees but unpaid on December 31, 1973, totaled $500.
7. Property taxes of $300 for 1973 are unpaid.
8. An invoice of $300 from the Packing Materials Company, dated December 14, 1973, for shipping cartons is discovered and is to be recorded as a Miscellaneous Selling Expense.
9. Shipping cartons on hand at December 31 were worth $300.
10. The Notes Payable account consists of a 90-day, 6-percent note dated November 1, 1973, issued to a bank.
11. The merchandise inventory at December 31, 1973 was $45,000. Income taxes for the year were estimated at $11,500.

Required:

In schedule form given, show:

a. The adjusting entries.
b. The section of the position statement affected by the adjusting entry.
c. The section of the income statement affected by the adjusting entry.
d. The amount reported on the appropriate financial statement.

Item 1 has been entered as an example.

Item	Explanation	Adjusting Entries		Financial Statement Classification	Amount Reported on Financial Statement
		Dr	Cr		
1	Prepaid Advertising Advertising Expense	800	800	Current Asset (PS) Selling Expense (IC)	800 2,900
2					
3					
4					
5					

P5-2. The following balances, arranged in alphabetical order, were taken from the Adjusted Trial Balance columns of the worksheet of the Bauer Corporation for the fiscal year ended June 30, 1973. The inventory on that date was $20,800.

Accounts Payable	$ 7,520
Accounts Receivable	10,500
Accumulated Depreciation–Delivery Equipment	3,500
Advertising Expense	1,100
Capital Stock	38,000
Cash	3,000
Delivery Equipment	10,500
Delivery Expense	2,200
Depreciation Expense–Delivery Equipment	1,650
Dividends	3,000
Gain on Disposal of Marketable Securities	350
Heat and Light Expense	890
Income Tax Expense	2,150
Income Taxes Payable	2,150
Insurance Expense	1,720
Interest Earned	250
Interest Expense	160
Loss on Disposal of Land	200
Marketable Securities	21,830
Merchandise Inventory, July 1, 1972	22,400
Notes Payable	2,000
Office Supplies	705
Prepaid Advertising	900
Prepaid Insurance	1,420
Purchases	59,700
Purchases Discounts	725

Purchases Returns and Allowances	$ 1,230
Rent Earned	1,800
Rent Expense	2,500
Retained Earnings	10,000
Sales	92,500
Sales Discounts	1,600
Sales Returns and Allowances	4,300
Salesmen's Salaries Expense	6,300
Transportation In	1,300

Required: 1. Prepare an income statement for the year ended June 30, 1973.
2. Prepare a statement of financial position as of June 30, 1973.
3. Prepare a statement of retained earnings for the year ended June 30, 1973.

P5-3. The trial balance of the Battle Corporation as of March 31, 1973, is shown:

BATTLE CORPORATION
Trial Balance
March 31, 1973

Account Title	Debits	Credits
Cash	$ 7,500	
Accounts Receivable	14,300	
Notes Receivable	1,525	
Merchandise Inventory, January 1, 1973	21,200	
Prepaid Insurance	850	
Prepaid Rent	4,200	
Office Supplies	190	
Store Equipment	2,500	
Accumulated Depreciation–Store Equipment		$ 1,600
Delivery Equipment	4,500	
Accumulated Depreciation–Delivery Equipment		1,560
Accounts Payable		8,950
Notes Payable		4,200
Capital Stock		25,000
Retained Earnings		10,610
Dividends	2,600	
Sales		107,095
Sales Returns and Allowances	3,175	
Sales Discounts	1,295	
Purchases	77,050	
Purchases Returns and Allowances		2,290
Transportation In	1,635	
Advertising Expense	5,540	
Miscellaneous General Expense	635	
Salesmen's Salaries Expense	7,950	
General and Administrative Expense	4,660	
Totals	$161,305	$161,305

Additional information on March 31 is given:

a. Merchandise inventory	$19,500
b. Insurance expired during the three-month period	300
c. The Prepaid Rent represents a payment made for the first six months of 1973	
d. Office supplies inventory	75
e. Depreciation of store equipment	60

f. Depreciation of delivery equipment $ 250
g. Estimated income taxes for the period   1,000

> Required: 1. Prepare a worksheet for the three months ended March 31, 1973.
> 2. Using the worksheet, prepare the closing entries in general journal form.

P5 4. The following information was taken from the general ledger of the Dado Corporation on December 31, 1973.

Account Title	Amount
Cash	$ 7,000
Marketable Securities	18,600
Accounts Receivable	41,000
Notes Receivable	7,000
Accrued Interest Receivable	–0–
Merchandise Inventory, January 1, 1973	50,000
Store Supplies	–0–
Advertising Supplies	–0–
Prepaid Insurance	2,500
Store Equipment	40,500
Accumulated Depreciation–Store Equipment	10,000
Accounts Payable	22,000
Notes Payable	23,000
Accrued Interest Payable	–0–
Accrued Wages Payable	–0–
Income Taxes Payable	–0–
Accrued Mortgage Interest Payable	–0–
Unearned Rent	–0–
Mortgage Payable (due 1977)	15,000
Capital Stock	50,000
Retained Earnings	15,000
Dividends	5,500
Sales	250,000
Purchases	141,500
Transportation In	2,500
Advertising Expense	4,900
Miscellaneous Selling Expense	7,500
Depreciation Expense–Store Equipment	–0–
Heat, Light, and Power Expense	5,000
Insurance Expense	–0–
Miscellaneous General Expense	8,800
Income Tax Expense	–0–
Rent Expense	4,800
Wages Expense	38,000
Interest Expense	1,500
Interest Earned	400
Rent Earned	1,200
Revenue and Expense Summary	–0–

Data for the end-of-period adjustments are as follows:

a. The Prepaid Insurance account consists of the following:

Policy Number	Date of Policy	Life of Policy	Premiums
A648	January 1, 1973	3 years	$1,500
P832	July 1, 1973	2 Years	1,000

b. The Notes Receivable account consists of a 60-day, 6-percent note dated December 1, 1973, for $7,000.

c. The Notes Payable consists of a 90-day, 6-percent note dated December 1, 1973.

d. Purchases of store equipment were as follows:

Purchase Date	Cost	Useful Life	Salvage Value
January 1, 1968	$22,000	10 years	$2,000
April 1, 1973	10,000	20 years	–0–
July 1, 1973	8,500	8 years	500

e. Wages earned by employees but unpaid as of December 31, 1973, totaled $400.

f. Income taxes for the year were estimated at $3,500.

g. On August 1, 1973, the Dado Corporation rented some store equipment to the O'Leary Company for 12 months and received a check for $1,200 representing the entire year's rental fee.

h. Interest on the mortgage payable is $800 per year, paid in semiannual installments on May 1 and November 1, 1973.

i. Inventories on December 31, 1973 were

Merchandise	$36,000
Advertising Supplies	1,200
Store Supplies (the original debit was made to Miscellaneous General Expense)	300

Required: 1. Prepare a worksheet for the year ended December 31, 1973.
2. Prepare (a) an income statement, (b) a statement of financial position, and (c) a statement of retained earnings.
3. Prepare the closing entries.

6

The Processing
of Data

1 83 — 2 11

The system of recording, classifying, summarizing, and reporting accounting information that is discussed in the preceding chapters has been satisfactory for teaching the fundamentals of the accounting process; but a business of any size will usually find it necessary to modify the methods of capturing the flow of accounting data to meet the needs of the particular business firm.

This chapter describes briefly the manner in which a system is designed or changed for a business. First, the function of the systems analyst and the aids and criteria for designing a system are presented. Flow charting, a basic tool for analyzing a system, a program or a job step, is then illustrated and described. Following this the various ways of processing data—manually, mechanically, and electronically—are considered. The division of the general journal into special journals is the model used to illustrate manual processing. A brief discussion of simple accounting machines, punched-card equipment, and electronic data processing follows. As an example of a language that may be used to instruct a computer, BASIC (Beginner's All-purpose Symbolic Instruction Code) is introduced.

DESIGN OF THE RECORD SYSTEM

The transaction is the basic source of accounting data; it is central to the collection process. Before data processing by any system can begin, some evidence that a transaction has occurred must exist. Source documents such as purchase invoices, sales invoices, and receipts indicate the occurrence of transactions. The data must then be introduced into the system. Data can be captured and processed from these transactions by handwritten procedures, by accounting machines, punched-card equipment, electronic equipment, or by a combination of these methods. The similarity of these methods of data collection is shown in Figure 6-1. The primary difference is in the

187

Figure 6-1. Information Flow Chart

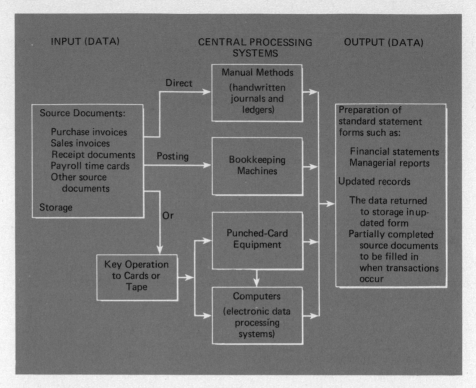

methods of collection; however, the more sophisticated the collection process, the more sophisticated, detailed, and elaborate is the information that is reported.

The information flow then is from input to output. It is the function of the systems analyst to create a method of collecting these data that will permit management to measure and control its human and physical resources to its best advantage. This design requires a thorough examination of the company's table of organization, its personnel and job descriptions, the current forms in use, the procedures and policies of the organization, and the legal constraints on the business or industry if the analyst is to gauge the integrity and accuracy of the measurement of the flow of information.

The development of the system generally will be in three stages: (1) *study and design*, (2) *implementation*, and (3) *operation*. The company's operation is studied and a method of collection is proposed for adoption. Once adopted it is then put into operation for verification, for review for improvements and redesign, and to test if the controls are effective. The flow of information from the source of input to the disposition of the output is examined with the following considerations:

1. *Where* will the information be found and stored?
2. *Who* will use the information?
3. *What* will be the application of the information?
4. *When* will the information be needed?

The criteria for selection of the method of collecting the flow of information are listed below.

1. *Speed:* Information should be available when it is needed. The size of the organization is a significant factor in the requirement for timely access to information. The larger the business, the greater will be the amount of data flow. The speed of electronic processing has enlarged the amount of data available to management, since the computer can organize, manipulate, and present timely information in a manner that is beyond human capability.

2. *Accuracy and Reliability of Information:* Error controls should be established in all methods. The more times information is written or manipulated, the greater the opportunity for error. Electronic processing has proved dependable; however, the input of data and the instructions (program) to the computer provide ample room for error in the use of this, the most reliable of methods.

3. *Volume of Data:* Storage areas or files of data are a major consideration in business data processing because of the mass of data flow. Quick retrieval of this information in usable form is a distinctive feature of electonic equipment designed for business use.

4. *Cost Balanced against Benefits:* The critical criterion is *cost.* The return is not always easily observed or measured; however, the cost is measured per unit or transaction. For instance, the computer is expensive as a system, but its efficiency and volume of usage are making it less expensive per transaction processed. The improvement in the design brought about by the systems examination can bring about economies by eliminating duplication of unneeded services, by increasing productivity, by reducing inventories and capital outlay, and by the improvement of operations. These are important factors in consideration of cost benefit. Clearly, a business should strive for the system that provides the necessary information at the least cost.

5. *Time Cycle:* The frequency of the transactions, the peak periods, and the deadlines are important areas to be determined in the examination.

6. *Priorities and Sequence of Events:* The establishment of the priorities for reports, the needs for reports, and the order in which events occur are integral parts of a study of information flow.

7. *Media:* The most efficient type of media for the input, output, and storage must be examined. Can the information be stored on disk or tape or must it be stored on paper? Is the source document on paper?

Thus, setting up a system for collecting and processing data in a business requires a total examination of the business and its environment. One of the tools that an analyst uses in this study is a flow chart.

FLOW CHARTING—AN AID IN THE ANALYSIS

Flow charting is a visual or pictorial plan that shows the steps required in the solution of a problem. By the use of rectangles, diamonds, circles, and other shapes connected by lines, a picture may be drawn that logically solves a problem. There are two basic types of flow charts—a *systems* and a *program.* The systems flow chart uses a broad or general approach and is useful for showing a picture of the total flow of information and the sequence of operations in a business. The systems flow chart will indicate which program must be developed. A program

Figure 6-2. Comparison of a Flow Chart for a System, a Job Step, and a Computer Program

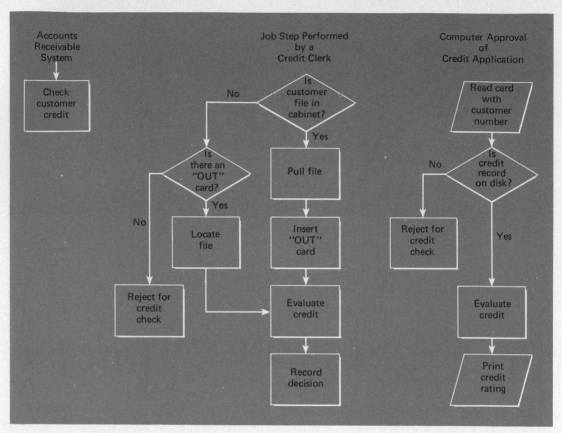

flow chart depicts specific processing steps in the solution of an individual problem. The word *program* suggests a machine, or more specifically, a computer. A program has a broader usage in flow charting, hence a program flow chart can graphically solve a task or job step in a system as well as display the logic of a computer program. Flow charting, however, is a preliminary step in the development of a computer program. Figure 6-2 compares the use of flow charting a task in a system, a job step, and a computer program.

Development of a Flow Chart

The first step in creating a flow chart is to define carefully the problem that is to be charted. The beginning and end of each step must be clearly shown, and an attempt must be made to develop a logical relationship between steps.

Next, the steps must be charted by using the basic symbols shown in Figure 6-3. This is a partial list, but flow charting a problem can be accomplished with these. Within each symbol, a comment should be made in order that a reader can understand and follow the solution. The comment must be brief, as there is little room within the symbol, particularly in the decision symbol.

Figure 6-3. Flow Chart Symbols

SYMBOL   FUNCTION

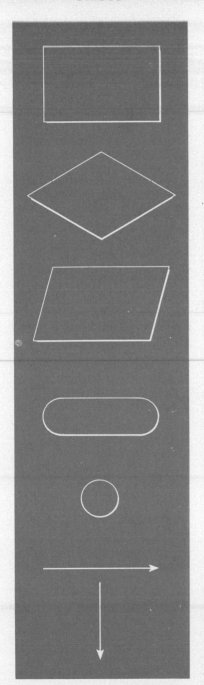

The rectangle is the process symbol, for example, moving data within the computer, arithmetic operations, a change of form, location, or value of the data being manipulated.

The diamond shows a decision is to be made and an alternative action is to be taken. This jumping or changing of sequence is called "branching." Examples of questions presented in the decision symbol are yes-no; high-low-equal; greater than; less than.

The parallelogram is the Input/Output symbol. Reading data into the computer is Input; Output is returning data to storage and communicating the results of processing. The commands usually are READ and WRITE or PRINT.

The oval is a terminal. The beginning of the problem is indicated by this symbol with START comment. HALT written in the symbol signals the end of the flow chart.

The small circle with a letter or number denotes the point is connected at another place on the page. It is an on-page connector.

Flow lines show the flow of the data. Arrows ordinarily are attached, particularly if the flow is in a direction other than top to bottom and left to right.

To illustrate the application of this technique to an accounting problem presented in Chapter 3, assume that the problem to be charted is to find the balances in the accounts in the general ledger preparatory to taking a trial balance as in Figure 6-4.

Figure 6-4. Flow Chart for Balancing Accounts in the General Ledger

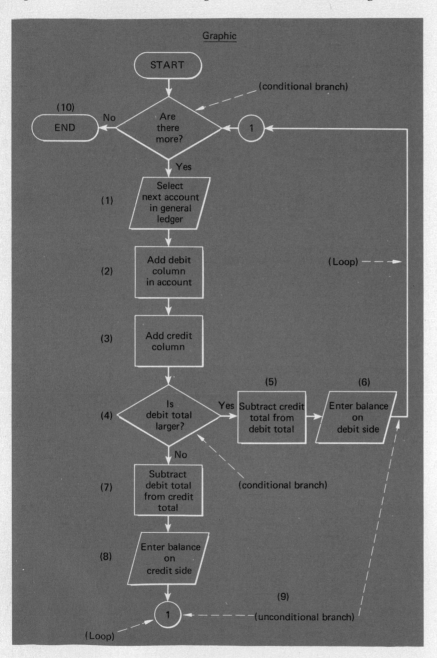

DESCRIPTIVE

1. Select next account in the general ledger.
2. Add the amounts in the debit column.
3. Add the amounts in the credit column.
4. Is the debit side larger?
5. If yes, subtract the credit total from the debit total.
6. Enter the balance on the debit side.
7. If the credit total is larger, subtract the debit total from the credit total.
8. Enter the balance on the credit side of the account.
9. Repeat the procedure on subsequent accounts until all accounts are balanced.
10. After the last account is balanced, end of job.

Important steps in the flow chart illustrated:

1. This program provides for the repetition of a series of steps until all the accounts in the general ledger have been balanced. This repetitive process is the hallmark of the computer. Repeating a set of instructions is called *looping*. There are two methods of charting the loop. Both are illustrated in the figure. Lines and arrows direct the procedure back to the beginning point; on-page connectors, as shown, will do the same thing.
2. Switching the sequence of processing is accomplished by *branching*. There are two kinds of branches—*conditional* and *unconditional*. The conditional branch provides for a change in the sequence of processing if the circumstances answer the question or condition properly. The condition is expressed in the decision symbol. The figure has the first condition in the question, "Are there more . . . (accounts to be processed)?" This conditional branch provides for the termination of the loop; its absence would leave an endless or infinite loop—that is, one without termination. The second condition, "Is debit total larger?" may initiate the second conditional branch.
3. There are also two unconditional branches in the figure. The first provides for proceeding to the next account after the debit balance is entered on the last account processed. The second is seen after the credit balance is entered.

It is helpful in making a flow chart to use a template of symbols on flow-charting worksheets.

In summary, a flow chart provides a working guide to enable a person to see the basic flow of logic and information in writing a program or designing or changing a system. It permits experimentation with a variety of approaches. The flow chart is a part of the documentation of the problem. A flow chart is an individual creation and will vary slightly from those drawn by others. It is used as an alternative or supplement to the descriptive method of stating a solution of a procedure.

MANUAL PROCESSING

Manually recording accounting data in a general journal and posting to preselected accounts in a general ledger and subsidiary records severely limit the scope and quantity of information that can be collected. This limitation is imposed by the time required to record, classify, and summarize the data; the cost necessary to obtain information beyond the minimum significant information; and the limited number of employees who can work at one time on the books.

A manual system will be illustrated that will provide savings in time of recording the transactions and posting. This system also enables a business to divide the collection process among several employees. Small businesses, or those businesses with limited transactions, find this type of system or adaptations of it useful. Modifying some of the journals and subsidiary ledgers for use in mechanical equipment improves its utility.

Special Journals

The procedures in the preceding chapters can be modified principally by making several journals to record special classes of transactions. Grouping transactions into classes and using a special journal to record each class offer the opportunity for the rapid and efficient processing of accounting data. The number and kinds of journals used are influenced by the type of business and the information desired. The model used in this text is shown in the following chart:

Journal	Kind of Transaction	Symbol
Sales Journal	Sale of merchandise on account	S
Purchases Journal	Purchase of merchandise on account	P
Cash Receipts Journal	Receipt of cash	CR
Cash Payments Journal	Payment of cash	CP
General Journal	All transactions that will not be grouped in the four classes above—for example, closing and adjusting entries, purchase of merchandise by note, purchase of equipment or supplies on account or by note, sales and purchases returns and allowances.	J

Special journals offer the following advantages:

1. Similar transactions are grouped in chronological order in one place. All credit sales of merchandise, for example, are entered in the sales journal.
2. The repeated writing of each account title—Sales, Purchases, Cash, and so on—is eliminated.
3. Postings are made from column footings in total only—rather than item by item—thereby reducing the volume of work. The general ledger is relieved of unnecessary detail since fewer postings are made. As a result of the fewer postings, the general ledger is more compact and easier to use, thus reducing the probability of error.
4. Bookkeeping duties may be divided up by function. For example, one person may enter information regarding charge sales, taken from *sales slips*, in the sales journal; a second person may post either from the sales journal or directly from the sales slips to the accounts receivable ledger; a third person may enter cash received from charge customers in the cash receipts journal and post to the accounts receivable ledger; and a fourth person may verify the accuracy of the work by comparing the accounts receivable ledger with the Accounts Receivable controlling account in the general ledger.

This division of responsibilities not only facilitates and accelerates the work flow but also creates some protection against errors and the misappropriation of assets. An essential feature of *internal control*—the built-in safeguards for the protection of the assets of an enterprise—is the careful planning and supervision of the recordkeeping of a company and a division of the work so that no one employee has complete control both of an operation of the business and of the recording of that operation.

The Sales Journal

All sales of merchandise on account are recorded in the sales journal. To illustrate the use of the sales journal, assume that the following transactions took place at the Hayward Casuals during June, 1973:

1973
June 3 Sold merchandise to Ella Gray, $400; terms 1/15, n/60.

    4 Sold merchandise to William Ramey, $600; terms 2/10, n/30.

    5 Sold merchandise to Arthur James, $300; terms 1/5, n/30.

   30 Sold merchandise to Byron Butts, $800; terms 2/10, n/30.

Figure 6-5. Simple Sales Journal

SALES JOURNAL					Page 1
Date	Sales Slip No.	Account Debited	Terms	F	Amount
1973 June	3	Ella Gray	1/15, n/60		400
	4	William Ramey	2/10, n/30		600
	5	Arthur James	1/5, n/30		300
	30	Byron Butts	2/10, n/30		800
	30	Accounts Receivable, Dr.—Sales, Cr.			2,100

When merchandise is sold on account, the transaction is recorded in the sales journal as follows:

1. The date of the transaction is entered in the Date column.
2. Sales slips or invoices are numbered in sequence; the numbers are entered in chronological order in the Sales Slip No. or Sales Invoice No. column.
3. The name of the customer to whom the sale was made is entered in the Account Debited column.
4. The terms of the sale are listed in the Terms column.
5. If the subsidiary ledger account has a folio, or reference number, it is entered in the folio (F) column when posting is complete; otherwise, a check mark is entered.
6. The amount of the sale is entered in the Amount column.

A simple sales journal is illustrated in Figure 6-5, which shows the entries for the transactions of Hayward Casuals listed above.

Each entry in the sales journal is a debit to the Accounts Receivable account and to the customer's account in the accounts receivable ledger and a credit to the Sales account. Expressed in the form of a two-column general journal entry, the entry for the sale made on June 1, for example, would be:

Accounts Receivable—Ella Gray	400	
Sales		400

The transaction is *not* actually recorded in both the general journal and the sales journal. It is shown in this manner only to illustrate the difference between the two forms.

Each amount is posted separately as a debit to the accounts receivable ledger, supporting the single debit that is posted at the end of the month to the Accounts Receivable controlling account in the general ledger. Posting to the subsidiary ledger accounts is usually done daily. It is important to have the up-to-date balance of each customer's account readily available so that requests for this information from the customer, the credit department, or others may be readily fulfilled.[1]

The daily posting is usually done in the following sequence:

1. The amount of the sale is posted to the Debit column of the customer's account and is added to the balance, if any, in the Balance column.
2. The journal symbol (S1) is written in the folio (F) column.
3. The date of the sale is recorded in the Date column.
4. A check mark is placed in the folio (F) column of the sales journal to indicate that the entry has been posted.

At the end of the month, the Amount column of the sales journal is footed. The total, the date of the transfer, and the sales journal page number are then posted to the debit side of the Accounts Receivable controlling account and the credit side of the Sales account in the general ledger. The general ledger account numbers are recorded in the sales journal immediately below the footing. To minimize errors, a systematic procedure should be followed in posting. The following sequence is suggested:

Debit posting:
1. The amount is posted to the Debit money column of the Accounts Receivable account in the general ledger.
2. The journal symbol (S1) is written in the folio (F) column of the account.
3. The date is recorded in the Date column.
4. The Accounts Receivable account number is written in parentheses below and to the left of the double rule in the Amount column of the journal.

Credit posting:
5. The amount is posted to the Credit money column of the Sales account in the general ledger.
6. The journal symbol (S1) is written in the folio (F) column of the account.
7. The date is recorded in the Date column.
8. The Sales account number is written in parentheses below the double rule in the Amount column of the journal, to the right of the debit posting reference number.

Postings from the sales journal of the Hayward Casuals for the month of June, 1973, are shown in Figure 6-6.

The Purchases Journal

The relationship of the purchases journal and the accounts payable ledger is similar to that of the sales journal and the accounts receivable ledger. All purchases

---

[1] A common form of subsidiary ledger account has three money columns—all on the right-hand side—for debits, credits, and balance. This form is introduced on page 35, and is illustrated for machine posting in Figure 6-14.

Figure 6-6. Posting Flow from the Sales Journal

of merchandise on account are recorded in the purchases journal. The transactions of the Hayward Casuals during June, 1973, illustrate the use of this journal.

1973

June 3 Purchased merchandise on account from Oakland Clothing Company, $900; terms 2/10, n/20.

8 Purchased merchandise on account from Southland Apparel, $400; terms, 2/10, n/60.

16 Purchased merchandise on account from San Francisco Clothiers, $500; terms 3/5, n/30.

28 Purchased merchandise on account from the Dexter Custom Tailors, $700; terms 1/20, n/60.

Figure 6-7 shows how these transactions are recorded in the purchases journal and posted to the general and subsidiary ledger accounts.

Expressed as a two-column general journal entry, the first entry in the purchases journal would be

Purchases	900	
Accounts Payable—Oakland Clothing Co.		900

The transaction is *not* actually recorded in both the general journal and the purchases journal. It is shown in this manner to illustrate the difference between the two recording forms.

Each transaction is posted separately as a credit to the accounts payable ledger to support the credit posted at the end of the month to the Accounts Payable controlling account in the general ledger. Transactions are usually posted to the subsidiary ledger daily. The date of the entry in the subsidiary ledger account is the invoice date, which is significant in determining if a discount may be taken. At the end of the month, the Amount column of the purchases journal is footed. This total is posted to the Purchases account in the general ledger as a debit. The same total is posted to the Accounts Payable controlling account in the general ledger as a credit.

The Cash Receipts Journal

All transactions involving the receipt of cash are entered in the cash receipts journal. A multicolumn cash receipts journal form is illustrated in Figure 6-8. The column headings typically provide the flexibility necessary to record cash receipts from customers or any other source and to record sales discounts. The form may be varied, particularly in the number and headings of the columns, to meet the needs of the individual business.

Explanation of the various columns in the cash receipts journal:

1. The date of the transaction is entered in the Date column.
2. The explanation of the transaction is written in the Explanation column.
3. There are three debit columns. Cash debits are entered in the first Debit column.
4. The Sales Discount Debit column is used for recording discounts granted to customers for paying within the discount period.
5. The Other Accounts Debit column is for debits to general ledger accounts for which no special columns have been provided.

Figure 6-7. Posting Flow from the Purchases Journal

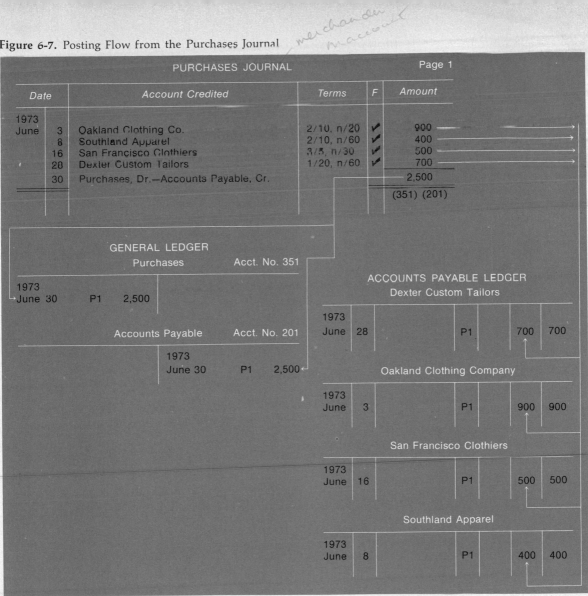

Date		Account Credited	Terms	F	Amount
1973 June	3	Oakland Clothing Co.	2/10, n/20	✔	900
	8	Southland Apparel	2/10, n/60	✔	400
	16	San Francisco Clothiers	3/5, n/30	✔	500
	28	Dexter Custom Tailors	1/20, n/60	✔	700
	30	Purchases, Dr.—Accounts Payable, Cr.			2,500

PURCHASES JOURNAL — Page 1

(351) (201)

GENERAL LEDGER

Purchases — Acct. No. 351

| 1973 June 30 | P1 | 2,500 |

Accounts Payable — Acct. No. 201

| | | | 1973 June 30 | P1 | 2,500 |

ACCOUNTS PAYABLE LEDGER

Dexter Custom Tailors

| 1973 June | 28 | | P1 | 700 | 700 |

Oakland Clothing Company

| 1973 June | 3 | | P1 | 900 | 900 |

San Francisco Clothiers

| 1973 June | 16 | | P1 | 500 | 500 |

Southland Apparel

| 1973 June | 8 | | P1 | 400 | 400 |

Figure 6-8. Column Headings of the Cash Receipts Journal

CASH RECEIPTS JOURNAL — Page 1

Date	Explanation	Debits					Account Credited	Credits				
		Cash	Sales Disc.	Other Accounts				Accounts Receivable		Sales	Other Accounts	
				Account Title	F	Amount		✔	Amount		F	Amount
1 2 3 4												1 2 3 4

6. There are three folio columns, two labeled (F), one, (✔); a posting symbol indicating that the amount has been posted to the general ledger or to the accounts receivable ledger is placed in the folio column.

7. The name of the general or subsidiary ledger account to be credited is written in the Account Credited column.

8. When a charge customer makes a payment on account, an entry is made in the Accounts Receivable Credit column, the first of three credit columns. The amount entered is the actual amount of cash received plus any sales discounts properly taken by the customer.

9. Sales of merchandise for cash are entered in the Sales Credit column.

10. The Other Accounts Credit column is for credits to general ledger accounts for which no special columns have been provided.

The Hayward Casuals' cash receipts journal for June, 1973, is illustrated in Figure 6-9.

Figure 6-9. Cash Receipts Journal

CASH RECEIPTS JOURNAL													Page 1
		Debits						Credits					
Date	Explanation	Cash	Sales Disc.	Other Accounts			Account Credited	Accounts Receivable		Sales	Other Accounts		
				Account Title	F	Amount		✔	Amount		· F	Amount	
1973 June 1	Invested in business	2,500					W. Ray, Capital					2,500	
10	Payment in full	588	12				William Ramey		600				
15	Cash sales	1,000					Sales			1,000			
18	Payment in full	396	4				Ella Gray		400				
22	Borrowed from bank	600					Notes Payable					600	
30	Cash sales	950					Sales			950			
30	Payment on account	100		Notes Receivable		200	Arthur James		300			·	
30	Totals	6,134	16			200			1,300	1,950			3,100

In previous chapters, transactions involving the receipt of cash were recorded in a simple two-column general journal. Similar transactions are recorded in a cash receipts journal in Figure 6-9. Although each transaction is entered on a single line, the equality of debits and credits is still maintained through the use of multiple columns. The transactions are analyzed in terms of debits and credits to indicate their effect on the accounts. These transactions, however, are *not* actually recorded in both the cash receipts journal and the general journal.

TRANSACTION:

1973
June 1 William Ray, the owner, invested $2,500 in the Hayward Casuals.

ANALYSIS OF DEBITS AND CREDITS:

Cash	2,500	
W. Ray, Capital		2,500

Cash is debited by entering the amount in the Cash Debit column. Since there is no special column for W. Ray, Capital, the amount is entered in the Other Accounts credit column.

TRANSACTION:

1973
June 10   Received payment in full from William Ramey

ANALYSIS OF DEBITS AND CREDITS:

Cash	588	
Sales Discounts	12	
Accounts Receivable		600

      The sales journal shows that on June 4 merchandise with an invoice price of $600 was sold to William Ramey; terms 2/10, n/30. Since payment was made within 10 days, Ramey deducted $12 from the invoice price and paid $588. Entering the three amounts in the special columns as shown has the same effect on the general ledger as the explanatory debit and credit analysis does. The customer's name is entered in the Account Credited column for posting to the accounts receivable ledger. If cash receipts from charge customers are numerous, a daily total may be entered from an adding machine tape; posting to the subsidiary ledger is done from supporting documents.

TRANSACTION:

1973
June 15   Cash sales for the first half of the month were $1,000.

ANALYSIS OF DEBITS AND CREDITS:

Cash	1,000	
Sales		1,000

The word *Sales* is written in the Account Credited column to fill the space. However, it can be omitted, since both the debit and the credit amounts are entered in the special columns.

TRANSACTION:

1973
June 18   Received full payment from Ella Gray.

ANALYSIS OF DEBITS AND CREDITS:

Cash	396	
Sales Discounts	4	
Accounts Receivable		400

The sales journal shows that on June 3 merchandise with an invoice price of $400 was sold to Ella Gray; terms 1/15, n/60. Since payment was made within 15 days, Gray deducted $4 from the invoice amount and paid $396.

TRANSACTION:

1973
June 22   Borrowed $600 from the bank on a notes payable.

ANALYSIS OF DEBITS AND CREDITS:

Cash	600	
Notes Payable		600

Since there is no special column for the Notes Payable account, the amount is entered in the Other Accounts credit column and the name of the account is written in the Account Credited column.

TRANSACTION:

1973
June 30   Cash sales for the last half of the month were $950.

ANALYSIS OF DEBITS AND CREDITS:

Cash	950	
Sales		950

1973
June 30   Received $100 from Arthur James on account and a promissory note payable in 30 days for the balance in his account.

ANALYSIS OF DEBITS AND CREDITS:

Cash	100	
Notes Receivable	200	
Accounts Receivable		300

The sales journal shows that on June 5 merchandise with an invoice price of $300 was sold to Arthur James; terms 1/5, n/30. The Sales Discounts account is not involved in this partial payment because the discount period has expired.

At the end of the month, the columns in the cash receipts journal are footed. Since each line contains equal debits and credits, it follows that the total of the Debit column footings should equal the total of the Credit column footings. This equality should be proved for each special journal before the column totals are posted to the general ledger; otherwise, errors in the special journals may not be detected, the posting to the ledger will not be equal, the ledger will not have equal balances, and the trial balance will not balance. Moreover, the controlling accounts may not agree with their corresponding subsidiary ledgers. The cash receipts journal of the Hayward Casuals is proved as shown:

	Debits		Credits
Cash	$6,134	Accounts Receivable	$1,300
Sales Discounts	16	Sales	1,950
Other Accounts	200	Other Accounts	3,100
Total	$6,350	Total	$6,350

Postings from the cash receipts journal of Hayward Casuals are shown in Figure 6-10 (page 204).

Individual credit postings are made to the accounts receivable ledger to support the $1,300 credit posting to the Accounts Receivable controlling account in the general ledger. A check mark is entered in the folio (✔) column of the cash receipts journal on the line of the entry to indicate that the item has been posted to the customer's account in the subsidiary ledger. Note that the balance of each account is either a debit or zero. Transactions have already been posted to these accounts from the sales journal.

The totals of the Cash Debit column ($6,134) and the Sales Discounts Debit column ($16) are posted to the respective general ledger accounts. The regular sequence for transferring an amount from a journal to a ledger is followed. The general ledger account number is entered in parentheses below the double rule in each column.

The (X) below the Other Accounts debit column means that the individual amounts contained in the column total have already been posted to the general ledger. The $200 debit to Notes Receivable was posted individually during the month. The account number of Notes Receivable (112) is entered in the folio (F) column of the journal at the time the posting is done.

The Accounts Receivable account is credited for $1,300 and the Sales account is credited for $1,950. These postings are also dated June 30. No posting symbol is used in the folio (F) column on the line of the entry for a cash sale because the item does not require individual posting.

The (X) below the double rule in the Other Accounts credit column indicates that the column total is not to be posted to the general ledger. The total is not posted because the $2,500 credit to W. Ray, Capital, and the $600 credit to Notes Payable were posted separately during the month. The ledger page numbers of these accounts are entered in the folio (F) column of the journal when the posting is done. Note that account numbers 251 and 205 are written in the folio column of the cash receipts journal in Figure 6-10. Postings from the Other Accounts credit column are dated as of the date of the entry.

The Cash Payments Journal

All transactions involving the payment of cash are entered in the cash payments journal. Most cash payments should be made by check. When payments in currency are required they may be recorded in a *petty cash journal,* discussed in Chapter 7.

A typical cash payments journal is illustrated in Figure 6-11 (page 205). The columns provide for recording cash payments, either to creditors or for any other purpose, and for recording purchases discounts.

Explanation of the various columns:

1. The date of the disbursement of cash is entered in the Date column.
2. Detailed information is initially recorded on the check stub, which bears the same number as the check. Entries in the cash payments journal then are made from the check stub and the check number is listed in the Check No. column.

Figure 6-10. Posting Flow from the Cash Receipts Journal

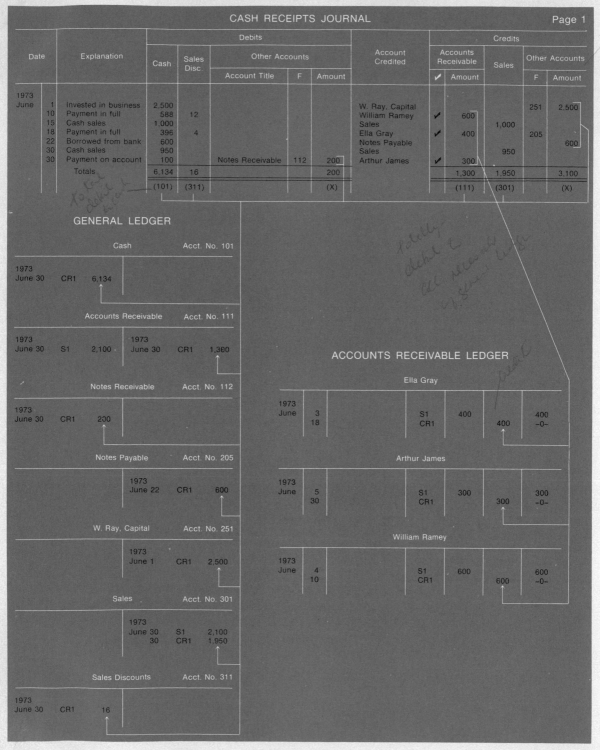

Figure 6-11. Column Headings of the Cash Payments Journal

			Credits						Debits				
Date	Check No.	Explanation	Cash	Purchases Discounts	Other Accounts			Account Debited	Accounts Payable		Purchases	Other Accounts	
					Account Title	F	Amount		✔	Amount		F	Amount

CASH PAYMENTS JOURNAL — Page 1

3. An explanation of the transaction is entered in the Explanation column.
4. There are three credit columns; they are located to the left of the debit columns. In a special journal the sequence of columns need not follow the traditional placement. Cash is the first credit and will be used in each transaction entered in this journal.
5. The Purchases Discounts Credit column is used for recording discounts taken on invoices paid within the discount period.
6. Credits to general ledger accounts other than Cash and Purchases Discounts are recorded in the Other Accounts Credit column.
7. There are three folio columns, two labeled (F), one, (✔); a posting symbol indicating that the amount has been posted to the general ledger or to the accounts payable ledger is placed in the folio column.
8. The name of the general ledger or subsidiary ledger account to be debited is written in the Account Debited column.
9. When a creditor is paid in full or on account, the amount is entered in the Accounts Payable Debit column. The amount entered is the actual amount of the check plus any purchases discounts taken.
10. The purchase of merchandise for cash is entered in the Purchases Debit column.
11. The Other Accounts Debit column is used for entries to general ledger accounts which have no special column.

The cash payments journal of Hayward Casuals is illustrated in Figure 6-12.

Although each transaction is entered on a single line, the equality of debits and credits is maintained through the use of multiple columns. The transactions are analyzed in terms of debits and credits to indicate their effect on the accounts. These transactions, however, are *not* actually recorded in both the cash payments journal and the general journal.

TRANSACTION:

1973
June 1   Issued Check 1 in the amount of $150 for the June rent.

ANALYSIS OF DEBITS AND CREDITS:

Rent Expense	150	
Cash		150

Figure 6-12. Cash Payments Journal

			Credits						Debits				
					Other Accounts				Accounts Payable			Other Accounts	
Date	Check No.	Explanation	Cash	Purchases Discounts	Account Title	F	Amount	Account Debited	✓	Amount	Purchases	F	Amount
1973 June 1	1	June rent	150					Rent Expense					150
11	2	Payment in full	882	18				Oakland Clothing Co.		900			
13	3	Payment in full	392	8				Southland Apparel		400			
15	4	Cash purchases	200					Purchases			200		
30	5	Partial payment	300		Notes Payable		200	San Francisco Clothiers		500			
30	6	Withdrawal of cash	400					W. Ray, Drawing					400
30	7	Various items	100					Misc. General Expense					100
		Totals	2,424	26			200			1,800	200		650

CASH PAYMENTS JOURNAL — Page 1

TRANSACTION:

1973
June 11   Paid Oakland Clothing Co. in full.

ANALYSIS OF DEBITS AND CREDITS:

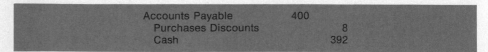

Accounts Payable	900	
Purchases Discounts		18
Cash		882

The purchases journal shows that on June 3 merchandise with an invoice price of $900 was purchased from Oakland Clothing Company; terms 2/10, n/30. Since payment was made within 10 days, a 2-percent discount, or $18, is taken, and a check for $882 is issued. Entering the three amounts in the special columns has the same effect on the general ledger as the explanatory debit and credit analysis does. The creditor's name is entered in the Account Debited column for posting to the accounts payable ledger.

TRANSACTION:

1973
June 13   Paid the Southland Apparel in full.

ANALYSIS OF DEBITS AND CREDITS:

Accounts Payable	400	
Purchases Discounts		8
Cash		392

The explanation for this entry is similar to that for the entry of June 11.

TRANSACTION:

1973
June 15   Purchased merchandise and issued a check for the full amount of the invoice.

Analysis of Debits and Credits:

Purchases	200	
Cash		200

Purchases of merchandise on account are entered in the purchases journal. A company may occasionally purchase merchandise for cash, probably from another company with which no credit relationship exists. These cash purchases are recorded directly in the cash payments journal. If cash purchases of merchandise occur frequently, a special Purchases Debit column may be provided in the cash payments journal.

Transaction:

1973
June 30   Paid the San Francisco Clothiers $300 on account and issued a promissory note for the balance, to be paid in 30 additional days.

Analysis of Debits and Credits:

Accounts Payable	500	
Cash		300
Notes Payable		200

Reference to the purchases journal shows that on June 16 merchandise with an invoice price of $500 was purchased from the San Francisco Clothiers; terms 3/5, n/30. Since the discount period has expired, no discount is taken.

Transaction:

1973
June 30   W. Ray, the owner, withdrew $400 for his personal use in anticipation of earned income.

Analysis of Debits and Credits:

W. Ray, Drawing	400	
Cash		400

Since there is no special column for personal withdrawals, the cash withdrawal is entered in the Other Accounts Debit column. If such withdrawals are numerous, a special column with the heading W. Ray, Drawing Debit could be provided.

Transaction:

1973
June 30   Issued Check 7 in the amount of $100 for miscellaneous general expenses

Analysis of Debits and Credits:

Miscellaneous General Expense	100	
Cash		100

The expense account is debited for various items purchased and consumed during the month.

Before the end-of-the-month postings are made, the columns of the cash payments journal should be footed, and the equality of debits and credits proved as shown.

	Debits		Credits
Accounts Payable	$1,800	Cash	$2,424
Purchases	200	Purchases Discounts	26
Other Accounts	650	Notes Payable	200
Total	$2,650	Total	$2,650

The total debit and total credit postings from this journal to the general ledger are equal.

Posting from the cash payments journal of Hayward Casuals is shown in Figure 6-13.

The individual debit postings to the accounts payable ledger support the $1,800 debit posting to the Accounts Payable controlling account in the general ledger. A check mark in the folio (✔) column of the cash payments journal indicates that the posting has been made to the supplier's account in the subsidiary ledger. Note that the balance of each account is either a credit or zero.

The Accounts Payable account is debited for $1,800 as of June 30. The total of the Purchases Debit column, $200, is posted to the Purchases account in the general ledger.

The total of the Other Accounts Debit column is not posted because it is used to record debits to accounts for which no special columns have been provided; each amount must be posted separately. The numbers of these accounts—703, 252, and 712—are entered in the folio (F) column. The (X) below the double rule in the Other Accounts Debit column indicates that the column total is not posted to the general ledger.

The totals of the Cash Credit column ($2,424) and the Purchases Discounts Credit column ($26) are posted to the general ledger. The basic posting steps are followed. The general ledger account numbers are placed in parentheses below the double rules in the columns to indicate that the postings have been performed.

The total of the Other Accounts Credit column is not posted since each entry in the column has been individually posted at the time the entry is made in the journal. The folio (F) column indicates the account to which the entry was posted.

Other Special Journals

Other special journals may be adopted as the need for them becomes apparent. Such a need is indicated if labor may be saved or if the special journal provides an element of flexibility in the accounting system. Examples of other special journals are the *sales returns and allowances journal*, the *purchases returns and allowances journal*, the *notes receivable register*, the *notes payable register*, and the *voucher register*.

Figure 6-13. Posting Flow from the Cash Payments Journal

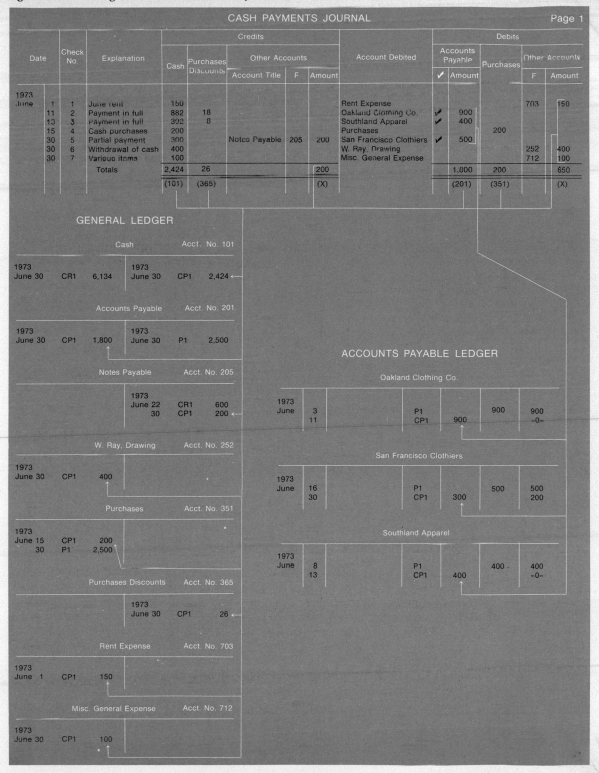

Entries in the General Journal

Although special journals provide for recording frequently recurring transactions, a need for recording (1) unusual current transactions, (2) correcting entries, and (3) adjusting and closing entries remains. For these purposes, a simple two-column general journal is used in conjunction with the special journals.

Unusual Current Transactions. All the transactions that cannot be entered in the special journals are recorded in the general journal. Sales returns and allowances and purchases returns and allowances, for example, are entered in the general journal if special journals for these transactions are not maintained. Other typical current transactions recorded in the general journal include (1) purchases on account of assets other than merchandise inventory, such as plant and equipment or supplies, and the incurrence of liabilities for services; (2) notes received from customers to apply toward accounts receivable; and (3) notes issued to creditors to apply toward accounts payable. The recording of a typical general journal entry is shown below.

GENERAL JOURNAL			Page 35
1973 July 7	Notes Receivable	115	350
	Accounts Receivable—S. Lee	111/✔	350
	To record receipt of 30-day note in full settlement of account.		

The amount, $350, is posted to the general ledger as a debit to Notes Receivable and a credit to Accounts Receivable. The other posting is to the subsidiary ledger to support the corresponding credit to the Accounts Receivable controlling account. A dual credit posting is necessary because the simple two-column general journal—unlike the special journals—does not have classified columns allowing end-of-period posting of column totals.

Note that the detailed explanation of the transaction, which is omitted from special journals (the type of special journal and a reference to an invoice date or number generally suffice to explain a special journal entry), is retained in the general journal because of the unusual nature of the transactions recorded there.

Correcting Entries. If it is discovered that an error has been made in the process of journalizing and posting, it may be corrected by a general journal entry. Erasures should be avoided because they may create doubt in the minds of persons who examine the records regarding the reason for the erasure. This becomes particularly important when the records are audited, and in cases of litigation when the records may be offered as evidence.

Assume that the following entry, recording the payment of an invoice for repairs to machinery, has been posted (actually recorded in the cash disbursements journal but for simplicity is shown here in general journal form):

1973 July 19	Machinery and Equipment	15	
	Cash		15

The debit should have been to an expense account; the error may be corrected by the following entry in the general journal:

GENERAL JOURNAL		Page 40
1973 July 20	Maintenance and Repairs Expense	15	
	Machinery and Equipment		15
	To correct entry of July 19 in		
	cash disbursements journal.		

If an error in a journal entry is discovered before it is posted, it may be corrected by drawing a line through the incorrect account or amount and entering the correction immediately above it.

Adjusting and Closing Entries. Adjusting and closing entries are always recorded in the general journal. These entries were discussed and illustrated in Chapter 4.

Direct Posting from Business Documents

In many business firms, data can be processed more efficiently and rapidly by posting from the original documents—sales invoices, sales slips, purchase invoices, and so on—directly to the subsidiary ledgers instead of first copying the information in special journals and then posting to the accounts. For example, if sales slips are serially numbered, a binder file of duplicate slips arranged in numerical order could take the place of a more formal sales journal. Amounts from the individual slips could be posted daily to the accounts receivable ledger; at the end of a designated period—a week or a month—the sales slips in the binder file are totaled and the following general journal entry is made:

GENERAL JOURNAL		Page 8
1973 Aug. 31	Accounts Receivable	120,000	
	Sales		120,000
	To record charge sales for the		
	month of August, 1973.		

A similar procedure may be used to record purchases on account.

If the postings are made from sales slips to the accounts receivable ledger, and if for any reason a special sales journal is still desired, a streamlined journal can be constructed by simply eliminating the Account Debited, Terms, and folio (F) columns, as shown below.

SALES JOURNAL		
Date	Sales Slip No.	Amount

These changes in procedure and the increasing use of direct posting from original documents are discussed here to add emphasis to a statement made earlier in this chapter: Accounting records and procedures should be designed to meet the needs of the particular business firm.

MACHINE PROCESSING

Bookkeeping Machines

The simple *posting machine* and similar electromechanical equipment can perform the two basic operations involved in the distribution of business transaction information to appropriate accounts: (1) *listing*—that is, writing such information as cross-reference, date, and amount, and (2) *adding* or *subtracting* amounts. Depending on the complexity of the machine—whether it has one or more *registers*, which allow it to accumulate amounts for further computation, and whether it has a built-in *program* (set of instructions for performing manipulations of data)—it may perform many additional tasks.

In a growing business, as the number of customers and charge transactions increases, the cost of hand posting to the accounts receivable ledger becomes excessive. It may be economical for such a company to buy or rent a simple posting machine that has a *horizontal register* (cross-footer) that can compute the difference between debits and credits on a single line. This type of machine can be used to post debits from sales slips or invoices and credits from receipts to each customer's account in the subsidiary ledger. The operator punches into the machine both debits and credits, if applicable, to the account. The machine records this information and prints out a new balance automatically.

The typical ledger account used in machine accounting is the balance-form card shown in Figure 6-14.

A similar procedure is followed to post entries to the accounts payable ledger.

Many firms have ADP systems that permit posting by machine to all ledgers, including the general ledger. Economies can be achieved by machine

Figure 6-14. Typical Machine Ledger Card

Date	Explanation	F or Code	Debit	Credit	Balance

accounting when the volume of similar accounting routines is large enough to enable the bookkeeper to gain speed through repetitive motions that can eventually become habitual. Accuracy and legibility of accounting records are attained by the use of electromechanical machines. These machines facilitate proofs of the accuracy of journalizing and posting. The more complex machines perform several stages of accounting—the preparation of source documents, journal entries, and ledger posting—in one operation.

Punched-Card Equipment

As a business engages in a larger number of transactions of similar nature, it may be economical to acquire punched-card equipment. This equipment rapidly, accurately, and automatically completes the three basic stages of distributing the details of accounting transactions to the appropriate accounts and reports: (1) recording information on a source document; (2) classifying the information according to the accounts affected; and (3) summarizing the resulting account balances. This kind of equipment is also useful for recording, classifying, and summarizing nonfinancial statistical data that help management to make decisions.

Recording Transactions. Punched cards are used to record transaction information. The accounting and statistical information is recorded on the card by the means of punched holes. There are 80 columns on each card in which information can be punched. One or more columns may be designated for recording each class of information. For example, in a sales analysis card, Column 1 may be used for a cross-reference code; Columns 2 through 6, the client number; Columns 7 through 12, the invoice number; Columns 13 through 18, the date; and so on. A single punch in a column indicates that a number has been recorded; two punches indicate a nonnumerical character.

The punched card may be the original source document of a business transaction, or the information can be transferred to punched cards from sales invoices, purchase invoices, or receipts. Several punched cards may be used to record the information contained on a single original source document; for example, a separate card may be required for each debit to the accounts receivable ledger and another card for the total credit to Sales.

The *key-punch machine* used to punch the cards is operated by a keyboard similar to that of a typewriter. With more complex machinery, cards can be punched automatically from other cards or paper tape, or as a by-product of other machine operations.

Classifying Information. A *sorter* is used to classify the information contained on the punched cards according to the accounts affected. The machine senses the holes punched in the cards electrically and causes them to drop into appropriate slots. Since the machine can only sort for one vertical column of information at a time, it is necessary to run the cards through the sorter several times to accomplish a complete classification.

Summarizing Information. A *tabulator*, by means of an electrically wired control panel, can list items, select items of a given type, add, and subtract. Thus, the information contained on the punched cards, now classified according to the accounts affected, can be summarized by running the cards through a tabulator.

All the typical accounting records and reports can be prepared by the tabulator. For example, many of the journals can be printed by passing all the punched cards for a given class of transactions through the tabulator, which lists the items and obtains totals. Posting to the accounts receivable ledger and the general ledger, and even the preparation of a trial balance and financial statements, can be accomplished by the use of punched cards and the tabulator.

One distinct advantage of punched cards is that the information contained in a single set of cards can be used to accumulate several different types of reports and records. In addition to the typical accounting records that can be prepared by successive runs of the punched cards through the sorting and tabulating equipment, other financial and statistical analyses can be prepared, such as an analysis of sales by product or by territory.

ELECTRONIC DATA PROCESSING

Electronic data processing (EDP) systems, which offer the greatest speed, volume, and reliability, consist of combinations of electronic equipment centered around digital computers. These machines are designed to receive a large mass of input data, perform basic arithmetic operations on the data, make comparison-type decisions regarding the data, update the previously stored data, almost immediately supply the information or output that results from these operations, and then store the data for later use.

What the Computer Can Do

The main advantage of electronic data processing is the computer's ability to compute at high rates of *speed* and to *store* data externally and retrieve them automatically. These abilities allow results of recent operations to be made available in time to help management make decisions. The computer assists in the maintenance of inventory, helps to facilitate control over costs and revenue, and thus speeds up the preparation of operating budgets and other forecasts.

As the equipment has become more diverse, efficient, and less expensive per unit, more applications have become practical. The Internal Revenue Service is using the computer to process tax returns. Instant credit and credit cards could lead to an almost cashless economy. Automated billing is quite ordinary. Airline reservation systems are handled by an integrated system.

In accounting, many certified public accounting firms throughout the country are installing computer systems as part of their management services departments. These systems perform a total accounting operation for the clients, including the billing of customers, as well as the preparation of a multitude of managerial analyses and reports. Smaller accounting firms have turned to time-sharing to offer these services to their clients.

Time-sharing can serve a wide variety of users who cannot afford a large computer installation. It is the kind of information processing that is making great strides for the simple reason that it is possible for a central processing unit, at a reasonable cost per unit, to accommodate many users who may be miles apart.

These users communicate with the computer by means of a teletypewriter (TWX) or a portable typewriter hooked up to a telephone. The computer operates so much faster than the operator can type that it can time-share many users with this type of input/output device. In summary, time-sharing is an almost simultaneous access to a central computer system by remote and diversified users. Delays caused by other users are insignificant, lasting only a few seconds.

For many companies, mini computers are an intermediate step between the manual and the large-size EDP system. These systems are used successfully when the manual system becomes burdensome. These small units by-pass punched-card equipment and provide low-cost, low-speed, more efficient, and more economical service. An example is the IBM System 3, which was developed for this market.

Banks are beginning to use *on-line real-time* computer systems. An on-line real-time computer is designed to capture data immediately from an operational center, such as a teller's window. When a deposit is made, the teller punches the information into a machine that transmits it immediately to the main computer center for processing. In this kind of system, the delay in recording information and making it available is substantially reduced by combining data processing, decentralized input and output, and communications. In one bank, for example, all its operations are included in the system—savings and checking accounts, mortgages, Christmas club and school accounts, payroll, payroll savings, general ledger posting, cost accounting, and trust operations.

Another example of the trend in computer usage is that of a gas company that acquired a computer capable of adding 16,000 five-digit figures in a second for processing meter readings into completed bills and making up-to-the-minute statistics available to management. The computer also handles inventory accounting for 20,000 items—from gas jets to 36-inch pipeline—that the company uses, payroll accounting for about 4,000 employees, accounting for the appliances sold by the company, and the preparation of dividend checks and proxy notices.

With this increased efficiency, however, the computer brings a number of difficulties and weaknesses. Some of these are listed below.

1. *Internal Control of Assets.* Skills in manipulating computers can provide a means of committing fraud or theft. This possibility demands control over the input and output in order that it may be independently reviewed. Printout of typical journals and ledgers may be necessary. The use of traditional accounting records would help to implement the internal control of assets. A systems analyst can make a significant contribution in providing audit trails to assist in the control. An *audit trail* involves the maintenance or printout of visual records which will enable the accountant to verify accounting data.

2. *Public Relations.* Mistakes in billing are legion and have created customer resentment, hostility, and dismay. There has not been adequate attention given to customer disagreement with the billing data. Letter after letter from a customer may disappear seemingly into the electronic maze without answer or modification in the billing.

3. *Loss of Records.* It is conceivable that valuable records stored on disk or tape could be destroyed by mistake or accident.

4. *Hazards of Down Time.* If a company's operations are geared to electronic records, the failure of the computer can halt the operations until service is restored. Backup equipment would generally be prohibitive because of cost.

5. *Invasion of Privacy.* The growth of data banks storing credit, health and employment information is attributable to the computer. Secrecy and use of the information have been the subject of increasing concern and legislative inquiry.

6. *Software Crisis.* The need to improve languages, processors, and compilers, the demand for more sophisticated analysis of the output, and the general lack of ability to utilize fully the capability of the computer all point to the problem that the hardware has outdistanced the knowledge of its use.

7. *Skilled Personnel.* Enough trained personnel is not available to satisfy the demand for analysts, programmers, operators, computer technicians to maintain the equipment, EDP supervisors or management personnel with an understanding of the use of electronic processing. There is also an acute shortage of skilled personnel to train this kind of people.

In summary, the advent of the computer has had a revolutionary effect on the collection of data and their use in the decision-making process. The future offers widespread use of the computer principally by reason of cost reductions, time-sharing, and the demands of competition.

How the Computer Functions

There are two types of electronic computers—*analog* and *digital.* An analog computer measures data directly, without converting the data to a code or storing them. A slide rule and a thermometer are examples of analog devices. An analog computer is used to control equipment in industry and weapons systems in the military. A digital computer has memory and solves problems by making comparisons and by arithmetic functions. Business has found the characteristics of the digital computer best suited for its uses. Thus the analog computer measures and the digital computer counts and compares.

The development of the digital computer is referred to in time by *generations* of computers. The first computers used commercially had vacuum tubes and entered the commercial market approximately in 1954; they are typically referred to as *first-generation* computers. Then the transistor transformed the computer from a large piece of equipment to a smaller component, reduced its cost of operation, and improved the speed of manipulating data. This transistorized *second-generation* computer was introduced in 1958. Mounting electronic circuits on small silicon chips brought about additional reductions in cost per transaction, size, increased memory, and speed. These *third-generation* computers appeared in 1965 and permitted greater flexibility in use of the hardware and software. The *fourth generation* of computers is being developed now, with the expectations of continuing the refinements that have been accomplished previously. These computers are expected to be placed on the market in the near future.

The developments reviewed above refer to the hardware—the physical equipment. Improvements in software, the techniques for using the equipment, have also been made.

In the early computers communication with the computer was in machine language. Each computer design had its own language, which was difficult to learn and understand. This led to the development of a symbolic language that made it easier to instruct the computer (write a program). This is called an *assembly* language. It converts the symbolic language on a one-to-one basis into machine language. Examples of assembly language are Symbolic Programming System

(SPS), Assembler Language Coding (ALC), and Autocoder. The languages were machine oriented—that is, generally restricted to use on one type of computer. An endeavor has been made to develop languages that would be problem or procedure oriented and that generally could be used on many different models of computers. These languages are commonly referred to as being independent of the machine and are written in statements and equations that are more comprehensible. These languages have to be translated into machine language also. To provide this translation each computer manufacturer has developed such a translator or processor, called a *compiler*. This results in the generation of many machine-language instructions for one source-program instruction. Programs are now being written in a freer form that is closer to human language. These languages are spoken of as being "high level" compared to machine language or assembly languages which are considered "low level." The chart below lists the more common programming languages and describes them briefly.

LANGUAGE	MEANING AND USE
Problem Oriented	
RPG	Report Program Generator was developed to print reports and keep the data up to date—file maintenance. This language will provide the maximum of data manipulation for the minimum of programmer coding.
COBOL	COmmon Business Oriented Language source language statements closely resemble English notation. This language permits a program to be written that management can read and follow. This is called "good documentation."
PL/1	Programming Language One was developed by IBM for the System/360. It is designed to serve the needs of both scientific and business users and is regarded as combining the best features of COBOL and FORTRAN.
FORTRAN	FORmula TRANslating was developed by IBM and has become the most universally used scientific language. It has widespread use in business as well.
BASIC	Beginner's All-purpose Symbolic Instruction Code is a language that has an algebraic basis. It is easy to learn and use and is the language that is used in this text to illustrate coding. It is limited in its ability to produce well-formated reports; it also lacks advanced features should the programmer need them. The language has been used extensively to write programs at remote typewriter terminals in time-sharing systems.
Machine Oriented	
SPS	Symbolic Programming System is an example of an assembly language. These languages are one for one, that is, one source language statement results in one machine language statement.
AUTOCODER	An assembly language that is an extension of SPS.
ALC	Assembler Language Coding is an assembly language for the S/360 and requires the programmer to think more in terms of the computer rather than the problem to be programmed. The assembly languages referred to above are outmoded, that is, SPS and Autocoder.
Binary or BCD	Binary or Binary Coded Decimal are machine languages.

Figure 6-15. Manually Processing Data

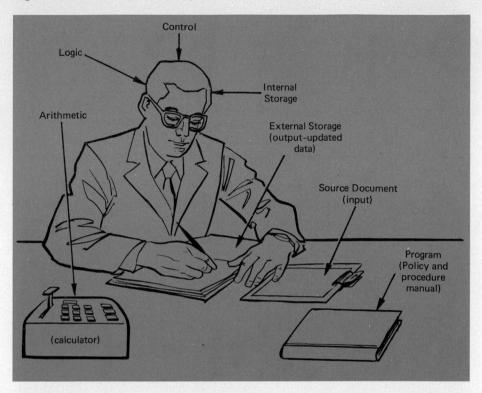

Figure 6-16. Structure of a Computer

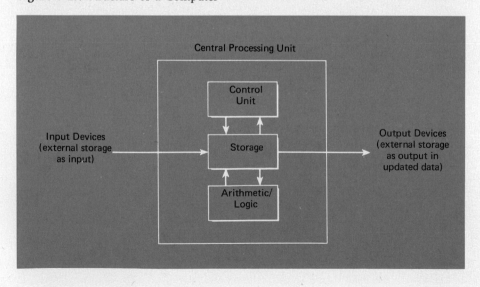

Hardware and software function together to produce for modern man solutions to many problems. How this is accomplished may be explained by comparing the manipulation of data by the computer to the approach that man uses in solving a similar problem. Figure 6-15 outlines the manual processing of data and Figure 6-16 illustrates the analogous structure of a computer and the data flow.

An explanation of Figure 6-16 follows:

Central Processing Unit: This comprises the computer in fact. It has three sections—control, memory (internal storage), and arithmetic/logic. The *control* unit is the traffic director—the brains of the computer. It takes the instructions from internal storage, follows them sequentially, directs the arithmetic/logic section to perform, and initiates any output. It is the key to the computer and its chief functions are supervision and coordination of the other sections in the CPU. The arithmetic/logic unit performs the mathematical operations in the program. The logic unit compares two items and makes a decision.

Storage: Data may be stored internally or externally. Internal storage is referred to as the *memory*. All data and instructions introduced to the computer as input are placed in internal storage. As the processing proceeds, the control unit can store intermediate data in the memory. External storage is the output and is placed on a disk or tape for later use. When the data are to be updated, they are introduced back into the computer as input. This storage characteristic is the feature of the digital computer that serves business so well.

Input Devices: Getting information in and out of the computer is the function of the input and output devices. Man communicates with the computer through an input device. This communication takes the form of *program instructions* and *data* to be processed and is translated by the input unit into electric signals or pulses. Input devices use many media—punched cards, punched paper tapes, magnetic tapes and disks, light pens, and typewriters. Use of the human voice as an input device is the object of current research. Optical scanners are in current use and can read pencil marks and magnetic characters enscribed on such items as checks.

Output Devices: The computer talks back to man through output devices. Generally the same media used by input devices are found in the output units. Both units have presented problems because they are relatively slow in comparison to the computer.

At this point the languages and the flow of data and instructions through the computer have been introduced. For a clearer picture of the dialogue between man and the computer and the translations required, Figure 6-17 is presented on page 220.

In summary, a set of instructions to the computer is written up (source program) in a high-level language. The manufacturer has supplied a compiler which processes these instructions into machine or absolute language. This is called the *object program* and is the source program translated into machine language for the control unit in the computer to read. To complete the survey of electronic processing of information, an illustration of coding a computer program is presented.

Figure 6-17. Languages, Programs, and Translators

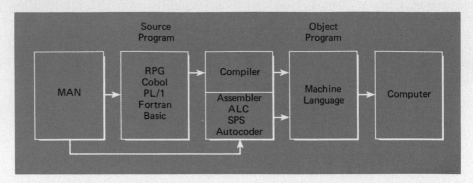

An Illustration of Coding a Program

There are three phases in developing a program for a computer.

1. State the problem in detail, carefully developing the steps; this is the descriptive phase.
2. Draw a flow chart of the problem. Sometimes, it is helpful to draw first a general chart and then design another with details. Precision and detail at this point are essential.
3. Code the instruction to the computer by following the flow chart.

BASIC is used in this text because it can be learned quickly by the student. It is also valuable as an aid to understanding the computer as well as making the task of learning another language easier. The saying that the best way to understand a computer is to learn a source language is a truism.

A more complete statement of BASIC is found in the *Student's Self-Study Guide* that accompanies this text. In the bibliography at the end of the chapter there are several references which should prove helpful to the reader in mastering this language.

Generally, there are three things that a program should provide.

1. Giving the computer information.
2. Telling the computer what calculations and comparisons to make.
3. Getting information out of the computer.

With these general objectives, consider this program for calculating the working capital for three firms. In Chapter 1 the formula used is $WC = CA - CL$. Assume you are given the following data on three firms to process:

Firm	CA	CL
A	100	50
B	15,000	5,000
C	75,000	25,000

The program should instruct the computer to process this data repetitively and solve for the working capital of each firm.

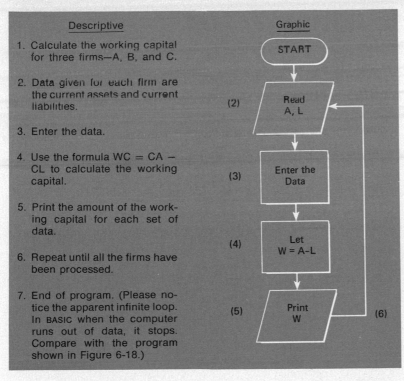

Descriptive

1. Calculate the working capital for three firms—A, B, and C.

2. Data given for each firm are the current assets and current liabilities.

3. Enter the data.

4. Use the formula WC = CA − CL to calculate the working capital.

5. Print the amount of the working capital for each set of data.

6. Repeat until all the firms have been processed.

7. End of program. (Please notice the apparent infinite loop. In BASIC when the computer runs out of data, it stops. Compare with the program shown in Figure 6-18.)

Graphic

START

(2) Read A, L

(3) Enter the Data

(4) Let W = A−L

(5) Print W (6)

Coding

```
   10   READ A, L

   20   DATA 100, 50, 15000

   30   DATA 5000, 75000, 26000

   40   LET W = A−L

   50   PRINT W

   60   GØ TØ 10

99999   END
```

Printout of Solution

```
50
10000
50000
```

The complete program illustrated above provides for all three functions. Study them carefully. Recognize, also, that this program satisfies the general criteria related earlier.

1. The computer acquires the information by the READ command and the DATA statement.
2. The computer is told the calculations to make by the LET command. The GØ TØ command provides an unconditional branch for looping back and processing additional data. When the computer runs out of data, it will stop.
3. The solution is obtained from the computer by the PRINT command.

There are many interesting things to learn from this program.

1. There is a statement on each line and each line is numbered. Each statement begins with an English word.
2. You may skip line numbers or have them out of order; the computer will process them sequentially. Please note the END statement is the highest number that possibly will be processed.
3. The names used in the program may consist of one or two characters. If a name has one character, it must be a letter. If it has two, the name must be a letter followed by a digit. The names used are

    A (current assets)
    L (current liabilities)
    W (working capital)

4. The calculations are indicated by these operators:

multiplication	*
division	/
addition	+
subtraction	—

5. The form of the LET command is

$$\text{LET variable} = \text{expression.}$$

This command causes the expression on the right side of the equals sign to be evaluated. An expression is a constant, or a variable, or a string of variables and constants, each separated by operators. If a statement is correct, it is said to be "legal."

6. The READ, DATA statements are used together to provide input into the storage of the computer. The READ command contains the names of variables. For each variable in the READ command, there is a corresponding constant in the DATA statement.

Figure 6-18. An Alternative Method of Ending a Program

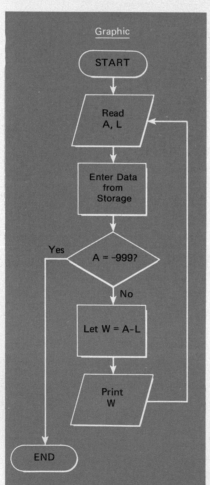

Coding

```
10 READ A, L

20 IF A = -999 THEN 9999

30 DATA 100, 50, 15000, 5000, 75000, 25000, -999

40 LET W = A-L

50 PRINT W

9999 END
```

By using the IF/THEN command, the program can be ended. The IF/THEN command takes this form:

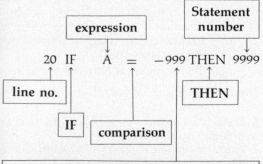

A dummy or fictional value is placed after the last set of values. The computer is instructed to test for this number. If the number is found, then it branches to the end of the program.

Both the variables and the constants are separated by commas. For this reason, data with a value of one thousand or more is not expressed with commas.

7. The READ statement says each set of data will have two numbers, there may be more than two in other programs. The first data will be assigned to A, the next to L. On the first loop, the computer will assign the first number in the second set to A and the second value to L. It will process the data sequentially even though the set is divided on two lines. Observe that the end of the DATA statement does not have a comma, even if the set is divided on two lines.

8. The names are defined in the READ statement prior to the LET command; that is, all of the names shown on the right side of the equals sign must have been given values earlier in the program. This is satisfied by placing the READ, DATA statements before the LET command.

9. The G$\emptyset$ T$\emptyset$ command and the READ statement form a loop that will continue to branch unconditionally until there are no more data. The computer will stop at this point. There are other methods of ending this program. From reading the flow chart, it appears there is an infinite loop; that is, the processing will not terminate. An alternative way of ending the program is shown in Figure 6-18.

A program for calculating accrued interest expense on the following three notes payable is shown below.

DATA:

Note #1 Principal of $5,750; interest rate, 10%; time elapsed, 32 days
Note #2 Principal of $775; interest rate, 12%; time elapsed, 15 days
Note #3 Principal of $1,200; interest rate, 10%; time elapsed, 20 days

PROGRAM:

```
10    PRINT "ERIN CARROLL"
15    PRINT
20    REMARK PROGRAM FOR ACCRUED INTEREST EXPENSE
25    PRINT
30    READ P, R, T
40    DATA 5750, 10, 32, 775, 12, 15, 1200, 10, 20
50    LET I = P * (R/100) * (T/360)
55    LET A = 0
60    LET A = A + I
70    PRINT "ACCRUED INTEREST EXPENSE FOR 1973"
75    PRINT
80    GO TO 30
90    PRINT A
9999  END
```

The output from this program would be:

ACCRUED INTEREST EXPENSE FOR 1973
61.66

This program introduces several new statements.

1. REMARK statement is a labeling device that a programmer can use to identify and clarify his program. This statement does not affect the output or the program. The form is quite simple:

REMARK any string of alphameric characters.

2. PRINT is a versatile command. In line 15 and others it is inserted to make the computer skip lines on the output paper. It can also be used to label by enclosing the statement in quotation marks. It also can be used to evaluate an expression and print the results.
3. After each calculation, a new value is obtained for A, the total. This is accomplished by adding the new interest calculation to the old balance to arrive at the new balance. The interest on the first note ($51.11) is stored. When the amount is calculated on the second note, it is added to the interest on the first note to get a new balance of $54.99. The last note is computed and added to the $54.99 to bring the total to $61.66. With each total, it eliminates the old balance and stores the new figure.
4. The operator / indicates division. The amounts must be written on one line; there are no fractions. To help make it clear to the computer what is to be done, parentheses are sometimes used.
5. A is initialized to assure that A has an initial balance of zero before the program is run.
6. There are five zones of 15 characters in each zone of BASIC output. If more than five variables and constants are given in a PRINT command, the sixth and remaining ones are printed on the next line beginning with the first zone. Print zones can be skipped by printing a blank in quotation marks. Labels follow the same rules. First one is in zone 1-15 and the next starts at column 16. If the label is longer than 15 characters, it will simply run over into the next zone.

An opportunity to apply flow charting and coding to the solution of problems will be found in selected areas of the *Student's Self-Study Guide* and at the end of several chapters in the remainder of the book. The intent in this chapter has been to introduce a source language and illustrate its utility.

SUMMARY

The design of a record system to capture financial data focuses on the *transaction.* With the aid of criteria and information about the business, a systems analyst designs a recordkeeping function that will satisfy the special needs of that business. He uses flow charts as one of the methods of depicting the flow of information through the business.

Flow charting is described and illustrated by the use of uniform symbols.

There are three broad methods used to gather and process data. A business ordinarily will use a combination of these. The remainder of the chapter examines manual, machine, and electronic processing.

The model used to show manual processing is special journals. Transactions are entered in the journals and posted to the ledgers.

Machine processing of data is briefly described.

A brief description of what can be done with electronic processing is given prior to illustrating how the hardware and the software function in a computer system.

BIBLIOGRAPHY

Farina, Mario V., *Programming in BASIC*. Englewood Cliffs, New Jersey; Prentice-Hall, 1968.
An excellent paperback with emphasis on time-sharing.
General Electric, *BASIC Language—Reference Manual* (Rev.). Bethesda, Maryland; General Electric, 1969, Cat. No. 202026B, 4-69.

————, *Introduction to BASIC Programming.* Bethesda, Maryland; General Electric, 1966. Both these manuals concentrate on time-sharing.

Gleim, George A., *Program Flow Charting.* New York: Holt, Rinehart and Winston, 1970. An up-to-date paperback on flow charting.

International Business Machines Corporation, *Fundamentals of Programming Text.* New York: IBM Corp., 1968, Cat. No. R29.0019-2. An excellent programmed instruction book on flow charting.

Nolan, Richard L. *Introduction to Computing through the BASIC Language.* New York: Holt, Rinehart and Winston, 1969. A well-written paperback that is complete as a resource for BASIC.

QUESTIONS

Q6-1. (a) What is the function of the systems analyst? (b) What are the considerations of the analyst in system design? (c) In selecting the method or combination of methods of data collection, what criteria are used? (d) What are the three methods of data collection?

Q6-2. (a) What is a flow chart? (b) What are the types of flow charts and how do they compare? (c) What are the steps in constructing a flow chart. (d) Draw the basic flow-charting symbols and explain the function of each.

Q6-3. (a) What is branching? (b) What is a conditional branch? (c) Distinguish an unconditional branch from a conditional branch. (d) Why is it important in flow charting to establish clearly the conditions that exist in the problem to be solved? (e) What is a loop? (f) What is an infinite loop?

Q6-4. (a) What is the function of special journals? (b) What determines the types of special journals to be used? (c) Do the special journals entirely eliminate the need for a general journal? (d) How do special journals save time and labor? (e) Are there other advantages in using special journals?

Q6-5. What is the rule for entering a transaction in the (a) sales journal? (b) purchases journal? (c) cash receipts journal? (d) cash payments journal? (e) general journal?

Q6-6. The Jensen Company uses sales, purchases, cash receipts, cash payments, and general journals. State the journal in which each of the following transactions and events should be recorded:

a. A sale of merchandise on account
b. A purchase of store supplies on account
c. A return of a cash sale
d. A purchase of delivery equipment on account
e. A payment to a creditor
f. A sale of merchandise for cash
g. Adjusting entries
h. A purchase of merchandise on account
i. A note receivable issued by a customer in full settlement of his account
j. A return of a credit purchase
k. A withdrawal of cash by owner for his own use
l. Closing entries
m. A payment of rent
n. A purchase of merchandise for cash
o. A note payable given to a creditor to apply on account
p. A withdrawal of merchandise by the owner for his own use

Q6-7. (a) When are postings made from the purchases journal to (1) the general ledger and (2) the accounts payable ledger? (b) What is the relationship of the amounts posted? (c) How is it possible to trace postings from the journals to the ledgers? (d) What is the significance of the check mark in the folio (F) column of the purchases journal? (e) Would it be advisable to use code numbers as posting references for creditor's accounts rather than check marks?

Q6-8. The following questions relate to the cash receipts journal illustrated in this chapter: (a) What are the special columns? (b) What is the purpose of the Other Accounts columns? (c) Why is the journal cross footed at the end of each month? (d) Explain the postings from this journal to (1) the general ledger and (2) the accounts receivable ledger.

Q6-9. (a) What are the two types of computers? (b) What has been the historical development of hardware? (c) What is machine language? (d) What function does an assembly language perform? (e) What is a compiler?

Q6-10. (a) What is problem-oriented language? (b) What is machine-oriented language? (c) In what other terms are these languages called? (d) Name and define the languages in common usage.

Q6-11. Explain the fundamental operation of a computer.

Q6-12. (a) What is a LET command? (b) What is a legal statement? (c) What is the function of READ, DATA statements? (d) What command and statement form a loop? (e) How may the loop be terminated?

Q6-13. (a) Explain the IF/THEN command. (b) Explain the REMARK statement and its function. (c) Explain the versatility of the PRINT command.

Q6-14. (a) What is BASIC language? (b) What are its advantages and disadvantages?

EXERCISES

E6-1. Describe the steps involved in analyzing a transaction to determine the debit and credit for a journal entry; then construct a flow chart that will logically illustrate this procedure.

E6-2. In Chapter 2 a procedure is described for the location of the error if the trial balance does not balance. Construct a flow chart that will display this sequence.

E6-3. Figure 5-7 illustrates the procedure for using the work sheet in making closing entries. Describe this procedure in logical steps and then construct a flow chart that will graphically illustrate the steps.

E6-4. The Heintz Company made the following credit sales during March, 1973:

1973
Mar. 2   Sold merchandise on account to Frank Fail, $140.

     3   Sold merchandise on account to Nathan Nome, $100.

     4   Sold merchandise on account to Melvin Baker, $200.

     7   Sold merchandise on account to Sumner Carter, $350.

     7   Sold merchandise on account to Frank Fail, $160.

   12   Sold merchandise on account to Nathan Nome, $50.

   20   Sold merchandise on account to Melvin Baker, $70.

   31   Sold merchandise on account to Sumner Carter, $150.

a. Record the transactions in a sales journal similar to the one illustrated in this chapter. The terms on credit sales are 1/10 EOM, n/30. Number the sales, starting with 101.
b. Open the customers' accounts in the accounts receivable ledger.
c. Open the following accounts in the general ledger: Accounts Receivable 111 and Sales 301.
d. Post from the sales journal to the accounts receivable ledger and the general ledger.

E6-5. The Seiler Tack Shop made the following credit purchases during December, 1973:

1973
Dec. 1 Purchased merchandise from the Hale Company on account, $400.

2 Purchased merchandise from the Raymond Company on account, $160.

5 Purchased merchandise from the Vatter Company on account, $325.

13 Purchased merchandise from the Sanderson Supply Company on account, $400.

17 Purchased merchandise from the Vatter Company on account, $210.

19 Purchased merchandise from the Hale Company on account, $230.

22 Purchased merchandise from the Raymond Company on account, $198.

26 Purchased merchandise from the Hale Company on account, $175.

30 Purchased merchandise from the Sanderson Supply Company on account, $205.

a. Record the transactions in a purchases journal similar to the one illustrated in this chapter. The terms on all purchases of merchandise on account are 2/10, n/30.
b. Open the following accounts in the general ledger: Accounts Payable 201 and Purchases 351.
c. Open the creditors' accounts in the accounts payable ledger.
d. Post from the purchases journal to the accounts payable ledger and the general ledger.

E6-6. The Allison Corporation received its charter on February 1, 1973. During the month of February, it completed the following cash receipt transactions:

1973
Feb. 1 Capital stock of $25,000 was issued at par for cash.

8 Received a check for $98 from Norman Lang in settlement of a $100 sales invoice.

15 Cash sales for February 1 through 15 were $1,200.

17 Received $50 in cash from Robert Sampson (no discount).

23 Borrowed $1,000 in cash from the State Street Bank and gave a note payable due March 24, 1973.

25 Received a check for $194 from Richard Burroughs in settlement of a $200 sales invoice.

28 Cash sales for February 16 through 28 were $1,500.

28 Sold a parcel of land purchased on February 1 at its cost of $4,000.

28 Received $2,000 in cash and a note receivable for the balance.

a. Record the transactions in a cash receipts journal similar to the one illustrated in this chapter.
b. Open the following general ledger accounts:

> Cash 101
> Accounts Receivable 111
> Notes Receivable 115
> Land 121
> Notes Payable 205
> Capital Stock 251
> Sales 301
> Sales Discounts 311

Post a debit of $600 to Accounts Receivable, dated February 28. This amount is from the sales journal.

c. Open the following accounts in the accounts receivable ledger and record the amounts given in the Debit and Balance columns (these are summary totals posted from the sales journal): Richard Burroughs, $300; Norman Lang, $200; Robert Sampson, $100.

d. Post from the cash receipts journal to the accounts receivable ledger and the general ledger.

e. Prepare a schedule of accounts receivable.

E6-7. The Cooper Company was organized on March 1, 1973. The following cash payments were made during the month:

1973

March 1 Purchased land and building for $30,000. Paid $10,000 in cash and a note for $20,000. Land is appraised at $5,000; building at $25,000.

10 Paid the Matterhorn Company $490 in settlement of a purchase made on March 2; the invoice price was $500.

15 Cash purchases for March 1 through 15 were $6,000.

17 Paid the Nelson Company $1,000 on account (no discount).

20 Purchased office equipment for $2,000 in cash.

31 Paid the Peters Company $500 on account (no discount).

31 Paid a 6-percent, 30-day note due this date. Face value of the note was $5,000; interest was $25.

31 Cash purchases for March 16 through 31 were $10,000.

a. Record the transactions in a cash payments journal similar to the one illustrated in this chapter.

b. Open the following general ledger accounts:

> Cash 101
> Land 201
> Building 202
> Office Equipment 203
> Accounts Payable 301
> Notes Payable 302
> Purchases 401
> Purchases Discounts 402
> Interest Expense 501

Enter the following account balances:
1. Debit balance in Cash, $100,000—posted from the cash receipts journal.
2. Credit balance in Accounts Payable, $4,000—posted from the purchases journal.
3. Credit balance in Notes Payable, $5,000—posted from the cash receipts journal.

c. Open the following accounts in the accounts payable ledger and record the amounts given in the Credit and Balance columns (these are summary totals posted from the purchases journal); Matterhorn Company, $500; Nelson Company, $1,600; Peters Company, $1,900.

d. Post from the cash payments journal to the accounts payable ledger and the general ledger.

e. Prepare a schedule of accounts payable.

E6-8. The Garcia Company uses sales, purchases, cash receipts, cash payments, and general journals. On January 31, 1973, it had the following accounts in its general ledger after the books had been closed:

Cash				Accounts Receivable			
1	58,000	2	38,000	3	60,000	4	20,000

Accounts Payable

	5	8,000			6	19,500	

Sales

	7	78,000			8	60,000	
					9	18,000	

Purchases

	10	19,500			12	25,500	
	11	6,000					

Purchases Returns and Allowances

	13	1,800			14	1,800	

On a sheet of paper opposite numbers 1 through 14 corresponding to the numbers that appear in the folio columns of the accounts, indicate the most probable journal source for each posting. Use the abbreviations J, S, P, CR, and CP to identify the journals, as shown in the following example:

Number	Journal Source
1	CR

E6-9. Are these names "legal"? Indicate yes or no. If no, state what is wrong with the name.
a. A   b. 2A   c. 5   d. AB   e. a5   f. 22   g. C10

E6-10. Are each of the following statements correct? If not, make the correction:

a. 10   LET A + B = 2 * C
b. 10   LET X14 = Y
c. 10   A = B + C7
d. 30   IF A = B10 THEN
e. 30   IF A + B THEN 50
f. 30   IF A * B THEN 50
g. 30   PRINT A, B,
h. 30   PRINT A, B
i. LET A = 3½
j. 30   IF A = 50 GO TO 999

E6-11. Debug the following program:

```
100   READ A, B, C, D          400   PRINT X
200   READ E                   500   DATA 1, 2, 3, 4,
300   LET X = A + B + C + D + E 600   END
```

E6-12. Debug the following program and show the printout:

```
10   DATA 1, 2, 3, 4, 5, 999   50   PRINT Y, X
20   IF X = 999 THEN           60   GO TO 40
30   LET Y = X + 10            999  END
40   READ X
```

E6-13. What will be the printout from the following program? If it does not compute the proper solution, what changes would be necessary in the program?

```
100   LET W = A - L            400   PRINT W
200   LET A = 100              999   END
300   LET L = 50
```

DEMONSTRATION PROBLEMS

DP6-1. (*Flow chart design*) Construct a flow chart that will illustrate the rules for selecting a special journal to enter a transaction. See page 194 for a summary of the special journals and the classifications of transactions that each special journal will accept.

DP6-2. (*Special journals*) The Rayher Company has been in operation for five years, selling merchandise for cash only. Beginning in January, 1973, it plans to start making sales on account. The general ledger of the Company shows the following account balances on January 1, 1973.

101	Cash	$20,000
121	Accounts Receivable	–0–
122	Notes Receivable	–0–
131	Merchandise Inventory	30,000
141	Prepaid Insurance	–0–
201	Store Equipment	10,000
201A	Accumulated Depreciation–Store Equipment	4,000
301	Accounts Payable	–0–
302	Notes Payable	–0–
401	Capital Stock	50,000
402	Retained Earnings	6,000
501	Sales	–0–
502	Sales Returns and Allowances	–0–
503	Sales Discounts	–0–
601	Purchases	–0–
602	Purchases Returns and Allowances	–0–
603	Purchases Discounts	–0–
701	Salesmen's Salaries Expense	–0–

Transactions during the month of January were

1973

Jan. 2 Sold merchandise to Aaron Johnson on account, $800; terms 2/10, n/30.

4 Sold merchandise to William Barker on account, $200; terms 2/10, n/30.

6 Sold merchandise to Walter Carson on account, $400; terms 2/10, n/30.

7 Sold merchandise to David Kirk on account, $900; terms 2/10, n/30.

8 Purchased merchandise from the Nelson Company on account, $1,000; terms 1/10, n/30.

9 Purchased merchandise from the Owen Company on account, $1,500; terms 1/10, n/30.

10 Purchased merchandise from the Parsons Company on account, $600; terms n/45.

11 Purchased merchandise from the Queens Company on account, $1,100; terms n/60.

12 Received a check from Aaron Johnson for the amount due from the sale of January 2.

13 Issued additional capital stock for $5,000 in cash.

14 Purchased store equipment, $2,000, making a down payment of $300 and issuing a 120-day, 8-percent note payable for the balance.

15 Cash sales of $4,000 were made.

16 Received a check from William Barker for $50 and a 60-day, 10-percent promissory note for the balance.

17 Received a check for $196 from Walter Carson in partial settlement of his account—invoice price $200 less discount of $4. Because the check was mailed before the expiration of the discount period, the discount was allowed.

18 Cash sales of $2,000 were made.

18 Paid $240 for a comprehensive insurance policy for two years, dating from January 1, 1973.

1971

Jan. 18 Paid the amount due the Nelson Company for the purchases made on January 8.

19 Paid $990 in partial settlement of the amount due the Owen Company: invoice price of $1,000 less discount of $10.

20 Paid salesmen's salaries of $300.

20 Cash purchases totaled $3,000.

28 Issued a 6-percent, 90-day note to the Owen Company in settlement of account.

30 Returned merchandise to the Parsons Company and received credit, $100.

31 Credited David Kirk for $75 for merchandise returned.

Required:

1. Set up general and subsidiary ledgers.
2. Journalize all the charge sales in a sales journal and post them to the accounts receivable ledger. Summarize the sales journal and make the January 31 postings to the general ledger.
3. Journalize all the charge purchases in a purchases journal and post them to the accounts payable ledger. Summarize the purchases journal and make January 31 postings to the general ledger.
4. Journalize all the cash receipts in a cash receipts journal and post them to the accounts receivable ledger. Summarize and cross foot the journal and make January 31 postings to the general ledger.
5. Journalize all the cash payments in a cash payments journal and post them to the accounts payable ledger. Summarize and cross foot the journal and make January 31 postings to the general ledger.
6. Journalize any other transactions in a two-column general journal.
7. Prove the balances of the Accounts Receivable and Accounts Payable accounts by preparing a schedule of accounts receivable and a schedule of accounts payable.

DP6-3. (*Computer programming and flow charting*) The following is a program written in BASIC. The purpose of the program is to find the sum of the digits 1, 2, 3, 4, 5, 6, 7, 8, 9, 10.

```
 1   DATA 1, 2, 3, 4,              30   LET T = T + X
 8   REMARK SHANNA LEE            50   PRINT T
10   PRINT SUM-OF-THE-YEARS DIGITS   60   8, 9, 10,
20   5, 6, 7,                     70   GO TO 40
20   LET T = 0                    99   END
40   READ X
```

Required:

1. List the errors in the program.
2. Rewrite the program so that it will obtain the sum of the digits.
3. Construct a flow chart that illustrates the corrected program.
4. What will be the printout of the corrected program?

PROBLEMS

P6-1. Using Figure 6-6 as a model, construct a flow chart that will illustrate the posting flow from the sales journal.

P6-2. Using Figure 6-10 as your guide, construct a flow chart that will illustrate the posting flow from the cash receipts journal.

P6-3. The Cerrudo Company started operations on July 1, 1973. During July, the Company used the following accounts:

Cash 101	Sales 501
Accounts Receivable 111	Sales Discounts 521
Notes Receivable 115	Sales Returns and Allowances 531
Prepaid Insurance 117	Purchases 601
Office Supplies 118	Purchases Discounts 611
Land 131	Purchases Returns and Allowances 621
Store Building 141	Transportation In 631
Store Fixtures 151	Salaries Expense 701
Office Equipment 154	Delivery Expense 711
Accounts Payable 201	Office Expense 721
Mortgage Payable 231	Utilities Expense 731
Capital Stock 401	

The following transactions took place during July:

1973

July 1 Issued capital stock worth $25,000 for cash.

1 Purchased a store building and site for $45,000, of which $11,000 is considered land cost. Paid $5,500 in cash and issued a mortgage of $39,500 for the balance.

1 Purchased store fixtures from the National Company for $6,500 on account; terms n/60. G J   c P

2 Purchased merchandise from Jones, Inc., on account, $6,000; invoice date, July 1; terms 2/10, n/60.

2 Purchased merchandise from Hill Baker on account, $7,000; invoice date, July 2; terms 2/10, n/60.

6 Purchased a six-year fire insurance policy for $840 in cash.

8 Purchased merchandise for $4,000 in cash.

9 Returned unsatisfactory merchandise to Jones, Inc., and received credit for $1,500. G J

13 Sold merchandise to David Evans on account, $7,700; Invoice 1; terms 1/10, n/30.

14 Paid Jones, Inc., and Hill Baker the amounts due.

15 Cash sales from July 1 through 15 were $1,400.

16 Sold merchandise to Kenneth Johnson on account, $6,000; Invoice 2; terms 1/10, n/30.

16 Sold merchandise to George Hooker on account, $5,500; Invoice 3; terms 1/10, n/30.

16 Paid salaries for July 1 through 15 totaling $1,800.

19 Sold merchandise to Stephen Gold on account, $6,000; Invoice 4; terms 1/10, n/30.

21 Purchased merchandise from the Sanders Company on account, $3,700; invoice date, July 21; terms 1/10, n/30. P

21 Received a bill for $130 from the Office Supply Company for items chargeable to Office Expense; terms, n/30. G

23 Received merchandise returned by Stephen Gold; issued Credit Memo 1 for $1,200. G

23 Received cash from David Evans for Invoice 1, less discount. C R

26 Received cash from Kenneth Johnson for Invoice 2, less discount. C R

1973

July 26　Purchased merchandise from Dumont, Inc., on account, $8,000; invoice date, July 24; terms 3/10, n/30. Paid transportation charges of $90.

28　Received $500 cash from George Hooker and an 8-percent, 30-day note for the balance.

28　Sold merchandise to Mason Wills on account, $3,000; Invoice 5; terms 1/10, n/30.

29　Paid $140 in cash for electricity. C P

29　Paid the Sanders Company on the invoice of July 21, less discount. C P

29　Received cash from Stephen Gold for the balance of Invoice 4, less discount. C R

31　Cash sales from July 16 through 31 were $1,700. C R

31　Paid salaries for July 16 through 31 totaling $2,200. C P

31　Received a bill for $66 from the Canter Company for delivery service for the month. G J Purchased two filing cabinets and a typewriter at a cost of $600 and various office supplies at a cost of $200; paid $300 in cash and issued $500 par value capital stock for the balance. C P

Required:

1. Record the transactions in a general journal, a cash receipts journal, a cash payments journal, a sales journal, and a purchases journal.
2. Indicate how the postings would be made from the journals by entering the appropriate posting references.

P6-4. Frye Furniture, Inc., uses a sales journal, a two-column general journal, and a cash receipts journal that includes an Accounts Receivable column. A monthly trial balance is prepared. The accounts receivable ledger is shown:

Rankin Stores

1973						
Jan.	1	Balance	✔			600
	10		S5	300		900
	19		CR3		600	300
	25		J8		50	250
	28		S5	400		650

Stonackers, Inc.

1973						
Jan.	1	Balance	✔			250
	5		CR3		250	—
	11		S5	310		310
	20		S5	450		760
	27		CR3		200	560
	30		J8		10	550

Thomas, Inc.

1973						
Jan.	1	Balance	✔			200
	12		J8		20	180
	15		S5	800		980
	31		CR3		180	800

Required:

1. Reconstruct the Accounts Receivable controlling account exactly as it appeared in the general ledger of Frye Furniture, Inc., after all postings from the journals had been completed, including dates and posting references.
2. Rule and balance the Accounts Receivable account.
3. Verify the ending account balance by preparing a schedule of accounts receivable.

P6-5. The general ledger of Parr Company shows the following account balances on November 1, 1973:

101	Cash	$16,000	205	Notes Payable	$ –0–
111	Accounts Receivable	2,200	251	Capital Stock	60,000
115	Notes Receivable	225	252	Retained Earnings	7,825
125	Merchandise Inventory	32,000	301	Sales	–0–
141	Prepaid Insurance	–0–	305	Sales Returns and	
162	Delivery Equipment	8,000		Allowances	–0–
162A	Accumulated Deprecia-		311	Sales Discounts	–0–
	tion–Delivery		351	Purchases	–0–
	Equipment	800	361	Purchases Returns and	
164	Store Equipment	14,000		Allowances	–0–
164A	Accumulated Deprecia-		365	Purchases Discounts	–0–
	tion–Store Equip-		703	Rent Expense	–0–
	ment	2,000	705	Heat and Light Expense	–0–
201	Accounts Payable	1,800	714	Wages Expense	–0–

The following information was taken from the subsidiary ledgers on October 31, 1973.

Accounts Receivable

Customer	Date of Sale	Terms	Amount
Applebee Company	October 24	2/10, n/30	$ 600
Hillory Company			–0–
Munsin Company	October 14	2/10, n/30	875
Zurback Company	October 31	2/10, n/30	725
Total			$2,200

Accounts Payable

Creditor	Date of Purchase	Terms	Amount
Danvers Company	October 15	1/10 EOM, n/60	$ 465
Jarvis Supply Company	October 6	n/30	835
Kelly Company	October 20	1/15, n/30	500
Total			$1,800

Transactions for November were:

1973

Nov. 1   Purchased merchandise from the Jarvis Supply Company on account, $800; terms n/30.

2   Issued Check 300 in the amount of $300 for a one-year insurance policy.

2   Issued a credit memorandum for $35 to the Zurback Company for the return of merchandise on the sale of October 31.

3   Received a check from the Applebee Company in payment for the sale made on October 24.

1973

Nov. 3 Paid the Kelly Company for the purchase of October 20.

     3 Purchased merchandise from the Danvers Company on account, $800; terms 1/10 EOM, n/60.

     4 Paid the Jarvis Supply Company $335 on account and issued a 60-day, 6-percent promissory note for the balance due on the purchase of October 8.

     4 Paid $180 for the November rent.

   10 Paid the Danvers Company for the purchase of October 15.

   10 Sold merchandise to the Hillory Company on account, $1,500; terms 2/10, n/30.

   11 Issued additional capital stock for $10,000 in cash.

   12 Received a check for $375 from the Munsin Company for the sale of October 14 and an 8-percent, 30-day note for the balance due.

   12 Sold merchandise to the Applebee Company on account, $1,600; terms 2/10, n/30.

   13 Purchased merchandise from the Kelly Company on account, $1,200; terms 1/15, n/30.

   14 Paid semimonthly salaries totaling $360.

   15 Cash sales from November 1 through 15 were $2,750.

   17 Sold merchandise to the Munsin Company on account, $1,550; terms 2/10, n/30.

   18 Received a credit memorandum for $25 from the Kelly Company for the return of defective merchandise.

   19 Received a check from the Hillory Company for $400 on account; no discount was allowed.

   20 Purchased merchandise for $1,800 in cash.

   21 Received a check for $200 from the Applebee Company and a note for the balance due; no discount was allowed.

   27 Received a check from the Munsin Company for the sale of November 17.

   28 Paid the Kelly Company for the purchase made on November 13.

   30 Paid semimonthly salaries totaling $360.

   30 Paid $70 for heat and light for November.

   30 Cash sales from November 16 through 30 were $3,250.

   30 Purchased merchandise from the Kelly Company on account, $1,100; terms 1/15, n/30.

Required:

1. Record the transactions in a sales journal, a purchases journal, a general journal, a cash receipts journal, and a cash payments journal.
2. Open the accounts listed in the general ledger. Using the date November 1, record the account balances.
3. Open the listed accounts in an accounts receivable ledger and an accounts payable ledger. Record the appropriate dates and amounts.
4. Post from the journals to the appropriate ledgers.
5. Prepare a trial balance.
6. Prepare a schedule of accounts receivable and a schedule of accounts payable.

P6-6. The following flow chart and explanation of required symbols are given:

DESCRIPTIVE	FLOW CHART

1. Document the program with your name and date.

2. Print the heading for the report: Gross pay for employees.

3. Read the employee number and hours worked.

4. If employee number is equal to or less than 2,000, calculate the gross pay at $7.00 per hour.

5. If the employee number is greater than 2,000, calculate the gross pay at $5.00 per hour.

6. Print the amount of gross pay for the employee.

7. Repeat until all employees are processed.

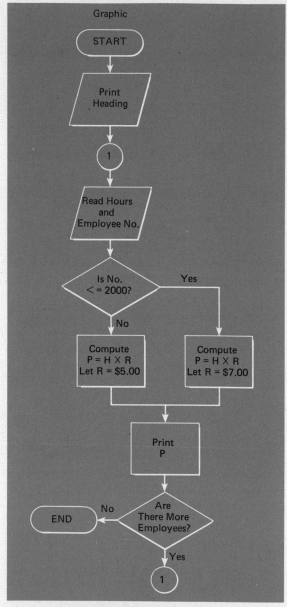

Symbols and their meaning:

$=$ equal to $<$ less than
$>$ greater than $<=$ less than or equal to
$>=$ greater than or equal to

Required: Using the foregoing flow chart as your guide, write a program coded in BASIC. Document the program with your name and the current date. Entitle the report Gross Pay for Employees.

Note. See page 415 for comment about the practice set.

Income
Measurement
and Valuation
Problems
Related
to Sources
and Uses
of Invested
Capital

part

7

The Control of
Cash Receipts
and Disbursements:
Payroll Accounting

Cash includes any item that a bank customarily accepts for deposit. Coins, *currency* (paper money), bank drafts, cashier's checks, money orders, and bank balances are included in the Cash account. Postdated checks and I.O.U.'s are receivables, not cash; postage stamps are prepaid expenses.

Effective management and control of cash is of the greatest importance because cash represents instantly available purchasing power and because nearly every transaction ultimately involves the exchange of cash. The problems of good cash management are twofold: (1) a proper cash balance must be maintained at all times, and (2) adequate safeguards must be established to prevent the theft, or misappropriation, of cash. While emphasizing the control of cash, this chapter deals with *petty cash, bank reconciliation, cash forecasting,* the control of cash disbursements through the use of a *voucher system,* and *payroll control.*

INTERNAL CONTROL

One of the primary functions of management is to protect the assets of a business against avoidable loss. As a business grows in size and complexity, it becomes increasingly important to organize the supervision of the book-keeping and accounting records to control the receipt of cash, to minimize or prevent the unauthorized disbursement of cash, and to eliminate errors. Employees must be carefully selected and trained, and their duties, responsibilities, and authority clearly defined. Adequate organization also requires the separation of duties, so that no one person is in complete charge of any business transaction. An error—whether intentional or not—is more likely to be discovered if a transaction is handled by two or more persons, so that, as far as possible, the work of each employee who records property is checked automatically by some other employee. It is customary business

239

practice, for example, for one person to make the sale and prepare a sales slip and for another person to receive the cash or record the charge to the customer's account; one person may prepare the payroll and another person make the actual payments to employees; one employee may prepare the check for payment to a creditor, another employee or an officer may sign the check, and a third employee may post the debit to the creditor's account. Adequate organization also provides for a regular follow-up to see how well the accounting work is being done. This system of self-policing is referred to as *internal control.*

Cash Control

Cash is naturally vulnerable to theft or misuse. If cash is handled and controlled properly, both the employer and the employee benefit—the employer safeguards the asset and the employee avoids suspicion of inaccuracy or dishonesty. Embezzlers often begin their criminal careers by temporarily borrowing funds from the company, intending to replace the cash. The intention usually falters. It is to the advantage of both employer and employee to institute such safeguards as will deter employees from misappropriating funds. The safeguards must be designed to prevent the following:

1. Misappropriation of cash on receipt and failure to record the transaction in the cash receipts journal. For example, scrap and waste material may be sold by an employee to a scrap dealer for cash and not reported.
2. Delay in recording the receipt of cash (the cash being withheld during the interval), or recording false entries. For example, cash may be pocketed on receipt of a payment from a customer but his account may be credited with an offsetting debit to Sales Returns and Allowances.
3. The recording of fictitious charges to expense accounts or other accounts to cover fraudulent cash withdrawals. For example, a branch supervisor may carry a terminated employee's name on the payroll for several additional pay periods, forging the endorsement of the former employee and appropriating the cash.

Certain basic controls must be instituted to prevent the misuse of funds. The individual responsibility for the flow of cash must be clearly established. An entry to record the receipt of cash must be made promptly. All checks should be rubber-stamped *For deposit only* on receipt to prevent their misuse. All cash receipts should be deposited intact daily; payments should be made by company check and not out of receipts. Mechanical accounting control devices should be used wherever possible.

The protection of cash against losses through fraud, error, and carelessness requires certain fundamental steps, including:

1. A clear segregation of duties and responsibilities.
2. Provision of the necessary facilities, such as cash registers, and furnishing definite instructions with respect to authorization for the removal of property or the payment of cash.
3. Organization of the flow and recording of documents so that, whenever possible, the work of one employee is subject to automatic verification

by another employee. The handling and recording of cash should be so planned that no one person both receives or disburses cash and records it in the cash journals.

4. Periodic testing to see if internal controls are operating effectively. Recorded cash receipts, for example, should be compared at unannounced times with cash on hand and deposits made.

Petty Cash

For adequate internal control, all cash receipts should be deposited intact daily and all disbursements should be made by check. There are occasions, however, when payment by check is impractical, such as for postage, small contributions, express charges, carfare, and minor supplies. A special fund, called the *petty cash fund*, should be set up for these purposes. The fund is placed in the charge of one person, and payments should be supported by signed receipts, called *petty cash vouchers*, that show the purpose of the expenditures, the dates, and the amounts.

To set up the petty cash fund, a check is drawn and cashed for the amount to be placed in the fund. The journal entry is

Petty Cash	50	
Cash		50

The money and the signed vouchers should be secured in the *petty cash box* or *cash register*.

When the cash on hand approaches a stated minimum, or at the end of each month, the fund is replenished; the signed petty cash vouchers serve as evidence of the disbursements. The entry in the cash disbursements journal to record a check for $43 issued to replenish the petty cash fund for certain expenditures made is

Postage Expense	12.00	
Telephone and Telegraph Expense	4.00	
Miscellaneous Selling Expense	14.50	
Miscellaneous General Expense	3.75	
Transportation In	4.25	
Stationery and Printing Expense	4.50	
Cash		43.00

The Petty Cash account in the general ledger remains at its original balance of $50. It does not change unless the amount of the fund itself is either increased or decreased. It is for this reason that the method described here is called the *imprest* (or fixed) petty cash system. The fund should be replenished at the end of each accounting period to record all the expenses incurred during the period and to bring the amount of cash on hand in the fund up to the balance of the Petty Cash account in the general ledger.

The Bank Statement

It is customary for banks to send depositors a monthly statement together with the canceled checks and notices of bank charges and credits. The statement shows the activities for the month; it should list:

1. The beginning balance
2. The deposits received
3. The checks paid
4. Other charges and credits to the account
5. The ending balance

Frederick Hall's bank statement for September, 1973, is shown in Figure 7-1.

The letter combinations listed in the lower section of the bank statement form identify certain entries on the statement.

Certified Check (CC). When the depositor requests a check to be certified, the bank immediately deducts the amount of the check from the depositor's balance.

Total of Listed Checks (LS). A number of checks issued by the depositor may be presented to the bank for payment on the same day. To conserve space, the bank shows only one entry for the total and attaches a listing of the individual amounts to the checks themselves.

Figure 7-1. Bank Statement

```
                    STATEMENT OF ACCOUNT
                           WITH
              UNITED STATES TRUST COMPANY      Frederick Hall
                      BOSTON, MASS.            14 Billings Street
                                               Boston, Mass., 02115
                   Acct. No. 037-325079
```

Checks and Other Debits			Deposits	Date	Balance
Balance forward from last statement.				Sept. 1, 1973	7,320.00
			450.00	Sept. 1	7,770.00
49.00	1,237.00			Sept. 2	6,484.00
			48.00	Sept. 3	6,532.00
175.00	1,300.00 CC			Sept. 6	5,057.00
14.00			1,650.00	Sept. 11	6,693.00
			762.00	Sept. 15	7,455.00
28.50	27.25	275.00	1,312.00	Sept. 18	8,436.25
2,000.00	367.00	2.00 DM	500.00 CM	Sept. 29	6,567.25
4.00 SC				Sept. 30	6,563.25

CC—Certified Check   DM—Debit Memo
LS—Total of Listed Checks   CM—Credit Memo
NSF—Not Sufficient Funds   OD—Overdraft
SC—Service Charge

Not Sufficient Funds (*NSF*). Deposits generally include checks received from trade customers. A customer's check that has been deposited may not clear on presentation for payment because the customer's bank balance is less than the amount of the check. If so, the check is deducted from the depositor's balance, the entry is identified by the letters NSF, and the check is returned to the depositor. The legal authority for this deduction is that credit to the depositor's account for checks deposited is conditional on their being honored on presentment.

Service Charge (*SC*). A service charge is a charge by the bank for acting as a depository for funds. The charge is based on the activity of the account in terms of number of items deposited and checks presented for payment. Credit is generally allowed for interest on the average daily balance.

Debit Memo (*DM*). A debit memo is a deduction from the depositor's account for additional services rendered (or an adjustment of an error); for example, the charge for collecting a note receivable is reported in a debit memo.

Credit Memo (*CM*). A credit memo is a credit, usually shown in the Deposits column, for items collected (or an adjustment of an error); for example, the collection of a note receivable left at the bank by a depositor is reported in a credit memo.

Overdraft (*OD*). An overdraft is the amount by which withdrawals exceed the depositor's available balance. The overdraft, if permitted, is usually entered in red in the Balance column. Because of automatic bank loan renewal arrangements or for other reasons, a bank may pay checks even when an overdraft results. The amount of the overdraft is a current liability.

Depositor's Monthly Bank
Reconciliation Procedure

The use of a checking account facilitates the control of cash. If all cash receipts are deposited intact and all cash payments are made by check, the records of the bank can be *reconciled* regularly with those of the depositor. The *bank reconciliation* underscores the reciprocal relationship between the bank's records and the depositor's. For each entry in the depositor's books, there should be a counterpart in the bank's books. All debits to Cash in the depositor's books should be matched by credit entries to the depositor's account in the bank's books; all credit entries to Cash in the depositor's books should be matched by debit entries to the depositor's account. For instance, cash received from a customer is recorded in the company's books by debiting Cash and crediting Accounts Receivable; the bank, on receiving the cash, debits Cash and credits the depositor's account. The company records a payment to a creditor by debiting Accounts Payable and crediting Cash; the bank debits the depositor's account and credits Cash.

Assuming that every item was properly recognized, no errors were made, and the beginning balances were equal, the reciprocal accounts would show the following:

DEPOSITOR'S BOOKS

Cash (Name of Bank)   Acct. No. 101

Opening balance Deposits made to bank Bank credit memos	Checks issued Bank debit memos

BANK'S BOOKS

Frederick Hall   Acct. No. 037-325079

Checks cleared Debit memos	Opening balance Deposits received Credit memos

The records of the depositor and of the bank will not normally agree at the end of the month because of items that appear on one record but not on the other. It is necessary, therefore, to reconcile the two balances and to determine the *adjusted*, or true, cash balance. Discrepancies between the balances may be due to the time lag in recording debits and credits, special charges and credits of which either the depositor or the bank is unaware, or to errors and irregularities.

The bank reconciliation is prepared as follows:

1. The deposits shown on the bank statement are compared with those entered in the cash receipts journal. Deposits made too late in the month to be credited by the bank on the current statement are referred to as *deposits in transit*. The bank reconciliation for the previous month should be inspected for any deposits in transit at the end of that period; they should appear as the initial deposits of the current period. Any items not on the statement should be reconciled.

2. Checks paid and returned by the bank (*canceled checks*) are arranged in numerical order and compared with the entries in the cash disbursements journal. Checks that have not yet been presented for payment are called *outstanding checks*. The previous bank reconciliation should be inspected for outstanding checks.

3. Special debits and credits made by the bank—usually reported in debit or credit memos—are compared with the depositor's books to see if they have already been recorded.

4. Any errors in the bank's or the depositor's records that become apparent during completion of the prior steps are listed.

A pro forma bank reconciliation is given in Figure 7-2. Errors and adjustments in the Per Books section require entries in the general journal to correct the books; adjustments in the Per Bank section do not require entries.

Frederick Hall's August bank reconciliation is shown in Figure 7-3. Note that the ending cash balance per the bank is the same as the beginning balance of the September statement (Figure 7-1).

Figure 7-2. Pro Forma Bank Reconciliation

```
                              NAME
                        Bank Reconciliation
                              Date

                           Per Books

Cash Balance per Ledger                                          $xxx
   Add:      (1) Any proper increases in cash already recorded
                 by the bank that have not been recorded as yet
                 by the firm
                    Example: Collection of note by bank          $xx
             (2) Any error in the firm's books that failed to reveal
                 a proper increase in cash or that improperly
                 decreased cash
                    Example: Check from customer for $90 entered
                             as $70                               xx      xx
                    Total                                                $xxx
   Deduct:   (1) Any proper decreases in cash already recorded
                 by the bank that have not been recorded as yet
                 by the firm
                    Example: Bank service charges                $xx
             (2) Any error in the firm's books that failed to reveal
                 a proper decrease in cash or that improperly
                 increased cash
                    Example: Check issued in payment to a creditor
                             for $462 entered as $426             xx      xx
Adjusted Cash Balance                                                   $xxx


                           Per Bank

Cash Balance per Bank Statement                                         $xxx
   Add:      (1) Any proper increases in cash already recorded
                 by the firm that have not been recorded as yet
                 by the bank
                    Example: Deposits in transit                 $xx
             (2) Any error by the bank that failed to reveal a
                 proper increase in cash or that improperly
                 decreased cash
                    Example: Another depositor's check incorrectly
                             charged to this depositor's account  xx      xx
                    Total                                                $xxx
   Deduct:   (1) Any proper decreases in cash already recorded
                 by the firm that have not been recorded as yet
                 by the bank
                    Example: Outstanding checks                  $xx
             (2) Any error by the bank that failed to reveal a
                 proper decrease in cash or that improperly
                 increased cash
                    Example: Firm's deposit of $679 entered by
                             bank as $697                         xx      xx
Adjusted Cash Balance                                                   $xxx
```

Figure 7-3. Bank Reconciliation

FREDERICK HALL
Bank Reconciliation
August 31, 1973

Cash Balance per Ledger, August 31, 1973		$6,400
Adjusted Cash Balance, August 31, 1973		$6,400
Cash Balance per Bank Statement		
August 31, 1973		$7,320
Add: Deposit in transit, August 31, 1973		450
Total		$7,770
Deduct: Outstanding checks		

Check	Amount	
680	$ 49	
694	1,237	
701	84	$1,370

Adjusted Cash Balance, August 31, 1973 $6,400

Hall's cash records for September show the following:

Cash Deposits

1973		
Sept. 3		$ 48.00
10		1,650.00
14		762.00
18		1,312.00
30		1,050.00
		$4,822.00

Checks Issued

1973		
Sept. 2	702	$ 175.00
5	703	1,300.00
8	704	14.00
15	705	82.50
15	706	312.25
18	707	27.25
26	708	2,000.00
26	709	367.00
30	710	103.00
		$4,381.00

The statement received from the bank (Figure 7-1) shows a balance of $6,563.25 as of September 30, 1973. The following items were received from the bank together with the bank statement:

Canceled Checks:	Check	Amount
	680	$ 49.00
	694	1,237.00
	702	175.00
	703	1,300.00
	704	14.00
	705	28.50
	707	27.25
	708	2,000.00
	709	367.00
	Check of Frederick Hale	275.00

Memos:

Credit memo, $500, for a note receivable collected by the bank on September 29.

Debit memo, $2, dated September 29, for collection fee charged by bank.

Notification of a certified check for $1,300 deducted on September 6. (Even if the certified check, Check 703, had not been canceled by the bank during September it would not be listed as outstanding, because it has been entered on both Hall's and the bank's records and would therefore not need to be reconciled.)

Service charge notification, $4, dated September 30.

Figure 7-4. Bank Reconciliation

FREDERICK HALL
Bank Reconciliation
September 30, 1973

Per Books

Cash Balance per Ledger, September 30, 1973		$6,841.00
Add: Customer's note collected by bank		500.00
Error in entering Check 705:		
Entered as	$82.50	
Correct amount	28.50	54.00
Total		$7,395.00
Deduct: Bank service charge	$ 4.00	
Collection fee	2.00	6.00
Adjusted Cash Balance, September 30, 1973		$7,389.00

Per Bank

Cash Balance per Bank Statement, September 30, 1973		$6,563.25
Add: Deposit of Sept. 30 in transit to bank		1,050.00
Check of Frederick Hale deducted by bank in error		275.00
Total		$7,888.25
Deduct: Outstanding checks		

	Check	Amount	
	701	$ 84.00	
	706	312.25	
	710	103.00	499.25
Adjusted Balance, September 30, 1973			$7,389.00

Following receipt of the bank statement, Hall prepares the bank reconciliation statement shown in Figure 7-4 (see Figures 7-1 and 7-3 for support data).

The following points should be emphasized:

1. The beginning balance in the Per Books section is taken from the general ledger Cash account; it was determined as follows:

Cash Balance per Ledger, August 31, 1973 (Figure 7-3)	$ 6,400
Add deposits	4,822
Total	$11,222
Deduct checks issued	4,381
Cash Balance per Ledger, September 30, 1973	$ 6,841

2. Check 705 was incorrectly recorded as $82.50 instead of $28.50 in Hall's books. The error overstated cash disbursements and therefore understated the ending cash balance by $54 ($82.50 — $28.50).

3. The beginning balance in the Per Bank section is the last amount in the Balance column of the bank statement for the month of September (Figure 7-1).

4. The deposit of $1,050 made on September 30 was not credited on the bank statement because it was in transit.

5. While determining the outstanding checks, Hall discovered that the bank had deducted in error a check for $275 signed by another depositor, Frederick Hale. This resulted in an understatement of the bank balance on the bank statement. The bank was notified about this error.

6. Check 701 was listed as an outstanding check on the bank reconciliation of August 31 (Figure 7-3). Since it has not yet been presented to the bank for payment, it continues to be listed as an outstanding check.

All the items that appear in the Per Bank section of the bank reconciliation for the previous month must be traced to the current month's bank statement. For example, a deposit not credited in the prior month should appear with the initial deposits for the current month; similarly, improper charges or credits of the preceding month should be adjusted on the current month's statement.

All additions to, and deductions from, the balance per books must be entered on Hall's books to bring the general ledger Cash account balance into agreement with the adjusted cash balance. The Cash account balance of $6,841 should be increased by $548 ($500 + $54 — $6) to show the actual cash balance of $7,389 as of September 30, 1973.

The required entries are

Cash	498	
Bank Service and Collection Charges Expense	2	
Notes Receivable		500
To record collection of sight draft by bank and related charge.		
Cash	54	
Accounts Payable		54
To record correction for error in entering Check 705 as $82.50 instead of $28.50.		
Bank Service and Collection Charges Expense	4	
Cash		4
To record bank service charge for September.		

These entries may be made in the cash journals for September if the journals have not been footed and posted, or the following compound entry may be made in the general journal:

Cash	548	
Bank Service and Collection Charges Expense	6	
Notes Receivable		500
Accounts Payable		54
To adjust the Cash account per		
bank reconciliation for		
September.		

After the entry is posted, Hall's Cash account appears as shown. Note that the beginning balance for the new period (October) agrees with the adjusted cash balance in the bank reconciliation.

	Cash					Acct. No. 101
1973				1973		
Sept. 1	(beginning balance)	6,400		Sept. 30	(checks issued)	4,381
30	(cash deposits)	4,822		30	Balance	7,389
30	(adjustment)	548				
		11,770				11,770
1973						
Oct. 1	Balance	7,389				

Only those items that either increase or decrease the balance per books need to be entered in the journal. Those items that increase or decrease the balance per bank already have been recorded on the depositor's books. If a running cash balance is maintained in the checkbook, the necessary adjustments must also be made there.

The form of bank reconciliation shown in Figure 7-4 is commonly used because the adjusted cash balance is a significant figure; it represents the true cash balance, the amount subject to withdrawal. The form also may be prepared in advance and the items entered directly into the appropriate sections as they are determined.

Cash Short or Over

The daily count of cash in the cash registers may differ from the cash register readings. If the records do not disclose a clerical error, it may be assumed that the shortage or overage was caused by an error in making change. The discrepancy may be entered temporarily in the books as a debit or credit to Cash Short or Over. To illustrate, assume that the cash register tape shows cash sales for the day of $100 but the count shows the cash on hand to be $101.50. The journal entry to record the cash sales and the cash overage is

Cash	101.50	
Sales		100.00
Cash Short or Over		1.50

If the cash count showed $98.50, the entry would be

Cash	98.50	
Cash Short or Over	1.50	
Sales		100.00

Cash Short or Over is classified on the income statement as General Expense if a debit or Other Revenue if a credit.

MANAGEMENT CONTROLS—CASH FORECASTS

The managers of a business must make certain that adequate cash funds are available at all times. Good management requires that sufficient cash be available for the timely payment of invoices, payrolls, and other costs and operating expenses. An adequate cash balance is also essential to maintain a good credit rating. But excessive cash balances, particularly during inflationary period when cash suffers a loss of purchasing power, indicate ineffective management of cash resources.

The regular cash needs of the business should be anticipated to ensure that purchases and expenses can be met promptly; that bank loans can be paid at maturity; that taxes and dividend payments can be met; that funds will be available for additional machinery, equipment, and buildings; and that excess funds, if any, are appropriately invested. All this requires a projected plan, or *cash forecast*, for a number of months in advance. The period covered by the forecast may be one month, three months, six months, or a year, depending on how accurately a company is able to forecast its receipts and disbursements. Some companies make fairly accurate forecasts for the next three-month period and rougher approximations for the remaining nine months. If the cash balance is low and sales are erratic, weekly forecasts may be desirable.

A cash forecast is a projection based on a careful analysis of prior periods, with appropriate adjustments for anticipated changes. The forecast deals exclusively with estimates involving *cash*. Noncash items such as depreciation are excluded. The cash forecast is a summary of projected cash receipts, cash disbursements, and resulting cash balances for the budgeted periods. Cash receipts from customers are projected on the basis of estimated sales and collection patterns experienced in prior periods. Other cash collections are generally lesser in amount and can be readily identified as to period of collectibility. When cash disbursements are forecast, consideration must be given to the various goods and services to be purchased and the timing of the required payments. Detailed operating forecasts are prepared for such items as materials and supplies, utilities, rent, payrolls, and taxes, from which the required cash disbursements are determined. The forms and schedules used should provide for the comparison of actual results with estimates so that any *variances* may be analyzed. If the variances indicate significant errors in the original estimates, corresponding revisions should be made in future forecasts.

The cash forecast of the Sterns Company for the first quarter of 1974 (Figure 7-5) is prepared from the following estimates:

	January	February	March
Cash sales	$ 7,500	$ 8,750	$ 9,200
Credit sales	30,000	35,000	37,000
Purchases of merchandise on account	22,000	20,000	30,000
Selling expenses	5,000	7,000	7,500
General and administrative expenses	6,000	6,500	7,000
Interest earned on investments	300	300	300
Taxes	350	400	425
Miscellaneous expenses	1,000	1,100	1,300

Estimated cash balance, January 1, is $12,500

Estimated purchases of merchandise on account for December, total $25,000

Sales are billed on terms of 2/10, n/30, but collections are expected as follows:
   80% within the month of billing and also within the discount period
   10% in the month following billing and after discount period
   8% in the second month following billing
   2% generally prove to be uncollectible

Estimated credit sales for November are $26,000; and for December, $29,000

The company buys merchandise on terms of 1/15, n/30. It is expected that discounts will be taken on all payments, which are made as follows:
   60% in the month of purchase
   40% in the month following purchase

Figure 7-5 Cash Forecast

STERNS COMPANY
Cash Forecast
For Three Months Ending March 31, 1974

	January	February	March
Cash balance at beginning of month	$12,500	$13,482	$19,700
Add: Estimated cash receipts			
Cash sales	7,500	8,750	9,200
Collections on accounts receivable (Schedule A)	28,500	32,760	34,908
Interest earned on investments	300	300	300
Total available cash	$48,800	$55,292	$64,108
Deduct: Estimated disbursements			
Payments on purchases of merchandise (Schedule B)	$22,968	$20,592	$25,740
Selling expenses	5,000	7,000	7,500
General and administrative expenses	6,000	6,500	7,000
Taxes	350	400	425
Miscellaneous expenses	1,000	1,100	1,300
Total disbursements	$35,318	$35,592	$41,965
Cash balance at end of month	$13,482	$19,700	$22,143

To compute the cash balance at the end of the month, the beginning balance is added to the estimated cash receipts for that month and the anticipated disbursements for the month are deducted. The ending cash balance of any month is the beginning cash balance of the next month.

Figure 7-6. Forecast of Collections from Customers

		January	February	March
STERNS COMPANY				*Schedule A*
Forecast of Collections on Accounts Receivable				
For Three Months Ending March 31, 1974				
November credit sales:				
$26,000 × 0.08		$ 2,080		
December credit sales:				
$29,000 × 0.10		2,900		
$29,000 × 0.08			$ 2,320	
January credit sales:				
$30,000 × 0.80	$24,000			
Deduct discounts	480	23,520		
$30,000 × 0.10			3,000	
$30,000 × 0.08				$ 2,400
February credit sales:				
$35,000 × 0.80	$28,000			
Deduct discounts	560		27,440	
$35,000 × 0.10				3,500
March credit sales:				
$37,000 × 0.80	$29,600			
Deduct discounts	592			29,008
Total monthly collections		$28,500	$32,760	$34,908

Figure 7-7. Forecast of Payments to Creditors

	January	February	March
STERNS COMPANY			*Schedule B*
Forecast of Payments of Purchases of Merchandise			
For Three Months Ending March 31, 1974			
December purchases:			
$25,000 × 0.40	$10,000		
January purchases:			
$22,000 × 0.60	13,200		
$22,000 × 0.40		$ 8,800	
February purchases:			
$20,000 × 0.60		12,000	
$20,000 × 0.40			$ 8,000
March purchases:			
$30,000 × 0.60			18,000
Totals	$23,200	$20,800	$26,000
Deduct discounts	232	208	260
Total monthly payments	$22,968	$20,592	$25,740

Management uses the cash forecast to determine whether sufficient cash will be available for tax payments, dividends, acquisition of equipment, or purchases of securities as investments. At the end of each month, the actual amount of each item is entered in an extra column headed Actual to provide a month-by-month comparison with the budgeted figures.

CASH DISBURSEMENTS CONTROL

INTRODUCTION

Two separate but related issues are now considered: (1) control of cash disbursements through the use of a *voucher system* and (2) payroll. These two areas have a high degree of practical significance. Some system of authorizing and verifying cash disbursements—the basic elements of a voucher system—is used by nearly all businesses. Also, virtually all businesses are required by law to withhold specified amounts from their employees' earnings. Businesses in turn are subject to various tax levies based on the payroll.

THE VOUCHER SYSTEM

The accounting system must be designed not only to enable the recording of transactions and the preparation of financial statements but also to achieve other managerial objectives: (1) to furnish analyses and reports of past, current, and projected events and (2) to establish internal controls to protect the assets of the business against loss through errors or fraud. The achievement of these objectives goes hand in hand with the achievement of maximum operating efficiency and maximum earnings. A properly functioning voucher system plays a key role in establishing and maintaining effective internal control.

The voucher system is a method of accumulating, verifying, recording, and disbursing all the expenditures of a business. The system covers any transaction that will require the payment of cash, including the purchase of merchandise, services, supplies, and plant and equipment, and the payment of expenses. Expenditures are verified, classified, and recorded when they are incurred. All expenditures must be properly authorized and, except for petty cash transactions, are paid by check.

Reference has been made to the importance of having a built-in system to protect the assets of a business against loss through fraud or error. The voucher system is designed to achieve this internal control by assigning the duties of authorizing expenditure, reporting the receipt of goods or services, and signing checks in settlement of the liability to different persons or different departments. This division of duties prevents cash being disbursed from the business without the knowledge and approval of several members of the organization.

The Voucher

The *voucher* is a serially numbered form that is the written authorization for each expenditure. It is prepared from the seller's invoice or group of invoices or from other documents that serve as evidence of the expenditure. The voucher form is tailored to meet the needs of the particular business.

The voucher, not the invoice, is the basis for the accounting entry. The invoice together with acknowledgments or approvals of the receipt of goods or services and other supporting papers are the underlying documents for the voucher. Some of these documents are discussed in detail later in this chapter. The voucher form provides space for:

1. A summary of the invoice data
2. The accounts to be debited
3. The details of payment
4. The signature of the person who authorizes the payment
5. The signature of the person who records the voucher

The Voucher Jacket

The *voucher jacket* is a folded voucher form or envelope that serves both as a voucher and as a cover for the invoice, or group of invoices from a particular vendor, and related documents. Space is provided on the outside of the jacket form for the details needed for the accounting entry.

Assume that during January, 1973, the Ajax Company received ten invoices from a creditor, the Silver Company, with terms of 2/10 EOM, n/30. Upon receipt, the invoices are verified for quantities, prices, and extensions and are filed in a voucher jacket. The total price of the invoices, shown on the voucher jacket, is entered in the journal to record the liability and to classify the expenditures. The unpaid vouchers are then filed according to their due date so that payment will be made within the discount period. Another advantage of filing unpaid vouchers according to due date is that the amount of cash needed daily to pay vouchers due may be readily determined. Paid vouchers are filed alphabetically.

The Voucher Register

The *voucher register*[1] is an elaboration of the purchases journal. It is a journal for recording all liabilities approved for payment. The register is ruled in columns for the frequently used accounts to be charged or credited. The precise form of the register and the number and arrangement of the column headings vary with the needs of the particular business.

The function of the Vouchers Payable account is the same as that of the Accounts Payable account. It is a controlling account—its balance represents the total of the unpaid vouchers recorded in the voucher register. Unpaid vouchers may, therefore, be readily determined to be those without entries on the corresponding line of the Paid column or those in the *unpaid voucher* file. At the end of the period, a list of the unpaid vouchers should be prepared for reconciliation with the balance of the Vouchers Payable account in the general ledger.

The voucher register is used for recording all transactions—of whatever category except petty cash—requiring a cash payment. Each transaction is entered in the voucher register first, followed by an entry in the check register when

[1] A voucher register is illustrated in the *Student's Self-Study Guide* which accompanies this text.

payment is made. The check register is a book of original entry for all cash disbursements except petty cash. The vouchers are entered in the voucher register in numerical order. Transactions involving liabilities that are not initially credited to Vouchers Payable—notes payable and accrued expenses, for example—are usually not entered in the voucher register until payment is due. Vouchers are not prepared for accrued expenses; rather, a voucher is prepared for the full amount when the invoice is received or when payment is to be made.

An entry is made in the Credit Vouchers Payable column for the amount due on each voucher. The account or accounts to be debited are indicated on the voucher, and entries are made in one of the special debit columns or in the Other General Ledger Accounts column if no special column is available.

The Check Register

No payment is made until a specific voucher has been prepared, recorded, and approved. Hence, each entry is a debit to Vouchers Payable, a credit to Cash, and a credit to Purchases Discounts, if any. No other columns are needed because the transaction already has been classified under an appropriate heading in the voucher register. Checks are entered in the check register in numerical sequence, one line to each check. At the time that the check is entered in the check register, a notation must also be made in the Paid column of the voucher register showing the date of payment and the check number.

Use of the Voucher Register and the Check Register

The voucher register form must be tailored to meet the needs of the particular enterprise. The register provides columns for each general class of expenditure—Selling Expense Control, and General and Administrative Expense Control, for example—with space to the left of each general column for the account number of the specific detail account to be debited. This gives the advantage of virtually unlimited flexibility combined with economy of space.

The check register will include a Purchases Discounts column if the vouchers are recorded in the voucher register at gross amounts. This register shows not only the serial number of the check but also the number of the voucher being paid.

Some companies prepare each voucher for the net amount due. This means that if payment is not made within the discount period, an additional voucher will be required, underscoring the expense for lost discounts. The entry in the voucher register for the additional voucher is (the amount is assumed)

Purchases Discounts Lost	5	
Vouchers Payable		5

One check is made out for the full amount due as shown by the two vouchers.

The Control of Unpaid Vouchers

The unpaid vouchers can be readily determined—they are the ones that have not been marked either "Paid" or "Canceled" in the Paid column. A schedule of unpaid vouchers is prepared at the end of the month; the total should correspond to the balance of the Vouchers Payable account in the general ledger and should equal the total of the vouchers in the unpaid file.

Elimination of the Accounts Payable Ledger

When the voucher system is used, the subsidiary accounts payable ledger can be eliminated. Each numbered voucher is entered on a separate line in the voucher register and may be considered as a credit to a separate account. When the liability is settled and a notation is made in the Paid column, it is equivalent to a debit to that account. The file of unpaid vouchers replaces the accounts payable ledger. The total of the unpaid vouchers must agree with the total of the Vouchers Payable controlling account.

Paying the Voucher—the Voucher Check

If a company pays all its invoices within the discount period, it may use the voucher check system. This system involves the use of a two-part form in triplicate prepared on the vouchering date. One part is the check; the other part, separated by a perforation, is in the form of a remittance letter ruled to indicate the invoices being paid, the discounts taken, and the amount of the check. The first copy—an exact copy of the original but not perforated—may serve as the voucher jacket; invoices and other related documents are attached to it. This voucher copy is filed alphabetically and provides a complete credit file. The second copy may be filed either numerically or chronologically and provides a record of all authorized paid vouchers. This copy may be modified to provide additional columns for the accounts and amounts debited and credited.

Advantages of the Voucher System

In a properly functioning voucher system, all invoices must be verified and approved for payment. As a result, responsibility is fixed and the possibility of error or fraud is reduced. The recording of all vouchers in a single journal (the voucher register) provides for prompt recognition and proper distribution of assets, liabilities, costs, and expenses. Economy in recording is effected by the elimination of the accounts payable ledger and by grouping invoices under a single voucher. The maintenance of a chronological unpaid voucher file facilitates the payment of invoices when they are due. This file also enables management to determine its future cash needs for the settlement of liabilities without loss of discounts. The systematic filing of paid vouchers provides a ready reference source for data and underlying documents in support of all disbursements.

On the other hand, the voucher system has certain limitations. The difficulties in handling special transactions and the need for the preparation of separate vouchers or voucher jackets involve extra clerical and accounting work. The elimination of the accounts payable ledger results in a loss of valuable reference data, although this may be overcome by maintaining an alphabetical file by vendor of copies of all vouchers.

THE ROLE OF SUPPORTING DOCUMENTS IN THE ACCOUNTING SYSTEM

Supporting business forms are basic to any accounting system. Much time and effort is devoted by the employees of the enterprise in preparing, using, and filing these forms, which vary widely in shape, size, color, and content. These forms—sales slips, invoices, vouchers, cash register tapes, bank statements, insurance policies, contracts, leases, pension plans, labor agreements, negotiable instruments, mortgages—constitute the starting point as well as the evidence for the recording of accounting transactions in the journals. If the entry is cross referenced to the supporting documents, the need for a detailed explanation accompanying each entry in the journals is eliminated.

The forms are not only evidence of the accounting transaction, they are also a means of transmitting information and a basis for analyses, studies, and special reports. The sales slip, for example, authorizes the withdrawal of merchandise from stock, serves as the basis for recording the sales and the inventory reduction, and also may be used as a source of data for a special study of sales by type and quantity of product sold.

Three supporting documents commonly used in the voucher system are:

1. The purchase order
2. The receiving report
3. The vendor's invoice

Purchase Order

The purchase order originates in the purchasing department. It is the written authorization to the vendor to supply goods, setting forth the descriptions and quantities, delivery dates, shipping and billing instructions, and specific terms and conditions: in effect, it is the legal contract between buyer and seller. Multiple copies of the order are prepared and distributed to several departments to inform them of what is on order. The original and one copy are sent to the vendor; the copy is signed by the vendor as an acknowledgment of receipt of the purchase order and returned to the buyer. Other copies may be distributed to the receiving department, the accounting department, the department or person who requested that the purchase be made, and others, depending on the existing conditions.

Receiving Report

The receiving report is prepared in the receiving department and is a record of the quantity, quality, condition, and description of the goods received. The receiving report may consist simply of notations on a copy of the purchase order or the *packing slip* sent by the vendor with the shipment. Larger companies prepare multiple copies of receiving reports for distribution to the purchasing department, accounting department, and any other departments or persons involved.

Invoice

The invoice is the form sent by the seller to the buyer and is the charge, or *bill*, for the materials or services supplied. The invoice shows the quantity, description, and price of the merchandise shipped; the buyer's name and address; the date and the invoice number; and the terms of payment. It is held until the goods are received, at which time it is compared with the purchase order and the receiving report for the quantity and quality of goods received, the charges, and the terms. Upon approval of the invoice, a voucher is prepared and the purchase is recorded.

Figure 7-8 illustrates the role of documents in the accounting system.

Figure 7-8. An Accounting Flow

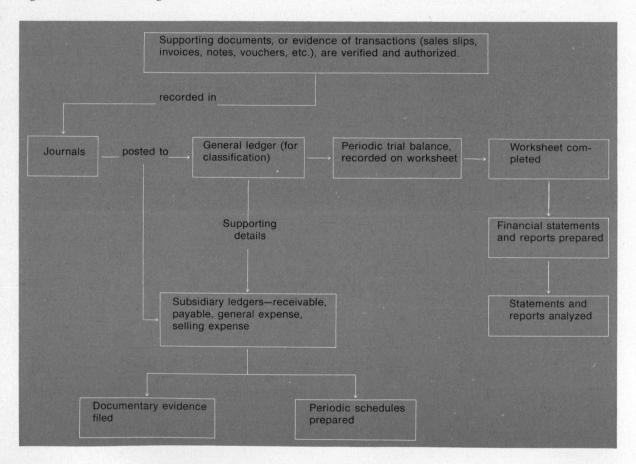

MANAGERIAL CONTROL OF PAYROLL

The payroll of a firm is a significant part of total expense, making continuous management control essential. The availability of machines and high-speed electronic equipment has facilitated the processing of payroll data and the establishment of effective controls at a reasonable cost.

Effective managerial control of payroll requires that

1. Management has properly authorized the payroll payment.
2. Wages paid are correct and have been received by authorized employees; that is, for example, that no fictitious names or names of persons no longer employed have been listed on the payroll.
3. The numerous reports based on payroll information that are made to governmental agencies, union organizations, and employees are reliable.

Payroll Deductions

It is unusual for an employee to receive the full (*gross*) amount of his salary or wages. Some deductions are required by law and must be *withheld* by the employer from the employee's regular pay. These include the following:

1. Federal income taxes of the employee
2. Old-Age, Survivors, and Disability Insurance (OASDI) and Hospitalization Insurance Tax (both often referred to as *F.I.C.A.*, for Federal Insurance Contributions Act, or the social security tax)
3. State unemployment tax (in some states)

Other deductions are optional with the employee, such as for the purchase of U.S. savings bonds or corporate stock; group, life, accident, and hospitalization insurance; and savings clubs. Deductions may also be required under union agreements or to settle other claims. The deductions are paid to the Federal and state governments and other designated agencies. Adequate records must be maintained to account for the deductions and their related liabilities and to prepare the required reports to the agencies involved.

Fair Labor Standards Act

The Fair Labor Standards Act—popularly known as the "Federal Wage and Hour Law"—relates to industries engaged directly in the production of goods for interstate commerce. It currently requires that workers not specifically exempted be paid a minimum hourly rate and an overtime wage of *time and one half*, or one and one-half times the hourly rate, for time worked over 40 hours a week. If no more than 40 hours are worked in a week, no overtime compensation need be paid regardless of the number of hours worked in any one day. Employers and employees may, of course, agree to more favorable terms, such as time and one half for all work over eight hours in any day and double time for Sunday or holiday work. The act does not place a limitation on total working time; it fixes the 40-hour work week as the basis for overtime pay.

The Social Security Act and Payroll Deductions

The Social Security Act (approved on August 14, 1935) is a Federal law, operated in part by the states with assistance from the Federal government. The act includes programs to provide funds for payments to employees who have lost their jobs and for the payment of benefits to retired workers, their families, and their survivors, and health insurance for the aged (Medicare). These programs are financed by taxes on wages and on self-employment income at rates and maximum annual amounts as specified and as changed from time to time by Congress. Funds for the payment of benefits to retired workers are provided by a tax imposed on both employers and employees, at the same rate. Funds for the payment of unemployment benefits are provided by a tax on the employer. These financing programs are commonly referred to as the "Federal Unemployment Tax Act" (F.U.T.A.) and the "Federal Insurance Contributions Act" (F.I.C.A.). Since all the states have their own state unemployment compensation laws, there is a tie-in between the federal and the state unemployment compensation systems.

The Federal Insurance Contributions Tax. Under the provisions of the Federal Insurance Contributions Act, the employer is required to continue to withhold the employee's share of the tax during each calendar year until the currently prevailing maximum amount has been withheld. An employee who works for more than one employer during the year may, as a result, pay more than the annual maximum. The excess may be treated as income tax withheld by the employee when he files his Federal income tax return (Form 1040). Some groups are exempt from the F.I.C.A. withholding requirement, and some who are exempted from the Federal income tax withholding requirements are subject to F.I.C.A. tax withholding. The reader should keep informed of all recent amendments or provisions that may have altered rates, amounts, and eligible groups. Current tables of F.I.C.A. tax withholding rates are available in Circular E, *Employer's Withholding Tax Guide,* published by the Internal Revenue Service.

Because the F.I.C.A. tax rate and the applicable maximum earnings base may be changed by Congress at any time,[2] and to simplify the computations, a combined rate of 10 percent—5 percent each on employer and on employee—applicable to the first $10,000 paid to an employee during a calendar year is used in all illustrations and problems in this textbook. The accounting principles and recording procedures are the same irrespective of the rates used.

Federal Income Tax Withholding. Employers are required by the Federal Revenue Act to make deductions from each employee's earnings for Federal income taxes. The amount that the employer is required to withhold (certain classes of wage payments are exempt) depends on the total number of exemptions that the employee claims, the employee's earnings, and the frequency of the payroll period. Upon being hired, the employee fills out an Employee's Withholding Exemption Certificate, Form W-4, indicating the number of exemptions he wishes to claim. A new form is filed when there is a change in the number of exemptions. The employee may claim exemptions for (1) himself, (2) his wife (unless she is employed and claims her own exemption), and (3) each qualified dependent.

---

[2]Projected tax rates are as follows:

Period	Rates (percent)
1971–1972	5.2
1973–1975	5.65
1976–1979	5.85
1980–1986	5.95
1987 and after	6.05

Additional exemptions may be claimed for old age (65 years or older) and blindness of the claimant or his wife. Since tax rates are subject to change, persons responsible for payrolls should be acquainted with the latest tax rates and regulations, both Federal and state, and in some cases, municipal. The Internal Revenue Service furnishes withholding tables for different payroll periods in its circular E.

Other Deductions. In some states, employees as well as employers are taxed under the state unemployment insurance programs. A number of states and some cities levy income taxes on the gross earnings of the employee. In some states, employees are taxed to provide funds for the cost of disability benefits. Such additional tax assessments are generally deducted from gross earnings by the employer and forwarded to the designated agencies.

Recording and Paying the Payroll

Accurate payroll records are necessary to determine operating expenses and to report earnings information to employees and to Federal, state, and other agencies. The records must show the names, earnings, and payroll deductions of all employees for each pay period. An individual record for each employee showing his earnings and deductions must also be kept. A general journal entry is made to record the payroll for the pay period. Assume that the Burns Company payroll entry for the week ended January 28, 1973, was as follows:

Salesmen's Salaries Expence	1,018.00	
Executive Salaries Expense	750.00	
Office Salaries Expense	320.00	
F.I.C.A. Taxes Payable (assumed rate of 5%)		104.40
Income Tax Withholding Payable		218.80
Bond Deductions Payable		47.50
Salaries and Wages Payable		1,717.30
To record the payroll for the week ended January 28.		

The debits are to a selling expense account for $1,018 and to two general and administrative expense accounts for $1,070, or a total payroll of $2,088, of which the employees' *take-home* pay is $1,717.30.

Employer's Payroll Taxes

In addition to the amounts that he must withhold from employees' pay, the employer must also pay payroll taxes.

F.I.C.A. Tax. The Federal Insurance Contributions Act levies a tax on employers to help finance the social security program. The rates and maximum amounts are applicable equally to employer and employee.

Federal Unemployment Compensation Tax. The Federal Unemployment Compensation Tax Act provides for an additional tax on the employer at a specified rate and up to a limited amount on wages paid. To simplify the computations, it will be assumed that the maximum rate is 5 percent on the first $5,000 paid to each employee covered during each calendar year with 4 percent payable to the State and 1 percent to the Federal government.

State Unemployment Compensation Tax. All the states have laws requiring the payment of an unemployment compensation tax. Funds are provided by a payroll tax levy on the employer and, in several states, on both the employer and the employees. Unemployed persons who qualify for benefits are paid by a state agency from funds acquired through the tax.

State unemployment tax laws vary in their detail and application. There are maximum rates which may be reduced on a *merit basis* if the employer's annual contributions are sufficiently in excess of withdrawals for unemployment payments made to discharged employees. The *merit-rating plan* provides an incentive to employers to maintain steady employment.

Recording the Employer's Payroll Tax Expense

The employer's payroll tax expense may be recorded at the end of each payroll period or at the end of each month. Assuming that the Burns Company records the payroll tax expense for each payroll and that, due to its merit-rating record, it is subject to a state unemployment tax rate of only 2 percent, the accrued payroll tax liability for the week ended January 28 is computed as follows:

F.I.C.A. tax ($2,088 $\times$ 0.05)	$104.40
State unemployment compensation tax ($2,088 $\times$ 0.02)	41.76
Federal unemployment compensation tax ($2,088 $\times$ 0.01)	20.88
Total	$167.04

The general journal entry to record the expense is:

Payroll Tax Expense	167.04	
F.I.C.A. Taxes Payable		104.40
State Unemployment Taxes Payable		41.76
Federal Unemployment Taxes Payable		20.88
To record accrued payroll taxes for week ended January 28.		

The debit is to the Payroll Tax Expense account; the three credits are the accrued liabilities to the Federal and state agencies. The liability for F.I.C.A. taxes ($104.40) matches the amount deducted from the employees' wages. In this entry, payroll taxes were based on $2,088, assuming that all the earnings were subject to payroll taxes. Earnings of any employee in excess of current maximums are not subject to payroll taxes. Assume, for example, that the Burns Company payroll for the week ended October 27 was $3,050, including $1,200 of nontaxable F.I.C.A. earnings and $2,000 of nontaxable unemployment compensation earnings. The accrued payroll tax liability is computed as follows:

	F.I.C.A. Tax	Unemployment Taxes
Total payroll	$3,050	$3,050
Payroll (in excess of maximum) not subject to F.I.C.A. tax	1,200	
Payroll (in excess of maximum) not subject to unemployment taxes		2,000
Payroll subject to taxes	$1,850	$1,050

Payroll taxes	
F.I.C.A. tax ($1,850 × 0.05)	$ 92.50
State unemployment compensation	
tax ($1,050 × 0.02)	21.00
Federal unemployment compensation	
tax ($1,050 × 0.01)	10.50
Total tax liability	$124.00

The entry to record the payroll taxes and the accrued liability is:

Payroll Tax Expense	124.00	
F.I.C.A. Taxes Payable		92.50
State Unemployment Taxes Payable		21.00
Federal Unemployment Taxes Payable		10.50
To record accrued payroll taxes		
for week ended October 27.		

Reporting and Payment of Payroll Taxes

The reporting and payment requirements for the employer's payroll taxes and the amounts withheld from employees' earnings are discussed in the following sections.

Income Taxes Withheld and F.I.C.A. Taxes. The Federal income taxes withheld and F.I.C.A. taxes withheld from the employees' earnings and the employer's F.I.C.A. taxes are reported quarterly. The tax report form is filed during the month following the close of each calendar quarter; for the months of October, November, and December, for example, the form must be filed by January 31. The amounts required to be paid are the amounts accumulated in the Income Taxes Withholdings Payable account and in the F.I.C.A. Taxes Payable account. If the sum of Income Tax Withholdings Payable and F.I.C.A. Taxes Payable is $200 or more and less than $2,000 in either the first or the second month of each quarter, the employer is required to deposit the amount due for that month in a Federal depositary bank. The deposit must be made by the fifteenth day of the following month. The form (Federal Tax Deposit Form 501) used for this purpose is receipted and returned for submittal with the quarterly tax report (Form 941). Assume that the accounts of the Burns Company show the following tax liabilities on October 31:

Income Tax Withholdings Payable (October)	$910.70
F.I.C.A. Taxes Payable (October)	295.50

Payment of these tax liabilities must be made to a Federal Reserve Bank or an authorized commercial bank before November 15. The entry to record the deposit is

Income Tax Withholdings Payable	910.70	
F.I.C.A. Taxes Payable	295.50	
Cash		1,206.20
To record payment of tax liabilities.		

The amount due for the third month of each quarter may either be deposited or be sent in with the quarterly tax report. If the Burns Company remits the December liability with the quarterly return, two depositary receipts covering the taxes for October and November and a check for the taxes for December must accompany the return. Monthly deposits are not required for the first or second month of any quarter if the sum of the income taxes withheld from employees' earnings and the total F.I.C.A. taxes on the employer and the employees does not exceed $200. Payment for these months accompanies the quarterly return. Amounts due of $2,000 or more must be deposited within three banking days after the end of each pay period.

By January 31 of each year, the employer is required to give each employee a Withholding Statement, Form W-2, showing his gross earnings and the amounts withheld during the previous calendar year. The employee, in turn, is required to submit a copy of this statement with his Federal income tax return.

State Unemployment Compensation Tax. The employer's state unemployment compensation tax liability is accumulated in the State Unemployment Taxes Payable account. The employer files a tax report form—the form varies with the states— and pays the required tax. Timing of the payments, monthly or quarterly, varies with the states. Assume that the balance of the State Unemployment Taxes Payable account of the Burns Company was $84.50 on December 31, for the fourth quarter (October through December), and that the tax report form must be filed and payment must be made to the proper collecting agency by January 31. The entry to record the payment of the accrued liability is

State Unemployment Taxes Payable	84.50	
Cash		84.50
To record payment of tax liability.		

Federal Unemployment Compensation Tax. The employer must pay the Federal unemployment compensation tax annually. The tax liability is accumulated during the year in the Federal Unemployment Taxes Payable account. Assume that the Federal Unemployment Taxes Payable account for 1973 (January through December) on the books of the Burns Company shows an accumulated tax liability of $319.50. The tax report form must be filed and payment must be made to the proper Federal agency by January 31, 1974. The entry to record payment of the accrued liability is

Federal Unemployment Taxes Payable	319.50	
Cash		319.50
To record payment of tax liability.		

Accrual of Salaries and Wages

If the end of the payroll period does not coincide with the end of the accounting period, an adjusting entry is made for salaries and wages earned but not paid. Assume that the Burns Company closes its books on October 31, and that the last payroll period ended on October 27 (Friday). The entry to accrue the salaries for the partial pay period is

Salesmen's Salaries Expenses	406	
Executive Salaries Expenses	300	
Office Salaries Expenses	128	
Accrued Salaries and Wages Payable		834
To record salaries and wages accrued from October 28 to 31.		

The entire credit for the accrued payroll is made to a single liability account rather than to separate liability accounts for the government and the employees. Amounts to be withheld from employees' earnings for income taxes and for F.I.C.A. taxes are based on the earnings for an entire payroll period. Insofar as the employer is concerned, the total liability is $834; its breakdown into the several liability accounts does not provide additional useful information and may, therefore, be deferred until the date of payment. Although the employer's payroll taxes are levied only on amounts actually paid, the employer's payroll tax expense on the accrued payroll for the partial pay period should be recognized. The entry for the Burns Company is

Payroll Taxes	66.72	
Accrued Payroll Taxes Payable		66.72
To record the employer's payroll tax liability on the accrued payroll from October 28 to 31:		
F.I.C.A. ($834 × 0.05)	$41.70	
State Unemployment Insurance ($834 × 0.02)	16.68	
Federal Unemployment Tax ($834 × 0.01)	8.34	
Total	$66.72	

SUMMARY

Cash includes those items that a bank customarily accepts for deposit—coins, paper money, bank drafts, cashier's checks, money orders, and bank balances.

Basic controls must be instituted to prevent the misuse of funds. These controls include a clear segregation of duties and responsibilities, use of mechanical aids, the furnishing of definite authorization for cash payments, and organization of the flow and recording of documents so that the work of one employee is subject to automatic verification by another employee. No one person should both receive and disburse cash. All cash receipts should be deposited intact daily and all disbursements should be made by check. When payment by check is impractical, a petty cash fund should be set up.

Control of cash is further facilitated by the use of checking accounts. Since the records of the depositor and the bank will not normally agree at the end of the month, it is necessary to reconcile the two balances and to determine the adjusted, or true, cash balance. Differences between the balances may be due to the time lag in recording debits and credits, to special charges and credits of which either the depositor or the bank is unaware, or to possible errors or irregularities. A statement is prepared to reconcile the two balances. Amounts entered on one set of records only, and all errors and irregularities, constitute the items that will reconcile the two balances to the adjusted balance. All additions to and deductions from the balance per books must be recorded to bring the general ledger cash balance into agreement with the adjusted cash balance.

The regular cash needs of a business should be anticipated to ensure that funds will be available when needed and that excess funds are invested. This requires a cash forecast for a number of months in advance, based on a careful study and analysis of prior periods with appropriate adjustments for anticipated changes. The forecast is a summary of projected cash receipts and disbursements and the resulting cash balance for the budgeted periods.

The voucher system is a method of accumulating, verifying, recording, and disbursing all the expenditures of a business. It covers any transaction that requires a cash payment. The voucher is a serially numbered form that serves both as the written authorization for each expenditure and as the basis for the accounting entry. Invoices, receiving reports, and other forms serve as supporting documents for vouchers.

The voucher register is a journal for recording all liabilities approved for payment. It is ruled in columns headed by the proper accounts to be charged. Each appropriate transaction is entered in the voucher register first, followed by an entry in the check register when payment is made. The check register is the book of original entry for all cash disbursements. At the same time that the check is entered in the check register, a notation is made in the Paid column of the voucher register, showing the date of payment and the check number. The posting procedure is the same as for other special journals.

The total of unpaid vouchers—those that have not been marked either Paid or Canceled in the Paid column of the voucher register—should equal the balance of the Vouchers Payable account in the general ledger and, correspondingly, the total of the vouchers in the unpaid vouchers file. This file replaces the accounts payable ledger.

Both employer and employees are subject to certain taxes on wages. The employer must deduct from each employee's pay amounts for income, F.I.C.A., and state unemployment insurance taxes (in some states). Deductions may also be required under union agreements or to meet other claims. The employer, in turn, is subject to F.I.C.A. taxes, a state unemployment tax, and a Federal unemployment tax on a limited amount of wages paid during each calendar year.

Withheld income taxes and F.I.C.A. taxes are deposited in a Federal depositary bank and reported quarterly to the Internal Revenue Service on Form 941. State unemployment taxes are reported and paid quarterly to the appropriate state agency. Federal unemployment taxes are reported on Form 940 and paid annually to the Internal Revenue Service.

QUESTIONS

Q7-1. The Stenn Company employs an office manager, a cashier, an accounts receivable bookkeeper, two clerk-typists, and 10 salesmen. The bookkeeper records all charge sales made to customers; she also opens the mail each day and credits the customers' accounts for remittances, turning the money over to the cashier. The monthly bank statement is received directly by the bookkeeper, who prepares the bank reconciliation.

Collections from cash sales are turned over by the salesmen to the cashier together with a cash sales invoice. The cashier compares these invoices daily with the cash register tapes. Disbursements for petty cash items are made by the cashier out of cash receipts. The cashier fills out a petty cash slip, which is signed by the person receiving the cash. All other disbursements are by check, signed by either the office manager or the owner of the company. Entries in the cash receipts journal and in the cash disbursements journal are generally made by the office manager. In his absence, the cashier handles the cash receipts journal and the accounts receivable bookkeeper handles the cash disbursements journal.

(a) What is wrong with this system? (b) What basic internal controls are lacking? (c) Can the system be improved without increasing the present staff?

Q7-2. Why is it advantageous to deposit all cash receipts intact and to make all disbursements by check?

Q7-3. (a) What is a petty cash fund? (b) How does it operate? (c) Why should the petty cash fund always be replenished at the end of each accounting period?

Q7-4. Explain the reciprocal relationships between the cash records of the bank and of the depositor.

Q7-5. Explain the following:

a. Certified check
b. Total of listed checks
c. Service charge
d. Not sufficient funds

e. Debit memorandum
f. Credit memorandum
g. Overdraft

Q7-6. Explain the effect, if any, on the bank statement balance of each of the following bank reconciliation items:

a. Outstanding checks total $323.
b. The bank recorded a $650 deposit as $560.
c. The service charge for the month was $7.
d. Deposits in transit total $800.
e. A note payable of $500 made to the bank by the depositor became due.

Q7-7. (a) What is the purpose of a cash forecast? (b) Describe the basic steps in the preparation of a cash forecast. (c) What are some of the problems that may be encountered in its preparation?

Q7-8. (a) What is the voucher system? (b) What is a voucher? (c) What is a voucher jacket? (d) What is a voucher register? (e) What is a check register? (f) What are the advantages of the voucher system? (g) What are the disadvantages of the voucher system?

Q7-9. What is the function of the various business forms in an accounting system?

Q7-10. (a) What two types of Federal taxes are most employers required to withhold from their employees' wages? (b) When do taxes withheld become liabilities to the employer? (c) When and in what manner is the employer required to pay to the responsible Federal agency the amounts withheld?

Q7-11. (a) What are three common payroll taxes levied on an employer? (b) What is the rate of each tax? (c) When and in what manner does the employer pay the tax?

Q7-12. (a) What are the main purposes of the Federal Wage and Hour Law? (b) Does it limit the number of hours an employee may work? (c) Are all businesses subject to the provisions of this law?

Q7-13. (a) What classes of employees are subject to the Federal unemployment compensation tax? (b) What is the tax rate? (c) When is a Federal unemployment tax liability incurred? (d) When is the liability paid to the proper governmental agency?

Q7-14. (a) What is a state unemployment merit-rating plan? (b) Why are merit ratings assigned by the several states? (c) What are the maximum state unemployment tax rates? (d) How was the maximum rate initially established in the Federal Unemployment Compensation Act? (e) When does the employer become subject to a state unemployment tax liability? (f) When and to whom is the liability paid?

Q7-15. A company may pay its employees in (a) cash, (b) checks drawn on the regular checking account, or (c) checks drawn on a special payroll bank account. Discuss the advantages and disadvantages of each form of payment.

EXERCISES

Unless indicated otherwise, the following rates and amounts are to be used in solving the payroll exercises and problems in this chapter:

a. *F.I.C.A. tax:* 5 percent each on employer and employee, applicable to the first $10,000 paid to an employee during a calendar year.

b. *Federal unemployment compensation tax:* A maximum of 5 percent on the first $5,000 paid to each covered employee during each calendar year with 4 percent payable to the state and 1 percent to the Federal government.

E7-1. State the underlying reason for each of the following procedures:

a. The ticket-taker at the theater tears each ticket presented for admission in two and returns one part to the theater goer.

b. The clerk in the department store gives the customer his cash register receipt.

c. After the company treasurer signs a batch of checks, he retains the attached supporting documents, but not the checks (which he mails), to the accounting department.

E7-2. (*Managerial policy decision problem*) The bookkeeper of the Carlbey Company, in need of money to pay off debts, "borrows" $500 by pocketing some cash and checks mailed in by customers. He enters appropriate credits to each customer's account for payment made. Can this misappropriation be concealed for a short period? Indefinitely? What measures should a company take to prevent the misappropriation of cash or other assets?

E7-3. On April 1, 1973, the Allied Company established a petty cash fund of $225. On April 30, 1973, the fund consisted of cash and other items as follows:

Coins and currency	$47.50
Postage stamps	47.00
Freight and express invoices	64.00
Salvation Army contribution receipt	25.00
Postdated check from an employee	41.50

Make the entries to (a) establish the fund; (b) replenish the fund; (c) increase the fund from $225 to $300 on April 30; (d) reduce the fund from $225 to $150 on April 30.

E7-4. The George Carriere Company has an imprest petty cash fund of $500. On December 31, 1973, the fund consisted of cash and other items as follows:

Coins and Currency		$265.00
Vouchers for:		
Transportation In	$112.62	
Telephone	10.75	
Postage Expense	108.16	
Stationery	0.50	232.03
Total		$497.03

Assuming that the petty cash fund was not replenished, make the necessary adjusting entry at December 31, 1973.

E7-5. The Alden Company's general ledger Cash account shows a balance of $6,939.49 as of April 30, 1973. The balance on the bank statement on that date is $7,778.09. Checks for $250, $177.82, and $42.18 are outstanding. There is a charge for a check made out by the Alten Company for $25. The bank statement shows a credit of $400 for a customer's note that had been left with the bank for collection. Service charges for the month were $6.40. What is the true cash balance as of April 30?

E7-6. Prepare a bank reconciliation and entries to adjust the books of the Greene-Land Company as of January 31, 1973, from the following data:

Balance on bank statement	$4,733.46
Balance on books	4,387.71
Bank service charge	8.35
Credit for a customer's note collected by the bank (includes interest of $5.60)	130.60
Deposit made on January 31, not credited by the bank	254.10
Check 786 for $261.54 was entered in the cash disbursements journal as $216.45.	
A customer's check for $12.90 was returned marked NSF on January 30.	
Outstanding checks were	

Check	Amount
817	$ 50.00
818	75.05
825	410.54

E7-7. The bookkeeper for the Weily Company prepared the following statement:

WEILY COMPANY
Bank Reconciliation
May 31, 1973

Cash balance per ledger, May 31, 1973	$4,341.10
Deduct bank service charges	4.12
Adjusted cash balance, May 31, 1973	$4,336.98
Cash balance per bank statement, May 31, 1973	$5,590.38
Add deposit in transit	1,314.15
Total	$6,904.53
Deduct outstanding checks	

Check	Amount	
680	$ 476.10	
690	891.44	
695 Certified check for $500		
701	1,200.01	2,567.55
Adjusted Cash Balance, May 31, 1973		$4,336.98

a. How did the bookkeeper determine the amounts to be added or deducted?
b. Why is check 695 excluded from the total of outstanding checks?
c. What journal entry is necessary to adjust the books at May 31, 1973?

E7-8. Gross sales of the Gaines Company for the year 1973 were $825,000. Accounts receivable were $75,000 at the beginning of the year and $59,000 at the end of the year. Accounts receivable written off during the year were $2,050 and the year's provision for uncollectible accounts was $1,650. Customers returned merchandise for $4,600 in credit and took cash discounts of $8,900. Compute the cash collections made from customers during 1973.

E7-9. The following statement was made by the treasurer of the Horton Corporation: "As nearly as I can determine, 60 percent of our customers pay within the discount period. Our terms are 3/10, n/30; 80 percent of the amount due is collected within the 30-day period; 5 percent of the delinquent receivables remains uncollected at the end of a 60-day period. As a matter of collection policy, at that point I consider such outstanding receivables as doubtful of collection."

Sales on account for April, May, June, and July were $13,000, $10,000, $12,000, and $16,000, respectively. On the basis of the company's collection experience, compute the monthly forecast of collections on accounts receivable for May, June, and July.

E7-10. The Elegant Corporation has been formed to sell appliances on the installment plan. The following estimates are made for the first year of operations:

a. Selling price per unit	$85
b. Cost to produce per unit	$35
e. Selling and administrative expenses per unit	$20
d. Sales (units):	
First month	50
Second month	100
Third month	150
Monthly during rest of year	200
e. Terms of sale:	
Down payment	$20
Monthly for 13 months	$ 5
f. All costs and expenses are paid in the month of sale.	

Prepare a statement showing estimated monthly and cumulative cash requirements for the first twelve months.

E7-11. From the following data, prepare a cash forecast for the Richard Company for January, February, and March, 1974. Actual balances as of December 31, 1973 are:

Cash	$22,000
Accounts Receivable	25,000
Accounts Payable	35,000

Estimates for the first quarter of 1974 are

	Jan.	Feb.	March
Sales on account	$30,000	$20,000	$22,000
Cash sales	12,000	17,000	13,000
Purchases on account	39,000	23,000	27,000
Cash operating expenses	15,000	12,000	9,000
Depreciation expense	2,000	2,000	2,000

Terms of sales and purchases on account are n/30.

E7-12. Actual and projected sales data for the J. Jencken Company follow:

	Cash Sales	Credit Sales
November, 1972–Actual		$21,000
December, 1972–Actual		24,000
January, 1973–Estimated	$12,000	22,000
February, 1973–Estimated	10,000	33,000
March, 1973–Estimated	21,000	54,000

The cash balance on January 1, 1973, was $18,000.

Experience indicates that 50 percent of the credit sales are collected in the month of the sale, 40 percent in the month following the sale, and 10 percent in the second month following the sale. Compute the cash collections by months for the first quarter of 1973.

E7-13. The James Company records all vouchers at the net amount. Record the following transactions in general journal form, indicating the proper book of original entry.

1973

Oct. 2   Issued a voucher payable to the Snow Company for $1,200 worth of merchandise; terms 2/10, n/30.

   5   Issued a voucher payable to White's, Inc., for $1,500 worth of merchandise; terms 3/10, n/30.

  12   Issued a check to the Snow Company in payment of the October 2 voucher.

Nov. 4   Issued a voucher payable to White's, Inc., for the discount not taken on the transaction of October 5.

   4   Issued a check payable to White's, Inc., for the amount due.

E7-14. Finer, Inc. completed the following transactions, among others, during October, 1973:

1973

Oct. 1   Issued Voucher 45 payable to the McGill Company for $750 worth of merchandise; terms 2/10, n/30.

   6   Received a credit memorandum for $75 from the McGill Company for unsatisfactory merchandise returned. Canceled Voucher 45 and issued Voucher 61 for the proper amount.

  10   Issued Check 25 in payment of Voucher 61, less a 2-percent discount.

Record the transactions in general journal form, indicating the journal in which each transaction would be properly recorded.

E7-15. The Mellono Company uses a voucher system. During May, 1973, the following selected transactions were completed:

1973

May 1   Issued Voucher 171 payable to the Hanscom Company for $3,000 worth of merchandise, terms n/10.

  11   Gave the Hanscom Company a 20-day, 4-percent note in payment of Voucher 171.

  31   Issued Voucher 189 payable to the Hanscom Company for the maturity value of the note of May 11.

  31   Issued Check 97 in payment of Voucher 189.

Record the transactions in general journal form, indicating the journal in which each transaction would be properly recorded.

E7-16. John Hills pays his 10 employees weekly. The payroll summary for the week ended January 15 is given as

Total earnings		$1,050.00
Deductions		
F.I.C.A. tax	$ 52.50	
Federal income tax	210.00	
Union dues	20.00	
Total deductions		282.50
Net amount paid		$ 767.50

Journalize (a) the payment of the payroll and (b) the employers' liability for payroll taxes.

E7-17. All the 30 employees of the Labco Company earned over $10,000 during the calendar year 1973. (a) What was the state unemployment tax expense for 1973? (b) Compute the tax expense based on a tax reduced by a merit rating to 0.5 percent. (c) Compute the Federal unemployment tax expense for 1973.

E7-18. From the payroll records of Leo Crowne for the week ended September 10 the following information is obtained:

Total earnings	$2,100
Earnings subject to unemployment compensation tax	750
Earnings subject to F.I.C.A. tax	1,200
Deductions	
F.I.C.A. tax	60
Federal income tax	215
Accounts receivable	50

Record (a) the payroll and (b) the employer's payroll tax liability.

E7-19. The payroll records of the Walltins Company for the week ended January 20 showed the following:

Total wages earned		$2,000
Deductions		
F.I.C.A. tax	$100	
Federal income tax	220	
Accounts receivable	100	420
Net amount paid		$1,580

Assuming that a voucher system is used, record in general journal form: (a) the total payroll, (b) the payment of the payroll, (c) the employer's payroll tax expense. Indicate the journal in which each entry would be properly reported.

E7-20. The following payroll data for the year 1973 were taken from the records of the Rolland Company:

Total wages expense	$90,000
Wages to employees with earnings in excess of $5,000	35,000
Wages to employees with earnings in excess of $10,000	15,000

Calculate the employer's payroll tax expense for the year.

E7-21. The Hilltop Company had 10 employees who worked during an entire calendar year. One of them, J. Downey, earned $10,500. What was the employer's total expenditure for Downey's services for the year?

DEMONSTRATION PROBLEMS

DP7-1. (*Recording petty cash fund transactions*) The transactions of the petty cash fund of the Wilding Company during the month of July, 1973, were

1973
July 1 Established an imprest petty cash fund in the amount of $70.

10 Replenished the fund and increased it to $150. The following items were in the petty cash box:

Coins and currency	$ 2.50
Vouchers for:	
Telephone and telegraph	24.86
Advances to employees	10.00
Postage stamps	20.00
Miscellaneous office supplies	12.64
Total	$70.00

1971

July 31   Replenished the fund again at the close of the Wilding Company's fiscal year. The potty cash box contained the following items:

Coins and currency		$ 44.22
Vouchers for:		
Telephone and telegraph	$31.34	
Office supplies	21.00	
Postage	37.44	
Traveling expense	1.60	
Entertainment expense	11.20	
Repairs	.80	
Hardware supplies	2.40	105.78
Total		$150.00

Required: Journalize the transactions.

DP7-2. (*Bank reconciliation*) The cash account of the Itec Company showed a balance of $2,123.31 on March 31, 1973. The bank statement showed a balance of $2,302.94. Other differences between the information in the firm's Cash account and the bank's records were

1. A deposit of $118.60 made on March 31 was not recorded by the bank before the bank statement was issued.
2. The following items were returned with the bank statement:
   a. A credit memo for $112.30, the proceeds of a draft for $115 drawn on the George Company and accepted by the drawee 60 days ago. The bank deducted $2.70 from the total collected for the cost of collection.
   b. A debit memo for $4.80 for annual rental of a safety deposit box.
   c. A customer's check for $7.50 received on account, which the firm had included in its deposit on March 27, was returned marked NSF.
   d. A canceled check in the amount of $205 drawn by the Itek Company and charged by the bank against the account of the Itec Company by mistake. The check is being returned to the bank.
3. Check 298 was made out correctly for $17.67 in payment of office supplies, but was entered in the cash disbursements journal as $17.76.
4. Outstanding checks on March 31 totaled $403.14.

Required: 1. Prepare a bank reconciliation as of March 31, 1973.
2. Prepare the journal entries to adjust the Cash account as of March 31, 1973.

DP7-3. (*Cash forecast*) The Eastend Company estimates the following sales, purchases, and operating expenses for the first four months of 1973:

	Operating Expenses	Purchases	Sales
January	$6,000	$ 50,000	$160,000
February	7,000	100,000	200,000
March	9,500	80,000	180,000
April	8,500	220,000	220,000

Balances on January 1, 1973 were:

Accounts Receivable	$30,000
Accounts Payable	20,000

Required:

1. Prepare a schedule of estimated monthly cash collections for the first four months of 1973. Approximately 25 percent of sales are for cash; sales on account are on terms of n/30 and are collected in the month following the sale.
2. Prepare a schedule of estimated monthly cash disbursements for the period. Purchases are made on terms of n/15, so that half the purchases are paid for in the month of purchase and the remainder in the following month. Operating expenses are paid for in the month in which they are incurred.

DP7-4. (*Voucher register*) A portion of a voucher register, showing the unpaid vouchers as of April 30, 1973, is given:

Date		Vou. No.	Name	Paid		Credit Vou. Pay.	Debit Purch.	Other General Ledger Accounts		
				Date	Ck. No.			Account	Debit	Credit
1973 April	5	270	Gilbert Spack				900			
	10	272	William Murphy				800			
	21	291	Baldwin Company				1,000			
	30	305	Norman Geller				600			

The following transactions, among others, occurred during May:

1973
May 1 Issued Check 651 in payment of Voucher 270, less 2 percent.

1 Issued Voucher 309 to Herbert Sedlin for $1,500 worth of merchandise, terms n/15.

5 Received a credit memorandum from the Baldwin Company for $300 for unsatisfactory merchandise returned. Canceled Voucher 291 and issued Voucher 310 for the proper amount.

8 Issued Check 652 in payment of Voucher 305, less 1 percent.

15 Issued Check 653 in payment of Voucher 310, less 1 percent.

16 By special agreement with Herbert Sedlin, the purchase of May 1 is to be paid for in installments; $500 immediately and the balance by June 16. Canceled Voucher 309 and issued Vouchers 311 and 312. Check 654 was issued in payment of Voucher 311.

Required:

1. Enter the unpaid vouchers in a voucher register similar to the one shown (draw double rules under the last entry to exclude these amounts from the May totals); record the May transactions in the voucher register and a check register.
2. Enter the total of unpaid vouchers as of April 30, $3,300, as a credit in the Vouchers Payable general ledger account; post to Vouchers Payable from the voucher register and check register.
3. Prepare a schedule of unpaid vouchers.

DP7-5. (*Recording transactions in special journals*) The Atlas Company uses a voucher system. During June, 1973, the following selected transactions were completed:

1973

June   1   Purchased $2,000 worth of merchandise from the Roche Company; terms 2/10, n/30.

10   Made a partial payment on the June 1 purchase. The check is made out for $837.90, representing a partial payment on which a discount is allowed.

15   Paid a 45-day, 6-percent note for $4,000 due today (the Company closed its books on May 31).

20   Returned merchandise with an invoice price of $200 to the Roche Company and received credit.

25   Paid $500 in rent for June.

30   Accrued, vouchered, and paid the following payroll:

	Gross Wages	F.I.C.A. Tax	Employees' Income Tax Withheld
Sales Staff	$2,000	$100	$155.00
Office Staff	1,000	50	77.50

30   Recorded the employer's total payroll tax expense, based on the payroll given.

Required: Record the transactions in general journal form and indicate the journal in which each transaction would be properly recorded.

DP7-6. (*Recording payroll*) The partially completed payroll register of the Bland Company for the week ended December 12 is given below.

Payroll Register

Name	Earnings		Deductions		Net Amount	Distribution		
	Week Ending December 12	Cumu- lative Through December 5	F.I.C.A. Tax	Federal Income Tax		Sales- men's Salaries	Exec- utive Salaries	Office Salaries
Bates, John	85	3,035		6.10		85		
Hanlon, Robert	110	3,050		11.00		110		
Perry, John	250	9,950		21.00			250	
Silver, Clifford	90	4,995		4.80				90
Totals								

Required: 1. Prepare a payroll register similar to the one shown, filling in all the blank columns.
2. Record the Bland Company's payroll for the week.
3. Record the Bland Company's payroll tax expense.

DP7-7. (*Managerial policy decision problem*)

a. The manager of a shoe department employing six salesmen has found on a number of occasions that the cash in the register at the end of the day is less than the amounts shown on the record of sales for that day. Each salesman rings up his own sales. What recommendations would you make to the manager?

b. How do the use of a petty cash system and the regular reconciliation of the bank account protect the company against mistakes and losses?

c. You note that the independent auditor, when making his examination, reconciles (1) total deposits shown on the bank statements with total receipts shown in the cash receipts journal, and (2) total disbursements shown on the bank statements with total checks drawn as recorded in the cash disbursements journal. Explain why the auditor makes these reconciliations.

d. It is essential for a business to establish internal controls to prevent the misappropriation of cash. Does management have other responsibilities relating to cash? Explain.

PROBLEMS

P7-1. The following data are taken from the records of Pride, Inc., and from the monthly bank statement furnished them by the Boston Trust Company:

a.	Balance per bank statement, June 30, 1973 *ADD Bank*	$84,159.86
b.	Balance per books, June 30, 1973 *ADD Book*	54,673.40
c.	Outstanding checks, June 30, 1973 *D Bank*	32,108.42
d.	Receipts of June 30, 1973, deposited July 2, 1973 *ADD bank*	5,317.20
e.	Service charge for June, per debit memo *D book*	3.85
f.	Proceeds of bank loan, June 15, 1973, discounted for 3 months at 5% per annum, omitted from the company's books *ADD book*	9,875.00
g.	Deposit of June 30, 1973, omitted from bank statement *ADD Bank*	2,892.41
h.	Error on bank statement in entering deposit of June 25, 1973:	

	Correct amount	$3,182.40	
	Entered as	3,181.40 *ADD bank*	1.00

i.	Check of Prime, Inc., charged in error *ADD bank*	2,690.00
j.	Proceeds of a customer's note collected by bank on June 16, 1973; not entered in the company's books:	

	Principal	$2,000.00	
	Interest	20.00	
	Total	$2,020.00 *ADD books*	
	Less collection fee	5.00	2,015.00

k. Error on bank statement in entering deposit of June 10, 1973:

	Entered as	$4,817.10	
	Correct amount	4,807.10 *D bank*	10.00

l.	Deposit of Preed Corporation, credited in error *bank*	1,800.00
m.	Debit memo for noninterest-bearing note not recorded by the company *D book*	5,000.00
n.	A check from Brown, Inc., was returned marked NSF; no entry has been made on the company's records *book*	417.50

Required: 1. Prepare a bank reconciliation as of June 30, 1973.
2. Prepare the journal entries necessary to adjust the books of Pride, Inc., as of June 30, 1973. The books are closed annually June 30.

P7-2. The Wall Company prepared the following bank reconciliation as of July 31, 1973:

WALL COMPANY
Bank Reconciliation
July 31, 1973

Balance per bank		$12,463.75
Less outstanding checks		

Check	Amount	
580	$2,025.50	
599	98.00	
600	3.40	2,126.90
Balance per books		$10,336.85

The bank statement for the month of August was as follows:

SECOND NATIONAL BANK
Statement of account with Wall Company

Checks			Deposits	Date	Balance
				1973	
				August 1	12,463.75
2,025.50				2	10,438.25
98.00	12.00	115.00	785.00	6	10,998.25
100.00			195.00	11	11,093.25
62.23	198.50	3.40		16	10,829.12
1,110.00	90.00 NSF			21	9,629.12
860.00	15.40		2,500.00	25	11,253.72
2.75 SC			760.80	29	12,011.77

Cash receipts for the month were:

Date	Amount
August 5	$ 785.00
10	195.00
23	2,500.00
28	760.80
31	500.00

Cash disbursements for the month were:

Check	Amount	Check	Amount
601	$ 12.00	607	$682.21
602	860.00	608	49.90
603	115.00	609	20.00
604	100.00	610	760.00
605	1,110.00	611	62.23
606	143.50	612	198.50

The canceled checks returned by the bank included a check for $15.40 made out by the Wall Company and charged to the Wall Company in error. The NSF check had been received from a customer on account.

Required: 1. Prepare the bank reconciliation as of August 31, 1973.
2. Make the necessary adjusting journal entries.

P7-3. (*Accounting policy decision problem*) The Wind Company has an imprest petty cash fund of $500. On June 30, 1973, the end of the company's fiscal year, the composition of the fund was as follows:

Currency and coins		$ 97.94
Vouchers for:		
Postage	$106.08	
Stationery	25.00	
Transportation out	153.62	
Telephone and telegraph	115.30	400.00
Total		$497.94
Cash shortage		2.06
Total		$500.00

Required:

1. Prepare the entry to replenish the fund on June 30.
2. Assuming that the fund was not replenished, (a) What adjusting entry should be made on June 30? (b) What amount will be reported in the June 30 position statement?
3. Should the custodian of the petty cash fund have the authority to withdraw cash from the bank whenever he needs to replenish the fund?

P7-4. According to the statement that John Markson received from his bank as of March 31, 1973, his balance was $2,700. He noted the following discrepancies between the bank statement and his records:

a. A deposit of $500 that was made on March 31 was credited by the bank on April 1.
b. Outstanding checks as of March 31 were: 652, $100; 689, $51; 701, $59; and 710, $86.
c. Check 655 for $350, issued on March 10 for advertising expense, was not recorded in the cash disbursements journal but was paid by the bank on March 16.
d. A 6-percent, 90-day note of Thomas Field for $400 maturing on March 31, was discounted by Markson on March 12, and dishonored at maturity. No entry has been made in Markson's records. The bank charged Markson's account for the note plus a $2.50 protest fee. Bank service charges for March were $3.

Required:

1. Determine the cash balance on the books before adjustments and prepare a bank reconciliation showing the true cash balances as of March 31, 1973.
2. Prepare the journal entries necessary to adjust the books.

P7-5. (*Accounting policy decision problem*) You have prepared the financial reports for the Baxter Corporation, which include the following amounts:

Cash balances:	
April 30, 1973	$35,000
April 30, 1972	22,000
Net income:	
For the fiscal year ending	
April 30, 1973	55,000
For the fiscal year ending	
April 30, 1972	60,000

Mr. Baxter, the company's president, says that you must have made a mistake, because you report an increase in the cash balance of $13,000 although earnings for the fiscal year declined by $5,000 from the year before. (a) Is he right? Explain. (b) He asks you what the effect on the cash balance would have been if the company had reported a $5,000 net loss for the period?

P7-6. (*Financial policy decision problem*) Estimates of the Flack Manufacturing Company for the first four months of 1973 are as follows:

	January	February	March	April
Sales	$50,000	$60,000	$70,000	$65,000
Purchases	36,000	40,000	40,000	45,000
Payrolls	10,000	12,000	14,000	9,500
Other expenses	5,000	6,000	7,000	6,500

The general ledger includes the following account balances at January 1, 1973:

Cash	$10,000
Accounts Receivable	45,000
Accounts Payable	30,000

All sales are on account on terms of n/30; 90 percent are collected in the month following the sale; 8 percent in the second month following the sale; and 2 percent are ultimately written off as bad debts. All payments on purchases and other expenses are made in the month following the month of purchase. Payrolls are paid during the month. The Accounts Receivable balance of January 1 represents total sales for December of the prior year, and the Accounts Payable balance represents purchases for that month.

Required:

1. Prepare a cash forecast by months for the first four months of 1973.
2. Based on the forecast, what financial policy decisions should the company make.

3. (a) Would you recommend daily or weekly cash forecasts? (b) What would be the costs and the benefits of more frequent forecasts?

P7-7. The general ledger of the Browne Manufacturing Company included the following account balances as of January 1, 1973:

Cash	$20,000
Accounts Receivable	35,000
Accounts Payable	18,000

Projected sales, purchases, and cash operating expenses for the first three months of 1973 were:

	January	February	March
Sales	$30,000	$40,000	$45,000
Purchases	20,000	30,000	25,000
Cash operating expenses	8,000	10,000	7,500

All sales and purchases are on terms of n/30, so that remittances by customers are received in the month following the sale, and all payments for merchandise are made during the month following the purchase. Cash operating expenses are paid for during the month in which they are incurred.

Required: Prepare a schedule showing cash requirements by months for the first quarter of 1973.

P7-8. The Alton Company prepares its vouchers for the net amount due. A portion of the voucher register, showing the unpaid vouchers as of June 30, is given below.

Date	Vou. No.	Name	Paid		Credit Vou. Pay.	Debit Purch.	Debit Purch. Disc. Lost	Other General Ledger Accounts		
			Date	Ck. No.				Account	Debit	Credit
1973 June	1	78	Robert Doyle				49			
	3	81	Bennett Co.				980			
	5	82	Gates & Son				196			

1973

July 1   Issued Check 110 in payment of Voucher 78.

5   Issued Voucher 83 payable to Gates & Son for $4 discount lost on the purchase of June 5.

6   Issued Check 111 in payment of Vouchers 82 and 83.

10   Issued Voucher 84 to the Giles Company for $500 worth of merchandise; terms 2/10, n/30.

14   Issued Voucher 85 to Warren's, Inc., for $750 worth of merchandise; terms 1½/10, n/30.

16   By special arrangement with the Bennett Company the purchase of June 3 (invoice $1,000; terms 2/10 EOM, n/30) is to be paid for in installments; $400 immediately and the balance on August 16. Issued Voucher 86 for the purchase discount lost. Canceled Vouchers 81 and 86 and issued Vouchers 87 and 88. Check 112 was issued in payment of Voucher 87.

20   Issued Check 113 in payment of Voucher 84.

Required:

1. Enter the unpaid vouchers as of July 1 in a voucher register similar to the one shown; record the July transactions in the voucher register and a single-column check register.
2. Enter the total amount of unpaid vouchers as of July 1 ($1,225) as a credit to the Vouchers Payable general ledger account; post to a Vouchers Payable T account from the voucher register and the check register.
3. Prepare a schedule of unpaid vouchers.

P7-9. The Madison Sales Company pays its salesmen monthly. On November 30, the following information was available:

F.I.C.A. Taxes Payable	Income Tax Withholdings Payable

State Unemployment Taxes Payable	Federal Unemployment Taxes Payable
1973 (Oct.–Nov. 200	1973 (Jan.–Nov.) 360

The December payroll was:

Total earnings		$9,500
Deductions		
F.I.C.A. taxes	$230	
Federal income taxes	990	1,220
Net amount due		$8,280

Required: Copy the T accounts with the November 30 balances and enter the following:

1. The December payroll.
2. The December employer's payroll tax expense. The taxable portion of the December payroll for state and Federal unemployment taxes is $2,500.
3. Checks and appropriate report forms mailed on January 31, 1974, as follows:
   a. To the Internal Revenue Service: a check for December and depositary receipts for October and November.
   b. To the Internal Revenue Service: a check for the Federal unemployment tax liability for 1973.
   c. To the State Division of Employment Security: a check for the state unemployment tax liability for the fourth quarter of 1973.

P7-10. The following information regarding the payroll of the Wenton Corporation for the week ended July 27, 1973, is given:

Employee	Type of Work	Cumulative Gross Wages to July 20, 1973	Gross Wages for Week ended July 27
James P. Morris	Salesman	$5,000	$400
Frederick M. Phillips	Salesman	9,950	350
Jane Dolittle	Office Clerk	2,460	100
Thomas O. Waters	Office Clerk	4,950	150

Deductions Other than F.I.C.A.

	Federal Income Taxes Withheld	State Income Taxes Withheld	Group Life Insurance Premiums Withheld
James P. Morris	$50	$10	$10
Frederick M. Phillips	30	6	6
Jane Dolittle	12	2	5
Thomas O. Waters	20	5	8

Required:

1. Prepare a journal entry on July 27, 1973, to record and classify the payroll expense.
2. Prepare a journal entry on July 27, 1973, to record the employer's payroll taxes.
3. Prepare a journal entry on July 29, 1973, to record the payment of the payroll.

P7-11. The general ledger of the Meade Company showed the following on November 30, 1973:

Name of Account	Period Covered	Amount
Accrued Salaries and Wages Payable		None
F.I.C.A. Taxes Payable	November	$ 180.00
State Unemployment Taxes Payable	October–November	98.20
Federal Unemployment Taxes Payable	January–November	201.72
Income Tax Withholdings Payable	November	150.20
Bond Deductions Payable		320.00
United Fund Payable		125.00
Salaries and Wages Expense	January–November	97,800.00
Payroll Tax Expense	January–November	3,010.00

Following is the payroll summary for December. The last pay period ended December 27.

Total earnings		$8,900.00
Deductions		
F.I.C.A. taxes	$182.50	
Federal income taxes	860.00	
U.S. bonds	150.00	
United fund	75.00	
Total deductions		1,267.50
Net amount paid		$7,632.50

Additional information taken from the records follows:

a. December earnings (through the last pay period) of $2,050.75 were subject to a state unemployment tax rate of 2 percent.
b. On December 5 a check was issued to Merchants National Bank for the purchase of four U.S. savings bonds at $37.50 and two at $18.75.
c. On December 29, a check was mailed to the United Fund for contributions withheld from employees' earnings through December 27.
d. Wages accrued on December 31 were $1,010.50; the taxable portion for state and Federal unemployment taxes is $350, with rates of 2.0 percent and 0.4 percent, respectively; the taxable portion for F.I.C.A. tax is $500.

Required:

1. Record the transactions relating to payroll, payroll deductions, and payroll tax expense for December. Checks are mailed on due date to the proper agencies.
2. List the affected ledger accounts and their balances as of December 31, after all entries have been posted.

P7-12. Marie's Fashions, a woman's clothing store, has five employees with the following payroll data for a period of a week:

Employee Number	Total Hours Worked	Hourly Rate	Income Tax Withheld	F.I.C.A. Tax Withheld
1	40	$10.00	$55.00	$20.00
2	40	6.00	37.00	12.00
3	30	4.00	15.00	6.00
4	15	3.00	9.00	2.25
5	20	3.00	5.00	3.00

Required:

1. Design a flow chart to compute and print the net pay for each of the employees in the weekly payroll given above.
2. Write a program coded in BASIC that will print the net pay for each employee. *Suggestion:* Assign a letter to each of the columnar headings (variables) of the data.

P7-13. Design a flow chart that will incorporate the following payroll procedures.

a. Print the following headings:

Name of Employee	Identification Number	Regular Pay	Overtime Pay	Total Pay	Federal Income Tax	F.I.C.A Tax	Net Pay

b. Read the name of the employee, identification number, rate of pay, hours worked, income tax withheld, F.I.C.A. tax withheld.
c. If hours worked are equal to or less than 40 hours, then multiply hours worked times regular rate of pay for the amount of regular pay.
d. If hours worked are greater than 40 hours, multiply 40 times regular rate of pay. Add this amount to the product of the overtime rate (1.5 times regular rate) times the overtime hours (total hours worked minus 40).
e. From the gross pay (sum of item d) subtract the Federal income tax withheld and F.I.C.A. tax withheld to arrive at the net pay for the employee.
f. Repeat until each employee's pay is computed.

P7-14. (*Financial policy decision problem*) The Endeco Company has two notes payable of $60,000 each with due dates of May 31 and June 30, 1973. The company wishes to arrange in advance for any refinancing that may be needed (a) to pay the notes on their due dates and (b) to provide a minimum end-of-month cash balance of $20,000. You are furnished with the following projected data:

Sales		Purchases	
February	$60,000	March	$51,000
March	85,000	April	39,000
April	60,000	May	45,000
May	63,000	June	36,000
June	70,000		

a. The cash balance on April 1 was $16,000.
b. All sales are on terms of 2/10 E.O.M. (a 2-percent discount is allowed if the invoice is paid by the tenth of the month following the sale). Past experience indicates that 70 percent of the sales are collected within the first 10 days of the first month following the sale, 20 percent during the remainder of the first month following the sale, and 8 percent in the second month following the sale. Bad debts losses are estimated at 2 percent of sales.
c. Terms of purchases are 2/10, n/30. Since all payments are made within the discount period, two thirds of the invoices will be paid in the month of the purchase and one third in the month following the purchase.

d. Operating expenses are $6,000 per month and are paid for when they are incurred. The Endeco Company receives $1,500 monthly from property rentals; $2,500 will be realized in June from the sale of obsolete equipment.

Required:

1. Prepare a report, with supporting schedules, advising management of the amount of additional borrowing that will be necessary.
2. Explain to management the usefulness and limitations of the forecast.
3. What specific steps can management take in planning their cash requirements.
4. To what other cash planning and control problems should the management of the Endeco Company direct its attention.
5. What suggestions would you offer for improving the cash position of the company.
6. After reviewing your report, one of the officials said: "But these are predictions about the future, and in this business you cannot predict what will happen the next week, or even the next day, so that I personally cannot rely on them." Write a brief answer to this official.

8

The Measurement
and Control
of Receivables

Making sales and purchases on account has become standard practice in the modern American System. Individuals and businesses alike buy and sell merchandise, invest in stocks and bonds, and even acquire plant and equipment on credit. Consequently, the increasing trend toward the extension of credit terms for transactions involving all types of goods and services has led to a greater need for control and analysis of receivables by management.

SOURCES AND CLASSIFICATION OF RECEIVABLES

There are two classes of trade receivables: accounts receivable, which are claims against customers for sales made on open account, and notes receivable, which are claims against customers supported by written formal promises to pay. From a legal point of view, a note receivable is probably better security than an account receivable because it is a written acknowledgement of the debt; however, in the United States, the unsecured open account form of credit is well established and will be widely used for a long time to come. Nontrade receivables arise from money lent, from deposits made, and from other sources.

The various claims should be properly recorded in several separate accounts, one possible classification of which appears below:

1. Accounts Receivable–Trade. This account represents claims against customers for goods sold or for services rendered.

2. Accounts Receivable–Nontrade. This group of accounts represents claims arising from sources other than normal trade transactions, including:
   a. Loans to officers or employees
   b. Deposits made on contract bids with public utilities or government agencies
   c. Claims against common carriers for loss or damage to goods in shipment, loss claims against insurance companies, and claims against the U.S. Treasury for tax refunds
   d. Amounts due from affiliated companies
   e. Amounts due or accrued from rentals, interest, and royalties

Notes are similarly classified as trade or nontrade receivables. Nontrade notes receivable should be carried in accounts specifically designated as to source (officers, affiliated companies, rental property) and properly classified on the statement of financial position.

Receivables that are due and collectible within a year should be shown in the Current Assets section of the statement of financial position. The terms *Accounts Receivable* and *Notes Receivable*, if unqualified, should be understood to represent trade receivables collectible within one year or operating cycle. Nontrade receivables that are not due or are not collectible within a year should be shown under Long-Term Investments.

RECOGNITION OF LOSSES ON UNCOLLECTIBLE ACCOUNTS

▼ A basic principle in accounting is that the earned revenue of any accounting period and the actual expense incurred in realizing that revenue should be related. ▼ The cost of the goods sold and all other expenses incurred during the period should be related or deducted from the revenue of that period. Hence, the cost of a machine is spread over the period during which the machine is used to arrive at a fair measure of the net income for each period. It would be inaccurate to charge the entire cost at the time of purchase or disposal of the machine.

Accounting Concept: ▼
Matching Revenue and
Expenses

Similarly, since the balance in the Accounts Receivable account represents uncollected amounts included in revenue, losses that may arise through failure to collect any of the receivables should be recognized as an expense of doing business during the period when the sales were made. Thus, accounts receivable originating from sales made on credit in 1973 and determined to be uncollectible in 1974 represent a bad debts expense of the year 1973. It also follows that the Accounts Receivable account in the statement of financial position should be shown at the amount expected to be realized through actual cash collections from customers. If accounts receivable are shown at their gross amount without any accompanying adjustment for the estimated uncollectible portion, then the total assets and the total stockholders' equity would be overstated to the extent of the failure to recognize an expense that arises out of the sale of goods on account.

Recording the Bad Debts Adjustment

To illustrate the recording of a bad debts adjustment, assume that on December 31, 1973, the credit department of the Greene Corporation, having analyzed sales during 1973 and past-due accounts, determines that out of the current year's sales, $550 will be uncollectible. This amount represents a bad debts expense to be shown in the General and Administrative Expense section of the income statement as a deduction from revenue. The estimated losses pertain to accounts receivable resulting from sales of the current period; therefore, in accordance with the principle of the periodic matching of expenses and revenues, estimated bad debts losses should be charged against revenue.

The adjusting general journal entry recorded on December 31, 1973, and the posting of the entry to the general ledger are shown below.

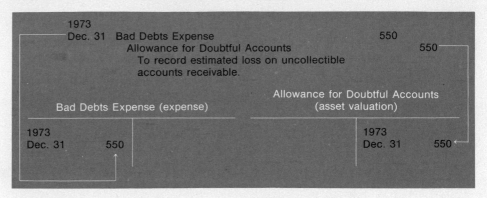

It is assumed that there was no balance before adjustments in Allowance for Doubtful Accounts and that no account receivable had been written off during the year 1973. These complications are discussed in more detail later in this chapter.

Since the amount of $550 is an estimate and is not related to specific customers' accounts, the credit must be made to a contra (valuation) account. If the credit were to be made directly to Accounts Receivable without corresponding credits to subsidiary accounts, the equality of the controlling account and the subsidiary accounts would no longer exist. The use of the valuation account Allowance for Doubtful Accounts permits a reduction in the asset account without destroying this essential equality. Allowance for Doubtful Accounts is shown in the statement of financial position as a deduction from the related asset account.

Assets		
Current Assets		
Cash		$1,210
Accounts Receivable	$6,945	
Deduct Allowance for Doubtful Accounts	550	6,395
Notes Receivable		1,000

The amount of $6,395 represents the anticipated net realizable value of the accounts receivable.

As actual accounts receivable are determined to be uncollectible during subsequent accounting periods, Allowance for Doubtful Accounts is debited instead of Bad Debts Expense, with offsetting credits to the controlling account and the specific customers' accounts involved. This procedure is required since the loss already has been recognized by the bad debts adjusting entry. A debit to Bad Debts Expense at the time of write-off would cause the loss to be recorded twice.

Assume that on May 1, 1974, the Greene Corporation decides that a claim of $75 against John Landry for a sale made on March 1, 1973, is uncollectible. The entry is

```
1974
May  1   Allowance for Doubtful Accounts              75
              Accounts Receivable–John Landry                75
              To write off the uncollectible account.
```

Estimating the Amount of Bad Debts Expense

It is necessary for management to make a careful estimate, based on judgment and past experience, of the amount of its uncollectible accounts. Accurate records must be kept and overdue accounts must be carefully analyzed.

There are two alternative approaches commonly used in estimating bad debts. In this text, these methods are referred to as (1) *the income statement approach*, based on the dollar volume of sales, and (2) *the statement of financial position approach*, based on the amount of receivables.

The Income Statement Approach. The income statement method associates the bad debts expense directly with dollar volume of sales. Typically the estimate is based on a percentage of sales less sales returns and allowances. The percentage is based on information derived from the company's past experience. It may be desirable to establish the percentage on the basis of charge sales only, excluding cash sales, particularly if the proportion of cash sales to total sales fluctuates from year to year. The method is simple to apply and furnishes an equitable basis for distributing bad debts losses. Since the computation used in this method yields the amount of the bad debts expense for the year, any existing balance in the Allowance for Doubtful Accounts is ignored. It should be noted, however, that even though the Bad Debts Expense item on the income statement may be quite close to reality, the Allowance for Doubtful Accounts on the statement of financial position may be greatly distorted. A small error in the same direction over the years will accumulate to a large amount in the Allowance for Doubtful Accounts since its balance is ignored in the adjustment process.

To illustrate the adjustment by this approach, assume that an examination of the accounts of a given company for the preceding five years shows that approximately one-half of 1 percent of credit sales have proved to be uncollectible. Assume further that credit sales for a particular year are $100,000 and that there is a credit balance of $85 in Allowance for Doubtful Accounts before adjustments are made. The bad debts expense for the year is $500 (0.005 × $100,000), and in recording the adjustment the $85 balance in the Allowance for Doubtful Accounts is ignored. The adjusting entry is

```
        Bad Debts Expense                    500
            Allowance for Doubtful Accounts              500
```

The Statement of Financial Position Approach. The statement of financial position method requires an adjustment of the existing balance of Allowance for Doubtful Accounts to an amount that, when deducted from Accounts Receivable on the statement of financial position, will show accounts receivable at their net realizable value. In the statement of financial position approach, the amount of accounts receivable rather than sales volume is used as the base for the adjustment. The necessary adjustment for the balance of Allowance for Doubtful Accounts is determined by either of two procedures: (1) the balance necessary to maintain the Allowance for Doubtful Accounts is established by *aging* the accounts receivable (that is, analyzing them by the amount of time they have remained unpaid) and adjusting the existing balance of Allowance for Doubtful Accounts to the proper amount, or (2) the balance of Allowance for Doubtful Accounts is adjusted to an amount equal to an estimated percentage of current accounts receivable. Aging the accounts receivable involves consideration of such factors as the date on which payment was due, the number of days that have elapsed since the due date, and any other available data of a financial nature that give some clue as to collectibility of the accounts. A columnar worksheet like the one shown in Figure 8-1 is often used to facilitate the analysis of the Accounts Receivable account. It is sometimes referred to as an *aging schedule.*

Figure 8-1. Analysis of Accounts Receivable by Age

Customer's Name	Total Balance	Not Yet Due	1–30 Days Past Due	31–60 Days Past Due	61–90 Days Past Due	Over 90 Days Past Due
WALTER CARTER CORPORATION Analysis of Accounts Receivable by Age December 31, 1973						
Walter G. Arnold	$ 880	$ 800	$ 80			
Allan Conlon	1,800	1,000	500	$ 300		
Charles Peacock	50				$ 50	
Richard C. Smith	320	100	200	20		
Jerome Werther	960				900	$ 60
[Others]	51,990	27,220	15,460	5,280	730	3,300
Totals	$56,000	$29,120	$16,240	$5,600	$1,680	$3,360
Percent of Total	100	52	29	10	3	6

All the accounts in the subsidiary accounts receivable ledger with their corresponding account balances are listed in the Customer's Name and Total Balance columns. The component charges that make up each balance in the Total Balance column are then extended to the appropriate columns. The aging method yields a more satisfactory Allowance for Doubtful Accounts than does any other method because the estimate is based on a study of individual customers' accounts rather than on a blanket percentage of a single general ledger account balance. Only a detailed analysis will disclose those accounts that are not past due but that may be uncollectible and those long overdue accounts that may give indication of eventual collectibility. Yet, if recoveries of accounts receivable previously written off or the write-off in the current year of accounts receivable arising from prior years' sales are run through the Allowance for Doubtful Accounts without any designation of which of these items affect prior years' net income, the bad debts expense of the current year could be greatly distorted.

Management should also compare the current analysis of accounts receivable by age with those of earlier periods, especially the age-group percentages. Presently, 52 percent of the total accounts receivable are not yet due, 29 percent are past due from 1 to 30 days, and so on. When compared with earlier years, percentage increases in the lower age classifications with offsetting decreases in the older classes are favorable.

The analysis in Figure 8-1 may be used to determine the proper balance to be established in Allowance for Doubtful Accounts. To make this determination, companies may apply a sliding scale of percentages based on previous experience to the total amount shown in each column. The computation to determine expected losses for the Walter Carter Corporation is shown below.

	Amount	Estimated Percentage Uncollectible	Allowance for Doubtful Accounts
Not yet due	$29,120	2	$ 582.40
1–30 days past due	16,240	4	649.60
31–60 days past due	5,600	10	560.00
61–90 days past due	1,680	20	336.00
Over 90 days past due	3,360	50	1,680.00
Totals	$56,000		$3,808.00

On the basis of this summary, $3,808 of the outstanding accounts receivable on December 31 may become uncollectible. Consequently, an Allowance for Doubtful Accounts with a balance of $3,808 should be established. Before the adjusting entry is made, the existing balance in the account must be considered. The Walter Carter Corporation has a present credit balance in Allowance for Doubtful Accounts of $200, a provision remaining from earlier periods. The adjusting entry amount will be for $3,608 ($3,808 − $200); when it is transferred to the allowance account, it will bring that account up to $3,808, the estimated probable uncollectible accounts. The adjusting journal entry is

1973			
Dec. 31	Bad Debts Expense	3,608	
	Allowance for Doubtful Accounts		3,608
	To increase the asset valuation account to the estimated loss.		

Assume, however, that the Allowance for Doubtful Accounts had a debit balance of $300 before adjustment, rather than a credit balance of $200. The adjusting entry would be for $4,108 ($3,808 + $300); after it is posted the allowance account will contain the desired credit balance of $3,808.

An analysis of accounts receivable by age is time-consuming; if there is a reliable pattern, the Allowance for Doubtful Accounts may be based on a single percentage of Accounts Receivable computed as follows for the Gnu Corporation:

End of Year	Balance of Accounts Receivable	Total Losses from Uncollectible Accounts
1970	$20,000	$ 800
1971	24,000	480
1972	22,000	700
Totals	$66,000	$1,980

The average loss of the past three years has been 3 percent ($1,980 ÷ $66,000). Assume that at the end of 1973 total accounts receivable are $25,000 and a credit balance of $150 is in the allowance account. Estimated uncollectible accounts at 3 percent of Accounts Receivable are $750 ($25,000 × 0.03). The following adjusting entry at the end of 1973 on the books of the Gnu Corporation increases the Allowance for Doubtful Accounts to the desired amount of $750.

1973			
Dec. 31	Bad Debts Expense	600	
	Allowance for Doubtful Accounts		600
	To increase the asset valuation account to the estimated uncollectible account.		

A portion of the information for the following partial statement of financial position is taken from the preceding data.

GNU CORPORATION
Partial Statement of Financial Position
December 31, 1973

Assets

Current Assets		
Cash		$ 3,200
Accounts Receivable	$25,000	
Less Allowance for Doubtful Accounts	750	24,250
Notes Receivable		$18,000

Promissory notes receivable arising from the sale of merchandise may also prove to be uncollectible. The amount due from the customer on a dishonored note is removed from Notes Receivable and transferred to Accounts Receivable. The amount will remain in the Accounts Receivable account until it either is collected or is determined to be uncollectible and written off in the usual manner. When notes receivable specifically arise from the sale of merchandise, the current provision for estimated bad debts losses should be adequate to cover outstanding notes receivable and accounts receivable. The following partial statement of financial position presentation shows that the allowance covers Notes Receivable and Accounts Receivable jointly:

GNU CORPORATION
Partial Statement of Financial Position
December 31, 1973

Assets

Current Assets		
Cash		$ 3,200
Accounts Receivable	$25,000	
Notes Receivable	18,000	
Total	$43,000	
Deduct Allowance for Doubtful Accounts and Notes	750	42,250

Writing Off Uncollectible Accounts

When it is decided that a customer's account is definitely uncollectible, the amount due should be written off. Assuming that on February 15, 1974, the Gnu Corporation definitely determined that the account of a customer, Joseph Sacks, is uncollectible, the entry to record the write-off is

1974			
Feb. 15	Allowance for Doubtful Accounts	50	
	Accounts Receivable–Joseph Sacks		50

This entry has no effect on the net realizable value of the receivables; it only adjusts the balances of the two reciprocal accounts. The entry does not affect expenses because no expense was incurred on February 15, 1974, the expense was recorded by the adjusting entry of December 31, 1973. Assume that immediately before this entry was made, the books of the Gnu Corporation showed the following balances:

Accounts Receivable	$25,000
Allowance for Doubtful Accounts (credit)	750

When the entry to write off Sacks's account is posted, the result is

	Balances Before Write-Off	Write-Off	Balances After Write-Off
Accounts Receivable	$25,000	$50	$24,950
Allowance for Doubtful Accounts	750	50	700
Estimated Realizable Value	$24,250		$24,250

This points up the fact that since the loss was recorded in the period when the sale was made, the subsequent write-off does not change assets, liabilities, or stockholders' equity.

Recovery of Bad Debts

An account that is written off as uncollectible may later be recovered in part or in full. In that event, the entry that was made to write off the account is reversed to the extent of the amount recovered or expected to be recovered. Assuming that Joseph Sacks settles with his creditors for 50 cents on the dollar and that a check for $25 is received, the required journal entries are

1974			
Nov. 15	Accounts Receivable–Joseph Sacks	25	
	Allowance for Doubtful Accounts		25
	To restore the collectible portion of the account previously written off.		
	Cash	25	
	Accounts Receivable–Joseph Sacks		25
	To record payment received.		

The debit and the credit to Accounts Receivable–Joseph Sacks cancel each other, but they are necessary if a complete record of all transactions with the customer is to be maintained. Such a record may be of considerable aid if further extension of credit to Joseph Sacks comes up for consideration at some future date.

CORRECTION OF ERRORS IN ALLOWANCE FOR DOUBTFUL ACCOUNTS

Because of changing economic conditions and the very fact that the percentage is based on past losses, errors can and do occur. Assume, for example, that the accountant of the Fountainhead Corporation, after analyzing Sales and Accounts Receivable determined the following information:

1. Correct bad debts expense for 1973, $4,000
2. Actual balance in Allowance for Doubtful Accounts before adjustment, $1,000 debit balance
3. Correct balance which should be in Allowance for Doubtful Accounts before adjustment, $100 credit balance
4. Cumulative error as a result of past understatement of the Allowance for Doubtful Accounts, $1,100
5. Required balance in Allowance for Doubtful Accounts, $4,100

The adjusting entry to record the bad debts expense for 1973 and to correct the error in the Allowance for Doubtful Accounts is

1973			
Dec. 31	Corrections of Prior Years' Income	1,100	
	Bad Debts Expense	4,000	
	Allowance for Doubtful Accounts		5,100
	To correct a material underestimate of uncollectibles and to provide for an adequate allowance balance.		

After the foregoing information is posted to the Allowance for Doubtful Accounts, its balance will yield the estimated correct amount needed for future uncollectibles, $4,100. The correction account is a deduction from revenue in arriving at net income.

Allowance for Doubtful Accounts				
1973 Dec. 31	Balance before Adjustment	1,000	1973 Dec. 31 Adjustment 4,100	5,100

Direct Write-Offs in Period of Discovery

A company that uses the direct write-off method postpones recognition of a bad debts expense until the receivable is definitely known to be uncollectible. In this case, an Allowance for Doubtful Accounts is *not* used, and no end-of-period adjusting entry for estimated losses is made. The February 15, 1974 entry on the books of the Gnu Corporation to remove Joseph Sacks's account in full under the direct write-off method is:

1974 Feb. 15	Bad Debts Expense	50	
	Accounts Receivable–Joseph Sacks		50

By this method, the loss is recognized in the period of write-off rather than in the period when the sale is made. The direct write-off method, as well as the methods previously illustrated, is acceptable for Federal income tax reporting purposes. This method, however, does not charge each accounting period with the losses arising out of sales made in that period and therefore violates the principle of matching expenses and revenue in each accounting period.

An account previously written off in the period of discovery may be subsequently collected in part or in full. Assume again that on November 15, 1974, Sacks makes a settlement of 50 cents on the dollar and issues a check for $25. The required journal entries are:

1974 Nov. 15	Accounts Receivable–Joseph Sacks	25	
	Bad Debts Recovered		25
	To restore the collectible portion of the account previously written off.		
	Cash	25	
	Accounts Receivable–Joseph Sacks		25
	To record payment received.		

Bad Debts Recovered is a revenue account; its balance may be reported in the Other Revenue section of the income statement.

Comparison of the Two Recording Procedures

The two methods of recording bad debts expense are shown in Figure 8-2, assuming the following data:

Allowance for Doubtful Accounts (credit balance, January 1)	$ 4,200
All sales on account	410,000
Cash collections on account	395,000
Sales returns and allowances	4,000
Accounts receivable written off as uncollectible	3,950
Bad debts recovered	250
The basis for estimating bad debt losses is 1 percent of Sales minus Sales Returns and Allowances.	

Figure 8-2. Two Methods of Accounting for Bad Debts Expense

Transactions (Jan. 1–Dec. 31, 1973)	Estimating Bad Debts Expense		Direct Write-off	
All sales on account.	Accounts Receivable Sales	410,000 410,000	Accounts Receivable Sales	410,000 410,000
Cash received on account.	Cash Accounts Receivable	395,000 395,000	Cash Accounts Receivable	395,000 395,000
Sales returns and allowances.	Sales Returns and Allowances Accounts Receivable	 4,000 4,000	Sales Returns and Allowances Accounts Receivable	 4,000 4,000
Accounts receivable determined to be uncollectible.	Allowance for Doubtful Accounts Accounts Receivable	 3,950 3,950	Bad Debts Expense Accounts Receivable	3,950 3,950
Bad debts recovered.	Accounts Receivable Allowance for Doubtful Accounts Cash Accounts Receivable	250 250 250 250	Accounts Receivable Bad Debts Recovered Cash Accounts Receivable	250 250 250 250
Adjusting entry, December 31, 1973 ($410,000 − $4,000 = $406,000 × 0.01 = $4,060.	Bad Debts Expense Allowance for Doubtful Accounts	4,060 4,060	(No entry is made)	
Closing entry, December 31, 1973.	Sales Sales Returns and Allowances Bad Debts Expense Revenue and Expense Summary	410,000 4,000 4,060 401,940	Sales Bad Debts Recovered Bad Debts Expense Sales Returns and Allowances Revenue and Expense Summary	410,000 250 3,950 4,000 402,300

Allowance Accounts for Returns and Allowances and Cash Discounts

The net realizable amount of receivables on the statement of financial position indicates the amount of collections available to the firm after allowing for bad debts losses. For example, Accounts Receivable of $15,000 and a corresponding Allowance for Doubtful Accounts of $1,000 should result in a company's collecting approximately $14,000. In reality, other types of deductions may be made that will decrease this amount. Typical deductions are sales returns, sales allowances, cash discounts granted to customers for prompt payments, and collection expenses.

Ideally, all these additional deductions should have corresponding valuation accounts, so that Accounts Receivable in the statement of financial position will be stated at an amount closer to the net amount that will be collected. However, such valuation accounts as Allowance for Sales Returns and Allowances and Allowance for Sales Discounts are rarely used because, as a practical matter, the adjusting entry to debit the expense account will have no significant effect on net income. Also, these adjustments are not recognizable for income tax purposes.

Opposite Balances in Accounts Receivable and Accounts Payable

In the accounts receivable ledger, the customers' accounts normally have debit balances. Sometimes an overpayment, a sales return, a sales allowance, or an advance payment may convert the balance into a credit.

Assume that there is a net debit balance of $14,800 in an accounts receivable ledger consisting of 100 accounts, as follows:

98 accounts with a debit balance	$15,000
2 accounts with a credit balance	200
Net debit balance of 100 accounts receivable	$14,800

The debit amount of $15,000 and the credit amount of $200 should appear on the statement of financial position as follows:

Current Assets		Current Liabilities	
Accounts Receivable	$15,000	Credit Balances in Customers' Accounts	$200

The controlling account balance of $14,800 should not be used in the statement of financial position because it would conceal the current liability of $200. Similarly, if the accounts payable ledger contains creditors' accounts with debit balances, the statement of financial position should show the total credit balances and the total debit balances of accounts payable. For example, if a company has a net balance in the Accounts Payable controlling account of $44,300, with certain subsidiary ledger accounts having debit balances that total $700, it should disclose this information in its statement of financial position as follows:

Current Assets		Current Liabilities	
Debit Balances in Creditors' Accounts	$700	Accounts Payable	$45,000

ACCOUNTS RECEIVABLE—MANAGERIAL ANALYSIS

The manager of a business that sells on credit must watch carefully for past-due accounts and guard against possible losses. A detailed analysis of the due date of each customer's account is desirable and should be secured periodically by preparing an aging statement similar to Figure 8-1. Two guides to the overall condition of the accounts receivable are the average collection period and the receivable turnover per year. If goods are sold on terms of 2/10, n/30, the amount of accounts receivable outstanding at any time should be less than the credit sales for the last 30 days because many of the sales will have been paid within the discount period. If allowance is made for slow-paying accounts, the receivables may represent 30 to 35 days' sales. If the receivables exceed this limitation, a careful analysis of all the accounts should be made.

To illustrate the computation of the average collection period, or number of days' sales uncollected, and the receivable turnover per year, the following data for the Morton Company are assumed:

	1974	1973	1972
Credit sales for year	$183,600	$165,600	$160,000
Trade accounts and notes receivable (net) at end of year	14,420	17,200	$15,000

Only receivables (accounts and notes) arising out of sales of merchandise on account are used. The balance of Allowance for Doubtful Accounts is deducted in computing the average trade receivables balance.

Figure 8-3. Managerial Analysis of Receivables

	1974	1973
1. Net credit sales	$183,600	$165,600
2. Days in year	365	365
3. Net credit sales per day (line 1 ÷ line 2)	$503	$454
4. Average trade receivables (balance at beginning of year + balance at end of year ÷ 2)	15,810	16,100
Average collection period (line 4 ÷ line 3)	31 days	35 days
Receivable turnover per year (line 1 ÷ line 4)	11.6 times	10.3 times

If line 1 covered sales for a period of less than one year, then line 2 would be changed accordingly. Thus, if the sales were for a three-month period, line 2 would show 91 days (one-fourth of 365 days).

Average collection periods vary with the line of business. Wholesalers of shoes may average 45 days, compared with grocery wholesalers whose average is approximately 15 days. In the illustration in Figure 8-3, assuming that sales are on terms of 2/10, n/30, both years show a healthy situation, with 1974 particularly good.

The receivables turnover per year or the ratio of credit sales to receivables is calculated by dividing net credit sales by the average balance of trade receivables. In Figure 8-3, the receivables for the year 1973 have been collected at a rate of approximately 10.3 times per year. For a standard of comparison, the preceding year's rate or the industry rate may be used. An increasing turnover of receivables as exhibited in Figure 8-3 indicates an improvement and reflects a decreasing relative amount of investment of working capital in receivables.

INTERNAL CONTROL—ACCOUNTS RECEIVABLE

As in the case of cash, adequate safeguards must be established for accounts receivable. It is important that persons who maintain the accounts receivable records should not have access to cash. Returns and allowances, discounts, and bad debts write-offs should be authorized by an officer and should be separated from the cash receipt and disbursement functions. Statements of account should be checked and mailed to customers by someone other than the accounts receivable bookkeeper. An independent check should be established to see that the statements sent to customers are in agreement with the accounts receivable records. Delinquent accounts should be reviewed periodically by a responsible official. Adequate control over receivables begins with the approved sales order and continues through the remaining stages in the credit sales process: approval of credit terms, recording of shipment, customer billing, recording the receivable and its collection, and approval of subsequent adjustments.

SUMMARY

Receivables represent amounts due from others for goods sold, services rendered, money lent, and deposits made. Those due within the year or the operating cycle, whichever is longer, should be classified as current assets; those not due within this period of time should be disclosed as long-term investments on the statement of financial position. Receivables should be segregated into Accounts Receivable–Trade, representing claims against customers for goods sold or services rendered, and nontrade accounts receivable, a group of receivables representing claims arising from sources other than normal sales of its regular product or service. These nontrade receivables include loans to officers or employees, deposits made on contract bids or with public utilities and public agencies, claims against common carriers for loss or damage to goods in shipment, loss claims against insurance companies, claims against the U.S. Treasury for tax refunds, amounts due from affiliated companies, and amounts due or accrued from rentals, interest, and royalties.

The balance of the Accounts Receivable–Trade account represents uncollected sales that have previously been recognized as revenue. Thus, to match properly revenues and expenses, any amounts that are expected to be uncollectible should be recognized as an expense in the period in which the related sales were realized as revenue. On the statement of financial position, Accounts Receivable–Trade should be valued at their net realizable value, or the amount that is ultimately expected to be collected. To accomplish this, an adjusting entry debiting Bad Debts Expense and crediting Allowance for Doubtful Accounts is made at the end of each accounting period. Bad Debts Expense is classified as a general and administrative expense in the income statement and Allowance for Doubtful Accounts is a contra account to Accounts Receivable in the statement of financial position. Two methods of estimating the amount of the bad debts adjustment are: (1) Income Statement Approach—the estimate of the bad debts expense is based on a specific percentage of sales or charge sales during the year; (2) Statement of Financial Position Approach—the estimate of the uncollectible accounts is determined by aging the accounts receivable or by taking a specific percentage of the total balance of Accounts Receivable. Regardless of the method of estimating the bad debts adjustment employed, the percentages should be based on previous years' experience amended for any developments expected to change the relationship. If the income statement approach is used, the adjusting entry is made for the amount of the estimated bad debts expense without reference to the balance of the Allowance for Doubtful Accounts. If the statement of financial position approach is followed, Allowance for Doubtful Accounts is adjusted to the balance determined in the analysis of the accounts receivable. The income statement approach yields a better estimate of the bad debts expense and thus a better measurement of net income; whereas the statement of financial position approach yields a better valuation of Accounts Receivable.

When a specific account proves to be uncollectible, it is written off by a debit to Allowance for Doubtful Accounts and a credit to Accounts Receivable. No expense is recognized at this time, because the expense was previously recorded by the bad debts adjustment. If an account previously written off as uncollectible is collected, Accounts Receivable is debited with an accompanying credit to Allowance for Doubtful Accounts. The collection of the account is then recorded in the normal manner. Any material error in estimating the bad debts adjustment that results in a material over or understatement in Bad Debts Expense or Allowance for Doubtful Accounts should be corrected.

An alternative method of accounting for losses from uncollectible accounts is the direct write-off method. Under this procedure, no allowance account is utilized and losses are recognized in the period in which the accounts prove uncollectible. This method violates the matching principle since the expenses relating to the uncollectible accounts are not recorded in the period in which the related revenue is recognized.

Other possible valuation accounts to Accounts Receivable–Trade include deductions for sales returns and allowances, cash discounts, and collection expenses. In practice these adjustments are very rarely used since the amount involved is generally immaterial and none of these adjustments is allowed for Federal income tax purposes.

Any credit balances in customers' accounts in the accounts receivable ledger should be disclosed as current liabilities and not as offsets against the debit balances in the Accounts Receivable account.

Two devices that aid management in determining the effectiveness of internal control over Accounts Receivable are the receivables turnover and the average collection period (number of days' sales outstanding).

Internal control over receivables requires the segregation of the maintenance of accounts receivable and related records, handling of cash, and sending of statements to customers; the proper authorization of returns and allowances, discounts, and bad debts written off; reviews of delinquent accounts; and an independent check to determine that statements mailed to customers are in agreement with the customers' accounts.

QUESTIONS

Q8-1. List eight different categories of receivables and state the probable financial position statement classification of each. The following format is suggested:

| | Probable Financial Position |
| Receivable Item | Statement Classification |

Q8-2. Discuss the general principle of the valuation of trade receivables.

Q8-3. (a) Explain the function of the Allowance for Doubtful Accounts account. (b) What methods may be used to estimate the Allowance for Doubtful Accounts? (c) How is Allowance for Doubtful Accounts shown on the position statement?

Q8-4. Distinguish between the income statement approach and the statement of financial position approach in estimating the bad debts expense.

Q8-5. A company attempting to state its accounts receivable at their net realizable value may have to establish accounts other than the Allowance for Doubtful Accounts. Name three other valuation accounts for Accounts Receivable.

Q8-6. How would you interpret each entry in the following account?

ALLOWANCE FOR DOUBTFUL ACCOUNTS

1973				1972				
Mar.	10		J58	1,260	Dec.	31		J50	3,650
1974				1973				
Jan.	5		J68	750	Dec.	31		J65	3,420
					1974				
					Apr.	6		J70	555

Q8-7. The following entry was made to record the recovery of a bad debt:

Cash   365
      Allowance for Doubtful Accounts   365

Discuss the validity of this method of recording the recovery.

Q8-8. (a) Discuss the reasons for credit balances occurring in Accounts Receivable accounts. (b) How are such balances presented in the statement of financial position?

Q8-9. (a) Why is management concerned with the average collection period of Accounts Receivable? (b) Describe its computation.

Q8-10. The Slavon Company, which had Accounts Receivable of $56,850 and an Allowance for Doubtful Accounts of $2,610 on January 1, 1973, wrote off in 1973 a past due account of N. Healy for $575. (a) What effect will the write-off have on the total current assets of the company immediately before and after the write-off? (b) On net income for 1973? Explain.

EXERCISES

E8-1. The Jimson Company maintains a controlling account entitled Receivables, the balance of which at December 31, 1973, was $48,650. Subsidiary ledger and other information reveal the following:

       a. 306 trade accounts (debit balances) $36,000
       b. 4 trade accounts (credit balances) $650
       c. 5 trade notes $8,000
       d. 2 loans to the president and vice president $5,300
       e. Allowance for Doubtful Accounts $3,000

Show how this information should be reported on the statement of financial position.

E8-2. The Adam Company, which uses an Allowance for Doubtful Accounts, had the following transactions involving worthless accounts in 1973 and 1974.

1973
Dec. 31   Recorded bad debts expense of $2,200.

1974
Mar.   5   Wrote off N. O. Girard's account of $520 as uncollectible.

Apr. 10   Wrote off A. M. Stanley's account of $560 as uncollectible.

Sept. 6   Recovered $560 from A. M. Stanley.

Journalize the transactions.

E8-3. The Catawba Company uses the direct write-off method of accounting for bad debts. It had the following transactions involving worthless accounts in 1973:

1973
Feb. 13   Wrote off Joseph White's account of $375 as uncollectible. The merchandise had been sold in 1972.

Aug. 13   Wrote off Alfred Green's account of $513 as uncollectible.

Dec. 10   Recovered $375 from Joseph White.

Journalize the transactions.

E8-4. The Bowan Trading Company had charge sales of $550,000 during 1973 and Accounts Receivable of $52,500 and a credit balance of $150 in Allowance for Doubtful Accounts at the end of the year. Record the bad debts expense for the year, using each of the following methods for the estimate: (a) The Allowance for Doubtful Accounts is to be increased to 5 percent of Accounts Receivable. (b) Bad debts expense is estimated to be 0.5 percent of charge sales. (c) The Allowance for Doubtful Accounts is to be increased to $3,100, as indicated by an aging schedule. (d) Which method would you choose and why?

E8-5. The trial balance of the Hathaway Company included the following accounts on August 31, 1973, the end of its fiscal year:

Accounts Receivable	$ 53,000
Allowance for Doubtful Accounts (credit)	300
Sales	383,000

Uncollectible accounts are estimated at 5 percent of Accounts Receivable. (a) Make the adjusting entry to record the bad debts expense. (b) State the bad debts expense for the year. (c) Show the presentation of Accounts Receivable and Allowance for Doubtful Accounts in the August 31, 1973, position statement. (d) Give the entry to write off the account of an insolvent customer, James Whitney, for $710.

E8-6. The accounts receivable ledger of the Vought Distributing Company shows the following data on December 31, 1973. The general ledger showed a $100 debit balance in Allowance for Doubtful Accounts before adjustments.

Name of Customer	Invoice Date	Amount
Modesto Fruit Company	May 2, 1973	$ 600.00
Neri Brothers	August 15, 1973	335.50
Paley Fruitrees, Inc.	October 2, 1973	719.85
	December 8, 1973	275.00
Temple Grapefruit Company	March 3, 1973	445.00
Royal Fruit Company	November 11, 1973	822.50
Yosemite Produce Company	November 20, 1973	250.00
	September 4, 1973	465.75
	July 10, 1973	922.00
[Others]	December 5, 1973	20,000.00

Terms of sale are n/30.

a. Prepare an analysis of accounts receivable by age.

b. Compute the estimated loss based on the following fixed percentages:

		Estimated Percentage Uncollectible
Accounts not due		0.5
Accounts past due:	1–30 days	1.0
	31–60 days	3.0
	61–90 days	10.0
	91–120 days	25.0
	121–365 days	50.0

c. Record the bad debts expense.

E8-7. The Cash account page in the general ledger of the Webster Corporation has been temporarily misplaced. The following data are available:

	December 31		Year
	1973	1972	1973
Accounts Receivable, Trade	$73,000	$59,000	
Allowance for Doubtful Accounts	5,200	3,100	
Sales			$605,000
Sales Discounts			10,350

During 1973, accounts receivable of $4,350 were written off as uncollectible and one account of $700, written off in 1971, was collected and recorded in the following manner:

Accounts Receivable	700	
Allowance for Doubtful Accounts		700
Cash	700	
Accounts Receivable		700

Compute the cash received from customers during 1973.

E8-8. The following transactions of the Summer company occurred during 1973:

1973

Jan.   2   Sold merchandise with a list price of $7,000 subject to a trade discount of 20%, 10%, and 10%, terms 2/10, n/30, to John Olesum

     10   Received a check from John Olesum in settlement of his account.

     20   Sold merchandise worth $6,000 to Arthur Samuelson on account, terms n/10.

Feb.   1   Received a 6-percent, 120-day note from Samuelson in settlement of account.

     19   Discounted Samuelson's note at the Bank of Chapel Hill at 4 percent. Endorsed the note in blank and followed the practice of recording the contingent liability.

June   2   Samuelson dishonored his note. The bank charged for the note and interest plus a protest fee of $3.00.

a. Journalize the transactions. Use the gross methods of recording receivables and handling cash discounts.

b. What is the equivalent lump-sum trade discount to a 20%, 10%, and 10% chain trade discount? Show computations.

E8-9. The records of the Gunderson Company show that amounts due from customers were $200,000 and $260,000 at the beginning and the end of the year 1973, respectively, and that sales for that period were $2,000,000. What conclusions can be drawn regarding the collection of accounts receivable, assuming that (a) terms of sale are 2/10, n/30; (b) terms of sale are 2/10, n/40; (c) terms of sale are 2/10, n/40, and 25 percent of the sales are for cash?

E8-10. The Plymouth Company sells on terms of 2/10, 1/20, n/60. Approximately 40 percent of its sales are for cash. The Accounts Receivable account shows a balance of $31,384 as of December 31, 1973. Total sales for the year were $365,200. What is the average collection period?

DEMONSTRATION PROBLEMS

DP8-1. (*Use of Allowance for Doubtful Accounts*) The following transactions of the Eason Company occurred in 1972, 1973, and 1974. The company uses the estimating procedure in accounting for bad debts.

1972
Dec. 31   Recorded bad debts expense of $4,650 for 1972.

1973
Mar. 10   Wrote off O. N. Collier's account of $650 as uncollectible.

Nov. 10   Wrote off various other accounts of $3,150 as uncollectible.

Dec. 31   Recorded bad debts expense of $4,265 for 1973.

1974
Feb.   6   O. N. Collier remitted $450 of the amount he owed the firm and agreed to pay the remainder in 30 days.

Required: Journalize the transactions.

DP8-2. (*Direct write-off method*) The following transactions of the Dawson Company occurred in 1973 and 1974. The company uses the direct write-off method of accounting for bad debts.

1973
Jan. 13   Wrote off B. E. Goodson's account of $313 as uncollectible.

Nov. 13   Wrote off O. N. Fair's account of $213 as uncollectible.

    20   Recovered the $313 from B. E. Goodson.

Dec. 13   Wrote off S. P. Santee's account of $613 as uncollectible.

1974
Mar. 10   Recovered the $213 from O. N. Fair.

Required: Journalize the transactions.

DP8-3. (*Adjusting entries for bad debts*) The partial trial balance of the Deborah Company at December 31, 1973, before any adjustments are made, is given below.

DEBORAH COMPANY
Partial Trial Balance
December 31, 1973

	Debits	Credits
Accounts Receivable	$80,000	
Notes Receivable	30,000	
Allowance for Doubtful Accounts and Notes	600	
Sales		$112,500
Sales Returns and Allowances	2,500	

Required: Prepare the adjusting entries for the bad debts expense under the following assumptions: (a) Allowance for Doubtful Accounts and Notes is to be increased to 4 percent of trade receivables; (b) the bad debts expense is estimated to be 1.8 percent of net sales.

PROBLEMS

P8-1. The balance of Allowance for Doubtful Accounts of the Richland Company on January 1, 1973, was $3,200. During 1973, uncollectible accounts totaling $2,900 were written off. The Company collected $300 on one of these accounts after it had been written off. The balance of the Accounts Receivable account on December 31, 1973, was $82,000.

Required:

Make the journal entries to (a) charge off the worthless accounts during 1973, (b) record the collection of the $300, and (c) make the adjusting entry on December 31, 1973, for the bad debts expense. Assume that uncollectible accounts average 4 percent of the uncollected accounts.

P8-2. (*Accounting policy decision problem*) The Nunnly Company uses a cash receipts journal, a cash disbursements journal, a single-column purchases journal, a single-column sales journal, and a two-column general journal. The Accounts Receivable account in the general ledger at May 1, 1973, is given (posting references have been omitted).

Accounts Receivable

1973			1973		
May 1	Balance	23,500	May 5		1,500
25		1,502	10		125
31		26,200	28		1,502
			31		19,750

During the month, the general journal was used to record transactions with only two customers. The subsidiary ledger accounts of these two customers are shown below.

William Duncan

1973					
May 1	Balance	✔			(300) cr.
6		S2	700		400
10		J4		125	275

Allen Younce

1973					
May 1	Balance	✔			1,500
5	(20-day note)	J4		1,500	–0–
25		CD6	1,502		1,502
28		J4		1,502	–0–

Required:

1. Explain the $300 credit balance on May 1 in William Duncan's account.
2. What would the posting references for the May 31 entries in the Accounts Receivable controlling account be?

3. What should be the total of the schedule of accounts receivable on May 31?
4. Explain the transaction that resulted in the debit of $1,502 on May 25 in Allen Younce's account.
5. State in narrative form the transactions that resulted in each of the following credits to the Accounts Receivable controlling account: May 5, $1,500; May 10, $125; May 28, $1,502.

P8-3. The Allowance for Doubtful Accounts of the Boston Company showed a credit balance of $300 on December 31, 1973, before adjustments were made. The bad debts expense for 1973 is estimated at 2 percent of the charge sales of $100,000 for the year.

The following transactions occurred during the next two years:

1974

May 1   Wrote off George Shaw's $900 account as uncollectible.

Oct. 15 Wrote off John Foley's $1,200 account as uncollectible.

Nov. 30 Received a check from George Shaw for $100 in final settlement of the account written off on May 1. He had been adjudged bankrupt by the courts.

Dec. 31 An analysis of accounts receivable by age indicated that accounts doubtful of collection totaled $1,900.

1975

Aug. 21 Wrote off Joseph Sack's $1,800 account as uncollectible.

Dec. 31 Estimated that uncollectible accounts receivable totaled $2,400.

Required: 1. Record transactions in general journal form.
2. Post to a T account for Allowance for Doubtful Accounts. Rule and balance the account at the end of each year.

P8-4. The balance of the Accounts Receivable account of the Reynolda Company at December 31, 1973, was $73,360. Two customers' accounts in the subsidiary ledger show credit balances of $3,160 and $1,200.

Required: 1. What is the amount that would be shown on the position statement as Accounts Receivable under Current Assets?
2. How would the credit balances in the customers' accounts be disclosed?

P8-5. The Accounts Receivable controlling account of the Winter Corporation shows a balance of $345,000 on June 30, 1973. A summary of the analysis of accounts receivable by age shows accounts outstanding from the date of the invoice as follows:

Accounts not due		$260,000
Accounts past due:	1–30 days	40,000
	31–60 days	25,000
	61–150 days	15,000
	151 days and over	5,000
	Total	$345,000

Allowance for Doubtful Accounts has a debit balance of $210 on June 30, before adjustments. The adjustment of the allowance account is to be based on the following schedule of percentages estimated uncollectible:

Accounts not due		½ of 1%
Accounts past due:	1–30 days	3%
	31–60 days	6%
	61–150 days	20%
	151 days and over	50%

Required: 1. Prepare the necessary adjusting entry.
2. Prepare a partial position statement, showing Accounts Receivable and Allowance for Doubtful Accounts.

P8-6. The accounts receivable ledger of the Lawter Company showed the following information on March 31, 1974:

Franklin Durce

1973									
Aug.	12		S27	4,250	00			4,250	00
Sept.	10		S33	743	00			4,993	00
	30		CR15			4,250	00	743	00
Oct.	12		S45	1,407	00			2,150	00
Nov.	4		S52	415	00			2,565	00
Dec.	10		CR27			415	00	2,150	00
1974									
Jan.	12		S6	500	00			2,650	00
	13		CR4			1,407	00	1,243	00
	15		S7	783	00			2,026	00
	17	Allowance on 1/15 invoice	J2			93	00	1,933	00

M. Katherson

1973									
Nov.	12		S51	1,000	00			1,000	00
Dec.	12		CR28			500	00	500	00
1974									
Jan.	29		S9	761	00			1,261	00
Mar.	10		S17	550	00			1,811	00
	31		CR11			550	00	1,261	00

Peter Wombly

1973									
Dec.	12		S56	5,401	00			5,401	00
1974									
Jan.	12	Note	J2			3,000	00	2,401	00
Feb.	26		S14	1,800	00			4,201	00
Mar.	26		S22	2,000	00			6,201	00

Paul Wulmer

1973									
Aug.	1		S24	973	00			973	00
Oct.	12		S45	76	00			1,049	00
1974									
Jan.	2	Return	J2			700	00	349	00
Feb.	3		S10	699	00			1,048	00
	12		S13	200	00			1,248	00
Mar.	30		CR11			899	00	349	00

Required:

1. Prepare an analysis of accounts receivable by age as of March 31, 1974. Assume that the terms of sale are n/30.
2. Make the adjusting entry for the bad debts expense on the basis of the age of the accounts as follows:

Accounts not due		½%
Accounts past due:	1–30 days	2%
	31–60 days	5%
	61–90 days	10%
	91 days and over	33⅓%

There is a debit balance of $200 in Allowance for Doubtful Accounts on March 31, 1974, before adjustments.

P8-7. On December 31, 1973, Jay Duce's trial balance showed the following:

Accounts Receivable	$72,000
Allowance for Doubtful Accounts (debit)	300

After making an analysis of the accounts receivable, estimate the accounts doubtful of collection at $3,000.

During the year 1974, the following transactions occurred:

a. Sales on account were $320,000.
b. Accounts written off as uncollectible totaled $3,300.
c. Collections from customers on account were $308,900. This includes a receipt of $100 that had been written off during the year as uncollectible.

On December 31, 1974, the accounts doubtful of collection were estimated at $3,400.

Required:

1. Set up T accounts for Accounts Receivable and Allowance for Doubtful Accounts, post the balances as of December 31, 1973, and make the entries for 1973 and 1974 directly into the T accounts.
2. Compute the bad debts expense deduction in the income statement for the year 1974, using: (a) the direct write-off method; (b) the Allowance for Doubtful Accounts method.

P8-8. During November and early December, 1973, the Capitol Hill Sales Company had the following sales and receivables transactions. All sales were made on account and carried terms of 2/10, n/30.

1973
Nov. 1 Sold merchandise to Jay Swan for $390 on Invoice 1001.

2 Sold merchandise to Ray Faulk for $2,150 on Invoice 1002.

7 Credited Ray Faulk for returned merchandise with an invoice price of $350.

9 Received a check for the amount due from Jay Swan on Invoice 1001.

10 Sold merchandise to the Scuppernong Company for $460 on Invoice 1003.

13 Received $205.80 in cash from the Scuppernong Company in partial payment of Invoice 1003. Discounts are allowed on partial payments.

14 Received a check for the amount due from Ray Faulk.

15 Sold merchandise to the Albermarle Company for $3,000 on Invoice 1004.

23 Received a check for the amount due from the Albermarle Company on Invoice 1004.

30 Sold merchandise to the Paris Company for $2,850 on Invoice 1005.

1973

Nov. 30 Sold merchandise to the Ronson Company for $3,250 on Invoice 1006.

30 Estimated the bad debts expense for November to be 2.5 percent of charge sales less sales returns and allowances.

Dec. 8 Received notice that the Scuppernong Company had been adjudged bankrupt. The balance of its account is therefore regarded as uncollectible.

Required:

1. Journalize the transactions.
2. Post all entries to the Accounts Receivable controlling and subsidiary accounts.
3. Prepare a schedule of accounts receivable at November 30, 1973.

P8-9. Design a flow chart that will graphically illustrate the procedures in aging accounts receivable that are necessary to solve Problem 8-6.

1. Print the headings illustrated in Figure 8-1.
2. Read customer's name, total balance, amount not due, amount 1–30 days past due, amount 31–60 days past due, amount 61–90 days past due, and amount over 90 days past due.
3. Print the data for each customer in the table under the appropriate headings.
4. Accumulate the total amount in each column for all customers.
5. Repeat until all the customers' accounts have been processed.
6. Print the totals in each column for all customers.
7. End of job.

9

The Measurement
and Control
of Inventory

Inventory in a wholesale or retail business—that is, a nonmanufacturing business—is generally understood to mean goods owned by the business for sale to customers. Alternative terms are *merchandise* and *merchandise inventory*. Up to this point in the text, the amount of the merchandise inventory was specified and, therefore, assumed to be correct. The factors involved in arriving at the value of the inventory—classification of items, determination of physical quantities on hand, and techniques of assigning costs—were not stated. These factors, however, are indispensable in valuing the merchandise inventory for the preparation of financial statements.

THE IMPORTANCE OF INVENTORY VALUATION

The proper valuation, or *costing*, of the merchandise inventory is of considerable importance for income measurement and position statement valuation. The inventory is often large in proportion to the other items in the financial statements; a misstatement of the inventory will cause a misstatement of the cost of goods sold, gross margin on sales, and net income for the period in which the error occurred, and will also misstate current assets, and stockholders' equity as of the end of that period. Furthermore, since the ending inventory of one accounting period is the beginning inventory of the next period, any over or understatement will also misstate the cost of goods sold, gross margin on sales, and net income of the next period.

The following information is taken from the income statements of a retail store for 1972 and 1973.

308

	1973		1972	
Sales		$300,000		$250,000
Cost of Goods Sold				
Beginning Inventory	$ 90,000		$ 80,000	
Purchases	150,000		120,000	
Total	$240,000		$200,000	
Deduct Ending Inventory	105,000	135,000	90,000	110,000
Gross Margin on Sales		$165,000		$140,000
Expenses		130,000		120,000
Net Income		$ 35,000		$ 20,000

If it is assumed that the ending inventory for 1972 should have been valued at $85,000 rather than $90,000, the effect of the error on the income statements is evident from the corrected statements.

	1973		1972	
Sales		$300,000		$250,000
Cost of Goods Sold				
Beginning Inventory	$ 85,000		$ 80,000	
Purchases	150,000		120,000	
Total	$235,000		$200,000	
Deduct Ending Inventory	105,000	130,000	85,000	115,000
Gross Margin on Sales		$170,000		$135,000
Expenses		130,000		120,000
Net Income		$ 40,000		$ 15,000

The $5,000 overstatement of the ending inventory in 1972 resulted in the following errors of $5,000 in the two income statements:

	1973	1972
Cost of Goods Sold	Overstated	Understated
Gross Margin	Understated	Overstated
Net Income	Understated	Overstated

Since the misstatements cancel each other, the error has no overall effect on the two-year span covered by the statements. That fact, however, does not diminish the seriousness of an inventory valuation error. The interpretation and analysis of the income statement for each period may influence some basic management decisions. Since both income statements are in error, their reciprocal canceling effect does not cancel management errors caused by reliance on two incorrect statements.

THE BASIS OF INVENTORY VALUATION

Inventories are recorded at cost. The term *cost* includes all expenditures "incurred in bringing an article to its existing condition and location."[1] Cost consists of the invoice price of the merchandise (less purchase discounts) plus transportation

[1] AICPA, *Accounting Principles*, Vol. 2. Chicago: Commerce Clearing House, Inc., 1970, p. 6014.

in, insurance while in transit, and any other expenditures made by the buyer to get the merchandise to his place of business. In the interest of simplifying the clerical task of prorating these other costs to the various items of inventory purchased, they are frequently carried in separate accounts and the Purchases account shows only the invoice price. If these amounts are significant in relation to the invoice price of the merchandise, a proportionate part should be added to the cost of the goods on hand at the end of the period. The cost of the inventory may be determined in several different ways. The method used to determine cost should be the one that "most clearly reflects periodic income."[2]

The term *value* is defined as "the amount at which an item is stated, in accordance with the accounting principles related to that item."[3] "Since accounting is predominantly based on cost, the proper uses of the word *value* in accounting are largely restricted to the statement of items at cost, or at modifications of cost."[4]

Accounting Concept: ▼
Valuation of Assets at
Cost

▼ The accountant, therefore, usually expresses *value* in terms of *cost.* ▼ There are, of course, other concepts of value; the accountant's valuation is *historical*, or prior cost, which is objective, being subject to measurement. It is this objectivity that accounts for the predominance of historical cost as a valuation basis. The economist, on the other hand, relates value to current and anticipated prices for better comparability and matching of expired costs with revenue. The distinction between these two concepts is especially important during periods of rapidly rising prices with their concomitant effect on financial statement valuations. Many persons in and out of the profession question the usefulness of cost as a valuation concept when prices are unstable. Nevertheless, the cost concept is thoroughly established in accounting.

Periodic and Perpetual Inventory Methods

There are two methods used for determining inventory quantities on hand: periodic (physical count) and perpetual (continuous record).

Periodic Inventory. With the periodic inventory method, the value of the inventory for statement of financial position presentation and for the determination of the cost of goods sold is determined at the end of each accounting period by a complete physical count and pricing of all inventory items. Acquired goods not on hand are assumed to have been sold. Possible merchandise losses through misappropriation, breakage, or other causes are reflected in the cost of goods sold as a deduction from revenue, although these goods do not actually create revenue. Small retail businesses often use the periodic method as a matter of expedience since it does not require a continuous record of inventory balances.

Perpetual Inventory. The perpetual inventory method provides for a continuous book inventory of items on hand; it is a method of recordkeeping. A card or sheet may be kept for each inventory item acquired; when units are purchased or sold, the inventory record for the item must be adjusted accordingly to show the quantity on hand at any time. The maintenance of continuous inventory records

[2]*Ibid.*, p. 6015.
[3]*Ibid.*, p. 9509.
[4]*Loc. cit.*

does not preclude the need for a complete annual physical inventory. Some companies that use the perpetual inventory method take physical counts of portions of the inventory during the course of the year to test whether the records are in agreement with quantities actually on hand. This practice may be followed instead of taking a complete annual physical inventory.

A perpetual inventory may be costly to maintain, especially when the inventory includes numerous items of small value. A company may, therefore, maintain continuous records for only certain classifications of its inventory. A hardware supply company, for example, may find it feasible to use the perpetual inventory method only for items with a high unit selling price and the periodic inventory method for all other items.

Assigning the Cost of the Merchandise

The total cost of goods available for sale must be allocated between the cost of goods sold and the cost of goods on hand. With the periodic inventory method, this allocation takes place at the end of each accounting period; with the perpetual inventory method, it takes place after each sale and each acquisition.

The process of assigning costs would be relatively simple if each item acquired could be marked and identified with a specific invoice cost. Such a procedure is possible in certain businesses in which the items are large or otherwise readily traceable. In most instances, however, specific identification of each inventory item is neither feasible nor practical, particularly when successive acquisitions are commingled in common storage facilities. The problem is complicated further by the fact that acquisitions of like items are usually made at fluctuating prices. Consequently, a method of assigning costs to merchandise items—with either a perpetual or periodic inventory method—based on an assumed flow of goods and expired costs must be adopted and followed consistently for inventory valuation purposes and for matching costs with revenues. (The principle of consistency is discussed later in this chapter.) The most commonly used methods of assigning costs to inventory items are

Perpetual Inventory Method	Periodic Inventory Method
1. First-in, first-out (FIFO)	1. First-in, first-out (FIFO)
2. Last-in, first-out (LIFO)	2. Last-in, first-out (LIFO)
3. Moving average	3. Weighted average
4. Specific identification	4. Specific identification

When costs are determined by either the FIFO or the LIFO procedure, it is essential that the inventory method used—periodic or perpetual—be clearly stated. This is especially significant with LIFO costing because the resulting cost assignments may be different.

To illustrate the various methods of assigning costs to inventories, the following information pertaining to a single inventory item, a steel coil, stock item number 7004 is given. Prior to April 1, 1973, the specific identification method of inventory valuation was in use.

1973
April 1 Inventory on hand consisted of 20 units, purchased at $2.20 each.

    5 Purchased 60 units at $2.60 each.

1973

April 10   Purchased 35 units at $2.80 each.

    11   Sold 30 units.

    15   Purchased 40 units at $3.50 each.

    19   Sold 50 units.

    22   Purchased 100 units at $3.20 each.

    30   Sold 60 units.

For convenience, the data are rearranged as follows:

	Units	Unit Cost		Total Cost
Inventory, April 1	20	$2.20		$ 44
Purchases				
April 5	60	2.60	$156	
10	35	2.80	98	
15	40	3.50	140	
22	100	3.20	320	714
Totals	255			$758
Sales				
April 11	30			
19	50			
30	60			
Total	140			
On hand, April 30	115	(255 − 140)		

First-In, First-Out (FIFO) Costing. The FIFO method of determining the cost of goods on hand and the cost of goods sold is based on the assumption that the units are sold in the order in which they were acquired; that is, the oldest units on hand are sold first, the units acquired next are the next to be sold, and so on. This assumption relates only to the method of accounting and not to the actual physical movement of the goods although it may approximate the actual physical flow. What is significant, however, is the monetary value. The unsold units on hand at the date of the inventory are assumed to be the units acquired most recently. Consequently, for income measurement, earlier costs are matched with revenue and the most current costs are used for position statement valuation.

Perpetual Inventory Method—FIFO Costing. A detailed perpetual inventory card illustrating the FIFO procedure for assigning costs is shown in Figure 9-1.

As each shipment of goods is received, the quantity, unit cost, and total cost are recorded in the appropriate columns. When goods are issued, the unit cost of the oldest goods on hand is recorded in the Unit Cost column; this cost is then multiplied by the number of units, and the total is written in the Total Cost column. For instance, 30 units were issued on April 11 on Stock Requisition 401 (a document authorizing the stockroom to issue 30 coils to a designated person or place); 20 units are recorded at the cost of the 20 units on hand at April 1, and the rest at the cost of the shipment received on April 5 on Purchase Order 673 (a document numbered 673 that authorizes the seller to deliver 60 coils at $2.60 each). The balance on hand, unit cost, and total cost for each

Figure 9-1. Perpetual Inventory Card (FIFO)

| Item: Coil, Steel   Part No. 7004   Location S-5 | | | | | | | | | | |
| Date | Ref. | Received (or Purchased) | | | Issued (or Sold) | | | Balance | | |
		Quantity	Unit Cost	Total Cost	Quantity	Unit Cost	Total Cost	Quantity	Unit Cost	Total Cost
1973 April 1	Balance							20	2.20	44.00
5	P.O. 673	60	2.60	156.00				20	2.20	44.00
								60	2.60	156.00
10	P.O. 678	35	2.80	98.00				20	2.20	44.00
								60	2.60	156.00
								35	2.80	98.00
11	S.R. 401				20	2.20	44.00	50	2.60	130.00
					10	2.60	26.00	35	2.80	98.00
15	P.O. 690	40	3.50	140.00				50	2.60	130.00
								35	2.80	98.00
								40	3.50	140.00
19	S.R. 407				50	2.60	130.00	35	2.80	98.00
								40	3.50	140.00
22	P.O. 701	100	3.20	320.00				35	2.80	98.00
								40	3.50	140.00
								100	3.20	320.00
30	S.R. 409				35	2.80	98.00	15	3.50	52.50
					25	3.50	87.50	100	3.20	320.00

shipment from which units are assumed to remain are recorded in the Balance column.

The inventory on April 30 is assumed to consist of

```
 15 units at $3.50 = $ 52.50
100 units at $3.20 =  320.00
───                 ────────
115 units          = $372.50
═══                 ════════
```

Periodic Inventory Method—FIFO Costing. When FIFO costing is used with the periodic inventory method, a continuous record of balances on hand is not kept. Rather, a physical count of the units is taken on April 30; they are valued on the assumption that they consist of the most recent acquisitions as follows:

Date Acquired	Quantity	Unit Price	Total Price
April 22	100	$3.20	$320.00
15	15	3.50	52.50
Total	115		$372.50

The cost of the units sold is decided on the assumption that the sales of April 11 (30 units) and April 19 (50 units) came from the 20 units on hand on April 1 and the 60 units purchased on April 5. The 60 units sold on April 30 are assumed to be the 35 units acquired on April 10 and 25 units of those acquired on April 15. Therefore, the 115 units on hand on April 30 are assumed to consist of the 15 unsold units from the April 15 purchase and the 100 units acquired on April 22. The cost of the units sold may be summarized as follows:

Cost of goods available for sale (beginning inventory plus purchases)			$758.00
Cost of April 30 ending inventory			
	15 units at $3.50	$ 52.50	
	100 units at $3.20	320.00	
Total	115 units		372.50
Cost of goods sold			$385.50

When FIFO costing is used, the amount of the ending inventory as well as the amount of the cost of goods sold is identical with either the periodic or the perpetual inventory method because in each instance the goods on hand are assumed to consist of the most recently acquired units.

Last-In, First-Out (LIFO) Costing. LIFO costing is based on the assumption that the cost of goods sold should be based on prices paid for the most recently acquired units and that the inventory consists of the oldest units on hand. The major advantage claimed for this procedure is that during periods of continuously rising prices, the higher prices of the most recent purchases are included in the cost of goods sold, thereby reducing the gross margin on sales and the taxable income. It is further claimed that the cost of goods sold is more realistic because LIFO costs most nearly approximate current replacement costs thereby achieving a closer matching of costs with revenue.

Perpetual Inventory Method—LIFO Costing. The application of LIFO costing to the perpetual inventory method is illustrated in Figure 9-2.

Issued goods are listed at the unit cost of the latest acquisition, up to the amount assumed to be still on hand. For instance, of the 50 units sold on April 19, 40 are recorded at the cost of the 40 units received on April 15, 5 at the cost of the 5 units remaining of those received on April 10, and 5 at the cost of the units received on April 5. The balance on hand, unit cost, and total cost for each shipment from which units are assumed to remain are recorded in the Balance column.

The inventory on April 30 is assumed to consist of:

20 units at $2.20	$ 44
55 units at 2.60	143
40 units at 3.20	128
115 units	$315

The cost of goods sold is $443 (goods available for sale, $758, less ending inventory, $315).

Figure 9-2. Perpetual Inventory Card (LIFO)

Date	Ref.	Received (or Purchased)			Issued (or Sold)			Balance		
		Quantity	Unit Cost	Total Cost	Quantity	Unit Cost	Total Cost	Quantity	Unit Cost	Total Cost
1973 April 1	Balance							20	2.20	44.00
5	P.O. 673	60	2.60	156.00				20	2.20	44.00
								60	2.60	156.00
10	P.O. 678	35	2.80	98.00				20	2.20	44.00
								60	2.60	156.00
								35	2.80	98.00
11	S.R. 401				30	2.80	84.00	20	2.20	44.00
								60	2.60	156.00
								5	2.80	14.00
15	P.O. 690	40	3.50	140.00				20	2.20	44.00
								60	2.60	156.00
								5	2.80	14.00
								40	3.50	140.00
19	S.R. 407				40	3.50	140.00	20	2.20	44.00
					5	2.80	14.00	55	2.60	143.00
					5	2.60	13.00			
22	P.O. 701	100	3.20	320.00				20	2.20	44.00
								55	2.60	143.00
								100	3.20	320.00
30	S.R. 409				60	3.20	192.00	20	2.20	44.00
								55	2.60	143.00
								40	3.20	128.00

Item: Coil, Steel   Part No. 7004   Location: S-5

Periodic Inventory Method—LIFO Costing. Under the periodic inventory method, the 115 units in the ending inventory on April 30 are assumed to consist of the beginning inventory of 20 units and, following the chronological sequence of purchases, the receipts of April 5, 60 units, and April 10, 35 units, for a total cost of $298. The cost of the units sold may be summarized as follows:

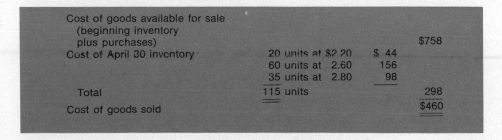

Cost of goods available for sale (beginning inventory plus purchases)			$758
Cost of April 30 inventory	20 units at $2.20	$ 44	
	60 units at 2.60	156	
	35 units at 2.80	98	
Total	115 units		298
Cost of goods sold			$460

Note that, unlike FIFO costing, the valuations of the cost of goods sold and ending inventory under LIFO costing may be different, depending on whether the perpetual or the periodic inventory method is used. When LIFO costing is used with the perpetual inventory method, prices at the beginning of the period that would be reflected in the ending valuation with the periodic inventory method may be dropped from the running balance as goods are issued. When the inventory is taken only at the end of the period, the various dates of sales are ignored. The LIFO procedure may be used appropriately with either periodic inventories or perpetual inventories even though the results may be different; the method selected, however, should be followed consistently. The following tabulation illustrates the different results of LIFO costing with the perpetual and the periodic inventory methods:

	Perpetual Inventory	Periodic Inventory
Inventory, April 1	$ 44	$ 44
Purchases	714	714
Total	$758	$758
Inventory, April 30	315	298
Cost of goods sold	$443	$460

Perpetual Inventory Method—Moving Average Costing. Under moving average costing, the cost of each purchase is added to the cost of units on hand, and the total cost is divided by the total quantity on hand to find the average price. Units issued are priced at the average price until additional units are purchased; then a new average price is computed. This method tends to level off price fluctuations. The application of moving average costing is shown in Figure 9-3.

Figure 9-3. Perpetual Inventory Card (Moving Average Costing)

Item: Coil, Steel   Part No. 7004   Location: S-5

Date	Ref.	Received (or Purchased)			Issued (or Sold)			Balance		
		Quantity	Unit Cost	Total Cost	Quantity	Unit Cost	Total Cost	Quantity	Unit Cost	Total Cost
1973										
April 1	Balance							20	2.20	44.00
5	P.O. 673	60	2.60	156.00				80	2.50	200.00(a)
10	P.O. 678	35	2.80	98.00				115	2.5913	298.00(b)
11	S.R. 401				30	2.5913	77.74	85	2.5913	220.26
15	P.O. 690	40	3.50	140.00				125	2.882	360.26(c)
19	S.R. 407				50	2.882	144.10	75	2.882	216.16
22	P.O. 701	100	3.20	320.00				175	3.06377	536.16(d)
30	S.R. 409				60	3.06377	183.83	115	3.06377	352.33

Computations

(a)	(b)	(c)	(d)
20 at $2.20 = $ 44	80 at $2.50 = $200	85 at $2.5913 = $220.26	75 at $2.882 = $216.16
60 at 2.60 = 156	35 at 2.80 = 98	40 at 3.50 = 140.00	100 at 3.20 = 320.00
80 $200	115 $298	125 $360.26	175 $536.16
Average $2.50	Average $2.5913	Average $2.882	Average $3.06377

The inventory valuation as of the end of the month is $352.33

Periodic Inventory Method—Weighted Average Costing. Under weighted average costing—not to be confused with moving average costing—the ending inventory is priced at the end of each accounting period at a unit cost computed by dividing the total cost of goods available for sale by the physical units available for sale. Similarly, all quantities sold are stated at a uniform price—the computed average price for the period. The assignment of costs to goods sold during the month must be delayed until the end of the month so that the weighted average cost computation can be made.

The average cost for the period, the inventory valuation, and the cost of goods sold is computed as follows:

Date		Units	Unit Cost	Total
1973				
April 1	Beginning inventory	20	$2.20	$ 44
5	Purchase	60	2.60	156
10	Purchase	35	2.80	98
15	Purchase	40	3.50	140
22	Purchase	100	3.20	320
	Totals	255		$758

$$\text{Average unit cost} = \frac{\text{Cost of goods available for sale}}{\text{Units available for sale}} = \frac{\$758}{\$255} = \$\ 2.9725$$

Units on hand, April 30	115
Inventory valuation (115 × $2.9725)	$341.85
Units sold	140
Cost of goods sold (140 × $2.9725)	$416.15

SPECIFIC IDENTIFICATION COSTING

The specific identification method of inventory valuation may be used if the goods purchased can be identified specifically with the related underlying documents. Some businesses mark the specific cost in code on every unit so that each item of inventory as well as each unit sold may be valued. Valuation by specific identification can be used with either the perpetual or the periodic inventory method. In either case, the cost of units sold as well as the cost of units remaining on hand is determined by reference to the related specific invoices.

Assume that the 115 units in the ending inventory consisted of 25 units purchased at $3.50 and 90 units purchased at $3.20, identified by the invoice numbers as being from the acquisitions of April 15 and April 22. The inventory valuation is computed as follows:

25 units at $3.50 =	$ 87.50
90 units at 3.20 =	288.00
115 units	$375.50

The valuation of the units sold is computed as follows:

20 units at $2.20 =	$ 44.00
60 units at 2.60 =	156.00
35 units at 2.80 =	98.00
15 units at 3.50 =	52.50
10 units at 3.20 =	32.00
140 units	$382.50

In many instances, whether due to the volume of items involved or because the items are of a kind that make individual coding impossible, the method of specific identification is impracticable. Similar items acquired on different dates and at different prices may be commingled, or *fungible* (interchangeable) items—wheat in bins, coal in piles—might be matched with unrelated invoices, thereby misstating net income. Furthermore, some costs are common to groups of items—shipping, insurance, handling—and may not be readily identifiable with specific items. Another disadvantage of this method is that income measurement can be changed arbitrarily by charging an item to income based on its cost rather than its operational significance.

PERPETUAL AND PERIODIC INVENTORY METHODS COMPARED

With the periodic inventory method assumed in the preceding chapters, the beginning inventory is shown in a Merchandise Inventory account, and all purchases are entered in a Purchases account. The cost of goods sold does not appear as an account balance in the general ledger but is determined only after the physical inventory is taken at the end of the period. With the perpetual inventory method, however, the beginning inventory and all purchases are shown as debits in a Merchandise Inventory (asset) account. The cost of all goods sold is debited to a Cost of Goods Sold Account and credited to the Merchandise Inventory account. The balance of the Merchandise Inventory account is the cost of the goods remaining in the inventory, provided there have been no shrinkages or other losses. The Merchandise Inventory account is a controlling account supported by a subsidiary inventory ledger made up of inventory record cards for all items.

The entries in summary journal form for both methods, based on the data in Figure 9-1, are

Periodic Inventory			Perpetual Inventory		
(1)			**(1)**		
Purchases	714		Merchandise Inventory	714	
Accounts Payable		714	Accounts Payable		714
To record April purchases.			To record April purchases.		
(2)			**(2)**		
Accounts Receivable	770		Accounts Receivable	770	
Sales		770	Sales		770
To record April sales of			To record April sales		
140 units at $5.50 each.			of 140 units at $5.50 each.		
			(3)		
			Cost of Goods Sold	385.50	
			Merchandise Inventory		385.50
			To record the cost of		
			140 units sold (amounts from		
			Issued column, Figure 9-1).		

After entries 1 and 3 under the perpetual inventory method are posted, the affected accounts in the general ledger appear as shown below.

Cost of Goods Sold			
April 30	385.50		

Merchandise Inventory			
April 1 Balance	44.00	April 30 Cost of Goods Sold	385.50
30 Purchases	714.00		

The Merchandise Inventory account shows a balance of $372.50, which is the cost of goods on hand to be reported in the statement of financial position for April 30.

The perpetual inventory cards (Figures 9-1, 9-2, and 9-3) combine a system of control of inventory quantities with a method of assigning costs. Some companies employ the perpetual inventory card form only for controlling quantities: Receipts, issues, and running balances are recorded, but the procedure for determining the cost of the inventory is the same as with the periodic method. One advantage of using perpetual inventory cards is that financial statements may be prepared without taking a physical inventory; this is an important advantage to businesses that require frequent, usually monthly, statements.

INVENTORY VALUATION METHODS COMPARED AND ANALYZED

The most common cost methods of inventory valuation have been discussed in this chapter; others may be used in special circumstances. In a particular business, the method selected should be the one that will best measure net income.

If there are no significant price changes in the merchandise handled during a given period, and the quantity held does not change, FIFO, LIFO, and moving average costing will produce approximately the same results. If, however, the prices of the goods acquired fluctuate significantly during the period and the inventory turnover is rapid, the method of inventory valuation used will have a direct effect on the financial statements. In Figure 9-1, the price of the item fluctuated from $2.20 to $3.50 during the month. To illustrate the comparative effect of rising prices on the financial statements under perpetual FIFO, moving average, and LIFO costing, the basic data (page 312) for the preceding discussions are used again. Two additional assumptions are made: (1) The selling price of each unit is $5.50, and (2) the operating expenses for the month are $100. These computations of income are for a single inventory item. The effect of the different methods on net income would be proportionately increased with increasing volume and number of items. The effect of the three methods of allocating inventory cost and cost of goods sold under the stated assumptions is further high lighted in Figure 9-4, which is abstracted from the preceding income computations.

Figure 9-4. Summary Tabulation

	Perpetual—FIFO	Perpetual—Moving Average	Perpetual—LIFO
Sales (140 units × $5.50)	$770.00	$770.00	$770.00
Cost of Goods Sold (see Figures 9-1, 9-2, and 9-3 for computations)	385.50	405.67	443.00
Gross Margin on Sales	$384.50	$364.33	$327.00
Deduct Operating Expenses	100.00	100.00	100.00
Net Income	$284.50	$264.33	$227.00

	FIFO	Moving Average	LIFO
Ending inventory	$372.50	$352.33	$315.00
Cost of goods sold	385.50	405.67	443.00
Gross margin on sales	384.50	364.33	327.00
Net income	284.50	264.33	227.00

During a period of rising prices, FIFO costing results in the highest ending inventory valuation, gross margin on sales, and net income and the lowest cost of goods sold. Given the same rising market conditions, the LIFO inventory method gives the opposite results: lowest ending inventory valuation, gross margin on sales, and net income and highest cost of goods sold. During a period of falling prices, FIFO results in the lowest ending inventory valuation, gross margin on sales, and net income and the highest cost of goods sold; LIFO gives the opposite results.

The major advantage of LIFO costing is that during a prolonged period of generally rising prices, lower year-to-year earnings are reported with a concomitant income tax advantage. A major disadvantage is that during inflationary periods LIFO costing results in a significant understatement of current assets, which limits the significance and usefulness of the position statement. Its purpose is to match revenue with current cost, rather than with earliest cost, as is done under FIFO costing.

Figure 9-4 shows that the amounts for the four income statement items listed under moving average costing fall between the corresponding amounts for FIFO and LIFO costing. The same position would be maintained in a falling market. Moving average costing reduces the effect of widely fluctuating prices and results in a valuation closer to FIFO than to LIFO.

The position statement classifies the ending inventory as a current asset; consequently, this statement as well as the income statement is affected by the method of inventory valuation used. The ending inventory is often the largest single item in the Current Assets section and has, therefore, a decided effect on the current ratio, the reported amount of working capital, the merchandise inventory turnover, the total stockholders' equity, and related ratios.

Historical cost is the primary basis used for inventory valuation. Some accountants recommend the use of replacement cost for inventory valuation. This may be defined as the current cost of replacing the inventory items at the inventory date, in the ordinary course of business, assuming access to the usual sources of supply and at volumes in which the goods are usually purchased. The accountants who criticize the use of historical cost argue that FIFO does not segregate gains from changing price levels and that LIFO eliminates the effects of changing price levels from income. Others recommend reporting parallel figures showing both historical cost and current costs, thereby providing the user with a better basis for evaluating past performance and for predicting future performance. The use of current costs would eliminate the need for a cost-flow assumption—LIFO, FIFO, average—and would result in a better matching of expired cost and revenue. The position statement valuation would also be more significant.

LOWER OF COST OR MARKET (LCM)

The various methods of inventory valuation discussed thus far in this chapter are methods of arriving at the cost of the inventory. ▼ However, a long-standing convention in accounting holds that inventories may be valued at the *lower of cost or market*. ▼ The position of the American Institute of Certified Public Accountants is that

Accounting Procedure: ▼
Lower of Cost or Market

> A departure from the cost basis of pricing the inventory is required when the utility of the goods is no longer as great as its cost. Where there is evidence that the utility of goods, in their disposal in the ordinary course of business, will be less than cost, whether due to physical deterioration, obsolescence, changes in price levels, or other causes, the difference should be recognized as a loss of the current period. This is generally accomplished by stating such goods at a lower level commonly designated as *market*.[5]

The term *market* generally means the cost of replacing the goods as of the position statement date. For Federal income tax purposes, market means the current bid price (current replacement cost) prevailing on the inventory date for the particular items for the volume usually purchased by the taxpayer.

Application of Lower of Cost or Market

The process of valuing the inventory at LCM takes place at the end of the accounting period, when financial statements are prepared. It may be done in any one of three ways:

1. By pricing each item individually at the lower of cost or market
2. By comparing the total cost with the total market price of each major inventory category and using the lower figure
3. By comparing the total cost with the total market price of the entire inventory and using the lower figure

Based on the inventory tabulations in Figure 9-5 (FIFO costing is assumed), the valuation under each procedure is as follows (Items A and B are assumed to constitute Category X and the remaining items constitute Category Y):

---

[5] AICPA, *op. cit.*, p. 6015.

Figure 9-5. Application of LCM

Item	Quantity	Unit Cost	Unit Market Price	Total Cost	Total Market	Lower of Cost or Market Basis Unit	Lower of Cost or Market Basis Major Category	Lower of Cost or Market Basis Total Inventory
Category X:								
Item A	100	$10	$9.00	$1,000	$ 900	$ 900		
Item B	200	4	6.00	800	1,200	800		
Subtotal				$1,800	$2,100		$1,800	
Category Y:								
Item C	400	1	1.25	$ 400	$ 500	400		
Item D	600	6	5.00	3,600	3,000	3,000		
Item E	250	3	2.50	750	625	625		
Subtotal				$4,750	$4,125		4,125	
Totals				6,550	6,225			$6,225
Ending Inventory-LCM						$5,725	$5,925	$6,225

1. If each item is valued individually, the inventory is reported as $5,725.
2. If the inventory is valued by major categories, it is reported as $5,925.
3. If the inventory is valued in total, it is reported as $6,225.

Evaluation of LCM

The reason for LCM inventory valuation is to avoid the anticipation of profits and to provide for all foreseeable losses. This principle was developed when the influence of the grantor of credit was paramount and when primary emphasis was on the statement of financial position and on conservative asset valuations. It is based on the assumption that a drop in the purchase price of goods will be followed by a corresponding drop in the selling price of those goods, thereby reducing or eliminating the normal profit margin.

LCM lacks theoretical support. The arguments against it are (1) it is a departure from the cost concept; (2) it is inconsistent because presumed losses are anticipated but potential gains from an increase in the purchase price of goods are ignored, and some goods may be priced at cost and others at market when LCM is applied to individual items or categories; (3) the expectation of lower selling prices may not materialize, thereby distorting the income of several periods. This is not to say that a serious decline in inventory valuation should be ignored, but rather to challenge the arbitrariness of the LCM rule and its reliance on the dubious assumption of a normal profit margin.

The rule of lower of cost or market is generally applied to individual items—the required procedure for Federal income tax reporting—rather than to the whole inventory. Pricing each item individually results in a lower inventory valuation of those items for which the market value is below cost. The loss is typically absorbed in the cost of goods sold. The application of LCM to the total inventory, however, may be more useful for accounting purposes, either because (1) the value of the entire inventory is of greater significance than the value of the parts or (2) goods in inventory with a market value less than cost are counter-balanced by equal quantities whose market value exceeds cost. A consistent procedure must be followed from year to year. ▼ For Federal income tax purposes, greater emphasis is placed on *consistency of method* than on the particular method. ▼ Either cost or the lower of cost or market is acceptable for tax purposes, except for goods valued under LIFO costing. The Federal income tax regulations state that on adoption of LIFO costing, no other method of inventory valuation may be used in annual statements, including reports to stockholders or creditors. The use of LCM is not permitted in conjunction with LIFO costing, although this does not preclude the disclosure, by footnote or parenthesis, of the excess of the FIFO valuation of the inventory over the LIFO valuation.

Accounting Concept: ▼
Consistency of
Reporting for Tax
Determination

POSITION STATEMENT DISCLOSURE—INVENTORY

Studies of financial reports prepared by leading corporations show that LCM is the most commonly used basis of valuation for inventories, the only other common basis being cost. Cost, of course, includes LIFO, FIFO, and weighted average valuations, by either the perpetual or the periodic inventory method. LIFO costing is the method most frequently used.

Some typical examples of how inventories are reported in statements of financial position from the published annual reports of business corporations are shown below.

(1)

Current Assets
    Merchandise Inventories—at lower of cost or market $2,500,000

Note: Inventories are reported at the lower of FIFO cost or estimated market on the basis of specific items and classes of merchandise. Obsolete stock is carried at estimated salvage value.

(2)

Current Assets
    Merchandise Inventories $3,250,549

Note: Inventories are stated at cost, certain inventories at average cost and others at FIFO cost. These costs are not in excess of market value.

(3)

Current Assets
    Merchandise Inventories $552,100

Note: Inventories are stated at the lower of cost or market. During 1973, the company adopted LIFO costing for a portion of its inventories. The effect of this change was to reduce net income by $27,000, and Federal income taxes by $12,000. FIFO costing is used for the balance of the inventories.

THE GROSS MARGIN METHOD OF ESTIMATING INVENTORIES

Taking a physical inventory or maintaining perpetual inventory records is often costly and time-consuming. For some purposes—preparing monthly financial statements, checking the accuracy of a physical inventory, or estimating inventory value when an accurate valuation cannot be made, as in the case of a fire loss—the *gross margin* method of estimating the inventory is used.

Assume that during the previous three years the Needham Company has averaged a gross margin rate on sales of 30 percent, as shown below.

| | Prior Years | | | |
	1	2	3	Totals
Sales	$124,000	$142,000	$154,000	$420,000
Cost of Goods Sold	87,420	97,980	108,600	294,000
Gross Margin	$ 36,580	$ 44,020	$ 45,400	$126,000
Gross Margin Rate	29.5%	31%	29.5%	30%

For the current year, the following data are available from the records of the company:

Inventory–January 1, 1973	$ 20,000
Purchases during 1973	110,000
Sales during 1973	160,000

Under the gross margin method, the estimated inventory on December 31, 1973, would be computed as follows:

Inventory–January 1, 1973		$ 20,000
Purchases		110,000
Total goods available		$130,000
Deduct estimated cost of goods sold		
Sales	$160,000	
Deduct gross margin (30% of $160,000)	48,000	112,000
Estimated inventory, December 31, 1973		$ 18,000

An alternative procedure is to arrange the data for the current year in conventional income statement form, and then to fill in the missing items as follows:

			Percent of Sales
Sales		$160,000	100
Cost of Goods Sold			
Inventory–January 1, 1973	$ 20,000		
Purchases	110,000		
Total	$130,000		
Estimated Inventory, December 31, 1973	? **(d)**	? **(c)**	? **(a)**
Gross Margin		$? **(b)**	30

a. If the gross margin is 30 percent of sales, the cost of goods sold must be 70 percent.
b. If the gross margin is 30 percent of sales, then the gross margin is 30 percent of $160,000, or $48,000.
c. If the gross margin is $48,000, then the cost of goods sold must be $160,000 $48,000, or $112,000.
d. If cost of goods sold is $112,000, then the ending inventory must be

Total goods available	$130,000
Cost of goods sold	112,000
Ending inventory	$ 18,000

This method is based on the assumption that the rate of gross margin on sales is substantially the same in every period. It is accurate, therefore, only to the extent that the assumed gross margin rate reflects the experience of the current period. It is essential that a careful study be made of possible differences between the past data from which the assumed rate is derived and the corresponding current data. Appropriate adjustments should be made for significant differences. The inventory on hand at the end of the current period computed by this method is the amount that would result at a gross margin rate equal to the assumed rate.

RETAIL METHOD OF ESTIMATING INVENTORIES

Another method of estimating the ending inventory, commonly used by chain and department stores, is the *retail inventory* method. Its value is twofold: It serves as a means of computing the ending inventory without a physical count and also provides a method of centrally controlling inventories that consist of a variety of items dispersed over several departments or several branch stores. Goods are charged to the departments or branches at their selling price, records of both cost and selling price are kept centrally, and records of sales are kept in the usual manner. From these records, the inventory valuation may be prepared at any time as shown in Figure 9-6.

A company may find it necessary to increase or decrease previously estab-

Figure 9-6. Retail Inventory Method

	Cost	Retail
Inventory of beginning of period	$ 20,000	$ 30,000
Purchases during period	180,000	270,000
Total goods available	$200,000	$300,000
Cost percentage (ratio of cost to retail)		
$\dfrac{\$200,000}{\$300,000} = 66\frac{2}{3}\%$		
Sales during period		258,000
Estimated inventory at retail		$ 42,000
Estimated inventory at cost (66⅔% of $42,000)	$ 28,000	

lished retail prices. Increases, called *markups*, are added in arriving at the total goods available for sale. Decreases, called *markdowns*, are excluded in arriving at the cost percentage but are combined with sales for the period. This results in a lower cost percentage and, therefore, a lower inventory when that percentage is applied to the retail figure. It is also a logical procedure because it assumes that goods that have been marked down have been sold, given away, or reduced to nominal value. It is also consistent with the principle that inventories should be valued at the lower of cost or market. Markups and markdowns are included in the computation as shown below.

	Cost	Retail
Inventory at beginning of period	$ 20,000	$ 30,000
Purchases during period	179,000	270,000
Transportation in during period	1,000	
Markups during period		10,000
Total goods available	$200,000	$310,000
Cost percentage (ratio of cost to retail)		
$\dfrac{\$200,000}{\$310,000} = 64.516\%$		
Sales during period	$258,000	
Markdowns during period	8,000	
Total sales (at intended retail)		266,000
Estimated inventory at retail		$ 44,000
Estimated inventory at cost (64.516% of $44,000)	$ 28,387	

Both the gross margin method and the retail inventory method are based on a calculation of the gross margin rate: The gross margin method uses past experience as a basis; the retail inventory method uses current experience. The gross margin method is, therefore, less reliable because past experience may be different from the current experience.

A physical inventory should be taken periodically. This inventory is first computed at the retail selling prices marked on the goods, reduced to cost by using the cost percentage, and then compared with the inventory value computed in the manner shown in Figure 9-6. If there have been losses due to thefts or shrinkage, the valuation based on the physical inventory will be less than that shown by the records, and an adjustment is made for the decrease.

The retail inventory method offers a means of determining a company's inventory at frequent intervals without taking a physical count—a valuable tool for purposes of preparing financial statements or other reports that require an inventory valuation. Its reliability rests on the assumption that the percentage of cost to retail is fairly uniform within the several departments of the company and for all the various items sold, and that the percentage is equally applicable to the goods sold and the goods unsold. If that is not the case, separate records should be maintained for the different departments and for the different items handled. Use of the retail inventory method is permissible for Federal income tax purposes.

MARKON COMPUTATIONS

Pricing goods held for sale requires an addition to the cost of the merchandise of a *markon* to cover operating expenses and profit. In most industries, percentage comparisons of markon, costs, and expenses are expressed in terms of net sales, but in some industries the comparisons are in terms of cost. It is essential, therefore, that the basis used—cost or sales—be clearly understood, particularly in quoting prices and in making internal and external income statement comparisons.

Assume, for example, that $25 is marked on an item costing $100, so that the item sells for $125. Using cost as the base (100 percent), the percentage of markon is computed as follows:

	Amount	Percent
Sales	$125	125
Cost	100	100 (base)
Gross margin (markon)	$ 25	25

$$\frac{\$125}{\$100} = 1.25 \text{ or } 125\% \qquad \frac{\$25}{\$100} = 0.25 \text{ or } 25\%$$

The use of the selling price as the base (100 percent) gives the following percentages of markon:

	Amount	Percent
Sales	$125	100 (base)
Cost	100	80
Gross margin (markon)	$ 25	20

$$\frac{\$100}{\$125} = 0.80 \text{ or } 80\% \qquad \frac{\$25}{\$125} = 0.20 \text{ or } 20\%$$

CONSISTENCY IN THE APPLICATION OF PROCEDURES

Different procedures may be used in different areas of accounting. ▼ It is of paramount importance, therefore, that the selected method should be followed consistently from year to year. ▼ Lack of consistency in inventory pricing, cost allocations, and financial statement presentation would make year-to-year comparisons of operating results and financial position meaningless. Since such comparisons often serve as the basis for managerial decisions, the importance of consistency becomes evident.

Accounting Concept: ▼
Consistency

The concept consistency may be applied at several levels. Consistency is important not only in the matter of valuation procedures followed but also with respect to the classification of items in financial statements. Consistency in classification applies to the grouping of items within each statement as well as to year-to-year consistency. The principle of consistency does not preclude required changes properly made and fully disclosed. A change from FIFO to LIFO inventory costing, for example, requires an explanation accompanying the financial statements of the year of change, giving the nature of the change and its effect.

INVENTORY CONTROL

Lack of control over inventories can be a serious detriment to the successful management of a business. An excessive inventory is expensive to carry. Studies made indicate that the costs of carrying an inventory—taxes, insurance, warehousing, handling, and inventory taking—may be as high as 25 percent of the original purchase price. This is exclusive of lost potential earnings (interest) on the funds tied up in inventories. On the other hand, sufficient items and quantities must be stocked to provide customers with good service.

Maintaining a proper balance, to avoid both shortages and excesses of inventory, requires organization and planning. Control plans must provide for day-to-day comparisons of projected inventory acquisitions with current sales volume. A reduction in sales volume will result in excess inventories unless adjustments are made.

Inventory Turnover

The cost of goods sold divided by the average inventory gives the *inventory turnover,* a useful guide in inventory control (see page 167). The turnover rate may be computed for individual items or for major categories in order to establish item-by-item control.

Ratio of Inventory to Working Capital

The ratio of inventory to working capital is an indication of the amount of working capital invested in inventory and the amount of currently maturing obligations that will have to be met with proceeds from the sale of the inventory. If, for example, a firm's ending inventory is $330,000 and its working capital is $300,000, the ratio is

$$\frac{\text{Ending inventory}}{\text{Working capital}} = \frac{\$330,000}{\$300,000} = 110\%$$

This ratio, being greater than 100 percent, indicates that the current debt cannot be paid in full from cash on hand and proceeds from receivables, but will require, in addition, part of the proceeds from the sale of inventory.

Maximum and Minimum Levels

It is customary to establish maximum and minimum stock levels for inventory items, so that the purchasing agent is automatically notified when the balance on hand is at the minimum quantity and the item must be replenished. Minimum levels should be set to allow for anticipated sales requirements during the time required for placing the replenishment order and receiving the goods, with a margin for unforeseen delay. Maximum balances should be set, based on sales requirements, minimum stock point, and the most economical buying quantities.

Economical Buying Quantities

Deciding the quantity to purchase involves considering the cost of acquisition and the cost of carrying the items. Ordering large quantities often results in a lower unit purchase price and lower transportation costs per unit, but the saving is offset by the increased cost of carrying the inventory. Carrying cost includes taxes, insurance, storage, losses due to obsolescence and deterioration, interest on the investment, and so on. The point at which the aggregate of all the cost elements—cost to order, carrying cost, and purchase cost—is lowest indicates the most economical quantity to order or the number of orders to place each year.

Assume, for example, that a quantity of steel parts is to be purchased; the company normally uses 24,000 of these parts each year. Assume further that freight, clerical, and other costs of placing one order is $150 and that the average carrying cost is 40 cents per unit in inventory. Normal usage is 2,000 parts each month. Assuming a reasonably consistent pattern of usage, the average inventory may be figured at one half the lot size ordered. The computation of the most economical buying quantity is shown in Figure 9-7.

Figure 9-7. Schedule for Determining Most Economical Buying Quantity

(1) Orders per Year	(2) Quantity per Order (12,000 ÷ Col. 1)	(3) Order Cost (Col. 1 × $150)	(4) Carrying Cost (½ of Col. 2 × $0.40)	(5) Total Annual Cost (Col. 3 + 4)
12	1,000	$1,800	$ 200	$2,000
6	2,000	900	400	1,300
4	3,000	600	600	1,200
3	4,000	450	800	1,250
2	6,000	300	1,200	1,500
1	12,000	150	2,400	2,550

The most economical buying quantity is the 3,000 lot size four times a year.

PERIODIC PHYSICAL INVENTORIES— SPECIAL CONSIDERATIONS

A periodic physical count of the entire inventory is an essential element of inventory control. A physical count (that is, a count by weight or measure) and valuation serve to confirm perpetual inventory records. If perpetual records are not maintained, an annual physical inventory is an absolute necessity for the preparation of financial statements. A physical count also aids in reviewing the condition of the goods on hand and detecting errors or laxity in the system of accounting for, storing, and handling merchandise.

The taking of a physical inventory requires careful planning—setting the date, selecting and instructing the inventory takers, and establishing controls and procedures. It is advantageous to select a business year that ends when quantities are low and when the inventory taking will interfere least with the regular operations of the business. When necessary, technically trained personnel must be available to assist in identifying items; others must be available to move bulky items or to reach items not easily accessible.

It is common practice to attach consecutively numbered tags to all inventory items for recording the counts as they are made. On completion of the count, the filled-in tags are removed and checked to ensure that they have all been returned. The inventory items and quantities are then accumulated on inventory sheets showing descriptions, quantities, unit costs, and total costs. If tags are not used, the inventory count is entered directly on the inventory sheets. The unit costs to be shown on the inventory sheets depend on the costing method employed—LIFO, FIFO, and so on. If there is a discrepancy between the records and the count, the inventory records are brought into agreement with the physical count. The cause of the discrepancy should be traced so that steps may be taken to prevent a recurrence.

Item descriptions on the inventory tags must be complete and accurate. To eliminate confusion resulting from incorrect or inadequate item descriptions, the tags may be prepared in advance from the stock records.

Some inventory items cannot be counted, measured, or weighed conveniently, such as piles of coal, large quantities of nails dumped in bins, and partially used tanks or containers of materials. Other appropriate means must be devised to estimate the quantities of such items on hand. Obsolete or damaged merchandise must be identified clearly and excluded from the inventory if it is unsalable. If such goods are salable at a reduced price, they should be valued at the reduced price less any selling costs.

Since the inventory is taken as of a specific date, a careful record must be kept of acquisitions, withdrawals, and goods in transit during the inventory period. Goods on hand for which the liability has been recorded are included in the inventory; goods held for shipment and charged to the customer must be excluded. Goods owned but physically elsewhere—at a branch warehouse or under *consignment*—must be included in the inventory.

SUMMARY

The proper valuation and costing of merchandise inventory is of considerable importance. Inventory includes goods owned by the business held for sale to customers. Cost includes the invoice price of the merchandise less purchase discounts plus transportation in, insurance while in transit, and any other costs paid by the buyer to get the merchandise to his place of business.

There are two methods for inventory and cost of goods sold valuations: periodic, based on a complete physical count and pricing of all inventory items, and perpetual, based on a continuous book inventory of items on hand.

Since specific identification of each inventory item is usually neither feasible nor practical, and since similar items are normally acquired at fluctuating prices, a method of assigning costs to merchandise items—under either a perpetual or periodic inventory system—based on an assumed flow of goods and flow of cost must be adopted and consistently followed. The commonly used methods based on actual cost include FIFO, LIFO, moving average, weighted average, and specific identification.

The FIFO method is based on the assumption that units are sold in the order in which they were acquired. The assumption relates only to the method of accounting and not to the actual physical movement of the goods. The LIFO method is based on the assumption that the cost of goods sold should reflect the prices paid for the most recently acquired units and that the inventory consists of the oldest units on hand.

Under the moving average method, the cost of each purchase is added to the cost of the units on hand, and their total cost is then divided by the total quantity on hand for a new average price. Units issued are priced at the newest average price until additional units are purchased and another new average price is computed. Under the weighted average method, the ending inventory is priced at a unit cost computed by dividing the total cost of goods available for sale by the physical units available for sale. Units issued are stated at a uniform price—the computed average price for the period.

The primary basis for the valuation of inventories is cost. In a particular business, the method that will best measure net income should be used.

Inventories may be valued at the lower of cost or market—cost as computed by any of the methods discussed, and market meaning the cost of replacing the goods as of the position statement date. Lower of cost or market may be applied to each item individually, to the total inventory, or to each major inventory category.

Two methods are available for estimating the ending inventories: the gross margin method and the retail method. The gross margin method is based on the assumption that the rate of gross margin on sales is substantially the same during each period. It is accurate only to the extent that the assumed gross margin rate reflects the experience of the current period. The inventory is computed by deducting the estimated cost of goods sold (sales minus estimated gross margin on sales) from sales.

The retail method is also based on a calculation of the gross margin rate but whereas the gross margin method is based on past experience, the retail method uses current experience for its gross margin relationship. The inventory is computed first at the retail selling prices of the goods, and then reduced to cost by using the cost-to-retail percentage.

Whatever the method used, a periodic physical count of the entire inventory is an essential element of inventory control.

QUESTIONS

Q9-1. Distinguish between the terms *cost* and *value* when used in connection with inventory valuations. Is this distinction imperative during periods of price stability? during periods of rising prices? during periods of falling prices?

Q9-2. Why are accountants reluctant to abandon the assumption that the dollar is a stable unit of valuation?

Q9-3. Why is it important that the selected method of inventory valuation be applied consistently from year to year? Does strict compliance with the principle of consistency preclude a change from FIFO to LIFO?

Q9-4. Distinguish between the perpetual and periodic inventory methods. Does the perpetual inventory method eliminate the need for a physical inventory count?

Q9-5. How do over or understatements of inventory affect net income in the period when the error is made? in the following period?

Q9-6. What effect do the different methods of inventory valuation have on the financial statements?

Q9-7. Compare the gross margin method with the retail inventory method.

Q9-8. An audit of the records of the Lebanon Corporation showed that the ending inventory on December 31, 1972, was overstated by $5,200 and that on December 31, 1973, the inventory was understated by $8,400. What was the effect of the errors on the income statement for each year? What was the overall effect for the two-year period?

Q9-9. The Kraft Company maintains perpetual inventory cards for all merchandise items. An inventory is taken annually. Serially numbered perforated tags are placed on or alongside the various items. The inventory is taken by teams of two employees: One fills in the description and quantity of the item on each section of the tag; the second checks both the description and the count and removes the second half of the tag. The removed portions of the tags are then sent to the office, where the information is entered on inventory sheets and priced on the basis of lower of cost or market. Explain the purpose of each step of this procedure. Criticize the procedure followed. State what precautionary steps must be taken prior to the actual inventory count, during the count, and immediately following the completion of the count.

Q9-10. Explain the effect on the statement of financial position valuation and on the income determination of the use of LIFO as compared with FIFO (a) if prices have risen during the year; (b) if prices have fallen during the year.

Q9-11. (a) Define the term *market* as used in lower of cost or market inventory valuation. (b) What is the rationale for LCM? (c) Does LCM always produce conservative financial statements?

Q9-12. Explain the means by which a company can protect itself against errors, theft, or the improper use of inventory items.

Q9-13. (a) What is the relationship between the actual physical flow of goods in and out of inventory and the method used for inventory valuation? (b) What inventory valuation method should a company use if, as new shipments of inventory items are received, they are commingled with identical items on hand in storage bins?

Q9-14. As a stockholder, how would you evaluate the adoption of LIFO by your company?

EXERCISES

E9-1. The records of the Stop Company show the following data as of December 31, 1973.

a. Cost of merchandise on hand, based on a physical count	$45,000
b. Merchandise sold to a customer, but held for him pending receipt of shipping instructions (included in Item a)	1,500
c. Merchandise shipped out on December 30, F.O.B. destination; expected delivery time is 8 days	2,500
d. Merchandise purchased on December 28, F.O.B. shipping point, delivered to a carrier on December 29; expected delivery date is January 5	500
e. Cost of spoiled merchandise (to be given away); not included in Item a	250

What is the value of the inventory on December 31, 1973, for financial statement reporting purposes?

E9-2. The following items were included in the income statements of the Josephson Company for the years ending December 31, 1973 and 1972:

	December 31	
	1973	1972
Cost of goods sold	$ 65,000	$ 70,000
Gross margin	130,000	120,000
Net income	40,000	32,000

An audit of the records revealed that the merchandise inventory at December 31, 1972, was understated by $5,000. What was the effect of the error on the amounts given?

E9-3. The year-end inventory of the Kidd Company consisted of the following groups of items, priced at cost and at market:

Item	Cost	Market
A	$45,000	$48,000
B	37,000	37,000
C	86,000	78,000
D	42,000	35,000

What inventory amount should be used in the financial statements? Why?

E9-4. The inventory of the Lustro Company on January 1 and December 31, 1973, consisted of 17,000 and 25,000 units, respectively, of Commodity X-1. The beginning inventory was priced at $1,360. The following purchases were made during the year:

Date		Quantity	Cost
January	10	10,000	$ 900
April	15	17,000	1,445
July	5	24,000	2,280
October	2	6,000	600
December 15		16,000	1,280

Determine the cost of the December 31, 1973, inventory by each of the following methods: (a) LIFO; (b) FIFO; (c) weighted average. Assume that the periodic inventory method is used.

E9-5. The beginning inventory, purchases, and sales of the Wend Company for the month of August, 1973, were

1973
August   1   Inventory on hand consisted of 50 units at $1.05 each.

   12   Sold 25 units.

   15   Purchased 20 units at $1.00 each.

   17   Purchased 30 units at $.90 each.

   19   Sold 15 units.

   25   Purchased 25 units at $1.15 each.

   29   Sold 20 units.

What was the value of the units on hand on August 31 under (a) the perpetual inventory moving average method, and (b) the periodic inventory weighted average method?

E9-6. The following information was taken from the books of the Lossey Corporation:

1973

January	1	On hand	5,000 units at $8.00
February	14	Purchase	6,000 units at 8.60
June	12	Purchase	7,000 units at 8.40
November 12		Purchase	5,000 units at 8.50
December 31		On hand	6,000 units

The periodic inventory method is used. Compute the value of the inventory on December 31, 1973, under (a) FIFO and (b) LIFO.

E9-7. The Olde Company calculates its inventory by the gross margin method for interim statement purposes. The inventory on January 1 was $40,000, net purchases during January were $105,000, and net sales for the month were $150,000. The gross margin rate is estimated at 32 percent of net sales. What was the estimated inventory on January 31?

E9-8. The entire stock of the Aco Appliance Company was destroyed by fire on August 22, 1973. The books of the company (kept in a fireproof vault) showed the value of goods on hand on August 1 to be $80,000. Transactions for the period August 1 through August 22 resulted in the following amounts:

Sales	$197,560
Sales Returns	4,210
Purchases	159,600
Purchases Returns	3,625
Transportation In	2,950

The rate of gross margin on sales for the previous three years averaged 40 percent. Determine the cost of the inventory destroyed by the fire.

E9-9. The books of Juggs Department Store show the following data for the leather goods department for the year 1973, its first year of operations:

Purchases (at cost)	$19,612
Purchases (at original selling price)	34,580
Markups	2,250
Markdowns	1,110
Sales	32,670

Compute the inventory on December 31, 1973, by the retail method.

E9-10. (a) From the following data, compute the cost of the ending inventory:

Sales	$12,000
Beginning inventory (cost)	5,000
Beginning inventory (retail)	7,000
Purchases (cost)	7,000
Purchases (retail)	9,000

(b) Recompute the ending inventory, assuming the following additional items:

Transportation In	$300
Purchases Returns (cost)	200
Purchases Returns (retail)	300
Sales Returns	400
Markups	350
Markdowns	250

E9-4, 7, 9   P9-1

DEMONSTRATION PROBLEMS

DP9-1. (*Accounting policy decision problem*) (*Inventory valuation*) On January 1, 1973, the Fullton Company had an inventory of 50 units of a product that cost $25 each. January receipts and issues were as follows:

	Received			Issued	
January 2	20 units at $26	$ 520	January 1	10 units	
January 10	30 units at 30	900	January 8	20 units	
January 23	10 units at 27	270	January 17	30 units	
			January 25	20 units	
Total	60	$1,690	Total	80	

Required:

1. Compute the January 31 inventory using (a) FIFO based on a periodic inventory, (b) LIFO based on a perpetual inventory, and (c) weighted average.
2. Prepare summary journal entries for the transactions, assuming the use of LIFO and the perpetual inventory method, and post to the following T accounts: Merchandise Inventory, Accounts Receivable, Accounts Payable, Cost of Goods Sold, and Sales. The unit selling price was $40.
3. What is the purpose of a perpetual inventory system?
4. Would you recommend recording quantities only on the perpetual records and eliminating unit costs and total costs.
5. (a) Does the use of a perpetual inventory system eliminate the need for taking periodic physical inventories? (b) How will differences between the physical count and the amounts shown on the perpetual records be accounted for? What are some causes for such differences?
6. Which method of inventory valuation would you recommend to Fullton Company management giving (a) reasons for your choice, and (b) the effect of your recommendation on the financial statements.

DP9-2. (*Managerial policy decision problem*) (*Inventory valuation: retail inventory method*) The records of the Hallmark Company show the following information on January 31, 1973:

	Cost	Sales Price
Merchandise Inventory–January 1, 1973	$ 6,700	$ 9,500
Purchases during January	62,000	92,600
Transportation In	850	
Purchases Returns and Allowances	2,345	3,500
Markups		9,150
Markdowns		950
Sales		95,000

Required:

1. Find the lower of cost or market value of the January 31 inventory, using the retail inventory method.
2. Why are markdowns excluded in arriving at the cost-to-retail ratio? How would you describe the valuation if markdowns are not excluded? If both markups and markdowns are excluded?
3. The Hallmark Company has had frequent inventory shortages in certain of its departments. What steps should management take to eliminate these shortages?

DP9-3. (*Accounting policy decision problem*) (*Inventory valuation: gross margin method*) A fire destroyed the entire inventory of the Blue Corporation on December 23, 1973. The following information is available for the years 1972 and 1973 (to the date of the fire):

	1973	1972
Merchandise Inventory, January 1	$ 27,850	$ 26,500
Sales	109,862	105,100
Sales Returns and Allowances	2,105	2,360
Purchases	92,308	79,460
Purchases Returns and Allowances	4,873	5,610
Transportation In	3,672	4,201

Required: 1. Estimate the amount of the inventory destroyed by the fire.
2. How reliable is the estimate?
3. Should this method be used for financial reporting purposes to eliminate the need for physical inventory taking?

PROBLEMS

P9-1. (*Accounting policy decision problem*) Purchases and sales data for the first three years of operation of the Groton Company were as follows (purchases are listed in order of acquisition):

	1971	1972	1973
Sales	12,000 units at $50	15,000 units at $60	18,000 units at $65
Purchases	4,000 units at $22	5,500 units at $32	7,000 units at $40
	6,000 units at 25	6,000 units at 34	4,500 units at 43
	5,000 units at 30	4,000 units at 37	5,000 units at 45

Required:

1. Prepare a schedule showing the number of units on hand at the end of each year.
2. Compute the year-end inventories under the periodic inventory method for each of the three years, using (a) FIFO and (b) LIFO.
3. Prepare income statements for each of the three years through Gross Margin on Sales based on (a) FIFO, (b) LIFO, and (c) weighted average.
4. Which method of inventory valuation do you think is the most logical? Why?
5. (a) As a manager, which method would you prefer assuming that you are paid a bonus based on earnings? (b) which method would you prefer if you were (1) a present shareholder; (2) a prospective shareholder.

P9-2. The following data are from the inventory records of a single item of the Richard Lindhe Company:

Purchases	Sales	Balance
		50 units at $1.00
100 units at $1.10		
50 units at 1.20		
	60 units at ?	
20 units at 1.30		
	30 units at ?	
	20 units at ?	
50 units at 1.40		

Required:

Determine the ending inventory and the cost of goods sold using:
1. FIFO and (a) the periodic inventory method, (b) the perpetual inventory method.

2. LIFO and (a) the periodic inventory method, (b) the perpetual inventory method.
3. Weighted average and the periodic inventory method.

P9-3. The Drew Machine Company buys and sells planers. Purchases and sales during April, 1973, were

	Purchases	Sales
April 2	44 units at $200	
3		80 units
9	42 units at 250	
15	46 units at 225	
20		30 units
25	44 units at 240	
30		86 units

The inventory on April 1 consisted of 50 units at $300 each.

Required:

1. Compute the cost of goods sold during April, using LIFO and the periodic inventory method.
2. Compute the cost of goods sold during April, using FIFO and the perpetual inventory method.

P9-4. (*Accounting policy decision problem*) In January, 1973, the David Jackson Company began buying and selling a recently patented stamping machine. Transactions for the month were:

1973
January 2 Purchased a machine at $3,300.

7 Purchased a machine at $3,500.

15 Sold a machine at $7,000.

20 Purchased a machine at $4,000.

28 Sold a machine at $7,000.

Operating expenses for January were $4,000.

Required:

1. Record the information on perpetual inventory records, using each of the following methods: (a) FIFO, (b) moving average, and (c) LIFO.
2. Prepare an income statement based on each of the three methods of inventory valuation.
3. Give reasons for the variations in the cost of goods sold and the net income in the three statements.
4. What factors should be considered when choosing a method of inventory valuation?
5. Assume that Mr. Jackson was about to purchase another machine before the month end but asks you first (a) how that will affect the net income for the month, and (b) whether he should defer the purchase until early in February. The price will not change. What would you recommend?

P9-5. (*Accounting policy decision problem*) The inventory of the Floyd Upholstering Company on December 31, 1973, consisted on the following items:

		Unit	
	Quantity	Cost	Market
Frames			
Type F-1	220	$28.50	$31.00
Type F-12	150	52.00	45.00
Type F-15	120	43.00	42.00

Springs (sets)

Type S-1	1520	14.50	17.00
Type S-12	1250	21.00	23.00
Type S-15	680	17.25	12.00

Required:

1. Compute the ending inventory at the lower of cost or market, applied to (a) each item, (b) each category, and (c) the entire inventory.
2. What is the effect of each application of LCM on the gross margin in the current year? in the following year?
3. It is maintained by some that LCM pricing is inherently inconsistent and that its application may result in income distortions. Discuss.

P9-6. (*Accounting policy decision problem*) The following data are taken from the books of the Jamison Company:

	Units	Unit Cost
Beginning balance	60	$1.00
First purchase	100	1.00
Second purchase	200	1.10
First sale	175	
Third purchase	250	1.20
Second sale	275	
Fourth purchase	100	1.25
Third sale	50	

Required:

1. Compute the cost value of the ending inventory under each of the following methods: (a) Weighted average—periodic, (b) FIFO—perpetual, (c) LIFO—perpetual, (d) FIFO—periodic, and (e) LIFO—periodic.
2. Assume that the current replacement costs of all the items in the inventory have increased significantly since they were acquired. How would this change your answer? What would be the effect of using the current replacement costs?

P9-7. The records of the Famous Clothing Company show the following information for the month of July, 1973:

Sales	$80,000
Markups	6,000
Markdowns	10,500
Transportation In	1,200
Purchases at cost	57,000
Purchases at retail	84,000
Inventory–July 1, at cost	21,000
Inventory–July 1, at retail	30,000

Required: Compute the July 31 inventory at the lower of cost or market, using the retail inventory method.

P9-8. (*Accounting policy decision problem*) The Rockwell Company estimates its merchandise inventory when preparing monthly financial statements. The following information is available on June 30:

	Cost	Retail
Merchandise Inventory, June 1	$ 80,000	$ 130,000
Purchases during June (net)	650,000	1,100,000
Transportation In during June	4,000	
Sales during June (net)		640,000

Required:

1. Compute the estimated inventory on June 30, using the gross margin method. Based on past experience, the Rockwell Company estimates a rate of gross margin of 38 percent for the current year.
2. Compute the estimated inventory on June 30, using the retail inventory method.
3. (a) Give the reason for the difference in the ending inventory under the two methods. (b) Which method is more reliable? Why?

P9-9. The Welt Company closes its books annually on December 31, at which time the merchandise inventory is determined by a physical count. For its monthly interim statements, however, inventory estimates based on the gross margin method are used. Condensed partial income statements for the years 1970, 1971, and 1972 are given as follows:

	1970	1971	1972
Sales	$175,000	$200,000	$220,000
Cost of Goods Sold	105,000	118,000	127,600
Gross Margin	$ 70,000	$ 82,000	$ 92,400

The merchandise inventory on December 31, 1972, was $35,000. During January, 1973, sales were $22,000 and purchases were $20,000.

Required:

1. Compute the inventory on January 31, 1973, based on (a) the gross margin rate for the prior three years and (b) the average annual gross margin rate.
2. Which gross margin rate should be used? Why?

P9-10. John Flynn, the owner of a retail store, has always carried fire insurance on his inventory. Under the terms of the policy, he is to collect from the insurance company 80 percent of any loss of merchandise inventory from fire.

On the morning of July 16, 1973, Flynn's store was destroyed by fire. The fixtures and inventory were a total loss. The records, which were kept in a fireproof safe, were not destroyed.

Operations for the period January 1 through July 15 resulted in the following balances:

Sales	$85,800
Heat, Light, and Water Expense	255
Inventory–January 1, 1973	12,000
Transportation In	1,500
Salaries and Wages	18,200
Purchases	59,500
Sales Returns and Allowances	280
Salesmen's Commissions	5,200
Purchases Returns and Allowances	1,150
Sales Discounts	1,520
Purchases Discounts	1,850

His records also include an Income Statement for the year ended December 31, 1972, which is condensed as follows:

Sales		$172,000
Cost of Goods Sold		120,400
Gross Margin		$ 51,600
Expenses		
Selling	$15,000	
General	19,400	34,400
Net Income		$ 17,200

Required:

Compute the amount of merchandise inventory lost in the fire and the amount that Flynn may expect to collect from the insurance company.

P9-11. The ordering costs for a product are $112.50 per order and the annual carrying costs per unit are $.30. Sales for the year are estimated to be 9,000 units.

Required:

1. (a) How many units should be ordered? (b) How often should orders be placed.
2. What is the effect on total costs if it later turns out that the actual ordering costs were $150 an order?

P9-12. (*Accounting policy decision problem*)

Part I

On November 1, 1973, Edward Herson established the Herson Company with an investment of $20,000 in cash. Purchases and sales during the month were

1973
Nov. 1 Purchased 3,600 units at $24.

10 Sold 2,100 units at $40.

13 Purchased 3,000 units at $25.50.

17 Sold 3,300 units at $40.

22 Purchased 4,500 units at $26.50.

30 Sold 2,700 units at $40.

Operating expenses were $28,000. Cash settlements on all transactions were completed by the end of the month.

Required: 1. Prepare perpetual inventory schedules, using (a) FIFO, (b) LIFO, and (c) moving average.
2. Prepare income statements and statements of financial position based on each method of inventory valuation.

Part II

Assume the same facts as in Part I, except that the units purchased on November 13 cost $22 each and those purchased on November 22 cost $21 each.

Required: The same as for Part I.

Part III

Assume the same facts as in Part I.

Required:

1. Discuss the effect of the three methods of inventory valuation on the ending inventory, the cost of goods sold, the gross margin on sales, the net income, and the total current assets during a period of (a) rising prices and (b) falling prices.
2. Explain why the different methods yield different results. Which method is correct?
3. What other factors should Herson consider in his choice of a method of inventory valuation?
4. Which method would you recommend? Explain.
5. FIFO reflects price increases on goods on hand in net income but these are not real profits because, as the inventory is depleted, replacement costs will be higher. Do you agree? Explain.

P9-13. (*Accounting policy decision problem*)

Part I

The following note accompanied the 1969 annual report of Engelhard Minerals and Chemicals Corporation:

> (2) Inventories
>
> Inventories are stated at the lower of cost or market. The inventories at December 31, 1969, Include $67,427,160 of precious metals of the Engelhard Industries Division, of which amount approximately 78 percent is valued at cost prices under the last-in, first-out method of valuation. At December 31, 1969, the market value of such precious metal inventories exceeded the carrying value by $26,234,000. Taxes on income would become payable on any realization of this excess by reason of reduction of precious metals inventories.

Required:

1. Discuss the purpose of this note?
2. (a) Would you recommend that the precious metal inventories be stated at their market values? (b) If so, what entry would you make? (c) What would be the effect on the balance sheet and income statement? (d) What accounting principles are involved.
3. What inventory management policies would be needed to avoid the additional taxes on income referred to in the last sentence?

Part II

The following note accompanied the 1968 annual report of the Glen Alden Corporation:

Inventories
Inventories consist of the following:

| | December 31, | |
	1968	1967
At the lower of cost (principally first-in, first-out, and average) or market:		
Finished goods	$ 65,980,338	$ 57,537,105
Work in process	21,083,916	21,593,530
Raw materials and supplies	55,443,458	31,025,601
At cost (whiskey, other spirits, and wine):		
Tax paid	28,721,162	
In bond	293,599,775	
	$464,828,649	$110,156,236

A substantial portion of in bond inventories of whiskey, other spirits, and wine in storage for aging over a period of several years are classified as current assets in accordance with general practice prevailing in the distilling industry.

Inventories of whiskey, other spirits, and wine, under existing Federal and other applicable laws, are subject to payment of excise taxes and other levies upon removal from bonded or other Government-controlled premises.

Required:

1. What principle supports the classification of inventories "in storage for aging" as a current asset?
2. What caused the quadrupling of its inventory during the year?
3. Are the inventory valuation procedures used by the company "conservative?" Explain.

Part III

The following note accompanied the 1970 annual report of Gulf-Western Industries, Inc.

NOTE D. Inventories
The amounts of inventories
were determined using the
following methods:

Lower of cost or market	$348,165,000
Cost, less amortization (primarily theatrical and television films)	124,664,000
Estimated net sales price (commodities, primarily sold but not shipped)	15,403,000
	$488,232,000

Required: Discuss the inventory valuation procedures of this company. Indicate the existing conditions justifying the use of amortized cost and estimated selling price for parts of the inventory.

P9-14. Draw a flow chart that illustrates the procedures to follow to update a perpetual inventory card using the moving-average method of costing.

Required:

1. Print headings for perpetual inventory card (Figure 9-3).
2. Read Balance—quantity, unit cost, and total cost.
3. Is the next entry a purchase of the item?
4. If yes, calculate a new unit cost by adding the cost of the units purchased to the cost of units on hand and then the total cost is divided by the total quantity of units on hand to find the new average price.
5. If no, the units issued are priced at the average price until new units are purchased.
6. Print the entry on the card.
7. If last entry, end of job.

Plant and Equipment—
Acquisition, Depreciation,
and Disposal

Industrial expansion often requires large expenditures for land, buildings, machinery, and equipment. When such expenditures must be made in an economic environment marked by sweeping technological changes, inflation, and high levels of taxation, the accounting problems become both more complicated and more controversial. This chapter deals with the determination of and accounting for the cost of plant assets, the allocation of asset costs to the appropriate accounting periods, the disposal or retirement of plant assets, and related problems of management planning and control.

The term *plant and equipment* denotes all types of land, structures, and equipment of a tangible and relatively permanent nature, acquired for use in the regular operations of the business, not for resale, and whose use or consumption will cover more than one accounting period. This classification includes land, buildings, machinery, trucks, fixtures, tools, office machines, furniture and furnishings, patterns, and dies. The terms *plant assets, capital assets, fixed assets, tangible assets,* and *noncurrent assets* are often used as synonyms for plant and equipment.

COST OF PLANT AND EQUIPMENT

The cost of plant and equipment includes the purchase price (less any discount) plus all other expenditures required to secure title and to get the asset ready for operating use. Hence the cost of land includes brokers' fees, legal fees, and transfer taxes. The cost of buildings includes permit fees, engineering fees, and remodeling costs. The cost of machinery includes transportation, installation, and all other costs incurred in preparing the machinery for operations.

Assume that a company purchases a machine for $5,000 at terms of 2/10, n/60, with freight to be paid by the buyer. Installation of the machine requires specialized electrical wiring and the construction of a cement foundation. All these expenditures are charged to the asset account. The total asset cost includes the following:

Purchase price	$5,000
Deduct 2% cash discount	100
Net purchase price	$4,900
Transportation	125
Cost of wiring	75
Construction of a special foundation	110
Total asset cost	$5,210

The entry for the purchase of the machine is the net cash paid on purchase.

Machinery	4,900	
Cash		4,900

The entry for the freight payment is

Machinery	125	
Cash		125

The entry to record the payment for installation of the machine is

Machinery	185	
Cash		185

When these entries are posted, the Machinery account shows a total cost for the machine of $5,210. If the discount of $100 is not taken, it should still be deducted from the purchase price of $5,000 and charged to Discounts Lost—Nonmerchandise Items. An asset acquired in some manner other than by cash payment—for example, by gift or issuance of securities—is valued on the basis of the amount of cash that would be required for its acquisition (*fair market value*). When a used plant asset is acquired, all expenditures incurred in getting the asset ready for use—paint, replacement parts, and so on—are charged to the asset account.

DEPRECIATION OF PLANT AND EQUIPMENT

Accounting Concept: ▼
Allocation of Costs

Depreciation is not necessarily a measure of the decline in the value of an asset, but rather a recognition of the fact that depreciable assets used in the business have a predictable and limited service life, over which asset costs should be allocated for income measurement. The emphasis is on the periodic charge to expense rather than the resulting position statement valuation. ▼ Since most plant and equipment assets have a limited useful life, their cost is properly allocable as an expense to the accounting periods in which the assets are used. ▼ Although the serviceable life of the asset cannot be definitely known at the time of its acquisition, the cost of the asset cannot be considered as an expense chargeable entirely either to the period of acquisition or to the period of disposal. It is better to make an estimation of the useful life of the asset for purposes of making the periodic charge to expense than to omit the charge on the grounds that there is no strictly scientific way of making such an estimation.

Depreciation should be distinguished from *depletion*. Depletion (discussed later in this chapter) refers to the process of estimating and recording the periodic charges to operations due to the exhaustion of a natural resource, such as coal, oil, or standing timber. *Amortization* is often used as a general term to cover depreciation, depletion, and write-downs of certain other assets.

There are several factors that limit the serviceability of plant assets, chiefly wear and tear through ordinary use, accidental damage, inadequacy, level of repairs of maintenance, and obsolescence. Inadequacy may be due to changes in the nature of the business—method of manufacture, location, or type or design of product—that necessitate the disposition or replacement of plant assets. Obsolescence is due to technological advances that necessitate replacement of an existing asset with a new model.

Estimated Useful Life (EUL)

It is often difficult to predict the useful service life of an asset. The estimate is important because the amount of cost assigned to each period (depreciation for a period) is deducted from current revenue, thereby affecting net income for the period. Past experience, standard operating policies, and equipment replacement policies may be used in estimating the period during which the asset can or will be used by the business. A machine may be able to withstand wear and tear for perhaps 20 years, but it may be used for only 10 years because it has become too slow or too small for current requirements; or it may have to be replaced because the particular model becomes obsolete. In any case, the cost is allocated over *estimated useful life* (EUL) of the asset.

The Internal Revenue Service provides guidelines to the acceptable estimation of useful lives of about 75 broad classes of assets. In most cases, a single industry guideline class covers all the production machinery and equipment typically used in the industry. For example, the aerospace industry, which includes manufacturers of aircraft, spacecraft, rockets, missiles, and component parts, has for its plant assets a guideline life of eight years.

Estimated Salvage Value

The cost of the asset to be depreciated is its acquisition cost minus the amount that is expected to be recovered when the asset is ultimately scrapped, sold, or traded in. If an expenditure will be required in dismantling or removing the asset, the estimated gross salvage value is reduced by the anticipated removal cost. It is frequently assumed that the salvage value will be offset by the removal cost; in this case, depreciation is computed on the total cost of the asset. Also, total cost may be depreciated when the salvage value is known to be negligible. A company may trade in any assets that have a market value. For example, some businesses trade in cars, trucks, and office equipment for new models after a period of use. In such instances, the estimated cash market value at the date of trade-in should be deducted in arriving at the depreciable amount. Experience will enable the company to arrive at a salvage value factor.

Methods of Computing Depreciation

A number of methods are used to calculate periodic depreciation charges; they may give significantly different results. The method selected in any specific instance should be based on a careful evaluation of all the factors involved including estimated useful life, intensity of use, rapidity of changes in the technology of the industry and of the equipment, and revenue-generating potential. The objective is to charge each period in proportion to the benefits received during that period from the total pool of expected benefits over the asset's useful life. Procedures for allocating the cost of the asset to each accounting period within its service life are based on either uniform or varying charges. By the use of certain methods, the amounts charged to each period may be irregular, or they may follow a regularly increasing or decreasing pattern.

Straight-line Method. Under the straight-line method, depreciation is considered a function of time, and a uniform portion of the cost is allocated to each accounting period. Degrees of use or age or efficiency factors are not considered in determining the amount of depreciation to be assigned to each period. The straight-line method may be expressed as follows:

$$\frac{\text{Cost less salvage value}}{\substack{\text{Number of accounting periods in the}\\ \text{estimated useful life of the asset}}} = \text{Depreciation for each accounting period}$$

Assume that a machine costing $5,210, with an estimated service life of five years and an estimated net salvage value of $210, is purchased on January 2, 1973. The annual depreciation charge is

$$\frac{\$5,210 - \$210}{5} = \$1,000$$

The straight-line method is popular primarily because it is simple to use. It assumes, however, level operating efficiency, repair and maintenance, and revenue contributions.

Production Methods. Production methods relate depreciation to usage or to results rather than time, recognizing either working hours or units of output with each unit being charged with an equal amount regardless of decline in service effectiveness, decline in revenue generated, or level of repair and maintenance requirements.

The *working-hours method* requires an estimate of service hours in the life of the asset. The charge to depreciation for an accounting period is determined as follows:

$$\frac{\text{Cost less salvage value}}{\text{Total estimated working hours}} = \frac{\text{Depreciation expense}}{\text{per hour}}$$

$$\substack{\text{Depreciation expense}\\ \text{per hour}} \times \substack{\text{Working hours for}\\ \text{the period}} = \substack{\text{Depreciation expense}\\ \text{for the period}}$$

Assume, for example, that a machine costing $21,000 with a salvage value of $1,000 is expected to render 40,000 hours of service. If it is used for 5,000 hours during an accounting period, the computation for that period would be

$$\frac{\$21,000 - \$1,000}{40,000 \text{ hrs.}} = \$.50 \text{ per service hour}$$

$.50 \times 5,000$ hrs. = $2,500 depreciation expense for the period

Under the *production-unit method,* depreciation is computed on units of output, and therefore an estimate of total units of output is required. If the machine in the previous example had an estimated productive life of 10,000 units and 1,500 units were processed during the current period, the charge to depreciation for the period would be

$$\frac{\$21,000 - \$1,000}{10,000 \text{ units}} = \$2 \text{ per unit produced}$$

$2 \times 1,500$ units = $3,000 depreciation expense for the period

The production methods allocate cost in proportion to the use that is made of the asset, the assumption being that there is a correlation between units of use and revenue generated. The straight-line method ignores use, emphasizing the fact that the asset is available; depreciation expense is regarded as a measure of such availability, irrespective of the extent of use.

Declining-amount Methods. The use of a declining-amount method results in larger depreciation charges during the early years with gradually decreasing charges in later years. Some commonly used forms are the *declining-balance method* and the *sum of the years-digits method.*

Under the *declining-balance method,* a uniform depreciation rate is applied in each period to the remaining *carrying value* (cost less accumulated depreciation). For Federal income tax purposes, the rate may not exceed twice the straight-line rate (*double-rate* declining balance) for most new assets. The computation is made without an adjustment for salvage, even though the asset cannot be depreciated below a reasonable salvage value, presumably because the arithmetic of this formula is such that it will never reduce the asset balance to zero. At the end of the EUL, therefore, the remaining balance (less salvage) may be depreciated under the straight-line method over a period determined at that time or by an adjustment in the amount of the depreciation for the final period, or it may continue to be reduced at the fixed percentage of the carrying value until it is retired from use.

Assume that a $10,000 machine is purchased on January 2, 1973, with an estimated life of 10 years and an estimated net salvage value of $500. A 20-percent depreciation rate—twice the straight-line rate of 10 percent—applied to the remaining carrying value gives the following results for the first three years:

Year	Computation	Annual Depreciation	Accumulated Depreciation	Carrying Value
1973	20% × $10,000	$2,000	$2,000	$8,000
1974	20% × 8,000	1,600	3,600	6,400
1975	20% × 6,400	1,280	4,880	5,120

The entry to record the depreciation charge for 1975 and the position statement presentation of the machine at the end of that year are as follows:

Depreciation Expense–Machinery and Equipment	1,280	
Accumulated Depreciation–Machinery and Equipment		1,280
Plant and Equipment		
Machinery and Equipment	$10,000	
Deduct Accumulated Depreciation	4,880	$5,120

Under the *sum-of-the-years-digits method*, depreciation for any year is determined by multiplying the cost less salvage of the asset by a fraction, the denominator of which is the sum of the numbers of the years or months of estimated useful life of the asset and the numerator of which is the number of the specific period applied in reverse order, or the number of years remaining, including the current year.

Assume that a machine costing $15,300 is purchased on January 2, 1973; the EUL is five years and the estimated salvage value is $300. The denominator of the fraction used is 15 (1 + 2 + 3 + 4 + 5). The annual depreciation is computed as follows:

Year	Years Digits	Fraction	Annual Depreciation
1973	5	$5/15 \times $15,000$	$ 5,000
1974	4	$4/15 \times 15,000$	4,000
1975	3	$3/15 \times 15,000$	3,000
1976	2	$2/15 \times 15,000$	2,000
1977	1	$1/15 \times 15,000$	1,000
Total	15		
Total depreciation for 5 years			$15,000

The denominators of the fraction used in the sum-of-the-years-digits method can be computed by multiplying the number of years of estimated useful life by the midpoint of the series. The midpoint is found by adding the first and the last years and dividing by two. In the previous example, the computation would be

$$\text{Number of years in series} = 5\left(\frac{\text{first year} + \text{last year}}{2}\right) = 5\left(\frac{1 + 5}{2}\right) = 15$$

Based on the same facts, the results under the double-rate declining-balance method (20% $\times$ 2) are as follows (amounts are rounded to nearest dollar):

Year	Computation	Annual Depreciation	Accumulated Depreciation	Carrying Value
1973	40% of $15,300	$6,120	$ 6,120	$9,180
1974	40% of 9,180	3,672	9,792	5,508
1975	40% of 5,508	2,203	11,995	3,305
1976	40% of 3,305	1,322	13,317	1,983
1977	40% of 1,983	793	14,110	1,190

A comparison of the three methods shows the following depreciation under each:

Year	Straight Line	Double-Rate Declining Balance (40%)	Sum of Years Digits
1973	$ 3,000	$ 6,120	$ 5,000
1974	3,000	3,672	4,000
1975	3,000	2,203	3,000
1976	3,000	1,322	2,000
1977	3,000	793	1,000
Totals	$15,000	$14,110	$15,000

The double-rate declining-balance method results in a higher depreciation in the first year due to the higher rate and the higher base ($15,300 as compared with $15,000). However, an undepreciated balance of $1,190 ($15,300 − $14,110) remains at the end of the fifth year.

Group Rates and Composite Rates

Some companies simplify the computation of depreciation and charge depreciation uniformly to all service years including the final one by use of a *blanket group* or *composite* rate, applied either to all the assets owned or to each major asset category. The term *group* refers to a number of homogeneous assets. When a group rate is applied to a number of nonhomogeneous assets, it is called a *composite* rate; it is a special application of the group rate. The group rate is especially useful if there are a large number of individual units with similar service lives and relatively low costs (for example, railroad tracks and ties, telephone poles and cables, and restaurant and hotel furniture). The use of a group rate eliminates the clerical work necessary to compute individual periodic depreciation and the need for detailed records of accumulated amounts. Its use is satisfactory if the assets are kept for relatively long periods and if variations in individual rates, either over or under the group rate, tend to cancel out.

Several methods may be used to develop a composite rate; one is illustrated below.

Asset	Cost	Estimated Salvage Value	Depreciable Cost	EUL (Years)	Annual Depreciation (Straight-Line)
A	$20,000	$2,000	$18,000	6	$3,000
B	15,000	–0–	15,000	10	1,500
C	10,200	600	9,600	12	800
	$45,200	$2,600	$42,600		$5,300

The *composite life* for this group of assets is 8.04 years, computed as follows:

$$\frac{\text{Depreciable cost}}{\text{Annual depreciation}} = \frac{\$42,600}{\$5,300} = 8.04 \text{ years of average life}$$

A group rate may be used with either straight-line depreciation or a declining-amount method. Assuming that the straight-line method is used, the annual rate to be applied is

$$\frac{\text{Annual depreciation}}{\text{Total cost}} = \frac{\$5,300}{\$45,200} = 11.72\%$$

Total depreciation at a mean rate of 11.72 percent, applied each year for 8.04 years to the total cost of $45,200, will be $42,600 ($45,200 × 11.72 × 8.04, adjusted for rounding), the amount to be depreciated. The annual depreciation charge is $5,297.44 ($45,200 × 11.72%).

When any unit in the group is disposed of, it is assumed that it has been fully depreciated and no gain or loss on disposal is recognized. Underdepreciation on items in the group that are used for less than their estimated useful lives is assumed to be offset by overdepreciation on items used longer than their EUL's. Although accumulated depreciation records on the individual units in the group are not kept, a record of original costs is kept.

Assume that Asset A is retired at zero salvage value after four years of service. The entry to record the retirement is

Accumulated Depreciation	20,000	
Asset Account		20,000
To record retirement of Asset A; salvage value is zero.		

If $4,000 in salvage value were realized, the entry would be

Accumulated Depreciation	16,000	
Cash	4,000	
Asset Account		20,000
To record sale of Asset A for $4,000.		

The debit to Accumulated Depreciation is the cost of the asset less proceeds from the sale.

Given accurate estimates of EUL and salvage values, the carrying value of the group is zero when the last item in the group is retired and there is indeed no gain or loss on disposal. But because errors in forecasting are likely and because an error made on one item affects the rate used on all the items in that group, it is essential that the rate be revised whenever acquisitions or disposals change the composition of the group with respect to types of assets, estimated useful lives, and so on.

Revenue Procedure 62-21 issued by the Internal Revenue Service permits the application of a single rate to groups of accounts, composite accounts, and accounts classified as to use.

Depreciation for Partial Accounting Periods

A consistent method should be followed for recording depreciation on assets acquired or retired during the accounting period. A variety of procedures are used. One that is popular because of its simplicity is to consider that a plant asset is purchased as of the beginning of the month of acquisition if it is purchased on or before the fifteenth of the month and to consider that it is purchased on the first day of the following month if the asset is purchased on or after the sixteenth of the month, the minimum measurable unit of time for the depreciation expense charge being one month.

Assume that a machine costing $6,500 with an estimated life of 10 years and salvage value of $500 was purchased on November 10, 1973. Depreciation on the machine for the calendar year 1973 is

$$\frac{\$6,500 - \$500}{10} \times \frac{2}{12} = \$100$$

The year-end entry to record depreciation on the machine for two months is

Depreciation Expense–Machinery and Equipment	100	
Accumulated Depreciation–Machinery and Equipment		100

If the machine had been acquired on or after November 16, the amount in the entry would be $50. Depreciation may have to be recorded for a partial accounting period when an asset is sold, discarded, or exchanged for another asset. In these situations, depreciation must be recorded to the date of the event, assuming that the asset has not already been fully depreciated. The amount of depreciation to be charged for the month of disposal is based on the method followed for acquisitions. The rules must be applied consistently.

DEPRECIATION METHODS COMPARED— MANAGEMENT CONSIDERATIONS

▼ The process of recording depreciation gives recognition to the expiration of asset costs through use. Depreciation is not a process of valuation; that is, its purpose is not to report the asset at the amount for which it could be sold at the time since the asset was not acquired for resale. ▼ The method that is most practical and meaningful for the user should be selected. Since the amount of the depreciation deduction has a direct effect on net income and since the alternative methods of calculating depreciation result in different amounts, the choice of method may significantly affect the income tax liability. The declining-amount methods, in contrast to the straight-line method, reduce the tax liability and conserve working capital during the early life of the asset.

Accounting Concept: ▼ *Purpose of Depreciation*

The straight-line method is simple to apply and is satisfactory under conditions of fairly uniform usage. Two objections to the method are

1. The straight-line depreciation charge results in a uniform deduction from revenue without adjustment for variation in sales volume or rate of output during the period.
2. If expenditures for repairs increase gradually with continued use of the asset, the deduction from revenue for the combined expenses of repairs and depreciation will increase annually, thus distorting the reported income.

The production methods allocate depreciation in proportion to usage or output. This is important if usage is the dominant cause of loss in value of the asset. It should be emphasized that the estimate of useful life is based on anticipated total usage before disposal of the asset regardless of the reason—wear and tear, obsolescence, or inadequacy.

The declining-amount methods are based on the hypothesis that the service rendered by a plant asset is greatest in the early years of use; hence, that depreciation charged under these methods results in a more accurate matching of expense and revenue. The rapidity of the decline in service value varies with the demand for the product and the rate of technological progress. If revenues drop significantly during the early years of use and if rapid changes in technology shorten the economic life of the asset, then the deduction of larger amounts of depreciation in early years is matched by the relatively larger revenues and the concomitant diminishing depreciation deductions in later years are matched against the diminishing revenues of those years.

Another reason for using the declining-amount methods is that as an asset gets older, it requires more maintenance. The increasing maintenance expenses in later years are offset by the diminishing depreciation expense, thus equalizing, to some extent, the total expenses of the asset and thereby achieving a better matching of expense with revenue. The declining-amount methods more closely reflect the economic fact that an investment in an asset is made for the purpose of realizing a desired annual rate of return on the unrecovered portion of the investment. "Entrepreneurs . . . buy the asset to make a profit; hence, conceptually, they discount the bundles of future net services which they purchase. Therefore, by inference, an *ideal depreciation* method is one which allocates cost in such a way as to produce a uniform return on remaining unamortized investment in all periods at the rate of return implicit in the original transaction by which the asset was acquired."[1] The difficulty here is to measure the revenue contribution of a particular asset from a group of assets that collectively generate the revenue for the period.

When a plant and equipment item is depreciated, the depreciable cost of the asset is written off over its useful life. Depreciation expense is included in the income statement as a deduction from revenue. The process of recording depreciation does not provide or segregate funds for the replacement of the property at the end of its EUL; an asset should be depreciated even if there is no intention of replacing it. The acquisition of a new asset creates a new series of depreciation charges. Of course, depreciation deductions reduce income taxes, but the amount by which the tax liability is reduced does not necessarily remain in the business as cash available for the replacement of equipment. It may be employed for a multitude of other purposes—inventory expansion, dividends, and so on. It is possible for a business to segregate an amount of cash equal to the periodic depreciation charges, but such funds, if available, probably would result in a greater return when used in the regular operations of the business.

CAPITAL AND REVENUE EXPENDITURES

The term *expenditure* refers to a payment or a promise to make a future payment for benefits received—that is, for assets or services. Expenditures made on plant and equipment assets during the period of ownership may be classified as *capital*

---

[1]Isaac N. Reynolds, Selecting the proper depreciation method, *Accounting Review*, April, 1961, pp. 243–44.

expenditures or *revenue* expenditures. A capital expenditure results in an addition to an asset account; a revenue expenditure results in an addition to an expense account.

Capital expenditures are payments for asset alterations, additions, and replacements that are significant in amount and which will benefit future accounting periods only; therefore, through the depreciation process, these expenditure are allocated to such future accounting periods. They prolong the useful life of the asset, making it more valuable or more adaptable by increasing the quality of the product, the quantity, or both, and are recorded as increases in plant and equipment; the expenditure is said to have been *capitalized*. Purchases of land, buildings, machinery, and office equipment are also capital expenditures.

Expenditures for extraordinary repairs made to equipment during its life are also classified as capital expenditures if they extend the useful life or capacity of the asset or otherwise make the asset more serviceable (for example, replacing a manually operated elevator with a fully automated one). Some accountants view an extraordinary repair as a restorative process; they record the increase in the asset by debiting Accumulated Depreciation, thereby cancelling past depreciation charges.

Revenue expenditures benefit a current period and are made for the purpose of maintaining the asset in satisfactory operating condition. A routine repair or the replacement of a minor part that has worn out is an expense of the current accounting period, to be deducted from the revenue for the period. These expenditures do not increase the serviceability of the asset beyond the original estimate, but rather represent normal maintenance costs.

Careful distinction between capital and revenue expenditures is one of the fundamental problems of accounting; it is essential for the matching of expenses and revenue and, therefore, for the proper measurement of net income. A capital expenditure that is recorded as a revenue expenditure, as, for example, a purchase of office equipment charged to Office Expense, causes an understatement of net income in that year. If the error is not corrected, net income for the following years will be overstated by the amount of depreciation expense that would otherwise have been recognized. Conversely, a revenue expenditure that is recorded as a capital expenditure, as, for example, an office expense charged to Office Equipment, overstates net income for that year. If the error is not corrected, net income for the following years will be understated by the depreciation charge on the overstated portion of the Office Equipment account.

DISPOSAL OF PLANT AND EQUIPMENT

An asset may be disposed of by sale, by being *traded in* as part of the purchase price of a replacement, or by simply being discarded. The accounting treatment of sales and of discards is similar; the treatment of *trade-ins* is somewhat different.

An asset may still be in use after it is fully depreciated—that is, when the balance of the Accumulated Depreciation account, assuming that the salvage value is zero, is equal to the cost of the asset. In this case, no further depreciation is taken and no further entries are required until the asset is disposed of. In the statement of financial position, the Accumulated Depreciation or Plant and Equipment account may be followed by a notation of the portion of the account that represents fully depreciated assets still in use.

Sale or Discard of Plant and Equipment

When an asset is sold or discarded, the entry for the transaction must remove the appropriate amounts from the asset and the accumulated depreciation accounts. Assume, for example, that a company acquires a truck on January 2, 1973, at a cost of $5,000. Depreciation is recorded on a straight-line basis at the rate of $1,000 annually (salvage value is assumed to be zero). Five possible situations, together with the methods of accounting for the disposal of the truck, are illustrated.

Example 1—*Discard of fully depreciated asset:* The truck is discarded on March 1, 1978 (in the sixth year).

Accumulated Depreciation–Trucks	5,000	
Trucks		5,000

The purpose of this entry is to eliminate the accumulated charges from the Accumulated Depreciation account and to reduce the asset account by the original cost of the truck. No depreciation expense would be recorded for the truck for the time it was in use during 1978 because the truck has been completely depreciated by December 31, 1977, the end of its fifth year of use.

Example 2—*Sale of fully depreciated asset:* The truck is sold on March 1, 1978, for $50.

Cash	50	
Accumulated Depreciation–Trucks	5,000	
Trucks		5,000
Gain on Disposal of Equipment		50

Gains and losses on disposal of plant assets are measured by the difference between the carrying value of an asset and the proceeds from its disposal: a gain results when the proceeds are greater than the carrying value; a loss results when the proceeds are less than the carrying value. If the asset is fully depreciated, as in the example, the carrying value is zero and the gain is the full amount realized from the sale. A gain or a loss may be indicative of errors in estimating the asset's useful life, salvage value, or both, in which case the gain or loss is, in fact, a correction of prior years' earnings. Also, the carrying value of the asset and, therefore, the gain or loss on disposal are affected by the depreciation procedure used. The Gain on Disposal of Equipment is shown in the income statement under Other Revenue. A loss would be shown under Other Expenses.

Example 3—*Sale of asset at a price equal to carrying value:* The truck is sold on July 1, 1977, for $500. The first entry is to record the depreciation for the current year, up to the date of the sale.

Depreciation Expense–Trucks	500	
Accumulated Depreciation–Trucks		500
To record depreciation on trucks for the six-month period 1/1/77 to 7/1/77.		

The Accumulated Depreciation account now has a credit balance of $4,500, as shown below.

Accumulated Depreciation–Trucks

	12/31/73	1,000
	12/31/74	1,000
	12/31/75	1,000
	12/31/76	1,000
	7/1/77	500

The entry to record the sale is

Cash	500	
Accumulated Depreciation—Trucks	4,500	
Trucks		5,000

Example 4—*Sale of asset at a price above carrying value:* The truck is sold on July 1, 1977, for $600. The entry to record the depreciation for the current year, up to the date of the sale, is the same as in Example 3 and is assumed to have been made. The following entry is made to record the sale:

Cash	600	
Accumulated Depreciation—Trucks	4,500	
Trucks		5,000
Gain on Disposal of Equipment		100

The gain of $100 is computed as follows:

Cost of truck	$5,000
Deduct accumulated depreciation	4,500
Carrying value of truck	$ 500
Amount received	600
Gain on disposal	$ 100

Example 5—*Sale of asset at a price below carrying value:* The truck is sold on July 1, 1977, for $400 in cash. Again, the entry to record the depreciation applicable to the year of sale is the same as in Example 3 and is assumed to have been made. The entry to record the disposal is

Loss on Disposal of Equipment	100	
Cash	400	
Accumulated Depreciation—Trucks	4,500	
Trucks		5,000

The loss of $100 is computed as follows:

Cost of truck	$5,000
Less accumulated depreciation	4,500
Carrying value of truck	$ 500
Amount received	400
Loss on disposal	$ 100

Loss on Disposal of Equipment is shown in the income statement under Other Expenses.

Trade-in of Plant and Equipment— Recognition of Gain or Loss

It is common practice to exchange, or trade in, used property when new property is acquired. If the trade-in allowance is not arbitrarily excessive (as a partial offset to an unrealistic list price of the new asset), it may be considered the proper selling price of the old asset, and the new asset is recorded at its list price. After the accumulated depreciation up to the date of the trade-in is recorded, the carrying value of the old asset is compared with its trade-in allowance. A gain is recognized if the trade-in allowance is greater than the carrying value, and a loss is recognized when the trade-in allowance is less than the carrying value. When the carrying value and the trade-in allowance are equal, however, there is no recognized gain or loss. If the list price or trade-in allowance is not realistic, the new asset should be recorded at its *cash market price,* or the cash payment plus the fair market value of the asset traded in. The gain or loss can then be measured by the difference between the cash market price of the new equipment and the total of the cash outlay and the carrying value of the old equipment.

Example 1—*Trade-in allowance greater than fair market value:* A truck with a cost of $5,000 and accumulated depreciation up to the date of the trade-in of $4,500 is exchanged for a new truck listed at $6,000. A trade-in allowance of $1,000 is granted on the old truck. The fair market value of the old truck, however, is only $600. The entry to record the trade-in is

Truck (new)	5,600	
Accumulated Depreciation—Trucks	4,500	
Truck (old)		5,000
Cash		5,000
Gain on Disposal of Equipment		100

The new truck is recorded at its cash market price—the cash payment ($5,000) plus the fair market value ($600) of the old truck. The inflated list price is reduced by the excess ($400) of the trade-in allowance ($1,000) over the fair market value ($600) of the old truck, as shown below.

List price	$6,000
Deduct trade-in allowance	1,000
Cash payment	$5,000
Fair market value of old truck	600
Fair market price of new truck	$5,600

The gain on the trade-in is computed in either of the following ways:

1. Cost of old truck	$5,000
Accumulated depreciation to date of trade-in	4,500
Carrying value	$ 500
Fair market value	600
Gain on trade-in	$ 100

2. Cash market price of new truck		$5,600
Cash outlay for new truck	$5,000	
Carrying value of old truck	500	5,500
Gain on trade-in		$ 100

The following three examples illustrate the possibilities involved in trade-ins when the trade-in allowance is *equal* to the fair market value of the truck traded in.

Example 2—*Trade-in allowance greater than carrying value:* A truck that cost $5,000 with accumulated depreciation up to the date of the trade-in of $4,500 is exchanged for a new one listed at $4,000; the trade-in allowance is $800. The fair market value of the old truck is $800. Again, the new truck is recorded at its cash market price—the cash payment plus the fair market value of the old truck. The transaction is recorded as follows:

Truck (new)	4,000	
Accumulated Depreciation—Trucks	4,500	
Cash		3,200
Truck (old)		5,000
Gain on Disposal of Equipment		300

The gain on disposal of the truck is computed as follows:

Cost of old truck	$5,000
Accumulated depreciation to date of trade-in	4,500
Carrying value—unrecovered cost	$ 500
Trade-in allowance	800
Gain on trade-in	$ 300

Example 3—*Trade-in allowance less than carrying value:* The old truck in Example 2 is traded in for an allowance of $400.

Truck (new)	4,000	
Accumulated Depreciation—Trucks	4,500	
Loss on Disposal of Equipment	100	
Cash		3,600
Truck (old)		5,000

The loss on disposal of the truck is computed as follows:

Cost of old truck	$5,000
Accumulated depreciation to date of trade-in	4,500
Carrying value—unrecovered cost	$ 500
Trade-in allowance	400
Loss on trade-in	$ 100

Example 4—*Trade-in allowance the same as carrying value:* The old truck in Example 2 is traded in for an allowance of $500.

Truck (new)	4,000	
Accumulated Depreciation—Trucks	4,500	
Cash		3,500
Truck (old)		5,000

There is no gain or loss in this case because the trade-in allowance is the same as the carrying value.

Trade-in of Plant and Equipment— Nonrecognition of Gain or Loss

An alternative procedure for recording exchanges of assets is required by the Internal Revenue Service. The cost of the new asset for income tax purposes must consist of the carrying value of the old asset plus the required additional expenditure (cash paid or its equivalent), or

$$\text{Cost of new asset} = \text{Carrying value of old asset} + \text{Expenditure}$$

The excess of trade-in allowance over carrying value is viewed not as a gain but as a reduction from an inflated list price, whereas the excess of carrying value over trade-in value is viewed not as a loss but as an addition to the cost of the new asset. List prices and trade-in values are not recognized in the accounts. They only enter into the computation of the required cash outlay. Under this rule, the unrecognized gain or loss on the exchange is absorbed in the cost valuation of the new asset. An objective of the Internal Revenue Service's rule of nonrecognition of gain or loss on the trade-in of assets of like kind is to prevent the shifting of income for income tax purposes from one year to the next. A company with a large gain on a trade-in could defer trading the asset until the following tax year, thereby shifting the gain to that year. ▼ The income tax method of recording asset exchanges violates the accounting principle that plant and equipment, like inventories, should be recorded at actual cash (or equivalent) cost. Future periodic charges for depreciation should be based on cost rather than on a conglomerate figure that may reflect a sales price adjustment of the new asset as well as the unrecovered cost of the old asset. A gain or loss on an asset exchange is an integral part of the complete transaction cycle and should, therefore, be recognized. ▼ The income tax method is frequently used to account for exchanges so that further analysis and adjustment may be avoided when income tax returns are prepared, but this tendency to adjust accounting principles to conform with tax rules for the sake of expediency should not be condoned.

Accounting Concept: ▼
Recording of Assets at Cost

CHANGING DEPRECIATION CHARGES

The periodic depreciation charge may require revision as the result (1) of a capital expenditure that does not prolong the useful life of the original asset and (2) of errors in the original EUL. In either case, the new depreciable cost is typically allocated over the remaining life of the property on which the expenditure was made. Assume, for example, that an additional wing costing $8,000 is added to a five-year-old factory building. The original cost of the building was $33,000, the estimated salvage value was $3,000, and the estimated useful life was 25 years.

The straight-line method of depreciation has been used. The calculation of the revised annual depreciation charge is

Original cost	$33,000
Deduct five years' accumulated depreciation	
($30,000 × 0.04 = $1,200 per year × 5 years)	6,000
Carrying value	$27,000
Additional cost	8,000
New carrying value	$35,000
Deduct estimated salvage value	3,000
New depreciable cost	$32,000
New annual depreciation charge, based on a remaining useful life of 20 years	$ 1,600

If the improvement prolongs the life of the asset or increases its salvage value, the calculations must be altered to give effect to such changes. For example, if after the addition of the wing the remaining useful life was estimated to be 24 years and the estimated salvage value was $3,800, the revised annual depreciation charge would be determined as follows:

New carrying value	$35,000
Deduct estimated salvage value	3,800
New depreciable cost	$31,200
New annual depreciation charge, based on a remaining useful life of 24 years	$ 1,300

DEPLETION OF NATURAL RESOURCES

Natural resources, or wasting assets, such as oil wells, mines, or timber tracts, should be recorded in the asset account at cost. As the resource is extracted, its asset value is reduced. This reduction in value, or expiration of the cost, of the asset resulting from production is called *depletion* and is recorded on the books by a debit to the Depletion Cost account and a credit to the Accumulated Depletion account. Theoretically, the depletion cost item becomes a part of the cost of the merchandise inventory and ultimately becomes an expense chargeable against revenue on the income statement when the goods are sold. In the statement of financial position, accumulated depletion is deducted from the cost of the resource.

The periodic depletion charge is usually calculated on an output basis similar to the production-unit method of recording depreciation. The cost of the wasting asset is divided by the estimated available units of output to arrive at a per-unit depletion charge. The number of units removed during the accounting period multiplied by the per-unit depletion charge represents depletion for that period. The computation is

$$\frac{\text{Cost} - \text{Salvage}}{\text{Estimated tons to be mined}} = \text{Depletion}$$

Assume that a mine costs $180,000 and contains an estimated 400,000 tons of ore. It is estimated that the net salvage value will be $20,000. The per-unit depletion charge is

$$\frac{\$180,000 - \$20,000}{400,000} = \$0.40 \text{ per ton}$$

If 10,000 tons are mined during an accounting period, the depletion charge is 10,000 × $0.40, or $4,000, and the entry to record the depletion for that period is

Depletion Cost–Mine	4,000	
Accumulated Depletion–Mine		4,000

The amount of the recorded depletion cost to be transferred to the Inventory account is the number of units on hand multiplied by the per-unit depletion charge. Assume that 2,000 tons remain unsold at the end of the period. The required entry is

Ore Inventory	800	
Depletion Cost–Mine		800

The balance of the Depletion Cost account, $3,200 ($4,000 − $800), is deducted in the income statement from the revenue realized from the sale of 8,000 tons of ore. The balance of the Ore Inventory account includes not only the allocated portion of mine depletion cost but also labor and other costs of extracting the ore (*overhead*). This is illustrated in the following T-account flow chart:

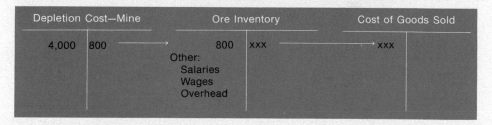

For income tax purposes, the deduction for a tax year may also be figured as a percentage of the gross income subject to maximum and minimum limits. These limits do not, however, preclude deductions over the life of the asset greater than the cost of the asset.

INTANGIBLE ASSETS

Intangible assets are nonphysical rights that are of future value to the business. Some intangibles, whether purchased or self-developed, such as patents, copyrights, franchises, and leaseholds, can be readily identified and their cost measured. Others, such as goodwill, are not specifically identifiable or measurable.

The procedure for the amortization, or periodic write-off of a portion of the cost, of an intangible asset is the same as for computing and recording depreciation on a plant and equipment item by the straight-line method. The amount to be amortized annually is computed by dividing the asset cost by the legal life or the estimated useful life, whichever is shorter. The entry is a debit to an amortization account and a credit to the asset account. The straight-line method is generally used in view of the difficulties and uncertainties in estimating useful economic life and future benefits.

Difficulties and uncertainties arise from the uniqueness of intangibles. The estimated useful life may be limited by law (copyright), by contract, by legislation (franchise), or by the economic factors of demand and competition (patents). Other intangibles (goodwill, trademarks) have an unlimited or indefinite life. Furthermore, some can be separately identified (franchise), whereas others cannot be, because they relate to the total entity (goodwill); finally, some intangibles are purchased, while others are developed within the firm.

In its Opinion Number 17, the AICPA Accounting Principles Board concluded, "That a company should record as assets the costs of intangible assets acquired from others, including goodwill acquired in a business combination. A company should record as expenses the costs to develop intangible assets which are not specifically identifiable. The Board also concludes that the cost of each type of intangible asset should be amortized by systematic charges to income over the period estimated to be benefited. The period of amortization should not, however, exceed forty years." [2]

Patents

The U.S. Patent Office grants *patents*, or exclusive rights to the owners to produce and sell their inventions or discoveries, for a period of 17 years. All the costs involved in developing and acquiring a patent are included in the intangible asset Patents account. The cost of a patent may be large and should be capitalized and amortized over the life of the asset or 17 years, whichever is shorter. The Patents account may be credited directly for the amortized portion; the account debited is called Amortization of Patent Cost.

Copyrights

A *copyright* is an exclusive right to publish a literary or artistic work, granted by the government. The copyright is recorded at cost and is subject to amortization either over its legal life—28 years—or its useful economic life. If the copyright is obtained directly, the cost is small and is usually written off entirely in the first year. If it is purchased, the cost may be large enough to warrant periodic amortization. In practice, however, since revenues from copyrighted material are uncertain and are often limited to a relatively brief period, the cost of a copyright is added to the other costs of the first printing and enters into the inventory cost of the books or other printed materials.

Franchises

A *franchise* is a monopolistic right granted by a government to render a service. A right to operate a bus line or railroad or the exclusive use of a television

[2] APB Opinion No. 17, published in *AICPA Accounting Principles,* Chicago: Commerce Clearing House, Inc., Vol. II, p. 6662.

transmitting channel is a valuable asset to the owner. The cost of obtaining the franchise is amortized over its life.

Leaseholds and Leasehold Improvements

Leaseholds are rights to the use of land, buildings, or other property. They are frequently paid for in advance and should be classified as capital expenditures. Leasehold improvements, such as buildings, are sometimes constructed on leased property. Leaseholds and leasehold improvements should be amortized over the life of the lease or over the estimated useful life of the asset, whichever is shorter.

Goodwill

Goodwill is a general term embodying a variety of intangible factors relating to the reputation of a firm and its ability to realize above-normal net income returns on an investment. Such factors as favorable customer relations, loyal and competent employees, possession of valuable patents, franchises, or copyrights, a high-quality product, and efficient management all aid in the development of goodwill. Self-developed goodwill is not recorded on the books. However, if the assets and goodwill of one company are purchased by another, the purchased goodwill should be recorded as an asset at cost.

The amount to be paid for goodwill is usually a product of a bargaining process between the buyer and the seller. The debit to Goodwill is the excess of the cost over the amounts allocable to the other assets.

"Cost is measured by the amount of cash disbursed, the fair value of other assets distributed, the present value of amounts to be paid for liabilities incurred, or the fair value of consideration received for stock issued. . . ."[3]

Research and Development

Current expenditures for research and development should be capitalized to the extent that they will benefit future periods whether in the form of new or better products, reduced costs, or other benefits. When future benefits are uncertain, research and development costs are usually expensed when incurred. Arguments against the immediate expensing of research and development costs are (1) that income is distorted, since all research and development expenditures are intended to benefit future periods, (2) that this accounting method is influenced more by its short-term effect on earnings than by the need to recognize future benefits, and (3) that capitalization and systematic allocation over future periods result in a better matching of revenue and expense, even in the presence of uncertainty, than arbitrary immediate write-off.

Organization Costs

This is an intangible asset resulting from expenditures made incidental to incorporation and is discussed further in Chapter 11.

[3] *Op. cit.*, p. 6665.

PLANT AND EQUIPMENT—MANAGERIAL ANALYSIS

The investment by a company in plant and equipment assets may vary considerably, depending on the nature of the business. Manufacturing concerns require a greater investment in machinery and equipment than do retail or wholesale firms. The relationship of the plant and equipment to total assets and to sales should be in proper proportion for the industry. If the amount invested in plant and equipment is too high, fewer funds are available for working capital purposes. Depreciation charges will also be high, resulting in either higher sales prices or lower profits. Finally, the long-term liabilities will be greater, resulting in greater interest costs and the need for funds to pay off debts as they mature.

The following ratios are used to determine whether there has been an overinvestment in plant and equipment:

1. Plant and equipment to long-term liabilities
2. Plant and equipment to stockholders' equity
3. Net sales to plant and equipment

The condensed comparative position statement of the Hassett Corporation (Figure 10-1) is used to illustrate these ratios.

Figure 10-1. Comparative Statement of Financial Position

	Line No.	1970 Amount	1970 Percent	1971 Amount	1971 Percent	1972 Amount	1972 Percent	1973 Amount	1973 Percent
HASSETT CORPORATION Comparative Statement of Financial Position December 31, 1970–1973 (In Thousands of Dollars)									
Assets									
Current Assets	1	$240	74	$260	72	$295	65	$300	59
Plant and Equipment (net)	2	85	26	100	28	160	35	210	41
Total Assets	3	$325	100	$360	100	$455	100	$510	100
Liabilities and Stockholders' Equity									
Liabilities									
Current Liabilities	4	$120	37	$130	37	$145	32	$170	33
Long-Term Liabilities	5	50	15	55	15	90	20	140	27
Total Liabilities	6	$170	52	$185	52	$235	52	$310	60
Stockholders' Equity									
Capital Stock	7	$ 80	25	$ 80	22	$ 80	18	$ 80	16
Retained Earnings	8	75	23	95	26	140	30	120	24
Total Stockholders' Equity	9	$155	48	$175	48	$220	48	$200	40
Total Liabilities and Stockholders' Equity	10	$325	100	$360	100	$455	100	$510	100
Net Sales	11	$255		$325		$400		$420	

The ratio of plant and equipment to long-term liabilities is obtained by dividing the total carrying value of the plant and equipment by the long-term liabilities (line 2 ÷ line 5). The ratios for the Hassett Corporation, given in percentages, are

December 31	Percent
1970	170
1971	182
1972	178
1973	150

This comparison is of particular significance to the long-term creditors if any of the plant and equipment has been mortgaged as security for loans. On December 31, 1970, the corporation owned $1.70 in plant and equipment assets for every $1 of long-term debt; on December 31, 1973, there was only $1.50. The reduced ratio reflects an increased dependence on long-term borrowing to finance plant and equipment acquisitions. It is apparent, for example, that the additional plant and equipment assets acquired in 1973 were paid for by long-term borrowing.

The ratio of plant and equipment to stockholders' equity is obtained by dividing the total carrying value of the plant and equipment by the stockholders' equity (line 2 ÷ line 9). The ratios for the Hassett Corporation are

December 31	Percent
1970	55
1971	57
1972	73
1973	105

On December 31, 1973, investment in plant and equipment exceeded the stockholders' equity in the corporation. This indicates a possible overinvestment in plant and equipment, resulting in higher interest, taxes, maintenance expenses, and depreciation charges, and lower working capital. A heavy investment in land, buildings, and machinery greatly restricts the mobility of a company if a change in plant location or type of product manufactured is desirable.

The ratio of net sales to plant and equipment, or *plant and equipment turnover,* is found by dividing net sales by the total carrying value of the plant and equipment (line 11 ÷ line 2). The ratios for the Hassett Corporation are

Year	Percent
1970	300
1971	325
1972	250
1973	200

In 1970, sales were 300 percent of plant and equipment; that is, for every $1 of plant and equipment there were sales of $3; in 1973, there were only $2 in sales for every $1 of plant and equipment. This, too, underscores a possible overinvestment in plant and equipment, especially during 1972 and 1973. Although sales have increased each year, the investment in plant and equipment has increased at a greater rate. The following comparison shows that a 147-percent increase in plant and equipment resulted in only a 65-percent increase in sales.

	Line	Sales	Plant and Equipment
1973	1	$420	$210
1970	2	255	85
Net change	3	$165	$125
Percent of change (line 3 ÷ line 2)		65	147

These results are based on historical cost. The amounts—net after depreciation—do not reflect the effect of changing economic and technological conditions and market price fluctuations. The use of current cost would improve income measurement and position statement reporting. The difficulty is in developing acceptable techniques for measuring current valuations.

PLANT AND EQUIPMENT REPLACEMENT— MANAGEMENT CONSIDERATIONS

The decision to replace plant and equipment items and the timing of the replacement is often a complex matter requiring careful analysis by management. The decision is particularly difficult when it involves not merely the replacement of a worn-out or obsolete unit, but the acquisition of a machine with a different purchase price, capacity, or operating cost. The problem of asset replacement involves a careful study of the expense of doing the given task with the present unit as compared with the expense of using the new unit. Generally, a replacement is advisable if the larger profits resulting from the use of the new equipment will justify the additional investment required. This consideration is discussed in detail in Chapter 24.

SUMMARY

The term "plant and equipment" includes land, natural resources, structures, and equipment of a tangible and relatively permanent nature acquired for use in the regular operations of the business. Intangible assets include copyrights, franchises, leaseholds, goodwill, and organization costs.

The cost of plant and equipment includes the purchase price less any discounts plus all other expenditures required to secure title and to get the asset ready for use. Plant and equipment, except land, is subject to depreciation in recognition of the predictable limited service life over which the cost of the asset should be allocated as an expense of each period in which the asset is used. Depreciation should be distinguished from depletion, which relates to natural resources, and from amortization, which relates to intangible assets.

There are several depreciation methods; they may give significantly different results. The straight-line method considers depreciation to be a function of time and allocates a uniform portion of the cost to each accounting period. The production methods relate depreciation to usage or results. The declining-amount methods—double-rate declining-balance and sum of the years-digits—result in larger depreciation charges during the early years with gradually decreasing charges in later years. These methods are based on the assumption that the service received from the asset is greatest in the early years of use. Some companies use a blanket group or composite rate applied either to all assets owned or to each major category of assets.

Expenditures made on plant and equipment during the period of ownership may be classified as (1) capital expenditures or (2) revenue expenditures. Capital expenditures are recorded as increases of the asset account because they benefit future accounting periods by prolonging the useful life of the asset or by making it more valuable or more serviceable. Revenue expenditures benefit only the current period and are made to maintain the asset in satisfactory operating condition.

A gain or loss on the disposal of a plant asset is measured by the difference between the carrying value of the asset and the proceeds from the sale. A new asset acquired by trade-in of an existing asset is recorded at (1) list price if the trade-in allowance is not arbitrarily excessive, (2) cash market price of the new asset if the list price or trade-in allowance is not realistic, or (3) the carrying value of the old asset plus the cash paid. Method 3—the income tax method—assumes that list prices and trade-in allowances are inflated—essentially, disguised trade discounts—and does not, therefore, recognize the difference between the trade-in value and the carrying value as either gain or loss.

The periodic depreciation charge may require revision due to additional capital expenditures made subsequent to acquisition. The additional expenditure is allocated over the remaining life of the asset.

Natural resources are recorded at cost; periodic depletion is calculated on an output basis similar to the production method. Copyrights are recorded at cost and amortized over either the legal life or the useful economic life. A franchise is recorded at cost and is amortized over its life. Leaseholds are amortized over the life of the lease or over the useful life of the property, whichever is shorter. Goodwill—the ability of a firm to realize above average normal earnings on the investment—is recorded at cost if it was purchased. Self-developed goodwill is not recorded on the books.

QUESTIONS

Q10-1. What does the term *plant* and *equipment* encompass?

Q10-2. (a) List some expenditures other than the purchase price that make up the cost of plant and equipment. (b) Why are cash discounts excluded from the cost of plant and equipment? (c) What problems in cost determination arise when used plant assets are acquired?

Q10-3. (a) What distinguishes a capital expenditure from a revenue expenditure? (b) What is the effect on the financial statements if this distinction is not properly drawn?

Q10-4. Student A maintains that if a plant asset has a fair market value greater than its cost after one year of use, no depreciation need be recorded for the year. Student B insists that the fair market value is irrelevant in this context. Indicate which position you support and give your reasons.

Q10-5. (a) What are some of the factors that must be considered when the depreciation method to be used is chosen? (b) When depreciation is recorded?

Q10-6. The basis for depreciation is generally original (historical) cost. Is there any other basis that could logically be used?

Q10-7 Since the total amount to be depreciated cannot exceed the cost of the asset, does it make any difference which method is used in calculating the periodic depreciation charges?

Q10-8. Describe the conditions that might require the use of each of the following methods of depreciation: (a) straight-line, (b) production, (c) declining-amount.

Q10-9. (a) Distinguish between the composite rate and the group rate of depreciation. (b) Give reasons to support the use of these procedures and state their underlying assumptions.

Q10-10. What procedures may be followed in recording depreciation on assets acquired during the accounting period?

Q10-11. What is the relationship, if any, between the amount of the annual depreciation charges on plant assets and the amount of money available for the new plant assets?

Q10-12. (a) What are the accounting problems resulting from the trade-in of one like plant asset for another? (b) from the sale of a plant asset?

Q10-13. (a) Distinguish between the terms depreciation, depletion, and amortization. (b) How is the periodic depletion charge determined?

Q10-14. (a) What are intangible assets? (b) What factors must be considered when the acquisition of intangibles is recorded? (c) When intangibles are amortized?

Q10-15. What ratios are useful in evaluating the level of investment in plant assets?

Q10-16. It has been argued that with proper maintenance certain equipment will last almost indefinitely, in which case depreciation is not necessary. Do you agree? Explain.

EXERCISES

E10-1. For each of the following items, indicate the account to be debited:

a. Expenditure for installing machinery
b. Expenditure for trial run of new machinery
c. Expenditure for conveyor system for machinery
d. Payment of delinquent taxes on land (taxes were delinquent at the date of purchase of the land)
e. Expenditure for extensive plumbing repairs on a building just purchased
f. Sales tax paid on new machinery just purchased
g. Payment of incorporation fees to the state
h. Expenditure for a major overhaul that restores a piece of machinery to its original condition and extends its useful life
i. Expenditure for an addition to a building leased for 20 years
j. Amount paid for a purchased business in excess of the appraised value of the net assets

E10-2. The Albee Company made the following expenditures on the acquisition of a new machine:

Invoice cost ($10,000) less 2% cash discount	$9,000
Transportation charges	300
Installation charges	500
Property insurance—premiums for three years	300
Materials and labor used during test runs	150

What is the cost of the machine?

E10-3. The Fleet Manufacturing Company acquired an old building for $50,000 and spent $20,000 to put it into usable condition. One year later, an additional expenditure of $1,150 was made for painting, plumbing, and electrical repair work. Record all the expenditures.

E10-4. The Floyd Corporation purchased a machine for $15,000; terms 1/10, n/60. Record (a) the acquisition of the machine and (b) payment of the invoice within the discount period.

E10-5. The Rose Corporation solicited bids for a new wing for its factory building. The lowest bid received was $20,000. The corporation decided to do the work with its own staff, and the wing was completed for a total cost of $18,000. Record the expenditure.

E10-6. On April 1, 1973, a calculating machine used in the office of the Cowan Company was sold for $250. The sale was recorded by a debit to Cash and a credit to Office Equipment for $250. The machine had been purchased on October 1, 1969, for $750 and had been depreciated at the rate of 10 percent annually (no salvage value) through December 31, 1972. The Cowan Company closes its books annually on June 30. Make an entry to correct the accounts as a result of the transaction.

E10-7. On August 1, 1973, the Merchant Corporation acquired a truck costing $7,500 with an estimated useful life of five years and a salvage value of $500. On August 1, 1976, the truck was traded in for a new one with a cash market price of $10,000. The dealer allowed $2,100 on the old truck, and the balance was paid in cash. Record the trade-in on the books of the Merchant Corporation, based on (a) recognition of gain or loss and (b) nonrecognition of gain or loss. (c) Contrast the entries in (a) and (b) and state how the nonrecognition of the gain or loss in (b) is compensated for.

E10-8. The Excel Corporation purchased a truck on January 2, 1973, for $4,200. It had an estimated useful life of four years and a trade-in value of $400. Compute the depreciation charge for the year 1973 under the following methods: (a) straight line, (b) sum of the years-digits, (c) double-rate declining-balance, and (d) production, assuming an operating life of 50,000 miles and 12,000 miles of actual use the first year.

E10-9. On January 2, 1973, the Byrd Company purchased land and an old building for $125,000. The land is appraised at $20,000; the building is estimated to have a useful life of 10 years and a salvage value of $5,000. After three years' use, the building was remodeled at a cost of $55,000. At this time, it was estimated that the remaining useful life of the building would be 20 years with a salvage value of $10,000. Using the straight-line method of depreciation, give the entries for (a) the purchase of the land and building, (b) depreciation for 1973, (c) remodeling costs, and (d) depreciation for 1976.

E10-10. The Stimson Corporation acquired a building for $100,000 with an estimated useful life of 20 years and an estimated salvage value of $5,000. Four years later, an addition to the building was constructed at a cost of $15,000. Using straight-line depreciation, compute the annual depreciation charges before and after the construction of the addition to the building.

E10-11. The Exeter Company acquired three machines as follows:

	Machine		
	A	B	C
Cost	$50,000	$35,000	$47,000
Estimated salvage value	4,000	3,000	5,000
Estimated life (years)	9	8	6

Assuming that the straight-line method is used, compute (a) the composite life for the three machines and (b) the annual depreciation rate.

E10-12. The unadjusted trial balance of the Cartor Company at December 31, 1973, includes the following accounts:

Patents (granted January 2, 1973)	$12,000
Copyrights (acquired July 1, 1973)	3,125
Goodwill	2,700
Research and Development (new products)	5,000
Organization Costs	1,500

(a) What is the basis of valuation of each of these accounts? (b) What adjustments should be made on December 31, 1973? (c) What additional information is needed to complete Requirement (b)?

E10-13. The Capital Corporation reported a net income of $50,000 for the year 1973. The president of the corporation noted that the beginning and ending inventories were $200,000 and $250,000, respectively, although the physical quantities on hand were relatively stable. He also noted that deductions for depreciation averaged 10 percent on plant and equipment costing $450,000, although the current dollar value of the assets is estimated at $600,000. The president suggests that the reported net income is erroneous. Comment.

E10-14. The Delta Company purchased a mine for $210,000. It was estimated that the land contained 700,000 tons of a recoverable mineral deposit, and that after recovery of the deposits the land would have a salvage value of $10,000. During the first year, 60,000 tons were recovered and 50,000 tons were sold. Labor and overhead costs were $100,000. Determine (a) the cost of goods sold and (b) the ending inventory valuation.

E10-15. The comparative financial statements of the Ball Corporation show the following information:

	Plant and Equipment	Long-Term Liabilities	Stockholders' Equity
December 31, 1973	$110,000	$ 50,000	$150,000
1972	100,000	48,000	115,000
1971	85,000	42,500	105,000
1970	90,000	45,000	100,000

Sales: 1973	$300,000
1972	220,000
1971	200,000
1970	180,000

(a) Compute the appropriate ratios and (b) evaluate the significance of the ratios.

E10-16. The condensed income statement of the Stern Company for the year ended June 30, 1973, was as follows:

Sales	$100,000
Cost of Goods Sold	60,000
Gross Margin	$ 40,000
Operating Expenses	
(includes depreciation expense of $3,500)	25,000
Net Income	$ 15,000

(a) Assuming that beginning and ending Accounts Receivable, Accounts Payable, and Merchandise Inventory balances were approximately the same, how much cash was generated by operations? (b) Did the depreciation expense deduction result in a direct cash increase of $3,500? Explain.

E10-17. (*Accounting policy decision problem*) (a) "The government gave away $2.7 billion in tax revenue." (b) "An unwarranted windfall." (c) "A bonanza."

These are some of the statements made by some public officials and economists following an announcement by the U.S. Treasury Department on January 11, 1971, reducing the depreciation provision period by about 20 percent.

Required:

1. Do you agree with the above quotations? Explain.
2. What is the Treasury Department's motive in permitting faster write-offs.
3. What is the effect of the Treasury Department's action on net income after taxes.

DEMONSTRATION PROBLEMS

DP10-1. (*Computing depreciation expense*) The Currier Company began business on January 2, 1973, with three new machines. Data for the machines are given:

Machine	Cost	Estimated Salvage Value	EUL (Years)
A	$66,000	$ 6,000	10
B	90,000	10,000	8
C	24,000	4,000	5

Required: Compute the depreciation expense for the first two years by each of the following methods: (a) straight-line, (b) sum of the years-digits, (c) double-rate declining-balance, and (d) composite rate based on straight-line depreciation.

DP10-2. (*Capital and revenue expenditures*) On January 2, 1973, the Violo Construction Company purchased a machine for $20,000. Its estimated useful life was 10 years with no salvage value. Additional expenditures were made for transportation, $300, and installation costs, $600. On June 30, 1979, repairs costing $5,000 were made, increasing the efficiency of the machine and extending its useful life to two years beyond the original estimate. On December 1, 1981, some minor worn-out parts were replaced for $200. On October 1, 1983, the machine was sold for $2,500.

Required: Give the journal entries to record (a) the purchase, (b) annual depreciation for 1973, (c) the extraordinary repair on June 30, 1979, (d) annual depreciation for 1979, (e) the ordinary repair on December 1, 1981, and (f) the disposal on October 1, 1983.

DP10-3. (*Asset sale; trade-in*) On January 2, 1973, the Dorne Corporation purchased a machine costing $12,000 with a useful life of 10 years and salvage value of $800. Assume that the sum of the years-digits method is used to record depreciation.

Required: Give the journal entries to record the sale or trade-in of the machine, based on each of the following assumptions:

1. Sale of the machine for $2,000 at the end of the sixth year.
2. Sale of the machine for $3,000 at the end of the fourth year.
3. Trade-in of the machine at the end of the sixth year for a new machine listed at $14,000. The corporation paid $8,400 in cash to acquire the new machine. (Recognize the gain or loss on the exchange.)
4. Assuming the same facts as in (3), record the trade-in under the income tax method.

DP10-4. (*Managerial policy decision problem*) The board of directors of the Arteck Corporation, after reviewing the following data taken from the firm's records, is concerned about a possible overinvestment in plant and equipment.

	1971	1972	1973
Current Assets	$65,000	$ 73,750	$ 75,000
Plant and Equipment	25,000	40,000	55,000
Current Liabilities	32,500	36,250	42,500
Long-Term Liabilities	13,750	22,500	24,000
Capital Stock	20,000	20,000	33,500
Retained Earnings	23,750	35,000	30,000
Net Sales	81,250	100,000	105,000

Required:

1. You have been asked to prepare a report on this matter to the board of directors. Include appropriate analyses and computations to support your conclusions.
2. Assume you are a prospective shareholder. How would this report influence your evaluation of the company?

PROBLEMS

P10-1. The Bowdoin Corporation purchased land and buildings for $300,000: the buildings were demolished at a cost of $8,500, salvaged materials were sold for $2,000, and a new building was constructed on the site for $2,000,000. The following additional expenditures were incurred during construction:

Fees for permits and licenses	$ 500
Interest on money borrowed for payment of construction costs	750
Architectural fees	10,000
Insurance	650
Real estate taxes	850
Land grading and leveling	4,000
Promotional literature describing the new facility	500
Trees, shrubs, and other landscaping costs	2,500

Required: Open T accounts for (a) Land, (b) Buildings, and (c) Operating Expenses. Post the transactions to the accounts.

P10-2. A piece of machinery was acquired by Fullington, Inc., for $6,000 on January 2, 1973. It was estimated to have a five-year life and a salvage value at the end of that time of $300.

Required: Prepare tables showing periodic depreciation over the five-year period, for each assumption listed:

1. Depreciation is to be calculated by the straight-line method.
2. Depreciation is to be calculated by the sum of years-digits method.
3. Depreciation is to be calculated by the double-rate declining-balance method.
4. Repair charges are estimated at $200 for the first year and are estimated to increase by $100 in each succeeding year; depreciation charges are to be made on a diminishing scale so that the sum of depreciation and estimated repairs is the same over the life of the asset.

P10-3. The Nile Corporation purchased a machine on January 3, 1973, at a cost of $46,000. In addition, the corporation paid $400 to have the machine delivered and $1,600 to have it installed. The estimated useful life of the machine is six years with a trade-in value of $9,000 at the end of that time.

Required: Prepare four separate schedules, showing the annual depreciation charge for the six-year period under each of the following methods: (a) straight-line; (b) production, assuming a total operating life of 30,000 hours with actual annual hours of use as follows: 4,000; 5,000; 6,000; 5,700; 4,600; 4,700; (c) double-rate declining-balance; and (d) sum of the years-digits.

P10-4. On January 2, 1973, the Merit Company purchased a new machine for $70,000 with an estimated salvage value of $4,000 and an estimated useful life of five years, or 6,000 machine hours. The plant manager expects to use the machine for 1,500 hours during 1973, and 1,300 hours during 1974.

Required:

1. Compute the depreciation expense for each of the first two years by the following methods: (a) straight-line, (b) production, (c) sum of the years-digits, and (d) double-rate declining-balance.
2. Assume that the Merit Company is in an industry in which rapid changes in technology have, in the past, made existing equipment obsolete. How does this affect the estimate of the asset's useful life?

P10-5. The following information was taken from the books of the Gruen Corporation.

	Machine A	Machine B	Machine C
Date acquired	January 2, 1973	January 2, 1974	January 2, 1975
Cash payment	$15,400	$4,400	$19,800
Estimated salvage value	1,000	1,200	2,200
Estimated useful life in years	4	5	6
Method of depreciation	Sum of the years-digits	Straight-line	Double-rate declining-balance

On January 2, 1974, machine A, with a value of $9,400, was traded for machine B which listed for $14,000.

Required:

1. Give all the necessary entries to record the transactions through December 31, 1975. The books are closed annually on December 31.
2. What is the entry for the trade-in of machine A for machine B when the income tax method is used?

P10-6. The Weil Corporation acquired two factory buildings. Subsequently, major improvements were made to roofs and foundations, extending the useful life of each building. The following information was taken from the records:

	Building A	Building B
Date acquired	1/2/73	7/1/73
Original cost	$92,000	$135,000
Estimated salvage value	$ 4,000	$ 10,000
Estimated useful life	20 years	25 years
Date improvements completed	7/1/74	7/1/74
Improvement costs	$10,000	$26,000
Revised estimated salvage value	$ 3,000	$7,000
Revised estimated useful life	25 years	25 years
Method of depreciation	Straight-line	Straight-line

Required:

1. Give the journal entries to record the transactions, including year-end adjustments through December 31, 1975. The books are closed annually on December 31.
2. What factors influence the estimate of the useful life of the buildings.
3. (a) What other methods of depreciation can be used? (b) What additional information would be needed?

P10-7. The general ledger of the McGowan Company includes the following accounts:

Machinery and Equipment

1969 Jan. 2	A	5,000	
1970 Apr. 1	B	5,500	
1972 June 1	C	7,500	

Accumulated Depreciation–Machinery and Equipment

1969 Dec. 31	833.33
1970 Dec. 31	1,245.83
1971 Dec. 31	1,383.33
1972 Dec. 31	1,820.83

The straight-line method is used, the machines have no salvage value, and gains and losses on trade-ins are recognized. Details regarding the computation of depreciation expense are summarized as follows:

Machine No.	Date Acquired	Cost	EUL (Years)	Accumulated Depreciation (12/31/1972)
A	1/2/1969	$5,000	6	$3,333.32
B	4/1/1970	5,500	10	1,512.50
C	6/1/1972	7,500	10	437.50

On January 2, 1973, machine A was traded in for machine D, with a cash outlay of $4,500. The cash value of the new machine is $6,500. Its estimated useful life is ten years.

On August 1, 1973, machine B was traded in for machine E. The new machine lists for $8,000 and its estimated useful life is six years. A trade-in allowance of $4,000 is received on the old machine; the fair market value of the old machine is $3,500.

Required:

1. Record all the necessary entries for the year 1973 through December 31.
2. Record the trade-in of machine B, assuming that it had been depreciated under the sum of the years-digits method instead of the straight-line method.

Note: Computations for depreciation for machine B for the years 1970 and 1971, using the sum of the years-digits method, would be as follows:

	Year 1970	Year 1971
April 1, 1970 through March 31, 1971:		
$^{10}/_{55} \times \$5,500 = \$1,000$, allocable to:		
1970: $^{3}/_{4} \times \$1,000$	$750	
1971: $^{1}/_{4} \times \$1,000$		$250
April 1, 1971 through March 31, 1972:		
$^{9}/_{55} \times \$5,500 = \$900$, allocable to:		
1971: $^{3}/_{4} \times \$900$		675
Totals	$750	$925

P10-8. The Machinery and Equipment account of the Wagner Corporation shows the following at the beginning of 1973:

Asset	Cost	Estimated Salvage Value	EUL (Years)
A	200	–0–	4
B	500	–0–	5
C	1,000	100	9

During 1973, the company acquired 25 pieces of small machinery to perform a repetitive machining operation. The machines cost $200 each, had no salvage value, and had an estimated weighted average useful life of four years. The company uses a blanket rate for all machinery and equipment.

Required:

1. Record the retirement during the year of Asset C which had been acquired six years ago.
2. Record the sale of one of the small machines for $100.
3. Record depreciation expense for the year.

P10-9. (*Managerial policy decision problem*) The 1969 annual report of the Cummins Engine Company, Inc. includes the following data:

	December 31	
	1969	1968
Net sales	$410,633,000	$366,489,000
Net earnings	18,350,000	13,153,000
Total shareholders' investment	130,205,084	115,762,810
Working capital	87,208,000	72,153,000
Property, plant and equipment at net book value	104,445,000	103,955,000
Total assets	278,065,000	251,342,000
Shares of common stock outstanding at end of year	6,045,864	5,475,103

Required:

1. Prepare such ratios as you consider useful by a present or prospective shareholder in evaluating the company.
2. Based on these ratios, (a) What is your assessment of the company? (b) Why might these ratios be misleading? (c) Why do you consider them useful?

P10-10. (*Accounting policy decision problem*)

a. Cutler-Hammer, Inc. explains in its report to its shareholders that depreciation provisions were generally computed using the sum of the years-digits method "which distributes the greatest cost of the assets to the early years of their estimated lives." Do you agree with the apparent rationale for using sum of the years-digits method of depreciation? Explain fully.

b. Assume that Cutler-Hammer had been using the straight-line method. Would its adoption of the sum of the years-digits method be more likely to insure the availability of funds that will be needed to replace assets when they are no longer useful.

c. What is the relationship between the balance in the Accumulated Depreciation–Machinery account and the availability of funds for replacing machinery. What is the relationship between the quantity and quality of a company's repair and maintenance programs and the amount and rate of the provisions for depreciation.

d. Growth International, Inc. reported to its shareholders that effective January 1, 1968, two subsidiary companies, for financial reporting purposes, changed from an accelerated method to the straight-line method of computing depreciation. Indicate (a) the probable reason for the changeover, (b) which accounts are affected, and (c) the effect on the financial statements.

P10-11. A $10,000 machine is purchased on January 2, 1973, with an estimated life of 10 years and an estimated net salvage value of $500. The double-declining balance method of depreciation is to be used.

    Required:

1. Construct a flow chart that will compute the depreciation expense for each year. Use these headings in the table:

Year	Annual Depreciation	Accumulated Depreciation	Carrying Value

2. Write a program coded in BASIC to compute the depreciation expense for each year.

P10-12. A machine costing $15,300 is purchased on January 2, 1973. The estimated useful life is five years and the estimated salvage value is $300. Depreciation is to be calculated by the sum of the years-digits method.

    Required:

Write a BASIC program to compute the annual depreciation expense for the machine.

P10-13. (*Accounting policy decision problem*) The following statements were extracted from notes accompanying annual reports:

a. Trade names and goodwill acquired through purchases prior to 1968 are being amortized over a 25-year period; subsequent purchases aggregating $1,530,000 will be amortized when it becomes evident that the value of the asset has diminished (Alberto-Culver Company, 1970).

b. Television and feature film costs are amortized in the proportion of rentals earned to date to management's estimate of ultimate rentals. If management's estimate indicates a loss, the full amount of the loss is charged against income (Filmways, Inc. 1968).

c. Franchises consist of Schenley contracts to import whiskeys, liquors, and other distilled spirits which, in the opinion of the management of Glen Alden, have continuing value and accordingly are not amortized. Other intangibles of $3,670,363 are being amortized over periods not exceeding 20 years (Glen Alden Corporation, 1969).

d. The Company follows the practice of accumulating costs applicable to immature fruit crops including caretaking expenses and depreciation. Costs during the year are capitalized and charged to earnings when the fruit crop is sold.

Required:

1. Comment critically on each of the foregoing notes and state your suggestions.
2. Do any of the methods used violate the proper matching of revenue and expense?
3. What alternative methods might have been used in each instance?
4. Do the methods used indicate an explicit attempt to influence reported net income? If so, in what way?
5. What are some specific circumstances underlying the choice of accounting method in each case?

P10-14. (*Accounting policy decision problem*) The Charcoal Briquet Company recently began operations as a manufacturer and wholesaler of charcoal briquets. Management has been holding regular meetings at which decisions are made regarding various company policies. One of the items on the agenda for the next scheduled meeting is the depreciation policy of the company. Kenneth Willis, the company treasurer and controller, is responsible for developing relevant supporting data. As a staff assistant to Willis, you are responsible for gathering the information that he requests.

You select from the Plant and Equipment section of the general ledger the following data:

Land	$ 10,000
Buildings	100,000
Furniture, fixtures, machinery, and equipment	150,000
Transportation equipment	8,000
Kilns	14,000

Based on information that has been obtained from reliable sources, you suggest to Willis the following useful lives and salvage values for the assets:

Buildings	45 years and $15,000
Furniture, fixtures, machinery, and equipment	10 years and $10,000
Transportation equipment	6 years and $ 1,200
Kilns	6 years and no salvage value

Based on comprehensive forecasts of sales and expenses, management estimates net income before depreciation and income taxes as follows:

First year of operations	$45,000
Second year of operations	60,000
Third year of operations	90,000

The company is subject to a Federal corporate income tax rate of 22 percent on the first $25,000 of taxable income and 48 percent on all taxable income in excess of $25,000. Also, management plans to use the same depreciation amounts on both the corporate financial statements and the corporate tax returns.

Required:

As preparation for Willis's presentation at the forthcoming meeting, you are instructed to do the following:

1. Using the straight-line, sum of the years-digits, and double-rate declining-balance methods, prepare depreciation schedules for the first three years of operations.
2. Calculate the net income under each method.
3. Describe the effect of each method on the company's cash balance during the first three years of operations.

4. Describe the effect of each depreciation method on the cash balance after the first three years.
5. Identify the difficulties of estimating useful lives and salvage values.
6. List the criteria for determining the company's depreciation policy.
7. Explain briefly what depreciation expense is and why it is included in the measurement of net income.
8. Explain briefly what accumulated depreciation is and why it is included in the preparation of statements of financial position.

P10-15. (*Accounting policy decision problem*) On January 2, 1969, the Neale Corporation purchased a group of machines for $120,000 for the manufacture of a new product. The machines have an estimated useful life of 10 years, during which time management plans to produce 440,000 units of the new product. The estimated salvage value of the machines is $10,000.

The following projections were prepared for use in selecting the depreciation method to be followed:

Year	Units of Output	Equipment Maintenance and Repairs	Net Taxable Income Before Depreciation
1969	36,000	$ 6,000	$24,500
1970	40,000	7,000	24,900
1971	44,000	9,000	25,200
1972	48,000	12,000	26,000
1973	52,000	16,000	30,000

All operating expenses have been deducted including equipment maintenance and repairs but excluding depreciation expense on the machine, to arrive at net taxable income.

Required:

1. Prepare separate depreciation schedules for the five-year period based on the following methods of depreciation: (a) straight line, (b) production, based on units of output, (c) double-rate declining balance, (d) sum of the years digits. Use the following headings for each schedule:

Year Ending December 31	Annual Depreciation Expense	Accumulated Depreciation	Carrying Value at End of Year

2. Write a report to management, stating the advantages and disadvantages of each method of depreciation and giving your recommendations as to choice of method. Support your conclusions with schedules showing the total annual cost of operating the machines. Compute the net income before and after income taxes and evaluate the tax consequences of the different methods of depreciation. (Assume a corporate income tax rate of 30 percent.)
3. Write a supplement to your report, based on any pertinent assumptions you wish to make. For example, (a) the machines can be leased for an annual rental of $25,000, (b) a favorable statement of financial position is essential in connection with an anticipated bank loan.

11

Contributed Capital—
Single Proprietorships,
Partnerships,
and Corporations

The owner's, partners', or stockholders' equity of a business results from assets contributed by the proprietor, partners, or stockholders and from earnings reinvested in the business. The characteristics of single proprietorships, partnerships, and corporations and the accounting for single proprietorship, partnership, and corporate capital contributions are presented in this chapter. The entries for the regular operating transactions are the same for all forms of business organization; only the entries for the formation of the business, the withdrawal of funds, and the closing process are different. The accounts used for recording the contributed capital in a single proprietorship, a partnership, and a corporation are shown in Figure 11-1.

SINGLE PROPRIETORSHIPS

The accounting procedures applicable to the capital accounts of single proprietorships were discussed and illustrated in the introductory chapters of this text. A brief review follows.

To illustrate the accounts used for recording the contributed capital in a single proprietorship, assume that on January 1, 1973, James Leary formed the Leary Appliance Company with a cash investment of $20,000. On June 15, he withdrew $6,000 in anticipation of earnings; a summary of the accounts on December 31 showed the net income for the year to be $10,000. The entries to record these events are

1973				
Jan.	1	Cash	20,000	
		James Leary, Capital		20,000
		To record investment by proprietor to form a retail appliance business to be called the Leary Appliance Company.		

June 15	James Leary, Drawing	6,000	
	Cash		6,000
	To record withdrawal		
	by proprietor in		
	anticipation of		
	earned income.		
Dec. 31	Revenue and Expense Summary	10,000	
	James Leary, Drawing		10,000
	To close net income		
	to the Drawing account.		
31	James Leary, Drawing	4,000	
	James Leary, Capital		4,000
	To close the balance		
	of the Drawing account.		

The James Leary, Drawing account is debited for all withdrawals in anticipation of earned income and is credited at the end of the period with the actual net income. It is then closed by transferring its balance to the Capital account.

Figure 11-1. Accounts for Recording Capital

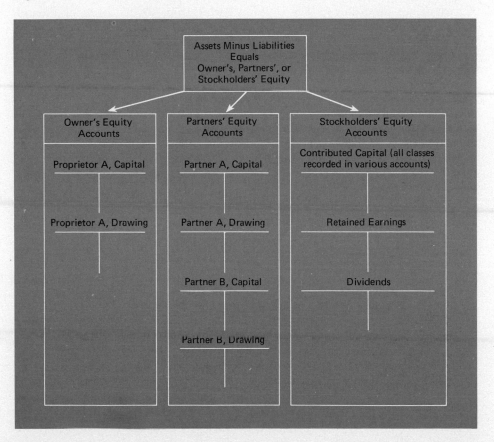

The Owner's Equity section of the statement of financial position as of December 31, 1973, would appear as follows:

> Owner's Equity
> James Leary, Capital $24,000

The statement of owner's equity for 1973 would appear as shown below.

> **LEARY APPLIANCE COMPANY**
> Statement of Owner's Equity
> For Year Ended December 31, 1973
>
> | | |
> |---|---:|
> | James Leary, Capital (investment, January 1, 1973) | $20,000 |
> | Add Net Income for the Year | 10,000 |
> | Total | $30,000 |
> | Deduct Withdrawals | 6,000 |
> | James Leary, Capital, December 31, 1973 | $24,000 |

PARTNERSHIPS

A partnership, according to The Uniform Partnership Act, is "an association of two or more persons to carry on, as co-owners, a business for profit." It is a contractual association whereby the partners pool their financial resources, services, skill, and knowledge and as a result hope to accomplish together what any one of them could not achieve individually. This association of two or more persons should be effected by a written contract called the *articles of copartnership*. The law, however, does not require any written agreement and, in the absence of any evidence to the contrary, considers the partners to share equally in profits or losses. Any other method of distributing profits or losses must be clearly agreed upon by all the partners.

The partnership form of business organization is the least common of the three principal forms. It is most often found in the professional fields, primarily medicine, accounting, and law, in which a personal responsibility exists. Professional practice in corporate form is recognized by most states and by the Internal Revenue Service for federal income tax purposes.

Types of Partnerships

Most trading partnerships are *general partnerships*. In this type of association, the members are called *general partners*. They take an active part in the business, and each one is subject to unlimited liability. If the partnership is unable to meet its obligations, the creditors may look to the personal assets of any of the partners for the full payment of the partnership debts.

The Limited Partnership Act allows some partners, but not all, a limited personal liability equal to the amounts that they have agreed to contribute to the business. Once they have made the agreed contributions, neither the partnership nor the creditors can expect to receive any further financial aid from them. *Limited partners* cannot have their names appear as a part of the firm name, cannot act as agents for the firm, and cannot withdraw any part of their agreed investment. Not all states permit this form of partnership organization. *Silent partners* do not participate in the firm management and are not known to be members. They do have a financial interest in the partnership. *Secret partners* do participate in the management of the firm and have a financial interest but their association with the firm is not revealed to persons outside the partnership. *Nominal partners* differ from general partners in that they have made no financial contributions. They take an active part in management and do not conceal their association with the firm. As a result of open participation in the affairs of the firm, they incur the same liability status as general partners. *Joint venture partnerships* are formed to accomplish a single objective. The partnership is liquidated on completion of the objective.

Advantages of Partnerships

Some advantages of the partnership form of business are listed below.

1. The money, skill, and knowledge of two or more persons can be combined.
2. Partnerships can be formed easily and quickly.
3. Government regulations do not limit the sphere of activity of a partnership. Partnerships may change from one type of business to another at will or may expand without limitation, whereas a corporation is limited to the sphere of activity stated in its charter, although if stated broadly enough, it too may engage in multiple activities.
4. A partnership can act promptly as a business enterprise in all matters (withdrawal of funds, for example). A corporation may be restricted in its actions on certain matters by its charter or bylaws.
5. Many of the formal governmental reports required of the corporation are not required of the partnership.
6. Federal income taxes are not levied against partnerships, although they are required to file information returns. The partners, however, report their distributive shares of partnership income, as shown on the partnership information return, on their individual tax returns. The partnership itself is not an income taxable entity.

Disadvantages of Partnerships

Some disadvantages of the partnership form are given below.

1. The liability of general partners is unlimited. Each member is jointly and individually liable for all the debts of the partnership.
2. The life of the partnership is limited. Death, withdrawal, or admission of a partner; agreement to terminate; bankruptcy; and incapacity are major causes for the termination of a partnership relationship. By amending the existing partnership agreement, a new partnership can be brought into existence without cessation of the actual business carried on by the enterprise.
3. The general partnership is a mutual agency; that is, each partner may act in business matters as the agent of the partnership, and the remaining

partners will be bound by his actions. If a partner purchases, in the name of the firm, merchandise used in the course of business, the other partners are also liable, although they may not have consented to or even been aware of the purchase.

4. The partners may find it difficult to cooperate, thus leading to dissolution of the partnership.
5. Partial or entire partnership interests may be difficult to transfer to another individual.
6. The ability of a partnership to raise funds is limited.

Nature of Partnership Accounting

The partnership type of business organization presents no new problems in accounting for assets, liabilities, expense, and revenue. The primary difference between a single proprietorship and a partnership is that the accounts of the partnership must show the equities of the individual partners of the partnership.

Each partner's share of ownership is recorded in an equity account, and its balance is in turn reported on the statement of financial position. On formation of a partnership, the contribution of each partner is also recorded in an equity account. To illustrate, assume that Robert Walsh and John Snow form a partnership, each investing $8,000 in cash. The opening entry is shown below.

Cash	16,000	
Robert Walsh, Capital		8,000
John Snow, Capital		8,000
To record the investments of the partners in the Walsh and Snow Company.		

It is not necessary that each partner invest the same amount of cash. If it is assumed that Walsh contributed $5,000 and Snow $10,000, the following entry is required:

Cash	15,000	
Robert Walsh, Capital		5,000
John Snow, Capital		10,000

Neither is it necessary that the original contributions be limited to cash. Assume that Walsh contributed land worth $3,000, a building worth $20,000, and merchandise costing $6,200, and that the partnership assumed a mortgage payable of $10,000 and $200 in interest accrued on the mortgage. Snow invested $15,000 in cash. The opening entry is shown below:

Cash	15,000	
Merchandise Inventory (or Purchases)	6,200	
Land	3,000	
Building	20,000	
Mortgage Payable		10,000
Accrued Mortgage Interest Payable		200
Robert Walsh, Capital		19,000
John Snow, Capital		15,000

The Function of Partnership Equity Accounts. It is possible to record all equity changes in the partnership Capital accounts. Since several individuals are involved, it is generally desirable to detail the reasons for equity changes in *capital subdivision accounts,* referred to as *personal, current,* or *drawing* accounts. The functions of partnership equity accounts are explained in the following paragraphs.

The following T account shows the recording of transactions in the Capital accounts:

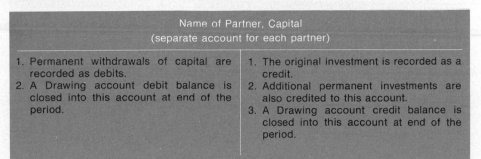

Name of Partner, Capital (separate account for each partner)	
1. Permanent withdrawals of capital are recorded as debits. 2. A Drawing account debit balance is closed into this account at end of the period.	1. The original investment is recorded as a credit. 2. Additional permanent investments are also credited to this account. 3. A Drawing account credit balance is closed into this account at end of the period.

After the closing entries have been posted, the Capital account normally has a credit balance showing the partner's equity in the net assets of the firm. A debit balance indicates the minimum additional investment that must be made by the partner to provide for the cumulative excess of his withdrawals and losses over his investments and profits.

The following types of transactions are recorded in the Drawing account:

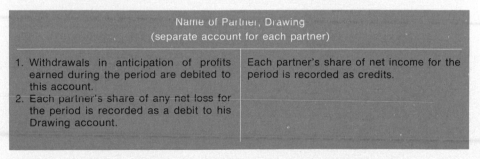

Name of Partner, Drawing (separate account for each partner)	
1. Withdrawals in anticipation of profits earned during the period are debited to this account. 2. Each partner's share of any net loss for the period is recorded as a debit to his Drawing account.	Each partner's share of net income for the period is recorded as credits.

The balance of the Drawing account is transferred periodically to the partner's Capital account. A partner's Drawing account is similar to the Drawing account of a single proprietor.

Sharing of Profits and Losses. The allocation of profits and losses to the partners is based on mutual agreement. If no articles or other evidence of agreement exist, the law assumes that profits and losses are to be divided equally even when the factors of investment, ability, or time are unequal. Since allocation is based on mutual agreement, there are many ways to distribute profits and losses. The more common are

1. Earnings are divided in an agreed ratio.
2. Interest is allowed on the capital investments and the balance is distributed in an agreed ratio.

3. Salaries are allowed to the partners, interest is allowed on capital investments, and the balance is distributed in an agreed ratio.

To illustrate these methods of sharing profits and losses, assume the following figures:

Robert Walsh, Capital				John Snow, Capital			
	1973				1973		
	Jan.	1	19,000		Jan.	1	15,000
	July	1	6,000		July	1	5,000

Revenue and Expense Summary		
1973		
Dec. 31	12,000	

1. *Agreed Ratio.* The partners may agree to divide the net income in any ratio. If, for example, Walsh contributed twice as much time to the business as Snow, and if earnings are distributed accordingly, the entry to distribute the net income is

Revenue and Expense Summary	12,000	
Robert Walsh, Drawing		8,000
John Snow, Drawing		4,000
To distribute the net income		
for the year in 2 to 1 ratio.		

2. *Interest and Agreed Ratio.* The partners may agree to allow for differences in capital investments as well as for differences in services rendered by allowing interest on capital balances and distributing the remainder in an agreed ratio. Interest, as it is used here, is not an expense but rather a mechanism for dividing a portion of the earnings in the ratio of contributed capitals, with the remainder divided in some other ratio. If 6 percent interest is allowed on opening capital balances, the division is as follows:

	Walsh	Snow	Total
Interest on opening capital			
6% of $19,000	$1,140		
6% of $15,000		$ 900	
Total interest			$2,040
Remainder: ⅔ and ⅓	6,640	3,320	9,960
Totals	$7,780	$4,220	$12,000

The entry to record this distribution of net income is

```
Revenue and Expense Summary        12,000
    Robert Walsh, Drawing                      7,780
    John Snow, Drawing                         4,220
        To distribute the net income
        for the year divided 2:1
        after allowing for 6% in-
        terest on opening capital
        balances.
```

3. *Salaries, Interest, and Agreed Ratio.* A part of the net income may be divided to recognize differences in capital balances, another part to recognize differences in the value of services rendered, and the remainder in an agreed ratio. Such a computation follows:

	Walsh	Snow	Total
Salaries	$4,000	$2,000	$ 6,000
Interest on opening capital			
6% on $19,000	1,140		
6% on $15,000		900	
Total			2,040
Remainder divided equally	1,980	1,980	3,960
Totals	$7,120	$4,880	$12,000

The entry to record the distribution is

```
Revenue and Expense Summary        12,000
    Robert Walsh, Drawing                      7,120
    John Snow, Drawing                         4,880
        To distribute the net income
        for the year equally after
        allowing for salaries and
        interest on capital balances.
```

In the absence of an agreement to the contrary, the salary and interest distributions must be made even though the net income is less than the total of such distributions. The excess is divided in the same ratio used for dividing an excess of net income over total salaries and interest. To illustrate, assume the same facts as in the previous example except that the net income for the year is $7,000. The computation is

		Walsh	Snow	Total
Salaries		$4,000	$2,000	$6,000
Interest on opening capital				
6% on $19,000		1,140		
6% on $15,000			900	2,040
Totals		$5,140	$2,900	$8,040
Deduct excess of salary and interest				
allowances over net income				
Net income	$7,000			
Deduct allowances	8,040			
Excess divided equally		(520)	(520)	(1,040)
Distribution of net income		$4,620	$2,380	$7,000

The entry to record the distribution is

Revenue and Expense Summary	7,000	
Robert Walsh, Drawing		4,620
John Snow, Drawing		2,380
To distribute the net income for the year.		

Partnership Financial Statements. The changes in partners' equity accounts during the year are shown in a statement of partners' equities. Its form is similar to the statement of owner's equity for a single proprietorship and the statement of retained earnings for a corporation. It is a supporting statement for the total partners' equities reported in the statement of financial position. Assume that Walsh and Snow each withdrew $3,000 during the year. The statement of partners' equities for the Walsh and Snow Company is shown as

WALSH AND SNOW COMPANY
Statement of Partners' Equities
For the Year Ended December 31, 1973

	Walsh	Snow	Total
Balances, January 1, 1973	$19,000	$15,000	$34,000
Add additional investments	6,000	5,000	11,000
Net income	4,620	2,380	7,000
Totals	$29,620	$22,380	$52,000
Deduct withdrawals	3,000	3,000	6,000
Balances, December 31, 1973	$26,620	$19,380	$46,000

The entries to close the partners' Drawing accounts are as follows:

Robert Walsh, Drawing	1,620	
Robert Walsh, Capital		1,620
To close the partner's drawing account (net income credit, $4,620, minus withdrawals debit, $3,000).		
John Snow, Capital	620	
John Snow, Drawing		620
To close partner's drawing account (withdrawal debit, $3,000, minus net income credit, $2,380).		

The financial statements of a partnership are similar to those of a single proprietorship. The allocations of net income to the partners may be shown below the Net Income line of the income statement or, if they are too numerous, in a supplementary statement. The statement of financial position shows the individual Capital account balances as of the end of the period and their total; or, if they are too numerous, the individual balances are shown in the supplementary statement of partners' equities.

Admission of a New Partner

The admission of a new partner technically dissolves the old partnership although, in the absence of complete dissolution or winding up, the business continues as before. A new partner either (1) may purchase his interest from one or more of the other partners, or (2) may be admitted as a partner by making an investment in the partnership.

If the new partner buys his interest from one of the original partners, partnership assets are unchanged because the transfer of assets is directly between the persons involved. The only entry on the partnership books is a transfer of the agreed share from the old partner's capital account to a capital account opened for the new partner. Assume that A and B are partners, each with capital balances of $50,000 and that A, with B's consent, sells one half of his interest to C for $30,000. The entry required to record C's admission is

A, Capital	25,000	
C, Capital		25,000

The amount paid by C to A has no effect on this entry since there is no change in partnership assets or total capital.

C may be admitted by making a contribution of cash or other assets directly to the firm, thereby increasing partnership assets and total capital. The amount credited to the incoming partner's capital account may be measured by the value of his investment. The admission of a new partner is often the occasion for recognizing goodwill—attributable to either the new partner or the old partnership—or a bonus may be allowed the old partners or the incoming partner. If the old partnership has been successful, the new partner may agree, as a condition, that part of his investment be considered a bonus from him to the old partners or he may agree to the recognition of goodwill being credited to the old partners. On the other hand, if the old partners need additional resources—the funds, the skills, or both—that the new partner will contribute, they may agree to credit the new partner with an amount greater than his investment in the form of either a bonus or goodwill.

Assume A and B are partners sharing gains and losses equally with capital account balances of $15,000 and $21,000. Some conditions under which C, a new partner, may be admitted, and the resulting journal entries, are illustrated below.

1. C is admitted to a one-third interest by investing $20,000, total capital to be $60,000.

Cash	20,000	
Goodwill	4,000	
A, Capital		2,000
B, Capital		2,000
C, Capital		20,000

Goodwill is recognized and is credited to the old partners in their profit and loss sharing ratios.

2. C is admitted to a one-third interest by investing $24,000, total capital to be $60,000.

Cash	24,000	
A, Capital		2,000
B, Capital		2,000
C, Capital		20,000

C pays $24,000 but is credited with $20,000, the excess being credited to the old partners as a bonus.

3. C invests $15,000 for a one-third interest, total capital to be $51,000.

Cash	15,000	
A, Capital	1,000	
B, Capital	1,000	
C, Capital		17,000

In this illustration, the old partners provide a special inducement to C by crediting him with $2,000 more than his actual investment as a bonus.

Liquidation of a Partnership

A partnership may be terminated by selling the assets, paying the creditors, and distributing the remaining cash to the partners. This process is called *liquidation* of a partnership; conversion of assets to cash is called *realization*. Gains and losses resulting from the sale of assets must first be distributed in profit and loss sharing ratios before making any distribution to the partners. If, after distributing all gains and losses, a partner's capital account shows a debit balance, that partner must make up the deficiency from his personal resources.

To illustrate, assume that A, B, and C, whose statement of financial position is shown below, decide to sell their noncash assets, pay their creditors, and distribute the remaining cash to themselves.

A, B, AND C
Statement of Financial Position
August 31, 1973

Assets

Cash	$ 25,000
Other Assets	125,000
	$150,000

Liabilities and Partners' Equities

Liabilities	$ 50,000
A, Capital	50,000
B, Capital	30,000
C, Capital	20,000
	$150,000

The noncash assets are sold for $140,000, profits and losses are shared equally. The summary below shows the liquidation sequence.

	Cash	Other Assets	Liabilities	Capital A	B	C
Balances before realization	26,000	125,000	50,000	50,000	30,000	20,000
① Sale of assets at a gain	140,000	(125,000)		5,000	5,000	5,000
Balances	165,000		50,000	55,000	35,000	25,000
② Payment of creditors	(50,000)		(50,000)			
Balances	115,000			55,000	35,000	25,000
③ Cash distribution to partners	(115,000)			(55,000)	(35,000)	(25,000)

Amounts to be distributed to the partners ③ are the balances in their capital accounts after crediting each partner with his share of the gain on the sale of the assets ①.

Sale of assets at a loss in the process of liquidation may result in a capital deficiency in a partner's capital account. If the partner cannot cover the deficiency from his personal assets, it is allocated to the other partners as an additional loss in the profit and loss sharing ratio that exists between themselves. If, for example, the assets in the foregoing illustration are sold for $50,000, C's one-third share of the resulting loss of $75,000 ($125,000 − $50,000) is $25,000 or $5,000 more than the balance in his capital account. The payments to A and B must be such as to leave credit balances in their accounts that will exactly absorb each partner's share of C's $5,000 deficiency if C is unable to cover it. This is accomplished by treating C's deficiency as an additional loss and distributing it to A and B in their profit and loss sharing ratio (33⅓ ÷ 66⅔) or $2,500 to each partner.

A summary statement follows:

	Cash	Other Assets	Liabilities	Capital A	B	C
Balances before realization	25,000	125,000	50,000	50,000	30,000	20,000
Sale of assets at a loss	50,000	(125,000)		(25,000)	(25,000)	(25,000)
Balances	75,000		50,000	25,000	5,000	(5,000)
Payment to creditors	(50,000)		(50,000)			
Balances	25,000			25,000	5,000	(5,000)
Cash distribution to partners	(25,000)			(22,500)	(2,500)	
Balances				2,500	2,500	(5,000)

If C subsequently pays the $5,000 to the partnership, the amount will be distributed equally to A and B and all the accounts will be reduced to zero balances. Failing that, the $5,000 debit balance in C's account will be distributed to A and B and all accounts reduced to zero balances.

THE CHARACTERISTICS OF A CORPORATION

John Marshall, Chief Justice of the United States, gave this classic definition of a corporation in a famous 1819 decision, "A corporation is an artificial being, invisible, intangible, and existing only in contemplation of law." The corporation is, from both the legal and the accounting point of view, a special and separate being, or separate *legal entity*, created by law. That is the characteristic that makes it almost ideally suited to doing business. The weaknesses inherent in single proprietorships and partnerships do not generally exist with the corporate form. The death or retirement of a single proprietor or of a partner may terminate the business, whereas the corporate form continues indefinitely irrespective of changes in stockholders.

A stockholder may sell his stock whenever he chooses without the prior consent of other stockholders, with the corporation simply recording the change in ownership; whereas a partner wishing to sell his interest must first get the consent of all the other partners. The purchase and sale of stock is a relatively simple matter because of the existence of stock exchanges (the New York Stock Exchange, for example). The sale and transfer of a block of stock from one holder to another is a private matter between the buyer and the seller. The transfer does not affect the issuing corporation.

Single proprietors and partners are fully liable to the firm's creditors. Their personal fortunes—in addition to their investments in the business—may have to be used. A stockholder, on the contrary, having paid for his stock in full, is not further liable either to the corporation or to satisfy the creditors' claims. For example, the possible losses of an investor who pays $500 to a corporation for 10 shares of $50 par value stock is limited to $500. This is a distinct advantage to the investor in a corporation. It may also be a disadvantage, especially to the smaller corporation seeking credit. Since satisfaction of creditor claims is limited to the assets of the corporation, the extent of credit tends to be limited to the level of corporate assets.

Because the corporation is treated as a legal entity, separate and distinct from the stockholders who own it, it enjoys the same legal rights and privileges as do single proprietorships and partnerships, and may therefore engage in almost any type of business activity, provided it is authorized by the charter. The corporate form of business organization is of great advantage for a large business because it may sell its stock to anyone willing to invest his money and is, therefore, able to raise large sums of capital. Although most large-scale businesses are incorporated and do a much larger volume of business than all other forms of business organization, there are many small businesses that are also incorporated—frequently with only a few stockholders—because of the advantages that the corporate form offers.

The corporate form also has its disadvantages. Because it is an artificial legal being created by the state, it must file reports with the state in which it was organized; it may engage in only that type of business for which it was chartered; it cannot distribute profits arbitrarily as do partnerships but must treat all shares of stock of the same class alike; and it is subject to special taxes and fees. Corporate laws vary from state to state and are often complex and undefined. The rights and obligations of corporations, directors, and stockholders are therefore often difficult to determine. The corporation is taxed as a business entity, and its prorata distributions of earnings to stockholders in the form of dividends are taxed as personal income. The earnings of single proprietorships and partnerships, on the other hand, are taxed only once, as the personal income of the owners.

Ownership of Corporations

Ownership in a corporation is represented by shares of stock, which may be owned by individuals or by other corporations or estates and trusts. Each share of stock represents a fractional part of the ownership. Ownership of a corporation may be vested in a single individual who owns all the stock, in a family whose members own all the stock, or by hundreds of thousands of stockholders. The holders of stock in a corporation are entitled to certain rights, including the right to participate in the distribution of earnings and the right to vote at elections of members of the board of directors, thereby participating, albeit indirectly, in the management of the corporation.

Organizing a Corporation

A corporation may be organized for a number of reasons. The purpose may be to start a new business or to buy a previously existing single proprietorship or partnership. It should be emphasized that the work of organizing a corporation must be done by competent attorneys since it involves legal matters.

To form a corporation it is first necessary for at least three incorporators to file a form known as the "Articles of Incorporation" with the Secretary of State or Corporation Commissioner (or other designated official), setting forth the name and address of the proposed corporation, the nature of the business it is to operate, a description of the stock and the amount to be authorized, and any other information required by the state in which incorporation takes place. On approval of the application, a charter is issued by the state.

The incorporators then hold the initial stockholders' meeting. Capital stock certificates are issued, the stockholders elect a board of directors, and a set of rules and regulations (known as *bylaws*) governing the internal activities of the corporation is approved. The directors in turn elect the officers of the corporation, who execute the policies approved by the board of directors for the operation of the business.

State laws pertaining to incorporation vary widely among the several states. Approximately one third of the corporations whose stock is listed on the New York Stock Exchange are incorporated in the State of Delaware because its laws are more liberal than most other states with respect to the taxation of corporations, the classes of shares a corporation may issue, the valuation of property or services exchanged for stock, the establishment of stated values, and the bases for dividend declarations.

Organization Costs. The formation of a corporation makes certain expenditures necessary, including legal fees, fees and commissions paid to promoters, and statutory fees and taxes. Since these expenditures are made to bring the corporation into existence, they may be regarded as of benefit during the entire life of the corporation and may therefore be charged to Organization Costs, which is classified as an intangible asset in the position statement. Since the life of a corporation is indefinite, there is theoretical justification for retaining the account on the books indefinitely. In practice, however, organization costs are often amortized over the early years of the corporation because they are considered as having limited potential for generating future earning power. Under the Internal Revenue Code, organization costs may be written off over a period of not less than five years. The entry to record the periodic amortization of organization costs is

Amortization of Organization Costs	xxx	
Organization Costs		xxx

The Stockholders. The stockholders occupy the top position in the corporate organization chart. The stockholders may attend annual and special meetings and participate in the management of the company by voting on matters presented for their consideration. If a stockholder is unable to attend the meeting, he may designate someone else—often the Secretary of the corporation—to cast his vote by *proxy.* A stockholder is entitled to one vote for each share of voting stock he holds. The meeting of stockholders need not be a routine affair, particularly if conflicting groups are attempting to gain control. On such occasions, each group seeks to obtain the largest number of proxy votes to assist it in acquiring control.

The Board of Directors and Officers. The stockholders elect the board of directors, who are then primarily responsible for the affairs of the corporation. All decisions reached by the board as a unit are recorded in a *minute book;* the recorded decisions are referred to as *minutes of meetings of the board of directors.* The accountant makes frequent reference to these minutes as the underlying authority for transactions affecting the accounts, particularly the capital stock accounts.

The board of directors selects the officers—president, vice presidents, treasurer, auditor, and so on—who carry on the daily activities of the corporation. But the responsibility of the board of directors does not end with the selection of officers. Directors are in effect trustees with responsibility to stockholders and creditors alike; they are legally liable for any acts they may perform that are not authorized by the corporate charter or bylaws. Only the board of directors may declare dividends.

Capital Stock

Ownership in a corporation is represented by its stock, which is divided into shares representing fractional ownership. There may be more than one type of stock, each in turn divided into shares. Each share in a class of stock must be treated like every other share in that class with respect to whatever rights and privileges attach to it.

Whenever there is more than one class of stock, one of the classes may enjoy the right, for example, to receive dividends before the other classes of stock. By the same token, certain restrictions, such as not having the right to vote, may be placed on a particular class of stock. If only one class of stock is issued, it is refered to as *common stock;* if two classes of stock are issued, they are usually referred to as common stock and *preferred stock.* There may be subclasses of stock within each major class, also with specific rights, privileges, and restrictive provisions.

The rights and privileges attached to common stock are

1. The stockholder's right to sell his stock or to dispose of it in any way he sees fit
2. The stockholder's so-called *pre-emptive right* to participate in any additional issues of stock in proportion to his holdings in the class of stock being issued
3. The right to vote
4. The right to participate in dividend distributions

Stock Certificate. A *stock certificate* is a printed or engraved serially numbered document issued to the stock purchaser as evidence of his ownership of the stated number of shares of capital stock of the issuing corporation. Transfer of the shares from one person to another is accomplished by filling in the assignment section on the reverse of the stock certificate. The buyer sends the assigned stock certificate to the corporation or to its transfer agent, who records the transfer on the corporation's capital stock records, cancels the old certificate, and issues a new one. Stock certificates are often bound with attached stubs in the same manner as checkbooks. The perforated stock certificate is removed, and the stub is filled in and retained as a permanent record.

Stockholders' Ledger. The *stockholders' ledger* furnishes the detail for the Capital Stock controlling accounts in the general ledger. An account is opened for each stockholder to show the certificates issued or canceled and the number of shares held. This record is used for purposes of establishing the voting and dividend rights of each stockholder. Only those persons whose names appear in the stockholders' ledger are recognized as share owners.

Stock Transfer Journal. The purpose of the *stock transfer journal* is to record transfers or exchanges of stock from one person to another. The date, certificate numbers (old and new), and number of shares exchanged are recorded in it. The work is often done by independent *transfer agents*—banks or trust companies—who handle the recording of the sale and transfer of stock. The stock transfer journal may be used for posting to the subsidiary stockholders' ledger. The function of recording all certificates issued and canceled is often done by a *registrar*, also usually a bank or trust company.

Sources of Capital

Operating transactions of corporations are recorded in the same manner as those of single proprietorships and partnerships. Care must be taken, however, to distinguish between the primary sources of corporate capital. These sources are from (1) investments by stockholders and (2) retained earnings from operations. This distinction is essential because state laws provide that earnings may be distributed to the stockholders but that the investments must not be distributed, both for the protection of corporate creditors and for the continued operation of the business. Hence, separate accounts should be kept for

1. The par or stated value of each class of stock
2. Each type of contributed capital other than the par or stated value of stock, including premiums (by class) on issuance of stock, proceeds from sale of treasury stock in excess of cost, and donated capital

3. Equity arising from revaluation of assets
4. The discount (by class) on stock issued below par value
5. Retained earnings (explained in Chapter 12)

These separate accounts must be clearly set forth in the Stockholders' Equity section of the corporate statement of financial position.

Authorized and Unissued Capital Stock

The charter granted by the state of incorporation authorizes the newly formed corporation to issue a designated number of shares of capital stock. The corporation usually secures authorization to issue more shares than it anticipates issuing at the outset. This allows for additional sales in the future without further authorization by the state. The total number of shares issued, however, cannot exceed the number of shares authorized.

General ledger accounts for authorized but unissued stock need not be opened. Detail with respect to the number of shares authorized is customarily included as a part of the description in the Stockholders' Equity section of the position statement. The position statement presentation may be as shown below.

```
Stockholders' Equity
  Contributed Capital
    Common Stock, $100 par value, authorized 1,000 shares,
    issued 500 shares                                        $50,000
```

Classes of Stock

Stock is usually issued in two classes, *common* and *preferred.*

Preferred Stock. One of the reasons for issuing two or more classes of stock is to endow one class with certain features that will make it more salable. The attractive feature of preferred stock is that when a dividend declaration is made by the board of directors, the preferred stockholders must be paid at the stated rate and amount for the class of stock before payments are made to other stockholders. The same preference applies when a corporation is dissolved: assets remaining for distribution to stockholders are used first to redeem the claims of preferred stockholders; the remainder, if any, is paid to the other stockholders. Preferred stockholders, on the other hand, are often restricted to a specific dividend rate and do not, therefore, benefit from extra earnings. A preferred stockholder is usually denied the right to vote.

Common Stock. If a corporation issues only one class of stock, then all shares are treated alike, and, there being no preferences, that class of stock is called "common stock." If there is more than one class, the class that does not have preferences and that shares only in the remainder of earnings or assets distribution is known as "common stock." This class of stock does have voting privileges.

Par Value

The term *par value* refers to a specific dollar amount per share, which is printed on the stock certificate, representing the minimum amount that must be paid to the issuing corporation by the purchaser of the stock; otherwise the purchaser may be held liable for the *discount,* or difference, in case of future claims by the corporate creditors. This contingent liability for the discount passes from the original buyer to successive buyers, provided each buyer in the chain is made aware of the fact that the particular stock had been acquired in the first instance at a discount. The par value may be any amount set forth in the corporation's charter and is not necessarily an indication of what the stock is actually worth. Par value is used as the basis for recording the stock on the corporate books; beyond that, it may have little or no significance. It is often established at a nominal value to preclude contingent stockholder liability.

The use of par value stock used to be considered advantageous to the stockholder and creditor, since it requires payment in full or the assumption of a liability for the discount. The value of stock, however, is determined not by its par value but rather by the value of the corporation's net assets and by its earnings. Furthermore, in some cases, evasive schemes were evolved to by-pass the par value rule, and creditors also found it difficult to recover the stock discount from stockholders in a bankrupt company. The evasive schemes usually involved the issuance of *watered* stock—that is, the transfer of property or the rendering of services to the corporation for its capital stock at highly inflated values, thereby overstating the stockholders' equity in the position statement. Sometimes this stock would then be given back to the corporation for sale at whatever price it would bring without any liability for the discount because the stock had already been fully paid for. The Securities and Exchange Commission of the Federal government may and does interfere when obviously inflated values are assigned to assets being turned over in payment for capital stock, so that the flagrant abuses of past periods have been checked. The investor and the creditor, therefore, enjoy a high degree of protection against unprincipled promoters.

No-Par Value

Par value was often misleading. *No-par value* stock began to be used widely in order to overcome some of the abuses and disadvantages of par value stock. The use of no-par value stock made it unnecessary to resort to evasive schemes for by-passing the contingent liability arising from a sale of par value stock at a discount. The attempted evasion of the par value rule through overvaluation of assets or services would no longer be necessary. Differences of opinion can and do exist, however, with regard to the proper value to be placed on an asset in exchange for stock, and resort to the use of no-par value stock has not eliminated this problem.

When no-par value stock is issued, the directors often assign a *stated,* or uniform, value to each share. This value becomes the basis for recording the stock on the corporate books, and the accounting is the same as for par value stock. Since, in most cases, the directors may change the stated value—unlike the par value—at will, there is usually no occasion for recording a discount on the sale of no-par value stock.

To illustrate the entries for the issuance of stock, assume that the King Corporation issues 1,000 shares of common stock for $110,000.

1. Assuming that the par value of the stock is $100,

Cash	110,000	
Common Stock		100,000
Premium on Common Stock		10,000

2. Assuming that the stock is no-par value with a $75 stated value,

Cash	110,000	
Common Stock		75,000
Contributed Capital—Excess over Stated Value of Common Stock		35,000

3. Assuming that the stock is no-par value and has no stated value,

Cash	110,000	
Common Stock		110,000

There are several other terms denoting the concept of value, which give a more direct indication of the worth of the stock. The term *book value* is used to indicate the value per share based on net assets (assets minus liabilities), or stockholders' equity. The book value of a share of stock is derived by dividing the total stockholders' equity by the number of shares of stock issued and outstanding. If the market value of the assets is either above or below their recorded cost values, then the book value per share computed in the above manner is not a fair indication of its value. The term *market value* is used to indicate the amount that a share will bring the seller if the stock is offered for sale. Such prices can be determined readily for many stocks by reference to the stock market quotations carried in daily newspapers or to a financial magazine or financial service publication.

Legal or Stated Capital

The term *legal capital*, or *stated capital*, is incorporated in the laws of a number of states for the purpose of placing a restriction on the return of capital to the stockholders. The purpose of this restriction is to protect the creditors because it prevents the stockholders from withdrawing their investment, either as dividends or by the reacquisition of capital stock, to the point where there may be insufficient funds left to satisfy creditors' claims. The creditors of a corporation do not have access to the personal resources of the stockholders thereby facilitating ready transferability of the shares; their only protection is in the corporate assets. Stated capital is the minimum amount of capital that must be left in the corporation and that cannot be withdrawn by the stockholders. Since there is a legal limit on stockholder withdrawals, creditors are assured that in the event of corporate losses the investors as a group will absorb the losses up to the amount of the stated capital.

There is considerable variation in the several state laws as to the method of determining and applying such provisions; the accountant may require the assistance of an attorney on questions involving legal capital. In some states, for example, legal capital is considered to be the total proceeds from the sale of stock. In other states, the directors of a corporation that has issued no-par value stock may, by resolution, designate a portion of the contributed capital as the stated capital, or the state may designate a minimum amount. On par value stock, the stated capital is the par value of all the shares issued. When, as is often the case, the par value is low in relation to the issue price, the stated capital will be much less than the total contributed by shareholders. This means, therefore, that legal capital is not a significant constraint on amounts to be distributed to stockholders, and the security of the creditors depends rather on the firm's operating and financial policies and resources.

Recording Stock Transactions

Great care needs to be taken to record stock transactions in strict compliance with the corporate laws of the state of incorporation, keeping in mind the interests of the stockholders and creditors. The entries should show clearly the sources of capital invested in the corporation. Enough accounts should be created so that the Stockholders' Equity section shows in adequate detail the sources of the corporate capital.

The Authorization and Issuance of Stock. The initial entry on a corporate set of books may be a simple narrative statement setting forth certain basic data taken from the corporate charter, including the name and date of incorporation, the nature of the business, and the number and classes of shares authorized to be issued. Assume that the following three transactions took place at the Crown Corporation, which is organized as a wholesale hardware supply business with an authorized capital of $200,000 consisting of 2,000 shares at $100 par value.

1. One half the stock is issued at par value for cash.

Cash	100,000	
Common Stock		100,000

2. A total of 900 shares are issued for $40,000 in cash plus land and buildings having a fair cash value of $10,000 and $40,000, respectively.

Cash	40,000	
Land	10,000	
Buildings	40,000	
Common Stock		90,000

3. A total of 100 shares are issued to the organizers of the corporation in payment for their services.

Organization Costs	10,000	
Common Stock		10,000

The Stockholders' Equity section of the Crown Corporation statement of financial position after the foregoing transactions shows the following:

Stockholders' Equity	
Contributed Capital	
Common Stock, $100 par value; authorized and issued	
2,000 shares	$200,000

Issuance of Stock at a Premium. Assume that a corporation is organized with an authorized capital of $100,000 consisting of 1,000 shares of $100 par value stock, which are issued for $108,000. The entry is

Cash	108,000	
Common Stock		100,000
Premium on Common Stock		8,000

When capital stock is offered for sale, the price it will bring depends not only on the condition and reputation of the corporation, but also on the availability of funds for investment and other external factors. When stock is issued above its par value, the difference is credited to Premium on Common Stock or to Excess over Par Value of Common Stock. The account represents the excess of the issue price per share over the par value per share. Although the premium appears in a separate account, it is part of the total capital contributed by investors. By using a separate account for the excess over par value paid in on the stock, the par value may be shown readily in the statement of financial position. Premium on Common Stock should be kept separate from the account showing corporate earnings. If more than one class of stock has been issued at a premium, separate premium accounts should be kept.

The Stockholders' Equity section immediately following the issue of the 1,000 shares for $108,000 appears as shown below.

Stockholders' Equity		
Contributed Capital		
Common Stock, $100 par value; authorized		
and issued 1,000 shares	$100,000	
Premium on Common Stock	8,000	
Total Contributed Capital		$108,000

Issuance of Stock at a Discount. Assume that a corporation is organized with an authorized capital of $100,000 consisting of 1,000 shares of $100 par value stock, which are issued for $90,000. The entry is

Cash	90,000	
Discount on Common Stock	10,000	
Common Stock		100,000

When the issue is for less than par value—that is, the stock has been issued at a discount—the difference between the par value and the issue price of the stock is charged to Discount on Common Stock. Purchasers of stock at a discount are contingently liable to the corporation's creditors for the amount of the discount. When such stock is transferred, the discount liability is noted on the stock certificate as foreknowledge that the liability passes to the new owner. In most states, par value stock may not be issued at a discount. The account appears as a deduction in the stockholders' equity section of the position statement and designates the existence and amount of the contingency as shown on page 399.

Stockholders' Equity
  Contributed Capital
    Common Stock, $100 par value; authorized
      and issued 1,000 shares $100,000
    Discount on Common Stock   10,000*
      Total Contributed Capital $ 90,000

*Deduction.

The use of premium and discount accounts makes it possible to show in the position statement the par value, or stated value, as well as the amount actually contributed. Premiums and discounts should not be offset. If, for example, a corporation that is authorized to issue 1,000 shares of $100 par value common stock issues 500 shares at $105 a share and later issues 250 shares at $98 a share, separate premium and discount accounts should be set up. The position statement presentation would be as shown.

Stockholders' Equity
  Contributed Capital
    Common Stock, $100 par value; authorized 1,000
      shares; issued 750 shares $75,000
    Premium on Common Stock   2,500
    Discount on Common Stock   500*
      Total Contributed Capital $77,000

*Deduction.

If only the net excess of $2,000 ($2,500 premium less $500 discount) is reported, the existence of the discount liability is concealed from readers of the statement.

Stock Subscriptions

The descriptions of stock issuance transactions in the previous sections were based on the assumption that full payment for the stock was received and the stock certificates issued at once. This condition normally exists for small or closely held corporations. In the following transactions, *subscriptions*, or pledges to buy the stock, are taken first, and payment is made later in single lump sums or in installments. The purchaser signs a formal, legally enforceable *subscription contract* in which he agrees to buy a certain number of shares of stock and to make certain specified payments. The stock certificates are issued upon completion of the payment.

The Subscriptions Receivable account is similar in nature and function to the Accounts Receivable account. It is a current asset and shows the amount due on stock that has been subscribed but has not been fully paid for. It is debited for the issue price, not necessarily the par or stated value, of the stock and is credited for collections as they are received. Like the Accounts Receivable account, it is a controlling account with supporting detail kept in a subsidiary *subscribers' ledger*, which contains the accounts of the individual subscribers. When more than one class of stock is issued, separate Subscriptions Receivable accounts should be kept for each class.

The Capital Stock Subscribed account is a temporary capital stock account.

It shows the amount of stock that has been subscribed, but the stock certificates for the amount in the account have not been issued pending receipt of the balance still due on the stock as shown in the Subscriptions Receivable account. The account is credited for the par or stated value of the subscribed stock and is debited for the par or stated value when the stock is issued, with the permanent Capital Stock account being credited. If no-par value shares without a stated value are issued, the Capital Stock Subscribed account is debited or credited for the full subscription price.

The subscriber to stock normally acquires the full status of a stockholder with all rights and privileges even though he is not in possession of the stock certificate. The stock subscription agreement, however, may restrict such rights until full payment is received.

Issuance By Subscription at Par Value. The Reed Corporation is authorized to issue 6,000 shares of $100 par value common stock. On July 1, 5,000 shares are issued at par value for cash and subscriptions are received for 1,000 shares. A 60-percent down payment is received; the remaining 40 percent is payable in two installments of $20,000 each on August 1 and September 1. The journal entries are

1973					
July	1	Cash		500,000	
		Common Stock			500,000
		To record the issuance of 5,000 shares for cash at par value.			
July	1	Subscriptions Receivable—Common Stock		100,000	
		Common Stock Subscribed			100,000
		To record the receipt of subscriptions for 1,000 shares of $100 par value stock at $100 per share.			
	1	Cash		60,000	
		Subscriptions Receivable—Common Stock			60,000
		To record the receipt of a 60% down payment on subscriptions to stock.			
Aug.	1	Cash		20,000	
		Subscriptions Receivable—Common Stock			20,000
		To record the receipt of the first 20% installment on the stock subscription of July 1.			
Sept.	1	Cash		20,000	
		Subscriptions Receivable—Common Stock			20,000
		To record the receipt of the second and final installment on the stock subscription of July 1.			

```
1973
Sept.   1   Common Stock Subscribed              100,000
                Common Stock                               100,000
                    To record the issuance of
                    stock certificates for
                    1,000 shares of stock.
```

Partial statements of financial position as of July 1 and September 1 are shown:

```
                        July 1, 1973

                          Assets

Current Assets
    Subscriptions Receivable–Common Stock          $ 40,000

                    Stockholders' Equity

Contributed Capital
    Common Stock, $100 par value; authorized 6,000 shares;
        issued 5,000 shares                          $500,000
    Common Stock, subscribed but not issued, 1,000 shares   100,000


                    September 1, 1973

                    Stockholders' Equity

Contributed Capital
    Common Stock, $100 par value; authorized and issued
        6,000 shares                                 $600,000
```

Issuance by Subscription at a Premium. Assume the same facts as in the previous example, except that the Reed Corporation issued the stock at a price of $105 per share.

```
1973
July    1   Cash                                   525,000
                Common Stock                               500,000
                Premium on Common Stock                     25,000
                    To record the issuance of
                    5,000 shares of $100 par value
                    stock for cash at
                    $105 per share.

        1   Subscriptions Receivable—Common Stock  105,000
                Common Stock Subscribed                    100,000
                Premium on Common Stock                      5,000
                    To record the receipt of
                    subscriptions for 1,000 shares
                    of $100 par value stock
                    at $105 per share.

        1   Cash                                    63,000
                Subscriptions Receivable—Common Stock       63,000
                    To record the receipt of a
                    60% down payment on
                    the stock subscription
                    of July 1.
```

```
1973
Aug.    1  Cash                                                  21,000
               Subscriptions Receivable—Common Stock                        21,000
                  To record the receipt of
                  the first 20% installment
                  on the stock subscription
                  of July 1.

Sept.   1  Cash                                                  21,000
               Subscriptions Receivable—Common Stock                        21,000
                  To record the receipt of
                  the second and final
                  installment on the
                  stock subscription
                  of July 1.

        1  Common Stock Subscribed                              100,000
               Common Stock                                                100,000
                  To record the issuance of
                  stock certificates for
                  1,000 shares of stock.
```

When stock is issued at a premium, the entire excess over par or stated value is credited to the Premium on Stock account at the time the stock is subscribed (see the entry of July 1). The premium is considered to be fully realized at the time of subscription—not proportionately as installments are collected. The amount of the entry for the issuance of the stock certificates is the par or stated value of the stock; the existence of a premium or discount does not affect the amount recorded.

Partial statements of financial position as of July 1 and September 1 are shown below.

July 1, 1973

Assets

Current Assets	
Subscriptions Receivable–Common Stock	$ 42,000

Stockholders' Equity

Contributed Capital	
Common Stock, $100 par value; authorized 6,000	
shares, issued 5,000 shares	$500,000
Common Stock, subscribed but not issued, 1,000 shares	100,000
Premium on Common Stock	30,000

September 1, 1973

Stockholders' Equity

Contributed Capital	
Common Stock, $100 par value; authorized and issued	
6,000 shares	$600,000
Premium on Common Stock	30,000

Issue by Subscription at a Discount. Assume the same facts as in the previous example, except that the Reed Corporation issued the stock at $95 a share.

```
1973
July  1   Cash                                         475,000
          Discount on Common Stock                      25,000
            Common Stock                                           500,000
              To record the issuance of
              5,000 shares of $100 par value
              stock for cash at $95 per share.

      1   Subscriptions Receivable—Common Stock         95,000
          Discount on Common Stock                       5,000
            Common Stock Subscribed                               100,000
              To record the receipt of
              subscriptions for 1,000 shares
              of $100 par value stock
              at $95 per share.
```

All the remaining entries are the same as in the previous example, except that the amount of the down payment is $57,000 (60 percent of $95,000) and the amount of each installment is $19,000 (20 percent of $95,000). The amount of the entry to record the issuance of the stock remains the same—that is, $100,000. The discount, like the premium, is recorded in full on July 1 when the subscription is received and is not involved when the payments are made. The Stockholders' Equity section of the statement of financial position as of July 1 is shown.

```
                              July 1, 1973

                                Assets

Current Assets
    Subscriptions Receivable—Common Stock                    $ 38,000

                          Stockholders' Equity

Contributed Capital
    Common Stock, $100 par value, authorized 6,000 shares,
      issued 5,000 shares                                    $500,000
    Common Stock, subscribed but not issued, 1,000 shares     100,000
    Discount on Common Stock                                   30,000*

    *Deduction.
```

If preferred stock is issued in addition to common stock, special accounts would be opened up as required for Subscriptions Receivable—Preferred Stock, Preferred Stock Subscribed, Discount on Preferred Stock, and Premium on Preferred Stock.

SUMMARY

The capital contributions of single proprietors and partners are credited to their Capital accounts; profits, losses, and withdrawals are entered in Drawing accounts; the balances in the Drawing accounts are closed to the Capital accounts at the end of the period. The Owner's Equity section of the statement of financial position shows only the owners' Capital accounts. These figures are supported by a statement of owner's equity for a single proprietorship, or by a statement of partners' equity for a partnership, showing the changes in the equity accounts during the period because of additional investments, withdrawals, and earnings or losses.

Partnerships can be formed easily and quickly and permit combining the money, skill, and knowledge of two or more persons. Each partner may act as agent for the partnership and is jointly and individually liable for its debts. The partnership should be effected by a written agreement called the "articles of copartnership." Partners share equally in profits and losses unless the partnership agreement provides otherwise.

There are many ways to distribute profits and losses; provision for salaries and interest on capital are common. Such provisions are not to be considered as deductions from revenue but rather as mechanisms for dividing a part of the net income. The remainder can be distributed in any manner agreed on.

A new partner may be admitted by either purchasing his interest from one or more of the other partners or by making an investment in the partnership directly. Goodwill or a bonus, credited to either the new partner or to the old partners depending on the agreement, may be recognized on the admission of a new partner. A partnership may be terminated by selling the assets, paying the creditors, and distributing the remaining cash to the partners. Gains, losses, and expenses resulting from the termination are distributed in profit and loss sharing ratios before making any distribution to the partners.

The corporation is, from both the legal and accounting points of view, a legal entity. The corporation continues indefinitely, irrespective of changes in stockholders; a stockholder may sell all or a part of his holdings without the prior consent of the other stockholders; and the stockholder, having paid for his stock in full, is not further liable either to the corporation or to its creditors.

A corporation is formed when at least three incorporators file articles of incorporation with the appropriate state office, receive the charter, hold a stockholders' meeting, issue stock, elect a board of directors, prepare bylaws, and elect corporate officers. Legal fees and other expenditures necessary to organize the corporation are charged to Organization Costs, which is classified as an intangible asset in the statement of financial position.

The stockholder's rights and privileges include selling his stock, participating in additional issues, voting, and participating in dividend distributions.

Separate capital accounts should be kept for (1) each class of stock, (2) contributions in excess of par or stated value for each class or source, (3) the discount—by class—on stock issued below par value, and (4) retained earnings.

More than one class of stock may be issued, endowing one class with certain preferences over another. The term "par value" refers to a specific dollar amount per share, printed on the stock certificate, representing the minimum that must be paid by the purchaser. When no-par value stock is issued, the directors often assign a stated value to each share.

When stock is issued for cash or other assets, the Capital Stock account is credited. If the issuing price is above par value, the excess is credited to a Premium on Capital Stock account; if the issuing price is less than par value, the deficiency is charged to a Discount on Capital Stock account. When payment is not received in full at once, issuance of the stock certificates is deferred until completion of the payments. The amount due is debited to a Subscriptions Receivable account, a current asset; the par or stated value is credited to a Capital Stock Subscribed account, a temporary capital stock account that is closed to Capital Stock when the certificates are issued.

QUESTIONS

Q11-1. (a) What are some of the distinct features of the partnership form of business organization? (b) What are its advantages? (c) What are its disadvantages?

Q11-2. Describe each of the following: (a) general partner, (b) limited partner, (c) secret partner, (d) nominal partner.

Q11-3. Compare the partnership form of business organization with the single proprietorship and corporate forms.

Q11-4. Why should agreements reached in forming a partnership be in writing? What are some of the matters that should be specifically covered in a partnership agreement?

Q11-5. Can a partnership business continue after the death or retirement of one of the partners? Explain.

Q11-6. James Brown and Cedric Lee formed a partnership. Brown invested $10,000 in cash; Lee invested land and a building with a cash market value of $25,000. Five years later they agree to terminate the partnership, and Lee demands the return to him of the land and building. Is he justified in his demand?

Q11-7. D. Myers and S. Sacks agreed orally to form a partnership as of January 10, 1969. They postponed formalization of their agreement pending the return of their attorney, who was out of town. D. Myers invested $40,000 in cash; S. Sacks invested land and buildings worth $20,000 and $80,000, respectively. On January 11, the building was completely destroyed by an accidental explosion, and they terminated their partnership. Sacks claims that both the land and the $40,000 belong to him. Is he right? Explain.

Q11-8. Frank Fish and Homer Little are partners with capital account balances of $40,000 each. They share profits one third and two thirds, respectively. (a) Is this an equitable arrangement? (b) Assume that 5-percent interest on capital balances is agreed on. How will profits of $12,000 be distributed? (c) What account should be charged for the interest on the capital balances?

Q11-9. Douglas Evans and Stanley Byrd form a partnership by oral agreement. The matter of profit distribution was not discussed. Evans invests $15,000 and Byrd, $10,000. At the end of the first year, Evans contends that he should be credited with 60 percent of the profits of $10,000. Byrd disagrees. (a) Is Evans right? (b) How could this disagreement have been avoided?

Q11-10. What books and records do corporations have that are not necessary for single proprietorships or partnerships? What is meant by the following terms: authorized capital stock, stock certificate, share of stock, par value stock, no-par value stock?

Q11-11. What is meant by preferred stock? common stock? stockholders' equity? retained earnings?

Q11-12. What is the purpose and function of the following corporate records: subscription ledger, stockholders' ledger, stock transfer journal, minute book?

Q11-13. Distinguish between authorized and unissued stock and issued and outstanding stock.

Q11-14. Student A says that if he were buying stock, he would purchase only stock having a par value. Student B takes the opposite viewpoint. Discuss.

Q11-15. What is legal capital? How is it determined? How does it differ from contributed capital? retained earnings? stockholders' equity? Why should the state of incorporation regulate the amount that may be distributed to stockholders in the form of dividends?

Q11-16. Student A says that Subscriptions Receivable is a current asset; Student B argues that the account belongs in the Stockholders' Equity section. Discuss.

Q11-17. Define and give the significance of each of the following terms: (a) par value of stock; (b) pre-emptive right; (c) market value of stock; (d) preferred stock; (e) corporation.

EXERCISES

E11-1. Enter the following transactions in appropriate T accounts:

a. Thomas Fine and James Lewis form a partnership with cash investments of $14,000 and $11,000, respectively.
b. Fine and Lewis withdrew $3,000 and $5,000, respectively, in anticipation of earnings.
c. Fine made an additional cash investment of $2,000, and Lewis turned over to the partnership the title to a parcel of land with a fair market value of $6,000.
d. The net income for the period was $13,000 (profits and losses are shared equally).

E11-2. In their partnership agreement, Richard Barker and Ernest Jones agreed to divide profits and losses as follows: (a) 5-percent interest on average capital balances, (b) salaries of $6,000 each, and (c) the remainder shared equally. Prepare a schedule showing the distribution of net income of $19,500, assuming average capital balances of $10,000 and $20,000 for Barker and Jones, respectively.

E11-3. The following information relates to the partnership of Bernice and Mark.

Average capital balances for 1973	
Bernice	$60,000
Mark	70,000
Net income for 1973	8,000

The partnership agreement states that profits shall be divided as follows:

Salary allowances:	
Bernice	$8,000
Mark	6,000
Interest allowance: 6 percent on average capital balances	
Remainder:	
Bernice ¾	
Mark ¼	

Prepare the closing journal entries (make three separate entries) to distribute the net income in accordance with the partnership agreement.

E11-4. J. Frohm, owner of the Burger Diner, asks you to determine his equity in the business at December 31, 1973. You determine his net income for the year from the diner to be $13,000. In addition, the following transactions occurred during the year:

Original investment	$15,000
Additional investment	2,000
Personal withdrawals	8,000

(a) Post the transactions to appropriate T accounts, and (b) prepare a statement of owner's equity.

E11-5. Frank Kane and Ralph Rizzo formed a partnership on June 8, 1973. Kane contributed $5,000 in cash, land worth $3,000, a building appraised at $20,000 (the land and the building are encumbered by a mortgage of $4,000, which is assumed by the partnership), and a truck valued at $1,000. Ralph Rizzo contributed $5,000 in cash. (a) Make the entries to record the formation of the partnership. (b) Why may Frank Kane be willing to enter into a partnership in which he contributes five times as much as his partner?

E11-6. The Granada Corporation, organized on September 30, 1970, was authorized to issue 12,000 shares of $15 par value common stock.

1973

Oct. 1   Issued 120 shares to an attorney for services, valued at $2,000, in organizing the corporation.

     15   Received subscriptions for 4,000 shares at $20 a share with a down payment of 50 percent, the balance due on December 15.

     25   Issued for cash 2,000 shares at $21 a share.

Nov. 10   Issued for cash 1,000 shares at $19.50 a share.

Dec. 15   Received amounts due from subscribers and issued the stock certificates.

Record the transactions.

E11-7. The Hurd Corporation was authorized to issue 30,000 shares of no-par value common stock with a $10 stated value and 5,000 shares of 5-percent preferred stock, $100 par value. At the end of one year of operations, the Hurd Corporation's trial balance included the following account balances:

Preferred Stock	$300,000
Common Stock	200,000
Subscriptions Receivable–Common	48,000
Subscriptions Receivable–Preferred	125,000
Preferred Stock Subscribed	150,000
Common Stock Subscribed	75,000
Premium on Common Stock	35,000
Discount on Preferred Stock	20,000

How much cash has been collected from the stock transactions?

E11-8. The W. E. Stimson Corporation acquired the plant and equipment of the J. Leibfried Company in exchange for 15,000 shares of its $20 par value common stock. Record the acquisition, assuming that if the assets had been acquired for cash, the purchase price would have been (a) $310,000; (b) $285,000.

E11-9. The Lynd Corporation is authorized to issue 10,000 shares of $100 par value common stock. The following transactions occurred:

1. Issued for cash 2,000 shares at par value.
2. Issued 100 shares to the promoters for services valued at $10,000.
3. Issued 50 shares to attorneys for services, valued at $5,000, in organizing the corporation and securing the corporate charter.
4. Issued 900 shares in exchange for a factory building and land valued at $80,000 and $10,000, respectively.
5. Issued for cash 1,000 shares at $95 per share.
6. Issued for cash 2,000 shares at $110 per share.

Record the transactions.

E11-10. The Atlantic Corporation was authorized to issue 10,000 shares of common stock. Record the issue of 8,000 shares at 14½, assuming that (a) the shares have a $10 par value; (b) the shares have no-par and no stated value; (c) the shares have a stated value of $8.00.

E11-11. The Georgia Corporation was authorized to issue 10,000 shares of no-par value common stock and 10,000 shares of $10 par value preferred stock. Organizers of the corporation received 1,500 shares of the no-par value common stock for services valued at $7,500. A total of 2,000 shares of the preferred stock were issued for cash at $9 a share, and 1,500 shares of common stock were issued for cash at $6 a share. A total of 2,000 shares of preferred stock were subscribed at $14 a share. One half of the subscribers paid in full. (a) Record the transactions in T accounts. (b) Prepare a statement of financial position.

E11-12. The Stockholders' Equity section of the Peabody Corporation's position statement as of December 31, 1973, shows the following:

Common Stock, $100 par value; authorized 1,000 shares;	
subscribed but not issued 800 shares	$80,000
Discount on Common Stock	2,000
Premium on Common Stock	8,000

The Current Assets section shows:

Subscriptions Receivable $40,000

How much cash has been collected from the stock subscribers?

E11-13. (*Financial policy decision problem*) The 1969 annual report of M. H. Fishman Company includes the following note to its financial statements:

During the year the stockholders approved a change in the authorized capital stock of the company from 15,000 shares, $100 par value preferred stock to 500,000 shares, no-par value and from 2,000,000 shares, $1 par value common stock to 3,000,000 shares, $1 par value common stock. (a) What was the effect of these changes on the company's financial statements? (b) What was the purpose of the changes?

DEMONSTRATION PROBLEMS

DP11-1. (*Recording partnership transactions*) The following selected transactions took place in the partnership of Jorgensen and Smith:

1973

Jan. 1   John Jorgensen and Samuel Smith formed a partnership on this date, making the following investments:

Jorgensen invested $55,000 in cash. Smith contributed his equity in a building and lot. The partners agreed that the building was worth $60,000 and the land, $10,000; there was, however, a mortgage on the land and building with a face value of $18,000; the mortgage carried an interest rate of 6 percent, and the interest was last paid on October 1, 1972. The partnership assumed all liabilities relative to the investment.

Mar. 1   Jorgensen withdrew $500 cash in anticipation of income to be earned.

Apr. 1   Smith withdrew merchandise from the business. The merchandise cost $450 and had a selling price of $600. The firm uses the periodic inventory system.

Oct. 1   Jorgensen was allowed to withdraw $10,000 in cash to pay a personal debt. This amount far exceeds any anticipated income to be earned.

Required: Record the transactions.

DP11-2. (*Distribution of partnership profits and losses*) Edward Herson and Maurice Slight formed a partnership on January 1, 1973, with investments of $20,000 and $35,000, respectively.

On July 1, 1973, Slight invested an additional $10,000. On October 1, 1973, Herson and Slight withdrew $5,000 and $5,500, respectively, in anticipation of earnings.

Required: Make the appropriate journal entries to record the distribution of profits and losses based on each of the following assumptions:

1. Net income is $10,000; profits and losses are shared equally.
2. Net loss is $4,500; the partnership agreement provides that profits are to be distributed 60 percent to Herson and 40 percent to Slight; the method of distributing losses was not specified.
3. Net income is $8,000; to be distributed in the ratio of capital balances as of December 31, 1973.
4. Net income is $15,000, to be distributed as follows: salaries of $8,000 to Herson and $9,000 to Slight; interest of 5 percent on ending capital balances; remainder to be distributed equally.

DP11-3. (*Recording capital stock issuance; stockholders' equity*) The Web Company was organized on July 1, 1973, with authority to issue 25,000 shares of $100 par value preferred stock and 15,000 shares of no-par value, $30 stated value common stock. The following transactions occurred during the year:

1973
July 1 Issued for cash 12,000 shares of preferred stock at $101 a share.

10 Issued for cash 8,000 shares of common stock at $40 a share.

15 Issued for cash 2,000 shares of preferred stock at $99 a share.

20 Received subscriptions for 4,000 shares of common stock at $35 a share with a down payment of 50 percent and the balance due on September 30.

31 Received subscriptions for 6,000 shares of preferred stock at $102 a share; one half the price was received upon subscription, with the remainder due on September 30.

Aug. 22 Issued 50 shares of preferred stock to an attorney in payment for services rendered in organizing the corporation.

Sept. 15 Issued 1,000 shares of common stock in exchange for land and a building appraised at $10,000 and $30,000, respectively.

30 Collected the installment due on the subscriptions of July 20 and July 31.

30 Net income from operations, after income taxes for the period July 1 to September 30, was $40,000 (debit Other Assets).

Required: 1. Record the transactions in appropriate T accounts.
2. Prepare the Stockholders' Equity section of the statement of financial position as of September 30, 1973.

PROBLEMS

P11-1. Donald Warren and Sheldon Rich form a partnership.

Required: Journalize their investments, based on each of the following assumptions:

1. Each partner invests $4,000 in cash.
2. Warren invests $4,000 in cash, and Rich invests $6,000 in cash.
3. Warren invests $1,000 in cash, land worth $5,000, a building worth $15,000, and merchandise worth $2,000. Rich invests $20,000 in cash.

4. Warren invests $2,000 in cash, land worth $3,000, and a building worth $10,000. The partnership agrees to assume a mortgage payable of $6,000 on the land and building. Rich invests $2,000 in cash, store equipment worth $4,000, and merchandise worth $1,500.

5. Before the formation of the partnership, Warren and Rich were competitors. They decide to form the partnership for their mutual advantage; the partnership assumes their existing assets and liabilities at book values as follows:

	Warren	Rich
Cash	$ 3,000	$ 3,500
Accounts Receivable	6,500	8,000
Merchandise Inventory	15,200	11,100
Delivery Equipment (net)	3,500	5,200
Store Equipment (net)	6,000	10,000
Totals	$34,200	$37,800
Accounts Payable	$13,400	$12,200
Notes Payable	5,000	6,000
Warren, Capital	15,800	
Rich, Capital		19,600
Totals	$34,200	$37,800

6. Assume the same facts as in assumption 5, except that the merchandise and equipment are to be recorded at their fair market valuations as follows:

	Warren	Rich
Merchandise Inventory	$14,000	$11,000
Delivery Equipment (net)	4,000	5,000
Store Equipment (net)	5,000	7,000

P11-2. James Bridges and Walter Kell form a partnership to operate a food brokerage business.

Required: Record their initial investments, based on each of the following assumptions:

1. Bridges and Kell each invest $7,500 in cash.
2. Bridges and Kell invest $3,000 and $2,000 in cash, respectively.
3. Bridges invests $3,000 in cash, merchandise worth $5,000, a building worth $20,000, and land worth $6,000. Kell invests $8,000 in cash, office equipment worth $5,000, and store equipment worth $7,000.
4. Bridges and Kell transfer the following assets and liabilities to the partnership as their initial investments:

	Bridges	Kell
Cash	$ 4,500	$ 2,000
Accounts Receivable	8,000	10,000
Merchandise Inventory	16,500	14,200
Delivery Equipment (net)	8,500	–0–
Store Equipment (net)	–0–	10,000
Accounts Payable	12,000	10,000
Notes Payable to Bank	10,000	15,000

P11-3. Walter Kwang, Raymond O'Connel, and John Stewart formed a partnership on May 1, 1972, with investments of $12,000, $8,000, and $10,000, respectively. Profits and losses were to be shared equally. During the next 12 months, Kwang and O'Connel made additional investments of $3,000 each; Stewart invested an additional $4,000 and withdrew $1,500. Net income for the period was $25,000.

Required: Prepare (a) a statement of partners' equities for the year ended April 30, 1973, and (b) entries to close the partners' Drawing accounts.

P11-4. Michael Pinto and Raymond Stone formed a partnership on January 1, 1973. Certain relevant accounts are given as of December 31, 1973.

Michael Pinto, Capital					Raymond Stone, Capital		
1973		1973				1973	
Aug. 1	5,000	Jan. 1	40,000			Jan. 1	50,000
		July 1	10,000			Dec. 1	6,000

Michael Pinto, Drawing			Raymond Stone, Drawing	
1973			1973	
Dec. 31	3,000		Dec. 31	4,000

The net income for 1973 was $5,000. The following provisions appeared in the articles of copartnership:

Net income shall be divided as follows:
Salary allowances: Pinto, $3,000; Stone, $4,000
Interest allowances: 6 percent on beginning-of-year capital balances
Remainder: divided 60 percent to Pinto and 40 percent to Stone

Required: Prepare the journal entries to distribute the net income to the partners' accounts and to complete the closing process.

P11-5. Assume that A and B are equal partners, each with capital balances of $30,000. Record the admission of C under each of the following assumptions:

a. A sells his interest to C for $40,000.
b. C invests $30,000 for a one-fourth interest.
c. C invests $30,000 for a one-fourth interest, total capital to be $100,000.
d. C invests $30,000 for a one-third interest, total capital to be $90,000.
e. C invests $35,000 for a one-third interest, total capital to be $105,000.
f. C invests $20,000 for a one-third interest, total capital to be $90,000.
g. C invests $36,000 for a one-fourth interest, total capital to be $96,000.
h. C invests $36,000 for a one-half interest, total capital to be $96,000.

P11-6. A, B, and C, whose statement of financial position is shown below, have decided to liquidate their partnership. Their general ledger shows the following balances on March 31, 1973:

Cash	$ 4,000
Accounts Receivable	5,000
Inventories	20,000
Machinery	25,000
Accounts Payable	4,000
A, Capital	10,000
B, Capital	15,000
C, Capital	25,000

Proceeds from the sale of noncash assets were as follows:

Accounts Receivable	$3,000
Inventories	9,000
Machinery	5,000

Required:

Prepare a schedule in good form showing the final distribution of the remaining cash following the sale of the assets and the payment of creditors.

P11-7. On December 31, 1973, the ledger of the Ell Company included the following accounts:

Notes Receivable	$ 10,000
Merchandise Inventory	50,000
Marketable Securities–U.S. Government Bonds	5,000
Common Stock ($100 par value)	200,000
Retained Earnings	65,000
Subscriptions Receivable–Common Stock	25,000
Preferred Stock ($10 par value)	100,000
Goodwill	20,000
Common Stock Subscribed	100,000
Organization Costs	15,000
Premium on Preferred Stock	8,000
Building	150,000
Premium on Common Stock	21,000
Notes Receivable Discounted	5,000
Cash	60,000
Research and Development Costs	75,000

Required: Prepare the Stockholders' Equity section of the statement of financial position as of December 31, 1973.

P11-8. John Downes, an investor, and Richard England, an inventor, decided to form Rentron, Inc., to manufacture and sell a product developed by England. The corporation is chartered by the state, with 5,000 shares of $100 par value common stock authorized.

a. Downes invests $160,000 and England invests $100,000 in cash for stock at par value. England is issued an additional $50,000 in stock at par value in payment for his patent on the product to be manufactured.
b. The corporation issues 100 shares of common stock at par value to each promoter as payment for promotion and incorporation fees.
c. Rentron, Inc., sells stock on a subscription basis to five investors. Each investor subscribes to 100 shares of the common stock at $110 per share, making a down payment of 40 percent of the subscription price. The remainder is to be paid at a later date.
d. Four of the five subscribers pay the remaining installment.

Required: Journalize the transactions.

P11-9. The Hewlett Corporation was organized on January 2, 1973, with authority to issue 5,000 shares of $100 par value common stock. The following transactions occurred during the year:

1973
Jan. 10   Issued for cash 100 shares at $101 per share.

Feb. 15   Issued for cash 100 shares at $99.50 per share.

Mar.   1   Issued 1,000 shares for land and a building with a fair market value of $100,000. One tenth the total valuation was allocable to the land.

June   1   Received subscriptions for 500 shares at $102 per share, payable 40 percent down and the balance in two equal installments due on August 1 and October 1.

      10   Paid $2,000 for legal fees incurred in organizing the corporation.

1973

July 5 Purchased equipment for $50,000 in cash.

Aug. 1 Received the installment due on the subscription of June 1.

Oct. 1 Received the installment due on the subscription of June 1.

Dec. 15 Received subscriptions for 500 shares at $90 per share payable 40 percent down and the balance in two equal installments due on February 15, 1974, and April 15, 1974.

31 Recorded the following entry, summarizing the results of operations before income taxes for the year:

Cash	27,000	
Accumulated Depreciation–Building		4,500
Accumulated Depreciation–Equipment		2,500
Revenue and Expense Summary		20,000

31 Recorded the income tax liability of $4,500.

31 Closed the Revenue and Expense Summary account.

Required: 1. Record the transactions in appropriate T accounts.
2. Prepare a statement of financial position as of December 31, 1973.

P11-10. The following selected transactions took place at the newly formed Curry Corporation:

1973

July 1 Received a charter authorizing the issuance of 10,000 shares of $100 par value preferred stock and 100,000 shares of no-par value common stock with a stated value of $10 per share.

2 Issued 50,000 shares of common stock at $20 per share for cash.

2 Issued 1,000 shares of common stock to an incorporator for a patent that he had perfected.

3 Received subscriptions from four investors for 500 shares each of preferred stock at $105.

5 Received 60-percent down payments on the subscriptions from all four subscribers.

20 Received payment in full from three of the preferred subscribers, and issued the stock.

31 Received payment in full from the fourth preferred subscriber, and issued the stock.

Aug. 10 Received a subscription from Richard Ring for 1,000 shares of the preferred stock at $98 per share.

12 Collected 70 percent of Richard Ring's subscription total. The balance is due on September 1, 1973.

Required: Record the transactions.

P11-11. (Tumble Products, Inc.) (*Financial and accounting policy decision problem*) Until 12 years ago, William Hoyle was employed as production manager for a large manufacturer of metal furniture; at that time he decided to begin his own firm, which he named the Tumble Products Company. The main activity of his company was the fabrication of baby furniture, sold directly to retailers.

After managing all phases of the business for six years, Hoyle decided to admit as partners, Thomas Smith and John Draper, in whom he had a lot of confidence. Hoyle retained a 52-percent equity in the firm. Each of the other partners was allowed a 24-percent equity in exchange for investments of cash. With the admission of the partners, Hoyle was relieved of some of his responsibilities. Smith was designated as the sales manager, and Draper was the production manager. Hoyle's title was general manager.

The partners now wish to expand the production facilities. They wish to add metal lawn furniture, dinette sets, wrought iron furniture, and metal office furniture to their line of products. Preliminary to expanding the facilities, the partners applied for and received a corporate charter. They plan to dissolve the partnership and to transfer all partnership assets and liabilities to the corporation. The charter authorizes the corporation, to be known as Tumble Products, Inc., to issue 1,000,000 shares of $1 par value voting common stock and 10,000 shares of $100 par value, 6-percent, nonvoting preferred stock. Amounts received in excess of the par value of shares issued are to be credited to appropriately titled accounts. According to the laws of the state of incorporation, these amounts do not become a part of the legal capital.

The new corporation has engaged in the following transactions:

1. Three separate notes payable for $1,200 each were issued to the incorporators for cash they had loaned to the corporation.
2. Incorporation fees of $75 were paid.
3. Fees of $150 for legal services were paid.
4. Stock certificate printing costs of $400 were paid.
5. The assets and liabilities of the partnership were transferred to the corporation. The trial balance of the partnership at that time was

	Debit	Credit
Cash	$ 5,400	
Accounts Receivable	12,000	
Allowance for Doubtful Accounts		$ 360
Inventories	19,000	
Prepaid Expenses	400	
Land	12,000	
Building	60,000	
Accumulated Depreciation		10,000
Equipment	40,000	
Accumulated Depreciation		10,000
Accounts Payable		15,000
Accrued Liabilities		700
William Hoyle, Capital		58,625
Thomas Smith, Capital		27,057
John Draper, Capital		27,058
Totals	$148,800	$148,800

It was agreed that the amounts were to be recorded as shown, except that the depreciable assets were to be recorded at their carrying values and that the corporation should begin with zero balances in the Accumulated Depreciation accounts. Each partner was to be issued common stock at par value in an amount equivalent to his equity in the partnership.

6. A local investor subscribed to 400 shares of preferred stock at $102 per share.
7. A number of local citizens subscribed to 12,000 shares of common stock at $1.25 per share.
8. The local investor paid for one half of his subscribed shares, and a certificate was issued.
9. The local citizens remitted $6,500 in cash in payment of their subscriptions, consisting of payment in full for 2,500 shares and partial payment on the remaining 9,500 shares. Certificates were issued for the fully paid shares.
10. The three incorporators agreed to accept at par value common stock certificates for the notes that they hold (see transaction 1), and the certificates were issued.

The new management, consisting of Hoyle as president-secretary-treasurer, Smith as vice-president in charge of sales, and Draper as vice-president in charge of production, plans to raise more funds by issuing additional stock. However, before proceeding further, they wish to know how they stand.

Required:

1. Record the transactions in general journal form.
2. Prepare a statement of financial position for the corporation upon completion of the transactions.
3. This entity has changed from a single proprietorship to a partnership and then to a corporation. What are the characteristics—advantages and disadvantages—of each form of organization so far as Tumble Products, Inc., is concerned?
4. Describe the legal relationships between the stockholders, the board of directors, and the
   company officers of Tumble Products, Inc.
5. What portion of the total stockholders' equity belongs to each of the three officers?
6. What portion of the voting power belongs to each of the three officers?
7. If all the voting common stock were issued, how many additional shares must be obtained
   collectively by the three officers for them to retain control of the organization?
8. What is the significance of the term "legal capital"?
9. What is the preferred accounting treatment of the organization costs? Why?

Note. The practice set, containing transactions of the Pineland Wholesale Furniture Company, a single proprietorship, may be assigned after Chapter 6, 7, 8,
9, 10, or 11. This is a short set and can be worked in about ten hours. The practice set, which contains the narrative of transactions and working papers, is available in a separate package.

12

Dividends, Retained Earnings, and Treasury Stock

The stockholders' equity in a corporation arises from a number of sources. It is of the utmost importance that these sources be clearly distinguished and stated. It is equally important that the terminology used to designate them be precise and meaningful.

The various sources of the stockholders' equity discussed in this chapter and in Chapter 11 are outlined in Figure 12-1.

CONTRIBUTED CAPITAL

As implied in the previous chapter, contributed capital, also referred to as *paid-in capital*, may include items other than the par or stated value of stock. Among these, in addition to premiums on common or preferred stock, may be donations and amounts transferred from the Common Stock account if the board of directors revises the stated value of no-par value stock.

Excess over Par or Stated Value

The premium on stock, or excess over par or stated value, is that part of the capital contributed by stockholders that is not credited to the capital stock accounts. Some accountants refer to it as *capital surplus*, but this term may be confusing, as other accountants use it to designate retained earnings. Separate contributed capital accounts are kept so that the position statement shows the specific sources of capital. Such precise source accounts are also desirable to establish the availability of source of funds for dividends or other distributions to stockholders, in states that permit such distributions.

Donations

A gift or donation to a corporation increases the assets and the stockholders' equity and is credited to Contributed Capital–Donations. Gifts of land,

416

Figure 12.1. Sources of Stockholders' Equity

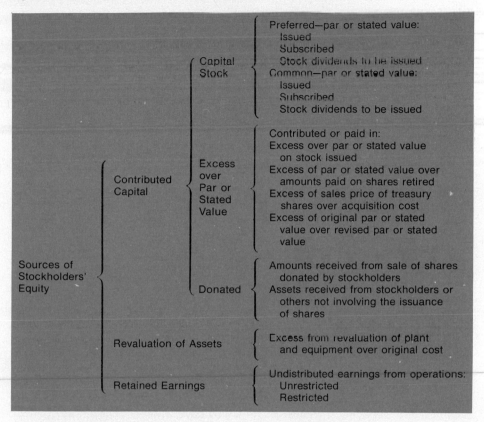

buildings, or other facilities are sometimes made by a local organization to encourage a corporation to do business in the area. Sometimes donations of assets or stock are made by the stockholders to a company in financial difficulties to enable it to raise funds.

A contribution of land and buildings by a town to a newly established firm is recorded by the receiving corporation at the fair market value of the assets contributed as shown (the fair market values are assumed) below.

Land	80,000	
Buildings	20,000	
Contributed Capital—Donations		100,000

To assist a corporation in raising needed working capital, its stockholders, instead of investing additional funds, may donate a portion of their fully paid stock to the corporation. Such stock is known as *treasury stock*, explained later in this chapter. Sales of the donated stock for cash are recorded by a debit to Cash and a credit to Contributed Capital–Donations.

Revaluations

The upward revaluation of corporate assets, generally following a continuing increase in price levels, results in an increase in the stockholders' equity. The practice of revaluing assets to reflect current market values is not common. There is a natural reluctance to replace historical (cost) data, which are readily verifiable, with amounts based on individual judgments requiring continuing and complex adjustments. There are, however, circumstances in which market or reproduction values are more significant than original cost, particularly when there is a wide disparity between these values. A financial statement prepared, for example, pursuant to a proposed sale of a business, as a basis for establishing insurance coverages or for certain credit purposes, is more informative to the user if it is based on replacement, rather than depreciated cost, values. When assets are revalued, the increase should be debited to a specifically designated Asset–Appreciation in Value account and credited to a specifically designated Revaluation Capital account. Increases in the stockholders' equity from asset revaluations are not a result of earnings and, in most states, may not properly be used as a basis for cash dividends.

RETAINED EARNINGS

Undistributed earnings from regular operating transactions, gains from sale of plant, equipment assets, and from sale of investments are classified as *retained earnings.* These are sources of stockholders' equity other than transactions involving the company's own stock and revaluations. Such terms as *earned surplus, retained income, accumulated earnings,* and *earnings retained for use in the business* are also used to designate the earnings that have not been distributed to the stockholders as dividends. The account should not be interpreted as an indicator of expected dividend distributions by the company. If losses and dividend distributions exceed earnings, the Retained Earnings account will have a debit balance and will be shown in the position statement under the caption *Deficit.*

The creation of special Restricted Retained Earnings accounts indicates that a portion of the earnings of the corporation is not available for dividend distribution. This does not mean that a special cash fund has been set up, nor does the restriction provide cash funds. The restrictions do not in any way alter the total retained earnings or the stockholders' equity. The segregation of retained earnings is a bookkeeping device by which a corporation, following a resolution of the board of directors, intentionally reduces the amount of earnings available for dividend distributions, thus indicating its intention to conserve corporate assets for other purposes. The restriction of retained earnings does not reduce the overall retained earnings but merely *earmarks,* or sets aside, a portion of the earnings in an account specifically designated to indicate its purpose. The same information can be communicated by a footnote or by a parenthetical notation.

Each restricted account, although separated from the parent Retained Earnings account, is nevertheless a part of retained earnings and is so classified in the Stockholders' Equity section of the position statement. When the special account has served its purpose and the requirement for which it was set up no longer exists, the amount in the restricted account is returned to the Retained Earnings account.

Restrictions may be either voluntary or involuntary. A restriction for plant expansion, for example, may be set up by voluntary action of the board of directors. The purpose of this restriction is to show management's intention to retain cash or other assets for use in connection with a projected plant expansion program rather than to distribute them in the form of dividends. When cash dividends are paid, the assets of the corporation are depleted. To the degree, then, that dividend declarations are restricted, assets are retained for other business purposes such as plant expansion. Involuntary restrictions may be required either by state statute, covered later in this chapter, or by contract. When a corporation enters into an agreement for a long-term loan, the terms of the contract may require periodic restrictions of retained earnings, accumulating over the term of the loan to an amount equal to the loan. The purpose of the restriction is to reduce the amount of earnings that might otherwise be distributed to the stockholders as dividends, thereby improving the corporation's ability to make periodic interest payments and any other payments required under the terms of the loan. The restriction does not ensure the availability of working capital; it does, however, limit the use of working capital for dividend distributions. The journal entry to record this type of restriction is a debit to Retained Earnings and a credit to Retained Earnings–Restricted for Long-Term Loan Retirement.

DIVIDENDS

The term *dividend* refers to the distribution by a corporation of cash, stock, or other corporate property to the stockholders. A dividend must be declared formally by the board of directors and entered in the minute book; the entry should indicate the date the dividend was declared, the *record date* to determine the eligibility of *stockholders of record* on that date, and the date of the payment. For a dividend distribution to be made, there must be accumulated unrestricted earnings and there must be assets available for distribution. If there are no earnings, the dividend becomes a reduction in contributed capital, which is normally illegal. There may be adequate earnings but insufficient cash or other readily distributable type of assets. A corporation may have a good earnings record but no cash available for dividends because the cash may have been used to acquire other assets (land, buildings, machinery, or inventory), or funds are being accumulated for an anticipated expansion program or other corporate needs. Only the board of directors has the authority to determine whether a dividend distribution is to take place, to which classes of stock it is to be paid, and the time, manner, and form of payment. This applies to all classes of stockholders, preferred and common.

The board of directors is the ultimate authority in regard to dividend declaration. There have been court cases in which stockholders have attempted to force a dividend declaration that they felt was being deliberately withheld by the board of directors. Except in rare instances, courts have been reluctant to interpose and order dividend payments. Once formal action has been taken by the board, however, the declaration immediately becomes a current liability of the corporation. The state corporation laws contain dividend provisions that must be observed by the board of directors. It is customary, for example, particularly for larger corporations with numerous stockholders, to make a public announcement of the dividend declaration in newspapers or magazines.

The term *dividend* is most often used to designate a cash distribution out of corporate earnings. A dividend may be paid in property other than cash; a company may, for example, distribute marketable securities or merchandise. A well-known distillery once declared a dividend and made a pro rata distribution of whiskey late in December. The term *stock dividend* is used to designate the distribution of additional shares of stock to existing stockholders. The term *liquidating dividend* refers to a distribution of assets by a company being liquidated, or a distribution whose effect is to reduce the stockholders' equity from contributed or revaluation capital. Thus, a liquidating dividend is a distribution of contributed capital when there are no accumulated retained earnings, or when a deficit exists. The term *ex-dividend* indicates that the quoted price of the shares is exclusive of a dividend declared and payable on a specified future date to shareholders of record as of a specified date prior to the payment date.

Declaration of a Dividend

The dividend may be stated as a percent of par or as a specified amount per share. Following is a typical dividend notice:

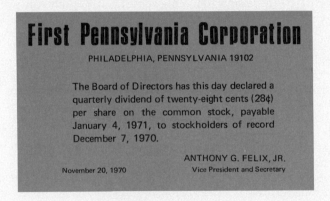

First Pennsylvania Corporation

PHILADELPHIA, PENNSYLVANIA 19102

The Board of Directors has this day declared a quarterly dividend of twenty-eight cents (28¢) per share on the common stock, payable January 4, 1971, to stockholders of record December 7, 1970.

November 20, 1970

ANTHONY G. FELIX, JR.
Vice President and Secretary

The holder of 100 shares of common stock of the First Pennsylvania Corporation will receive $28 on January 4, 1971. An investor who is recorded as owner of common stock of this company prior to December 7, the record date, will receive the dividend. An investor who buys stock of this company after December 7, 1970 is said to buy the stock *ex-dividend*—that is, without the right to receive the latest declared dividend. Stock traded on the stock exchanges are quoted ex-dividend two or three days prior to the record date to allow time for the recording and delivery of the securities. During the interval between December 7, 1970 and January 4, 1971, the company prepares the list of eligible stockholders and performs all other tasks incident to the mailing of the dividend checks.

Recording Cash Dividends

To illustrate the recording of a cash dividend, assume that on August 2, 1973, the board of directors of Magnetics, Inc., declared a quarterly dividend of $3,000 on 2,000 shares of $100 par value 6-percent preferred stock, and a $2,000 dividend on 10,000 shares of $10 par value common stock. The dividends are payable on September 1, 1973, to stockholders of record at the close of business on August 15, 1973. The entries to record the dividend declaration and the payment are as follows:

```
1973
Aug.  2  Dividends–Common Stock                      2,000
         Dividends–Preferred Stock                   3,000
            Dividends Payable–Common Stock                    2,000
            Dividends Payable–Preferred Stock                 3,000
            To record the declaration of a dividend on the
            outstanding preferred and common
            stock, payable September 1, 1973, to
            stockholders of record on August 15,
            1973: 1.5 percent on $200,000 preferred,
            and 2 percent on $100,000 common.

Sept. 1  Dividends Payable–Common Stock              2,000
         Dividends Payable–Preferred Stock           3,000
            Cash                                              5,000
            To record payment of dividends
            to stockholders of record on
            August 15, 1973.
```

The Dividends accounts are closed out at the end of the accounting year to Retained Earnings. The use of a Dividends account has the advantage of segregating dividends declared during the year; it also keeps Retained Earnings clear of charges that would require analysis at the end of the year. The Dividends account is a temporary stockholders' equity account; it has a debit balance and represents a reduction in the stockholders' equity. It is shown on the statement of retained earnings as a deduction from the total of the beginning balance of Retained Earnings plus net income and other credits to Retained Earnings. Dividends Payable, on either common or preferred stock, is a current liability.

Dividends on Preferred Stock

As mentioned in Chapter 11, preferred stock enjoys certain dividend preferences. The right to a dividend of a preferred stockholder must await a formal declaration by the board of directors. On declaration, the preferred stockholders are entitled to a stated amount per share before any dividend distribution is made to holders of common stock.

If the preferred stock is *cumulative,* undeclared dividends are accumulated and must be paid together with the current dividend before any dividend payment is made on common stock. If the preferred stock is *noncumulative,* a dividend by-passed in any one year is lost forever. Preferred stock may be either *participating* or *nonparticipating.* If the preferred stock is participating, it receives its specified dividend rate and a share of any additional dividends declared. The manner of determining the amount of the additional dividend depends on the terms of the stock contract. If the preferred stock is fully participating, it participates on a pro rata basis with the common stock in dividend distributions after the common stock has received an amount equal to the stipulated preference rate on the preferred stock. The participation may be limited in the stock contract to a specified rate or amount per share. If the preferred stock is nonparticipating, it receives the stipulated rate only, and the balance of the dividend distribution, irrespective of amount, is paid to the common stockholders. Most preferred stock issues are cumulative and nonparticipating.

The extent to which preferred stockholders participate in distributions above the regular rates depends on the specific provisions of the corporate charter. The following examples illustrate the application of the dividend preference of preferred stock.

1. *Cumulative and Nonparticipating.* A corporation has outstanding 1,000 shares of 5-percent cumulative preferred stock and 2,000 shares of common stock, each with a par value of $100. Undistributed earnings are $75,000, there are no dividends in arrears, and a $27,000 dividend is declared. Assuming that the preferred stock is nonparticipating, the required journal entry for the dividend declaration is shown as

Dividends—Preferred Stock	5,000	
Dividends—Common Stock	22,000	
Dividends Payable—Preferred Stock		5,000
Dividends Payable—Common Stock		22,000

2. *Cumulative and Fully Participating.* Assume the same facts as in illustration 1, except that the preferred stock is cumulative and fully participating—that is, the preferred stock shares at an equal rate with the common stock in the amount distributed in excess of the 5-percent preferred dividend and a comparable dividend on the common stock. The required journal entry is shown below.

Dividends—Preferred Stock	9,000	
Dividends—Common Stock	18,000	
Dividends Payable—Preferred Stock		9,000
Dividends Payable—Common Stock		18,000

The allocation is computed as follows:

	To Preferred	To Common
Current rate at 5%, or $5 per share:		
To preferred stock: 1,000 shares × $5	$5,000	
To common stock: 2,000 shares × $5		$10,000
Participation at 4%, or $4 per share:		
To preferred stock: 1,000 shares × $4	4,000	
To common stock: 2,000 shares × $4		8,000
Total distribution	$9,000	$18,000

Note that each stockholder receives $9 per share because the preferred stock is fully participating, and the common stock receives a current rate equal to the preference rate on preferred stock.

3. *Cumulative and Partly Participating.* Assume the same facts as in illustration 2, except that the preferred stock participates to a maximum of 2 percent, or $2 per share, above its preference rate; the allocation of the $27,000 is computed as follows:

	To Preferred	To Common
Current rate	$5,000	$10,000
Participation:		
Preferred stock: 1,000 shares × $2	2,000	
Common stock: remainder		10,000
Total distribution	$7,000	$20,000

Preferred stock participates at the stated maximum only if the proportionate distribution to the common stock—at a rate on the par value, or in an amount per share on no-par value stock—equals or exceeds the distribution to the preferred stock. In this illustration, the preferred rate per share is $7 and the common rate is $10. The amount actually received on participation may be less than $2 a share, as shown in the following illustration.

4. *Dividend Arrearage.* This illustration is based on the same facts as in illustration 3, except that there is a dividend *arrearage* (amounts owed from previous periods) on the preferred stock of $9,000. The dividend distribution is computed as follows:

To preferred stock:	
Arrearage	$ 9,000
Current year's preference dividend	5,000
Participation	1,000
Total to preferred	$15,000
To common stock:	
Remainder	12,000
Total distribution	$27,000

The distribution to the preferred stock due to the participation provision is computed as follows:

Total dividend		$27,000
Deduct: Arrearage payment	$ 9,000	
Current year's preference—preferred stock	5,000	
Current year's rate—common stock	10,000	24,000
Available for participation		$ 3,000
Number of shares outstanding		3,000
Rate per share on participation		$ 1
To preferred stock: 1,000 × $1		$ 1,000

Preferred stock may also be preferred in distributing assets; this means that if the corporation is liquidated, the preferred stockholders must be paid before any liquidating payments are made to the common stockholders. The manner of the preference application depends on the wording in the stock contract. The preference may be for the par value of the preferred stock, the par value and accumulated dividends, or some other stipulated amount. If the preferred stock is not preferred as to assets, then the assets are usually distributed to all classes of stockholders on an equal basis proportionate to the respective par values.

Stock Dividends

The term *stock dividend* refers to the issuance by a corporation of additional shares of its authorized stock without additional payment of any kind by the stockholders. There are various occasions for the declaration of a stock dividend, such as

1. A large unappropriated retained earnings balance
2. A desire by the directors to reduce the market price of the stock
3. A desire to increase the permanent capitalization of the company by converting a portion of the retained earnings into capital stock
4. A need to conserve available cash

A stock dividend does not change the total stockholders' equity in the corporation; it simply effects a transfer of retained earnings to contributed capital. A cash dividend, on the other hand, decreases both the assets and the stockholders' equity. A stock dividend has no effect on either total assets or total stockholders' equity; the change is entirely within the Stockholders' Equity section (Retained Earnings decreases and contributed capital increases). To illustrate, assume that the Truro Corporation, with $500,000 common stock, $100 par value, outstanding and retained earnings of $80,000 declares a $50,000 stock dividend. The effect of the declaration on the stockholders' equity is shown below.

	Stockholders' Equity		
	Immediately before Declaration	Immediately after Declaration	Immediately after Stock Issuance
Stockholders' equity:			
Common stock, $100 par value	$500,000	$500,000	$550,000
Stock dividends to be issued		50,000	
Retained earnings	80,000	30,000	30,000
Total stockholders' equity	$580,000	$580,000	$580,000

The Stock Dividends to Be Issued account is part of the stockholders' equity. It is not a liability because its reduction will result not in a reduction of a current asset but rather in an increase in capital stock. The account should therefore be shown under Capital Stock in the Stockholders' Equity section of the position statement.

It is evident that a stock dividend has no effect on the total stockholders' equity; the relative interest of each stockholder is, therefore, unchanged. For example, John Green, a stockholder with 100 shares before the stock dividend, will have 110 shares after the stock dividend. His proportionate holdings remain unchanged at 2 percent of the total stock outstanding. Hence, all his rights and privileges are unaltered, as shown below.

	Line	Before Declaration	After Declaration
Total stockholders' equity	1	$580,000	$580,000.00
Number of shares outstanding	2	5,000	5,500.00
Stockholders' equity per share (line 1 ÷ line 2)	3	$ 116	$ 105.45
Shares owned by John Green	4	100	110.00
Green's equity (line 4 × line 3)	5	$ 11,600	$ 11,600.00

A stock dividend, nevertheless, is significant to the stockholder. The dividend does not alter the recipients' equity in the company and is not, therefore, considered income. There is no income tax on a stock dividend. If the stock dividend does not cause a significant decline in the price of stock, the stockholder's gain is equal to the market value of the new shares received. If, in addition, the corporation continues to pay its customary cash dividends per share, the stockholder gains the dividends on the additional shares. It is this aspect—the expectation of greater dividends as well as the availability of more shares for possible ultimate profitable resale—that creates a favorable reception for a stock dividend.

A stock dividend provides certain advantages to the corporation. Its earnings are capitalized (that is, earnings are transferred to capital stock accounts); there is no reduction in working capital; and the corporation may plow back its earnings for expansion or other purposes. The corporation also may wish to reduce the market price of its shares in order to attract more buyers; by issuing more shares, the price per share will decrease. At the same time, it makes possible larger total dividend distributions without a change in the regular dividend rate.

When there are two classes of stockholders, the stock dividend normally applies only to the common stockholders. Payment, however, may be in either preferred or common stock. The various court rulings are not consistent with respect to the rights of preferred stockholders to participate in a stock dividend, although generally no such rights inhere in preferred stock.

The AICPA has recommended that for small dividends—those involving the issuance of less than 20 or 25 percent of the number of shares previously outstanding—the corporation should "transfer from earned surplus to the category of permanent capitalization (represented by the capital stock and capital surplus accounts) an amount equal to the fair value of the additional shares issued." [1] To illustrate, assume that the market value of the shares issued by the Truro Corporation was $60,000 (500 shares at $120 a share) and that the board of directors, in authorizing the stock dividend, directed that the dividend be recorded at market value. The entries to record the declaration and stock issuance are

Retained Earnings	60,000	
Stock Dividends to Be Issued		50,000
Contributed Capital–Excess Over		
Par or Stated Value on Stock Dividends		10,000
Stock Dividends to Be Issued	50,000	
Common Stock		50,000

For large stock dividends—those involving the issuance of more than 25 percent of the number of shares previously outstanding—the AICPA recommends that "there is no need to capitalize earned surplus, other than to the extent occasioned by legal requirements." [2] This means that for large stock dividends, the amount of retained earnings capitalized is represented by the par or stated value of the shares issued. To illustrate, assume that the Truro Corporation declares a stock dividend of 2,500 shares or 50 percent of the 5,000 shares previously outstanding. The entry to record the stock issuance is shown on page 426.

[1] AICPA, *Accounting Principles*, Vol. II. Chicago: Commerce Clearing House, 1970, p. 6024.
[2] *Ibid.*, p. 6025.

Retained Earnings	250,000	
Common Stock		250,000
To record the issuance of 2,500 shares of additional common stock as a stock dividend.		

The AICPA's rationale with respect to small stock dividends is that since the market value of the shares previously held remains substantially unchanged and since "many recipients of stock dividends look upon them as distributions of corporate earnings and usually in an amount equivalent to the fair value of the additional shares issued"—that is, as a cash dividend—the accounting should be such as to show the amount of retained earnings available for future dividend distribution. The rationale with respect to large stock dividends is that the effect is to reduce materially the share market value, and the transaction is "a split-up effected in the form of a dividend." There is, therefore, no need to capitalize retained earnings beyond the legal requirements.

Stock Split-Ups

A corporation may wish to reduce the par value of its stock, or it may desire to reduce the price at which the stock is being issued to make it more salable. This is accomplished by a stock split-up whereby the shares outstanding are increased and the par or stated value per share is reduced; there is no change, however, in the total par or stated value of the outstanding shares. No journal entries are required, and *there is no change in retained earnings.* The capital stock ledger account headings are changed to show the new par or stated value per share and the subsidiary stockholders' ledger is revised to show the new distribution of shares.

Assume, for example, that a corporation has outstanding 100,000 shares of $50 par value common stock. The current market price of the stock is $175 per share. The corporation, wishing to reduce this high market price to create a broader market for a forthcoming additional stock issue, reduces the par value from $50 to $25 and increases the number of shares from 100,000 to 200,000. this is called a "2-for-1 split-up" because the number of shares owned by each shareholder is doubled. The split in shares may be accomplished by calling in all the old shares and issuing certificates for new shares on a 2-for-1 basis or by issuing an additional share for each old share previously owned. This action is recorded either by a memorandum notation in the capital stock account or by the following journal entry:

Common Stock, $50 par value	5,000,000	
Common Stock, $25 par value		5,000,000
To record a 2-for-1 split-up, increasing the number of outstanding shares from 100,000 to 200,000 and reducing par value from $50 to $25.		

It may be assumed that the market price of the shares will now be reduced sufficiently to enhance the marketability of the new issue.

TREASURY STOCK

A corporation may reacquire some of its own stock, preferred or common, either by purchase or gift, or in settlement of a debt. Such stock is known as *treasury stock*. Treasury stock, if it has been fully paid for originally, may be issued at a price below par or stated value without the assumption of the usual contingent discount liability by the purchaser of discount stock to the corporation's creditors for the amount of the discount. Another feature of treasury stock is that it need not first be offered to present stockholders in compliance with their pre-emptive rights to participate in any additional issues. Treasury stock does not fall into the category of new issues; it is the corporation's own stock that has been issued and later reacquired. It is issued, but not outstanding, stock and therefore does not have voting or dividend rights.

A corporation may purchase some of its own stock to bolster a sagging market, or to meet the needs under a plan whereby the company's own stock is distributed to its employees in lieu of other compensation, at or below the market price. Sometimes the stock is purchased because it is available at a favorable price. Acquisition of treasury stock has the effect of reducing the assets and the stockholders' equity. The Treasury Stock account, therefore, should appear in the Stockholders' Equity section as a deduction from the total contributed capital. Since the acquisition of treasury stock results in a distribution of corporate assets to stockholders, some states have enacted restrictive provisions pertaining to this kind of stock to protect the corporate creditors. If a corporation faces financial difficulties, certain influential stockholders could have the corporation buy back their shares, thereby reducing the amount available for the creditors and other stockholders. The restrictive provisions vary widely among the states. Some states require a restriction of retained earnings to the extent of the disbursement for the treasury stock.

Recording the Purchase of Treasury Stock

When a corporation reacquires shares of its own stock, the Treasury Stock account is debited for the cost of the shares acquired. To illustrate, assume that the Lee Corporation reacquires 10 shares of its own stock at $55 per share. The entry is as shown below.

Treasury Stock—Common	550	
Cash		550

The purchase of the 10 shares of stock reduces cash by $550 and the stockholders' equity by $550. It also reduces the number of shares outstanding. It does not reduce the amount of issued stock because the purchase of the shares is recorded not by a debit to Common Stock but by a debit to a special Treasury Stock account, which is shown in the Stockholders' Equity section as a deduction from Total Contributed Capital and Retained Earnings.

Issuance of Treasury Stock—Above Cost

The reissuance of treasury stock is recorded by a credit to Treasury Stock for the cost of the shares. The difference between the cost and the issue price of treasury stock when it is issued above cost is credited to Contributed Capital from Treasury Stock Transactions. To illustrate, assume that the Lee Corporation reissues five shares for $65 per share. The entry is shown as

Cash	325	
Treasury Stock—Common		275
Contributed Capital from Treasury Stock		
Transactions—Common		50

The Stockholders' Equity section of the Lee Corporation's position statement after the reissuance of the five shares is shown below (other amounts are assumed).

Stockholders' Equity	
Contributed Capital	
Common Stock, $50 par value; authorized and issued	
1,000 shares of which five shares are held	
in treasury	$50,000
Premium on Common Stock	2,500
From Treasury Stock Transactions	50
Total Contributed Capital	$52,550
Retained Earnings	20,000
Total Contributed Capital and Retained Earnings	$72,550
Deduct Cost of Treasury Stock—Common	275
Total Stockholders' Equity	$72,275

Issuance of Treasury Stock—Below Cost

The entry to record the issuance of treasury stock below cost depends on the existence of capital accounts that are not considered to be a part of the stated capital. To illustrate, assume that the Lee Corporation issues the five remaining shares of treasury stock (which cost $275) for $225. The "loss" of $50 is charged to Contributed Capital from Treasury Stock Transactions, as follows:

Cash	225	
Contributed Capital from Treasury Stock Transactions	50	
Treasury Stock—Common		275

If the "loss" on the issue of the shares exceeds the amount in Contributed Capital from Treasury Stock Transactions–Common, the excess is charged to any other contributed capital account arising from the original issuance of the same class of stock and not a part of the stated capital (Excess over Par or Stated Value, for example). In the absence of such accounts, the difference between the cost and the selling price of the treasury stock is charged to Retained Earnings.

Treasury Stock Donated

One or more shareholders may donate a portion of their shares to the corporation for reissuance to raise needed cash. Shares acquired by donation do not affect the position statement, as there is no change in the assets, liabilities, or stock-holders' equity. On acquisition, a memorandum is made in the Treasury Stock account indicating the date and the number of shares donated. When the shares are reissued, the proceeds are credited to Contributed Capital–Donations. Assume that 100 shares are donated to the Lee Corporation by its principal stockholder on May 1. The shares are reissued on June 15 at $45 per share. Upon receipt of the shares, the following memorandum is made in the Treasury Stock account:

Treasury Stock	
May 1 100 shares donated	

The journal entry to record the reissuance is shown below.

Cash	4,500	
Contributed Capital–Donations		4,500
To record the reissuance for cash of 100 shares of donated treasury stock.		

A memo entry should also be made in the Treasury Stock account to record the reissuance of the shares.

Book Value of Capital Stock

The value of a share of stock may be expressed in terms of par, market, or book value. The book value of a share of stock, or the stockholders' equity per share, assuming that there is only one class of stock outstanding, is computed as follows:

	Line	Amount
Total stockholders' equity	1	$750,000
Number of shares outstanding	2	6,000
Book value per share (line 1 ÷ line 2)	3	$ 125

When there is more than one class of stock outstanding, it becomes necessary to determine the claims of each class in the net assets of the corporation (assets minus liabilities). If, for example, the preferred stock is cumulative and non-participating and there are dividends in arrears, the stockholders' equity is divided between the two classes based on the preferences accorded to the preferred stock. Assume that a corporation has the following capital structure:

Common stock, $100 par value; issued 1,000 shares	$100,000
Preferred stock (6%), $100 par value; cumulative, nonparticipating; issued 1,000 shares	100,000
Retained earnings	45,000
Retained earnings–restricted for plant addition	10,000
Excess over stated value of no-par common stock	5,000
Total stockholders' equity	$260,000

Dividends are in arrears for the prior and the current year. The book value of a share of preferred stock at the end of the year is computed as follows:

Preferred stock, $100 par value; issued 1,000 shares	$100,000
Dividends in arrears (2 years × $6,000)	12,000
Total equity of preferred stockholders	$112,000
Number of shares outstanding	1,000
Book value per share	$ 112

The book value of a share of common stock is computed as shown:

Total stockholders' equity	$260,000
Deduct equity of preferred stockholders	112,000
Total equity of common stockholders	$148,000
Number of shares outstanding	1,000
Book value per share	$ 148

If the preferred stock is participating, an additional portion of the retained earnings is allocated to the preferred stockholders' equity based on the participation provisions. Hence, in computing the book value of preferred stock, its preference rights—dividends in arrears, dividend participation rights, and preference in dividing the assets on dissolution—must be known.

The book value and the market value of a share of stock may be and usually are different in amount. The market value of a share of stock—the price that a share of stock commands on the stock exchange—reflects price level changes, available investment funds, economic, political, and psychological factors, and so on. Since these factors are not reflected in the accounts, there is often a disparity between book and market values. The book value per share is what each stockholder would receive for each share held in the theoretical event of liquidation after the assets are sold without gain or loss. Since the valuations on the books—especially for inventories and plant and equipment—do not necessarily reflect market conditions, the book value of a share of stock may be of little significance as an indicator of the resale value of the stock.

Of greater usefulness to the investor are the ratios of earnings and dividends to the market value of the shares, because it is the cash represented by the market value of the shares that can be put to other uses. Three such ratios are

$$\text{Earnings yield rate} = \frac{\text{Earnings per share}}{\text{Market value per share}}$$

$$\text{Dividend yield rate} = \frac{\text{Dividends per share}}{\text{Market value per share}}$$

$$\text{Price-earnings ratio} = \frac{\text{Market price per share}}{\text{Earnings per share}}$$

A careful analysis of the relationship and trend of these ratios indicates the profitability of the firm as related to the market value of its shares, its ability to pay dividends, and its growth prospects.

Earnings per Share

Reported earnings, earnings per share, and the selling price of shares expressed as a multiple of earnings per share are of primary interest to most investors. These figures are not a satisfactory substitute for a thorough financial analysis, but, investors consider them key tools in their investment decisions.

The introduction and popularity in the past decade of securities that were, in substance, the equivalent of common stock resulted in the issuance of APB Opinions Numbers 9 and 15 by the Accounting Principles Board of the American Institute of Certified Public Accountants (AICPA). These opinions require that earnings per share (EPS) be presented on the face of the income statement and provide specific guidelines for earnings per share calculations.

Prior to the issuance of Opinions 9 and 15, earnings per share were calculated by dividing net income applicable to common stock by the number of common shares outstanding. Opinion Number 15 calls for a dual reporting of EPS—primary EPS and fully diluted EPS—when convertible securities exist which, if exercised, would materially decrease the amount reported as EPS. Thus, convertible securities, stock options, warrants, stock purchase contracts, participating securities, two-class common stock, and agreements to issue stock in the future are included in EPS calculations on an "as if" converted basis. The calculations are based on the assumption that common stock is issued for those securities which are considered to be either (1) common stock equivalents (warrants, stock options) or (2) other securities with conversion privileges (convertible preferred stock, convertible debt) which would dilute reported EPS when converted.

The opinions have thus converted EPS from a historically oriented figure to a pro forma and predictive figure. Calculations are twofold—(1) primary EPS based on the outstanding common stock plus common stock equivalents, and (2) fully diluted EPS based on primary EPS plus the number of common shares represented by convertible securities not included in primary EPS.

To illustrate, assume a company with the following earnings and equities:

Net income	$100,000
6-percent convertible bonds, convertible three common shares for each $100 bond	$ 60,000
6-percent convertible preferred stock, $100 par, convertible one common share for each share of preferred.	1,000 shares
Common stock	10,000 shares
Calculation of primary EPS:	
Actual net income (A)	$100,000
Adjusted shares outstanding:	
Actual shares outstanding	10,000
Additional shares issuable to preferred stockholders	1,000
Adjusted shares outstanding (B)	11,000
Primary EPS (A ÷ B)	$ 9.09

Calculation of fully diluted EPS:

Adjusted net income:	
Actual net income	$100,000
Interest reduction if bonds converted; 6-percent net of 50-percent tax effect (0.06 × $60,000) .5	1,800
Adjusted net income (A)	$101,800
Adjusted shares outstanding:	
Actual shares outstanding	10,000
Additional shares issuable:	
To preferred shareholders	1,000
To bondholders (600 × 3)	1,800
Adjusted shares outstanding (B)	12,800
Fully diluted EPS (A ÷ B)	$7.95

CONTRIBUTED CAPITAL IN THE STATEMENT OF FINANCIAL POSITION

The Stockholders' Equity section of the Dwight Corporation's statement of financial position as of December 31, 1973, is shown in Figure 12-2. Each item in the statement is numbered and is discussed in the following paragraphs. Duplicate numbers are used for related items. Brief technical account titles may be used, for convenience, in journal and ledgers because these records are for internal use only and the functions of the accounts are understood by the users. However, for external reporting, these account titles should either be replaced or be supplemented by descriptive language to minimize possible misunderstanding by nontechnical readers of the statement. The nature and significance of the items should not be obscured by the use of jargon or the absence of supporting detail.

(1) On the date of its organization, the Dwight Corporation issued 2,000 shares of preferred stock at $105 per share. The total par value of these shares (2,000 × $100 = $200,000) is labeled Preferred Stock. This amount represents part of the legal, or stated, capital. The excess ($5 × 2,000) over the par value of the preferred stock is reported separately as Premium on Preferred Stock.

(2) The Dwight Corporation also issued 5,000 shares of no-par value common stock at $60 per share. The stated value of the shares—originally $50 per share but reduced to $40 per share on December 31—multiplied by the number of shares issued ($40 × 5,000) is shown as Common Stock. The excess of the issue price ($60) over the original stated value ($50) multiplied by the number of shares issued ($10 × 5,000), not being a part of the stated capital, is shown separately as Excess over Stated Value on Common Stock. The excess of the original stated value ($50) over the revised stated value ($40), multiplied by the number of shares issued ($10 × 5,000), is also entered separately, for the same reason; it is labeled Excess from Reduction of Stated Value of 5,000 Shares of Common Stock from $50 to $40 Per Share.

(3) On July 10, the Dwight Corporation acquired 1,000 shares of its own common stock for $55 per share. On August 2, it sold 500 shares for $60 per share. The excess of the issue price over the cost is shown as Contributed Capital from Treasury Stock Transactions.

Figure 12-2. Partial Statement of Financial Position–Stockholders' Equity

DWIGHT CORPORATION
Partial Statement of Financial Position
December 31, 1973

Stockholders' Equity
  Contributed Capital

(1) Preferred Stock, 5 percent cumulative, nonparticipating, $100 par value, authorized 2,500 shares; issued 2,000 shares $200,000
(1) Premium on Preferred Stock 10,000

        Total Contributed by Preferred Stockholders $210,000
(2) Common Stock, no par value, $40 stated value, authorized 7,000 shares, issued 5,000 shares of which 500 shares are held in treasury $200,000
(2) Excess over Stated Valued on Common Stock 50,000
    Excess from Reduction of Stated Value of 5,000 shares of Common Stock from $50 to $40 per share 50,000
(3) From Treasury Stock Transactions—Common 2,500
(5) Common Stock Subscribed but not Issued 12,000

        Total Contributed by Common Stockholders 314,500
    Other Contributed Capital
(7)   Donation of Land by Town of Needham 50,000

        Total Contributed Capital $574,500
(8) Excess of Appraised Value of Land over Cost 10,000
(6) Retained Earnings (of which $27,500 is restricted for treasury stock acquisitions and $45,000 for anticipated plant expansion) 200,000

        Total $784,500
(4) Deduct cost of Treasury Stock—Common 27,500
        Total Stockholders' Equity $757,000

DWIGHT CORPORATION
Statement of Retained Earnings
For Year Ended December 31, 1973

(6) Retained Earnings, January 1, 1973 .... $130,000
(6) Net Income for 1973 120,000

    Total $250,000
(6) Dividends 50,000
    Retained Earnings, December 31, 1973 .... $200,000

(4) On July 10, the Dwight Corporation reacquired 1,000 shares of its own common stock for $55,000. The laws of the state in which it is incorporated limit the payment of dividends to the extent of the amount in the unrestricted Retained Earnings account. Since the effect of a purchase of treasury stock is the same as a cash dividend—a reduction in corporate assets and in the stockholders' equity—the limitation applies equally to dividend payments and to treasury stock acquisitions. A company with free retained earnings of $25,000, for example, may either reacquire treasury stock or declare cash dividends, or do both, provided the total disbursement is not over $25,000. Such a restriction prevents a corporation from by-passing restrictions on dividend distributions and improves the protection of the corporate

creditors. The amount of $27,500 ($55,000 from the transaction of July 10 less $27,500 from the transaction of August 2) appears twice in the Stockholders' Equity section: (1) as a parenthetical note following retained earnings and (2) as a reduction in the stockholders' equity resulting from a distribution of $27,500 in cash to the stockholders from whom the stock was acquired.

(5) Subscriptions have been received from key employees under a stock option plan for 300 shares of common stock. Stock certificates will be issued on receipt of the uncollected portion of the subscription price as shown in the asset account, Common Stock Subscriptions Receivable.

(6) The beginning retained earnings balance represents undistributed earnings from prior years. The corporation earned $120,000 from operations for the year; $50,000 was to be distributed to the stockholders on January 15, 1974; $72,500 was restricted for specific purposes; and the remainder, $127,500, is unrestricted.

(7) A building site with an estimated cash market value of $50,000 was donated by the town of Needham as an inducement to the Dwight Corporation to establish itself there. This gift increased the assets and the contributed capital.

(8) The $10,000 increase in the Land account following an appraisal of the current market value of the land increased the assets and the stockholders' equity.

SUMMARY

The sources of the stockholders' equity are contributed capital, retained earnings, and asset revaluations. The sources of contributed capital are (1) the par or stated value of capital stock issued or subscribed, or a stock dividend to be issued, (2) the excess over the par or stated value of capital stock, and (3) donations.

Donated assets are recorded at the fair market value of the assets received. When assets are revalued to reflect current market values—not a common practice—the increase should be credited to a special stockholders' equity account. Earnings from regular operating transactions—that is, increases in the stockholders' equity other than from transactions involving the company's own stock and from revaluations—are classified as retained earnings. A portion of the retained earnings may be segregated from the Retained Earnings account to indicate the intention of the board of directors to conserve corporate assets for purposes other than dividend distributions. Such restrictions may be voluntary or they may be required by state statute or by contract.

The term *dividend* refers to the distribution of cash, stock, or other corporate property to the stockholders. The charge is to accumulated unrestricted Retained Earnings. Preferred stockholders are entitled to a stated amount per share before any distribution is made to common stockholders. If the preferred stock is cumulative, undeclared dividends accumulate and must be paid together with the stated preference rate before any dividend payment is made on common stock. If the stock is participating, it receives its specified dividend rate and a share of any additional dividends declared. If the stock is preferred as to assets on liquidation of the firm, preferred stockholders must be paid before any liquidating payments are made to the common stockholders.

The term *stock dividend* refers to the issuance by a corporation of additional shares of its authorized stock without payment of any kind by the stockholders. The charge is to Retained Earnings. Hence, a stock dividend, unlike a cash dividend, has no effect on assets or the total stockholders' equity. Its effect is to transfer from Retained Earnings to Contributed Capital an amount equal to the fair value of the additional shares issued. If the additional shares are issued to reduce substantially the price at which the stock is being traded, or to reduce the par value, the action is termed a *stock split up*. There is no charge to retained earnings, and only a memorandum notation is made in the stock accounts.

Treasury stock is a corporation's own stock that has been issued and later reacquired. It is issued, but not outstanding, stock. Its acquisition reduces the assets and the stockholders' equity, and is reported in the position statement as a deduction from total contributed capital.

When treasury stock is reissued, the difference between the cost and the reissue price is recorded in a Contributed Capital from Treasury Stock Transactions account. In the absence of such an account, an excess of cost over selling price is debited to Retained Earnings. Shares acquired through donation are recorded by memorandum only; upon reissue, the proceeds are credited to Contributed Capital—Donations. In some states, a corporation must reduce the amount of retained earnings available for dividends by the cost of the shares issued and then reacquired.

The book value of a share of stock, when there is only one class of stock outstanding, is the total stockholders' equity divided by the number of shares outstanding. When there is more than one class outstanding, it is necessary to determine the claims of each class against the net assets of the corporation, taking into consideration preference rights—dividends in arrears, dividend participation rights, and preference as to assets on liquidation.

The ratios of earnings and dividends to the market value of the shares— earnings yield rate, dividend yield rate, and the price-earnings ratio—are more useful to the investor than book values. APB Number 15 requires a dual reporting of EPS—primary EPS and fully diluted EPS—when convertible securities exist which, if exercised, would materially decrease the amount reported as EPS.

QUESTIONS

Q12-1. (a) What are the major subdivisions of the Stockholders' Equity section of the statement of financial position? (b) Why must particular care be taken in subdividing the Stockholders' Equity section?

Q12-2. (a) What is the purpose of restricting retained earnings? (b) Is the restriction of retained earnings tantamount to the establishment of a special cash fund?

Q12-3. The following quotation is adapted from the notes to the financial statements of a large company, "Retained earnings of $28,500,000 are restricted from payment of cash dividends on common stock because of a promissory note agreement. Further restrictions of $1,700,000 are made to cover the cost of the company's own common stock reacquired." What is the significance of this note to (a) a short-term creditor, (b) a long-term creditor, (c) a stockholder?

Q12-4. What is meant by the term *book value*? How is book value computed? Has it any real significance as a financial measure of the worth of stock?

Q12-5. The unclassified statement of financial position of the Quality Corporation is shown on page 436.

QUALITY CORPORATION
Statement of Financial Position
December 31, 1973

Assets

Cash	$ 15,000
Accounts Receivable	35,000
Merchandise Inventory	40,000
Other Assets	10,000
Total Assets	$100,000

Liabilities and Stockholders' Equity

Liabilities		
Accounts Payable		$ 15,000
Notes Payable		5,000
Total Liabilities		$ 20,000
Stockholders' Equity		
Common Stock, $100 par value	$50,000	
Retained Earnings	30,000	80,000
Total Liabilities and Stockholders' Equity		$100,000

The members of the board of directors are considering several dividend distribution plans. They seek your advice with respect to these alternatives: (a) a cash dividend of 20 percent, (b) a stock dividend of 50 percent, (c) no dividend distribution. Discuss.

Q12-6. Preferred stock enjoys certain preferences. (a) What are these preferences? (b) How do they affect dividend distributions?

Q12-7. (a) What is a stock dividend? (b) What conditions prompt the declaration of a stock dividend? (c) How does a stock dividend affect (1) the total stockholders' equity, (2) the total assets, (3) the book value per share, (4) the taxable income of the recipient, (5) the market price per share?

Q12-8. (a) What is accomplished by a stock split-up? (b) How is it recorded? (c) How does it affect (1) the total stockholders' equity, (2) the book value per share, (3) the market price per share?

Q12-9. (a) What is treasury stock? (b) Why do corporations buy back their own shares? (c) How does the reacquisition of its own shares affect a company's financial position? (d) Why do some states place certain restrictions on treasury stock acquisitions? (e) How is the purchase of treasury stock recorded? (f) How is the issuance of treasury stock recorded? (g) How does the issuance of treasury stock affect the financial statements?

Q12-10. *Limited liability* is one of the distinguishing characteristics of the corporate form of organization. In state corporation law it is recognized in a number of the provisions relating to financial aspects of the corporation. Indicate three such provisions that are relevant to the financial and accounting aspects of the stockholders' equity.

EXERCISES

E12-1. The outstanding capital stock of the Jaspers Corporation consisted of the following:

5 percent Preferred Stock, par value $100 (3,000 shares)	$300,000
Common Stock, par value $50 (9,000 shares)	450,000

Earnings from operations for the year 1973 were $80,000. Compute the earnings per share on the preferred and common stock.

E12-2. The Stockholders' Equity section of the Slater Company's statement of financial position shows the following:

Common Stock, no-par value, issued 10,000 shares	$330,000
Retained Earnings	70,000
Total	$400,000

What is the cumulative effect on stockholders' equity of each of the following events, occurring in sequence: (a) the declaration of a 10-percent stock dividend; (b) the distribution of the dividend; (c) the acquisition of 100 shares of the company's own stock for $20 per share; (d) the issuance of these shares for $22 per share; (e) the declaration of a $2-per-share cash dividend; (f) the payment of the dividend.

E12-3. The Truro Corporation, having 100,000 shares of $15 par value common stock authorized and issued, finds itself in need of working capital. The stockholders agree to donate 10 percent of their holdings to the corporation. The shares are then reissued at $15 per share. Record the transactions.

E12-4. The Whole Milk Company restricted retained earnings of $25,000 to cover a lawsuit by a customer. The lawsuit was ultimately settled for $18,750. Make all the necessary journal entries.

E12-5. The Wheaton Corporation has issued and outstanding 2,000 shares of $100 par value common stock and 1,000 shares of $100 par value 6-percent cumulative and nonparticipating preferred stock. Jerome Calmos owns 10 shares of the common stock, which he purchased at $55 per share; Leon Curley owns 10 shares of preferred stock, which he acquired for $110 per share. (a) What basic rights and privileges does Calmos have? (b) Curley? (c) How are these shares reported on the Wheaton Corporation's statement of financial position? (d) How much will Calmos and Curley each receive if over a three-year period the corporation distributes earnings of $5,000, $12,000, and $30,000? (e) How much would Curley receive if the preferred stock were cumulative and participating?

E12-6. The Staht Corporation entered into an agreement with the town of Danville to build a plant there. The town donated land and buildings valued at $25,000 and $75,000, respectively. Record the transaction.

E12-7. The Creek Corporation was authorized to issue 100,000 shares of $2 par value common stock, all of which was issued to the principal incorporator in payment for machinery and equipment he sold to the corporation. Shortly thereafter, the incorporator donated 50,000 shares to the corporation. The shares were then reissued for cash at an average price of $1.75 per share.

a. Make all the necessary journal entries.
b. Prepare statements of financial position immediately before and immediately after the reissuance of the donated shares.

E12-8. The capital stock of the Fishman Corporation consists of no-par value common stock with a $10 stated value. Record: (a) the issuance of 500 shares at $15 per share, (b) the reacquisition of 100 shares at $12 per share (restriction of retained earnings is not required), (c) the reissuance of the treasury stock at $16 per share, (d) a reduction in the stated value to $5 per share, (e) a 2-for-1 stock split-up.

E12-9. The Drew Corporation has issued and outstanding 2,000 shares of common stock and 1,000 shares of 5-percent preferred stock, each with a par value of $100. Retained earnings are $50,000, and the directors declare a $25,000 cash dividend. Record the dividend declaration, assuming that (a) the preferred stock is cumulative and nonparticipating and there are no dividends in arrears; (b) the preferred stock is cumulative and participates up to $3 per share above the regular 5-percent rate; (c) the preferred stock is cumulative and fully participating, and there was no dividend declaration during the previous year.

E12-10. The Georgia Mining Company's statement of financial position shows the following:

Common Stock, par value $100; 6,000 shares	$600,000
Retained Earnings	200,000

Give the effect on these accounts of each of the following situations: (a) All the stock is called in and 12,000 shares of no-par value stock is issued, the entire proceeds constituting legal capital. (b) The old shares are replaced by 12,000 shares of no-par value, $60 stated value common stock. (c) Each stockholder receives a stock dividend of one additional share for every three shares he now holds.

E12-11. Indicate the effect, if any, of each of the following transactions on total retained earnings of the Bowe Company.

1. The board of directors declared a stock dividend to be issued one month from the current date.
2. Issued the stock dividend declared in transaction 1.
3. Wrote off accounts receivable against the Allowance for Doubtful Accounts.
4. Paid accounts payable.
5. Collected accounts receivable.
6. Issued $100 par value common stock at $97 per share.
7. Restricted retained earnings for contingencies.
8. Issued $100 par value preferred stock at $103 per share.
9. Purchased machinery on open account.
10. Issued long-term notes and received cash in return.

E12-12. On July 31, 1973, the directors of the Budlow Corporation, after a successful year with its new products, declared $60,000 in dividends on all classes of stock. There are outstanding 4,000 shares of $50 par value, 6-percent cumulative preferred stock participating to 9 percent, and 20,000 shares of no par common stock. Dividends are in arrears for the preceding two years on the preferred stock. Common stock also has not received any dividends for the preceding two years. The same number of shares of preferred stock was outstanding on July 31, 1972; however, on July 31, 1971, only 3,000 shares of preferred stock were outstanding. The Common Stock account has remained unchanged for more than three years. Compute the amount of dividends each class will receive as a result of the dividend declaration.

E12-13. The following is part of note 8 accompanying the August 31, 1970, balance sheet of the Gordon Jewelry Corporation:

Capital Stock

Each holder of Class A Stock or Class B Stock has one vote per share. Each and all shares vote as one class except that they are entitled to vote separately by classes in cases of certain amendments to the certificate of incorporation affecting the rights of the capital stock, and except as may be required by law. The holders of the Class A Stock and the Class B Stock are entitled to receive dividends when and as declared by the Board of Directors. Cash dividends must be declared and paid on each class at the same time but dividends on Class B Stock shall be 5 percent (or $\frac{1}{20}$th) per share of the dividends per share on Class A Stock. The holders of Class A Stock and Class B Stock participate equally share for share in any stock or liquidating dividends to stockholders. The shares of Class B Stock are convertible into Class A Stock at any time at the option of the holder on a share-for-share basis. On June 1, 1980, should any share of Class B Stock be outstanding, they shall each, without further action of the company or the holder thereof, become one share of Class A Stock.

Give some reasons why a company might issue more than one class of capital stock. What are the advantages to the stockholders? to the corporation?

DP12-1. (*Recording corporate transactions; stockholders' equity*) Following is the Stockholders' Equity section of the statement of financial position of the Benson Corporation as of December 31, 1972:

Common Stock, no-par value; Issued and outstanding 25,000 shares		$300,000
Retained Earnings		
Restricted		
For Lawsuit Damages	$ 25,000	
For Plant Expansion	125,000	
Unrestricted	75,000	225,000
Total Stockholders' Equity		$525,000

The following transactions occurred during the year 1973 (restriction of retained earnings is required).

1. Acquired 5,000 shares of its own common stock at $10 per share.
2. Paid $5,000 in settlement of the lawsuit for injuries.
3. Issued 2,500 shares of treasury stock at $15 per share.
4. One of the stockholders donated land and a building worth $20,000 and $80,000, respectively.
5. Paid a cash dividend of $1 per share.
6. Reduced the retained earnings restriction for plant expansion by $100,000.
7. Wrote off organization costs of $10,000.
8. Net income for the year after income taxes was $50,000 (make the closing entry).

Required:

1. Enter the December 31, 1972, balances in T accounts.
2. Journalize the transactions and post to the appropriate accounts.
3. Prepare the Stockholders' Equity section of the statement of financial position as of December 31, 1973.
4. What is the effect of the retained earnings restrictions on (a) the financial statements, and (b) the individual shareholders?
5. Why did the company write off its organization costs?

DP12-2. (*Effect of cash and stock dividends*) The Stockholders' Equity section of the Brightman Corporation's statement of financial position consists of the following accounts:

Common Stock, $100 par value; issued 1,000 shares	$100,000
Retained Earnings	25,000
Total Stockholders' Equity	$125,000

Required:

1. (a) Prepare the journal entries to record the declaration and the payment of a $10-per-share cash dividend. (b) Compute the book value per share of the common stock immediately before the declaration of the dividend and immediately after the payment of the dividend.
2. Assume that the corporation declares a stock dividend instead of a cash dividend, each stockholder to receive one dividend share for each 10 shares he now holds. Complete Requirements 1a and 1b based on this assumption.
3. John Fellner owns 20 shares of Brightman Corporation stock. What was his equity (a) before the stock dividend and (b) after the stock dividend?
4. Discuss the purpose, advantages, and disadvantages of a stock dividend from the viewpoint of (a) the stockholder and (b) the issuing corporation.

5. Suppose the board of directors declared a 2-for-1 stock split which the stockholders approved. How would this affect John Fellner? The company's position statement? The earnings per share?

DP12-3. (*Computing dividend distributions*) The Loew Corporation has outstanding 5,000 shares of $100 par value common stock and 5,000 shares of $100 par value 5-percent preferred stock. The board of directors declared a cash dividend of $100,000.

Required:

Journalize the declaration of the cash dividend based on each of the following assumptions:

1. The preferred stock is cumulative and nonparticipating.
2. The preferred stock is cumulative and fully participating.
3. The preferred stock is cumulative and nonparticipating, and dividends have not been declared for the current year or for the two years preceding the current year.
4. The preferred stock is cumulative and fully participating, and dividends have not been declared for the current year or the preceding year.
5. Assume the same facts as in Requirement 4 except that the board of directors declared a cash dividend of $65,000.

DP12-4. (*Financial policy decision problem*) The 1969 annual report of Boise Cascade states in a note to its financial statements that "The terms of certain note agreements restrict the payment of cash dividends on common stock. The amount of retained earnings not so restricted on December 31, 1969, was approximately $122,000,000.

Required:

1. Of what usefulness is the statement regarding the amount of restricted retained earnings? of the amount not restricted?
2. The cash dividend distributions during 1969 were $14,908,000; net income for the year was $84,010,000. Do the stockholders have the right to dividends up to $14,908,000? up to $122,000,000?
3. Total shareholders' equity at December 31, 1969, was $860,703,000. Does this indicate what the shareholders would receive in the event of liquidation? of sale? Explain.

PROBLEMS

P12-1. On February 1, 1973, the McCormack Corporation was authorized to issue 20,000 shares of $20 par value common stock and 1,000 shares of 6-percent preferred stock, $100 par value. The following transactions occurred between February 1 and December 31, 1973:

1. Received subscriptions for 5,000 shares of common stock at $20 per share and 1,000 shares of preferred stock at $101 per share.
2. Purchased the assets of the Heinch Company at their fair cash value; the assets consisted of land worth $15,000, buildings worth $125,000, and plant and equipment worth $175,000. Issued 15,000 shares of common stock in payment.
3. Collected in full for the stock subscribed in transaction 1.
4. Purchased 500 shares of its own common stock at $18.75 per share. (The laws of the state of incorporation require a restriction of retained earnings equal to the cost of treasury stock.)
5. Established a restriction on retained earnings for contingencies of $10,000.
6. Issued 200 shares of treasury stock for $19 per share.
7. Earnings through December 31 after Federal income taxes were $72,000 (make the closing entry).
8. Declared a $.50-per-share dividend on the common stock and a $3 dividend on the preferred stock.

Required:

1. Record the transactions in appropriate T accounts.
2. Prepare the Stockholders' Equity section of the statement of financial position as of December 31, 1973.

P12-2. The Stockholders' Equity section of the Dunn Corporation's statement of financial position as of June 30, 1972, is shown below.

Stockholders' Equity

Common Stock, $100 par value; issued 1,000 shares	$100,000
Retained Earnings	50,000
Total Stockholders' Equity	$150,000

The following transactions occurred during the next 12 months:

1. Established a retained earnings restriction of $8,000 for a pending lawsuit.
2. Received, as a donation from the town of Lee, land and a building worth $10,000 and $90,000, respectively.
3. Received 100 shares of stock as a gift from one of the stockholders of the corporation.
4. Declared a 2-percent stock dividend. The shares to be issued are currently quoted at $110 per share.
5. Purchased 50 shares of its own stock for $108 per share.
6. Issued the stock certificates for the stock dividend.
7. Issued 50 of the donated shares for $5,500.
8. Issued 25 shares of treasury stock for $3,000.
9. Net income for the year after income taxes was $25,000 (make the closing entry).

Required:

1. Enter the balances as of June 30, 1972, in T accounts.
2. Record the transactions directly into the T accounts.
3. Prepare the Stockholders' Equity section of the statement of financial position as of June 30, 1973.

P12-3. The condensed statement of financial position of the Glass Corporation as of December 31, 1973, was as follows:

Total Assets	$725,000
Liabilities	$200,000
Preferred Stock, 7-percent, $100 par value; cumulative	100,000
Common Stock, no-par value; stated value $10	300,000
Retained Earnings	50,000
Premium on Preferred Stock	10,000
Excess over Stated Value of Common Stock	15,000
Retained Earnings–Restricted for Plant Expansion	50,000
Total Liabilities and Stockholders' Equity	$725,000

Required:

1. Find the book value per share of common stock, assuming that there are no dividend arrearages. The liquidating value of the preferred stock is equal to the par value.
2. Find the book value per share of common stock, assuming that dividends on the preferred stock are in arrears for the years 1972 and 1973.
3. What is the significance of the book value per share?
4. What is the interrelationship between book value per share and market value per share?

P12-4. (*Accounting policy decision problem*) The following information is taken from the Stockholders' Equity section of the Lynn Corporation's statement of financial position as of December 31, 1973:

Preferred Stock, 6-percent, cumulative and nonparticipating, $100 par value; authorized and issued 1,500 shares	$150,000
Common Stock, no-par value; stated value $20; authorized 20,000 shares; issued 10,000 shares	200,000
Excess over Stated Value of Common Stock	420,000
Retained Earnings–Restricted for Plant Expansion	40,000
Retained Earnings–Restricted for Bond Redemption	20,000
Retained Earnings–Unrestricted	150,000
Total Stockholders' Equity	$980,000

Dividends on the preferred stock are in arrears for 1972 and 1973.

Required:

1. Compute the book value per share of the common stock.
2. Assume that the market value of the Lynn Corporation stock was twice the book value per share. Does this indicate that faulty accounting principles or procedures were used? Give some reasons for the difference in book and market values per share.

P12-5. The following account balances were taken from the ledger of the Spark Company as of December 31, 1973:

Excess from Revaluation of Building	$ 30,000
Premium on Preferred Stock	25,000
Contributed Capital–Donated	60,000
Contributed Capital from Treasury Stock Transactions–Common	5,000
Preferred Stock, 6-percent, $100 par value; issued 4,000 shares	400,000
Retained Earnings–Restricted for Plant Additions	80,000
Retained Earnings–Restricted for Contingencies	10,000
Contributed Capital–Excess of Original Stated Value over Revised Stated Value of Common Stock	75,000
Common Stock, no-par value; stated value $20; issued 10,000 shares	200,000
Retained Earnings	165,000
Treasury Stock–Common	50,000
Contributed Capital–Excess over Stated Value of Common Stock	20,000
Estimated Income Taxes Payable	48,000
Organization Costs	10,000

Required:

1. Prepare the Stockholders' Equity section of the statement of financial position as of December 31, 1973.
2. Give a brief statement of the origin and function of each account.

P12-6. A listing of the balances of all the Stockholders' Equity accounts, taken from the statement of financial position of Tappan Inc., at December 31, 1973, is given below.

Preferred stock, $100 par value; 6-percent, cumulative; entitled to $105 per share plus cumulative dividends in arrears in liquidation; authorized 10,000 shares, issued 8,000 shares of which 500 are held in treasury	$800,000

Paid-In capital in excess of par value of preferred stock	24,000
Paid-In capital from treasury stock transactions–preferred	2,000
Common stock, no-par value; stated value $40; authorized 20,000 shares, issued 16,000 shares	640,000
Stock dividend, to be issued at stated value 4,000 common shares	160,000
Paid In capital in excess of stated value of common stock	56,000
Paid-In capital from stock dividend–common stock	16,000
Discount on common stock	1,000
Land donated by Suffolk County	15,000
Retained earnings	
Restricted in the amount of treasury stock purchased at cost	41,500
Unrestricted	100,300
Treasury stock, preferred—at cost	41,500

Required:

1. Prepare a properly classified Stockholders' Equity section.
2. Compute (a) the amount contributed by the preferred stockholders, (b) the amount contributed by the common stockholders, (c) the book value per share of common stock, (d) the book value per share of preferred stock, assuming that one year's preferred dividends are in arrears.
3. How does the reacquisition by a company of its own shares affect (a) the financial statements, and (b) the individual shareholders?

P12-7. The Stockholders' Equity section of the Jersey Corporation's statement of financial position as of December 31, 1972, was as follows:

Stockholders' Equity	
Capital Stock	
Preferred Stock, 5-percent, $100 par value; authorized and issued 2,000 shares	$200,000
Common Stock, $40 par value; authorized and issued 10,000 shares	400,000
Premium on Common Stock	50,000
Retained Earnings	200,000
Total Stockholders' Equity	$850,000

Transactions for the year 1973 were

1. Declared a $60,000 cash dividend for 1973. (The preferred stock is cumulative and non-participating; there are no dividends in arrears.)
2. Paid the dividend declared in transaction 1.
3. Purchased 500 shares of its own preferred stock for $100 per share (a restriction of retained earnings is not required).
4. Established a restriction on retained earnings of $10,000 for contingencies.
5. Issued 300 shares of treasury stock for $105 per share.
6. Earnings from operations for the year after income taxes were $185,000 (make the closing entry).
7. Issued 200 shares of treasury stock for $90 per share.
8. The principal stockholder donated a warehouse valued at $35,000 to the corporation.

Required:

1. Prepare journal entries to record the transactions.
2. Post to T accounts.
3. Prepare the Stockholders' Equity section of the statement of financial position as of December 31, 1973.
4. Why do you think the principal stockholder donated his warehouse to the corporation?

P12-8. (*Accounting policy decision problem*) The following information was taken from the ledger of Scott, Inc., as of June 30, 1973:

Cash	$ 50,000
Accounts Receivable	200,000
Cash Dividends Payable	40,000
Organization Costs	1,500
Common Stock Subscribed	100,000
Preferred Stock Subscribed	200,000
Common Stock, $5 par value	300,000
Preferred Stock, $10 par value	500,000
Subscriptions Receivable–Common Stock	20,000
Subscriptions Receivable–Preferred Stock	50,000
Premium on Preferred Stock	45,000
Premium on Common Stock	25,000
Retained Earnings	125,000
Retained Earnings–Restricted for Contingencies	15,000
Contributed Capital–Donated	20,000
Contributed Capital from Treasury Stock Transactions—Common	9,000
Retained Earnings–Restricted for Retirement of Preferred Stock	35,000
Discount on Common Stock	15,000
Allowance for Doubtful Accounts	11,000
Retained Earnings–Restricted for Plant Addition	45,000
Estimated Income Taxes Payable	23,000
Accumulated Depreciation–Building	18,000

Required:

1. Prepare the Stockholders' Equity section of the statement of financial position as of June 30, 1973.
2. Give several possible alternatives in the manner of grouping and sequencing the accounts when preparing the stockholders' equity section of the statement of financial position.
3. Which of the subtotals in the stockholders' equity section are most significant to the reader? Why?

P12-9. The Bellow Corporation was organized on January 2, 1973, with authority to issue 10,000 shares of no-par value common stock and 5,000 shares of 6-percent preferred stock, $100 par value. During 1973, the following transactions occurred:

1. Received subscriptions to 500 shares of preferred stock at $103 per share. Collected down payments of $10,000.
2. Issued 4,000 shares of common stock for cash at $13 per share. A stated value of $10 per share is set by the board of directors for the common stock.
3. Issued 100 shares of common stock, in lieu of a $10,000 fee, to the corporation's attorneys for their services in drafting the articles of incorporation and a set of bylaws.
4. Received additional payments of $33,000 from subscribers to preferred stock; 310 shares are issued to the subscribers who paid in full.
5. Acquired 200 shares of common stock for $2,500 from the estate of a deceased stockholder.
6. Received the balance of subscriptions due and issued the shares.
7. Reissued the 100 shares of the treasury stock acquired in transaction 5 at $16 per share.
8. Declared a 6-percent dividend on preferred stock and a $0.30-per-share dividend on common stock. The dividends are payable on January 15, 1974, to stockholders of records on December 31, 1973. The board also authorized the restriction of retained earnings of $6,000 for plant expansion.

Required:

Prepare the journal entries to record the transactions.

P12-10. (*Financial policy decision problem*) An analysis of the Treasury Stock account of Karl, Inc., shows the following debit entries during 1973:

Date	Lot No.	Description	No. of Shares	Class of Stock	Amount
1973					
Jan. 10	1	Purchase	120	Common	$4,800
Feb. 15	2	Purchase	80	Preferred	1,600
Apr. 20	3	Purchase	50	Common	2,100
May 2	4	Gift	25	Preferred	625
2	5	Gift	25	Common	800

The following credit entries were made:

1973					
Feb. 5	1	Sale	50	Common	$2,200
11	1	Sale	20	Common	860
16	1	Sale	20	Common	780
29	2	Sale	70	Preferred	1,750
Apr. 20	3	Sale	40	Common	1,840
22	1	Sale	20	Common	700
July 20	4	Sale	25	Preferred	500
26	5	Sale	20	Common	400

The bookkeeper has followed the policy of debiting the account at cost for purchases and at the prevailing market price for gifts; all credits to the account are for the net proceeds from sales. The common stock was originally issued at a substantial premium; the preferred stock was originally issued at par value.

Required:

1. Give the journal entries to correct the Treasury Stock account (compute costs by specific identification).
2. Give the journal entry to restrict an amount of retained earnings equal to the cost of the shares on hand.
3. Is it appropriate for a company to trade in its own stock?
4. Give some reasons why a company may want to reacquire its own shares.

P12-11. (*Financial policy decision problem*) The 1969 annual report of the AMK Corporation included explanatory note 5, a portion of which is shown below:

Shareholders' Equity

The Board of Directors on June 3, 1968 declared a 100-percent common stock distribution on common shares, payable July 15, 1968. The per share amounts in the consolidated statement of income have been adjusted retroactively to reflect this July 1968 stock distribution.

Series preference stock, no par value, amounting to 1,000,000 shares have been authorized. The initial series of such series preference stock is the $3.20 preference stock of which 215,000 shares are authorized and 76,654 are outstanding. This preference stock ranks junior as to dividends and in liquidation to the $3.00 preferred stock of which 112,254 shares are authorized and 47,088 are outstanding.

The $3.00 preferred and the $3.20 preference shares are each convertible into 3.6 common shares, have liquidating preferences of $65 and $100 per share, respectively, redeemable beginning in 1972 at $68 and $103 per share, respectively, and are entitled to one vote per share. The company has been advised by counsel that there are no restrictions on income retained in the business as a result of the excess of liquidating preference over stated value of the preferred stocks.

In January 1969, the company increased the number of authorized shares of common stock from 7,000,000 to 45,000,000 shares. Of the common shares authorized but unissued at December 31, 1969, a total of 15,949,307 were reserved for conversion of preferred stocks and convertible subordinated debentures and for exercise of stock options and warrants.

Required:

1. What was achieved by the 100% common stock distribution (a) from the corporation's viewpoint, and (b) from the stockholders' viewpoint?
2. How did the stock distribution affect the statement of financial position?
3. What is the purpose of the conversion privilege attaching to the preferred shares.
4. What is the significance of the advice by counsel regarding retained earnings restrictions?
5. Give some reasons for the large increase in the number of authorized shares of common stock.

P12-12. (*Financial policy decision problem*) The income statement of the Champion Corporation for the year ended December 31, 1973 was as follows:

Revenue		$100,000
Costs and expenses		
(exclusive of interest		
on bonds)	$75,000	
Interest on bonds	5,000	80,000
Net income before taxes		$ 20,000
Income taxes (50%)		10,000
Net income		$ 10,000

The following securities were outstanding:

	Units
No-par common stock (shares)	1000
5-percent bonds, $1000 maturity value,	
each convertible into	
10 shares of common	
stock.	100

Required:

1. Compute the primary and fully diluted earnings per share (assume the bonds do not qualify as common stock equivalents).
2. Assume that, in addition to the above, there are outstanding 500 shares of 5-percent preferred stock, $100 par, each convertible into one share of common stock. Compute primary and fully diluted earnings per share.
3. Calculate primary and fully diluted earnings per share, assuming the bonds qualify as common stock equivalents.

P12-13. (*Financial policy decision problem*) Comment on each of the following statements extracted from published annual reports:
a. Alberto-Culver Company (1970):

Earnings Per Share

Per share computations are based on the average number of shares outstanding during the year, adjusted to include shares issued in poolings of interests. Conversion of convertible debt, exercise of stock options and warrants, and issuance of contingent shares would not result in a material dilution of earnings per share.

b. AMK Corporation (1969):

Per Share Income Data

Per share income amounts have been calculated in accordance with Opinion Number 15 of the Accounting Principles Board of the American Institute of Certified Public

Accountants. In compliance with this opinion the company has elected to classify as common stock equivalents (common shares assumed to be outstanding for the calculation of primary earnings per share) only those securities issued prior to June 1, 1969, which were classified as residual securities under Accounting Principles Board Opinion Number 9. As a result, the company's preferred stocks are considered common stock equivalents and the computation of primary earnings per share gives effect to the full conversion of the preferred stocks into common shares. Fully diluted earnings per share assume, in addition to full conversion of preferred stocks, exercise of the outstanding warrants and the outstanding stock options with the proceeds applied in the following steps:

(a) Purchase 20 percent of the company's common stock outstanding at average market price during the period.
(b) Payment of all long and short-term obligations including convertible subordinated debentures and,
(c) The balance invested in government securities.

The weighted average number of shares for the primary computation was 8,352,000 and 4,959,000 for 1969 and 1968, and for the fully diluted computation was 16,675,000 and 5,421,000 shares, respectively.

c. Electronic Memories & Magnetics Corporation (1969):

Earnings per Common and
Common Equivalent Share

Earnings per common and common equivalent share is based on the weighted average number of common and common equivalent shares outstanding during the periods. The number of shares used in the calculation of earnings per common and common equivalent share in 1969 and 1968 (adjusted for the 1969 2-for-1 split) is 4,498,398 and 4,583,686, respectively. Earnings per common share—assuming full dilution is based upon the common and common equivalent shares outstanding plus the common shares that would have been issued had the 5½-percent subordinated bonds been converted when issued in 1969 and, in 1968, had the 4¾-percent convertible subordinated debentures been converted when issued. Conversion of the preferred stock and issuance of contingent shares have not been assumed as their effect on earnings per share is antidilutive.

　　In computing the per share effect of assumed exercise of dilutive stock options, proceeds from the exercise of stock options are assumed to have been used to purchase shares of the company's common stock and the net increase in the number of shares outstanding has been added to the weighted average of shares outstanding. Interest charges (less applicable income tax) on the bonds and debentures have been added to income in computing the per share effect of the assumed conversions.

P12-14. (*Accounting and financial policy decision problems*) The Martin Development Corporation was formed 10 years ago to acquire real estate for the development of suburban housing and shopping areas. It was originally organized as a closed corporation, financed by the investments of five businessmen. During the first years of operations, the board of directors, which consisted of the five original stockholders, voted to restrict the payment of dividends and to reinvest all earnings, if any, in the expanding projects of the corporation. This policy was favored by all the members of the board of directors, although one of them, Peter Holt, was reluctant. To placate him, the other members did agree on different occasions to issue two stock dividends and a stock split-up.

　　After another year of operations, the board of directors agreed, except for Holt, to issue some preferred stock to a number of individuals who had indicated an interest in the organization. Holt, being suspicious of the motivations of the new investors, offered his stock to the corporation. The other members of the board of directors voted to buy all his shares at 10 percent more than their book value. Holt accepted the offer. Shortly thereafter, preferred stock was issued to the new investors.

A review of the sequence of events affecting the Stockholders' Equity section of the corporation's statement of financial position is given:

1. The corporate charter was received, authorizing the issuance of 20,000 shares of $100 par value voting common stock and 40,000 shares of $50 par value cumulative, 5-percent, participating to 6-percent (for the latest year only), nonvoting preferred stock. The preferred stock can become fully voting on a per-share basis when preferred dividends are in arrears, beginning with the third year of arrearage.
2. Each of the five original stockholders purchased 500 shares of common stock at par value.
3. The corporation reported a net loss of $8,500 for the first year of operations.
4. The corporation reported a net income of $17,500 for the second year of operations.
5. The directors voted to restrict all retained earnings for the expansion of operations.
6. The corporation reported a net income of $40,000 for the third year of operations.
7. The directors voted to restrict all retained earnings for the expansion of operations.
8. The directors voted to issue a 10-percent stock dividend and to release the appropriate amount of restricted retained earnings.
9. The corporation reported a net income of $55,000 for the fourth year of operations.
10. The directors voted to issue a 20-percent stock dividend.
11. The corporation reported a net income of $65,000 for the fifth year of operations.
12. The corporate charter was changed, authorizing the issuance of 50,000 shares of $50 par value voting common stock (the preferred stock authorization was not changed).
13. The directors voted a 2-for-1 common stock split-up.
14. The corporation reported a net income of $75,000 for the sixth year of operations.
15. Holt sold all his shares of common stock to the corporation for 110 percent of book value. The directors voted to restrict an equal amount of retained earnings.
16. New investors purchased 5,000 shares of preferred stock at par value.
17. The corporation reported a net income of $90,000 for the seventh year of operations.
18. At the end of the first two full years since the preferred stock was issued, the directors declared a $65,000 cash dividend.
19. The directors voted to sell one fourth of the treasury stock to another local investor for 5 percent more than its cost. An equal amount of retained earnings was released. The other three fourths of the treasury stock was canceled.
20. The corporation reported a net income of $80,000 for the eighth year of operations.

Required:

Answer the following questions in terms of the Martin Development Corporation.

1. Record the events in the corporation's general journal.
2. Describe the meaning of the following terms relating to capital stock: (a) capital stock authorized, (b) capital stock issued, (c) par value, (d) voting and nonvoting, (e) cumulative, (f) participating to 6-percent, (g) outstanding.
3. What purpose is served by restricting the retained earnings?
4. What is a stock dividend; what function does it normally serve?
5. What is a stock split-up; what function does it normally serve?
6. What is the book value? How is it determined?
7. Based on the information given, why did the directors decide to pay a cash dividend? What was the cash dividend amount per share? Show your calculations.
8. What was the amount of treasury stock? Is it an asset, a liability, part of the stockholders' equity, or a contra to one of these classifications? Why?
9. What are retained earnings? What is the source of retained earnings? Why is the amount of retained earnings not equal to the amount of cash on hand?
10. Prepare a partial statement of financial position that will disclose the stockholders' equity after all 20 events have been completed.

13

Short-Term Business Financing: Simple and Compound Interest

In periods of high interest rates, it is extremely important for managers to know the rudiments of both simple and compound interests. This chapter discusses the problems of simple interest and compound interest, and primarily how they are related to short-term business financing.

INTEREST: COMPOUND AND SIMPLE

Definition of Interest

Interest is the price of credit, a payment made (or collection received) for the use of money or the equivalent of money. Because it is similar to the price of merchandise, interest to the maker—the debtor—is an expense; to the payee—the creditor—interest is a revenue.

Simple Interest versus Compound Interest

Simple interest is interest on the original principal of a note or a time draft, regardless of interest amounts that may have accrued on the principal in past periods; whereas *compound interest* is interest that accrues on unpaid interest of past periods as well as on the principal. In other words, compound interest is interest earned on a principal sum that is increased at the end of each period by the interest for that period.

Illustration of Simple Interest Calculation

Assume that Richard Baldwin gives Edward Fenn a 6-percent, 60-day note that has a principal amount of $2,000.

449

The interest specified on a note or draft, unless otherwise indicated, is an annual rate on the principal, or face amount, of the instrument. Thus, in Richard Baldwin's note (see Figure 3-2), the price, or charge for the use of $2,000 for one year, is $120 ($2,000 × 0.06). Since the term of the note is less than one year, the interest must be computed by multiplying the interest amount for one year by a fraction; the numerator is the term of the note in days and the denominator, the number of days in a year. The formula is

$$\text{Principal} \times \text{Rate} \times \text{Time} = \text{Interest}$$

This is usually stated as $P \times R \times T = I$. In Baldwin's note, the interest calculation for the 60-day period is

$$\$2,000 \times 0.06 \times \frac{60}{360} = \$20$$

It is common commercial practice to assume that the year contains 360 days (or 12 months of 30 days each) in computing interest. This practice is followed here, but it should be understood that the amount of bias in the final interest calculation is 1/73, that is,

$$\frac{365 - 360}{365} = \frac{1}{73}$$

Time can be saved through various short-cut methods of computing interest. Two of these are referred to as the *6-percent, 60-day method* and the *6-percent, 6-day method*. Since the interest at 6 percent for 60 days on any principal is 1 percent (60/360 × 6%), interest at 6 percent for 60 days on any principal can be figured by moving the decimal point two places to the left in the principal, which is the same as multiplying the principal by 1 percent. Similarly, the interest at 6 percent for 6 days can be figured by moving the decimal point three places to the left in the principal. Either or both of these short methods may be used for note terms other than 6 or 60 days. The term of the note can be stated as a fraction or multiple of 6 or 60 days, and the interest may then be quickly computed.

Short methods can also be applied when the interest rate is other than 6 percent. The interest calculation is first made at 6 percent, then an adjustment is made for the difference between 6 percent and the particular rate.

The following two examples illustrate interest computation by the short methods:

1. Interest at 7 percent on $3,600 for 90 days:

Interest at 6% for 60 days	$36
Interest at 6% for 30 days (½ of $36)	18
Interest at 6% for 90 days	$54
Interest at 1% for 90 days (⅙ of $54)	9
Interest at 7% for 90 days	$63

2. Interest at $4\frac{1}{2}$ percent on $4,800 for 30 days:

Interest at 6% for 60 days	$48
Interest at 6% for 30 days (½ of $48)	$24
Less interest at 1½% for 30 days (¼ of $24)	6
Interest at 4½% for 30 days	$18

An advantage of the short methods is that they often require relatively simple arithmetical computations, thereby reducing the possibility of error. This is true when interest rates and terms are such that the mathematical manipulations are obvious, but if rates and terms require elaborate adjustments for the use of these methods (for example, 4.25 percent for 27 days), the calculation time will not be reduced, but increased. In such cases it is better to use the basic interest formula, $PRT = I$.

The Amount of a Single Sum at Compound Interest

A simple illustration of the interest compounded annually on a single sum of $100 for four years at 6 percent per year is

(1) Year	(2) Amount at Beginning of Year	(3) Annual Amount of Interest (Col. 2 × 0.06)	(4) Accumulated Amount at End of Year (Col. 2 + Col. 3)
1	$100.00	$ 6.00	$106.00
2	106.00	6.36	112.36
3	112.36	6.74	119.10
4	119.10	7.15	126.25
Total		$26.25	

The principal of $100 at the beginning of year 1 has by year 4 grown to $126.25, the *compound amount*.

Each amount in column 4 is 106 percent of the corresponding amount in column 2. This means that 106 percent, or 1.06, has been used as a multiplier four times; 1.06 has been raised to the fourth power. The compound amount is, therefore, $100 multiplied by 1.06 to the fourth power, as shown below.

1.06^1	1.2625
Multiplied by principal	$ 100
Compound amount	$126.25

The compound amount of 1 for n periods is expressed by the following formula:

$$a = (1 + i)^n$$

where a = compound amount of 1 ($1, or any other monetary unit) at interest for n periods

n = number of periods

i = periodic interest rate

The difference between the compound amount and the original principal is the compound interest. The compound interest (I) on 1 for four periods at 6 percent is computed as follows:

$$I = (1 + i)^n - 1$$
$$= (1 + 0.06)^4 - 1$$
$$= 1.2625 - 1$$
$$= 0.2625$$

The calculation of compound interest on $100 for four years at 6 percent compounded annually is

$$\$100 \times 0.2625 = \$26.25$$

Present Value

If $100 is worth $126.25 when it is left at 6-percent compound interest each year for four years, then it follows that $126.25 four years from now is worth $100 now; that is, $100 is the *present value* of $126.25. The present value is the amount that must be invested now to produce the known future value. In compound-amount problems, the future value of a known present value must be determined; in present-value problems, the present value of a known future value must be determined. If the known future value is $126.25, then the amount that must be invested now at 6 percent compounded annually to produce $126.25 is $100. The computation is as shown.

$$\frac{\$126.25}{(1 + 0.06)^4} = \frac{\$126.25}{1.2625} = \$100$$

The general formula for the present value (p) of 1 due in any number of periods is as follows:

$$p = \frac{1}{(1 + i)^n}$$

The present value of 1 at 6-percent interest compounded annually for four years is computed as shown.

$$p = \frac{1}{(1 + i)^n} = \frac{1}{(1 + 0.06)^4} = \frac{1}{1.2625} = 0.79208$$

If the present value of 1 is 0.79208, then the present value of $126.25 is computed as follows:

$$\$126.25 \times 0.79208 = \$100$$

If $100 is deposited at 6-percent interest compounded annually, it will amount to $126.25 in four years.

Compound Discount

Compound discount (D) is the difference between the future value and the present value; it is expressed by the following formula:

$$D = 1 - \frac{1}{(1 + i)^n}$$

The compound discount on 1 at 6-percent interest, compounded annually, is

$$D = 1 - \frac{1}{(1 + i)^n} = 1 - 0.79208 = 0.20792$$

Ordinary Annuity—Amount

An *ordinary annuity* is the sum of a series of equal payments or deposits (also called *rents*) at the end of equal intervals of time plus compound interest on these payments. The value of the annuity at the end of the successive time periods is the *amount of the annuity*. The calculation of the amount of an ordinary annuity of four payments of $100 each at 6 percent is shown in Figure 13-1.

Figure 13-1. Amount of an Ordinary Annuity

(1) Period	(2) Beginning Balance	(3) Interest Earned (6% × Col. 2)	(4) Periodic Payment	(5) Accumulated at End of Period (Col. 2 + Col. 3 + Col. 4)
1	$ –0–	$ –0–	$100	$100.00
2	100.00	6.00	100	206.00
3	206.00	12.36	100	318.36
4	318.36	19.10	100	437.46

The formula for finding the amount (A) of an ordinary annuity of 1 is as follows:

$$A = \frac{(1 + i)^n - 1}{i}$$

Since the numerator of this equation is the compound interest (I), the equation may be restated as

$$A = \frac{I}{i}$$

The amount of an ordinary annuity of $100 for four years at 6-percent interest compounded annually may be computed directly as follows.

$$A = \frac{I}{i} = \frac{0.2625}{0.06} \times \$100 = \$437.50$$

Figure 13-1 shows the amount to be $437.46. The $0.04 difference is due to rounding.

Ordinary Annuity—Present Value

The present value of an ordinary annuity is the present value of a series of payments to be made at equal intervals in the future; that is, it is the single sum that, if invested at compound interest now, provides for a stated series of payments or withdrawals at equal time intervals. The formula for the present value of an ordinary annuity of 1 is as follows:

$$P = \frac{1 - \dfrac{1}{(1 + i)^n}}{i}$$

Since the numerator of this equation is the compound discount, the equation may be restated as shown.

$$P = \frac{D}{i}$$

The present value of an ordinary annuity of four payments of $100 at 6 percent is calculated as follows:

$$P = \frac{D}{i} = \frac{0.20792}{0.06} \times \$100 = \$346.53$$

The proof that the present value of an ordinary annuity of four payments of $100 at 6 percent is $346.53 is shown.

Amount invested	$346.53
Interest earned, 1st period (6% × $346.53)	20.79
Amount at end of 1st period	$367.32
Deduct 1st payment	100.00
Balance of investment at beginning of 2d period	$267.32
Interest earned, 2d period (6% × $267.32)	16.04
Amount at end of 2d period	$283.36
Deduct 2d payment	100.00
Balance of investment at beginning of 3d period	$183.36
Interest earned, 3d period (6% × $183.36)	11.00
Amount at end of 3d period	$194.36
Deduct 3d payment	100.00
Balance of investment at beginning of 4th period	$ 94.36
Interest earned, 4th period (6% × $94.36)	5.66
Amount at end of 4th period	$100.02
Deduct 4th payment	100.00
Total (difference is due to rounding)	$000.02

The four basic formulas may be summarized in chart form, using the abbreviated notations, as follows:

$$\text{Present value} \longleftarrow p = \frac{1}{a} \longrightarrow \boxed{\text{Single payment}} \longrightarrow a = (1 + i)^n \longrightarrow \text{Future value}$$

$$\text{Present value} \longleftarrow P = \frac{D}{i} \longrightarrow \boxed{\begin{array}{c}\text{Series} \\ \text{of} \\ \text{payments}\end{array}} \longrightarrow A = \frac{I}{i} \longrightarrow \text{Future value}$$

Since $p = 1/a$, $D = 1 - p$, and $I = a - 1$, the formula for the amount of 1, $a = (1 + i)^n$ is the source for the derivation of the other formulas.

Use of Compound Interest Tables

Compound interest tables are available and are in common use in banking, industry, and elsewhere. Tables of a, p, A, and P of $1 for different periods and at various interest rates are illustrated in the Appendix tables on pages 853–856.

To illustrate how these tables are used, refer to page 853, which shows the present value of $1, ($p$). The figure in the 10-percent column for Period 10 is 0.386. This means that $1 due at the end of 10 years, compounded annually at 10-percent interest, if discounted, has a present worth or present value of $0.386; that is, if $0.386 were invested today at 10-percent interest compounded annually, it would accumulate to $1 in 10 years. The figures in the table are *discount factors* that produce the present value equivalent of any known future amount when multiplied by that amount. For example, 10 years from now to produce $6,750 at 10-percent interest compounded annually, $6,750 × 0.386, or $2,605.50, must be deposited.

The table on page 855 shows the present values of series of payments to be made at equal intervals in the future (P). For example, the figure in the 10-percent column for period 10 is 6.145. This means that $1 due at the end of each year for 10 years, compounded annually at 10-percent interest, has a present value of $6.145. The same result can be obtained by using the discount factors from the table on page 853 to accumulate each present value in the series. The table on page 855 shortens the process by giving a single discount factor for an entire series. The figures in the present value tables are discount factors that, when multiplied by any series of uniform amounts due at regular intervals in the future, produce the present equivalent of that series of amounts. For example, to produce $1,250 at the end of each year for 10 years at 10-percent interest compounded annually, $1,250 × 6.145, or $7,681.25, must be deposited.

The precomputed formula values for a and A as shown on pages 854 and 856 are used in a manner similar to that described for p and P above.

Uses of Compound Interest Techniques

Compound interest must be used to solve complex problems of calculating insurance probabilities, to determine values of investments at given interest yield rates, and to equate the time value of future sums of many management-type decisions. Elementary problems involving compound interest are illustrated in this chapter and Chapters 14, 24, and 25. Suggestions are made in several other chapters as to how the compound interest techniques could be used.

SHORT-TERM BUSINESS FINANCING

Types and Description of Short-Term Financing Devices

Business firms often find it more economical to use some means of short-term financing than to pay cash for various purchases. An extremely popular form of short-term financing is the purchase of merchandise, supplies, and equipment on 30-, 60-, or 90-day open charge accounts. Cash terms—no carrying charges are assigned—are often extended for a period of 90 days or more. During this period, cash may be obtained from new sales and used to pay for merchandise obtained on the open charge accounts. This form of financing has already been discussed in Chapter 5. Several other short-term financing devices are considered in this chapter, as follows:

1. Issuance of notes to trade creditors
2. Borrowing from banks on a company's own notes
3. Discounting notes receivable from customers

Managers faced with the decision as to which method to choose must consider for each method both its current and expected future availability and its effective cost. In general, a financial manager should choose the method or methods that will produce and continue to produce the desired short-term funds at the lowest long-run cost. In applying this general rule to specific financial decisions, management must consider such related variables as the availability of collateral, financial institutional connections, and the attendant effect on long-term debt financing.

MORE ABOUT PROMISSORY NOTES

A *negotiable promissory note* may be defined as an unconditional written promise to pay a specified sum of money to the order of a designated person, or to bearer, at a fixed or determinable future time or on demand.

A typical note is illustrated in Figure 13-2. Richard Baldwin, the *maker*, gives Edward Fenn, the designated *payee*, a 6-percent, 60-day note for $2,000, dated April 19, 1973, in payment for a purchase of merchandise.

Figure 13-2. A Promissory Note

> $ 2,000.00   Boston, Mass.   April 19, 1973
>
> Sixty days   after date   I   promise to pay
>
> to the order of   Edward Fenn
>
> Two Thousand and no/100   Dollars
>
> Payable at   First National Bank
>
> Value received   with interest at 6%
>
> No. 40   Due   June 18,   1973   *Richard Baldwin*

The outstanding characteristics of a note are the following:

1. The instrument must be in writing, signed by the maker.

2. The instrument must contain an unconditional promise to pay a sum certain in money.
3. The instrument may be payable to the order of a designated person, the payee, or it may be payable to bearer (that is, anyone who holds the note).
4. The instrument must be payable either on demand or at a determinable time in the future.
5. The instrument may or may not be interest bearing.

The ownership of a negotiable promissory note is transferred simply by delivery if it is payable to the bearer; otherwise, it is transferred by endorsement and delivery.

A *blank endorsement* consists of a signature of the owner, or the payee, on the back of the instrument. A *full endorsement* consists of a notation on the back of the document, "Pay to the order of the Blank Company," accompanied by the signature of the owner. If the endorser—the owner who is transferring the document—wishes to pass title to the instrument and at the same time to relieve himself of any further liability, he places his signature on the back of the note and adds the phrase "without recourse" (this is a *qualified endorsement*).

From the viewpoint of the maker, Richard Baldwin, the note illustrated in Figure 13-2 is a liability and is recorded by crediting Notes Payable. From the viewpoint of the payee, Edward Fenn, however, the same note is an asset and is recorded by debiting Notes Receivable. At the maturity date, Edward Fenn, or his *agent* the First National Bank, will expect to receive $2,020 in cash for the note and interest, and Richard Baldwin will expect to pay $2,020 in cash.

Maturity Dates of Notes and Their Determination

The *term* of a note may be expressed in years, months, or days. To determine the maturity of a note expressed in months or years, count the number of months or years from the issuance date. For example, a two-year note dated April 3, 1973, is due on April 3, 1975, and a two-month note dated April 3, 1973, is due on June 3, 1973. Occasionally, when time is expressed in months, there may be no corresponding date in the maturity month, in which case the last day of the month of maturity is used; a three-month note dated March 31 is due on June 30, and a one-month note dated January 29, 30, or 31 is due on the last day of February. If the term of the note is expressed in days, the maturity is found by counting forward the specified number of days after the date of the note, excluding the date of the note but including the maturity date. The note of Richard Baldwin in Figure 13-2 has an issuance date of April 19; the due date of June 18 is determined as follows:

Total days in April	30
Date of note in April	19
Number of days note runs in April (excluding April 19)	11
Total days in May	31
Total number of days note has run through May 31	42
Due date in June (60 days minus 42 days)	18
Term of the note	60

If the term of a note that is expressed in days includes an entire month, count the actual number of days in that month. The determination of the number of calendar days in a term expressed in months is the same as the calculation for a term expressed in days. Thus, a two-month note dated April 19 is due 61 days later on June 19. Interest may be computed for either 60 or 61 days. Though banks generally compute interest by using the exact number of days—61 days in the example—on their direct loans, the usual commercial practice is to calculate interest (as in the example) for two months of 30 days each, or 60 days rather than 61 days. The typical commercial practice is followed in this text; that is, the interest computation on a one-month note is based on 30 days; on a two-month note, 60 days; and so on.

Recording Procedure Involving Notes Payable

All notes payable may be recorded in a single Notes Payable account in the general ledger as shown below.

		GENERAL LEDGER				
		Notes Payable				Acct. No. 111
1973 Dec.	24	F. T. Anson (paid)	450	1973 Nov.	15	B. B. Baker, 5%, 60 days	2,000
					24	F. T. Anson, 6%, 30 days	450
				Dec.	3	C. L. Jones, 6%, 90 days	800
					10	F. E. Merrick, 6%, 60 days	1,000
					18	P. O. Paulson, 6%, 90 days	950

The Notes Payable account may be used to record many of the supplementary details of the notes, including the name of the payee, the interest rate, the maturity date, and the term of the note. The credit entries in the account represent the issuance of notes payable, and the debit entry indicates the payment of a note. In addition to this record, carbon copies of the notes may be placed in a *tickler file* in order of maturity dates. When the maker pays the note and receives the canceled original (either perforated or marked *Paid*), he may destroy the carbon copy and place the canceled original in a *paid note file.* It is important that a record of paid notes be maintained in case of later disputes. The files of unpaid and paid notes can serve as subsidiary records of notes payable.

If the volume of notes payable becomes large, however, a special notes payable register may be created. This register can serve both as a special journal and as a subsidiary record of notes payable. In addition to Debit and Credit money columns, memorandum columns can be provided for supplementary information.

Issuance of Notes for Plant and Equipment. The following examples illustrate the use of notes payable in the acquisition of plant and equipment.

Assume that on July 10, 1973, the Able Company buys a bookkeeping machine at a cost of $2,000 from the Bourrim Machine Company; the creditor agrees to take a 90-day, noninterest-bearing note for the purchase price. This transaction is recorded as follows:

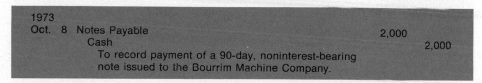

1973
July 10   Office Equipment   2,000
          Notes Payable   2,000
               To record the purchase of a bookkeeping machine
               and the issuance of a 90-day, noninterest-hearing
               note to the Bourrim Machine Company.

On the maturity date, 90 days later, the payment of the note is recorded as follows:

1973
Oct.   8   Notes Payable   2,000
           Cash   2,000
                To record payment of a 90-day, noninterest-bearing
                note issued to the Bourrim Machine Company.

Although the transaction of October 8, 1973, should be entered in the Able Company's cash disbursements journal, a general journal entry is shown to illustrate the *effect* of the transaction. (With very few exceptions, the general journal form is used to show the effect of transactions throughout the remainder of the text.)

Few creditors accept noninterest-bearing notes. Therefore, in the second example, assume that the Able Company purchases the same bookkeeping machine, but gives the Bourrim Machine Company a 6-percent, 90-day note. The journal entry is similar to the previous one.

1973
July 10   Office Equipment   2,000
          Notes Payable   2,000
               To record the purchase of a bookkeeping machine
               and the issuance of a 6%, 90-day note to the
               Bourrim Machine Company.

On October 8, 1973, the payment of the note and interest to the Bourrim Machine Company is recorded as follows:

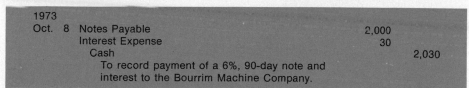

1973
Oct.   8   Notes Payable   2,000
           Interest Expense   30
           Cash   2,030
                To record payment of a 6%, 90-day note and
                interest to the Bourrim Machine Company.

Issuance of Notes for Merchandise. A business may use notes as a means of postponing payment for merchandise purchased for resale. These transactions could be recorded as were those in the preceding section; but since the volume of business done with a particular supplier or customer must be known for managerial purposes, such as applying for quantity discounts, it is helpful to have a subsidiary ledger account showing the total history of all transactions with a particular firm. To supply management with this information, the accountant may wish to record all merchandise transactions involving notes through the Accounts Payable account and the individual creditors' accounts in the subsidiary ledger. For example, assume that on October 10, 1973, the Able Company purchases merchandise costing $1,800 from the Baldwin Company and issues a 6-percent, 45-day note to the creditor. The note and interest are paid on November 24, 1973. These transactions are recorded as follows:

1973			
Oct. 10	Purchases	1,800.00	
	Accounts Payable–Baldwin Company		1,800.00
	To record merchandise purchased.		
10	Accounts Payable–Baldwin Company	1,800.00	
	Notes Payable		1,800.00
	To record the issuance of a 6%, 45-day note to the Baldwin Company.		
1973			
Nov. 24	Notes Payable	1,800.00	
	Interest Expense	13.50	
	Cash		1,813.50
	To record payment of a note and interest to the Baldwin Company.		

Issuance of Notes in Settlement of Open Accounts. A firm may issue a note to an open account creditor as a means of postponing payment further, or a creditor may require a debtor to give a note if the account is past due. Legally, a note is no more binding or collectible than an open account. Businessmen, however, prefer to hold notes because they are better legal evidence of the existence of debts, they are negotiable, and most makers of notes have a strong aversion to defaulting. They fear that the default of a note indicates a weak financial position to the business world more than failure to pay an open account does, and therefore does more damage to their credit standing.

The entry for the issuance of a note in settlement of an open account payable is similar to the second entry dated October 10 in the previous section.

Issuance of Notes to Borrow from Banks. A business faced with the possibility of losing cash discounts may find it advantageous to borrow money from a bank to pay the open accounts within the discount periods. A 2/10, n/30 cash discount, for example, represents an annual cost saving of 36 percent, as was illustrated in Chapter 5. It is a sound financial decision to borrow money at 6 percent, for example, to prevent the loss of a 36-percent cost saving.

There are two ways in which banks and other grantors of credit handle notes: (1) money may be borrowed on an interest-bearing note signed by the borrower, or (2) money may be advanced on a noninterest-bearing note *discounted* by the borrower. In the first case, the borrower receives the face value of the note and pays the face value plus the accumulated interest on the maturity date. In the second case, the note is noninterest bearing because the interest, or *discount,* is deducted in advance, and the borrower receives only the discounted value. At the maturity date, the borrower pays the face value of the note. The element of interest is present in either case: the difference is primarily one of form. There may also be notes that are noninterest bearing as far as both the maker and the payee are concerned.

Assume that on March 1, 1973, the Able Company borrows $5,000 from the First National Bank, giving a 6-percent, 60-day note, and that on April 30 it pays the bank for the note and interest. The issuance and payment of the note are recorded in the Able Company's books as follows:

```
1973
Mar.  1  Cash                                              5,000
            Notes Payable                                          5,000
               To record a 6%, 60-day note issued to the First
               National Bank.

Apr. 30  Notes Payable                                     5,000
            Interest Expense                                  50
               Cash                                                5,050
               To record payment of a 6%, 60-day note to the
               First National Bank.
```

Assume that on May 1, 1973, the Able Company borrows money from the City National Bank, discounting its own $5,000, 60-day, noninterest-bearing note at the *discount rate* of 6 percent. The amount of cash received in this case is $4,950, or $5,000 less a discount of $50 computed by applying the discount rate to the face value for the discount period of 60 days. If the maturity date falls within the current accounting period—the calendar year is assumed—the following entries are made in the Able Company's books:

```
1973
May   1  Cash                                              4,950
            Interest Expense                                 50
               Notes Payable                                       5,000
               To record a noninterest-bearing note issued to the
               City National Bank discounted at 6% for 60 days.

June 30  Notes Payable                                     5,000
            Cash                                                   5,000
               To record payment of a noninterest-bearing note
               to the City National Bank.
```

Assume that the Able Company had issued the note on December 16, 1973. Since the maturity date falls in the accounting year 1974 the following entry would be made:

```
1973
Dec. 16  Cash                                              4,950
            Discount on Notes Payable                        50
               Notes Payable                                       5,000
               To record a noninterest-bearing note discounted at
               6% for 60 days.
```

The $50 discount is not prepaid and should not be debited to Prepaid Interest, as is sometimes done. The interest is not paid until the note matures. At that time, the net amount borrowed of $4,950 plus total interest of $50 is paid; therefore, the balance of Discount on Notes Payable represents a potential interest expense. Accordingly, an adjusting entry is required at December 31, 1973, to transfer the expense portion of the balance of Discount on Notes Payable to the Interest Expense account; the entry is illustrated later in this chapter.

Discount on Notes Payable should be shown in the statement of financial position as a contra account to Notes Payable under current liabilities to indicate clearly the source of the net amount of funds received from creditors. Later, as adjustments are made to the Discount on Notes Payable account, the difference between the Notes Payable account and the balance of the Discount on Notes Payable account shows the net amount borrowed plus accrued interest on that amount.

In reference to the March 1 and May 1 bank loans, the amount paid at maturity was $50 more than the amount received from the bank by the borrower. However, the borrower had the use of $5,000, or the full face value of the interest-bearing note (March 1 bank loan), whereas only $4,950 was available from the noninterest-bearing discounted note. The *effective interest* (*i*) on a discounted note may be computed by the following formula:

$$\frac{D}{P} \times \frac{12}{T} = i$$

where D = the amount of the discount
$\quad\ \ P$ = the net proceeds
$\quad$ 12 = months in the year, and
$\quad\ \ T$ = the term of the note in months

The effective interest in the example is not 6 percent; rather, it is

$$\frac{\$50}{\$4,950} \times \frac{12}{2} = 1.01\% \times 6 = 6.06\%$$

The accountant should carefully determine the effective interest rate of a loan since this is relevant to making any short-term financial decision.

A discount may be defined as a deduction made from a gross future sum. The amount of the discount on a note is the difference between its value on the date of discount and its future value at maturity. Since discount and interest are similar in that each represents the charge for the use of money, the Interest Expense account is used in this text to record the incurred portion of expense for each of these items. The use of the Interest Expense account is further extended when a firm discounts customers' notes receivable, another short-term financing device discussed in this chapter.

End-of-Period Adjustments

Since interest is incurred continuously throughout the life of a note payable, it is necessary to make adjusting entries for the interest expense on those notes payable that mature in a later accounting period. Two kinds of adjustment are considered: the accrual of interest on an interest-bearing note payable and the expense apportionment on a discounted note payable.

Assume that the Boston Company has the following accounts in its general ledger as of December 31, 1973:

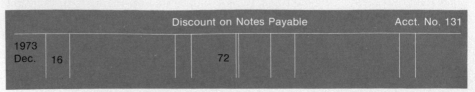

Discount on Notes Payable						Acct. No. 131
1973 Dec. 16			72			

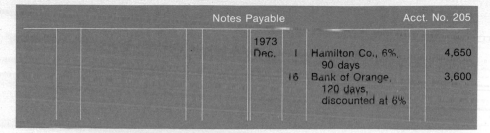

Notes Payable				Acct. No. 205
	1973			
	Dec.	1	Hamilton Co., 6%, 90 days	4,650
		16	Bank of Orange, 120 days, discounted at 6%	3,600

At December 31, 1973, the following two adjusting entries are made:

1973			
Dec. 31	Interest Expense	23.25	
	Accrued Interest Payable		23.25
	To record accrued interest on the note issued to the Hamilton Co.: Interest for 30 days at 6% on $4,650 is $23.25.		
31	Interest Expense	9.00	
	Discount on Notes Payable		9.00
	To record the transfer of $9 interest from the Discount on Notes Payable account to the Interest Expense account on the note discounted at the Bank of Orange.		

Comments on these two entries are

1. The amount of the accrued interest on a note issued to the Hamilton Company is figured at 6 percent for 30 days, the number of days after December 1, including December 31. Of course, no interest for the time period after December 31, 1973, should be recorded as an expense of 1973.
2. The second adjusting entry transfers interest from the Discount on Notes Payable account to the Interest Expense account. There are two methods by which the interest expense of $9 for 1973 can be determined. First, the amount of the discount may be multiplied by a fraction consisting of the age of the note as of the adjustment date divided by the term—in the example, $15/120 \times \$72 = \$9$. Second, an ordinary interest computation may be made—interest at 6 percent on $3,600 for 15 days is $9.

On March 1, 1974, when the Boston Company pays the Hamilton Company for the note and interest, the following journal entry is made:

1974			
Mar. 1	Notes Payable	4,650.00	
	Accrued Interest Payable	23.25	
	Interest Expense	46.50	
	Cash		4,719.75
	To record payment of a 6%, 90-day note and interest to the Hamilton Co.		

The credit to Cash of $4,719.75 represents the payment of two liabilities already on the books, Notes Payable and Accrued Interest Payable, and a payment of interest expense of $46.50 ($6\% \times 60/360 \times \$4,650$) entirely applicable to 1974.

The payment of the $3,600 on April 15, 1974, to the Bank of Orange is recorded in the following journal entry:

1974		
Apr. 15 Notes Payable	3,600	
Cash		3,600
To record payment of a note to the Bank of Orange.		

Since the note is noninterest bearing, no interest is recorded at the time of payment. However, there is a $63 balance in the Discount on Notes Payable account, which represents an expense of the year 1974. The following adjusting entry is made as of December 31, 1974, to transfer this amount to the Interest Expense account:

1974		
Dec. 31 Interest Expense	63	
Discount on Notes Payable		63
To apportion the amount of interest expense		
applicable to the year 1974.		

NOTES RECEIVABLE FINANCING PROBLEM

Another financial device that is often employed to obtain short-term funds is discounting customers' notes receivable. Before this is discussed, however, it would be helpful to understand the accounting for notes received from customers.

In general, the accounting for notes receivable is similar to that for notes payable; however, some procedures warrant additional discussion.

Recording Procedures

Many businesses make use of promissory notes to establish a legal basis for their claims against a customer and to create a legal document that may be easily discounted at a bank should the need for funds arise. They include firms selling high-priced durable goods such as furniture, farm machinery, and automobiles. Notes receivable are also received by a financial institution when it loans money.

It is perhaps even more important to keep good accounting records for notes receivable than it is for notes payable. After all, the payee of a note payable will send a statement to the maker that a note is due, so there is little danger that the maker will overlook the due date. The holder of notes receivable must have his records arranged so that he can notify the debtor that the note is due. This requires that notes receivable be filed chronologically by maturity date in a tickler file.

All notes receivable are usually recorded in a single general ledger account. The tickler file of notes receivable plus the general ledger account containing such information as the maker, the term, the interest rate, and any collateral pledged make it unnecessary for a firm to maintain a subsidiary notes receivable ledger. The Notes Receivable account of the Carson Company is shown.

Notes Receivable							Acct. No. 111
1973 Nov.	1	C. Adams, 45 days, 6%	775	1973 Dec.	16	C. Adams	775
Dec.	20	B. Baker, 00 days, 7%	425				
	20	L. Wilson, 60 days, 6%	500				

Each debit posting indicates that an asset, Notes Receivable, has been acquired from a customer; each credit entry indicates that a particular note has been settled by payment or renewal, or has been dishonored. In addition to the dollar amounts in the money columns, the Explanation columns give the maker's name, the term of the note, the interest rate, and any other relevant information.

If the volume of transactions warrants it, a special notes receivable register, like a notes payable register, could be created. Special Debit and Credit money columns could be inserted, along with memorandum columns for supplementary information. This register could serve as both a journal and a subsidiary record of notes receivable.

Receipt of a Note for a Sale

Assume that on March 5, 1973, the Dawson Company sells merchandise to John Roch and receives a 6-percent, 90-day note for $650. The following entries are made:

1973				
Mar.	5	Accounts Receivable–John Roch	650	
		Sales		650
		To record sale of merchandise.		
	5	Notes Receivable	650	
		Accounts Receivable–John Roch		650
		To record the receipt of a 6%, 90-day note from John Roch		

The first entry is made so that the customer's account in the subsidiary ledger will contain a complete record of all credit sales transactions. This information is useful to management in making decisions as to collection efforts and further extension of credit.

On June 3, 1973, when the Dawson Company receives payment from John Roch, the following entry is made:

1973				
June	3	Cash	659.75	
		Notes Receivable		650.00
		Interest Earned		9.75
		To record receipt of payment from John Roch for note and interest due today.		

The Interest Earned account is a revenue account. The balance of this account is closed at the end of the accounting period to the Revenue and Expense Summary account.

Receipt of a Note in Settlement of an Open Account. Assume that Ralph Towne owes the Dawson Company $1,850, due on July 10, 1973. On August 1, the Dawson Company agrees to accept a 60-day, noninterest-bearing note with a face value of $1,868.50 (the amount receivable, $1,850, plus interest at 6% for 60 days) in settlement of the open account. This procedure is common among retailers who plan to discount their notes at banks. Banks prefer that most, if not all, of their notes be noninterest bearing. Since the maturity date of this note falls within the current accounting period—the calendar year is assumed—the following entry is made:

```
1973
Aug.  1  Notes Receivable                          1,868.50
             Accounts Receivable–Ralph Towne                    1,850.00
             Interest Earned                                       18.50
                 To record receipt of a 60-day, noninterest-
                 bearing note, with interest of $18.50
                 included in the face value, from Ralph
                 Towne.
```

The credit of the entire $18.50 to the revenue account, Interest Earned, is permissible since that amount will become revenue by the time the books are closed on December 31.

On September 30, when payment is received, the following entry is made:

```
1973
Sept. 30  Cash                                     1,868.50
              Notes Receivable                                  1,868.50
                  To record collection of note from Ralph
                  Towne.
```

If the note of August 1, 1973, had been received on December 1, 1973, all the interest would not be earned by December 31, 1973. The following entry is required:

```
1973
Dec.  1  Notes Receivable                          1,868.50
             Accounts Receivable–Ralph Towne                    1,850.00
             Unearned Interest (included in face of notes
                 receivable)                                      18.50
                 To record receipt of a 60-day, noninterest-
                 bearing note, with interest of $18.50
                 included in the face value, from Ralph
                 Towne.
```

The Unearned Interest account, credited for $18.50, represents the interest that will be partly earned in 1973 and partly earned in 1974. Since the interest is not received in the form of cash, it should *not* be classified as a current liability, as is sometimes done. Rather, it should be shown as a contra account to Notes Receivable, to reduce that account to an estimate of its present value—the amount that could be received by discounting the note at a bank. The Unearned Interest account will require an adjusting entry at December 31, 1973, to apportion the amount of revenue earned in 1973 to the operations of the period. This procedure is described later in this chapter.

Renewal of a Note Receivable. A customer who has given a note to a business firm may not be able to pay at the maturity date, but may be willing to renew the old note by the issuance of a new note, thus extending the time of the payment of the debt. To illustrate, assume that Samuel Thompson gives a 6-percent, 60-day note for $1,540 to the Dawson Company on April 1, 1973. On May 31, Thompson agrees to pay the Dawson Company cash for the interest on the old note and to give a new 6-percent, 90-day note for the principal. The May 31 transaction is recorded on the Dawson Company's books as follows:

1973			
May 31	Notes Receivable (new 90-day note)	1,540.00	
	Cash	15.40	
	Notes Receivable (old 60-day note)		1,540.00
	Interest Earned		15.40
	To record the collection of cash for interest on the old note and to record the receipt of a new 6%, 90-day note in renewal of the old note.		

Since there is an equal debit and credit to the same account, there might be some question as to the propriety of including Notes Receivable in the journal entry. However, the omission of the debit and the credit would fail to disclose the action taken and would leave a gap in the permanent records of the Dawson Company. For example, the new note would still carry an entry date of April 1, 1973, and would appear to be past due. The entry as shown is the only way that a permanent record of this transaction can be achieved and the only way to avoid possible confusion.

Dishonor of a Note Receivable by the Maker. If a note cannot be collected at maturity, it is said to be *dishonored* by the maker. Another term that is often used is *defaulting* on a note. Once the maturity date of a note passes without the note being collected, an entry should be made transferring the face value of the note plus any uncollected accrued interest to the Accounts Receivable account.

Assume that Ronald Ronson issued a 6-percent, 90-day note for $2,000 to the Dawson Company on June 1, 1973. At the maturity date, August 30, 1973, Ronson fails to pay the amount of the note and interest, at which time the following entry is made on the books of the Dawson Company:

1973			
Aug. 30	Accounts Receivable–Ronald Ronson	2,030	
	Notes Receivable		2,000
	Interest Earned		30
	To record the dishonor by Ronald Ronson of a 6%, 90-day note.		

Two questions arise in connection with this entry: (1) Why should $30 be recognized as revenue and credited to the Interest Earned account? and (2) why should the amount of the note and interest not be written off to Allowance for Doubtful Accounts?

Under the accrual concept, the interest has been earned. It represents a valid claim against the maker of the note; if the face of the note is collectible, so is the interest. This leads to the answer to the second question: The fact that a note is uncollectible at its maturity is not a definite indication that it will never be collected. Unless there is some evidence to the contrary, most business firms assume that notes will ultimately be collected. Certainly, if the amounts involved are material, all possible steps including legal action will be taken to collect both accounts and notes receivable, and only after such steps have failed will an account be written off to Allowance for Doubtful Accounts.

The transfer of dishonored notes and interest to Accounts Receivable accomplishes two things: (1) the Notes Receivable account is relieved of past due notes, reflects only the current notes, and therefore represents a highly liquid asset; and (2) use of the Accounts Receivable account emphasizes the legal fact of dishonor (legally, a past due note is the same as an open account claim against a customer) and presents a complete picture of all transactions with the customer.

End-of-Period Adjusting Entries

The adjusting entries for interest on notes receivable parallel the adjusting entries for interest on notes payable. The major problem is accurate measurement of the revenue Interest Earned and the asset Accrued Interest Receivable, or the contra account Unearned Interest. To illustrate the adjusting entries and the effect they have on the accounting for notes and interest in the next accounting period, assume that the Eason Company has the following accounts in its general ledger as of December 31, 1973:

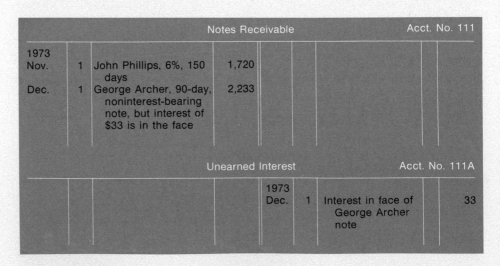

			Notes Receivable				Acct. No. 111
1973							
Nov.	1	John Phillips, 6%, 150 days	1,720				
Dec.	1	George Archer, 90-day, noninterest-bearing note, but interest of $33 is in the face	2,233				

			Unearned Interest				Acct. No. 111A
				1973			
				Dec.	1	Interest in face of George Archer note	33

At December 31, 1973, the accountant for the Eason Company makes the following adjusting entries:

```
1973
Dec. 31   Accrued Interest Receivable              17.20
              Interest Earned                              17.20
                  To record the accrued interest on the John
                  Phillips note at 6% for 60 days.

       31   Unearned Interest                       11.00
              Interest Earned                              11.00
                  To record the transfer of ⅓ of $33 interest on
                  the note from George Archer from the
                  Unearned Interest account to the revenue
                  account.
```

Comments about these adjustments follow:

1. The accrued interest receivable on the note from John Phillips is figured at 6 percent for 60 days, the number of days after November 1 including December 31. No interest for the period after December 31, 1973, should be recorded as revenue in the year 1973.
2. The second adjustment involves the apportionment of interest revenue earned in a given period, 1973, to that period.

On March 1, 1974, when the Eason Company collects the George Archer note, the following entry is made:

```
1974
Mar.  1   Cash                                    2,233
              Notes Receivable                           2,233
                  To record collection of a note from George
                  Archer.
```

Since the note is noninterest bearing, no interest is recorded at the time of collection. However, a balance of $22 remains in the Unearned Interest account, representing revenue earned in the year 1974. Thus, an adjusting entry is necessary as of December 31, 1974, to transfer this amount to the Interest Earned account:

```
1974
Dec. 31   Unearned Interest                         22
              Interest Earned                             22
                  To apportion the amount of interest revenue
                  applicable to the year 1974.
```

A slightly different problem is associated with the collection of the note from John Phillips. The following entry is made on March 31, 1974, when the note is collected:

```
1974
Mar. 31   Cash                                   1,763.00
              Notes Receivable                         1,720.00
              Accrued Interest Receivable                  17.20
              Interest Earned                              25.80
                  To record collection of a 6%, 150-day note
                  and interest from John Phillips.
```

The debit to cash of $1,763 represents the collection of two receivables already on the books, Notes Receivable and Accrued Interest Receivable, and of a revenue, Interest Earned of $25.80, which was earned in and is entirely applicable to the year 1974.

DISCOUNTING CUSTOMERS' NOTES RECEIVABLE

For a business that receives a large number of notes from customers, it may be economically advantageous to obtain short-term funds by discounting these notes at a bank rather than holding them to maturity. If the credit rating of the firm is good, most banks will usually discount customers' notes receivable because they are secured loans. If the maker fails to pay the maturity value when it is due, the firm that has discounted the note—having previously endorsed it—must make payment to the bank. This obligation is referred to as a *contingent liability.*

Determining the Cash Proceeds

As far as the bank is concerned, it is making a loan to the borrower based on the maturity value of the note, including any interest, because that is the amount the bank will collect from the maker at the maturity date. The discount that the bank deducts is based on a stipulated rate of the maturity value for the period of time the note has to run.

The sequence for computing the proceeds of a discounted note is

1. The maturity value, or the principal plus the total interest to maturity, is determined.
2. The discount period, or the number of days the note still has to run after the date of the discount, is found.
3. The discount is computed at the stipulated bank rate for the discount period.
4. The discount is deducted from the maturity value to find the cash proceeds.

This sequence may be stated as

$$MV - (MV \times D \times RL) = P$$

where MV = the maturity value
    D = the rate of discount
   RL = the remaining life of the note
    P = the cash proceeds

Assume that on April 19, 1973, the Faison Company receives a 6-percent, 60-day note for $2,000 from Edward Goodson in settlement of a past-due open account. This transaction is recorded as follows:

1973			
Apr. 19	Notes Receivable	2,000	
	Accounts Receivable–Edward Goodson		2,000
	To record receipt of a 6%, 60-day note from Goodson in settlement of a past-due open account.		

On May 1, 1973, the Faison Company, needing short-term funds, decides to discount Goodson's note at the bank's rate of 5 percent. Calculation of the proceeds follows:

1. Maturity value of note (principal of $2,000 plus total interest of $20)		$2,020.00
2. Due date	June 18	
3. Period of discount:		
May 1–May 31 (not counting May 1)	30 days	
June 1–June 18 (including June 1)	18 days	
	48 days	
4. Discount at 5% for 48 days on the maturity value:		
Interest on $2,020 at 6% for 60 days	$20.20	
Less interest on $2,020 at 6% for 12 days		
($\frac{1}{5}$ × $20.20)	4.04	
Interest on $2,020 at 6% for 48 days	$16.16	
Less interest on $2,020 at 1% for 48 days		
($\frac{1}{6}$ × $16.16)	2.69	
Discount (or interest) on $2,020 at 5% for 48 days		13.47
Total cash proceeds		$2,006.53

Recording the Proceeds

The entry on the Faison Company's books is

```
1973
May  1  Cash                                        2,006.53
           Notes Receivable Discounted                          2,000.00
           Interest Earned                                          6.53
              To record the discounting of Edward
              Goodson's 6%, 60-day note at the bank at 5%.
```

The Notes Receivable Discounted account is used to indicate that the Faison Company, having endorsed the note before turning it over to the bank, is now obligated to pay the bank if Goodson fails to do so; that is, the Faison Company would have to pay the $2,000 contingent liability plus the $20 interest at 6 percent for 60 days, plus any *protest fee* charged by the bank. The obligation assumed by the Faison Company is contingent on Goodson's payment, and the account is therefore referred to as a *contingent liability account.* This account brings the existence of the contingent liability to the attention of the reader of the statement of financial position. ▼ In preparing financial statements, full disclosure of all essential facts is of paramount importance. ▼ Goodson does not need to be informed that the note has been discounted, and no entry is required on his books; his obligation to pay the maturity value of the note on its presentation by the legal holder in due course remains unchanged.

Accounting Concept: ▼
Full Disclosure

Presentation on the Statement of Financial Position

Assume that on May 31 the Notes Receivable account shows a balance of $3,500 (including the $2,000 note discounted on May 1). The statement of financial position prepared on that date may disclose the existence of the contingent liability by a footnote or supplementary note to the statement of financial position as follows:

Assets	
Current Assets	
Notes Receivable (see Note 1)	$1,500
Note 1: The Company is contingently liable for notes receivable discounted in the amount of $2,000.	

Disclosure of the contingent liability can also be made by offsetting Notes Receivable Discounted against Notes Receivable in the statement of financial position in the following manner:

Assets		
Current Assets		
Notes Receivable	$3,500	
Deduct Notes Receivable Discounted	2,000	
Net Notes Receivable		$1,500

Payment of a Discounted Note

If notification of dishonor is not received from the bank (the bank normally does not notify the borrower of payment by the maker), it is assumed that the maker has paid the note at the maturity date, and the borrower is released from his contingent liability. The entry on the Faison Company's books to eliminate the contingent liability is

1973			
June 18	Notes Receivable Discounted	2,000	
	Notes Receivable		2,000
	To eliminate the contingent liability on Goodson's note, which was discounted on May 1, 1973.		

The entry on Edward Goodson's books on the date of payment is

1973			
June 18	Notes Payable	2,000	
	Interest Expense	20	
	Cash		2,020
	To record payment to the bank for a 6%, 60-day note issued to the Faison Company on April 19, 1973.		

The debit to Interest Expense is for the full 60-day period. It is assumed that no adjusting entry has been made for any interest expense.

Nonpayment of a Discounted Note

If Edward Goodson dishonors the note at the maturity date, the bank must follow a certain formal procedure involving the preparation of notarized protest documents to establish the legal basis for the collection of the full amount from the Faison Company. Assuming that the bank charges a protest fee of $5, the following entries are made on the Faison Company's books when the Company pays the bank the face value of the note, the interest, and the protest fee.

1973			
June 18	Accounts Receivable—Edward Goodson	2,025	
	Cash		2,025
	To record payment of Edward Goodson's note, which was discounted and is now dishonored by Goodson:		

Face value	$2,000
Interest	20
Protest Fee	5
Total	$2,025

18	Notes Receivable Discounted	2,000	
	Notes Receivable		2,000
	To record the elimination of the contingent liability and Goodson's discounted and dishonored note.		

Note that Accounts Receivable is debited in the entry recording the cash payment, instead of Notes Receivable Discounted. This procedure avoids the error of treating discounted notes as though they were actual liabilities; since payment is made as soon as the contingency is realized, no book liability need be recorded. The second journal entry is necessary to remove the contingent liability after the cash payment is made for the dishonored note.

The fact that a note is dishonored does not mean that it will be definitely uncollectible or that it should be written off to Allowance for Doubtful Accounts. Goodson, in this case, may pay at a later date, either voluntarily or on a court order. The account remains open in the accounts receivable ledger until it is settled or definitely determined to be uncollectible and written off.

Use of Compound Interest in Installment Payments

A very popular form of short-term debt is the obligation that requires installment payments. Often this kind of obligation provides that it be liquidated by a series of equal payments that are to include both principal and accrued interest. The future principal obligation represents the present value of an annuity, the equal payments being calculated by dividing the principal sum owed by the present value of an annuity of $1. To illustrate, assume a debt of $1,000 incurred as of August 1, 1973, is to be paid off by 12 equal *monthly* installments including both principal and interest. Interest at the annual rate of 18 percent, or monthly rate of $1\frac{1}{2}$ percent, accrues on the unpaid balance, and the first payment is to be made on August 31, 1973. The monthly payments are determined by dividing $1,000 by 10.908, the present value of an annuity of 12 rents of $1 each at $1\frac{1}{2}$ percent. The equal payments, then, are $91.68.

Under the assumption that the obligation is represented by the issuance of an installment notes payable, entries that would be made on August 31 and September 30, 1973, appear below. Similar entries would be made in subsequent periods.

Transaction	Books of Party Issuing Note		Books of Party Receiving Note	

August 1, 1973. Note for $1,000 is issued.	Purchases (or Cash) 1,000.00
	   Notes Payable[1]
		1,000.00	Notes Receivable[1] 1,000.00
			   Sales (or Cash)
				1,000.00

August 31, 1973. Monthly payment is made.	Notes Payable 76.68
	Interest Expense 15.00
	   Cash
		91.68	Cash 91.68
			   Notes Receivable
			   Interest Earned
				76.68
				15.00

September 30, 1973. Monthly payment is made.	Notes Payable 77.83
	Interest Expense 13.85
	   Cash
		91.68	Cash 91.68
			   Notes Receivable
			   Interest Earned
				77.83
				13.85

[1] If the item arises out of a transaction involving the sale of merchandise, it should first be recorded in open Accounts Payable and Accounts Receivable accounts.

DRAFTS

A *draft* is a written order to pay, such as a bank check, with the same negotiability as a note for which it is often used as a substitute. Commercial drafts, excluding checks, are used to enforce the collection of open accounts, to obtain the advantages of both a written acknowledgment and a negotiable instrument, and for C.O.D. (collect on delivery) shipments.

The person who issues the order and draws the draft is the *drawer*; the person to whom it is addressed and who is to make payment is the *drawee*; and the person to whom payment is to be made is the *payee*. If the drawer names himself as the payee—a common occurrence with commercial drafts—the draft becomes a two-party document similar to a note. The types of drafts used in business are (1) *ordinary checks*, (2) *certified checks*, (3) *cashier's* or *treasurer's checks*, (4) *sight drafts*, (5) *time drafts*, and (6) *trade acceptances*.

Ordinary Check

The most common form of the three-party draft is the ordinary check. It is used by most firms to make business payments. A check is a written order by a depositor for his bank to pay a specific sum of money to a designated person when the check is presented to the bank. The Cash account is credited when a check is written and debited when a check is received.

Certified Check

An ordinary bank check, personal or business, that has been stamped *Certified* and signed by an official of the bank is called a *certified check.* The bank official, having certified that the money is in the bank, immediately reduces the drawer's account and holds the amount in a special fund so as to pay the check on presentation. The check may be certified on the request of the drawer (to assure the payee of the availability of sufficient funds at the bank to pay the check) or of the holder (to insure prompt payment of the check when it is presented later by an ultimate *endorsee*). Certified checks are often used as a type of warranty deposit when a firm is bidding for a contract or ordering a special shipment of goods for the first time. As with the ordinary check, Cash is credited when a certified check is given and debited when a certified check is received.

Cashier's Check

A cashier's, or treasurer's, check is drawn by a bank against its own funds and may be purchased in the same manner as a money order or travelers' check. The treasurer of a state-chartered bank issues a treasurer's check, the cashier of a national bank issues a cashier's check—otherwise they are the same. The buyer pays the bank the full amount of the check plus a nominal fee and tells the bank to whom the check is to be made out—to himself, a business firm, or another person. Since it is a bank check, it is signed by the bank; the name of the buyer of the check does not appear on it. Such checks are used either when a debtor does not have a checking account or when a personal check is not acceptable. Again, a cashier's check is treated from an accounting point of view as cash.

Sight Draft

A sight draft is a demand for payment drawn by the person to whom money is owed. Sight drafts may be used effectively when merchandise is shipped to another city to a new customer without an established credit rating. The sight draft, attached to the *order bill of lading* (the document authorizing the passage of title to the goods and a receipt given by the common carrier), is mailed to the customer's bank. Since the customer cannot get the merchandise without the bill of lading, the payment of the draft must precede receipt of the bill of lading and delivery of the goods by the warehouse or the transportation firm. To help account for the shipment of merchandise, a journal entry may be made at the time the sight draft is drawn, debiting Accounts Receivable and crediting Sales. No entry would be made for the draft itself at this time because the drawing of a draft is simply an intent until the draft is accepted. When the draft is honored by payment and the drawer is notified of the fact, Cash and any collection expense that may be charged by the bank are debited and Accounts Receivable is credited.

Time Draft

A time draft is due after the passage of a specified period of time. The drawer presents the instrument to the drawee, who indicates his agreement to pay the draft at maturity by writing "Accepted" across the face of the draft and signing it properly. The accounting entry is usually made on the drawee's book when the drawee accepts a time draft drawn by a creditor for an amount of a past-due open account is a debit to Accounts Payable and a credit to Notes Payable. When he receives the accepted draft from the debtor, the drawer debits Notes Receivable and credits Accounts Receivable. The accounting for any interest that the draft bears would be similar to that for notes. The interest may accrue from the date of the draft—*60 days from date*—or from the date the draft was accepted by drawee—*60 days from sight*.

Trade Acceptance

A trade acceptance is a special form of time draft used in connection with a specific sales transaction. The document is drawn by the seller of merchandise. Its acceptance by the buyer serves as an acknowledgment of the purchase, and it then assumes the same status as a note. Trade acceptances may be used to ensure prompt payment and to borrow money.

THE COST OF BORROWING MONEY

An essential factor in all short-term financial decisions is the effective cost of the particular means of financing. Even though recent legislation requires the disclosure of the effective annual interest cost of borrowed funds, debtors should be familiar with the computations involved in the determination of these rates. This knowledge is particularly important when individuals are faced with the decision for selecting a single method from among several alternative short-term financing methods.

To illustrate the calculation of the effective interest rate involved in an installment purchase plan, assume that an item may be purchased either for $3,580 in cash or for $80 down and $83.33 per month for 48 months. This is equivalent to borrowing $3,500 ($3,580 less $80 down payment). The absolute amount of total interest for four years is

$$\$499.84 = (48 \times \$83.33) - \$3,500$$

The cost of buying on the installment plan and the effective interest rate may be calculated by the use of the following formula.[2]

$$\frac{2MC}{P(N + 1)} = i$$

where M = 12 if payments are monthly, 4 if payments are quarterly, or 52 if payments are weekly (M = 12, 4, or 52 even if the number of payments are less than or more than 12, 4, 52)

C = the absolute amount of interest or carrying charge

P = the principal sum (cash price less down payment)

N = the total number of payments

i = the effective annual rate of interest

[2]This formula will produce an approximation of the effective interest rate as calculated by using the compound interest techniques.

Substituting the values in the example

$$\frac{2 \times 12 \times \$499.84}{\$3,500(48 + 1)} = \frac{\$11,996.16}{\$171,500.00} = 6.99\%$$

The effective interest rate varies depending on the financial reputation of the customer, the size of the loan, the region, and cyclic fluctuations in interest rates. Although in a particular case the borrower may not be able to bargain for favorable terms, he should be fully aware of the effective cost involved and, whenever possible, choose the cheapest alternative means of short-term financing.

SUMMARY

Interest is the cost of obtaining money or credit: to the maker of a note, it is a cost for the use of money and thus an expense; to the payee of a note, it is compensation for lending the money and thus revenue. The amount of simple interest to be paid on an interest-bearing note is computed by multiplying the three factors of (1) the face value of the note, (2) the specified interest rate, and (3) the term of the note stated as a fraction on an assumed commercial year of 360 days.

Compound interest is interest that accrues on unpaid interest of past periods as well as on the principal. The formulas for the various compound interest techniques are: The Compound Amount

Formula: $$a = (1 + i)^n$$

The Present Value of a Single Sum

Formula: $$p = \frac{1}{(1 + i)^n}$$

The Amount of an Ordinary Annuity

Formula: $$A = \frac{(1 + i)^n - 1}{i}$$

and The Present Value of an Ordinary Annuity

Formula: $$P = \frac{1 - \frac{1}{(1 + i)^n}}{i}$$

These formulas are used in the solution of a number of business problems. For example, a knowledge of compound interest is an essential ingredient in calculating insurance probabilities, in determining values of investments at given interest rates, and in equating the time value of future sums in many management-type decisions.

Firms often find it more economical to obtain short-term financing rather than to pay cash for purchases. The particular type of short-term financing is dependent on current and future availability and effective cost of the funds. The method or methods chosen should produce the desired short-term funds at the lowest long-run cost.

Perhaps the most common form of short-term financing is the purchase of goods on open account. The issuance of notes to creditors is another popular short-term financing device. A promissory note is a negotiable instrument that constitutes an unconditional written promise to pay a sum certain in money to the order of a designated person, or to bearer, at a fixed or determinable future time or on demand. On the books of the maker, the liability for a note is recorded by a credit to Notes Payable; on the books of the payee, the asset reflecting the right to receive a fixed sum of money at a future time is recorded by a debit to Notes Receivable. If the term of a note is expressed in months or years from the issuance date, the maturity date is determined by counting the months or years. If the term of the note is expressed in days, the maturity date is determined by counting forward the number of days—the issuance date is excluded and the maturity date included in the count.

If a note is issued for the purchase of merchandise, it should first be recorded as a credit to the Accounts Payable account; then the amount is removed from this account by a debit and recorded as a credit in the Notes Payable account. If money is borrowed from a bank or other financial institution by the issuance of an interest-bearing note, then the borrower receives the face value of the note and at maturity must pay the face value plus the accrued interest. The accounting for a note of this type parallels the accounting for the issuance of a note for the settlement of an open account. If money is advanced from the bank, however, on a noninterest-bearing note discounted by the borrower, the borrower receives the face value of the note less the discount amount and at maturity must repay only the face value of the note. If the issuance and maturity dates are in the same accounting period, Interest Expense is debited for the discount amount. If the maturity date falls within a future accounting period, the discount amount is debited to Discount on Notes Payable, and at the end of the current accounting period an adjusting entry is made transferring the expense portion to Interest Expense. If a note payable is issued in the current accounting period but is not due until a future period, an adjusting entry recognizing the interest expense applicable to that period and the related liability is required on the maker's books at the end of the current period. On the books of the payee of the note, an adjusting entry recognizing the interest earned during the period and the related asset is required.

The accounting for notes receivable is typically the mirror image of the accounting for notes payable. For emphasis, however, these points should be reiterated: (1) The receipt of a note for the sale of merchandise should first be recorded in the Accounts Receivable account for managerial purposes. (2) If a note receivable is renewed, an entry recognizing the issuance of the new note and the cancellation of the old is required. (3) If a note is dishonored at maturity, the face value of the note and any uncollected accrued interest—if the note is interest bearing—should be transferred to the Accounts Receivable account.

Another short-term financing device is the discounting of customers' notes at a bank or other financial institution. The maker of the note, at maturity, pays the face value of the note and any interest accrued thereon to the bank. The discounter is liable for the amount due at maturity if the maker defaults. The cash obtained from the discounting of a note is the maturity value of the note less the discount amount, the bank charge for the loan. When a customer's note is discounted, the resultant contingent liability is recognized by a credit to Notes

Receivable Discounted. This contingent liability may be reflected on the statement of financial position by showing only the net notes on hand as a current asset and disclosing the contingent liability in a footnote, or by deducting Notes Receivable Discounted from the total Notes Receivable, thus deriving the net notes on hand in the Current Assets section.

A draft is a three-party instrument with the same negotiable characteristics of a note; some types of draft are often used as substitutes for promissory notes. Common forms include checks, certified checks, cashier's checks, sight drafts, time drafts, and trade acceptances.

Even though recent legislation requires the disclosure of the effective annual interest cost of borrowed funds, debtors should be familiar with the computations involved in the determination of these rates. Thus, in appraising the merits of various financing devices, one must be aware of the effective rates to make valid comparisons.

QUESTIONS

Q13-1. Distinguish between simple and compound interest.

Q13-2. Distinguish between the amount of 1 and the amount of an annuity of 1.

Q13-3. What is the interest rate per period and the frequency of compounding per year in each of the following:

a. 6 percent compounded semiannually?
b. 5 percent compounded quarterly?
c. 9 percent compounded monthly?

Q13-4. Distinguish between the amount of 1 and the present value of 1.

Q13-5. Distinguish between the present value of 1 and the present value of an annuity of 1.

Q13-6. Explain how each of the following would be solved without tables:
a. The present value of $1,000 for five years at 6 percent compounded annually.
b. The present value of $2,000 for four years at 5 percent compounded semiannually.
c. The compound discount on $1,000 for 12 years at 4 percent compounded quarterly.

Q13-7. Explain the following terms or procedures: (a) negotiable instrument, (b) the 6-percent, 60-day method, (c) interest-bearing note, (d) the maker of a note, and (e) the payee of a note.

Q13-8. Explain the following terms or procedures: (a) discounting a note, (b) bank discount rate, (c) contingent liability, (d) proceeds, (e) maturity value, and (f) a dishonored note.

Q13-9. The accountant for the Nashua Company recorded the receipt of a note on a sale to John Lane as follows:

Notes Receivable	750	
Sales		750

State how you think the transaction should have been recorded and give your reason.

Q13-10. The Norman Company negotiated a 90-day loan (reference 1) with the Beacon Bank, which was paid on its due date (reference m). It arranged for another 90-day loan (reference x) with the Astor Bank, which was also paid when due (reference y).

Cash		Notes Payable to Bank		Interest Expense	
(1) 3,000	(m) 3,045	(m) 3,000	(1) 3,000	(m) 45	
(x) 2,955	(y) 3,000	(y) 3,000	(x) 3,000	(x) 45	

(a) Describe the type of negotiable instrument used by the Beacon Bank; (b) the Astor Bank. (c) Which loan is more favorable to the Norman Company? Why?

Q13-11. The following account balances appear in the general ledger of the Goodwin Company:

Notes Receivable	Notes Payable	Notes Receivable Discounted
35,000	20,000	15,000

(a) What is the amount of customers' notes outstanding? (b) What amount of customer notes are in the Goodwin Company's possession? (c) What amount of customers' notes have been discounted? (d) What is the Goodwin Company's contingent liability on discounted notes? (e) Do the accounts furnish enough data to compute the company's working capital position? (f) How would these accounts be shown in the position statement?

Q13-12. Six transactions related to a sale to a customer are recorded in the T accounts. Describe each transaction.

Cash		Accounts Receivable		Notes Receivable	
(c) 904	(d) 911	(a) 900	(b) 900	(b) 900	(e) 900
(f) 916		(d) 911	(f) 911		

Notes Receivable Discounted		Sales		Interest Earned	
(e) 900	(c) 900		(a) 900		(c) 4
					(f) 5

Q13-13. (a) What is a contingent liability? (b) May there be more than one person contingently liable on a particular note? Explain. (c) What amounts must a person who is contingently liable on an interest-bearing note pay if the maker dishonors the note on its due date?

Q13-14. Discuss the managerial factors that a company must consider in determining what method of short-term financing it should choose.

EXERCISES

E13.1. Using the amount tables on pages 854 and 856, solve the following:

a. What is the amount on January 1, 1977, of a deposit of $10,000 left on January 1, 1973, to accumulate interest at 6 percent compounded annually?
b. What is the amount on January 1, 1977, of a deposit of $1,500 left on July 1, 1973, to accumulate interest at 6 percent compounded quarterly?
c. What is the compound interest on an investment of $2,500 left for five years at 10 percent compounded annually?

E13-2. Stan Smith deposited $5,000 in a special savings account that provides for interest at the rate of 18 percent compounded monthly if the deposit is maintained for four years. Using the amount tables on pages 854 and 856, calculate the balance of the savings account at the end of the four-year period.

E13-3. Five equal annual contributions are to be made to a fund, the first deposit to be made on December 31, 1973. Using the amount tables on pages 854 and 856, determine the equal contributions that, if invested at 6 percent compounded annually, will produce a fund of $10,000, assuming that this sum is desired on December 31, 1977.

E13-4. Using the present value tables on pages 853 and 855, solve each of the following problems:

a. What is the present value on January 1, 1973, of $10,000 due January 1, 1977, and discounted at 6 percent compounded annually?
b. What is the present value on July 1, 1973, of $2,500 due January 1, 1977, and discounted at 6 percent compounded quarterly?
c. What is the compound discount on $1,000 for five years at 10 percent compounded annually?

E13-5. B. B. Fitch borrows $1,000 that is to be repaid in 24 equal monthly installments with interest at the rate of 1½ percent per month. Using the tables on pages 853 and 855, calculate the equal installments.

E13-6. Information regarding five notes is given below.

Date of Note	Term of Note	Interest Rate	Principal
(1) March 1, 1973	60 days	4%	$1,250
(2) April 4, 1973	90 days	6%	1,500
(3) August 24, 1973	15 days	8%	3,965
(3) September 12, 1973	3 months	5%	1,560
(5) November 3, 1973	2 months	6%	675

Determine the maturity date and maturity value of each note.

E13-7. The following were among the transactions of the Baltimore Company for 1973 and 1974:

1973

Jan. 2   Purchased $4,500 worth of merchandise from the Alston Company, and issued a 6%, 45-day note.

Feb. 16   Paid note and interest due the Alston Company.

Mar. 15   Issued a 6%, 90-day note to the Peters Company in settlement of an open account of $5,000.

June 13   Paid the Peters Company $2,000 on principal and all the interest for the preceding 90 days; issued a new 7%, 60-day note for the balance of the principal.

Aug. 12   Paid the remaining amount due the Peters Company.

Nov. 25   Issued a 6%, 75-day note to the Milton Company in settlement of an open account of $6,600.

1974

Feb. 8   Paid the amount due the Milton Company.

Journalize the transactions, including any necessary adjusting entries on December 31, 1973.

E13-8. The following were among the transactions of the Dawson Company for 1973 and 1974:

1973

June 10   Discounted its own 90-day, noninterest-bearing note, made out to the Bank of Columbia in the principal amount of $8,000, at a discount rate of 4%.

Sept. 8   Paid the Bank of Columbia amount due.

1973

Dec. 1 Discounted its own 90-day, noninterest-bearing note, made out to the National Bank in the principal amount of $4,000, at a discount rate of 6%. (Assume that the books are closed on December 31.)

1974

Mar. 1 Paid the amount due the National Bank.

Journalize the transactions including any necessary adjusting entries on December 31, 1973 and 1974.

E13-9. The following were among the transactions of the Finn Corporation for 1973 and 1974:

1973

Jan. 18 Sold merchandise worth $850 to H. Hawser and received a 6%, 70-day note.

Mar. 29 Collected the amount due from H. Hawser.

May 12 Received a 6%, 120-day note from B. Newton in settlement of an open account of $2,400.

Sept. 9 B. Newton dishonored his note.

Nov. 15 Received a 6%, 90-day note from R. Hoode in settlement of an open account of $3,000.

1974

Feb. 13 Collected the note and interest from R. Hoode.

Journalize the transactions, including any necessary adjusting entries as of December 31, 1973.

E13-10. The following were among the transactions of the Grunderson Company for 1973 and 1974:

1973

Mar. 1 Received a 90-day, noninterest-bearing note from Albert Irons, the principal amount of which included a past due open account of $3,600 plus interest at 6% for 90 days. (The books are closed annually on December 31.)

May 30 Collected the amount due from Irons.

Dec. 1 Received a 120-day, noninterest-bearing note from Malcolm Sullivan, the principal amount of which included a past due open account of $4,840 plus interest at 5% for 120 days.

1974

Mar. 31 Collected the amount due from Sullivan.

Journalize the transactions, including any necessary adjusting entries on December 31, 1973 and 1974.

E13-11. Phipps Company completed the following transactions in 1973 and 1974:

1973

Aug. 1 Sold $600 worth of merchandise to the Rampart Company on account.

Oct. 8 Received a 90-day, 6% note in full settlement of account.

Dec. 5 Discounted the note at 5% at the Merchants Bank.

1974

Jan. 6 The note was paid at maturity.

Journalize the transactions on the books of Phipps Company and the Rampart Company, including any necessary adjusting entries on December 31, 1973.

E13-12. On September 5, 1973, the Adolph Television Company sold $1,800 worth of merchandise to Milton Company on account and received a 5-percent, 60-day note. This note was discounted at 6 percent on October 20, 1973, at the Roxboro Trust Company. At maturity date the note was dishonored by the Milton Company and the Adolph Television Company paid the maturity value plus a $2.50 protest fee. Journalize the transactions on the books of the Adolph Television Company.

E13-13. Ransom Evarts received a 6-percent, 120-day note for $3,000 from Edward Lawson, dated March 3, 1973. Evarts discounted Lawson's note 30 days later at 8 percent with William Reynoldo. Lawson paid the note at maturity.

Journalize the transactions on the books of Evarts and of Reynolds.

E13-14. Kaye Sawyer owed the Frix Marta Company $850 for merchandise that she had purchased. Since the debt was past due, Marta drew a sight draft and sent it to Miss Sawyer's bank for collection. Miss Sawyer paid the sight draft. The bank charged $1.50 for its services.

Journalize the transactions on the books of Kaye Sawyer and the Frix Marta Company.

E13-15. The Master's Company accepts trade notes from its customers. As of December 31, 1973, it had accepted only one: a 5-percent, 90-day note on December 1, 1973. At the end of the year, the following adjusting entry was made:

```
1973
Dec. 31   Accrued Interest Receivable            20.50
             Interest Earned                              20.50
                 To record interest at 5% for 30 days on
                 the note received from T. S. Balls
                 December 1 in settlement of an open
                 account receivable.
```

Reconstruct the entry made on December 1 to record the receipt of the note from T. S. Balls. Show all your calculations.

DEMONSTRATION PROBLEMS

DP13-1. (*Compound interest*) The following four cases are given:

Case A. John Jones invests $10,000 on January 1, 1973, in a savings account that earns interest at 6 percent compounded quarterly. What will be the amount in the fund at December 31, 1978?

Case B. Sam Smith receives a bonus of $2,000 each year on December 31. He starts depositing his bonus on December 31, 1973, in a savings account that earns interest at 10 percent compounded annually. What will be the amount in the fund on December 31, 1978, after he deposits his bonus received on that date?

Case C. James Johnson owes $10,000 on a noninterest bearing note due January 1, 1983. He offers to pay the amount on January 1, 1973, provided that it is discounted at 6 percent on a compound annual discount basis. What would he have to pay on January 1, 1973, under this assumption?

Case D. Thomas Paine purchased an annuity on January 1, 1973, which would yield at a 12 percent annual rate, $5,000 each June 30 and December 31 for the next six years. What must have been the cost of the annuity to Thomas Paine?

DP13-2. (*Computing maturity dates*) The following notes were received by Amity, Inc.:

Date of Note	Term of Note
March 10, 1973	60 days
April 4, 1973	90 days
March 10, 1973	2 months
April 4, 1973	3 months
January 31, 1973	1 month

Required: Determine the maturity date of each note.

DP13-3. (*Computing interest by short-cut methods*) The following information pertains to five notes:

1. $3,200 at 6% for 60 days
2. $4,600 at 6% for 30 days
3. $2,400 at 6% for 72 days
4. $6,600 at 5% for 60 days
5. $9,000 at 7½% for 45 days

Required: Using the short-cut methods discussed in this chapter, compute the amount of interest on each note.

DP13-4. (*Journalizing notes payable transactions*) The Turlington Company completed the following transactions during 1973 and 1974:

1973
Jan. 2 Purchased $3,680 worth of merchandise from the Nolta Company; issued a 6%, 60-day note.

Mar. 3 Paid the Nolta Company the amount due for the note and interest.

3 Issued a 6%, 45-day note for $4,000 to Owens, Inc., in settlement of an open account.

Apr. 17 Paid Owens, Inc., $3,000 on the March 3 note plus all the interest; issued a new 7%, 30-day note for the balance of the principal.

May 17 Paid Owens, Inc., for the April 17 note.

June 1 Discounted its own 30-day, noninterest-bearing note, made out to the first National Bank in the amount of $8,000, at a discount rate of 6%.

July 1 Paid the First National Bank the amount due.

Dec. 1 Issued a 6%, 90-day note for $5,680 to the Petersen Company in settlement of an open account.

Dec. 16 Discounted its own 60-day, noninterest-bearing note, made out to the Second National Bank in the amount of $10,000, at a discount rate of 6%.

1974
Feb. 14 Paid the Second National Bank the amount due.

Mar. 1 Paid amount due to Petersen Company for the note issued on December 1, 1973.

Required:

Journalize the transactions, including any necessary adjusting entries on December 31, 1973 and 1974.

DP13-5. (*Journalizing notes receivable transactions*) The following were among the transactions of the Quarter's Company for 1973 and 1974:

1973
Jan. 6 Sold merchandise worth $1,860 to I. Rose and received a 6%, 45-day note.

Feb. 20 Collected the amount due from I. Rose.

Mar. 1 Received a 6%, 75-day note for $3,400 from N. Richards in settlement of an open account.

May 15 N. Richards dishonored his note.

June 1 Sold merchandise worth $2,000 to W. Walters and received a 90-day, noninterest-bearing note for the amount of the sale plus interest at 6%.

Aug. 30 Collected the amount due from W. Walters.

Nov. 16 Received a 6%, 120-day note for $4,860 from J. Aikens in settlement of an open account.

1973
Dec. 1 Received a 90-day, noninterest-bearing note from H. Barrow in settlement of an open
         account of $4,400. The note had interest of $60 included in the face value.

1974
Mar. 1 Received the amount due from H. Barrow.

     16 Received the amount due from J. Aikens.

         Required:

Journalize the transactions, including any necessary adjusting entries on December 31, 1973
and 1974.

DP13-6. (*Journalizing notes discounted transactions*) Record in general journal form the following notes transactions on the books of S. Yaeger, the maker, and W. Hines, the payee:

1. On July 1, S. Yaeger purchased $4,900 worth of merchandise on account from W. Hines.
2. S. Yaeger gave a 6%, 90-day note, dated August 21, to W. Hines in settlement of his account.
3. On August 31, W. Hines discounted S. Yaeger's note at the First Street Bank at a discount
   rate of 6%.
4. On the maturity date, S. Yaeger paid the bank the maturity value of the note.

DP13-7. (*Effective interest computation*) The following transactions took place at the Henderson
Company:

1. Discounted its own 90-day, noninterest-bearing note for $5,000 at a bank at 6%.
2. Borrowed $4,800 in cash from a bank; interest at 5% on $4,800 is added to the note, making
   the principal amount of the note $5,040; the note is to be paid off in monthly installments
   over 12 months ($420 each month).

         Required: Compute the effective interest cost in each case.

DP13-8. (*Application of compound interest techniques*) B. Burton purchases a new refrigerator
at a cost of $600. He pays $100 down and issues an installment notes payable which promises
to pay the balance during the next year in 12 equal monthly installments which include interest
at 18 percent on the remaining unpaid balance at the beginning of each month.

         Required: 1. Compute the equal installment payments.
                   2. Prepare the journal entries to record the first two installment
                      payments.

PROBLEMS

P13-1. Five equal withdrawals are to be made beginning December 31, 1973. Using the proper
table, determine the equal annual withdrawals if $10,000 is invested at interest of 6 percent
compounded annually on December 31, 1973. (Tables are on pages 853–856.)

P13-2. Using the tables given on pages 853–856 solve each of the following problems:

a. Ten payments of $1,000 are due at annual intervals beginning June 30, 1974. What amount
   will be accepted in cancellation of this series of payments on June 30, 1973, assuming a
   discount rate of 6 percent compounded annually.

b. Ten payments of $1,000 are due at annual intervals beginning December 31, 1973. What
   amount will be accepted in cancellation of this series of payments on January 1, 1973,
   assuming a discount rate of 10 percent compounded annually?

P13-3. Parks borrows $25,000 on December 31, 1973, promising to repay this amount together
with accrued interest at 6 percent compounded annually on December 31, 1983. Parks plans

to make five equal deposits at annual intervals in a special savings fund in order to retire the obligation at its maturity, the first deposit to be made on January 1, 1975. He believes that the fund will earn 10 percent compounded annually. What amounts are to be deposited?

P13-4. Thurmon Royce purchases a new automobile at a cost of $3,600. He pays $600 down and issues an installment notes payable that promises to pay the balance during the next year in 12 equal monthly installments which include interest at 18 percent on the remaining unpaid balance at the beginning of each month.

> Required: 1. Compute the equal installment payments.
> 2. Prepare the journal entries to record the first two installment payments.

P13-5. The San Marko Company completed the following transactions with Goode Larson:

1973

Jan. 10   Sold $1,250 worth of merchandise to Larson on account.

Mar. 1   Received a 6%, 60-day note in full settlement of the account.

  17   Discounted the note at 4% at the First Union Bank.

May   5   Received a notice from the bank that Larson failed to honor the note.

   5   Paid the bank the maturity value of the note plus a protest fee of $4.00.

  19   Received a check from Larson for the full amount due, plus interest at 6% on the maturity value of the old note from the due date to the present.

> Required:

Record the transactions in general journal form on the books of the San Marko Company.

P13-6. (*Financial policy decision problem*) Marta Ames borrowed $3,500 from the Plymouth Trust Company, giving her 6-percent, 60-day note. On the same day, Miss Ames borrowed from the United Trust Company by discounting her $3,500 note for 60 days at 6 percent.

> Required: 1. Give the entries in general journal form to: (a) record both bank loans, and (b) record the payments of the loans on the maturity date.
> 2. Explain which loan was more favorable to Miss Ames.

P13-7. During 1973, the Wilbur Hinton Company completed the following transactions, among others:

1973

Jan. 5   Sold merchandise worth $2,800 to C. T. Perkins on account.

   7   Received a 6%, 30-day note, dated January 7, from C. T. Perkins, payable at the National Shawmut Bank.

   8   Purchased $3,400 worth of merchandise from the E. Beale Company, giving a 4%, 45-day note payable at the Second National Bank.

  10   Purchased $2,000 worth of merchandise from the J. A. Nelson Company on account.

  15   Gave the J. A. Nelson Company a 4½%, 60-day note in settlement of the account, payable at the Second National Bank.

  17   Sold merchandise worth $900 to the A. F. Duling Company on account.

  19   Sold merchandise worth $3,400 to Charles J. Collins on account.

  21   Received a 3%, 20-day note, dated January 20, from the A. F. Duling Company, payable at the Merchants Trust Company.

  22   Received a 4%, 50-day note from Charles J. Collins, payable at the First National Bank.

1973

Jan. 28   Purchased $5,500 worth of merchandise from the C. A. Gerden Company, giving a 6%, 75-day note, payable at the National Chawmut Bank, in full payment.

30   Discounted its own $6,000 note for 30 days at 6% with the Second Federal Bank.

Feb. 1   Discounted Charles J. Collins' note of January 22 at the Acton National Bank at 6%.

6   Received payment from C. T. Perkins for his note of January 7.

10   The A. F. Duling Company dishonored its note of January 21.

23   Paid the E. Beale Company for the note of January 8.

Mar. 1   Paid the Second Federal Bank for the loan made on January 30.

15   Charles J. Collins paid the bank for his note due on March 13.

Required: Record the transactions in general journal form.

P13-8. During 1973, the Ideal Manufacturing Company completed the following transactions, among others:

1973

Jan. 3   Purchased merchandise worth $4,500 from the A. L. Kalman Company giving a 6%, 30-day note, payable at the First National Bank.

4   Sold $3,000 worth of merchandise to S. M. Friedberg on account.

6   Sold $4,500 worth of merchandise to C. D. Burch on account.

8   Purchased merchandise worth $500 from McDermott & Company on account.

10   Gave McDermott & Company a 4%, 30-day note, payable at the Merchants Trust Company.

12   C. D. Burch gave a 4%, 20-day note, payable at the First National Bank.

15   S. M. Friedberg gave a 5%, 30-day note, payable at the National Shawmut Bank.

16   Sold $3,200 worth of merchandise to E. Hazelwood, Inc., on account.

24   Received a 6%, 20-day note, payable at the Worcester County Trust Company, from E. Hazelwood, Inc.

24   Sold $7,500 worth of merchandise to Fenn & Company and received a 4%, 30-day note, payable at the Second National Bank.

Feb. 1   C. D. Burch's note of January 12 was dishonored.

2   Paid the A. L. Kalman Company for the note due today.

9   Paid the McDermott Company for the note due today.

13   Received a check from E. Hazelwood, Inc., for $1,200 plus interest, and accepted a new 6%, 90-day note payable at the Worcester County Trust Company for the balance of the note of January 24.

14   Received payment from S. M. Friedberg in payment of his note due today.

23   Received a check from Fenn & Company for $3,500 plus interest, and accepted a new 4%, 30-day note payable at the Second National Bank for the balance of the note of January 24.

28   Discounted Fenn & Company's note of February 23 at the Lynn Bank at 6%.

Mar. 25   Received notice that Fenn & Company had dishonored its note of February 23. Paid the bank the maturity value of the note plus a $3 protest fee.

Required: Record the transactions in general journal form.

P13-9. On November 1, 1973, the Edenton Company adopted a policy of requesting customers whose accounts have become past due to substitute interest-bearing notes for the open account. In many cases, the company discounts the notes receivable obtained from customers. The bank charges a 6-percent discount on such transactions.

The following ledger accounts reflect the note transactions, interest expense, and interest earned during November and December. The company closes its books at the end of the calendar year, December 31.

Notes Receivable — Acct. No. 111

1973					1973				
Nov.	6	J. Johns, 30-day	J2	700	Dec.	6	J. Johns	J4	700
	24	D. M. Bell, 60-day	CD1	1,500					
Dec.	12	A. G. Lee, 90-day	J6	4,000					
	18	K. Murray, 5%, 30-day	J7	1,200					

Notes Receivable Discounted — Acct. No. 111A

					1973				
					Dec.	9	D. M. Bell	CR1	1,500
						20	K. Murray	CR1	1,200

Notes Payable — Acct. No. 202

					1973				
					Nov.	18	B. E. Ray, 5%, 90-day (settle open account)	J3	2,100

Interest Earned — Acct. No. 311

					1973				
					Dec.	6	J. Johns	J4	3.50
						9	D. M. Bell	CR1	3.64
						31	Adjustment	J10	12.67

Interest Expense — Acct. No. 713

1973									
Dec.	20	K. Murray	CR1	.62					
	31	Adjustment	J10	12.54					

Required:

1. Prepare in general journal form all the entries made by the Evans Company to record the information in the ledger accounts. Assume that all the notes bear interest at the rate of 6 percent, unless otherwise indicated. Also assume that the accounts include the necessary adjustments for interest at December 31. For the two notes receivable discounted, determine whether the bank in fact charged interest at an annual rate of 6 percent (show your computation).

2. Show how the facts regarding all the notes should be disclosed in the statement of financial position.

P13-10. On June 30, the Moonglo Company's trial balance included the following accounts:

Notes Receivable	$12,600
Notes Receivable Discounted (credit)	5,000

The notes receivable register showed the following supporting details:

Note No.	Face Value	Date of Note	Term of Note	Interest Rate	Remarks
1	$3,000	May 29, 1973	60 days	5%	Discounted at bank on June 30, 1973. Bank discount rate, 4%.
2	2,000	May 1, 1973	120 days	6%	Discounted at bank on June 16, 1973. Bank discount rate, 4%.
3	4,000	June 16, 1973	30 days	4%	
4	3,600	June 21, 1973	90 days	6%	

The disposition of the four notes was:

Note 1: Paid at the bank by the maker on the maturity date.

Note 2: Dishonored by the maker. The Moonglo Company paid the bank the maturity value of the note plus a $3 protest fee.

Note 3: Paid by the maker on the maturity date.

Note 4: On July 10, 1973, the Moonglo Company had its own $3,000 noninterest-bearing note due at the bank. Moonglo Company paid its $3,000 note by discounting Note 4 (the bank discount rate was 4%) and received the balance due in cash. The maker of Note 4 paid the bank on the maturity date.

      Required: Prepare dated general journal entries to record the disposition of each note.

P13-11. (*Financial policy decision problem*) The Hudson Appliance Company sells a standard refrigerator for $240 in cash or on terms of $25 down and $40 a month for six months. In order to meet competition, the company is considering changing its credit terms to a $25 down payment and $20 a month for 12 months.

      Required: Compute the real annual interest rate under (a) the present plan and (b) the proposed plan. Carry your computations to two decimal places. Assume that each installment includes a uniform monthly reduction in the carrying charge. (c) Which financing method should be chosen?

P13-12. At December 31, 1973, the Reynoldo Appliance Company's ledger contained the following information in the Notes Receivable and Notes Payable accounts:

Analysis of Notes Receivable:

Maker	Date of Note	Principal	Term of Note	Interest Rate	Remarks
	1973				
A. Able	November 2	$ 2,380	90 days	6%	
W. Cutler	December 8	3,460	60 days	5%	
M. Bower	December 16	4,488	90 days		Interest of
Total		$10,328			$88 included in face value.

Analysis of Notes Payable:

Payee	Date of Note	Principal	Term of Note	Interest Rate	Remarks
Dawer Company	November 10, 1973	$ 3,670	120 days	4½%	
Evart Company	November 20, 1973	2,860	90 days	6%	
State Bank	December 1, 1973	3,600	120 days		Discounted at 6%.
Total		$10,130			

Required: Prepare the adjusting journal entries. Show your calulations, properly labeled.

14

Managerial
Financial Decisions—
Debt

The financial managers of modern corporations are constantly faced with the problem of how and where to get corporate capital for both short-term and long-term needs. The various alternative sources are outlined as follows:

1. Investments of the owners (discussed in Chapter 11)
2. Retention of earnings (discussed in Chapter 12)
3. Financing by creditors, which may create current or long-term liabilities (discussed in Chapter 13 and in this chapter)

Only summary consideration is given to current liabilities in this chapter since they have been discussed in various other parts of this text, particularly Chapter 13. More detailed attention is paid to various long-term liabilities, such as Bonds Payable, Mortgage Payable, and Liabilities Under Pension Contracts.

CURRENT LIABILITIES

As previously defined, current liabilities represent obligations, the liquidation of which requires the use of current assets or the creation of other current liabilities within a year or an operating cycle, whichever is the longer period of time. Various kinds of current liabilities have been discussed elsewhere in this text, including

Bank overdrafts
Accounts payable, trade;
  or vouchers payable
Notes payable, trade
Notes payable, bank
Maturing bonds payable

Current installments of
  serial bonds payable
Credit balances in
  customers' accounts
Accrued interest payable
Sales taxes payable

491

F.I.C.A. taxes payable

State unemployment compensation
taxes payable

Federal unemployment compensation
taxes payable

Federal income taxes payable

Employees' income tax
withholdings payable

Unearned subscriptions

Bonds Payable, though they may have been originally issued with lives as long as 50 years or more, are classified as a current liability on the statement of financial position prepared at the end of the fiscal year immediately preceding the date of retirement. Unearned Subscriptions are not liquidated by the use of current assets but are earned within the next year or cycle; current assets are consumed in the earning process. Current liabilities are generally presented on the statement of financial position at their full maturity value.

All these current liabilities provide cash or some other asset, such as merchandise. They are significant to a financial manager since payment or refunding must be accomplished; but the management of current liabilities may also influence decisions made in regard to long-term debt financing. For example, if there is a large amount of unsecured accounts payable outstanding, these short-term creditors may bring pressure to bear to prevent the issuance of long-term secured bonds payable.

BONDS PAYABLE

One of the means used by businesses to acquire funds that will not be repaid for many years is the issuance of bonds. A *bond*, or *bond certificate*, is a written promise under the corporate seal to pay a specific sum of money on a specified or determinable future date to the order of a person named in the certificate or to the order of the bearer. An example of a corporate bond is the $2\frac{7}{8}\%$ First Mortgage Callable Bond Payable, Series A, due 1996, issued by the Bessemer and Lake Erie Railroad Company, a subsidiary of the United States Steel Corporation. Bonds are issued in denominations of $100, $500, $1,000, or $5,000 each; this enables the issuing company to obtain funds from many different classes of investors. The smaller denominations, for example, are used by the United States Government in its Series E Savings Bond issues. On the other hand, municipal bond issues in $5,000 denominations are also common.

Bonds may be issued directly by the borrowing corporation or they may be transferred to banks, brokers, or other underwriting syndicates who, in turn, market the bonds through their own channels. *Bondholders* are creditors of the corporation; with the exception noted above, the Bonds Payable account is a long-term liability. Bonds contain provisions for interest to be paid at regularly stated intervals. Interest is usually paid semiannually on industrial bonds.

A bond, like a promissory note, represents a corporate debt to the lender, which must be satisfied from the assets of the corporation in preference to stockholders' equity claims. The main functional difference between bonds and promissory notes is that bonds are used in long-term financing, whereas promissory notes are used in short-term financing.

Bonds Compared with Capital Stock

A better knowledge of bonds may be obtained if they and related concepts are compared with capital stock. The following parallel listing should help the reader understand more fully the nature of bonds.

Bonds	Capital Stock
Bondholders are creditors.	Stockholders are owners.
Bonds Payable is a long-term liability account.	Capital Stock is a stockholders' equity account.
Bondholders, along with other creditors, have primary claims on assets in liquidation.	Stockholders have residual claims on assets in liquidation.
Interest is typically a fixed charge; it must be paid or the creditors can institute bankruptcy proceedings against the debtor corporation.	Dividends are not fixed charges; even preferred dividends are at best only *contingent charges.*
Interest is a valid expense.	Dividends are not expenses; they are distributions of net income.
Interest is deductible in arriving at both taxable and business income.	Dividends are not deductible in arriving at taxable and business income.
Bonds do not carry voting rights.	All stock carries voting rights unless they are expressly denied by contract, as is usually the case with preferred stock.

Classifications of Bonds

There are many types of bonds, each tailored to meet the particular financial needs of the issuing corporation. Some common classifications of bonds are described in the following paragraphs.

Registered Bonds. Registered bonds are issued in the name of the bondholder. They require proper endorsement on the bond certificate to effect a transfer from one owner to another. The debtor corporation or its transfer agent, usually a bank or trust company appointed by the corporation, maintains complete ownership records. Bonds may be registered both as to principal and interest, in which case interest checks are issued only to bondholders of record. It is possible, however, to register the principal only (*coupon bonds*); the owner detaches *interest coupons* from the bond certificate and deposits them at the stated interest dates at his bank, or at a designated bank.

Bearer Bonds. Bonds may be issued without being registered in the name of the buyer; title to them is vested in the *bearer.* The procedure for making interest payments is the same as with coupon bonds. This method is least burdensome to the issuing corporation, but the owner must take particular care against loss or theft of the certificates, or unauthorized removal of the coupons attached to the bonds.

Secured Bonds. A *secured* bond is one that pledges some part of the corporate property as security for the bond. The property pledged may consist of land and buildings (*real estate mortgage* bonds), machinery (*chattel mortgage* bonds), negotiable securities (*collateral trust* bonds), or other corporate property. Several loans may use the same property for collateral; this gives rise to *first mortgage* bonds and *second mortgage* bonds. The numbers indicate the order to be followed in satisfying the mortgageholders' claims if the corporation fails to meet its obligations under the *bond indenture*—the contract between the corporation and the bondholder. In the event of default *foreclosure* and sale of the property follow. Second and third mortgage bonds necessarily carry a higher interest rate than first mortgage bonds because of the order of priority of payment in the event of a default; thus, they are not as marketable as first mortgage bonds and are more costly to the borrowing company. It is, therefore, desirable for the borrower to raise the required funds through a single, large first mortgage bond issue.

Unsecured Bonds. Unsecured bondholders rank as general, or ordinary, creditors of the corporation and rely upon the corporations' general credit. Such bonds are commonly referred to as *debenture* bonds, or often simply as *debentures*. Sometimes debenture bonds are issued with a provision that interest payments will depend on earnings; such bonds are called *income* bonds.

Bonds may have other special features; for instance, the bonds may mature serially (*serial* bonds), which means that specified portions of the outstanding bonds will mature in installments and be paid at stated intervals. Sometimes the issuing corporation retains an option to call in the bonds before maturity (*callable* bonds); or, in other cases, the bondholder may be given an option to exchange his bonds for capital stock (*convertible* bonds). The bond indenture may require the issuing corporation to deposit funds, often to a trustee for the bondholders, at regular intervals to insure the availability of adequate funds for the redemption of the bonds at maturity (*sinking fund* bonds).

Managerial Reasons for Issuing Bonds Instead of Capital Stock

Among the many factors that influence management in regard to the issuance of bonds instead of capital stock is that management may be enabled to tap another market source of creditor funds that it would not be able to tap by the issuance of stock. For example, many banks and other financial institutions are not permitted by law or regulation to buy stocks, but they are allowed to buy bonds.

A second factor is *leverage,* or *trading on the bondholders' equity.* This practice can be described very simply: if funds can be borrowed at an interest rate of 6 percent and utilized in the business to earn 14 percent after taxes, then the additional earnings of 8 percent (14% − 6%) accrue to the common stockholders. However, there is always the possibility of the opposite reaction taking place; in other words, the borrowed funds may earn less than the cost of borrowing —an instance of unfavorable leverage.

A third reason why corporations decide to issue bonds rather than capital stock is that there is a high income tax rate on corporate net income. If a corporation pays out at least half its net income in Federal and state income taxes, it naturally considers the issuance of bonds as a means of effecting a considerable tax saving.

To illustrate the way that leverage and heavy income taxes affect financial decision making involving the choice of alternative methods of fund raising, assume that the Hunt Corporation, which has $100 par value common stock outstanding in the amount of $1,000,000, needs $500,000 to purchase additional plant and equipment. Three plans are under consideration: Plan 1 is to issue additional common stock at $100 par value; Plan 2 is to issue 6% preferred stock at $100 par value, cumulative and nonparticipating; Plan 3 is to issue 5% bonds.

	Plan 1	Plan 2	Plan 3
Common stock	$1,000,000	$1,000,000	$1,000,000
Additional funds	500,000	500,000	500,000
Total	$1,500,000	$1,500,000	$1,500,000
Net income before bond interest and income taxes	$ 300,000	$ 300,000	$ 300,000
Deduct bond interest expense	–0–	–0–	25,000
Net income after bond interest expense	$ 300,000	$ 300,000	$ 275,000
Deduct income taxes (assumed rate of 50%)	150,000	150,000	137,500
Net income after income taxes	$ 150,000	$ 150,000	$ 137,500
Deduct dividends on preferred stock	–0–	30,000	–0–
Available for common stock dividends	$ 150,000	$ 120,000	$ 137,500
Pro forma earnings per share on common stock (15,000 shares outstanding under Plan 1; 10,000 shares under Plans 2 and 3)	$10	$12	$13.75

All the plans assume that the securities will be issued at par value, that earnings of $300,000 annually before the bond interest expense is deducted will be maintained, and that an income tax rate of 50 percent will prevail.

Assuming that earnings per share on common stock is an accepted decision-making criterion, Plan 3 appears to be the most promising for the common stockholders, particularly if the annual earnings exceed $300,000, because the bond interest rate is fixed. If the annual earnings fall below $300,000, one of the other plans may become more advantageous. Since the securities market and corporate net earnings remain uncertain, there is no exact mathematical formula to solve this financial problem. The decision requires sound judgment based on past experience and projected future needs.

A fourth reason for the issuance of bonds instead of common stock is the fact that bonds, and to a lesser extent preferred stock, aid in offsetting losses due to shrinkage in the purchasing power of the funds invested in assets. Bonds, for example, carry fixed contract maturity values in terms of the monetary unit at the maturity date. If the value of the dollar decreases before the bonds are paid, a gain resulting from the use of the more valuable money received at the time of borrowing accrues to the owners of the business.

A fifth factor is control. The issuance of additional common stock may result in a loss of management control because the ownership of the corporation is distributed over a larger number of stockholders. Bondholders, on the other hand, are creditors and do not participate in managerial decisions, except in the rare instances when this is a specific provision of the bond indenture.

Other reasons may influence the decision of management to issue bonds; but these five factors indicate the scope of the problem.

Authorizing the Bond Issue

Even after management decides that bonds should be issued, it is faced with months of preliminary work before the bonds can actually be *floated*, or sold. For example, the exact amount to be borrowed, the *contract* or *nominal interest rate* (the rate on the bond certificate that applies to the face value), the maturity date, and the assets, if any, to be pledged must be determined. The provisions of the bond indenture must be chosen with extreme care: For instance, should the bonds be callable, and should they be convertible into some other form of security? Careful long-range financial planning helps to reduce the cost of securing the long-term funds. For example, if there is any chance that the company will need additional funds in the near future, management should not close the door on the possibility of marketing additional bonds by pledging the company's total mortgageable assets. In this case, management probably should seek authority for a bond issue large enough to meet all foreseeable needs.

The financial vice president, working with other corporate officers, is responsible for finding answers to these and other questions. He prepares a written report for the board of directors, summarizing the proposed features of the bond financing and stating why the funds are needed, how they are to be used, and the means of ultimately retiring the bond issue. Various alternative methods of raising funds, such as those shown in the example of the Hunt Corporation, no doubt, are presented to point up the financial advantage of issuing the bonds.

The board of directors studies this written report, along with the laws of the state of incorporation, the corporate charter, and the corporate bylaws, before passing a resolution recommending to the stockholders that bonds be issued; a record of the resolution is entered in the minute book of the corporation. Next, the proposal is presented to the stockholders for their approval. Once this approval has been gained, the board of directors prepares a resolution instructing the proper corporate officers to issue the bonds and sign the necessary documents. The final step is the issuance of a formal certified statement that the approval of the board of directors and the stockholders has been obtained. Approval by the stockholders is required since the bondholders have a preferred position; as creditors, they have a prior claim to the assets of the corporation in the event of liquidation.

Accounting for the Issuance of Bonds

No formal journal entry is required to record the authorization of the bond issue by the stockholders, but a memorandum should be made in the Bonds Payable account indicating the total amount authorized. This information is needed when the statement of financial position is prepared since it should disclose the total authorization as well as the amount issued.

The issue price, usually stated as a percentage of the face value, is affected primarily by the prevailing market interest rate on bonds of the same grade. Bonds are graded by various financial institutions; the grade depends on the financial condition of the issuing corporation. The highest grade is AAA; the next, AA; and in descending order: A, BBB, BB, B. If, on the issue date, the stated interest rate applicable to the face value of the bonds—also called *contract,* or *nominal,* rate—is established at the prevailing market interest rate for the particular grade of bonds, the authorized bonds will sell at face value. On the other hand, if there is a disparity between the contract bond interest rate and the prevailing market rate for that grade of bonds, the bonds will sell at a price above or below face value, that is, at a *premium* or a *discount.*

Bonds Issued at Face Value. The first example involves the simple situation in which a corporation issues bonds at face value on an interest date. The same sequence is followed in each of the first three illustrations: First, an entry is made to record the issuance of the bonds; next, any peculiarity of financial statement presentation is discussed; after this, the accounting procedure for interest payments is described; and, finally, the recording of the *retirement* of the bonds at the maturity date is shown.

Assume that on July 1, 1973, the Grogan Corporation is authorized to issue 5% debenture bonds with a face value of $200,000 and a maturity date of June 30, 1993. Interest is paid semiannually on June 30 and December 31. All the bonds are issued on July 1, 1973, at 100, or face value, and the following entry is made:

```
1973
July  1   Cash                                            200,000
              Debenture Bonds Payable                                  200,000
              To record the issuance of all the authorized
              5% bonds due on June 30, 1993.
```

The similarity between this entry and that for the issuance of notes, discussed in Chapter 13, is clear.

A statement of financial position prepared after this transaction would report the bond issue as follows:

```
              Long-Term Liabilities
                  5% Debenture Bonds Payable, due June 30, 1993      $200,000
```

The following entry records the payment of interest on December 31, 1973, (the bond issue and interest payment entries are normally made in the cash receipts and cash disbursements journals):

```
1973
Dec. 31   Bond Interest Expense                           5,000
              Cash                                                     5,000
              To record the payment of the semiannual
              interest on the 5% bonds payable.
```

A similar entry is made each June 30 and December 31 until the bonds are retired. It is possible for all the interest paid by the corporation to be recorded in a single Interest Expense account; however, in the present case, the interest on bonds payable is considered to be material enough to warrant a separate general ledger account.

On June 30, 1993, the bonds are retired by the payment of cash to the bondholders. The following compound entry is made on that date to record the last interest payment and the retirement of the bonds:

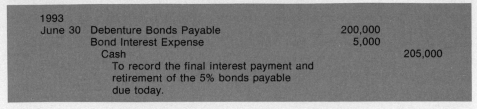

1993			
June 30	Debenture Bonds Payable	200,000	
	Bond Interest Expense	5,000	
	Cash		205,000
	To record the final interest payment and retirement of the 5% bonds payable due today.		

Issuing Bonds at a Discount or a Premium. If the average effective market interest rate on bonds of any particular grade exceeds the contract interest rate of bonds of the same grade being issued, investors will offer less than the face value of the bonds in order to make up the difference between the rates. The difference between the issue price and the face value, which the investors will receive at maturity, plus receipts of the semiannual interest, will give them a return on their investments approximating the yield of similar amounts invested at the prevailing market interest rate. By the same token, if the stated interest rate is more favorable than the current market rate, investors will tend to offer more than the face value because they know that the premium paid will, in effect, be returned to them to the extent that the periodic interest payments exceed the amount that they would otherwise receive on investments made at the current market rate.

Two examples are presented to emphasize the reasons for bonds selling at a premium or discount. First, assume that the Strong Company has an AAA financial rating and is planning to issue debenture bonds. Assume also that all the AAA debenture bonds on the market have an effective average market interest rate of 5 percent. If the Strong Company issues debenture bonds with a 5-percent contract interest rate, it will receive the face value of the bonds; if it issues bonds with a 6-percent contract interest rate, it will receive an amount in excess of the face value; but even with its excellent credit rating, if it issues bonds with a 4-percent contract rate, it will receive an amount less than the face value.

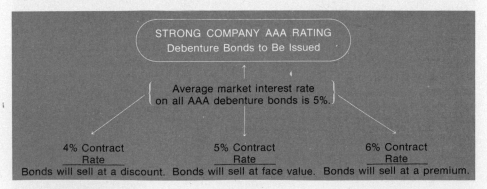

The second example will help to show that the financial condition of a company is not the basic determinant of the issue price of the company's bonds.

Assume that the Weak Company, with a BB financial rating, intends to issue first mortgage bonds. Further assume that the average effective market interest rate on BB first mortgage bonds is 7 percent. If the Weak Company issues its bonds with a 7-percent contract interest rate, it will receive the face value of the bonds. Even with its relatively poor credit rating if it issues bonds with an 8-percent contract interest rate, it will receive an amount in excess of the face value; but if it issues bonds with a 6-percent contract interest rate, it will receive an amount less than the face value.

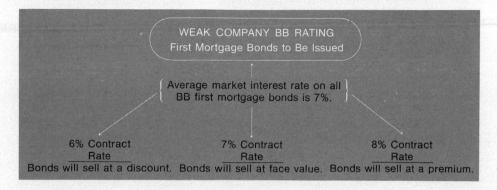

The Calculation of the Exact Price of Bonds to Yield a Given Rate. The exact price that an investor must pay for the bonds to yield a given effective rate can be determined by a compound interest computation, or by reference to a *bond yield table*. To illustrate the compound interest computation, assume that a 10-year (20 semiannual periods), 6%, $1,000 bond with interest paid semiannually is to yield 4 percent (or 2 percent every six months). The issue price is calculated as shown below.

Present value of $1,000 for 20 periods at 2%:	
$1,000 × 0.673	$ 673.00
Add present value of 20 interest payments of $30 each at 2%:	
$30 × 16.351	490.53
Total price to yield 4% annually	$1,163.53

Accounting for Bonds Issued at a Premium—Straight-Line Amortization Method. Assume that on July 1, 1973, the Hunt Corporation is authorized to issue 5% first mortgage bonds with a face value of $300,000 and a maturity date of June 30, 1988. Interest is paid semiannually on June 30 and December 31. All the bonds are issued on July 1, 1973, at 103; that is, at 103 percent of their face value; and the following entry is made:

1973		
July 1 Cash	309,000	
First Mortgage Bonds Payable		300,000
Premium on Bonds Payable		9,000
To record the issuance of 5% first mortgage bonds due June 30, 1988.		

A statement of financial position prepared on July 1, 1973, would show Bonds Payable and Premium on Bonds Payable as follows:

Long-Term Liabilities		
5% First Mortgage Bonds Payable, due June 30, 1988	$300,000	
Premium on Bonds Payable	9,000	
Total Long-Term Liabilities		$309,000

The assets pledged as security for the bonds payable would be disclosed in the following footnote:

> Land and buildings costing $600,000 (market value $650,000) are pledged as security for the bonds payable.

This method of disclosure is consistent with the concept that the right side of the statement of financial position describes the sources of business funds. Of course, the Premium account will be reduced by periodic amortization and thus will be smaller on each subsequent statement; but, again, this procedure is consistent with the concept that when bonds are issued at a premium, each interest payment contains, in effect, a payment of the interest earned on the investment and also a partial return of the amount borrowed from the investor. If part of the $309,000 borrowed is repaid, a statement of financial position prepared at a later date would naturally show a smaller amount. The footnote describing the assets pledged as security for the long-term debt is a disclosure of important information that may influence the decision of an investor to buy or not to buy the company's bonds.

The amount received from the issuance of the bonds is $9,000 greater than the amount that must be repaid at maturity. This amount is not a gain, for it is illogical to assume that revenue can result directly from the borrowing process. The premium arose because the contract rate of interest on the bonds issued was higher than the prevailing market rate on similar grade bonds; therefore, it is sound accounting practice to allocate part of the Premium on Bonds Payable to each period as a reduction of the periodic bond interest expense. The straight-line method of allocation is most commonly used, and will be emphasized in this text; however, the compound interest method of premium and discount amortization is illustrated later in this chapter. In summary, the total bond interest expense over the life of a bond issue is equal to the total amount of cash paid in interest minus the amount of the premium.

The bond interest expense of the Hunt Corporation is recorded on December 31, 1973, as follows:

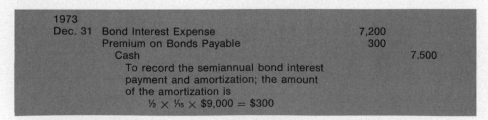

1973			
Dec. 31	Bond Interest Expense	7,200	
	Premium on Bonds Payable	300	
	Cash		7,500
	To record the semiannual bond interest payment and amortization; the amount of the amortization is		
	½ × ⅟₁₅ × $9,000 = $300		

If the $9,000 premium on the bonds payable represents a reduction in interest over the entire 15-year life of the bonds, it is evident that by the straight-line amortization method the reduction in interest for the six months ended December 31, 1973, is $9,000 divided by 30 semiannual periods (calculated as $\frac{1}{2} \times \frac{1}{15} \times$ $9,000 in the journal entry), or $300.

This compound entry emphasizes that the $7,500 constitutes the payment of effective bond interest expense of $7,200 and a partial return of the amount borrowed, the $300 amortized. (It is suggested for the problems in this text that premiums or discounts on bonds payable be amortized each time the bond interest expense is recorded to emphasize that this amortization is an adjustment of the bond interest expense.)

Even though the compound entry is acceptable, two separate entries are generally made to record the payment of the semiannual bond interest and the semiannual amortization of the premium, as shown below.

1973			
Dec. 31	Bond Interest Expense	7,500	
	Cash		7,500
	To record the semiannual bond interest payment.		
31	Premium on Bonds Payable	300	
	Bond Interest Expense		300
	To record the semiannual amortization of the premium on bonds payable: $\frac{1}{2} \times \frac{1}{15} \times$ $9,000 = $300		

When the debit of $7,500 and the credit of $300 to Bond Interest Expense are combined, the net expense is $7,200, the amount of the effective interest for six months. Assuming the use of straight-line amortization of the premium on bonds payable, the validity of the $7,200 semiannual bond interest figure can be established as follows:

Cash payments	
Face value of bonds at maturity	$300,000
Total interest—5% $\times$ 15 years $\times$ $300,000	225,000
Total cash payments	$525,000
Cash receipts	
Bonds with face value of $300,000 issued at 103	309,000
Net interest expense for 15 years	$216,000
Net semiannual interest expense	
$\dfrac{\$216,000}{30 \text{ semiannual periods}}$	$ 7,200

A formula for the approximation of effective interest rate (i) on bonds issued at a premium can be stated as follows:

$$i = I \div \left(F + \frac{P}{2} \right)$$

where I = annual absolute interest, adjusted for amortization of premium
F = face value of bonds
P = total premium
$\dfrac{P}{2}$ = average premium

The effective interest rate on the Hunt Corporation bonds is approximately 4.73 percent [$14,400 ÷ ($300,000 + $9,000/2)]—that is, the absolute effective amount of annual interest divided by the average carrying value (face value plus unamortized premium) of the bonds issued. Exact effective rates may be determined readily from bond yield tables or by using compound interest techniques. The effective interest rate computation emphasizes the fact that the premium on the bonds results in a downward adjustment of the 5-percent contract rate to the effective rate.

Assume that the 5% first mortgage bonds payable are retired on June 30, 1988. After the first two of the following entries—the last semiannual interest payment and last semiannual amortization of the Premium on Bonds Payable account—are made, the Premium on Bonds Payable account has a zero balance. The third entry, recording the retirement of the bonds at maturity, is similar to the one that records the retirement of the Grogan Company bonds in the first bond example.

1988			
June 30	Bond Interest Expense	7,500	
	Cash		7,500
	To record the last semiannual interest payment on the 5% bonds payable.		
30	Premium on Bonds Payable	300	
	Bond Interest Expense		300
	To record the semiannual amortization of bond premium.		
30	First Mortgage Bonds Payable	300,000	
	Cash		300,000
	To record the retirement of the 5% bonds payable at maturity.		

Accounting for Bonds Issued at a Discount—Straight-Line Amortization Method. Assume that on July 1, 1973, the Ironson Company is authorized to issue 4% debenture bonds with a face value of $400,000 and a maturity date of June 30, 1983. Again, assume that interest is paid semiannually on June 30 and December 31. All the bonds are issued on July 1, 1973, at 97. The discount is due to the influence of the prevailing market interest rate on similar grades of debenture bonds. In the case of the Ironson Company's debenture bonds, their contract interest rate is lower than the prevailing market rate on a similar grade of securities. The issuance of these bonds may be recorded as follows:

1973			
July 1	Cash	388,000	
	Discount on Bonds Payable	12,000	
	Debenture Bonds Payable		400,000
	To record the issuance of 4% debenture bonds due June 30, 1983.		

A statement of financial position prepared on July 1, 1973, would disclose the Bonds Payable and Discount on Bonds Payable as follows:

Long-Term Liabilities:		
4% Debenture Bonds Payable, due June 30, 1983	$400,000	
Deduct Discount on Bonds Payable	12,000	
Total Long-Term Liabilities		$388,000

Note the similarity of this method to the disclosure of a premium on bonds payable.

The following compound entry records the first semiannual interest payment by the Ironson Company and semiannual amortization of the Discount on Bonds Payable account.

1973			
Dec. 31	Bond Interest Expense	8,600	
	Cash		8,000
	Discount on Bonds Payable		600
	To record semiannual bond interest payment and amortization; the amount of amortization is $\frac{1}{2} \times \frac{1}{10} \times \$12,000 = \$600$		

This entry indicates that the effective semiannual interest expense is $8,600, not $8,000. Assuming that the straight-line method of amortization is used, the effective interest is equal to the cash interest payment plus a pro rata share of the discount, which is, in effect, a part of the total interest cost over the entire life of the bonds. This accounting procedure, therefore, recognizes the reason for the discount on the bonds: That the contract rate of interest was lower than the prevailing market interest rate on similar grades of securities.

Instead of a compound entry, *two* journal entries may be made as follows:

1973			
Dec. 31	Bond Interest Expense	8,000	
	Cash		8,000
	To record the semiannual bond interest payment on the 4% bonds.		
31	Bond Interest Expense	600	
	Discount on Bonds Payable		600
	To record the semiannual amortization of discount on bonds payable.		

The two debits to Bond Interest Expense total $8,600, the amount of the effective interest expense for the six months ended December 31, 1973. Assuming the use of straight-line amortization of the discount on bonds payable, the proof of this semiannual bond interest expense can be established as follows:

Cash payments		
Face value of bonds at maturity		$400,000
Total interest—4% × 10 years × $400,000		160,000
Total cash payments		$560,000
Cash receipts		
Bonds with face value of $400,000 issued at 97		$388,000
Net interest expense for 10 years		$172,000
Net semiannual interest expense		
$\dfrac{\$172,000}{20 \text{ semiannual periods}}$		$ 8,600

A formula for the approximation of effective interest rate (i) on bonds issued at a discount can be stated as follows:

$$i = I \div \left(F - \frac{D}{2} \right)$$

where I = annual absolute interest, adjusted for amortization of discount
$\quad F$ = face value of bonds
$\quad D$ = total discount
$\quad \dfrac{D}{2}$ = average discount

The effective interest rate is approximately 4.37 percent [$17,200 ÷ ($400,000 − $12,000/2)]. Again, an exact effective interest rate may be determined readily from bond yield tables or by using compound interest techniques. The bond discount results in an upward adjustment of the 4-percent contract rate to its effective yield rate of 4.37 percent.

On June 30, 1983, the 4% debenture bonds payable are retired. After the first two of the following entries—the last semiannual interest payment and the last semiannual amortization of the Discount on Bonds Payable account—are made, the Discount on Bonds Payable account has a zero balance. The third entry records the retirement of the bonds at maturity.

1983			
June 30	Bond Interest Expense	8,000	
	Cash		8,000
	To record the last semiannual interest payment on the 4% bonds payable.		
30	Bond Interest Expense	600	
	Discount on Bonds Payable		600
	To record the final amortization of bond discount.		
30	Debenture Bonds Payable	400,000	
	Cash		400,000
	To record the retirement of the 4% bonds payable at maturity.		

Amortization and End-of-Period Adjustments. The preceding examples emphasized the basic accounting procedures and the reasons for amortizing bond premiums and discounts. A more complex problem involving the issuance of bonds between interest dates, bond premium amortization, and end-of-year adjustments is presented in the following paragraphs.

Bonds may be authorized by the stockholders but not issued for several months or even years because market conditions are not favorable. Some of the bonds may be issued and the rest held until a specific need for the additional funds arises. Often the time needed for clerical work delays issuance past an interest date. The interest on bonds issued between interest dates will have accrued from the last interest date to the date of issuance. Since the bonds carry an inherent promise to pay not only the face value at maturity but six months' interest at each interest date, it is customary in these cases for the investor to pay the issue price of the bonds plus an amount equal to the accrued interest. In turn, the first interest payment will be for one full interest period—six months' interest—thereby returning to the purchaser the accrued interest that he paid plus the interest earned from the date of purchase to the current interest date.

Assume that on October 1, 1971, the Johnson Company is authorized to issue 6% debenture bonds with a face value of $1,000,000 and a maturity date of October 1, 1981. The semiannual interest dates are April 1 and October 1.

The bonds are held until June 1, 1973, when bonds with a face value of $400,000 are floated at 105 plus accrued interest. The amount of cash that the Johnson Company receives is $424,000: $420,000 for the bonds plus $4,000 for accrued interest. Note that the promise to pay six months' interest is not retroactive beyond April 1, 1973, the interest date preceding the date of issuance. On October 1, 1973, the purchaser of the bonds receives an interest payment of $12,000, although the interest on $400,000 at 6 percent from June 1 to October 1 is only $8,000. The payment includes a return of the $4,000 that the investor paid for accrued interest on June 1, as illustrated in Figure 14-1.

Figure 14-1. Accumulation of Interest

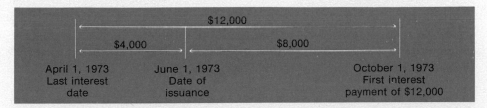

The Johnson Company records the bond issuance as shown below.

```
1973
June  1  Cash                                        424,000
              Debenture Bonds Payable                          400,000
              Premium on Bonds Payable                          20,000
              Accrued Bond Interest Payable                      4,000
                  To record the issuance of bonds
                  at 105 plus accrued interest.
```

The accrued interest is credited to a current liability account since it must be repaid on the next interest date.

The entries to record the payment of semiannual interest and the amortization of bond premium are shown below.

```
1973
Oct.  1  Bond Interest Expense                         8,000
         Accrued Bond Interest Payable                 4,000
              Cash                                               12,000
                  To record the payment of semiannual
                  interest on 6% bonds payable.

      1  Premium on Bonds Payable                        800
              Bond Interest Expense                                 800
                  To record the amortization of the bond
                  premium for four months:
                      $20,000 ÷ 100 mos. × 4 = $800
```

The entry for the interest payment reflects the amounts shown in Figure 14-1; that is, the semiannual cash payment includes a return of $4,000 for the accrued interest that was sold to the investor plus $8,000 for interest actually earned by the investor for the four months' use of his money.

The amortization covers only the period from the date of issuance to the maturity date. The date of authorization and even the preceding interest date are not relevant to the start of the amortization period. For the bonds of the Johnson Company, the amortization periods begin on June 1, 1973, and end on October 1, 1981, a total of 100 months. The amount of bond premium to be amortized each month is $200 ($20,000 ÷ 100 mos.); the amount for four months is $800 ($200 × 4).

Assuming that the Johnson Company closes its books on a calendar-year basis, the following adjusting entries are made on December 31, 1973:

1973		
Dec. 31 Bond Interest Expense	6,000	
Accrued Bond Interest Payable		6,000
To record the accrual of bond interest for three months.		
31 Premium on Bonds Payable	600	
Bond Interest Expense		600
To record the amortization of bond premium for three months: 3 × $200 = $600		

The effect of the end-of-year adjustments is that the Bond Interest Expense account reflects the correct interest expense ($12,600) incurred for the seven months during which the bonds were outstanding (June 1 to December 31). The Bond Interest Expense account is closed to Revenue and Expense Summary. The Accrued Bond Interest Payable account is shown as a current liability on the statement of financial position and remains on the books until the next regular interest date.

On April 1, 1974, the next regular interest date, the following entries are made to record the payment of interest and the amortization of the bond premium:

1974		
Apr. 1 Bond Interest Expense	6,000	
Accrued Bond Interest Payable	6,000	
Cash		12,000
To record the payment of semiannual bond interest.		
1 Premium on Bonds Payable	600	
Bond Interest Expense		600
To record the amortization of bond premium for three months.		

Note that only three months' amortization of the bond premium is recorded. This coincides with the three months' bond interest expense incurred and recorded to April 1, 1974.

Compound Interest Method of Premium and Discount Amortization

The computation by use of present-value techniques of the exact price of a 6% 10-year $1,000 bond sold to yield 4 percent was determined to be $1,163.53 as calculated on page 499. If this bond were authorized and issued by the Edwards

Corporation on January 1, 1973, with a maturity data of December 31, 1982, and with interest dates of June 30 and December 31, it would be recorded as follows:

1973				
Jan.	1	Cash	1,163.53	
		Bonds Payable		1,000.00
		Premium on Bonds Payable		163.53
		To record issuance of		
		6% bonds to yield 4%.		

An alternative to the straight-line method of amortization is the compound interest method, sometimes called the *effective-yield* method of amortization. In other words, the interest expense is reported at the effective or yield rate times the carrying value of the bonds with the amount of amortization being the difference between the effective interest so computed and the nominal interest, calculated by multiplying the nominal interest rate times the face value of the bonds.

The effective-interest calculation and attendant compound interest amortization for June 30 and December 31 appear below.

1973			
June 30	Bond Interest Expense (2% × $1,163.53)	23.27	
	Premium on Bonds Payable ($30.00 − $23.27)	6.73	
	Cash		30.00
	To record payment of interest and		
	amortization of premium on a 4% annual		
	yield basis.		
Dec. 31	Bond Interest Expense [2% × ($1,163.53 − $6.73)]	23.14	
	Premiun on Bonds Payable ($30.00 − $23.14)	6.86	
	Cash		30.00
	To record payment of interest and		
	amortization of premium on a 4% annual		
	yield basis.		

A similar procedure is used when the compound interest method of amortization is applied to bonds issued at a discount.

It should be noted that the foregoing procedure will produce a constant yield on the carrying value of the bonds payable, face plus unamortized premium or face minus unamortized discount. Compare this with the results achieved with the straight-line method of amortization: a constant absolute interest amount related to bond carrying value that will be reduced over time will produce an "effective" interest rate that increases in subsequent years. The compound interest method of amortization is superior to the straight-line method because of this peculiarity; but due to the complexity of the compound interest calculation, the attendant effective-yield method of amortization is seldom used in practice.

Underwriting Bond Issues

Brokers, banks, or investment syndicates often *underwrite* the flotation of a bond issue, just as in the issuance of capital stock. The entire authorized bond issue of a corporation may be turned over to the *underwriter* at a specified price, say 103; the underwriter then offers the bonds to the public at a slightly higher market price, say 104. This arrangement ensures that the issuing corporation will receive the full specified amount of funds on a given date. The amount of premium or discount is based on the net amount that the issuing corporation receives from the underwriter, not on the market price paid by the investors for the bonds.

Consider, for example, the case of a company that plans to issue 6% bonds with a face value of $1,000,000. The company turns the bonds over to the underwriter at 103, for a total price of $1,030,000. The underwriter, according to the underwriting agreement, plans to sell the bonds at 104. Even though the investors pay $1,040,000 for the bonds, the issuing company receives only $1,030,000 and hence considers that the bonds are issued at a premium of $30,000.

Retirement and Refunding of Bonds Payable

The borrowing company may retire its outstanding bonds at the maturity date by paying the contract face value in cash. Even if the bonds were originally issued at a premium or discount, the entry to record the retirement is a debit to Bonds Payable and a credit to Cash for the face value. Serial bonds are retired in serial installments. Assume, for example, a $500,000, 10-year serial bond issue, $50,000 to be retired at face value at the end of each year. The annual retirement entry is again a debit to Bonds Payable and a credit to Cash for $50,000. The retirement schedule is established by the issuing corporation and may provide for several retirement dates beginning a fixed number of years after the date of issue.

Other methods of retiring bonds include (1) the retirement of all or part of a bond issue by call, or purchase on the open market before the bonds are actually due, (2) the retirement of bonds by *refunding*, or refinancing by issuing new bonds on new terms, (3) the conversion of bonds payable into capital stock, and (4) the retirement of bonds with sinking fund assets and the attendant problem of accumulating the sinking fund.

Retirement of Bonds before Maturity. A corporation that has issued bonds may find itself with more cash than it expects to need for operations, permitting it to retire all or part of its outstanding bonded indebtedness prior to maturity date. Management may decide to retire the bonds immediately if the cash is available, if there appears to be no better alternative use now or in the future for the excess cash, and if they wish to decrease the fixed charges for the bond interest. For bonds to be retired by a corporation before maturity, they must contain a *call provision*, permitting the issuing corporation to redeem the bonds by paying a specified price, usually slightly above face value; or if the bonds are not callable, the issuing company may redeem them before the maturity date by purchasing them on the open market. Retirement of bonds below the carrying value results in a gain; a loss is incurred if the purchase price exceeds the carrying value. An important point to remember in bringing the carrying value of the bonds up to date is the fact that the premium or discount accounts must be properly amortized up to the point of retirement. In recording the amortization of premium or discounts on bonds retired by purchase in between an interest period, it may be helpful first to place the bond interest expense on the books by an accrual-type entry. This entry could then be followed by the amortization entry. The details of this structural form is quite complex; it, therefore, is covered in more advanced textbooks.

Gains and losses on the retirement of bonds payable are classified in the income statement under Other Revenue or Other Expense.

Refunding. Bonds also may be retired by refunding, or refinancing by issuing new bonds on new terms. The proceeds from the new issue are specifically designated for the retirement of the old bond issue. The old bondholders may be given the option of exchanging their bonds for the new bonds at the call price. This procedure helps reduce the refinancing costs of the issuing corporation. A refunding decision may be warranted if it is possible to redeem bonds with a relatively high interest rate and substitute bonds with a lower interest rate. Other reasons for refunding are to replace an issue about to mature with a new issue, thus extending the maturity date, or to retire outstanding bonds containing such stringent restrictive provisions as a closed mortgage lien or a requirement that funds be accumulated to retire the bonds.

In the accounting procedure for refunding, the retirement should be recorded in entries similar to those described in the preceding section. Accounting for the new issue is the same as described earlier in this chapter.

Conversion of Bonds into Common Stock. To make certain bonds more attractive to investors, and thus to increase their marketability, the bond agreement may give investors the option of exchanging bonds on a given interest date, or dates, for a certain number of shares of stock, usually common, of the issuing company. These securities, referred to as convertible bonds, have the advantage of offering the investor an initial fixed return on his investment combined with an opportunity to share in profitable operations of the issuing company by later conversion of the bonds to stock. The terms and conditions for conversion are designated in the bond indenture. Conversion is at the option of the bondholder, so that if earnings are unfavorable he does not need to exercise the conversion privilege and may retain the fixed return and greater security of the bonds. The conversion of bonds into stock changes the legal and accounting status of the security holder from creditor to owner.

Assume, for example, that the Avon Corporation has bonds outstanding on July 1, 1973 of $300,000. Interest dates are January 1 and July 1, and the bonds are convertible at the rate of a $1,000 bond for nine shares of the Avon Corporation's $100 par value common stock on any interest date after January 1, 1973. After the July 1, 1973, interest payment had been made, bonds with a face value of $100,000 are surrendered for conversion by bondholders because, let us assume, the market price of the common stock that would be received in exchange is higher than the market price of the bonds held. The entry to record these facts is shown below.

1973			
July 1	Bonds Payable	100,000	
	Common Stock		90,000
	Premium on Common Stock		10,000
	To record the conversion of 100 bonds into 900 shares of common stock.		
	Face value of bonds converted	$100,000	
	Par value of common stock issued:		
	900 shares × $100	90,000	
	Premium on common stock	$ 10,000	

In this illustration, the carrying value identified with the converted bonds, $100,000, is transferred to contributed capital, which includes Common Stock and Premium on Common Stock. It is as if the Avon Corporation had sold 900 shares of common stock for $100,000 and used the proceeds to redeem the bonds.

Bond Sinking Fund. The borrowing corporation may agree in the bond indenture to accumulate funds to retire the bonds at maturity. Periodic cash payments are made to a sinking fund trustee, usually a bank or a trust company. These payments are ordinarily invested in revenue-producing securities. When the bonds mature, the sinking fund trustee sells the securities, and the proceeds are used to pay the bondholders. In some instances the corporation itself may act as trustee, thereby retaining control over the activities of the sinking fund.

To illustrate the operation of a simple sinking fund managed by a trustee, assume that on the authorization date, January 1, 1973, Wells, Inc., issues 10-year sinking fund bonds with a face value of $500,000. The bond indenture provides that at the end of each year a deposit of $50,000—reduced by any net earnings of the funds from its investments—be made to the trustee. The entry to record the initial deposit with the trustee is shown below.

1973			
Dec. 31	Bond Sinking Fund	50,000	
	Cash		50,000
	To record the initial sinking fund deposit with the trustee.		

The bond sinking fund account is a controlling account. The trustee must invest all the available cash in the fund in revenue-producing securities. As a practical matter, it would not always be possible for the trustee to invest odd amounts of cash or to purchase securities immediately on the receipt of cash. Hence, the bond sinking fund is composed of a number of individual items, such as cash, securities, and accrued interest receivable. It is unnecessary for Wells, Inc., to maintain a separate general ledger account for each asset contained in the bond sinking fund.

If, at the end of the second year, the trustee reports net earnings of $1,500 from investments in bonds, the following entries record the second deposit:

1974			
Dec. 31	Bond Sinking Fund	1,500	
	Interest Earned		1,500
	To record net earnings of the bond sinking fund per report of the trustee.		
31	Bond Sinking Fund	48,500	
	Cash		48,500
	To record the second sinking fund deposit with the trustee; the amount is $50,000 less earnings of $1,500, or $48,500.		

The following entry is made to record the retirement of the bonds at maturity by the payment of assets in the bond sinking fund:

```
1983
Jan.  1  Sinking Fund Bonds Payable          500,000
             Bond Sinking Fund                               500,000
                 To record the retirement of bonds
                 by the trustee.
```

The Bond Sinking Fund account is classified in the Assets section as a long-term investment on each statement of financial position except the one prepared at the end of the year preceding the date of the retirement of the bonds. On this statement, the amount in the bond sinking fund should be shown as a current asset and Sinking Fund Bonds Payable should be disclosed as a current liability.

Another method of accumulating a sinking fund provides for a fixed amount to be deposited periodically with the trustee. It is assumed that these deposits, accumulating at compound interest, will equal the principal sum needed to retire the debt at maturity. If, at the retirement date, the accumulated funds exceed the required amount, the excess is returned by the trustee to the corporation; a shortage, on the other hand, requires an additional deficiency payment from the corporation.

Restriction on Retained Earnings for Bond Redemption. In addition to the requirement for sinking fund deposits, the bond indenture may require a restriction on retained earnings up to the amount in the sinking fund. The bondholders thus are provided with twofold protection: the sinking fund ensures the availability of adequate cash for the redemption of the bonds, and the restriction on retained earnings for bond redemption reduces the amount available for distribution as dividends to the stockholders. This restriction enhances the company's working capital position and its ability to meet its regular needs as well as its requirements for bond interest and bond sinking fund payments. An improved working capital position also is advantageous in enabling the company to meet its regular operational cash requirements and to maintain a favorable credit standing.

To illustrate, assume that the bond indenture of Wells, Inc., provides for a restriction of retained earnings. The entry at the end of each year is

```
Dec. 31  Retained Earnings                            50,000
             Retained Earnings–Restricted for Bond
             Redemption                                           50,000
                 To record the restriction of retained earnings
                 equal to the annual increase in the bond
                 sinking fund.
```

Retained Earnings–Restricted for Bond Redemption is shown in the Stockholders' Equity section of the statement of financial position under Retained Earnings. The restriction reduces the amount of retained earnings available for dividends. Earnings in excess of the annual restriction are, of course, available for dividends. There is not necessarily a direct relationship between the bond sinking fund and the restriction on retained earnings for bond redemption. The provisions of the bond indenture may require the creation of (1) a bond sinking fund, (2) a restriction on retained earnings until the bonds are redeemed, or (3) both a bond sinking fund and a restriction on retained earnings. When the bonds are redeemed at maturity, the contractual restriction on retained earnings is removed. The journal entry to record the removal of the restriction is

```
1983
Jan.  1  Retained Earnings–Restricted for Bond
            Redemption                               500,000
            Retained Earnings                                    500,000
               To remove the restriction on retained
               earnings on retirement of the bonds.
```

The unrestricted Retained Earnings account now has been increased by an amount equal to the maturity value of the bonds. The equivalent amount in funds may not be available for distribution to the stockholders because it has been permanently committed to the operations of the business in the form of plant expansion or debt retirement. In essence, the stockholders have been contributing capital to the corporation through earnings retained in the business that might otherwise have been distributed as dividends. Formal recognition of this fact is often made in the form of a stock dividend; that is, the increase in retained earnings resulting from the removal of the bond redemption restriction is capitalized permanently by issuing additional shares of stock to the stockholders.

The net effect on the accounts to record the stock dividend is

```
1983
Jan.  1  Retained Earnings                           500,000
            Common Stock                                      500,000
               To record the declaration and issuance of a
               stock dividend equal in amount to retained
               earnings previously restricted for bond
               redemption.
```

OTHER LONG-TERM LIABILITIES

Among long-term liabilities found on the statement of financial position are those arising from the use of long-term financing devices such as secured or unsecured long-term notes and continuing obligations incurred under employee profit-sharing and pension plans and similar forms. Brief comments are made about each of these.

Instead of issuing bonds, a corporation may borrow from financial institutions, such as banks or insurance companies. A group of banks or insurance companies may jointly finance the transaction. By this arrangement, the corporation eliminates the need for dealing with many bondholders. The corporation issues long-term notes to the lending institutions. Such notes may also provide for a sinking fund and for a restriction on retained earnings. Notes are usually issued at face value; hence the accounting for these items is similar to that for short-term notes. They may be for a short period with optional renewal provisions. Renewable notes are often used when the bond interest rate is unfavorable.

Long-term financing may involve the pledging of specific assets. A corporation may, for example, acquire funds for plant expansion or other purposes by placing a mortgage on its plant and equipment. This creates a long-term liability—Mortgage Payable. Sometimes the lending institution advances funds for the construction of the plant and upon completion takes a mortgage on the newly constructed plant. This is known as a *Construction Mortgage Payable*. The title of the liability account should clearly indicate the nature and type of instrument used.

Accounting for liabilities under pension contracts and similar forms is rather complex and specialized; therefore, only very brief comments are made in this text. The accounting for employees' pension costs and the related liability depends on whether the employees' rights in such plans are forfeitable or non-forfeitable. Under the forfeitable plans, a separate trust must be established; hence the company's long-term liability is usually limited to the cumulative amount of each year's contribution to the pension or profit-sharing trust. Under the nonforfeitable plan, the company simply accrues the liability on the books and records the offsetting expense. The amounts involved are usually determined by the use of compound actuarial tables.

SUMMARY

Sources of capital for a corporation include investments by owners, retention of corporate earnings, and investments by creditors. One of the primary sources of long-term capital from creditors arises through the issuance of bonds.

A bond is a written promise under the corporate seal to pay a specific sum of money on a specified or determinable future date to the order of a person named in the certificate or to the bearer. Registered bonds are registered in the name of the owner and thus require endorsement of the certificate to transfer ownership. If bonds are registered as to principal and interest, interest checks are mailed only to bondholders of record; however, if bonds are registered as to principal only (coupon bonds), interest coupons are detached from the certificate and presented by the holder to a bank for payment. Bearer bonds are not registered as to principal or interest and title is passed by delivery only. If specific corporate property is pledged as security for bonds, the bonds are said to be "secured." Bonds that are backed by only the general credit of the corporation are referred to as "unsecured" bonds or "debentures."

Although the decision whether to raise needed funds through the issuance of capital stock or bonds is a difficult one in which many factors must be considered, often the issuance of bonds is desirable for the following reasons: (1) bonds offer sources of funds that cannot be obtained through the issuance of capital stock because of regulations and legal restrictions; (2) if the funds resulting from the issuance of bonds can be used to yield a return that is higher than the interest rate on the bonds, the marginal earnings will accrue to the stockholders; (3) income taxes are one of the primary costs of operating a business, and bond interest, unlike dividends, may be deducted as an expense for income tax purposes; (4) bonds aid in offsetting a loss due to shrinkage in the purchasing power of funds invested in assets; and (5) the issuance of stock is more likely to result in a loss of present control over the corporation's affairs.

The issue price of bonds is primarily determined by the stated interest rate and the prevailing interest rate on bonds of the same grade. If the stated interest rate is higher than the market rate, the bonds will sell at a premium; if it is lower, the bonds will sell at a discount. The issuance of bonds requires a credit to Bonds Payable for the face value of the bonds. If bonds are issued for an amount higher than the face value, the excess is credited to Premium on Bonds Payable; if they are issued for an amount less than the face value, the deficiency is debited to Discount on Bonds Payable. If the bonds are issued at face value and one of the semiannual interest payments falls on the last day of the accounting period, the entire interest payment is debited to Bond Interest Expense. The normal rules for accruing interest apply if the end of the accounting period does not coincide with an interest date. If bonds are issued at a premium or a discount, the charge to Bond Interest Expense is based on the effective interest cost of the bonds; that is, the total interest cost of the bonds over their life is the total of the cash interest payments minus the amount of the premium or plus the amount of the discount. Therefore, the semiannual interest expense is the cash payment minus a proportion of the premium or plus a proportion of the discount. The proportion of premium or discount entering into the bond interest expense of a period is determined by amortizing the premium or discount over the period, beginning with the date of issuance of the bonds and ending with the date of retirement. If interest expense is accrued at the end of an accounting period, the amortization of the premium or discount element for a similar time period must also be recorded. If bonds are issued between interest dates, the purchaser pays the interest accrued to the date of issuance and the company pays interest at the stated rate to the purchaser on the next interest date, thereby returning to the purchaser the accumulated interest that he paid to the corporation. If bonds are issued through an underwriter or other financial agency, the amount of premium or discount is based on the net amount that the issuing corporation receives from the underwriter and not on the market price paid by the investors.

If bonds are retired at maturity, the retirement is recorded by a debit to Bonds Payable and a credit to Cash. If bonds are retired before maturity on a date other than an interest date, the bond interest applicable to the bonds being retired must be accrued to the date of retirement. The difference between the carrying value and the retirement price of the bonds is recognized as a gain or a loss, and the balances of the Accrued Bond Interest Payable, Bonds Payable, and Premium or Discount on Bonds Payable accounts applicable to the bonds being retired are eliminated from the books in the retirement entry.

Convertible bonds contain a provision allowing the investor to exchange his bonds on a specific interest date or dates for a predetermined number of shares of stock, usually common, of the issuing company. To record the conversion of bonds to par value common stock, the amounts of the Bonds Payable and Premium or Discount accounts applicable to the bonds being converted are eliminated; the Common Stock account is credited for the par value of the shares issued, and the excess of the carrying value of the bonds over the par value of the stock is credited to Premium on Common Stock.

The bond indenture may require the corporation to accumulate a sinking fund over the life of the bonds to provide for the retirement of the bonds at maturity. Periodic payments are made to a sinking fund trustee, who invests the assets in securities. Bond Sinking Fund is disclosed as a long-term investment on the statement of financial position. The corporation may also agree to a restriction of retained earnings for the bond redemption, which reduces the amount of retained earnings available for dividend distribution. Although the restriction does not automatically provide money for the retirement of the bonds, it may increase the company's working capital position, thus making it more likely that there will be funds available for the retirement of the bonds. When the bonds are retired, the restriction is eliminated.

QUESTIONS

Q14-1. In light of the definition of a current liability stated in this chapter, justify the classification of Unearned Magazine Subscriptions as a current liability.

Q14-2. (a) What is the difference between a stock certificate and a bond? (b) A bond and a promissory note?

Q14-3. Identify the following terms: (a) registered bonds; (b) bearer bonds; (c) secured bonds; (d) unsecured bonds; (e) serial bonds; (f) convertible bonds; (g) coupon bonds; (h) income bonds.

Q14-4. A corporation needs cash for the acquisition of plant and equipment. It is considering three alternative sources: additional common stock, 6 percent preferred stock, and 4 percent bonds. (a) What are some of the factors involved in this decision? (b) Will the decision affect the present common stockholders? Discuss.

Q14-5. (a) What are the general requirements for the approval of a bond issue? (b) Should the stockholders always approve a bond issue? Why?

Q14-6. (a) Why does the buyer of a bond purchased between interest dates pay the seller for accrued interest on the bond? (b) Is the accrued interest included in the stated purchase price of the bond?

Q14-7. (a) What is the difference to the issuing corporation between common stock issued at a premium and bonds issued at a premium? (b) Does revenue result from either?

Q14-8. Before its bonds mature, a corporation may retire them by: (a) paying cash; (b) refunding; or (c) conversion. Explain each of these methods.

Q14-9. On December 31, 1973, a corporation has serial bonds with a face value of $500,000 outstanding. These bonds mature annually in $100,000 amounts, beginning June 30, 1974. How will this be shown on the position statement as of (a) December 31, 1973, (b) December 31, 1974, and (c) December 31, 1975?

Q14-10. Why are bonds not always issued at the prevailing interest rate, thereby eliminating bond discount or bond premium?

EXERCISES

E14-1. On the date of authorization, January 1, 1973, the Walters Corporation issued 10-year, 5% bonds with a face value of $500,000 at 100. Interest is payable each January 1 and July 1.

1. Record the issuance of the bonds.
2. Record the first interest payment.
3. Record the accrued interest expense on December 31, 1973.
4. Record the retirement of the bonds on January 1, 1983, by the payment of cash.

E14-2. On the date of authorization, January 1, 1973, the Jamestown Corporation issued 20-year, 6% bonds with a face value of $600,000 at 102. Interest is payable each January 1 and July 1.

1. Record the issuance of the bonds.
2. Record the first interest payment and amortization of the premium by the straight line amortization method.
3. Record the accrued interest expense and amortization of the premium on December 31, 1973.
4. Open a Bond Interest Expense account and post the transactions.
5. Prepare a schedule proving the interest cost for 1973 by the straight line amortization method.
6. Compute the approximate effective interest rate.

E14-3. On the date of authorization, January 1, 1973, the Dowdy Corporation issued 10-year, 4% bonds with a face value of $200,000 at 97. Interest is payable each January 1 and July 1.

1. Record the issuance of the bonds.
2. Record the first interest payment and amortization of the discount by the straight line amortization method.
3. Record the accrued interest expense and amortization of the discount on December 31, 1973.
4. Open a Bond Interest Expense account and post the transactions.
5. Prepare a schedule proving the interest cost for 1973 by the straight line amortization method.
6. Compute the approximate effective interest rate.

E14-4. On October 1, 1973, the Winterhaven Corporation issued 6% bonds with a face value of $800,000 at 103 plus accrued interest. The bonds mature on June 1, 1981, and interest is paid each June 1 and December 1. The straight line amortization of premium is recorded each time Bond Interest Expense is recorded. Prepare all the entries relating to the bond issue during 1973.

E14-5. On June 1, 1975, the Winterhaven Corporation (see Exercise E14-4) purchased its own bonds with a face value of $400,000 at 101 on the open market. Assuming that the proper entries have been made on June 1, 1975, to record the payment of interest and related information, record the purchase and retirement of the bonds.

E14-6. On the authorization date, January 1, 1973, the Welbourne Corporation issued 10-year bonds with a face value of $1,000,000. Under the terms of the bond indenture, a sinking fund is to be maintained to provide for the retirement of the bonds at maturity. Deposits are to be made with a trustee at the end of each year in amounts that, when added to the sinking fund earnings, will total $100,000. Record (a) the deposit with the trustee on December 31, 1973; (b) earnings of $4,360 during the second year; (c) the deposit with the trustee on December 31, 1974 and (d) the retirement of the bonds at maturity by the trustee.

E14-7. Assume that the bond indenture (see Exercise E14-6) requires a restriction on retained earnings equal to the amount of the sinking fund. Record (a) the restriction at the end of 1973 and 1975 and (b) the removal of the restriction at the maturity date.

E14-8. (*Financial policy decision exercise*) In addition to 6% bonds with a face value of $800,000 outstanding, the total capitalization of the Eden Corporation at December 31, 1973, is

6% Preferred Stock, Nonparticipating	$1,200,000
Common Stock	1,600,000
Retained Earnings	400,000

1. Prepare a schedule showing the distribution of net income of $280,000 before bond interest expense but after income taxes, and compute the rate of return on the investment of each of the equity groups—bondholders, preferred stockholders, and common stockholders.

2. Prepare a similar schedule, assuming a distribution of $160,000.
3. Which rate of return reflects a favorable leverage position?

E14-9. On the date of authorization, January 1, 1973, the Fulton Company issued 20-year, 4% bonds. Interest is paid semiannually on January 1 and July 1. On July 1, 1973, the accountant for the Fulton Company prepared the following journal entry to record the payment of bond interest and the straight line amortization of the discount:

```
1973
July  1   Bond Interest Expense            3,960
            Cash                                     3,600
            Discount on Bonds Payable                 360
              To record the bond interest expense
              for the preceding six months.
```

From this information, reconstruct the journal entry that was made to record the issuance of the bonds. Show all your calculations.

DEMONSTRATION PROBLEMS

DP14-1. (*Accounting for the issuance of bonds*) In each of the following cases, assume (a) 6% bonds with a face value of $400,000; (b) date of authorization, January 1, 1973; (c) interest payable each January 1 and July 1; (d) maturity date of bonds, January 1, 1983; and (e) year ends December 31.

	Case A	Case B	Case C	Case D	Case E
Date of issuance	Jan. 1, 1973	Jan. 1, 1973	Jan. 1, 1973	Mar. 1, 1973	Jan. 1, 1973
Issue price	100	102	97	101 plus accrued interest	at a price to yield 8%

Required:

1. For Cases A, B, C and D, prepare all journal entries for 1973, assuming the use of the straight line amortization method.
2. For Case E, prepare all journal entries for 1973, assuming the use of the compound interest method of amortization. (Given: p of $1 for 20 periods at 4% is 0.456; P of $1 for 20 periods at 4% is 13.590.)
3. For Cases B and C, prepare a schedule proving the interest cost for 1973 by the straight-line amortization method.
4. For Cases B and C, calculate the approximate effective interest rate.

DP14-2. (*Retirement of bonds before maturity*) On April 1, 1973, the Raleigh Company issued 6% bonds with a face value of $300,000 at 106 plus accrued interest. The bonds have a maturity date of August 1, 1981, and interest is paid each February 1 and August 1.
On December 1, 1974, the Raleigh Company purchased its own bonds with a face value of $100,000 on the open market at 102 plus accrued interest.

Required:

Assuming that the books of the Raleigh Company are closed each December 31, prepare all the entries relevant to the bonds for the years 1973 and 1974.

DP14-3. (*Accounting for bond sinking fund*) On the date of authorization, January 1, 1973, the Fountain Corporation issued four-year sinking fund bonds with a face value of $200,000 at 100. The sinking fund indenture requires an annual contribution at the end of each of the four years to provide for the retirement of the bonds at maturity. As an added protection, the terms of the bond indenture requires that retained earnings be restricted in an annual amount equal to the total addition to the sinking fund. The Fountain Corporation is to make a deposit to the North Carolina Bank, which has been named trustee of the sinking fund, of amounts that when added to the sinking fund earnings will total $50,000 each year. The North Carolina Bank guaranteed the Fountain Corporation a return of 4 percent annually. The bank will credit the sinking fund account with this return each December 31.

Required:

1. Record the issuance of the sinking fund bonds.
2. Give all the entries for the four years to record the deposits to the sinking fund and the related restrictions on retained earnings.
3. Record the retirement of the sinking fund bonds by the trustee on the maturity date and the removal of the retained earnings restriction.

PROBLEMS

P14-1. On the date of authorization, January 1, 1973, the Benson Corporation issued 6%, 20-year bonds with a face value of $2,000,000 at 100. Interest is payable each January 1 and July 1.

Required:

1. Record the issuance of the bonds.
2. Record the first interest payment.
3. Record the accrued interest payable on December 31, 1973.
4. State how the bonds payable should be shown on the statement of financial position, assuming that (a) the bonds are unsecured debenture bonds and (b) the bonds are secured by a first mortgage on land and buildings.

P14-2. On the date of authorization, March 1, 1973, the Potter Corporation issued 20-year, 6% bonds with a face value of $400,000 at 103. Interest is payable each March 1 and September 1.

Required:

1. Record the following transactions during 1973: (a) The issuance of the bonds. (b) The first interest payment and straight line amortization of the premium. (c) The accrual of interest on December 31, 1973, and amortization of the premium.
2. Calculate the approximate effective interest rate paid.
3. State how Bonds Payable and Premium on Bonds Payable should be shown on the statement of financial position prepared as of December 31, 1973, assuming that the bonds are unsecured debenture bonds.

P14-3. On the date of authorization, April 1, 1973, the Powell Company issued 10-year, 4½% bonds with a face value of $400,000 at 97. Interest is payable each April 1 and October 1.

Required:

1. Record the following transactions during 1973: (a) The issuance of the bonds. (b) The first interest payment and straight line amortization of the discount. (c) The accrual of interest on December 31, 1973, and amortization of the discount.
2. Calculate the approximate effective interest rate paid.
3. State how the bonds payable and discount on bonds payable should be shown on the statement of financial position as of December 31, 1973, assuming that the bonds are first mortgage bonds with land and buildings pledged as security.

P14-4. On April 1, 1973, the stockholders of the Nathan Corporation authorized the issuance of 10-year, 4% first mortgage bonds with a face value of $600,000. The bonds mature on April 1, 1983, and interest is payable each April 1 and October 1.

Required: Make journal entries to record the following transactions:

1973

June   1   Issued the bonds at 104 plus accrued interest.

Oct.   1   Paid the semiannual interest. (Assume that Premium on Bonds Payable is amortized by the straight line method each time Bond Interest Expense is recorded.)

Dec. 31   Accrued the bond interest.

  31   Closed the Bond Interest Expense account.

1974

Apr.   1   Paid the semiannual interest.

Oct.   1   Paid the semiannual interest.

Dec. 31   Accrued the bond interest.

P14-5. On March 1, 1973, the authorization date, the Millsboro Company issued 10-year, 3% debenture bonds with a face value of $500,000 at 101½. Interest is payable each March 1 and September 1. The company closes its books on December 31. The following selected transactions and adjustments were made:

1973

Mar.   1   Issued all the bonds for cash.

Sept.   1   Paid the semiannual interest.

Dec. 31   Accrued the bond interest.

1974

Mar.   1   Paid the semiannual interest.

Sept.   1   Paid the semiannual interest.

Dec. 31   Accrued the bond interest

1978

Mar.   1   Paid the semiannual interest.

Sept.   1   Paid the semiannual interest.

  1   Purchased for retirement bonds with a face value of $250,000 on the open market at 100.

Dec. 31   Accrued the bond interest.

1983

Mar.   1   Paid the semiannual interest.

  1   Paid the bonds outstanding at maturity.

      Required: 1. Record the transactions. (Assume that the premium is amortized by the straight line method each time the bond interest expense is recorded.)
         2. Set up a Premium on Bonds Payable T account and post all entries to that account for the entire 10-year period.

P14-6. On January 1, 1973, the Hilton Corporation authorized and issued 10-year, 4% sinking fund bonds with a face value of $2,000,000. The bond indenture provided for (a) an annual deposit with a trustee at the end of each year of $200,000 less sinking fund earnings since the previous deposit and (b) an annual restriction on retained earnings.

Required: Record the following selected transactions relating to the bond issue:

1973

Dec. 31   Made the initial deposit with the sinking fund trustee.

     31   Made the restriction on retained earnings.

1974

Dec. 31   Received a report of sinking fund earnings of $7,800.

     31   Made the deposit with the sinking fund trustee.

     31   Made the restriction on retained earnings.

1982

Dec. 31   Paid the bonds at maturity.

     31   Removed the contractual restriction on retained earnings.

P14-7. (*Financial policy decision problem*) The Fenton Corporation, with 20,000 shares of $100 par value common stock outstanding, needs an additional $2,000,000 for plant expansion. Three plans for raising the funds have been proposed to the board of directors: (a) the issuance of additional common stock at $100 par value; (b) the issuance of 6% nonparticipating preferred stock; and (c) the issuance of 20-year, 5% bonds. It is estimated that the corporation will earn $800,000 annually before bond interest and income taxes of 50 percent.

Required: 1. Determine the earnings per share of common stock under each plan. Assume that the securities will be issued at par or face value.
2. Using earnings per share as a basis for your decision, which plan should the Fenton Corporation employ?

P14-8. Selected accounts from three trial balances of the Lenton Corporation are presented.

	Adjusted		Unadjusted
	12/31/71	12/31/72	12/31/73
Debits			
Bond Interest Expense	$ 900	$ 5,400	$ 3,600
Loss on Retirement of Bonds Payable	–0–	–0–	630
Credits			
Accrued Bond Interest Payable	2,000	2,000	–0–
6% Bonds Payable—issued 11/1/71	100,000	100,000	90,000
Premium on Bonds Payable	8,800	8,200	7,800

The data from the adjusted trial balances are correct. The bonds were issued between interest-payment dates. On September 1, 1973 the corporation retired bonds with a face value of $10,000 by a disbursement of $10,630.

Required:

1. Compute the following: (a) Original issue price as of November 1, 1971, (b) Maturity date, (c) Semiannual interest payment dates.
2. Reconstruct the journal entry to record the issuance of the bonds on November 1, 1971.
3. Prepare any required adjusting or correcting entries as of December 31, 1973.

P14-9. The Borden Company issued 4% bonds on September 1, 1973, at a certain price plus accrued interest. The bonds mature on June 1, 1983. Interest is paid each June 1 and December 1. The accountant for the company recorded the first semiannual bond interest payment as follows:

1973
Dec.   1   Bond Interest Expense   3,137
           Accrued Bond Interest Payable   2,657
               Discount on Bonds Payable   480
               Cash   5,314
               To record the payment of semiannual
               bond interest and the straight line
               amortization of the discount for
               three months.

> Required. 1. Compute the following: (a) Face value of bonds issued, (b) Original issue price and discount.
> 2. Reconstruct the journal entry to record the issuance of the bonds on September 1, 1973.

P14-l0. (*Financial policy decision problem*) The board of directors of the Ramsey Corporation has approved the recommendation of the management to expand the production facilities. The firm currently manufactures only heavy machinery, but plans are being developed for diversifying the corporation's activities through the production of smaller and more versatile equipment.

The directors have concluded that whereas a number of factors should influence their choice as to the method of financing to be used in obtaining the $1,500,000 needed, prime attention should be devoted to observing the expected income effect on the corporate equity of the common stockholders. They are considering the following methods of providing the necessary funds:

1. They can issue 25,000 shares of $50 par value common stock at a net price of $60 per share.
2. They can issue 15,000 shares of $100 par value, 5½%, cumulative, nonparticipating preferred stock at a net price of $100 per share.
3. They can issue $1,500,000 face value of 20-year, 5% bonds at a net price of 102.50.
4. They can issue $1,500,000 face value of 20-year, 4¾% bonds at a net price of 97.50.

The corporation's current liability and stockholders' equity structure is

Current liabilities	$ 120,000
4% bonds payable due in 10 years	180,000
5½% preferred stock, cumulative and nonparticipating, $100 par value; authorized 50,000 shares; issued 8,000 shares	800,000
Common stock, $50 par value; authorized 100,000 shares; issued 20,000 shares	1,000,000
Excess over par value received–common stock	100,000
Retained earnings	400,000

Management expects that the investment of $1,500,000 will yield a return of 12 percent before income taxes, which will be computed at a 48-percent rate. The corporation is currently realizing a return of 10 percent on all long-term capital before income taxes.

Required:

1. Using a form like the following, compare the expected effect of each proposed financing method on the corporate equity of the common stockholders.

	Currently (before expansion)	After Issuing Common Stock	After Issuing Preferred Stock	After Issuing 5% Bonds	After Issuing 4¾% Bonds
Cash proceeds available for investment					
Net income before bond interest and income taxes					
Less: Bond interest expense					
Net income before income taxes					
Less: Income tax expense					
Net income					
Less: Full dividend to preferred stockholders					
Portion of net income applicable to common stockholders					
Net income applicable to each share of outstanding common stock					
Portion of net income applicable to common stockholders as a percentage of common stockholders' equity					

2. Applying the single expressed criterion established by the directors, what method of financing should be employed? Why?

3. Discuss other factors that must influence a decision of this type.

4. Assuming that the directors decide to issue the 5% bonds, prepare the general journal entries: (a) To record the issuance of the bonds; (b) To record the periodic interest payment six months after the issuance of the bonds; (c) To record the adjusting entry immediately prior to closing the books four months after entry (b); (d) To record the periodic interest payment two months after entry (c); (e) To record the periodic interest payment and the retirement of the bonds at maturity.

5. A decrease in the tax rate will tend to favor which method of financing? An increase will tend to favor which method? Explain why.

15

Managerial Financial Decisions—Investments

Management may wish to invest excess funds not needed for current operations because of temporary reductions in inventory and accounts receivable. Available temporary excess cash is often invested in the securities of other companies for a favorable return in the form of interest or dividends; the investments should be made in securities for which a ready market exists so that they can be sold when cash is required. Such investments are classified as current assets because they can be and will be converted into cash in a relatively short period of time when there is a seasonal shortage of cash. If the securities are to be held until they mature, or if they are not readily salable, the investments are classified as long-term investments on the statement of financial position. Investments are often also made for the purpose of obtaining control of another company, whose productive or other facilities are needed by the investing company. Such investments must always be shown on the statement of financial position as long-term investments.

MARKETABLE SECURITIES

A firm should give serious consideration to the investment of any seasonal excess of cash as it becomes available. In this way, it tends to maximize its income by putting idle, nonrevenue-producing funds to work when they are not needed in the operations of the business. If it is expected that the funds will be needed in the near future, they must be invested in readily marketable securities. These securities should be high-grade, *blue-chip* stocks or bonds that will not fluctuate widely in price and, hence, on future sales will yield approximately the amount that was originally invested or, better, a larger amount. Of course, this kind of security yields a relatively low rate of return, a common characteristic of readily marketable, high-grade

523

securities. Only a few securities qualify as marketable; these are United States Government bonds, AAA industrial bonds, and certain blue-chip stocks that are listed on the various stock exchanges. The accounting examples that follow illustrate the recording of the purchase of bonds accompanied by the receipt of interest and the purchase of stock accompanied by the receipt of dividends.

Temporary Investment in Bonds

For example, consider the financial decision of the Owens Company on March 1, 1973, to purchase as temporary investments 4% bonds of Peters Company with a face value of $30,000 at 102 plus accrued interest. Interest is paid on January 1 and July 1. The brokerage fee and other costs incident to the purchase are $60. This information is recorded as follows:

1973			
Mar. 1	Marketable Securities–Bonds of Peters Company	30,660	
	Accrued Bond Interest Receivable	200	
	Cash		30,860
	To record the purchase of bonds of Peters Company as temporary investments.		

Accounting Concept: ▼
Recording Assets
at Cost

1. ▼ In accordance with the generally accepted principle of recording all assets at cost, Marketable Securities are recorded at full cost, including the brokerage fee and other incidental costs. ▼
2. The account title, Marketable Securities–Bonds of Peters Company, includes the general ledger control account, Marketable Securities, and the name of the individual bond for posting to a subsidiary record, typically in the form of an *investment register*.
3. The transaction involves the purchase of two different assets: the bonds and the accrued bond interest. The amount of the accrued interest should be set up in a separate account (and not merged with Marketable Securities) since it is a different asset and has a maturity date different from the marketable securities.

The receipt of semiannual interest on July 1, 1973, is recorded as follows:

1973			
July 1	Cash	600	
	Accrued Bond Interest Receivable		200
	Bond Interest Earned		400
	To record the receipt of semiannual bond interest on bonds of the Peters Company.		

1. The six months' interest represents a collection of the receivable that was purchased on March 1 and the amount of interest that was earned for the four-month period from March 1 to July 1.
2. Note that the premium element of the cost of the bonds is not amortized. Neither the premium element nor the discount element of the cost of bonds purchased as *temporary investments* is amortized because the purchasing firm is uncertain as to how long it will hold the temporary investments. On the other hand, the premium or discount on bonds purchased as long-term investments *is amortized*.

To complete the cycle, assume that on August 1, 1973, the Owens Company found that it had a shortage of cash and decided to sell the bonds of Peters Company. They were sold at $101\frac{3}{4}$ (net of brokerage fees and other costs) plus accrued interest; the transaction is recorded as follows:

1973			
Aug. 1	Cash	30,625	
	Loss on Disposal of Marketable Securities	135	
	Marketable Securities–Bonds of Peters Company		30,660
	Bond Interest Earned		100
	To record the sale of marketable securities.		

1. The computation of the Loss on Disposal of Marketable Securities is

Original full cost of bonds	$30,660	
Selling price of bonds ($30,000 × 101.75%)	30,525	
Loss on disposal of marketable securities	$ 135	

2. The cash received comes from two sources: the sale of the bonds, $30,525, and the sale of the accrued interest, $100.

3. Note that the Marketable Securities account must be credited with the same amount, the cost, for which it was originally debited.

Loss on Disposal of Marketable Securities is shown in the income statement under Other Expenses. Management must consider this loss along with the Bond Interest Earned in evaluating the success of its decision to invest in the bonds of Peters Company.

Temporary Investment in Stocks

To illustrate the recording of a purchase of stock as a temporary investment, assume that on April 1, 1973, the Arlex Company purchases 200 shares of Hurley Corporation $100 par value preferred stock at $105 per share. Brokerage fees are $108. The entry to record the purchase is

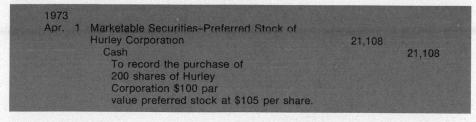

1973			
Apr. 1	Marketable Securities–Preferred Stock of		
	Hurley Corporation	21,108	
	Cash		21,108
	To record the purchase of		
	200 shares of Hurley		
	Corporation $100 par		
	value preferred stock at $105 per share.		

1. The amount of the debit to the asset is the full cost. The par value is of no significance to the investor except as a possible base to measure the amount of dividends to be received when the dividend rate is stated as a percentage of par value.

2. Dividends do not legally accrue; therefore, no recognition is given to this feature even for preferred stock until the dividend is actually declared. If the Hurley Corporation had declared a dividend on its preferred stock, and the Arlex Company had purchased the 200 shares between the declaration date and

the dividend record date, then the Arlex Company should divide the purchase price between Marketable Securities and Dividends Receivable. One important facet of stock market behavior should be mentioned. The market price of both common and preferred stock reflects investors' anticipation of the ultimate declaration of dividends. In other words, if all other variables were constant, the market price of stock on which dividends are regularly declared would go up gradually from one dividend date to the next in approximately the same manner that interest accrues on bonds. On the dividend record date, the market price per share would drop by the amount of the dividend per share.

Assume that on July 1, 1973, a quarterly dividend of $1.50 per share is received on the Hurley Corporation stock. The entry to record the dividend is

```
1973
July  1  Cash                                             300
             Dividends Earned                                      300
                 To record the receipt of a quarterly dividend
                 from the Hurley Corporation.
```

Dividends Earned is classified under Other Revenue on the income statement.

Again, to meet a seasonal cash shortage, on September 15, 1973, the preferred stock of the Hurley Corporation is sold for $106.50 per share (net of brokerage fees and other costs). The sale is recorded as follows:

```
1973
Sept. 15  Cash                                            21,300
              Marketable Securities–Preferred Stock of
              Hurley Corporation                                   21,108
              Gain on Disposal of Marketable Securities              192
                  To record the sale of preferred stock of
                  Hurley Corporation at $106.50
                  per share.
```

Gain on Disposal of Marketable Securities is determined as follows:

Selling price of preferred stock (200 × $106.50)	$21,300
Original full cost	21,108
Gain on disposal of marketable securities	$ 192

Gain on Disposal of Marketable Securities is shown on the income statement under Other Revenue. Management must consider this amount along with Dividends Earned in evaluating the success of its decision to buy the preferred stock as a temporary investment, for often in reality it represents the sale of nonrecognized accumulated dividends.

Valuation of Marketable Securities

Ideally, all current assets should be shown at current market price on the statement of financial position. However, this represents a departure from another generally accepted accounting principle, the cost principle. Only rarely do firms use the current market price in the valuation of marketable securities, mainly because in a rising market, writing up the marketable securities would mean recording an unrealized gain. Specific attention is given here to (1) the cost and (2) the lower of cost or market methods of valuation, the two methods most often used.

Temporary investments are recorded at cost and may be presented on the statement of financial position at the same figure. Even if they are carried at cost, the current market value of the securities, obtainable from the financial page of any daily newspaper, should be disclosed in the statement of financial position by a parenthetical notation as shown to enable the reader to evaluate the item for purposes of financial position analysis.

Assets		
Current Assets		
Cash		$562,000
Marketable Securities (shown at cost; current market price, $175,000)		158,000
Accounts Receivable	$200,000	
Deduct Allowance for Doubtful Accounts	8,000	192,000
Merchandise Inventory		300,000
Prepaid Insurance		2,000
Total Current Assets		$1,214,000

Note that even though the current market value is disclosed parenthetically, the securities are valued at cost; that is, only the original cost is added into the figures that are totaled. The cost method is consistent with the fundamental principle of matching expired costs (or expenses) and revenues as well as with income tax requirements.

Many firms value their marketable securities at the lower of cost or market. In effect, these firms value their securities at cost or *realizable cost*, whichever is the lower. The objective of this valuation method is to recognize the effect of market price declines without recognizing market price increases. ▼ Thus, it adheres to the concept of conservatism, the recognition of all anticipated losses without the recognition of unrealized gains. ▼ Although there are two possible methods of applying the lower of cost or market method to marketable securities (the *unit* method and the *total securities* method), the unit method—taking the lower of cost or market for each security owned—is the most conservative and the only method discussed in this text. To illustrate, assume that the lower of cost or market unit method is applied to the securities owned by the Duncan Company as of December 31, 1973, as shown.

Accounting Concept: Conservatism

Marketable Securities	Cost (at time securities were acquired)	Market (December 31, 1973)	Lower of Cost or Market
Preferred Stock of Anison Company	$12,550	$12,000	$12,000
Common Stock of Bassom Company	16,470	16,200	16,200
Bonds of Connors Company	20,000	20,500	20,000
Totals	$49,020	$48,700	$48,200

If the lower of cost or market unit method is applied to these three securities, the amount to appear in the statement of financial position for

Marketable Securities is $48,200, which represents the December 31, 1973, market price of the stocks of Anison and Bassom Company plus the cost of the bonds of Connors Company. The adjusting entry necessary to give recognition to the valuation may take one of two forms: (1) direct asset reduction or (2) creation of a valuation account. Since cost must be retained for income tax requirements and other managerial evaluations, it is suggested that the second method is desirable and that the following valuation adjusting entry is proper:

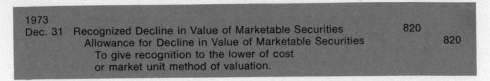

```
1973
Dec. 31   Recognized Decline in Value of Marketable Securities          820
              Allowance for Decline in Value of Marketable Securities          820
                  To give recognition to the lower of cost
                  or market unit method of valuation.
```

The statement of financial position then shows the following:

```
                                        Assets
        Current Assets
            Marketable Securities (at cost)                  $49,020
            Deduct Allowance for Decline in Value of
            Marketable Securities                                820
                Marketable Securities at Lower of Cost
                or Market                                                    $48,200
```

The account Recognized Decline in the Value of Marketable Securities is closed to the Revenue and Expense Summary, and the $820 loss is reported on the income statement under Other Expenses.

To complete the cycle, suppose that on January 15, 1974, the Duncan Company sells the preferred stock of Anison Company for $12,060. This transaction is recorded as follows:

```
1974
Jan. 15   Cash                                                    12,060
              Allowance for Decline in Value of Marketable
              Securities                                             550
                  Marketable Securities–Preferred Stock of
                  Anison Company                                            12,550
                  Gain on Sale of Marketable Securities                         60
                      To record the sale of preferred stock of Anison
                      Company.
```

Observe that the gain or loss on the sale must be determined by comparing the selling price with the lower of cost or market figure used for the statement of financial position valuation. For the Anison Company stock, the gain is computed by comparing the $12,060 received with the $12,000 carrying value. It should be understood that the $60 gain is not recognized for tax purposes; instead a $490 loss is reported on the tax return for 1974 since securities that had cost $12,550 were sold for $12,060.

LONG-TERM INVESTMENTS

In addition to its primary operational activities, a firm may make investments in stocks, bonds, and other securities that are expected to contribute to the success of the business largely by making independent contributions to business revenue. These investments may be temporary or long term. As suggested in the preceding section, investments are called *Marketable Securities* and classified as current assets only when they are readily marketable and it is the *intention of management* to convert them into cash when there is a seasonal need for such action. Investments that do not qualify as Marketable Securities are classified as long-term investments on the statement of financial position.

Investment in Stocks

A company may buy stock in another company for the dividend revenue, or it may acquire control of another company—a *subsidiary*—thereby expanding its operations and gaining a more prominent competitive position, possibly accompanied by a steady supply of merchandise or the creation of sales outlets. The acquisition of a controlling interest in one or more subsidiary corporations frequently leads to the combining of the financial statements of the affiliated companies into single consolidated statements. Accounting concepts and procedures appropriate to such circumstances are discussed in Chapter 17.

    Stock may be acquired directly from the issuing company, but it is more likely to be purchased through a broker on the New York Stock Exchange, the American Stock Exchange, or other exchanges in this or other countries. If shares of stocks are not listed on an exchange—that is, sold through securities dealers— they are said to be sold *over the counter.*

    Long-term investment in stocks as well as temporary investments are recorded at full cost including brokerage fees and postage. If cash is paid for the purchase of stock, there is no problem in establishing cost. In other cases, problems of valuation may arise. A sound accounting rule is to record the investment in stocks at the most objective measurement of the cash equivalent cost of the securities. Since dividends do not legally accrue, no recognition is given to the purchase of Dividends Receivable unless the issuing corporation has officially declared a dividend and the investing corporation purchases the stock between the dividend declaration date and the record date. To illustrate both cases, assume, first, that on July 1, 1973, the Satterfield Company purchases 1,000 shares of $100 par value common stock of James Corporation at 105 with a broker's fee of $440. The investor's total cost is $105,440, and the following entry is made:

1973		
July 1 Investment in Stocks—Common Stock of James		
Corporation	105,440	
Cash		105,440
To record the purchase of 1000 shares of		
$100 par value common stock of James		
Corporation.		

Observe that the asset, Investment in Stocks, is debited for the cost, not the par value, of the stock. The account title shows the general ledger controlling account, Investment in Stocks, and the subsidiary account title, Common Stock of James Corporation. The information about the specific stock is transferred to an investment register, which serves in place of a more formal subsidiary ledger.

To illustrate the handling of declared dividends, consider the purchase on July 20, 1973, by the Satterfield Company of 100 shares of common stock of Iser Company at 102½ plus a brokerage fee of $42. On July 10, 1973, the board of directors of the Iser Company had declared a $1 per share dividend, payable on August 10, 1973, to stockholders of record on July 25, 1973. The purchase price of $102.50 per share includes the cost of all rights. An analysis of this price, therefore, reveals that $101.50 is the cost of each share of stock, excluding the brokerage fees, and $1 per share is the cost of the Dividends Receivable purchased. This transaction is recorded in the journal as follows:

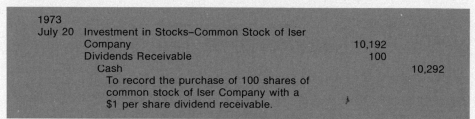

1973			
July 20	Investment in Stocks–Common Stock of Iser Company	10,192	
	Dividends Receivable	100	
	Cash		10,292
	To record the purchase of 100 shares of common stock of Iser Company with a $1 per share dividend receivable.		

When the dividend is received on August 10, an entry is made debiting Cash and crediting Dividends Receivable for the $100. Similarly, if a firm sells its stock in a company that has declared a cash dividend before the dividend record date, it should give recognition to a dividend revenue.

Normally, for convenience, a cash dividend is not recorded until the cash is actually received. For example, if the Satterfield Company receives a $0.60 per share quarterly dividend on the stock of James Corporation on November 10, 1973, it records this information as follows:

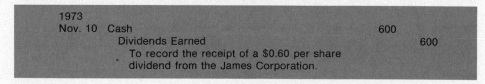

1973			
Nov. 10	Cash	600	
	Dividends Earned		600
	To record the receipt of a $0.60 per share dividend from the James Corporation.		

Accounting Procedure: Recognizing Declared Dividends ▼

A necessary exception to the foregoing rule is the case of a dividend declared in one year and payable in another year. ▼ Sound accrual accounting theory dictates that the dividend revenue be recognized in the year in which the dividend is declared, not in the year in which it is paid. ▼ In this case, an entry is made on or before the last day of the fiscal year in which the dividend is declared, debiting Dividends Receivable and crediting Dividends Earned. Then, when the dividend is actually received in the subsequent accounting period, an entry is made debiting Cash and crediting Dividends Receivable.

Today, frequent use is made of stock dividends and stock split-ups to reduce the market price per share and thus to put the stock in a more favorable price range. The additional shares received by an investing company are not revenue to the stockholder. Only a memorandum entry is necessary to record the increase in the number of shares owned. The unit cost is decreased, however, because of the larger number of shares held after the stock dividend is issued. For example, assume that the James Corporation declares a 100-percent stock dividend (a 2-for-1 split-up would be treated in the same way). The receipt of the additional 1,000 shares on December 12, 1973, by the Satterfield Company is noted in the journal as follows (the original 1,000 shares had cost $105,440):

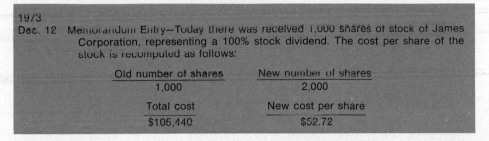

1973
Dec. 12　Memorandum Entry—Today there was received 1,000 shares of stock of James Corporation, representing a 100% stock dividend. The cost per share of the stock is recomputed as follows:

Old number of shares	New number of shares
1,000	2,000
Total cost	New cost per share
$105,440	$52.72

The gain or loss per share on any subsequent sale of James Corporation stock is determined by comparing the selling price with the new cost of $52.72 per share.

The Dividends Earned balance is disclosed in the income statement under Other Revenue, whereas the Investment in Stocks account is reported in the statement of financial position under Long-Term Investments, a noncurrent caption appearing between Current Assets and Plant and Equipment. The most commonly used method of valuation for long-term investments is cost. When, however, there is a material and presumably permanent decline in the market value of the investment, an adjustment may be made crediting the investment account and debiting the Loss from Decline in Market Value of Investment in Stocks account.

Investment in Bonds—Straight Line Amortization

A number of institutional investors are prohibited by law from buying common stock; others are restricted in the amount of common stock that they may buy. Organizations such as banks, insurance companies, some trusts, and pension funds acquire bonds as sound investments. Industrial companies, either for the interest revenue to be received or for reasons of business connection, also frequently buy bonds.

Accounting for the purchase of long-term bonds is practically the mirror image of accounting for the issuance of bonds, with one exception: *no premium or discount accounts are used when the bonds are purchased above or below face value*. To measure the bond interest revenue properly, the amount of the discount or premium is amortized, however, with offsetting debits or credits to the Bond Interest Earned account. Two examples are presented to illustrate the accounting for investment in bonds; the second example involves more complex issues than the first.

In the first example, assume that on May 1, 1973, the Aman Company places a 4%, $300,000 bond issue with the Boston Finance Company at 98. The interest is payable on May 1 and November 1 and the bonds mature on May 1, 1983. The entries on both the issuing company's and the investing company's books for the year 1973 are shown in Figure 15-1.

Figure 15-1. Entries for Bonds on Books of Issuer and Investor Assuming the Use of the Straight Line Amortization Method

Transaction	Books of Aman Company (Issuer)			Books of Boston Finance Company (Investor)		
1973	**1973**			**1973**		
May 1 Aman Company issued the bonds to Boston Finance Company at 98.	May 1 Cash Discount on Bonds Payable Bonds Payable To record the issuance of bonds at 98.	294,000 6,000	300,000	May 1 Investment in Bonds— Aman Company Bonds Cash To record the purchase of bonds at 98.	294,000	294,000
Nov. 1 Aman Company paid semiannual interest to Boston Finance Company.	Nov. 1 Bond Interest Expense Cash To record payment of semiannual interest	6,000	6,000	Nov. 1 Cash Bond Interest Earned To record the receipt of semiannual interest.	6,000	6,000
1 Amortized discount for six months.	1 Bond Interest Expense Discount on Bonds Payable To record the amortization of bond discount for six months: 6/120 × $6,000 = $300	300	300	1 Investment in Bonds— Aman Company Bonds Bond Interest Earned To record the discount accumulated for six months.	300	300
Dec. 31 Accrued interest for two months.	Dec. 31 Bond Interest Expense Accrued Bond Interest Payable To record the accrual of interest for two months.	2,000	2,000	Dec. 31 Accrued Bond Interest Receivable Bond Interest Earned To record the accrual of interest earned for two months.	2,000	2,000
31 Amortized discount for two months.	31 Bond Interest Expense Discount on Bonds Payable To record the amortization of bond discount for two months: 2/120 × $6,000 = $100	100	100	31 Investment in Bonds— Aman Company Bonds Bond Interest Earned To record the discount accumulated for two months.	100	100

Observe that the discount accumulation (comparable to the discount amortization for the issuer) results in a debit to the asset account and a credit to the Bond Interest Earned account. For better measurement of periodic revenue from the securities on the investor's books, the discount on long-term investments is accumulated over the outstanding life of the bonds, starting with the date of purchase and ending with the maturity date. Otherwise, the amount of the discount would have to be recognized as a gain in the accounting period during which the bonds mature. Such a gain would reflect only the failure to adjust the Bond Interest Earned account in prior accounting periods.

The income statement of the Boston Finance Company for the year ended December 31, 1973, includes Bond Interest Earned of $8,400 ($8,000 + $400). Accrued Bond Interest Receivable of $2,000 is shown in the December 31, 1973, statement of financial position under Current Assets. The Investment in Bonds is shown under Long-Term Investments on the statement of financial position at $294,400 ($294,000 + $400). At maturity, the investment account will have a balance of $300,000. It will have been increased by periodic discount accumulation entries to the $300,000 figure.

Only the investor's entries are shown in the more complex example. Assume that on March 1, 1973, the Western Company purchases 6% bonds of the Malcolm Company with a face value of $200,000 at 104 plus accrued interest. Interest is paid on May 1 and November 1. The bonds mature on November 1, 1989. The Western Company holds the bonds until August 1, 1977, at which time it sells them at 103½ plus accrued interest. The 1973 entries for the purchase of the bonds, receipt of interest, straight line amortization of premium element of cost and accrual of bond interest, and the 1977 entries to record the sale are presented as follows:

1973				
Mar.	1	Investment in Bonds–Malcolm Company Bonds	208,000	
		Accrued Bond Interest Receivable	4,000	
		Cash		212,000
		To record the purchase of 6% bonds at 104		
		plus accrued interest.		
May	1	Cash	6,000	
		Bond Interest Earned		2,000
		Accrued Bond Interest Receivable		4,000
		To record the receipt of semiannual interest		
		from the Malcolm Company.		
	1	Bond Interest Earned	80	
		Investment in Bonds–Malcolm Company Bonds		80
		To record the premium amortization for		
		two months:		
		$2/200 \times \$8000 = \$80$		
Nov.	1	Cash	6,000	
		Bond Interest Earned		6,000
		To record the receipt of semiannual interest		
		from the Malcolm Company.		

1973			
Nov. 1	Bond Interest Earned	240	
	Investment in Bonds–Malcolm Company Bonds		240
	To record the premium amortization for		
	six months:		
	6/200 × $8000 = $240		
Dec. 31	Accrued Bond Interest Receivable	2,000	
	Bond Interest Earned		2,000
	To record the accrual of interest for two		
	months on the Malcolm Company Bonds.		
31	Bond Interest Earned	80	
	Investment in Bonds–Malcolm Company Bonds		80
	To record the premium amortization for		
	two months:		
	2/200 × $8000 = $80		
1977			
Aug. 1	Accrued Bond Interest Receivable	3,000	
	Bond Interest Earned		3,000
	To accrue the interest for three months on		
	the bonds to be sold.		
1	Bond Interest Earned	120	
	Investment in Bonds–Malcolm Company Bonds		120
	To record the premium amortization for		
	three months:		
	3/200 × $8000 = $120		
1	Cash	210,000	
	Investment in Bonds–Malcolm Company Bonds		205,880
	Accrued Bond Interest Receivable		3,000
	Gain on Sale of Bonds		1,120
	To record the sale of bonds of Malcolm		
	Company at 103½ plus accrued interest.		

1. On March 1, 1973, two assets are purchased; separate accounts are maintained for each asset, particularly since Accrued Bond Interest Receivable is a current asset and Investments in Bonds is a noncurrent asset.
2. For better measurement of periodic bond interest revenue, the premium element of the cost of the bonds is amortized over the outstanding life of the bonds. The amortization credit is made to the Investment in Bonds account.
3. The gain on the sale of bonds is determined as follows:

Selling price of bonds ($200,000 at 103.50%)		$207,000
Deduct: Book value at date of sale		
Original cost	$208,000	
Total amortization to August 1, 1977		
(53 months × $40 per month)	2,120	
Book value at date of sale		205,880
Gain on sale of bonds		$ 1,120

Investment in Bonds—Compound Interest Amortization

The method of accounting for the amortization of the premium or discount elements involved in the investment in bonds described in the previous section is referred to as the straight line method. If an investor buys bonds to yield a given effective interest rate, he may want to reflect in his records this constant rate of return on the book value of the investment. In this case, he would use the compound interest or effective yield method of amortizing the premium or discount elements of the investment in bonds.

To illustrate this particular method of accounting, assume that on January 1, 1973, Harold Baskin purchased the one 6%, 10-year, $1,000 bond issued by the Edwards Corporation described in Chapter 14 (see pages 499 and 507) to yield 4 percent. Baskin would pay $1,163.53 for the bond as calculated on page 499. The purchase of the bond on January 1, 1973, and the compound interest or effective interest calculation and attendant compound interest amortization for June 30 and December 31, 1973, appear below:

```
1973
Jan.  1  Investment in Bonds—Edwards Corporation Bond        1,163.53
            Cash                                                          1,163.53
               To record the purchase of the Edwards Corporation
               bond to yield an annual rate of 4 percent.

Jun. 30  Cash                                                  30.00
            Bond Interest Earned (2% × $1,163.53)                            23.27
            Investment in Bonds—Edwards Corporation Bond
            ($30.00 − $23.27)                                                 6.73
               To record the receipt of semiannual interest
               and the amortization of the premium
               element on a 4 percent annual yield basis.

Dec. 31  Cash                                                  30.00
            Bond Interest Earned [2% × ($1,163.53 − $6.73)]                 23.14
            Investment in Bonds—Edwards Corporation Bond
            ($30.00 − $23.14)                                                 6.86
               To record the receipt of semiannual interest
               and the amortization of the premium
               element on a 4 percent annual yield basis.
```

A similar procedure is used when the compound interest method of amortization is applied to the investment in bonds purchased at a discount.

Two comments should be made about the foregoing procedure.

1. To reiterate, the procedure will produce a constant rate of return on the book value of the investment in bonds.
2. The accounting is essentially the mirror image of the accounting for the issuance of bonds described in Chapter 14 except that separate premium and discount accounts are not maintained; therefore, the amount of the premium amortization is credited to the Investment in Bonds account and the amount of the discount accumulation is debited to the Investment in Bonds account.

Long-Term Investment in Secured and Unsecured Notes

Other types of long-term investments may be made, particularly by financial institutions. Notes secured by mortgages or deeds of trust and unsecured notes are typical. The accounting principles and procedures applicable to these investments are similar to those for investment in bonds. For example, mortgage notes are often acquired at a discount, in which case accounting theory dictates that the mortgage note be recorded at cost and the amount of the discount be accumulated (amortized) over the remaining outstanding life of the note. After the entry is made to record the periodic cash interest, the discount accumulation entry is made, debiting Investment in Mortgages and crediting Interest Earned.

MANAGERIAL ANALYSIS

In addition to the effective interest yield computations discussed in Chapter 14, there is another very important ratio used by investors in bonds—the *number of times bond interest expense is earned.* This ratio is of special interest to bond investors as a measure of the safety of their investment; it is an indication of a firm's ability to meet its annual bond interest requirement. To illustrate, assume that the Analee Corporation has bonds outstanding with a face value of $1,000,000, and that in 1973 it reports bond interest expense of $40,000, income taxes of $60,000, and net income (after income taxes) of $80,000. Since bond interest expense is deductible in determining taxable income, the following formula seems appropriate:

Number of times bond interest expense is earned

$$= \frac{\text{Net income} + \text{Income tax} + \text{Annual bond interest expense}}{\text{Annual bond interest expense}}$$

Substituting the amounts given for the Analee Corporation,

Number of times bond interest expense is earned

$$= \frac{\$80,000 + \$60,000 + \$40,000}{\$40,000}$$

$$= 4.5 \text{ times}$$

A ratio of 4.5 times appears to be relatively safe for the investors holding bonds of Analee Corporation, although there are no established universal standards of safety. The safety margin depends in part on the type of collateral used, the type of business in which the firm is engaged, and the liquidity of the firm. Investors in a private utility with mortgageable plant assets, for example, may feel secure with a ratio of 2.5 times; whereas investors in other businesses without mortgageable assets may feel insecure with a ratio smaller than 5 times.

Another investor-oriented ratio similar to the foregoing one is the *number of times preferred dividends is earned.* This ratio is of particular interest to investors in preferred stock as a safety measure for their investment. To illustrate, assume that the Analee Corporation has 6% preferred stock outstanding with a par value of $1,000,000. Since preferred dividends are *not* deductible in determining taxable income, the following formula seems appropriate:

$$\text{Number of times preferred dividends is earned} = \frac{\text{Net income (after taxes)}}{\text{Annual preferred dividends}}$$

Substituting the amounts given for the Analee Corporation,

$$\text{Number of times preferred dividends is earned} = \frac{\$80,000}{\$60,000}$$

$$= 1.33 \text{ times}$$

The adequacy of this ratio must be interpreted in the same manner as that described for the number of times bond interest expense is earned; that is, the safety margin that is acceptable will depend in part on the type of business in which the firm is engaged, the liquidity of the firm, and other factors.

SUMMARY

Marketable securities are temporary investments in high-quality securities that are readily marketable at approximately the amount that was originally invested. Marketable securities are often purchased when there is a seasonal excess of cash and subsequently liquidated when there is a cash shortage. Investments that do not qualify as marketable securities are classified as long-term investments. Such long-term investments may be made to increase earnings by gaining a more competitive market position or through the dividends or interest earned on the investments.

The purchase of marketable securities and long-term investments is recorded by debiting the appropriate asset accounts for the total cost to the company, exclusive of any accrued interest or declared dividends purchased. No discount or premium account is maintained for an investment in bonds; the discount or premium element is recorded in the asset account.

If a temporary investment is made in bonds, neither the premium nor the discount element is amortized since the purchasing firm is uncertain as to the length of time the investments will be held. The premium or discount element included in the total cost of a long-term investment in bonds, however, is amortized by an offsetting debit or credit to the investment account.

On the statement of financial position, marketable securities may be valued at cost or the lower of cost or market, and long-term investments are generally valued at cost. If marketable securities are valued at the lower of cost or market, the adjusting entry to effect this valuation is a debit to an expense account and a credit to a valuation account that is subtracted from the cost of marketable securities on the statement of financial position.

QUESTIONS

Q15-1. What are marketable securities? How are they classified on the statement of financial position?

Q15-2. List four types of investments that may qualify as marketable securities.

Q15-3. Name and discuss the methods of valuation of marketable securities.

Q15-4. Discuss the accounting involved in the lower of cost or market method of valuation of marketable securities; give journal entries to illustrate your discussion.

Q15-5. Why do firms acquire stock as a long-term investment?

Q15-6. Do dividends legally accrue? Can a firm buy dividends receivable? Explain.

Q15-7. What is a stock split-up? Discuss the accounting for a stock split-up from the point of view of the investor. Would there be any difference in the accounting for a stock dividend as compared to the accounting for a stock split-up from the point of view of the investor?

Q15-8. Name the various groups of investors who typically buy bonds as a long-term investment.

Q15-9. State the financial position statement classifications of (a) Bond Sinking Fund; (b) Bonds Payable; (c) Accrued Bond Interest Receivable; (d) Discount on Bonds Payable; (e) Premium on Bonds Payable; (f) Accrued Bond Interest Payable; (g) Retained Earnings–Restricted for Bond Redemption.

EXERCISES

E15-1. The Indow Company had the following transactions in temporary investments during 1973:

1973

March 1   Purchased 4% bonds of Able Company with a face value of $200,000 at 103 plus accrued interest. Interest is paid on January 1 and July 1. Brokerage fees and other costs incident to the purchase were $75. The bonds have a maturity date of July 1, 1993.

April 10   Purchased 300 shares of $100 par value, 6% preferred stock of Baker Company at $108 per share. Dividends are paid semiannually on January 1 and July 1. Brokerage fees and other costs incident to the purchase were $60.

July 1   Received the semiannual interest from the Able Company.

5   Received the semiannual dividends from the Baker Company.

Aug. 1   Sold the bonds of Able Company at 103½ plus accrued interest.

Journalize the transactions.

E15-2. The Valle Company had the following temporary investments as of December 31, 1973:

	Cost	Market Price at December 31, 1973
Bonds of Carson Company	$20,000	$19,200
Preferred Stock of Dawson Company	10,000	10,100

On February 1, 1974, immediately after receiving and recording the semiannual interest, the Valle Company sold the bonds of Carson Company for $19,000. Assuming the use of a valuation offset account, record the necessary adjusting entry under the lower of cost or market unit method as of December 31, 1973, and the sale on February 1, 1974.

E15-3. The Papaw Company had the following transactions in long-term investment in stocks during 1973:

1973

Jan. 5   Purchased 2,000 shares of $100 par value common stock of Sunno Company at 108. The Sunno Company had declared a $1 per share dividend on January 1, 1973, payable on January 20, 1973.

20   Received the cash dividend from the Sunno Company.

1973

Mar. 10 Purchased 1,000 shares of $100 par value common stock of Sunno Company at 112.

July 1 Received a $1.10 per share cash dividend from the Sunno Company.

Dec. 1 The Sunno Company split up its stock two for one. The Papaw Company exchanged 3,000 shares of $100 par value stock for 6,000 shares of no-par value stock.

31 The Sunno Company declared a $1 per share cash dividend payable January 10, 1974, to stockholders of record on December 31, 1973.

Journalize the transactions.

E15-4. On January 1, 1973, the Edison Corporation purchased as a long-term investment 6% bonds of Charles Corporation with a face value of $300,000 at 102½. The bonds have a maturity date of January 1, 1983. Interest is payable each January 1 and July 1.

Record (a) the purchase of the bonds by the Edison Corporation, and (b) all the necessary remaining entries for 1973. Use the straight line method of amortization.

E15-5. Assume that the Edison Corporation (see Exercise E15-4) purchased the Charles Corporation bonds at 98 instead of 102½.
Prepare all the required entries for 1973. Use the straight line method of amortization.

E15-6. On May 1, 1973, the Goodson Company purchased as a long-term investment 6% bonds of Celler Company. Interest is paid semiannually on May 1 and November 1. The bonds mature on May 1, 1985. On November 1, 1973, the accountant for the Goodson Company prepared the following entry to record the receipt of bond interest and the amortization of the premium:

1973			
Nov. 1	Cash	3,765	
	Investment in Bonds–Celler Company Bonds		180
	Bond Interest Earned		3,585
	To record the receipt of bond interest from the Celler Company and to amortize the premium for six months by the straight line method.		

From this information, reconstruct the journal entry that was made to record the purchase of the bonds. Show all your calculations.

DEMONSTRATION PROBLEMS

DP15-1. (*Accounting for marketable securities*) The Doris Monroe Company had the following transactions in temporary investments during 1973:

1973

Feb. 1 Purchased 6% bonds of Zulla Company with a face value of $200,000 at 120 plus accrued interest. Interest is paid each May 1 and November 1. Brokerage fees and other costs incident to the purchase were $150. The bonds have a maturity date of November 1, 1993.

Mar. 15 Purchased 400 shares of $100 par value, 5% preferred stock of Yardley Corporation at $110 per share. Dividends are paid semiannually on March 15 and September 15. The Yardley Corporation had declared the regular semiannual cash dividend on their preferred stock on March 10, 1973, payable on March 20, 1973. Brokerage fees and other costs incident to the purchase were $80.

20 Received the semiannual dividend from the Yardley Corporation.

May 1 Received the semiannual interest on the bonds of Zulla Company.

1973

Sept. 20 Received the semiannual dividends on the preferred stock of Yardley Corporation.

Oct. 1 Sold bonds of Zulla Company with a face value of $100,000 at 118 plus accrued interest.

Nov. 1 Received semiannual interest on the remaining bonds of Zulla Company.

Dec. 31 Accrued the interest on the bonds of Zulla Company.

Required: Journalize the transactions.

DP15-2. (*Valuation of marketable securities*) The Lawrence Company had the following temporary investments as of December 31, 1973:

	Cost	Market Price at December 31, 1973
Bonds of Meeson Company	$15,740	$15,890
Preferred Stock of Newton Company	7,500	7,400
Preferred Stock of Owers Company	16,710	16,560

On February 1, 1974, the Lawrence Company sold the preferred stock of Newton Company for $7,280. On March 1, 1974, the company sold the preferred stock of Owers Company for $16,600.

Required:

1. Assuming that a valuation offset account is used, record the necessary adjusting entry under the lower of cost or market unit method.
2. Show how the investments should be shown on the end-of-period financial statement.
3. Record the sales of marketable securities in 1974.

DP15-3. (*Accounting for long-term investment in stocks*) The Parento Company had the following transactions involving long-term investment in stocks in 1973:

1973

Jan. 6 Purchased 2,000 shares of $100 par value common stock of Sun Company at 120.

May 1 Received a $2 per share cash dividend from the Sun Company.

June 1 Purchased 1,000 shares of $100 par value common stock of Sun Company at 128.

Sept. 1 The Sun Company split up its stock four for one. The Parento Company exchanged 3,000 shares of $100 par value stock for 12,000 shares of no-par value stock.

Oct. 10 The Parento Company sold 1,000 shares of the stock of Sun Company for $40 per share. On October 5, the Sun Company declared a $1 per share cash dividend payable on October 25 to stockholders of record on October 20.

25 Received the cash dividend on the remaining shares of stock of Sun Company.

Required: 1. Journalize the transactions.
2. Show how the long-term investment in stocks should be shown on the statement of financial position at December 31, 1973.

DP15-4. (*Accounting for the purchase of bonds as a long-term investment*) Assume that Ames, Inc., purchased 6% bonds of Pearson Corporation under each of the following conditions (the authorization date is January 1, 1973).

	Case A	Case B	Case C	Case D
Face value of each bond	$500	$1,000	$10,000	$1,000
Term of bond issue (years)	10	20	20	10
Interest payable	Jan. 1 and July 1	Jan. 1 and July 1	Jan. 1 and July 1	Jan. 1 and July 1
Date of purchase	Jan. 1, 1973	Jan. 1, 1973	Mar. 1, 1973	Jan. 1, 1973
Number of bonds purchased	20	10	10	20
Purchase price	100	98½	102 (plus accrued interest)	at a price to yield 8%

Required: For each case, record (a) the purchase of the bonds, (b) the receipt of the first interest payment, accompanied by the entry to record proper amortization, and (c) the adjusting entry for interest accrual on December 31, 1973, accompanied by the entry to record proper amortization. (In cases B and C use the straight line amortization method, and in case D use the compound interest method. Given: p of $1 for 20 periods at 4% is 0.456; P of $1 for 20 periods at 4% is 13.590.)

PROBLEMS

P15-1. The Tarlton Company had the following transactions involving temporary investments during 1973:

1973

Jan. 1   Purchased 4% bonds of Zoom Company with a face value of $200,000 at 102 plus accrued interest. Interest is paid each March 1 and September 1. Brokerage fees and other costs incident to the purchase were $160. The bonds have a maturity date of September 1, 1982.

Mar. 1   Received semiannual interest on bonds of Zoom Company.

     15   Purchased 600 shares of $50 par value, 6% preferred stock of Suskin Company at $40 per share. Dividends are paid semiannually on February 15 and August 15. Brokerage fees and other costs incident to the purchase were $60.

Aug. 15   Sold 200 shares of preferred stock of Suskin Company at $52 per share. On August 10, the board of directors of the Suskin Company declared the regular semiannual dividend on this stock payable on August 25 to stockholders of record on August 20.

     25   Received the dividend on the remaining preferred stock of Suskin Company.

Sept. 1   Received semiannual interest on the bonds of Zoom Company.

Oct. 1   Sold the bonds of Zoom Company at 103 plus accrued interest.

Required: Journalize the transactions.

P15-2. The Rankin Company had the following temporary investments as of December 31, 1973:

	Cost	Market Price at December 31, 1973
Bonds of Sampson Company	$42,000	$42,500
Preferred Stock of Thompson Company	37,500	37,400
Preferred Stock of Uriah Company	53,650	53,575

The following transactions involving the investments took place in 1974:

1974

Jan. 15   Sold the preferred stock of Thompson Company for $37,480.

1974

Feb. 15   Sold the preferred stock of Uriah Company for $53,520.

Required:

1. Assuming the use of a valuation offset account, record the necessary adjusting entry under the lower of cost or market unit method.
2. Show how the temporary investments should be shown on the end-of-period financial statement.
3. Record the sales of the temporary investments in 1974.

P15-3. The Peters Company had the following transactions involving long-term investment in stocks in 1973:

1973

Jan.   4   Purchased 2,000 shares of $50 par value common stock of Sunner Company at 60.

Feb.   10   Purchased 3,000 shares of $50 par value common stock of Sunner Company at 67. On February 2, the Sunner Company declared a $1 per share cash dividend payable February 26 to stockholders of record on February 21.

26   Received the cash dividend on the stock of Sunner Company.

Mar.   2   Purchased 2,000 shares of $50 par value common stock of Sunner Company at 68.

Sept. 10   The Sunner Company declared a 100% stock dividend. The Peters Company received 7,000 additional shares of $50 par value common stock from the Sunner Company.

Nov.   1   Sold 2,500 shares of the common stock of Sunner Company at 35.

Dec. 31   The Sunner Company declared a 75 cent per share cash dividend payable January 16, 1974 to stockholders of record on December 31, 1973.

Required: 1. Journalize the transactions.
2. Show how the long-term investment in stock should be shown on the statement of financial position of the Peters Company as of December 31, 1973.

P15-4. On May 1, 1973, the Isaacs Company purchased 6% bonds of Barley Company with a face value of $160,000 at 103. The bonds mature on May 1, 1983, and interest is paid each May 1 and November 1. The books are closed each December 31.
Required: Journalize all necessary entries on the books of the Isaacs Company for 1973 and 1974, assuming that proper straight line amortization is recorded each time bond interest is recorded.

P15-5. On April 1, 1973, the Roughton Company purchased 4½% bonds of Sparrow Company with a face value of $400,000 at 98 plus accrued interest. The bonds mature on August 1, 1981, and interest is paid each February 1 and August 1. On July 1, 1977, the Roughton Company sold bonds with a face value of $100,000 at 99 plus accrued interest. The books are closed each December 31.

Required:

1. Journalize all necessary entries on the books of the Roughton Company for 1973, assuming that proper straight line amortization is recorded each time bond interest is recorded.
2. Assuming that the proper accounting is carried out in the years 1974 through 1976, prepare all the entries for the year 1977, including the receipt of interest on February 1 and August 1, the proper discount accumulation, the sale of the bonds on July 1, and the accrual of interest and other necessary adjusting and closing entries at December 31.

P15-6. On June 1, 1973, the Eton Company purchased as a long-term investment 6% bonds of Hamilton Company at a certain price plus accrued interest. Interest is payable semiannually on April 1 and October 1. The bonds mature on October 1, 1992. On October 1, 1973, the accountant for the Eton Company prepared the following entry to record the receipt of bond interest and the amortization of the premium:

1973			
Oct. 1	Cash	5,550	
	Investment in Bonds–Hamilton Company		60
	Accrued Bond Interest Receivable		1,850
	Bond Interest Earned		3,640
	To record the receipt of semiannual bond interest from the Hamilton Company and to amortize the premium for four months by the straight line method.		

Required:

1. Compute and state separately (a) the face value of bonds, (b) the original purchase price of bonds.
2. From the information given, reconstruct the journal entry to record the purchase of the bonds by the Eton Company.

P15-7. (*Accounting policy decision problem*) The Goodwin Corporation has only common shares outstanding, owned by the following three stockholders:

R. A. Goode	3,000 shares
B. E. Deale	3,000 shares
I. M. Inman	4,000 shares

Inman has agreed to sell his shares at book value (based on generally accepted accounting principles) to the Newco Corporation provided past profits have been recorded with reasonable accuracy. A review of past records of the Goodwin Corporation indicates the following:

The bad debts expense of the corporation has been estimated to be 1 percent of credit sales. The Allowance for Doubtful Accounts appears as follows since the corporation was formed:

Allowance for Doubtful Accounts

1970				1969			
July 10	Write-off	760		Dec. 31	Adjustment	1,500	
1971				1970			
Nov. 18	Write-off	1,000		Dec. 31	Adjustment	1,800	
1972				1971			
Sept. 2	Write-off	1,400		Dec. 31	Adjustment	2,400	
1973				1972			
Aug. 8	Write-off	1,360		Dec. 31	Adjustment	2,300	
				1973			
				Dec. 31	Adjustment	2,600	

In addition, five years ago the Goodwin Corporation made an investment in Reynoldo Corporation bonds with a face value of $20,000. The bonds cost $16,400 and had 18 years of life remaining at the time of purchase. The discount was never amortized because the corporation had always intended to sell the bonds in the following year, but for one reason or another had not done so.

The corporation had also made an investment in the stock of Ronson Corporation four years before, and it appears on the books at its original cost of $47,400. The stock has increased in market value steadily each year and is presently worth approximately $64,000. The Goodwin Corporation's net income has averaged $80,000 during the past five years, and average stockholder's equity has been $400,000. Goodwill of $12,000 appears on the corporation's books.

Required:

1. As an accounting consultant for the Newco Corporation, would you feel that the determination of past net income has been reasonably accurate?
2. If you were adjusting the assets of the Goodwin Corporation preparatory to the sale of Inman's stock, how much would the adjustment be? Discuss.
3. If you believe that the income has been incorrectly computed, state how you would change the corporation's accounting policies.

Financial Reporting: Analysis and Interpretive Problems

16

Corporate Financial Reporting: Interpretation and Analysis

The accounting department of a business organization is responsible for preparing a number of different kinds of reports, which may be classified as follows:

1. Primarily for use by outside groups: (a) annual (or periodic) financial reports, (b) prospectuses, and (c) special reports to grantors of credit.
2. Primarily for use by management: various managerial reports and analyses.

These reports are discussed in this chapter in terms of their history and functions.

DEVELOPMENT OF FINANCIAL REPORTING TO OUTSIDE GROUPS

The importance of financial reporting to outside groups has paralleled the growth of the corporate type of enterprise. Early American corporations revealed very little financial information to anyone outside of internal management. Annual financial reports to stockholders were meager and consisted usually of condensed and unaudited financial statements.

With the growth of corporations, the New York Stock Exchange became interested in the type of information that was being furnished to stockholders. In 1898, for example, the Exchange, in reviewing the application of a particular company for a listing of its stock, requested that the applicant present detailed statements to the stockholders prior to each annual meeting. This was the genesis of the detailed annual corporate reports that are made available today to the stockholders. These reports, in addition to a summary letter from the president or the chairman of the board of directors, contain detailed audited comparative statements of financial position and income and other descriptive and analytical information about the present and future outlook for the corporation.

The Securities and Exchange Commission (SEC), an independent quasi-judicial agency of the United States Government, created by the Securities Act of 1933 and strengthened by the Securities Exchange Act of 1934 and the Securities Acts Amendments of 1964 and other years, requires prior registration with the SEC of all securities to be sold on a public exchange and unlisted securities that are sold over the counter of companies with total assets of over $1,000,000 and 500 or more stockholders. The SEC may exempt from the registration requirements certain offerings, particularly those of governmental agencies and certain common carriers such as interstate railroads.

The registration of securities with the SEC requires the filing of a registration statement and a *prospectus,* including detailed financial statements with a report and opinion of an independent public accounting firm. These data must be kept current by the filing of annual financial reports prepared in accordance with the rules and regulations of the SEC. The agency does not appraise the registered securities; it attempts to safeguard the investing public by requiring that all material facts be presented properly and that no important information be withheld. The SEC may require that any speculative features of a particular offering be made clearly evident. It has made a signal contribution to the improvement in financial reporting procedures of corporations and to the scope and nature of the data available to investors. Its influence has been far-reaching and salutary; the reporting requirements have been carried over into the annual reports to stockholders and thus have contributed to a degree of standardization in financial reporting.

Corporate financial reports may take a slightly different form when a corporation requests a loan from a bank or establishes a line of credit. The grantor of credit under these circumstances will dictate the type and form of reports. Often, only a statement of financial position will be required. In other cases, in addition to the statement of financial position, an income statement, a statement of sources and uses of funds (discussed in Chapter 19), and other narrative-type statistical and financial reports may be required.

MANAGEMENT NEEDS FOR FINANCIAL DATA

If business executives are to make intelligent decisions based on accounting data, they must understand these data. A major function of the accounting department of a corporation, therefore, is to supply the necessary financial reports to management in meaningful form. The accounting department records the data, prepares the financial statements, and also may prepare ratio, trend, and percentage analyses. The financial data are used by the corporate executives, who are responsible for the stewardship of the business, to measure past performance in terms of costs and revenue, to determine the efficiency and effectiveness of the various departments, to determine future business policies, and to report to the stockholders.

The format of managerial reports often cannot be predetermined. The particular form depends on the decision that is to be made. If these reports are to be most beneficial, however, they should (1) be current, (2) contain sufficient details regarding the particular problem to be solved, and (3) present acceptable alternatives.

There is a constantly increasing reliance by business executives on financial reports. Large-scale production, wide geographical distribution, the increasing trend toward corporate business expansion with a concomitant delegation of authority, complex income tax legislation, and increasing governmental regulation of business are some of the factors requiring management reliance on corporate financial reports.

THE PURPOSE OF FINANCIAL STATEMENTS

Financial statements, whether in an annual report to stockholders, a prospectus for investors, or a report to grantors of credit or to management, should be prepared carefully. They should furnish the reader with enough information to enable him to make an intelligent decision concerning some aspect of the entity.

Over three and one-half decades ago the purpose of financial statements appearing in annual corporate reports was stated rather well by a group of very forward-thinking accountants as follows:

> Financial statements are prepared for the purpose of presenting a periodical review or report on progress by the management and deal with the status of the investment in the business and the results achieved during the period under review. They reflect a combination of recorded facts, accounting conventions, and personal judgments; and the judgments and conventions applied affect them materially. The soundness of the judgments necessarily depends on the competence and integrity of those who make them and on their adherence to generally accepted accounting principles and conventions.[1]

Recorded facts refer to the data in financial statements as taken from the accounting records. The amounts of Cash, Accounts Receivable, and Plant and Equipment, for example, represent recorded facts. *Accounting conventions* are basic assumptions or conditions accepted by common consent. These conventions are concerned with the problems of asset valuation, allocation of expenditures between asset and expense classifications in the accounting period, and the proper measurement of income. ▼ Accounting statements are prepared on the assumption that each enterprise is a separate entity, that all business transactions can be expressed in dollars, that the enterprise will continue in business indefinitely, and that reports will be prepared at regular intervals. ▼

Accounting Concepts: ▼
Three Concepts Forming Basis of Reports: Entity Concept, Transactions Price, Going Concern Concept

▼ Accounting is ultimately an art and not an exact science, and financial statements must therefore reflect the opinion and judgment of the accountant and of management. ▼ For example, the estimated life and the method of depreciation to be used in the valuation of plant and equipment, the method of inventory valuation, the valuation of intangibles (patents, goodwill, and so on) are some areas that require opinion and judgment. Equally competent accountants, given the same set of facts, may arrive at different results. Thus, the element of personal judgment and preference affects the financial statements.

Accounting Concept: ▼
Importance of Personal Judgment

[1] Examination of Financial Statements by Independent Public Accountants, *Bulletin of American Institute of Certified Public Accountants*, Jan., 1936, p. 1.

Accounting Concept: ▼
Basic Purpose of
Financial Statements

▼ In short, the basic purpose of financial statements is to transmit reliable and useful information to interested groups, both external and internal. Proper use of the information by these groups should result in their making sound decisions. ▼

INTERPRETIVE FINANCIAL STATEMENT PRESENTATION

If the purpose of financial statements, as stated in the previous section, is to be achieved, these statements must be constructed in a manner that will make them as understandable and useful as possible to the reader. In preparing financial statements, the accountant should do his best to obtain an interpretative presentation of the information included therein. The following four basic devices are commonly utilized to achieve the desired interpretative statement presentation:

1. *Classification.* Items are presented together in classes to emphasize the similarity of the items within each class and to arrive at meaningful class totals.
2. *Arrangement.* Individual items, classes, totals, and other information are arranged within a statement to indicate important relationships in the data. The disclosure of total current assets and total current liabilities in juxtaposition helps in evaluating the ability of a business to meet its current obligations.
3. *Order.* The order in which figures are shown directs attention to the most important data and reinforces the arrangement. For instance, the final figure on a typical income statement is the net income—the most important amount.
4. *Description.* Accountants have been accused of using out-dated, stereotyped account titles in statements. This has been true in the past, but modern financial reports do not necessarily carry titles taken verbatim from the general ledger. Rather, serious consideration is given to the selection of words to ensure that descriptions of dollar amounts are both accurate and understandable.

The Statement of Financial Position

The statement of financial position, or balance sheet, shows the financial position—the cost (or cost less accumulated amortization) of assets, the liabilities, and the equity of the owner or owners—as of a specific point in time. As previously explained, the statement may be prepared in one of two forms—account or report. A skeleton of the account form of position statement is shown.

Heading	
Assets	**Liabilities and Stockholders' Equity**
Current Assets	Current Liabilities
Long-Term Investments	Long-Term Liabilities
Plant and Equipment	Deferred Credits
Intangible Assets	Total Liabilities
Deferred Charges	Stockholders' Equity
Total Assets	Total Liabilities and Stockholders' Equity

The chief advantage of this form of statement of financial position is that the juxtaposition of subgroups helps to show the relationship of certain data and therefore facilitates statement analysis and interpretation.

An outline of a typical report form of position statement follows:

Heading

Assets

Current Assets
Long-Term Investments
Plant and Equipment
Intangible Assets
Deferred Charges
Total Assets

Liabilities and Stockholders' Equity

Current Liabilities
Long-Term Liabilities
Deferred Credits
  Total Liabilities
Stockholders' Equity
Total Liabilities and Stockholders' Equity

The advantages of this form include (1) ease of preparation and (2) expansibility. Since the totals do not have to be placed on the same line, this form of the statement is easier to prepare. In addition, a large number of items may be presented in an orderly manner.

The lists of class headings include several new terms. These are defined and illustrated on the following pages. The traditional class headings also are re-examined in light of the large number of items that have been introduced since classified statements were first discussed in Chapter 1.

Current Assets. "The term *current assets* is used to designate cash and other assets or resources commonly identified as those which are reasonably expected to be realized in cash or sold or consumed during the normal operating cycle of the business," or one year, whichever is the longer period of time.[2] A normal operating cycle is the length of time it takes a business to purchase an entire stock of goods, convert them to accounts receivable, and collect the accounts receivable. One business may complete a single operating cycle in two years, whereas another business may have four cycles within a single year. In the latter case, the year is normally chosen as the length of time for determining the currency of assets; in the former case it would be two years.

Included in Current Assets are Cash, Marketable Securities, Accounts Receivable, Accrued Interest Receivable, Notes Receivable, Merchandise Inventory, Prepaid Insurance, and other prepaid expenses that will be consumed within an operating cycle. Even though short-term prepaid expenses are not converted into cash as such, it is logical to include them among the current assets since in a break-even or profit-making operation their total cost will be recovered through revenue within the year or operating cycle.

[2] American Institute of Certified Public Accountants, *Accounting Principles*, Vol. II. Chicago: Commerce Clearing House, Inc., 1970, p. 6010.

Current assets are often subdivided into *quick current assets* and *trading current assets*. The quick current assets include Cash and the items that will normally be converted into cash rather rapidly, such as Marketable Securities and the receivables. The trading current assets include the inventories and prepaid expenses. This method of subdividing Current Assets is useful in financial statement analysis; for example, the acid-test ratio (Chapter 1) is determined by dividing quick current assets by total current liabilities.

Long-Term Investments. The second asset caption is generally Long-Term Investments; it includes stocks and bonds purchased from other companies, long-term funds, long-term receivables, the cash surrender value of life insurance policies owned by the company, and land held for future use. To restrict the name "long-term investments" to this particular group of assets is somewhat misleading, since all assets represent investments. Nevertheless, it is a commonly accepted practice to include only the nonoperating, long-term assets under this caption.

Plant and Equipment. This group of assets includes those tangible, long-lived assets that are used in the operations of the business rather than being held for resale. Among these assets are land, buildings, machinery and equipment, and delivery equipment. Often called *fixed assets* or *fixed tangible assets*, these assets usually are disclosed on the statement of financial position in order of decreasing permanence, beginning with land and buildings.

A word of caution should be injected at this point. A generally accepted principle is that plant and equipment should be carried at original cost in the case of land and original cost less accumulated depreciation in the case of depreciable assets. Since this brief description is preparatory to the discussion of financial statement analysis, it should be kept in mind that most plant and equipment accounts contain a commingling of dollars with different purchasing powers. Sound financial statement analysis must take this fact into account, or perhaps even require that necessary price-level adjustments be made to the data that are being used in analysis relationships.

Intangible Assets. This group includes the long-term assets that have no form or substance but make a significant contribution to the production of revenue, typically by legally sheltering the company from competition. There are many intangible assets owned by entities. Some of them are current, such as Accounts Receivable; others are noncurrent, such as investments in bonds and stocks. The only items generally listed under Intangible Assets are goodwill, trademarks, copyrights, organization costs, patents, leaseholds, and leasehold improvements. Since only fixed assets appear under the caption Intangible Assets, it seems that the more descriptive caption *Intangible Fixed Assets* should be used.

Deferred Charges. Long-term unallocated debits against future operations commonly are referred to as *Deferred Charges*. This title to some extent describes all assets. Buildings depreciate and are allocated to future operations; merchandise is sold and its cost is allocated against future revenue; and even cash is held to acquire the assets that, in turn, become expenses, thus being allocated against future operations. Despite this fact, only a few items are generally shown under Deferred Charges, for instance, Research and Development Costs, Long-Term Prepaid Expenses, and Discount on Bonds Payable. Each of these items would be better disclosed under some other statement of financial position caption. The first two are intangible fixed assets; the third should be offset against Bonds Payable under Long-Term Liabilities. There is little in accounting theory to justify the use of the classification Deferred Charges.

Current Liabilities. Current liabilities represent obligations the liquidation of which requires the use of current assets or the creation of other current liabilities within a year or operating cycle, whichever is longer. Accounts Payable, Notes Payable, Accrued Expenses Payable, Sales Taxes Payable, and Unearned Revenue are typically carried under this caption, as well as currently maturing installments of long-term debts, such as the installment of serial bonds that is due within the coming year or operating cycle.

In much financial statement analysis, current liabilities are related either to current assets or to some subdivision of current assets. Thus it is important that any obligation that does not require the use of a current asset to liquidate it should not be classified as a current liability or else the resulting analyses will be misleading.

Long-Term Liabilities. Obligations that will not be liquidated until after the current year or operating cycle are referred to as Long-Term Liabilities, or Long-Term Debt. Shown under this caption are Bonds Payable, Mortgage Payable, Long-Term Contracts Payable, Liability under Pension Contracts, and Long-Term Leases Payable. Proper disclosure dictates that maturity dates and other relevant information concerning these liabilities be clearly shown on the statement of financial position.

Deferred Credits. Appearing on many statements of financial position is the caption *Deferred Credits,* or *Deferred Revenue,* which represents long-term unallocated credits to future operations. As with the term Deferred Charges, Deferred Credits does not properly describe the items generally appearing under it, which are long-term unearned revenues such as Unrealized Gross Profit on Installment Sales, Premium on Bonds Payable, and similar items. Typically, this kind of caption becomes a catch-all classification for amounts that do not precisely fit under another caption. In attempting to analyze financial statements, it is extremely important to recognize this fact. Often a statement may have to be recast before it can be analyzed properly. As with Deferred Charges, there is little in financial reporting theory to justify this statement of financial position category.

Stockholders' Equity. The Stockholders' Equity section of a statement of financial position for a corporation should not only disclose the major sources of capital, but should also show certain legal restrictions that are imposed on capital withdrawals. The following two outlines emphasize slightly different points of view.

```
                       Sources of Capital Approach
     Stockholders' Equity
        Contributed Capital
          Preferred Stock
          Add Premium on Preferred Stock
             Total Capital Contributed by Preferred Stockholders
          Common Stock
          Deduct Discount on Common Stock
             Total Capital Contributed by Common Stockholders
          Other Contributed Capital
             Donation of Land by City of X
                Total Contributed Capital
        Retained Earnings
          Restricted for
             Contingencies
             Purchase of Treasury Stock
          Unrestricted
                Total Retained Earnings
        Deduct Treasury Stock–Common (at cost)
        Total Stockholders' Equity
                        Legal Capital Approach
     Stockholders' Equity
        Capital Stock (legal capital)
          Preferred Stock
          Common Stock
             Total Legal Capital
        Other Contributed Capital (not legal capital)
          Premium on Preferred Stock
          Donation of Land by City of X
             Total
          Deduct Discount on Common Stock
             Total Other Contributed Capital
        Retained Earnings
          Restricted for
             Contingencies
             Purchase of Treasury Stock
          Unrestricted
                Total Retained Earnings
        Deduct Treasury Stock–Common (at cost)
        Total Stockholders' Equity
```

Footnotes to Statements

Footnotes are used quite liberally to disclose methods of inventory pricing, depreciation methods, contingent liabilities, long-term lease provisions, and many other items. Some accounting theoreticians prefer to disclose contingent liabilities short, as shown below.

```
                            Liabilities
     Current Liabilities
        Accounts Payable                                    $ 50,000
     Long-Term Liabilities
        Bonds Payable, due July 1, 1999                      100,000
     Contingent Liabilities
        Pending Damage Lawsuits               $10,000
        Total Liabilities                                   $150,000
```

Since the amount of the contingent liabilities is not included in the total liabilities, this method of presentation is similar to a footnote; it is a memorandum included in the body of the statement of financial position. A criticism of this method of disclosure is that some readers will interpret these items to be actual liabilities.

The Income Statement and the Statement of Retained Earnings

Three other financial statements that typically appear in annual reports are the income statement, the statement of retained earnings, and the statement of sources and uses of working capital. The first two statements are discussed in this chapter. The latter one is discussed in Chapter 19. Up until December, 1966, when the Accounting Principles Board (APB) of the American Institute of Certified Public Accountants (AICPA) issued *Opinion No. 9*, there was quite a controversy about whether the income statement or the statement of retained earnings should be used to report extraordinary items such as losses from fires or natural hazards, nonrecurring gains or losses on the retirement of bonds payable or the disposal of assets, and corrections of errors in the net income of prior periods. One group argued that if these items are substantial and if they are included in the income statements, they would distort net income; thus this group of advocates stated that these extraordinary items should be disclosed in the statement of retained earnings. This view was referred to as the *current operating performance concept.* Opponents argued that all items affecting the calculation of net income should appear in the income statement. Extraordinary items most certainly would affect the long-run income of a firm; thus they should be disclosed in the income statement. This view was labeled the *all-inclusive income statement concept.*

Illustration of the Pre-1966 Current Operating Performance Concept and All-Inclusive Concept

To illustrate the variation that could occur in net income under the two historical concepts assume, for example, that the Baxter Company earns an ordinary income of $50,000 for each of the three years 1973 through 1975; in addition, in the first year, it sells a patent that it developed but did not use for a gain of $100,000; in the second year, it sells other plant assets for a gain of $70,000; and in the third year, it experiences an uninsured fire loss in the plant of $50,000. Under the current operating performance concept, the Baxter Company's net income would be reported as $50,000 each year. However, under the all-inclusive concept, the net income would be reported as shown below.

	1973	1974	1975
Ordinary Income	$ 50,000	$ 50,000	$50,000
Extraordinary Gain (loss)	100,000	70,000	(50,000)
Net Income before Income Taxes	$150,000	$120,000	$ –0–

Advocates of the current operating concept argued that under this theory, net income reflects what took place under normal business conditions and that the income statement comparability is thereby enhanced. On the other hand, adherents of the all-inclusive concept maintain that the periodic income statement should record the total income history of the company; that allowing the omission of extraordinary items from the income statement furnishes an opportunity to conceal pertinent information; and that the omission or inclusion of certain items in borderline cases may make possible the manipulation of reported net income.

APB Opinion No. 9—Present Policy of the AICPA

With the issuance of *APB Opinion No. 9*, the AICPA virtually ended the controversy over the current operating and all-inclusive concepts. In this opinion, the AICPA states that all items of gain or loss recognized during the period with the single exception of "prior period adjustments" (carefully defined by the AICPA)[3] should be disclosed in the income statement. The extraordinary items, described carefully in terms of nature and amount, should be segregated from the results of recurring, normal operations and disclosed separately in the income statement. Those few items which qualify as "prior period adjustments" should be shown as adjustments of the opening balance of retained earnings in the statement of retained earnings.

Accounting Concepts: Extraordinary Items ▼

▼ *Extraordinary gains and losses* are defined in *APB Opinion No. 9* as those arising from events and transactions which are significantly different from the customary business activities of the entity, have a material effect on the operating results, and are not considered recurring factors in any evaluation of the ordinary operating process of the business. Examples are material gains and losses resulting (1) from the disposal of assets not acquired for resale; (2) from fire, floods, riots, war damages, or embezzlements; (3) from litigation in which special damages are at issue; (4) from the involuntary conversion of assets; or (5) from the settlement of debts at more or less than carrying value.▼

Prior period adjustments are limited to

> . . . those material adjustments which (a) can be specifically identified with and directly related to the business activities of particular prior periods, and (b) are not attributable to economic events occurring subsequent to the date of the financial statements for the prior period, and (c) depend primarily on determination by persons other than management, and (d) were not susceptible of reasonable estimation prior to such determination.[4]

The AICPA goes on to say, "Such adjustments are rare in modern financial accounting."[5] Then it lists examples of prior period adjustments as

> material, nonrecurring adjustments or settlements of income taxes, or renegotiation proceedings, or of utility revenues under rate processes. Settlements of significant amounts resulting from litigation or similar claims may also constitute prior period adjustments.[6]

[3] American Institute of Certified Public Accountants, *Accounting Principles*, Vol. II. Chicago: Commerce Clearing House, Inc., 1970, p. 6561.
[4] *Ibid.*, p. 6561.
[5] *Ibid.*
[6] *Ibid.*

In the vast majority of cases *APB Opinion No. 9* has moved virtually all the way toward the all-inclusive income statement concept. For this reason, the illustrations in this chapter will emphasize only the all-inclusive income statement concept. The income statement in Figure 16-1 and the supporting statement of retained earnings in Figure 16-2 are prepared in accordance with the all-inclusive income statement concept.

Figure 16-1. Income Statement under the All-Inclusive Income Statement Concept

EVANS COMPANY		
Condensed Income Statement		
For the Year Ended December 31, 1973		
Net Sales Revenue		$390,000
Cost of Goods Sold		200,000
Gross Margin on Sales		$190,000
Deduct Operating and General Expenses		60,000
Net Income before Income Taxes		$130,000
Income Taxes		65,000
Net Income before Extraordinary Items		$ 65,000
Add Adjustment of Cost of Machinery Charged to Equipment Repairs		10,000
Total		$ 75,000
Deduct: Understatement of Depreciation		
Loss from Flood	$ 1,000	
Loss from Sale of Land	5,000	
	10,000	16,000
Net Income after Extraordinary Items		$ 59,000

Figure 16-2. Statement of Retained Earnings under the All-Inclusive Income Statement Concept

EVANS COMPANY	
Statement of Retained Earnings	
For the Year Ended December 31, 1973	
Retained Earnings, December 31, 1972	$220,000
Net Income after Extraordinary Items per Income Statement	59,000
Total	$279,000
Deduct Dividends Declared	15,000
Retained Earnings, December 31, 1973	$264,000

Combined Statement of Income and Retained Earnings. Many accountants favor combining the statements of income and retained earnings to show within one statement both the recurring and the nonrecurring items. By placing the nonrecurring items in a separate section of the income statement, operating income as well as net income may be shown. A disadvantage of the combined statement is that it does not end with the amount of Net Income. If care is exercised in distinguishing between recurring and nonrecurring charges and credits, the combined statement is convenient and useful. Figure 16-3 illustrates the combined statement of income and retained earnings under the all-inclusive income statement concept. Some figures are omitted to avoid duplication of material in the previous statements.

Figure 16-3. Combined Statement of Income and Retained Earnings under the All-Inclusive Income Statement Concept

EVANS COMPANY Statement of Income and Retained Earnings For the Year Ended December 31, 1973	
Net Sales Revenue	$390,000
Net Income after Extraordinary Items (see Figure 16-1)	$ 59,000
Add Retained Earnings, December 31, 1972	220,000
Total	$279,000
Deduct Dividends Declared	15,000
Retained Earnings, December 31, 1973	$264,000

All-Inclusive Single-Step Income Statement. The all-inclusive single-step income statement shows all the revenue items and the amount of total revenues, followed by a listing of all costs and expenses the total of which is deducted from total revenue to determine net income. This type of statement has the advantage of easy readability. There are no intermediate additions and deductions, with accompanying labeled subtotals that may confuse the untrained reader. It is primarily for this reason that this form has become increasingly popular in recent years. The single-step statement is best adapted for annual reports to stockholders since they are not vitally interested in operating details.

Certain intermediate figures that are important for management purposes, such as the cost of goods sold, the gross margin on sales, and the net income before income taxes, are not shown. Furthermore, only a skilled reader is able to determine operating income because nonrecurring items are intermingled with recurring items. The single-step statement does not furnish management with sufficient data for decision making. The income statement of the Evans Company is illustrated in single-step form in Figure 16-4.

All-Inclusive Multiple-Step Income Statement. The all-inclusive multiple-step income statement was illustrated in Figure 16-1. The groupings in this statement furnish the following essential data: gross margin on sales, operating income, net income before income taxes, and extraordinary items. These figures are valuable in making statistical analyses, in comparing current data with prior periods of the company and with data of the industry, and in financial planning. The usefulness of this form of statement to management justifies its popularity.

Figure 16-4. All-Inclusive Single-Step Income Statement

EVANS COMPANY
Income Statement
For the Year Ended December 31, 1973

Revenue		
Net Sales Revenue	$390,000	
Adjustment for Cost of Machinery Charged to Equipment Maintenance and Repairs	10,000	$400,000
Revenue Deductions		
Cost of Goods Sold	$200,000	
Selling and General Expenses	60,000	
Income Taxes	65,000	
Understatement of Depreciation	1,000	
Loss from Flood	5,000	
Loss from Sale of Land	10,000	341,000
Net Income		$ 59,000

THE INTERPRETATION AND ANALYSIS OF FINANCIAL DATA

Before an individual can adequately understand and evaluate financial statement data, he must (1) understand the nature and limitations of accounting, (2) understand the terminology of accounting and business, (3) have some knowledge of business, and (4) be acquainted with the nature and tools of financial statement analysis. The major problem for current consideration is a further look at item 4, the tools of financial statement analysis.

The Tools of Financial Statement Analysis

The figures in financial statements may be said to have significance in at least three different respects. First, in themselves they are measures of absolute quantity. When an analyst sees that a company has $50,000 in cash, he understands that figure in terms of current purchasing power. However, the absolute amount does not tell him whether it is adequate for the current needs of the particular company. Some other means of determining its significance is required. Second, a degree of significance is indicated when figures are compared with similar amounts for other years and other companies. If $50,000 in cash was shown on the statement of financial position at the end of the previous year, if that amount was sufficient at that time, and if no changes in needs are foreseen, then it may be assumed that a Cash balance of $50,000 is adequate now. A third determinant of significance is the consideration of financial data in conjunction with related figures. When current assets are compared with current liabilities, the margin of safety—the dollars of current assets behind each dollar of current liabilities—can be determined.

The various tools of financial statement analysis are related to the ways in which financial data have significance. These tools are (1) comparative statements, (2) percentage analyses, (3) ratio analyses, and (4) a combination of the three. A brief review of the various standards of comparisons will indicate methods of using these tools of financial statement analysis. The central theme of any analysis is the evaluation of financial data through comparisons and measurement by some consistent standard to determine performance. Three types of standard have been proposed: (1) a company's past performance, (2) performance of companies in the same field, and (3) industry comparisons. In using each of these standards, the analyst should be aware of certain basic limitations. For example, if a company earned only $100 last year and earns $200 during the current year, it has improved 100 percent; yet it is still not a growth-type company. In a like manner, the performance of other companies and the industry standards have similar pitfalls. Even with these difficulties, these standards of comparison can be extremely beneficial as a means of revealing improvements and regressions, and thus can be helpful in the interpretation of statement data.

Percentage and ratio analyses have been illustrated throughout this text, but little has been said about comparative statements as such. In the following discussion, emphasis is placed on comparative statements; then a summary chart of the major ratios that have been discussed is presented.

Comparative Financial Statements

A study of the financial position of a company and the results of its operations for a period is more meaningful if the analyst has available the statements of financial position and the income statements for several periods. Trends can be better ascertained when three or more financial statements are compared. It is not uncommon to find comparative statements for at least three years in annual reports. One large corporation in its recent annual report showed comparative financial statements covering a period of 15 years.

Accounting Concept: ▼
Comparability of Data
on Statements

▼ For effective analysis, the statements being compared must be based on the consistent application of generally accepted accounting principles over the period of time covered by the comparison. If there is an absence of comparability, it should be made known in the accountant's report. ▼ The effect on net income, for example, of a changeover from FIFO to LIFO in valuing inventories must be clearly disclosed in the report.

The AICPA makes the following recommendations regarding comparative financial statements:

> The presentation of comparative financial statements in annual and other reports enhances the usefulness of such reports and brings out more clearly the nature and trends of current changes affecting the enterprise. Such presentation emphasizes the fact that statements for a series of periods are far more significant than those for a single period and that the accounts for one period are but an installment of what is essentially a continuous history.
>
> In any one year it is ordinarily desirable that the balance sheet (statement of financial position), the income statement, and the surplus statement (statement of retained earnings) be given for one or more preceding years as well as for the current year. Footnotes, explanations, and accountant's qualifications which appeared on the statements for the preceding years should be repeated, or at least referred to, in the comparative statements to the extent that they continue to be of significance . . . . This procedure is in conformity with the well-recognized principle that any change in practice which affects comparability should be disclosed.[7]

---

[7] American Institute of Certified Public Accountants, *Accounting Principles*, Vol. II. Chicago: Commerce Clearing House, Inc., 1970, pp. 6008–6009.

The use of comparative information in annual corporate reports to stock-holders is nearly universal. Other devices are also used to present the entire financial story as clearly and attractively as possible. Although there is no uniformity in the type of visual and statistical aids used, some of the more common are comparative statements with accompanying *trend percentages; common-size* statements, which present individual figures as percentages of a base total or some other established norm; pictorial statements using bar or line graphs to emphasize particular trends, ratios, or relationships; and pie charts showing the allocation of each company sales dollar. Any of these methods of presentation can make an interesting and informative report, aimed at perhaps the largest audience in the history of corporate reporting. Some of these devices are illustrated in this chapter.

The Comparative Statement of Financial Position. Successive statements of financial position of a company may be given side by side, showing only the dollar amounts. These statements can be made more meaningful if the dollar amount of increase or decrease and the percentage of increase or decrease are also shown. This is illustrated in Figure 16-5, the comparative position statement of the Melvin Company. In this illustration, the year 1972 is the base year and represents 100 percent. Accounts Receivable increased by 30.8 percent ($8,000 ÷ $26,000) during 1973; Notes Payable decreased by 5 percent ($1,000 ÷ $20,000); and Cash increased by $16,000, or 100 percent. The December 31, 1973, cash balance is twice the December 31, 1972, balance; Retained Earnings as of December 31, 1973, are almost twice the amount shown on December 31, 1972. No additional plant and equipment assets were acquired; the decreases reflect the annual depreciation deductions.

The change that took place during 1973 for the Melvin Company is apparently favorable. Current assets have increased by 42.3 percent, whereas current liabilities have increased by only 18.5 percent. The total stockholders' equity has increased by 20 percent; this is reflected by an increase in all the current assets. The favorable position of Retained Earnings, accompanied by an increase in working capital, was accomplished without resort to long-term borrowing because Mortgage Payable and Notes Payable have decreased during the period. Additional working capital was acquired by the sale of stock.

The Comparative Income Statement. A single income statement is just one link in a continuous chain reporting the operating results of the business. Comparative income statements are required for an analysis of trends and for making decisions regarding possible future developments. An income statement showing the results of operations for a single year is inadequate for purposes of analyzing the significance of the changes that have occurred.

The comparative statement of income and retained earnings of the Melvin Company is shown in Figure 16-6. The year 1972 is again used as the base year. Gross Margin on Sales increased by 25.4 percent, Net Income before Income Taxes increased by 67.2 percent; and Total Operating Expenses decreased by 0.6 percent. These favorable changes resulted primarily from an increase in sales. The provision for income taxes increased by 106.4 percent due to the sharp change in the Federal corporate tax rate on earnings in excess of $25,000. In 1972, it was assumed that the entire net taxable income of $23,000 was subject to only the normal

Figure 16-5. Comparative Statement of Financial Position

MELVIN COMPANY
Comparative Statement of Financial Position
December 31, 1973 and 1972

	December 31 1973	December 31 1972	Amount of Increase or (Decrease) during 1973	Percent of Increase or (Decrease) during 1973
Assets				
Current Assets				
Cash	$ 32,000	$ 16,000	$16,000	100.0
Accounts Receivable (net)	34,000	26,000	8,000	30.8
Inventories	45,000	36,000	9,000	25.0
Total Current Assets	$111,000	$ 78,000	$33,000	42.3
Plant and Equipment				
Land	$ 7,000	$ 7,000	$ –0–	–0–
Building (net)	116,000	119,000	(3,000)	(2.5)
Store Equipment (net)	23,000	25,000	(2,000)	(8.0)
Total Plant and Equipment	$146,000	$151,000	$(5,000)	(3.3)
Total Assets	$257,000	$229,000	$28,000	12.2
Liabilities and Stockholders' Equity				
Current Liabilities				
Accounts Payable	$ 34,000	$ 26,000	$ 8,000	30.8
Notes Payable	19,000	20,000	(1,000)	(5.0)
Accrued Payables	11,000	8,000	3,000	37.5
Total Current Liabilities	$ 64,000	$ 54,000	$10,000	18.5
Long-Term Liabilities				
Mortgage Payable	55,000	60,000	(5,000)	(8.3)
Total Liabilities	$119,000	$114,000	$ 5,000	4.4
Stockholders' Equity				
Capital Stock	$109,000	$100,000	$ 9,000	9.0
Retained Earnings	29,000	15,000	14,000	93.3
Total Stockholders' Equity	$138,000	$115,000	$23,000	20.0
Total Liabilities and Stockholders' Equity	$257,000	$229,000	$28,000	12.2

corporate tax rate; whereas, in 1973, $13,450 ($38,450 — $25,000) was assumed to be subject to both the normal and the surtax rates.

There is a close relationship between the cost of goods sold, the volume of sales, and net income before income taxes. In periods of exceptionally high sales volume, net income before income taxes tends to rise (percentage of increase, 67.2) at a faster rate than do sales (percentage of increase, 30.5). In periods of declining sales volume, earnings fall more sharply than sales. This is because a significant part of the operating expenses are constant (or fixed)—they are not affected by the current sales volume. Such fluctuations in net income can be eliminated if unit sales prices are increased in periods of low sales volume and reduced

Figure 16-6. Comparative Statement of Income and Retained Earnings

MELVIN COMPANY
Comparative Statement of Income and Retained Earnings
For the Years Ended December 31, 1973 and 1972

	Years Ended December 31		Amount of Increase or (Decrease) during 1973	Percent of Increase or (Decrease) during 1973
	1973	1972		
Sales (net)	$197,000	$151,000	$46,000	30.5
Cost of Goods Sold	123,000	92,000	31,000	33.7
Gross Margin on Sales	$ 74,000	$ 59,000	$15,000	25.4
Operating Expenses				
Selling Expenses				
Advertising	$ 1,200	$ 1,100	$ 100	9.1
Sales Salaries	18,300	17,900	400	2.2
Depreciation Expense–Store Equipment	2,000	2,000	–0–	–0–
Total Selling Expenses	$ 21,500	$ 21,000	$ 500	2.4
General Expenses				
Depreciation Expense–Building	$ 3,000	$ 3,000	$ –0–	–0–
Insurance Expense	675	650	25	3.8
Miscellaneous General Expenses	425	350	75	21.4
General Salaries	7,200	8,000	(800)	(10.0)
Total General Expenses	$ 11,300	$ 12,000	$ (700)	(5.8)
Total Operating Expenses	$ 32,800	$ 33,000	$ (200)	(0.6)
Operating Income	$ 41,200	$ 26,000	$15,200	58.5
Other Expenses				
Interest Expense	2,750	3,000	(250)	(8.3)
Net Income Before Income Taxes	$ 38,450	$ 23,000	$15,450	67.2
Income Taxes	14,450	7,000	7,450	106.4
Net Income After Income Taxes	$ 24,000	$ 16,000	$ 8,000	50.0
Retained Earnings, January 1	15,000	9,000	6,000	66.7
Total	$ 39,000	$ 25,000	$14,000	56.0
Dividends Declared	10,000	10,000	–0–	–0–
Retained Earnings, December 31	$ 29,000	$ 15,000	$14,000	93.3

in periods of high sales volume. Such a pricing policy, however, would be undesirable from the customers' viewpoint and impracticable from the company's viewpoint. It becomes important, therefore, that management knows the volume at which profits begin. This figure, the *break-even point*, is that volume of sales at which the business will neither make a profit nor incur a loss. Break-even analysis is discussed and illustrated in Chapter 23.

Percentage increases or decreases are calculated only when the base figure is positive. When there is no figure for the base year or when base year amounts are negative, there is no extension into the Percent of Increase or (Decrease) column. When there is a positive amount in the base year and none in the following year, the percent of decrease is 100, as shown on page 564.

	1973	1972 (Base Year)	Amount of Increase or (Decrease)	Percent of Increase or (Decrease)
Notes Receivable	$3,000	–0–	$3,000	
Notes Payable	–0–	$2,000	(2,000)	(100)
Net Income or (Loss)	4,000	(1,000)	5,000	

Trend Percentages

Comparative financial statements for several years may be expressed in terms of trend percentages. Management can more readily study changes in financial statements between periods by establishing a base year and expressing the other years in terms of the base year. The base year may be any typical year in the comparison—the first, the last, or any of the others. To illustrate, a partial comparative income statement is presented in Figure 16-7.

The amounts in Figure 16-7 are converted into trend percentages with 1972 as the base year, as shown in Figure 16-8.

Each item in the 1972 column of Figure 16-7 is assigned a weight of 100 percent. All the amounts in other years are expressed as trend percentages, or percentages of the figures for the base year. Each base year amount is divided into the same item for the other years. Trend percentages for Sales, for example, are calculated as follows: 1973: $95,000 ÷ $100,000 = 95; 1974: $120,000 ÷ $100,000 = 120; and 1975: $130,000 ÷ $100,000 = 130. When the base year amount is larger than the corresponding amount in another year, the trend percentage is less than 100 percent; conversely, when the base year amount is the lesser of the two, the trend percentage is over 100 percent.

The trend percentage statement is an analytical device for condensing the absolute dollar data of comparative statements. The device is especially valuable to management because readability and brevity are achieved by substituting percentages for large dollar amounts, which in themselves are difficult to compare. Trend percentages are generally computed for the major items in the statements; minor amounts are omitted, the objective being to high light the significant changes.

Figure 16-7. Partial Comparative Income Statements for Four Years*

	1972	1973	1974	1975
Sales (net)	$100,000	$95,000	$120,000	$130,000
Cost of Goods Sold	60,000	58,900	69,600	72,800
Gross Margin on Sales	$ 40,000	$36,100	$ 50,400	$ 57,200
Total Selling Expenses	$ 10,000	$ 9,700	$ 11,000	$ 12,000
Net Income before Income Taxes	$ 5,000	$ 3,800	$ 8,400	$ 10,400

*The years in this figure are listed in reverse order to facilitate analysis when data for three or more years are given.

Figure 16-8. Comparative Trend Percentages for Four Years*

	1972	1973	1974	1975
Sales (net)	100%	95%	120%	130%
Cost of Goods Sold	100	98	116	121
Gross Margin on Sales	100	90	126	143
Total Selling Expenses	100	97	110	120
Net Income before Income Taxes	100	76	168	208

*The years in this figure are listed in reverse order to facilitate analysis when data for three or more years are given.

An evaluation of the trend percentages requires a careful analysis of the interrelated items. Sales, for example, may show increases over a four-year period leading up to a trend percentage of 150 percent for the fourth year. This is unfavorable if it is accompanied by trend percentages of 200 percent for cost of goods sold, 175 percent for selling expenses, and 95 percent for net income before income taxes. Other unfavorable trends include an upward trend in receivables and inventories accompanied by a downward trend in sales and a downward trend in sales accompanied by an upward trend in plant and equipment. Favorable trends would be an increase in sales accompanied by a decrease in cost of goods sold and selling expenses or an increase in current assets accompanied by a decrease in current liabilities.

Trend percentages show the degree of increase and decrease; they do not indicate the causes of the changes. They do, however, single out unfavorable developments for further analysis and investigation by management. A marked change may have been caused by inconsistency in the application of accounting principles, by fluctuating price levels, or by controllable internal factors (for example, an unnecessary increase in merchandise inventory or a decrease in operating efficiency).

Common-Size Statements

Trend percentages provide for *horizontal statement analysis;* common-size statements provide for *vertical analysis* (see Figure 16-9). It is important for the analyst to compare changes on the financial statements that occur from period to period with certain base totals within those periods. Thus total assets, total liabilities and stockholders' equity, and total sales are each converted to a base of 100 percent. Each item within each classification is expressed as a percentage of the base; each asset, for example, is expressed as a percentage of total assets. Since these bases represent 100 percent in all the statements in the comparison, there is a common basis for analysis; therefore, the statements are referred to as "common-size statements." Comparisons can be made within the company, with other companies in the same industry, or with entire industry figures. Thus, important relationships can be discerned even when comparisons are made with companies of unlike size; and any significant differences may indicate that a

Accounting Concept: ▼
Uniformity of Data
for Comparisons

decision should be made. The common-size statement supplemented by additional analytical financial data are effective tools for a historical financial study of a business or industry. ▼ If comparisons are to be made of one company with one or more other companies or with an entire industry, it must first be carefully established that the data in the comparison are based on reasonably uniform and consistent accounting methods and principles. ▼

Figure 16-9. Comparative Common-Size Statement of Financial Position

MELVIN COMPANY
Comparative Common-Size Statement of Financial Position
December 31, 1973 and 1972

	December 31		Common-Size Percentages December 31	
	1973	1972	1973	1972
Assets				
Current Assets				
Cash	$ 32,000	$ 16,000	12.5	7.0
Accounts Receivable (net)	34,000	26,000	13.2	11.4
Inventories	45,000	36,000	17.5	15.7
Total Current Assets	$111,000	$ 78,000	43.2	34.1
Plant and Equipment				
Land	$ 7,000	$ 7,000	2.8	3.0
Building (net)	116,000	119,000	45.1	52.0
Store Equipment (net)	23,000	25,000	8.9	10.9
Total Plant and Equipment	$146,000	$151,000	56.8	65.9
Total Assets	$257,000	$229,000	100.0	100.0
Liabilities and Stockholders' Equity				
Current Liabilities				
Accounts Payable	$ 34,000	$ 26,000	13.2	11.4
Notes Payable	19,000	20,000	7.4	8.7
Accrued Payables	11,000	8,000	4.3	3.5
Total Current Liabilities	$ 64,000	$ 54,000	24.9	23.6
Long-Term Liabilities				
Mortgage Payable	55,000	60,000	21.4	26.2
Total Liabilities	$119,000	$114,000	46.3	49.8
Stockholders' Equity				
Capital Stock	$109,000	$100,000	42.4	43.7
Retained Earnings	29,000	15,000	11.3	6.5
Total Stockholders' Equity	$138,000	$115,000	53.7	50.2
Total Liabilities and Stockholders' Equity	$257,000	$229,000	100.0	100.0

Common-Size Statement of Financial Position. The common-size position statement of the Melvin Company is shown in Figure 16-9. The method of converting dollar amounts into common-size percentages, using data from Figure 16-9, is shown below.

$$\frac{\text{Accounts Receivable (1973)}}{\text{Total Assets (1973)}} = \frac{\$34,000}{\$257,000} = 13.2\%$$

Accounts Receivable in 1973 represent 13.2 percent of the total assets. For each dollar of total assets there were 13.2 cents of accounts receivable.

$$\frac{\text{Accounts Payable (1972)}}{\text{Total Liabilities and Stockholders' Equity (1972)}} = \frac{\$26,000}{\$229,000} = 11.4\%$$

Accounts Payable for 1972 represents 11.4 percent of total liabilities and stockholders' equity. For each dollar of total liabilities and stockholders' equity there were 11.4 cents of accounts payable.

Each current asset item has increased both in dollar amount and as a percentage of the total assets. Total current assets for 1973 have increased by 9.1 percent (43.2% − 34.1%) over 1972; total current liabilities for 1973 have increased by only 1.3 percent. Thus, the working capital position has been strengthened. Increases in net income and proceeds from the sale of stock are reflected by increases in each current asset item. The company did not invest in plant and equipment; the decreases in Store Equipment and Building are due to deductions for annual depreciation charges.

The ratio of stockholders' equity to total assets has increased, with corresponding decreases in the ratio of total liabilities to total assets. On December 31, 1972, the ratio of total liabilities to total assets was 49.8 percent; a year later this decreased to 46.3 percent. The overall financial position of the Melvin Company has improved.

Common-Size Income Statement. The common-size income statement of the Melvin Company is shown in Figure 16-10. Examples of the conversion of income statement dollar amounts into common-size percentages are shown below.

$$\frac{\text{Gross margin on sales (1973)}}{\text{Net sales (1973)}} = \frac{\$74,000}{\$197,000} = 37.6\%$$

Gross margin on sales for 1973 represents 37.6 percent of net sales; for each dollar of net sales there was a margin of 37.6 cents.

$$\frac{\text{Total operating expenses (1972)}}{\text{Net sales (1972)}} = \frac{\$33,000}{\$151,000} = 21.8\%$$

Total operating expenses for 1972 represent 21.8 percent of net sales; for each dollar of net sales there were 21.8 cents of total operating expenses.

A comparison of the cost of goods sold for the two years shows an increase of 1.5 percent (62.4% − 60.9%) and a corresponding decrease in the gross margin. This relatively modest change may indicate an increase in markdowns from original sales prices. Increases in amounts and percentages of inventories accompanied by a decrease in gross margin may indicate an overinvestment in inventories.

The change in total operating expenses is favorable: sales increased by $46,000 ($197,000 − $151,000), whereas total operating expenses remained approximately the same. The Melvin Company has increased the efficiency of its operations by increasing dollar sales without increasing its operating costs—a favorable development. The amount of increase in income taxes is at best a semi-uncontrollable factor.

Figure 16-10. Comparative Common-Size Income Statement

MELVIN COMPANY
Comparative Common-Size Income Statement
For the Years Ended December 31, 1973 and 1972

	Year Ended December 31		Common-Size Percentages Year Ended December 31	
	1973	1972	1973	1972
Sales (net)	$197,000	$151,000	100.0	100.0
Cost of Goods Sold	123,000	92,000	62.4	60.9
Gross Margin on Sales	$ 74,000	$ 59,000	37.6	39.1
Operating Expenses				
Selling Expenses				
Advertising	$ 1,200	$ 1,100	0.6	0.7
Sales Salaries	18,300	17,900	9.3	11.9
Depreciation Expense–Store Equipment	2,000	2,000	1.0	1.3
Total Selling Expenses	$ 21,500	$ 21,000	10.9	13.9
General Expenses				
Depreciation Expense–Building	$ 3,000	$ 3,000	1.5	1.9
Insurance Expense	675	650	0.4	0.4
Miscellaneous General Expenses	425	350	0.2	0.2
General Salaries	7,200	8,000	3.7	5.4
Total General Expenses	$ 11,300	$ 12,000	5.8	7.9
Total Operating Expenses	$ 32,800	$ 33,000	16.7	21.8
Net Operating Margin	$ 41,200	$ 26,000	20.9	17.3
Other Expenses				
Interest Expense	2,750	3,000	1.4	2.0
Net Income before Income Taxes	$ 38,450	$ 23,000	19.5	15.3
Income Taxes	14,450	7,000	7.3	4.7
Net Income	$ 24,000	$ 16,000	12.2	10.6

Use of the Company's Revenue Dollar

Annual reports often include graphic presentations of the disposition of each revenue dollar. These may take the form of a pie chart, bar graph, or simple statement. Such a presentation is often more meaningful to the reader than a detailed income statement and is popular for its simplicity and effectiveness. A revenue-dollar statement for Melvin Company is shown below.

	1973	1972
Each sales dollar was allocated as follows:		
Cost of Goods Sold	$0.624	$0.609
Selling Expenses	0.109	0.139
General Expenses	0.058	0.079
Interest Expense	0.014	0.020
Income Taxes	0.073	0.047
Net Income	0.122	0.106
Total Sales Dollar	$1.000	$1.000

Ratios

A tabulation of twenty significant ratios arranged in an outline of their primary measurements is shown in Figure 16-11, indicating the range of possibilities in the analysis of financial statements. With the aid of these ratios, the skilled analyst is better able to evaluate the managerial efficiency and financial stability of a company.

Figure 16-11. Major Ratios

TWENTY SIGNIFICANT RATIOS

Chapter Reference	Page Number	Ratio	Computing Ratio	Indicates
A. Short-Run Solvency Measurements				
1	14	Current Ratio	$\dfrac{\text{Current Assets}}{\text{Current Liabilities}}$	The ability of a business to meet its current obligations
1	14	Acid-Test Ratio	$\dfrac{\text{Quick Current Assets}}{\text{Current Liabilities}}$	The ability of a business to meet quickly unexpected demands for working capital
8	296	Average Number of Days' Sales Uncollected	$\dfrac{\text{Average Accounts Receivable}}{\text{Net Sales}} \times 365$ OR (1) Net Sales ÷ 365 = Net Sales Per Day (2) $\dfrac{\text{Average Trade Receivables}}{\text{Net Sales per Day}}$	The rapidity with which the accounts receivable are collected; the average number of days elapsing from the time of sale to the time of payment
5	167	Merchandise Inventory Turnover	$\dfrac{\text{Cost of Goods Sold}}{\text{Average Inventory}}$	The number of times the merchandise inventory was replenished during the period, or the number of dollars in the cost of goods sold for each dollar of inventory
20	693	Materials Turnover	$\dfrac{\text{Materials Used}}{\text{Average Materials Inventory}}$	The number of times the materials inventory was replaced during the period, or the number of dollars of materials used in manufacturing for each dollar of inventory on hand.
20	693	Finished Goods Turnover	$\dfrac{\text{Cost of Goods Sold}}{\text{Average Finished Goods Inventory}}$	The number of times the finished goods inventory was sold and replaced during the period, or the number of dollars of cost of finished goods sold for each dollar of finished goods on hand
B. Long-Run Solvency Measurements				
4	132	Creditors' Equity Ratio	$\dfrac{\text{Total Liabilities}}{\text{Total Assets}}$	The amount of creditor sources of total assets
4	133	Stockholders' Equity Ratio	$\dfrac{\text{Stockholders' Equity}}{\text{Total Assets}}$	The amount of owner sources of total assets
10	364	Plant and Equipment to Long-Term Liabilities	$\dfrac{\text{Plant and Equipment (net)}}{\text{Long-Term Debt}}$	The adequacy of protection to long-term debtors
10	364	Plant and Equipment to Stockholders' Equity	$\dfrac{\text{Plant and Equipment (net)}}{\text{Stockholders' Equity}}$	The extent to which owner sources are being used to finance plant and equipment acquisitions

Figure 16-11 (continued)

Chapter Reference	Page Number	Ratio	Computing Ratio	Indicates
15	537	Number of Times Preferred Dividend Is Earned	$$\frac{\text{Net Income}}{\text{Annual Preferred Dividend}}$$	The primary measure of the safety of an individual's investment in preferred stock—the ability of a firm to meet its preferred dividend requirement
15	536	Number of Times Bond Interest Is Earned	$$\frac{\text{Net Income} + \text{Income Taxes} + \text{Annual Bond Interest Expense}}{\text{Annual Bond Interest Expense}}$$	The primary measure of the safety of an individual's investment in bonds—the ability of a firm to meet its bond interest requirement

C. Earning Power and Growth Potential Measurements

5	165	Net Income to Stockholders' Equity	$$\frac{\text{Net Income}}{\text{Average Stockholders' Equity}}$$	The profitableness of the business expressed as a rate of return on the stockholders' equity
5	166	Operating Ratio	$$\frac{\text{Cost of Goods Sold} + \text{Operating Expenses}}{\text{Net Sales Revenue}}$$	The number of cents needed to generate one dollar of sales
10	364	Sales to Plant and Equipment (Plant Turnover)	$$\frac{\text{Net Sales}}{\text{Average Plant and Equipment (net)}}$$	Dollar of sales per dollar of investment in plant and equipment assets
12	431	Earnings Per Share of Common Stock	$$\frac{\text{Net Income minus Annual Preferred Dividend}}{\text{Outstanding Common Shares}}$$	The company's earning power as related to common stockholders' equity
5	166	Return on Total Investment	$$\frac{\text{Net Income} + \text{Bond Interest Expense}}{\text{Average Total Assets}}$$	The profitableness of the business expressed as a rate of return on total investments by both owners and creditors.
12	430	Earnings Yield Rate	$$\frac{\text{Earnings per Share}}{\text{Market Value per Share}}$$	Earnings as related to market value of the shares
12	430	Dividends Yield Rate	$$\frac{\text{Dividends per Share}}{\text{Market Value per Share}}$$	Dividend payout as related to market value of the shares
12	430	Price-Earnings Ratio	$$\frac{\text{Market Price per Share}}{\text{Earnings per Share}}$$	Profitability of the firm as related to market value of each share

D. Financial Structure Measurements: These measurements can be determined from common-size statements of financial position, which shows the composition of items on each side of the position statement.

FINANCIAL STATEMENT ANALYSIS—INFLUENCES

The techniques and procedures for the analysis of financial statements discussed thus far are useful tools for gaining an insight into the financial affairs of a business. The analyst must, however, evaluate many other influences that, although not specifically reflected in the statements, may nevertheless influence the future of the company. Careful evaluation must be made of the possible effect on the company of sudden changes in key management personnel, shifts in employee or customer loyalty, development of new competing products, as well as broad shifts in the social, political, or economic environment. Another factor that must be evaluated with care is the impact of changing price levels on the statements. Also, differences in financial statements may be due to the wide variations that exist within the framework of generally accepted accounting principles and procedures—in the valuation of inventories, the selection of depreciation bases, the treatment of intangibles, and the method of disclosing extraordinary and nonrecurring items, for example.

SUMMARY

One of the fundamental responsibilities of an accounting department is the preparation of various financial reports to be used by management and interested outside parties, including stockholders, potential investors, and grantors of credit.

The increase in the number of stockholders and the diversity of ownership that accompanied the immense growth in the size of corporations resulted in the adoption of regulations by the New York Stock Exchange and the Securities Exchange Commission as a means of protecting the investments of these stockholders. As a result of the efforts of these organizations and other groups, the quality of the information included in financial statements has vastly improved. Factors such as large-scale production, wide geographical distribution, the increasing trend toward corporate business expansion with a concomitant delegation of authority, complex income tax legislation, and increasing governmental regulations have necessitated a comprehensible medium of communication within an organization. To satisfy this demand, management has relied on various accounting and financial reports. To be of maximum usefulness, reports for management must be specifically tailored to fit the decisions to be based on the reports. They should be current, contain sufficient detail of the particular problem to be solved, and present acceptable alternatives. The purpose of financial statements, particularly the annual reports to stockholders, is the communication of the progress made by management, the status of the investment in the business, and the results achieved during the period under review. These statements are not a compilation of absolute truths; rather, they are an incorporation of recorded facts, accounting conventions and principles, and personal judgments. Knowledge of the assumptions on which the statements are based is mandatory to a thorough understanding of the significance of the statements.

The comprehensibility of financial statements is augmented by these four basic devices: (1) the grouping of similar items to accentuate their resemblance; (2) the arrangement of the items to indicate important relationships; (3) the ordering of the items to focus attention on the most important data; and (4) the description of items in an understandable manner. The statements most commonly included in annual corporate reports are the statement of financial position, the income statement, the statement of retained earnings, and statement of sources and uses of working capital.

The statement of financial position is a static statement, showing the resources of an enterprise and the equities in these resources at a specific point of time. This statement may be prepared in the account form, which facilitates financial analysis, or in the report form, which is easily prepared and can be readily expanded. In the statement of financial position, assets are generally classified under Current Assets, Long-Term Investments, Plant and Equipment, Intangible Assets, and Deferred Charges. The use of the caption Deferred Charges has little justification in accounting since the items generally listed in this category may be more appropriately disclosed under another heading. Liabilities are commonly subdivided into Current Liabilities, Long-Term Liabilities, and Deferred Credits. Items that do not fit neatly under another category often appear as Deferred Credits; they must be reclassified before a meaningful analysis of the statement can be made. On the corporate statement of financial position, the Stockholders' Equity section should reveal the major sources of equity capital as well as certain legal restrictions on capital withdrawals. Adequate disclosure may require the use of footnotes to describe accounting procedures, explain items not readily understandable, or show contingent liabilities. Prior to December, 1966, when the AICPA issued *APB Opinion No. 9*, the appropriate disclosure of extraordinary, nonrecurring gains and losses and corrections of prior years' income led to the controversy between the current operating performance and all-inclusive income statement concepts of income reporting. The philosophy of the current operating performance concept is that the net income of a period should be an accumulation of items that are related to the ordinary operations of the business. Advocates maintain that extraordinary items and corrections of prior years' income should have no effect on the current income and therefore should appear in the statement of retained earnings. The all-inclusive income statement is prepared to show all the items of gain and loss for the period on the supposition that a series of income statements should reveal the entire income history of a company. Advocates maintain that permitting the deletion of extraordinary items from the income statement may allow the concealment of pertinent information. Also, it is argued that the manipulation of net income is made possible by the omission of certain borderline items from the income statement. *APB Opinion No. 9* virtually ended the controversy over the two concepts; it moved very close to the all-inclusive income statement concept. If this opinion is adhered to, only a few prior period adjustments would be eliminated from the income statement. A combined statement of income and retained earnings offers the possibility of including both ordinary and extraordinary items in the same statement. A disadvantage of this arrangement is that attention is not focused on net income, which is one of the most significant figures in financial statements. An income statement may be arranged in either the single-step or multiple-step form. The single-step statement is simple to prepare and easy to understand; but it does not facilitate statement analysis as does the multiple-step statement.

An adequate understanding and analysis of financial statement data can be achieved only if the analyst (1) understands the nature and limitations of accounting; (2) understands the terminology of accounting and business; (3) has some knowledge of business; and (4) is acquainted with the nature and tools of financial analysis. The figures in a financial statement are significant (1) as measures of absolute quantity; (2) in relation to similar figures of prior years and comparable companies; and (3) in conjunction with other related figures. The tools of financial analysis are comparative statements, percentage analysis, ratio analysis, and combinations of these. Comparative financial statements, or those covering a period of two or more years, review the progress of a business, thereby emphasizing that statements and the figures contained therein are not isolated data but fragments of a continuous history. The consistent application of generally accepted accounting principles in the comparative statements is a prerequisite for an effective analysis and interpretation of the data contained in the statements. Comparative statements may be made more meaningful by showing, in addition to absolute figures, the dollar amount and the percentage of increase or decrease between the absolute figures. Trend percentages, or the reduction of the absolute figures for different years to a common denominator, high light significant changes and are thus especially valuable to management in the decision-making process. Trend percentages are often misleading if viewed as isolated figures. To be of maximum benefit, they must be analyzed in the light of the trend percentages of related items.

Common-size financial statements, or those in which a group of items is expressed as percentages of the total of the items, may reveal significant relationships.

Financial ratios and other analytical devices must be considered in relation to the nature of the company, the economical environment, the accounting methods employed, and similar ratios and devices of previous years and similar companies that are relevant to the current situation. Otherwise, the interpretation of the statements will yield useless, if not misleading, results.

QUESTIONS

Q16-1. (a) What are some limitations of financial statements? (b) List and discuss some factors contributing to the development of financial reporting to outside groups.

Q16-2. (a) Discuss the characteristics of a good managerial report. (b) Discuss the purposes of financial statements.

Q16-3. Discuss the four basic devices that are commonly used to achieve interpretative statement presentation.

Q16-4. What major classifications may be applied to (a) assets, (b) liabilities, and (c) stockholders' equity items? Indicate the nature of the data that are reported within each classification.

Q16-5. 1. Give an example of (a) an asset offset, (b) a liability offset, and (c) a stockholders' equity offset. 2. When is an offset improperly applied?

Q16-6. (a) Define the term *contingent liability*. (b) State three ways in which Notes Receivable Discounted may be disclosed on the financial statements.

Q16-7. How has the AICPA's *APB Opinion No. 9* altered the accountant's view of the (a) current operating concept of income reporting and (b) all-inclusive income statement concept?

Q16-8. "The financial statement analyst should have available comparative statements, showing changes in absolute amounts and percentage changes." Explain.

Q16-9. Comment on the significance of each of the following factors to the financial statement analyst:

1. A steadily increasing price level
2. An increase in inventory
3. An increase in plant and equipment
4. An increase in sales
5. An increase in sales and a decrease in accounts receivable
6. An increase in liabilities

Q16-10. Trend percentages are of limited usefulness because (a) they do not indicate whether the change is favorable or unfavorable, (b) the change may be in relation to a year that is not typical or normal, and (c) they do not measure the effectiveness of management. Discuss.

Q16-11. What are the advantages and limitations to the analyst of the following: (a) comparative statements, (b) trend percentages, and (c) common-size percentages?

Q16-12. Explain how each of the following would be determined:
1. A company's earning power
2. The extent to which owner sources have been used to finance plant and equipment acquisitions

3. The adequacy of protection to long-term debtors
4. The rapidity with which the accounts receivable are collected
5. The ability of a business to meet quickly the unexpected demands for working capital

Q16-13. What ratios or other analytical devices will help to answer the following questions?

1. Is there an overinvestment in plant and equipment?
2. Are the assets distributed satisfactorily?
3. Is there adequate protection for creditors?
4. How is the business being financed?
5. Are earnings adequate?
6. Is there a satisfactory relationship between creditor and owner financing?
7. Are costs and expenses too high? Are sales adequate?

Q16-14. (a) What knowledge must an analyst possess to enable him to evaluate financial statement data successfully? (b) What are some of the influences that are not specifically reflected in financial statements but that an analyst must evaluate to draw correct inferences from his analysis of financial statements?

EXERCISES

E16-1. The following items are among those that would appear on the statement of financial position as of December 31, 1973, for the Gleason Company:

1. Marketable Securities
2. Subscriptions Receivable–Common Stock
3. Notes Receivable
4. Notes Receivable Discounted
5. Discount on Notes Payable
6. Discount on Bonds Payable
7. Discount on Common Stock
8. Unearned Interest Included in Face Value of Notes Receivable
9. Treasury Stock–Common
10. Stock Dividend to be Issued–Common

Indicate the statement of financial position classification of each item.

E16-2. The following information is available for the Rossell Company as of December 31, 1973:

Gain from Sale of Equipment	$ 30,000
Net Sales Revenue	900,000
Income Taxes–1973	110,000
Selling and Administrative Expenses	225,000
Cost of Goods Sold	440,000
Loss on Write-Off of Abandoned Equipment	4,000
Uninsured Loss through Fire	5,000
Adjustment for Cost of Maintenance and Repairs charged to Plant and Equipment	3,500
Retained Earnings, Dec. 31, 1972 (credit)	60,000
Dividends Declared	50,000
Income Tax Refund for Prior Years	15,000

Prepare (a) an all-inclusive income statement and (b) a statement of retained earnings for the Rossell Company for the year ended December 31, 1973.

E16-3. Refer to Exercise E16-2. (a) Prepare a combined all-inclusive statement of income and retained earnings. (b) Prepare an all-inclusive single-step income statement.

E16-4. Assume that you have been hired as chief accountant for the Golden Company on December 31, 1973, before the books were closed. In looking back over the accounting records, you discover the following errors:

1. The December 31, 1972, merchandise inventory was overstated by $2,500 because some merchandise items had been included twice.
2. On December 31, 1972, accrued interest payable of $250 had not been recorded; this amount was recorded as an expense in 1973 when it was paid.
3. The liability for invoices from merchandise suppliers is not recorded until the goods are inspected and marked, although merchandise in the Receiving and Marking department is correctly included in the physical inventory taken at the end of the year. The cost of the uninspected and unmarked merchandise in the Receiving and Marking department at end of 1972 and 1973 was:

December 31, 1972	$3,420
December 31, 1973	$4,500

Assuming that the all-inclusive income statement concept is followed, prepare correcting journal entries as of December 31, 1973.

E16-5. The following groups of items are presented for various companies as of December 31, 1973 and 1974, or for the years then ended:

	1974	1973
1. Sales	$ 620,000	$ 480,000
Cost of Goods Sold	400,000	320,000
Operating Expenses	100,000	80,000
Net Income	90,000	60,000
2. Current Liabilities	300,000	200,000
Mortgage Bonds Payable	450,000	500,000
3. Common Stock	1,200,000	1,000,000
Preferred Stock	300,000	400,000
Retained Earnings (deficit)	(10,000)	100,000
4. Cash	142,000	212,000
Accounts Receivable	130,000	140,000
Inventories	60,000	80,000
Other Current Assets	3,000	2,000
Land	20,000	20,000
Buildings	500,000	420,000
Accumulated Depreciation–Buildings	72,000	60,000

Compute the percentage increase or decrease for each item, and indicate possible reasons for the changes.

E16-6. Assume the following transactions:

1. Borrowed cash from the bank; issued a $5,000, 60-day, 5-percent note.
2. Purchased machinery for $60,000; paid $25,000 in cash and issued a 120-day note for the balance.
3. Sold for $25,000 some plant and equipment items that had a book value of $30,000.
4. Wrote off $1,500 of uncollectible accounts.
5. Declared a stock dividend of $35,000.
6. Paid $4,800 to trade creditors.

Indicate the effect of the foregoing transactions on the working capital.

E16-7. The following information is given:

	1974	1973
Net Sales	$635,000	$510,000
Cost of Goods Sold	425,000	370,000
Selling Expenses	70,000	55,000
General Expenses	40,000	35,000
Other Revenue	2,000	3,500

	1974	1973
Other Expenses	1,000	4,000
Income Taxes	61,000	30,000

(a) Prepare a comparative income statement with common-size percentages. (b) Indicate the favorable and unfavorable changes.

E16-8. The following condensed information is taken from the statement of the Warner Company:

	December 31	
	1974	1973
Current Assets	$228,000	$170,000
Plant and Equipment (net)	290,000	300,000
Current Liabilities	130,000	122,000
Long-Term Liabilities	100,000	120,000
Capital Stock	225,000	200,000
Retained Earnings	63,000	28,000

Prepare a condensed comparative statement of financial position, showing the dollar amounts and the percentages of increase or decrease during 1974.

E16-9. The following balances were taken from the books of the Baucom Corporation as of June 30, 1973 and 1974:

	June 30	
	1974	1973
Current Assets	$230,000	$170,000
Plant and Equipment	290,000	305,000
Current Liabilities	130,000	110,000
Long-Term Liabilities	115,000	130,000
Common Stock	225,000	200,000
Retained Earnings	50,000	35,000

Prepare a comparative statement of financial position showing common-size percentages.

E16-10. The following revenue and expense data of the Baylor Company for the year 1973 are given:

Sales	$210,000
Cost of Goods Sold	130,000
Selling Expenses	18,000
General Expenses	12,000
Interest Expense	2,500
Income Taxes	23,750
Net Income	23,750

Prepare a revenue-dollar statement.

E16-11. In the left-hand column a series of transactions is listed; in the right-hand column, a series of ratios:

Transaction	Ratio
1. Declaration of a cash dividend	Current ratio
2. Write-off of an uncollectible account receivable	Receivables turnover
3. Purchase of inventory on open account	Acid-test ratio
4. Issuance of 10-year mortgage bonds	Rate of return on total assets
5. Issuance of additional shares of stock for cash	Creditor equity ratio

Transaction	Ratio

6. Issue of stock dividend on
   common stock   Earnings per share
7. Appropriation of retained earnings   Rate of return on
                                                          stockholders' equity

8. Purchase of supplies on open
   account   Current ratio
9. Payment to short-term creditor in full   Acid-test ratio
10. Payment of accounts payable, taking
    the cash discount   Inventory turnover

State whether each transaction will cause the indicated ratio to increase, decrease, or remain unchanged. For the current ratio, receivables turnover, acid-test ratio, and inventory turnover, assume that the ratio is greater than 1:1 before each transaction occurred.

DEMONSTRATION PROBLEMS

DP16-1. (*Statement of financial position*) The following terms appear on various statements of financial position:

Current Assets	Deferred Charges
Long-Term Investments	Current Liabilities
Plant and Equipment	Long-Term Liabilities
Intangible Assets	Stockholders' Equity

Required: 1. Define and give several examples of each term.
2. Indicate three ways of grouping the items in formal statements of financial position.

DP16-2. (*Correcting errors*) Assume that you are hired as chief accountant of the Ernest Company as of December 31, 1973, before the books are closed. To familiarize yourself with the accounting procedures, you review the records for the two preceding years and discover the following errors:

1. The depreciation on the building was recorded as $1,000 in 1972; it should have been $10,000.
2. The December 31, 1972, inventory was understated by $1,850.
3. The company purchased a typewriter on July 1, 1972, at a cost of $300. This amount was debited to Office Expense. Normally, the Ernest Company depreciates office equipment by the straight-line method, using a five-year life.
4. The liability for a $2,450 purchase was not recorded as of December 28, 1973, when the purchase was made, although the amount was correctly included in the December 31, 1973, periodic inventory.

Required:

Assuming the use of the all-inclusive income statement concept, prepare correcting and adjusting entries as of December 31, 1973.

DP16-3. (*Financial statements prepared by all-inclusive income statement concept*) The following information is taken from the books of the Butkus Company on December 31, 1973:

Retained Earnings, December 31, 1972 (credit)	$ 65,000
Loss from Sale of Land	6,000
Sales	560,000
Loss from Flood	8,000
Cost of Goods Sold	280,000
Adjustment for Cost of Machinery Charged to	
Equipment Repairs	7,000
Income Taxes	85,000

Understatement of Depreciation in Prior Years	12,000
Selling and General and Administrative Expenses	90,000
Dividends Declared	50,000

Required:

1. Prepare an income statement and a statement of retained earnings, following the all-inclusive income statement concept.
2. Prepare a combined statement of income and retained earnings, following the all-inclusive income statement concept.
3. Prepare an all-inclusive single-step income statement.

DP16-4. (*Comparative statements: amount and percentage of increase or decrease*) The following condensed comparative statements of Brafford, Inc., are given:

BRAFFORD, INC.
Comparative Statement of Financial Position
December 31, 1974 and 1973

	December 31	
	1974	1973
Current Assets	$180,000	$155,000
Plant and Equipment	190,000	205,000
Total Assets	$370,000	$360,000
Current Liabilities	$ 69,000	$ 54,500
Long-Term Liabilities	70,000	75,000
Total Liabilities	$139,000	$129,500
Capital Stock	$200,000	$200,000
Retained Earnings	31,000	30,500
Total Stockholders' Equity	$231,000	$230,500
Total Liabilities and Stockholders' Equity	$370,000	$360,000

BRAFFORD, INC.
Comparative Statement of Income and Retained Earnings
For the Years Ended December 31, 1974 and 1973

	Years Ended December 31	
	1974	1973
Sales (net)	$495,000	$550,000
Cost of Goods Sold	376,000	410,000
Gross Margin on Sales	$119,000	$140,000
Operating Expenses	82,000	95,000
Net Income Before Income Taxes	$ 37,000	$ 45,000
Income Taxes	18,500	22,500
Net Income	$ 18,500	$ 22,500
Retained Earnings, January 1	30,500	30,000
Total Net Income and Retained Earnings	$ 49,000	$ 52,500
Dividends Declared	18,000	22,000
Retained Earnings, December 31	$ 31,000	$ 30,500

Required:

1. Prepare a comparative statement of income and retained earnings, showing the amount and percentage of increase or decrease during 1974.

2. Prepare a comparative position statement, showing the amount and percentage of increase or decrease during 1974.
3. Write a report indicating whether the financial condition and operating results are favorable or unfavorable and stating your reasons.

DP16-5. (*Comparative statements—trend percentages*) The following information is taken from the books of the York Company:

	1973	1974	1975	1976
Sales (net)	$135,000	$147,500	$156,250	$168,750
Cost of Goods Sold	78,000	86,840	91,600	98,400
Accounts Receivable	20,000	23,000	24,400	26,800
Merchandise Inventory	35,000	40,600	43,050	45,850
Net Income	12,000	12,240	12,600	12,960

Required: 1. Calculate the trend percentages (1973 is the base year).
2. Point out the favorable and unfavorable tendencies.

DP16-6. (*Common-size statements: revenue-dollar statements*) The comparative condensed financial statements of the Boston Company are given as follows:

BOSTON COMPANY
Comparative Statement of Financial Position
December 31, 1974 and 1973

	December 31	
	1974	1973
Current Assets	$ 80,000	$ 97,500
Plant and Equipment	210,000	162,500
Total Assets	$290,000	$260,000
Current Liabilities	$ 52,000	$115,000
Long-Term Liabilities	126,000	60,000
Total Liabilities	$178,000	$175,000
Capital Stock	$ 98,000	$ 75,000
Retained Earnings	14,000	10,000
Total Stockholders' Equity	$112,000	$ 85,000
Total Liabilities and Stockholders' Equity	$290,000	$260,000

BOSTON COMPANY
Comparative Income Statement
For the Years Ended December 31, 1974 and 1973

	Years Ended December 31	
	1974	1973
Sales (net)	$320,000	$285,000
Cost of Goods Sold	183,600	161,250
Gross Margin on Sales	$136,400	$123,750
Operating Expenses		
Selling Expenses	$ 68,200	$ 55,000
General Expenses	40,300	27,500
Total Operating Expenses	$108,500	$ 82,500
Net Income	$ 27,900	$ 41,250

Required: 1. Prepare (a) a comparative common-size statement of financial position, (b) a comparative common-size income statement, and (c) a comparative revenue-dollar statement.
2. Discuss the financial condition and operating results of the company, emphasizing favorable and unfavorable trends.

PROBLEMS

P16-1. The post-closing trial balance of the R. Blanton Corporation is given.

R. BLANTON CORPORATION
Post-Closing Trial Balance
December 31, 1973

Cash	$ 180,000	
Marketable Securities (at cost; market value is $56,000)	50,000	
Accounts Receivable	144,000	
Allowance for Doubtful Accounts		$ 6,000
Merchandise Inventory	450,000	
Accrued Bond Interest Receivable	12,000	
Prepaid Insurance	6,000	
Bond Sinking Fund	20,000	
Investment in Bonds–Excel Company Bonds	200,000	
Delivery Equipment	16,000	
Accumulated Depreciation–Delivery Equipment		4,000
Machinery and Equipment	900,000	
Accumulated Depreciation–Machinery and Equipment		100,000
Accounts Payable		244,000
Estimated Income Taxes Payable		100,000
Accrued Bond Interest Payable		12,000
First Mortgage 3% Bonds Payable		200,000
Discount on First Mortgage Bonds Payable	2,400	
Second Mortgage 6% Bonds Payable		100,000
Premium on Second Mortgage Bonds Payable		2,000
Preferred Stock, 6%, $100 par value		400,000
Common Stock, $25 par value		600,000
Retained Earnings		116,400
Prepaid Rent	4,000	
Retained Earnings–Restricted for Plant Addition		80,000
Retained Earnings–Restricted for First Mortgage Bond Redemption		20,000
Totals	$1,984,400	$1,984,400

Required: Prepare the statement of financial position for the R. Blanton Corporation as of December 31, 1973, showing working capital and net assets on the left-hand side balanced by stockholders' equity on the right-hand side.

P16-2. Assume that you are hired as chief accountant of the Newman Company as of December 31, 1973, before the books are closed. To familiarize yourself with the accounting procedures of the firm, you review the records for the two preceding years and discover the following errors:

1. The depreciation of the building was recorded as $50,000 in 1972; it should have been recorded as $5,000.

2. The December 31, 1972, inventory was overstated by $2,160.
3. An unrecorded bill in the amount of $1,670 for a 1972 purchase was paid in 1973; Purchases was debited.
4. The freight cost of $500 incurred for the purchase of machinery was debited to Transportation In on July 1, 1972, when the amount was paid. No part of this cost was assigned to the December 31, 1972, Inventory. Machinery is depreciated by the straight-line method, assuming a 10-year life.
5. Merchandise costing $1,200 was sold on credit for $1,800 on December 21, 1972; it was returned on December 29, 1972. No entry was made in 1972 to record the return; the entry debiting Sales Returns and Allowances was made on January 5, 1973. The merchandise was included in the December 31, 1972, inventory at the selling price.

Required: Assuming that the all-inclusive income statement concept is followed, prepare correcting journal entries.

P16-3. The following information is taken from the books of the Raymond Company on December 31, 1973.

Retained Earnings, December 31, 1972 (credit)	$ 85,000
Sales	750,000
Dividends Declared	65,000
Selling and General and Administrative Expenses	280,000
Loss on Sale of Securities	5,000
Income Taxes	33,000
Cost of Goods Sold	390,000
Loss on Disposal of Equipment	7,000
Overstatement of Depreciation in Prior Years	8,000
Gain from Disposal of Building	15,000

Required:

1. Prepare an income statement and a statement of retained earnings, following the all-inclusive income statement concept.
2. Prepare a combined statement of income and retained earnings, following the all inclusive income statement concept.
3. Prepare an all-inclusive single-step income statement.

P16-4. (*Financial policy decision problem*) The Yancey Company presents the following comparative information as of December 31, 1973 and 1974:

	1974	1973
Cash	$ 38,000	$ 35,000
Accounts Receivable	42,000	25,000
Notes Receivable	38,000	10,000
Inventories	65,000	70,000
Machinery and Equipment (net)	90,000	100,000
Building (net)	100,000	120,000
Land	40,000	40,000
Accounts Payable	55,000	47,000
Notes Payable (current)	15,000	29,000
Mortgage Payable (long-term)	70,000	100,000
Capital Stock ($100 par value)	250,000	200,000
Retained Earnings, January 1 (credit)	?	20,000
Sales (net)	385,000	300,000
Cost of Goods Sold	250,000	185,000
Operating Expenses	72,000	70,000
Income Taxes	34,000	23,000
Dividends Declared	30,000	18,000

Required: 1. Prepare comparative financial statements, including the amounts and the percentages of change during 1974.
2. Write a report to management indicating the favorable and unfavorable financial and operating trends.

P16-5. Condensed comparative financial statements for the Bay Manufacturing Company appear below.

BAY MANUFACTURING COMPANY
Comparative Statements of Financial Position
October 31, 1975, 1974, and 1973
(in thousands of dollars)

Assets	1975	1974	1973
Current Assets	$ 1,360	$1,500	$2,000
Plant and Equipment (net of accumulated depreciation)	8,400	7,200	6,000
Intangible Assets	600	800	1,000
Total Assets	$10,360	$9,500	$9,000

Liabilities and Stockholders' Equity	1975	1974	1973
Liabilities			
Current Liabilities	$ 1,040	$1,000	$ 800
Long-term Liabilities (net of discount)	1,960	1,920	1,880
Stockholders' Equity			
Capital Stock ($50 par)	4,800	4,000	4,000
Capital in Excess of Par Value	360	200	200
Retained Earnings	2,200	2,380	2,120
Total Liabilities and Stockholders' Equity	$10,360	$9,500	$9,000

BAY MANUFACTURING COMPANY
Comparative Income Statements
For the Years Ended October 31, 1975, 1974, and 1973
(in thousands of dollars)

	1975	1974	1973
Net Sales	$28,000	$24,000	$20,000
Cost of Goods Sold	21,000	17,400	14,000
Gross Margin on Sales	$ 7,000	$ 6,600	$ 6,000
Selling Expenses	$ 2,760	$ 2,480	$ 2,000
Administrative Expenses	2,940	2,880	2,800
Interest Expense	98	96	94
Total Expenses	$ 5,798	$ 5,456	$ 4,894
Net Income Before Income Taxes	$ 1,202	$ 1,144	$ 1,106
Provision for Income Taxes	614	592	566
Net Income After Income Taxes	$ 588	$ 552	$ 540

Required:

1. Compute the trend percentages for all statement of financial position items, using 1973 as the base year.
2. Prepare common-size comparative income statements for the three-year period, expressing all items as percentage components of net sales.
3. Comment on the significant trends and relationships revealed by the analytical computations in requirements 1 and 2.

P16-6. In the following schedule, certain items taken from the income statements of the Munson Company have been expressed as percentages of net sales:

| | Percentage of Net Sales | |
	1974	1973
Net Sales	100	100
Beginning Inventory	10	16
Net Purchases	68	60
Ending Inventory	8	12
Selling Expenses	13	15
Administrative Expenses	8	9
Provision for Income Taxes	2.7	3.6

Net sales were $200,000 in 1973; they increased by 20 percent in 1974. Average accounts receivable were $21,000 in 1974 and $20,000 in 1973. Credit sales were 80 percent of total sales in both years.

Required:

1. Did the net income increase or decrease in 1974 as compared with 1973, and by how much? Prepare a comparative income statement to support your answer.
2. Compute the average length of the company's receivables turnover days for both years, showing the basis of your computation.

P16-7. Statements for the Jamestown Company as of December 31, 1973, follow.

JAMESTOWN COMPANY
Income Statement
For the Year Ended December 31, 1973

Gross Sales	$295,800
Sales Returns and Allowances	4,500
Net Sales	$291,300
Cost of Goods Sold	208,000
Gross Margin on Sales	$ 83,300
Operating Expenses	65,300
Net Income from Operations	$ 18,000
Interest on Mortgage Payable	800
Net Income before Income Taxes	$ 17,200
Federal Income Taxes	6,200
Net Income after Income Taxes	$ 11,000

JAMESTOWN COMPANY
Statement of Financial Position
December 31, 1973

Assets

Current Assets			
Cash		$12,000	
Accounts Receivable	$95,000		
Deduct Allowance for Doubtful Accounts	6,000	89,000	
Inventory		80,000	
Total Current Assets			$181,000
Plant and Equipment			
Land		$20,000	
Building	$60,000		
Deduct Accumulated Depreciation	12,000	48,000	
Store Equipment	$15,000		
Deduct Accumulated Depreciation	7,000	8,000	
Total Plant and Equipment			76,000
Total Assets			$257,000

Liabilities and Stockholders' Equity

Current Liabilities		
Accounts Payable	$86,600	
Accrued Expenses Payable	29,000	
Total Current Liabilities		$115,600
Long-Term Liabilities		
Mortgage Payable		20,000
Total Liabilities		$135,600
Stockholders' Equity		
Preferred Stock, 6%, $100 Par Value	$20,000	
Common Stock, $100 Par Value	80,000	
Retained Earnings	21,400	
Total Stockholders' Equity		121,400
Total Liabilities and Stockholders' Equity		$257,000

On December 31, 1972, the inventory was $100,000 and the total stockholders' equity was $115,000.

Required: Compute the following (carry to two decimal places):

Current ratio
Acid-test ratio
Inventory turnover
Percent of year's net sales uncollected
Ratio of stockholders' equity to total assets
Ratio of net sales to stockholders' equity
Ratio of plant and equipment assets to long-term debt
Earnings per share of common stock
Percent of net income to average stockholders' equity
Number of times preferred dividends is earned
Number of times mortgage interest is earned

P16-8. (*Financial policy decision problem*) Certain financial information for the Ames Company and the Buttress Company as of the end of 1973, and additional information, are shown.

	Ames Company	Buttress Company
Current Assets	$ 240,000	$220,000
Plant and Equipment	1,016,000	770,000
Accumulated Depreciation	(160,000)	(120,000)
Patents	4,000	–0–
Goodwill	–0–	10,000
Total Assets	$1,100,000	$880,000
Current Liabilities	$ 130,000	$ 68,000
Bonds Payable, 5%, due in 10 years	200,000	240,000
Preferred Stock, 7%, $100 par value	240,000	160,000
Common Stock, $25 par value	400,000	300,000
Retained Earnings	90,000	60,000
Retained Earnings Restricted for Contingencies	40,000	–0–
Premium on Common Stock	–0–	52,000
Total Liabilities and Stockholders' Equity	$1,100,000	$880,000
Analysis of Retained Earnings:		
Balance, beginning of year	$ 91,200	$ 49,600
Net Income for year	74,800	39,600
Dividends: Preferred	(16,800)	(11,200)
Dividends: Common	(19,200)	(18,000)
Additions to Retained Earnings Restricted for Contingencies	(40,000)	–0–
	$ 90,000	$ 60,000
Market price of common stock per share	$ 30	$ 30
Market price of preferred stock per share	105	102

Required: Under the assumption that the two companies are generally comparable, write a brief answer to each of the questions given. Use only the ratios that will most reasonably substantiate your answer and indicate why. Compute the amount of each ratio and percentage indicated (carry your computations to one place beyond the decimal point).

1. Since the market prices of the bonds are not given, what ratios would aid potential investors to determine which bonds would probably sell at the higher price and which bonds would probably yield the higher return?
2. What ratio(s) would aid potential investors in preferred stock to determine which company's preferred stock is the safer investment?
3. To what extent is each company benefiting from the leverage factor inherent in the existence of the bonds? of preferred stock?
4. What are the dividend yield rates and earnings per share for the common stock of each company?

P16-9. (*Financial policy decision problem*) The Schuler Corporation has issued convertible bonds under an agreement to maintain net assets, defined in the agreement as assets minus all liabilities except the convertible bonds, at an amount not less than 230 percent of the convertible bonds outstanding; to maintain current assets at not less than 200 percent of the current liabilities; and to maintain working capital at not less than 100 percent of the convertible bonds outstanding.

On December 31, 1973, the corporation's adjusted trial balance was as follows:

SCHULER CORPORATION
Adjusted Trial Balance
December 31, 1973

	Debits	Credits
Cash	$ 10,000	
Marketable Securities	75,000	
Accounts Receivable	74,000	
Allowance for Doubtful Accounts		$ 3,000
Inventory	113,000	
Prepaid Expenses	6,000	
Land	18,000	
Building	156,000	
Accumulated Depreciation–Building		21,000
Equipment	224,000	
Accumulated Depreciation–Equipment		42,000
Accounts Payable		69,000
Notes Payable, 4-Year (due 12/20/76)		75,000
Accrued Expenses Payable		6,000
Convertible Bonds Payable		200,000
Common Stock		150,000
Retained Earnings		110,000
Totals	$676,000	$676,000

In January, 1974, it was discovered that title had passed as of December 31, 1973, on incoming merchandise costing $40,000. Since the merchandise was not on hand, it was not included in the inventory. The corporation had recorded $28,000 of collections from customers received on January 2, 1974, under the date of December 31, 1973, on the theory that such collections in all probability were in the mail before midnight, December 31, 1973. In the afternoon of January 2, 1974, the corporation wrote and mailed checks to creditors, dating and recording the checks as of December 31, 1973; the checks amounted to $28,000, equal to the collections in transit.

Required:

1. Contrast, by means of comparative ratios, the reported conditions with those you believe more fairly indicate the status of the corporation. Limit your comparison to the ratios mentioned in the agreement with the bondholders.
2. Comment briefly on your findings.

17

Corporate Financial Reporting: Business Combinations and Consolidated Statements

BUSINESS COMBINATIONS

The last two decades have witnessed a great acceleration in the number and size of business combinations. Companies with widely differing products and activities have been combined into new single units for a variety of reasons, but primarily to achieve certain advantages such as increased control of the market, a steady flow of raw materials from a reliable source at a favorable price, acquisition of operating companies with a minimum investment, minimization of income taxes, increased efficiency and economy in managerial operations and control, increased earnings from large-scale operations, and restriction of possible financial loss through diversification.

Business combinations may be classified as either *mergers* or as *consolidations*. A *merger* results when two or more previously separate legal entities are combined through the acquisition by one of the companies of the net assets of the other companies. The acquired companies lose their separate legal identities in the process and are dissolved. A *consolidation* results when the net assets of all the previously separate legal entities are transferred to a different entity.

Some of the advantages sought through mergers and consolidations are often achieved more simply through *acquisitions*, whereby a company acquires a controlling portion of the voting stock of another company but—unlike mergers and consolidations—each component unit retains its separate legal and individual identity.

ACCOUNTING PROCEDURE—PURCHASE AND POOLING

Two methods of accounting are used for the business combinations that result from either mergers or consolidations, and for business acquisitions.

These are referred to as (1) *purchase* and (2) *pooling of interests.* The differences in accounting exemplified by these two methods are not a consequence of the legal form—merger, consolidation, or acquisition—but rather arise from the point of view regarding the nature of the transaction with respect to the former ownership. The purchase viewpoint is that the former ownership is eliminated as a result of the combination, whereas the pooling viewpoint is that former ownership is continued.

Under the purchase method of accounting, the valuation of the assets acquired is based on their market value. Although stock of the acquiring company is commonly issued for the stock or assets of the acquired company, the exchange is assumed to be the result of free bargaining between independent parties and is, therefore, recorded at cost as represented by the market value of the acquired stock. The value of the assets is assumed to be equal to the market value of the stock issued in the exchange. Any portion of the total purchase price not represented by specific assets acquired is assumed to represent goodwill. Under the pooling-of-interests method of accounting, the combination is viewed as a continuation of the formerly separate companies, combined into a new entity through the exchange of stock between the groups of stockholders involved. The assets and equities, including retained earnings balances, are combined and carried forward at their existing book values on the assumption that this is not a "market exchange" type of transaction requiring new accountability. In the typical case, accounting for the business combination using the purchase alternative resulted in higher asset values with concomitant higher depreciation charges and lower net income for a period of years following the combination. As a result, and in the absence of clear and precise guidelines, the choice of alternatives was frequently arbitrary and was influenced more by the accounting consequences than by the attendant facts. With the issuance of APB Opinion No. 16,[1] fairly explicit criteria and definitions are now available for the choice of alternatives. The Board concluded that "The purchase method and the pooling-of-interest method are both acceptable in accounting for business combinations, although not as alternatives in accounting for the same business combination. A business combination that meets specified conditions requires accounting by the pooling-of-interests method." All other combinations are to be accounted for as a purchase at cost.

To illustrate the accounting for the purchase and pooling alternatives in a merger, assume the following statements of financial position for Companies A and B:

	Company A	Company B	Total
Assets (net)	$650,000	$500,000	$1,150,000
Capital Stock	$500,000	$300,000	$ 800,000
Contributed Capital in Excess of Par	50,000	150,000	200,000
Retained Earnings	100,000	50,000	150,000
	$650,000	$500,000	$1,150,000

[1] *Opinion No. 16 of the Accounting Principles Board,* American Institute of Certified Public Accountants, *Accounting Principles,* Vol. II. Chicago: Commerce Clearing House, Inc., 1970, pp. 6637–6660.

Company C acquires the assets and assumes the liabilities of Companies A and B. It issues 10,000 shares of its own stock to shareholders of Company A and 7,500 shares to shareholders of Company B. Shares of Company C are currently selling at $70 a share. The effects on consolidated position statements under the purchase and pooling alternatives on completion of the combination are shown below (it is assumed that the situation permits either alternative).

	Purchase	Pooling
Assets		
Assets (net) based on current market value of 17,500 shares of Company C at $70 a share	$1,225,000	
Total net assets per books of Companies A and B		$1,150,000
Equities		
Capital Stock, no par, 17,500 shares	$1,225,000	
Capital Stock, per books of Companies A and B		$ 800,000
Contributed Capital in Excess of Par		200,000
Retained Earnings		150,000
	$1,225,000	$1,150,000

Note that accounting for the combination as a purchase resulted in $75,000 excess assets. Under pooling there is no excess because prior book values are carried forward, the market value of Company C's shares being ignored. If Company C had issued 17,500 shares of $40 par value stock, the statements would be as follows:

	Purchase	Pooling
Net Assets	$1,225,000	$1,150,000
Capital Stock	$ 700,000	$ 700,000
Contributed Capital in Excess of Par	525,000	300,000
Retained Earnings		150,000
	$1,225,000	$1,150,000

Under the pooling alternative in this illustration, the decrease in the capital stock account is offset by an equivalent increase in Contributed Capital in Excess of Par. The Retained Earnings amount is unchanged.

CONSOLIDATED STATEMENTS

When a company acquires a controlling portion of the voting shares of another company, unified managerial control is achieved just as if the two companies were a single larger unit, even though each component unit retains its separate legal and individual identity. The corporation that holds the voting stock and controls the operations of other companies is known as the *parent company;* the companies that are controlled by the parent are called *subsidiaries.* The portion of the stock of the controlled companies held by persons outside of the parent company is referred to as the *minority interest.*

▼ When financial and managerial control exists, the parent company may prepare consolidated financial statements. ▼ Consolidated statements present the financial affairs of the parent company and its subsidiaries as if they were a single economic unit. The major published financial reports for such families of corporations are in consolidated form. The terms "consolidation" and "consolidated" are commonly used, and they are used in the rest of this chapter not in their legal sense denoting a form of business combination but rather to describe the accounting process of *combining* the accounts of a controlling parent company with the accounts of its subsidiary companies.

Consolidated statements should be prepared when (1) the parent company owns over 50 percent of the voting stock of the subsidiaries; (2) the business activities of the companies are related or similar; and (3) the financial condition of the group as a single economic unit is of greater significance than the fact of their separate existence.

In certain instances, consolidation may be appropriate when the parent company has less than a majority of ownership. The existence, for example, of leasehold and patent arrangements, interlocking directorates, and a satisfied group of majority stockholders are factors that create a unified managerial policy and control and provide the rationale for consolidation. Conversely, a parent company may own a majority of the voting shares, but such factors as the following may preclude consolidation: materially different business activities; differences in accounting periods; weak financial position of the subsidiary (particularly insolvency or bankruptcy); and the location of a subsidiary in a foreign country where assets may be subject to severe exchange restrictions.

Membership in a consolidated group does not eliminate the legal responsibilities of each unit to its own creditors and stockholders. Each corporation, as a separate legal entity, is responsible for its own decisions and its own obligations. Hence, even when consolidated statements are prepared, each separate legal entity prepares its own financial statements.

Consolidated Position Statements— Basic Illustrations

The fundamental techniques of consolidated financial statement preparation are illustrated below in a series of problems. Assets and liabilities are shown in total only to eliminate unnecessary details and to focus attention on the consolidation procedures.

Acquisition of 100 Percent of Stock at Book Value. On July 1, 1973, Company P (parent company) acquires 100 percent of the stock of Company S (subsidiary company) at a cost of $130,000. The first two columns of the work sheet (Figure 17-1) present the debit and credit items of the financial position statements of Companies P and S *immediately after* the stock acquisition; the third and fourth columns present the intercompany elimination entries; the last column is for the extension of the consolidated position statement amounts.

The work sheet is used to convert the separate financial position statements of Companies P and S into a consolidated statement showing the combined assets, liabilities, and stockholders' equity. Reciprocal accounts representing intercompany relationships are eliminated to avoid the double counting that would otherwise result. Since Company S's actual assets are to be extended into the consoli-

Figure 17-1

COMPANY P AND SUBSIDIARY COMPANY S
Work Sheet for Consolidated Position Statement
July 1, 1973

Debits	Company P	Company S	Intercompany Eliminations Debit	Intercompany Eliminations Credit	Consolidated Position Statement
Investment in Company S Stock	130,000			(a) 130,000	
Other Assets	220,000	190,000			410,000
	350,000	190,000			410,000
Credits					
Liabilities	100,000	60,000			160,000
Capital Stock, Company P	200,000				200,000
Retained Earnings, Company P	50,000				50,000
Capital Stock, Company S		100,000	(a) 100,000		
Retained Earnings, Company S		30,000	(a) 30,000		
	350,000	190,000	130,000	130,000	410,000

dated position statement column, the reciprocal amount on Company P's books represented by the Investment in Company S's Stock account must be eliminated. Similarly, Company S's stockholders' equity accounts are eliminated to avoid double counting a similar amount included in Company P's stockholder equity total.

Intercompany elimination entry (a) in Figure 17-1 cancels the parent company's investment account and the subsidiary stockholders' equity accounts. These reciprocal accounts are not extended in the consolidated position statement columns because they express the intercompany relationships only. The effect of the elimination is to convert the parent acquisition of Company S stock into the analogous purchase of Company S assets and the assumption of Company S liabilities. By eliminating intercompany relationships, the consolidated position statement presents Companies P and S as a single economic entity to the outside world. *All intercompany elimination entries are for work sheet purposes only;* they are not entered on the books of either Company P or Company S.

The formal consolidated statement of financial position is prepared from the Consolidated Position Statement column of the work sheet as follows:

COMPANY P AND SUBSIDIARY COMPANY S
Consolidated Statement of Financial Position
July 1, 1973

Assets	$410,000
Liabilities	$160,000
Capital Stock	200,000
Retained Earnings	50,000
	$410,000

The actual statement would, of course, show the details of assets owned and the nature of debt and stockholders' equity.

Acquisition of 100 Percent of Stock at More Than Book Value. Assume that Company P acquired 100 percent of the stock of Company S for $140,000 rather than for $130,000. The worksheet elimination entry is

Capital Stock, Company S	100,000	
Retained Earnings, Company S	30,000	
Excess of Cost over Book Value	10,000	
Investment in Company S Stock		140,000

The $10,000 excess of cost over the book value of the subsidiary interest may be due to an understatement of assets, unrecognized appreciation in asset values, superior earning power, or simply the result of a negotiated price paid to acquire the company. Although superior earning power is properly designated by the account title Goodwill, the presence of the other factors and the difficulty of allocating the $10,000 excess to the several factors giving rise to it require that a broader designation be used. The account title Excess of Cost over Book Value of Subsidiary Interest is used. It is classified as the final item in the position statement as an addition to total assets.

In this and in the remaining illustrations and problems, it is assumed that when the subsidiary interest is acquired at other than book value, the difference is not related, wholly or partially, to specific assets. These differences appear only on the consolidated work sheets and consolidated statement of financial position. They do not appear on the separate statements of the affiliated companies. It is also assumed that they are not amortized.

Acquisition of 100 Percent of Stock at Less Than Book Value. Assume the same data as in Figure 17-1 except that Company P acquires 100 percent of the stock of Company S for $125,000 instead of $130,000. The work sheet elimination entry is

Capital Stock, Company S	100,000	
Retained Earnings, Company S	30,000	
Investment in Company S Stock		125,000
Excess of Book Value over Cost		5,000

The classification of the Excess of Book Value over Cost account is determined by the reasons for its presence. If it is determined that the excess reflects an overvaluation of the assets of the subsidiary, then the account should be classified as an offset to those specific accounts that are overvalued; or if such specific identification is not possible, then the excess is classified as a general contra or valuation account to total assets. The excess, although not specifically identifiable, may relate to either or to both overstated assets and understated liabilities and may therefore be classified as the last item in the liability section of the consolidated statement of financial position. This is the classification used in this chapter. It is further assumed that it is not an amortizable account.

Acquisition of Less Than 100 Percent of Stock. Assume the same data as in Figure 17-1 except that Company P acquires 90 percent of Company S stock at book value of $117,000 ($130,000 × 0.90 = $117,000). The minority interest of $13,000 ($130,000 × 0.10) represents the interest of an outside group and is classified on the consolidated position statement under a separate caption immediately above the stockholders' equity section. The worksheet elimination entries are

	(a)		
Capital Stock, Company S	10,000	
Retained Earnings, Company S	3,000	
Minority Interest		13,000

	(b)		
Capital Stock, Company S	90,000	
Retained Earnings, Company S	27,000	
Investment in Company S Stock		117,000

Continuing this illustration, work sheet elimination entries—assuming the acquisition prices above and below book value—are now shown. For each assumption, entry (a) eliminates 10 percent of the subsidiary capital stock and retained earnings and establishes the minority interest, and entry (b) eliminates the reciprocal amounts represented by the parent company investment account and the subsidiary company stockholders' equity accounts. If an acquisition price of $118,000 is assumed, the work sheet elimination entries are

	(a)		
Capital Stock, Company S	10,000	
Retained Earnings, Company S	3,000	
Minority Interest		13,000

	(b)		
Capital Stock, Company S	90,000	
Retained Earnings, Company S	27,000	
Excess of Cost over Book Value	1,000	
Investment in Company S Stock		118,000

Or, assuming an acquisition price of $115,000:

	(a)		
Capital Stock, Company S	10,000	
Retained Earnings, Company S	3,000	
Minority Interest		13,000

	(b)		
Capital Stock, Company S	90,000	
Retained Earnings, Company S	27,000	
Investment in Company S Stock		115,000
Excess of Book Value over Cost		2,000

Consolidation in a Subsequent Period. The preparation of consolidated statements immediately after subsidiary acquisition has been presented in the foregoing illustrations. When consolidated statements are prepared at a later date, the elimination of the Investment in Company S Stock is unchanged because the amount—cost at acquisition—is unchanged. The elimination of the Retained Earnings of the subsidiary company at date of acquisition, however, requires the recognition of the increase or decrease since date of acquisition. The change is allocated to the parent and minority interests in proportion to stock ownership.

If, for example, Company S's retained earnings increased by $10,000 one year after acquisition, the consolidated retained earnings is increased by 90 percent of $10,000, or $9,000, and the minority interest is increased by 10 percent of $10,000, or $1,000. It is not necessary to separate the minority interest in retained earnings prior to and since acquisition, but consolidated retained earnings includes the parent company's interest in the subsidiary company's retained earnings only since acquisition.

Additional Intercompany Eliminations. Up to this point, the discussion of intercompany eliminations has been limited to the Parent's Investment in Stock of Subsidiary account and to the reciprocal subsidiary stockholder equity accounts. The preparation of consolidated statements—income statement as well as statement of financial position—requires the elimination of all reciprocal accounts stemming from intercompany transactions. Such transactions include accounts receivable and accounts payable, interest receivable and interest payable, dividends receivable and dividends payable, as well as sales and purchases or cost of goods sold, interest earned and interest expense, and dividend income and dividends declared. The reciprocal asset and liability amounts and revenue and expense amounts are eliminated consistent with the goal of representing the affiliated companies as if they constituted a single entity.

Consolidated Income Statement

A consolidated income statement of affiliated companies, assuming no intercompany transactions, may be prepared by combining the amounts on each separate income statement. Assuming intercompany transactions, the reciprocal revenue and expense amounts must first be eliminated. Such intercompany transactions are analogous to transfers made between the several departments of one company.

Because consolidated statements present the financial position and operating results of several business units as if they constituted a single entity, all intercompany gains included in the accounts must be eliminated. Intercompany gains included in inventory or other assets are eliminated. The amount of intercompany gain or loss to be eliminated is not affected by the existence of a minority interest. Assume that a parent company with a 90-percent interest in a subsidiary purchases a tract of land from the subsidiary for $50,000. The land cost the subsidiary $40,000. The intercompany gain to be eliminated is the entire $10,000. This is consistent with the basic objective of consolidated statements—to show the financial position and operating results of two or more companies as if they were a single entity.

Work Sheet for Consolidated Statements

A work sheet for the consolidated financial statements of Company P and subsidiary Company S is shown in Figure 17-2. All the adjusting and eliminating entries are explained below.

a. Company P acquired 90 percent of the stock of Company S on January 1, 1972, for $240,000. Capital stock of Company S on this date was $200,000, retained earnings were $60,000. Ninety percent of the capital stock and 90 percent of the retained earnings of Company S as of January 1, 1972, are eliminated against

Figure 17-2. Worksheet for Consolidated Statements

COMPANY P AND SUBSIDIARY COMPANY S
Worksheet for Consolidated Statements
For the Year Ended December 31, 1973

Debits	Company P	Company S	Eliminations Debit	Eliminations Credit	Income Statement Debit	Income Statement Credit	Retained Earnings Debit	Retained Earnings Credit	Position Statement Debit	Position Statement Credit
Cash	5,000	6,000							11,000	
Accounts Receivable	39,000	48,000		(c) 10,000					77,000	
Merchandise Inventory	72,000	60,000		(f) 2,000					130,000	
Machinery and Equipment (net)	127,000	206,000							333,000	
Investment in Stock of Company S (cost)	240,000			(a) 240,000						
Excess of Cost over Book Value			(a) 6,000						6,000	
Cost of Goods Sold	340,000	150,000	(f) 2,000	(g) 90,000	402,000					
Other Operating Expenses	160,000	60,000			220,000					
Dividends, Company P	50,000						50,000			
Dividends, Company S		20,000		(d) 18,000					2,000(M)	
	1,033,000	550,000								
Credits										
Accounts Payable	85,000	30,000	(c) 10,000							105,000
Minority Interest				(b) 26,000 (e) 1,000						27,000(M)
Capital Stock, Company P	300,000									300,000
Capital Stock, Company S		200,000	(a) 180,000 (b) 20,000							
Retained Earnings, 1/1/73, Company P	80,000							89,000		
Retained Earnings, Company S At 1/1/72 (date of acquisition)		60,000	(a) 54,000 (b) 6,000							
Increase from 1/1/72 to 1/1/73		10,000	(e) 10,000	(e) 9,000						
Sales	550,000	250,000	(g) 90,000			710,000				
Dividend Income	18,000		(d) 18,000							
	1,033,000	550,000	396,000	396,000						
Consolidated Net Income					88,000					
					710,000	710,000				
Income to Minority Interest, 10% of Net Income per Company S Books of $40,000 (see computation below)										4,000(M)
Balance to Controlling Interest								84,000		
Consolidated Retained Earnings							123,000			123,000
							173,000	173,000	559,000	559,000

Co. S

Sales		250,000
Deduct: Cost of Goods Sold	150,000	
Other Operating Expenses	60,000	210,000
Net Income		40,000
To Minority Interest—10% of $40,000		4,000
Total Minority Interest (4,000 + 27,000 − 2,000)		29,000(M)

the investment account. The entry is

Capital Stock, Company S	180,000	
Retained Earnings, Company S	54,000	
Excess of Cost over Book Value	6,000	
Investment in Stock of Company S		240,000

The excess of cost over book value is determined as follows:

Amount paid		$240,000
Subsidiary interest acquired		
on January 1, 1972:		
Capital Stock (90% of $200,000)	$180,000	
Retained Earnings (90% of $60,000)	54,000	234,000
Excess of Cost over Book Value		$ 6,000

The difference between the amount paid and the equity acquired is assumed to remain unchanged until such time as the parent's interest in the subsidiary changes.

b. The 10-percent minority interest in the capital stock and the retained earnings of the subsidiary at January 1, 1972, are transferred to a separate account. The entry is

Capital Stock, Company S (10% of $200,000)	20,000	
Retained Earnings, Company S (10% of $60,000)	6,000	
Minority Interest in Company S (10% of $260,000)		26,000

c. On December 31, 1973, Company S owed Company P $10,000 for merchandise purchased. The reciprocal accounts are eliminated as follows:

Accounts Payable (Company S)	10,000	
Accounts Receivable (Company P)		10,000

d. Company S declared a cash dividend of $20,000 during the year. Company P's portion—90 percent of $20,000 or $18,000—is eliminated by the following entry:

Dividend Income (Company P)	18,000	
Dividends (Company S)		18,000

e. Retained Earnings of Company S has increased $10,000 as follows:

Company S Retained Earnings on Consolidation Date, December 31, 1973	$70,000
Company S Retained Earnings on Acquisition Date, January 1, 1973	60,000
Increase since acquisition	$10,000
Accruing to parent company (90% of $10,000)	$ 9,000
Accruing to minority interest (10% of $10,000)	1,000
	$10,000

The entry to allocate the increase as shown above is as follows:

Retained Earnings, Company S	10,000	
Retained Earning of Company S		
Accruing to Parent		9,000
Retained Earnings of Company S		
Accruing to Minority Interest		1,000

f. During the year, Company P sold merchandise to Company S for $90,000. The ending inventory of Company S included $10,000 of this merchandise which cost Company P $8,000.

The presence of a Cost of Goods Sold account in the trial balance indicates that a perpetual inventory system is used; the merchandise inventory amounts are, therefore, the ending inventories. The intercompany profit of $2,000 in the ending inventory is eliminated by the following entry:

Cost of Goods Sold	2,000	
Merchandise Inventory		2,000

This entry reduces the asset account to cost and, concomitantly, increases Cost of Goods Sold by the same amount since the deduction of an overstated ending inventory from total cost of goods automatically understates the resulting Cost of Goods Sold by the same amount.

g. The intercompany sales and purchases are eliminated by the entry below.

Sales	90,000	
Cost of Goods Sold		90,000

The $90,000 is included in both Company P's sales and Company S's purchases (or Cost of Goods Sold when a perpetual inventory system is used). But because only transactions with third parties are relevant for consolidated statements, the entire amount is eliminated. This entry avoids the double counting of the $90,000 as both revenue and expense and treats the transaction as if it were merely a transfer between two departments of a single company.

The amounts in the first two columns are from the individual statements in preclosing trial balance form. Company S Retained Earnings on January 1, 1973 was $70,000. The increase of $10,000 during 1972 is shown on a separate line to high light its allocation to minority and controlling interests (entry e). The dividends declared during the year are also entered on a separate line.

Amounts in the first four columns are combined and extended to the appropriate Income Statement, Retained Earnings, and Position Statement columns. The consolidated net income of $88,000 consists of

Company S's separate net income		$10,000
Company P's separate net income	$50,000	
Deduct intercompany profit		
in Company S's ending inventory	2,000	48,000
Consolidated net income		$88,000

Figure 17-3. Consolidated Income Statement

COMPANY P AND SUBSIDIARY COMPANY S
Consolidated Income Statement
For the Year Ended December 31, 1973

Sales	$710,000
Deduct cost of goods sold	402,000
Gross margin on sales	$308,000
Deduct other operating expenses	220,000
Consolidated net income	$ 88,000
Deduct minority interest in net income of Company S	4,000
Net income to controlling interest	$ 84,000

Figure 17-4. Consolidated Retained Earnings Statement

COMPANY P AND SUBSIDIARY COMPANY S
Consolidated Retained Earnings Statement
For the Year Ended December 31, 1973

Consolidated retained earnings, Jan. 1, 1973	$ 89,000
Add consolidated net income for the year	84,000
Total	$173,000
Deduct dividends	50,000
Consolidated retained earnings, Dec. 31, 1973	$123,000

Figure 17-5. Consolidated Financial Position Statement

COMPANY P AND SUBSIDIARY COMPANY S
Consolidated Financial Position Statement
December 31, 1973

Assets

Current Assets:		
Cash	$ 11,000	
Accounts Receivable	77,000	
Merchandise Inventory	130,000	
Total Current Assets		$218,000
Machinery and Equipment (net)		333,000
Excess of Cost over Book Value of Subsidiary Interest		6,000
Total Assets		$557,000

Liabilities

Current Liabilities:		
Accounts Payable		$105,000
Minority Interest in Company S		29,000
Total Liabilities		$134,000

Stockholders' Equity

Capital Stock	$300,000	
Retained Earnings	123,000	423,000
Total Liabilities and Stockholders' Equity		$557,000

The minority interest in Company S's net income is extended into the Position Statement credit column. The several amounts comprising minority interest are identified by the letter (M) following each such amount.

The consolidated financial statements prepared from Figure 17-2 are shown in Figures 17-3, 17-4, and 17-5.

Limitation in the Use of Consolidated Financial Statements

The basic principles and procedures for the preparation of consolidated financial statements have been discussed and illustrated. A number of complex problems are, however, beyond the scope of this chapter.

The reader of consolidated financial statements must understand the accounting alternatives used in their preparation and their limitations. The amounts are composites of the several separate legal entities in the combination, and any weakness—in working capital or earnings, for example—of any single entity in the groups is not revealed. This is of especial significance when the companies combined are a conglomeration of companies in a wide variety of industries and activities.

Financial ratios based on the consolidated amounts may not be very useful if the reader is seeking information regarding sources of earnings or of working capital, or information as to parent retained earnings and dividend prospects. For such purposes, the user must have available the individual statements of the separate companies. This is especially true of the creditors of such companies. On the other hand, when a composite view of all of the companies as a single economic unit is needed and the individual statements of the separate companies are not available or are not useful, then consolidated financial statements serve their intended purpose.

SUMMARY

The merger or consolidation of separate legal entities into larger single units offers the advantages of increased earnings through large-scale operations and through diversification. Similar advantages are often achieved through the acquisition of a controlling portion of the voting stock of another company.

The business combination may be viewed as a purchase transaction and accounted for at cost based on the market value of the shares issued. Any excess of total purchase price over specific asset valuation is charged to the asset account "Excess of Cost over Book Value." Or the combination may be viewed as a pooling of interests with no new accountability being recognized, in which case the separate accounts are combined and carried forward at their existing book values. APB Opinion No. 16 has concluded that both methods are acceptable, the choice depending on certain specified criteria.

The term "consolidation" is used not only in its legal form but also to describe the accounting process of combining or consolidating the accounts of a controlling company with its subsidiary companies, and to present the affairs of the separate entities as if they were a single economic unit.

The combining of the accounts of a parent company with its subsidiaries requires the elimination of reciprocal accounts represented by the Investment in Subsidiary account on the books of the parent company and the stockholder equity accounts on the books of the subsidiary, as well as all other intercompany accounts.

Stock of the subsidiary company may be acquired at book value or at an amount above or below book value; in which case if the difference is an excess, it is debited to the account "Excess of Cost over Book Value," and if it is a deficiency, the difference is credited to "Excess of Book Value over Cost." In each instance, the assumption is that the difference is not related to specific assets and is classified in the statement of financial position as an asset if an excess or as a liability if a deficiency. The acquisition of less than 100 percent of the subsidiary company stock requires the recognition of a minority interest, which is classified in the consolidated position statement immediately above the stockholder equity section.

A consolidated income statement of affiliated companies is prepared by combining the amounts on each separate statement after reciprocal intercompany revenue and expense accounts are eliminated. The increase in the retained earnings of the subsidiary after acquisition is allocated to controlling and minority interests, and the minority interest's share of the earnings of the subsidiary for the current year is credited to the minority interest.

The user of consolidated financial statements must be aware of their limitations. Because the amounts are combined, the performance and position of any single company in the group is blurred. The creditors must look to the individual company statements for useful information. But separate statements either may not be available or may not present the overall view that the reader is seeking.

QUESTIONS

Q17-1. What are the factors responsible for the continual trend toward consolidated financial and managerial control?

Q17-2. What is meant by (a) consolidated financial statement, (b) parent company, and (c) subsidiary company?

Q17-3. What are the relevant factors for the inclusion of a subsidiary company in a consolidated statement of financial position?

Q17-4. Intercompany elimination entries are not formally recorded in the parent company journals. Why?

Q17-5. Identify the following terms: (a) excess of cost over book value; (b) excess of book value over cost; and (c) minority interest.

Q17-6. Why is it necessary to eliminate all intercompany items from the individual statements of parent and subsidiary companies when preparing consolidated statements?

Q17-7. Describe the procedure for distributing an increase or decrease in Retained Earnings of the subsidiary after acquisition to the parent company and to the minority interest.

Q17-8. How are the following items classified on the consolidated statement of financial position: (a) Excess of Cost over Book Value; (b) Excess of Book Value over Cost; and (c) Minority Interest?

Q17-9. Describe the procedure for eliminating intercompany profits in beginning and ending inventories.

E17-1. Below are eight unrelated assumptions concerning Company P's acquisition of stock in Company S.

	Investment by Company P		Subsidiary Stockholders' Equity Balances	
	Amount Paid	Percent of Stock Acquired	Capital Stock	Retained Earnings (Deficit)
a.	$250,000	100	$200,000	$50,000
b.	255,000	100	200,000	50,000
c.	247,000	100	200,000	50,000
d.	157,000	90	200,000	(25,000)
e.	160,000	90	200,000	(25,000)
f.	156,500	90	200,000	(25,000)
g	209,000	90	200,000	30,000
h.	206,000	90	200,000	30,000

For each assumption give the eliminating entry or entries for a consolidated statement of financial position prepared immediately after acquisition.

E17-2. Company P prepares a consolidated statement of financial position immediately after purchasing 1,000 shares of Company S stock at $120 a share. What is the eliminating entry assuming that (a) the stockholders' equity of Company S consists of 1,000 shares, $100 par, and retained earnings (credit balance) of $25,000; (b) retained earnings (debit balance) of $5,000.

E17-3. On January 1, 1973, Company P acquired an 80 percent interest in Company S at a cost of $91,000. On acquisition date, the Capital Stock and Retained Earnings amounts of Company S were $100,000 and $10,000 (credits), respectively. During the year, Company S earned $5,000; no dividends were declared. (a) What are the eliminations on the consolidated work sheet on December 31, 1973? (b) What portion of the $5,000 accrues to Company P? (c) What is the minority interest to be shown on the consolidated statement of financial position?

E17-4. Following are the condensed statements of financial position of Companies P and S on December 31, 1973:

	Company P	Company S
Total Assets (excluding Investment)	$218,000	$200,000
Investment in Company S Stock (950 shares)	122,000	
	$340,000	$200,000
Total Liabilities	$ 80,000	$ 60,000
Capital Stock ($100 par)	200,000	100,000
Retained Earnings	60,000	40,000
	$340,000	$200,000

On January 1, 1973, Company P acquired the stock of Company S when the retained earnings of Company S were $30,000 (credit). (a) Prepare a consolidated statement of financial position as of December 31, 1973. (b) Prepare a consolidated statement of financial position assuming that the acquisition price of $122,000 was for 930 shares.

E17-5. Company P acquired all of the stock of Company S 10 years ago. On December 31, 1973, certain account balances were

	Company P	Company S
Investment in Company S Stock	$45,000	
Accounts Receivable	80,000	$70,000

	Company P	Company S
Notes Receivable	90,000	15,000
Accounts Payable	30,000	40,000
Notes Payable	50,000	70,000
Capital Stock	75,000	50,000
Retained Earnings	40,000	20,000

On acquisition date, Retained Earnings of Company S showed a credit balance of $5,000. On January 1, 1973, Company S issued a $50,000 noninterest-bearing note to Company P. On December 31, 1973, Company P owed Company S $15,000 on open account. What eliminations are required at December 31, 1973.

E17-6. What eliminations are necessary on the consolidated work sheet for the year ended December 31, 1973, as a result of the following:

a. On January 1, 1973, Company P purchased 1,200 shares of Company S $100 par value stock at $145 when Company S had 2,000 shares outstanding and a Retained Earnings credit balance of $80,000.
b. Company P sold merchandise at cost to Company S, $22,000.
c. Company S issued a note for $50,000 payable to Company P. Company S paid $2,000 interest. Each company accrued $500 interest on December 31, 1973.
d. Company S declared a $10,000 dividend.

E17-7. Company P owns 95 percent of the stock of Company S. What are the eliminations for the following items:

COMPANY P's BOOKS

Account	Amount
a. Accounts Receivable	$ 5,000
b. Advances to Company S	10,000
c. Notes Payable	50,000
d. Dividends Receivable from Company S	9,500

COMPANY S's BOOKS

Account	Amount
a. Accounts Payable	$ 5,000
b. Advances from Company P	10,000
c. Notes Receivable	50,000
d. Dividends Payable	10,000

E17-8. The parent company who owns 80 percent of the stock of the subsidiary company sells merchandise to the subsidiary company which *costs* the parent company $12,640. This merchandise is in the December 31, 1973 inventory of the subsidiary company at the price it paid the parent company. The parent company makes a gross profit of 20 percent of sales on the merchandise it sells to the subsidiary company. Present in general journal form the consolidating work sheet entry that is necessary to eliminate the intercompany profit contained in the December 31, 1973, inventory.

DEMONSTRATION PROBLEMS

DP17-1. (*Consolidated work sheet, consolidated statements of financial position*) The statements of financial position of Companies P and S on July 1, 1973, follow.

	Company P	Company S
Cash	$275,000	$ 60,000
Other Assets	175,000	270,000
	$450,000	$330,000
Liabilities	$ 90,000	$ 80,000
Capital Stock	300,000	200,000
Retained Earnings	60,000	50,000
	$450,000	$330,000

On July 2, 1973, Company P acquired all of the stock of Company S for cash.

Required:

1. Prepare a consolidated position statement work sheet immediately after the stock acquisition, assuming the amount paid was (a) $250,000; (b) $255,000; (c) $247,000.
2. Prepare consolidated statements of financial position based on each assumption.
3. Assume Company P combines with Company S by issuing stock with a market value of $275,000 in exchange for the shares of Company S. Show the position statement accounts immediately after the combination (a) by the purchase method of accounting and (b) by the pooling-of-interest method of accounting.

DP17-2. (*Consolidated work sheet; consolidated statement of financial position*) On August 1, 1973 Company P acquired all of the stock of Companies A and B. The statements of financial position of the three companies immediately after the acquisition were

	Company P	Company A	Company B
Cash	$ 30,000	$ 20,000	$ 15,000
Accounts Receivable (net)	80,000	150,000	200,000
Merchandise Inventory	50,000	70,000	90,000
Buildings (net)	120,000	190,000	
Land	20,000	50,000	
Investment in Company A Stock	350,000		
Investment in Company B Stock	240,000		
	$890,000	$480,000	$305,000
Accounts Payable	$190,000	$130,000	$ 65,000
Capital Stock	500,000	300,000	200,000
Retained Earnings	200,000	50,000	40,000
	$890,000	$480,000	$305,000

Required:

1. Consolidated work sheet.
2. Consolidated statement of financial position.
3. What conditions or criteria should be present to justify the preparation of consolidated statements of financial position?
4. (a) Why does one corporation acquire the stock of another corporation? (b) What are the advantages and disadvantages to (1) the shareholders of the acquiring company and (2) the shareholders of the acquired company.

DP17-3. (*Consolidated work sheet; consolidated statements*) On January 1, 1972, Company P purchased all of the stock of Company S for $107,000 when Company S's Retained Earnings account was $15,000. The preclosing trial balances of Companies P and S on December 31, 1973 follow.

Debits	Company P	Company S
Cash	$ 10,000	$ 6,000
Accounts Receivable (net)	150,000	40,000
Notes Receivable	80,000	60,000
Merchandise Inventory, January 1, 1973	95,000	80,000
Plant and Equipment (net)	112,000	50,000
Investment in Company S stock	107,000	
Purchases	250,000	200,000
Operating Expenses	220,000	190,000
Interest Expense	3,000	1,500
Dividends Declared by Company P	40,000	
Dividends Declared by Company S		15,000
	$1,067,000	$642,500

Credits		
Accounts Payable	$ 80,000	$ 82,500
Notes Payable	40,000	30,000
Capital Stock	350,000	90,000
Retained Earnings, January 1, 1973	50,000	18,000
Sales	525,000	420,000
Interest Earned	3,000	2,000
Rent Earned	4,000	
Dividends Earned, Company S Stock	15,000	
	$1,067,000	$642,500

Inventories, December 31, 1973	$ 110,000	$ 90,000

Other data:

a. During 1973, Company S purchased merchandise from Company P for $75,000.

b. The January 1, 1973, inventory of Company S included merchandise purchased from Company P at an intercompany profit of $1,500.

c. The December 31, 1973, inventory of Company S also included merchandise purchased from Company P at an intercompany profit of $3,500.

d. Company S issued a note for $30,000 payable to Company P. Company S paid $1,500 interest on the note during 1973.

e. Included in Operating Expenses of Company S is rent paid to Company P for the use of certain equipment, $2,400.

> Required: 1. Consolidated work sheet.
> 2. Consolidated income statement.
> 3. Consolidated statement of financial position.
> 4. Consolidated statement of retained earnings.
> 5. Do consolidated statements violate the entity concept? Explain.

DP17-4. (*Accounting policy decision problem*) The 1968 annual report of Lewis Business Forms, Inc. includes the following note:

Intangibles

> Intangible assets consist of the excess of the purchase price over the net book value of the assets of businesses at dates of acquisitions. Amounts applicable to businesses acquired in 1960 and 1962 are being amortized over 10-year periods by charges to earnings. The remainder ($461,821) is deemed to have continuing value and, accordingly, is not being amortized.

> Required: 1. Comment on the dual amortization policy being followed.
> 2. What are the attributes of the remainder not being amortized by which it is deemed to have continuing value?

P17-1. Following are the statements of financial position of Companies P and S as of February 1, 1973, immediately after Company P acquired stock of Company S.

	Company P	Company S
Investment in Company S Stock	$ 54,000	
Other Assets	120,000	$90,000
	$174,000	$90,000
Liabilities	$ 10,000	$30,000
Capital Stock ($100 par)	150,000	50,000
Retained Earnings	14,000	10,000
	$174,000	$90,000

Required: 1. Prepare a work sheet for statement of financial position assuming that the number of shares acquired were (a) 450, (b) 440, (c) 455.
2. Prepare consolidated statements of financial position based on each assumption.

P17-2. On December 31, 1973, the condensed statements of financial position of Companies P and S were

	Company P	Company S
Cash	$ 6,000	$ 3,000
Accounts Receivable (net)	22,000	30,000
Advances to Company S	12,000	
Dividends Receivable from Company S	9,000	
Merchandise Inventory	25,000	40,000
Machinery and Equipment (net)	180,000	150,000
Investment in Company S Stock (900 shares)	110,000	
	$364,000	$223,000
Accounts Payable	$ 74,000	$ 61,000
Advances from Company P		12,000
Dividends Payable	30,000	10,000
Capital Stock ($100 par)	200,000	100,000
Retained Earnings	60,000	40,000
	$364,000	$223,000

Retained Earnings of Company S at acquisition was $20,000.

Required: 1. Consolidated work sheet.
2. Consolidated statement of financial position.

P17-3. The condensed position statements of Companies P and S as of December 31, 1973 follow.

	Company P	Company S
Current Assets	$130,000	$120,000
Plant and Equipment	280,000	300,000
Investment in Company S Stock	170,000	
	$580,000	$420,000
Current Liabilities	$ 50,000	$ 60,000
Long-Term Liabilities	200,000	100,000
Capital Stock ($100 par)	300,000	200,000
Retained Earnings	30,000	60,000
	$580,000	$420,000

Company P acquired the stock of Company S on January 1, 1973, when the stockholders' equity of Company S was

Capital Stock	$200,000
Retained Earnings	40,000
	$240,000

Required: Prepare consolidated work sheets assuming that the number of shares acquired was (a) 1,400; (b) 1,500.

P17-4. Statements of financial position on April 1, 1973, immediately after Company P acquired stock in Companies X and Y follow.

	Company P	Company X	Company Y
Investment in Company X Stock (1,000 shares)	$145,000		
Investment in Company Y Stock (1,500 shares)	178,000		
Other Assets	87,000	$180,000	$210,000
	$410,000	$180,000	$210,000
Liabilities	$160,000	$ 40,000	$ 30,000
Capital Stock ($100 par)	200,000	100,000	150,000
Retained Earnings	50,000	40,000	30,000
	$410,000	$180,000	$210,000

Required: 1. Consolidated work sheet.
2. Consolidated statement of financial position.

P17-5. Statements of financial position for Company P and its subsidiary Company S as of December 31, 1973 follow.

	Company P	Company S
Cash	$ 3,000	$ 6,000
Accounts Receivable (net)	62,000	25,000
Advances to Company P		5,000
Merchandise Inventory	70,000	23,000
Plant and Equipment (net)	150,000	110,000
Investment in Company S Stock (1,800 shares)	90,000	
	$375,000	$169,000
Accounts Payable	$ 90,000	$ 65,000
Advances from Company S	5,000	
Capital Stock (no par)	200,000	
Capital Stock ($50 par)		100,000
Retained Earnings	80,000	4,000
	$375,000	$169,000

The investment in Company S was made on January 1, 1972, when its Retained Earnings showed a credit balance of $3,000. No dividends have been paid by Company S since acquisition. On consolidation date, Company P owes Company S $10,000 for merchandise purchased by Company P from Company S at cost.

Required: 1. Consolidated work sheet.
2. Consolidated statement of financial position.

P17-6. Company P acquired a 60-percent interest in Company S two years ago when S had Retained Earnings of $36,000. Data on the financial condition of the companies at June 30, 1973, and other information follow.

Balances, June 30, 1973

	Company P		Company S	
	Debit	Credit	Debit	Credit
Cash	$ 44,000	$	$ 26,000	$
Notes Receivable	60,000		—	
Accrued Interest Receivable	2,700		—	
Accounts Receivable	116,000		84,000	
Inventory	194,000		168,000	
Investment in Stock of S Company	160,000			
Land	64,000		30,000	
Buildings	370,000		112,000	
Notes Payable		28,000		60,000
Accrued Interest Payable		—		2,700
Accounts Payable		134,000		84,000
Capital Stock		600,000		200,000
Retained Earnings		248,700		73,300
	$1,010,700	$1,010,700	$420,000	$420,000

Additional information: Company S owes Company P $60,000 on a 6-percent one-year promissory note that has been outstanding nine months. P's inventory includes $60,000 of goods purchased from Company S. Company S's gross margin on the sale was 30 percent.

Required: Work sheet for consolidated statements.

P17-7. Following are the preclosing trial balances of Companies P and S as of December 31, 1973:

Debits	Company P	Company S
Cash and Receivables	$ 65,000	$115,000
Merchandise Inventory, Jan. 1, 1973	50,000	45,000
Investment in Company S Stock (acquired 800 shares on January 1, 1973)	85,000	
Purchases	190,000	155,000
Operating Expenses	140,000	55,000
Dividends Declared by Company P	30,000	
Dividends Declared by Company S		5,000
	$560,000	$375,000

Credits	Company P	Company S
Accounts Payable	$ 16,000	$ 30,000
Capital Stock, Company P	100,000	
Retained Earnings, Company P, January 1, 1973	60,000	
Capital Stock, Company S ($100 par)		100,000
Retained Earnings, Company S, January 1, 1973		10,000
Sales	380,000	235,000
Dividends Earned, Company S Stock	4,000	
	$560,000	$375,000

Company P acquired the stock of Company S on January 1, 1973. The merchandise inventories on December 31, 1973 are Company P, $70,000 and Company S, $60,000. During 1973, Company P sold merchandise to Company S, $15,000. The December 31, inventory includes an intercompany profit of $1,200.

Required: 1. Work sheet for consolidated statements.
2. Consolidated income statement.
3. Consolidated statement of financial position.
4. Consolidated statement of retained earnings.

P17-8. On January 1, 1972, Henry Company acquired a 90-percent interest in George Company for $155,000. At the date of acquisition, George Company had a shareholders' equity of $150,000.

The statements of financial position of each company on December 31, 1973, follow.

Debits	Henry Company	George Company
Cash	$ 20,000	$ 15,000
Accounts receivable	55,000	15,000
Inventories	60,000	50,000
Investments in stock	155,000	
Investments in notes		10,000
Fixed assets (net)	440,000	105,000
Totals	$730,000	$195,000

Credits		
Accounts payable	$ 40,000	$ 30,000
Long-term liabilities	90,000	
Capital Stock	400,000	100,000
Retained Earnings	200,000	65,000
Totals	$730,000	$195,000

George Company acquired 60 percent of its present inventories from Henry Company at 50 percent above cost, one half of which has not been paid for.

Henry Company borrowed $10,000 from George Company; the latter accepted a noninterest-bearing note due on July 1, 1975.

Required: 1. Work sheet for consolidated statements.
2. List four reasons for acquiring control of a subsidiary.

P17-9. Preclosing trial balances for Company P and its subsidiary Company S, as of December 31, 1973, were as follows:

	Company P		Company S	
Cash	$ 6,000		$ 1,000	
Accounts Receivable	90,000		40,000	
Allowance for Doubtful Accounts		$ 1,000		$ 500
Merchandise Inventory, January 1, 1973	100,000		60,000	
Plant and Equipment	400,000		250,000	
accumulated Depreciation		45,000		25,000
Investment in Company S Stock (2,250 shares)	243,000			
Accounts Payable		113,000		15,500
Capital Stock ($100 par)		600,000		300,000
Retained Earnings, January 1, 1973		10,000		20,000
Sales		450,000		130,000
Purchases	300,000		90,000	
Operating Expenses	80,000		50,000	
	$1,219,000	$1,219,000	$491,000	$491,000

The merchandise inventories on December 31, 1973 were Company P, $90,000 and Company S, $80,000. The investment in Company S stock was made on January 1, 1973. There were no entries in retained earnings accounts during the year.

Required: 1. Consolidated work sheet.
2. Consolidated income statement.
3. Consolidated statement of financial position.
4. Consolidated statement of retained earnings.

P17-10. Financial statements for Companies P and S as of December 31, 1973, and for the year then ended follow.

Position Statements, December 31, 1973:

Assets	Company P	Company S
Cash	$ 85,000	$ 50,000
Merchandise Inventory	160,000	145,000
Investment in Company S stock (900 shares)	113,000	
Total Assets	$358,000	$195,000

Liabilities and Stockholders' Equity	Company P	Company S
Accounts Payable	$ 60,000	$ 40,000
Capital Stock ($100 par)	200,000	100,000
Retained Earnings	98,000	55,000
Total Liabilities and Stockholders' Equity	$358,000	$195,000

Income Statements for Year Ended December 31, 1973

	Company P		Company S	
Sales		$650,000		$550,000
Cost of Goods Sold:				
Merchandise Inventory, January 1, 1973	$110,000		$ 75,000	
Purchases	390,000		330,000	
Total	$500,000		$405,000	
Merchandise Inventory, December 31, 1973	160,000	340,000	145,000	260,000
Gross Margin		$310,000		$290,000
Operating Expenses		240,000		240,000
Net Operating Margin		$ 70,000		$ 50,000
Dividends Earned, Company S Stock		18,000		
Net Income		$ 88,000		$ 50,000

Statement of Retained Earnings for Year Ended December 31, 1973:

	Company P	Company S
Retained Earnings, January 1, 1973	$ 40,000	$25,000
Net Income	88,000	50,000
Total	$128,000	$75,000
Deduct: Dividends Declared	30,000	20,000
Retained Earnings, December 31, 1973	$ 98,000	$55,000

Other Data:

a. Company P acquired 90 percent of the stock of Company S on January 1, 1973.
b. During the year, Company P sold merchandise at cost to Company S, $25,000.

Required: 1. Consolidated work sheet.
2. Consolidated income statement.
3. Consolidated statement of financial position.
4. Consolidated statement of retained earnings.

P17-11. Following are the statements of financial position of companies A and B on December 31, 1973.

	Company A	Company B
Assets (net)	$7,000,000	$5,000,000
Capital Stock ($100 par)	$4,000,000	$3,500,000
Contributed Capital in Excess of Par	2,000,000	1,000,000
Retained Earnings	1,000,000	500,000
	$7,000,000	$5,000,000

Company A combines with Company B by issuing 50,000 shares of its own stock with a current market value of $5,500,000 in exchange for the shares of Company B.

Required:

1. Show the position statement accounts on completion of the combination if it is viewed as a purchase of Company B by Company A.
2. Show the position statement accounts on completion of the combination if it is accounted for by the pooling-of-interest method.

P17-12. (*Accounting policy decision problem*) The December 31, 1965, consolidated balance sheet of the Houston Oil Field Material Company, Inc. included a "deferred credit resulting from acquisition of subsidiary" of $2,437,418. The accompanying explanatory note was

The company's investments in subsidiaries are carried at cost plus equity in undistributed earnings since dates of acquisition and, in the case of BS&B, plus amortization of a portion of the excess of equity in net assets at dates of acquisition over cost of the investment. The amount being amortized (over four years from the respective dates of acquisition by the sum of the years-digits method) is the balance remaining after direct charges in 1964 for certain revaluations and losses. Of the balance of $2,437,418 at December 31, 1965, amortization for 1966 will approximate that for 1965; thereafter, such amortization will be in declining amounts through 1969.

Required:

1. Comment on the company's accounting for its investments in subsidiaries.
2. Prepare proforma journal entries (without amounts) for (a) acquisition, (b) revaluations and losses, and (c) annual amortization.

P17-13. (*Accounting policy decision problem*) in 1968, International Controls Corporation acquired 59 percent of the common stock of Electronic Specialty Company. An accompanying note read as follows:

An independent appraisal and determination of remaining depreciable lives of the property, plant, and equipment of Electronic Specialty Company is presently in process. On completion of the appraisal, the excess of appraised values over the depreciated amounts of the property, plant, and equipment will be transferred from cost of investment in excess of net assets acquired to the applicable asset categories.

Required:

1. How will the results of the appraisal affect reported earnings?
2. How should the company amortize the cost of the investment in excess of net assets acquired to the extent not allocated to property, plant, and equipment.
3. Why did the company not allocate the entire cost of investment in excess of net assets acquired to specific asset items?

P17-14. The following is a part of Note 1 accompanying the financial statements included in the 1969 annual report of the AMK Corporation:

> . . . the company acquired 6,810,278 common (83% of the outstanding) and 99,424 preferred (78% of the outstanding) shares of United. Since the acquisition of United stock was treated as a purchase, AMK's investment was recorded at the market value of the AMK securities issued based on the quoted market prices of convertible debentures and warrants on the first date when these securities traded and the price of AMK common stock on such date. The cost of investment and the excess of cost of investment over equity in net assets (as recorded on books of United) acquired are summarized below:

	in thousands
Issuance of $254,597,818 principal amount of 5½% convertible debentures, at 96.5%	$245,687
Issuance of 3,684,967 shares of AMK common stock at $47.75 per share	175,957
Issuance of 10,049,913 warrants, each to purchase one share of AMK common stock, at $17.25 per warrant	173,361
Payment to Zapata of $6,800,500 in cash and issuance of subordinated note for $17,605,965	24,406
Costs of tender offer	10,214
Investment in United at December 31, 1968, of $41,778,000, less proceeds of $40,695,000 received on rescission of purchase	1,083
Total cost of investment	$630,708
Less—AMK equity in net assets (as recorded on books of United) acquired at dates of acquisition	286,262
Excess of cost of investment over equity in net assets (as recorded on the books of United) acquired	$344,446

The company has undertaken a study to determine whether any portion of the excess cost of this investment should be allocated to specific assets acquired or liabilities assumed. This study, representing a major undertaking, was commenced in 1969 and is not expected to be completed before late 1970. Based on preliminary reports from its appraisers, the company is of the opinion that the effect of this allocation will not result in a material change in currently reported earnings. Pending completion of this study the assets and liabilities of United have been included in the consolidated financial statements at the values recorded on the books of United. Since it is the opinion of the company that the benefits to be derived from the investment in United will be of indefinite duration, no amortization has been provided for the excess of cost of the investment in United over the equity in the net assets (as recorded on books of United) acquired.

The company is also of the opinion that the excess of cost over related equities of businesses acquired amounting to about $41,522,000 in the accounts of United is attributable to intangibles with continuing values and accordingly no amortization has been provided.

The company purchased a portion of its interest in John Morrell & Co. for cash in late 1966. The equity of the purchased shares in Morrell's net assets exceeded their cost by $6,413,000. This amount is being amortized by credits to income over the ten year period ending October 31, 1976. Income in 1969 and 1968 includes approximately $612,000 and $646,000, respectively, for this amortization.

The comparative balance sheets as of December 31, 1969 and 1968, included the following as the final asset item:

Excess of Cost of Investments Over Equity in Net Assets of Subsidiary Companies at Dates of Acquisition, including $344,446 arising on the purchase of United Fruit Company (Note 1)	385,968	—
	$1,063,480	$223,689

See Notes to Financial Statements.

Required:

1. If you were conducting the study referred to above, what guidelines or criteria would you establish, and what direction would your study take to determine whether to allocate any portion of the excess to assets acquired or liabilities assumed?

2. What general conclusion in the appraiser's preliminary report provided the basis for the company's opinion that the effect of the prospective allocations will not materially change current earnings?

3. Comment on the company's amortization procedure of the excess of equity acquired over cost of its interest in John Morrell and Company.

4. Compare and contrast AMK's accounting for the excess of cost of the investment in United over the equity in the net assets acquired with the following differing views regarding intangibles.[2]

    a. Allocating the cost of goodwill or other intangible assets with an indeterminate life over time is necessary because the value almost inevitably becomes zero at some future date. Since the date at which the value becomes zero is indeterminate, the end of the useful life must necessarily be set arbitrarily at some point or within some range of time for accounting purposes.

    b. The amortization of intangible assets should be based on professional judgment, rather than arbitrary rules.

    c. Amortizing the cost of goodwill and similar intangible assets on arbitrary bases in the absence of evidence of limited lives or decreased values may recognize expenses and decreases of assets prematurely, but delaying amortization of the cost until a loss is evident may recognize the decreases after the fact.

5. Give your own views in this matter and the reasons for your position.

[2] *Opinion No. 17 of the Accounting Principles Board,* American Institute of Certified Public Accountants, *Accounting Principles,* Vol. II, Chicago: Commerce Clearing House, Inc., 1970, pp. 6662–6667.

18

Corporate
Financial Reporting:
Changing Price Levels

INTRODUCTION—THE HISTORICAL COST DOLLAR AND CHANGING PRICE LEVELS

The use of historical cost as the primary recording basis is a generally accepted principle of accounting. This principle has furnished a readily determinable and objective accounting measure reflecting the independent positions of the buyer and the seller in the market place. Recording transactions in terms of dollars of cost developed quite naturally as a basis for reporting the results of business operations and the financial position of the enterprise. Because dollars constitute the economic medium of exchange and all property, goods, and services can be equated in terms of this common denominator, the dollar has been a convenient accounting device.

The continued use of the cost dollar is, however, under severe test because of its instability. It is unstable because the value of the dollar, as expressed in terms of its purchasing power, changes from year to year. Financial statements prepared in terms of historical dollar cost reflect, therefore, dollars with varying degrees of purchasing power and fail to reflect the effect of price-level changes on the financial position of the firm and the results of its operations. This is considered by many to be a serious shortcoming in accounting because the financial statements may show not the results of management's skill and judgment, but rather a commingling of the results of management decision making with the results of inflation or deflation—of changing price levels.

Furthermore, if the nature of the resulting reported earnings and dividend distributions is not a reliable indicator of the firm's potential, then the usefulness of the statements is limited. Certainly, the usefulness of the comparative statements of prior periods is severely limited if material price changes occurred during the time span covered by such statements.

To overcome these shortcomings, and to avoid this commingling of "shoes and ships and sealing wax"—that is, of dollars of different sizes with different purchasing power dimensions—a conversion to a uniform or "common dollar" basis is necessary. An expenditure of $10,000 for a tract of land, for example, represents a commitment of $10,000 of current purchasing power. The subsequent reporting of that item in financial statements should be in terms of dollars of purchasing power as of statement date. If, a year later, prices in general have increased by 10 percent, the land should then be reported at $11,000 or $10,000 × 110/100. Thus, the land will be stated in dollars of uniform size or in "common dollars"—that is, in dollars with a purchasing power size prevailing at statement date. The cost remains at $10,000 but it has been restated in more units of lesser purchasing power. The $1,000 increase is a recognition of the change in the value of the measuring unit, a recognition of the fact that there has been a 10-percent increase in the *general* level of prices, so that $11,000 is now required to buy all kinds of goods and services that could have been bought for $10,000 a year before. The $1,000 increase is not a gain, but its recognition means that assets and contributed capital will have been increased by an amount sufficient to maintain the general purchasing power of the contributed capital at its original level. The purchasing power needed to replace the specific tract of land may be greater than, or less than, $11,000 depending on the currently prevailing market conditions for that specific asset. The discussions in this chapter related only to general, not specific, price-level changes. If the tract of land has a current market value of $15,000, it will still be restated at $11,000. The additional $4,000 ($15,000 − $11,000) is due to a specific price change and is not recognized in statements adjusted for general price-level changes.

SHORTCOMING OF HISTORICAL COST— SOME ILLUSTRATIONS

The problems created by changing price levels and the use of historical cost are presented below in three illustrations.

Illustration 1—Effective Gain or Loss on Sale of Assets. Assume that Ace Realty Corporation purchased a building for $20,000 and later sold it for $30,000. The proceeds were then used to buy a similar building. This transaction would be reported in conventional income statement form as follows:

Sales	$30,000
Cost of Sales	20,000
Gain	$10,000

If it is assumed that the price level increased 50 percent during the time the building was held, it may be reasoned that Ace Realty Corporation has realized no real gain because the proceeds of $30,000 represent exactly the same amount of purchasing power as did the $20,000 invested in the building originally. The two amounts are not stated in comparable terms because they were incurred at different general price levels. The reported gain is the result of matching two unlike items and is not, therefore, a real gain in an economic sense. When the cost of the building is restated in current dollars, the gain is wiped out.

Sales (in current dollars)	$30,000
Cost of Sales (in common dollars, or $20,000 × 150/100)	30,000
Gain	–0–

Illustration 2—Noncomparability of Items. Assume that Towne Corporation constructed a building at a cost of $200,000. Ten years later a similar building was constructed at a cost of $400,000, at which time the position statement shows total cost of the two buildings as follows:

Building 1	$200,000
Building 2	400,000
Total Cost	$600,000

It is true, of course, that the total outlay was $600,000, but the items are not comparable. Adding together dollars that represent different purchasing powers is similar to adding together cups, pints, quarts, and gallons without converting these items to a common denominator. The amounts express asset values in terms of past dollars for Building 1. The statement does not indicate costs in terms of purchasing power as of the date of the position statement. The reader or analyst must search elsewhere in his efforts to evaluate the current position of the company.

A further distortion is introduced through the periodic charges for depreciation. Assuming an annual rate of 5 percent, deductions for depreciation on the buildings are

Building 1 (0.05 × $200,000)	$10,000
Building 2 (0.05 × $400,000)	20,000
Total	$30,000

Although both buildings are identical, depreciation charges for Building 2 are $10,000 greater than for Building 1 only because of the decline in the purchasing power of the dollar when Building 2 was constructed.

Illustration 3—Effect of Changing Price Levels on Certain Assets. Assume that Company A acquires a tract of land for $10,000 and Company B invests $10,000 in corporation bonds. Assume further that during the next 10 years, the prices of goods and services have doubled. Although Companies A and B have assets on their books at $10,000 each, Company A can sell its land for $20,000 and be as well off as before. Company B, on the other hand, has only half the purchasing power it had 10 years ago.

INDEX NUMBERS

If the essence of the financial reporting process is to measure and report purchasing power, then the items being compared must be expressed in terms of a common, stabilized, or comparable purchasing power yardstick. Clearly, a $100 investment that matures when the price level has doubled cancels the investment but the two $100 amounts cannot be compared to measure the result of the investment. The investor's original $100 is worth $200 now (200/100 × $100) and he has lost $100 in terms of dollars at maturity. Similarly, the $100 he receives at maturity is worth only $50 in terms of dollars at the time the investment was made (100/200 × $100).

It is necessary to distinguish between the amount of dollars (money value) and the kind and amount of goods and services those dollars command (real value). Such distinction is necessary because changing price levels cause changes in purchasing power, which in turn create the gap between money values and real values. To illustrate, assume a person earns $100 a year over a three-year period as follows:

	1971	1972	1973
a. Money value (current dollars)	$100	$100	$100
b. Price index (base year: 1971)	100	125	150
c. Real value (divide a by b and multiply by 100)	$100	$ 80	$ 66.67
d. Adjusted value (divide b by a)	$100	$125	$150

A dollar in 1972 buys only as much as 80 cents bought in 1971; $100 in 1973 buys only as much as $66.67 bought in 1971. To maintain his purchasing power over the period, this person would need to receive $125 in 1972 and $150 in 1973. He needs $1.50 in 1973 to buy what $1.00 would have bought in 1971. The dollar will buy more goods and services when prices fall; the dollar will buy fewer goods and services when prices rise. This fluctuation in the purchasing power of the dollar results from fluctuating price levels. Changes in price levels may be measured by index numbers.

A price index is a statistical average of prices expressed as a percentage of a base period. It describes the changes in a group of items and measures the impact of price-level changes on purchasing power. The consumer price index, for example, is made up of a list of items that are weighted and expressed as a percentage in terms of their relative importance to all items in the index—food, housing, apparel, transportation, and medical care. The subdivisions of the wholesale price index include farm products, processed foods, textile products and apparel, leather products, fuel, chemicals, metals, machinery, and furniture. Several price indexes are available for use in measuring price-level changes. The Accounting Principles Board (APB) of the AICPA in its statement No. 3 recommends the use of the Gross National Product Implicit Price Deflator (GNP Deflator) "to prepare, general price-level statements in U.S. dollars."[1] The U.S. Bureau of Labor Statistics publishes the Consumer Price Index and the Wholesale Price Index, and the U.S. Department of Commerce prepares the GNP Deflator. A number of specific industry indexes are compiled privately.

---

[1] Statement of the Accounting Principles Board, *Financial Statements Restated for General Price-Level Changes.* New York: American Institute of Certified Public Accountants, June, 1969, p. 14.

Use of Index Numbers to Adjust Costs

The steps to convert historical cost dollars into dollars of a uniform purchasing power are listed below.

1. Convert to base-year dollars by dividing by the price index of the date on which the amount was incurred.
2. Convert the amount in step (1) to year-end dollars by multiplying by the current year-end index.

The foregoing steps may be expressed by the formula,

$$\text{Historical cost} \times \frac{\text{Current index}}{\text{Index at date of origin}} = \frac{\text{Cost measured in current}}{\text{year-end dollars}}$$

Assume that equipment that cost $200,000 was acquired four years ago when the price index was 90; the current price index is 180. The carrying value of the equipment based on both historical cost and converted cost is shown below. An annual depreciation rate of 10 percent is assumed.

	Historical Cost	Converted Cost	
Cost	$200,000	$400,000	($200,000 × 180/90)
Accumulated depreciation	80,000	160,000	($ 80,000 × 180/90)
Carrying value	$120,000	$240,000	

The accumulated depreciation on each basis is computed as follows:

$$\begin{pmatrix} \text{Elapsed time in} \\ \text{years from date} \\ \text{acquired} \end{pmatrix} \times \begin{pmatrix} \text{Annual rate (\%)} \\ \text{of} \\ \text{depreciation} \end{pmatrix} \times \text{(Cost)} = \begin{matrix} \text{Accumulated} \\ \text{depreciation} \end{matrix}$$

4	× 0.10	× $200,000 =	$ 80,000
4	× 0.10	× 400,000 =	160,000

The conversion of the historical-based accumulated depreciation may also be computed as follows:

$$\begin{pmatrix} \text{Accumulated depreciation} \\ \text{based on historical cost} \end{pmatrix} \times \begin{pmatrix} \text{Current index} \\ \text{Index on date acquired} \end{pmatrix} =$$

$$\$80,000 \qquad \times \qquad 180/90 \qquad = \$160,000$$

The effect on reported net income for 1973 is

Converted cost depreciation (0.10 × $400,000)	$40,000
Historical cost depreciation (0.10 × $200,000)	20,000
Overstatement of net income if historical amounts not converted	$20,000

Use of Index Numbers in Sales Analysis

Assume sales and the corresponding price index for a three-year period as follows:

Year	Unadjusted Sales	Price Index	Multiplier	Adjusted Sales
1971	$50,000	100	200/100	$100,000
1972	60,000	150	200/150	80,000
1973	70,000	200	200/200	70,000

In terms of the 1973 purchasing power of the dollar, sales for the years 1972 and 1973, rather than increasing, actually decreased in each successive year. The adjusted sales figures provide a more meaningful and a more significant basis for comparison because they are stated in a common measure—the purchasing power of the 1973 dollar. Because the yardstick is the same, the amounts are comparable. The unadjusted sales figures, representing dollars with different quantities of general purchasing power, are not comparable with each other; nor are the adjusted and unadjusted amounts comparable, the one being a restatement of the other in terms of a common yardstick.

MONEY ITEMS AND CHANGING PRICE LEVELS

The problems of price-level changes as related to the basic matching concept have been discussed thus far. A somewhat different problem arises in connection with monetary assets or money items—cash, notes and accounts receivable, accrued receivables, notes and accounts payable, accrued payables, and bonds payable. These items are fixed in terms of the total number of dollars that will be collected on the assets and the number of dollars that must be paid to creditors on the liabilities regardless of changes in prices. The purchasing power, however, of the cash to be collected or to be paid fluctuates. Cash or claims to cash are worth or will buy less during periods of rising prices and, conversely, in periods of falling prices, they are worth more and will buy more. By the same token, the reduction of indebtedness during periods of rising prices is eased by payment in current or cheaper dollars. The opposite is true if prices are falling. The relative effect of changing price levels on monetary assets and liabilities will result in a purchasing power monetary gain or loss depending on the relative balance in existence and the movement of the price level, whether rising or falling. These gains and losses constitute a part of the net income for the period.

To illustrate monetary or purchasing power gain or loss, assume the following (Figure 18-1) taken from the statements of financial position of Andover Corporation.

To simplify the illustration, it is assumed that the average price levels during 1972 and 1973 were 100 and 150 and that end-of-year levels were 120 and 165, respectively. The relevant multipliers and related conversion factors to restate to dollars of general purchasing power as at December 31, 1973, are computed by dividing the index number at December 31, 1973, by each of the

Figure 18-1. Andover Corporation Net Monetary Assets

	December 31, 1972	December 31, 1973	Increase
Cash	$412,000	$570,000	$158,000
Accounts Receivable	300,000	368,000	68,000
Totals	$712,000	$938,000	$226,000
Accounts Payable	$209,000	$260,000	$ 51,000
Bonds Payable	300,000	300,000	0
Totals	$509,000	$560,000	$ 51,000
Net Monetary Assets	$203,000	$378,000	$175,000

Assumed Price Index:	1972–average	100
	1972–end of year	120
	1973–average	150
	1973–end of year	165

other index numbers. Thus, for items originating during 1972, the index number for the current position statement date, December 31, 1973, is divided by the average index for 1972 (165 ÷ 100 or 1.65). An item acquired during 1972 at a cost of $100 is restated in current dollars as at December 31, 1973, as $100 × 1.65 or $165. The $100 cost in 1972 is equal to a cost of $165 at December 31, 1973. Conversion factors are computed as follows:

1. For items originating during 1972:

$$\frac{\text{December 31, 1973}}{\text{Average for 1972}} = 165/100 = 1.65$$

2. For 1972 year-end:

$$\frac{\text{December 31, 1973}}{\text{December 31, 1972}} = 165/120 = 1.375$$

3. For items originating during 1973:

$$\frac{\text{December 31, 1973}}{\text{Average for 1973}} = 165/150 = 1.10$$

4. For 1973 year-end:

$$\frac{\text{December 31, 1973}}{\text{December 31, 1973}} = 165/165 = 1.00$$

All items in Figure 18-2 are converted in terms of December 31, 1973 dollars as follows:

1. All amounts as at the end of 1972 are multiplied by 165/120, or by the conversion factor, 1.375.
2. All amounts originating during 1973—the changes during the year— are multiplied by 165/150 or 1.10.
3. The amounts in (1) and (2) are compared with the appropriate December 31, 1973, balances to measure the purchasing power gain or loss.
4. The net loss or net gain is computed by deducting gains from losses or losses from gains.

Figure 18-2. Purchasing Power Gains and Losses

ANDOVER CORPORATION
Purchasing Power Gains and Losses
For Year Ended December 31, 1973

	Amount (From Figure 18-1)	Conversion Factor	Converted to 12/31/73 Dollars	
Conversion of monetary assets:				
Balance, December 31, 1972	$712,000	1.375	$ 979,000	
Increase during 1973	226,000	1.100	248,600	
Total	$938,000		$1,227,600	
			938,000	
Purchasing power loss				$289,600
Conversion of monetary liabilities:				
Balance, December 31, 1972	$509,000	1.375	$ 699,875	
Increase during 1973	51,000	1.100	56,100	
Total	$560,000		$ 755,975	
			560,000	
Purchasing power gain				195,975
Net purchasing power loss				$ 93,625

The purchasing power loss of $93,625 resulting from the conversion of money assets reflects the extent to which money asset growth has failed to keep pace with the increase in the price level during 1973. The required increase in money assets to maintain purchasing power parity in the face of price-level increase during 1973 is as follows:

On 1972 year-end balances (37.5% of $712,000)	$267,000
On increases during 1973 (10% of $226,000)	22,600
Total	$289,600

The purchasing power gain of $195,975 resulting from the conversion of money liabilities reflects a reduction in the debt burden due to the decline in the purchasing power of the dollar. The $509,000 indebtedness as of December 31, 1972, is fixed by contractual agreement. But repayment will be in dollars that have lost 37.5 percent of their purchasing power. It may be reasonably assumed that the Andover Corporation has used creditor funds in the manufacture and sale of a product whose selling price has been increased to correspond with the increasing price level. Repayment of debt, however, is fixed at the amounts owed prior to the price-level increase. The excess, therefore, represents a purchasing power gain. If the $509,000 indebtedness as of December 31, 1972, were to be repaid in terms of December 31, 1973, dollars, the required payment would be $699,875, computed as follows:

Liabilities (unadjusted)	$509,000
Adjustment for price level increase (509,000 × 37.5%)	190,875
Total (adjusted)	$699,875

The adjusted total of $699,875 has the same purchasing power as $509,000 had one year earlier. If all 1972 year-end debts were paid on December 31, 1973, the creditors will have incurred a purchasing power loss of $190,875, and Andover Corporation will have realized a corresponding purchasing power gain. The adjustment for the increase in liabilities during 1973 is $51,000 × 0.10 or $5,100. The total of the two adjustments ($190,875 + $5,100) represents a purchasing power gain of $195,975 from the conversion of money liabilities.

NONMONEY ITEMS AND CHANGING PRICE LEVELS

The money items, being fixed by the customary legal relationship between banks, customers, and creditors, *are not* restated in the current statements. They are already stated in current dollars (when comparative statements are presented, money items for prior periods *are* restated). Regardless of changing price levels, there is no quantitative change in the dollars on deposit in the bank, or the numerical amount of the settlement between debtors and creditors. Only the purchasing power of these items changes and this is what gives rise to gains and losses. The opposite is true of the other position statement items—merchandise inventory, land, plant and equipment, common stockholders' equity, and so on. It is necessary to convert or restate the nonmoney items. The purchasing power that the dollar amount of these items represents is not fixed contractually, and they are not stated in terms of current dollars; rather, the purchasing power of the dollar amount of these items fluctuates with changes in price levels and must, therefore, be converted to the current dollar basis. Such conversion does not give rise to purchasing power gains and losses, however; the change is due only to a change in the measuring yardstick—it is not an economic event such that gives rise to a real gain or loss. Contrariwise, the money items are not converted because they are already stated in current dollars, but the qualitative change in their purchasing power while they are being held does give rise to gains and losses.

Illustrative Problem

The financial statements of the Andover Corporation illustrate, in summary form, the procedure for the price-level conversion of such statements (Figures 18-3 and 18-4). The multipliers used are based on the same price index assumptions as in Figure 18-1. The explanation of the conversions follows the presentation of the unconverted and converted statements.

The derivation of the purchasing power loss of $93,625 is shown in Figure 18-2. Amounts for the changes in the monetary items during 1973 were taken from the statements of financial position. A similar schedule is shown in Figure 18-5 except that the changes in the monetary items during 1973 are taken from the income statement for that year.

Conversion of Combined Statement of Income and Retained Earnings.
Sales. Sales were made uniformly throughout the year. The conversion is, therefore, at the average price index for 1973, or

$$\$750,000 \times 1.100 = \$825,000$$

Cost of Goods Sold. The computation and conversion for the cost of goods sold is shown in Figure 18-6.

Figure 18-3. Comparative Statements of Financial Position

ANDOVER CORPORATION
Comparative Statements of Financial Position
as of December 31, 1973 and 1972

Assets	Unconverted Year Ended December 31		Converted Year Ended December 31	
	1973	1972	1973	1972
Cash	$ 570,000	$ 412,000	$ 570,000	$ 566,500
Accounts Receivable	368,000	300,000	368,000	412,500
Merchandise Inventory	50,000	30,000	55,000	49,500
Land	40,000	40,000	66,000	66,000
Plant and Equipment	1,150,000	1,150,000	1,897,500	1,897,500
Accumulated Depreciation	(465,000)	(350,000)	(767,250)	(577,500)
	$1,713,000	$1,582,000	$2,189,250	$2,414,500
Liabilities and Stockholders' Equity				
Accounts Payable	$ 260,000	$ 209,000	$ 260,000	$ 287,375
Bonds Payable	300,000	300,000	300,000	412,500
Capital Stock	975,000	975,000	1,608,750	1,608,750
Retained Earnings	178,000	98,000	20,500	105,875
	$1,713,000	$1,582,000	$2,189,250	$2,414,500

( ) Deduction

Figure 18-4. Combined Statement of Income and Retained Earnings

ANDOVER CORPORATION
Combined Statement of Income and Retained Earnings
For the Year Ended December 31, 1973

	Unconverted	Converted
Sales	$750,000	$825,000
Costs and Expenses:		
Cost of Goods Sold	$430,000	$489,500
Depreciation	115,000	189,750
Other Expenses	125,000	137,500
Total	$670,000	$816,750
Operating Income	$ 80,000	$ 8,250
Purchasing Power Loss		(93,625)
Net Income (Loss)	$ 80,000	$ (85,375)
Retained Earnings, January 1, 1973	98,000	105,875
Retained Earnings, December 31, 1973	$178,000	$ 20,500

Figure 18-5. Purchasing Power Gains and Losses

ANDOVER CORPORATION
Schedule of Purchasing Power Gains and Losses
For the Year Ended December 31, 1973

	Unconverted	Conversion Factor	Converted
Net Monetary Assets, December 31, 1972			
(Figure 18-1)	$203,000	1.375	$ 279,125
Add: Sales (Figure 18-4)	750,000	1.100	825,000
	$953,000		$1,104,125
Deduct:			
Purchases (Figure 18-6)	$450,000	1.100	$ 495,000
Other Expenses (Figure 18-4)	125,000	1.100	137,500
	$575,000		$ 632,500
Net Monetary Assets, December 31, 1973	$378,000		$ 471,625
			378,000
Purchasing Power Loss			$ 93,625

Figure 18-6. Conversion of Cost of Goods Sold

Inventory, January 1	$ 30,000 × 1.65 = $ 49,500
Purchases	450,000 × 1.100 = 495,000
Total	$400,000 $544,500
Inventory, December 31	50,000 × 1.100 = 55,000
Cost of Goods Sold	$430,000 $489,500

The beginning inventory was acquired during 1972 and the purchases were made uniformly during 1973. The Andover Corporation uses the first-in, first-out method of inventory valuation.

Depreciation. The converted cost of plant and equipment is $1,897,500. Assuming a straight-line rate of 10 percent, the converted depreciation expense is 10 percent of $1,897,500 or $189,750. An alternative method is to multiply the unconverted depreciation expense by the same factor used in converting the related asset, or

$$\$115,000 \times 1.65 = \$189,750$$

Other Expenses. Other expenses were incurred during the year. The conversion computation is

$$\$125,000 \times 1.100 = \$137,500$$

Conversion of Position Statement as of December 31, 1972. The monetary items—cash, Accounts Receivable, Accounts Payable, and Bonds Payable are converted from year end 1972 to their December 31, 1973, equivalent by the factor 1.375. All other items except Retained Earnings are assumed to have originated when the price index was 100; the applicable conversion factor is, therefore, 1.65. Retained Earnings is a balancing figure arrived at by subtracting total liabilities and capital stock from total assets.

Conversion of Position Statement as of December 31, 1973. The monetary assets and liabilities are, by definition, payable in current dollars and need not, therefore, be converted. All other items except Retained Earnings are assumed to have orginated when the price index was 100; the application conversion factor is, therefore, 1.65. The Retained Earnings amount of $20,500 is detailed in Figure 18-4.

Analysis of Unconverted and Converted Statements

A comparison of some ratios in the converted and unconverted statements underscores the striking effect of the conversion of the statements into current dollar terms. The ratio of operating income to sales, for example, is

$$\text{Unconverted: } \frac{\$80,000}{\$750,000} = 10.67\%$$

$$\text{Converted: } \frac{\$8,250}{\$825,000} = 1\%$$

Position statement ratios for the nonmoney items also change drastically. For example: Ratio of operating income to stockholders' equity is

$$\text{Unconverted: } \frac{\$80,000}{\$1,153,000} = 6.94\%$$

$$\text{Converted: } \frac{\$8,250}{\$1,629,250} = 0.5\%$$

Book value per share (assume 9,000 shares outstanding)

$$\text{Unconverted: } \frac{\$1,153,000}{9,000} = \$128.11$$

$$\text{Converted: } \frac{\$1,629,250}{9,000} = \$181.03$$

Managerial Uses and Limitations

Researchers into the problem of adjusting accounting data for price-level changes also have concerned themselves with the uses and limitations of such data. Professor Jones who directed the price-level study of the American Accounting Association[2] suggests the following specific managerial uses of uniform-dollar figures: profit planning, price policies, analyzing divisional or branch results, plant management, dividend policies, expansion policies, capital structure, explaining financial policies to employees and stockholders, and contract renegotiation.

[2]Ralph Coughenaur Jones, *Effects of Price Level Changes on Business Income, Capital, and Taxes.* Columbus, Ohio: American Accounting Association, 1956, Chapter 8.

Perry Mason observed that

Unless these limitations of conventional accounting are recognized and taken into account, it will be difficult for management to make properly informed decisions as to such things as dividend policy, price policy, and expansion programs. (It is recognized that additional specific information may be needed in settling a particular problem.) Although income taxes under the present law will not be changed if adjusted income figures are prepared, evidence will be obtained that income taxes are now based upon a concept of income which is questionable and which, in particular, discriminated against companies with large investments in plant and equipment when the price level is rising and in their favor when prices are falling.[3]

The Accounting Principles Board (APB) of the AICPA

believes that general price-level financial statements or pertinent information extracted from them present useful information not available from basic historical-dollar financial statements. General price-level information may be presented in addition to the basic historical-dollar financial statements, but general price-level financial statements should not be presented as the basic statements.[4]

SUMMARY

Financial statements prepared in terms of historical cost do not reflect the effects of changing price levels—that is, the effects of inflation and deflation. This omission limits the usefulness of the statements both for purposes of comparison with prior periods and for the evaluation of performance. One remedy is to restate the accounts to reflect general price-level changes and thereby distinguish between the amount of dollars—money value—and the kind and amount of goods and services those dollars command—real value. The restatement of the amounts to measure the changes in the general price level is by means of a price index, which is a statistical average of prices expressed as a percentage of a base period. A number of price indexes are available. The APB in its statement No. 3, dealing with general price-level financial statements, recommends the use of the Gross National Product Implicit Price Deflator index.

A careful distinction must be drawn between money items such as cash, receivables, and payables, which are fixed in amount, and nonmoney items such as inventory, plant and equipment, and stockholders equity items which are nonmoney items. Since there is no quantitative change in the money items, they are not restated, but purchasing power does change, giving rise to a monetary gain or loss. The conversion of the nonmonetary items is a measurement change only and does not result in either gain or loss.

Historical cost multiplied by the ratio of the current index over the index at date or origin converts historical cost into cost measured in current year-end dollars. The effect of changing price levels on monetary assets and liabilities is a purchasing power gain or loss depending on (1) the relative balance in existence and (2) whether the prices were rising or falling.

[3] Perry Mason, *Price-Level Changes and Financial Statements.* Columbus, Ohio: American Accounting Association, 1956, p. 11.
[4] Statement of the Accounting Principles Board, *Financial Statements Restated for General Prive-Level Changes.* New York: American Institute of Certified Public Accountants, June, 1969, p. 12.

Researchers into this problem have concluded that accounting data adjusted for general price level changes are useful in decisions involving dividend policy, price policy, profit planning, and evaluation of management performance.

QUESTIONS

Q18-1. Why should accountants concern themselves with price-level fluctuations?

Q18-2. Give three illustrations of distortions or inaccuracies in conventional financial statements resulting from changes in dollar purchasing power.

Q18-3. Why is the historical-cost dollar not always reliable as a basis for management decision?

Q18-4. What are the probable effects of rising costs on earnings? Illustrate.

Q18-5. A member of the board of directors of Allyn Corporation refused to vote for a proposed $250,000 dividend declaration. He contended that the reported net earnings of $300,000, after adjustments for price-level changes, would be inadequate to justify the proposed declaration. Comment on his position.

Q18-6. Zolite Corporation constructed Plant A in 1963 at a cost of $1,000,000. Ten years later, it built Plant B, a similar plant, in another city at a cost of $2,000,000. What are the competitive advantages of Plant A over Plant B?

Q18-7. How may changes in price levels be measured?

Q18-8. What is a price index? How is it constructed? How may it be used?

Q18-9. Does the use of LIFO resolve the problem of inventory price fluctuation? What is the effect of LIFO on (a) net income, and (b) working capital?

Q18-10. What is the relationship between rising prices and accumulated depreciation?

Q18-11. It has been said that the central problem of accounting is the proper matching of expense and revenue. How do rising prices affect this problem?

Q18-12. What is the relative effect of changing price levels on monetary assets and liabilities?

Q18-13. What gives rise to a monetary purchasing power gain or loss? Illustrate.

Q18-14. In what specific areas of decision making may accounting data adjusted for price level changes be used to advantage? In what areas is the use of such data of no advantage?

Q18-15. What is the effect of adjusting accounting data for rising prices on the financial statement ratios?

Q18-16. Summarize the arguments for and against the conversion of historical dollar amounts into "real" dollars by the use of price index numbers. Should the converted amounts supplement or replace the historical amounts in financial statements?

Q18-17. A corporation issued $5,000,000 in bonds on July 1, 1948, to mature on June 30, 1973. What is the relative gain or loss position of the (a) issuing corporation, and (b) the bondholders on June 30, 1973? How do the financial statements reflect such gains and losses.

EXERCISES

E18-1. Students A and B each received cash birthday gifts of $750. Student A purchased a bond with a maturity value of $1,000 in 10 years. Student B purchased a tract of land. Prepare adjusted statements of financial position for A and B 10 years later assuming the price index has doubled during the interval.

E18-2. Stone Corporation acquired the following plant and equipment assets:

Year	Cost	Index
1953	$200,000	100
1963	150,000	150
1973	350,000	200

Convert the foregoing amounts using the 1973 index as the base. Discuss the significance of the converted amounts.

E18-3. Ryder Corporation constructed a plant in 1954 at a cost of $400,000 when the price level stood at 100. A similar plant was built in 1973 when the price level was 198. What was the approximate cost of the second plant? What is the effect of the increased cost of the new plant on this company's competitive position? Should the depreciation base on the original plant be changed? Comment on the effect of such a change.

E18-4. Lexigraph Corporation sales for the years 1972 and 1973 were $350,000 and $475,000, respectively. Price indexes were

	1972	1973
January 1	150	200
December 31	200	250

Assuming no seasonal fluctuations in sales and uniform price-level changes, what significant conclusions may be drawn from the sales data for the two years?

E18-5. Lally Corporation began business on July 1, 1973, by acquiring merchandise costing $100,000. On July 31, 1973, 60 percent of the merchandise was sold. The price index rose from 120 to 130 during the month. Compute the adjusted cost of goods sold and cost of goods on hand as of July 31.

E18-6. Granger Corporation was formed to operate an office building that cost $200,000. Operating data for the first year were

Income from rentals	$40,000
Operating costs (exclusive of depreciation)	20,000
Depreciation	8,000

Assume all transactions are for cash and are incurred or received uniformly throughout the year. The price level doubled during the year. Prepare a statement of financial position as of December 31, 1973, and an operating statement for the year.

E18-7. Wallace Corporation had on hand on January 1, 1973, 6,000 units of merchandise costing $60,000 that was acquired when the price level was 115. During 1973, 7,500 units were acquired at a cost of $90,000 when the price level was 120. Sales for the period totaled 10,000 units. The index at the end of the period was 140. Compute, in terms of year-end dollars, (a) cost of goods sold and cost of goods on hand using FIFO, and (b) cost of goods sold and cost of goods on hand using the conventional LIFO procedure.

E18-8. Ellison Corporation's Notes Receivable Register shows the following outstanding notes as of December 31, 1973:

Date Acquired	Amount	Price Level at Acquisition
February 10	$10,000	110
April 21	4,000	125
September 30	15,000	150
December 4	20,000	176
	$49,000	

At year end, the price level stood at 180; the average price level for the year was 140. (a) Convert the total amount of notes held using the average price index; (b) convert each specific amount on the basis of the index number prevailing at acquisition.

E18-9. The machinery and equipment account of Mann Corporation consisted of two separate acquisitions: (1) 10 machines costing a total of $160,000 with an estimated service life of 20 years, no salvage value, acquired when the price level was 90; and (2) five machines costing $125,000, with an estimated service life of 10 years, no salvage value, acquired when the price level was 120. The first group of machines has been in use six years; the second group, four years. Straight-line depreciation is used. The index now stands at 150. Compute (a) the adjusted and unadjusted carrying value of the machines, and (b) the adjusted and unadjusted depreciation expense for the current year.

E18-10. The sales manager and the financial vice-president of the Polaride Company disagree as to the significance of the company's sales increases during the last three years. Gross sales were as follows:

1971	$5,000,000
1972	6,000,000
1973	7,000,000

Relevant price indices were, respectively, 100, 140, and 180. The sales manager is satisfied with the level of "growth" in sales during the three-year period. The financial vice-president argues to the contrary that there has been a steady decline in sales. Who is correct? Why?

DEMONSTRATION PROBLEMS

DP18-1. (*Preparation of converted income statement*) The following trial balance was taken from the books of Reis Company as of December 31, 1973:

			Price Level
Cash	$ 60,000		115
Notes and Accounts Receivable	90,000		115
Merchandise Inventory (beginning)	55,000		100
Plant and Equipment	400,000		100
Notes and Accounts Payable		$ 75,000	115
5% Mortgage Bonds Payable		125,000	100
Common Stock ($100 par)		350,000	100
Retained Earnings		40,000	100
Sales		800,000	115
Purchases	600,000		115
Operating Costs (excluding depreciation)	150,000		115
Depreciation	28,750		100
Interest Cost	6,250		115
	$1,390,000	$1,390,000	

Merchandise Inventory, December 31, 1973, $90,000 (price level, 115). Indicated price levels at acquisition dates are based on the following assumptions:

January 1	100
December 31	140
Year's Average	120

Required

1. Prepare conventional income statement for year and statement of financial position as of December 31, 1973.
2. Prepare converted statements.

3. Compute the following ratios for each set of statements: (a) net income to net sales; (b) book value per share of common stock; (c) current ratio; (d) net income to stockholders' equity.

DP18-2. (*Computing monetary purchasing power gain or loss*) The position statements of Jones Company as of December 31, 1972 and 1973, included the following:

	December 31	
	1972	1973
Cash	$550,000	$600,000
Notes and Accounts Receivable	400,000	450,000
Notes and Accounts Payable	225,000	300,000
5% Mortgage Bonds Payable	250,000	250,000

Price levels were

	1972	1973
Beginning of year	100	120
Average for year	110	130
End of year	120	140

Required: Prepare a schedule showing the monetary purchasing power gain or loss during 1973.

PROBLEMS

P18-1. During the period 1940–1968, the Kresge Corporation acquired five parcels of land in the area surrounding its home plant (all parcels were approximately equal in size) as follows:

Lot No.	Year	Cost	Price Index*
1	1940	$10,000	43.9
2	1950	12,000	80.2
3	1958	20,000	100.0
4	1965	30,000	110.9
5	1968	40,000	117.6

*Gross National Product Implicit Price Deflator

Required:

1. How should these parcels be shown in the company's statement of financial position as at the end of 1968?
2. Indicate some alternative methods of presentation.
3. State the method you consider as being the most useful, explaining your choice fully.
4. What additional information is needed?

P18-2. Refer to Problem P18-1. Assume that the Kresge Corporation sold lot number 4 for $50,000 when the price index was 150. What was the gain or loss on the sale? Explain fully.

P18-3. The Kroll Corporation acquired machinery costing $100,000 two years ago when the price index was 110. The current price index is 150. The estimated useful life of the equipment is 10 years.

Required:

1. How should the equipment be shown in the Kroll Corporation's statement of financial position?
2. What is the effect on the company's results of operations for the current year if price-level change is ignored? on total assets?

P18-4. The Leroy Corporation's merchandise inventory, on January 1, 1973 was $50,000. Merchandise purchases during the year were as follows:

June 20	$300,000
September 1	200,000

Goods on hand as of December 31 cost $100,000. Prevailing price indexes were as follows:

January 1	120
June 20	130
September 1	135
December 31	140

Required: Cost of goods sold for the year.

P18-5. The net monetary assets of the Gilbert Corporation were $200,000 on January 1, 1973, and $400,000 on December 31, 1973. Price indexes were

January 1	125
Average during year	140
December 31	150

Required:

1. Calculate the purchasing power gain or loss for the year.
2. Calculate the purchasing power gain or loss, assuming no change in net monetary assets.

P18-6. Refer to Problem P18-5. Assume that net monetary assets increased $400,000 during the year and that its nonmonetary assets increased by an equal amount.

Required: Calculate the company's purchasing power gain or loss for the year.

P18-7. The machinery account of the Zinn Corporation shows the following:

Year	Acquisitions	Disposals	Average Price Index
1970	$100,000	$10,000	110
1971	75,000	25,000	120
1972	125,000	30,000	125
1973	50,000	20,000	130
12/31/73			140

Required:

1. Restate the machinery account in terms of the December 31, 1973, price index.
2. What is the balance in the accumulated depreciation account assuming (a) 10-year life, straight-line depreciation, no end-of-life value; (b) full year's depreciation in year of acquisition and none in year of disposal.

P18-8. Following is the condensed income statement of Douglas Company for the year 1973:

Sales		$200,000
Cost of Goods Sold:		
Inventory, January 1	$ 20,000	
Purchases (net)	130,000	
Total	$150,000	
Inventory, December 31	30,000	120,000
Gross Margin on Sales		$ 80,000
Operating Expenses:		
Depreciation	$ 10,000	
General and Administrative	50,000	60,000
Net Income		$ 20,000

Price index assumptions:

January 1	110
December 31	140
All plant and equipment	100
Inventory, January 1	105
All other items (average index for year)	120

      Required: Prepare a corrected income statement based on the end-of-year price index.

P18-9. Following is the post-closing trial balance of Olds Company as of December 31, 1973:

			Price Level at Acquisition
Cash	$ 40,000		126
Notes Receivable	20,000		*
Accounts Receivable (net)	80,000		125
Prepaid Insurance	2,000		100
Merchandise Inventory	125,000		120
Plant and Equipment	350,000		100
Accumulated Depreciation		$ 70,000	100
Notes Payable		25,000	†
Accounts Payable		50,000	125
Common Stock ($100 par)		400,000	100
Retained Earnings		72,000	100
	$617,000	$ 617,000	

* Notes Receivable consist of:

        $12,000 acquired when price level was 110
         8,000 acquired when price level was 125

†Notes Payable consist of:

        $ 5,000 note issued when price level was 116
        20,000 note issued when price level was 122

Additional price level data:

January 1, 1973	100
December 31, 1973	130
Average for year	118

      Required:

1. Prepare an unadjusted statement of financial position.
2. Prepare an adjusted statement of financial position based on the end-of-year price level.
3. Prepare, for each statement, the following ratios: (a) current ratio, (b) ratio of plant and equipment to total assets, (c) stockholders' equity ratio, (d) book value per share of common stock.
4. What conclusions may be drawn from the two sets of ratios?

P18-10. The Fox Company was formed on January 1, 1973, with the following investments for which capital stock was issued:

Cash	$ 50,000
Merchandise Inventory	40,000
Land	10,000
Buildings	100,000
Machinery and Equipment	20,000

The post-closing trial balance on December 31, 1973, was as follows:

Cash	$ 30,000	
Accounts Receivable (net)	46,000	
Merchandise Inventory	65,000	
Prepaid Expenses	1,000	
Machinery and Equipment	45,000	
Accumulated Depreciation– Machinery and Equipment		$ 3,000
Buildings	100,000	
Accumulated Depreciation–Buildings		4,000
Land	10,000	
Accounts Payable		40,000
Common Stock (par $100)		220,000
Retained Earnings		30,000
	$297,000	$ 297,000

Summary of operations incurred at the average price level for the year, except for depreciation and for beginning inventory included in cost of goods sold, follows:

Sales	$200,000
Cost of Goods Sold	130,000
Operating Costs (other than depreciation)	33,000
Depreciation	7,000

Price level data:

1. Beginning of year	100
2. End of year	120
3. Average for year	115
4. Cash, Accounts Receivable, Inventory, and Accounts Payable	116
5. Prepaid Expenses	100
6. Additional machinery and equipment acquired when price level was (depreciation on the additions: $1,000)	112

Required: 1. Prepare unadjusted and adjusted position statements as of December 31, 1973.

2. Prepare for each set of statements the following ratios: (a) current ratio, (b) earnings per share, (c) rate of return on stockholders' equity.

P18-11. Following are the comparative trial balances of East Corporation as of December 31, 1973 and 1972:

		December 31			
		1973		**1972**	
Cash	140 (note 2)	$ 300,000		$ 225,000	130 (note 2)
Accounts Receivable (net)	142	700,000		600,000	132
Merchandise Inventory	142	1,540,000		1,365,000	132
Machinery and Equipment	Note 1	2,490,000		2,490,000	Note 1
Accumulated Depreciation–Machinery and Equipment	Note 1		$ 1,100,000		$ 950,000	Note 1
Buildings	100	1,200,000		1,200,000	100
Accumulated Depreciation–Buildings	100		500,000		450,000	100
Land	100	200,000		200,000	100
Accounts Payable	142		750,000		750,000	132
Mortgage Bonds Payable	110		500,000		500,000	110

		December 31			
		1973		1972	
Common Stock ($100 par)	100		3,000,000	3,000,000	100
Retained Earnings	Note 6		350,000	300,000	Note 6
Sales	110		7,000,000	5,800,000	130
Cost of Goods Sold	140 (note 4)	5,450,000		4,600,000	130 (note 3)
Selling Expenses	140	625,000		500,000	130
General and Administrative Expenses	140	525,000		400,000	130
Depreciation Expense	140 (note 1)	150,000		150,000	130 (note 1)
Interest Expense	140	20,000		20,000	130
		$13,200,000	$13,200,000	$11,750,000	$11,750,000

Notes and supplementary data:

1. The machinery and equipment consists of the following three separate acquisitions:

	(a)	(b)	(c)
Cost	$1,500,000	$500,000	$490,000
Accumulated Depreciation:			
December 31, 1972	700,000	200,000	50,000
December 31, 1973	775,000	250,000	75,000
Price level on acquisition date	100	110	115

2. Includes $100,000 acquired when price level was 100; balance at average price levels.
3. Includes $1,000,000 acquired when price level was 120.
4. Includes $2,000,000 when price level was at 142.
5. Other price level data:

	1973	1972
Beginning of year	135	125
Average for year	140	130
End of year	145	135

6. Retained Earnings:

	December 31, 1973		December 31, 1972	
Acquisition	Amount	Price Level	Amount	Price Level
1	$125,000	100	$125,000	100
2	75,000	110	75,000	110
3	100,000	120	100,000	120
4	50,000	130	—	
	$350,000		$300,000	

All dividends were charged against the earnings of the year in which they were paid.

Required:

1. Prepare unadjusted and adjusted income statements (in terms of December 31, 1973 dollars).
2. Prepare unadjusted and adjusted position statements (in terms of December 31, 1973 dollars).
3. Compute for each set of statements the following ratios: (a) net income to sales, (b) net income to total assets, (c) net income to stockholders' equity, (d) current ratio, (e) book value per share of common stock.

19

Sources and Uses of Funds—Working Capital; Cash

The income statement and the statement of retained earnings disclose the causes of part, but not all, of the changes that take place in the items appearing in the statements of financial position at the beginning and end of a given period. Businesses engage in a variety of financial transactions, the details of which are not disclosed in either the income statement or the statement of retained earnings. Information regarding the changes in working capital, cash, and other financial items are summarized in various *funds statements*, considered in this chapter.

FUNDS

The term "funds" has a variety of meanings, including working capital, cash, cash and securities, current assets, quick assets, and total resources. It is essential to know the sense in which the term is used when reading or preparing a funds statement. The term "funds" is used here first in the sense of working capital—current assets minus current liabilities. Alternative uses are discussed later. To be explicit, the word *funds* will be used sparingly; instead, the name of the specified fund concept will be used—that is, *working capital, cash,* or another concept.

FUNDS EQUAL WORKING CAPITAL

The chief sources of working capital are operations, additional investments by owners, long-term borrowing, and the sale of assets. The chief uses of working capital are to increase noncurrent assets, retire long-term debt, reduce the owner's or stockholders' equity, and provide for the declaration of dividends. The statement of sources and uses of working capital emphasizes the interrelationship of the sources (inflows) and uses (outflows) of working capital. A chart of working capital inflows and outflows based on an analogy between the flow of working capital through a business and the flow of water into and out of a container is shown in Figure 19-1.

634

Figure 19-1. Working Capital Inflows and Outflows

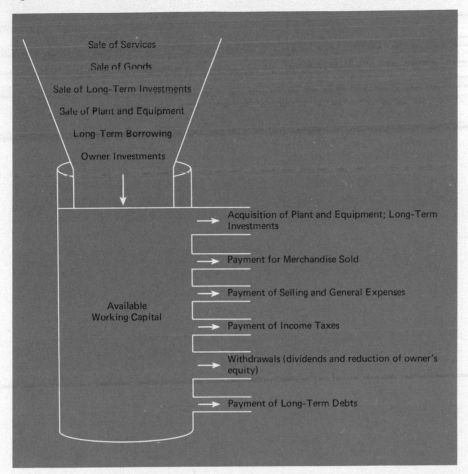

The Statement of Sources and Uses
of Working Capital

The income statement and the statement of financial position report the results
of operations of a business during a period and the financial condition of that
business as of the end of the period. The *statement of the sources and uses of working
capital* supplements the two conventional statements by reporting changes relating
to the financial activities of the firm that are not otherwise readily discernible.
Its purpose is to show the source of working capital from operations and other
financing and the use of such working capital during the period covered by the
statement.

Purpose of the Statement of Sources and Uses of Working Capital

It is often difficult for management and others to understand how the net income for a period was disposed of and the effect of the flow of working capital through the business. Readers of the conventional financial statements often ask such questions as: Where did the working capital come from? What was done with it? What happened to the various asset items during the period? Why did working capital decrease although earnings were favorable? Why were dividends not larger? Is the company solvent? Where did the working capital for replacement or expansion come from? What kind of financial decisions were made during the period? The statement of sources and uses of working capital helps to answer these questions.

The smooth flow of working capital into and out of a business is the result of a continuing series of managerial decisions, often requiring a high level of skill and judgment. The statement of sources and uses of working capital helps the reader to understand not only the financial well-being of the company but also the effectiveness of the financial policies of its management.

Understanding the Statement of Sources and Uses of Working Capital

Proper preparation of the statement of sources and uses of working capital requires an analysis of the relationships among the items in the financial statements.[1] This involves two basic steps: (1) an analysis of the current accounts— current assets and current liabilities—to determine the net change in working capital during the period and (2) a determination of the causes of the net change in working capital by an analysis of the changes in the noncurrent accounts. The relationships among the various items in a position statement are expressed in the basic accounting equation,

$$\text{Assets} = \text{Liabilities} + \text{Owners' Equity}$$

The equation for a classified position statement is

Current Assets + Noncurrent Assets
$$= \text{Current Liabilities} + \text{Noncurrent Liabilities} + \text{Owners' Equity}$$

Since the purpose of the statement of sources and uses of working capital is to show the causes of the changes in working capital, the equation is rewritten to show the current accounts on one side of the equation and the noncurrent accounts on the other side (the initial letters of the terms in the basic equation are used for brevity).

(1) $$CA - CL = NCL + OE - NCA$$

Since the analysis involves comparative position statements, the beginning statement may be represented by

(2) $$CA_1 - CL_1 = NCL_1 + OE_1 - NCA_1$$

The subscripts indicate that the amounts in Equation 2 are from the beginning

---

[1] This discussion is based on Ching-Wen Kwang and Albert Slavin, "The Mathematical Unity of Funds-Flow Analyses," *NAA Bulletin*, Section 1, January, 1965, pp. 49–56.

of the period. Similarly, the ending position statement can be represented by

(3) $$CA_2 - CL_2 = NCL_2 + OE_2 - NCA_2$$

Equations 2 and 3 may be combined to obtain

(4) Net change in working capital
$$= (CA_2 - CL_2) - (CA_1 - CL_1) = (CA_2 - CA_1) - (CL_2 - CL_1)$$
$$= (NCL_2 - NCL_1) + (OE_2 - OE_1) - (NCA_2 - NCA_1)$$

Equation 4 proves that the net change in the current accounts is equal to the algebraic sum of the changes in all noncurrent accounts. All financial transactions for the period can be described within this system of equations. Any single transaction causes a change in one or more items in Equation 2. The cumulative effect of all transactions for the year is to bring about such changes in the terms of Equation 2 that the financial position of the company at the end of the year is shown in Equation 3. The statement of sources and uses of working capital explains the changes in working capital by listing the changes that appear on the right side of Equation 4. Equations 2, 3, and 4, therefore, constitute the analytical framework within which all transactions occurring between the comparative position statement dates can be analyzed in terms of their effect on working capital.

Classification of Transactions

Since there is great variety in the transactions that enter into the inflow and outflow of working capital, it is helpful to classify them in distinctive categories, based on their effect on working capital.

1. *Transactions that change a current and a noncurrent account.* For example, the acquisition of a tract of land for cash changes working capital and is, therefore, reported in the statement of sources and uses of working capital.
2. *Transactions that change current asset or current liability accounts but have no effect on net working capital.* For example, the purchase of merchandise on account and the settlement of an account receivable change the current accounts but do not change the amount of working capital; hence, they are not reported in the statement of sources and uses of working capital.
3. *Transactions that change noncurrent accounts only.* For example, the acquisition of a tract of land by a company in exchange for its own stock does not change working capital and is, therefore, not reported in the statement of sources and uses of working capital. Other transactions in this category include restrictions on retained earnings, the declaration and issuance of stock dividends, and plant and equipment revaluations. It should be noted, however, that when assets of a material amount are acquired by the use of nonworking capital items, a footnote to the statement of sources and uses of working capital indicating this transaction is warranted.

Working Capital Provided by Operations

A primary source of working capital is the regular operating activities of the business. The determination of working capital from this source is complicated by the fact that the change in working capital may be greater than, or less than, the net income shown in the income statement. To illustrate, assume that the Cowan Company's income statement for the year ended December 31, 1973, is as follows:

Sales		$10,000
Cost of Goods Sold		7,000
Gross Margin on Sales		$ 3,000
Operating Expenses		
Depreciation–Plant and Equipment	$ 400	
Other	2,100	2,500
Net Income		$ 500

An analysis of this statement in terms of the change in working capital resulting from operations shows:

	Income Statement	Working Capital Increase or (Decrease)	Explanation
Sales	$10,000	$10,000	Increase in cash or accounts receivable
Cost of Goods Sold	7,000	(7,000)	Decrease in inventories
Gross Margin on Sales	$ 3,000	$ 3,000	
Operating Expenses			
Depreciation–Plant and Equipment	$ 400	–0–	Decrease in net income and the carrying value of Plant and Equipment
Other	2,100	(2,100)	Decrease in Cash or increase in Accounts Payable
Total Operating Expenses	$ 2,500		
Total Outflow of Working Capital		$ (2,100)	
Net Income	$ 500		
Net Increase in Working Capital		$ 900	

For brevity, the net increase in working capital from operations may be determined by working backwards as follows:

Working Capital Provided by Operations	
Net Income	$500
Add Nonworking Capital Charges to Revenue and Expense Summary:	
Depreciation Expense–Plant and Equipment	400
Increase in Working Capital	$900

It must not be inferred from the mechanics of this procedure that the $400 depreciation expense increased working capital and is thereby a source of working capital. The deduction of depreciation expense merely decreased net income without effecting a corresponding decrease in working capital. An income statement is likely to include several items of this kind—for example, depreciation, amortization of intangible assets, and loss on disposal of plant assets representing costs and expenses that enter into income determination but do not affect working capital in the current period. The relevant expenditures either were made in a prior period or will be made in a future period. The recognition of depreciation is essential to income measurement, but it does not change the amount of working capital.

To illustrate the preparation of a simple form of the statement of sources and uses of working capital, the position statement of the Fairfield Company, Inc., is given.

FAIRFIELD COMPANY, INC.
Comparative Statement of Financial Position
December 31, 1973 and 1972

	December 31 1973	December 31 1972	Increase or (Decrease)
Assets			
Current Assets			
Cash	$ 30,000	$ 32,000	$ (2,000)
Accounts Receivable (net)	65,000	52,000	13,000
Merchandise Inventory	112,000	92,000	20,000
Unexpired Insurance	3,000	4,000	(1,000)
Total Current Assets	$210,000	$180,000	$ 30,000
Plant and Equipment	$470,000	$438,000	$ 32,000
Deduct Accumulated Depreciation	105,000	98,000	7,000
	$365,000	$340,000	$ 25,000
Total Assets	$575,000	$520,000	$ 55,000
Liabilities and Stockholders' Equity			
Current Liabilities			
Accounts Payable	$ 60,000	$ 81,000	$(21,000)
Bank Loans Payable (short-term)	31,500	26,500	5,000
Accrued Payables	3,500	2,500	1,000
Total Current Liabilities	$ 95,000	$110,000	$(15,000)
Stockholders' Equity			
Capital Stock	$410,000	$350,000	$ 60,000
Retained Earnings	70,000	60,000	10,000
Total Stockholders' Equity	$480,000	$410,000	$ 70,000
Total Liabilities and Stockholders' Equity	$575,000	$520,000	$ 55,000

Step 1 in preparing the statement of sources and uses of working capital is to determine the changes in working capital.

FAIRFIELD COMPANY, INC.
Schedule of Changes in Working Capital
For the Year Ended December 31, 1973

| | December 31 | | Changes in Working Capital | |
	1973	1972	Increase	Decrease
Current Assets				
Cash	$ 30,000	$ 32,000		$ 2,000
Accounts Receivable (net)	65,000	52,000	$13,000	
Merchandise Inventory	112,000	92,000	20,000	
Unexpired Insurance	3,000	4,000		1,000
Total Current Assets	$210,000	$180,000		
Current Liabilities				
Accounts Payable	$ 60,000	$ 81,000	21,000	
Bank Loans Payable (short-term)	31,500	26,500		5,000
Accrued Payables	3,500	2,500		1,000
Total Current Liabilities	$ 95,000	$110,000		
Working Capital	$115,000	$ 70,000		
Net Increase in Working Capital				45,000
			$54,000	$54,000

Step 2 is to analyze the changes in all the noncurrent accounts.

FAIRFIELD COMPANY, INC.
Analysis of Changes in Noncurrent Accounts
For the Year Ended December 31, 1973

| | (Debit) or Credit | Effect on Working Capital | |
		Increase	Decrease
Plant and Equipment			
Balance, 12/31/72	$(438,000)		
Acquisitions during 1973	(32,000)		$ 32,000
Balance, 12/31/73	$(470,000)		
Accumulated Depreciation—Plant and Equipment			
Balance, 12/31/72	$ 98,000		
Depreciation for 1973	7,000	$ 7,000*	
Balance, 12/31/73	$ 105,000		
Capital Stock			
Balance, 12/31/72	$ 350,000		
Stock Issued	60,000	60,000	
Balance, 12/31/73	$ 410,000		
Retained Earnings			
Balance, 12/31/72	$ 60,000		
Net Income for 1973	35,000	35,000	
Dividends declared	(25,000)		25,000
Balance, 12/31/73	$ 70,000		
		$102,000	$ 57,000
Net Increase in Working Capital			45,000
		$102,000	$102,000

*Nonworking capital charge to Revenue and Expense Summary.

Step 3 is to prepare a statement summarizing the sources and uses of working capital during 1973, as follows:

FAIRFIELD COMPANY, INC.
Statement of Sources and Uses of Working Capital
For the Year Ended December 31, 1973

Sources of Working Capital		
Stock Issued		$ 60,000
Operations		
Net Income	$35,000	
Add Depreciation of Plant and Equipment	7,000	42,000
Total		$102,000
Uses of Working Capital		
Purchase of Equipment	$32,000	
Payment of Dividends	25,000	57,000
Net Increase in Working Capital		$ 45,000

The T-Account Method

Although a statement of sources and uses of working capital can be prepared directly from a comparative position statement as in the preceding example, it becomes more difficult to prepare as the number of transactions and accounts to be analyzed increases. Some systematic method is needed to facilitate the analysis of the transactions required for the preparation of the formal statement. Several techniques may be used for this purpose, all of which lead to the same result. The technique known as the *direct,* or *T-account,* method[2] is often used because of its relative simplicity and clarity. The basic steps are as follows:

Step 1. A schedule of changes in working capital is prepared.

Step 2. A T account is opened for each noncurrent position statement item and the amount of the net increase or decrease, obtained from the comparative position statement, is entered in each account. Increases in assets and decreases in liabilities and stockholders' equity accounts are debit changes and are entered on the debit side; decreases in assets and increases in liabilities and stockholders' equity accounts are credit changes and are entered on the credit side. A single horizontal line is then drawn under each amount, across the account. The amounts entered in the T accounts are added to make sure that total debits equal total credits.

Step 3. Two additional T accounts, Working Capital Summary and Revenue and Expense Operating Summary, are opened. The Working Capital Summary account represents all the current asset and current liability accounts; the amount entered in this account is, therefore, the net change in working capital as determined in Step 1: it is a debit if there is a net increase; a credit if there is a net decrease. The Revenue and Expense Operating Summary account is used to determine the amount of working capital provided by operations. No entry is made in this account at this point.

Step 4. The net changes entered in the T accounts in Steps 2 and 3 represent, in summary form, all the transactions that occurred during the period. These

[2]Based on William J. Vatter, "A Direct Method for the Preparation of Fund Statements," *The Journal of Accountancy,* June, 1946, pp. 479–489.

transactions are now reconstructed by separate entries below the horizontal lines in the appropriate T accounts. An offsetting debit or credit to a noncurrent account may be to

   a. *Another noncurrent account.* Although such a transaction does not affect working capital, the entry is made so that all changes may be explained.
   b. *Working Capital Summary.* This account is debited or credited for transactions other than revenue and expense that affect working capital and noncurrent accounts.
   c. *Revenue and Expense Operating Summary.* This account is debited or credited for transactions affecting revenue, expense, and noncurrent accounts.

Step 4 is completed only when the balance of the amounts below the horizontal line in each account is equal to the net change entered above the horizontal line in Steps 2 and 3. This ensures that all the transactions that affect working capital have been accounted for. Each entry should be identified by a letter or number, together with a brief notation giving the source of the entry to facilitate the preparation of the formal statement.

Step 5. The balance of Revenue and Expense Operating Summary is transferred to Working Capital Summary.

Step 6. The formal statement of sources and uses of working capital is prepared. Revenue and Expense Operating Summary shows the amount of working capital provided by operations. Working Capital Summary contains details of sources and uses of working capital; the debit entries represent sources; the credit entries are uses.

The comparative position statement of the Plymouth Corporation and related supplementary data are used to illustrate the step-by-step T-account method for the preparation of a statement of sources and uses of funds.

PLYMOUTH CORPORATION Comparative Position Statement December 31, 1973 and 1972	December 31		Increase or (Decrease)
	1973	1972	
Assets			
Current Assets			
Cash	$ 16,000	$ 21,000	$ (5,000)
Accounts Receivable (net)	19,600	16,600	3,000
Merchandise Inventory	31,000	21,000	10,000
Total Current Assets	$ 66,600	$ 58,600	$ 8,000
Long-Term Investments (at cost)	$ 22,000	$ 19,000	$ 3,000
Plant and Equipment			
Land	$ 18,000	$ 18,000	$ -0-
Buildings	126,000	110,000	16,000
Accumulated Depreciation–Buildings	(38,000)	(35,000)	(3,000)*
Machinery	152,000	125,000	27,000
Accumulated Depreciation– Machinery	(37,000)	(25,000)	(12,000)
Total Plant and Equipment	$221,000	$193,000	$28,000
Intangible Assets	$ 9,000	$ 10,000	$ (1,000)
Total Assets	$318,600	$280,600	$38,000

* These items represent increases to contra asset accounts, which in turn represent decreases in assets.

	December 31		Increase or (Decrease)
	1973	1972	
Liabilities and Stockholders' Equity			
Current Liabilities			
Accounts Payable	$ 23,000	$ 19,000	$ 4,000
Notes Payable	3,500	4,000	(500)
Total Current Liabilities	$ 26,500	$ 23,000	$ 3,500
Long-Term Liabilities			
Mortgage Payable	32,000	35,000	(3,000)
Total Liabilities	$ 58,500	$ 58,000	$ 500
Stockholders' Equity			
5% Preferred Stock, $100 par value	$ 55,000	$ 50,000	$ 5,000
Common Stock, no par value, $10 stated value	125,000	110,000	15,000
Premium on Common Stock	13,000	10,000	3,000
Retained Earnings	67,100	52,600	14,500
Total Stockholders' Equity	$260,100	$222,600	$37,500
Total Liabilities and Stockholders' Equity	$318,600	$280,600	$38,000

PLYMOUTH CORPORATION
Income Statement
For the Year Ended December 31, 1973

Sales		$125,000
Cost of Goods Sold		70,000
Gross Margin on Sales		$ 55,000
Operating Expenses		
Depreciation–Machinery	$12,000	
Depreciation–Building	3,000	
Amortization of Intangibles	1,000	
Other	20,675	36,675
Operating Margin		$ 18,325
Gain on Sale of Investments		1,000
Net Income		$ 19,325

An analysis of the income statement, the statement of retained earnings, and the changes in the noncurrent items discloses the following supplementary information:

1. Net income per income statement — $19,325
2. Depreciation
   a. Machinery — 12,000
   b. Building — 3,000
3. Amortization of intangible assets — 1,000
4. Dividends declared and paid — 4,825
5. Payment on mortgage payable — 3,000
6. Investments costing $4,000 were sold for $5,000 (the gain of $1,000 was included in net income). Since investments increased by $3,000, additional investments costing $7,000 ($4,000 + $3,000) must have been acquired.

7. Plant and Equipment
   a. No machinery was sold during the period. Acquisitions, therefore, must have cost $27,000.
   b. No buildings were disposed of during the period. Acquisitions, therefore, must have cost $16,000.
8. Issuance of Stock
   a. Preferred—50 shares at par value
   b. Common—1,500 shares at $12 per share

Step 1. A schedule of changes in working capital is prepared.

PLYMOUTH CORPORATION Schedule of Changes in Working Capital For the Year Ended December 31, 1973				
	December 31		Changes in Working Capital	
	1973	1972	Increase	Decrease
Current Assets				
Cash	$16,000	$21,000		$ 5,000
Accounts Receivable (net)	19,600	16,600	$ 3,000	
Merchandise Inventory	31,000	21,000	10,000	
Total Current Assets	$66,600	$58,600		
Current Liabilities				
Accounts Receivable	$23,000	$19,000		4,000
Notes Payable	3,500	4,000	500	
Total Current Liabilities	$26,500	$23,000		
Working Capital	$40,100	$35,600		
Net Increase in Working Capital				4,500
			$13,500	$13,500

Step 2. A T account is opened for each noncurrent position statement item and the amount of change during the year is entered. A single horizontal rule is drawn under each amount, as shown below.

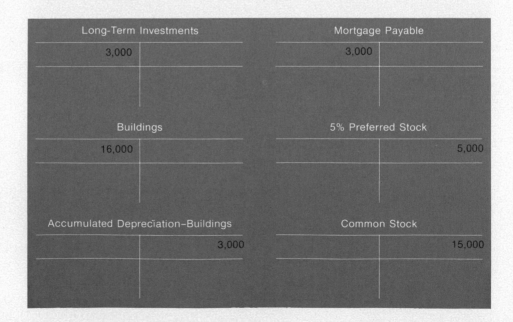

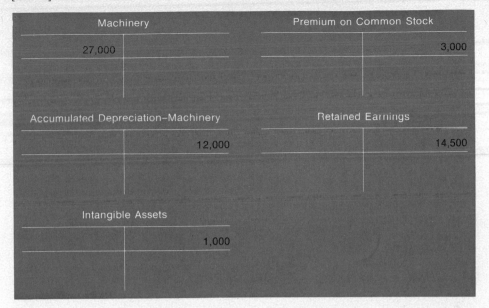

Step 3. Two additional T accounts are opened—Working Capital Summary and Revenue and Expense Operating Summary. The net change in working capital is entered in the Working Capital Summary account, and a rule is drawn. It is suggested that before proceeding to Step 4 the accountant test the accuracy of the debit and credit changes in the T accounts: the sum of the debit changes should equal the sum of the credit changes.

Revenue and Expense Operating Summary		Working Capital Summary	
		4,500	
		Increases in working capital	Decreases in working capital

Step 4. All the transactions for the year are reconstructed in separate summary entries below the horizontal rules. The entries indicated by the net changes in the comparative position statements and the supplementary data are made directly to the T accounts. They are shown in general journal form only to facilitate the explanation. They are posted to the T accounts only—*not to the regular general ledger accounts.*

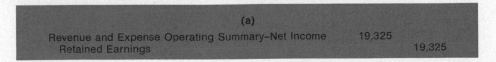

(a)		
Revenue and Expense Operating Summary—Net Income	19,325	
Retained Earnings		19,325

The net income figure is a summary of all the entries made during the period to the revenue and expense accounts. The amount of $19,325, the net income for the period, was originally recorded as a closing entry by a debit to Revenue and Expense Summary and a credit to Retained Earnings. In this entry, Revenue and Expense Operating Summary is debited in place of Revenue and Expense Summary. Since the balance of the Revenue and Expense Operating Summary account will show the amount of working capital provided by operations, this entry assumes a net increase in funds of $19,325 resulting from the revenue and expense transactions for the period.

(b)		
Revenue and Expense Operating Summary–Depreciation of Machinery	12,000	
Accumulated Depreciation–Machinery		12,000

This entry represents the annual depreciation charge, the original debit being to Depreciation Expense–Machinery, an expense account. It is evident that the assumption made in entry (a), that all expenses decrease working capital, is not valid. Working capital is used to acquire machinery, but the periodic allocation of this cost as a deduction from revenue does not affect working capital. The debit in this entry will, therefore, be added to the debit from entry (a) in determining the amount of working capital provided by operations.

(c)		
Revenue and Expense Operating Summary–Depreciation of Buildings	3,000	
Accumulated Depreciation–Buildings		3,000

The reason for this entry is the same as for entry (b).

(d)		
Revenue and Expense Operating Summary–Amortization of Intangibles	1,000	
Intangible Assets		1,000

This entry represents the amortization of a cost incurred in a prior period. The reason for the entry is the same as for entry (b).

(e)		
Retained Earnings	4,825	
Working Capital Summary—Declaration of Dividends		4,825

Dividends were declared and paid, resulting in a decrease in working capital. If the dividends were declared but not paid, the credit to Dividends Payable would increase current liabilities and decrease working capital. Entry (e) would, therefore, be the same.

(f)		
Working Capital Summary—Sale of Investments	5,000	
Long-Term Investments		4,000
Revenue and Expense Operating Summary—Gain on Sale of Investments		1,000

Securities that cost $4,000 were sold for $5,000. The gain on the sale is included in the reported net income of $19,325, and in Revenue and Expense Operating Summary through entry (a). But the effect of the sale was to increase working capital by a total of $5,000; hence, the debit to Working Capital Summary for $5,000 in entry (f). Furthermore, the increase in working capital resulting from the gain ($1,000) should be reported as an integral part of the total increase in Working Capital from sale of investments ($5,000) and not as a part of working capital provided by operations. The credit of $1,000 to Revenue and Expense Operating Summary, therefore, cancels a like amount included in Revenue and Expense Operating Summary through entry (a).

The T account for Long-Term Investments now appears as shown.

Long-Term Investments		
3,000		
	(f)	4,000

Since the balance below the horizontal line must be the same as the balance above the line, a debit entry of $7,000 must be made. It may be assumed that securities costing $7,000 were acquired. In practice, reference would be made to the records to confirm this assumption.

(g)

Long-Term Investments	7,000	
Working Capital Summary—Purchase of Investments		7,000

(h)

Machinery	27,000	
Working Capital Summary—Purchase of Machinery		27,000

The explanation for entry (h) is the same as for entry (g).

Since no machinery was sold during the period, it may be assumed that the net change represents acquisitions.

(i)

Buildings	16,000	
Working Capital Summary—Acquisition of Building		16,000

(j)

Working Capital Summary—Issuance of Preferred Stock	5,000	
5% Preferred Stock		5,000

A total of 50 shares of preferred stock were issued at par value.

(k)		
Working Capital Summary—Issuance of Common Stock	18,000	
Common Stock		15,000
Premium on Common Stock		3,000

A total of 1,500 shares of common stock were issued at $12 per share.

(l)		
Mortgage Payable	3,000	
Working Capital Summary—Payment of Mortgage Payable		3,000

The decrease in Mortgage Payable is assumed to be due to a cash payment.

At this point, the balance below the horizontal line in each noncurrent account is equal to the net change above the line, all the transactions affecting funds having been reproduced.

Step 5. The balance in the Revenue and Expense Operating Summary account is now $34,325, representing the working capital provided by operations. This balance is transferred to Working Capital Summary.

(m)		
Working Capital Summary—Working Capital Provided by Operations	34,325	
Revenue and Expense Operating Summary		34,325

The completeness and accuracy of the work is verified by the equality of the balances above and below the rule of the Working Capital Summary account.

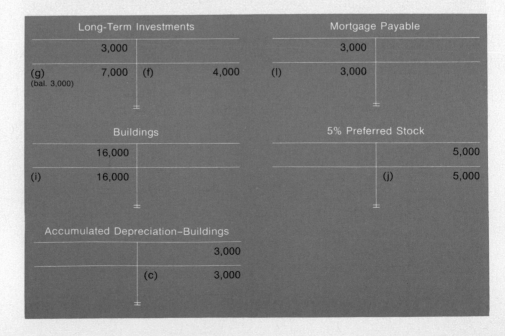

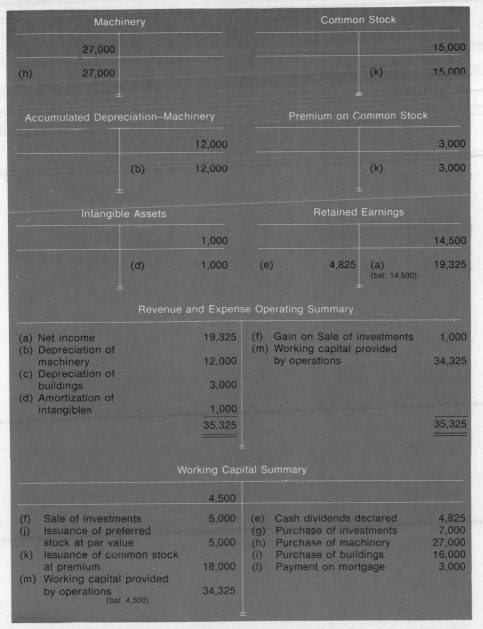

Machinery				Common Stock	
	27,000				15,000
(h)	27,000		(k)		15,000

Accumulated Depreciation–Machinery				Premium on Common Stock	
		12,000			3,000
(b)		12,000	(k)		3,000

Intangible Assets				Retained Earnings	
	1,000				14,500
(d)	1,000	(e)	4,825	(a)	19,325
				(bal. 14,500)	

Revenue and Expense Operating Summary

(a) Net income	19,325	(f)	Gain on Sale of investments	1,000
(b) Depreciation of machinery	12,000	(m)	Working capital provided by operations	34,325
(c) Depreciation of buildings	3,000			
(d) Amortization of intangibles	1,000			
	35,325			35,325

Working Capital Summary

	4,500			
(f) Sale of investments	5,000	(e)	Cash dividends declared	4,825
(j) Issuance of preferred stock at par value	5,000	(g)	Purchase of investments	7,000
		(h)	Purchase of machinery	27,000
(k) Issuance of common stock at premium	18,000	(i)	Purchase of buildings	16,000
		(l)	Payment on mortgage	3,000
(m) Working capital provided by operations	34,325			
(bal. 4,500)				

It is suggested that the accountant place some symbol in the noncurrent accounts to indicate that he has explained all the changes that have occurred in these accounts during the year. An equals sign (=) written across the vertical line of the T account is an excellent symbol to describe that the accountant has completed his task. When all the T accounts have an equals sign (=) written across the vertical line of the T, the accountant can quickly ascertain that he has completed the total work requirement on the T accounts. He can then proceed to Step 6, the preparation of the formal statement.

Step 6. The formal statement of sources and uses of working capital can now be prepared directly from the Working Capital Summary account: the debits represent sources of working capital; and the credits represent uses of working capital. Supporting figures for Working Capital received from operations may be taken from the Revenue and Expense Operating Summary Account. The statement is shown below.

PLYMOUTH CORPORATION
Statement of Sources and Uses of Working Capital
For the Year Ended December 31, 1973

Sources of Working Capital		
Operations		$34,325
Sale of Investments		5,000
Issuance of Stock		
Preferred	$ 5,000	
Common	18,000	23,000
Total		$62,325
Uses of Working Capital		
Purchase of Investments	$ 7,000	
Purchase of Machinery	27,000	
Purchase of Buildings	16,000	
Declaration of Dividends	4,825	
Payment on Mortgage	3,000	57,825
Net Increase in Working Capital		$ 4,500

The Statement of Sources and Uses of Working Capital—Managerial Analysis

The statement of sources and uses of working capital of the Plymouth Corporation, arranged in common-size form, is shown in Figure 19-2. An analysis in question and answer form to indicate how this statement may be used by management, investors, and other interested persons follows.

1. What was the net change in working capital? An increase of $4,500.

2. What was the effect of plant and equipment acquisitions on working capital? The purchase of additional machinery and buildings decreased available working capital by $43,000, or 69 percent of available working capital ($43,000 ÷ $62,325). Note, however, that net income per the income statement was $19,325, whereas the working capital provided by operations was $34,325; the difference is represented by the deductions from revenue for depreciation on machinery ($12,000) and buildings ($3,000).

3. What Working Capital was made available from investment by owners? from operations? These two sources thus provided approximately 92 percent of the available working capital ($57,325 ÷ $62,325). The remaining 8 percent came from the sale of investments for $5,000.

	Amount	Percent of Total
From operations	$34,325	60
From issuance of preferred and common stock	23,000	40
Total	$57,325	100

Figure 19-2. Common-Size Statement of Sources and Uses of Working Capital

PLYMOUTH CORPORATION
Statement of Sources and Uses of Working Capital
For the Year Ended December 31, 1973

		Amount	Percent
Sources of Working Capital			
Operations		$34,325	55.1
Sale of Investments		5,000	8.0
Issuance of Stock			
Preferred	$ 5,000		
Common	18,000	23,000	36.9
Totals		$62,325	100.0
Uses of Working Capital			
Purchase of Investments		$ 7,000	11.2
Purchase of Machinery		27,000	43.3
Purchase of Buildings		16,000	25.7
Declaration of Dividends		4,825	7.8
Payment on Mortgage		3,000	4.8
Net Increase in Working Capital		4,500	7.2
Totals		$62,325	100.0

4. What working capital came from outside borrowing? None.
5. What working capital came from the sale of noncurrent assets? The sale of investments increased working capital by $5,000.
6. What was the effect of the dividend declaration on working capital? Dividends declared totaled $4,825, which was the amount by which Plymouth decreased working capital. The declaration of dividends represents approximately 25 percent of net income ($4,825 ÷ $19,325) and 8 percent of available working capital ($4,825 ÷ $62,325).

ALTERNATIVE DEFINITIONS OF FUNDS

Much of the attention given to the statement of sources and uses of funds in recent years[3] has centered on alternative definitions of the term *funds* and on increasing the flexibility of presentation of the statement. "Types of transactions reflected in the statement of source and application of funds may vary substantially in relative importance from one period to another. As a result, consistency of arrangement of items from period to period and uniformity of arrangement as between reporting enterprises are of less significance than in the case of balance sheet or income statement."[4]

In *APB Opinion No. 19, Reporting Changes in Financial Position*, issued in March, 1971, the AICPA concludes that "a statement summarizing changes in financial position should also be presented as a basic financial statement for each period for which an income statement is presented,"

[3]Perry Mason, "'Cash Flow Analysis' and the Funds Statement," *Accounting Research Study No. 2*, New York: American Institute of Certified Public Accountants, 1961. *Opinion No. 3 of the Accounting Principles Board*, "The Statement of Sources and Application of Funds." New York: American Institute of Certified Public Accountants, October, 1963.
[4]*Opinion No. 3 of the Accounting Principles Board*, "The Statement of Source and Application of Funds," New York: American Institute of Certified Public Accountants, October, 1963.

8. The Board also concludes that the statement summarizing changes in financial position should be based on a broad concept embracing all changes in financial position and that the title of the statement should reflect this broad concept. The Board therefore recommends that the title be Statement of Changes in Financial Position. . . The Statement of each reporting entity should disclose all important aspects of its financing and investing activities regardless of whether cash or other elements of working capital are directly affected. For example, acquisitions of property by issuance of securities or in exchange for other property, and conversions of long-term debt or preferred stock to common stock, should be appropriately reflected in the statement.[5]

The foregoing concept of funds is often referred to as the *total resources* concept. Essentially it represents a combination of the previously discussed working capital concept plus the addition of the items noted in the conclusion of the AICPA in *APB Opinion No. 19.*

The common definition of funds as *working capital* limits the usefulness of the report. Since preparation of the statement involves an analysis of the relationships of the items in the financial statements, the logic of the analysis is the same regardless of the assumed meaning of funds. The mathematical relationships of the accounting quantities are the same; the form of reporting these relationships may vary. A change in the definition of funds simply means a different way of grouping the various items on the right-hand side of Equation 4 (page 637). An important advantage of examining the flow of funds in algebraic terms is that it becomes clearly evident that the underlying mathematical relationships can be readily reported in a variety of statement forms. If, for example, inventories are to be excluded from the definition of funds, Equation 1 (page 636) is rewritten as shown.

(1A)   Funds = Current Assets (other than inventories) − Current Liabilities
= Noncurrent Liabilities + Owners' Equity
− (Noncurrent Assets + Inventories)

Equation 4 now becomes

(4A)   Net change in funds
$$= [CA_2 \text{ (excluding inventories)} - CA_1 \text{ (excluding inventories)}]$$
$$- (CL_2 - CL_1)$$
$$= (NCL_2 - NCL_1) + (OE_2 - OE_1) - [(NCA_2 - NCA_1)$$
$$+ (\text{Inventories}_2 - \text{Inventories}_1)]$$

Equation 4A means that a change in inventories will now appear as a specific element in explaining the change in funds.

FUNDS DEFINED AS CASH

The first concept of *funds* illustrated in the preceding pages of this chapter was working capital. For many short-run purposes, a funds statement based on this meaning of the term may be too inclusive. The flow of cash—as contrasted

---

[5] *Opinion No. 19 of the Accounting Principles Board,* "Reporting Changes in Financial Position," New York: American Institute of Certified Public Accountants, March, 1971, pp. 373–374.

with the flow of working capital—is often of particular interest to management, credit grantors, investors, and others. A statement of changes in cash is useful to management and analysts in budgeting cash requirements.

The basic logic of the analysis for a funds-equals-cash statement is the same as for a funds-equals-working-capital statement; an analysis of the relationships of the items in the financial statements. The causes of the changes in cash—the sources and the uses of cash—are determined by analyzing the changes in all accounts other than Cash. Figures from the income statement are used to determine the changes in cash as a result of operations, and figures from the position statement together with supplementary data will reveal the remaining causes for the changes in cash.

The procedure for analyzing the transactions for a funds-equals-cash statement are the same as for a funds-equals-working-capital statement except that the changes in current asset and current liability accounts are treated separately instead of being netted as a single amount (working capital). The determination of the cash generated by operations, however, is complicated by the fact that the revenue and expense figures used for income measurement are different from cash receipts and disbursements. The time lag in the settlement of accounts with customers and creditors and the prepayment of certain expenses, for example, make necessary the conversion of accrual-basis revenue and expense amounts to the cash equivalent.

The income statement of the Plymouth Corporation (page 643) is analyzed in terms of the changes in cash resulting from operations, as shown.

PLYMOUTH CORPORATION Income Statement Converted to Show Cash Generated by Operations For the Year Ended December 31, 1973		Income Statement	Cash Increase or (Decrease)
Sales		$125,000	$122,000 (a)
Cost of Goods Sold			
Inventory, 12/31/72	$ 21,000		
Purchases	80,000		
Total	$101,000		
Inventory, 12/31/73	31,000		
Cost of Goods Sold		$ 70,000	$(76,500) (b)
Operating Expenses			
Depreciation–Machinery	$ 12,000		–0–
Depreciation–Building	3,000		–0–
Amortization of Intangibles	1,000		–0–
Other	20,675	36,675	(20,675)
Total Costs and Expenses		$106,675	$(97,175)
Operating Margin		$ 18,325	
Gain on Sale of Investments		1,000	
Net Income		$ 19,325	
Cash Generated by Operations			$ 24,825

	Income Statement	Cash Increase or (Decrease)
(a) Sales		$125,000
Accounts Receivable, 12/31/72		16,600
Total		$141,600
Accounts Receivable, 12/31/73		19,600
Cash Collections from Customers		$122,000
(b) Cost of Purchases		$ 80,000
Notes and Accounts Payable, 12/31/72		23,000
Total		$103,000
Notes and Accounts Payable, 12/31/73		26,500
Cash Payments to Creditors		$ 76,500

The T-account method illustrated earlier in this chapter can also be used in the preparation of a sources and uses of cash statement. Again, the data for the Plymouth Corporation are used. Since, by definition, cash is the only fund account, all other accounts are nonfund; hence, T accounts must be opened for those current accounts that are netted under the working capital definition of funds. In the partial T-account ledger shown, only the additional accounts and the two summary accounts are given. All the other accounts would be unchanged from the earlier example (page 648). New entries are designated by double letters; all the other entries carry the original letter notations.

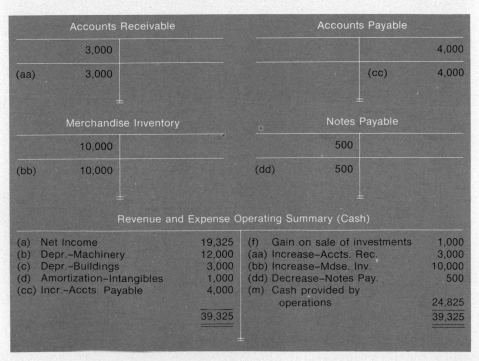

Accounts Receivable

	3,000		
(aa)	3,000		

Accounts Payable

			4,000
		(cc)	4,000

Merchandise Inventory

	10,000		
(bb)	10,000		

Notes Payable

	500		
(dd)	500		

Revenue and Expense Operating Summary (Cash)

(a) Net Income	19,325	(f) Gain on sale of investments	1,000
(b) Depr.–Machinery	12,000	(aa) Increase–Accts. Rec.	3,000
(c) Depr.–Buildings	3,000	(bb) Increase–Mdse. Inv.	10,000
(d) Amortization–Intangibles	1,000	(dd) Decrease–Notes Pay.	500
(cc) Incr.–Accts. Payable	4,000	(m) Cash provided by operations	24,825
	39,325		39,325

Cash Summary				
				5,000
(f)	Sale of investments	5,000	(e) Cash dividends paid	4,825
(j)	Issuance of pfd. stock	5,000	(g) Purch. of investments	7,000
(k)	Issuance of common stock	18,000	(h) Purch. of machinery	27,000
(m)	Cash from operations	24,825	(i) Purch. of buildings	16,000
			(l) Payment on mortgage	3,000
			(bal. 5,000)	

The statement of sources and uses of cash is prepared from the data in the Cash Summary account. The Revenue and Expense Operating Summary (Cash) account provides the details of cash received from operations ($24,825).

PLYMOUTH CORPORATION
Statement of Sources and Uses of Cash
For the Year Ended December 31, 1973

Sources of Cash		
Operations	$24,825	
Issuance of stock	23,000	
Sale of investments	5,000	$52,825
Uses of Cash		
Purchase of securities	$ 7,000	
Purchase of machinery	27,000	
Purchase of buildings	16,000	
Dividend payments	4,825	
Mortgage payments	3,000	57,825
Net Decrease in Cash		$ 5,000

SUMMARY

The purpose of the various funds statements is to furnish information regarding sources and uses of working capital, cash, or other financial items.

The chief sources of working capital are operations, long-term borrowing, and the sale of assets. The chief uses are to increase noncurrent assets, retire long-term debt, reduce the stockholders' equity, and provide for the declaration of dividends.

The preparation of the statement of sources and uses of working capital requires (1) an analysis of the current assets and current liabilities to determine the net change in working capital during the period and (2) a determination of the causes of the net change by an analysis of the changes in all the other accounts. Transactions that do not change working capital are not reported in the statement of sources and uses of working capital (for example, transactions that change only current assets or current liabilities and transactions that change only noncurrent accounts). Transactions that change working capital are reported (for example, transactions that change a current and a noncurrent account).

Regular operating activities are primary sources of working capital, but the change in working capital may be greater than the net income as shown in the income statement. Adjustments must be made for nonworking capital charges to Revenue and Expense Summary, representing costs and expenses that affect net income but not the working capital of the current period (for example, depreciation, a loss on a disposal of assets, or the amortization of intangible assets). Preparation of the statement of sources and uses of working capital requires the following steps:

1. The change in working capital is determined.
2. The changes in all the noncurrent accounts are analyzed.
3. The statement is prepared.

The statement can be prepared directly from a comparative position statement, but if there are a number of transactions and accounts to analyze, some systematic method is needed. The T-account method is one such method.

The flow of cash—as contrasted with the flow of working capital—and a statement of changes in cash are useful to management and analysts in forecasting cash requirements. The causes of the changes in cash are determined by analyzing the changes in all accounts other than Cash. The income statement is converted to determine the changes in cash from operations, and the changes in the position statement together with underlying data reveal the remaining causes for the changes in cash. The procedures for analyzing the transactions for a funds-equals-cash statement are the same as for funds-equals-working capital statement except that the changes in current asset and current liability accounts are treated separately instead of being netted as a single amount (working capital).

QUESTIONS

Q19-1. What is meant by the term *funds?*

Q19-2. What is the purpose of the statement of sources and uses of working capital?

Q19-3. How may working capital provided by operations be determined?

Q19-4. What are the chief sources of working capital from operations? The chief uses?

Q19-5. Certain transactions are eliminated from the statement of sources and uses of working capital. Why? Give some examples.

Q19-6. How may the statement of sources and uses of working capital be used to advantage by management? Investors? Others?

Q19-7. How may the statement of sources and uses of cash be used to advantage by management? Investors? Others?

Q19-8. What are the sources of information for the preparation of the statement of sources and uses of working capital?

Q19-9. What is the effect of a dividend declaration on working capital? Of the payment of a dividend?

Q19-10. What is the effect of depreciation of plant and equipment on (a) working capital? (b) cash?

Q19-11. The net income as shown on the income statement and the working capital provided by operations are different amounts. Why?

Q19-12. Does the statement of sources and uses of working capital eliminate the need for the statement of financial position? the income statement? Discuss.

Q19-13. What is the effect on working capital of a change to an accelerated method of depreciation?

Q19-14. In arriving at working capital provided by operations, certain items are added to net income and other items are deducted. Illustrate and explain.

Q19-15. It is alleged that the statement of sources and uses of cash is helpful to business management. (a) List the areas in which this information would be particularly useful. (b) What are the shortcomings of these data?

EXERCISES

E19-1. The following statements of Northeast Company are given.

NORTHEAST COMPANY
Income Statement
For the Year Ended December 31, 1973

Net Sales		$65,000
Cost of Goods Sold		47,300
Gross Margin on Sales		$17,700
Expenses:		
Salaries	$9,200	
Depreciation Expense	1,500	
Rent Expense	2,400	
Supplies Expense	1,000	14,100
Net income		$ 3,600

NORTHEAST COMPANY
Statement of Financial Position Accounts
December 31, 1973 and 1972

	December 31	
	1973	1972
Debits		
Cash	$16,170	$11,360
Accounts Receivable	6,110	7,220
Inventory	8,100	8,100
Supplies on Hand	300	700
Equipment	15,000	12,000
	$45,680	$39,380
Credits		
Accounts Payable—Inventory	$ 3,900	$ 3,100
Accrued Rent Payable	400	200
Accrued Salaries	300	100
Accumulated Depreciation	6,300	4,800
Capital Stock	25,000	25,000
Retained Earnings	9,780	6,180
	$45,680	$39,380

Prepare a statement of net cash generated by operations.

E19-2. For each of the following transactions, state whether it (a) was a source of working capital, (b) was a use of working capital, or (c) had no effect on working capital:

1. Purchased U.S. Treasury notes maturing in six months.
2. Issued a stock dividend to common stockholders.
3. Restricted retained earnings for anticipated plant expansion.
4. Issued common stock in exchange for a building.
5. Acquired machinery for $50,000; paid $20,000 in cash and issued a long-term note for the balance.
6. Wrote off an uncollectible account receivable against Allowance for Doubtful Accounts.
7. Reacquired some outstanding preferred stock for retirement.
8. Issued additional common stock at a premium for cash.
9. Wrote off a portion of the Goodwill account.
10. Issued bonds at a discount; the proceeds were used to retire preferred stock.

E19-3. Comparative financial statements of the Framison Corporation showed the following balances:

	December 31	
	1973	1972
Cash	$ 50,000	$ 52,000
Other Current Assets	110,000	115,000
Plant and Equipment (net)	140,000	110,000
Current Liabilities	110,000	115,000
Stockholders' Equity	190,000	162,000

There were no disposals of plant and equipment during the year. Dividend payments totaled $10,000. Prepare a schedule explaining the cause of the decrease in cash in spite of reported net income of $38,000.

E19-4. The Plant and Equipment section of the Ward Company's comparative statement of financial position shows the following amounts:

	December 31	
	1973	1972
Plant and Equipment		
Machinery	$550,000	$500,000
Deduct Accumulated Depreciation	250,000	240,000
Total Plant and Equipment	$300,000	$260,000

Acquisitions of new machinery during the year totaled $140,000. The income statement shows depreciation charges for the year of $70,000 and a loss from machinery disposals of $24,000. Determine the original cost and accumulated depreciation of machinery sold during the year and the proceeds of the sale; prepare a partial statement of sources and uses of working capital.

E19-5. For each of the following cases, compute the working capital generated by operations.

	a	b	c	d	e
Net income (loss) per income statement	$15,000	$(15,000)	$55,000	$45,000	$(20,000)
Depreciation of plant and equipment	2,000	2,000	4,500	3,000	1,000
Gain (loss) on sale of long-term investments			(1,000)	2,000	(500)

	a	b	c	d	e
Periodic amortization of discount on bonds payable			1,000	500	250
Periodic amortization of patents				500	300

E19-6. During the year 1973, the changes in the accounts of the Emory Company were as follows:

	Increases	Decreases
Cash		$10,000
Accounts Receivable	$ 6,000	
Merchandise Inventory	20,000	
Long-Term Investments	6,000	
Plant and Equipment	58,000	
Accumulated Depreciation	4,000	
Accounts Payable	7,500	
Taxes Payable		500
Mortgage Payable		6,000
Common Stock	46,000	
Retained Earnings	29,000	

Additional information is given:

1. Net income per income statement $38,650
2. Dividends declared   9,650
3. There were no disposals of plant or equipment during the year.

Prepare a statement of sources and uses of working capital.

E19-7. Determine the amount of cash received from customers in each of the following cases:

	1	2
Accounts Receivable–Beginning of Year	$ 27,000	$ 40,000
Accounts Receivable–End of Year	35,000	38,000
Sales	105,000	150,000
Uncollectible Accounts Written Off	500	750
Cash Discounts on Sales	1,000	2,500

E19-8. Determine the amount of cash disbursements for merchandise in each of the following cases:

	1	2
Beginning Inventory	$12,000	$15,000
Ending Inventory	10,000	18,000
Purchases	75,000	85,000
Beginning Accounts Payable	10,000	14,000
Ending Accounts Payable	12,000	10,000
Discounts on Purchases	1,000	1,500

E19-9. From the following data, taken from the ledger of the Windham Company, prepare a partial statement of sources and uses of working capital.

Machinery

1973				1973			
Jan.	1	Balance	250,000	Feb.	14	Sale	30,000
July	10	Purchase	33,000	June	21	Sale	25,000

Accumulated Depreciation–Machinery

1973				1973			
Feb.	14	Sale	20,000	Jan.	1	Balance	130,000
June	21	Sale	15,000	Dec.	31	Depreciation	42,000

Gain or Loss on Sale of Machinery

1973				1973			
June	21	Sale	3,500	Feb.	14	Sale	2,000

Revenue and Expense Summary

	1973			
	Dec.	31	Net income for year	60,000

E19-10. How would each of the following transactions be reflected in a statement of sources and uses of working capital? Classify each item as a use of working capital, a source of working capital, or a nonworking capital transaction.

1. Construction of a building
2. Issuance of bonds
3. Recording of depreciation on a building
4. Declaration of a cash dividend
5. Purchase of machinery, giving a 60-day note
6. Sale of land for cash at a loss
7. Acquisition of a patent by the issuance of capital stock
8. Amortization of a discount on bonds payable

E19-11. The accounts receivable of a business totaled $15,000 at the beginning of the year and $12,000 at the end of the year. Accounts receivable written off as uncollectible during the year amounted to $1,300, and cash discounts allowed to customers amounted to $600. The sales for the year were $35,000. What were the cash receipts during the year from sales of the current and prior periods?

E19-12. The purchase of merchandise of a business amounted to $50,000 during 1973. Accounts payable at the beginning and end of the year were $16,500 and $14,800, respectively; notes payable given to trade creditors in settlement of open accounts were $4,000 at the beginning of the year and $4,400 at the end of the year. Returns and allowances on purchases were $435. What were the cash payments during 1973 for purchases of 1973 and prior periods?

E19-13. For each of the following transactions, indicate whether it (a) was a source of working capital, (b) was a use of working capital, or (c) had no effect on working capital:

1. Restricted retained earnings for contingencies.
2. Issued common stock in exchange for a patent.
3. Wrote off an uncollectible account receivable against the Allowance for Doubtful Accounts.
4. Wrote off a portion of the Patent account.
5. Acquired machinery costing $50,000. Paid $20,000 in cash and issued a long-term note for the balance.
6. Declared a cash dividend of $5,000, payable in the following accounting period.
7. Purchased merchandise for cash.

8. Sold for $600 treasury stock purchased in the preceding accounting period at a cost of $500.
9. Sold for $5,000 in cash machinery with a book value of $9,000.
10. Received treasury stock as a donation. The treasury stock had a fair market value of $1,000
11. Issued common stock for cash.

E19-14. Assume that you are preparing a statement of cash generated by operations for Warner, Inc. One of the problems confronting you is to determine the amount of cash paid out in 1973 in connection with rent transactions. Rent expense of $62,500 is reported on the 1973 income statement. From a comparative statement of financial position, you discover the following items and amounts:

	December 31	
	1973	1972
Prepaid Rent Expense	$2,450	$1,890
Accrued Rent Payable	4,760	5,150

From the information given, compute the amount of cash paid out in 1973 in connection with all rent transactions.

E19-15. Assume that you are a prospective investor in Wear, Inc., and have assembled certain information relating to the operations of the company. From a comparative statement of financial position and a statement of sources and uses of cash, you decide to reconstruct an income statement on the accrual basis. The first item you desire to determine is Sales for 1973. The 1973 statement of sources and uses of cash reports Cash Received from Customers of $256,410. On the comparative statement of financial position, you find the following items and amounts:

	December 31	
	1973	1972
Accounts Receivable	$50,000	$52,000
Allowance for Doubtful Accounts	3,000	2,000

From other sources, you discover that in 1973 the company had written off $1,500 of the accounts receivable at December 31, 1972. You therefore calculated that the bad debts expense for 1973 was $2,500.

From the information given, compute the accrual sales figure for 1973.

DEMONSTRATION PROBLEMS

DP19-1. (*Statement of sources and uses of working capital*) The December 31, 1972 and 1973, statements of financial position of the Newton Company carried the following debit and credit amounts:

	December 31	
	1973	1972
Debits		
Cash	$ 10,200	$ 12,600
Accounts Receivable (net)	35,100	32,900
Merchandise Inventory	85,200	86,400
Prepaid Expenses	1,500	1,800
Office Equipment	5,000	5,600
Store Equipment	29,800	28,300
Totals	$166,800	$167,600

	December 31	
	1973	1972
Credits		
Accumulated Depreciation–Office Equipment	$ 2,500	$ 2,400
Accumulated Depreciation–Store Equipment	7,500	6,500
Accounts Payable	22,400	23,500
Notes Payable	10,000	5,000
Common Stock, $10 par value	110,000	100,000
Premium on Common Stock	6,500	5,500
Retained Earnings	7,900	24,700
Totals	$166,800	$167,600

Additional information is given:

1. The net loss for the year was $1,900.
2. Depreciation expense on office equipment was $500; on store equipment, it.was $1,700.
3. Office equipment that was carried at its cost of $600 with accumulated depreciation of $400 was sold for $300. The gain was carried directly to Retained Earnings.
4. Store equipment costing $2,200 was purchased.
5. Fully depreciated store equipment that cost $700 was discarded and its cost and accumulated depreciation were removed from the accounts.
6. Cash dividends of $4,000 were declared during the year.
7. A 1,000-share stock dividend was declared and issued. On the date of declaration, the common stock of the company had a fair market value of $11 per share.

Required: Prepare a statement of sources and uses of working capital.

DP19-2. (*Statement of sources and uses of working capital; of cash*) The following data are taken from the books of the Fuller Corporation (figures are in thousands of dollars):

	December 31	
	1973	1972
Debits		
Cash	$ 315	$ 285
Marketable Securities	106	50
Receivables (net)	145	125
Inventories	95	70
Long-Term Investments	70	110
Machinery	500	350
Buildings	600	200
Land	35	35
Totals	$1,866	$1,225
Credits		
Accumulated Depreciation	$ 275	$ 150
Accounts Payable	100	75
Notes Payable	50	25
Mortgage Bonds Payable	500	250
Common Stock	550	400
Premium on Common Stock	55	-0-
Retained Earnings	336	325
Totals	$1,866	$1,225

FULLER CORPORATION
Income Statement
For the Year Ended December 31, 1973

Sales		$600
Cost of Goods Sold		337
Gross Margin on Sales		$263
Operating Expenses		
Depreciation–Machinery	$ 50	
Depreciation–Buildings	80	
Other Expenses	100	230
Net Income from Operations		$ 33
Gain on Sale of Long-Term Investments		12
Total		$ 45
Loss on Sale of Machinery (proceeds were $15)		5
Net Income		$ 40

Required: 1. Prepare a statement of sources and uses of working capital.
2. Prepare a statement of sources and uses of cash.

DP19-3. (*Working capital generated by operations*) You are given the following single-step combined statement of income and retained earnings:

RANG COMPANY
Statement of Income and Retained Earnings
For the Year Ended December 31, 1973

Revenue and Other Credits		
Sales		$ 600,000
Interest Earned		10,500
Correction of Prior Years' Income–		
Overstatement of 1971 Depreciation of		
Machinery		5,000
Total		$ 615,500
Expenses, Losses, and Other Charges		
Cost of Goods Sold	$470,000	
Salaries and Wages Expense	40,000	
Bad Debts Expense	4,000	
Advertising Expense	10,000	
Depreciation Expense	60,000	
Office Expense	20,000	
Loss on Reduction of Marketable Securities		
to Market	5,000	
Loss on Sale of Machinery	8,000	
Interest Expense	4,000	
Total		621,000
Net Loss for the Year		$ (5,500)
Retained Earnings, December 31, 1972		1,010,500
Total		$1,005,000
Deduct: Dividends declared June 2, 1973		
and paid July 2, 1973	$100,000	
Dividends declared December 2,		
1973 to be paid January 2, 1974	150,000	
Stock dividends declared and		
issued in 1973	200,000	
Total		450,000
Retained Earnings, December 31, 1973		$ 555,000

Interest Earned represents a receipt of $10,000 in cash and the amortization of discount on bonds purchased for investments (long-term) of $500. The Interest Expense figure was increased by $350 for amortization of discount on bonds payable and was decreased by $200 for amortization of a premium on bonds payable.

Required: 1. Starting with the Net Loss for Year compute, in schedule or T-account form, the working capital provided (or used) by operations during 1973.

2. Compute the amount of working capital provided or used in connection with the dividend policy of the company.

PROBLEMS

P19-1. The comparative statements of financial position of the Simpson Company, as of December 31, 1973 and 1972, were as follows:

	December 31	
	1973	1972
Debits		
Cash	$ 48,000	$ 63,000
Accounts Receivable (net)	58,800	49,800
Merchandise Inventory	85,000	65,000
Long-Term Investments	68,000	60,000
Machinery	350,000	300,000
Buildings	270,000	225,000
Land	50,000	50,000
Patents	18,000	20,000 .
Totals	$947,800	$832,800
Credits		
Accumulated Depreciation–Machinery	$ 40,000	$ 30,000
Accumulated Depreciation–Buildings	35,000	20,000
Accounts Payable–Trade	55,000	50,000
Notes Payable–Trade	8,000	10,000
Mortgage Payable	50,000	60,000
Common Stock	550,000	500,000
Retained Earnings	209,800	162,800
Totals	$947,800	$832,800

Additional information is given:

1. Net income for the year was $47,000.
2. There were no sales or disposals of plant or equipment during the year.

Required: Prepare a statement of sources and uses of working capital.

P19-2. The following data of the Hull Company are given in three parts (figures are in thousands of dollars):

Part I

	December 31	
	1973	1972
Debits		
Current Assets	$105	$ 60
Plant and Equipment (net)	150	125
Totals	$255	$185

	December 31	
	1973	1972
Credits		
Current Liabilities	$ 40	$ 20
Common Stock	150	150
Retained Earnings	65	15
Totals	$255	$185

Depreciation for period is $5.

Part II

Assume the same facts, except that Plant and Equipment cost and Accumulated Depreciation are itemized as follows:

	December 31	
	1973	1972
Debits		
Current Assets	$105	$ 60
Plant and Equipment	170	140
Totals	$275	$200
Credits		
Accumulated Depreciation	$ 20	$ 15
Current Liabilities	40	20
Common Stock	150	150
Retained Earnings	65	15
Totals	$275	$200

Part III

Assume the same debit and credit amounts as in Part II. Assume further that during the year a machine having an original cost of $10,000 and accumulated depreciation of $5,000 was sold for $7,000.

Required: For each part, prepare a statement of sources and uses of working capital.

P19-3. Following is the comparative post-closing trial balance of the Trix Company:

TRIX COMPANY
Comparative Post-Closing Trial Balance
December 31, 1973 and 1972

	December 31	
	1973	1972
Debits		
Cash	$ 35,000	$ 50,000
Accounts Receivable (net)	95,000	80,000
Merchandise Inventory	260,000	195,000
Marketable Securities	–0–	110,000
Prepaid Expenses	4,000	2,500
Plant and Equipment	500,000	300,000
Patents	64,000	68,000
Totals	$958,000	$805,500

	December 31	
	1973	1972
Credits		
Accumulated Depreciation–Plant and Equipment	$135,000	$100,000
Accounts Payable	100,000	60,000
Common Stock	500,000	500,000
Retained Earnings	223,000	145,500
Totals	$958,000	$805,500

Additional data are given:

1. Net income for the period was $125,000.
2. Dividends declared were $47,500.
3. The marketable securities were sold at a gain (included in Item 1) of $15,000.
4. Equipment with an original cost of $20,000 and accumulated depreciation of $10,000 was sold at a loss (included in Item 1) of $2,000.
5. Patents are being amortized over their legal life of 17 years.

Required: Prepare a statement of sources and uses of working capital.

P19-4. The following data of Bannon, Inc., are given:

	December 31	
	1973	1972
Debits		
Cash	$ 60,000	$ 45,000
Accounts Receivable	90,000	80,000
Merchandise Inventory	40,000	32,000
Investments (Long-Term)	30,000	50,000
Machinery	40,000	25,000
Buildings	90,000	75,000
Land	10,000	10,000
Totals	$360,000	$317,000
Credits		
Allowance for Doubtful Accounts	$ 3,000	$ 2,000
Accumulated Depreciation–Machinery	7,500	3,000
Accumulated Depreciation–Buildings	18,000	12,000
Accounts Payable	40,000	33,000
Accrued Payables	4,500	3,500
Mortgage Payable	35,000	40,000
Common Stock	200,000	200,000
Retained Earnings	52,000	23,500
Totals	$360,000	$317,000

Additional data are given:

1. Net income for the year was $60,000.
2. Dividends declared during the year were $31,500.
3. Investments that cost $20,000 were sold during the year for $25,000. The gain is included in item 1.
4. Machinery that cost $5,000, on which $1,000 in depreciation had accumulated, was sold for $6,000. The gain is included in item 1.

Required: Prepare a statement of sources and uses of working capital.

P19-5. The following data of Lamm Company are given:

LAMM COMPANY

Comparative Position Statements

December 31, 1973 and 1972

	December 31	
	1973	1972
Debits		
Cash	$ 26,000	$ 37,000
Accounts Receivable (net)	90,000	96,000
Merchandise Inventory	100,000	80,000
Investments (Long-Term)	12,000	10,000
Machinery (net)	200,000	150,000
Buildings (net)	160,000	100,000
Land	20,000	15,000
Totals	$608,000	$488,000
Credits		
Accounts Payable	$ 75,000	$ 65,000
Accrued Payables	3,000	4,000
Mortgage Payable	70,000	58,000
Common Stock	300,000	250,000
Retained Earnings	160,000	111,000
Totals	$608,000	$488,000

LAMM COMPANY

Income Statement

For the Year Ended December 31, 1973

Sales		$810,000
Cost of Goods Sold		480,000
Gross Margin on Sales		$330,000
Operating Expenses		
Depreciation–Machinery	$ 20,000	
Depreciation–Buildings	10,000	
Other Operating Expenses	221,000	251,000
Net Income		$ 79,000

Additional data are given:

1. Dividends paid during year were $30,000.
2. The increase in long-term investments, machinery, buildings, and land were from purchases.
3. Common stock worth $50,000 was issued at par value.

    Required: Prepare a statement of sources and uses of cash.

P19-6. You are given the following comparative financial statements and supplementary information for the Mann Company:

MANN COMPANY
Comparative Position Statement
December 31, 1973, 1972, and 1971

	December 31		
Debits	1973	1972	1971
Cash	$ 30,000	$ 28,000	$ 26,000
Marketable Securities	25,000	18,000	–0–
Accounts Receivable (net)	65,000	79,000	60,000
Inventories	145,000	125,000	134,000
Plant and Equipment	550,000	400,000	435,000
Totals	$815,000	$650,000	$655,000
Credits			
Accumulated Depreciation	$235,000	$200,000	$170,000
Current Liabilities (trade)	130,000	90,000	105,000
Long-Term Liabilities	195,000	125,000	150,000
Common Stock	135,000	125,000	140,000
Retained Earnings	120,000	110,000	90,000
Totals	$815,000	$650,000	$655,000

MANN COMPANY
Comparative Income Statement
For the Years Ended December 31, 1973 and 1972

	1973	1972
Sales	$735,000	$785,000
Cost of Goods Sold	490,000	510,000
Gross Margin on Sales	$245,000	$275,000
Operating Expenses		
Depreciation	$ 60,000	$ 40,000
Selling and Administrative Expenses	154,000	190,000
Total Operating Expenses	$214,000	$230,000
Net Margin from Operations	$ 31,000	$ 45,000
Gain (Loss) on Disposal of Plant and Equipment	4,000	(5,000)
Net Income	$ 35,000	$ 40,000

Additional data are given:

	1973	1972
Dividends declared and paid	$ 25,000	$20,000
Plant and equipment acquisitions	175,000	50,000

Required: 1. Prepare statements of sources and uses of working capital for (a) 1972; (b) 1973.

2. Prepare statements of sources and uses of cash for (a) 1972; (b) 1973.

P19-7. You are given the following information from the books of the Atlas Corporation:

ATLAS CORPORATION
Statement of Financial Position
December 31, 1973 and 1972

| | December 31 | | Increase |
	1973	1972	(Decrease)
Debits			
Cash	$ 13,200	$ 15,600	$ (2,400)
Accounts Receivable	47,600	32,400	15,200
Merchandise Inventory	22,000	28,000	(6,000)
Machinery	82,400	87,400	(5,000)
Sinking Fund Cash	10,000	–0–	10,000
Totals	$175,200	$163,400	$ 11,800
Credits			
Allowance for Doubtful Accounts	$ 2,800	$ 2,500	$ 300
Accumulated Depreciation–Machinery	16,200	18,200	(2,000)
Accounts Payable	21,000	24,200	(3,200)
Dividends Payable	2,000	–0–	2,000
Bonds Payable	20,000	–0–	20,000
Premium on Bonds Payable	950	–0–	950
Capital Stock	100,000	100,000	–0–
Retained Earnings	2,250	18,500	(16,250)
Retained Earnings–Restricted for Sinking Fund	10,000	–0–	10,000
Totals	$175,200	$163,400	$ 11,800

ATLAS CORPORATION
Statement of Retained Earnings
For the Year Ended December 31, 1973

Balance, December 31, 1972		$18,500
Add: Net Income for year ended December 31, 1973		750
Total		$19,250
Deduct: Dividends Declared and Paid in Cash	$ 5,000	
Dividend Declared Payable January 15, 1974	2,000	
Appropriation for Sinking Fund	10,000	17,000
Balance, December 31, 1973		$ 2,250

ATLAS CORPORATION
Income Statement
For the Year Ended December 31, 1973

Sales		$85,450
Cost of Goods Sold		65,000
Gross Margin on Sales		$20,450
Operating Expenses		
Salaries	$14,700	
Bad Debts Expense	300	
Depreciation of Machinery	3,500	
Taxes	400	
Insurance	300	19,200
Net Income from Operations		$ 1,250
Other Expenses		
Bond Interest Expense	$ 1,050	
Deduct Amortization of Bond Premium	50	
Net Bond Interest Expense	$ 1,000	
Other Revenue		
Gain on Sale of Machinery	500	500
Net Income to Retained Earnings		$ 750

Additional data are given:

Bonds payable in the amount of $20,000 were sold on April 30, 1973, at 105. Machinery that cost $7,000, and had accumulated depreciation of $5,500, was sold for $2,000 in cash.

Required: Prepare a schedule of working capital changes and a statement of sources and uses of working capital by the T-account approach. Submit all supporting computations, including the T accounts.

P19-8. The comparative statements of financial position of the Durham Company as of December 31, 1973 and 1972, and related supplementary data are as follows:

DURHAM COMPANY
Comparative Position Statements
December 31, 1973 and 1972

	December 31	
	1973	1972
Assets		
Current Assets		
Cash	$ 25,000	$ 23,000
Marketable Securities	40,000	35,000
Accounts Receivable (net)	65,000	62,000
Merchandise Inventory	60,000	50,000
Total Current Assets	$190,000	$170,000
Investments (at cost)	$ 80,000	$ 10,000
Plant and Equipment		
Machinery (net)	$200,000	$140,000
Buildings (net)	225,000	175,000
Land	50,000	50,000
Total Plant and Equipment	$475,000	$365,000
Total Assets	$745,000	$545,000

	December 31	
	1973	1972
Liabilities and Stockholders' Equity		
Current Liabilities		
Accounts Payable–Trade	$ 95,000	$ 90,000
Notes Payable–Trade	10,000	25,000
Total Current Liabilities	$105,000	$115,000
Long-Term Liabilities		
Mortgage Bonds Payable	75,000	25,000
Total Liabilities	$180,000	$140,000
Stockholders' Equity		
5% Preferred Stock, $100 par value	$100,000	$ –0–
Common Stock, $10 par value	350,000	350,000
Retained Earnings	115,000	55,000
Total Stockholders' Equity	$565,000	$405,000
Total Liabilities and Stockholders' Equity	$745,000	$545,000

Additional data are given:

1. Net income for the year 1973 was $70,000.
2. Dividends declared during year were $10,000.
3. Depreciation was:
   Machinery $20,000   Buildings $10,000
4. There were no plant and equipment disposals during the year.
5. The Company issued 1,000 shares of 5% preferred stock at par value.
6. Investments costing $10,000 were sold for $14,000. The gain is included in Item 1.

Required:

Prepare the following statements:

1. Net change in working capital
2. Working capital provided by operations
3. Sources and uses of working capital.

P19-9. You are given the following partial statement and other information for the Kimzey Company:

	December 31	
	1973	1972
Debits		
Plant and Equipment	$1,100,000	$800,000
Credits		
Accumulated Depreciation	470,000	400,000
Bonds Payable	100,000	–0–
Premium on Bonds Payable	5,000	–0–

	1973
Income Statement Data	
Depreciation Expense	$120,000
Gain on Disposal of Plant and Equipment	8,000

Additional data are given:

1. Plant and Equipment acquisitions during the year were $350,000.
2. Bonds Payable were issued on December 31, 1973, at 105 for a total of $105,000.

Required: Set up T accounts for Plant and Equipment, Accumulated Depreciation, Bonds Payable, Premium on Bonds Payable, Revenue and Expense Operating Summary, and Working Capital Summary. Place the net changes that occurred during 1973 in the first four accounts. Then make all the necessary entries in the accounts to accumulate information for the statement of sources and uses of working capital.

P19-10. (*Accounting policy decision problem*) The following information was extracted from the books of the Watson Company:

	December 31	
	1973	1972
Working Capital	$366,700	$442,000
Tools	14,000	12,000
Machinery	39,000	45,000
Delivery Equipment	18,000	15,000
Buildings	100,000	100,000
Accumulated Depreciation—All Plant and Equipment	90,500	84,500
Land	25,000	40,000
Patents	3,500	4,500
Goodwill	-0-	50,000
Discount on Bonds Payable	-0-	6,000
Bonds Payable	-0-	100,000
Capital Stock	350,000	250,000
Treasury Stock	30,000	-0-
Retained Earnings	155,700	180,000
Retained Earnings—Restricted for Bond Retirement	-0-	100,000

Retained Earnings

Stock dividend	100,000	Balance, Jan. 1, 1973	180,000
Loss on scrapping of machinery; cost $6,000 accumulated depreciation $4,500	1,500	Gain on sale of land; cost $15,000, sold for $18,000	3,000
Goodwill written off	50,000	Gain on trade of delivery equipment; cost $4,000, book value $2,500; an allowance of $3,200 was received on purchased new equipment costing $7,000	700
Unamortized discount ($4,000) and call premium ($2,500) on bond retirement	6,500		
Cash dividends	10,000	Retained earnings restricted for bond retirement	100,000
Balance, Dec. 31, 1973	155,700	Net income for the year	40,000
	323,700		323,700
		Balance, Dec. 31, 1973	155,700

The income statement reports depreciation of buildings of $6,000; depreciation of machinery of $4,000; depreciation of delivery equipment of $2,000; tools amortization of $4,000; patents amortization of $1,000; and bond discount amortization of $2,000.

Required:

1. Prepare a statement of sources and uses of working capital.
2. Based on the information given, which concept of or approach to net income does the company apply? Support your answer. (The cash basis or the accrual basis is not relevant in answering this question.)
3. Identify the alternative concept or approach, and compute net income according to this other concept.
4. State briefly two arguments supporting each concept.

Cost
Accumulation,
Cost Control, and
Financial Planning

part

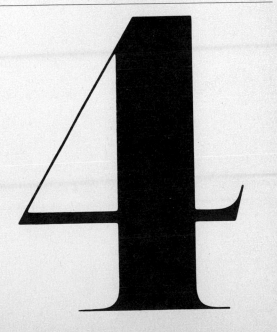

20

Cost Accumulation and Control— General Manufacturing Operations

Up to this point, only the accounting for service and trading businesses has been considered. A trading business buys merchandise in finished form and sells it in the same form. A manufacturing company, on the other hand, buys materials that it converts into finished products by the application of labor and other factory costs. The accounting principles and procedures, however, are the same for both manufacturing and nonmanufacturing businesses. Additional accounts are opened to record the activities involved in the manufacturing process—the conversion of materials into finished goods. From these accounts the schedule of cost of goods manufactured may be prepared; this shows the cost of materials consumed, direct labor costs, and the other factory costs incurred in the manufacture of the finished product over a stated period.

MATERIALS USED

All materials that are economically traceable to the finished product are referred to as *materials, raw materials,* or *direct materials.* Because many of these materials are fabricated by other manufacturers, the titles "materials" and "direct materials" are used here rather than "raw materials." The cloth used in the manufacture of a suit, for example, is classified as a "direct material." Some materials, although an integral part of the finished product, are not classified as direct materials because the cost or the quantity used is small or because it would be uneconomical to trace and determine the cost and amount of certain materials that are incorporated in the finished product. The thread used in manufacturing a garment, for example, may not be regarded as a direct material although it can otherwise be clearly identified with the end product. The cost of the thread would be accounted for, as are certain other indirect factory costs, which are discussed later in this chapter.

675

The cost of materials used during an accounting period in the manufacture of a product may be determined by the periodic inventory method in the same manner as is the cost of goods sold in a trading business. The procedure necessary to account for *materials, direct labor,* and *manufacturing overhead* in a manufacturing company may be illustrated by the following sequence of transactions.

The Acme Manufacturing Company had materials on hand on January 1, 1973, costing $8,200. During the month of January, entries and postings were made as follows (only the general ledger accounts necessary for the illustration are shown):

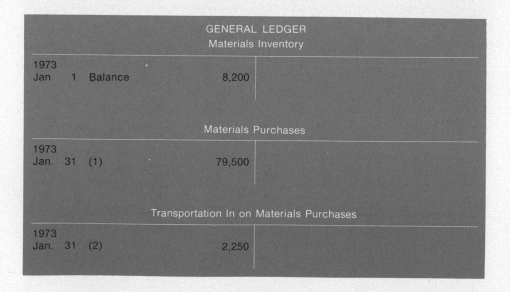

	(1)		
Materials Purchases		79,500	
Vouchers Payable			79,500
To record purchases of materials on account.			
	(2)		
Transportation In on Materials Purchases		2,250	
Vouchers Payable			2,250
To record freight charges on materials purchased.			
	(3)		
Vouchers Payable		3,250	
Materials–Purchases Returns and Allowances			3,250
To record credit received for materials returned.			
	(4)		
Vouchers Payable		80,000	
Materials–Purchases Discounts			1,600
Cash			78,400
To record payment of vouchers for materials purchased.			

GENERAL LEDGER
Materials Inventory

1973				
Jan.	1	Balance	8,200	

Materials Purchases

1973				
Jan.	31	(1)	79,500	

Transportation In on Materials Purchases

1973				
Jan.	31	(2)	2,250	

Materials—Purchases Returns and Allowances		
	1973	
	Jan. 31 (3)	3,250

Materials—Purchases Discounts		
	1973	
	Jan. 31 (4)	1,600

Materials on hand on January 31 were $9,700. The Materials Used section of the schedule of cost of goods manufactured for the month of January is shown in Figure 20-1.

Figure 20-1. Computation of Materials Used

ACME MANUFACTURING COMPANY
Partial Schedule of Cost of Goods Manufactured
For the Month Ended January 31, 1973   Schedule A-1

Materials Used			
Materials Inventory, January 1, 1973			$ 8,200
Materials Purchases		$79,500	
Transportation In on Materials Purchases		2,250	
Gross Cost of Materials Purchases		$81,750	
Deduct Purchases Returns and Allowances	$3,250		
Purchases Discounts	1,600	4,850	
Net Cost of Materials Purchases			76,900
Cost of Materials Available for Use			$85,100
Deduct Materials Inventory,			
January 31, 1973			9,700
Cost of Materials Used			$75,400

DIRECT LABOR

The wages paid to employees performing operations directly on the product being manufactured are referred to as *direct labor*. Direct labor is the cost of wages paid for work involving the construction, composition, or fabrication of the end product.

The following journal entries demonstrate the recording of direct labor:

(5)		
Direct Labor	58,300	
Vouchers Payable (and payroll tax withholding		
liabilities)		58,300
To record the direct labor costs vouchered during		
January (payroll deduction details have been omitted).		

(6)		
Direct Labor	2,700	
Accrued Wages and Salaries Payable		2,700
To record direct labor costs accrued.		

The debit total of $61,000 ($58,300 + $2,700) is the direct labor cost for the month. This amount is entered in the schedule of cost of goods manufactured on one line immediately following the amount for materials used.

MANUFACTURING OVERHEAD

All factory costs incurred in the manufacturing process other than the cost of materials used and direct labor are classified as *manufacturing overhead*. Other terms used for this group of costs are *indirect manufacturing costs* and *manufacturing burden*. For a manufacturing company, manufacturing overhead is a product cost and not a period expense; that is, these costs are incorporated in the inventory of manufactured goods. Selling expenses and general and administrative expenses are not considered manufacturing overhead because they reflect the administrative and distributive functions of the business and are not part of the manufacturing function. Most of the accounts listed in the schedule of cost of goods manufactured (see Figure 20-2) are self-explanatory. Others are explained in the following paragraphs.

Indirect labor is the labor cost for those workers whose efforts are not directly identified with the conversion of specific materials into specific finished products. Wages paid to employees who schedule and supervise the work of others, for example, would be classified as indirect labor. The term also includes the wages of repair and maintenance crews, guards, janitors, and cost accounting clerks assigned to the manufacturing function.

Amortization of patents represents that part of the cost of patents allocable to the current accounting period. It is assumed that these patents are for manufacturing processes. The cost of the patents should be amortized over the economically useful life or the remaining legal life of the asset, whichever is shorter. The Patents account may be credited directly for the amortized portion. The amortized portion is debited to Amortization of Patents, listed under Manufacturing Overhead. The unamortized balance of Patents is reported on the statement of financial position as an intangible asset.

Small tools used represents the cost of special small tools used up by workmen during the accounting period. It is possible to depreciate small tools by methods similar to those used for machinery and equipment. This procedure is difficult, however, because of the great variety of tools used and their relatively small value. In addition, small hand tools are easily lost or broken, and their useful life is difficult to predict. To overcome this practical difficulty, small tools may be accounted for as follows: The acquisition cost is debited to the asset account Small Tools; at the end of each accounting period an inventory of tools on hand is taken and priced; the discrepancy between the balance in the asset account and the inventory count represents the cost of tools broken, discarded, or lost. The entry to adjust the Small Tools account to the inventory amount is a debit to Small Tools Used, manufacturing overhead item, and a credit to Small Tools, plant and equipment item.

A separate account may be opened in the general ledger for each manufacturing overhead item; however, if these accounts are numerous, a subsidiary *manufacturing overhead ledger* may be set up. Its controlling account in the general ledger is Manufacturing Overhead.

The journals of the Acme Manufacturing Company showed the following additional entries (entry 7 was made during the month; the others represent end-of-period adjustments):

(7)		
Factory Rent	2,000	
Heat, Light, and Power	12,000	
Indirect Labor	9,100	
Equipment Maintenance and Repairs	2,900	
Miscellaneous Factory Costs	2,950	
Vouchers Payable (and payroll tax withholding liabilities)		28,950
To record overhead costs vouchered during the		
month. (There was no accrued indirect labor, and payroll		
deduction details have been omitted.)		
(8)		
Depreciation—Machinery and Equipment	3,500	
Accumulated Depreciation—Machinery and Equipment		3,500
To record one month's depreciation of machinery and		
equipment.		
(9)		
Factory Insurance	1,100	
Prepaid Insurance		1,100
To record the expiration of one month's insurance.		
(10)		
Factory Property Tax	1,600	
Accrued Property Taxes Payable		1,600
To record property taxes accrued on the factory building.		
(11)		
Amortization of Patents	950	
Patents		950
To amortize the patent cost for January.		
(12)		
Small Tools Used	250	
Small Tools		250
To adjust the asset account to the inventory valuation.		

GENERAL LEDGER
Depreciation—Machinery and Equipment

1973			
Jan. 31	(8)	3,500	

GENERAL LEDGER
Factory Rent

1973 Jan. 31	**(7)**	2,000	

Heat, Light, and Power

1973 Jan. 31	**(7)**	12,000	

Amortization of Patents

1973 Jan. 31	**(11)**	950	

Small Tools Used

1973 Jan. 31	**(12)**	250	

Factory Insurance

1973 Jan. 31	**(9)**	1,100	

Factory Property Tax

1973 Jan. 31	**(10)**	1,600	

Indirect Labor

1973 Jan. 31	**(7)**	9,100	

Equipment Maintenance and Repairs

1973 Jan. 31	**(7)**	2,900	

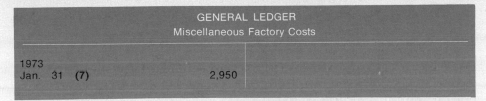

TOTAL PERIOD MANUFACTURING COSTS

Total period manufacturing costs are made up of the costs of materials used, direct labor, and manufacturing overhead, as shown below.

THE WORK-IN-PROCESS INVENTORY

The fabrication of a product is a continuing and repetitive process. At any time, therefore, partly finished products will be on hand in various stages of completion; they are known as *work in process*, or *goods in process*. At the end of the accounting period, the work in process is inventoried and its value determined. Since the cost of these partly finished units is included in the total period manufacturing costs, the end-of-period work-in-process inventory is deducted from the total costs to arrive at the cost of goods manufactured. Work-in-Process Inventory is classified as a current asset in the statement of financial position. The ending inventory of one period is the beginning inventory of the next period and enters into the cost of goods manufactured for that next period.

The Acme Manufacturing Company had a beginning work-in-process inventory on January 1 of $2,900. On January 31, the ending work-in-process inventory was $3,600. Note that the inventories include the costs of materials, labor, and overhead assignable to the unfinished product.

The completed schedule of cost of goods manufactured is shown in Figure 20-2.

FINISHED GOODS AND COST OF GOODS SOLD

The Cost of Goods Sold sections of the income statements of a merchandising business and of a manufacturing business are compared in Figure 20-3. The amounts are from the statements of the King Corporation (Figure 5-1) and the Acme Manufacturing Company. The cost of goods manufactured in the Acme Manufacturing Company statement is equivalent to the net cost of purchases in the King Corporation statement. The significant difference, however, is that the

Figure 20-2. Completed Schedule of Cost of Goods Manufactured

ACME MANUFACTURING COMPANY
Schedule of Cost of Goods Manufactured
For the Month Ended January 31, 1973

Schedule A-1

Materials Used			
Materials Inventory, January 1, 1973			$ 8,200
Materials Purchases		$79,500	
Transportation In on Materials Purchases		2,250	
Gross Cost of Materials Purchases		$81,750	
Deduct Purchases Returns and Allowances	$3,250		
Purchases Discounts	1,600	4,850	
Net Cost of Materials Purchases			76,900
Cost of Materials Available for Use			$ 85,100
Deduct Materials Inventory,			
January 31, 1973			9,700
Cost of Materials Used			$ 75,400
Direct Labor			61,000
Manufacturing Overhead			
Depreciation–Machinery and Equipment		$ 3,500	
Factory Insurance		1,100	
Factory Rent		2,000	
Factory Property Tax		1,600	
Heat, Light, and Power		12,000	
Indirect Labor		9,100	
Amortization of Patents		950	
Equipment Maintenance and Repairs		2,900	
Small Tools Used		250	
Miscellaneous Factory Costs		2,950	
Total Manufacturing Overhead			36,350
Total Period Manufacturing Costs			$172,750
Add Work-in-Process Inventory, Jan. 1, 1973			2,900
Total			$175,650
Deduct Work-in-Process Inventory,			
January 31, 1973			3,600
Cost of Goods Manufactured			$172,050

Figure 20-3. Comparison of Cost of Goods Sold Sections

Merchandising Business		Manufacturing Business	
Cost of Goods Sold		Cost of Goods Sold	
Merchandise Inventory,		Finished Goods Inventory,	
1/1/1973	$15,400	1/1/1973	$ 12,100
Purchases (net)	63,280	Cost of Goods Manufac-	
		tured (Schedule A-1)	172,050
Cost of Merchandise		Cost of Finished Goods	
Available for Sale	$78,680	Available for Sale	$184,150
Merchandise Inventory,		Deduct Finished Goods	
12/31/1973	11,480	Inventory, 1/31/1973	10,150
Total Cost of Goods Sold	$67,200	Total Cost of Goods Sold	$174,000

cost of goods manufactured is supported by a detailed schedule that presents three distinct cost elements, a variety of accounts, and two inventories. The calculation of net cost of purchases, on the other hand, involves only four accounts.

It is assumed in Figure 20-3 that the Acme Manufacturing Company had a beginning finished goods inventory of $12,100 and an ending inventory of $10,150. The term *finished goods* means the completed goods ready for sale and corresponds to the merchandise inventory of a trading business.

MANUFACTURING SUMMARY

It is possible to close all the manufacturing accounts directly into the Revenue and Expense Summary account. However, since the determination of the cost of goods manufactured is in part a process of adjusting, it is helpful to indicate this fact by showing the cost of goods manufactured in a temporary general ledger account called *Manufacturing Summary*. All account balances that enter into the calculation of the cost of goods manufactured are transferred to this account. In turn, the final balance of this account, which is the cost of goods manufactured, is closed into the Revenue and Expense Summary account. The closing entries are entered in the general journal, and the procedure followed is the same as for a trading concern. The closing entries may be made directly from the work-sheet.

The closing entries for the Acme Manufacturing Company are given as follows:

Closing Entries		
(13)		
Manufacturing Summary	190,200	
Materials Inventory (beginning)		8,200
Work-In-Process Inventory (beginning)		2,900
Materials Purchases		79,500
Transportation In on Materials Purchases		2,250
Direct Labor		61,000
Depreciation–Machinery and Equipment		3,500
Factory Insurance		1,100
Factory Rent		2,000
Factory Property Tax		1,600
Heat, Light, and Power		12,000
Indirect Labor		9,100
Amortization of Patents		950
Equipment Maintenance and Repairs		2,900
Small Tools Used		250
Miscellaneous Factory Costs		2,950
To close all the manufacturing accounts with debit balances.		
(14)		
Materials Inventory (ending)	9,700	
Work-in-Process Inventory (ending)	3,600	
Materials–Purchases Returns and Allowances	3,250	
Materials–Purchases Discounts	1,600	
Manufacturing Summary		18,150
To record the ending inventories and to close all the manufacturing accounts with credit balances.		

(15)

Revenue and Expense Summary	172,050	
Manufacturing Summary		172,050
To close the Manufacturing Summary account and to transfer the cost of goods manufactured to Revenue and Expense Summary.		

(16)

Revenue and Expense Summary	12,100	
Finished Goods Inventory (beginning)		12,100
To close the beginning finished goods inventory into Revenue and Expense Summary.		

(17)

Finished Goods Inventory (ending)	10,150	
Revenue and Expense Summary		10,150
To record the ending finished goods inventory.		

Entries 16 and 17 may be recorded as part of the compound entries closing out the remaining income statement accounts. If they are made separately, the balance of Revenue and Expense Summary after entries 16 and 17 are posted shows the cost of goods sold.

GENERAL LEDGER
Manufacturing Summary

1973				1973			
Jan.	31	**(13)**	190,200	Jan.	31	**(14)**	18,150
					31	**(15)**	172,050
			190,200				190,200

Finished Goods Inventory

1973				1973			
Jan.	1	Bal.	12,100	Jan.	31	**(16)**	12,100
	31	**(17)**	10,150				

Revenue and Expense Summary

1973				1973			
Jan.	31	**(15)**	172,050	Jan.	31	**(17)**	10,150
	31	**(16)**	12,100				

The $174,000 balance of the Revenue and Expense Summary account is the cost of goods sold, as shown in Figure 20-3. The remaining closing entries for the Acme Manufacturing Company are the same as for a merchandising business.

THE WORKSHEET FOR A MANUFACTURING COMPANY

There is only one essential difference between a worksheet for a manufacturing company and one for a merchandising company. In the worksheet for a manufacturing company, a pair of columns is added, headed Manufacturing, into which are extended the debit and credit account balances representing the elements of the cost of manufacturing—that is, all the accounts that enter into the preparation of the schedule of cost of goods manufactured. The difference between the totals of these columns is the cost of goods manufactured, which is then transferred to the Income Statement Debit column.

The function of the other worksheet columns is the same as in a merchandising company. The remaining illustrations and discussion in this chapter are based on the worksheet of the Carol Manufacturing Company, shown in Figure 20-4. It should be observed that a different illustration is used here in order to add complexities that were not appropriate to the elementary illustration of the Acme Manufacturing Company.

Ending Inventories on the Manufacturing Worksheet

The materials inventory on December 31, 1973, was $51,500. This amount is entered on the Materials Inventory line as a debit in the Position Statement columns and as a credit in the Manufacturing columns. The ending inventory is a current asset; furthermore, it must be deducted from the cost of materials available to determine the cost of materials used. This deduction is effected on the worksheet by entering the amount in the Manufacturing Credit column.

The work-in-process inventory at the end of the year was $47,000; it is entered on the Work-in-Process Inventory line. The debit in the Position Statement columns sets up the new inventory (a current asset), and the credit in the Manufacturing columns is used in computing the cost of goods manufactured.

The finished goods inventory on December 31, 1973, was $19,600; it is entered on the Finished Goods Inventory line. Again, the debit in the Position Statement columns establishes the new inventory (a current asset); the credit in the Income Statement columns is deducted from the cost of goods available to derive the cost of goods sold.

Adjusting Entries on the Manufacturing Worksheet

The entries in the Adjustments columns of the worksheet are based on the information that follows. The numbers correspond to those used on the worksheet.

(1)

The Bad Debts Expense was estimated at $\frac{1}{4}$ of 1 percent of gross sales less sales returns and allowances. The amount of the adjustment was computed as indicated on page 687:

Figure 20-4. Worksheet for a Manufacturing Company

CAROL MANUFACTURING COMPANY
Worksheet
For the Year Ended December 31, 1973

Account Title	Trial Balance Dr.	Trial Balance Cr.	Adjustments Dr.	Adjustments Cr.	Manufacturing Dr.	Manufacturing Cr.	Income Statement Dr.	Income Statement Cr.	Position Statement Dr.	Position Statement Cr.
Cash	12,000								12,000	
Accounts Receivable	78,350								78,350	
Allowance for Doubtful Accounts		650		(1) 1,037						1,687
Materials Inventory	58,300				58,300	51,500			51,500	
Work-in-Process Inventory	31,725				31,725	47,000			47,000	
Finished Goods Inventory	23,200						23,200	19,600	19,600	
Prepaid Insurance	2,100			(2) 1,500					600	
Office Equipment	6,050								6,050	
Accumulated Depreciation—Office Equipment		2,000		(4) 605						2,605
Store Equipment	10,000								10,000	
Accumulated Depreciation—Store Equipment		4,000		(4) 1,000						5,000
Machinery and Equipment	51,000								51,000	
Accumulated Depreciation—Machinery and Equipment		10,000		(3) 10,200						20,200
Accounts Payable		29,200								29,200
Capital Stock		180,000								180,000
Retained Earnings		12,855								12,855
Dividends	10,000								10,000	
Sales		420,000						420,000		
Sales Returns and Allowances	5,200						5,200			
Sales Discounts	2,400						2,400			
Materials Purchases	91,000				91,000					
Materials—Purchases Returns and Allowances		2,800				2,800				
Materials—Purchases Discounts		2,650				2,650				
Direct Labor	98,530		(5) 3,500		102,030					
Indirect Labor	21,200		(5) 1,400		22,600					
Rent	12,000				9,600		{1,800 S / 600 G}			
Heat, Light, and Power	8,100				7,290		{405 S / 405 G}			
Advertising Expense	6,500						6,500			
Salesmen's Salaries Expense	50,000		(5) 5,100				55,100			
Executive Salaries Expense	60,500						60,500			
Office Salaries Expense	26,000						26,000			
	664,155	664,155								
Bad Debts Expense			(1) 1,037				1,037			
Insurance			(2) 1,500		1,050		{300 S / 150 G}			
Depreciation—Machinery and Equipment			(3) 10,200		10,200					
Depreciation Expense—Office Equipment			(4) 605				605			
Depreciation Expense—Store Equipment			(4) 1,000				1,000			
Accrued Wages and Salaries Payable				(5) 10,000						10,000
Income Tax Expense			(6) 7,368				7,368			
Income Taxes Payable				(6) 7,368						7,368
			31,710	31,710	333,795	103,950				
Cost of Goods Manufactured						229,845	229,845			
					333,795	333,795	422,415	439,600	286,100	268,915
Net Income							17,185			17,185
							439,600	439,600	286,100	286,100

Legend: S = Selling expenses
G = General and administrative expenses

Gross Sales	$420,000
Deduct Sales Returns and Allowances	5,200
	$414,800
Bad Debts Expense Percentage	× 0.0025
Bad Debts Expense	$ 1,037

The entry is as shown below.

1973			
Dec. 31	Bad Debts Expense	1,037	
	Allowance for Doubtful Accounts		1,037

The debit records the estimated bad debts charge; the credit increases Allowance for Doubtful Accounts to $1,687 ($650 + $1,037).

(2)

Insurance of $1,500 has expired; this is recorded by the following entry.

1973			
Dec. 31	Insurance	1,500	
	Prepaid Insurance		1,500

The debit records the cost of the expired insurance; the credit decreases the asset account.

(3)

The annual depreciation rate for factory machinery and equipment is 20 percent. Since all the equipment was acquired prior to 1973, a full year's depreciation is taken, based on the amount shown in the trial balance. The computation is as follows:

Cost of machinery and equipment	$51,000
Annual depreciation rate	× 0.20
Depreciation for 1973	$10,200

The entry is as shown below.

1973			
Dec. 31	Depreciation–Machinery and Equipment	10,200	
	Accumulated Depreciation–Machinery and Equipment		10,200

The debit records the depreciation of the machinery and equipment; the credit increases the Accumulated Depreciation–Machinery and Equipment account.

(4)

The annual depreciation rate for both office equipment and store equipment is 10 percent. All the office and store equipment was acquired prior to 1973, consequently a full year's depreciation is taken, based on the amount of each account shown in the trial balance. The computations are as follows:

	Office Equipment	Store Equipment
Cost	$6,050	$10,000
Annual depreciation rate	×0.10	×0.10
Depreciation for 1973	$ 605	$ 1,000

The entry is

1973			
Dec. 31	Depreciation Expense–Office Equipment	605	
	Depreciation Expense–Store Equipment	1,000	
	Accumulated Depreciation–Office Equipment		605
	Accumulated Depreciation–Store Equipment		1,000

The debits record the depreciation expense for the office and store equipment; the credits increase the corresponding Accumulated Depreciation accounts.

(5)

The accrued wages and salaries payable as of December 31, 1973, were

Direct labor	$ 3,500
Indirect labor	1,400
Salesmen's salaries	5,100
Total	$10,000

The entry is

1973			
Dec. 31	Direct Labor	3,500	
	Indirect Labor	1,400	
	Salesmen's Salaries Expense	5,100	
	Accrued Wages and Salaries Payable		10,000

The debits record all the wages and salaries incurred but not paid; the credit records the accrued liability.

(6)

The estimated income tax liability is $7,368. The entry is as shown below.

1973			
Dec. 31	Income Tax Expense	7,368	
	Income Taxes Payable		7,368

The debit records the estimated income tax; the credit records the estimated income tax liability.

Allocation of Costs and Expenses
on the Worksheet

In the Trial Balance and Adjustments columns, there are certain accounts representing cost incurred partly in the manufacturing processes and partly in the selling and general and administrative functions. Assume that a study was made late in 1972 to find an equitable method for allocating these items. As a result of this study, the following bases for allocation were decided on:

Item	Basis for Allocation
Rent	Square footage of building space used
Heat, light, and power	Actual readings from meters in the factory, in the sales rooms, and in the general and administrative areas
Insurance	Cost of comprehensive policies covering the buildings allocated on the basis of square footage; other insurance costs charged directly to manufacturing, selling, or general and administrative expense

From these bases, converted to percentages, the following allocations were made:

		Allocation						
			Manufacturing		Selling		General	
Item	Total	%	Amount	%	Amount	%	Amount	
Rent	$12,000	80	$9,600	15	$1,800	5	$600	
Heat, light, and power	8,100	90	7,290	5	405	5	405	
Insurance	1,500	70	1,050	20	300	10	150	

On the line of the worksheet for each of these items, the total of the Trial Balance and Adjustments columns is extended to the appropriate column. The Rent debit balance of $12,000, for example, is distributed as follows: $9,600 ($12,000 × 0.80) is extended to the Manufacturing Debit column; $1,800 ($12,000 × 0.15) and $600 ($12,000 × 0.05) are extended to the Income Statement Debit column. Note that the $9,600 is classified as manufacturing overhead under Factory Rent (Figures 20-4 and 20-6); the $1,800 is classified as a selling expense, Rent Expense (Figures 20-4 and 20-5). The $9,600 portion is carried as a product cost and not as an expense because it is part of the cost of the finished product; it becomes an expense only when the product is sold. Until such time, overhead costs are assets; that is, they are part of either work in process (asset) or finished goods (asset). The $1,800 portion of the rent is classified as Rent Expense because it does not enter into the cost of goods manufactured (finished goods) but is rather an expense of the period in which it is incurred. This distinction also applies to heat, light, and power and to insurance. All the overhead accounts and all the portions of accounts allocated to manufacturing are product cost accounts.

The letters S and G after the amounts identify the specific income statement classifications of selling or general and administrative expenses. These letters may be further used for amounts extended as a lump sums in a single column to facilitate the precise classification of the accounts if the formal income statement is prepared directly from the worksheet.

FINANCIAL STATEMENTS

The Manufacturing columns of the worksheet contain all the amounts required for the preparation of the schedule of cost of goods manufactured in their proper debit or credit relationship; each amount is used once. Similarly, the Income Statement and Position Statement columns of the worksheet contain all the figures needed for the preparation of the income statement, statement of retained earnings, and statement of financial position. The financial statements are illustrated in Figures 20-5, 20-6, 20-7, and 20-8.

Figure 20-5. Income Statement

CAROL MANUFACTURING COMPANY			Exhibit A
Income Statement			
For the Year Ended December 31, 1973			
Sales Revenue			
Sales			$420,000
Deduct Sales Returns and Allowances		$ 5,200	
Sales Discounts		2,400	7,600
Net Sales Revenue			$412,400
Cost of Goods Sold			
Finished Goods Inventory, January 1, 1973		$ 23,200	
Add Cost of Goods Manufactured (Schedule A-1)		229,845	
Cost of Finished Goods Available for Sale		$253,045	
Deduct Finished Goods Inventory,			
December 31, 1973		19,600	
Cost of Goods Sold			233,445
Gross Margin on Sales			$178,955
Operating Expenses			
Selling			
Rent Expense	$ 1,800		
Heat, Light, and Power Expense	405		
Advertising Expense	6,500		
Salesmen's Salaries Expense	55,100		
Insurance Expense	300		
Depreciation Expense–Store Equipment	1,000		
Total Selling Expenses		$ 65,105	
General and Administrative			
Rent Expense	$ 600		
Heat, Light, and Power Expense	405		
Executive Salaries Expense	60,500		
Office Salaries Expense	26,000		
Bad Debts Expense	1,037		
Insurance Expense	150		
Depreciation Expense–Office Equipment	605		
Total General and Administrative Expenses		89,297	
Total Operating Expenses			154,402
Net Income Before Income Taxes			$ 24,553
Income Tax Expense			7,368
Net Income After Income Taxes			$ 17,185

Figure 20-6. Schedule of Cost of Goods Manufactured

CAROL MANUFACTURING COMPANY Schedule of Cost of Goods Manufactured For the Year Ended December 31, 1973			Schedule A-1
Materials Used			
Materials Inventory, January 1, 1973			$ 58,300
Materials Purchases		$91,000	
Deduct Purchases Returns and Allowances	$2,800		
Purchases Discounts	2,650	5,450	
Net Cost of Materials Purchases			85,550
Cost of Materials Available for Use			$143,850
Deduct Materials Inventory,			
December 31, 1973			51,500
Cost of Materials Used			$ 92,350
Direct Labor			102,030
Manufacturing Overhead			
Indirect Labor		$22,600	
Factory Rent		9,600	
Heat, Light, and Power		7,290	
Factory Insurance		1,050	
Depreciation—Machinery and Equipment		10,200	
Total Manufacturing Overhead			50,740
Total Period Manufacturing Costs			$245,120
Add Work-in-Process Inventory,			
January 1, 1973			31,725
Total			$276,845
Deduct Work-in-Process Inventory,			
December 31, 1973			47,000
Cost of Goods Manufactured (to Exhibit A)			$229,845

MANUFACTURING ACCOUNTING—MANAGERIAL ANALYSIS

A company must control its inventories and its cost of operations. Excessive inventories must be avoided because they may result in losses due to changes in style, obsolescence, and price fluctuations. Several ratios and comparisons are indicators of such potential losses. Ratios and trends vary from industry to industry, but within any given industry, or especially within a single company, valuable trends and ratios can be established. Amounts for the year 1972 for the Carol Manufacturing Company have been assumed. Amounts for 1973 are from the statements in Figures 20-5, 20-6, 20-7, and 20-8.

Turnover of Materials

An overinvestment or underinvestment in materials may be brought to management's attention by comparing the materials turnover with that of prior periods or of other similar companies. An overinvestment in materials inventory should be avoided because it ties up working capital and storage space and creates the possibility of loss through shrinkage, style and price changes, and so on. Conversely, an underinvestment in inventory must be avoided to ensure a steady flow

Figure 20-7. Statement of Financial Position

	CAROL MANUFACTURING COMPANY		Exhibit B
	Statement of Financial Position		
	December 31, 1973		
	Assets		
Current Assets			
Cash		$ 12,000	
Accounts Receivable	$78,350		
Deduct Allowance for Doubtful Accounts	1,687	76,663	
Materials Inventory		51,500	
Work-in-Process Inventory		47,000	
Finished Goods Inventory		19,600	
Prepaid Insurance		600	
Total Current Assets			$207,363
Plant and Equipment			
Office Equipment	$ 6,050		
Deduct Accumulated Depreciation	2,605	$ 3,445	
Store Equipment	$10,000		
Deduct Accumulated Depreciation	5,000	5,000	
Machinery and Equipment	$51,000		
Deduct Accumulated Depreciation	20,200	30,800	
Total Plant and Equipment			39,245
Total Assets			$246,608
	Liabilities and Stockholders' Equity		
Current Liabilities			
Accounts Payable		$ 29,200	
Accrued Wages and Salaries Payable		10,000	
Income Taxes Payable		7,368	
Total Current Liabilities			$ 46,568
Stockholders' Equity			
Capital Stock		$180,000	
Retained Earnings (Exhibit C)		20,040	
Total Stockholders' Equity			200,040
Total Liabilities and Stockholders' Equity			$246,608

Figure 20-8. Statement of Retained Earnings

	CAROL MANUFACTURING COMPANY	Exhibit C
	Statement of Retained Earnings	
	For the Year Ended December 31, 1973	
Retained Earnings, January 1, 1973	$12,855	
Net Income for the Year (Exhibit A)	17,185	
Total	$30,040	
Deduct Dividends	10,000	
Retained Earnings, December 31, 1973	$20,040	

of materials into production and to prevent the possible incurrence of higher costs through a "shoe-string" buying policy. The turnover of materials inventories is shown in Figure 20-9.

Figure 20-9. Materials Turnover

		1973	1972
Materials used	**(a)**	$92,350	$86,670
Materials inventories			
Beginning of year		$58,300	$61,900
End of year		51,500	58,300
Average	**(b)**	$54,900	$60,100
Materials turnovers (a ÷ b)		1.68	1.44

In 1973, for every $1 in the average materials inventory there was $1.68 worth of materials used in the manufacture of the finished products. The numbers 1.68 and 1.44 represent the number of times the materials were replaced during the year. These turnover rates may be converted to days by dividing the number of days in a year by the turnover.

		1973	1972
Number of days in year	**(a)**	365	365*
Turnover (from Figure 20-9)	**(b)**	1.68	1.44
Number of days' inventory (a ÷ b)		217	253

*For purposes of comparability, it is assumed that each year has 365 days, even though there are 366 days in the leap year 1972.

The number 217 for 1973 means that during that year the company had, on the average, materials on hand sufficient for 217 days' use. This information, together with such factors as available sources of supply and the length of time required to obtain the material, makes it possible to recognize and to initiate action to control overstocking or understocking of inventories.

Turnover of Finished Goods

The computation of the finished goods turnovers for the Carol Manufacturing Company for the years 1973 and 1972 is shown in Figure 20-10.

Figure 20-10. Turnover of Finished Goods

		1973	1972
Cost of goods sold	**(a)**	$233,445	$197,142
Finished goods inventories			
Beginning of year		$ 23,200	$ 24,650
End of year		19,600	23,200
Average	**(b)**	$ 21,400	$ 23,925
Finished goods turnovers (a ÷ b)		10.91	8.24

In 1973, for every $1 in the average finished goods inventory there was $10.91 worth of finished goods sold. The computation for converting these turnover rates to days is

		1973	1972
Number of days in year	(a)	365	365*
Turnover (from Figure 20-10)	(b)	10.91	8.24
Number of days' inventory (a ÷ b)		33	44

*For purposes of comparability, it is assumed that each year has 365 days, even though there are 366 days in the leap year 1972.

The Carol Manufacturing Company had improved the finished goods inventory turnover in 1973 as compared to 1972. In terms of the number of days' sales requirements, the inventory has been decreased from 44 days to 33 days.

There are a variety of factors that influence the finished goods inventory turnover trend and that must be considered before any conclusions are drawn. The ratio is influenced by actual or anticipated changes in prices, volume, basis of inventory valuation, the presence of obsolete or unsalable goods in the inventory, and so on. If, for example, a higher turnover is the result of an increased volume of sales due to lowered prices, gross margin may not increase. If, however, the amount of the inventory and the rate of gross margin are relatively stable, an increased turnover will result in an increase in gross margin. Again, such increases in gross margin may not result in increased earnings if the more rapid turnover is accompanied by increases in advertising and other costs of distributing the product.

Manufacturing Costs

The percentage relationships of materials used, direct labor, and manufacturing overhead to total period manufacturing costs also provide significant information about the business. These percentages may indicate to management the need for investigation if they are disproportionate to those of prior periods or similar companies. The computations of the relationships for the Carol Manufacturing Company for 1973 are:

		Percentage
$\dfrac{\text{Materials used}}{\text{Total period manufacturing costs}} = \dfrac{\$92,350}{\$245,120} =$		38
$\dfrac{\text{Direct labor}}{\text{Total period manufacturing costs}} = \dfrac{\$102,030}{\$245,120} =$		41
$\dfrac{\text{Manufacturing overhead}}{\text{Total period manufacturing costs}} = \dfrac{\$50,740}{\$245,120} =$		21
Total		100

Each dollar of the total period cost of manufacturing consisted of materials, 38 cents; direct labor, 41 cents; and manufacturing overhead, 21 cents.

Unit Cost Analysis

An important measure of management efficiency is the cost to manufacture each unit. It is in the interest of management to keep the unit cost of the product as low as possible. Any increase in unit cost results in either a decrease in gross margin or an increase in the selling price. Assume that the Carol Manufacturing Company manufactures a single product and that it manufactured 20,000 units in 1973. The unit cost is computed as shown in Figure 20-11.

Figure 20-11. Unit Cost Computation

$$\frac{\text{Cost of goods manufactured}}{\text{Number of units manufactured}} = \frac{\$229,845}{20,000} = \$11.49 \text{ (cost per unit)}$$

MEASURING AND RECORDING INVENTORIES

To determine operating results in manufacturing accounting, it is necessary to take physical inventories of materials, work in process, and finished goods. The valuation of the work-in-process and finished goods inventories is difficult to accomplish because the cost of the components that are incorporated in these inventories cannot be easily associated with the physical articles. The next two chapters deal with the more elaborate methods used in cost accounting, which enable management to trace the flow of unexpired costs directly to the products.

If the Carol Manufacturing Company produced only a single product and manufactured 20,000 units (see Figure 20-11), management could cost each inventory unit at $11.49. However, if the Company produced several different products, it would have to install a device for costing the ending work-in-process and finished goods inventories. The cost of materials per unit of the product can usually be measured accurately by reference to materials requisitions.[1] Direct labor cost per unit can also be determined satisfactorily by observation coupled with the keeping of time and cost records. The unit cost of factory overhead is difficult to determine directly. It is necessary to determine a causal relationship between factory overhead cost and some common measure to the commodities produced. Direct labor cost is usually a fair indicator because the passage of time is an element in both direct labor and factory overhead costs. More direct labor time implies more use of factory facilities, which results in more factory overhead cost for that product. This relationship of factory overhead and direct labor cost—called the *overhead rate*—for the Carol Manufacturing Company (see Figure 20-6) is as shown.

$$\frac{\text{Total manufacturing overhead}}{\text{Direct labor}} = \frac{\$50,740}{\$102,030} = 49.7\%$$

For each dollar of direct labor cost incurred on a given product, 49.7 cents worth of manufacturing overhead will be allocated to it. For example, the per unit cost of the ending inventories of finished goods and work in process of Products A and B were computed as shown on page 696.

---

[1] A materials requisition is a written request for materials from the storeroom.

Finished Goods Inventory	Product A	Product B
Materials (from requisitions)	$ 5.00	$ 4.00
Direct labor (from payroll records)	4.00	6.00
Manufacturing overhead ($4 × 0.497)	1.99	
($6 × 0.497)		2.98
Total inventory cost per unit	$10.99	$12.98

Work-in-Process Inventory	Product A	Product B
Materials (from requisitions)	$ 3.00	$ 2.00
Direct labor (from payroll records)	2.30	1.20
Manufacturing overhead ($2.30 × 0.497)	1.14	
($1.20 × 0.497)		.60
Total inventory cost per unit	$ 6.44	$ 3.80

SUMMARY

The accounting system for a manufacturing firm is an elaboration of the system employed in trading concerns. Since a manufacturing firm purchases materials and converts them into finished products, additional accounts must be employed for costing the conversion process. General accounting for a manufacturing firm utilizes the periodic inventory system; the cost accounting systems discussed in subsequent chapters use the perpetual inventory system.

Direct materials are all the materials of a significant nature that are incorporated in the finished product. Materials used represents the cost of the direct materials consumed during a given period of time. Direct labor is the cost of all the wages paid to employees performing operations directly on the product being manufactured. Manufacturing overhead is all the manufacturing costs other than direct materials and direct labor. Materials used, direct labor, and manufacturing overhead are product costs, since they reflect the cost of the finished product and become expenses only when the product is sold—that is, when they become a part of cost of goods sold. General and administrative expenses and selling expenses are period expenses because they are deducted from revenues in the period in which they are incurred.

A manufacturing concern has three inventory accounts: Materials, Work in Process, and Finished Goods. All are classified as current assets in the statement of financial position. The total period manufacturing costs are the costs of all materials and efforts expended in the manufacturing process during the period. The cost of goods manufactured is the cost of all goods that were completed during the period, regardless of the period in which the costs were incurred. The computation of the cost of goods manufactured is shown in the manufacturing schedule, which supplements the income statement. The only difference in the computation of the cost of goods sold for a manufacturing concern and for a trading concern is that the cost of goods manufactured is substituted for the net cost of purchases.

Manufacturing Summary is a temporary intermediary account into which all the account balances that enter into the determination of the cost of goods manufactured are closed at the end of an accounting period. The balance of Manufacturing Summary is then closed to Revenue and Expense Summary.

The only essential difference between the worksheet of a manufacturing concern and that of a nonmanufacturing concern is the addition of Manufacturing Debit and Credit columns, in which all the amounts for the determination of the cost of goods manufactured are entered. The balance of these columns is transferred to the Income Statement columns. Certain costs that are incurred partially in the manufacturing process and partially in the administrative or selling functions must be allocated in a reasonable manner between the Manufacturing and Income Statement columns of the worksheet.

Comparisons of the turnover of materials and the turnover of finished goods with the ratios of previous years and the equivalent ratios of similar firms yield valuable information to management concerning the propriety of the investment in inventories. The percentage relationships of materials used, direct labor, and manufacturing overhead to total period manufacturing costs may reveal useful information to management when compared with the relationships of previous years and of similar companies.

The valuation of the work-in-process and finished goods inventories is a difficult task when the periodic inventory system is employed. If more than one product is manufactured, an estimation of the materials, direct labor, and manufacturing overhead incorporated in the inventories must be made. These estimates, which are inherently inexact, may result in a material over or understatement of the inventories and thus a corresponding error in net income.

QUESTIONS

Q20-1. "The accounting principles and procedures are the same for both the manufacturing and the nonmanufacturing types of business," Justify this statement by showing that accounting in the two types of business is the same in regard to inventory items.

Q20-2. Explain each of the following terms: (a) materials used, (b) direct labor, and (c) manufacturing overhead.

Q20-3. What are the criteria for distinguishing between direct labor and indirect labor?

Q20-4. (a) How is the cost of a patent determined? (b) What part of the cost of the patent should be assigned to the current accounting period? (c) Discuss the nature of the Amortization of Patents account.

Q20-5. Describe the purpose and function of the Manufacturing columns in the worksheet. Where in the worksheet would the amounts normally contained in the Manufacturing columns be entered if the Manufacturing columns were eliminated?

Q20-6. The following accounts appear on the ledger of Haley Company, Inc.:

Manufacturing Summary		Revenue and Expense Summary	
96,000	23,200	72,800	14,200
	72,800	10,600	

Reconstruct in summary form the journal entries that resulted in these postings.

Q20-7. The books of the Sampson Corporation showed the following information:

Inventories	12/31/1973	12/31/1972
Finished goods	$16,000	$12,000
Work in process	11,500	7,000
Materials	10,600	12,700

Explain how each amount will be shown in (a) the worksheet, (b) the schedule of cost of goods manufactured, (c) the income statement, and (d) the statement of financial position.

Q20-8. When a given cost is applicable partly to manufacturing and partly to the administrative or selling function, how is the amount allocated in the worksheet? Discuss a possible alternative method.

Q20-9. State the formula and purpose of (a) the turnover of materials and (b) the turnover of finished goods.

Q20-10. Identify some of the problems involved in the measurement of the periodic inventories of work in process and finished goods.

EXERCISES

E20-1. The following data are taken from the books of the Godwin Company for the year 1973:

Materials purchases	$100,000
Direct labor	200,000
Manufacturing overhead	200,000
Materials inventory change (amount of increase of ending inventory over beginning inventory)	30,000
Work-in-process inventory (net change—decrease)	20,000
Finished goods inventory (net change—increase)	10,000

Determine (a) the cost of goods manufactured and (b) the cost of goods sold.

E20-2. Compute the missing amounts in the following tabulation:

	Beginning Inventory of Materials	Materials Purchases	Transpor-tation In on Materials	Materials Purchases Returns And Allow-ances	Materials Purchases Discounts	Net Cost of Materials Purchases	Cost of Materials Available for Use	Ending Inventory of Materials	Cost of Materials Used
1.	$1,500	$8,600	$?	$300	$150	$9,500	$?	$?	$8,500
2.	?	2,500	300	200	?	2,500	5,500	?	3,600
3.	3,500	?	700	200	400	?	19,900	5,000	?

E20-3. Compute the missing amounts in the following tabulation:

	Net Sales	Beginning Inventory of Finished Goods	Cost of Goods Manufactured	Cost of Finished Goods Available for Sale	Ending Inventory of Finished Goods	Cost of Goods Sold	Gross Margin on Sales
1.	$41,000	$?	$30,000	$40,000	$?	$25,500	$?
2.	?	25,000	?	?	10,000	81,000	20,000
3.	60,000	?	40,000	60,000	?	?	10,500

E20-4. Compute the missing amounts in the following tabulation:

	Cost of Materials Used	Direct Labor	Manufacturing Overhead	Total Period Cost of Manufacturing	Beginning Work-in-Process Inventory	Ending Work-in-Process Inventory	Cost of Goods Manufactured
1.	$ 10,500	$?	$ 12,000	$ 37,000	$ 5,000	$?	$ 35,000
2.	?	50,000	60,000	135,500	100,000	125,000	110,500
3.	250,500	400,000	300,000	?	100,000	150,000	?

E20-5. The Brunswick Corporation acquired certain patent rights for $90,000 and spent an additional $46,000 in further developing them.

1. Record the acquisition and development of the patents.
2. Record the patent amortization for one year, based on a full legal life.
3. Record the patent amortization, based on an assumed useful economic life of eight years.

E20-6. The following Small Tools account is from the books of the Windsor Corporation:

Small Tools

1973				
Jan.	1	Balance	10,400	
Aug.	3	Purchase	2,600	

The inventory of small tools on hand on December 31, 1973, was priced at $6,750, based on a physical count.

1. How is the cost of small tools used determined? What part of the Small Tools account is allocated to the current accounting period?
2. Prepare the entry to adjust the Small Tools account.

E20-7. The adjusted trial balance of the Holly Corporation included the following items:

Rent	$3,500
Heat, light, and power	2,100
Insurance	1,200
Taxes	1,000
Depreciation	2,000

The accountant for the Holly Corporation determined the following allocation percentages:

	Manufacturing	Selling	General
Rent	80%	15%	5%
Heat, light, and power	83	10	7
Insurance (plant and equipment)	60	20	20
Taxes	70	20	10
Depreciation	77	12	11

Enter the account balances in the Adjusted Trial Balance columns of a manufacturing worksheet and, using the allocation percentages given, extend the items to the appropriate columns of the worksheet.

E20-8. The following data are taken from the books of the Axiom Manufacturing Company:

	1973	1972
Materials used	$47,000	$45,000
Materials inventories		
Beginning of year	29,000	32,000
End of year	26,000	29,000

	1973	1972
Cost of goods sold	$117,000	$112,000
Finished goods inventories		
Beginning of year	13,750	14,500
End of year	11,500	13,750

1. Compute the turnover of materials and finished goods.
2. What were the average inventories in terms of days, on the basis of a 365-day year?

E20-9. The following data are revealed by the financial statements of the Raleigh Corporation:

Materials Inventory, December 31, 1972	$232,000
Materials Purchases, 1973	364,000
Materials Inventory, December 31, 1973	204,000
Direct Labor, 1973	400,000
Manufacturing Overhead, 1973	200,000
Work-in-Process Inventory, December 31, 1972	132,000
Work-in-Process Inventory, December 31, 1973	170,000
Finished Goods Inventory, December 31, 1972	92,000
Finished Goods Inventory, December 31, 1973	80,000

What significant relationships may be determined from these figures?

DEMONSTRATION PROBLEMS

DP20-1. (*Computation of materials used*) The following information is available from the records of the Rocky Mount Manufacturing Company:

Materials inventory, December 31, 1972	$ 12,750
Materials inventory, December 31, 1973	10,000
Materials purchases, 1973	200,000
Transportation in on materials purchases, 1973	4,000
Materials purchases returns and allowances, 1973	5,000
Materials purchases discounts, 1973	3,500

Required: In schedule form, compute the cost of materials used in 1973.

DP20-2. (*Computation of cost of goods sold*) The following information is available from the records of the Swanee Company:

Finished goods inventory, December 31, 1972	$ 25,000
Cost of goods manufactured in 1973	300,000
Finished goods inventory, December 31, 1973	30,000
Work-in-process inventory, December 31, 1972	10,500
Work-in-process inventory, December 31, 1973	12,650

Required: In schedule form, compute the cost of goods sold in 1973.

DP20-3. (*Journal entries; schedule of cost of goods manufactured; analysis*) The Greensboro Manufacturing Company uses a voucher register. During 1973, the firm completed certain transactions as follows:

1. Purchased materials on account for $154,000.
2. Paid transportation charges amounting to $5,100 on materials.
3. Received $8,000 credit for materials returned.
4. Issued checks for $133,000 in payment of vouchers for materials purchased for $135,000 (discounts taken were $2,000).
5. Paid direct labor wages of $80,000 (ignore payroll taxes).
6. Paid the following items: factory rent, $6,000; heat, light, and power, $7,000; indirect labor, $5,000; and miscellaneous factory costs, $1,500.

7. Made year-end adjusting entries to record expired factory insurance of $2,000; small tools costs of $2,000; and depreciation on machinery and equipment of $8,000.

Required:

1. Journalize the transactions and post to T accounts.
2. Prepare a schedule of cost of goods manufactured for the Greensboro Manufacturing Company. Inventories were as follows:

	Beginning	Ending
Materials	$11,000	$9,000
Work in process	3,000	4,000

3. Journalize the entries to close the nominal manufacturing accounts.
4. Compute the materials turnover in terms of (a) rate and (b) days.
5. Determine the percentage relationship of materials used, direct labor, and manufacturing overhead to total period manufacturing costs.

DP20-4. (*Worksheet, statements, and closing entries*) The condensed adjusted trial balance of the Anson Corporation on December 31, 1973, after adjustment, consisted of the following:

Cash	$20,000
Accounts Receivable	14,000
Finished Goods, December 31, 1972	12,000
Work in Process, December 31, 1972	8,000
Materials, December 31, 1972	10,000
Plant and Equipment	50,000
Accumulated Depreciation–Plant and Equipment	10,000
Vouchers Payable	24,000
Common Stock	50,000
Retained Earnings	18,000
Sales	84,000
Materials Purchases	30,000
Direct Labor	20,000
Manufacturing Overhead	16,000
Selling Expenses	4,000
General Expenses	2,000

Inventories on December 31, 1973, were:

Finished goods	$10,000
Work in process	12,000
Materials	14,000

Required: Prepare (a) a manufacturing worksheet, (b) a schedule of cost of goods manufactured, (c) an income statement, (d) a statement of financial position, and (e) the closing entries.

PROBLEMS

P20-1. The following information is available for the Franklin Corporation:

	12/31/1972	1973	12/13/1973
Inventories			
Materials	$12,000		$11,000
Work in Process	14,000		18,000
Finished Goods	22,000		21,500
Materials purchased during year		$37,000	
Direct labor		22,000	
Manufacturing overhead		17,000	

Required: Prepare a schedule of cost of goods manufactured for 1973.

P20-2. The Tyson Manufacturing Company's partial statement of financial position as of December 31, 1972, is given:

Materials Inventory		$ 6,300
Work-in-Process Inventory		8,200
Finished Goods Inventory		9,500
Prepaid Insurance		950
Patents		2,000
Machinery and Equipment	$25,000	
Deduct Accumulated Depreciation	3,000	22,000
Office Equipment	$10,000	
Deduct Accumulated Depreciation	1,000	9,000

Condensed transactions for 1973 are shown:

1. Sales on account for the year were $250,000.
2. Collections from customers were:

Accounts receivable	$210,000
Deduct discounts taken	2,400
Total	$207,600

3. Materials purchases on account were $78,300.
4. Freight and other transportation charges on materials purchases were $2,300.
5. Credit received for materials returned was $3,750.
6. Vouchers payable were paid as follows:

Vouchers payable	$60,000
Deduct discounts taken	1,500
Checks issued	$58,500

7. Direct labor vouchered and paid for the year was $62,000 (ignore payroll taxes).
8. Insurance vouchered and paid for the year was $4,500.
9. The following additional items were vouchered and paid for:

Rent	$ 5,200
Property taxes	1,100
Indirect labor (ignore payroll taxes)	9,300
Building maintenance and repairs	3,000
Miscellaneous factory overhead costs	1,500
Office salaries	10,400
Heat, light, and power	6,500
Salesmen's salaries (ignore payroll taxes)	13,800

Inventory and adjustment data are given:

a. Depreciation rates are: machinery and equipment, 5 percent; office equipment, 4 percent.
b. Amortization of patents is $500.
c. Prepaid insurance is $800.
d. Wages and salaries payable (not yet recognized) were

Direct labor	$ 850
Indirect labor	150
Salesmen's salaries	1,200
Office salaries	1,000

e. Ending Inventories include materials, $6,600; work in process, $7,500; and finished goods, $8,800.
f. Allocation data:

Item	Allocation		
	Manufacturing	Selling	General
Rent	80%	15%	5%
Property Taxes	85	10	5
Maintenance and Repairs	90	5	5
Heat, Light, and Power	70	10	20
Insurance	80	5	15

Required:

1. Enter the December 31, 1972, balances in T accounts.
2. Record the transactions for 1973, including the adjusting entries, in general journal form and post to the T accounts.
3. Prepare a schedule of cost of goods manufactured.
4. Prepare the closing entries to accumulate the cost of goods manufactured and to transfer the balance to the appropriate account.

P20-3. The Gray Manufacturing Company was created on January 1, 1973. Selected transactions that took place during the year are given below.

1. Received a charter authorizing the issuance of 30,000 shares of $75 par value common stock.
2. Issued 20,000 shares of common stock at $79 per share for cash.
3. Purchased machinery and equipment for $41,250 in cash (assume that this purchase was made on January 1, 1973).
4. Purchased materials on account for $260,000.
5. Paid $8,500 in transportation charges on materials.
6. Received $7,250 credit for materials returned.
7. Issued checks for $240,000 in payment of vouchers for $248,000 (discounts taken were $8,000).
8. Paid the following factory payrolls:

	Gross Wages	F.I.C.A. Taxes Withheld	Employees' Federal Income Taxes Withheld	Employees' State Income Taxes Withheld
Direct labor	$100,000	$5,000	$15,150	$3,100
Indirect labor	10,000	500	1,200	300

Record the employer's payroll taxes (use assumed rates: 5% for FICA taxes, 2.7% for state unemployment, and 0.4% for Federal unemployment taxes).

The gross wages were subject to all payroll taxes. Debit Payroll Taxes–Factory for the total and include this in manufacturing overhead.

9. Paid factory rent of $8,950 and miscellaneous factory costs of $12,000.
10. Made year-end adjustments to record expired factory insurance of $4,500 and depreciation of machinery and equipment, computed under the sum of the years-digits method, assuming a 10-year life and no salvage value.
11. The December 31, 1973, inventories were as follows: materials, $14,000; work in process, $4,500; and finished goods, $16,400.

Required: 1. Journalize the transactions, assuming general manufacturing operations and the use of periodic inventories.

2. Prepare the journal entries to record the three ending inventories.

P20-4. Following are the Manufacturing columns from the worksheet of the Baldwin Corporation for the year ended December 31, 1973:

	Manufacturing	
	Debits	Credits
Materials Inventory	$ 30,000	$ 29,000
Work-in-Process Inventory	20,000	25,000
Materials Purchases	70,000	
Direct Labor	35,000	
Indirect Labor	7,500	
Rent	3,200	
Heat, Light, and Power	2,400	
Depreciation–Plant and Equipment	3,000	
Miscellaneous Factory Costs	2,500	
	$173,600	$ 54,000
Cost of Goods Manufactured (40,000 units)		119,600
	$173,600	$173,600

Required:

1. Prepare a schedule of cost of goods manufactured for 1973.
2. Compute the significant ratios and percentages.
3. Journalize the closing entries pertaining to the manufacturing functions.

P20-5. The following accounts and amounts, arranged in alphabetical order, were taken from the completed worksheet of the Carolina Manufacturing Corporation:

Accounts Receivable	$ 28,500
Accumulated Depreciation–Machinery and Equipment	9,800
Advertising Expense	1,450
Allowance for Doubtful Accounts	600
Bad Debts Expense	550
Cash	2,550
Depreciation–Machinery and Equipment	1,100
Direct Labor	15,500
Factory Insurance	1,500
Factory Rent	3,000
Finished Goods Inventory, December 31, 1972	23,500
Finished Goods Inventory, December 31, 1973	21,200
Heat, Light, and Power–Factory	1,450
Indirect Labor	4,300
Machinery and Equipment	23,000
Materials Inventory, December 31, 1972	18,500
Materials Inventory, December 31, 1973	18,750
Miscellaneous Factory Costs	1,970
Prepaid Insurance	1,100
Purchases–Materials	46,150
Purchases Discounts–Materials	1,500
Purchases Returns and Allowances–Materials	1,200
Sales	148,500
Sales Discounts	2,100
Salesmen's Salaries Expense	13,500
Sales Returns and Allowances	1,400
Small Tools	6,200
Small Tools Used	650
Transportation In–Materials	750
Work-in-Process Inventory, December 31, 1972	15,000
Work-in-Process Inventory, December 31, 1973	12,000

Required:

1. Prepare the schedule of cost of goods manufactured for 1973.
2. Prepare a partial income statement through Gross Margin on Sales for 1973.
3. Prepare the Current Assets section of the statement of financial position.

P20-6. The adjusted trial balance of the Easley Company for the year ended December 31, 1973, is shown below.

EASLEY COMPANY
Adjusted Trial Balance
December 31, 1973

	Debits	Credits
Cash	$ 16,300	
Accounts Receivable	39,890	
Allowance for Doubtful Accounts		$ 1,200
Materials Inventory	29,600	
Work-in-Process Inventory	1,590	
Finished Goods Inventory	12,100	
Prepaid Insurance	425	
Machinery and Equipment	45,300	
Accumulated Depreciation—Machinery and Equipment		20,320
Office Equipment	8,010	
Accumulated Depreciation—Office Equipment		3,800
Accounts Payable		14,600
Income Taxes Payable		3,500
Accrued Wages and Salaries Payable		5,500
Capital Stock		60,000
Retained Earnings		35,100
Sales		220,000
Sales Returns and Allowances	2,700	
Sales Discounts	1,250	
Purchases—Materials	45,800	
Purchases Returns and Allowances—Materials		1,375
Purchases Discounts—Materials		1,500
Direct Labor	51,070	
Depreciation—Machinery and Equipment	5,200	
Indirect Labor	10,900	
Rent	7,200	
Heat, Light, and Power	4,600	
Insurance	1,750	
Advertising Expense	3,800	
Salesmen's Salaries Expense	51,300	
Executive Salaries Expense	22,700	
Bad Debts Expense	1,100	
Depreciation—Office Equipment	810	
Income Taxes Expense	3,500	
Totals	$366,895	$366,895

Additional data.

The December 31, 1973, inventories were

Materials	$12,525
Work in Process	1,125
Finished Goods	28,600

Allocation percentages are

Item	Manufacturing	Selling	General
Rent	80	10	10
Heat, light, and power	85	10	5
Insurance	70	20	10

Required:

1. Prepare a schedule of cost of goods manufactured for 1973.
2. Prepare an income statement.
3. Prepare a statement of financial position.

P20-7. The post-closing trial balance of the Ormon Manufacturing Company on December 31, 1972, is shown below.

ORMON MANUFACTURING COMPANY
Post-Closing Trial Balance
December 31, 1972

	Debits	Credits
Cash	$ 25,250	
Accounts Receivable	13,000	
Allowance for Doubtful Accounts		$ 650
Materials Inventory	18,000	
Work-in-Process Inventory	24,000	
Finished Goods Inventory	22,000	
Prepaid Insurance	1,200	
Supplies Inventory	425	
Patents	1,000	
Small Tools	675	
Machinery and Equipment	25,000	
Accumulated Depreciation		8,000
Vouchers Payable		28,000
Accrued Wages and Salaries Payable		6,000
Dividends Payable		20,000
Income Taxes Payable		13,500
Common Stock, $100 par value; issued 400 shares		40,000
Retained Earnings		14,400
Totals	$130,550	$130,550

Condensed transactions for 1973 were

1. The accrued wages and salaries payable as of December 31, 1972, consisted of (no entry is required; this detailed information is needed for a later entry)

Direct Labor	$2,000
Indirect Labor	1,500
Salesmen's Salaries	1,200
Executive Salaries	1,300

2. Sales on account for the year were $150,000.
3. Collections from customers were:

Accounts receivable	$130,000
Deduct discounts allowed	1,300
Amount collected	$128,700

4. Purchased materials on account for $36,000.
5. Dividends due stockholders were paid in the amount of $20,000.
6. Freight and other transportation charges on materials were vouchered and paid in the amount of $600.
7. Credit received for materials returned totaled $1,100.
8. Vouchers for materials were paid as follows:

Vouchers payable	$39,500
Deduct discounts taken	790
Amount paid	$38,710

9. Payrolls vouchered and paid during year were (ignore the payroll taxes):

Direct labor	$16,000
Indirect labor	7,300
Salesmen's salaries	9,500
Executive salaries	10,300

10. The following items were also vouchered and paid:

Small Tools	$ 300
Insurance (debit Prepaid Insurance)	1,200
Supplies	720
Rent	6,000
Repairs and Maintenance	2,500
Miscellaneous General Expenses	1,200
Miscellaneous Selling Expenses	420
Heat, Light, and Power	1,800

11. Dividends declared by the board of directors were $8,000.
12. Accounts receivable written off during year amounted to $900.
13. Merchandise returned by customers and credit granted totaled $2,300.
14. Vouchered and paid income taxes were $13,500.

Inventory and adjustment data are given:

1. Depreciation of machinery and equipment is 10 percent of original cost.
2. All patents had a legal and economic life of 10 years as of the beginning of the year.
3. Prepaid Insurance as of December 31, 1973, was $950.
4. Provision for doubtful accounts is estimated at ½ percent of net sales.
5. The small tools inventory as of December 31, 1973, was $810.
6. Supplies on hand as of December 31, 1973, amounted to $350.
7. Estimated income taxes were $26,500.
8. The December 31, 1973, inventories were

Materials	$19,000
Work in Process	21,000
Finished Goods	20,000

9. Allocation percentages are as follows:

Item	Manufacturing	Selling	General
Insurance	85	10	5
Supplies	80	10	10
Rent	80	15	5
Repairs and Maintenance	90	5	5
Heat, Light, and Power	80	15	5

Required:

1. Enter the December 31, 1972, post-closing trial balance amounts in appropriate ledger T accounts.
2. Record the condensed transactions for 1973 and post to T accounts (omit dates and posting references).
3. Prepare (a) a worksheet, (b) a schedule of cost of goods manufactured, (c) an income statement, (d) a statement of retained earnings, and (e) a statement of financial position.
4. Compute the turnover of materials.
5. Compute the turnover of finished goods.
6. Determine the percentage relationship of materials used, direct labor, and factory overhead to the total period costs of manufacturing.
7. Assume that the Ormon Manufacturing Company produced a single product. Determine the unit cost based on 50,000 units manufactured during the year.

P20-8. The following information is from the books of the Creswell Company:

	Inventories		
	June 30, 1972	June 30, 1973	Year Ended June 30, 1973
Materials	$20,000	$23,000	
Work in Process	29,800	28,700	
Finished Goods	73,500	70,900	
Materials Purchases			$275,500
Transportation In–Materials			13,700
Direct Labor			310,000
Manufacturing Overhead			263,000

Required: 1. Compute the total period cost of manufacturing.
2. Compute the cost of goods manufactured.
3. Compute the cost of goods sold.

P20-9. The following information is from the books of the Farmville Company as of December 31, 1973:

Cost of goods sold	$186,000
Total manufacturing overhead	36,000
Direct labor	72,000
Cost of goods manufactured	190,000
Materials inventory, 12/31/1972	17,000
Transportation in–materials	10,000
Work-in-process inventory, 12/31/1972	14,600
Materials used in production	90,000
Finished goods inventory, 12/31/1972	17,800
Materials purchases	84,000

Required: Compute the inventories of materials, work in process, and finished goods as of December 31, 1973.

P20-10. (*Accounting policy decision problem*) The Windfall Manufacturing Company produces a single commodity. A summary of its activities for 1973 follows.

	Units	Amount
Sales	60,000	$600,000
Materials inventory, 12/31/1972		32,000
Work-in-process inventory, 12/31/1972		40,000
Finished goods inventory, 12/31/1972	12,000	48,000
Materials inventory, 12/31/1973		24,000

	Units	Amount
Work-in-process inventory, 12/31/1973		$ 50,000
Finished goods inventory, 12/31/1973	16,000	?
Materials purchases		128,000
Direct labor		90,000
Manufacturing overhead costs		72,000

Required:

1. Prepare a schedule of cost of goods manufactured for 1973. Indicate on the schedule the number of units completed for the year and the cost per unit of finished goods.
2. Determine the gross margin on sales for the year, assuming that the transfer of the cost of finished goods to cost of goods sold is on the last-in, first-out basis. Show all your computations.
3. Discuss the accounting concepts underlying the selection of the LIFO basis vs. the FIFO basis. Which of these two methods should be chosen if sound accounting concepts are followed? Why?

P20-11. The accountant for the Rossell Manufacturing Company made several errors during 1973 and previous years, as indicated below.

1. Purchases of materials are not recorded until payment is made, although the company purports to be on the accrual basis. In January, 1973, $4,600 was paid for materials received in 1972. As of December 31, 1973, $2,750 worth of materials for which payment had not been made were on hand.
2. The December 31, 1972, inventory of materials was understated by $3,000.
3. Machinery used in manufacturing was purchased on January 1, 1972, at a cost of $5,500. This machinery was debited to Repairs and Maintenance and was reported as a part of the operating expenses for 1972. No depreciation has been taken on this machinery. Normally, the company depreciates factory machinery under the sum of the years'-digits method, using a 10-year life.

Required: Assuming that the all-inclusive income statement concept is followed and that the books have not been closed for 1973, prepare correcting and adjusting entries as of December 31, 1973.

21

Cost Accumulation and Control—Job Order and Process Cost Systems

Cost accounting, a tool of management, is concerned with three basic objectives: (1) unit cost determination, (2) cost control, and (3) cost analysis. The calculation of relevant unit product costs enables management to obtain better cost information; and this, in turn, enables management to determine more exactly the net income figure. In addition, this information helps management in making many decisions, particularly those involved in the determination of profitable selling prices and the development of means of reducing costs. The control of costs is achieved by the establishment and use of a system of perpetual inventory accounts, budgets, and other predetermined cost information. For example, when subsidiary perpetual inventory records related to the general ledger accounts are maintained, control is more constant and systematic, and inventory valuations are more accurate. Cost information is available at any time for managerial analysis, thereby permitting the observation and control of cost trends and cost movements.

COST ACCOUNTING SYSTEMS

The flow of the product and its related costs through the factory can be determined by a *job order cost system* or a *process cost system*. The job order cost system is used when each unit maintains its identity and costs can be specifically associated with the physical units in the job order, as in job printing. A process cost system is used for manufacturing processes in which one unit cannot be distinguished from another unit and production is largely continuous, as in the petroleum industry. Costs for the total output of a productive operation are determined over a period of time, and the unit cost is determined by dividing the total cost by the number of units produced.

A cost system under the job order or process approach may be either *historical* or *standard*. In a historical cost system, the actual costs of materials requisitioned and labor expended are recorded when they are used on the job. Manufacturing overhead is usually allocated on the basis of a predetermined overhead rate.

On the other hand, when a standard cost system is employed, predetermined costs are incorporated in the inventory accounts. Each product has an established standard cost for materials, labor, and overhead. The flow of costs through the production process is measured at both standard cost and actual cost and all variations are recorded in *variance accounts*. By constantly analyzing the variance accounts, management can quickly determine the reasons for variances and initiate proper remedial action. Standard costs are discussed in more detail in Chapter 22. The remainder of this chapter is concerned with the examination of historical cost systems.

GENERAL ACCOUNTING COMPARED WITH COST ACCUMULATION FOR A MANUFACTURING COMPANY

A manufacturing company may accumulate costs under a general accounting system as described in the preceding chapter, or it may accumulate costs under a cost accounting system. The difference between the two systems is the method of cost determination and control. In a general accounting system for a manufacturing firm, the cost of goods manufactured in any particular period is determined by assembling appropriate account balances in a schedule of cost of goods manufactured. The shortcoming of this procedure is that the cost of each product, process, job, unit, or department is not known. Furthermore, the use of a periodic inventory does not provide as satisfactory a means of controlling the cost of materials used in manufacturing as does the perpetual inventory approach.

A sound cost accounting system, therefore, involves the use of the perpetual inventory plan, which provides for (1) a system of inventory control through controlling accounts and (2) a flow of costs through ledger accounts for Materials Inventory, Factory Payroll, and Manufacturing Overhead, culminating in cost accumulations for work in process, finished goods, and cost of goods sold. In this flow and accumulation, it is necessary to reiterate between the distinguishment of *product costs* and expenses. Product costs are initially assets; they have been reclassified in form but maintain their basic identity. These asset costs become expenses when they expire and are released from the company, becoming deductions from revenue. In a trading business, sales salaries and all selling and general and adminstrative expenses are expired costs and are expenses of the period in which they are incurred. Factory wages and all other costs of manufacturing, on the other hand, are initially unexpired product costs (assets, not expenses) in the form of the finished product. When the finished product is sold, it becomes an expired cost, or an expense—cost of goods sold.

There are three stages in the flow of costs: (1) *recognition* (asset); (2) *transference*, or internal reclassification (asset)—transference of materials, direct labor, and manufacturing overhead through work in process into finished goods; and (3) *expiration*, or conversion of asset into expense—finished goods are sold and thus become expired costs or expenses, that is, the cost of goods sold.

THE JOB ORDER COST SYSTEM

Figure 21-1 shows the flow of job order costs through the general ledger accounts. The debits and credits represent current transactions; balances represent ending inventories.

The debits to Materials Inventory, Factory Payroll, and Manufacturing Overhead in Figure 21-1 reflect the recognition of assets. Transference, or the internal regrouping of assets, is reflected by the three debits to Work-in-Process Inventory with offsetting credits to Materials Inventory, Factory Payroll, and Manufacturing Overhead; the debit to Finished Goods Inventory and the credit to Work-in-Process Inventory are for the cost of work completed. Expiration is reflected by the debit to a *Cost of Goods Sold* account, set up to accumulate expired manufacturing costs, and the credit to Finished Goods Inventory for the cost of work completed and sold. The debit to Revenue and Expense Summary and the credit to Cost of Goods Sold for the expired cost of finished goods sold during the period is a closing entry and reflects the deduction of expired costs—expenses—from realized revenues for the period.

Figure 21-1. Flow Chart for Job Order Cost System

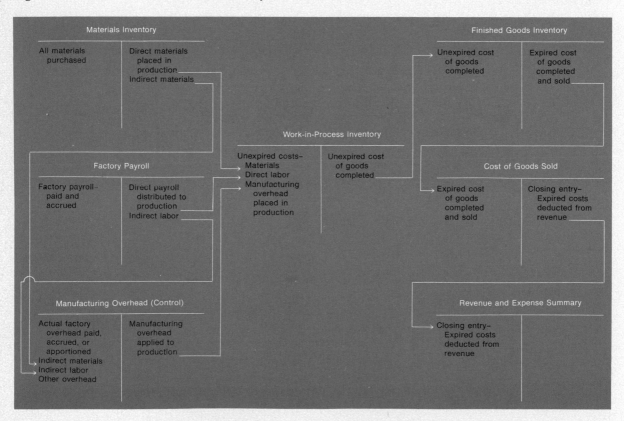

The flow of costs illustrated in Figure 21-1 can be summarized in journal form, as follows:

Materials Inventory	xx	
Vouchers Payable (or Accounts Payable)		xx
To record purchase of materials and supplies to be used in the manufacturing process.		
Work-in-Process Inventory	xx	
Manufacturing Overhead	xx	
Materials		xx
To record the issuance of direct and indirect materials to production.		
Factory Payroll	xx	
Cash or Accrued Factory Wages Payable (and payroll tax liabilities)		xx
To record the factory payroll for the period.		
Work-in-Process Inventory	xx	
Manufacturing Overhead	xx	
Factory Payroll		xx
To record the distribution of all factory wages—direct wages to production and indirect wages to Manufacturing Overhead.		
Manufacturing Overhead	xx	
Various Accounts (Cash, Accumulated Depreciation, and so on)		xx
To record actual factory overhead paid, accrued, or apportioned.		
Work-in-Process Inventory	xx	
Manufacturing Overhead		xx
To record the overhead applied to production by the use of a predetermined rate.		
Finished Goods Inventory	xx	
Work-in-Process Inventory		xx
To record the cost of goods completed in the current period.		
Cost of Goods Sold	xx	
Finished Goods Inventory		xx
To record the expired cost of goods sold during the period.		
Revenue and Expense Summary	xx	
Cost of Goods Sold		xx
To close the Cost of Goods Sold account at the end of the period.		

Cost Control Accounts

Cost control accounts are controlling accounts used with a cost system. The function of the cost control accounts is the same as that of the controlling accounts in a general accounting system—Accounts Receivable and Accounts Payable, for example. Some commonly used cost control accounts and the related subsidiary ledgers or records are

Cost Control Accounts	Subsidiary Ledgers or Records
Work-in-Process Inventory	Job order cost sheets
Finished Goods Inventory	Finished goods ledger cards
Materials Inventory	Material ledger cards
Factory Payroll	Individual employee payroll records
Manufacturing Overhead	Manufacturing overhead ledger cost accounts

Many forms and documents are used in conjunction with the flow and accumulation of costs. These are omitted here, except for the basic *job order cost sheet* (Figure 21-2), because they are usually tailored to meet specific needs and, therefore, vary widely in scope and content.

Work in Process. The Work-in-Process Inventory account and its subsidiary job order cost sheets accumulate production cost data for single items or a group of items. A job order cost sheet is kept for each job in process. During the accounting period, the costs of material, labor, and manufacturing overhead are entered on a cost sheet for each job in production. Work-in-Process Inventory is a summary controlling account, the details of which are shown on the job order cost sheets. A job order cost sheet for the Wilson Company is shown in Figure 21-2 (the amounts are assumed). The amount of manufacturing overhead costs applied is explained later in this chapter.

The summary entry to record the data that are entered on the cost sheet in Figure 21-2 is

Work-in-Process Inventory	753.00	
Materials		425.50
Factory Payroll		227.50
Manufacturing Overhead		100.00

The balance of the Work-in-Process Inventory account should correspond to the total charges for materials, labor, and overhead entered on the job order cost sheets for all jobs started but not yet completed.

The job order cost sheet provides management with each element of the cost per unit. Once the variances between actual and budgeted costs and their causes are known, required remedial action may be initiated. In addition, the job order cost sheets may serve as guides for future budgeting and pricing policies.

Finished Goods. The entry to record the transfer of work completed to the Finished Goods Inventory account is (two Type B Motors at $376.50 each).

Finished Goods Inventory	753	
Work-in-Process Inventory		753

A corresponding debit entry for $753 is made on the subsidiary *finished goods ledger card* for two Type B Motors. When finished goods are sold, entries are made to record (1) the selling price and (2) the cost of goods sold. The entries to record the sale by the Wilson Company of one Type B motor for $750 are as shown below.

Accounts Receivable	750.00	
Sales		750.00
Cost of Goods Sold	376.50	
Finished Goods Inventory		376.50

Corresponding entries would be made in the subsidiary finished goods ledger and the accounts receivable ledger.

The perpetual inventory records for finished goods are of value to management in furnishing current inventory data and in inventory control. The

Figure 21-2. Job Order Cost Sheet

Quantity and Description	2 Type B Motors				Job No.	53	
Date Started	1/2/1973				Date Completed	1/19/1973	
For	Stock						

Direct Materials			Direct Labor			
Date	Requisition Number	Amount	Date	Time Ticket Number	Hours	Amount
1973			1973			
1/2	475	125.00	1/2	892	8	40.00
1/5	481	75.50	1/4	901	8	34.00
1/19	490	225.00	1/10	909	6	25.50
			1/11	915	8	40.00
			1/12	917	6	24.00
			1/15	920	8	34.00
			1/19	925	6	30.00
	Total	425.50		Totals	50	227.50

Summary

	Amount	Per Unit
Materials	$425.50	$212.75
Labor	227.50	113.75
Overhead 50 hours at $2.00	100.00	50.00
Totals	$753.00	$376.00

availability of goods to fill telephone or across-the-counter orders, for example, may be determined without delay by reference to the perpetual inventory cards. The taking of a complete physical inventory at one time with its attendant interruption of normal operational activities is not necessary; the count of inventory items on hand may be compared with the finished goods ledger cards on a continuing basis.

Materials. Control of materials involves the recording, reconciling, efficient use, and verification of quantitative data; it is essential to effective management. The receipt of material is recorded from the approved vendor's invoice by a debit to Materials Inventory and a credit to Vouchers Payable or Accounts Payable; each different type of item purchased is entered on an individual *materials ledger card*, sometimes referred to as a *stores ledger card*. Transfer of materials from the storeroom is effected on receipt of an authorized materials requisition form, which shows quantity, stock and job numbers, unit price, and total price; a requisition for indirect materials refers to an identifying account in the manufacturing overhead ledger. Work-in-Process Inventory or Manufacturing Overhead is debited and Materials Inventory is credited for the transfers. On the subsidiary records, appropriate charges are made either to the job order cost sheet or to the manufacturing overhead ledger, with corresponding credits to the materials ledger cards. The pricing procedure used may be FIFO, moving average, or any other acceptable

Accounting Concept: ▼
Consistency

method. ▼ The selected pricing method must be used consistently. ▼ The reconciliation of material control is effected when the balances of the individual materials ledger cards agree in total with the balance of the Materials Inventory controlling account.

Under the perpetual inventory system for the control of materials, quantities of stock on hand may be determined readily from the records at any time; this eliminates the need for a complete physical inventory at the end of each accounting period. Verification by physical count of goods on hand and comparison with materials ledger cards can be a continuing process resulting in a minimum of interruption to plant operation.

Factory Payroll. *Time cards,* or *time tickets,* showing daily hours worked by employees are sorted by type of labor—direct and indirect. If an employee changes jobs during the day, a new time card is prepared. Time cards serve as the basis for the distribution of employee wages either to job order cost sheets (direct labor) or to manufacturing overhead accounts (indirect labor, such as supervision, factory clerical, idle time, or overtime). At the end of each pay period, a summary entry of the total labor costs incurred is made, usually from the factory payroll register, debiting Factory Payroll and crediting Accrued Factory Wages Payable. Payroll details are entered regularly on individual employees' earnings record cards from the factory payroll register. The total debits to the Factory Payroll controlling account should agree with the total earnings on the individual employees' earnings record cards. A summary entry is also made at the end of the accounting period, debiting Work-in-Process Inventory for direct labor and Manufacturing Overhead for indirect labor and crediting Factory Payroll, to distribute the total factory payroll costs. The Factory Payroll account thus serves as a clearing account—all the charges to it are redistributed to other accounts.

Manufacturing Overhead. Manufacturing overhead includes all costs incurred in the manufacturing process other than the costs of materials and labor charged directly to job order cost sheets. Generally, all actual manufacturing overhead costs incurred are first debited to the Manufacturing Overhead controlling account. Individual overhead items—factory supplies used, indirect labor, depreciation of factory machinery, and others—are also debited to the various accounts in the subsidiary manufacturing overhead ledger.

The specific identification of the direct material and labor costs incurred on a given job order can be determined readily. Manufacturing overhead, however, cannot be economically identified with a specific job order. Some manufacturing overhead items—depreciation, insurance, rent, and property taxes, for example— are related to the passage of time and are not affected by production volume, whereas other manufacturing overhead costs—power, cutting oil, and small tools, for example—vary with the volume of production. If completed product costs are to be currently available to management, it becomes necessary to apply manufacturing overhead to job order cost sheets on a predetermined, or estimated, basis.

The calculation of a predetermined overhead rate is based on (1) expected manufacturing overhead based on budgeted production and (2) an estimated cost factor related to expected future production. A cause and effect relationship should exist between the cost factor selected and the manufacturing overhead cost. To illustrate, assume that the Wilson Company estimates manufacturing overhead costs at $800,000 and expects a production level of 400,000 direct labor hours during 1973. In this plant, there is a close relationship between direct labor hours and manufacturing overhead. The predetermined overhead rate for 1973 is calculated as follows:

$$\frac{\text{Estimated manufacturing overhead}}{\text{Estimated direct labor hours}} = \frac{\$800,000}{400,000} = \$2 \text{ per direct labor hour}$$

If a given job requires 50 labor hours (see Figure 21-2), a charge of $100 (50 hours × $2) would be recorded on that job order cost sheet for overhead. The entry would be

Work-in-Process Inventory	100	
Manufacturing Overhead		100

If actual direct labor hours during 1973 are 400,000, as estimated, the Wilson Company will have charged $800,000 (400,000 hours × $2) in manufacturing overhead costs to the various job order cost sheets. If, as is likely, a variance exists between the actual and the estimated amounts, there will be a balance in the Manufacturing Overhead account; a debit balance indicates overhead underapplied (overhead applied is less than actual overhead) and a credit balance indicates overhead overapplied (overhead applied is more than actual overhead). Although the under- or overapplied manufacturing overhead affects work in process, finished goods, and cost of goods sold, it may, in practice, be treated as an adjustment to the largest of these items, the cost of goods sold; it is, therefore, closed into that account. The amount of over- or underapplied overhead should be relatively small at all times. Variances arise through variations in actual volume of production from budgeted volume, variations in actual price levels from budgeted, and errors or waste. Persistent variations may necessitate a revision of the predetermined rate. This, in turn, may involve adjustments of the sales price of the product, revisions of purchase commitments (for overhead services and supplies), and so on. Careful investigation should be made to trace specific causes so that proper remedial steps may be taken.

Other bases for applying manufacturing overhead are (1) material cost, (2) machine hours, (3) direct labor dollars, and (4) units of production. The computation of a predetermined overhead rate using any of these bases is the same as for direct labor hours. Assume that the Wilson Company selects the material cost basis and estimates the direct material cost to be $3,200,00 for budgeted production in 1973. The computation of the predetermined overhead rate based on material cost is as follows:

$$\frac{\text{Estimated manufacturing overhead}}{\text{Estimated material cost}} = \frac{\$800,000}{\$3,200,000} = 25\% \text{ of material cost}$$

The overhead to be applied to Job Order 53 (Figure 21-2) would be $106.38 (direct material cost of $425.50 × 0.25 predetermined overhead rate).

Selecting the Basis of Allocation. An important management decision is the selection of the proper basis for allocating overhead. The basis that should be selected is one that charges the job with an amount of manufacturing overhead most nearly corresponding to the actual manufacturing overhead costs incurred on the job. Each available basis—with due consideration for economy and practicability in application—has particular merits under particular circumstances. A detailed analysis should be made of all cost and production factors involved prior to the selection of a base, and should be continuously reconsidered. The direct labor hours method, for example, is used widely because it recognizes the causal relationship of time and overhead cost; an increase in direct labor hours on a job will result in a corresponding increase in the factory overhead charged to that job. Some may object to its use because of certain added clerical costs in recording and reconciling hours of direct labor by jobs.

The direct labor dollars method is economical to administer. Direct labor costs are readily available from the payroll records. Reference to direct labor hours may, therefore, be omitted from the job order cost sheets for clerical simplicity. The method may, however, result in an inequitable overhead charge when there are differentials in wage rates for employees performing the same type of operation with the same degree of skill. Assume, for example, that a factory with a predetermined overhead rate of 50 percent of labor costs has the following identical jobs in process concurrently:

Job No.	Materials	Labor	Overhead	Total Cost
110	$50	$30 (10 hours × $3)	$15 ($30 × 0.50)	$ 95
111	50	40 (10 hours × $4)	20 ($40 × 0.50)	110

Assume that the production process primarily uses automatic machines, with the cost of depreciation on machinery and equipment representing approximately 80 percent of the total overhead cost. Overhead is most equitably charged to production in this instance by using a machine hours basis. Additional clerical costs are incurred, however, in recording machine hours and allocating them to jobs.

A satisfactory predetermined rate should accomplish two objectives in distributing overhead to job order cost sheets: (1) accuracy, resulting in a minimization of over- or underapplied manufacturing overhead; (2) equitability, resulting in a charge to each job of a logically defensible share of overhead. If these objectives are met, the overhead applied to each job will correspond closely to the actual overhead costs incurred on those jobs.

Departmentalization of Manufacturing Overhead. Up to this point, a single predetermined overhead rate, or *blanket rate*, has been used to distribute factory overhead costs to jobs. If the operations are organized by departments, predetermined departmental overhead rates are desirable to achieve closer control of overhead costs and more accurate product and unit cost figures. Costs are accumulated for each department—both *service* and *producing*. Producing departments are the departments that are in actual contact with the job or product—milling, cutting, assembling, and others. A service, or *indirect*, department services the producing departments—power, maintenance, and storage, for example. Overhead rates are calculated only for the producing departments.

To establish predetermined overhead rates, each department head submits a budget of his anticipated direct overhead costs (costs incurred within the department) for the budget period. Estimated indirect overhead costs (costs incurred in more than one department) are then allocated to the producing and service departments. The allocation of indirect costs to all the departments and the reallocation of service department costs to the producing departments require the selection of appropriate bases for such allocations. The resulting estimated total is the budgeted departmental overhead. Total budgeted departmental overhead is then divided by the appropriate allocation base—the anticipated total direct labor dollars, probable total machine hours, and so on, to arrive at the predetermined rate to be used.

THE PROCESS COST SYSTEM

The process cost system is used by companies in which the manufacturing process is continuous and uniform—that is, where there is a continuous flow of units of a product through successive departments. Process costing is used by firms engaged in such diverse industries as pharmaceuticals, chemicals, petroleum, gas, electricity, plastics, and mining. Basic differences between job order costing and process costing are these: in job order costing, all costs are identified with specific jobs, and unit costs are computed when the job is completed; in process costing, there is a continuous flow of units of a product unrelated to specific jobs, and emphasis is placed on homogeneous output for a given period of time. Unit costs are computed for time intervals rather than for specific jobs. Material, labor, and manufacturing overhead costs are charged to the manufacturing department in which they are used, and at the end of a period—usually a month—the unit cost of the product in that department is determined by dividing the total manufacturing cost by the total number of units of the product processed through that department.

Flow of Costs in a Process Cost System

The distinction between direct and indirect materials and labor in a process cost system may be different from that in a job order cost system. In many cases, what was an indirect cost in a job order cost system may now be a direct cost because it can be specifically identified with a particular department; if it cannot, the cost becomes an element of manufacturing overhead.

In a number of cases, actual manufacturing overhead may be charged directly to the departments, thus eliminating the application of overhead by a predetermined rate; however, if certain manufacturing overhead costs, particularly those of a company that operates a seasonal business, cannot be assigned directly to departments, a predetermined rate may be used.

The flow of the three elements of cost through a hypothetical two-process pharmaceutical company that manufactures a single homogeneous product called Allegrow is illustrated in Figure 21-3. Certain basic materials used in the manufacture of this product are started first in the Cooking Department. After the drug

Figure 21-3. Flow Chart for Process Cost System

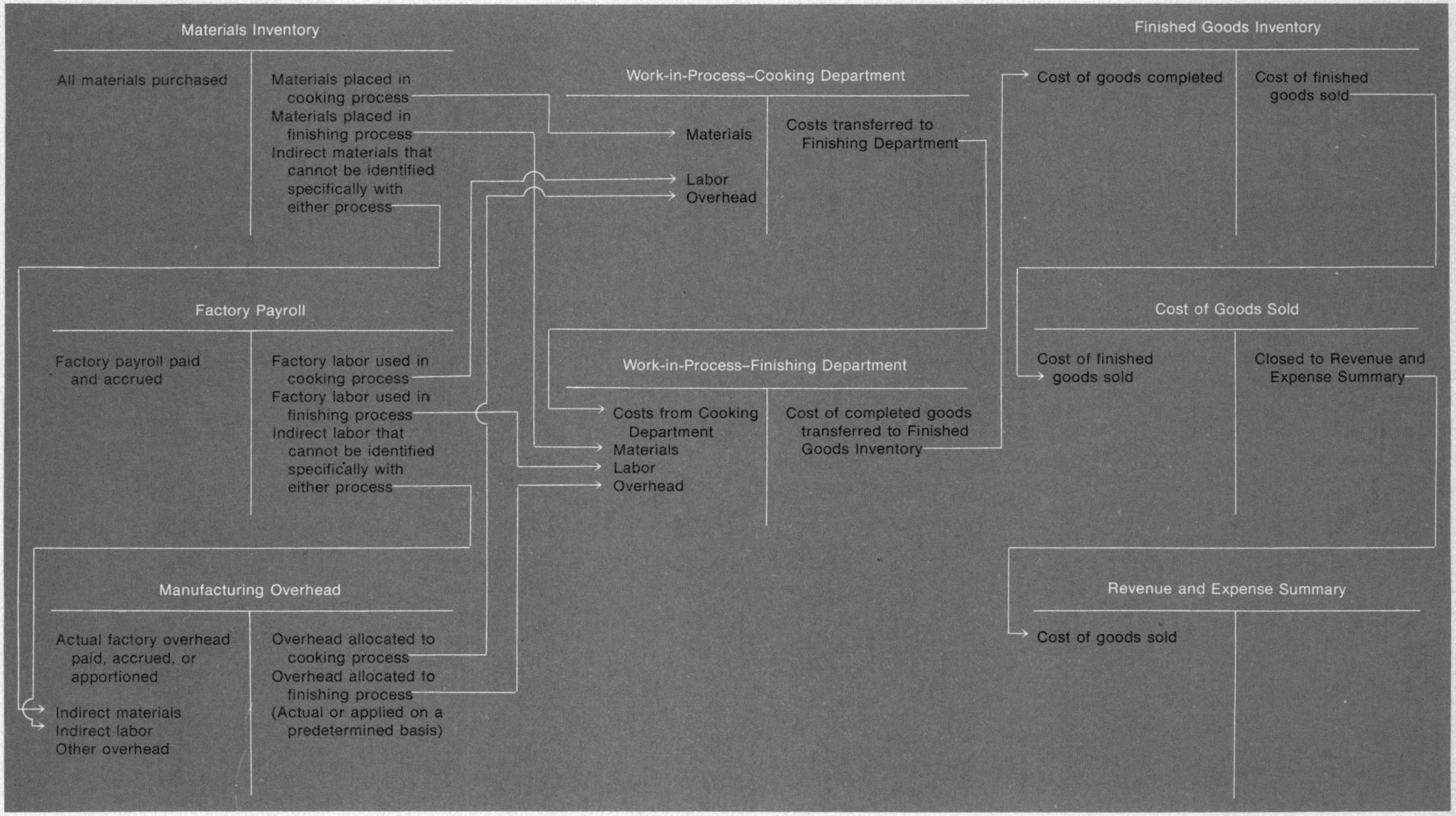

Materials Inventory

All materials purchased | Materials placed in cooking process
Materials placed in finishing process
Indirect materials that cannot be identified specifically with either process

Factory Payroll

Factory payroll paid and accrued | Factory labor used in cooking process
Factory labor used in finishing process
Indirect labor that cannot be identified specifically with either process

Manufacturing Overhead

Actual factory overhead paid, accrued, or apportioned
Indirect materials
Indirect labor
Other overhead | Overhead allocated to cooking process
Overhead allocated to finishing process
(Actual or applied on a predetermined basis)

Work-in-Process–Cooking Department

Materials
Labor
Overhead | Costs transferred to Finishing Department

Work-in-Process–Finishing Department

Costs from Cooking Department
Materials
Labor
Overhead | Cost of completed goods transferred to Finished Goods Inventory

Finished Goods Inventory

Cost of goods completed | Cost of finished goods sold

Cost of Goods Sold

Cost of finished goods sold | Closed to Revenue and Expense Summary

Revenue and Expense Summary

Cost of goods sold

is cooked for several hours, it is transferred to the Finishing Department, where additional materials are added and the product is finished and bottled in pint jars for sale.

The flow of costs illustrated in Figure 21-3 can be summarized in the following journal entries:

Work-in-Process—Cooking Department	xx	
Work-in-Process—Finishing Department	xx	
Manufacturing Overhead	xx	
Materials		xx
To record materials issued to processes and Manufacturing Overhead.		
Work-in-Process—Cooking Department	xx	
Work-in-Process—Finishing Department	xx	
Manufacturing Overhead	xx	
Factory Payroll		xx
To record the distribution of factory wages incurred during the period.		
Work-in-Process—Cooking Department	xx	
Work-in-Process—Finishing Department	xx	
Manufacturing Overhead		xx
To record the allocation of actual overhead to the producing departments.		
Work-in-Process—Finishing Department	xx	
Work-in-Process—Cooking Department		xx
To record the cost of Allegrow transferred to the Finishing Department from the Cooking Department.		
Finished Goods Inventory	xx	
Work-in-Process—Finishing Department		xx
To record the cost of Allegrow finished.		
Cost of Goods Sold	xx	
Finished Goods Inventory		xx
To record the cost of Allegrow sold.		
Revenue and Expense Summary	xx	
Cost of Goods Sold		xx
To close Cost of Goods Sold at the end of the period.		

Only the flow of costs involving the three major cost accounts is illustrated in the journal entries. The entries to record the debits to Materials, Factory Payroll, and Manufacturing Overhead are the same as those in the job order cost illustrations.

Process Cost Accounting Illustration—
The Atkins Chemical Company

The Atkins Chemical Company produces a single product, Bettergum, which is processed in two departments, Blending and Aging. On July 1, 1973, there is no beginning work-in-process inventory in the Blending Department. During July, 50,000 units of Bettergum are started in the Blending Department; of this amount, 40,000 units are finished and transferred to the Aging Department. As of July 31, 10,000 units are still in process—these are 100 percent complete as to materials and 50 percent complete as to labor and overhead. The July costs added in the Blending Department are

Materials	$10,000
Labor	13,500
Overhead	11,250

In the Aging Department, there is a beginning (July 1) work-in-process inventory of 4,000 units, 75 percent complete as to labor and overhead; no materials are added in the Aging Department. During July, 40,000 units are received from the Blending Department. Of the 44,000 units of Bettergum to be accounted for in the Aging Department, 38,000 units are finished and transferred to Finished Goods Inventory and on July 31, 6,000 units are in process, $33\frac{1}{3}$ percent complete as to labor and overhead. The work-in-process inventory and costs added in July in the Aging Department are

July 1 work-in-process inventory	$ 5,300
July costs	
Materials	–0–
Labor	14,800
Overhead	13,320

Generally, the detailed information regarding a process cost system is summarized on a *cost of production report*. The individual items that appear on this report are first discussed separately; then the entire cost of production report for July, 1973, is presented and summarized.

Quantity Schedule—Blending. A *quantity schedule* is prepared for each department, showing the number of units of the product processed during a given period of time. Such a schedule for the Blending Department is illustrated in Figure 21-4. The stage of completion for the July 31 work-in-process inventory is an average estimate; in other words, the Bettergum that has just entered the Blending Department has material added but no labor or overhead; the Bettergum that is almost ready to leave the department has almost all the labor and overhead absorbed; thus, the average work in process *in this case* has all the material cost and one half the labor and overhead cost.

Figure 21-4. Quantity Schedule, Blending Department

	Units
Quantity to be accounted for	
Units in process at beginning of period	–0–
Units started in process	50,000
Total	50,000
Quantity accounted for	
Transferred to Aging Department	40,000
Units still in process at end of period	10,000 (all material–½ L and O)
Total	50,000

Schedule of Equivalent Production—Blending. Equivalent production is the finished unit equivalent of the units completely and partially processed in a given period; in other words, it is the finished number of whole units that could have been completed if all the effort and costs for the period had been applied only to wholly finished units. The conversion of work-in-process units to equivalent whole units is necessary when computing unit costs because there may be a different number of units—called *equivalent production units*—for material, for labor, and for overhead. The schedule of equivalent production for the Blending Department is illustrated in Figure 21-5.

Figure 21-5. Schedule of Equivalent Production, Blending Department

	Materials	L and O
Beginning work-in-process inventory (to complete)	–0–	–0–
Units started and finished (this period)	40,000	40,000
Equivalent whole units contained in ending work-in-process inventory (stage of completion)	10,000 (10,000 × 100%)	5,000 (10,000 units × ½)
Equivalent production units	50,000	45,000

In the Blending Department, there is no beginning work-in-process inventory to complete; hence zeros are entered in the Materials column and in the L and O column (Figure 21-5). Units started and finished in this period (July) totaled 40,000 and are shown in both the Materials column and the L and O column. The ending work-in-process inventory consists of 10,000 units, its stage of completion is such that all the materials have been received (10,000 is entered in the Materials column), and one-half labor and overhead has been absorbed (5,000 is entered in the L and O column). This is based on the assumption that the costs expended in completing one half the work on 10,000 units are the same as the costs of completing 5,000 units.

Unit Cost Computation—Blending. Unit costs are computed for each element—materials, labor, and overhead. Each cost element in the Total Cost column is divided by the corresponding equivalent units produced to derive the unit costs indicated in Figure 21-6.

Figure 21-6. Unit Cost Computation, Blending Department

Element	Total Cost Amount	Equivalent Units	Unit Cost
Materials	$10,000	50,000	$0.20
Labor	13,500	45,000	0.30
Overhead	11,250	45,000	0.25
Totals	$34,750		$0.75

Accumulated Cost Distribution—Blending. The total accumulated cost distribution of the Blending Department ($34,750) is accounted for by the $30,000 (40,000 units × $0.75) transferred to the Aging Department and the $4,750 that appears in the ending work-in-process inventory; this is computed as follows:

Materials	10,000 units × $0.20	$2,000
Labor	10,000 units × ½ × $0.30	1,500
Overhead	10,000 units × ½ × $0.25	1,250
Work-in-Process Inventory–Blending Department (July 31, 1973)		$4,750

The same schedules and computations are now made for the second process in the Aging Department. Note that there is an added complication in this process, a beginning work-in-process inventory of 4,000 units.

Quantity Schedule—Aging. The quantity schedule for the Aging Department is shown in Figure 21-7.

Figure 21-7. Quantity Schedule, Aging Department

	Units*
Quantity to be accounted for	
Units in process at beginning of period	4,000 (¾ L and O)
Units received from Blending Department	40,000
Total	44,000
Quantity accounted for	
Transferred to Finished Goods Inventory	38,000
Units still in process at end of period	6,000 (⅓ L and O)
Total	44,000

*No materials are added in the Aging Department.

Schedule of Equivalent Production—Aging. The 4,000 units in the beginning work-in-process inventory were three fourths complete as to the elements of labor and overhead on July 1. Therefore, these 4,000 units receive one fourth of their labor and overhead during this cost period (July); each should be equated with one fourth of a unit of labor and of overhead. Consequently, 1,000 units (4,000 units × ¼) are entered in the L and O column, as shown in Figure 21-8. The number of units started and finished during this period is determined as follows:

$$\underset{38,000}{\underset{\text{finished goods inventory}}{\text{Units transferred to}}} - \underset{4,000}{\underset{\text{work-in-process inventory}}{\text{Units in beginning}}} = \underset{34,000}{\underset{\text{and finished}}{\text{Units started}}}$$

These 34,000 units are recorded in the L and O column. Each unit in the ending work-in-process inventory of 6,000 units received one third of its labor and overhead this month. The stage of completion of the ending work-in-process inventory, expressed in terms of whole units, is 2,000 (6,000 units × ⅓); this figure is recorded in the L and O column. The total of the L and O column (37,000 units) represents equivalent production units for the month of July.

Figure 21-8. Schedule of Equivalent Production, Aging Department

	Materials	L and O
Beginning work-in-process inventory (to complete)	–0–	1,000 (4,000 units × ¼)
Units started and finished	–0–	34,000
Equivalent whole units contained in ending work-in-process inventory (stage of completion)	–0–	2,000 (6,000 units × ⅓)
Equivalent production units	–0–	37,000

Unit Cost Computation—Aging. Since no materials are added in the Aging Department, the departmental unit cost is computed by dividing the cost of labor and overhead added in July by the equivalent production for July. This computation is shown in Figure 21-9.

Figure 21-9. Unit Cost Computation, Aging Department

	Total Cost		
Element	Amount	Equivalent Production	Unit Cost
Labor	$14,800	37,000	$0.40
Overhead	13,320	37,000	0.36
Totals	$28,120		$0.76

It should be noted, however, that the total unit cost of goods started, completed, and transferred to the finished goods inventory during July is $1.51 (the unit cost of $0.75 from the Blending Department plus the unit cost of $0.76 from the Aging Department).

Accumulated Cost Distribution—Aging. The total cost to be accounted for in the Aging Department is shown below:

Work-in-Process Inventory, July 1 (beginning)	$ 5,300
Cost from the preceding department, the Blending Department, transferred to the Aging Department during July: 40,000 units × unit cost of $0.75	30,000
Cost added to the foregoing units by the Aging Department during July (labor and overhead only)	28,120
Total cost for which an accounting must be made	$63,420

This cost is accounted for by the amount assigned to the 38,000 units finished and transferred to the storeroom and the amount assigned to the July 31 Work-in-Process Inventory. The beginning work-in-process inventory and the new July production (started and finished) are typically recorded separately and are costed on the first-in, first-out basis; that is, the beginning work-in-process inventory is assumed to be completed before the new production is completed and costed. The cost of the completed 4,000 units which were in the July 1 (beginning) work-in-process inventory, the cost of the new production of 34,000 units which were started and finished during July, and the cost of the 6,000 units in the July 31 (ending) work-in-process inventory are shown below:

Accumulated Cost Distribution			
The completed cost of the 4,000 units in the beginning work-in-process inventory:			
Cost of the July 1 Work-in-Process Inventory, from June		$5,300	
Added July cost to complete these 4,000 units:			
Labor added 4,000 × ¼ × $0.40	$400		
Overhead added 4,000 × ¼ × $0.36	360	760	
Total cost of the 4,000 units completed (unit cost, $1.515)			$ 6,060
The completed cost of the new production, the units started and finished during July:			
34,000 × $1.51			51,340
Total cost of the 38,000 units completed			$57,400
The cost of the Work-in-Process Inventory, July 31:			
Cost from the Blending Department 6,000 × $0.75		$4,500	
Labor added during July 6,000 × ⅓ × $0.40		800	
Overhead added during July 6,000 × ⅓ × $0.36		720	
The cost of the Work-in-Process Inventory, July 31			6,020
Total Accumulated Cost Distribution			$63,420

It should be observed that the total cost of the first 4,000 units finished and transferred to finished goods is $6,060, or $1.515 per unit, and that these units have a different cumulative unit cost from the cumulative unit cost of $1.51 for the new production which was started and finished during July. Thus there is a variation in the unit cost of the two groups of items. Also note that the total cost of the ending work-in-process inventory of $6,020 added to the total cost of the 38,000 units finished of $57,400 equals $63,420; which is the accumulated cost to be distributed and for which an accounting must be made.

Cost of Production Report

All the information described separately in the preceding paragraphs is combined in the cost of production report. This report for the Atkins Chemical Company is shown in Figure 21-10.

Flow of Process Costs—Summary Journal Entries

Summary entries to record the flow of costs for the Atkins Chemical Company are shown below.

(a)		
Work-in-Process Inventory–Blending Department	10,000	
Materials Inventory		10,000
(b)		
Work-in-Process Inventory–Blending Department	13,500	
Work-in-Process Inventory–Aging Department	14,800	
Factory Payroll		28,300

Figure 21-10. Cost of Production Report

ATKINS CHEMICAL COMPANY — COST OF PRODUCTION REPORT — FOR THE MONTH ENDED JULY 31, 1973

Accumulated costs

	Blending Department			Aging Department		
	Total Cost	Unit Cost	Comments and Computations	Total Cost	Unit Cost	Comments and Computations
Beginning work-in-process inventory	-0-			$ 5,300		(Given as June cost)
Costs from preceding department transferred in during period				$30,000	$ 0.75	($30,000 ÷ 40,000 units)
Costs added within department						
Materials	$10,000	$ 0.20	($10,000 ÷ 50,000 units)	$14,800	0.40	($14,800 ÷ 37,000 units)
Labor	13,500	0.30	($13,500 ÷ 45,000 units)	13,320	0.36	($13,320 ÷ 37,000 units)
Overhead	11,250	0.25	($11,250 ÷ 45,000 units)			
Total costs within department	$34,750	$ 0.75		$28,120	$ 0.76	
Total costs accumulated	$34,750	$ 0.75		$63,420	$ 1.51	

Accumulated costs distributed

	Blending Department			Aging Department		
	Total Cost	Unit Cost	Comments and Computations	Total Cost	Unit Cost	Comments and Computations
Transferred to next department or finished goods inventory	$30,000		(40,000 units × $0.75)			
From beginning work-in-process inventory						
Inventory value				$5,300		(Value brought down from preceding section)
Labor added				400		(4,000 units × ¼ × $0.40)
Overhead added				360		(4,000 units × ¼ × $0.36)
From current production, units started and finished				51,340		(34,000 units × $1.51)
Total	$30,000			$57,400		
Ending work-in-process inventory						
Costs from preceding department				$ 4,500		(6,000 units × $0.75)
Materials	$ 2,000		(10,000 units × $0.20)	800		(6,000 units × ⅓ × $0.40)
Labor	1,500		(10,000 units × ½ × $0.30)	720		(6,000 units × ⅓ × $0.36)
Overhead	1,250		(10,000 units × ½ × $0.25)			
Total	$ 4,750			$ 6,020		
Accumulated cost distribution	$34,750			$63,420		

Quantity Schedule

	Blending Department		Aging Department	
	Units		Units	
Quantity to be accounted for				
Units in process at beginning			4,000	(¾ L and O)
Units started in process or received from preceding department	50,000		40,000	
Total	50,000		44,000	
Quantity accounted for				
Transferred to next department or finished goods inventory	40,000		38,000	
Units still in process	10,000		6,000	(½ L and O)
Total	50,000		44,000	

Schedule of Equivalent Production

	Blending Department			Aging Department	
	Materials	L and O		L and O	
Beginning work in process inventory (to complete)	-0-	-0-		1,000	(4,000 units × ¼)
Started and finished (this period)	40,000	40,000		34,000	(38,000 units – 4,000 units)
Ending work in process inventory (stage of completion)	10,000	5,000	(10,000 units × ½)	2,000	(6,000 units × ⅓)
Equivalent production units	50,000	45,000		37,000	

(c)		
Work-in-Process Inventory–Blending Department	11,250	
Work-in-Process Inventory–Aging Department	13,320	
Manufacturing Overhead		24,570
(d)		
Work-in-Process Inventory–Aging Department	30,000	
Work-in-Process Inventory–Blending Department		30,000
(e)		
Finished Goods Inventory	57,400	
Work-in-Process Inventory–Aging Department		57,400
(f)		
Cost of Goods Sold	57,400	
Finished Goods Inventory		57,400

Work-in-Process Inventory–Aging Department has a debit balance on July 1 of $5,300, which is the value of the beginning work-in-process inventory. Entry (d) transfers costs from the Blending Department to the Aging Department. When the finished goods are sold, the costs are transferred to Cost of Goods Sold—entry (f)—and the customers are billed for the sales.

It should be noted that the accountant of the Atkins Chemical Company was able to assign all materials and labor costs to the applicable department; hence, none of these costs had to be considered as manufacturing overhead.

Managerial Uses of the Cost of Production Report

The cost of production report is a valuable aid in controlling costs; it may be used for comparisons with prior company costs, current industry costs, and predetermined estimates. The report can be expanded to include the description and total cost of each item of material, each labor operation, and each item of overhead, together with corresponding unit costs. A careful study and analysis of day-to-day variations in unit costs as shown on daily cost reports may reveal losses or inefficiencies that might otherwise continue for an indefinite period.

SUGGESTIONS FOR APPLICATIONS OF AUTOMATIC DATA-PROCESSING PROCEDURES

The cost accounting area affords an excellent opportunity to utilize the automatic data-processing procedures discussed in Chapter 6. For example:

1. In inventory control, punched cards could be used in the maintenance of the perpetual inventory of materials and finished goods.
2. Direct and indirect labor time cards could be prepunched with employee name, badge number, and job or department code and used to facilitate automatic data processing of the payroll and accumulating and distributing the costs to various functions.
3. In a similar manner, materials requisition cards could be prepunched with job or department code to facilitate the automatic data processing of materials costs.

SUMMARY

Although a manufacturing concern could use a general accounting system similar to the one discussed in the previous chapter, it should use a perpetual inventory system as a better means of controlling materials and of providing unit cost information of finished goods. A job order cost system is used if the units maintain their identity and the costs can be specifically associated with the physical units in the job order. A process cost system is used for manufacturing processes in which one unit cannot be distinguished from another unit and production is largely continuous. The three stages in the flow of manufacturing costs for either system are (1) recognition (asset); (2) transference, or internal reclassification (asset); and (3) expiration or conversion of assets into expense.

In a job order cost system, total production costs are debited to the Work-in-Process Inventory controlling account. In a subsidiary ledger consisting of separate job order cost sheets, the total cost of each job is accumulated. Thus, in the production process, entries must be made in both the control accounts and the subsidiary records. With the use of a perpetual inventory system, a materials ledger card is maintained, showing the quantity and cost of each item of material. When materials are purchased, Materials Inventory is debited for the total cost, and the quantity and price of each item are entered on the various materials ledger cards. As direct materials are withdrawn on the basis of materials requisitions, the costs are entered on job order cost sheets and credited to the materials ledger cards to reflect the transfer. The total cost of the materials withdrawn is credited to Materials Inventory and debited to Work-in-Process Inventory for direct materials and Manufacturing Overhead for indirect materials. During the period, the job order cost sheets (for direct labor) and Manufacturing Overhead (for indirect labor) are debited for an amount based on the time cards of all employees. At the end of each pay period, a summary of the total labor costs is made and debited to Factory Payroll. At the end of the accounting period, factory payroll costs are distributed by debiting Work-in-Process Inventory (for direct labor) or Manufacturing Overhead (for indirect labor) and crediting Factory Payroll. During the period, the total actual manufacturing overhead costs are debited to Manufacturing Overhead and the individual overhead costs are debited to the appropriate accounts in the Manufacturing Overhead subsidiary ledger. Since most items of manufacturing overhead cannot be identified specifically with a single job, it is necessary to apply overhead to the jobs on a predetermined basis if the costs of completed products are to be currently available to management. The calculation of a predetermined overhead rate is based on (1) expected manufacturing overhead cost based on budgeted production and (2) an estimated cost factor related to expected future production. The basis chosen for distributing overhead to jobs should be accurate, resulting in a minimization of over- or underapplied manufacturing overhead; and equitable, resulting in a charge to each job with a logically defensible share of overhead. As a practical expediency at the end of an accounting period, over- or underapplied overhead is closed to Cost of Goods Sold.

If business operations are organized by departments, more effective control over manufacturing overhead and more accurate product costs can be obtained if overhead costs are allocated on a departmental basis. Overhead costs are accumulated in service and producing departments, the service department overhead costs are allocated to the producing departments, and the overhead costs of the producing departments are applied to the products on a predetermined basis. As each job is completed, its cost is entered on a subsidiary finished goods ledger card, and the total cost of jobs completed is debited to Finished Goods Inventory and credited to Work-in-Process Inventory. When a completed unit of product is sold, an entry is made on the finished goods ledger card and the sale is recorded in the controlling accounts as it would be in a nonmanufacturing concern using the perpetual inventory system.

In process costing, costs are associated with departments or processes and not with specific jobs as in job order costing, and unit costs are computed for a specific period and not for a specific job. The unit cost of a product in a specific department is computed by dividing the total manufacturing costs incurred in that department by the total number of units of product processed through that department. Direct process costs are those that are economically traceable to the related department or process. All costs that are not direct process costs are included in factory overhead. In many instances, costs that are indirect in a job order cost system may be direct in a process cost system if they can be specifically identified with a department. The costs of all direct materials and direct labor are charged to the associated department's Work-in-Process Inventory account. Actual manufacturing overhead costs often can be allocated to departments on some reasonable basis.

At the end of a specified time period, the unit cost of each product in each department is computed for each cost component. If there is a beginning or ending work-in-process inventory in a department, the production of that department must first be converted to equivalent production, which is the number of whole units that could have been completed if all efforts and costs for the period had been applied to wholly finished units only. This must be done separately for each cost component since the work-in-process inventories may be in different stages of completion for each component. After completing the equivalent production, the unit cost of each component is computed by dividing the total cost of each component by the equivalent production for that component. The finished cost of items in the beginning work-in-process inventory is computed by adding the previous period's costs to the costs required to complete the goods in the current period. The cost of the items that were started and finished during the current period is computed by multiplying the units completed by the previously determined cost per unit. The cost of the ending inventory of each department is computed by (1) multiplying the unit cost of each component by the equivalent production of that component and (2) totaling the costs.

A cost of production report, which summarizes the detailed information in a process cost system, is a valuable aid in controlling costs. It serves as a basis for comparisons of actual costs with prior company costs, current industry costs, and predetermined estimates.

QUESTIONS

Q21-1. Name two types of cost systems. Which produces more meaningful information for management? Explain.

Q21-2. The three stages in the flow of costs are recognition, transference, and expiration. Explain these stages.

Q21-3. What is the difference between *product cost* and *expense?*

Q21-4. What subsidiary ledgers or records are controlled by each of the following general ledger accounts: (a) Work-in-Process Inventory; (b) Materials Inventory; (c) Factory Payroll; (d) Manufacturing Overhead; and (e) Finished Goods Inventory?

Q21-5. (a) What is the function of a job order cost sheet? (b) What documents may furnish direct material and direct labor costs for the job order cost sheet? (c) How is manufacturing overhead applied? (d) What controlling account in the general ledger controls the data on the job order cost sheets?

Q21-6. (a) Define the term *manufacturing overhead.* (b) What are the debit and credit functions of the Manufacturing Overhead controlling account? (c) Why is a predetermined overhead rate used in applying overhead to job order cost sheets? (d) Explain the causes and the significance of over- and underapplied overhead.

Q21-7. (a) How is a predetermined overhead rate computed? (b) What bases may be used in applying manufacturing overhead to job order cost sheets? (c) What are the objectives in distributing overhead to job order cost sheets?

Q21-8. (a) Distinguish between producing and service departments. (b) What are the advantages of departmental overhead rates?

Q21-9. (a) What types of industry are likely to use a process cost system? (b) What are the differences between a job order cost system and a process cost system? (c) Describe the accumulation of costs when a process cost system is used.

Q21-10. A given manufacturing cost may be indirect if a job order cost system is used, but may be direct if a process cost system is used. Explain and give two examples.

EXERCISES

E21-1. The following are among the transactions of the Rollie Manufacturing Company:

1. Issued $80,000 worth of materials for use on jobs and $4,000 for general factory use.
2. Distributed factory payroll, consisting of $100,000 of direct labor and $8,000 of indirect labor.
3. Applied manufacturing overhead at 60% of direct material cost.
4. Completed jobs that cost $96,000.

Prepare journal entries to record the transactions.

E21-2. The work-in-process inventory as of the end of a period is as follows:

Work-in-Process Inventory

Direct materials	40,000	Finished goods	116,000
Direct labor	56,000		
Manufacturing overhead	28,000		

There is one job in process at the end of the month. The direct materials charged to this job total $2,000.

Determine the amount charged to this job for direct labor and manufacturing overhead. Assume that manufacturing overhead is applied to production on the basis of direct labor cost.

E21-3. The following account is from the ledger of the Sanford Manufacturing Company:

Manufacturing Overhead (Control)

1973	Actual	204,670	1973	Applied	203,250

(a) Before this account is closed, three accounts are understated because of underapplied overhead. Name these three accounts. (b) Give the entry to close the account.

E21-4. Various cost data for the Jetson Company are given as follows:

Direct labor for 1973	$55,000
Direct material for 1973	20,000
Manufacturing overhead for 1973	55,550
Materials inventory, 12/31/73	12,000
Work-in-process inventory, 12/31/73	8,000
Finished goods inventory, 12/31/73	15,000

(a) Based on direct labor cost, what was the manufacturing overhead rate? (b) If the direct labor cost in the finished goods inventory was $6,000, what did the direct materials cost?

E21-5. The following information is taken from the records of a firm that produces one standardized product in a single process:

a. Beginning work-in-process inventory: 1,000 units, 75 percent complete as to materials and 40 percent complete as to direct labor and manufacturing overhead.
b. Finished and transferred to finished goods inventory: 30,000 units during the period.
c. Ending work-in-process inventory: 500 units, 60 percent complete as to materials and 20 percent complete as to direct labor and manufacturing overhead.

Compute the equivalent production for each element of cost for the period.

E21-6. The following information is taken from the books of the Profitt Company in May, 1973:

Schedule of Equivalent Production

	Materials	L and O
Equivalent production of Runtz	10,000	8,000

The beginning work-in-process inventory consisted of 1,000 units, 70 percent complete as to materials and 40 percent complete as to direct labor and overhead. The May, 1973, cost to manufacture was

Materials	$30,000
Direct Labor	24,000
Manufacturing Overhead	20,000
Total	$74,000

Cost of the beginning work-in-process inventory was $5,600. There were 5,000 units of Runtz started and finished during May.

Compute the total cost of only the 5,000 units that were started and finished during May, 1973.

E21-7. The Winterville Chemical Company manufactures its product in a single processing department. The costs of production for 1973 were

Materials	$200,000
Direct labor	141,000
Manufacturing overhead	117,500

During the year, 100,000 units were started in process, of which 92,000 units were transferred to the finished goods inventory. On December 31, 1973, 8,000 units were still in process, having received all materials and one quarter of labor and overhead. The finished goods inventory on December 31, 1972, consisted of 20,000 units costing $4.95 each. On December 31, 1973, there were 12,000 finished units on hand. There was no work-in-process inventory as of December 31, 1972. The finished goods inventory is costed on the first-in, first-out basis.

Calculate the cost of the December 31, 1973, inventories of finished goods and work in process.

E21-8. The Roundtree Manufacturing Company produces a single product requiring a single process. Following are data for the month of May, 1973:

a. Beginning work-in-process inventory: 12,000 units, 100 percent complete as to materials and 50 percent complete as to direct labor and manufacturing overhead; cost $18,000
b. Started in process: 48,000 units
c. Added within department during the period: materials, $144,000; direct labor, $48,000; overhead, $24,000
d. Completed: 54,000 units
e. Units in process on May 31, 6,000; all material; and one third completed as to labor and overhead.

Compute (a) the unit cost of material, direct labor, and overhead for May, 1973; (b) the total cost to be accounted for; (c) the cost of completed units; and (d) the cost of the ending work-in-process inventory.

DEMONSTRATION PROBLEMS

DP21-1. (*Job order cost system*) The Atlanta Manufacturing Company completed the following transactions during the month of April, 1973:

1. Purchased materials for $50,000.
2. Requisitioned materials for production as follows:

Job 1	$12,000
Job 2	8,000
Job 3	5,000
Job 4	3,000
Total	$28,000

3. Requisitioned materials for general factory use for $4,000 (charge Manufacturing Overhead).
4. Paid the factory payroll totaling $48,000 (ignore payroll taxes). The direct factory labor cost was distributed as follows:

	Hours	Amount
Job 1	5,000	$10,000
Job 2	3,000	6,000
Job 3	7,000	15,750
Job 4	6,000	13,500
Total		$45,250

Indirect labor used cost $2,750.
5. Incurred additional overhead costs of $42,750 (credit Vouchers Payable).
6. Applied manufacturing overhead to job order cost sheets at the rate of $1.75 per direct labor hour.
7. Completed Jobs 1, 2, and 3 and transferred them to finished goods.
8. Sold Jobs 1 and 2 on account for $90,000.
9. Transferred the balance of Manufacturing Overhead to Cost of Goods Sold.

Required: 1. Prepare journal entries to record the transactions.
2. Post to a Work-in-Process Inventory T account.
3. Post to a T account for each of the four jobs.
4. Verify the ending work-in-process inventory.

DP21-2. (*Process cost system with a single process*) The Griggs Manufacturing Company began operations on January 1, 1973. It plans to manufacture a single standardized product called Zex, which requires a single process.

During January it started and finished 8,000 units of Zex. There was no January 31 work-in-process inventory. The company's costs for January were

Materials	$ 52,000
Direct labor	68,000
Manufacturing overhead	81,600
Total	$201,600

During February, the company started and finished 9,000 units of Zex; it had 400 units in process as of February 28, 1973, in the following stage of completion:

Materials	75%
Direct labor and manufacturing overhead	50%

Costs for February were:

Materials	$ 57,660
Direct labor	75,440
Manufacturing overhead	90,528
Total	$223,628

During March, the company completed 10,000 units, including the beginning work-in-process inventory. It had 500 units in process as of March 31, in the following stage of completion:

Materials	100%
Direct labor and manufacturing overhead	60%

Costs for March were:

Materials	$ 61,200
Direct labor	80,800
Manufacturing overhead	96,960
Total	$238,960

Required: For each month, where applicable, (a) prepare a schedule of equivalent production; (b) compute the unit cost of materials, direct labor, and manufacturing overhead; (c) compute the total cost to be accounted for; (d) compute the cost of completed units; and (e) compute the cost of the ending work-in-process inventory.

DP21-3. (*Process cost system with two processes*) The Zoomby Company manufactures a product in two processes. In Process 1, all the material is added when the units of the product are started in process; in Process 2, materials are added as the last step in the processing. During July, 1973, the Company started 8,000 units in Process 1; 6,000 units were completed and sent to Process 2. The remaining 2,000 were one half complete in Process 1. There were 1,000 units three quarters complete in Process 2 at the beginning of the month; at the end of the month 1,800 were on hand, two thirds complete. The following costs were incurred:

	Process 1	Process 2
Beginning work-in-process inventory	$ –0–	$8,670
Materials	24,000	2,600
Labor	11,200	5,650
Manufacturing overhead	15,400	4,520

Required:

1. Calculate the equivalent units produced.

2. Calculate the unit cost of material, direct labor, and overhead for July.
3. Calculate the cost of the units completed and transferred.
4. Calculate the cost of the ending work-in-process inventory in each process.

PROBLEMS

P21-1. The following ledger accounts show certain cost flows for a period:

Materials Inventory

Inventory	36,000	Returned to vendors	1,800
Purchases	44,000	Direct	70,000
Returned from jobs	4,000	Indirect	2,000

Factory Payroll			Manufacturing Overhead		
60,000	Direct	54,000	Materials	2,000	
	Indirect	6,000	Labor	6,000	
			Other	29,100	

Finished Goods Inventory

145,620

Manufacturing overhead is applied to production on the basis of 70 percent of direct labor cost.

Required: Reconstruct the journal entries affecting the Work-in-Process Inventory account and post to a Work-in-Process Inventory T account.

P21-2. The following were among the transactions completed by the Potter Manufacturing Company during the month of December:

1. Purchased materials for $72,000.
2. Requisitioned materials for production as follows:

Job 80	$16,000
Job 81	14,000
Job 82	18,000
Job 83	10,000
Total	$58,000

3. Requisitioned materials for general factory use for $6,000 (charge Manufacturing Overhead).
4. Paid the factory payroll for December of $84,000 (ignore payroll taxes). Direct labor was distributed as follows:

Job 80	$20,000
Job 81	18,000
Job 82	23,000
Job 83	15,000
Total	$76,000

Indirect labor used cost $8,000.

5. Recorded additional actual overhead costs for December of $72,000 (credit Vouchers Payable).

6. Applies manufacturing overhead to job order cost sheets at the rate of 150% of direct material cost.

7. Completed Jobs 80, 81, and 83 and transferred them to finished goods inventory.

8. Sold Jobs 80 and 83 on account for $140,000.

9. Closed the balance of Manufacturing Overhead into Cost of Goods Sold.

Required:

1. Journalize the transactions.
2. Post to a Work-in-Process Inventory T account.
3. Post to T accounts for each of the jobs.
4. Verify the ending work-in-process inventory.

P21-3. The Dawson Manufacturing Company completed the following transactions during October:

1. Purchased materials on account for $104,000.
2. Requisitioned direct materials totaling $60,000 for job orders.
3. Used indirect materials worth $6,000.
4. Returned materials worth $2,000 to the vendor during October.
5. Returned materials to the storeroom: from job orders, $2,400; from indirect materials issued, $1,000.
6. Paid a total factory payroll for October of $130,000 (ignore payroll taxes).
7. Distributed the factory payroll as follows: direct labor, $128,400; indirect labor, $1,600.
8. Recorded additional actual overhead costs for October of $58,000.
9. Applied manufacturing overhead to production at 50% of direct labor cost.
10. Completed jobs during the month costing $230,000.
11. Sold finished goods on account as follows: selling price, $370,000; cost of finished goods sold, $222,000.
12. Allowed credit for finished goods returned by customers, $3,000. These finished goods cost $1,800.
13. Closed out the over- or underapplied manufacturing overhead to Cost of Goods Sold.

Required: Journalize the transactions.

P21-4. (*Managerial policy decision problem*) The Thompson Company uses a job order cost system for assigning manufacturing costs to its products. Management has decided to change from a system of allocating actual manufacturing overhead to jobs at the end of each month to a system of allocating overhead at a predetermined rate.

At the beginning of 1973, the following estimates of production costs for the year were made:

Direct materials	$ 750,000
Direct labor	900,000
Manufacturing overhead	1,350,000

There was no work-in-process on January 1, 1973. During the first three months of 1973, actual production costs were:

	January	February	March
Direct materials	$30,000	$44,250	$44,550
Direct labor	40,500	48,750	60,750
Manufacturing overhead	60,000	75,000	90,000

Required:

1. The company uses the direct labor dollar method to allocate manufacturing overhead to the various jobs. Based on the estimated production cost for 1973, what should the pre-

determined rate for allocating manufacturing overhead be? In light of the actual costs for the three months given, is this rate realistic? Support your answer by computations.

2. In summary form, record the materials requisitioned for the various jobs; the distribution of the direct labor payroll; and, using the rate derived in Requirement 1, the assignment of manufacturing overhead to the various jobs for the month of January.

3. All goods worked on during the three-month period were completed except for Job 1247, which had accumulated direct materials costing $1,200, and direct labor costing $900. All goods completed during the period were sold except for Job 1114, which had a total assigned cost of $3,000. Record, in general journal entry form, the completion of work during the period and the cost of goods sold during the period.

P21-5. (*Accounting policy decision problem*) The Dunstan Manufacturing Company prepared the following budgeted data for the year 1973:

Manufacturing overhead	$300,000
Direct material cost	$150,000
Machine hours	600,000
Direct labor hours	100,000
Direct labor cost	$300,000
Units of production	900,000

Required:

1. Calculate the predetermined overhead rate for the company for 1973 on each of the following bases: (a) direct material cost, (b) machine hours, (c) direct labor hours, (d) direct labor cost, and (e) units of production.

2. Data on Job 30, which was completed during 1973, are as follows: direct materials cost, $320; direct labor hours, 680; direct labor cost, $2,220; machine hours, 1,330; units, 2,000. (a) Compute the cost of Job 30, using each of the bases from Requirement 1. (b) Which method of applying overhead do you recommend? (c) Why?

P21-6. The Vinson Extract Company produces a product in a single process. Following are data for the month of May:

a. In process as of April 30: 2,000 units, 60 percent complete as to materials and 10 percent complete as to direct labor and manufacturing overhead

b. Started in process during May: 26,000 units

c. In process on May 31: 3,000 units, 75 percent complete as to materials and 20 percent complete as to direct labor and manufacturing overhead.

Required: Prepare a schedule in good form showing the equivalent units produced in May.

P21-7. The cost of production report for Department 2 of the Raymond Company for June is reproduced below in part (there was no beginning work-in-process inventory).

	Total Cost	Unit Cost
Production costs		
Costs from preceding department	$180,000	$1.80
Costs added during June within department		
Materials	$ 40,000	
Direct labor	55,200	
Manufacturing overhead	18,400	
Total costs added	$113,600	
Total costs	$293,600	

	Units
Quantity to be accounted for	
Units transferred from Department 1	100,000
Quantity accounted for	
Units completed and transferred to storeroom	88,000
Units unfinished at end of month	12,000
Total	100,000

The work in process in Department 2 at the end of June is complete as to materials and one third complete as to direct labor and manufacturing overhead.

Required:

1. Compute the equivalent units produced in June.
2. Compute the unit cost of production in Department 2 for materials, labor, and manufacturing overhead added in Department 2.
3. Compute the total cost and unit cost of goods transferred to finished goods inventory.
4. Compute the cost of the work-in-process inventory in Department 2 at the end of June. Show computations in good form.

P21-8. The Sutton Company started manufacturing a new product on November 1; it required processing in two departments, Baking and Drying. Total cost and unit data for the month were

	Department	
	Baking	Drying
Costs		
Materials	$ 92,160	$ –0–
Labor	50,032	84,185
Overhead	33,072	76,735
Totals	$175,264	$160,920
	Units	Units
Quantity to be accounted for		
Started in process	96,000	
Received from preceding department		82,000
Totals	96,000	82,000
Quantity accounted for		
Transferred to next department	82,000	72,000
Units in process (all materials added)		
$\frac{1}{5}$ complete as to labor and overhead	14,000	
$\frac{1}{4}$ complete as to labor and overhead		10,000
Totals	96,000	82,000

Required: Prepare a cost of production report for November.

P21-9. The Rumbly Chemical Company manufactures a product in two processes: preparation and blending. Materials are complete when a unit is started in the Preparation Department, but are added continuously in the Blending Department. During September, the company started 24,000 units in the Preparation Department; 4,000 of them were in the work-in-process inventory, one-quarter complete, at the end of the month. The others went to the Blending Department where there were 6,000 units, one-third complete, at the start of the month and 8,000 units, three-quarters complete, at the end. Costs were as follows:

| | Department | |
	Preparation	Blending
Work-in-process, August 31	$ -0-	$18,240
Direct materials	20,400	11,000
Direct labor	14,700	17,000
Manufacturing overhead	10,500	14,300

Required: Prepare a cost of production report for the two departments for the month of September.

22

Cost Accumulation and Control—Standard Costs; Direct Costing

A historical cost system furnishes information that often becomes available too late for many decisions. If data are to be received in time for most decisions, a system must be designed to yield predetermined or precomputed costs, the output of a *standard cost system*. This chapter deals with the rudiments of standard costs and the question of direct costing.

STANDARD COSTS

Standard costs are precomputed costs based on certain projected conditions and are used as a basis for comparison with actual costs, thereby serving as a criterion of the adequacy of a company's performance. Standard costs are similar to budgets in that both are predetermined. Both standard costs and budgets aim at the same objective—managerial control. Standard costs are the anticipated costs of a product; to be useful to management they must be computed with great care.

Each product has a *standard cost card* that shows what costs should be incurred under normal operating conditions. Actual costs of the product may also be recorded on the card. The basic objective is to compare each element of standard cost with each element of actual cost so that differences may be identified for study and remedial action.

The Principle of Management by Exception

Job order and process costing procedures, as described in the previous chapter, deal with actual historical costs except for the use of predetermined overhead rates. In many industries, the use of predetermined costs has been extended to all costs of manufacturing through the use of standard costs. The comparison of actual costs with standard costs or the analysis of actual cost variances from standard costs makes possible *management by exception*. It is the exceptions and their causes that must be determined and remedied. Costs can be controlled better when variances and their causes are known promptly. Standard costs may be used with either job order costing or process costing. They also may be used effectively for the control of selling and administrative costs of a company to measure the efficiency of those functions.

The use of overhead standards is related to the grouping of costs in the overhead budget. Budgetary control results when budgets and standards are harmonized effectively. One cannot function properly without the other, for the budget is, in effect, a summary of standard costs. The materials purchases budget, for example, can be prepared readily when production requirements are known and the standard quantity of material required for the end product has been determined.

The Fixed Manufacturing Overhead Budget

Budgeted overhead is sometimes based on the assumption of a *fixed* budget; that is, it is based on a predetermined level of production. The individual items in such a budget are often not even classified as to fixed or variable elements. A fixed overhead budget based on a production level of 10,000 units of the finished product of the Stetson Manufacturing Company is shown in Figure 22-1.

Figure 22-1. Fixed Manufacturing Overhead Budget

STETSON MANUFACTURING COMPANY
Fixed Manufacturing Overhead Budget
For the Month Ending July 31, 1973

Item	Amount
Depreciation–Factory Building	$ 3,000
Factory Property Taxes	200
Insurance–Factory Building	300
Other Fixed Costs	16,500
Factory Supplies	500
Light and Power	800
Indirect Labor	600
Other Variable Costs	8,100
Total	$30,000

Such a budget is of limited use to management in its control-exercising function because variations of actual costs from budgeted costs arise whenever the total number of units produced is different from that on which the budget was based.

The Flexible Budget

A budget that gives recognition to varying levels of production and to the costs that change with these levels, often called the *flexible budget*, overcomes the shortcomings of the fixed budget by providing management with a basis for analyzing—and, therefore, controlling—the variances between budgeted and actual costs. This is accomplished by comparing actual expenditures with previously established budgeted amounts, adjusted for varying levels of production. A series of budgets is prepared, showing estimated or standard costs at various levels of production. Since it is not practicable to set up budgets for every possible level of operation, interpolation may be necessary if, for example, the flexible budgets are at 5,000 unit intervals and actual production falls at a point between the intervals. The preparation of a flexible budget involves an analysis of the degree and extent to which each item of overhead cost is affected by changes in volume of production. The flexible budget, therefore, is essentially a series of fixed budgets. The preparation of any one budget in the series is the same as for a single fixed budget.

Cost Behavior Patterns. A prerequisite to this type of budget planning is a knowledge of the patterns of cost (cost behavior) within the various cost functions. Up to this point the assumption has been made that all costs are strictly fixed or strictly variable. This assumption does not hold true in a number of situations. In Figure 22-2, cost curves are given to illustrate diagrammatically four types of cost patterns. Some costs, for a given period, may be relatively fixed *in total*, regardless

Figure 22-2. Patterns of Cost Behavior

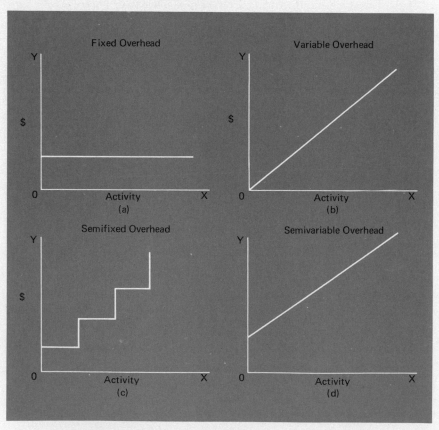

of changes in production. Depreciation, property taxes on factory buildings, and fire insurance may be examples of these costs. As indicated previously, these are referred to as fixed costs; they produce a curve similar to that indicated in Figure 22-2a.

Other costs, such as supplies, may be relatively variable; that is, they vary in total in proportion to changes in output. These costs are referred to as variable costs and produce a curve similar to that indicated in Figure 22-2b.

Certain other costs may change in total in the direction of changes in production, but these changes are not proportionate. Two examples of these kinds of costs are referred to as semifixed costs and semivariable costs. The semifixed costs vary in steps. For example, one inspector of finished goods may be needed for outputs of 0 to 10,000 units; two inspectors may be needed for outputs of 10,001 to 20,000 units, and so on. The salaries of the inspectors would be a semifixed cost (see the cost curve in Figure 22-2c). On the other hand, assume that a foreman receives a base salary of $10,000 plus a bonus of 2 percent of the revenue produced by sales of products made by his department. His salary would contain both a fixed component—the base salary—and a variable component—the bonus based on sales generated by his department. This kind of cost is referred to as a semivariable cost and produces a cost curve as indicated in Figure 22-2d.

Illustration of Flexible Budget. When the flexible budget is prepared, the fixed and variable components of each semivariable cost must be resolved. Also, the production range of the semifixed costs must be known so that the amounts may be indicated as being fixed for only that particular range. For example, indirect labor may remain constant for the 85 and 90 percent production capacity, but it may be indicated at a higher fixed amount for the 95 and 100 percent production capacity. To illustrate the flexible budget, assume that the Stetson Manufacturing Company produces a single, uniform product, and that its costs can be resolved into fixed and variable components. The flexible manufacturing overhead budget for the month of July is shown in Figure 22-3.

Figure 22-3. Flexible Manufacturing Budget

	90%	95%	100%	105%
Direct Labor Hours	27,000	28,500	30,000	31,500
Fixed costs				
Depreciation–factory building	$ 3,000	$ 3,000	$ 3,000	$ 3,000
Factory property taxes	200	200	200	200
Insurance–factory building	300	300	300	300
Other costs	16,500	16,500	16,500	16,500
Total fixed costs	$20,000	$20,000	$20,000	$20,000
Variable costs				
Factory supplies	$ 450	$ 475	$ 500	$ 525
Light and power	720	760	800	840
Indirect labor	540	570	600	630
Other costs	7,290	7,695	8,100	8,505
Total variable costs	$ 9,000	$ 9,500	$10,000	$10,500
Total costs	$29,000	$29,500	$30,000	$30,500

The 100 percent of capacity level used in Figure 22-3 is not intended to indicate the maximum plant capacity. Rather, it is the level at which it is considered theoretically sound to charge all fixed overhead costs to the finished products as being properly utilized; that is, no part of the fixed overhead costs should be considered as *idle time cost,* a lost cost. Hence, the Stetson Manufacturing Company may select 90 percent, 95 percent, or some other actual level as the standard level of output on which to base its predetermined overhead rate and the point from which to measure overapplied or underapplied overhead. It may be assumed that the level of 30,000 direct labor hours or 10,000 units of output represents the company's practical operating capacity over a relatively long period of time.

Figure 22-3 indicates that (1) fixed costs are constant at all four levels of capacity, (2) overhead is to be applied with direct labor hours as a basis, and (3) variable costs are in direct proportion to capacity levels. This is evident from the following computations relating to the 100 percent and 95 percent columns:

$$30,000 \text{ direct labor hours} \times 95\% = 28,500 \text{ hours}$$
$$\$500 \text{ in factory supplies} \times 95\% = \$475$$
$$\$10,000 \text{ in total variable costs} \times 95\% = \$9,500$$

The Stetson Manufacturing Company produces 10,000 units at its 100 percent of capacity level. Each unit requires three hours of direct labor.

Illustration of Standard Cost Accounting

A standard cost accounting system is illustrated by the continuation of the activities of the Stetson Manufacturing Company for the month of July, 1973.

The Standard Cost Card. The accountant working with engineers develops standards usually based on what the cost of each element should be, assuming average performance of laborers working under normal operating conditions. The standard cost card of the Stetson Manufacturing Company reveals the following standard cost per unit:

Materials: 2 pieces of Material K-12 at $5	$10
Labor: 3 hours at $3	9
Overhead: 3 hours at $1 (See Figure 22-3)	3
	$22

The predetermined overhead rate for the month of July, based on the 100 percent column (from Figure 22-3), is shown in Figure 22-4.

Figure 22-4. Predetermined Overhead Rate

$$\text{Variable cost per hour} = \frac{\text{Variable costs}}{\text{Total hours}} = \frac{\$10,000}{30,000} = \$0.33\frac{1}{3}$$

$$\text{Fixed cost per hour} = \frac{\text{Fixed costs}}{\text{Total hours}} = \frac{\$20,000}{30,000} = \$0.66\frac{2}{3}$$

$$\text{Predetermined overhead rate (per hour)} \qquad \underline{\$1.00}$$

The hourly rate also may be computed as follows:

$$\frac{\text{Total Budget Manufacturing Overhead}}{\text{Total Budgeted Direct Labor Hours}} = \frac{\$30,000}{30,000} = \$1 \text{ per hour}$$

Figure 22-5. Flow Chart of a Standard Cost System

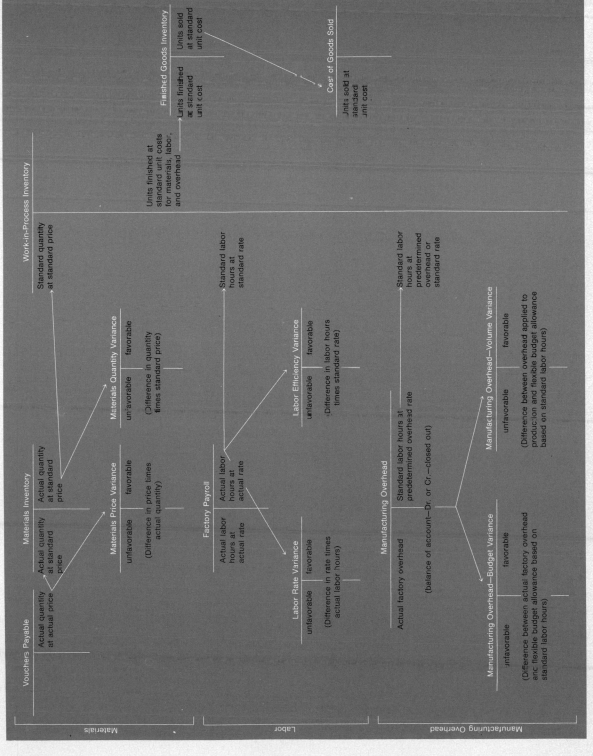

The Flow Chart of a Standard Cost System. Figure 22-5 shows the flow of standard costs through the hypothetical Stetson Manufacturing Company. Each of these indicated steps is illustrated and discussed in conjunction with the accounting for the activities and transactions described below.

July Cost Information for the Stetson Manufacturing Company. During July, 10,000 units were started and 9,880 units were completed; the beginning work-in-process inventory consisted of 80 units, which had received all the material and one fourth of the labor and overhead; there were 200 units in the ending work-in-process inventory, which had received all materials and one fifth of the labor and overhead. These data may be expressed in schedule form, as shown in Figure 22-6.

Figure 22-6. Quantity Schedule for July

	Units
Quantity to be accounted for	
Units in process at beginning	80 (all material–¼ L and O)
Units started in process	10,000
Total	10,080
Quantity accounted for	
Transferred to finished goods inventory	9,880
Units still in process	200 (all material–⅕ L and O)
Total	10,080

The equivalent production is computed as shown in Figure 22-7.

Figure 22-7. Schedule of Equivalent Production for July

	Materials	L and O
Beginning work-in-process inventory	–0–	60 (80 units × ¾)
Started and finished this period	9,800	9,800 (9,880 units − 80 units)
Units still in process	200	40 (200 × ⅕)
Equivalent production units	10,000	9,900

A summary of transactions for the month of July is given below.

1. Materials purchased: 20,200 pieces of Material K-12 at $4.98 each
2. Materials requisitioned for production: 20,100 pieces of Material K-12
3. Factory payroll incurred during July: 29,600 hours at $3.05 per hour
4. Direct labor applied: standard hours for 9,900 units of finished product times standard rate
5. Manufacturing overhead incurred: $29,850
6. Manufacturing overhead applied to production: $29,700 (9,900 × $3)

7. Units finished: 9,880

8. Units sold on account: 9,500 at $30

9. Manufacturing Overhead controlling account closed and variances entered in budget and volume variance accounts

The entries to record the transactions for the month are

(a)

Materials Inventory	101,000	
Materials Price Variance		404
Vouchers Payable (or Accounts Payable)		100,596

Quantity	Price	Amount
Actual: 20,200 × Standard: $5.00		$101,000
Actual: 20,200 × Actual: $4.98		100,596
Materials price variance (favorable)		$ 404

(b)

Work-in-Process Inventory	100,000	
Materials Quantity Variance	500	
Materials Inventory		100,500

Quantity	Price	Amount
Actual: 20,100 × Standard: $5.00		$100,500
Standard: 20,000 × Standard: $5.00		100,000
Materials quantity variance (unfavorable)		$ 500

10,000 equivalent production units (see Figure 22-7)
  ×2 standard pieces per unit
20,000 standard units of material

(c)

Factory Payroll	90,280	
Vouchers Payable (and payroll tax liabilities)		90,280
29,600 actual hours × $3.05 = $90,280		

(d)

Work-in-Process Inventory	89,100	
Labor Rate Variance	1,480	
Labor Efficiency Variance		300
Factory Payroll		90,280

Rate Variance

Hours	Rate	Amount
Actual: 29,600 × Actual: $3.05		$90,280
Actual: 29,600 × Standard: $3.00		88,800
Labor rate variance (unfavorable)		$ 1,480

Efficiency Variance

Standard: 29,700 × Standard: $3.00	$89,100
Actual: 29,600 × Standard: $3.00	88,800
Labor efficiency variance (favorable)	$ 300

9,900 equivalent production units (see Figure 22-7)
×3 standard hours per unit
29,700 total standard labor hours

(e)

| Manufacturing Overhead | 29,850 | |
| Prepaid Insurance and other accounts | | 29,850 |

(f)

| Work-in-Process Inventory | 29,700 | |
| Manufacturing Overhead | | 29,700 |

29,700 standard labor hours × $1 per hour
predetermined overhead rate = $29,700

(g)

| Finished Goods Inventory | 217,360 | |
| Work-in-Process Inventory | | 217,360 |

9,800 completed units × $22 standard unit cost = $217,360

(h)

Cost of Goods Sold	209,000	
Accounts Receivable	285,000	
Finished Goods Inventory		209,000
Sales		285,000

9,500 units × $22 standard unit cost = $209,000
9,500 units × $30 unit selling price = $285,000

(i)

Manufacturing Overhead—Volume Variance	200	
Manufacturing Overhead—Budget Variance		50
Manufacturing Overhead		150

The Manufacturing Overhead controlling account after entry (i) is posted appears as follows:

Manufacturing Overhead			
Entry (e)	29,850	Entry (f)	29,700
		Entry (i)	150
	29,850		29,850

The actual manufacturing overhead incurred ($29,850) exceeded the overhead applied ($29,700); therefore, the debit balance of $150 represents underapplied overhead. Further analysis indicates that the $150 is made up of (1) a credit budget variance of $50 and (2) a debit volume variance of $200. In deriving these two amounts, reference must be made to the flexible budget to determine the budget allowance based on standard labor hours for the actual work completed (29,700 units). Since a breakdown of the fixed and variable elements in the predetermined overhead rate is available, computations for the flexible budget allowances for 29,700 labor hours on work completed may be made as follows (see Figure 22-4):

Fixed costs	$20,000
Variable costs 29,700 hours × $0.33⅓	9,900
Flexible budget allowance	$29,900

If a breakdown of the fixed and variable elements is not available, the $29,900 may be derived directly from the flexible budget schedule (Figure 22-3):

$$\frac{\text{Standard labor hours for work done}}{\text{Budgeted direct labor hours}} = \frac{29,700}{30,000} = 99\%$$

The flexible budget allowance at this 99-percent level may now be interpolated as follows:

95% (28,500 hours)	$29,500
100% (30,000 hours)	30,000
5% difference	$ 500
1% difference	100
4%	$ 400

The flexible budget allowance at 99% level is

95%	$29,500
4%	400
99%	$29,900

The underapplied overhead of $150 may be analyzed as follows:

1. Budget variance:	
Flexible budget allowance for 99% capacity attained	$29,900
Actual overhead incurred	29,850
Budget variance (favorable)	$ 50
2. Volume variance:	
Flexible budget allowance for 99% capacity attained	$29,900
Overhead applied during July (29,700 hours × $1)	29,700
Volume variance (unfavorable)	$ 200

The budget variance is favorable because the actual overhead costs incurred are less than the flexible budget allowance at the 99 percent of actual capacity level. The volume variance is unfavorable because a portion (1%) of the available plant facilities were not used, resulting in a loss of $200, computed alternatively as follows:

Budgeted hours	30,000
Standard hours for capacity attained	29,700
Idle capacity hours	300
Fixed overhead rate per hour	$ 0.66⅔
Cost of idle capacity	$ 200

The idle capacity, or unfavorable volume variance, represents the portion of the fixed costs that was not absorbed due to the failure to achieve full production (30,000 hours). Had the volume of activity exceeded 100 percent (30,000 standard labor hours), an excess capacity, or favorable volume variance, would have resulted.

Practice varies with respect to the disposition of the variance accounts. Many accountants view standard costs as being realistic costs; therefore, they view the variances as losses or if they are favorable, as gains. They would close the variances to the Revenue and Expense Summary account. Another method is to treat the variances as costs of the period in which they are incurred—that is, to close all the variance accounts into Cost of Goods Sold. This may either be done monthly or be deferred until the end of the annual accounting period. Deferral may be practical if the variances tend to offset each other owing to seasonal volume fluctuations.

The standard cost of the 80 units (all material and one quarter of labor and overhead) in the beginning work-in-process inventory of the Stetson Manufacturing Company is comprised of the following cost elements:

Materials: 80 units × $10 standard cost =	$ 800
Labor: 80 units × ¼ × $9 standard cost =	180
Overhead: 80 units × ¼ × $3 standard cost =	60
Total	$1,040

The Work-in-Process Inventory ledger account appears as shown below.

Work-in-Process Inventory				
Beginning balance		1,040	Entry (g) finished goods	217,360
Entry (b) materials		100,000		
Entry (d) labor		89,100		
Entry (f) overhead	(2,480)	29,700		

The $2,480 debit balance in the account represents the standard cost of 200 units in the ending work-in-process inventory, which is verified as follows:

Cost Element	Units in Process	Stage of Completion	Standard Unit Cost	Total Standard Cost
Materials	200	100%	$10	$2,000 (200 × $10)
Labor	200	20%	9	360 (200 × ⅕ × $9)
Overhead	200	20%	3	120 (200 × ⅕ × $3)
Total work in process				$2,480

MANAGERIAL INTERPRETATION OF VARIANCES

As a first step in the managerial interpretation of variances, it is necessary to identify who has primary responsibility for each of the variances. For example, the purchasing department is responsible, in part at least, for the materials price variance. Supervisory factory personnel, however, may have some influence on materials prices when these individuals specify certain brand-named materials or materials of certain grade and quality. Factory supervisory personnel have primary responsibility for the materials quantity and labor efficiency variances. The personnel department is partly responsible for the labor rate variance (although others in the factory may have some influence here—for example, hiring policies). Top factory heads are responsible for the overhead volume variance; those who acquire and use overhead items are responsible for the overhead budget variance.

When any variance is large enough, an investigation should be made to see if corrective action should be taken. For example, if the actual price of materials is substantially above the standard, a study should be made—possibly by the accountant working with the individual (or individuals) who has primary responsibility for the materials price variance—to see if this cost could be reduced by buying in larger quantities, by the substitution of other materials, or by taking other measures. The other variances are analyzed in a similar manner. It is important, moreover, to know what variances *are not* large enough to justify an investigation, as these studies may be extremely costly and hence, for small differences, unprofitable for management.

DIRECT COSTING

A primary purpose of cost accounting is to furnish management with meaningful accounting data for use in decision making. With this in view, a number of companies have adopted a cost method referred to as *direct costing.* Direct costing is contrasted with absorption, or conventional, costing. Under direct costing, all manufacturing costs are segregated into product costs and period expenses based on the variability of costs with volume. For direct costing purposes, costs that vary with changes in volume are considered product costs; those that do not vary are treated as period expenses. The cost of goods sold and the cost of goods in inventory are valued on the basis of product costs alone—direct labor, direct material, and variable manufacturing overhead. Fixed manufacturing overhead costs are reported as expenses for the period and deducted from the gross margin. Thus, the reported excess of revenue over variable costs and expenses, or *marginal income,* under direct costing reflects directly the effect of sales volume. Costs that are incurred to make a given level of plant productive facilities available—that is, costs that do not vary with the amount of work done but expire with the passage of time—are excluded in valuing both the cost of goods sold and the cost of goods on hand. Absorption costing, which treats *all* manufacturing costs as product costs, on the other hand, reflects the factors of both sales and production volume.

The ledger accounts under direct costing provide for the segregation of costs into their fixed and variable elements; the income statement is prepared to show *marginal income*—sales minus variable costs—from which fixed costs are deducted to arrive at net income. This is in contrast to absorption costing, under which the fixed and variable elements are mingled within the individual accounts. The separation of costs into their fixed and variable elements enables management to analyze the effect of volume changes on these cost elements and on net income. Under direct costing, fixed costs are deducted in the period when they are incurred, whereas under absorption costing, a portion of the fixed costs remains in inventory; hence the reported net income will differ under the two systems. When production exceeds sales, a portion of the fixed costs will remain in inventory under the absorption costing method, cost of goods sold will be less, and net income will be higher than under the direct costing method. The results are reversed when sales exceed production. Reported earnings under absorption costing may, therefore, rise with falling sales volume if production volume is increased, and fall with rising sales volume if production falls.

The operating data of the Crane Corporation for the three years 1971 through 1973 are used to compare absorption costing with direct costing.

Sales price per unit		$13
Normal capacity	20,000 units per year	
Manufacturing costs at normal capacity		
	Total	Per Unit
Fixed	$ 80,000	$4.00
Variable	105,000	5.25
Total	$185,000	$9.25
Selling and administrative expenses		
Fixed	$ 9,000	$0.45
Variable	8,000	0.40
Total	$ 17,000	$0.85

Inventories, production, and sales, in units, are shown in Figure 22-8.

Figure 22-8. Inventories, Production, and Sales in Units

	Units			
	1973	1972	1971	For the 3-Year Period
Beginning finished goods inventory	6,000	10,000	–0–	–0–
Production	21,000	11,000	20,000	52,000
Sales	27,000	15,000	10,000	52,000
Ending finished goods inventory	–0–	6,000	10,000	–0–

The beginning and ending work-in-process inventories for each year were zero.

Comparative income statements based on the data in Figure 22-8 under the two cost reporting methods are shown in Figures 22-9 and 22-10. The statements are prepared under the assumptions that (1) volume is the only factor that

Figure 22-9. Comparative Income Statement—Absorption Costing

CRANE CORPORATION
Comparative Income Statement—Absorption Costing
For the Years Ended December 31, 1973, 1972, and 1971

	Year 1973	Year 1972	Year 1971	For the 3-Year Period
Sales	$351,000	$195,000	$130,000 (10,000 units × $13)	$676,000
Cost of Goods Sold (standard)				
Beginning Finished Goods Inventory	$ 55,500	$ 92,500	–0–	–0–
Cost of Goods Manufactured	194,250	101,750	$185,000 (20,000 units × $9.25)	$481,000
Total Goods Available for Sale	$249,750	$194,250	$185,000	$481,000
Ending Finished Goods Inventory	–0–	55,500	92,500 (10,000 units × $9.25)	–0–
Cost of Goods Sold	$249,750	$138,750	$ 92,500	$481,000
Gross Margin on Sales (standard)	$101,250	$ 56,250	$ 37,500 ($130,000 − $92,500)	$195,000
Selling and Administrative Expenses				
Variable Selling and Administrative Expenses	$ 10,800	$ 6,000	$ 4,000 (10,000 units × $0.40)	$ 20,800
Fixed Selling and Administrative Expenses	9,000	9,000	9,000	27,000
Total	$ 19,800	$ 15,000	$ 13,000	$ 47,800
Net Income (standard)	$ 81,450	$ 41,250	$ 24,500 ($37,500 − $13,000)	$147,200
Deduct Underapplied Manufacturing Costs	–0–	36,000 **(a)**	–0–	32,000 **(c)**
Add Overapplied Manufacturing Costs	4,000 **(b)**	–0–	–0–	–0–
Net Income (actual)	$ 85,450	$ 5,250	$ 24,500	$115,200

(a) 9,000 units (20,000 units − 11,000 units) × $4 = $36,000
(b) 1,000 units (21,000 units − 20,000 units) × $4 = $ 4,000
(c) 8,000 units (9,000 units − 1,000 units) × $4 = $32,000

Figure 22-10. Comparative Income Statement—Direct Costing

CRANE CORPORATION
Comparative Income Statement—Direct Costing
For the Years Ended December 31, 1973, 1972, and 1971

	Year 1973	Year 1972	Year 1971	For the 3-Year Period
Sales	$351,000	$195,000	$130,000 (10,000 units × $13)	$676,000
Cost of Goods Sold–Variable Costs	141,750	78,750	52,500 (10,000 units × $5.25)	273,000
Marginal Income from Manufacturing	$209,250	$116,250	$ 77,500	$403,000
Variable Selling and Administrative Expenses	10,800	6,000	4,000 (10,000 units × $0.40)	20,800
Marginal Income	$198,450	$110,250	$ 73,500	$382,200
Fixed Operating Costs and Expenses				
Manufacturing Costs	$ 80,000	$ 80,000	$ 80,000	$240,000
Selling and Administrative Expenses	9,000	9,000	9,000	27,000
Total	$ 89,000	$ 89,000	$ 89,000	$267,000
Net Income (or loss)	$109,450	$ 21,250	$(15,500) ($89,000 − $73,500)	$115,200

had an influence on net income or loss; (2) selling prices remain constant; (3) fixed costs of production and selling and administrative costs remain unchanged; (4) variable costs are directly proportionate to sales at any level, hence constant in terms of cost per unit; (5) volume variances (under and overapplied costs) are closed to Revenue and Expense Summary rather than apportioned between the cost of goods sold and the ending inventories; and (6) finished goods inventories are valued at standard costs.

The statements of the Crane Corporation show the effect of the two costing methods on the relationship of sales, volume of production, and cost of goods sold, as follows:

1. In any given year when units produced are greater than units sold, reported net income under direct costing is less than under absorption costing. Results for 1971 are

Absorption costing–net income (Figure 22-9)	$24,500
Direct costing–net loss (Figure 22-10)	(15,500)
Variation between methods	$40,000

Since there was no beginning finished goods inventory, the $40,000 variation results solely from the difference in the valuation of the ending finished goods inventories, which are

Absorption costing (10,000 units × $9.25)	$92,500
Direct costing (10,000 units × $5.25)	52,500
Difference	$40,000

This difference is due, in turn, to the $4 fixed manufacturing cost per unit:

Inventory including fixed manufacturing costs (10,000 × $9.25)	$92,500
Inventory excluding fixed manufacturing costs (10,000 × $5.25)	52,500
Difference	$40,000

2. When units produced are less than units sold, reported income under direct costing is greater than under absorption costing. Results for 1972 under these assumptions are

Direct costing (Figure 22-10)	$21,250
Absorption costing (Figure 22-9)	5,250
Variation between methods	$16,000

The variation is due to the difference in inventory valuations resulting from the inclusion (absorption) or exclusion (direct) of the $4 fixed manufacturing overhead cost per unit, as follows:

Beginning finished goods inventory		
Absorption costing (10,000 units × $9.25)		$92,500
Direct costing (10,000 units × $5.25)		52,500
Difference		$40,000
Ending finished goods inventory		
Absorption costing (6,000 units × $9.25)	$55,500	
Direct costing (6,000 units × $5.25)	31,500	24,000
Difference		$16,000

3. When units sold and units produced are the same, reported income is the same under both methods. This is evident from the tabulation that follows, in which the data for the three years are combined. Units produced and units sold were equal over the three years.

	Year			For the 3-Year Period
	1973	1972	1971	
Units produced	21,000	11,000	20,000	52,000
Units sold	27,000	15,000	10,000	52,000
Net income–absorption costing (Figure 22-9)	$ 85,450	$ 5,250	$24,500	$115,200
Net income (or loss)–direct costing (Figure 22-10)	$109,450	$21,250	($15,500)	$115,200

4. Under direct costing, increases and decreases in units sold result in proportionate increases and decreases in marginal income because only variable costs are assigned to the cost of units produced.

		Per Unit
Sales price		$13.00
Variable costs		
Manufacturing	$5.25	
Selling and Administrative	0.40	5.65
Marginal income		$ 7.35

Year	Units Sold	Marginal Income Per Unit	Marginal Income on Income Statement
1971	10,000	$7.35	$ 73,500
1972	15,000	7.35	110,250
1973	27,000	7.35	198,450

5. Under direct costing, the emphasis is on the number of units sold, and the net income or net loss will, therefore, move in the same direction as the sales volume. Net income or net loss cannot increase or decrease, however, in direct proportion to sales volume because unit fixed costs do not stay constant. Under absorption costing, emphasis is on both production and sales, and the net income and net loss do not, therefore, show the expected relationship to sales. This is illustrated by the comparison that follows of sales and net income (or loss) data for the Crane Corporation.

	Direct Costing			Absorption Costing		
	1973	1972	1971	1973	1972	1971
Sales	$351,000	$195,000	$130,000	$351,000	$195,000	$130,000
Net Income (or Loss)	109,450	21,250	(15,500)	85,450	5,250	24,500

Although sales during the second year increased by $65,000 ($195,000 — $130,000), net income under absorption costing decreased by $19,250 ($24,500 — $5,250).

6. Under direct costing, inventory valuations are determined with fixed costs excluded and are always smaller than inventory valuations computed under absorption costing, which includes fixed manufacturing overhead costs. Therefore, working capital (current assets less current liabilities) reported on the statement of financial position under the direct costing method will always be smaller. Ending finished goods inventories reported on the statement of financial position under both methods for 1971 and 1972 are as follows:

December 31	Direct Costing	Absorption Costing
1971	$52,500 (10,000 units × $5.25)	$92,500
1972	31,500 (6,000 units × $5.25)	55,500

In conclusion, note that the difference between the results under direct costing and absorption costing stems from the amount of fixed manufacturing costs allocated to finished goods and work-in-process inventories. The advocates of direct costing argue that these fixed costs are not a part of the cost of goods manufactured during a given period. Rather, these are the costs of having the capacity to produce; hence, they are expenses and should be charged against revenue irrespective of physical production. Proponents of absorption costing argue that fixed manufacturing costs are as essential to the production of goods as are variable costs. Moreover, net income from the sale of any unit of a product does not emerge until after the total cost of bringing that product to the point of sale has been recovered.

Unquestionably, the delineation of costs into their fixed and variable components is useful to management in studying cost-volume-income relationships; but to include only variable costs in finished goods and work-in-process inventories leaves some doubt about the validity of the valuation of those items for such purposes as securing loans and issuing capital stock; and the under-valuation of inventories leaves some doubt about the validity of subsequent income measurement. For these reasons, direct costing has not attained the status of a generally accepted accounting procedure. Some firms, however, have set up their records on a direct costing basis; then for financial reporting and tax purposes they convert their statements to an absorption costing basis.

SUMMARY

A standard cost is a predetermined estimate of the cost of each element of a product, based on an analysis of past experience and expected future developments. It shows what each product should cost if the assumptions on which the standard costs are based prove to be true. Standard costs provide a basis for comparison with actual costs and, therefore, serve as a criterion in measuring the adequacy or inadequacy of the actual performance.

To utilize standard costs effectively in connection with manufacturing overhead costs, a flexible budget that shows the expected standard cost of overhead at various levels of production should be used. A fixed budget is of little value, because variations of actual costs from budgeted costs will arise if actual production differs from budgeted production. To prepare a flexible budget, the behavior of each overhead cost in relation to changes in volume must be examined. A fixed overhead cost is unaffected by volume changes; a variable overhead cost varies proportionately with volume changes. A semivariable cost and a semifixed overhead cost change with volume changes, but not proportionately; in a flexible budget, the semivariable costs must be divided into their fixed and variable components. If a flexible budget is employed, one volume of production must be chosen on which to apply overhead to the various products during the period. Once the volume is selected, the overhead rate may be divided into two components—the variable overhead rate and the fixed overhead rate. During the period, actual overhead costs are accumulated in the Manufacturing Overhead account but overhead is charged to products based on the standard overhead rates. At the end of the period, the difference between the budgeted overhead at the standard volume and the actual overhead incurred can be broken down into the following variances: (1) budget variance—the difference between the budgeted amount at the attained capacity and the actual overhead incurred during the period; (2) volume variance—the difference between the budgeted amount at the attained capacity and the overhead applied during the period.

Under a standard cost system, purchased materials are charged to Materials Inventory at standard prices, and Work-in-Process Inventory is charged for the standard quantity of materials used at their standard prices. The difference between the standard cost and the actual cost of materials purchased is the materials price variance, and the difference between the actual quantity used and the standard quantity at the standard cost is the materials quantity variance.

Work-in-Process Inventory is charged for the standard number of labor hours at the standard rate under a standard cost system. The labor rate variance is the difference between the actual hours worked at the actual rate and at the standard rate. The labor efficiency variance is the difference between the standard labor hours and the actual labor hours at the standard rate.

A common method of diposing of the variances is to close them to the Revenue and Expense Summary account at the end of the accounting period; alternatively they may be closed to the Cost of Goods Sold account.

Absorption costing, or conventional financial costing, is based on the assumption that all factory costs, fixed and variable, should be charged to cost of goods manufactured during the period and should be recognized as expenses only as the related goods are sold. Since all manufacturing costs are treated as product costs, the gross margin reflects the effect of both sales and production volume. Direct costing rejects the assumption that all manufacturing costs are product costs and limits product costs to those that vary with changes in the volume of production—that is, direct materials, direct labor, and variable manufacturing overhead. Fixed costs are reported as expenses of the period. Thus, the marginal income (excess of sales revenue over variable costs) reflects only the effect of sales volume. Direct costing is often more valuable to management for decision-making purposes than absorption costing since variable cost and marginal income data are readily available from the accounting records and statements. It also helps to clarify the relationship between costs, volume, and income. When production exceeds sales, net income will be higher under absorption costing than under direct costing, because a portion of the fixed costs will be charged to the inventory account instead of being charged to expense during the period. when sales exceed production, the results are reversed. Under direct costing, reported earnings move in the same direction as sales volume; if the volume of sales increases, reported earnings increase, and if the volume of sales decreases, reported earnings decrease. However, under absorption costing, reported earnings do not necessarily move in the same direction as sales volume; for example, an increase in earnings may accompany a decrease in sales volume if production volume increases. The difference in reported net income under direct costing and absorption costing is due to the difference in inventory valuations resulting from the inclusion (absorption costing) or exclusion (direct costing) of the fixed overhead costs.

QUESTIONS

Q22-1. How does a standard cost system make possible the application of the principle of management by exception?

Q22-2. (a) What is the difference between a fixed budget and a flexible budget? (b) Why must all costs ultimately be classified either as fixed or variable when preparing a flexible budget? (c) Why is it desirable to establish the variable and fixed factors of the predetermined overhead rate?

Q22-3. (a) What is meant by the standard cost of a unit? (b) Why is a standard cost system an effective means of cost control? (c) Identify and explain six variance accounts used in a standard cost system.

Q22-4. (a) What is meant by "budget allowance based on standard costs"? (b) How may the budget and volume variances be analyzed? (c) When should the standard costs be changed?

Q22-5. Standard cost as discussed in this text applies to a manufactured product; is it possible to extend the general principle of standard cost to the cost of services? Explain and give examples.

Q22-6. What is the basic difference between an income statement based on direct costing procedures and one based on the absorption costing method?

Q22-7. Give the advantages and the disadvantages of direct costing to management.

Q22-8. On January 1, 1973, the Dowdee Company had on hand 1,000 units of a given product; it manufactured 10,000 units and sold 6,000 units. Which costing method—direct or absorption—will produce the smaller net income for 1973? Explain the reason for the difference.

Q22-9. State the production circumstances under which the absorption method as compared to the direct costing method will yield the lower net income figure for a given year.

Q22-10. When a nonmanufacturing trading firm determines the cost of its purchases by taking invoice price less cash discounts plus an applicable part of direct transportation cost, but ignoring any fixed cost of the purchasing department, is it not applying a direct costing principle? Identify and explain the appropriate absorption costs for purchases.

EXERCISES

E22-1. Five pounds of a given material at $0.65 per pound are standard for the production of a given product manufactured by the Jardin Company. During August, 14,000 pounds of the particular materials were purchased at $0.66 a pound; 12,000 pounds were put into process; 2,470 equivalent units of the finished product were produced.

Determine the materials price and quantity variances.

E22-2. Three gallons of a given material at $1.10 per gallon are standard for the production of a given product manufactured by the Mattheson Company. During March, 1973, the following transactions (in summary form) took place:

1. Materials purchased were 17,000 gallons at $1.08 per gallon.
2. Materials requisitioned for production totaled 15,765 gallons.
3. Equivalent production for March was 5,250 equivalent units of the finished product.

Journalize the transactions involving materials, including the materials price and quantity variances.

E22-3. The Lawrence Company's standard cost card for one of its products showed the following direct labor charge:

Direct labor: 2 hours at $2.75 per hour

Standard direct labor hours for production for the month of April were 2,400; actual direct labor hours were 2,360 at a total cost of $6,608.

Determine (a) the labor rate variance and (b) the labor efficiency variance.

E22-4. The Bardin Company's standard cost card for its product, Zoxine, showed the following direct labor charge:

Direct labor: 3½ hours at $2.00 per hour

The following were among the transactions that occurred during June, 1973:

1. Factory payroll incurred during June was 30,460 hours, at a total cost of $60,615.
2. The standard direct labor cost was assigned to 8,680 equivalent finished units.

Journalize the transactions involving direct labor, including the labor rate variance and the labor efficiency variance.

E22-5. The Dawson Company maintains a standard cost system and a flexible overhead budget, as shown:

	70%	80%	90%	100%
Variable costs	$ 56,000	$ 64,000	$ 72,000	$ 80,000
Fixed costs	100,000	100,000	100,000	100,000
Total costs	$156,000	$164,000	$172,000	$180,000

Normal capacity is budgeted at the 100-percent level of 400,000 direct labor hours; the standard overhead rate is $0.45 an hour. During the period, the company worked 392,000 actual direct labor hours. Overhead was applied to production on the basis of 394,000 standard hours. Actual overhead incurred was $176,000.

Determine the manufacturing overhead (a) volume variance and (b) budget variance. (c) Prove the volume variance, using alternative computations.

E22-6. The Lutz Company produced 20,000 units of a new product during 1973. 16,000 units were sold at $25 each. Cost of production and operating expenses were as follows:

Direct materials	$ 60,000
Direct labor	40,000
Manufacturing overhead–fixed	100,000
Manufacturing overhead–variable	120,000
(there was no ending work-in-process inventory)	
Selling and administrative expenses–fixed	30,000
Selling and administrative expenses–variable	20,000

Prepare an income statement, using the direct costing method.

E22-7. The Washington Company reported the following results for the year 1973: sales, $200,000; variable cost of goods sold, $96,000; variable selling expenses, $12,000; fixed manufacturing overhead, $64,000; and fixed selling expenses, $8,400.

Prepare an income statement, using the direct costing method.

E22-8. The Buttricks Company, which began operations on January 1, 1973, produced 2,000 more units than it sold in 1973. Its fixed manufacturing overhead cost was $5 per unit, and the variable manufacturing cost was $7 per unit. There was no ending work-in-process inventory.

From this information, compute the difference between the net income that would be reported under direct costing and compare it to the income that would be reported under absorption costing.

E22-9. The Rex Company had a finished goods inventory of 3,000 units of a given product as of January 1, 1973, with a cost of $24,300 under the absorption costing method, or a cost of $15,000 under the direct costing method. There was no beginning work-in-process inventory.

During 1973, the Rex Company manufactured 56,500 units of the particular product. The fixed manufacturing overhead cost totaled $169,500 during 1973 and the variable unit cost was the same as in 1972. The company sold 50,000 units of the product at $10 each and used the FIFO method of assigning costs to the cost of goods sold. There was no ending work-in-process inventory.

Operating expenses for the year were:

Selling and administrative expenses–fixed	$16,400
Selling and administrative expenses–variable	22,000

Prepare an income statement for 1973 using (a) the direct costing method and (b) the absorption costing method.

DEMONSTRATION PROBLEMS

DP22-1. (*Standard cost accounting with a flexible budget*) The Atlas Products Company used a standard cost system and a fixed manufacturing overhead budget in 1972, as follows:

Direct labor hours	40,000
Fixed costs	
Depreciation–factory building	$ 8,000
Factory taxes	600
Depreciation–machinery and equipment	16,000
Other costs (item data omitted)	35,400
Total fixed costs	$60,000
Variable costs	
Light and power	$ 2,000
Factory supplies	1,000
Other costs (item data omitted)	17,000
Total Variable Costs	$20,000
Total manufacturing overhead	$80,000

In 1973, the management decided to prepare a flexible overhead budget at 80, 90, 100, and 110 percent of capacity levels of production. The 1972 budget represents a normal capacity of 100 percent. The standard unit cost of the product is

Materials: 1 piece of Material Y-37	$ 3
Direct labor: 2 hours at $2.50	5
Manufacturing overhead: 2 hours at $2	4
Total	$12

Production data for 1973 were

There was no beginning work-in-process inventory.
19,800 units started in production.
19,000 units completed.
800 units in process (all materials added and one quarter of labor and overhead)

Condensed transactions for 1973 were:

1. Materials purchased totaled 20,000 pieces at $3.02.
2. Materials requisitioned for production were 19,810 pieces.
3. Direct labor was 38,500 hours at $2.48 per hour.
4. Manufacturing overhead totaled $77,200.
5. Manufacturing overhead was applied to production on the basis stated.
6. Units finished were 19,000.
7. Units sold were 18,800 at $22 each.
8. Manufacturing Overhead control account was closed and variances were entered in budget and volume variance accounts.

Required:

1. Construct the flexible budget.
2. Record the transactions for 1973.
3. Post to a Work-in-Process Inventory T account and prove the ending balance.
4. Prepare a schedule analyzing the manufacturing overhead volume variance.

DP22-2. (*Absorption and direct costing*) The Gorman Manufacturing Company produced 40,000 units of a new product during 1973 and sold 30,000 units at $25 each. Costs for 1973 were as follows:

	Fixed Costs	Variable Costs
Direct materials		$100,000
Direct labor		80,000
Manufacturing overhead	$220,000	160,000
Selling and administrative expenses	140,000	40,000

There was no ending work-in-process inventory.

Required:

1. Prepare comparative income statements for the year 1973, using: (a) the absorption cost method and (b) the direct cost method.
2. Give the reasons for the difference in reported net income or net loss in Requirements (a) and (b).

PROBLEMS

P22-1. The budgeted data for the Townsville Company at 100 percent of capacity are

Direct labor hours	120,000
Variable overhead costs	$60,000
Fixed overhead costs	$90,000

Required: 1. Prepare a flexible overhead budget at 85, 90, 95, 100, and 105 percent of capacity.
2. Compute the overhead rate at each capacity.

P22-2. Following are the budgeted data for the Roughton Company for the first three months of 1973, based on a normal capacity level of 100 percent:

Units	60,000
Direct materials	$180,000
Direct labor cost	$120,000
Direct labor hours	60,000
Fixed overhead costs	
Depreciation–machinery and equipment	$10,000
Factory taxes	4,000
Factory insurance	6,000
Miscellaneous	10,000
Variable overhead costs	
Light and power	5,000
Factory supplies	2,000
Miscellaneous	8,000

Required:

1. Construct a flexible manufacturing overhead budget at levels of 85, 90, 95, 100, and 105 percent.
2. Prepare standard cost cards for the product at each level of activity; compute separate variable and fixed cost rates per direct labor hour.

P22-3. The standard cost card for the Frautchi Company showed the following information in regard to its commodity, Plamb:

Materials: 2 gallons of Zunk at $2 each	$ 4
Direct labor: 3 hours at $3	9
Total materials and direct labor cost	$13

Production data for 1973 were:

Beginning work-in-process inventory: 100 units, 60 percent complete as to materials and 40 percent complete as to direct labor and manufacturing overhead

Completed during 1973: 20,000 units

Ending work-in-process inventory: 2,000 units, 80 percent complete as to materials and 50 percent complete as to direct labor and manufacturing overhead.

Transactions involving materials and labor during 1973 were

1. Purchased 48,000 gallons of Zunk at $2.02 per gallon.
2. Requisitioned 43,120 gallons of Zunk for production.
3. Factory payroll incurred during the period was 61,920 hours at a total cost of $186,379.20. In recording the factory payroll, ignore payroll taxes.
4. A standard direct labor cost was assigned to production on the basis of information contained on the standard cost card.

Required: Record in journal form the foregoing information clearly establishing all material and labor variances in appropriate accounts.

P22-4. The Eno Company manufactures a single product in several styles, all of which are uniform as to material quantity and production time requirements. The standard cost sheet for all products is as follows:

Materials: 16 pieces at $2	$ 32
Direct labor: 20 hours at $3	60
Manufacturing overhead: 20 hours at $1	20
Total	$112

The standard cost was the same for July and August. Overhead distribution is based on direct labor hours. The condensed flexible overhead budget for August, 1973, is

	50%	75%	100%	125%
Direct labor hours	1,200	1,800	2,100	3,000
Variable costs	$ 600	$ 900	$1,200	$1,500
Fixed costs	1,200	1,200	1,200	1,200
Total costs	$1,800	$2,100	$2,400	$2,700

Production data for August were as follows:

Beginning work-in-process inventory: 10 units, 80 percent complete as to materials and 50 percent complete as to direct labor and manufacturing overhead.

Completed during the period: 122 units

Ending work-in-process inventory: 6 units, 100 percent complete as to materials and 50 percent complete as to direct labor and manufacturing overhead.

Transactions for the month included the following:

1. Materials purchased totaled 2,050 pieces at $1.98.
2. Materials issued for production totaled 2,040 pieces.
3. Labor costs incurred were 2,510 direct labor hours at $2.95; standard labor cost was transferred to the work-in-process inventory.
4. Manufacturing overhead incurred was $2,600.
5. Manufacturing overhead was applied to production.
6. Recorded units completed.
7. Sold 130 units for $200 each.
8. Closed the Manufacturing Overhead controlling account and entered the variances in budget and volume variances accounts.

Required: 1. Give the journal entries for the month.
2. Post to a Work-in-Process Inventory T account and verify the ending balance.
3. Prepare a schedule to account for the manufacturing overhead volume variance.

P22-5. The Gnawson Company manufactures a single product in several styles, all of which are uniform as to quantity of materials and production time requirements. The standard cost card for all products reveals the following quantities and costs:

Materials:	6 pieces × $1	$ 6
Direct labor:	8 hours × $4	32
Manufacturing overhead:	8 hours × $4	32
Total		$70

The normal (100%) standard budgeted overhead costs consist of

Direct labor hours	2,000
Variable costs	$2,000
Fixed costs	6,000
Total costs	$8,000

Production data for July, 1973, are given (there was no June 30, 1973, work-in-process inventory):

Completed: 250 units

In process as of July 31: 10 units, 40 percent complete as to materials and 30 percent complete as to labor and overhead

Selected transactions for the month of July, 1973, included the following:

1. Materials purchased were 1,600 pieces at $0.98.
2. Materials issued for production totaled 1,530 pieces.
3. Manufacturing overhead incurred was $8,200.
4. Manufacturing overhead was applied to production.
5. Closed the Manufacturing Overhead controlling account and entered the variances in budget and volume variance accounts.

> Required: 1. Prepare the journal entries to record the transactions.
> 2. Prepare the end-of-period entries to close the four established variances.

P22-6. The standard cost card for the Ennis Company shows the following information in regard to its commodity, Zamblam:

Materials: 4 pounds of Dunker at $1.50	$ 6
Direct labor: 2 hours at $2	4
Total	$10

The schedule of equivalent production reveals the following figures:

	Materials	Direct Labor
Equivalent production	52,000 units	51,600 units

Selected transactions for the month of November, 1973, included the following:

1. Purchased 215,600 pounds of Dunker at $1.49 per pound.
2. Requisitioned for production 207,950 pounds of Dunker.
3. Factory payroll incurred during the period was 103,100 hours at a total cost of $205,100.
4. Standard direct labor costs were assigned to production at the standard rate.

> Required: 1. Prepare the journal entries to record the transactions.
> 2. Prepare the end-of-period entries to close the four established variances.

P22-7. (*Managerial policy decision problem*) The Calvin Manufacturing Company, having completed its first year of operations on December 31, 1973, reported the following:

Units sold	24,000
Units produced	36,000
Sales price per unit	$ 20.00
Variable manufacturing cost per unit	8.00
Fixed manufacturing overhead	216,000.00
Fixed manufacturing overhead cost per unit	6.00
(There was no ending work-in-process inventory)	
Variable selling and administrative expenses per unit sold	0.60
Fixed selling and administrative expenses	80,000.00

Required:

1. Prepare income statements for the year 1973, using (a) the absorption costing method and (b) the direct costing method.
2. Prepare a schedule to account for the difference in net income or net loss.
3. Which costing method gives the better cost and net income information assuming sound accounting principles are applied? Discuss.

4. Would your answer in Requirement 3 be the same in regard to the development of cost and income information for decision making? Discuss.

P22-8. (*Accounting policy decision problem*) On January 1, 1973, the Lampman Manufacturing Company began the manufacture of a new product. Management is disturbed because, in spite of a substantial increase in sales, profits decreased during 1974. The cost accountant explains that reported marginal income does not necessarily fluctuate in proportion to sales unless the statements are prepared on the direct costing basis. Operating data for 1973 and 1974 are

	1973	1974
Units sold	60,000	80,000
Units produced	100,000	50,000
Sales price per unit	$ 18.00	$ 18.00
Variable manufacturing cost per unit	6.00	6.00
Fixed manufacturing overhead	400,000.00	400,000.00
(There was no ending work-in-process inventory)		
Variable selling and administrative expenses per unit sold	0.20	0.20
Fixed selling and administrative expenses	32,000.00	32,000.00

Required:

1. Prepare income statements for 1973 and 1974, using the absorption costing method. In a parallel column, prepare an income statement for 1974 only, assuming sales of 90,000 units. Assume the use of FIFO.
2. Prepare income statements for 1973 and 1974, using the direct costing method. In a parallel column, prepare an income statement for 1974 only, assuming sales of 90,000 units.
3. Under what conditions will the net income be the same under either method?

P22-9. On January 1, 1973, the Buford Company had a finished goods inventory of 5,600 units of its commodity, Ortogum, which had a cost of $61,600 under the absorption costing method and a cost of $42,000 under the direct costing method.

During 1973, the Buford Company manufactured 175,650 units of Ortogum. The fixed manufacturing overhead costs totaled $702,600 during 1973 and the variable unit cost was the same as in 1972. The company sold 100,000 units of Ortogum at $20 each and used the LIFO method of assigning costs to the cost of goods sold.

Operating expenses for the year were

Selling and administrative expenses–fixed	$20,000
Selling and administrative expenses–variable	18,000

Required: 1. Prepare income statements for 1973, using (a) the absorption costing method and (b) the direct costing method.
2. Prepare a schedule to account for the difference in net income or net loss.

23

Special Cost Analyses and Control in Management Decisions

Before costs can be analyzed and interpreted for managerial use, a specific conception of the nature and content of various costs must be known. Therefore, certain basic cost concepts are reviewed or discussed here.

Fixed costs are the costs that, without change in present productive capacity, are not affected by changes in volume of output. For instance, rent on a factory building is a fixed cost because it does not change when productive volume increases or decreases.

Variable costs are costs that are affected in total by changes in the volume of output. The cost of materials, for example, is a variable cost because it increases in direct proportion to the increase in the number of units produced.

Semifixed costs are costs that vary in steps; they are not affected by changes in volume of output within a given range of output. For example, one inspector may be required for an output of 0 to 10,000 units; two may be required for outputs of 10,001 to 20,000 units; and on.

Semivariable costs are costs that include both a fixed and a variable component. An example is a foreman who receives a base salary plus a bonus determined by a percent of production.

Marginal costs (or *differential costs*) are the differences in cost between two levels of output, or the additional cost necessary to produce an additional unit.

Opportunity cost is the cost of foregoing one thing to get its next best alternative; for example, a company may make a large investment in plant and equipment, thereby giving up an opportunity to invest in bonds.

Out-of-pocket costs are costs that give rise to cash expenditures, such as wages, in contrast to depreciation, which requires no cash disbursement in the current period.

Sunk costs are costs that do not involve new cash expenditures and that therefore should not enter into a specific management decision. The difference between the undepreciated original cost of an old machine and what it would bring in the secondhand market is such a cost.

As a general rule, no single cost concept is relevant for all the decisions that must be made. Different kinds of decisions require different kinds of cost calculations. The problems of determining periodic net income are different from the problems met by management in day-to-day operations. Cost calculations that serve one purpose will not always serve another.

Business decisions are made after alternative courses of action are considered; the identification of the alternatives to be considered is itself a very important aspect of decision making. A rational decision depends on a determination of the expected consequences of each of the various alternatives. It is only the prospective differences in consequences that influence the choice. Only those factors that are affected by the choice should be viewed as relevant to the decision.

If a cost is the same for each alternative under consideration, that cost should have no bearing on the outcome of the decision. As a general rule, fixed costs are common to all alternatives and hence have little meaning to many managerial problems. The relevant costs for the majority of business decisions are variable costs; however, it must be realized that in the long run all costs are variable; hence, for long-run decisions, all costs are relevant. Also, in those short- and intermediate-run decisions involving the addition of an element of fixed cost, the cost that is added becomes, in effect, a variable cost for the particular decision to be made. In other words, marginal cost as defined is simply that cost which is variable for the specific decision under consideration—that is, the variable cost as such plus any additional fixed cost per unit, due to new facilities, that will be incurred in implementing the decision.

The average total absorption cost described in Chapters 21 and 22 is acceptable for measuring the amount of inventories for statement presentation, for the calculation of net income, and for decisions of long run effect; for example, a firm would not build a new plant unless it were sure of earning a return after the recovery of total expired costs. As a general rule, however, these average unit cost figures are unacceptable as a guide to short-run decisions.

In decision making, all relevant differences are necessarily future differences, starting from the moment of decision. Past events cannot be changed by a decision made today. Past costs in dollars of any size are not relevant costs. Present and estimated future costs are the only relevant costs. It should be emphasized, however, that sometimes the only guides to present and future costs are past book figures.

Some of the specific managerial decisions for which special cost analyses must be prepared are discussed in this chapter. As will be shown in the following discussion, these analyses may require the use of data that are not readily available from regular accounting records. The more complex decisions involving the acquisition of plant assets and those decisions requiring the use of quantitative techniques are discussed in Chapter 24.

BREAK-EVEN ANALYSIS

The *break-even point* is the volume of sales at which the business will neither earn income nor incur a loss; it is the point at which expired costs, or expenses, and revenue are exactly equal. The break-even point indicates to management the volume of sales needed to cover total costs and expenses, which must be broken down into only two basic components—fixed and variable. Sales in excess of the break-even point result in a net income because fixed costs have been recovered at the break-even sales volume.

Break-even analysis is an aid to management in policy making because it highlights the effect on income of changes in selling prices, volume of sales, *product mix* (changes in the type of products sold), variable costs, and fixed costs. An understanding of the interaction of these factors assists management in budgeting and income planning and in evaluating the effects of alternative courses of action.

Computation of the Break-Even Point

Since the break-even point is the volume of sales at which the business will neither earn net income nor incur a loss, the following basic formula is indicated:

$$S_{\text{BEP}} - (FC + VC_{\text{BEP}}) = 0$$

where S_{BEP} = sales at break-even point
FC = total fixed costs
VC_{BEP} = variable costs at break-even point

Further, since S_{BEP} is the unknown element in the equation and since VC_{BEP} depends on a knowledge of the sales at break-even point, VC_{BEP} has to be stated as a percentage of sales. With this in mind, the equation can be restated as follows:

$$S_{\text{BEP}} = FC + VC_{\text{BEP}}$$

and

$$VC_{\text{BEP}} = \frac{TVC}{TS} S_{\text{BEP}},$$

where TVC = total variable cost for whatever volume of actual or budgeted sales is used in the computation
TS = the total sales volume that corresponds to the total variable cost

Then the equation may be further restated, thus,

$$S_{\text{BEP}} = \frac{FC}{1 - \dfrac{TVC}{TS}}$$

To illustrate, assume that the budgeted data of Jackson Corporation are as shown in Figure 23-1.

Figure 23-1. Data for Break-Even Computation

	Fixed	Variable	Budgeted Net Income Calculation
Budgeted sales: 20,000 units $15 each			$300,000
Budgeted costs			
Direct materials		$ 25,000	
Direct labor		35,000	
Factory overhead	$ 50,000	40,000	
Selling expenses	30,000	15,000	
Administrative expenses	25,000	5,000	
Totals	$105,000	$120,000	$225,000
Budgeted Net Income			$ 75,000

The break-even point is $175,000, computed as follows:

$$\frac{\$105,000}{1 - (\$120,000)/(\$300,000)} = \frac{\$105,000}{1 - 0.40} = \frac{\$105,000}{0.60} = \$175,000$$

The mechanics of the break-even computation are further illustrated by the following equation:

$$\text{Variable cost percentage} = \frac{\text{Total variable costs}}{\text{Total sales}} = \frac{\$120,000}{\$300,000} = 0.40$$

Thus, 40 percent of sales is required to cover the variable costs.

	Percent
Break-even sales	100
Variable costs	40
Fixed costs at break-even point	60

Then 60 percent of each sales dollar (the *contribution percentage*) is available to cover the fixed costs.

$$S_{BEP} = \frac{\text{Fixed costs}}{\text{Contribution percentage}} = \frac{\$105,000}{0.60} = \$175,000 = \begin{array}{l}\text{Volume of sales at}\\\text{break-even point}\end{array}$$

The proof of this solution is as follows:

Break-even sales		$175,000
Costs		
Variable (40%)	$ 70,000	
Fixed (60%)	105,000	175,000
Net income		$ –0–

The Break-Even Chart

One effective means of presenting the relationship of fixed and variable costs to sales at different volume levels is the *break-even chart*. Two charts as shown (Figures 23-2 and 23-3) are based on data in Figure 23-1. In Figure 23-2, the vertical line (*y* axis) represents dollars from which both total sales and various costs can be read; the horizontal line (*x* axis) represents sales unit volume and percent of plant capacity. The fixed costs, assumed to be unaffected by volume changes, are, therefore, represented by a horizontal line running parallel to the *x* axis. Total costs, which are affected by volume changes, are represented by a straight line starting at the fixed cost point on the *y* axis and rising to the right of the chart. The point at which the two lines meet is the break-even point; at this point costs equal sales so that there is neither income nor loss. The spread between the lines above the intersection measures the amount of income; the spread between the lines below the intersection measures the amount of loss.

In Figure 23-2, the fixed costs line is below the variable costs line. In Figure 23-3, an inverted break-even chart, the fixed costs line is above the variable costs line to show clearly the portion of the fixed costs remaining to be recovered (loss area) before income is realized. The break-even point in the two forms is, of course, the same.

Both charts show the *relevant volume range*, which is the operating range

Figure 23-2. Typical Break-Even Chart

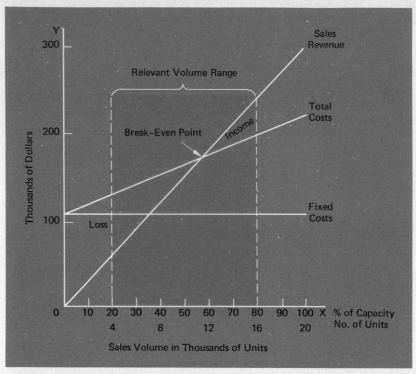

Figure 23-3. Inverted Break-Even Chart

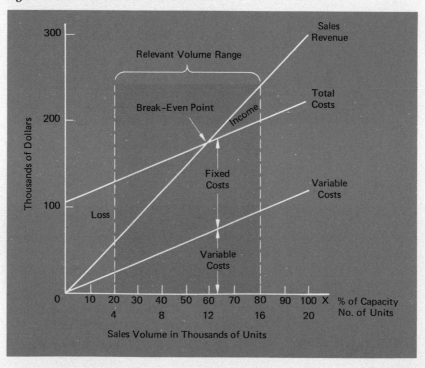

span over which all costs are likely to be either completely fixed or exactly variable. This range excludes extremely high and low levels of volume where the probability of the cost behavior patterns would most likely be different from those indicated for the output of the relevant volume range; for example, semifixed costs are lower at the lower volume range and are higher at the higher volume range. The information contained in the relevant volume range of the chart is, thus, more reliable for decision making than is the information contained in the nonrelevant range area of the chart.

The charts are based on certain assumptions regarding the relationship between prices and costs and the relative proportions of the various products sold. Further assumptions are that costs are either fixed or variable and that variable costs are affected proportionately by volume changes; and that beginning and ending inventories, price levels, product mix, and technical plant and labor efficiency will remain essentially unchanged. The degree and the effect of these factors on actual and assumed conditions must be carefully balanced and evaluated in break-even analysis. Break-even charts may be prepared from budgeting data as a forecast of costs and income, or they may be based on data taken from the books as a historical presentation of cost-volume-income relationships.

The break-even point in terms of units or in terms of percentage of plant capacity used may be determined from the x-axis scale. The amounts at the break-even point are as shown (see Figure 23-2):

Break-even percent of plant capacity	58.3
Break-even units (assuming a single product or a constant mix)	11,667

The break-even percentage of operating capacity may also be verified mathematically as follows:

$$\frac{\text{Break-even sales volume}}{\text{Budgeted sales volume}} = \frac{\$175,000}{\$300,000} = 58.3\%$$

The break-even point in units is proven in the following equation:

$$x = \text{number of units sold at break-even point at \$15 each}$$
$$15x = 15(0.4x) + 105,000$$
$$9x = 105,000$$
$$x = 11,667$$

The same computation may be made in the following terms:

Line		
1	Unit sales price (see Figure 23-1)	$ 15
2	Unit variable cost (0.40 × $15)	6
3	Unit contribution (amount available for the recovery of fixed costs and profit)	$ 9
4	Fixed costs	$105,000
5	Unit break-even sales (line 4 ÷ line 3)	11,667

The proof of this calculation is

Sales (11,667 × $15)		$175,000*
Costs		
Variable (11,667 × $6)	$ 70,000*	
Fixed	105,000	175,000
Net Income		$ –0–

*Adjusted for rounding.

As indicated, cost variability in break-even analysis has been based on the assumption that costs can be segregated into two groups—those that vary directly with volume and those that are unaffected by volume changes. This assumption is an oversimplification, and care must be taken against reaching possible erroneous conclusions, particularly for conclusions based on information outside of the relevant volume range area. The course of many costs as shown in Chapter 22 is quite erratic in relation to volume. This is particularly true of second-shift costs, fringe benefits, and so on. Few if any costs are uniform in terms of units of output or time except within relatively limited volume ranges, referred to here as the *relevant volume range*.

Other limitations, in summary, are (1) if the break-even chart is based on data of only one or just a few periods, the results obtained may not be typical of the company's experience; and (2) the chart is not well designed for firms that sell a great variety of products, the proportions of which may change.

MARGINAL INCOME STATEMENTS

Marginal income, or contribution to fixed cost, is the excess of revenue over variable costs and variable expenses. The marginal income statement, therefore, separates costs and expenses into their fixed and variable elements. It is a convenient means of presenting data to management when charts or other forms might not be as serviceable. The break-even sales volume can be calculated readily from such a statement. A marginal income statement and break-even computation for the Jackson Corporation is shown in Figure 23-4 (see Figure 23-1 for supporting data).

Figure 23-4. Marginal Income Statement

Sales (net): 20,000 units × $15 each	$300,000
Variable costs and expenses	120,000
Marginal income	$180,000
Fixed costs and expenses	105,000
Net income	$ 75,000
Marginal income (or contribution) percentage	60%
Break-even point: $105,000 ÷ 0.60	$175,000
Break-even point in units: $\dfrac{\$105,000}{\$15 - 0.4\,(\$15)}$	11,667

From this information, the following basic equations may be derived:

Sales − Variable costs = Marginal income

Marginal income − Fixed costs = Net income

Marginal income ÷ Sales = Marginal income, or contribution, percentage

Fixed costs ÷ Contribution percentage = Break-even point in sales dollars

Fixed costs ÷ Contribution per unit = Break-even point in units

A marginal income statement is prepared to emphasize the contribution of each sales dollar toward the recovery of fixed costs and toward net income. Marginal income must equal fixed costs if the firm is to break even; marginal income must exceed fixed costs if a net income is to be realized. Thus, in Figure 23-4, 60 cents out of each sales dollar contributes to the recovery of fixed costs up to sales of $175,000; out of each dollar of sales thereafter, 60 cents contributes to net income.

MARGIN OF SAFETY

The *margin of safety* is the dollar volume of sales above the break-even point, or the amount or percentage by which sales may decrease before losses are incurred. The margin of safety for the Jackson Corporation is

Sales	$300,000
Deduct break-even sales	175,000
Margin of safety	$125,000

A loss will not be incurred unless sales decrease by more than $125,000. The percentage of safety is computed as follows:

$$\frac{\text{Margin of safety}}{\text{Net sales}} = \frac{\$125,000}{\$300,000} = 0.4167$$

Any decreases in sales up to 41.67 percent can be absorbed before a loss is incurred.

MARGINAL INCOME PLANNING

The effect of any prospective changes in operations can be determined rapidly when data on costs are divided between the fixed and variable elements. This kind of evaluation and analysis is demonstrated in the following two cases.

Case 1. The Excel Manufacturing Company is considering the possibility of expanding the present plant facilities at a time when the plant is operating at full capacity. Two important factors that must be known before the decision is made are the sales volume required with the planned expansion to earn the current income and an appraisal from the marketing department of whether this figure can be reached and exceeded.

Assume the following data for the Excel Manufacturing Company:

	Under Present Plant Facilities		Under Proposed Plant Facilities	
Sales		$600,000		$800,000
Variable costs	$180,000		$240,000	
Fixed costs	350,000	530,000	462,000	702,000
Net income		$ 70,000		$ 98,000

The following basic formula (expanded from the break-even formula) is appropriate to determine the sales volume required with the planned expansion to earn a specified amount of income:

$$S = VC_S + FC + I$$

where I = specified income
VC_S = variable costs at the specifically required sales volume

Thus, the formula can be stated:

$$S = \frac{FC + I}{1 - \dfrac{TVC}{TS}}$$

The data for the company may be substituted in the foregoing formula,

$$S = \frac{\$462,000 + \$70,000}{1 - (\$240,000/\$800,000)} = \$760,000$$

This is verified in conventional income statement form as follows:

Sales (S)		$760,000
Variable costs (0.30S)	$228,000	
Fixed costs	462,000	690,000
Net income (currently being earned)		$ 70,000

It is assumed in this illustration that the variable cost rate will continue to be 30 percent of sales. It is possible that the additional facilities may permit an increase in the productivity of labor or purchasing economies, thus causing a decrease in the variable cost rate. Other factors must be considered in determining whether the proposed expansion is warranted. The acquisition of additional plant and equipment involves long-term investments, possible long-term financing, and increased taxes, insurance, maintenance, and other costs. Management should be reasonably assured that it will be able to make sustained use of the added facilities.

Case 2. A corporation is considering whether to purchase some special machines. Management will buy the machines if their cost can be recovered in three years—that is, if the marginal income (less out-of-pocket related fixed costs other than depreciation) generated by these machines over a three-year period is equal to their cost. Assume the following facts:

1. The machines cost $180,000.
2. The annual revenue generated by the machines will total $200,000.
3. The variable cost is 60 percent of sales.

The marginal income is $80,000 per year, computed as

$$[(1.00 - 0.60) \times \$200,000] - \$80,000$$

If the annual fixed cost on these machines other than depreciation—property taxes, insurance, and so on—amounts to $6,000 per year, then the remainder, or $74,000 ($80,000 − $6,000) per year, is a recovery of the cost of the machines. At this rate, the cost of the machines will be recouped in approximately 2.4 years, determined as follows:

$$\frac{\$180,000}{\$74,000} = 2.4 \text{ years}$$

If this is the only variable upon which the decision rests, then the special machines should be purchased. A more complete discussion of this and other problems involving investments in plant assets may be found in Chapter 24.

PRICING OF SPECIAL ORDERS

A decision with which management is often confronted is whether or not to accept a special order involving the production of additional units beyond outstanding commitments. An analysis of pre-existing cost patterns will not necessarily furnish the required data for such a decision. Each new situation requires a new cost analysis. The probable effect of the additional order on fixed manufacturing costs, selling and administrative expenses, selling price, and possible reduction in direct material costs resulting from increased volume buying must be analyzed carefully.

If the price of the special order exceeds its marginal costs—which will equal variable costs if unused capacity is available—and there are no alternative uses for this available capacity, the offer should be accepted. To illustrate, assume the following total unit cost data for the Jason Company, based on a budgeted annual production of 60,000 units:

Manufacturing costs		
Direct materials	$	2.00
Direct labor		2.50
Variable overhead costs		1.50
Total variable costs	$	6.00
Fixed overhead costs ($180,000 ÷ 60,000 units)		3.00
Total unit cost	$	9.00
Fixed selling and administrative expenses	$100,000.00	

The Jason Company has been offered a long-term contract for 20,000 additional units annually at a unit price of $8.50. Since the purchaser is to attach his own label to the product, the Jason Company's established price of $15 each will not be affected. Because fixed costs are not affected by the volume of production, fixed manufacturing, fixed selling, and fixed administrative expenses, $280,000 in this case, will not be increased by the new order. Therefore, since the special offer price of $8.50 exceeds the marginal costs of $6, the regular sales are not affected, and a gain of $50,000 is realized on the additional order, the offer should be accepted. The comparative budget data shown below verify this conclusion.

	JASON COMPANY Budgeted Comparative Income Statement For the Year Ending December 31, 1973		
	Budgeted Production	Additional Order	Totals
Sales			
60,000 units at $15.00	$900,000		
20,000 units at 8.50		$170,000	$1,070,000
Variable Costs			
60,000 units at $ 6.00	360,000		
20,000 units at 6.00		120,000	480,000
Marginal Income	$540,000	$ 50,000	$ 590,000
Fixed Costs	280,000		280,000
Net Income	$260,000	$ 50,000	$ 310,000

The data also indicate the possibility of developing a new market through price reductions made possible by the absorption of fixed costs in the regular volume of business. This may be particularly effective when a product is sold in a foreign market, or in any decisions involving levels of output or the cost of additional volume.

PRODUCT PRICING

An intricate relationship exists between the factors of price, cost, and volume. An understanding of this relationship is imperative because it underlies virtually every decision confronting management. It is essential, therefore, that management make continuing analyses of its selling prices, particularly for competitive products.

One of the knottiest problems is calculating the effect of price on the volume of sales in terms of both short-run and long-run effects. The cost analyst plays a significant role in pricing policy decisions by projecting the effect on costs and income of the sales volumes that may be expected at different prices.

The method of accumulating costs to arrive at total costs has been discussed in previous chapters. Total costs consist of direct costs (direct materials and labor), variable manufacturing overhead (power, supplies, maintenance), and fixed manufacturing overhead (insurance, taxes, depreciation). The process of establishing a predetermined overhead rate involves an allocation of the fixed manufacturing overhead on some arbitrary basis as well as an estimated volume factor that becomes the denominator in the overhead rate formula. The pricing of the product on this total cost basis is often considered unsatisfactory (1) because the allocation of overhead items is inherently imprecise, (2) because the projected volume on which the overhead rate is based is also imprecise, and (3) because total cost is not relevant to short-run decisions.

In general, however, the unit price that yields the greatest marginal income is the price that should be used for a particular product. Following this approach, therefore, a schedule should be prepared based on variable costs only, such as the one in Figure 23-5 showing the probable volume of sales and the marginal income that will result at each of the several price levels under consideration. It may be assumed that the volume-price relationships are estimated from the results of a market survey based on test sales in selected areas and on questionnaires.

Figure 23-5. Marginal Income at Various Prices

Quantity	Sales Price Per Unit	Projected Sales	Variable Costs ($40 per unit)	Marginal Income
40,000	$80.00	$3,200,000	$1,600,000	$1,600,000
45,000	78.00	3,510,000	1,800,000	1,710,000
55,000	75.00	4,125,000	2,200,000	1,925,000
57,000	72.50	4,132,500	2,280,000	1,852,500
65,000	67.00	4,355,000	2,600,000	1,755,000

A sales price of $75 per unit will provide the greatest marginal income—that is, $1,925,000. The $75 selling price does not provide the greatest margin on each unit sold; the unit marginal income is $35 compared with $40 at the $80 selling price. The increased sales volume at the lower price, however, results in a greater total marginal income.

When more than one product is priced, it is necessary to find a combination of price and volume that results in the greatest marginal income. Assume, for example, that the Baker Company manufactures two different products, X and Y, that require nearly identical production processes. Variable unit costs are $10 for Product X and $10 for Product Y. Facilities are available to produce a combined total of 11,000 units. The following schedule was prepared to aid management in its pricing policy:

	Sales Price Per Unit	Projected Sales	Variable Cost	Marginal Income
Product X				
Quantity				
4,000	$22	$ 88,000	$40,000	$48,000
5,000	20	100,000	50,000	50,000
7,000	16	112,000	70,000	42,000
Product Y				
3,000	$26	$ 78,000	$36,000	$42,000
5,000	23	115,000	60,000	55,000
7,000	22	154,000	84,000	70,000

A combination of 5,000 units of Product X and 7,000 units of Product Y results in the largest possible marginal income ($50,000 + $70,000 = $120,000). If, however, plant capacity cannot be efficiently expanded beyond the previously assumed level of 11,000 units, the most profitable combination is 4,000 units of Product X and 7,000 units of Product Y for a total marginal income of $118,000 ($48,000 + $70,000).

The establishment of prices based on marginal income is the customary practice in retailing. Prices are set on the basis of a percentage markup on cost. The markup must be delicately adjusted to gauge the responsiveness of consumer demand. Studies may be made to determine the percentage of change that results from each percentage price change (elasticity of demand) for products whose sales potential fluctuates inversely with changes in price.

In these examples, it is assumed that fixed costs remain the same at all the indicated sales levels and that net income is, therefore, maximized at prices that provide the greatest marginal income. Total unit costs (fixed and variable) depend, however, on total volume, and total volume in turn depends on the price charged. It is for this reason that cost studies also should be made showing estimates of total cost and net income at the various sales levels. Such studies might indicate maximum net income at levels different from the marginal income studies. In the last analysis, a firm must recover total costs, not just variable costs. Long-term pricing based on marginal income might result in prices set too close to the marginal income point, possibly resulting in needless cutthroat competition within the industry.

Another factor is that the firm may not be motivated exclusively by the maximum income objective. In the long run—or even in the short run—a just price resulting in a reasonable income may prove ultimately to be the best price. A short-run price based on maximized income may operate adversely in the long run by depressing future demand. There is also the possibility that competing costs and prices are such as to permit setting a price above the level indicated by the marginal income analysis should the firm so decide.

DECIDING TO MAKE OR TO BUY

Management must often decide whether to make or to buy a particular part, product, or plant asset. If the plant facilities have already been acquired, the capacity is available, quality can be assured, and there are no negative factors, the decision depends on a comparison of marginal costs, which in this case are equal to variable costs, with the outside purchase price of the item. (If other fixed costs have to be added, then marginal cost would be larger than variable cost.) If the variable production cost of the item—the marginal cost—is less than the quoted purchase price, then the item should be manufactured; if the quoted purchase price is less than the variable cost of the item, it should be purchased.

Assume that the Ames Company manufactures a particular part at a unit cost of $6.80, and that this cost consists of the following:

Direct materials	$1.50
Direct labor	2.50
Variable overhead costs	1.20
Total variable costs	$5.20
Fixed overhead costs	1.60
Total unit cost	$6.80

The Ames Company can purchase this part from a reliable manufacturer for $6.05. If the available plant facilities represent sunk costs that cannot be recovered by some other use of the facilities represented by the fixed overhead unit cost of $1.60, then the firm should continue to make the part. The variable costs of $5.20 are less than the quoted purchase price of $6.05 and the difference might be used to defray part of fixed overhead costs. If, on the other hand, the Ames Company can make an alternative and profitable use of those facilities for other purposes, it should buy the part. Under this assumption, fixed overhead costs must be included in the total cost of the part because the company is foregoing the opportunity of making an alternate use of the facilities. With fixed overhead costs included, the unit cost to make is greater than the cost to buy—that is, $6.80 compared with $6.05.

    This involves a decision whether to continue making a product or to buy it. The parallel problem—whether to manufacture a part or a product that is currently being purchased—involves essentially the same factors for consideration, together with such other relevant factors as the effect of the change on inventories and on working capital, on net income before and after taxes, on the rate of return on capital employed, and on the rate of return on sales. Finally, intangible factors at the top management level would also enter into the decision to make or to buy.

DEPARTMENT, TERRITORY, OR PRODUCT ABANDONMENT

The decision whether or not to abandon a supposedly unprofitable department, territory, or product involves a careful analysis of the effect of the abandonment on the fixed and variable costs and the marginal income. If a department, territory, or product produces any marginal income it should not be abandoned unless the newly created capacity—that is, a substituted new department, territory, or product—could be committed to a more profitable use.

    The departmental income statement of the Stevens Clothing Company is shown in Figure 23-6. The accountant for the company has been asked by the management to study the probable effect on total costs if the Children's Department is eliminated. Management is aware that although closing the department will entirely eliminate sales, cost of goods sold, and gross margin, certain other costs currently chargeable to the department will continue. A careful analysis reveals the cost tabulation shown in Figure 23-7.

    As a result of this study, the effect of discontinuing the Children's Department can be reasonably forecast as follows:

Net operating income of all departments (Figure 23-6)		$15,545
Reduction in gross margin on sales (Figure 23-6)	$7,770	
Reduction in variable costs (Figure 23-7)	4,454	
Reduction in net operating income		3,316
Combined net operating income with Children's Department eliminated		$12,229

Based on this calculation, the Children's Department should not be eliminated even though it shows a net loss. The department contributed to the earnings of

Figure 23-6. Departmental Income Statement

STEVENS CLOTHING COMPANY
Income Statement
For the Year Ended December 31, 1973

	Men's Department	Women's Department	Children's Department	Combined
Sales (net)	$78,910	$128,000	$34,400	$241,310
Cost of Goods Sold	53,656	90,444	26,630	170,730
Gross Margin on Sales	$25,254	$ 37,556	$ 7,770	$ 70,580
Deduct Operating Expenses				
Advertising Expense	$ 981	$ 1,590	$ 429	$ 3,000
Salesmen's Salaries	9,050	12,030	3,515	24,595
Commissions Expense	750	1,100	240	2,090
Rent Expense	2,160	3,600	1,440	7,200
Depreciation Expense–Store Equipment	400	500	100	1,000
Supervisor's Salary	2,603	5,196	1,301	9,100
Office Salary	1,158	2,313	579	4,050
Insurance Expense	480	600	120	1,200
Bad Debts Expense	75	175	50	300
Miscellaneous General Expenses	400	500	100	1,000
Heat and Light Expense	450	750	300	1,500
Total Operating Expenses	$18,507	$ 28,354	$ 8,174	$ 55,035
Net Operating Income or (Loss)	$ 6,747	$ 9,202	$ (404)	$ 15,545

Figure 23-7. Effect on Costs of Elimination of Children's Department

	Operating Costs Charged to Children's Department	Effect of Elimination of Children's Department	
		Eliminated	Not Eliminated
Variable Costs			
Advertising	$ 429	$ 429	
Salesmen's Salaries	3,515	3,515	
Commissions	240	240	
Insurance	120	120	
Bad Debts	50	50	
General	100	100	
Fixed Costs			
Rent	1,440		$1,440
Depreciation–Store Equipment	100		100
Supervisor's Salary	1,301		1,301
Office Salaries	579		579
Heat and Light	300		300
Totals	$8,174	$4,454	$3,720

the company by absorbing a part of the fixed expenses. Elimination of the department will reduce net operating income by $3,316.

Children's Department fixed costs (Figure 23-7)	$3,720
Deduct net loss (Figure 23-6)	404
Reduction in net operating income	$3,316

If this department were discontinued, the other departments would have to absorb the remaining $3,316 of fixed costs, resulting in a comparable decrease in the combined net income.

Another way of verifying this information is to compute the marginal income earned by the Children's Department: revenue of $34,400, less variable costs of $31,084 (cost of goods sold of $26,630 plus variable operating expenses of $4,454), equals $3,316, the advantage to the total firm of continuing the Children's Department.

In this example, the information used is net operating income (or income before income taxes and other expenses and revenue). Since a loss reduces income taxes, the value of the Children's Department to the total firm would be in reality larger than the $3,316 indicated. The effect of income taxes on the decision was ignored to simplify the problem. Of course, income taxes are pertinent to the problem, but their inclusion in this instance will not change the final decision.

There are, in addition, certain intangible factors that would result from the elimination of the Children's Department and that cannot be measured by an analysis of the income statement. This department brings in customers; business may be lost because some customers will not be able to buy clothing for the entire family in one location. Furthermore, customers who intend to purchase children's clothing only are exposed to the displays of the other two departments, which may result in additional purchases from these other departments. Also, the reduction in the volume of purchases may have a negative effect on the ability of the company to get quantity discounts.

SUMMARY

Although useful in measuring periodic net income, the costs reported in financial statements are often meaningless in the solution of short-run business decisions; therefore, other costs must be developed to satisfy management's requirements.

The word *cost* has many different meanings, some of which follow: (1) fixed costs are those costs that, without change in present productive capacity, are not affected by changes in volume of output. (2) Variable costs are those that change in proportion to changes in volume of output. (3) Semifixed costs are costs that vary in steps; they are not affected by changes in volume of output within a given range of output. (4) Semivariable costs are costs that include both a fixed and a variable component. (5) Marginal, or differential, cost is the difference in cost between two levels of output, or the additional cost necessary to produce an additional unit. In other words, the marginal cost for a specific decision is the variable cost plus any additional fixed cost that will result from the decision to be made. (6) Opportunity cost is the sacrifice involved in accepting one alternative under consideration rather than following another course of action. (7) Out-of-pocket costs are costs that require cash expenditures. (8) Sunk costs are costs that do not involve a new cash expenditure but have arisen from actions taken in the past, and thus are unaffected by a current decision.

There is no cost that is acceptable for all decision-making purposes; cost calculations that serve one purpose do not always serve another purpose. The calculation, therefore, must be tailored to fit the specific decision being analyzed. Most business decisions are results of comparisons of alternative courses of action. In comparing alternatives, costs that are the same under each alternative should be ignored; only those costs that are different under the alternatives are relevant to the decision. In decision making, all relevant costs are present costs or expected future costs; past events cannot be affected by a current decision and thus are irrelevant to current decisions.

The break-even point is the volume of sales at which a company neither realizes a net income nor incurs a net loss. The break-even chart graphically depicts the relationships between variable and fixed costs, revenue, and income. Break-even analysis is an aid to management in budgeting, income planning, and other decisions because it spotlights the effect on income of changes in volume, product mix, variable costs, and fixed costs. The relevant volume range area of a break-even chart contains information that is more reliable for decision making because it is restricted to a volume span in which certain costs are basically completely fixed and others are more likely to be strictly variable. The use of break-even analysis is subject to certain limitations: (1) the assumption that all costs are either fixed or variable is an oversimplification since many costs behave erratically with changes in volume, especially outside a relatively limited volume range; (2) if the break-even chart is based on one period or only a few periods, the results obtained may not be typical of the company's experience; and (3) a break-even chart assumes a specific product mix, and any change in the product mix invalidates the previous break-even chart.

In a marginal income statement, costs are divided into fixed and variable, rather than by the nature of the expenditure, as in the conventional income statement. Thus, the contribution of sales revenue toward the recovery of fixed costs and the earning of income is emphasized. The separation of costs in such a manner is useful for decision-making purposes, because the effect of any prospective changes can be quickly determined. The margin of safety is the dollar volume of sales above the break-even point or the percentage by which sales may decrease before a loss is incurred.

A special offer to produce additional units beyond outstanding plans and commitments should be accepted if there is a resultant marginal income (excess of revenue from the offer over the marginal cost of producing the additional units) and if there are no adverse effects on regular sales and business operations.

The determination of the optimum selling price of a product involves a thorough analysis of the intricate relationships between price, cost, and volume. Generally, the unit price of a product should be the one that yields the greatest marginal income.

If the marginal cost of producing an item is less than the outside purchase price of the item, the item should be manufactured. Fixed costs (other than the additional fixed costs created by the production of the item) should be omitted from the determination of the marginal cost if the available productive capacity cannot be utilized in any other manner.

A seemingly unprofitable department, product, or territory should be discontinued or abandoned only if it produces no marginal income or the capacity presently devoted to it could be committed to a more profitable use.

All factors involved in decision making cannot be reduced to simplified quantitative computations. Many intangible and qualitative factors that cannot be expressed in quantitative terms must also be analyzed and considered in conjunction with quantitative measures to reach the most appropriate decisions. The more factors, however, that can be reduced to quantitative terms, the less will be the area over which value judgments must be made. Chapter 24 explores the use of other quantitative methods that are now being used in decision making.

Q23-1. Define the following terms: (a) sunk costs, (b) variable costs, and (c) out-of-pocket costs.

Q23-2. What is meant by the saying, "Different costs for different purposes"? Illustrate by explaining how an element of depreciation might be treated differently, as a cost, for different purposes.

Q23-3. (a) Costs relevant to a decision must be present or estimated future costs. Explain. (b) Can past costs ever be relevant to a given decision?

Q23-4. (a) What is meant by the term *break-even point?* (b) How is it computed? (c) What are its practical applications? (d) What are its limitations?

Q23-5. Define the following terms: (a) operating capacity, (b) product mix, (c) margin of safety, and (d) marginal income statement.

Q23-6. Under what circumstances would it be advantageous for a manufacturer in this country to accept a long-term contract for his product from a foreign buyer?

Q23-7. The sales price of a product should be the amount that will result in the largest marginal income. Comment.

Q23-8. Is maximum income the sole objective in determining the sales price of a new product?

Q23-9. (a) What use does management make of cost data in deciding whether to make or buy a certain part? (b) Should fixed costs enter into the decision?

Q23-10. (a) Is it possible for one of three departments in a retail store to show a net loss even though its elimination would decrease the total net income of the entire store? (b) What other intangible factors must be considered when deciding whether or not a certain department should be eliminated?

E23-1. For the year 1973, the Tilson Company estimates fixed costs at $195,000 and variable costs at $1.30 per unit.

1. How many units must be sold to break even, assuming a unit sales price of $3.25?
2. Prepare an income statement in proof of your answer.

E23-2. The Rangoon Company has fixed costs of $440,000 per year. Its variable costs are $6.60 per unit and its sales price is $11 per unit. It is considering the purchase of machinery that will increase the fixed costs to $512,000 per year, but will enable the company to reduce variable costs to $4.84 per unit.

1. Compute the break-even point before and after the acquisition of the new machinery, giving it in both sales dollars and units of product.
2. If net income before the acquisition is $88,000, how many units will have to be sold after the machinery is acquired to maintain the net income?

E23-3. The fixed costs in the Edison Division of the Langer Company are now $736,000 per year. They are expected to increase to $760,000 next year. Variable costs will also go up from $4.40 to $4.80 per unit. Its product sells for $9.60 per unit.

How much sales revenue must be obtained to have a net income (before taxes) of $72,000 next year?

E23-4. A new machine costing $320,000 is under consideration. The product it makes sells for $10 per unit and requires materials costing $2.20, direct labor of $3.20, and other variable costs of $0.30 per unit. Sales of 40,000 units per year are assumed. Applicable annual fixed costs other than depreciation amount to $12,000.

Over what period of time would this investment be recovered?

E23-5. The Jaxson Company manufactures and sells 1,500,000 units of its product in the United States annually. The selling price per unit is $20, variable costs are $8 per unit, and fixed costs are $10 per unit.

Should the company accept an additional order to sell 500,000 units abroad at (a) $7.50 per unit? (b) $7.90 per unit; (c) $9.00 per unit; (d) $10.50 per unit? Explain your answer to each question.

E23-6. The Jason Company was organized early in 1973. During 1973, it produced 6,000 units and sold 5,600 units; costs for the year were

Variable costs	
Direct materials	$21,600
Direct labor	28,800
Manufacturing overhead	34,500
Selling and administrative expenses	9,000
Fixed costs	
Manufacturing overhead	13,500
Selling and administrative expenses	6,000

The selling price per unit is $22.

1. Calculate the break-even point.
2. Prepare a marginal income statement.
3. Compute the margin of safety, expressed as a dollar amount.

E23-7. Ronson, Inc., can sell 22,000 units of its product at $8 per unit. The variable costs of this product are $3 per unit. However, a reduction in sales price to $6 per unit would increase units sold to 35,000. The greater volume of production would reduce variable costs to $2.50 per unit; fixed costs are expected to increase by $15,000. Should Ronson, Inc., reduce its selling price? Explain and support with computations.

E23-8. The Columbia Company manufactures Parzine; unit costs are as follows:

Direct materials	$ 6
Direct labor	4
Variable overhead costs	2
Subtotal	$12
Fixed overhead costs	3
Total	$15

The Columbia Company can purchase this part for $13.40.

Should Parzine be purchased if (a) fixed overhead unit cost of $3 is a sunk cost? (b) an alternative and profitable use can be made of the plant facilities now devoted to making Parzine?

E23-9. The following operational information is available for the Glosson Department Store for 1973:

| | Department | | | |
	1	2	3	Total
Net operating income or (loss)	$10,000	$20,000	$(5,000)	$25,000
Marginal income	22,000	37,600	2,000	61,600

1. Should Department 3 be eliminated?
2. If Department 3 is eliminated and 1974's operating results for Departments 1 and 2 are the same as in 1973, how much higher (or lower) will the 1974 net operating income be?

DEMONSTRATION PROBLEMS

DP23-1. (*Break-even sales; income planning in conjunction with expansion of plant facilities*) The Hamm Manufacturing Company is operating at full capacity. It has under consideration a plan for the expansion of its plant facilities. Current and projected income statement data are as shown below.

	Under Present Plant Facilities		Under Proposed Plant Facilities	
Sales		$1,000,000		$1,500,000
Variable costs	$400,000		$600,000	
Fixed costs	480,000	880,000	720,000	1,320,000
Net income		$ 120,000		$ 180,000

Required:

1. What is the present break-even point?
2. What is the break-even point under the proposed plan?
3. What will be the amount of sales necessary to realize the current net income of $120,000 under the proposed plan?
4. Prepare an income statement to prove your answer to Requirement 3.

DP23-2. (*Acceptance or rejection of an offer*) The Boston Company is operating at 70 percent of capacity, producing 140,000 pairs of men's fancy boots annually. Actual unit cost and selling price data for the year 1973 are as follows:

Direct materials	$ 6
Direct labor	4
Variable overhead costs	2
Total variable costs	$12
Fixed overhead costs ($700,000 ÷ 140,000)	5
Total unit cost	$17
Selling price	$32

The company has been offered a long-term contract to sell 50,000 pairs of men's boots annually to a Canadian importing firm at $14.50 per pair. This will not affect domestic sales. Fixed overhead costs of $700,000 as well as fixed selling and administrative costs of $1,000,000 will not be affected by the new order.

Required: Prepare comparative statements for management indicating whether or not this long-term contract should be accepted.

DP23-3. (*Product pricing*) After conducting a market survey of its new product, the Colonial Company prepared the following estimates:

Sales Price Per Unit	Estimated Sales (units)
$25	36,000
24	46,000
22	54,000
21	58,000
16	64,000

Variable costs are estimated at $5 per unit.

Required: Determine the price that will result in the maximum marginal income and the maximum net income.

DP23-4. (*Make or buy decision*) The Balderash Manufacturing Company can produce a part for the following costs:

Direct materials	$ 4.50
Direct labor	6.00
Variable overhead costs	2.50
Subtotal	$13.00
Fixed overhead costs	4.00
Total unit costs	$17.00

The Company can purchase the part for $14.

Required: Should the part be purchased if (a) fixed overhead unit cost of $4 is a sunk cost? (b) an alternative and profitable use can be made of those plant facilities now devoted to making the part?

DP23-5. (*Department abandonment*) The following condensed marginal income statement is available for the Solomon Department Store for 1973:

	Department			
	A	B	C	Total
Sales (net)	$350,000	$300,000	$250,000	$900,000
Variable costs	180,000	270,000	120,000	570,000
Marginal income	$170,000	$ 30,000	$130,000	$330,000
Fixed costs	100,000	80,000	68,000	248,000
Net Operating Income (or Loss)	$ 70,000	$ (50,000)	$ 62,000	$ 82,000

Required:

1. Should Department B be eliminated? Explain.
2. Assume that none of the fixed costs can be eliminated if Department B is abandoned, and that the 1974 operational results for Departments A and C are the same as in 1973. Prepare a condensed marginal income statement for 1974, assuming that Department B is eliminated.

P23-1. The Winston Company estimates its costs at full capacity as follows:

Fixed	$210,000
Variable	120,000

Fixed costs are constant at all levels of operation; variable costs vary in direct proportion to sales. Sales at full capacity are estimated at $400,000.

Required:

1. Calculate the break-even point.
2. Determine the break-even percentage of operating capacity.
3. Prepare a marginal income statement assuming full capacity sales.
4. Compute the margin of safety, expressed as a dollar amount.
5. Compute the margin of safety, expressed as a percentage.

P23-2. The management of the Morton Corporation prepared the following budgeted income statement for the year 1973:

	Fixed	Variable	Budgeted Net Income Calculation
Estimated sales (70,000 units at $25)			$1,750,000
Estimated costs			
Direct materials		$266,000	
Direct labor		140,000	
Factory overhead	$410,000	320,000	
Selling	80,000	41,000	
Administrative	60,000	20,500	
Totals	$550,000	$787,500	1,337,500
Estimated net income			$ 412,500

Required:

1. (a) Compute the break-even point. (b) Prove the break-even point. (c) Compute the break-even point expressed as a percentage of operating capacity. (d) Compute the break-even point in units, assuming a constant product mix. (e) Compute the margin of safety, expressed both as a percentage and as a dollar amount.
2. Prepare a marginal income statement.
3. Prepare a break-even chart.

P23-3. The estimate of the Kooky Objects Manufacturing Company is that fixed costs will total $720,000 during 1973 and that variable costs will be $7 per unit.

Required:

1. At a selling price of $15 per unit, at what level of revenue will the company break even?
2. At a selling price of $16 per unit, at what level of revenue will the company break even?
3. In order to earn $500,000 before taxes, how many units will have to be sold at a price of $15.50?

P23-4. (*Managerial policy decision problem*) The Eastern Company can sell 44,000 units of its product at $16 per unit. The variable costs of this product are $6 per unit. However, a reduction in sales price to $14 per unit would increase units sold to 50,000. The greater volume of production would reduce variable costs to $5 per unit; fixed costs are expected to increase by $60,000.

Required: Should the Eastern Company reduce its selling price? Explain, showing supporting computations.

P23-5. The condensed income statement for Krog, Inc. is shown below.

KROG, INC.
Condensed Income Statement
For the Year Ended December 31, 1973

Net Sales		$500,000
Deduct Costs and Expenses		
Variable	$250,000	
Fixed	150,000	400,000
Net Income		$100,000

The directors of Krog, Inc., are considering a plant expansion program from the present 100-percent sales capacity of $500,000 to $750,000. The expansion would increase annual fixed costs by $75,000. Variable costs would remain directly proportional to sales, and the expansion would not change the current relationship of variable costs to sales.

Required:

1. What is the current break-even point?
2. What will the break-even point be under the proposed plan?
3. What dollar amount of sales is required under the proposed plan to produce a net income of $150,000?
4. Prepare an income statement to prove your answer to Requirement 3.

P23-6. (*Managerial policy decision problem*) The Banshee Corporation is considering whether to purchase some special machines. Management does not wish to buy the machines unless their cost can be recovered in three years. The following information is available:

1. Cost of the machines is $360,000.
2. Sales revenue generated by the new machines is estimated to be $400,000.
3. Variable cost is 60 percent of sales.
4. Annual fixed costs other than depreciation total $12,000.

Required:

1. Based on the criterion of the three-year recovery period, should the special machines be purchased? Support your answer with a computation of the period of time required for the investment of $360,000 to be recovered.
2. Discuss briefly any other factors that should be considered by management in deciding whether to acquire the special machines.

P23-7. (*Managerial policy decision problem*) The Lawton Company is currently operating at its full capacity of 200,000 units annually. Costs are as follows:

Direct materials	$400,000
Direct labor	200,000
Variable overhead	100,000
Fixed overhead	60,000
Variable selling and administrative expenses	40,000
Fixed selling and administrative expenses	30,000

The product is sold under Lawton Company brand for $6.15. Hamilton Distributors, Inc., offers to purchase 50,000 units annually for the next five years at $4.10 per unit. This offer, if accepted, will not affect the current selling price because Hamilton Distributors will sell under its own brand name. Acceptance of the offer will have the following results:

1. Labor costs on the additional 50,000 units will be 1½ times the regular rate.
2. Variable selling and administrative expenses will increase by $0.05 per unit on the additional units only.
3. The required additional materials can be purchased at a 5-percent volume discount.
4. All other cost factors will remain the same.

Required: Should Lawton Company accept the offer? Show all your computations in support of your conclusion.

P23-8. The Hamilton Company has the facilities to produce two additional products, Florex and Byxine, which require approximately the same production processes. The following data were made available to management to aid in establishing sales prices and product mix:

Florex		Byxine	
Estimated Sales Units	Sales Price Per Unit	Estimated Sales Units	Sales Price Per Unit
6,000	$65	4,500	$76
7,250	61	7,500	70
10,250	47	10,500	65
Variable costs per unit are $25.		Variable costs per unit are $35.	

Required: What product mix of Florex and Byxine will result in the largest marginal income?

P23-9. (*Managerial policy decision problem*) The Riggsbee Company is presently purchasing five parts used in the manufacture of its finished product. Comparative costs to manufacture the parts and to buy them outside are as shown below.

Part No.	Estimated Materials, Labor, and Variable Overhead to Make	Cost to Buy
1	$20.00	$18.00
2	7.50	8.50
3	5.50	6.50
4	7.00	5.00
5	10.00	9.00
Totals	$50.00	$47.00

The Riggsbee Company has the capacity to produce these parts, and at the present time it has no alternative profitable use for the facilities. Making the parts will not increase fixed costs.

Required:

1. What is the proper decision?
2. Assume that the Riggsbee Company is presently purchasing 20,000 units of each part annually, that it can use the available plant facilities to make and sell annually 10,000 units of a new product without increasing fixed costs, and that this will result in an estimated marginal income of $6.50 per unit. What is the proper decision under these circumstances?

P23-10. (*Managerial policy decision problem*) The management of the Wilson Company is considering the elimination of Department Z. The departmentalized income statement follows:

WILSON COMPANY
Income Statement
For the Year Ended December 31, 1973

	Dept. Y	Dept. Z	Combined
Sales (net)	$134,000	$45,000	$179,000
Cost of Goods Sold	68,000	30,000	98,000
Gross Margin on Sales	$ 66,000	$15,000	$ 81,000
Operating Expenses			
Advertising Expense	$ 4,200	$ 1,200	$ 5,400
Salesmen's Salaries	10,000	6,000	16,000
Office Salaries	3,500	1,700	5,200
Insurance Expense	900	600	1,500
Bad Debts Expense	1,000	500	1,500
Miscellaneous General Expenses	1,800	900	2,700
Rent Expense	11,000	5,000	16,000
Depreciation Expense–Store Equipment	2,000	1,200	3,200
Total Operating Expenses	$ 34,400	$17,100	$ 51,500
Net Operating Income or (Loss)	$ 31,600	$(2,100)	$ 29,500

The following additional data have been submitted to management relative to the proposed elimination of Department Z:

1. There will be a 10-percent decline in the sales of Department Y. The cost of goods sold varies directly with the sales volume.
2. The operating expenses of Department Y will decrease as follows:
   a. Insurance Expense by 5 percent
   b. Bad Debts Expense by 8 percent
   c. Miscellaneous General Expenses by 10 percent
3. The elimination of Department Z will have the following effect on the operating expenses of Department Z:
   a. Advertising Expense, Salesmen's Salaries, Insurance Expense, and Bad Debts Expense will be eliminated.
   b. Of the apportioned Miscellaneous General Expenses, 80 percent will not be incurred.
   c. Office salaries will be reduced by $900 through the dismissal of some part-time employees.
   d. There will be no reduction in Rent Expense or in Depreciation Expense–Store Equipment.

Required:

1. Prepare a statement showing the probable effect on operating costs if Department Z is eliminated.
2. Prepare a statement showing the effect on net income if Department Z is eliminated.
3. Should Department Z be eliminated?

P23-11. (*Managerial policy decision problem*) The Teague Company has three sales territories, A, B, and C. Management is considering the elimination of Territory A. The following condensed information has been prepared to aid in making this decision:

TEAGUE COMPANY
Marginal Income Statement
For the Year Ended December 31, 1973

	Territory			
	A	B	C	Total
Sales (net)	$176,000	$200,000	$300,000	$675,000
Variable Costs	105,000	80,000	120,000	305,000
Marginal Income	$ 70,000	$120,000	$180,000	$370,000
Fixed Costs	100,000	50,000	75,000	225,000
Net Operating Income (or Loss)	$(30,000)	$ 70,000	$105,000	$145,000

None of the fixed costs of Territory A can be eliminated.

Required: Prepare a report to aid management in deciding whether to discontinue Territory A.

P23-12. (*Managerial policy decision problem*) The Parker Oil Company operates a chain of service stations throughout the local area. Each station sells the usual service station products: gasoline, oil, tires, batteries, automobile accessories, and so on. All the products are purchased in bulk by the home office and delivered on a scheduled basis to each station. If a station manager foresees that the quantities he will need will vary by more than 5 percent from the scheduled quantities, he calls the home office at least twenty-four hours in advance of the anticipated delivery time and changes the standing order.

Being an astute businessman, Oman Lauter, the president and major stockholder of the company, has the accountant of the company prepare a separate income statement for each station. Also, he often asks for income statements by product line within each station. However, his main concern at this time is the poor overall operating results of the station located in Johnson City. This station was once considered profitable, but since a nearby military base was closed, business has declined. The most recent income statement is typical of each of the past three years.

Sales		$110,632
Cost of Goods Sold		86,293
Gross Margin on Sales		$ 24,339
Operating Expenses (listed alphabetically)		
Advertising (company-oriented and allocated equally to each station)	$ 950	
Attendants' Salaries (the number of attendants is adequate for the current volume)	10,500	
Depreciation--Building and Equipment	5,000	
Home Office Expenses (allocated to each station based on station sales)	4,500	
Insurance (fire and public liability)	700	
Interest on Average Book Investment (a book charge only; all long-term funds are provided by the stockholders)	4,800	
Local Property Taxes and Privilege Licenses	382	
Manager's Bonus	400	
Manager's Salary	4,800	
Payroll Taxes (attendants' salaries and manager's salary and bonus)	1,042	
Repairs and Maintenance (on building and equipment)	275	
Station Supplies	3,500	
Utilities (electricity, heat, telephone, and water)	310	
Total Operating Expenses		37,159
Net Loss		$(12,820)

Required:

1. As a management consultant with the local certified public accounting firm, what would you recomment to Lauter as the course of action regarding the station in Johnson City? Some possibilities are (a) to continue to operate as is, (b) to discontinue operation, (c) to initiate local advertising, and (d) to sell the station. If your recommendation is to sell the station, what is the minimum amount that Lauter should accept?
2. Give the reason(s) for your recommendation.
3. What overall business objective will your recommendation help to achieve? Justify this objective.
4. Support your recommendation with appropriate computations.
5. Identify some nonaccounting factors that could influence a decision of this type.
6. Which accounting techniques, if any, do you think should be changed? How should they be changed? Why should they be changed?
7. If the division into variable and fixed costs remains as it is and current accounting procedures are continued, by how much must sales increase in order for this station to break even?
8. How much must sales be in order for this station to report a net income of $10,000?

P23-13. Using the formulas and data below, write a program coded in BASIC to compute the break-even point in the three territories.

$$\text{Contribution margin} = \text{Sales price per unit} - \text{Variable cost per unit}$$

$$\text{Break-even point} = \frac{\text{Fixed cost}}{\text{Contribution margin}}$$

Territory X:
Fixed costs	$100,000.00
Sales price per unit	8.00
Variable cost per unit	6.00

Territory Y:
Fixed costs	$50,000.00
Sales price per unit	7.00
Variable costs per unit	6.00

Territory Z:
Fixed costs	$75,000.00
Sales price per unit	11.00
Variable costs per unit	6.00

24

Capital
Budgeting Decisions;
Quantitative Techniques
for Decision Making

Two separate but related topics are discussed in this chapter: capital budget decision making and quantitative techniques for decision making. An essential variable in decisions is compound interest and the time value of money discussed in Chapter 13. Reference to Chapter 13 is necessary for an improved understanding of this chapter.

BUDGETING CAPITAL EXPENDITURES

Capital budgeting refers to the allocation and commitment of funds to long-term capital investment projects. Such investments or expenditures are usually large in amount and are made in expectation of benefits to be received over a number of years. Capital budgeting concerns itself with the development, selection, and evaluation of proposals for plant expansion and modernization, equipment replacement, product development, and so on. The nature of these investments and their effect on the long-range welfare of a company make it imperative that they be analyzed and evaluated with the utmost care.

Types of Capital Expenditure

The types of capital expenditure can perhaps best be illustrated by questions involving capital investment decisions, such as the following:

1. *Expansion*. Shall we buy additional equipment to supply the actual or anticipated increase in demand for our product? Shall we expand our facilities to produce new products? Shall we acquire the necessary facilities to make parts that we are now buying from outside sources? Shall we conduct a new type of advertising campaign to boost our product?

793

2. *Replacement.* Shall we replace present equipment with new and more efficient equipment? Shall we automate our production lines? Shall we buy Machine A or Machine B? Shall we lease the new equipment or shall we buy it?

3. *Other.* Some investments are made on noneconomic grounds. Expenditures for recreational facilities for use by employees, for example, are not made to reduce costs or increase revenue, but rather to improve employer-employee relations. An investment to eliminate sound nuisances or smoke hazards may be made in compliance with local ordinances; but even if it is not mandatory, a company may choose to make such an investment to improve its relations with the local community.

Rate of Return

Businessmen make investments to get a satisfactory return. What constitutes a satisfactory rate of return depends on a number of factors, including available funds, available investment opportunities, the cost of obtaining funds, and the degree of uncertainty and risk. In the long run, the rate of return must be adequate to attract new capital.

The choice of an appropriate rate of return is central to the capital budgeting decision since it has a direct influence on the decision. The choice may be based on the *investment opportunity* concept, which is a subjective evaluation of the available investment opportunities and their respective earnings rates. The selected rate of return is the rate that the funds could earn if they were invested in the best available alternative project. Since funds used on Project A, for example, are not available for use on Project B, the amount that could have been earned on Project B is sacrificed. The amount or rate so sacrificed constitutes an opportunity cost, or the minimum rate that must be earned on Project A, the project chosen.

The choice of a cutoff rate may be based on a different concept, the *cost of capital.* The premise for the use of the cost of capital as the minimum rate of return is that the project ought to earn at least as much as the cost of the funds invested in the project. The minimum rate of return or the cost of capital is difficult to measure and varies with each company. Stated in its simplest terms, it represents a weighted average of the cost to the company of common stock equity capital as measured by the ratio of the market value of the stock to the dividend rate, and the cost of long-term debt as measured by the rate of interest on the debt. But other variables such as reinvested earnings, future dividend rates, and changes in the market value of the shares complicate the calculations.

Budgeting Decisions

The capital budgeting decision involves making a choice among alternatives. Available proposals usually exceed available funds, so that a system must be established for ranking the proposals and selecting the most desirable ones. Since the capital budgeting decision is an investment decision, it may be subjected to the same criterion that any prudent investor uses—that is, the gain or the rate of return to be realized on the investment. This, in turn, furnishes the rationale for the selection once the desired minimum rate of return has been fixed.

Present Value Concept

The present value concept refers to the conversion of cash inflows and outflows over a period of time to a common point in time for purposes of comparing capital expenditures. The concepts of compound amounts and present values are used in this conversion process: Since dollar amounts can be moved forward in time by compounding or backward in time by discounting, direct comparisons can be made of cash flows occurring in different periods. If, for example, an investment in a piece of equipment will reduce operating costs by $100 a year for four years, and the company has opportunities to invest its funds in other projects yielding a return of 10 percent a year, it can afford to pay $317 for this piece of equipment and still realize a 10-percent rate of return on the investment. The factor comes from the 10 percent column for Period 4 (Appendix A, Table 3). The computation is as follows:

$$\$100 \times 3.170 = \$317$$

The company could pay $317 for the equipment even if it had to borrow the $317 at 10-percent interest. The fact that the company could repay the loan and interest with the funds derived from the annual $100 costs savings and still be as well off as it would be before the equipment was purchased is demonstrated by the following calculation:

Amount borrowed	$317.00
Interest for 1st year	31.70
Total	$348.70
First payment	100.00
Amount due at beginning of 2d period	$248.70
Interest for 2d year	24.87
Total	$273.57
Second payment	100.00
Amount due at beginning of 3d period	$173.57
Interest for 3d year	17.36
Total	$190.93
Third payment	100.00
Amount due at beginning of 4th period	$ 90.93
Interest 4th year	9.09
Total	$100.02
Fourth payment	100.02

The discrepancy of $0.02 is due to rounding. Payments are assumed to have been made at the end of each year. The assumed saving of $100 each year in operating costs enables the company to recover the loan or the investment of $317 plus annual interest of 10 percent on the unrecovered balance.

Capital expenditures are subject to the same test as any other kind of investment: the earning of a satisfactory profit. Investments in government securities are, of course, qualitatively different from investments in machinery because the element of certainty of return on the investment is greater. But the essential objectives of the two types of investment are the same: a satisfactory rate of return. Since sums moved forward or backward in time can be converted to a comparable basis by the factor $(1 + i)^n$ or its reciprocal, $1/(1 + i)^n$, the application of present value factors to the solution of capital budgeting problems follows logically. The formulas that apply to the analysis of financial investments apply equally to the analysis of capital expenditures.

COMPARING CAPITAL EXPENDITURES

Determining the Relevant Cash Flows. A capital investment generates a flow of cash into and out of the business over a period of time. A comparison of several investment projects from which the best choice is to be made involves a comparison of the expected cash flows under the several alternatives. The concern is with future, not past, costs and with relevant costs—that is, the costs that will be different. Clearly, a cost or revenue amount that will be the same under all the alternatives from which a choice is to be made is not relevant since it will not change the decision. The appropriateness for the emphasis on cash flow to the exclusion of valuations based on generally accepted accounting principles must be considered within the context of the capital budgeting problem. The measurement of revenue and expense—the measurement of net income—*is not* relevant to the timing of the related cash flows. The measurement of a rate of return on a specific investment proposal *is* affected by the timing of the cash flows due to the time value of money. There is no conflict between conventional income measurements and rate of return measurements; the goals and end-uses of each are different.

Present Value Method

Under this method, the cash flows are discounted to the present, using the firm's cost of capital as the discounting rate. If the present value of the inflows exceeds the present value of the outflows, the investment is desirable. If the present value of the outflows exceeds the present value of the inflows, the investment is undesirable. The measurement of a proposed capital expenditure by the present value method requires a determination of the following:

1. The net cash investment
2. The net cash inflows
3. The estimated useful life of the investment
4. Excess present value

For example, assume that the West Company is planning to buy a new press for $25,000, with an estimated useful life of 10 years. Freight and installation costs will be $1,500. The press being replaced originally cost $20,000, has a carrying value of $8,000 and a remaining life of 10 years, and can be sold for $4,000. The new press is not expected to change revenue but is expected to reduce labor costs, including fringe benefits, by $5,500, and to increase power costs by $1,000. Maintenance, taxes, and insurance will be unchanged. The advisability of the replacement is being questioned. The company's cost of capital is 14 percent.

Step 1: Net Cash Investment. The initial step in the measurement of the rate of return is to determine the net amount of the initial cash investment required by the specific capital expenditure proposed. This usually consists of the purchase price of the asset, transportation, installation, and any other costs incurred to prepare the asset for operation. If the project involves the replacement of an old asset, the proceeds from the sale of the old asset are deducted in arriving at the amount of the net investment.

The net cash investment for the West Company is computed as follows:

Purchase price of new press	$25,000
Freight and installation	1,500
Total	$26,500
Deduct proceeds from sale of old press	4,000
Net investment	$22,500

The carrying value of the old press is irrelevant because it represents a past, or sunk, cost, not a future cost. Whatever the carrying value, the net investment is $22,500. What is relevant is the selling price of the old machine because it represents a future cash flow.

Step 2: Net Cash Inflows. The West Company proposal falls into the cost reduction category. The relevant cash outflows are those costs that will be different—the *differential costs*—if the proposal is adopted. The expected change in annual operating cash flows will be as follows:

Cost decreases—labor	$5,500
Deduct cost increases—power	1,000
Net annual saving	$4,500

This step involves a careful analysis of all operating costs to determine which costs will be increased and which decreased. Only those cost changes that will change cash flows are relevant. Changes in costs due, for example, to changes in cost allocations without corresponding changes in cash flow are irrelevant for this purpose even though they are essential to the accounting process.

Step 3: Estimated Useful Life. The rate of return on an investment project is directly affected by the estimated useful life of the project. The serviceable life of an asset cannot be definitely known at the time of its acquisition, and it may be difficult to estimate, but an approximation or judgment must be made. The estimate is based not on physical life but on economic life. The question to be answered is: How long will the project contribute earnings to the firm? A machine with an estimated physical life of 10 years may have to be replaced after only one year due to changes in the nature of the business—method of manufacture; location, type, or design of product; and so on. Advances in technology may necessitate replacement of an existing machine even if it is in perfect condition. The relevant factor is earning power, not necessarily physical life, the life used for financial reporting, or the life used for Federal income tax reporting.

Step 4: Excess Present Value. The relative desirability of an investment is indicated by the difference, at a common point of time, between the cost of the investment and the expected earnings from that investment discounted at the desired minimum rate. The greater the excess of the present value of the earnings over the net cash investment, the more desirable is the investment. Using the West Company figures, the excess present value is calculated as follows:

Present value of earnings at 14% rate: $4,500 ´ 5.216	$23,472
Net cash investment	22,500
Excess present value	$ 972

Since the present value of the earnings exceeds the investment, the project is desirable. If, however, the desired minimum is increased to 16 percent, the present value of the earnings is less than the investment; at 16 percent, therefore, the investment is undesirable. The computation is as follows:

Net cash investment	$22,500
Present value of earnings at 16%: $4,500 × 4.833	21,749
Excess of investment over present value	$ 751

Excess Present Value Index. The excess present value index is the ratio of the present value of the earnings to the required investment. This ratio, or *profitability index*, is useful as a ranking device for investments varying in size and economic life. An index of 1.00 or more indicates that the earnings equal or exceed the desired minimum rate. The higher the index, the more desirable is the project. The indexes for the West Company at 14 percent and 16 percent are shown.

$$\frac{\text{Present value of earnings at 14\%}}{\text{Investment}} = \frac{\$23,472}{\$22,500} = 1.04$$

$$\frac{\text{Present value of earnings at 16\%}}{\text{Investment}} = \frac{\$21,749}{\$22,500} = 0.967$$

The index at 16 percent, being less than 1.00, indicates that the earnings are not high enough to earn a 16-percent return on the $22,500 investment.

Rate of Return Method

The net cash investment of the West Company ($22,500), the annual net cash earnings ($4,500), and the economic life (10 years) having been determined, these relationships can now be combined to compute a rate of return on the investment and, concurrently, the return of the investment. In the language of compound interest, the rate of return will be that rate—the *internal rate of return* or the *time-adjusted rate of return*—at which the present values of the cash inflows and outflows offset each other. This means that if the company were to borrow funds to finance the investment at that internal rate of return, it would recover its investment as well as the interest on the borrowed funds. The computation on page 795 shows, for example, that an investment of $317 now is exactly equal to a future inflow of $100 at the end of each year for four years at 10 percent interest; that is, the present value of the inflows exactly offsets the present outflow. This means that the rate of return on the $317 investment is exactly 10 percent.

The rate of return computation for the West Company involves finding a discount rate that, applied to the net cash inflows of $4,500 over the 10-year period, equals $22,500, the net cash investment. This can be found by the process of trial and error. When positive and negative present values are found, the exact rate can be discovered by interpolation. This procedure is illustrated later in this chapter. However, when the cash flows are *uniform*, as in the West Company problem, the time-consuming trial and error method can be avoided. The predicted annual earnings of $4,500 must, in each of the 10 years, contribute to the recovery of a portion of the net cash investment of $22,500 and a return on the yet unrecovered portion of the investment. What is needed is a present value factor that, when applied to the annual cash inflows of $4,500, equals $22,500. This factor must be the net cash investment divided by the net cash inflow, or $22,500 ÷ $4,500 = 5.

The quotient 5 is the ratio of the investment to the annual earnings. The factors in Appendix A, Table 3 are likewise ratios of investments to earnings: of an investment of $1 to various rates and lives of earnings. Since the problem is to find a discount factor that, when applied to the earnings, exactly equals the investment, that factor must be the investment (numerator) divided by the earnings (denominator).

Appendix A, Table 3 lists combinations of three elements: (1) economic life, (2) interest rate, and (3) discount factor. Given any two of these elements, the third element can be read off directly. Given the factor 5 and the economic life, 10 years, the third element, the rate, can be read directly from the table.

The rate of return can now be found by looking at Appendix A, Table 3, in the row corresponding to the economic life, and for the factor closest to 5, the quotient of the investment divided by the earnings. The column heading under which this figure is found is the approximate rate. The factors in the 14 percent and 16 percent columns are 5.216 and 4.833. The rate may therefore be estimated at roughly 15 percent.

The trial-and-error method yields the same result. Assuming that the first rate tried was 14 percent and the next was 16 percent, the results would be as shown.

Net cash investment	$22,500
Present value of earnings at 14%: $4,500 × 5.216	23,472
Difference	$ 972
Net cash investment	$22,500
Present value of earnings at 16%: $4,500 × 4.833	21,749
Difference	$ (751)

The positive difference at 14 percent indicates a rate above 14 percent; the negative difference at 16 percent indicates a rate below 16 percent; the true rate is therefore between 14 percent and 16 percent. If an investment of $22,500 is made today with an estimated life of 10 years, and if the required minimum rate of return is 15 percent, then the project will have to produce annual cash earnings of $4,500 to repay the investment.

Depreciation, Income Taxes, and Capital Budgeting

For financial and income tax reporting, the costs of plant and equipment assets are amortized over the useful lives of the assets; a portion of the cost of the assets is deducted from revenue in measuring net income. Such revenue deductions, although essential to the income measurement process, are irrelevant to the capital budgeting decision because they do not represent actual cash outflows. The inclusion of the entire net cash investment as a cash outflow makes it unnecessary to allocate portions of the cost over the asset's useful life as revenue deductions. Only the actual acquisition of the asset, not its allocation to income, involves cash. But the periodic depreciation deduction does reduce net income and therefore the amount of the income tax, which does represent a cash outflow. Furthermore, the use of accelerated depreciation methods has a direct effect on the pattern of the income tax cash outflows and thereby influences the rate of return.

Assuming that the West Company is subject to an income tax rate of 50 percent, the loss on the sale of the old press will result in a $2,000 tax benefit as shown below.

Carrying value	$8,000
Selling price	4,000
Deductible loss	$4,000
Tax rate	0.50
Tax deduction	$2,000

Although the book loss is $4,000, the net after-tax effect of the sale is a loss of only $2,000 since if the sale did not take place, the West Company's cash outflow for income taxes would be $2,000 greater. In this case, the net cash investment would be as shown.

Cost of new press		$26,500
Proceeds from sale of old press	$4,000	
Tax deduction from loss on sale of old press	2,000	6,000
Net cash investment		$20,500

If the old press were sold at a gain, the tax on the gain would be deducted from the proceeds in computing the net cash investment.

The depreciation deduction and income taxes affect not only the net investment but also the net cash outflow. The change in the annual depreciation deduction changes taxable net income, which, in turn, changes the net cash earnings after taxes. The net cash earnings after taxes for the West Company, assuming the use of the straight-line depreciation method, is as follows:

Annual cash savings before taxes		$4,500	$4,500
Increase in annual depreciation deduction			
On new press: 10% of $26,500	$2,650		
On old press: 10% of $20,000	2,000	650	
Increase in taxable net income		$3,850	
Income taxes: 50% of $3,850			1,925
Net cash earnings after taxes			$2,575

Irregular Cash Flow Patterns

The capital budgeting proposals discussed thus far involved a single present net cash investment and uniform savings over the entire life span. Some projects, however, produce irregular cash flow patterns. The present value of a stream of earnings is influenced directly by both the amount and the timing of the inflow. The rate of discount increases with time, so that cash inflows of early years have a higher present value than corresponding inflows of later years. The analysis must, therefore, identify both the amount and the time pattern by years. To illustrate, assume that a company makes an immediate investment of $100,000 in a plant to manufacture a new product. Earnings rise in the second year as the market for the product is developed, then fall in the third year under the impact of competition. An additional investment is made in the third year for an intensive advertising campaign. Because of the uneven cash flow, each amount must be multiplied by the appropriate present value of 1 factor, as shown (assumed cost of capital is 20 percent).

Year	Cash Inflow (Outflow)	Present Value of $1 Discounted at 20% (Appendix A, Table 1)	Present Value
1	$40,000	0.833	$ 33,320
2	50,000	0.694	34,700
3	25,000	0.579	14,475
	(10,000)	0.579	(5,790)
4	45,000	0.482	21,690
5	30,000	0.402	12,060
Total			$110,455

The excess present value and index are computed as follows:

Present value of cash flows	$110,455
Present value of original investment	100,000
Excess present value	$ 10,455
Excess present value index: $110,455 ÷ 100,000	1.10455

The exact rate of return may be found by trial and error. The cash flows are discounted, using different trial rates, until a rate is found at which the net present value is zero. At this rate, the net inflows equal the amount of the investment. The trial-and-error computation, using trial rates of 20 and 25 percent, follows:

Year	Cash Inflow (Outflow)	Present Value Factors 20%	Present Value Factors 25%	Present Values of Cash Flows 20%	Present Values of Cash Flows 25%
1	$40,000	0.833	0.800	$ 33,320	$32,000
2	50,000	0.694	0.640	34,700	32,000
3	25,000	0.579	0.512	14,475	12,800
	(10,000)	0.579	0.512	(5,790)	(5,120)
4	45,000	0.482	0.410	21,690	18,450
5	30,000	0.402	0.328	12,060	9,840
Net Present Values				$110,455	$99,970

The second trial rate of 25 percent shows present value inflows of $99,970, which when compared with the net investment of $100,000 gives an approximate rate of return of 25 percent.

Annual Cost of an Investment

Businessmen customarily think in terms of annual costs. Statements of financial position and earnings reports are in annual terms. Capital budgeting problems may also be expressed in terms of annual costs. This is useful not only because it is a customary way of thinking but also because it provides a common basis for the comparison of two projects with different economic lives. The decision is based on whether the annual earnings expected from the investment exceed the annual cost of the investment over the estimated life.

The annual cost of an investment may be found by dividing the net investment by the present value factor corresponding to the desired rate of return and estimated life. Returning to the West Company proposal, if the Company used a cutoff rate of 16 percent, the annual cost, given the net investment of $22,500 and a useful life of 10 years, is:

$$\frac{\text{Investment}}{\text{Present value factor for } i = 16\%, n = 10} = \frac{\$22,500}{4.833} = \$4,655$$

Since the estimated savings are $4,500, the project will not earn the 16-percent rate. If, however, the desired minimum is 14 percent, the annual cost becomes

$$\frac{\text{Investment}}{\text{Present value factor for } i = 14\%, n = 10} = \frac{\$22,500}{5.216} = \$4,314$$

The annual cost at 14 percent is $4,314; this is less than the estimated annual earnings of $4,500. The project therefore meets the 14-percent minimum rate test.

Annual cost computations are useful for a variety of capital expenditure problems. To illustrate, assume that a company is considering the advisability of investing in data processing equipment that will reduce annual clerical costs from $30,000 to $18,000. The equipment costs $60,000 and has an estimated useful life of 10 years. Assuming that the desired rate of return is 10 percent, the annual cost comparison is as shown.

Present costs		$30,000
Proposed costs		
Clerical	$18,000	
Equipment	9,764	27,764
Annual saving		$ 2,236

The computation of the annual cost of the equipment is as follows:

$$\frac{\text{Investment}}{\text{Present value factor for } i = 10\%, n = 10} = \frac{\$60,000}{6.145} = \$9,764$$

The annual saving indicates (1) that the rate of return is greater than 10 percent, (2) that the 10-percent rate of return can be realized even if proposed costs increase by $2,236, or (3) that the company could pay up to $73,740

[($30,000 − $18,000) × 6.145] for the equipment and still realize a 10-percent rate of return, as shown.

Present costs		$30,000
Proposed costs		
Clerical	$18,000	
Equipment	12,000	30,000
Annual saving		$ –0–

In this situation, the computation of the annual cost of the equipment is as follows:

$$\frac{\text{Investment}}{\text{Present value factor for } i = 10\%, n = 10} = \frac{\$73,740}{6.145} = \$12,000$$

Payback

Payback, or *payout*, is a method of measuring the desirability of a project in terms of a single criterion: How soon will the cash invested in the project be returned? It is a measure of the time required for the accumulated cash earnings from a project to equal the cash investment, or

$$\frac{\text{Investment}}{\text{Annual net cash flow}} = \text{Payback}$$

In theory, the shorter the payback time, the less the risk. The popularity of payback is due to its simplicity and to its effectiveness as an initial screening measure, especially for high-risk investments in which the useful life is difficult to project. It is also useful in evaluating projects of such obvious merit that refined analysis is not needed, and projects showing no financial merit. Its limitations are that it ignores (1) the useful life, (2) the amount and pattern of cash flows beyond the payback point, (3) disposal values, (4) the time value of money, and (5) the profitability of the investment. To illustrate, assume the following figures:

Project	Net Investment	Annual Net Cash Savings
A	$10,000	$ 5,000
B	20,000	10,000

The payback on both projects is two years; on this basis they are equally desirable. However, if it is further assumed that Project A has a two-year life and Project B a five-year life, it becomes obvious that these proposals are not equally desirable.

LIMITATIONS

Although the rate-of-return method and the present-value method will often point to the same choice, in some situations the two methods yield conflicting results. Given two or more investments with only one to be undertaken, the rate-of-return method ignores the sizes of the investments. The rate of return on the incremental cash flows generated by the incremental investment may be below the acceptable rate. In such cases, the present-value method yields the more accurate rate and should be used.

The primary objective is to present an approach to the quantification of capital expenditures. The concept of present values has theoretical validity and practicability in the capital budgeting process. It provides the basis for a systematic analysis of available alternative investment proposals. But sophistication and refinement of procedure cannot insure a best choice if the data are wrong. The data used are projections of expectations—often long-range—involving revenue, costs, equipment life, human and material performance, and so on. Under such conditions of uncertainty, skillful managerial judgment is imperative. Finally, there are irreducible factors that cannot be quantified. An investment may have a direct or indirect effect on employee morale or on relations with the community, which, if not carefully judged, could cause irreparable harm. There is usually no single right answer. Sophisticated analytical procedures will not mitigate the effects of poor judgment as to market potential, available resources, and environmental factors—economic, political, and social.

QUANTITATIVE TECHNIQUES FOR DECISION MAKING

Decision Making—Introduction

The executive of a business—as well as all individuals—is involved in the continuous process of decision making. Some of the decisions that he makes will have a long-range effect and may be crucial to the very survival of the firm. When the executive makes the right decisions and executes them properly, he will have succeeded in his most important function. The purpose of this section of the chapter is to examine the decision-making process and to discuss several of the quantitative techniques or models useful in executive decision making. A model is a representation or an approximation of a real-life situation or process. The model makes it possible to project the possible consequences of a decision and to pretest that decision prior to making the actual commitment involved. Models may represent the ideal or the pragmatic, they may be concrete or abstract, they may be operating or nonoperating. Hence they describe and inform.

The executive makes his decisions and choices with the foreknowledge that he has control over only some of the factors involved, such as the amount of money required, the manpower requirements, and the amount of materials needed, but he cannot control such outside forces as the reaction of competitors, the state of the economy, the weather, and many others.

Decision making requires all kinds of information at each state of the decision-making process. The decision maker must be clear as to his objectives, must ask the right questions, and must gather data. He must examine past decisions and measure past performances as guides to the future, and he must make a careful evaluation of the risks involved and the probable gains and losses. He must know what the alternatives are as well as the constraints in men, money, materials, and technical and managerial expertise, and must compare these alternatives with the resources that will be required. He must make the best use of his resources. He does this by choosing the best of the available alternatives. If there are no alternatives, there is no choice and no decision to make. To choose, the decision maker must know what his (the firm's) goals and objectives are. If the decision maker knows his objectives, if he can measure the possible outcomes of each available alternative, he will then choose that alternative which comes closest to achieving his objective.

The Role of Accounting in Decision Making

The use of mathematical models may appear to be a departure from what is commonly recognized as the domain of accounting. But conventional accounting, with its reliance on historical cost, often does not furnish the kind of information needed by the business executive for making decisions. Accounting is not predictive. It does not search out optimal solutions and does not indicate what would have happened if an alternative decision had been made; that is, it does not measure the optimum allocation of resources—the opportunity cost of the decision. If fundamental concepts and models from mathematics, economics, and the natural and behavioral sciences provide tools for improving the decision-making process, then the accountant must integrate these into his work. Otherwise, he forfeits his role in the vital planning and control functions of the firm.

Since the decision maker must choose, he must formulate guidelines and criteria—cost minimization, optimum return on investment, maximum sales—by which to judge and measure each of the available alternatives from which he will make his choice. Scientific models and the computer provide the decision maker with the means for systematizing the choice process. This is the purpose of the models and techniques discussed below.

Probability

Since the decision maker must choose from several alternatives, he must measure the probable outcome of each alternative for comparison prior to the choice decision. But the outcome of an alternative cannot be predicted with certainty, and most decisions affecting the future involve uncertainty. The theories of probability provide the means for measuring the risk and uncertainty in the decision. Technically, a decision problem under risk is when the probabilities of each outcome is known; a decision problem under uncertainty is when the probabilities of each outcome is, by definition, unknown. The discussion and illustrations that follow are not hindered by treating the two conditions as one. The tossing of a coin provides a simple illustration. Numbers are assigned to all possible outcomes of an event. The scale used is 1 and the range is from 0 to 1 with 0 as the measure of an event that can never occur—two heads on the toss of a single coin—and 1 as the measure of an event that is certain to occur—either a head or a tail on the toss of a coin. If the event is the showing of a head on the toss of a fair coin, the only possible outcomes are either a head or a tail, and the number 1/2 is assigned to each outcome. Numbers are assigned based on logic, subjective judgment, or by experimentation and testing. Logic dictates assigning 1/2 to the probability of a head on the toss of a coin, 1/6 that the roll of a die will produce a 5, and 1/52 to the probability of a draw of the jack of clubs from a complete and well-shuffled deck of cards. Similarly, if two defective flashlight batteries are commingled with six good batteries in a container, the likelihood of selecting a good battery is 6/8 and the probability of selecting a defective battery is $8/8 - 6/8 = 2/8$. Subjective judgment or intuition dictates the probability to be assigned to the event that it will rain tomorrow or to the event of a rise in the Dow-Jones stock market averages. On the other hand, if the owner of a store wants to know the probability of there being more than 10 customers in his store during a particular hour of a particular day, he can make actual counts over a period of days and calculate the probability based on the number of times the event occurred over the number of tests he conducted. However evaluated, the same rules can be used for calculating all these probabilities.

From this it can be generalized that the probability of an equally likely event is 1 divided by the number of possible events $(1/n)$, the events being mutually exclusive—a single toss of a coin will not show *both* a head and a tail—and collectively exhaustive—on any single toss of the coin, it is certain that either a head or a tail will show.

Numbers can also be assigned to the event head on the first toss of a coin followed by a head on the second toss of the coin, or to the probability of three heads on three consecutive tosses of a coin. These are diagrammed in Figure 24-1.

Figure 24-1. Tree Diagram: 2 and 3 Coin Tosses

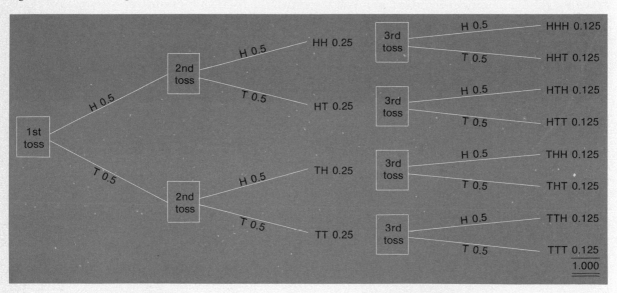

The sum of the probabilities on each toss is still the sum of the separate probabilities, but the probabilities of each of the possible outcomes of the two tosses combined is the product of their individual probabilities or $0.5 \times 0.5 = 0.25$. These can be read by tracing each of the four equally likely paths (HH, HT, TH, TT), the probability of any of the four paths being $1/4$. The first set of branches traces the two possible outcomes on the first toss of the coin and the second set traces the possible outcomes of the second toss. The possible outcomes on the second toss are not affected by the results of the first toss. To avoid having to show each item separately—a laborious task when the number of tosses is large and to avoid a possibly confusing array of numbers—a *frequency* distribution such as that shown in Figure 24-2 may be prepared.

The concepts discussed above can be applied to business decision making although frequency distributions such as those shown in Figure 24-2 are not as easily determinable and equally likely outcomes cannot be assumed. But if a decision is to be made—whether or not to market a new product, bid on a contract, or predict the weather or some other state of nature   it is better to gather the

Figure 24-2. Frequency Distribution: 2 and 3 Coin Tosses

Outcomes of 2 Tosses	Frequency	Probability
2 heads	1	0.25
1 head and 1 tail	2	0.50
2 tails	1	0.25
	4	1.00
Outcomes of 3 Tosses		
3 heads	1	0.125
2 heads and 1 tail	3	0.375
1 head and 2 tails	3	0.375
3 tails	1	0.125
		1.000

available information and establish the probabilities than to proceed purely from hunch. Systematization of the analytical process will, in itself, improve the decision-making process. If, further, the probability of each outcome is associated with a dollar value, an *expected value* can be derived. Expected value is the arithmetic average of all possible values and is calculated by multiplying the numerical value of each possible outcome by its related probability and summing the products.

To illustrate, assume that a salesman, in planning his calls for the next day, is undecided whether to call on Customer A in City X or Customer B in City Y. His decision is based on the maximum expected dollar value of the order. He cannot call on both A and B. The size of the order is directly affected by whether or not it is raining on the day of the call. The weather bureau predicts a 20 percent chance of rain the next day for both cities. A convenient means of structuring this information, together with the expected order sizes in dollars, is in the form of a *payoff matrix* with the rows representing the alternatives or strategies and the columns representing the risks and uncertainties or states of nature as shown in Figure 24-3. Since the salesman's goal is to maximize his expected value and since strategy S_1 has the higher expected value, he should visit Customer A.

Probabilities may be applied to both positive and negative values thereby making it possible to bring differing viewpoints to bear on a decision. Assume, for example, that there is a 70-percent chance that a certain decision will result

Figure 24-3. Payoff Matrix

State of Nature	N_1	N_2
Probability	20%	80%
Weather	Rain	Sunny
S1: Customer A	$100	$300
S2: Customer B	200	250

S1: EV = 0.2($100) + 0.8($300) = $260
S2: EV = 0.2($200) + 0.8($250) = $240

in a $10,000 gain and a 30-percent chance that it will result in a $5,000 loss. The expected value of the decision is calculated as follows:

$$
\begin{array}{lll}
0.7\ (\$10,\!000) & = & \$7,\!000 \\
0.3\ (-5,\!000) & = & -1,\!500 \\
\hline
\text{Expected value} & & \$5,\!500
\end{array}
$$

Inventory Models

How much of each size, style, or color, to carry in stock, how much and how frequently to order or how much to produce in a given production run are crucial policy decisions for the businessman. The extreme positions are (1) to stock enough so as to be able to fill all orders and never be out of stock or (2) to produce only on receipt of an order from a customer. But either of these extremes would be too costly or impractical for most businesses. What is needed is a policy that will balance supply and demand at an economical level consistent with the firm's goals, whether they be to maintain stable employment, maximum customer satisfaction, stable production runs, maximum earnings, or maximum sales.

The expenses involved in inventory decisions fall into two categories: (1) those which increase with increases in lot size ordered (handling and storing, spoilage and obsolescence, insurance, taxes, rent, heat, light, cost of capital) and (2) those expenses which decrease with increases in lot size (clerical, setup, backordering, loss of orders and customer goodwill, shipping). Thus, as one cost increases, the other decreases. The objective is to minimize total cost involved. This is achieved when the quantity ordered is that amount at which the cost of ordering is exactly equal to the cost of carrying the goods on hand. To illustrate, assume a company uses 12,000 units annually of a steel part that costs $5 each. It costs $150 to place an order, and the annual carrying costs are 8 percent of the cost of the part or $0.40 ($5 × 0.08) per unit on hand. The schedule in Figure 24-4 shows that the optimum ordering frequency is every three months and the optimum lot size is 3,000 parts.

In Figure 24-4, six different order sizes were tested to arrive at the optimum lot size. A much simpler way to solve this kind of a problem is to use a formula based on the general model shown in Figure 24-5. This model can be best explained by relating it to the specific data in Figure 24-4. The curves in Figure

Figure 24-4. Optimum Lot Size

(1) Orders per Year	(2) Quantity per Order (12,000 ÷ col. 1)	(3) Order Cost (col. 1 × $150)	(4) Carrying Cost (½ of col. 2 × $.40)	(5) Total Annual Cost (cols. 3 + 4)
12	1,000	$1,800	$ 200	$2,000
6	2,000	900	400	1,300
4	3,000	600	600	1,200
3	4,000	450	800	1,250
2	6,000	300	1,200	1,500
1	12,000	150	2,400	2,550

24-5 are not intended to represent the specific facts on which Figure 24-4 is based but rather as a picture of the general model.

Curve C_1 represents those costs which decrease with increases in lot size and is represented in part by column 3 of Figure 24-4. The amount represented by a point on this curve is a function of (a) the cost of placing one order, (b) the total demand for the year, and (c) the quantity per order. The number of orders per year is the annual demand divided by the quantity per order (12,000 ÷ column 1: orders per year).

Curve C_2 shows those costs which increase with increases in lot size and is represented in part by column 4 of Figure 24-4. The amount represented by a point on this curve is a function of (a) the annual carrying cost per unit and one half of the ordering quantity (one half of column 2 or average inventory).

Curve TC is the total annual cost, or the sum of curves C_1 and C_2 and is represented in part by column 5 in Figure 24-4 or the sum of columns 3 and 4.

Figure 24-5. Optimum Lot size

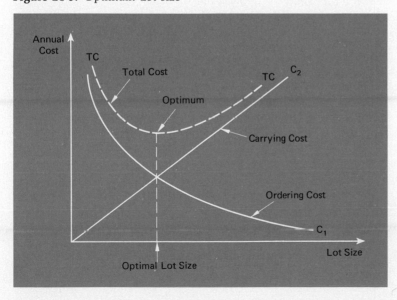

The actual shapes of the three curves will vary with the facts in any specific situation.

Since the objective is to minimize the total C_1 and C_2 costs and since curve TC represents that total, it follows that the optimum ordering quantity is represented by the lowest point on the curve TC, the point at which the slope is zero. It is directly above the crossover point of curves C_1 and C_2; that is, the sum of C_1 and C_2 must correspond to the lowest point on the TC curve. This point is represented by four orders per year and 3,000 units per order at which point columns 3 and 4 are equal (C_1 and C_2 costs) and is the lowest amount in column 5 (curve TC).

The purpose of the formula is to find that point on the TC curve whose cost is equal to the sum of the C_1 and C_2 curves at the point at which they cross over. The model assumes certainty as to ordering and carrying costs, demand, order lead time, receipt of order, and all orders being received when the inventory is zero.

The mathematical formula is as follows:

$$EOQ = \sqrt{\frac{2C_1 D}{i}} = \sqrt{\frac{2 \times 150 \times 12{,}000}{0.4}} = 3{,}000 \text{ units}$$

where EOQ = economic ordering quantity
$\quad\quad C_1$ = annual ordering cost
$\quad\quad D$ = annual demand
$\quad\quad i$ = annual carrying cost for one unit of inventory

The Inventory Cycle

Inventory decisions involve commitment of resources to meet future and uncertain demands. The amount committed must be justified by the return on the resources committed. This is accomplished by minimizing the costs involved in ordering and carrying the inventory. Figures 24-4 and 24-5 show that the economic ordering quantity or optimum lot size is the point at which ordering costs and carrying costs are equal. A diagram of the inventory cycle is shown in Figure 24-6. The solid vertical lines show the increase in inventory when an order is received, the height of the line being determined by the amount received or the EOQ. The downward sloping lines represent the gradual depletion of the inventory from time to time as goods are sold. A second order, represented by a broken vertical line, is placed at time T_1 and is received at time T_2, the interval between T_2 and T_1 representing the lead time needed for an order to be placed and delivered. When the second order is received, the units on hand will again be at the target level.

Linear Programming

Linear programming is a technique used for analyzing a problem so as to arrive at the optimum choice from related alternatives involving the allocation of scarce resources subject to certain constraints. The nature of the optimum solution depends on the objectives. Assuming that available resources in men, machines, and money are restricted, the decision to produce one product may limit the

Figure 24-6. Inventory Cycle

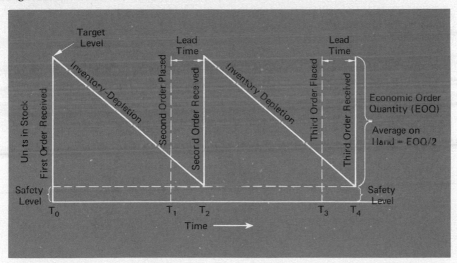

resources available for the production of another product because different products require a different mix of scarce resources as well as a different market demand and profit margins. The optimum solution is that which allocates the available resources so as to maximize profits or minimize expense.

The starting point is to state the *objective function,* which is a statement of the mathematical model for the solution to the problem of allocating scarce resources. It is a measurement of the expected outcome from a proposed strategy. When the number of alternatives is large, the computer and advanced linear programming models are used. When the problem involves two alternatives, it can be solved graphically by lines drawn on a quadrant representing equations expressing the objective function and related constraints. The optimum solution can then be read visually from the graph. The graph of the equations are straight lines connecting two indentified points, the assumption being that each production unit requires a fixed amount of a scarce resource. Thus, if one unit of product A requires two hours of machine time, then two units are assumed to require four hours; if one unit of product A contributes $5, then two units are assumed to contribute $10.

When all the lines have been drawn, the boundaries of the *technically feasible* or acceptable solution area will have been defined. Within this area there are a number of possible solutions that can be represented by parallel lines; that is, each line has the same slope. The highest one of these lines that still touches a point within the acceptable area is the optimum solution. The coordinates of that point representing the optimum mix of products are determined and the contribution is then calculated.

To illustrate, assume the Jordan Company makes products A and B. Product A requires two hours of cutting machine time and two hours of polishing machine time. Product B requires an hour of cutting machine time and three hours of polishing machine time. Daily available machine time capacity is restricted to 10 hours for the cutting department and 18 hours for the polishing department. Each item is sold separately; contribution margins (selling price less variable expenses) are $3 for product A and $2 for product B. The objective function is

$$3A + 2B = P$$

where A = the number of units of product A to be produced daily
    B = the number of units of product B to be produced daily
    P = profit to be maximized

The purpose is to find those numbers (coordinate points) which, when substituted for A and B in the objective function, will maximize profits. The next step is to introduce into the statement of the problem the constraints represented by the limited available machine hour capacity.

Constraint I—Cutting: 2A + 1B ≤ 10

One unit of A requires two hours of cutting capacity and a unit of B requires one hour of cutting capacity. The combined requirements cannot exceed 10 hours. Thus, if total cutting machine capacity were devoted to producing either A's or B's, the department could cut either five units of A ($5 \times 2 = 10$), or 10 units of B ($10 \times 1 = 10$).

Constraint II—Polishing: 2A + 3B ≤ 18

One unit of A requires two hours of polishing machine capacity and a unit of B requires three hours of polishing machine capacity. The combined capacity requirements for the production of A's and B's can be less than, or equal to, but cannot be greater than 18 hours. Thus, the firm could process either nine units of A or six units of B in this department ($9 \times 2 = 18$ or $6 \times 3 = 18$). Figure 24-7 summarizes these facts in the problem and the solution can be read from Figure 24-8.

There are several combinations that can be produced within the constraints—that is, within the area of technical feasibility. What is needed is that combination which provides the maximum contribution margin. The graph shows the feasibility area, the area within which all the possible combinations can be produced without violating the cutting and polishing department constraints. The boundaries for each constraint are drawn by identifying and connecting two points, one on each axis. The two points for the cutting department constraint are 10 on the vertical axis and 5 on the horizontal axis identified as follows:

Constraint: $2A + 1B = 10$
when A = 0, then B = 10   and
when B = 0, then A = 5

Similarly, the two points for the polishing department are 9 and 6 identified as follows:

Constraint: $2A + 3B = 18$
when A = 0, then B = 6   and
when B = 0, then A = 9

Any combination of A's and B's on the line will equal 18. This means that all such combinations will utilize the maximum available polishing department capacity of 18 hours daily.

The technically feasible area is bounded by the corner points identified

Figure 24-7. Summary Schedule for Linear Program

THE JORDAN COMPANY
Summary Schedule

	Department		Contribution Margin
	Cutting	Polishing	
1. Machine hours per unit:			
Product A	2	2	$3
Product B	1	3	2
2. Total hours available	10	18	
3. Maximum output and contribution margin if produce either all A's or all B's:			
Product A	10 ÷ 2 = 5 ①	18 ÷ 2 = 9	5 × $3 = $15 ①
Product B	10 ÷ 1 = 10	18 ÷ 3 = 6 ②	6 × $2 = 12 ②
4. Contribution margin if optimum mix is produced:			
Product A (3 units at $3 each)			$9
Product B (4 units at $2 each)			8
Total			$17

Notes

① Since only five A's can be cut, the available polishing capacity for four additional units cannot be used. Cutting is the bottleneck.

② Since only six B's can be polished, the available cutting capacity for four additional units cannot be used. Polishing is the bottleneck

Figure 24-8. Graph of Optimum Product Mix

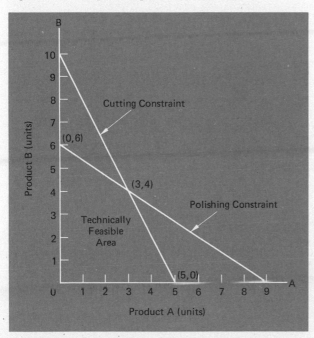

by the coordinates (0, 0) (0, 6), (3, 4), and (5, 0). The optimum product combination is at the corner (3, 4). Marginal contribution (*P*) for each of the corner points are

| Coordinates | Products | | Objective Function |
	A	B	($3A + $2B = P)
0, 0	0	0	$3(0) + $(0) = $ 0
0, 6	0	6	3(0) + 2(6) = 12
3, 4	3	4	3(3) + 2(4) = 17
5, 0	5	0	3(5) + 2(0) = 15

SUMMARY

Capital budgeting refers to the allocation and commitment of funds to long-term investment projects, most commonly involving the acquisition of plant and equipment. The measurement techniques give effect to the time value of money at compound interest—interest based on a principal sum that is increased at the end of each period by the interest for that period.

The concept of present value is especially relevant to capital budgeting. The present value of an amount is the amount that must be invested in the present to produce the known future value; the present value of a series of amounts is the present value of a series of payments to be made at equal intervals in the future. Tables of present value discount factors are commonly available to facilitate their application to capital budgeting valuations. Of especial relevance are the discount factors (1) for a single amount to be received at the end of *n* periods from the present, discounted at various interest rates, and (2) for a stream of uniform amounts to be received at the end of each period for the next *n* periods. The present value is the product of the discount factor multiplied by the amount.

The choice of an appropriate rate of return is central to the capital budgeting decision. This rate may be (1) the rate that the funds could earn if invested in the next best available alternative project and (2) the cost of capital—a weighted average of the cost of the funds obtained from the stockholders and the long-term debtors. Once the desired minimum rate of return has been fixed, the choice can be made based on the highest return.

The analysis of the cash flows must identify both amounts and the time pattern by years since these have a direct bearing on the present value. Investments and earnings are reduced to a net amount after taxes. Revenue deductions that do not represent actual cash outflows are irrelevant to the capital budgeting decision but the depreciation deduction reduces net income and therefore the amount of the cash outflow for income taxes. It is for this reason only that depreciation is significant in capital budgeting.

Discounting cash flows is a method of applying present-value factors to convert cash inflows and outflows over time to present values for comparisons. The relative desirability of an investment is indicated by the magnitude of the excess of the cost of the investment and the expected earnings from that investment discounted at the desired minimum rate to facilitate comparisons. The excess may be expressed as an index by dividing the present value of the earnings by the investment. This index is useful as a ranking device for investments varying in size and economic life.

Comparison may be based on the internal rate of return or the time-adjusted rate of return. This is the rate at which the present values of the cash inflows and outflows offset each other and can be found by a process of trial and error. The cash flows are discounted, using different trial rates, until a rate is found at which the net present value is zero.

A crude measure of the desirability of an investment is payback, or the time required for the accumulated cash earnings to equal the cash investment.

The primary responsibility of the decision maker is to make the best use of the firm's resources by choosing the best of the identified available alternatives. Scientific models and the computer provide the executive with the means for systematizing the choice process.

Decision making involves the future and therefore involves risk and uncertainty. The theories of probability provide the means for measuring risk and uncertainty in the decision-making process. Numbers are assigned to outcomes based on logic, subjective judgment, or experimentation depending on the nature of the event. When the probability of an event is associated with a dollar value, expected values—a weighted average of all possible values—can be calculated.

Mathematical techniques are useful in a number of recurring business decision situations. A common problem is to determine how frequently to place orders for goods in inventory and how many units to order. The optimum lot size model and its underlying formulas show that the most economical ordering quantity is at the point at which ordering costs and carrying costs are equal. Another common problem is to arrive at the optimum choice from related alternatives involving the allocation of scarce resources subject to certain constraints. The linear programming model provides the mathematical structures for the solution of problems involving the optimum allocation of scarce resources to maximize the firm's objective. For simple problems, a graphing technique can be used to locate the optimum solution point.

QUESTIONS

Q24-1. What is capital budgeting? Why are the principles of compound interest relevant to capital budgeting?

Q24-2. What is meant by (a) simple interest? (b) compound interest? (c) present value? (d) compound discount? (e) ordinary annuity amount? (f) present value of an ordinary annuity?

Q24-3. What kind of investment problems lend themselves to rate of return measurement techniques?

Q24-4. What constitutes a satisfactory rate of return? How is a rate selected? How is it determined?

Q24-5. What is meant by the term *discounted cash flow*?

Q24-6. Why is it appropriate in making capital budgeting decisions to emphasize the relevant cash flows rather than revenue and expense valuations based on generally accepted accounting principles?

Q24-7. What are the steps to be taken in measuring the rate of return on a proposed capital expenditure?

Q24-8. How is the annual cost of an investment measured? Of what use is such a measurement?

Q24-9. What is meant by (a) excess present value? (b) excess present value index?

Q24-10. What is the relevance of depreciation and income taxes to capital budgeting problems?

Q24-11. (a) Define *payback*. (b) What are its advantages? (c) Its disadvantages?

Q24-12. What limitations are inherent in the application of present value to capital budgeting problems?

Q24-13. "The excess present-value method is wrong because it ignores depreciation." Comment on this statement.

Q24-14. "The method of depreciation does not affect the capital budgeting decision." Comment on this statement.

Q24-15. (a) What is a model? (b) Identify some accounting models you are familiar with. (c) What purposes do accounting models serve? (d) What are their limitations?

Q24-16. (a) What is the role of accounting in decision making? (b) Of what concern is the work of behavioral scientists to the accountant?

Q24-17. (a) How may an executive apply probability theory to his decision making? (b) Does this preclude the use of intuition, hunch, or common sense?

Q24-18. (a) What is meant by "expected value? (b) What is a "payoff matrix." (c) How are these terms related?

Q24-19. (a) What is the central objective in inventory decisions? (b) What information is needed for inventory decisions? (c) Describe the optimal lot size inventory model.

Q24-20. (a) Describe the linear programming model. (b) What is meant by the terms "objective function," and "feasible solution?" (c) What is the criterion for determining the optimum product mix?

Q24-21. In problems that can be solved graphically when two products are involved, is there a limit to the number of constraining equations involved?

EXERCISES

Note: *For all exercises and problems, use an interest rate of 10 percent unless otherwise instructed.*

E24-1. Students A and B have expressed contrary views to you regarding each of the following matters and ask your help in settling their differences:

1. The amount of $70 today is more valuable than $100 five years from today.
2. It is worthwhile to invest $4,000 now in a canteen operation that will earn about $1,000 a year for the next five years.
3. It is better to invest $5,000 in food vending machines that will earn about $2,000 a year for five years than to invest $8,800 in a similar business that will earn about $3,000 a year for five years.
4. An investment of $30,000 in a business that will earn $5,000 a year for ten years will not earn a 10 percent return.
5. To justify a $50,000 investment in a 10-year concession operation, earnings would have to be at least $8,200 annually.
6. Projects A and B each involve a $2,000 investment but the net cash proceeds for the first year are $2,400 and $2,000, respectively. Project A should therefore be selected.

E24-2. What is the approximate rate of return on an investment with an initial cash outlay of $10,000 and net cash inflows of $2,770 a year for five years?

E24-3. A machine that costs $15,000 will reduce present operating costs by $3,000 a year (net). What is the approximate rate of return if the life of the machine is (a) 8 years? (b) 15 years? (c) What must the minimum useful life of the machine be if the required rate of return is 10 percent?

E24-4. A company has an opportunity to make one of three possible investments, as follows:

	1	2	3
Investment	$44,500	$57,300	$62,500
Estimated net cash inflow			
Year 1	12,000	18,000	22,000
Year 2	18,000	25,000	30,000
Year 3	25,000	35,000	40,000

Determine, for each investment, (a) the payback period, (b) the excess present value, (c) the excess present value index, and (d) the time-adjusted rate of return.

E24-5. The engineer for the Bouton Corporation has proposed the installation of certain equipment that he estimates will produce the following net after-tax savings over a five-year period:

Year	Savings
1	$1,500
2	1,800
3	2,000
4	2,200
5	2,200

What is the maximum amount that should be paid for the equipment? (Assume a minimum rate of return of 12 percent.)

E24-6. The Fleet Machine Company is considering replacing a machine presently in use and carried on the books at $10,000 with a new machine costing $20,000. The new machine will make possible cost reductions of $3,800 annually for 10 years. The old machine, which could otherwise be continued in use for another 10 years, can be sold for $5,000. Assuming the use of straight-line depreciation, a desired rate of return of 10 percent, and an income tax rate of 50 percent, should the replacement be made?

E24-7. What is the maximum amount that should be paid for a business that will earn $10,000 a year for five years, at the end of which time it can be sold for about $25,000?

E24-8. Some companies have long-run objectives other than profit maximization, such as service to the public or enhancing the power of the central management group. How does this affect the work of the accountant?

E24-9. Should the accountant include in his measurements of a company's performance the cost to society of the air or water pollutants being discharged by the company's production processes? Explain.

E24-10. A manufacturer produces products X and Y which are processed in two departments. Department I can process either 500 X's or 1000 Y's and Department II can process either 1000 X's or 500 Y's.

(a) Assuming contribution margins of $10 for each product, what is the optimum product mix? (b) Under what conditions will profits be maximized if (1) only X's are produced, or (2) only Y's are produced.

E24-11. Net cash earnings from the introduction of a new product are expected to be $80,000 for 10 years. An initial investment of $400,000 will have to be made.

(a) What is the internal rate of return? (b) Should the investment be made if the cost of capital is 12 percent?

E24-12. The Jackson Company uses 120,000 units of Product X which cost $0.50 each. The cost of placing an order is $200 and the average cost of carrying a unit is $0.05. What is the optimum ordering frequency assuming usage is spread evenly throughout the year?

DEMONSTRATION PROBLEMS

DP24-1. (*Payback; excess present value; internal rate of return*) Gilman, Inc., plans to invest $200,000 in certain improved metal fabrication equipment that is expected to save $70,000 (net after taxes) annually for 10 years. Additional working capital of $20,000 will be required. Assume a 50-percent income tax rate and straight-line depreciation with no salvage value.

> Required: 1. Compute the payback period.
> 2. Compute the excess present value.
> 3. Compute the internal rate of return.

DP24-2. (*Payback; excess present value; rates of return*) The New York Machine Company plans to spend $50,000 on land for the construction of a factory and an adjoining warehouse. Preparation of the site for construction (deductible as an expense) will be $25,000, construction of buildings will cost $825,000 and additional working capital of $50,000 will be needed. The new facilities are expected to bring savings of $200,000 (before taxes and depreciation) annually for 10 years. The sum of the years-digits method of depreciation is used. Assume a 50-percent income tax rate.

> Required: Determine whether the plan should be undertaken.

DP24-3. (*Payback, excess present value; rates of return*) The Murphy Company is considering a proposal to add an electro-zinc plating unit for finishing work now being done by outside contractors at an average cost of $0.027 per pound. Annual requirements are 2,000,000 pounds. Two types are available.

	Semiautomatic	Fully Automatic
Purchase price	$25,000	$50,000
Operating costs per unit	0.024	0.01955
Economic life	8 years	8 years

> Required: Determine which type of unit is preferable.

DP24-4. Thermiquetron, Inc., manufactures models AX and BY steam facial units. Production processes and available capacities for the coming month are

> Cutting   100 AX or 150 BY
> Wiring   200 AX or 100 BY
> Assembly   150 AX or 100 BY

Contributions margins are $50 for model AX and $70 for model BY.

> Required: Calculate the optimum product mix.

DP24-5. A company orders 6000 units a year at $20 a unit. Carrying costs average 6 percent of the cost of goods on hand. The cost of placing an order is $100.

> Required:

1. The optimum quantity to order and the number of orders to place each year.
2. What is the total inventory cost.
3. Prove your results by setting up a schedule similar to that shown in Figure 24-4.
4. What are the underlying assumptions of your solution?

P24-1. The Travers Company is considering the advisability of buying a new reactor that can handle products at high temperatures. The reactor will make possible annual savings in labor and maintenance costs of about $10,000. Data regarding the new reactor are as follows:

> Purchase price $75,000
> Salvage value   5,000
> Estimated life   15 years

Required: Determine whether the reactor should be purchased.

P24-2. The Kahn Corporation owns 32 concrete block buildings that house certain metering and control equipment. To maintain good public relations with the residents and officials of the towns in which the buildings are located, it is necessary to paint the buildings regularly at an annual cost of $6,400. It has been proposed that the buildings be covered with aluminum siding at a cost of $51,200; this will eliminate all further maintenance. The guarantee period is 20 years.

Required: Determine whether the proposal should be approved.

P24-3. The Burgoin Company is planning to buy a continuous gelatin dryer to replace the hand nets currently used to perform the drying operation. The useful life of the dryer is 10 years and its installed cost is $300,000. The old equipment has a carrying value of $50,000 and can be sold for $20,000.

The new dryer will reduce labor costs and fringe benefits by $70,000 annually and will eliminate the need for nets at a saving of $20,000 each year. Maintenance costs will increase by $10,000 annually. The new dryer is expected to improve the quality of the product and eliminate some presently existing sanitation problems.

The company uses the straight-line method of depreciation and is subject to a combined Federal and state income tax of 50 percent. The present equipment could have been used for another 10 years.

Required: Determine whether the dryer should be purchased to replace the old equipment.

P24-4. N. C. Jones, the plant engineer for the Smith Company, has been asked to procure equipment that will improve the present method used by the company for shearing bar stock. He finds three different systems, each of which will improve present methods and reduce space requirements. The costs of the systems are as follows:

> A $56,100
> B   86,100 (includes $30,000 for unscrambler)
> C   94,100 (includes $38,000 for unscrambler and unloading conveyor)

The work to be done by the new equipment currently requires 2,200 hours annually at an hourly variable cost of $24.02. The new systems will do the same work in 733 hours at the following rates:

> A $28.77
> B   25.90
> C   21.03

The company plans to depreciate the new equipment over eight years, using the straight-line method, and is subject to a 50-percent combined state and Federal income tax rate. No salvage value is expected.

The old equipment, which has a carrying value of $5,000, can be sold for $2,000. The new system will not require increased working capital.

Required: 1. Compute the payback period.
          2. Compute the internal rate of return.

P24-5. The Rosen Company is considering the replacement of conventional drilling equipment with a numerically controlled drilling machine. The purchase price of the machine, including controls, is $54,560. Freight and installation costs are $1,643. Other first-year expenses include a programmer at $8,500 and training fees of $1,500. The useful life of the machine is 10 years. Projected annual savings are as follows:

Reduction in tooling costs	$13,857
Reduction in tool wear and tear	600
Reduced scrap and rework costs	494
Reduced floor space: 160 square feet × $2.92 per square foot	467
Reduced maintenance	600
Reduction in labor and fringe benefits	7,775

After the first year, the part-time services of a programmer will be needed at an annual cost of $2,830.

Required: Compute the internal rate of return, assuming no salvage value, a 50-percent income tax rate, and straight-line depreciation.

P24-6. The Plimpton Company needs equipment to produce about 1,400 microcircuits per week for the next five years. Rapidly evolving microcircuit technology makes projections for any period longer than five years hazardous. Two methods are being considered, as follows:

	A	B
Investment for equipment	$24,000	$30,000
Variable costs per 1-inch microcircuit (exclusive of transistors and diodes)	0.80	0.77

The choice of method will not affect sales volume because the microcircuits are incorporated into a larger piece of equipment. No salvage value is expected.

Required: Determine which investment should be made.

P24-7. The Richard Lindhe Company has been using manually operated equipment to service its customers. Automatic equipment is now available and the company has conducted a cost-benefit study to determine whether to replace its conventional equipment.

The study indicates that annual revenue will continue at its present level of $50,000.

Comparative costs of using the conventional and automatic equipment are estimated as follows:

	Manual	Automatic
Equipment	$10,000	$12,000
Salvage	1,000	2,000
Supplies, annual	1,000	1,500
Maintenance, annual	100	150
Overhaul:		
End of year 2	500	
End of year 3		1,000

Assume that the estimated useful life for either type of equipment is five years and that the company's cost of capital is 10 percent.

Required:

1. Should the company invest in automatic equipment?
2. What are the underlying assumptions and the advantages and disadvantages of your analysis for this decision?

P24-8. The ABC Company is considering introducing a new product. Cost and marketing studies indicate that the item can be sold for $10 each. Production costs are uncertain because the company has no experience with this product, but the production manager provides the following estimates:

	Probability	Unit Cost
Most optimistic	0.10	$4
Most probable	0.75	6
Most pessimistic	0.15	8

The sales manager predicts that he can easily sell the entire projected output of 100,000 units for the first year.

Required: What is the expected profit the first year?

P24-9. A new design computer is being considered for the design engineering group of the automotive division of the Nielsen Manufacturing Company, Inc. The investment will have no effect on revenue but will reduce operating expenses by $1,000,000 a year for the next seven years.

The equipment will cost $3,500,000, has an estimated useful life of seven years, and a salvage value of $500,000 at the end of the seventh year. Annual fixed costs are $100,000. These will not change.

Required: Should the investment be made, assuming a desired rate of return of 10 percent?

P24-10. The Linhdie Company has the following two investment proposals under consideration

	Proposal	
	Product A	Product B
Investment	$225,000	$100,000
Salvage	$ 5,000	$ 15,000
Estimated life (years)	5	5
Unit selling price	$ 1.00	$ 0.75
Variable cost per unit	$ 0.60	$ 0.45
Fixed costs–annual	$180,000	$150,000

Projected unit sales and their probabilities are as follows:

Product A		Product B	
Units	Probability	Units	Probability
1,000,000	0.1	800,000	0.2
800,000	0.2	600,000	0.6
600,000	0.4	300,000	0.2
400,000	0.2		
200,000	0.1		
	1.0		1.0

Required: Which investment proposal should the company choose? Explain fully. Assume 10-percent cost of capital.

P24-11. Mr. Harry Kahn, developer and designer of a steam hair-waving machine, is prepared to distribute his product nationally. He asks you for a forecast of the number of units he might expect to distribute the first year. After surveying a number of large cities, you arrive at the following estimates:

Units	Probability
1000	0.1
1500	0.3
1800	0.4
2500	0.2
	1.0

The selling price of the machine is $300. A manufacturer has agreed to produce the machine for $150 each. Shipping expenses will average $10 a unit. Distribution will be through contractors' representatives who will receive a $100 commission on each unit. Mr. Kahn's other expenses are $25,000 annually.

Required: What are Mr. Kahn's expected earnings the first year.

P24-12. The Cowan Electric Company manufactures and distributes two models of epilators, the AG and the BG models. The major production processes are wiring and cutting. Available resources and required time in hours are as follows:

	Model		Available Capacity
Process	AG	BG	(hours)
Wiring	1	2	30
Cutting	4	3	100

Required:

1. Graph the technically feasible area for models AG and BG, identify all corner points, and determine the optimum mix assuming contribution margins of $150 for model AG and $200 for model BG.
2. Calculate the contribution of each model for each corner point.

P24-13. The Gaynor Corporation performs accurate light machining operations on numerous small parts for certain scientific instruments. Orders are for small lots, each requiring special jigs and fixtures. The company has been investigating the possible use of numerically controlled machining techniques, which would make possible multiple machining operations in one setup and eliminate the need for the special jigs and fixtures. This, in turn, would lessen the problems of quality control and reduce inventory requirements. Companies now using numerically controlled equipment report reductions in machining time of from 50 to 80 percent and can produce parts of a higher quality than with conventional machinery. Subsequent studies by the Gaynor Corporation indicate possible savings in the following areas:

1. Labor hours
2. Variable overhead
3. Inventory carrying costs
4. Scrap and rework
5. Inspection
6. Tolling costs

The company has made a study of the savings that would result on 195 parts suitable for numerically controlled machining to be phased into the new program in two stages: 98 parts at the beginning of the first year and the remainder at the beginning of the second year.

Labor Hours. The 195 parts currently require 11,000 machining hours annually at an average hourly rate of $2.80 (including fringe benefits). The same parts can be machined on numerically controlled equipment in 6,000 hours.

Variable Overhead. The present overhead rate is $7 per direct labor hour. This amount includes $0.20 for fringe benefits and $0.41 for depreciation and other nonvariable costs.

Inventory Carrying Costs. The average inventory cost of the 195 parts is $50,000, with an annual turnover ratio of 4 to 1. Use of numerically controlled equipment would require an average inventory cost of $16,250. Inventory carrying charges are presently 20 percent, but since present storage space and stores personnel would remain unchanged, annual savings of about $5,000 are anticipated.

Scrap and Rework. A review of the quality control records and monthly rework reports showed rework costs due to shop errors for the 195 parts of about $3,000. The built-in self-monitoring devices of the numerically controlled equipment should eliminate at least 90 percent of rework costs.

Inspection. Since the numerically controlled equipment is highly accurate within the guaranteed limits, it will be necessary to inspect only the first piece of each lot and one or two other pieces, instead of every piece. This will reduce inspection costs by $3,000 annually.

Tooling Costs. Anticipated savings relating to tooling result from (1) design and fabrication of tools for new parts and (2) maintenance of existing tools. Design and fabrication of new parts suitable for the numerically controlled equipment is expected to number 43, 85, and 85, respectively, for the first three years of use, after which the two-shift capacity of the machine will have been reached. Numerically controlled tooling is $75 per part, compared with $300 per part currently. Savings from general tool maintenance would continue on an annual basis at $5,000 yearly.

The cost of the numerically controlled equipment is $140,000, consisting of the following:

Basic machine price	$112,000
Tool holders and accessories	20,000
Installation	8,000
Total	$140,000

In addition, one-time costs of $11,000 would be incurred for the basic program for producing tapes and for training programmers and operators.

It is estimated that the equipment will be worth $14,000 at the end of its expected six-year life. The company uses the sum-of-the-years'-digits method of depreciation and is subject to a 50-percent income tax rate. Its cost of capital is 10 percent.

Required: Write a report to management, giving your recommendations and reasons for the action you recommend, together with supporting schedules and exhibits.

P24-14. The customary letter to the stockholders from the company president included in the firm's annual report typically includes a statement that its greatest asset is its employees. The 1970 annual report of Beatrice Foods Company, for example, includes the following statement:

> *The Future.* The progress of your company last year and all through the sixties primarily is the result of the superior performance and dedication of our management-employee team. It is their creativity, their production and marketing skills, and their abilities to capitalize on the potentials and facilities of Beatrice that encourage confidence of even greater growth of your company in this new decade.

It has been suggested that the company should quantify its human resources for inclusion in the financial statements.

The following methods have been proposed:

1. Cost of recruitment, training, and retraining.
2. Replacement cost
3. Capitalized value of excess earnings attributed to human resources
4. Present value of future employee earnings

Required:

1. Do you agree that a firm's human resources should be quantified? If you do, which method would you use?
2. How would this aid in the evaluation of the firm's performance and financial position.
3. Will readers or employees resent the idea of quantifying human beings in the manner of plant assets?
4. How will the amounts be amortized? What factors would have to be considered in establishing amortization policies?
5. What variables would have to be considered in constructing the measurement model?

25

Federal
Income
Taxes

The major justification for the inclusion of an introduction to Federal income taxes in an elementary text is the need to emphasize the primary differences between traditional business income and taxable income. Accordingly, in this chapter, consideration is given (1) to high lights of Federal income taxation, (2) to income tax planning problems as a foundation for observing some examples of differences between book net income and taxable income, and (3) to the impact of income taxes on business decisions.

THE FEDERAL INCOME TAX

To acquaint the student with a few of the intricacies of the Federal income tax structure, this section includes discussions of (1) classes of taxpayers, (2) tax accounting methods, (3) individual income taxes, (4) the partnership informational return, and (5) corporate income taxes.

Classes of Taxpayers

Four kinds of separate entities are subject to the income tax: individuals, corporations, estates, and trusts—each must file a return and, if applicable, pay a tax on its taxable income.[1] Single proprietorships and partnerships are not taxed as separate entities. Rather, the single proprietor reports his business income along with all his personal income on Form 1040, the U.S. Individual Income Tax Return. The partnership files a separate informational return, Form 1065, but each partner reports his share of net income together with his personal nonpartnership income on his Form 1040.

[1] Some trusts, all of whose income goes to beneficiaries, file tax returns for information purposes only. The income received from these trusts by the individual beneficiaries should be reported on their individual tax returns. Under these circumstances, the trust would not pay any income taxes.

Tax Accounting Methods

The Internal Revenue Code sets forth rules and the Internal Revenue Service establishes regulations regarding the inclusion and exclusion of certain revenue and expense items and the use of certain methods and procedures in computing taxable income.

The Internal Revenue Code, however, permits taxpayers to select certain options, among them the alternative to choose the cash or accrual basis of computing net income under certain circumstances. To reiterate, on the cash basis, income is recognized when cash is received and expenses are considered to be incurred when the cash expenditure is made. Although the cash basis is not a satisfactory method of measuring net business income, for tax purposes it is well-suited for individuals not engaged in business and also, to a lesser extent, for businesses in which inventories, payables, and receivables are not a major factor. An individual whose only income is a salary is required to use the cash basis.

The cash basis allowed for income tax purposes is modified in two ways: (1) the cost of a long-lived asset cannot be deducted in the year of its purchase: the taxpayer must treat the item as an asset and apportion its cost over its useful service life and (2) revenue is recognized when it is constructively received—that is, when the revenue is in the control of the taxpayer. For example, interest credited to a savings and loan account is deemed to be constructively received even though the cash is not yet in the hands of the taxpayer.

The taxpayer should choose the method permissible under the law that will postpone and avoid taxes, thereby conserving working capital and achieving the lowest long-run tax cost.

The accrual basis of measuring income has been discussed in preceding chapters of this text. Under this method, revenue is recognized in the period when a sale is made or a service is rendered, irrespective of when cash is received; and expenses are recognized in the period when services are received and utilized in the production of revenue. The accrual basis is required of those businesses in which production, purchases, and sales of merchandise are significant factors. Any taxpayer other than a salaried individual who maintains a set of accounting records may elect to use the accrual basis.

THE INDIVIDUAL INCOME TAX

The individual taxpayer computes his tax by following the outline provided on the U.S. Individual Income Tax Return, Form 1040. Figure 25-1 presents the basic content of Form 1040 and shows the tax formula for individuals.

Gross Income. All income not specifically excluded by law is includable in gross income. In addition to the items mentioned in Figure 25-1, gambling winnings and income from illegal activities must be included in gross income.

The following are specifically excluded by law, Treasury regulations, or court decisions:

1. Interest on state and municipal bonds and notes
2. Qualified dividends received by each spouse who actually owns stock, not to exceed $100 for each owner

Figure 25-1. Individual Income Tax Chart

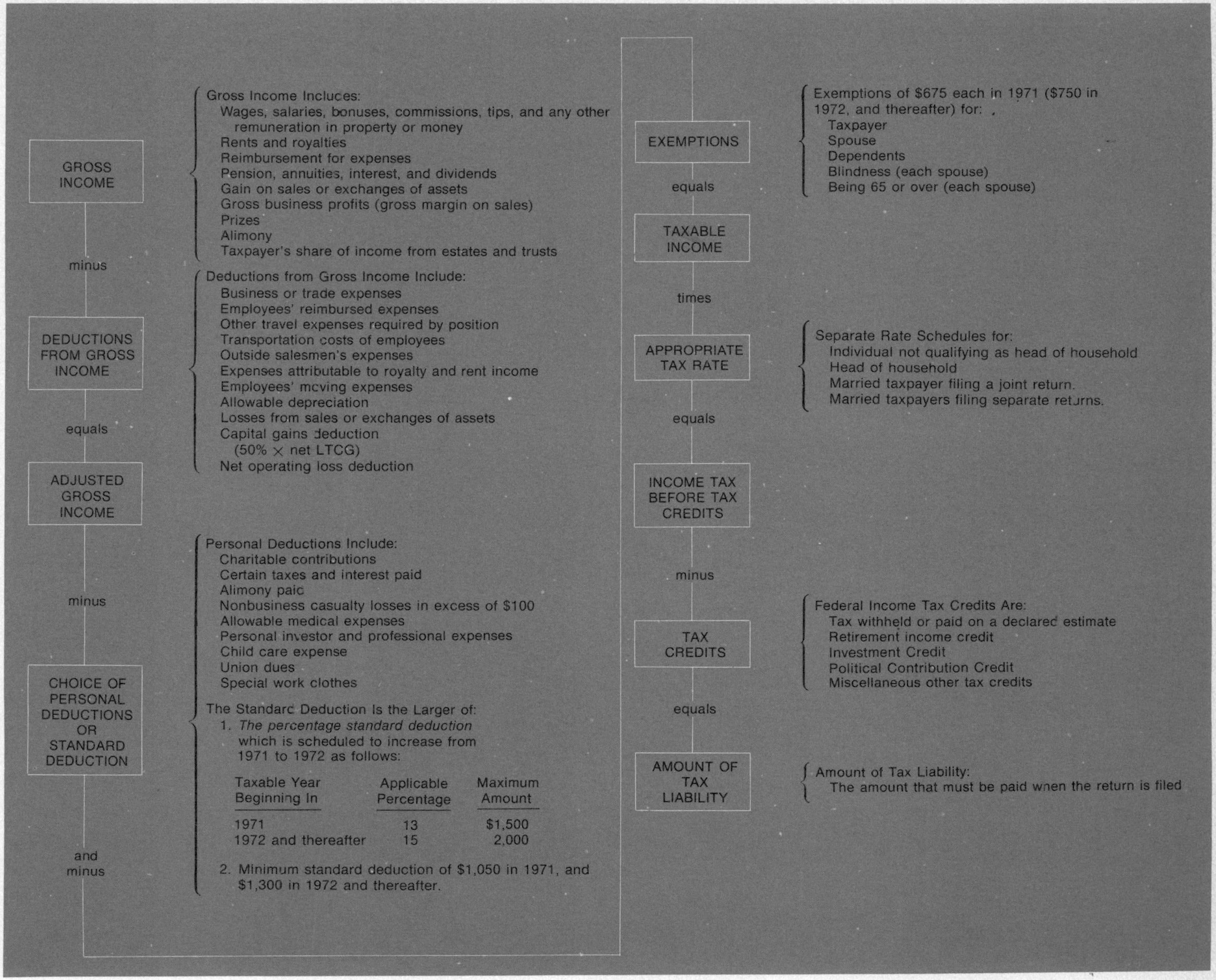

GROSS INCOME

Gross Income Includes:
Wages, salaries, bonuses, commissions, tips, and any other remuneration in property or money
Rents and royalties
Reimbursement for expenses
Pension, annuities, interest, and dividends
Gain on sales or exchanges of assets
Gross business profits (gross margin on sales)
Prizes
Alimony
Taxpayer's share of income from estates and trusts

minus

DEDUCTIONS FROM GROSS INCOME

Deductions from Gross Income Include:
Business or trade expenses
Employees' reimbursed expenses
Other travel expenses required by position
Transportation costs of employees
Outside salesmen's expenses
Expenses attributable to royalty and rent income
Employees moving expenses
Allowable depreciation
Losses from sales or exchanges of assets
Capital gains deduction
(50% × net LTCG)
Net operating loss deduction

equals

ADJUSTED GROSS INCOME

minus

CHOICE OF PERSONAL DEDUCTIONS OR STANDARD DEDUCTION

Personal Deductions Include:
Charitable contributions
Certain taxes and interest paid
Alimony paid
Nonbusiness casualty losses in excess of $100
Allowable medical expenses
Personal investor and professional expenses
Child care expense
Union dues
Special work clothes

The Standard Deduction is the Larger of:
1. *The percentage standard deduction* which is scheduled to increase from 1971 to 1972 as follows:

Taxable Year Beginning In	Applicable Percentage	Maximum Amount
1971	13	$1,500
1972 and thereafter	15	2,000

2. Minimum standard deduction of $1,050 in 1971, and $1,300 in 1972 and thereafter.

and minus

EXEMPTIONS

Exemptions of $675 each in 1971 ($750 in 1972, and thereafter) for: ,
Taxpayer
Spouse
Dependents
Blindness (each spouse)
Being 65 or over (each spouse)

equals

TAXABLE INCOME

times

APPROPRIATE TAX RATE

Separate Rate Schedules for:
Individual not qualifying as head of household
Head of household
Married taxpayer filing a joint return
Married taxpayers filing separate returns.

equals

INCOME TAX BEFORE TAX CREDITS

minus

TAX CREDITS

Federal Income Tax Credits Are:
Tax withheld or paid on a declared estimate
Retirement income credit
Investment Credit
Political Contribution Credit
Miscellaneous other tax credits

equals

AMOUNT OF TAX LIABILITY

Amount of Tax Liability:
The amount that must be paid when the return is filed

3. Gifts, inheritances, and bequests received
4. Life insurance proceeds received on the death of the insured
5. Amounts received from workmen's compensation and other kinds of insurance, with a limitation of usually $100 per week under certain conditions
6. Social security receipts
7. Return of investment portion of annuity receipts and other returns of capital investments
8. GI benefits and certain veteran's payments
9. Income earned by United States citizens while resident in a foreign country and from foreign sources up to $20,000 per year, provided the taxpayer remains in the foreign country at least 18 months

Capital Gains and Losses. The income tax treatment of gains and losses on sale of capital assets—stocks, bonds, and other qualifying property—is extremely important because net long-term capital gains are taxed at one half, or less than one half, the rates applicable to ordinary income. The amount of gain or loss is the difference between the selling price and the tax basis—cost when the asset was acquired by purchase, the basis in the hands of the donor and in some cases fair market value when the property was acquired by gift, fair market value at date of death (or the alternative valuation date used for estate tax purposes) when the property was acquired by inheritance, and other legally specified bases.

Gains or losses from capital assets held for six months or less are classified as short-term and 100 percent of the gain must be reported. Short-term gains are taxed as ordinary income. Gains and losses arising from capital assets held for more than six months are classified as long-term; only one half of net long-term gains are included in adjusted gross income. The maximum rate of tax applicable to the gross (before the 50-percent reduction) gain is 25 percent on the first $50,000 of gross gain plus

In 1971: 32½ percent of the excess above $50,000
In 1972 and thereafter: 35 percent of the excess above $50,000

In computing deductible capital losses, the sum of 100 percent of the short-term losses plus 50 percent of long-term losses may be deducted from other gross income up to a maximum of $1,000, or the taxable income, whichever is smaller. The unused portion of the capital loss, however, may be carried over to future years, without any limitation as to the number of years, and offset against the ordinary income of those years, not to exceed the maximum limitations per year as stated.

The income tax law requires that long- and short-term transactions be combined in a certain way in computing adjusted gross income. In the first place, all long-term gains and long-term losses must be offset against each other in order to determine the net long-term gain or loss. In a similar manner, short-term gains and losses must be combined. The combination and netting of long-term and short-term items produce a number of situations that require further explanation. For example, a taxpayer may have both a net long-term gain and a net short-term gain. In this case, he would treat the two items separately: the entire short-term gain would be included in gross income and treated as ordinary income. Similarly, if a taxpayer has net short-term losses and net long-term losses, he would combine 100 percent of the short-term capital loss plus 50 percent of the long-term capital loss into one figure, and would deduct up to $1,000 in the computation of adjusted gross income. Still further, it is possible for a taxpayer to have gains of either type greater than losses of either type. These must be combined to arrive at either a net long-term gain or a net short-term gain, depending on the characteristic of the dominant gain. These rules are illustrated in Figure 25-2.

Figure 25-2. Capital Gain and Loss Rules

Case A		Case B	
Net LTCG	$5,000	Net LTCL	$1,000
Net STCG	1,000	Net STCL	500
		Total Capital Loss	$1,500
		Less: 50 percent	
		of net LTCL	500
		Deductible Capital Loss	$1,000

Includable in AGI:

All of the STCG is included, but only half of LTCG; the total included in AGI is $3,500.

Deductible from Gross Income:

Only $1,000 is deductible in the current year to arrive at AGI.

Case C		Case D	
Net LTCG	$4,000	Net LTCL	$4,200
Net STCL	2,500	Net STCG	5,600
Net capital gain (long-term)	$1,500	Net capital gain (short term)	$1,400

Includable in AGI:

50 percent of the $1,500, or $750, is included.

Includable in AGI:

The entire $1,400 would be included and taxed as ordinary income.

Abbreviations used in this illustration are:
Net LTCG—Net long-term capital gain
Net STCG—Net short-term capital gain
Net LTCL—Net long-term capital loss
Net STCL—Net short-term capital loss
AGI—Adjusted gross income

Deductions from Gross Income. The various classes of deductions from gross income are indicated in Figure 25-1. In general, they are self-explanatory. A brief word about a few should suffice.

Business expenses are the ordinary and necessary expenses of carrying on a trade, business, or profession. In actual practice, business expenses are deducted from business revenue on a separate Schedule C to Form 1040, and only the net income from business is included in adjusted gross income.

Allowable employee expenses are necessary and must actually be incurred in connection with the employment.

Losses from sales or exchanges may qualify as capital losses and hence would follow the rules summarized in Figure 25-2.

The *capital gains deduction* is 50 percent of the net long-term capital gains (as determined in Figure 25-2). Legally, 100 percent of long-term capital gains qualifies as gross income. As indicated previously, however, in deriving the long-term capital gains to be included in adjusted gross income, it is necessary to deduct the capital gains deduction from the legal gross income item, the 100 percent amount of net long-term capital gain.

Personal Deductions or Percentage Standard Deduction and Minimum Standard Deduction. A taxpayer has the option of itemizing the personal deductions listed in Figure 25-1 or taking the standard deduction, whichever will benefit him most. Some of the personal deductions have limits. For example, contributions to recognized charitable, religious, educational, and other eleemosynary organizations are limited to a percentage that may vary from 20 to 50 percent of adjusted gross income. The limitation depends on whether the eleemosynary organization is publicly supported or is a certain type of private foundation. Publicly supported organizations include religious, educational, community chest, and other charitable organizations that derive the majority of their funds from the general public. The nonpublicly supported charities that have a limitation of 20 percent include private foundations that do not distribute all of their revenue within two and one-half months following the close of the year to qualifying charities. If the contributions to the publicly supported organizations are at least 30 percent of adjusted gross income, the limit is 50 percent of adjusted gross income; but if these contributions to the publicly supported organizations are not 30 percent of adjusted gross income, the limit is 20 percent of adjusted gross income plus the amount of the special contribution to the qualifying publicly supported organizations.

Gross medical expenses include doctor, hospital, dental fees, the cost of medicines and drugs in excess of 1 percent of adjusted gross income, travel to receive medical treatment, and medical and hospital insurance.

The *deductible* medical expense is one half of the medical and hospital insurance, not to exceed $150, plus the amount of medical and dental expense and remaining medical and hospital insurance in excess of 3 percent of adjusted gross income, with no maximum limit. To illustrate the computation of the deductible medical expense, assume that a taxpayer has an adjusted gross income of $20,000; medical and hospital insurance of $360; drugs of $310; and other medical, dental, and hospital expenses of $1,800.

Deductible Medical Expenses:			
One half of medical and hospital insurance,			
½ × 360 = 180; this exceeds $150, thus the			
deductible portion is			$ 150.00
Gross Medical:			
Remaining medical and hospital insurance		$ 210.00	
Allowable drugs:			
Gross drugs	$310		
Less: 1% of $20,000 (AGI)	200	110.00	
Other medical, dental, and			
hospital expenses		1,800.00	
Gross Medical		$2,120.00	
Less: 3% × $20,000 (AGI)		600.00	1,520.00
Deductible Medical Expense			$1,670.00

The 1971 Revenue Act modified the optional standard deduction by changing both the percentage applicable to adjusted gross income and the maximum allowable amount. The optional standard deduction is the larger of the allowable *percentage standard deduction* or the *minimum standard deduction.* The Act increased the percentage standard deduction from its 1970 level of 10 percent of adjusted gross income, with a maximum of $1,000, to 15 percent, with a maximum of $2,000, over a two-year period beginning on January 1, 1971.

Taxable Year Beginning In	Applicable Percentage of AGI	Maximum Amount
1971	13	$1,500
1972	15	2,000

A married taxpayer filing a separate return is allowed the same percentages as shown above, but only up to one half of the indicated maximum amounts.

The new minimum standard deduction is designed primarily to remove poverty level taxpayers from the tax rolls. For those taxpayers who are required to file a return and who elect to use the minimum standard deduction rather than the percentage standard deduction, the amount of the deduction is $1,050 in 1971 and $1,300 in 1972 and years thereafter. For a married taxpayer filing a separate return in 1971, the minimum standard deduction is $525; in 1972, it is scheduled to be $650.

Exemptions. A personal exemption in 1971 in the amount of $675 is allowed for the taxpayer, for his spouse if a joint return is filed, and for each person who qualifies as a *dependent* of the taxpayer. The value of each exemption is scheduled to increase to $750 in 1972 and for years thereafter. The taxpayer and spouse may claim special exemptions if he or she is blind, or if either is 65 years or over.

Under the law, a dependent is a person who (1) receives over one half his support from the taxpayer, (2) is closely related to the taxpayer or lives in his home, (3) has received less than $675 in gross income during the year 1971, unless the dependent is a child of the taxpayer who is under 19 years of age or a full-time student, and (4) has not filed a joint return.

Individual Income Tax Rates. Once the taxable income is properly determined, the income tax before credits is computed by multiplying the appropriate tax rates by the net taxable income. The tax rates that are applied depend on the rate qualification of the taxpayer. There is a separate tax schedule for a single person who does not qualify as head of household, a schedule for an individual who does qualify as head of household, a schedule for a married couple filing a joint return and still another schedule for married taxpayers filing separate returns. All these rates are progressive in nature; that is, those with the lowest taxable income are taxed at the lowest rate and those with larger taxable incomes are taxed at progressively higher rates. The progressive character of the individual tax rate can be observed from Figure 25-3, which shows the individual income tax rates, starting at 14 percent and rising gradually to 70 percent. (The taxpayer must consult the latest rates, which are furnished by the Internal Revenue Service, before he prepares his Federal income tax return.)

Figure 25-3. Individual Income Tax Rate Schedule

831

Individual Income Tax Rates for Filing in 1971

Taxable Income	Rate Schedule No. 1 Separate Returns (Unmarried taxpayers)		Rate Schedule No. 2 Joint Returns (Married taxpayers and surviving spouses)		Rate Schedule No. 3 Head of Household Returns		Rate Schedule No. 4 Separate Returns (Married taxpayers)	
	Tax	Rate on Excess	Tax	Rate on Excess	Tax	Rate on Excess	Tax	Rate on Excess
Up to $500		14%		14%		14%		14%
500	$ 70	15	$ 70	14	$ 70	14	$ 70	15
1,000	145	16	140	15	140	16	145	16
1,500	225	17	215	15	220	16	225	17
2,000	310	19	290	16	300	18	310	19
3,000	500	19	450	17	480	18	500	19
4,000	690	21	620	19	660	19	690	22
6,000	1,110	24	1,000	19	1,040	22	1,130	25
8,000	1,590	25	1,380	22	1,480	23	1,630	28
10,000	2,090	27	1,820	22	1,940	25	2,190	32
12,000	2,630	29	2,260	25	2,440	27	2,830	36
14,000	3,210	31	2,760	25	2,980	28	3,550	39
16,000	3,830	34	3,260	28	3,540	31	4,330	42
18,000	4,510	36	3,820	28	4,160	32	5,170	45
20,000	5,230	38	4,380	32	4,800	35	6,070	48
22,000	5,990	40	5,020	32	5,500	36	7,030	50
24,000	6,790	40	5,660	36	6,220	38	8,030	50
26,000	7,590	45	6,380	36	6,980	41	9,030	53
28,000	8,490	45	7,100	39	7,800	42	10,090	53
32,000	10,290	50	8,660	42	9,480	45	12,210	55
36,000	12,290	50	10,340	45	11,280	48	14,410	55
38,000	13,290	55	11,240	45	12,240	51	15,510	58
40,000	14,390	55	12,140	48	13,260	52	16,670	58
44,000	16,590	60	14,060	50	15,340	55	18,990	60
50,000	20,190	62	17,060	50	18,640	56	22,590	62
52,000	21,430	62	18,060	53	19,760	58	23,830	62
60,000	26,390	64	22,300	53	24,400	58	28,790	64
64,000	28,950	64	24,420	55	26,720	59	31,350	64
70,000	32,790	66	27,720	55	30,260	61	35,190	66
76,000	36,750	66	31,020	58	33,920	62	39,150	66
80,000	39,390	68	33,340	58	36,400	63	41,790	68
88,000	44,830	68	37,980	60	41,440	64	47,230	68
90,000	46,190	69	39,180	60	42,720	64	48,590	69
100,000	53,090	70	45,180	62	49,120	66	55,490	70
120,000	67,090	70	57,580	64	62,320	67	69,490	70
140,000	81,090	70	70,380	66	75,720	68	83,490	70
160,000	95,090	70	83,580	68	89,320	69	97,490	70
180,000	109,090	70	97,180	69	103,120	70	111,490	70
200,000	123,090	70	110,980	70	117,120	70	125,490	70

Examples of Use of Tax Tables

1. Unmarried taxpayer with taxable income of $23,000:

Tax on first $22,000	$5,990
Tax on excess:	
40% × $1,000	400
Total tax	$6,390

2. Married taxpayer filing joint return with taxable income of $84,000:

Tax on first $80,000	$33,340
Tax on excess:	
58% × $4,000	2,320
Total tax	$35,660

The separate tax schedule for married taxpayers is designed to eliminate tax inequity for married couples in states having community property laws that permit them to divide gross income and couples in states that do not have such laws. Married couples filing a joint return determine their income tax before credits by applying the rates indicated in Rate Schedule No. 2 of Figure 25-3, the tax rates that are specifically applicable to married taxpayers filing joint returns.

It should be noted that marital status is determined as of December 31 of a given taxable year. For example, if a couple were married on December 31, 1971, they would qualify to file a joint return for the entire taxable year of 1971.

The special tax schedule for head of household (Rate Schedule No. 3 of Figure 25-3) provides an element of relief for widows or widowers and others who qualify as head of household to compensate them partially for the additional family burden that they must carry. Only the following persons may qualify as head of household: (1) one who is unmarried (or separated) at the end of the taxable year, or (2) one who is married at the end of the year to an individual who was a nonresident alien at any time during the taxable year. In addition, the individual must have furnished over half the cost of maintaining as the taxpayer's home a household that during the entire year, except for temporary absences, was occupied as the principal place of abode and as a member of such household by (1) any related person, other than the taxpayer's unmarried child, grandchild, or stepchild for whom the taxpayer is entitled to a deduction for an exemption, unless the deduction arises from a multiple support agreement, or (2) the taxpayer's unmarried child, grandchild, or stepchild, even though such child is not a dependent. The rates, as shown in Rate Schedule No. 3 of Figure 25-3, are lower than for nonhead-of-household unmarried individuals but are higher than those for married couples filling joint returns.

Use of the Tax Tables. The Internal Revenue Service provides tax tables for taxpayers who have adjusted gross income of less than $10,000. The use of these tax tables is simply a short-cut method of figuring the income tax. The tables are based on the taxpayer's personal exemptions and the relevant standard deduction in place of itemized personal deductions and certain credits. It should be noted that a taxpayer desiring to make use of the minimum standard deduction must use the tax tables provided by the Internal Revenue Service. The special tax tables are prepared by the Internal Revenue Service and are mailed to the taxpayer at the same time Form 1040 is mailed.

Although there are four different classes of income tax payers, there are only two different basic rate structures, the individual and corporate structures. An estate or trust is subject to the income tax rates applicable to a single individual who does not qualify as head of household—that is, at the rates shown in Rate Schedule No. 1 of Figure 25-3. The corporate rate structure is considered in connection with the discussion of the corporate income tax.

Exceptions to the Schedule Tax Rates. There are two exceptions to the rates as published in Figure 25-3. First, the Revenue Act of 1969 imposed a new minimum tax on large taxpayers who have certain "tax preference items" such as accelerated depreciation, stock options, long-term capital gains, and other tax preference items. Form 4625, Computation of Minimum Tax, must be filed if a taxpayer has tax preference items in excess of $15,000 even though there may be no minimum tax due.

The other exception to the tax rate schedule is for large taxpayers who have large amounts of net long-term capital gains. To illustrate, assume that in 1971 Mr. and Mrs. Sam Samuelson have the following taxable income indicated on a joint return:

> $75,000 Net Taxable Income Excluding
> Net Long-Term Capital Gains
> 25,000 Net Long-Term Capital Gains
> before 50 percent reduction

By including $12,500 of net long-term capital gains in taxable income there would be $87,500 of taxable income and an indicated tax of $37,690, computed as follows:

Tax on first $80,000	$33,340
Add Tax on Remaining $7,500: 58% × $7,500	4,350
Indicated Tax	$37,690

Yet since long-term capital gains are subject to a maximum tax in 1971 of 25 percent on the first $50,000 and 32½ percent on the excess of the amount above $50,000, without giving consideration to the 50-percent reduction, the actual tax would be $36,720, computed as follows:

Tax on ordinary taxable income of $75,000	
Tax on first $70,000	$27,720
Tax on remaining $5,000: 55% × $5,000	2,750
Tax on ordinary taxable income	$30,470
Tax on capital gains of $25,000	6,250
Total Income tax for 1971	$36,720

The advantage of the alternate tax on capital gains would disappear as the amount of these gains became larger and subject to the possible higher alternate tax on capital gains in excess of $50,000 and the new minimum tax on tax preference items.

Tax Credits. After the income tax has been computed, certain special credits may be deducted from this amount in computing the amount of the tax liability currently outstanding. Typical tax credits are

1. Income Tax Withheld or Paid on Declared Estimate. A taxpayer takes credit for all salary withholding income taxes and for advance payments made on the basis of his Declaration of Estimated Income Tax, Form 1040-ES.

2. Retirement Income Credit. Persons who have worked for at least 10 years, in which at least $600 was earned in each year, who are now receiving qualifying retirement pay and individuals over 65 who meet the same earnings test and who receive primarily rents, interest, and dividends are entitled to a tax credit of 15 percent of qualifying retirement income—rents, interest, dividends, and other—up to $1,524, or a maximum credit of $228.60; however, if a husband and wife, both 65 or over, file a joint return and if either one meets the 10-year work test, then the tax credit of 15 percent may be applied to qualifying retirement income up to $2,286, or a maximum credit of $342.90. The maximum

allowable credit on a joint return where *both husband and wife* show retirement income of $1,524 is $457.20.

3. Investment Credit. The 1971 Revenue Act restored the 7 percent investment tax credit. This 7 percent tax credit applies to qualifying business equipment acquired since August 15, 1971, or ordered since April 1, 1971.

4. Political Contribution Credit or Deduction. The 1971 Revenue Act also provided a credit amounting to one half of a taxpayer's actual political contribution, made after December 31, 1971, with a maximum credit of $12.50, or $25 for a couple filing a joint return; alternatively the taxpayer could elect to take an itemized personal deduction for such actual contribution, made after December 31, 1971, up to a maximum $50, or $100 for a couple filing a joint return.

5. Miscellaneous Tax Credits. A few other rather infrequent tax credits are allowed. For example, a credit is allowed for taxes paid to foreign countries on income that is also taxed by the United States.

Illustrative Problem—Individual Income Tax

The following hypothetical case illustrates the major features of the individual Federal income tax computation:

John Thompson, who is 44 years old, is married to Faye Thompson, who is 40 years old. They have two children: a son, John, Jr., 10 years old; and Mary Kay, 20 years old, who is attending college. The Thompsons furnish over one half the support of both their children, although Mary Kay works as a summer camp counselor and earned $900 in 1971.[2] Thompson owns and operates a grocery store under the name of Thompson Groceries. Mrs. Thompson did not earn any income in 1971. Relevant business and personal information for the family is shown in Figure 25-4 on page 835.

The computation of the tax liability on a joint return filed by the Thompsons appears, in summary form, in Figure 25-5. Supporting information is shown in Schedules 1 through 5.

THE PARTNERSHIP INFORMATIONAL RETURN

Partnerships are not taxed as separate entities. Rather, the relevant revenues and expenses of the partnership are reported on an informational return, Form 1065, and the individual partners report their respective shares of operating income, net long-term and short-term capital gains, dividends received, contributions, tax-exempt income, and any other items that require special treatment on their own U.S. Individual Income Tax Returns.

Consider the partnership firm of Warren and Baker, which has an ordinary taxable income of $100,000 after salaries of $8,000 to George Warren and $10,000 to Peter Baker. Relevant items belonging to each partner are indicated in Figure 25-6 on page 837.

On his U.S. Individual Income Tax Return, Warren, for example, would consolidate the following items with his own personal income and deductions: salary received from partnership, $8,000; ordinary income from partnership,

---

[2] The year 1971 rather than 1973 is used in the discussion in this chapter because statements made are based on the law in effect during 1971. The Federal tax rates are subject to change at any time.

Figure 25-4. Tax Information—John and Faye Thompson

835

Income
　Net income from Thompson Groceries (gross margin on sales of $50,000
　　less operating expenses of $40,000) $10,000
　Interest on U.S. Bonds 1,000
　Interest on State of Massachusetts Bonds 1,800
　Dividends on stock jointly owned 3,200
　Net long-term capital gain from sale of 100 shares of National
　　Carbon Company stock:

Date Acquired	Date Sold	Tax Basis (Cost)	Selling Price	
2/10/63	3/6/71	$4,000	$5,000	1,000

　Net short-term capital gain from sale of 200 shares of United
　　Widgets Company stock:

Date Acquired	Date Sold	Tax Basis (Cost)	Selling Price	
1/10/71	4/1/71	$2,000	$2,500	500

Expenditures
　Contributions to church and university 800
　Contribution to Community Chest 200
　Interest paid on personal loans 300
　Property taxes paid on town and county 692
　State taxes paid
　　Sales tax 158
　　Automobile license tags 24
　　Gasoline tax 100
　Family medical expenses
　　Doctor and hospital fees 200
　　Drugs and medicine 100
　Amount paid in 1971 as a result of filing Form 1040-ES,
　　Declaration of Estimated Income Tax 1,700

Figure 25-5. Computation of the Tax Liability

JOHN AND FAYE THOMPSON
Computation of Income Tax Liability
Taxable Year 1971

Gross Income (Schedule 1)		$55,500
Deductions from Gross Income		
Operating Expenses of the Grocery Store (from Figure 25-4)	$40,000	
Capital Gains Deduction		
50% × Net LTCG of $1,000	500	
Total Deductions from Gross Income		40,500
Adjusted Gross Income		$15,000
Personal Deductions (Schedule 2)	$ 2,250	
Personal Exemptions (Schedule 3)	2,700	4,950
Taxable Income		$10,050
Federal Income Tax for 1971 (Schedule 4)		$ 1,831
Tax Credits (Schedule 5)		1,700
Net Tax Liability		$　131

Figure 25-5 (continued)

Schedule 1—Gross Income

Gross Margin on Sales of Thompson Groceries	$50,000
Interest on U.S. Bonds	1,000
Dividends received ($100 per owner-spouse is excluded)	3,000
Net long-term capital gains	1,000
Net short-term capital gains (100% included)	500
(Interest on State of Massachusetts Bonds is 100% excludable)	
Total Gross Income	$55,500

Schedule 2—Personal Deductions

Contributions (both apply since they do not exceed allowable limitation—all are qualifying special contributions)	$1,000
Interest paid on personal loans	300
Property taxes	692
Sales tax	158
Gasoline tax	100
(The $24 paid for license tags is not a deductible item in post-1963 years, and the medical expenses are not large enough to be included—only that part of the drugs that exceed $150 (1% of AGI of $15,000) would qualify as a gross medical expense and further only the medical expenses that exceed $450 (3% of AGI of $15,000) would qualify as a personal deduction.)	
Total Personal Deductions	$2,250

Schedule 3—Personal Exemptions

John Thompson	1
Faye Thompson	1
Mary Kaye (Under a special relief provision of the tax law, she qualifies as an exemption for Thompson even though she earned over $675 income—she would have to file a return and could claim an exemption for herself; but Thompson may also claim her as an exemption)	1
John, Jr.	1
Total	4

Value of Personal Exemptions; 4 × $675 = $2,700

Schedule 4—Computation of Federal Income Tax

Referring to Rate Schedule No. 2, Figure 25-3 for married couples filing joint returns:	
Income tax on first $10,000	$1,820
Plus 22% × $50	11
Total Federal Income Tax for 1971	$1,831

Schedule 5—Tax Credits

Amount Paid in 1971 as a result of filing Form 1040-ES, Declaration of Estimated Income Tax for Individuals	$1,700

Figure 25-6. Partnership Tax Information

WARREN AND BAKER PARTNERSHIP Tax Information—Taxable Year 1971			
	Total	Warren's Share	Baker's Share
Partnership ordinary income	$100,000	$70,000	$30,000
Net long-term capital gains	2,000	1,400	600
Net short-term capital gains	1,000	700	300
Dividends received	10,000	7,000	3,000
Contributions	(2,200)	(1,540)	(660)
Interest received on municipal bonds	1,100	770	330
Total partnership income per books	$111,900	$78,330	$33,570

$70,000; net long-term capital gains (only 50% included, but subject to special tax on capital gains), $700; net short-term capital gains, $700; dividends received (net of $100 exclusion, assuming that Warren is single and does not own any stocks personally), $6,900; and contributions, $1,540. The interest received on municipal bonds is tax-exempt and hence would be excluded from Warren's gross income. Warren's individual Federal income tax would then be computed in the manner described in Figure 25-5.

CORPORATE INCOME TAXES

The income of business corporations is subject to a separate income tax, and the corporations are not allowed to deduct dividends that are paid to stockholders. Also, the dividends are partially taxed to the individual stockholders who receive them. The special corporate tax rate schedule is a simple two-step progressive structure.

Taxable Income	Tax Rate
$0 to $25,000	22%
$25,000 and over	48%

In general, the taxable income of a corporation is computed in the same manner as the taxable income of an individual. Among the exceptions is the fact that a corporation may not take certain personal deductions allowed to individuals. For example, a corporation is not entitled to personal exemptions, the standard deduction, or such deductions as medical expenses. Since personal deductions are not allowed, the concept of adjusted gross income would be meaningless and, therefore, is not applicable to the corporation.

The $100 dividend exclusion is not applicable to corporations. Normally, they may deduct from gross income 85 percent of dividends received from domestic corporations. Under certain conditions, when a consolidated return is filed for qualifying affiliates, the consolidated group may, in effect, deduct 100 percent of dividends received by members of the group from each other, that is, the intercompany dividend amount.

Capital losses of a corporation can be deducted only against capital gains. Capital losses may be carried back three years and forward five years and offset against any capital gains earned during those years, not counting the year of the loss. The unlimited carryover of losses rules included in the 1964 Revenue Act apply only to individuals; carryovers by corporations are still limited to five years.

Net long-term capital gains are 100-percent includable in taxable income of corporations, but are subject to a maximum tax rate of 30 percent. For example, if the Carter Corporation reported a taxable income in 1971 of $100,000, composed entirely of net long-term capital gains, its tax would be only $30,000; but if it reported a normal business income of $100,000, its tax would be $41,500.

A maximum limit of 5 percent of net income, figured without regard to the contribution deduction, for corporate contributions is imposed on corporations. Any contribution in excess of this limit may be carried over, however, to the five succeeding years and deducted, provided the total contributions including the carried over amounts are within the 5-percent limit of the appropriate years.

The Corporate Income Tax Return, Form 1120, must be filed two and one-half months after the end of the taxable fiscal year. Corporations whose tax liability for the forthcoming year is expected to be in excess of $100,000 must file declarations of estimated tax on Form 1120-ES and prepay their income tax.

The major features of the corporate income tax are illustrated by the tax computation for the Dickens Corporation, shown in Figure 25-7.

Figure 25-7. Corporate Income Tax Computation

DICKENS CORPORATION Tax Computation—Taxable Year 1971		
Revenue		
Net Sales		$500,000
Expenses		
Cost of Goods Sold	$250,000	
Operating Expenses	100,000	350,000
Net Income per Books		$150,000
Add Items not Deductible for Tax Purposes		
Capital Losses Deducted as a Part of Operating Expenses	$ 7,200	
Charitable Contributions in Excess of 5% Limit	2,800	10,000
Net Taxable Income		$160,000
Tax Computation		
Tax on First $25,000 of Taxable Income at 22%		$ 5,500
Tax on Income over $25,000 ($135,000 × 48%)		64,800
Total Corporate Income Tax		$ 70,300

INCOME TAX PLANNING

Since 1913, the weight of the income tax has become heavier and heavier on individuals, estates, trusts, and corporations. Today, a large part of the income dollar of all taxpayers goes to various governmental agencies in the form of taxes, with the income tax taking one of the largest bites. Therefore, it behooves the management of taxpaying entities to plan certain controllable transactions in a manner that will minimize the tax cost in the long run. In other words, management should avoid all income taxes possible by the legal method of preventing a tax liability from coming into existence, referred to as *avoidance*; but it should never evade taxes by failure to report, illegal reporting, or the nonpayment of taxes.

The essence of tax planning is the predetermination of the income tax effect of transactions; with the effect thus determined, the taxpayer can make those transactions that will result in the minimization of the income tax. For example, the timing of revenue receipts and expenses is an excellent way of controlling taxable income. A few general rules illustrate this point: a taxpayer should avoid bunching taxable revenue in one year with related expenses falling in another; if he anticipates high revenue in a succeeding year, he should hold off discretionary expenses and make these in the high-revenue year in order to minimize taxable income; if a change in income tax rates is anticipated, he should accelerate or postpone revenue and expenses accordingly; and he should avoid, if possible, the offsetting of short-term capital losses against long-term capital gains in the same year, for only 50 percent of net long-term capital gains are includable in taxable income.

There are many relief provisions in the income tax law, which should be used by taxpayers to the fullest extent possible. Some examples follow.

1. The use of LIFO in inventory valuation when prices are rising (permission must be obtained from the Internal Revenue Service for a company to switch inventory pricing methods)
2. The use of allowable accelerated depreciation methods and the use of the shorter average estimated useful lives allowed under the new Asset Depreciation Range provision of the 1971 Revenue Act.
3. The required use of the percentage depletion allowance (a percent authorized by the Internal Revenue Service multiplied by revenue) if it exceeds cost depletion (explained in Chapter 10). The taxpayer has no option to choose between these two methods; he must use the method that yields the larger deduction.

In summary, these guidelines should be observed:

1. All controllable transactions should be planned in light of the tax consequences—a taxpayer may be able to do something about the tax effect before a transaction occurs, but he can legally do nothing except follow the tax law after the transaction has already taken place.
2. Evidence of transactions should be preserved; in other words, a set of books should be maintained. Even a cash-basis salaried individual taxpayer should establish as a minimum a simple columnar journal of cash receipts and expenditures. In case of an audit by a representative of the Internal Revenue Service, this kind of record would be invaluable.

THE IMPACT OF INCOME TAXES ON BUSINESS DECISIONS

With the present extremely high income tax rates, it is essential for prudent business managers to consider carefully the effect of income taxes on the various alternatives under review. There is an adage among businessmen, that a tax dollar saved, with a tax rate of approximately 50 percent, is as profitable as the earning of two dollars of net operating income. In the preceding section, certain suggestions were made regarding how to plan transactions so as to minimize the amount of the income tax; this planning is one aspect of decision making. In this section, however, the focus is on the impact of taxes on the choice of form of business organization, effect on financial arrangements, effect on adoption of accounting procedures, and the effect on hold-or-sell decisions.

When one or more individuals are deciding to create a business, one of the first decisions that must be made involves the selection of the legal form of organization that should be used. Income taxes, along with many other factors, may help to influence the choice of a form of business organization—sole proprietorship, partnership, or corporation. Tax provisions that must be kept in mind are: (1) a sole proprietor must pay a tax on the entire taxable income of his business; (2) a partner must pay a tax on his proportionate share of the taxable partnership income whether distributed or not; (3) a corporation (unless it elects *Subchapter S* treatment) must report and pay a tax on its income and the stockholders must include their dividend income on their individual return. From the viewpoint of one *individual* who is to be involved in the formation of a new business, a calculation must be made to estimate how he would fare from a tax standpoint under the alternative business forms. This calculation would require an estimated anticipated after-tax net income of the corporation, the salary to be received by the major stockholder, the net income of the sole proprietorship, and a calculation of the available disposable income for the proprietor. If the calculation shows one form to yield a larger disposable net income, that business form, holding all other items constant, *may* be the one that should be used.

As indicated in Chapter 14, income taxes may influence the particular financing arrangement that a firm used to obtain new long-term capital. The main thrust of this problem results from the fact that dividends are not deductible in arriving at taxable income, whereas interest expense is deductible. Thus, if a decision has to be made in regard to whether or not to issue bonds as compared to common or preferred stock, the calculation of taxable income and the resultant income taxes may be a deciding factor.

Certain accounting procedures may be adopted because of tax factors. For example, the LIFO inventory method may be chosen for tax purposes because it is anticipated that it will possibly yield a lower taxable income than would other inventory pricing methods. The tax law requires that LIFO be used for book purposes if it is used for tax purposes. This tax requirement thus forces firms to adopt a procedure that may not, in *most* cases, produce an income figure which is best for business decisions. Other examples of possible unsound accounting procedures involve the nonrecognition of gains and losses on trade-in of plant and equipment items and the percentage depletion method, discussed in Chapter 10.

Because of a difference between tax rate on ordinary income and capital gains rates on long-term capital gains under $50,000, particularly, the income tax may influence a decision of an owner to hold or to sell an income-producing asset. If the present value of the future after-tax income is higher than the after-tax income resulting from a sale, then the income-producing property should be held. On the other hand, if the after-tax gain resulting from the possible sale is greater than the present value of the after-tax income, then the property should be sold.

DIFFERENCES BETWEEN BUSINESS INCOME AND TAXABLE INCOME

Taxable income should be computed in accordance with statutes and administrative regulations of the Federal government, whereas the computation of business income should be based on generally accepted accounting principles. Any feature of the tax law that increases taxable income also increases the amount of tax; likewise, any feature of the law that decreases the amount of taxable income decreases the amount of tax. A summary of the major differences between traditional business income and taxable income follows.

1. Some items not considered to be revenue by generally accepted accounting principles are taxed as revenue by the law.
2. Some items considered as business expenses are not deductible for tax purposes.
3. Some items generally considered to be business revenue are exempt from tax by law.
4. Some items not generally considered to be business expenses are deductible for tax purposes.

A brief discussion of each of these differences is illustrated by examples. In general, the corporate net income is the basis for the comparison; however, many of the statements apply to net income earned by a single proprietor.

Taxable Nonbusiness Revenues

The most important taxable receipts that are not generally considered to be business revenues are certain unearned revenue items, such as advance receipts of rent, interest, or royalties. The Federal government levies the tax in the year of receipt, when the cash is presumably available for payment of the tax. Sound accounting, on the other hand, recognizes these items as revenue in the year in which they are earned. An exception to the general tax rule stated is the unearned subscriptions revenue received by publishing companies. These particular entities are permitted to report taxable revenue on the basis of the earning process as opposed to the time of cash receipt.

Nondeductible Business Expenses

Representative examples of items that would normally be considered business expenses but that are not allowed for tax purposes are as follows:

1. As indicated in the discussion of corporate income tax, charitable contributions in excess of 5 percent of net income, figured without regard to the contribution deduction, are not deductible even when they are made for an ostensible business purpose.
2. Interest on money borrowed to purchase tax-exempt securities is not deductible.
3. Premiums paid on life insurance policies carried by the corporation on the lives of its key personnel are not deductible if the corporation names itself as beneficiary—sound accounting would require that the amount

of the premium in excess of increases in cash surrender value (the investment in the policies) should be considered an expense.
4. The Federal income tax itself is not an expense for tax purposes.
5. Any amortization of an indefinite-life intangible fixed asset, particularly goodwill, is not deductible.

Business Revenue Items Exempt from Taxation

There are several revenue items that are exempt from taxation because of various reasons ranging from social desirability to administrative expediency. Representative examples of items specifically exempted by the Internal Revenue Code are as follows:

1. Interest received on state and municipal bonds and notes is specifically exempt from taxation.
2. Gains on plant assets traded in for similar assets to be held for the same purpose as the old assets are exempt; the bases of the new plant assets are reduced by the amounts of the nonrecognized gains (see page 358).
3. A portion of net long-term capital gains, in effect, is exempt since there is a maximum tax rate on such gains.
4. Life insurance proceeds received on the death of the insured are not taxed.

Deductions Allowed by Tax Law That Are Not Generally Considered to Be Expenses

The tax law provides special relief provisions and investment incentives that are not generally deducted from business revenue to measure net income. Among these are the following:

1. The part of depletion usually determined on a percentage of revenue basis that is in excess of cost.
2. In a similar manner, the part of allowable accelerated depreciation that is in excess of sound depreciation expense.
3. The net operating loss deduction—a special feature of the tax law designed to give taxpayers who suffer a loss in a given bad year some relief from taxes paid in the three years immediately preceding, or the five years following, the year of the loss.

FINANCIAL REPORTING PROBLEMS

The differences between taxable income and business income fall into two classes: (1) those that tend to result in a near-permanent difference between taxable and business income, and (2) those for which the difference between taxable income and business income is washed out in time. The latter class has caused some financial reporting problems that are magnified by the size of the current income tax. The controversy centers around the proper measurement of the Federal income tax expense. If the Federal income tax is a business expense, it appears that the matching concept dictates that it be computed on the basis of reported business income, taking into consideration the items in Class 2 above.

If the assumption is valid, the accountants of those companies which have material differences between taxable income and reported business income that tend to wash out in time should give serious consideration to the allocation of the income tax expense among the relevant periods. Since the problem is such a complex one and also since it is typically treated in depth in more advanced accounting texts, it is not further developed here.

SUMMARY

As provided by the Internal Revenue Code, Federal income taxes are levied on individuals, corporations, estates, and trusts. These taxes consume a significant portion of the taxpayer's income and therefore should be considered in all decisions of any consequence. The subject is broad and complicated; however, it is essential to realize the impact of taxes on individuals and various forms of business organizations and the problems its creates in financial reporting.

A taxpayer in certain instances may elect to report income for Federal income tax purposes on either the cash basis or accrual basis of accounting. When confronted with this decision, he should choose the method that postpones the payment of taxes for the longest period of time. The accrual basis is required of businesses in which production, purchases, and sales of merchandise are significant factors, and the cash basis is required of taxpayers whose only income is a salary. For income tax purposes, a taxpayer using the cash basis may not deduct the cost of long-lived assets in the year of purchase but must apportion the cost through depreciation deductions over the useful life of the assets. Revenue must be recognized when it is constructively received—that is, when it is in the control of the taxpayer.

All items of income except those specifically excluded by law must be included in gross income. Among the more common exclusions are interest on state and municipal bonds, the dividend exclusion, and gifts and inheritances. Deductions from gross income include expenses incurred in a trade or business or in the production of royalty or rental revenue, travel and entertainment expenses, certain expenses of employees, and the capital gains deduction. The distinction between these deductions and deductions from adjusted gross income is important since each may have a different effect on the income tax liability.

Capital gains and losses result from the sale of stocks, bonds, and other capital assets. If a capital asset held for over six months is sold, a long-term capital gain or loss results; if the capital asset was held for a shorter period of time, its sale results in a short-term capital gain or loss. A deduction of 50 percent of the net long-term capital gain is allowed for tax purposes. If short-term or long-term capital losses exceed the capital gains, 50 percent of the excess is the deductible loss if the loss is a long-term capital loss, or 100 percent of the loss is the deductible loss if the loss is a short-term capital loss. The amount of capital loss that may be deducted from ordinary income is the actual deductible loss up to a maximum of $1,000 or the taxable income, whichever is smaller. If the allowable capital losses exceed this limitation, the excess may be carried to future years and offset against capital gains or gross income not to exceed the maximum limitation.

A taxpayer has the option of taking the standard deduction or itemizing personal deductions, whichever will benefit him the most. The standard deduction is a stipulated percent of adjusted gross income or the minimum standard deduction. Itemized deductions include charitable contributions, medical expenses, interest, specific taxes, and various expenses of employees. Many of these deductions are subject to limitations specified by the Internal Revenue Code. Regardless of whether a taxpayer elects to take the minimum or percentage standard deduction, or to itemize personal deductions, a personal exemption of $675 in 1971 and $750 in 1972 and later years is allowed for the taxpayer, for his spouse if a joint return is filed, and for each person qualifying as a dependent. Additional exemptions are allowed if the taxpayer or his spouse is 65 years old or blind.

The income tax before credits is determined by multiplying the taxable income by the appropriate rates. The tax rates are progressive; that is, the applicable rate increases as the taxable income increases. Different rate structures apply to married couples filing a joint return, a single person qualifying as head of household, a single person not qualifying as head of household and married individuals filing separate returns. Tax credits are deducted from the income tax to determine the federal income taxes payable. Common tax credits are withheld taxes, payments made on declared estimates, the retirement income credit, the investment credit, the political contribution credit, and the foreign tax credit.

Although a partnership is not taxed as a separate entity, it is required to file an information return. Each partner reports his share of profits, dividends received, capital gains and losses, charitable contributions, and other items on his personal return.

The computation of the taxable income of a corporation is similar to that of the taxable income of an individual; however, a corporation is not allowed personal deductions, such as the standard deduction, or personal exemptions. An exclusion of 85 percent of the dividends received by a corporation is provided by law, and charitable contributions in any year are limited to 5 percent of the net income computed wihout regard to the contribution deduction. Net long-term capital gains are 100-percent includable in taxable income, but are subject to a maximum tax rate in 1971 of 30 percent. The allowable capital losses of a corporation can be offset only against capital gains, and any unused capital losses may be carried back three years and forward five years and offset against capital gains earned during those years.

Because of the existing high income tax rates, taxpayers should plan their financial affairs in such a manner as to avoid as much income taxes as possible by the legal method of preventing tax liabilities from coming into existence. If the income tax effects on proposed transactions are predetermined, then the taxpayer may choose the transaction or form of transaction that will result in the minimum tax. Tax planning also encompasses the full utilization of all relief provisions in the income tax law that are available to the taxpayer.

Since net income for accounting purposes is computed following generally accepted accounting principles, whereas taxable net income is computed according to statutes and regulations of the Federal government, in many cases, the two net income figures will differ. The differences are primarily caused by one or more of the following: (1) Items that are not considered to be revenue by generally accepted accounting principles but are taxed as revenue by the tax laws. (2) Items that are considered as business expenses but are not deductible for tax purposes. (3) Items that are generally considered to be business revenue but are exempt from tax by law. (4) Items that are not generally considered to be business expenses but are deductible for tax purposes.

Some of these factors may result in near-permanent differences; others result in differences that are washed out over a period. This latter class has caused a controversy concerning the proper measurement of Federal income tax expenses for financial accounting and the proper handling of the complex problem of income tax allocation, which is not discussed in this text.

QUESTIONS

Q25-1. (a) Distinguish between the cash and accrual bases of accounting. (b) What is a modified cash basis?

Q25-2. (a) Define the term *gross income* from an individual income tax point of view. (b) List six items that must be reported as gross income. (c) List four items that are excludable from gross income.

Q25-3. (a) What is the individual income tax standard deduction? (b) State its maximum and minimum limits.

Q25-4. Smith, a bachelor, earned $20,000 in taxable income in 1971. What amount of Federal income tax would be saved if he were to marry on December 31, 1971, a woman who had no taxable income in 1971?

Q25-5. (a) For tax purposes, what are capital assets? (b) Distinguish between short-term and long-term capital gains. (c) The timing of capital gains and losses is important in tax planning. Discuss.

Q25-6. John Allen, aged 21, is attending the State University. During the summer of 1971, he worked as a construction laborer and earned $850. His parents contributed $1,850 toward his support in 1971. Can Allen's parents claim him as an exemption?

Q25-7. Samuel Sawyer elected to use the cash basis for tax purposes. During 1971, he collected $12,000 from clients for services rendered in prior years, and billed clients for $30,000 for services rendered in 1971. His accounts receivable as of December 31, 1971, totaled $8,700. What is the amount of gross income he should report on his Form 1040 for 1971?

Q25-8. John and Susan Adams owned some shares of stock. During 1971, they received $700 in dividends. Dividends of $610 were received on stock owned by John Adams only. The remainder was received on stock owned by Susan Adams. What would be the dividends included in gross income on a joint return?

Q25-9. List and briefly discuss the computational differences between the individual income tax and the corporation income tax.

Q25-10. (a) State the objective of tax planning. (b) Discuss ways and means of accomplishing tax planning.

Q25-11. In outline form, state four ways that traditional business income may differ from taxable income, and under each way give two specific illustrations.

EXERCISES

E25-1. Saul Allison, a bachelor, had the following cash receipts during 1971:

Salary earned as a professor	$14,000
Receipt of insurance proceeds for fire damages to personal car	500
Dividends from domestic companies	2,000
Interest on U.S. Government bonds	600
Interest on North Carolina State bonds	700
Total Cash Receipts	$17,800

Compute the amount of gross income subject to the individual income tax.

E25-2. Dunn and Pauline Carson filed a joint return in 1971. They had the following taxable income after deductions and exemptions:

Ordinary taxable income	$100,000
Long-term capital gains (before reduction)	30,000
Total	$130,000

Compute the 1971 Federal income tax. Remember that the income tax on net long-term capital gains cannot exceed a certain percentage of the long-term gain.

E25-3. Sanders and Sally Dee filed a joint return in 1971, on which they reported an adjusted gross income of $12,000. The couple had allowable personal deductions of $1,500; they are both under 65 and have two small children, aged six and eight.
Compute the 1971 Federal income tax.

E25-4. Paul and Renee Eubanks filed a joint return in 1971, on which they reported an adjusted gross income of $5,000. The couple's itemized deductions totaled $600; they are both under 65 and have five children, aged one, three, five, seven, and nine.
Compute the 1971 Federal income tax.

E25-5. Tow and Alice Fountain filed a joint return and reported a 1971 correct income tax before credits of $4,600. Includable in taxable income was $1,000 of qualifying dividends—the couple had received $1,200 on stock jointly owned. They paid $4,100 in 1971 on a declaration of estimated tax for 1971.
Compute the amount of the remaining tax liability for 1971.

E25-6. The Goober Corporation reported a net income per books of $400,000. In addition, its records show capital losses deducted as operating expenses of $8,000 and charitable contributions in excess of the 5-percent limit of $3,000.
Compute the 1971 Federal income tax.

DEMONSTRATION PROBLEMS

DP25-1. (*Individual income tax computation*) Adam Kennedy, who is 66 years old, is married to Sara Kennedy, who is 63 years old. They have two children: John, 16 years old, and Susan, 21 years old, who is attending a university. The Kennedy's furnish over one half the support for both their children, although Susan works as a salesclerk in the summer and earned $950 in 1971. Kennedy owns and operates a service station under the name of Kennedy Service Station. Mrs. Kennedy did not have any earned income in 1971.

Relevant business and personal information for the family is shown:

Cash Receipts
Gross revenue from Kennedy Service Station	$100,000
Interest on U.S. bonds	1,000
Interest on State of Virginia bonds	3,450
Dividends on stock jointly owned	4,200
Cash proceeds from Insurance policy for fire damage on nonbusiness property which had an original cost of $1,800	1,800

Capital gains
Sale of 200 shares of National Fruit Company common stock:

Date Acquired	Date Sold	Cost	Selling Price
3/4/69	5/2/71	$24,000	$28,000

Sale of 100 shares of United Fusbits Company common stock:

Date Acquired	Date Sold	Cost	Selling Price
4/2/71	8/10/71	$10,000	$10,600

Expenditures
Cost of goods sold ($55,000) and operating expenses ($15,000) of Kennedy Service Station	70,000
Contributions to church and university	2,000
Contribution to Community Chest	800
Interest paid on personal loans	600
Property taxes paid to town and county	800
State taxes paid	
Sales tax	160
Automobile license tags	24
Gasoline tax	100
Family medical expenses	
Doctor and hospital fees	800
Drugs and medicine	120
Blue Cross–Blue Shield Hospital Insurance	280
Amount paid in 1971 on declared estimated tax for 1971	7,000

Required: In an orderly schedule form, compute the income tax liability remaining to be paid for 1971, assuming that a joint return is filed.

DP25-2. (*Information to be reported on partnership informational return*) Carter and Newton are partners sharing profits 2:1, respectively. The following information has been taken from the partnership records for the year 1971:

Taxable ordinary income (less partners' salaries)	$60,000
Long-term capital gains	9,000
Short-term capital gains	3,600
Short-term capital losses	(3,000)
Dividends received	1,800
Charitable contributions	(2,100)
Interest on Orange County bonds	900
Salaries to partners ($5,000 to Carter and $4,000 to Newton)	9,000
Net income per books before partner's salaries	$79,200

Assume that Carter is 40 years old and single, and that he has the following tax information from sources other than the partnership:

Dividends received	$8,000
Long-term capital losses	3,000
Itemized deductions	1,500

Required: 1. Prepare a schedule showing the information that should be presented on the partnership informational return.
2. Compute the 1971 income tax for Carter.

DP25-3. (*Corporate income tax computation*) The Lundee Corporation reported the following information for 1971:

Sales	$2,000,000
Cost of goods sold	1,100,000
Operating expenses other than capital losses and charitable contributions	500,000
Capital losses	20,000
Charitable contributions	25,000
(There were no capital gains)	

Required: Compute the corporate income tax for 1971.

PROBLEMS

P25-1. Roy and Abigail Butts had the following income and related information for 1971:

Salary to Roy Butts	$10,000
Dividends on stock owned by Roy Butts	2,000
Dividends on stock owned by Abigail Butts	1,000
Abigail Butts sold some stock she had acquired on April 1, 1964 on March 15, 1971 at a gain of	4,000
Roy Butts sold some stock he had acquired on July 1, 1971, on November 15, 1971, at a loss of	1,500

Required: Compute the adjusted gross income subject to tax on a joint return filed by Roy and Abigail Butts.

P25-2. Randolph Peters, who is 45 years old, is married to Alice Peters, who is 41 years old. They have two children: a son, Duncan, 9 years old, and a daughter, Sue, 14 years old. Peters owns and operates a hardware store under the name of the Peters Hardware Company. Mrs. Peters did not have any earned income in 1971.

Tax and other information for 1971 are as follows:

Cash Receipts	
Gross sales of Peters Hardware Company	$200,000
Interest on Dare County bonds	2,000
Dividends on stock owned by Alice Peters	6,000
Cash inherited by Alice Peters	20,000
Capital gains on stock sold by Alice Peters	
Long-term gains	10,000
Short-term gains	1,200
Expenditures	
Cost of goods sold of Peters Hardware Company	100,000
Operating expenses of Peters Hardware Company	40,000
Contribution to church	8,000
Contribution to Community Chest	1,000
Interest paid on personal loans	800
Personal property taxes	1,000

State taxes paid	
Sales taxes	175
Automobile license tags	30
Gasoline tax	120
Family medical expenses	
Doctor and hospital fees	1,200
Hospital insurance	320
Drugs and medicine	500
Amount paid in 1971 on declared estimated tax for 1971	20,000

Required: Compute the income tax liability remaining to be paid for 1971, assuming that a joint return is filed.

P25-3. Parm Quarles, who is 67 years old, and his wife Mimie Quarles, who is 64 years old, file a joint return. They have two children, Parm, Jr., who is 30 years old, and Vera, who is 21 years old and is attending college full time. Mr. and Mrs. Quarles furnish over one half the support for Vera although she earned $1,150 on a summer job in 1971. Various receipts and expenditures of Mr. and Mrs. Quarles are listed below.

Mr. Quarles

Cash Receipts

Withdrawal by proprietor from business (sales, $270,000; cost of goods sold, $154,000; operating expenses, $52,000)	$30,000
Cash dividends received	2,600
Gain on sale of stock purchased five years ago	4,000
Interest received on school district bonds	2,000

Expenditures

Contribution to church and university	6,000
Contribution to Community Chest	200
Personal property taxes	1,000
Insurance on residence	200
Automobile license plates	24
State sales taxes	150
State gasoline tax	100
Medical expenses	
Drugs and medicines	380
Hospital insurance	280
Doctor and hospital bills	1,050
Interest on personal loans	700
Payment on declaration of estimated tax	21,500

Mrs. Quarles

Cash Receipts

Rental of apartment building	$10,000
Dividends received on stock	850
Received from sale of stock purchased for $3,600 four months previously	2,900

Expenditures

Apartment building (original cost on January 1, 1963, was $63,000. Sum of the years'-digits depreciation is used for tax purposes, with an assumed life of 20 years and no salvage value)	
Interest on business indebtedness	900
Property taxes	1,600
Insurance for 1971	210
Repairs and maintenance	1,800
Contribution to church	300

Required: Compute the remaining tax liability for 1971 for Mimie and Parm Quarles on a joint return.

P25-4. Each of the following five cases represents a possible situation with respect to capital gains and losses. Assume that Allen Sims, a bachelor, has a salary income of $10,000 in addition to the items shown:

1. Long-term capital gains of $8,000; long-term capital losses of $4,000; short-term capital gains of $6,000; short-term capital losses of $3,000
2. Long-term capital gains of $8,000; short-term capital losses of $16,000
3. Long-term capital gains of $4,000; long-term capital losses of $8,000; short-term capital gains of $2,000; short-term capital losses of $7,000
4. Long-term capital gains of $10,000; short-term capital losses of $6,000
5. Long-term capital gains of $1,000; long-term capital losses of $500; short-term capital loss of $1,200

Required: Compute Allen Sims' adjusted gross income in each case for the year 1971.

P25-5. Greg Sands is single, aged 47; Robert Rand is also single, aged 38; both use the standard deduction. They reported the following tax information for 1971:

Tax information for Greg Sands	
Ordinary income	$30,000
Net long-term capital gains	1,000
Tax information for Robert Rand	
Ordinary income	$ 5,000
Net long-term capital gains	40,000

Required: Compute the amount of Sands' and Rand's income tax for 1971. (Remember that the tax on long-term capital gains cannot exceed a certain percentage of the long-term gain.)

P25-6. The following information relates to a taxpayer:

Gross revenue (including $1,000 in interest received on South Carolina bonds and $1,000 in dividends)	$13,900
Deductions to arrive at adjusted gross income	800
Payments made on declaration of estimated tax for 1971	1,200
Long-term capital gains	1,500
Short-term capital losses	2,900
Itemized deductions	1,060

Required:

1. Compute the remaining income tax liability, assuming that the taxpayer is married, that both he and his wife are under 65, that they have three dependent children, and that the wife did not receive any separate income.
2. Compute the remaining income tax liability, assuming that the taxpayer is single and under 65.

P25-7. King and Johnson are partners; they share profits 3:1, respectively. The following information has been taken from the partnership records for the year 1971:

Taxable ordinary income (less partners' salaries)	$24,000
Long-term capital gains	10,000
Short-term capital losses	(4,000)
Dividends received	2,000
Charitable contributions	(800)
Interest on Florida State bonds	1,000
Salaries to partners ($6,000 to King; $4,000 to Johnson)	10,000
Net income per books before partners' salaries	$42,200

Assume that King is 68 years old and single, and that he has the following tax information from sources other than the partnership:

Dividends received	$6,000
Long-term capital losses	1,600
Itemized deductions	2,000

Required: 1. Prepare a schedule showing the information that should be presented on the partnership informational return.
2. Compute King's 1971 income tax.

P25-8. The Heller Corporation reported the following information for 1971.

Sales	$1,890,000
Cost of goods sold	920,000
Operating expenses, other than capital losses and charitable contributions	380,000
Capital losses	18,000
Charitable contributions	21,000

Required: Compute the corporate income tax for 1971.

P25-9. (*Financial policy decision problem*) The Conners Production Company, a textile manufacturer, has recently had a change in ownership and top management. Robert Janes, the new president, is a retired military officer and is noted for being an excellent organizer and administrator. Janes is gaining a reputation around the office for asking hard questions and for requiring complete and logical answers.

During one of the mornings that Janes is devoting to familiarizing himself with the workings of the accounting department, he reviews the latest federal corporate tax return and the latest income statement in the corporate annual report. He immediately notices that the taxable income of $136,495 on the tax return and the net income before income taxes of $219,400 on the income statement are not the same amount. On closer examination he observes that the following items are not the same on each report.

1. Depreciation expense is $92,510 on the income statement and $147,250 on the tax return.
2. Cost of goods sold is $929,180 on the income statement and $951,200 on the tax return.
3. Interest earned is $1,200 on the income statement and $880 on the tax return.
4. Gain on disposal of machinery is $5,790 on the income statement and does not appear on the tax return.
5. Bad debt expense is $6,400 on the income statement and $6,350 on the tax return.
6. Amortization of organization costs does not appear on the income statement and is $85 on the tax return.

He also notes that the income tax expense on the income statement is not the same as the income tax on the tax report.

By this time he is confused and bewildered. He approaches you, an assistant accountant in the tax division, and questions the discrepancies. (He has a dual purpose in asking you questions. He wishes answers to his questions and he wishes to evaluate your knowledge of tax accounting.)

Required:

1. Reconcile the two different income amounts.
2. Identify what might be a complete and logical reason for each of the six differences. (Remember that you wish to convince the new president of your competence.)
3. (a) Why does income tax expense on the income statement differ from the income tax on the tax report? (b) What is the basis for each calculation? (c) Which would you expect to be the larger? Why?

4. What is the justification for permitting differences between business income and taxable income?

5. Identify the separate objectives of business accounting and tax accounting.

6. How would you explain to Mr. Janes that mistakes have not been made and that everything is correct?

P25-10. (*Financial policy decision problem*) Assume that the owner of a parking garage is in the 60-percent tax bracket. The parking garage has a tax basis of $30,000 and a remaining useful life of four years. The net income before income tax from the garage has been averaging $22,500 per year. The garage will have no salvage value after its useful life.

The owner receives a cash offer of $78,000 for the parking garage. Assume any gain on the sale will be taxed at 25 percent.

> Required: 1. Prepare a suitable analysis of the alternatives to assist the owner in deciding whether to sell or hold the asset.
> 2. Mention one consideration that could influence the decision.

P25-11. (*Financial policy decision problem*) (a) For each of the following forms of business organization, estimate the amount of gross income that John T. Adams will have to report on his individual tax return.

		Corporation	Partnership
Sales		$1,000,000	$1,000,000
Expenses			
Salary to John T. Adams	$ 30,000		
Other	870,000	900,000	870,000
Net operating income		$ 100,000	$ 130,000
Dividends		$ 40,000	
Drawings			$ 30,000

Under the corporate form of organization, Adams will own 60 percent of the outstanding stock. Under the partnership form of organization, he will have a 60 percent interest in the partnership.

(b) Assume the facts set forth in (a) and that the business is organized as a corporation. Assume further that the corporation can earn 12 percent before corporate income tax on an additional investment of $100,000.

Adams is willing to make an additional investment of $100,000 in the business and is considering the following alternative arrangements:

1. A long-term loan of $100,000 at 6-percent interest.
2. An investment of $100,000 for an additional 1,000 shares of stock. After the issuance of the additional 1,000 shares, 5,000 shares will be outstanding.

> Required: Assuming that the corporation will distribute as additional dividends all incremental after-tax income from its use of the $100,000, estimate the increase in Adams's taxable income under each alternative.

Appendix A

Compound Interest Tables

Table 1. Present Value of $1

Period	1½%	6%	8%	10%	12%	15%	20%	25%	30%	40%
1	.985	.943	.926	.909	.893	.870	.833	.800	.769	.714
2	.971	.890	.857	.826	.797	.756	.694	.640	.592	.510
3	.956	.840	.794	.751	.712	.658	.579	.512	.455	.364
4	.942	.792	.735	.683	.636	.572	.482	.410	.350	.260
5	.928	.747	.681	.621	.567	.497	.402	.328	.269	.186
6	.915	.705	.630	.564	.507	.432	.335	.262	.207	.133
7	.901	.665	.583	.513	.452	.376	.279	.210	.159	.095
8	.888	.627	.540	.467	.404	.327	.233	.168	.123	.068
9	.875	.592	.500	.424	.361	.284	.194	.134	.094	.048
10	.862	.558	.463	.380	.322	.247	.162	.107	.073	.035
11	.849	.527	.429	.350	.287	.215	.135	.086	.056	.025
12	.836	.497	.397	.319	.257	.187	.112	.069	.043	.018
13	.824	.469	.368	.290	.229	.163	.093	.055	.033	.013
14	.812	.442	.340	.263	.205	.141	.078	.044	.025	.009
15	.800	.417	.315	.239	.183	.123	.065	.035	.020	.006
16	.788	.394	.292	.218	.163	.107	.054	.028	.015	.005
17	.776	.371	.270	.198	.146	.093	.045	.023	.012	.003
18	.765	.350	.250	.180	.130	.081	.038	.018	.009	.002
19	.754	.331	.232	.164	.116	.070	.031	.014	.007	.002
20	.742	.312	.215	.149	.104	.061	.026	.012	.005	.001
21	.731	.294	.199	.135	.093	.053	.022	.009	.004	.001
22	.721	.278	.184	.123	.083	.046	.018	.007	.003	.001
23	.710	.262	.170	.112	.074	.040	.015	.006	.002	
24	.700	.247	.158	.102	.066	.035	.013	.005	.002	
25	.689	.233	.146	.092	.059	.030	.010	.004	.001	
26	.679	.220	.135	.084	.053	.026	.009	.003	.001	
27	.669	.207	.125	.076	.047	.023	.007	.002	.001	
28	.659	.196	.116	.069	.042	.020	.006	.002	.001	
29	.649	.185	.107	.063	.037	.017	.005	.002		
30	.640	.174	.099	.057	.033	.015	.004	.001		
40	.551	.097	.046	.022	.011	.004	.001			

Table 2. Amount of $1

Period	1½%	6%	8%	10%	12%	15%	20%
1	1.015	1.060	1.080	1.100	1.120	1.150	1.200
2	1.030	1.124	1.167	1.210	1.254	1.323	1.440
3	1.046	1.191	1.260	1.331	1.405	1.521	1.728
4	1.061	1.263	1.361	1.464	1.574	1.749	2.074
5	1.077	1.338	1.469	1.611	1.762	2.011	2.489
6	1.093	1.419	1.587	1.772	1.974	2.313	2.986
7	1.110	1.504	1.714	1.949	2.211	2.660	3.583
8	1.126	1.594	1.851	2.144	2.476	3.059	4.300
9	1.143	1.690	1.999	2.358	2.773	3.518	5.160
10	1.161	1.791	2.159	2.594	3.106	4.046	6.192
11	1.178	1.898	2.332	2.853	3.479	4.652	7.430
12	1.196	2.012	2.518	3.139	3.896	5.350	8.916
13	1.214	2.133	2.720	3.452	4.364	6.153	10.700
14	1.232	2.261	2.937	3.798	4.888	7.076	12.839
15	1.250	2.397	3.172	4.177	5.474	8.137	15.407
16	1.269	2.540	3.426	4.595	6.130	9.358	18.489
17	1.288	2.693	3.700	5.055	6.866	10.761	22.186
18	1.307	2.854	3.996	5.560	7.690	12.376	26.623
19	1.327	3.026	4.316	6.116	8.613	14.232	31.948
20	1.347	3.207	4.661	6.728	9.646	16.367	38.338
21	1.367	3.400	5.034	7.400	10.804	18.822	46.005
22	1.388	3.604	5.437	8.140	12.100	21.645	55.206
23	1.408	3.820	5.872	8.954	13.552	24.892	66.247
24	1.430	4.049	6.341	9.850	15.179	28.625	79.497
25	1.451	4.292	6.849	10.835	17.000	32.919	95.396
26	1.473	4.549	7.396	11.919	19.040	37.857	114.476
27	1.495	4.822	7.988	13.110	21.325	43.535	137.371
28	1.517	5.112	8.627	14.421	23.884	50.066	164.845
29	1.540	5.418	9.317	15.863	26.750	57.576	197.814
30	1.563	5.743	10.063	17.450	29.960	66.212	237.376
40	1.814	10.286	21.725	45.259	93.051	267.864	1469.772

Table 3. Present Value of Ordinary Annuity of $1

Period	1½%	6%	8%	10%	12%	14%	16%	20%	25%	30%
1	.985	.943	.926	.909	.893	.877	.862	.833	.800	.769
2	1.956	1.833	1.783	1.736	1.690	1.647	1.605	1.528	1.440	1.361
3	2.912	2.673	2.577	2.487	2.402	2.322	2.246	2.106	1.952	1.816
4	3.854	3.465	3.312	3.170	3.037	2.914	2.798	2.589	2.362	2.166
5	4.783	4.212	3.993	3.791	3.605	3.433	3.274	2.991	2.689	2.436
6	5.697	4.917	4.623	4.355	4.111	3.889	3.685	3.326	2.951	2.643
7	6.598	5.582	5.206	4.868	4.564	4.288	4.039	3.605	3.161	2.802
8	7.486	6.210	5.747	5.335	4.968	4.639	4.344	3.837	3.329	2.925
9	8.361	6.802	6.247	5.759	5.328	4.946	4.607	4.031	3.463	3.019
10	9.222	7.360	6.710	6.145	5.650	5.216	4.833	4.192	3.571	3.092
11	10.071	7.887	7.139	6.495	5.938	5.453	5.029	4.327	3.656	3.147
12	10.908	8.384	7.536	6.814	6.194	5.660	5.197	4.439	3.725	3.190
13	11.732	8.853	7.904	7.103	6.424	5.842	5.342	4.533	3.780	3.223
14	12.543	9.295	8.244	7.367	6.628	6.002	5.468	4.611	3.824	3.249
15	13.343	9.712	8.559	7.606	6.811	6.142	5.575	4.675	3.859	3.268
16	14.131	10.106	8.851	7.824	6.974	6.265	5.669	4.730	3.887	3.283
17	14.908	10.477	9.122	8.022	7.120	6.373	5.749	4.775	3.910	3.295
18	15.673	10.828	9.372	8.201	7.250	6.467	5.818	4.812	3.928	3.304
19	16.426	11.158	9.604	8.365	7.366	6.550	5.877	4.843	3.942	3.311
20	17.169	11.470	9.818	8.514	7.469	6.623	5.929	4.870	3.954	3.316
21	17.900	11.764	10.017	8.649	7.562	6.687	5.973	4.891	3.963	3.320
22	18.621	12.042	10.201	8.772	7.645	6.743	6.011	4.909	3.970	3.323
23	19.331	12.303	10.371	8.883	7.718	6.792	6.044	4.925	3.976	3.325
24	20.030	12.550	10.529	8.985	7.784	6.835	6.073	4.937	3.981	3.327
25	20.720	12.783	10.675	9.077	7.843	6.873	6.097	4.948	3.985	3.329
26	21.399	13.003	10.810	9.161	7.896	6.906	6.118	4.956	3.988	3.330
27	22.068	13.211	10.935	9.237	7.943	6.935	6.136	4.964	3.990	3.331
28	22.727	13.406	11.051	9.307	7.984	6.961	6.152	4.970	3.992	3.331
29	23.376	13.591	11.158	9.370	8.022	6.983	6.166	4.975	3.994	3.332
30	24.016	13.765	11.258	9.427	8.055	7.003	6.177	4.979	3.995	3.332
40	29.916	15.046	11.925	9.779	8.244	7.105	6.234	4.997	3.999	3.333

Table 4. Amount of Ordinary Annuity of $1

Period	1½%	6%	8%	10%	12%	15%	20%
1	1.000	1.000	1.000	1.000	1.000	1.000	1.000
2	2.015	2.060	2.080	2.100	2.120	2.150	2.201
3	3.045	3.184	3.247	3.310	3.375	3.473	3.641
4	4.091	4.375	4.507	4.642	4.780	4.994	5.369
5	5.152	5.638	5.867	6.106	6.353	6.743	7.442
6	6.230	6.976	7.336	7.716	8.116	8.754	9.930
7	7.323	8.394	8.923	9.488	10.090	11.067	12.916
8	8.433	9.898	10.637	11.436	12.300	13.727	16.500
9	9.559	11.492	12.488	13.580	14.776	16.786	20.799
10	10.703	13.181	14.487	15.938	17.549	20.304	25.959
11	11.863	14.972	16.646	18.532	20.655	24.350	32.151
12	13.041	16.870	18.978	21.385	24.134	29.002	39.581
13	14.237	18.883	21.496	24.523	28.030	34.352	48.497
14	15.450	21.016	24.215	27.975	32.393	40.505	59.196
15	16.682	23.276	27.153	31.773	37.280	47.581	72.036
16	17.932	25.673	30.325	35.950	42.754	55.718	87.443
17	19.201	28.213	33.751	40.545	48.884	65.076	105.931
18	20.489	30.906	37.451	45.600	55.750	75.837	128.117
19	21.797	33.760	41.447	51.160	63.440	88.212	154.740
20	23.124	36.786	45.762	57.275	72.053	102.444	186.688
21	24.471	39.993	50.423	64.003	81.699	118.811	225.026
22	25.838	43.393	55.457	71.403	92.503	137.632	271.031
23	27.225	46.996	60.894	79.544	104.603	159.277	326.237
24	28.634	50.816	66.765	88.498	118.156	184.168	392.485
25	30.063	54.865	73.106	98.348	133.334	212.794	471.982
26	31.514	59.157	79.955	109.182	150.334	245.712	567.378
27	32.987	63.706	87.351	121.100	169.375	283.569	681.853
28	34.481	68.529	95.339	134.210	190.699	327.105	819.224
29	35.999	73.640	103.966	148.631	214.583	377.170	984.068
30	37.539	79.059	113.284	164.495	241.333	434.746	1181.882
40	54.268	154.762	259.057	442.593	767.092	1779.091	7343.858

Development of Accounting Principles

Professional journals of accounting (the *Journal of Accountancy*, the *Accounting Review*, and others) contain much candid and critical discussions of the many unresolved problems of financial reporting. No effort is being made to conceal unresolved problems or existing shortcomings and inadequacies. Although much remains to be done, accountants have, over a relatively short period, established a practical, rational, and integrated structure of theory and methodology for the determination of financial position and income measurement. The measurement of income is not precise; neither is it a hit-or-miss matter (which may have unlimited possible results). Rather, the accountant is guided by an elaborate system of theory and procedures. The system is neither final nor complete; nor is it entirely consistent. However, research continues at several levels in matters of terminology, in standards of disclosure, and in the narrowing of differences in those areas of accepted practice where considerable latitude now exists. Accounting is continuously evolving; it is a dynamic art, not a static one.

The following organizations, as well as some notable scholars and writers, have been influential in the development and improvement of accounting theory and practice.

New York Stock Exchange. As early as 1900 the NYSE required proper financial statements from certain companies. In 1932 it required independent audit reports from all registrants.

Board of Governors of the Federal Reserve System. The board established minimum requirements and forms for the preparation and verification of financial statements.

Securities and Exchange Commission. Since 1937 the SEC has published a series of releases dealing with specific accounting principles and the development of uniform standards and practices.

American Accounting Association. In 1936 the association published a "Tentative Statement of Accounting Principles"; this was followed by a series of revisions and supplements under the title "Accounting and Reporting Standards for Corporate Financial Statements." In 1966 the association issued "A Statement of Basic Accounting Theory." It sponsors scholarly monographs, case studies, statements, and research studies in accounting theory and practice.

American Institute of Certified Public Accountants. Since 1939 the institute has published a series of *Accounting Research Bulletins, Terminology Bulletins,* and *Statements on Auditing Procedure.* Since 1947 it has published an annual survey of *Accounting Trends and Techniques.* It publishes *Accounting Research Studies;* of special interest are the following: No. 1, "The Basic Postulates of Accounting," by Maurice Moonitz; No. 3, "A Tentative Set of Broad Accounting Principles for Business Enterprises," by Robert T. Sprouse and Maurice Moonitz; and No. 7, "Inventory of Generally Accepted Accounting Principles for Business Enterprises," by Paul Grady. The institute also publishes for continuing reference a two-volume text of *APB* (Accounting Principles Board) *Accounting Principles,* which includes the *Opinions and Statements of the APB* as well as the *Accounting Research Bulletins* issued by its predecessor, the Committee on Accounting Procedure. In October 1970, the APB issued Statement No. 4 entitled "Basic Concepts and Accounting Principles Underlying Financial Statements of Business Enterprises."

GENERALLY ACCEPTED ACCOUNTING PRINCIPLES, DEFINITIONS, AND ASSUMPTIONS

Accounting. Accounting is the process of recording the changes, in terms of increases and decreases, in property or in the rights to property, and the analysis and interpretation of financial transactions. Its function is to provide general-purpose financial information about the business enterprise for the common needs of internal and external users in making economic decisions.

Generally Accepted Accounting Principles. Reliable financial statements are predicated on those principles on which there is reasonably general agreement.

The Statement of Financial Position. The financial position of a business consists of its assets, liabilities, and owners' equity. Their relationship may be expressed in equation form as follows:

$$\text{Assets} = \text{Liabilities} + \text{Owners' Equity}$$

Income Statement. The results of operations of a business consists of its revenues, expenses, and net income. Their relationship may be expressed as follows:

$$\text{Revenue} - \text{Expenses} = \text{Net Income}$$

Assets. Everything of value owned by the business as recognized and measured in accordance with generally accepted accounting principles.

Liabilities. The rights or the claims of the creditors of the business.

Owners' Equity. The owners' claims against the assets of a business or the excess of all assets over all liabilities.

Revenue. The source and amount of an inflow of assets resulting from services rendered, sales of product or merchandise, gains from sale or exchange of assets other than stock in trade, and earnings from interest and dividends on investments. Revenue is *realized* when the asset is sold or the service is rendered.

Expenses. Costs of services received during a specified period and utilized in the production of revenue during the same period.

Basic Assumptions. Financial statements are based on the following assumptions:

> *Accounting Entity.* Each specific business enterprise is a separate accounting entity.
>
> *Monetary Measure.* Business transactions can be measured and expressed in terms of money.
>
> *Going Concern.* The enterprise will continue in business indefinitely unless there is evidence to the contrary.
>
> *Time Periods.* Financial statements shall be prepared at regular specified time periods.
>
> *Estimates.* Accounting measurements involve informed judgments, opinions, and estimates.

Accrual Basis. The net income for a period is measured by relating the revenue (accomplishments) of a period with the properly applicable expenses (efforts) of that period without regard to the timing and the amount of cash receipts and cash payments.

Consistency. Since different procedures may be used in some areas, for comparability it is important that the selected method should be followed consistently. Changes should be fully disclosed to permit comparability.

Cost Allocation. The cost of assets whose benefits extend over more than one accounting period are allocated on a reasonable and systematic basis to the periods benefited.

Materiality. The need for adjusting entries and the need for full disclosure do not apply to insignificant, immaterial, or trivial items.

Conservatism. In matters of doubt and conflict where no clear-cut evidence is available and a value judgment, opinion, or estimate must be reached, the tendency is to minimize net income and owners' equity.

Exchange Price. The money exchange price at acquisition (historical cost) is the primary recording basis. Other money prices used are current replacement cost, current selling price, and discounted present value of future cash flows. Disclosure of the financial effects of price-level changes through supplementary statements is recommended.

Glossary

Absorption costing. A method of product costing in which all production costs, variable and fixed, are classified as product costs and are identified with inventory. These costs are then divided between inventory and cost of goods sold at the end of the period.

Accruals. The recognition of an expense or revenue and its related asset or liability that has not been recorded in the normal course of business.

Accumulated depreciation. That portion of an asset cost that has been charged as an expense in prior periods and is shown as a reduction in the long-term asset cost on the statement of financial position.

Adjusting entries. Entries made at the end of the accounting period to record the accrued effect of unfinished transactions.

Aging schedule. A classification of accounts receivable according to the age of the unpaid balances.

All-inclusive concept. Earnings include all nonrecurring and extraordinary items of gain or loss. Under this concept all changes in retained earnings except dividends will be shown in the income statement.

Allowance for doubtful accounts. An estimate of the amount of accounts receivable that will be uncollectible.

Amortization. The extinguishment of an amount over a period of time, for example, the periodic allocation of bond premium or discount to bond interest expense.

Analog computer. (a) A computer that operates on data represented in the form of continuously variable physical quantities by performing physical processes on the data. (b) A calculating device that operates on numbers represented by measurable physical quantities such as temperature, amount of voltage, or angular position.

Assembly program. A computer program that takes instructions in a nonmachine language and changes them to the language used by the machine on which the program is to be run.

Audit trails. (a) A means for identifying the actions taken in processing input data or in preparing an output. A system for tracing step by step from output back to the original source data. (b) The means for tracing the steps taken in processing input data or in preparing an output. Data on a source document can be traced to an output or an output can be followed back to the source document from whence it came.

Authorized shares. The shares of stock that a corporate charter specifies may be legally issued.

861

BRANCHING. A term that means a sequence of steps has been completed or is to be broken and that the sequence is to be repeated or changed to a new one.

BREAK-EVEN POINT. The point at which the revenue from sales exactly meets the total expenses, fixed and variable, to produce that revenue, without any profit or loss.

BUDGET VARIANCE. The variance calculated by subtracting the actual overhead incurred from the overhead in the flexible budget allowance for the capacity attained based on the actual work completed.

CAPITAL STOCK. The money value assigned to a corporation's issued shares which constitute the legal capital of the corporation. The value assigned is the par or stated value times the number of shares issued.

CLOSING ENTRIES. Entries that transfer the balances in revenue and expenses to a summary account and then to retained earnings.

COMMON STOCKHOLDER. One who owns the residual interest, after debt and other stock interests, in a corporation.

COMPILER. A program that converts a user-oriented computer language through one or more steps into a machine language. A different compiler is required for each computer language that may be used on a given machine.

COMPOSITE RATE. A group rate for depreciation applied to a number of assets with different service lives and costs.

COMPOUND INTEREST. The periodic addition of simple interest to principal, the sum being the new principal for computation of simple interest for the ensuing period.

CONDITIONAL BRANCHING. An instruction that may or may not cause a departure from the normal sequence of executing instructions depending on the result of the condition. This type of transfer is basic to the decision-making processes in computer programs.

CONSERVATISM. The accounting concept that states if there is reasonable doubt or uncertainty in measurement, net income and net assets should be understated rather than overstated.

CONSISTENCY. The treatment of items in a consistent manner from period to period so that reliable comparisons can be made. If there is a change in practice or procedures, full disclosure should be made.

CONSOLIDATED ACCOUNTING REPORT. A financial statement that combines the statements of earnings and financial position of a parent company and one or more subsidiaries.

CONSOLIDATION. The combination of two or more enterprises through the creation of a new corporation which acquires the net assets of the absorbed companies.

CONSUMERS' PRICE INDEX. An index published by the Bureau of Labor Statistics sometimes used to measure the changes in the purchasing power of the dollar.

CONTINGENT LIABILITY. An obligation that may arise as a consequence of a possible future event.

CONTRIBUTION MARGIN. The excess of sales revenues over variable expenses.

COST PRINCIPLE. The concept that assets are initially recorded at the acquisition or historical price. Modifications are made for expirations of original cost.

CURRENT ASSET. Cash and other assets that will be converted to cash or consumed during the normal operating cycle of the business. The usual subdivisions of current assets are cash, marketable securities, receivables, inventory and prepaid expenses.

CURRENT LIABILITY. A debt that is payable in the ensuing year, normally from current assets.

DEBUG. To locate and eliminate mistakes in a program.

DIFFERENTIAL COST. The difference in total cost between two alternatives. It is also called "incremental cost" or "marginal cost."

DIGITAL COMPUTER. A computer that performs arithmetic and logical operations on data and provides for storage.

EARNINGS PER SHARE. Earnings divided by the number of shares of stock outstanding.

ENTITY CONCEPT. The principle that limits the area of interest for which financial accounting is applied to the specific business enterprise. This area of interest is identified in the statements and may not be the same as the legal entity.

EXCESS PRESENT VALUE. The technique used to determine if the present value of estimated net future inflows at the company's desired rate of return is greater or less than the cost of the proposal.

EXPENSES. An expired cost the benefits from which do not extend beyond the present period.

FAIR PRESENTATION. The standard that financial statements should be a fair presentation based on generally accepted accounting principles and should fully reveal financial data and happenings that would influence a statement user's decisions.

FLEXIBLE BUDGET. A budget which can be adjusted to the actual level of output in order to compare budgeted costs at that level with actual costs incurred.

FLOW CHART. A diagram that shows graphically the structure and general sequence of operations of a program (program flow chart) or a system of processing (systems flow chart).

FULL DISCLOSURE. See *fair presentation*.

GNP IMPLICIT PRICE DEFLATOR. A price-level index used to state gross national product in common dollar terms and used to measure changes in purchasing power of the dollar.

GOING CONCERN. The concept that assumes the continuation of the entity long enough to experience the revenues generated by the assets suspended in the accounts.

GOODWILL. The excess of the price paid for a business as a whole over the book value or agreed value of all tangible net assets purchased.

GROUP RATE. A rate of depreciation applied to a group of assets with similar service lives and low costs.

HARDWARE. The physical equipment from which a computer is formed.

IDLE CAPACITY. The unfavorable volume variance represented in fixed costs not applied because of the failure to achieve 100 percent volume of activity.

INCREMENTAL COST. See *differential cost*.

LABOR EFFICIENCY VARIANCE. The variance calculated by the formula: (actual hours — standard hours) × standard rate.

LABOR RATE VARIANCE. Variance calculated by the formula: (actual rate — standard rate) × actual direct labor hours used.

LEGAL CAPITAL. The portion of net assets restricted as to withdrawal by law; paid-in capital which is the par or stated value of the capital stock.

LINEAR. Having the mathematical properties of a straight line or a plane surface.

LINEAR PROGRAMMING. A mathematical method of planning an operation.

LOOP. A sequence of instructions that can be executed repetitively.

MACHINE LANGUAGE. A set of instructions that a computer can directly recognize and execute.

MATCHING CONCEPT. The convention of matching with the revenue the expenses associated with, or necessary to, the rendering of that service or product.

MATERIALITY. The concept that financial reports should only be concerned with data that is relatively significant. The determination of that which is significant is governed by experience and judgment.

MATERIALS PRICE VARIANCE. The variance from standard cost that is the difference between actual and standard unit prices times the actual quantity purchased.

MATERIALS QUANTITY VARIANCE. The variance from standard cost that is the difference between actual and standard quantities used times the standard price.

MERGER. The combination of two or more enterprises through the acquisition by one company of the net assets of the other. There is no new concern created.

PARTNERSHIP. A form of business organization in which ownership is by two or more individuals who have unlimited liability, provide the capital, and manage the company.

POOLING OF INTERESTS. A business combination in which the book values of the acquired companies remain substantially unchanged since the elements of a purchase and sale are absent. Cf. with the alternative purchase method.

PREFERRED STOCK. The class of stock that has a prior claim to common stock on the earnings of a corporation and on the assets of the corporation in the event of liquidation.

PREPAID EXPENSE. An expenditure that will benefit future periods. They are classified as current assets for the reason that they will be converted to cash in the next period or, if they were not paid for in advance, they would require the disbursement of cash in the following period.

PRESENT VALUE. The current value of an amount of money to be received in the future which is calculated by discounting the future amount to the present.

PRESENT-VALUE METHOD. A means of determining the relative desirability of an expenditure by comparing the difference between the cost of the investment and the expected earnings from the investment discounted by the desired minimum rate. If the present value of the earnings exceed the investment, the investment is desirable.

RATE-OF-RETURN METHOD. That rate of return which exists when the present value of the future cash inflows equals the cost of the investment which produces them. It is also called "time-adjusted" rate of return.

PRICE-LEVEL CHANGE. A change in the purchasing power of the dollar usually measured by changes in the Consumer's Price Index or the GNP Implicit Price Deflator.

RETAIL INVENTORY METHOD. A method of valuing physical inventories at selling prices and reducing them to cost by a computed percentage.

RETAINED EARNINGS. Accumulated net earnings of a corporation less dividend distributions to stockholders.

SOFTWARE. Programs and routines that facilitate the programming and operation of the computer.

STANDARD COST. A predetermined cost per unit that should be attained. When compared with actual results, it affords management a basis of cost control.

SUNK COSTS. A cost of present assets that was incurred in the past and is irrelevant to a present decision regarding the sale or disposition of the asset.

SYSTEMS ANALYSIS. The examination of an activity, procedure, method, or business to determine what needs to be done and how it can best be accomplished.

TIME PERIODS. The principle that financial information is presented for specified time periods that are uniform to facilitate comparisons and that are shorter than the life of the enterprise to be useful in decisions.

TIME SHARING. The simultaneous use of a single computing facility by many persons at terminals with two distinct characteristics—lower cost to the users and the interchange of dialogue between user and computer.

TREASURY STOCK. Fully paid capital stock that has been reacquired by the issuing corporation through gift or purchase and held for resale or cancellation.

UNCONDITIONAL BRANCH. An instruction that always causes a departure from the normal sequence of executing instructions.

UNIFORM ACCOUNTING PERIOD. A uniform time period of a year or less for which statements reporting the economic activities of the entity have been prepared. The uniformity of time periods affords comparability of data.

UNIT-OF-MEASURE PRINCIPLE. The principle of using the dollar as the unit of measure in financial accounting. Price-level changes are not recognized in the basic financial statements.

VOLUME VARIANCE. A comparison of the overhead allowed in the flexible budget for capacity attained with the overhead applied or estimated using a predetermined rate times the capacity attained. This variance represents the fixed costs not absorbed for the reason of failing to achieve 100-percent volume of activity.

Index